America's
TEST KITCHEN

THE COMPLETE
AMERICA'S TEST KITCHEN
TV SHOW COOKBOOK

2001-2010

THE COMPLETE AMERICA'S TEST KITCHEN TV SHOW COOKBOOK

2001 / 2010

BY THE EDITORS AT **AMERICA'S TEST KITCHEN**

PHOTOGRAPHY **CARL TREMBLAY, KELLER + KELLER, AND DANIEL J. VAN ACKERE**

AMERICA'S TEST KITCHEN
17 Station Street, Brookline, MA 02445

Library of Congress Cataloging-in-Publication Data
The Editors at America's Test Kitchen

THE COMPLETE AMERICA'S TEST KITCHEN TV SHOW COOKBOOK:
Every recipe from 10 years of the hit TV show with product ratings and a look behind the scenes

1st Edition

ISBN-13: 978-1-933615-55-4   ISBN-10: 1-933615-55-9
Hardcover: $39.95 US
1. Cooking. 1. Title
2009

Manufactured in the United States of America

10 9 8 7 6 5 4 3 2

Distributed by America's Test Kitchen
17 Station Street, Brookline, MA 02445

EDITORIAL DIRECTOR: Jack Bishop

EXECUTIVE EDITOR: Elizabeth Carduff

SENIOR EDITORS: Lori Galvin and Rachel Toomey Kelsey

CONTRIBUTING EDITORS: Elizabeth Emery, Kate Hartke, Barbara Wood

EDITORIAL ASSISTANT: Elizabeth Pohm

DESIGN DIRECTOR: Amy Klee

ART DIRECTOR: Greg Galvan

DESIGNERS: Tiffani Beckwith and Matthew Warnick

STAFF PHOTOGRAPHER: Daniel J. van Ackere

ADDITIONAL PHOTOGRAPHERS: Elisabeth O'Donnell and Peter Tannenbaum

FOOD STYLISTS: Marie Piraino and Mary Jane Sawyer

PRODUCTION DIRECTOR: Guy Rochford

SENIOR PRODUCTION MANAGER: Jessica Lindheimer Quirk

SENIOR PROJECT MANAGER: Alice Carpenter

TRAFFIC AND PRODUCTION COORDINATOR: Laura Collins

COLOR AND IMAGING SPECIALIST: Andrew Mannone

PRODUCTION AND IMAGING SPECIALISTS: Judy Blomquist and Lauren Pettapiece

COPYEDITOR: Cheryl Redmond

PROOFREADER: Jeffrey Schier

SHOPPING GUIDE COPYEDITOR: Debra Hudak

SHOPPING GUIDE PROOFREADER: Holly Hartman

INDEXER: Elizabeth Parson

CONTENTS

PREFACE BY CHRISTOPHER KIMBALL   viii

WELCOME TO AMERICA'S TEST KITCHEN   x

CHAPTER 1   SOUP'S ON!   3

CHAPTER 2   SALAD DAYS   19

CHAPTER 3   EASY SKILLET SUPPERS   37

CHAPTER 4   ONE POT DINNERS   49

CHAPTER 5   SIMPLY CHICKEN   63

CHAPTER 6   TALKING TURKEY AND ALL THE TRIMMINGS   85

CHAPTER 7   WE'LL HAVE THE STEAK   107

CHAPTER 8   PORK CHOPS EVERY DAY   117

CHAPTER 9   ROASTS, MEATLOAF, AND MORE   129

CHAPTER 10   FAVORITE WAYS WITH FISH   149

CHAPTER 11   DINNER AT THE DINER   171

CHAPTER 12   WHO WANTS PASTA?   189

CHAPTER 13   BRINGING HOME ITALIAN FAVORITES   221

CHAPTER 14   THE FLAIR OF THE FRENCH   249

CHAPTER 15   TEX-MEX TONIGHT   277

CHAPTER 16   LET'S DO TAKEOUT   299

CHAPTER 17   IT'S GRILL TIME!   335

CHAPTER 18   SIDES OF PLENTY   385

CHAPTER 19   COME FOR BRUNCH   409

CHAPTER 20   PLEASE PASS THE BREAD   443

CHAPTER 21   COOKIE JAR FAVORITES   457

CHAPTER 22   A PIECE OF CAKE   485

CHAPTER 23   PUDDINGS AND SOUFFLÉS   525

CHAPTER 24   CLASSIC FRUIT DESSERTS   539

CHAPTER 25   KEEP YOUR FORK—THERE'S PIE!   557

THE AMERICA'S TEST KITCHEN SHOPPING GUIDE   583

CONVERSIONS & EQUIVALENCIES   618

2010 TV SHOW EPISODE DIRECTORY   620

INDEX   621

PREFACE

My first experience riding a horse ended badly. The animal in question was my own horse, a Morgan, who realized instantly that I had no idea how to control 1,200 pounds of horseflesh. So he did the natural thing, which was to lope at an easy pace up to a small embankment and then stop dead, sending me flying into space. The good news was that my 10-year-old bones bent rather than snapped. I dusted myself off and got back on.

Flying off of horses was a constant theme during my childhood. My most spectacular fall was precipitated by an act of such extreme stupidity that I could have won a Darwin Award. One summer, as an aspiring hippie in Oregon, I managed to rope-halter a horse I chanced upon while crossing a large pasture and then hopped on its back without the benefit of saddle or bridle. A furious gallop ended in a spectacular arc that, of course, brought me rather harshly back to terra firma, only inches away from a large boulder. One might say that I have lived a charmed life, at least if survival is the key criterion.

As the host of *America's Test Kitchen*, I know that we have had our share of stumbles in the early years but we have always gotten back on our feet to do another segment and another season. If practice makes perfect, or almost perfect, then we stuck to it and so did you. Hopefully, we can make a better claim than "We survived!" since we are now the most-watched cooking show on public television.

After well over 200 episodes and hundreds of recipes, we thought that the 10-year anniversary would be a good time to publish *The Complete America's Test Kitchen TV Show Cookbook*. We have included EVERY recipe (500 or so) from all 10 years as well as a comprehensive guide to our product tastings and equipment testings, organized by category for easy reference, including photos of each of the winners.

I am not as young as I was when I stood in front of the TV cameras for the first time (watching early episodes is something I avoid) which means that I had forgotten some of the died-and-gone-to-heaven highlights from our 10 years. So preparing this book was a true trip down memory lane. The list includes Skillet Lasagna (just 40 minutes from start to finish and better than the oven-baked version), Chicken and Dumplings, Pan-Seared Thick Cut Steaks (unusual oven/stovetop method), Poached Salmon with Herb and

Caper Vinaigrette (so little liquid it's almost braised), Easier French Fries (started in cold, not hot, oil), Weeknight Bolognese, Italian-Style Grilled Chicken, French Chicken in a Pot (incredibly flavorful, moist meat), Well-Done Grilled Hamburgers (still juicy and tender), Barbecued Pulled Pork (finished in the oven), Creamy Mashed Potatoes, Blueberry Muffins (with a blueberry swirl), Molasses Spice Cookies with Rum Glaze, Chocolate-Chunk Oatmeal Cookies with Pecans and Dried Cherries, Triple-Chocolate Mousse Cake, Applesauce Snack Cake, and our to-die-for Coconut Layer Cake.

Last weekend, I rode horseback with a neighbor through high mountain pastures that were just a few minutes from our farm. It was a neighbor's property and I had never ventured up the steep embankment just off the road and up into the hidden fields above. We loped through the high timothy, the Indian paintbrushes, and the daisies, rear ends firmly set in our saddles, boot heels down, comfortable with our horses and the ride. I had discovered another country, a magic valley that was just out my back door after a dozen years of similar rides just a stone's throw away.

Cooking is like that ride. It takes years to get comfortable, to figure out what you are doing, and to be certain that you can overcome almost any eventuality, whether it be a woodchuck hole or a substitute ingredient. Years of accumulated experience—other rides and other recipes—are the bits and pieces that turn one from tentative to confident, from novice to professional.

The joy of cooking is that experience brings with it unexpected pleasure, moments when a recipe turns from everyday to transcendent. This book is a container of sorts, it holds all the steps, all the preparation that can take one from good cook to great cook, from putting food on the table to really enjoying the ride. One day, when you least expect it, you will be out and about and realize that you've found a whole new world, just around the corner.

Christopher Kimball
Founder and editor, *Cook's Illustrated* and *Cook's Country*
Host, *America's Test Kitchen* and
Cook's Country from America's Test Kitchen

WELCOME TO AMERICA'S TEST KITCHEN

This book has been tested, written, and edited by the folks at America's Test Kitchen, a very real 2,500-square-foot kitchen located just outside of Boston. It is the home of *Cook's Illustrated* magazine and *Cook's Country* magazine and is the Monday-through-Friday destination for more than three dozen test cooks, editors, food scientists, tasters, and cookware specialists. Our mission is to test recipes over and over again until we understand how and why they work and until we arrive at the "best" version.

Our television show highlights the best recipes developed in the test kitchen during the past year—those recipes that our test kitchen staff makes at home time and time again. These recipes are accompanied by our most exhaustive equipment tests and our most interesting food tastings.

Christopher Kimball, the founder and editor of *Cook's Illustrated* magazine, is host of the show and asks the questions you might ask. It's the job of our chefs, Julia Collin Davison, Bridget Lancaster, Rebecca Hays, Yvonne Ruperti, and J. Kenji Alt, to demonstrate our recipes. The chefs show Chris what works and what doesn't, and they explain why. In the process, they discuss (and show you) the best examples from our development process as well as the worst: roast chicken with flabby skin, dry grilled salmon, and tempura so greasy no one wanted to eat it.

Adam Ried, our equipment guru, and Lisa McManus, our gadget guru, share the highlights from our detailed testing process in equipment corner segments. They bring with them our favorite (and least favorite) gadgets and tools. They tell you which blender performed best in a dozen kitchen tests and show you what's missing in most cookware sets and how to put together your own.

Jack Bishop is our ingredient expert. He has Chris taste our favorite (and least favorite) brands of common food products—everything from cinnamon and vanilla to premium butter and cottage cheese. Chris may not always enjoy these exercises (vegetable broth and mirin, Japanese rice wine, aren't always a whole lot of fun to taste), but he usually learns something as Jack explains what makes one brand superior to another.

Although just eight cooks and editors appear on the television show, another 50 people worked to make the show a reality. Producer Melissa Baldino conceived and developed each episode and organized many aspects of filming to ensure that taping would run smoothly. Meg Ragland conducted all the historical recipe research. Guy Crosby, our science consultant, researched the science behind the recipes. Along with the on-air crew, executive chefs Erin McMurrer and Keith Dresser helped plan and organize the 26 television episodes shot in May 2009 and ran the "back kitchen," where all the food that appeared on camera originated. Meredith Butcher and Peggy Collier organized the tasting and equipment segments.

During filming, chefs J. Kenji Alt, Matthew Herron, Suzannah McFerran, Paco Robert, Bryan Roof, Diane Unger, Lynn Clark, Andrea Geary, and Marcus Walser, and interns Mary Ting, Melissa Suderman, and Cheryl Mui cooked all the food needed on set. Additional cooks worked on-set developing recipes for our magazines and books—Cali Rich, Kristen Widican, David Pazmiño, J. Kenji Alt, Lisa McManus, Jennifer Lalime, Chris O'Connor, Maria del Mar Sacasa, and Meredith Butcher. Nadia Domeq was charged with making sure all the ingredients we needed were on hand. Kitchen assistants Maria Elena Delgado, Ena Gudiel, and Edward Tundidor also worked long hours. Chefs Adelaide Parker, Yvonne Ruperti, Meghan Erwin, and Dan Souza and intern Lilly Jan helped coordinate the efforts of the kitchen with the television set by readying props, equipment, and food. Meredith Smith led all tours of the test kitchen during filming.

The staff of A La Carte Communications turned our recipes, tastings, testings, and science experiments into a lively television show. Special thanks to Geoffrey Drummond, director and editor Herb Sevush, and director of photography Jan Maliszewski.

We also appreciate the hard work of the video production team, including Stephen Hussar, Michael McEachern, Peter Dingle, Ken Fraser, Roger Macie, Gilles Morin, Brenda Coffey, Elena Battista, Michael Andrus, Aaron Frutman, Lindsay More, and Ariana Johnston. Thanks also to Peter Tannenbaum, the second unit videographer.

We also would like to thank Christina Regan, Nancy Bocchino, and Bara Levin at WGBH Station Relations, and the team at American Public Television that presents the show: Cynthia Fenneman, Chris Funkhauser, Judy Barlow, and Tom Davison. Thanks also for production support from DGA Productions, Boston, and Zebra Productions, New York.

DCS by Fisher & Paykel, Woodbridge by Robert Mondavi, Kohler Company, VIVA Towels, Diamond Crystal Kosher Salt, and Cooking.com helped underwrite the show and we thank them for their support. We also thank Marcy McCreary, Ann Naya, and Bailey Vatalaro for handling underwriter relations and Deborah Broide for managing publicity.

Meat was provided by Scott Brueggeman of DiLuigi Sausage Company of Danvers, Massachusetts. Fish was supplied by Ian Davison of Constitution Seafood of Boston, Massachusetts. Live plants and garden items for the show were furnished by Mark Cutler at Mahoney's Garden Center of Brighton, Massachusetts. Aprons for Christopher Kimball were made by Nicole Romano and staff aprons were made by Crooked Brook. Props were designed and developed by Jay Layman, Christine Vo, and Erica Lee and Foam Props of Woburn, Massachusetts.

CHAPTER 1

SOUP'S ON!

Classic Chicken Noodle Soup 4

Hearty Chicken Noodle Soup 5

Quick Beef and Vegetable Soup 6

Classic Cream of Tomato Soup 7

Creamless Creamy Tomato Soup 8

   Classic Croutons

Creamy Pea Soup 9

Creamy Mushroom Soup 10

   Sautéed Wild Mushrooms

Butternut Squash Soup 11

Rustic Potato-Leek Soup 12

Hearty Lentil Soup 13

Ham and Split Pea Soup 14

Mulligatawny Soup 15

Classic Gazpacho 16

   Garlic Croutons

New England Clam Chowder 17

CLASSIC CHICKEN NOODLE SOUP

WHY THIS RECIPE WORKS: Classic chicken noodle soup is one of *the* all-time comfort foods. We eat it to nurse a cold or pair it with a simple sandwich for a satisfying meal. But making chicken noodle soup from scratch can take all day. We wanted a simple recipe but we wanted to make it the old-fashioned way—starting with a whole chicken— rather than cheating with store-bought broth.

We began by cutting the chicken into small pieces that could be browned in batches. To develop additional flavor, we sweated the browned pieces in a covered pot with an onion, then simmered them for less than half an hour. Now we had a stock that just needed some salt and a bay leaf to round out its flavor. We reserved some of the skimmed fat from the stock to sauté aromatics and carrots for the soup, and we added in tender chicken breast pieces that had already been poached in our stock. For extra flavor, we cooked the egg noodles right in the soup pot so they could absorb rich, meaty flavor from the stock. With a final sprinkling of chopped parsley, our chicken noodle soup was complete—rich, homemade broth, moist pieces of chicken, tender vegetables, and perfectly cooked noodles.

Classic Chicken Noodle Soup

SERVES 6 TO 8

Make sure to reserve the chicken breast pieces until step 2; they should not be browned. If you use a cleaver, you will be able to cut up the chicken parts quickly. A chef's knife or kitchen shears will also work. Be sure to reserve 2 tablespoons of chicken fat for sautéing the aromatics in step 4; however, if you prefer not to use chicken fat, vegetable oil can be substituted.

STOCK

- 1 tablespoon vegetable oil
- 1 (4-pound) whole chicken, breast removed, split, and reserved; remaining chicken cut into 2-inch pieces (see note)
- 1 medium onion, chopped medium
- 2 quarts boiling water
- 2 teaspoons table salt
- 2 bay leaves

SOUP

- 2 tablespoons chicken fat, reserved from making stock, or vegetable oil (see note)
- 1 medium onion, chopped medium
- 1 large carrot, peeled and sliced ¼ inch thick
- 1 celery rib, sliced ¼ inch thick
- ½ teaspoon dried thyme
- 3 ounces egg noodles (about 2 cups)
- ¼ cup minced fresh parsley leaves
  Table salt and ground black pepper

1. FOR THE STOCK: Heat the oil in a large Dutch oven over medium-high heat until shimmering. Add half of the chicken pieces and cook until lightly browned, about 5 minutes per side. Transfer the cooked chicken to a bowl and repeat with the remaining chicken pieces; transfer to the bowl with the first batch. Add the onion and cook, stirring frequently, until the onion is translucent, 3 to 5 minutes. Return the chicken pieces to the pot. Reduce the heat to low, cover, and cook until the chicken releases its juices, about 20 minutes.

2. Increase the heat to high; add the boiling water, reserved chicken breast pieces, salt, and bay leaves. Reduce the heat to medium-low and simmer until the flavors have blended, about 20 minutes.

3. Remove the breast pieces from the pot. When cool, remove the skin and bones from the breast pieces and discard. Shred the meat with your fingers or two forks and set aside. Strain the stock through a fine-mesh strainer into a container, pressing on the solids to extract as much liquid as possible; discard the solids. Allow the liquid to settle about 5 minutes and skim off the fat; reserve 2 tablespoons, if desired (see note). (The shredded chicken, strained stock, and fat can be refrigerated in separate airtight containers for up to 2 days.)

4. FOR THE SOUP: Heat the reserved chicken fat in a large Dutch oven over medium-high heat. Add the onion, carrot, and celery and cook until softened, about 5 minutes. Add the thyme and reserved stock and simmer until the vegetables are tender, 10 to 15 minutes.

5. Add the noodles and reserved shredded chicken and cook until just tender, 5 to 8 minutes. Stir in the parsley, season with salt and pepper to taste, and serve.

HEARTY CHICKEN NOODLE SOUP

WHY THIS RECIPE WORKS: Sometimes we prefer a simple bowl of chicken soup—a brothy soup modestly enriched with chicken, noodles, and vegetables. Other times, a heartier version of chicken noodle soup is what we crave—one chock-full of chicken, noodles, and vegetables—a true meal in a bowl. We also wanted to find a way to produce such a soup without relying on a whole chicken for the stock.

We began by jump-starting the flavor of our soup with a mixture of store-bought chicken broth and water, but the broth-and-water base had a distinctly flat flavor. A few pounds of chicken parts created a wonderfully rich stock, but the method—browning the parts and then simmering them—was just too fussy for what we wanted here. Instead, we turned to a somewhat unlikely but more convenient substitute—store-bought ground chicken. Ground chicken offers more surface area and exponentially more flavor, providing a great-tasting stock when sautéed with aromatics and then simmered with the broth and water. All the stock needed was some body and thickening, which we found by adding a little cornstarch. With our broth down, we were ready to add the chicken (breasts that had been poached in the stock until just cooked through and then shredded), vegetables, and noodles. Along with onion, celery, and carrots, we further enriched the soup with potato and Swiss chard. Our streamlined hearty chicken noodle soup was now rich, and satisfying.

Hearty Chicken Noodle Soup

SERVES 4 TO 6

When skimming the fat off the stock, we prefer to leave a little bit on the surface to enhance the soup's flavor.

STOCK

- 1 tablespoon vegetable oil
- 1 pound ground chicken
- 1 small onion, chopped medium
- 1 medium carrot, peeled and chopped medium
- 1 celery rib, chopped medium
- 2 quarts low-sodium chicken broth
- 4 cups water
- 2 bay leaves
- 2 teaspoons table salt
- 2 (12-ounce) bone-in, skin-on chicken breast halves, cut in half crosswise

SOUP

- ¼ cup cold water
- 3 tablespoons cornstarch
- 1 small onion, halved and sliced thin
- 2 medium carrots, peeled, halved lengthwise, and cut crosswise into ¾-inch pieces
- 1 medium celery rib, halved lengthwise and cut crosswise into ½-inch pieces
- 1 medium russet potato (about 8 ounces), peeled and cut into ¾-inch cubes
- 1½ ounces egg noodles (about 1 cup)
- 4–6 Swiss chard leaves, ribs removed, torn into 1-inch pieces (about 2 cups; optional)
- 1 tablespoon minced fresh parsley leaves
  Table salt and ground black pepper

1. FOR THE STOCK: Heat the oil in a large Dutch oven over medium-high heat until shimmering. Add the ground chicken, onion, carrot, and celery. Cook, stirring frequently, until the chicken is no longer pink, 5 to 10 minutes (do not brown the chicken).

2. Reduce the heat to medium-low. Add the broth, water, bay leaves, salt, and chicken breasts; cover and cook for 30 minutes. Remove the lid, increase the heat to high, and bring to a boil. (If the liquid is already boiling when the lid is removed, remove the chicken breasts immediately and continue with the recipe.) Transfer the chicken breasts to a large plate and set aside. Continue to cook the stock for 20 minutes, adjusting the heat to maintain a gentle boil. Strain the stock through a fine-mesh strainer into a container, pressing on the solids to extract as much liquid as possible; discard the solids. Allow the liquid to settle about 5 minutes and skim off the fat (see note). (The strained stock can be refrigerated in an airtight container for up to 2 days or frozen for up to 3 months. The chicken breasts can be stored in a zipper-lock bag with the air squeezed out.)

3. FOR THE SOUP: Return the stock to a Dutch oven set over medium-high heat. In a small bowl, combine the water and cornstarch until a smooth slurry forms; stir into the stock and bring to a gentle boil. Add the onion, carrots, celery, and potato and cook until the potato pieces are almost tender, 10 to 15 minutes, adjusting the heat as necessary to maintain a gentle boil. Add the egg noodles and continue to cook until all the vegetables and noodles are tender, about 5 minutes longer.

4. Meanwhile, remove the skin and bones from the reserved cooked chicken and discard. Shred the meat with your fingers or two forks. Add the shredded chicken, Swiss chard (if using), and parsley to the soup and cook until heated through, about 2 minutes. Season with salt and pepper to taste and serve.

QUICK BEEF AND VEGETABLE SOUP

WHY THIS RECIPE WORKS: Rich and hearty beef and vegetable soup with old-fashioned flavor is a snap to make—if you have a few hours free and several pounds of beef and bones hanging around. We wanted to find another way to develop the same flavors and textures in under an hour.

We knew the key to this recipe would be finding the right cut of meat, one that had great beefy flavor and that would cook up tender in a reasonable amount of time. Tender cuts, like strip steak and rib eye, became tough, livery, and chalky when simmered in soup. Sirloin tip steak was the best choice—when cut into small pieces, the meat was tender and offered the illusion of being cooked for hours, plus its meaty flavor imparted richness to the soup.

In place of labor-intensive homemade beef broth, we doctored store-bought beef broth with aromatics and lightened its flavor profile with chicken broth. To further boost the flavor of the beef, we added cremini mushrooms, tomato paste, soy sauce, and red wine, ingredients that are rich in glutamates, naturally occurring compounds that accentuate the meat's hearty flavor. To mimic the rich body of a homemade meat stock (made rich through the gelatin released by the meat bones' collagen during the long simmering process), we relied on powdered gelatin. Our beef and vegetable soup now had the same richness and flavor as cooked-all-day versions in a whole lot less time.

Quick Beef and Vegetable Soup
SERVES 4 TO 6
Choose whole sirloin tip steaks over ones that have been cut into small pieces for stir-fries. If sirloin tip steaks are unavailable, substitute blade or flank steak, removing any hard gristle or excess fat. Button mushrooms can be used in place of the cremini mushrooms, with some trade-off in flavor. If you like, add 1 cup frozen peas, frozen corn, or frozen cut green beans during the last 5 minutes of cooking. For a heartier soup, add 10 ounces red potatoes, cut into ½-inch pieces (2 cups), during the last 15 minutes of cooking.

- 1 pound sirloin tip steaks, trimmed of excess fat and cut into ½-inch pieces (see note)
- 2 tablespoons soy sauce
- 1 teaspoon vegetable oil
- 1 pound cremini mushrooms, stems trimmed, caps wiped clean, and quartered (see note)
- 1 large onion, chopped medium
- 2 tablespoons tomato paste
- 1 medium garlic clove, minced or pressed through a garlic press (about 1 teaspoon)
- ½ cup red wine
- 4 cups beef broth
- 1¾ cups low-sodium chicken broth
- 4 medium carrots, peeled and cut into ½-inch pieces
- 2 medium celery ribs, cut into ½-inch pieces
- 1 bay leaf
- 1 tablespoon unflavored powdered gelatin
- ½ cup cold water
- 2 tablespoons minced fresh parsley leaves
  Table salt and ground black pepper

1. Combine the beef and soy sauce in a medium bowl; set aside for 15 minutes.

2. Heat the oil in a large Dutch oven over medium-high heat until just smoking. Add the mushrooms and onion; cook, stirring frequently, until the onion is browned and dark bits form on the pan bottom, 8 to 12 minutes. Transfer the vegetables to a bowl.

3. Add the beef and cook, stirring occasionally, until the liquid evaporates and the meat starts to brown, 6 to 10 minutes. Add the tomato paste and garlic; cook, stirring constantly, until fragrant, about 30 seconds. Add the red wine, scraping the bottom of the pot with a wooden spoon to loosen any browned bits, and cook until syrupy, 1 to 2 minutes.

4. Add the beef broth, chicken broth, carrots, celery, bay leaf, and browned mushrooms and onion; bring to a boil. Reduce the heat to low, cover, and simmer until the vegetables and meat are tender, 25 to 30 minutes. While the soup is simmering, sprinkle the gelatin over the cold water and let stand.

5. When the soup is finished, turn off the heat. Remove and discard the bay leaf. Add the gelatin mixture and stir until completely dissolved. Stir in the parsley, season with salt and pepper to taste, and serve.

CLASSIC CREAM OF TOMATO SOUP

WHY THIS RECIPE WORKS: Canned cream of tomato soup is a childhood favorite. But grown-up tastes deserve something better—and let's face it, the canned soup's overly sweet flavors are just not all that appealing today. We wanted a well-balanced cream of tomato soup, one with rich color, great tomato flavor, and a silky texture.

Right away, we turned to canned tomatoes; fresh tomatoes are at their best just a few months out of the year and we didn't want to restrict our soup-making to just one season. To coax the most flavor from our canned whole tomatoes, it was essential to roast them in the oven. The intense dry heat worked to evaporate surface liquids and concentrate the flavor, and a sprinkling of brown sugar encouraged caramelization. We cooked our roasted tomatoes with shallots, chicken broth, and reserved tomato juice to develop robust flavor, then pureed the tomatoes (with broth) to keep the deep red flavor of the tomato broth intact. Finished with heavy cream and a splash of brandy, this cream of tomato soup will satisfy everyone at the table.

Classic Cream of Tomato Soup
SERVES 6

Make sure to use canned whole tomatoes packed in juice. To obtain 3 cups of juice, use the packing juice as well as the liquid that falls from the tomatoes when they are seeded.

 2 **(28-ounce) cans whole tomatoes packed in juice, drained, 3 cups juice reserved (see note)**
1½ **tablespoons dark brown sugar**
 4 **tablespoons (½ stick) unsalted butter**
 2 **large shallots, minced (about ½ cup)**
 1 **tablespoon tomato paste**
    Pinch ground allspice
 2 **tablespoons unbleached all-purpose flour**
1¾ **cups low-sodium chicken broth**
 ½ **cup heavy cream**
 2 **tablespoons brandy or dry sherry**
    Table salt and cayenne pepper

1. Adjust an oven rack to the upper-middle position and heat the oven to 450 degrees. Line a large rimmed baking sheet with foil. With your fingers, carefully open the whole tomatoes over a fine-mesh strainer set in a bowl and push out the seeds, allowing the juices to fall through the strainer into the bowl; discard the seeds. Spread the seeded tomatoes in a single layer on the foil and sprinkle evenly with the brown sugar. Bake until all the liquid has evaporated and the tomatoes begin to color, about 30 minutes. Cool the tomatoes slightly, then peel them off the foil; transfer to a small bowl and set aside.

2. Melt the butter in a large saucepan over medium heat. Add the shallots, tomato paste, and allspice. Reduce the heat to low, cover, and cook, stirring occasionally, until the shallots are softened, 7 to 10 minutes. Add the flour and cook, stirring constantly, until thoroughly combined, about 30 seconds. Gradually add the chicken broth, whisking constantly to combine; stir in the reserved tomato juice and roasted tomatoes. Cover, increase the heat to medium, and bring to a boil. Reduce the heat to low and simmer, stirring occasionally, for 10 minutes.

3. Pour the mixture through a fine-mesh strainer into a medium bowl; rinse and dry the saucepan. Transfer the tomatoes and solids in the strainer to a blender; add 1 cup of the strained liquid and puree until smooth. Add the pureed mixture and the remaining strained liquid to the saucepan. Add the cream and warm over low heat until hot, about 3 minutes. Off the heat, stir in the brandy, season with salt and cayenne to taste, and serve. (The soup can be refrigerated in an airtight container for up to 2 days. Warm over low heat until hot; do not boil.)

CREAMLESS CREAMY TOMATO SOUP

WHY THIS RECIPE WORKS: Creamy tomato soup boasts a bright, sweet tomato flavor when done right, but not everyone is a fan of rich cream soups. We wanted to keep the sharp tomatoey flavor in this classic soup, but ditch the dairy and tame the tartness in other ways.

Our first step was to choose canned tomatoes over fresh tomatoes—canned are simply more consistent in flavor than your average supermarket tomato. We mashed whole tomatoes (preferred over diced or crushed for their concentrated flavor) with a potato masher, then combined them with aromatics sautéed in extra-virgin olive oil, not butter, which guaranteed bright, clean flavor. Stirring in some olive oil before pureeing our soup added back vital flavor that was lost when we cooked the oil. To combat the acid in the tomatoes, we added full-flavored brown sugar. And for an ultra-creamy texture without the cream, we pureed sandwich bread into the soup. For a final touch, we stirred chicken broth into the pot and simmered the soup briefly to give our creamless creamy tomato soup a rich and velvety feel.

Creamless Creamy Tomato Soup

SERVES 6

If half of the soup fills your blender more than halfway, process the soup in three batches, but do not add more olive oil for the third batch. You can also use a hand-held blender to process the soup directly in the pot. Serve this soup topped with croutons (recipe follows), if desired. For an even smoother soup, strain the pureed mixture through a fine-mesh strainer before stirring in the chicken broth in step 2.

- ¼ cup extra-virgin olive oil, plus extra for drizzling (see note)
- 1 medium onion, chopped medium
- 3 medium garlic cloves, minced or pressed through a garlic press (about 1 tablespoon)
  Pinch red pepper flakes (optional)
- 1 bay leaf
- 2 (28-ounce) cans whole tomatoes
- 3 slices high-quality white sandwich bread, crusts removed, torn into 1-inch pieces
- 1 tablespoon brown sugar
- 2 cups low-sodium chicken broth
- 2 tablespoons brandy (optional)
  Table salt and ground black pepper
- ¼ cup chopped fresh chives

1. Heat 2 tablespoons of the oil in a large Dutch oven over medium-high heat until shimmering. Add the onion, garlic, red pepper flakes (if using), and bay leaf. Cook, stirring frequently, until the onion is translucent, 3 to 5 minutes. Stir in the tomatoes with their juice. Using a potato masher, mash until no pieces bigger than 2 inches remain. Stir in the bread and sugar and bring the soup to a boil. Reduce the heat to medium and cook, stirring occasionally, until the bread is completely saturated and starts to break down, about 5 minutes. Remove and discard the bay leaf.

2. Transfer half of the soup to a blender. Add 1 table-spoon more oil and process until the soup is smooth and creamy, 2 to 3 minutes. Transfer to a large bowl and repeat with the remaining soup and the remaining 1 tablespoon oil. Rinse and dry the Dutch oven and return the soup to the pot. Stir in the chicken broth and brandy (if using). Return the soup to a boil and season with salt and pepper to taste. Ladle the soup into bowls, sprinkle with the chopped chives, drizzle with olive oil, and serve. (The soup, minus the garnish, can be refrigerated in an airtight container for up to 2 days. Warm over low heat until hot; do not boil.)

Classic Croutons

MAKES ABOUT 1½ CUPS

- 3 slices high-quality white sandwich bread, crusts removed, cut into ½-inch cubes (about 1½ cups)
- 1½ tablespoons olive oil
  Table salt and ground black pepper

1. Adjust an oven rack to the upper-middle position and heat the oven to 400 degrees. Combine the bread cubes and oil in a medium bowl and toss to coat. Season with salt and pepper to taste.

2. Spread the bread cubes in an even layer on a rimmed baking sheet and bake, stirring occasionally, until golden, 8 to 10 minutes. Cool on the baking sheet to room temperature. (The croutons can be stored in an airtight container or a plastic bag for 3 days.)

CREAMY PEA SOUP

WHY THIS RECIPE WORKS: Sweet pea soup is a labor of love—fresh peas are shelled, blanched, cooked with other vegetables, then passed through a sieve. We were after a fuss-free but still elegant version of this special soup. Our goal was a streamlined approach that would produce a soup with silky texture and real pea flavor.

Both garden and grocery store peas can be disappointing; fresh pods often reveal tough, starchy pellets that require a significant amount of time spent shelling. Instead, we decided to use frozen peas, which are processed at the height of ripeness, so their freshness and flavor is completely preserved. For maximum pea flavor, we ground the frozen peas in a food processor before adding them to our simple soup base of chicken broth and shallots. Adding some Boston lettuce leaves gave the soup a wonderfully frothy texture. And a small dose of heavy cream added richness. Now the focus is on the peas, not the work, with this easy recipe for creamy pea soup that highlights the natural sweetness of peas (even frozen ones).

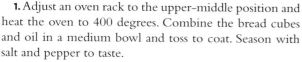
WHY OUR EQUIPMENT RATINGS ARE DIFFERENT

For many viewers, the equipment corner is the most valuable part of the TV show. Why? Besides the fact that we save you big bucks (more often than not the expensive model is beaten by a much cheaper option), viewers know they can trust our ratings. That's because we're independent (we don't accept advertising) and because we put equipment through real-world tests.

On the television show, Adam asks Chris to re-create some of the tests he and his team use in rating kitchen equipment. For example, Chris will wash dishes with various brands of liquid dish detergent to demonstrate which ones cut the grease and which ones don't. But that's just a sample of the work involved in our tests. Often, hundreds of kitchen hours go into each of our equipment ratings.

In testing blenders, Adam and his team whipped smoothies, crushed ice, pureed soup, ground peanuts into peanut butter, and processed pesto. (In all, they performed 11 separate kitchen tests to determine which blender you should own.) And to evaluate chef's knives, Adam enlisted four additional testers—a cook with large hands, a cook with small hands, a skilled cook, and a kitchen novice—and asked them to perform the same series of tasks. Each tester spent weeks working with eight knives, accumulating data that Adam analyzed to determine our winner.

And in case you're wondering, Chris doesn't regularly do the dishes in the test kitchen—lucky for him, there are professional dishwashers on hand to do the job.

Creamy Pea Soup

SERVES 4 TO 6

A few Classic Croutons (see page 8) are the perfect embellishment to this smooth soup.

- 4 tablespoons (½ stick) unsalted butter
- 4 large shallots, minced (about 1 cup), or 2 medium leeks, white and light green parts chopped fine and rinsed thoroughly (about 1⅓ cups)
- 2 tablespoons unbleached all-purpose flour
- 3½ cups low-sodium chicken broth
- 1½ pounds frozen peas (about 4½ cups), partially thawed at room temperature for 10 minutes
- 12 small leaves Boston lettuce (about 3 ounces), washed and dried
- ½ cup heavy cream
    Table salt and ground black pepper

1. Melt the butter in a large saucepan over low heat. Add the shallots and cook, covered, until softened, 8 to 10 minutes, stirring occasionally. Add the flour and cook, stirring constantly, until thoroughly combined, about 30 seconds. Whisking constantly, gradually add the chicken broth. Increase the heat to high and bring to a boil. Reduce the heat to medium-low and simmer 3 to 5 minutes.

2. Meanwhile, process the peas in a food processor until coarsely chopped, about 20 seconds. Add the peas and lettuce to the saucepan. Increase the heat to medium-high, cover, and return to a simmer; cook for 3 minutes. Uncover, reduce the heat to medium-low, and continue to simmer 2 minutes longer.

3. Working in batches, puree the soup in a blender until smooth, filling the blender jar only halfway for each batch. Strain the soup through a fine-mesh strainer into a large bowl; discard the solids in the strainer. Rinse and dry the saucepan; return the pureed mixture to the saucepan and stir in the cream. Warm the soup over low heat until hot, about 3 minutes. Season with salt and pepper to taste and serve. (The soup can be refrigerated in an airtight container for up to 2 days. Warm over low heat until hot; do not boil.)

CREAMY MUSHROOM SOUP

WHY THIS RECIPE WORKS: Mushroom soups have great potential, but they often disappoint with their lackluster taste and less-than-stellar texture. We knew this pureed soup could be richly textured, neither too thick nor too thin, and showcase the deep, earthy flavor of mushrooms.

We chose to use readily available white mushrooms, which are often underestimated; fresh wild mushrooms were shelved because they can be expensive and difficult to find. To bring out the most flavor from the mushrooms, we had to slice them by hand (processing made for uneven and bruised pieces) and then sweat them in a covered pot with butter and shallots; roasted mushrooms were nixed because the juices released during roasting had browned on the pan and were lost, making for flavorless soup. Chicken broth proved a better addition than water for the liquid base, and dried porcini mushrooms amplified the mushroom flavor. After pureeing the soup, we added cream and a splash of Madeira for body. Our creamy mushroom soup was now texturally light and full of deep, rich flavor.

Creamy Mushroom Soup

SERVES 6 TO 8

The garnish of sautéed mushrooms (recipe follows) adds visual and textural appeal to this creamy soup.

- 6 tablespoons (¾ stick) unsalted butter
- 3 large shallots, minced (about ¾ cup)
- 1 medium garlic clove, minced or pressed through a garlic press (about 1 teaspoon)
- ½ teaspoon freshly grated nutmeg
- 2 pounds white mushrooms, wiped clean and sliced ¼ inch thick
- 4 cups hot water
- 3½ cups low-sodium chicken broth
- ½ ounce dried porcini mushrooms, rinsed well
- 1 cup heavy cream
- ⅓ cup Madeira or dry sherry
- 2 teaspoons juice from 1 lemon
  Table salt and ground black pepper
- 1 recipe Sautéed Wild Mushrooms for garnish (recipe follows; see note)

1. Melt the butter in a large Dutch oven over medium-low heat. Add the shallots and sauté, stirring frequently, until softened, about 4 minutes. Stir in the garlic and nutmeg and cook until fragrant, about 30 seconds. Increase the heat to medium, add the mushrooms, and stir to coat with the butter. Cook, stirring occasionally, until the mushrooms release some liquid, about 7 minutes. Reduce the heat to medium-low, cover the pot, and cook, stirring occasionally, until the mushrooms have released all their liquid, about 20 minutes.

2. Add the water, chicken broth, and porcini mushrooms. Cover, bring to a simmer, then reduce the heat to low and simmer until the mushrooms are fully tender, about 20 minutes.

3. Working in batches, puree the soup in a blender until smooth, filling the blender jar only halfway for each batch. Rinse and dry the pot; return the soup to the pot. Stir in the cream and Madeira and bring to a simmer over low heat. Add the lemon juice and season with salt and pepper to taste. Ladle the soup into bowls, garnish with sautéed wild mushrooms, and serve. (The soup, minus the garnish, can be refrigerated in an airtight container for up to 2 days. Warm over low heat until hot; do not boil.)

Sautéed Wild Mushrooms

MAKES ENOUGH TO GARNISH 6 TO 8 BOWLS OF SOUP

  2 **tablespoons unsalted butter**
  8 **ounces shiitake, chanterelle, oyster, or cremini mushrooms, stems trimmed and discarded, mushrooms wiped clean and sliced thin**
      Table salt and ground black pepper

1. Melt the butter in a medium skillet over low heat. Add the mushrooms and season with salt and pepper to taste. Cover and cook, stirring occasionally, until the mushrooms release their liquid, about 10 minutes for shiitakes and chanterelles, about 5 minutes for oysters, and about 9 minutes for cremini.

2. Uncover and continue to cook, stirring occasionally, until the liquid released by the mushrooms has evaporated and the mushrooms are browned, about 2 minutes for shiitakes, about 3 minutes for chanterelles, and about 2 minutes for oysters and cremini. Serve immediately as garnish for the soup.

BUTTERNUT SQUASH SOUP

WHY THIS RECIPE WORKS: Butternut squash soup strikes a perfect balance between nuttiness and sweetness. But getting that balance right depends on selecting just a few key ingredients so the sweet squash flavor can take center stage.

We found our answer to intense squash flavor in the squash's seeds and fibers. We sautéed shallots and butter with the seeds and fibers, simmered them in water, then used the liquid to steam the unpeeled quartered squash (thereby eliminating the pesky task of peeling raw squash). Once cooled, we scooped the flesh from the skin and pureed the squash with the steaming liquid (strained of seeds and fibers) for a soup with a perfectly smooth texture.

A little dark brown sugar added to the soup also intensified the sweetness of the squash. Finally, we enriched the soup with a splash of heavy cream and a pinch of nutmeg to round out this velvety soup's rich flavors.

Butternut Squash Soup

SERVES 4 TO 6

Lightly toasted pumpkin seeds, drizzles of balsamic vinegar, or sprinklings of paprika make appealing accompaniments to this soup.

  4 **tablespoons (½ stick) unsalted butter**
  1 **large shallot, minced (about ¼ cup)**
  3 **pounds butternut squash (about 1 large squash), cut in half lengthwise, each half cut in half widthwise; seeds and fibers scraped out and reserved**
  6 **cups water**
      Table salt
  ½ **cup heavy cream**
  1 **teaspoon dark brown sugar**
      Pinch grated nutmeg

1. Melt the butter in a large Dutch oven over medium-low heat. Add the shallot and cook, stirring frequently, until translucent, about 3 minutes. Add the seeds and fibers from the squash and cook, stirring occasionally, until the butter turns a saffron color, about 4 minutes.

2. Add the water and 1 teaspoon salt to the pot and bring to a boil over high heat. Reduce the heat to medium-low, place the squash, cut side down, in a steamer basket, and lower the basket into the pot. Cover and steam until the squash is completely tender, about 30 minutes. Take the pot off the heat and use tongs to transfer the squash to a rimmed baking sheet. When cool enough to handle, use a large spoon to scrape the flesh from the skin. Reserve the squash flesh in a bowl and discard the skin.

3. Strain the steaming liquid through a fine-mesh strainer into a second bowl; discard the solids in the strainer. (You should have 2½ to 3 cups liquid.) Rinse and dry the pot.

4. Working in batches and filling the blender jar only halfway for each batch, puree the squash, adding enough reserved steaming liquid to obtain a smooth consistency. Transfer the puree to the clean pot and stir in the remaining steaming liquid, the cream, and brown sugar. Warm the soup over medium-low heat until hot, about 3 minutes. Stir in the nutmeg, season with salt to taste, and serve. (The soup can be refrigerated in an airtight container for up to 2 days. Warm over low heat until hot; do not boil.)

RUSTIC POTATO-LEEK SOUP

WHY THIS RECIPE WORKS: Rustic potato-leek soup often disappoints with soft, mealy potatoes and dingy, over-cooked leeks. We wanted to perfect this soup so both ingredients would be at their best and the dish would retain its textural integrity and bright flavor.

We quickly eliminated potatoes with high or medium starch levels because they broke down too quickly in the chicken broth. Waxy, low-starch red potatoes were perfect—they kept their shape and didn't become water-logged during cooking. To pump up the flavor of the soup, we used a substantial amount of leeks and sautéed both the white and light green parts in butter. Leeks and potatoes require different cooking times, so we staggered the cooking—leeks first, then potatoes, and then we removed the pot from the stove so the potatoes could gently cook through in the hot broth without becoming overcooked and mushy. We also added a bit of flour with the sautéed leeks to give our broth some body. At long last, we had a flavorful, oniony soup, full of perfectly cooked potatoes and sweet, tender leeks.

and bring to a boil. Reduce the heat to medium-low and simmer, covered, until the potatoes are almost tender, 5 to 7 minutes. Remove the pot from the heat and let stand, covered, until the potatoes are tender, 10 to 15 minutes. Discard the bay leaf, season with salt and pepper to taste, and serve. (The soup can be refrigerated in an airtight container for 2 days. Warm over low heat until hot; do not boil.)

Rustic Potato-Leek Soup

SERVES 6

Leeks can vary in size; if your leeks have large white and light green parts, use the smaller amount of leeks given.

- 6 tablespoons (¾ stick) unsalted butter
- 4–5 pounds leeks, white and light green parts only, halved lengthwise, sliced crosswise 1 inch thick and rinsed thoroughly (about 11 cups) (see note)
- 1 tablespoon unbleached all-purpose flour
- 5¼ cups low-sodium chicken broth
- 1¾ pounds red potatoes (about 5 medium), peeled and cut into ¾-inch chunks
- 1 bay leaf
  Table salt and ground black pepper

1. Melt the butter in a large Dutch oven over medium-low heat. Add the leeks, increase the heat to medium, cover, and cook, stirring occasionally, until the leeks are tender but not mushy, 15 to 20 minutes; do not brown them. Add the flour and cook, stirring constantly, until thoroughly combined, about 2 minutes.

2. Increase the heat to high; whisking constantly, gradually add the broth. Add the potatoes and bay leaf, cover,

HEARTY LENTIL SOUP

WHY THIS RECIPE WORKS: A hot bowl of lentil soup provides warm comfort on a cold day and, when properly prepared, tastes great—maybe even better—the next day. We wanted a hearty lentil soup worthy of a second bowl, not the tasteless variety we have so often encountered.

While *lentilles du Puy* are our top choice for lentil soup, almost any lentil (other than red lentils) can be used. To keep the lentils from losing their shape as they cooked, we sweated them with sautéed aromatic vegetables before adding chicken broth to the soup pot. These lentils stayed intact in our final soup, but their flavor was weak. Revisiting this step, we added canned tomatoes and crisp bacon, which gave our lentils a huge flavor boost. And because we cooked the bacon first, we could then use the rendered fat to sauté our vegetables and aromatics, which brought a nice smoky flavor to the soup. Looking for a not too smooth, or too thick, texture we pureed a few cups of the soup and added it back to the pot to warm through. Lentil soup needs plenty of acidity, so we used white wine as part of the broth and finished the soup with balsamic vinegar.

Hearty Lentil Soup

SERVES 4 TO 6

Lentilles du Puy, sometimes called French green lentils, are our first choice for this recipe, but brown, black, or regular green lentils are fine, too. Note that cooking times will vary depending on the type of lentils used. Be sure to rinse and then carefully sort through the lentils to remove any small stones.

- 3   ounces (3 slices) bacon, cut into ¼-inch pieces
- 1   large onion, minced
- 2   medium carrots, peeled and chopped medium
- 3   medium garlic cloves, minced or pressed through a garlic press (about 1 tablespoon)
- 1   (14.5-ounce) can diced tomatoes, drained
- 1   bay leaf
- 1   teaspoon minced fresh thyme leaves
- 1   cup (7 ounces) lentils, rinsed and picked over (see note)
- 1   teaspoon table salt
      Ground black pepper
- ½   cup dry white wine
- 4½ cups low-sodium chicken broth
- 1½ cups water
- 1½ teaspoons balsamic vinegar
- 3   tablespoons minced fresh parsley leaves

1. Fry the bacon in a large Dutch oven over medium-high heat, stirring occasionally, until the fat is rendered and the bacon is crisp, 3 to 4 minutes. Add the onion and carrots; cook, stirring occasionally, until the vegetables begin to soften, about 2 minutes. Add the garlic and cook until fragrant, about 30 seconds. Stir in the tomatoes, bay leaf, and thyme; cook until fragrant, about 30 seconds. Stir in the lentils, salt, and pepper to taste; cover, reduce the heat to medium-low, and cook until the vegetables are softened and the lentils have darkened, 8 to 10 minutes.

2. Uncover, increase the heat to high, add the wine, and bring to a simmer. Add the chicken broth and water; bring to a boil, cover partially, and reduce the heat to low. Simmer until the lentils are tender but still hold their shape, 30 to 35 minutes; discard the bay leaf.

3. Puree 3 cups of the soup in a blender until smooth, then return to the pot. Stir in the vinegar and heat the soup over medium-low heat until hot, about 5 minutes. Stir in 2 tablespoons of the parsley. Ladle the soup into bowls, garnish with the remaining parsley, and serve. (The soup, minus the garnish, can be refrigerated in an airtight container for up to 2 days. Warm over low heat until hot; do not boil.)

BEHIND THE SCENES

MAKING GOOD TV IN THE TEST KITCHEN

The process of creating our show begins several months before filming starts, in all-day script meetings. A group of six editors argues the merits of each recipe developed in the test kitchen for *Cook's Illustrated* magazine during the past year, choosing only the very best recipes to present on television. We're looking for recipes that not only taste great (obviously) but are also visually and editorially interesting. And coming to an agreement isn't always so easy or smooth. Passions run high and any fly on the wall might think some of us are in training to argue a case before the Supreme Court. One year, for a show on drive-in specials, some editors rooted for pairing frothy chocolate milk shakes with hamburgers. Sounds good, but in the end, the process of making the milk shakes—dump ingredients into a blender and press a button—turned out to be as interesting as watching paint dry. The result? Goodbye milk shakes, hello oven-fried onion rings.

Once the recipe lineup is settled, we then spend several months hammering out scripts. Instead of mapping out dialogue, these scripts detail what the camera is going to see—for example: "Julia chops onions and then sautés them in a 12-inch skillet with pinch of salt until golden, about 5 minutes." So why do we write our scripts this way? Cooking is the heart of the show and it's why, we hope, you tune in. And frankly, Chris, Julia, Bridget, and Becky don't need scripts to banter (or argue) with each other. They've had plenty of practice at script meetings.

HAM AND SPLIT PEA SOUP

WHY THIS RECIPE WORKS: Split pea soup tends to show up on the home cook's menu only when the previous meal (usually a holiday celebration) featured a big ham—and the leftovers are begging to be made into soup. We wanted a recipe for an old-fashioned ham and split pea soup that could be made anytime, with a readily available cut of meat that would also provide enough meat for the soup.

Ham stock is essential for this soup, and we found that you can get it with a picnic shoulder, a small, inexpensive cut that adds great flavor and provides plenty of meat for the soup and some leftovers too. As for soaking the peas beforehand, a step called for in many soup recipes, we found it wasn't necessary; they were easy enough to cook in the ham stock. Our vegetables, on the other hand, benefited from a sauté in a separate pan. We started out wanting a one-pot operation, but found that caramelized vegetables gave this straightforward soup a richness and depth of flavor that had been missing from traditional versions—it was well worth the time spent washing an extra pan. Finished with a splash of mildly sweet balsamic vinegar, this rich and meaty split pea soup was now perfectly balanced.

Ham and Split Pea Soup

SERVES 6

Use an entire small 2½-pound smoked picnic portion ham if you can find one. Otherwise, buy a half-picnic ham and remove some meat, which you can roast and use in sandwiches, salads, or omelets. To remove the meat, loosen the large comma-shaped muscles on top of the ham with your fingers, then use a knife to cut the membrane separating the comma-shaped muscles from the rest of the ham.

- 1 (2½-pound) smoked bone-in picnic ham (see note)
- 4 bay leaves
- 3 quarts water
- 1 pound (2½ cups) split peas, rinsed and picked through
- 1 teaspoon dried thyme
- 2 tablespoons extra-virgin olive oil
- 2 medium onions, chopped medium
- 2 medium carrots, peeled and chopped medium
- 2 celery ribs, chopped medium
- 1 tablespoon unsalted butter
- 2 medium garlic cloves, minced or pressed through a garlic press (about 2 teaspoons)
  Pinch sugar
- 3 small red potatoes (about ½ pound), scrubbed and cut into ½-inch chunks
  Ground black pepper
  Minced red onion (optional)
  Balsamic vinegar

1. Place the ham in a large Dutch oven, add the bay leaves and water, cover, and bring to a boil over medium-high heat. Reduce the heat to low and simmer until the meat is tender and pulls away from the bone, 2 to 2½ hours. Remove the ham meat and bone from the pot and set aside.

2. Add the split peas and thyme to the stock. Bring to a boil, reduce the heat, and simmer, uncovered, until the peas are tender but not dissolved, about 45 minutes. While the vegetables are cooking, shred the meat with your fingers or two forks and set aside. Discard the rind and bone.

3. Meanwhile, heat the oil in a large skillet over medium-high heat until shimmering. Add the onions, carrots, and celery and sauté, stirring frequently, until most of the liquid evaporates and the vegetables begin to brown, 5 to 6 minutes. Reduce the heat to medium-low and add the butter, garlic, and sugar. Cook the vegetables, stirring frequently, until deeply browned, 30 to 35 minutes; set aside.

4. Add the sautéed vegetables, potatoes, and shredded ham to the pot with the split peas. Simmer until the potatoes are tender, the peas dissolve, and the soup thickens to the consistency of light cream, about 20 minutes. Season with pepper to taste. Discard the bay leaves and ladle the soup into bowls. Sprinkle with red onion (if using) and serve, passing balsamic vinegar separately. (The soup, minus the garnishes, can be refrigerated in an airtight container for 2 days. Warm over low heat until hot; do not boil.)

MULLIGATAWNY SOUP

WHY THIS RECIPE WORKS: As with many other dishes of Indian origin, mulligatawny soup is mildly spicy and richly flavored, with a number of spices in its lineup. We wanted an elegant, but potent, rendition of this classic soup, not the thin, raw-tasting version found in many restaurants.

Chicken broth proved to be the best base for this pureed vegetable-laden soup; beef broth was too strong and vegetable broth gave us an overly vegetal soup. For the spices, good-quality curry powder is a must, and a little cumin and cayenne pepper made for the perfect spice mix. Garlic, ginger, and coconut were a given—essentials in mulligatawny—but the best way to incorporate them wasn't immediately clear. We ended up adopting a technique common in Indian cooking—we pureed the raw garlic and ginger with water so they could be mixed into the soup for fresh bites of garlic and ginger. The best source for true coconut flavor turned out to be shredded unsweetened coconut.

Finally, to give the finished soup the right amount of body, we made a roux with our aromatics and pureed the soup with a banana, which imparted a rich, sweet flavor to the dish (a potato worked fine, too). A dollop of yogurt and sprinkling of cilantro were the crowning touches on our richly spiced, velvety mulligatawny.

Mulligatawny Soup

SERVES 6 TO 8

Leave the garlic and ginger puree from step 1 in the blender while making the soup; when the finished soup is pureed in the same blender, it will pick up a hit of spicy raw garlic and ginger. For a heartier soup, stir in cooked white rice.

- 4 **medium garlic cloves, 2 peeled and 2 minced or pressed through a garlic press (see note)**
- 1½ **tablespoons minced or grated fresh ginger (see note)**
- ¼ **cup water**
- 3 **tablespoons unsalted butter**
- 2 **medium onions, chopped medium**
- 1 **teaspoon tomato paste**
- ½ **cup shredded unsweetened coconut**
- ¼ **cup unbleached all-purpose flour**
- 1½ **tablespoons curry powder**
- 1 **teaspoon ground cumin**
- ¼ **teaspoon cayenne pepper**
- 7 **cups low-sodium chicken broth**
- 2 **medium carrots, peeled and chopped medium**
- 1 **celery rib, chopped medium**
- 1 **medium very ripe banana (about 5 ounces), peeled, or 1 medium red potato (about 5 ounces), peeled and cut into 1-inch chunks**
  Table salt and ground black pepper
  Plain yogurt
- 2 **tablespoons minced fresh cilantro leaves**

1. Puree the 2 peeled whole garlic cloves, 2 teaspoons of the ginger, and the water in a blender until smooth; leave the mixture in the blender and set aside.

2. Melt the butter in a large Dutch oven over medium heat. Add the onions and tomato paste and cook, stirring frequently, until the onions are softened and beginning to brown, about 3 minutes. Stir in the coconut and cook until fragrant, about 1 minute. Add the minced garlic, the remaining 2½ teaspoons ginger, the flour, curry powder, cumin, and cayenne; stir until evenly combined, about 1 minute. Whisking constantly, gradually add the chicken broth.

3. Add the carrots, celery, and banana to the pot. Increase the heat to medium-high and bring to a boil. Cover, reduce the heat to low, and simmer until the vegetables are tender, about 20 minutes.

4. Working in batches, puree the soup in the blender with the garlic and ginger until smooth, filling the blender jar only halfway for each batch. Wash and dry the pot. Return the pureed soup to the pot and season with salt and pepper to taste. Warm the soup over medium heat until hot, about 1 minute. Ladle the soup into bowls, spoon a dollop of yogurt over each bowl, sprinkle with the cilantro, and serve. (The soup, minus the garnishes, can be refrigerated in an airtight container for up to 3 days. Warm over low heat until hot; do not boil.)

CLASSIC GAZPACHO

WHY THIS RECIPE WORKS: Spain's famous chilled soup, gazpacho, boasts bright flavors, distinct pieces of vegetables, and a bracing tomato broth. But all too often, gazpacho is either grainy with the addition of too much bread (a common thickener) or watery from an abundance of macerated vegetables. We were after a chunky gazpacho that was well seasoned with vibrant tomato flavor.

We had to figure out the best method for preparing the vegetables. Although it was a breeze to use, the blender broke down our vegetables beyond recognition. Next, we tried the food processor, but even this machine pulverized some of our tomatoes. We had better luck processing each vegetable individually, but the resulting soup was closer to a slushie than a good gazpacho. For the best texture, we had to chop the vegetables by hand.

Tomatoes are the star player in this dish, and early on we decided that full, ripe beefsteaks were the best option. As for peppers, we preferred red over green for their sweeter flavor. Onion and garlic are usually too overpowering in gazpacho, so we kept to modest levels. A combination of tomato juice and ice cubes—to help chill the soup—provided the right amount of liquid for our broth. And instead of using bread as a thickener, we saved it to make croutons. Now our gazpacho was nice and chunky, and brightly flavored.

Classic Gazpacho

SERVES 8 TO 10

This recipe makes a large quantity, but it can be easily halved if you prefer. Traditionally, the same vegetables used in the soup are also used as garnish. If that appeals to you, cut additional vegetables while you prepare those called for in the recipe. Other garnish possibilities include Garlic Croutons (recipe follows), chopped pitted black olives, chopped hard-cooked eggs (see page 23), and finely diced avocado.

- 3 medium ripe beefsteak tomatoes (about 1½ pounds), cored and cut into ¼-inch cubes (about 4 cups)
- 2 medium red bell peppers (about 1 pound), stemmed, seeded, and cut into ¼-inch cubes (about 2 cups)
- 2 small cucumbers (about 1 pound), one peeled and the other with skin on, both seeded and cut into ¼-inch cubes (about 2 cups)
- ½ small sweet onion (such as Vidalia, Maui, or Walla Walla) or 2 large shallots, minced (about ½ cup)
- 2 medium garlic cloves, minced or pressed through a garlic press (about 2 teaspoons)
- ⅓ cup sherry vinegar
  Table salt and ground black pepper
- 5 cups tomato juice
- 8 ice cubes
- 1 teaspoon hot pepper sauce (optional)
  Extra-virgin olive oil, for serving

1. Combine the tomatoes, peppers, cucumbers, onion, garlic, vinegar, 2 teaspoons salt, and pepper to taste in a large (at least 4-quart) nonreactive bowl. Let stand until the vegetables just begin to release their juices, about 5 minutes. Stir in the tomato juice, ice cubes, and hot pepper sauce (if using). Cover tightly and refrigerate to blend flavors, at least 4 hours and up to 2 days.

2. Season with salt and pepper to taste and remove and discard any unmelted ice cubes. Serve cold, drizzling each portion with about 1 teaspoon olive oil and topping with the desired garnishes (see note).

Garlic Croutons

MAKES ABOUT 3 CUPS

- 3 tablespoons extra-virgin olive oil
- 3 medium garlic cloves, minced or pressed through a garlic press (about 1 tablespoon)
- ¼ teaspoon table salt
- 6 slices high-quality white sandwich bread, cut into ½-inch cubes (about 3 cups)

1. Adjust an oven rack to the middle position and heat the oven to 350 degrees. Combine the oil, garlic, and salt in a small bowl; let stand 20 minutes, then pour through a fine-mesh strainer into a medium bowl. Discard the garlic. Add the bread cubes to the bowl with the oil and toss to coat.

2. Spread the bread cubes in an even layer on a rimmed baking sheet and bake, stirring occasionally, until golden, about 15 minutes. Cool on the baking sheet to room temperature. (The croutons can be stored in an airtight container or a plastic bag for 1 day.)

NEW ENGLAND CLAM CHOWDER

WHY THIS RECIPE WORKS: Good traditional chowder isn't that hard to make, but it can be daunting for the home cook. The biggest hurdle is a finicky ingredient that most people don't know how to work with—clams. We wanted to come up with a clam chowder that was economical, could be prepared quickly, and provided a simple method for working with the star ingredient.

We tested a variety of clams and ultimately found that medium-size hard-shell clams guaranteed the most clam flavor. Rather than shucking the raw clams (which can be tedious and time-consuming) and adding them to the pot, we steamed the clams to open them, then used the steaming liquid as our broth. The steamed clams had to be pulled from the pot when they had just opened; allowing them to open completely meant they would overcook quickly when returned to the soup to heat through. We found waxy red potatoes to be the best choice for our creamy chowder; high-starch potatoes, like russets, broke down too much. Bacon made a nice substitute for the traditional salt pork and gave our chowder great smoky flavor. As for the creaminess factor, using a modest amount of heavy cream instead of milk meant that we could use less dairy for a rich, creamy chowder that tasted distinctly of clams.

New England Clam Chowder

SERVES 6

Don't skip the step of scrubbing the clams; many clams have bits of sand embedded in their shells that can ruin a pot of chowder. To remove the sand, simply scrub them under cold, running water using a soft brush.

- 7 pounds medium-size hard-shell clams, such as cherrystones, washed and scrubbed clean (see note)
- 5 ounces (about 3 slices) thick-cut bacon, cut into ¼-inch pieces
- 1 large onion, chopped medium
- 2 tablespoons unbleached all-purpose flour
- 1½ pounds red potatoes (about 4 medium), cut into ½-inch chunks
- 1 bay leaf
- 1 teaspoon fresh thyme leaves or ¼ teaspoon dried thyme
- 1 cup heavy cream
- 2 tablespoons minced fresh parsley leaves
  Table salt and ground black pepper

1. Bring 3 cups water to a boil in a large Dutch oven. Add the clams and cover with a tight-fitting lid. Cook for 5 minutes, uncover, and stir with a wooden spoon. Quickly cover the pot and steam until the clams just open, 2 to 4 minutes. (Don't let the clams open completely.) Transfer the clams to a large bowl and cool slightly; reserve the broth. Open the clams with a paring knife, holding the clams over a bowl to catch any juices. With the knife, sever the muscle that attaches the clam to the bottom shell and transfer the meat to a cutting board; discard the shells. Mince the clams and set aside. Pour the clam broth into a large bowl, holding back the last few tablespoons of broth in case of sediment; set the clam broth aside. (You should have about 5 cups. If not, add bottled clam juice or water to make this amount.) Rinse and dry the pot, then return the pot to the burner.

2. Fry the bacon in the pot over medium-low heat until the fat renders and the bacon crisps, 5 to 7 minutes. Add the onion and cook, stirring occasionally, until softened, about 5 minutes. Add the flour and stir until lightly colored, about 1 minute. Gradually whisk in the reserved clam broth. Add the potatoes, bay leaf, and thyme and simmer until the potatoes are tender, about 10 minutes. Add the clams, cream, parsley, and salt and pepper to taste; bring to a simmer. Remove from the heat, discard the bay leaf, and serve.

CHAPTER 2

SALAD DAYS

Leafy Green Salad with Red Wine Vinaigrette 20

Leafy Green Salad with Rich and Creamy Blue Cheese Dressing 21

Spicy Salad with Mustard and Balsamic Vinaigrette 21

Arugula Salad with Figs, Prosciutto, Walnuts, and Parmesan 22

Wilted Spinach Salad with Warm Bacon Dressing 23

Foolproof Hard-Cooked Eggs

Salad with Herbed Baked Goat Cheese and Vinaigrette 24

Almond-Crusted Chicken with Wilted Spinach Salad 24

Pan-Seared Scallops with Wilted Spinach, Watercress, and Orange Salad 26

Cherry Tomato Salad with Feta and Olives 27

Classic Greek Salad 28

Sesame Lemon Cucumber Salad 28

Creamy Coleslaw 29

Creamy Buttermilk Coleslaw 30

Confetti Cabbage Salad with Spicy Peanut Dressing 30

Cool and Creamy Macaroni Salad 31

Pasta Salad with Pesto 32

Antipasto Pasta Salad 33

Rice Salad with Oranges, Olives, and Almonds 34

American Potato Salad with Hard-Cooked Eggs and Sweet Pickles 34

Austrian-Style Potato Salad 35

LEAFY GREEN SALAD WITH RED WINE VINAIGRETTE

WHY THIS RECIPE WORKS: A leafy green salad with red wine vinaigrette is a vital recipe to have in your arsenal. We wanted to develop a recipe for this basic salad—a mix of well-chosen greens tossed with a light vinaigrette that was neither harsh nor oily.

Leafy green salads sound simple, but in reality, the dressing often soaks the greens, resulting in a muddy salad that's too acidic from the vinegar. We went back to the basics and revisited standard vinaigrette proportions. In most cases, 4 parts oil to 1 part vinegar produces the best balance of flavors in a vinaigrette, so that's where we started. Red wine vinegar was the foundation of our vinaigrette; with a sharp but clean flavor, this vinegar is a great choice for dressing salads. Before whisking the vinaigrette ingredients together, we added salt and pepper to the vinegar. This step mutes these seasonings a bit and prevents them from becoming too overpowering. With the right mix of salad greens—we like a combination of mild, delicate greens and peppery greens—this leafy salad makes the perfect complement to any main dish.

Leafy Green Salad with Red Wine Vinaigrette
SERVES 4 TO 6

For the best results, use at least two kinds of greens. A blend of mild, delicate greens, such as Boston and leaf lettuces, and peppery greens, such as arugula and watercress, is ideal. Romaine adds crunch and texture. If you like, add mild fresh herbs, such as chives, tarragon, or basil, in small amounts.

- 2¼ teaspoons red wine vinegar
- ⅛ teaspoon table salt
   Pinch ground black pepper
- 3 tablespoons extra-virgin olive oil
- 8 cups mixed salad greens, washed, dried, and torn into bite-sized pieces (see note)

Combine the vinegar, salt, and pepper in a bowl; add the oil and whisk until combined. Place the greens in a large bowl, drizzle the vinaigrette over the greens, and toss to coat evenly. Serve.

LEAFY GREEN SALAD WITH RICH AND CREAMY BLUE CHEESE DRESSING

WHY THIS RECIPE WORKS: Cool and crunchy salad greens coated with creamy blue cheese dressing are simply irresistible. But getting the right proportion of dressing to greens can be tricky. Order this salad at a restaurant and it's likely you'll receive a plate of dressing-soaked greens. We wanted lettuce lightly napped with a creamy, tangy dressing.

Starting with the dressing, we found that the secret to proper flavor and texture was in using the right creamy components. We determined that three creamy ingredients were essential: mayonnaise to give the dressing body, sour cream to supply tang, and buttermilk to thin out and further reinforce the dressing's bold flavors. A bit of sugar brought some much-needed sweetness and white wine vinegar gave our dressing some zing. As for the main ingredient, we ruled out really pungent blue cheeses as too overpowering; a mild blue cheese works best. For the right chunky consistency, we mixed the crumbled blue cheese with the buttermilk before adding any other ingredients.

Leafy Green Salad with Rich and Creamy Blue Cheese Dressing

SERVES 4 TO 6

Sturdy romaine and curly leaf lettuce hold up well to this thick dressing. In a pinch, whole milk can be used in place of the buttermilk; the dressing will be a bit lighter and milder in flavor, but will still taste good.

- 2½ ounces blue cheese, crumbled (about ½ cup)
- 3 tablespoons buttermilk (see note)
- 3 tablespoons sour cream
- 2 tablespoons mayonnaise
- 2 teaspoons white wine vinegar
- ¼ teaspoon sugar
- ⅛ teaspoon garlic powder
- Table salt and ground black pepper
- 10 cups loosely packed sturdy salad greens, such as romaine or curly leaf lettuce, washed, dried, and torn into bite-sized pieces (see note)

1. Mash the blue cheese and buttermilk in a small bowl with a fork until the mixture resembles cottage cheese with small curds. Stir in the sour cream, mayonnaise, vinegar, sugar, and garlic powder and season with salt and pepper to taste.

2. Place the greens in a large bowl. Pour the dressing over the greens and toss to coat evenly. Serve. (The dressing can be refrigerated in an airtight container for up to 2 weeks.)

SPICY SALAD WITH MUSTARD AND BALSAMIC VINAIGRETTE

WHY THIS RECIPE WORKS: Some salads act as humble introductions to the main course, while other salads demand attention and pack a flavor punch all their own. We had a craving for a bold salad, one using spicy and bitter greens dressed in a pungent, mustardy vinaigrette.

We started by focusing on the greens, and chose peppery greens like arugula and watercress. We envisioned this salad as standing up to rich main dishes, like fettuccine Alfredo or a hearty meat stew, so we used both balsamic vinegar and Dijon mustard as the acidic components. Minced shallot provided another strong flavor and added a bit of texture to our vinaigrette. We mixed the greens and vinaigrette together a little at a time to ensure that all the greens were well covered. Boldly flavored, this spicy salad with mustard and balsamic vinaigrette will wake up any dulled palate.

STAYING GREEN IN THE TEST KITCHEN

It's not unusual for the test kitchen fridge to be packed with salad greens. And although we try to work with the greens the day they arrive, it's not always a possibility. As a result, we've come up with a couple of storage tips for greens. First, remove any rubber band or tie from the greens. Constriction only encourages rotting. Gently wash the greens and spin them dry in a salad spinner. Then depending on the type of greens, store them one of two ways:

For delicate greens, line an empty salad spinner with paper towels. Layer the dried greens in the bowl, covering each layer with additional towels, and refrigerate. Greens stored in this manner should keep for at least two days.

For sturdier greens, loosely roll the leaves in paper towels, then seal in a zipper-lock bag and refrigerate. Greens stored this way should keep for up to one week.

We applied our storage techniques to basil too, especially because recipes often call for just a few leaves. First, we found that it's essential not to wash the basil before storage. In our tests, washing basil before storage decreased its storage life by half. Instead, gently wrap basil in a damp paper towel. It should keep for up to one week.

Spicy Salad with Mustard and Balsamic Vinaigrette

SERVES 8 TO 10

This salad makes a perfect partner to rich main dishes, like lasagna, because its bitter greens and zesty vinaigrette help to cut the richness.

- 6 tablespoons extra-virgin olive oil
- 4 teaspoons balsamic vinegar
- 1 tablespoon Dijon mustard
- 1 teaspoon finely minced shallot
- ¼ teaspoon table salt
- ⅛ teaspoon ground black pepper
- 16 cups spicy greens, such as arugula, watercress, mizuna, and baby mustard greens, washed and dried

Whisk the oil, vinegar, mustard, shallot, salt, and pepper together in a bowl until combined. Place the greens in a large bowl, drizzle the dressing over the greens a little at a time, and toss to coat evenly, adding more vinaigrette if the greens seem dry. Serve.

ARUGULA SALAD

WHY THIS RECIPE WORKS: Unlike everyday iceberg lettuce, spicy arugula is more than just a leafy backdrop for salad garnishes. But arugula's complex, peppery flavor also makes it something of a challenge to pair with other ingredients. We wanted a truly outstanding arugula-based salad with co-starring ingredients that would stand up to these spicy greens.

Salad combinations with harsh, one-dimensional flavor profiles (adding radishes, and lemon-buttermilk dressing to arugula, for example) struck out, with too much abrasive flavor. What we did like were the salads containing fruit and cheese, so we decided to pair our arugula with sweet and salty ingredients. Fried prosciutto strips and shaved Parmesan fit the bill when it came to upping the saltiness of our salad. A spoonful of jam added to the vinaigrette helped to emulsify the dressing and provided a sweet contrast to arugula's peppery bite. For additional sweetness, dried figs worked well and toasted walnuts delivered just the right amount of crunch.

Arugula Salad with Figs, Prosciutto, Walnuts, and Parmesan

SERVES 6

Although frying the prosciutto adds crisp texture to the salad, if you prefer, you can simply cut it into ribbons and use it as a garnish. Honey can be substituted for the jam in either of these salads.

- 4 tablespoons extra-virgin olive oil
- 2 ounces thinly sliced prosciutto, cut into ¼-inch strips
- 3 tablespoons balsamic vinegar
- 1 tablespoon raspberry jam
- ½ cup dried figs, stems removed, fruit chopped into ¼-inch pieces
- 1 small shallot, minced (1 tablespoon)
  Table salt and ground black pepper
- 5 ounces loosely packed baby arugula (about 5 cups), washed and dried
- ½ cup walnuts, toasted and chopped
- 2 ounces Parmesan cheese, shaved into thin strips with a vegetable peeler

1. Heat 1 tablespoon of the oil in a 10-inch nonstick skillet over medium heat; add the prosciutto and fry until crisp, stirring frequently, about 7 minutes. Using a slotted spoon, transfer to a paper towel–lined plate and set aside to cool.

2. Whisk the vinegar and jam together in a medium microwave-safe bowl until combined; stir in the figs. Cover with plastic wrap, cut several steam vents in the plastic, and microwave on high until the figs are plump, 30 seconds to 1 minute. Whisk in the remaining 3 tablespoons oil, the shallot, ¼ teaspoon salt, and ⅛ teaspoon pepper until combined. Cool to room temperature.

3. Toss the arugula with the vinaigrette in a large bowl; season with salt and pepper to taste. Divide the salad among individual plates; top each with a portion of the prosciutto, walnuts, and Parmesan. Serve.

WILTED SPINACH SALAD

WHY THIS RECIPE WORKS: Traditional wilted spinach salad, tossed with warm bacon dressing, makes for an appealing and elegant salad. But too often, this salad is a soggy mess of slimy spinach, bogged down from too much oil and too much heat. We wanted perfectly wilted spinach, a rich, balanced dressing, and crisp pieces of meaty bacon throughout.

Baby spinach was preferred over the mature variety for its tender, sweet qualities. Fried thick-cut bacon provided more textural interest than regular sliced bacon. And using the bacon fat left in the skillet to cook our onion and garlic gave the finished salad a smoky flavor. For the vinaigrette, a generous amount of cider vinegar, enhanced with sugar, cut the richness of the bacon fat. We found that pouring the hot vinaigrette right over the baby spinach provided enough heat to wilt the spinach without saturating it. With wedges of hard-cooked egg for some heartiness, this wilted spinach salad delivers on all fronts.

Wilted Spinach Salad with Warm Bacon Dressing

SERVES 4 TO 6

This salad comes together quickly, so have the ingredients ready before you begin cooking. When adding the vinegar mixture to the skillet, step back from the stovetop—the aroma is quite potent.

- 6 ounces baby spinach (about 6 cups), washed and dried
- 3 tablespoons cider vinegar
- ½ teaspoon sugar
- ¼ teaspoon ground black pepper
  Pinch table salt
- 10 ounces (about 8 slices) thick-cut bacon, cut into ½-inch pieces
- ½ medium red onion, chopped medium
- 1 small garlic clove, minced or pressed through a garlic press (about ½ teaspoon)
- 3 hard-cooked eggs (recipe follows), peeled and quartered

1. Place the spinach in a large bowl. Whisk the vinegar, sugar, pepper, and salt in a small bowl until the sugar dissolves; set aside.

2. Fry the bacon in a medium skillet over medium-high heat, stirring occasionally, until crisp, about 10 minutes. Using a slotted spoon, transfer the bacon to a paper towel–lined plate. Pour off all but 3 tablespoons of the bacon fat left in the pan. Add the onion to the skillet and cook over medium heat, stirring frequently, until softened, about 3 minutes. Stir in the garlic and cook until fragrant, about 15 seconds. Add the vinegar mixture, then remove the skillet from the heat. Working quickly, scrape the bottom of the skillet with a wooden spoon to loosen the browned

bits. Pour the hot dressing over the spinach, add the bacon, and toss gently until the spinach is slightly wilted. Divide the salad among individual plates, arrange the egg quarters over each, and serve.

Foolproof Hard-Cooked Eggs

MAKES 3

You can double or triple this recipe as long as you use a pot large enough to hold the eggs in a single layer, covered by an inch of water.

- 3 large eggs

1. Place the eggs in a medium saucepan, cover with 1 inch of water, and bring to a boil over high heat. Remove the pan from the heat, cover, and let sit for 10 minutes. Meanwhile, fill a medium bowl with 1 quart water and one tray of ice cubes.

2. Transfer the eggs to the ice bath with a slotted spoon and let sit 5 minutes. Peel the eggs.

BAKED GOAT CHEESE SALAD

WHY THIS RECIPE WORKS: Warm goat cheese salad has been a fixture on restaurant menus for years, featuring artisanal cheeses, organic greens, barrel-aged vinegars, and imported oils. But too often what arrives is an unremarkable salad at a price that defies reason. We wanted to bring this restaurant favorite home with creamy cheese rounds infused with the flavor of fresh herbs and surrounded by crisp, golden breading, all cradled in lightly dressed greens.

Ground Melba toasts (those ultra-dry and crispy crackers) made the crispiest crust for the goat cheese. After dipping the cheese rounds in beaten egg and herbs, we coated them with the crumbs, shaped them into attractive disks, and froze them to set the cheese and the crust. With the oven superhot and the cheese very cold, the cheese developed a crispy crust (with no oozing) and kept its shape, and a quick brush of olive oil on the outside of the disks lent flavor to the crumbs without turning them oily. A mix of greens paired well with the tangy flavor of the goat cheese, and a simple, light vinaigrette was all that was needed to finish this elegant salad.

Salad with Herbed Baked Goat Cheese and Vinaigrette

SERVES 6

The baked goat cheese should be served warm. Prepare the salad components while the cheese is in the freezer, then toss the greens and vinaigrette while the cheese cools a bit after baking.

GOAT CHEESE

- 3 ounces white Melba toasts (about 2 cups)
- 1 teaspoon ground black pepper
- 3 large eggs
- 2 tablespoons Dijon mustard
- 1 tablespoon chopped fresh thyme leaves
- 1 tablespoon chopped fresh chives
- 12 ounces goat cheese
  - Extra-virgin olive oil

SALAD

- 6 tablespoons extra-virgin olive oil
- 2 tablespoons red wine vinegar
- 1 tablespoon Dijon mustard
- 1 teaspoon minced shallot
- ¼ teaspoon table salt
  - Ground black pepper
- 14 cups mixed delicate and spicy salad greens, such as arugula, baby spinach, and frisée, washed and dried

1. FOR THE CHEESE: In a food processor, process the Melba toasts to fine, even crumbs, about 1½ minutes; transfer the crumbs to a medium bowl and stir in the pepper. Whisk the eggs and mustard in a second medium bowl until combined. Combine the thyme and chives in a small bowl.

2. Using dental floss or kitchen twine, divide the cheese into 12 equal pieces by slicing the log lengthwise through the middle and each half into six even pieces. Roll each piece of cheese into a ball; roll each ball in the combined fresh herbs to coat lightly. Transfer 6 pieces to the egg mixture and turn each piece to coat; transfer to the Melba crumbs and turn each piece to coat, pressing the crumbs into the cheese. Flatten each ball gently with your fingertips into a disk about 1½ inches wide and 1 inch thick and set on a baking sheet. Repeat with the remaining 6 pieces of cheese. Transfer the baking sheet to the freezer and freeze the disks until firm, about 30 minutes. Adjust an oven rack to the top position and heat the oven to 475 degrees.

3. FOR THE SALAD: Meanwhile, whisk the oil, vinegar, mustard, shallot, and salt in a small bowl until combined; season with pepper to taste. Set aside.

4. Remove the cheese from the freezer and brush the tops and sides evenly with the oil. Bake until the crumbs are golden brown and the cheese is slightly soft, 7 to 9 minutes (or 9 to 12 minutes if the cheese is completely frozen). Using a thin metal spatula, transfer the cheese to a paper towel–lined plate and cool 3 minutes.

5. Place the greens in a large bowl, drizzle the vinaigrette over them, and toss to coat. Divide the greens among individual plates; place two rounds of goat cheese on each salad and serve.

NUT-CRUSTED CHICKEN WITH SALAD GREENS

WHY THIS RECIPE WORKS: When leafy greens are paired with sautéed chicken, a simple salad becomes a satisfying, one-dish meal. We wanted to create an easy recipe for such a dish, and thought incorporating nuts in the coating of the chicken would make for a heartier, more elegant meal.

We started by pounding store-bought chicken breasts to the same thickness to ensure that they would cook evenly. Ground almonds paired with panko (Japanese-style bread crumbs) created a rich-tasting crust that was both light and crisp. After dipping the chicken breasts in eggs and the nut and panko mixture, we let them sit for a few minutes so the coating could set. Much like regular breaded chicken, the breasts had to be pan-fried in a fair amount of oil. Pan-frying can make a mess in a traditional skillet, so we used a nonstick pan. To make a quick salad with bright flavors, we heated orange slices to create a dressing in the skillet, then used the hot dressing to wilt the spinach.

Almond-Crusted Chicken with Wilted Spinach Salad

SERVES 4

Don't process the nuts longer than directed or they will turn pasty and oily.

CHICKEN

- 4 (5 to 6-ounce) boneless, skinless chicken breasts, trimmed
  - Table salt and ground black pepper
- 1 cup sliced almonds

½ cup panko (Japanese-style bread crumbs)

2 large eggs

1 teaspoon Dijon mustard

1¼ teaspoons grated zest from 1 orange

¾ cup plus 2 tablespoons vegetable oil

SALAD

5 ounces baby spinach (about 5 cups)

2 medium oranges, peel and pith removed (see page 167), quartered and sliced ¼ inch thick

1 small shallot, minced (about 1 tablespoon)

1. FOR THE CHICKEN: Adjust an oven rack to the middle position and heat the oven to 200 degrees. Pound each breast between two sheets of plastic wrap to a uniform ½-inch thickness. Pat the chicken dry with paper towels and season with salt and pepper.

2. Process the almonds in a food processor to fine crumbs, about 10 seconds (do not overprocess; see note). Toss the nuts with the panko in a shallow dish. Whisk the eggs, mustard, 1 teaspoon of the orange zest, ½ teaspoon salt, and ¼ teaspoon pepper together in another shallow dish. Working with 1 chicken breast at a time, dip the chicken into the egg mixture, turning to coat well and allowing the excess to drip off, then coat with the nut mixture, pressing gently so that the nuts adhere. Place the breaded chicken in a single layer on a wire rack set over a rimmed baking sheet and let sit for 5 minutes.

3. Heat 6 tablespoons of the oil in a 12-inch nonstick skillet over medium heat until shimmering. Add 2 of the chicken breasts and cook until browned on both sides, 4 to 6 minutes total. Drain the chicken briefly on a paper towel–lined plate, then transfer to a clean wire rack set over a rimmed baking sheet and keep warm in the oven. Discard the oil and wipe out the skillet with paper towels. Repeat with 6 tablespoons more oil and the remaining chicken.

4. FOR THE SALAD: Place the spinach in a large bowl. Discard the oil and wipe out the skillet with paper towels. Heat 1 tablespoon more oil in the skillet over high heat until just smoking. Add the orange slices and cook until lightly browned around the edges, 1½ to 2 minutes. Remove the pan from the heat and add the remaining 1 tablespoon oil, the shallot, remaining ¼ teaspoon zest, ¼ teaspoon salt, and ⅛ teaspoon pepper and allow residual heat to soften the shallot, 30 seconds. Pour the warm dressing with the oranges over the spinach and toss gently. Divide the greens among individual plates. Remove the chicken from the oven and set a cutlet over each portion and serve.

WARM SPINACH SALAD WITH PAN-SEARED SCALLOPS

WHY THIS RECIPE WORKS: Attempts to make perfectly seared, caramelized sea scallops usually result in overcooking these tender mollusks, rendering them rubbery and tough. We wanted a concentrated, nutty, rich-colored crust encasing an interior of sweet, creamy, perfectly cooked scallop meat. And for a complete meal, we wanted to incorporate our scallops into a main course salad that would be both elegant and satisfying.

We tackled the scallops first: To get scallops with a crusty exterior, using the unprocessed variety is a must. We found it was essential to dry the scallops thoroughly before adding them to the pan, to further guard against the scallops steaming rather than searing. Equally important is to avoid crowding the pan. We cooked the scallops in batches, browning each batch on just one side, then returned them all to the skillet at once to cook through on the other side, so that each salad would have hot, not tepid, scallops.

For the salad, we liked baby spinach and watercress for easy prep and moist, tender greens. A bright dressing with sherry vinegar and fresh orange complemented the rich scallops. For a finishing touch, toasted sliced almonds lent our salad nutty flavor and welcome crunch.

Pan-Seared Scallops with Wilted Spinach, Watercress, and Orange Salad

SERVES 4

Sea scallops can vary dramatically in size from 1 to 1½ ounces each. A dinner portion, therefore, can range from four to six scallops per person. To ensure that the scallops cook at the same rate, be sure to buy scallops of similar size. Note that scallops have a small, rough-textured, crescent-shaped muscle that toughens once cooked. It's easy to remove—simply peel it from the side of each scallop before cooking.

SALAD

5 ounces baby spinach (about 5 cups)
4 ounces watercress or arugula (about 4 cups)
¾ cup sliced almonds, toasted

SCALLOPS

1½ pounds large sea scallops (16 to 24 scallops), tendons removed (see note)
Table salt and ground black pepper
¼ cup vegetable oil

DRESSING

3 tablespoons extra-virgin olive oil
½ medium red onion, sliced thin
1 teaspoon minced fresh thyme leaves
2 large oranges, peel and pith removed (see page 167), quartered and sliced ¼ inch thick
2 tablespoons sherry vinegar

1. FOR THE SALAD: Toss the spinach, watercress, and almonds together in a large bowl; set aside.

2. FOR THE SCALLOPS: Place the scallops on a dish towel–lined plate or baking sheet and season with salt and pepper. Lay a single layer of paper towels over the scallops; set aside.

3. Add 2 tablespoons of the vegetable oil to a 12-inch skillet and heat over high heat until just smoking. Meanwhile, press the paper towel flush to the scallops to dry. Add half of the scallops to the skillet, dry side facing down, and cook until evenly golden, 1 to 2 minutes. Using tongs, transfer the scallops, browned side facing up, to a large plate; set aside. Wipe out the skillet using a wad of paper towels. Repeat with the remaining 2 tablespoons oil and the remaining scallops. Once the first side is golden, turn the heat to medium, turn the scallops over with tongs, and return the first batch of scallops to the pan, golden side facing up. Cook until the sides on all the scallops have firmed up and all but the middle third of each scallop is opaque, 30 to 60 seconds longer. Transfer all the scallops to a clean, large plate; set aside.

4. FOR THE DRESSING: Wipe the skillet clean with a wad of paper towels. Add the olive oil, onion, thyme, and ½ teaspoon salt to the skillet and return to medium-high heat; cook until the onion is slightly softened, about 1 minute. Add the oranges and vinegar to the pan and swirl to incorporate. Remove from the heat.

5. TO FINISH THE SALAD: Pour the warm dressing over the salad mixture and gently toss to wilt. Divide the spinach salad among four plates and arrange the scallops on top. Serve immediately.

CHERRY TOMATO SALAD

WHY THIS RECIPE WORKS: Cherry tomatoes are sweet, juicy, and available year-round—and especially tempting during those cold winter months when summer seems eons away. We wanted an easy recipe that would make the most of their sweetness so we could enjoy fresh tomatoes anytime we wanted.

Simply slicing cherry tomatoes in half and sprucing them up with vinaigrette resulted in a waterlogged salad with no flavor at all. To prevent this soggy, watery outcome, we quartered the tomatoes, salted them, and then took them for a spin in a salad spinner to remove as much of the jelly and seeds as possible. Reducing the jelly with red wine vinegar concentrated its flavor, and adding olive oil made for a dressing that brought the tomato flavor to the forefront. The tomatoes and vinaigrette were well flavored, but the salad lacked texture. Cucumber contributed welcome crunch, while chopped olives and crumbled feta added a briny touch that brought the whole dish together.

Cherry Tomato Salad with Feta and Olives

SERVES 4 TO 6

If in-season cherry tomatoes are unavailable, substitute vine-ripened cherry tomatoes or grape tomatoes from the supermarket. Cut grape tomatoes in half along the equator (rather than quartering them). If you don't have a salad spinner, after the salted tomatoes have stood for 30 minutes, wrap the bowl tightly with plastic wrap and gently shake to remove seeds and excess liquid. Strain the liquid and proceed with the recipe as directed. The amount of liquid given off by the tomatoes will depend on their ripeness. If you have less than ½ cup juice after spinning, proceed with the recipe using the entire amount of juice and reduce it to 3 tablespoons as directed (the cooking time will be shorter).

2   pints ripe cherry tomatoes, quartered (about 4 cups)
    (see note)
½   teaspoon sugar
    Table salt
1   medium shallot, minced (about 3 tablespoons)
1   tablespoon red wine vinegar
2   medium garlic cloves, minced or pressed through a
    garlic press (about 2 teaspoons)
½   teaspoon dried oregano
2   tablespoons extra-virgin olive oil
    Ground black pepper

1   small cucumber, peeled, halved lengthwise, seeded, and
    cut into ½-inch pieces
½   cup chopped pitted kalamata olives
4   ounces feta cheese, crumbled (about 1 cup)
3   tablespoons chopped fresh parsley leaves

1. Toss the tomatoes, sugar, and ¼ teaspoon salt in a medium bowl; let stand for 30 minutes. Transfer the tomatoes to a salad spinner and spin until the seeds and excess liquid have been removed, 45 to 60 seconds, stirring to redistribute the tomatoes several times during spinning. Return the tomatoes to the bowl and set aside. Strain the tomato liquid through a fine-mesh strainer into a liquid measuring cup, pressing on the solids to extract as much liquid as possible.

2. Bring ½ cup of the tomato liquid (discard any extra), the shallot, vinegar, garlic, and oregano to a simmer in a small saucepan over medium heat. Simmer until reduced to 3 tablespoons, 6 to 8 minutes. Transfer the mixture to a small bowl and cool to room temperature, about 5 minutes. Whisk in the oil until combined and season with salt and pepper to taste.

3. Add the cucumber, olives, feta, parsley, and dressing to the bowl with the tomatoes; toss gently and serve.

GREEK SALAD

WHY THIS RECIPE WORKS: Most versions of Greek salad consist of iceberg lettuce, chunks of green pepper, and a few pale wedges of tomato, sparsely dotted with cubes of feta and garnished with one forlorn olive of questionable heritage. We wanted a salad with crisp ingredients and bold flavors—married with a lively, herb-infused dressing.

A combination of lemon juice, red wine vinegar, garlic, and olive oil made a rich, zesty vinaigrette and oregano lent it fresh herb flavor. To give our salad a flavorful foundation, we marinated onion and cucumber slices in the vinaigrette. This step also served to mute the sting of raw onion in the salad. We swapped in crisp, flavorful romaine for the iceberg. And along with sliced tomatoes, we added jarred roasted red peppers for a bit of sweetness. A handful of kalamata olives and tangy feta cheese lent the traditional touches, and torn mint and parsley leaves gave our salad a fresh finish.

Classic Greek Salad

SERVES 6 TO 8

Marinating the onion and cucumber in the vinaigrette tones down the onion's harshness and flavors the cucumber. For efficiency, prepare the other salad ingredients while the onion and cucumber marinate.

VINAIGRETTE

- 6 tablespoons extra-virgin olive oil
- 3 tablespoons red wine vinegar
- 2 teaspoons minced fresh oregano leaves
- 1½ teaspoons juice from 1 lemon
- 1 medium garlic clove, minced or pressed through a garlic press (about 1 teaspoon)
- ½ teaspoon table salt
- ⅛ teaspoon ground black pepper

SALAD

- ½ medium red onion, sliced thin (about ¾ cup)
- 1 medium cucumber, peeled, halved lengthwise, seeded, and sliced ⅛ inch thick
- 2 romaine hearts, washed, dried, and torn into 1½-inch pieces (about 8 cups)
- 2 medium, firm, ripe tomatoes (6 ounces each), cored, seeded, and each tomato cut into 12 wedges
- 6 ounces jarred roasted red bell peppers, cut into 2 by ½-inch strips (about 1 cup)
- ¼ cup loosely packed fresh parsley leaves, torn
- ¼ cup loosely packed fresh mint leaves, torn
- 20 large pitted kalamata olives, quartered
- 5 ounces feta cheese, crumbled (about 1¼ cups)

1. Whisk the vinaigrette ingredients in a large bowl until combined. Add the onion and cucumber and toss; let stand to blend the flavors, about 20 minutes.

2. Add the romaine, tomatoes, peppers, parsley, and mint to the bowl with the onions and cucumbers; toss to coat with the vinaigrette.

3. Transfer the salad to a serving bowl or platter; sprinkle the olives and feta over the salad and serve.

CUCUMBER SALAD

WHY THIS RECIPE WORKS: More often than not, by the time you eat a cucumber salad, the cucumbers have gone soft and watery, having lost their crunchy texture and released enough liquid to dilute the dressing enough to turn it flavorless. This phenomenon made the primary goal of our cucumber salad easy to identify: Maximize the crunch.

Because water makes cucumbers lose their texture, we had to salt and weight the seeded and sliced cucumbers to draw off excess moisture. For extra insurance, we also rinsed them and patted them dry. Then we tossed the cucumbers with a rice vinegar, lemon, and sesame oil vinaigrette, a flavorful combination that stood up to the superior crunch of our cucumbers. Toasted sesame seeds added even more textural interest.

Sesame Lemon Cucumber Salad

SERVES 4

Mild rice vinegar works well in this Asian-inspired dressing.

- 3 medium cucumbers (about 2 pounds), peeled, halved lengthwise, seeded, and sliced ¼ inch thick
- 1 tablespoon table salt
- ¼ cup rice vinegar (see note)
- 2 tablespoons toasted sesame oil
- 1 tablespoon juice from 1 lemon
- 1 tablespoon sesame seeds, toasted
- 2 teaspoons sugar
- ⅛ teaspoon red pepper flakes

1. Toss the cucumbers with the salt in a colander set over a large bowl. Weight the cucumbers with a gallon-sized plastic bag filled with water; drain for 1 to 3 hours. Rinse and pat dry.

2. Whisk the remaining ingredients together in a medium bowl. Add the cucumbers; toss to coat. Serve chilled or at room temperature.

CREAMY COLESLAW

WHY THIS RECIPE WORKS: No other food embodies an outdoor grillfest quite the same as coleslaw. This summery salad offers a nice crunch and creaminess that contrasts well with sweet and savory barbecued meats and vegetables. But, despite its simplicity, simple coleslaw can be tough for home cooks to get just right. Usually, the coleslaw ends up sitting in a pool of water, with limp cabbage floating around. We wanted a recipe for a crisp salad and a creamy dressing that wouldn't be waterlogged.

To prevent the salad from getting watery, we salted the cabbage until it wilted, then rinsed and dried it. Removing the excess water helped to keep our dressing thick and creamy, and ensured that the cabbage stayed crunchy in the slaw. For the dressing, we used a combination of mayonnaise and low-acidity rice vinegar; these made a creamy dressing that was flavorful but not too harsh. All our coleslaw needed now were a few grinds of black pepper and some shredded carrot for color and further crunch and a little sweetness.

Creamy Coleslaw

SERVES 4

If you like caraway or celery seeds, add ¼ teaspoon of either with the mayonnaise and vinegar. If you like a tangier slaw, replace some or all of the mayonnaise with an equal amount of sour cream. To serve the coleslaw immediately, rinse the salted cabbage and carrot in a large bowl of ice water, drain them in a colander, pick out any ice cubes, then pat the vegetables dry before dressing.

- 1 **pound red or green cabbage (about ½ medium head), shredded (about 6 cups; see the photos)**
- 1 **large carrot, peeled and shredded**
- 1 **teaspoon table salt**
- ½ **small onion, minced**
- ½ **cup mayonnaise**
- 2 **tablespoons rice vinegar**
  Ground black pepper

1. Toss the cabbage and carrot with the salt in a colander set over a medium bowl. Let stand until the cabbage wilts, at least 1 hour or up to 4 hours. Rinse the cabbage and carrot under cold running water (or in a large bowl of ice water if serving immediately). Press, but do not squeeze, to drain; pat dry with paper towels.

HOW TO SHRED CABBAGE

1. Cut the cabbage into quarters, then trim and discard the hard core.

2. Separate the cabbage into small stacks of leaves that flatten when pressed.

3. Use a chef's knife to cut each stack of cabbage leaves into thin shreds.

2. Combine the cabbage, carrot, onion, mayonnaise, and vinegar in a medium bowl; toss to coat and season with pepper to taste. Serve chilled or at room temperature. (The coleslaw can be refrigerated for up to 2 days.)

BUTTERMILK COLESLAW

WHY THIS RECIPE WORKS: Order barbecue down South, and you won't just get coleslaw on the side, you'll get buttermilk coleslaw. Unlike all-mayonnaise coleslaw, buttermilk coleslaw is coated in a light, creamy, and refreshingly tart dressing. We wanted a recipe that showcased the best attributes of this side salad: a pickle-crisp texture and a tangy dressing.

1. Toss the cabbage with 1 teaspoon salt in a colander set over a medium bowl. Let stand until the cabbage wilts, at least 1 hour or up to 4 hours. Rinse the cabbage under cold running water (or in a large bowl of ice water if serving immediately). Press, but do not squeeze, to drain; pat dry with paper towels. Transfer the cabbage to a large bowl; add the carrot.

2. Combine the remaining ingredients with ¼ teaspoon salt in a small bowl. Pour the buttermilk dressing over the cabbage and carrot and toss to coat. Serve chilled or at room temperature. (The coleslaw can be refrigerated for up to 2 days.)

To prevent watery coleslaw, we salted, rinsed, and dried our shredded cabbage. This also gave us the texture we wanted—as the salted cabbage sat, moisture was pulled out of it, wilting it to the right crispy texture. For a tangy dressing that clung to the cabbage and didn't pool at the bottom of the bowl, we supplemented the buttermilk with mayonnaise and sour cream. For finishing touches, we added shredded carrot, which contributed both color and sweetness. The mild flavor of shallot was a welcome addition, and sugar, mustard, and cider vinegar amped up the slaw's tanginess.

Creamy Buttermilk Coleslaw

SERVES 4

To serve the coleslaw immediately, rinse the salted cabbage in a large bowl of ice water, drain it in a colander, pick out any ice cubes, then pat the cabbage dry before dressing.

- 1 **pound red or green cabbage (about ½ medium head), shredded (about 6 cups; see page 29)**
  Table salt
- 1 **large carrot, peeled and shredded**
- ½ **cup buttermilk**
- 2 **tablespoons mayonnaise**
- 2 **tablespoons sour cream**
- 1 **small shallot, minced (about 1 tablespoon)**
- 2 **tablespoons minced fresh parsley leaves**
- ½ **teaspoon cider vinegar**
- ¼ **teaspoon Dijon mustard**
- ½ **teaspoon sugar**
- ⅛ **teaspoon ground black pepper**

CABBAGE SALAD

WHY THIS RECIPE WORKS: Cabbage makes a great salad—not just as coleslaw but as a crunchy, flavorful, dress-up kind of salad. We aimed to develop an Asian-inspired cabbage salad that incorporated spicy, sweet flavors for a salad side dish that was a refreshing change from the same old slaw.

Salting the cabbage and setting it over a colander helped to extract excess liquid, which otherwise would dilute the potent flavors of the dressing. Shredded carrot gave the salad some sweetness, and radishes brought a peppery crunch. For the dressing, we started with smooth peanut butter for its rich flavor and velvety texture. Rice vinegar and soy sauce provided bright, tangy notes. White sugar would have contributed too much sweetness, but a small amount of honey was just right. Last touches to the dressing came in the form of a spicy jalapeño chile and fresh ginger. Processed to a smooth consistency, our spicy peanut dressing provided the perfect lush coating to the crisp vegetables.

Confetti Cabbage Salad with Spicy Peanut Dressing

SERVES 6

Serve this Asian-inspired cabbage salad with simple pork or chicken dishes. To serve the salad immediately, rinse the salted cabbage and carrot in a large bowl of ice water, drain them in a colander, pick out any ice cubes, then pat the vegetables dry before dressing.

- 1 **pound red or green cabbage (about ½ medium head), shredded (about 6 cups; see page 29)**
- 1 **large carrot, peeled and shredded**
  Table salt

2 tablespoons smooth peanut butter

2 tablespoons peanut oil

2 tablespoons rice vinegar

1 tablespoon soy sauce

1 teaspoon honey

2 medium garlic cloves, minced or pressed through a garlic press (about 2 teaspoons)

1½ tablespoons minced or grated fresh ginger

½ jalapeño chile, seeds and ribs removed

4 medium radishes, halved lengthwise and sliced thin

4 scallions, sliced thin

1. Toss the cabbage and carrot with 1 teaspoon salt in a colander set over a medium bowl. Let stand until the cabbage wilts, at least 1 hour or up to 4 hours. Rinse the cabbage and carrot under cold running water (or in a large bowl of ice water if serving immediately). Press, but do not squeeze, to drain; pat dry with paper towels.

2. Process the peanut butter, oil, vinegar, soy sauce, honey, garlic, ginger, and jalapeño in a food processor until smooth. Combine the cabbage, carrot, radishes, scallions, and dressing in a medium bowl; toss to coat. Season with salt to taste. Cover and refrigerate; serve chilled. (The salad can be refrigerated for up to 2 days.)

MACARONI SALAD

WHY THIS RECIPE WORKS: Macaroni salad seems simple enough—toss elbow macaroni and a few seasonings with a mayo-based dressing. So why does this picnic salad often fall short, with mushy pasta and a bland, ho-hum dressing? We set out to make a picnic-worthy macaroni salad with tender pasta and a creamy, well-seasoned dressing.

First we had to get the pasta texture just right. To do this, we didn't drain the macaroni as thoroughly as we could have; the excess water is absorbed by the pasta as it sits and this prevents the finished salad from drying out. Also, cooking the macaroni to a point where it still has some bite left means the pasta won't get too soft when mixed with the mayonnaise. For the most flavor, we seasoned the pasta first—before adding the mayonnaise—so that the seasonings could penetrate and flavor the macaroni. Garlic powder added flavor to the salad (fresh garlic was too harsh), and lemon juice and Dijon mustard enlivened the creamy dressing.

Cool and Creamy Macaroni Salad

SERVES 8 TO 10

Don't drain the macaroni too well before adding the other ingredients—a little extra moisture will keep the salad from drying out. If you've made the salad ahead of time, simply stir in a little warm water to loosen the texture before serving.

Table salt

1 pound elbow macaroni

½ small red onion, minced

1 celery rib, chopped fine

¼ cup minced fresh parsley leaves

2 tablespoons juice from 1 lemon

1 tablespoon Dijon mustard

⅛ teaspoon garlic powder

Pinch cayenne pepper

1½ cups mayonnaise

Ground black pepper

1. Bring 4 quarts water to a boil in a large pot. Stir 1 tablespoon salt and the pasta into the boiling water and cook, stirring often, until nearly tender, about 5 minutes. Drain the pasta and rinse with cold water until cool, then drain briefly so that the macaroni remains moist. Transfer to a large bowl.

2. Stir in the onion, celery, parsley, lemon juice, mustard, garlic powder, and cayenne and let sit until the flavors are absorbed, about 2 minutes. Add the mayonnaise and let sit until the salad is no longer watery, 5 to 10 minutes. Season with salt and pepper to taste and serve. (The salad can be refrigerated for up to 2 days.)

PASTA SALAD WITH PESTO

WHY THIS RECIPE WORKS: Pasta salad with pesto should be light and refreshing, not dry and dull. We decided to perfect pesto pasta salad—and keep it fresh, green, garlicky, and full of herbal flavor.

Using a pasta shape with a textured surface, like farfalle, guaranteed that the pesto wouldn't slide off. To ensure that the pesto coated the pasta, we didn't rinse the pasta after cooking. Instead, we spread the pasta to cool in a single layer on a baking sheet; a splash of oil helped prevent the pasta from sticking. For the pesto, we blanched the garlic to tame its harsh bite. Lots of basil made for vibrant herb flavor, and to keep the green color from fading, we added mild-tasting baby spinach, which lent the salad a vivid green color but didn't overpower the basil. For a creamy, not greasy, pesto, we enriched it with mayonnaise. Lemon juice brightened the pesto's flavor, and extra pine nuts, folded into the salad, provided an extra hit of nutty flavor and a pleasant crunchy texture.

Pasta Salad with Pesto

SERVES 8 TO 10

This salad is best served the day it is made; if it's been refrigerated, bring it to room temperature before serving. The pesto can be made a day ahead—just cook the garlic in a small saucepan of boiling water for 1 minute.

2 medium garlic cloves, unpeeled
 Table salt
1 pound farfalle (bow-tie pasta)
¼ cup plus 1 tablespoon extra-virgin olive oil
3 cups packed fresh basil leaves (about 4 ounces)
1 cup packed baby spinach (about 1 ounce)
¾ cup pine nuts (3¾ ounces), toasted
2 tablespoons juice from 1 lemon
½ teaspoon ground black pepper
1½ ounces Parmesan cheese, finely grated (about ¾ cup), plus extra for serving
6 tablespoons mayonnaise
1 pint cherry tomatoes, quartered, or grape tomatoes, halved (optional)

1. Bring 4 quarts water to a boil in a large pot. Add the garlic to the boiling water and let cook 1 minute. Remove the garlic with a slotted spoon and rinse under cold water; set aside to cool. Stir 1 tablespoon salt and the pasta into the boiling water and cook, stirring often, until the pasta is just past al dente. Reserve ¼ cup of the pasta cooking water, drain the pasta, toss with 1 tablespoon of the oil, spread in a single layer on a rimmed baking sheet, and cool to room temperature, about 30 minutes.

2. Peel and mince the garlic or press it through a garlic press. Process the garlic, basil, spinach, ¼ cup of the nuts, lemon juice, pepper, remaining ¼ cup oil, and 1 teaspoon salt in a food processor until smooth, scraping down the sides of the workbowl as necessary. Add the Parmesan and mayonnaise and process until thoroughly combined. Transfer the mixture to a large serving bowl. Cover and refrigerate until ready to assemble the salad.

3. Toss the pasta with the pesto, adding the reserved pasta water, 1 tablespoon at a time, until the pesto evenly coats the pasta. Fold in the remaining ½ cup nuts and the tomatoes (if using). Serve, passing extra Parmesan separately.

ANTIPASTO PASTA SALAD

WHY THIS RECIPE WORKS: We love the traditional antipasto platter served at Italian restaurants, chock-full of cured meats, cheese, and pickled vegetables. It's a full-flavored and satisfying dish—and something that we thought would translate well to a hearty pasta salad.

We quickly decided that short, curly pasta was the best shape to use, as its curves held on to the salad's other components, making for a more cohesive dish. Quickly rendering the meats in the microwave helped to keep this

salad from becoming greasy. We used an increased ratio of vinegar to oil in the dressing—the sharp, acidic flavor cut the richness of the meats and cheese for a brighter-tasting salad. For well-seasoned pasta, we tossed the hot pasta with the dressing—hot pasta absorbs dressing better than cold pasta. Slicing the meat into thick strips meant that its hearty flavor wasn't lost among the other ingredients. And grating the cheese, rather than cubing it, made for evenly distributed sharp flavor throughout the salad.

Antipasto Pasta Salad

SERVES 6 TO 8

We also liked the addition of 1 cup chopped pitted kalamata olives or 1 cup jarred artichokes, drained and quartered, to this salad.

- 8 **ounces sliced pepperoni, cut into ¼-inch strips**
- 8 **ounces thick-sliced sopresatta or salami, halved and cut into ¼-inch strips**
- 10 **tablespoons red wine vinegar**
- 6 **tablespoons extra-virgin olive oil**
- 3 **tablespoons mayonnaise**
- 1 **(12-ounce) jar pepperoncini, drained (2 tablespoons liquid reserved), stemmed, and chopped coarse**
- 4 **garlic cloves, minced or pressed through a garlic press (about 4 teaspoons)**
- ¼ **teaspoon red pepper flakes**
  Table salt and ground black pepper
- 1 **pound short, curly pasta, such as fusilli or campanelle**
- 1 **pound white mushrooms, wiped clean and quartered**
- 4 **ounces aged provolone cheese, grated (about 1 cup)**
- 1 **(12-ounce) jar roasted red peppers, drained, patted dry, and chopped coarse**
- 1 **cup minced fresh basil leaves**

1. Bring 4 quarts water to a boil in a large pot. Place the pepperoni on a large paper towel–lined plate. Cover with another paper towel and place the sopresatta on top. Cover with another paper towel and microwave on high power for 1 minute. Discard the paper towels and set the pepperoni and sopresatta aside.

2. Whisk 5 tablespoons of the vinegar, the oil, mayonnaise, pepperoncini liquid, garlic, pepper flakes, ½ teaspoon salt, and ½ teaspoon pepper together in a medium bowl.

3. Stir 1 tablespoon salt and the pasta into the boiling water and cook, stirring often, until the pasta is just past al dente. Drain the pasta and return it to the pot. Pour ½ cup of the dressing and the remaining 5 tablespoons vinegar over the pasta and toss to combine; season with

salt and pepper to taste. Spread the pasta in a single layer on a rimmed baking sheet and cool to room temperature, about 30 minutes.

4. Meanwhile, bring the remaining dressing to a simmer in a large skillet over medium-high heat. Add the mushrooms and cook until lightly browned, about 8 minutes. Transfer to a large bowl and cool to room temperature.

5. Add the meat, provolone, peppers, basil, and pasta to the mushrooms and toss to combine. Season with salt and pepper to taste and serve.

RICE SALAD

WHY THIS RECIPE WORKS: Rice makes a light, refreshing salad when dressed properly and studded with vegetables—and it makes a nice change from pasta salad. But unlike pasta, rice can't stand up to assertive flavors or be bogged down by a heavy vinaigrette. To get rice salad just right, we would have to include a few bright, tangy ingredients and use a light hand when making the dressing.

To start out with as much flavor as possible, we toasted the rice to intensify its flavor and then boiled it in a large amount of water, as we would pasta. This method kept the rice tender when cool. To dry the rice, we spread it out on a large baking sheet—this guaranteed that the rice didn't clump or become waterlogged. As for the vinaigrette, restraint was key. We used small amounts of oil, vinegar, and seasonings to complement, but not overshadow, the grains of rice. Orange segments, slivered almonds, and chopped olives gave the salad character and textural interest. And a brief rest to blend the flavors yielded a rice salad that was bright and balanced.

Rice Salad with Oranges, Olives, and Almonds

SERVES 6 TO 8

Taste the rice as it nears the end of its cooking time; it should be cooked through and firm, but not crunchy. Be careful not to overcook the rice or the grains will be blown out.

- 1½ cups long-grain or basmati rice
    Table salt
- 2 tablespoons extra-virgin olive oil
- ¼ teaspoon grated zest plus 1 tablespoon juice from 1 orange
- 2 teaspoons sherry vinegar
- 1 small garlic clove, minced or pressed through a garlic press (about ½ teaspoon)
- ½ teaspoon ground black pepper
- 2 medium oranges, peel and pith removed (see page 167), cut into segments
- ⅓ cup chopped pitted green olives
- ⅓ cup slivered almonds, toasted
- 2 tablespoons fresh oregano leaves, minced

1. Bring 4 quarts water to a boil in a large pot. Heat a medium skillet over medium heat until hot, about 3 minutes; add the rice and toast, stirring frequently, until faintly fragrant and some grains turn opaque, about 5 minutes.

2. Stir 1½ teaspoons salt and the rice into the boiling water. Cook, uncovered, until the rice is tender but not soft, 8 to 10 minutes for long-grain rice or about

15 minutes for basmati (see note). Line a rimmed baking sheet with foil or parchment paper. Drain the rice in a colander and spread on the prepared baking sheet. Cool while preparing the salad ingredients.

3. Whisk the oil, orange zest and juice, vinegar, garlic, 1 teaspoon salt, and pepper together in a small bowl. Combine the rice, oranges, olives, almonds, and oregano in a large bowl; drizzle the dressing over the salad and toss to combine. Let stand 20 minutes to blend the flavors, and serve.

AMERICAN POTATO SALAD

WHY THIS RECIPE WORKS: Few salads make a splash at potlucks or picnics the way potato salad does—this classic, all-American side always seems to disappear first. We wanted a recipe for a traditional, creamy (read: mayonnaise-based) potato salad that looked good—no mushy, sloppy spuds—and tasted even better.

We began by choosing red potatoes. The skin adds color to a typically monochromatic salad. We boiled them whole for best flavor and then used a serrated knife to cut the potatoes into fork-friendly chunks—the serrated edge helps prevent the skins from tearing for a nicer presentation. While the potatoes were still warm, we drizzled them with vinegar and added a sprinkle of salt and pepper; this preseasoning gave the finished salad more flavor. When the potatoes were cool, we folded in the final traditional touches—mayonnaise, pickles, and red onion—for a perfect potluck potato salad, with a creamy dressing and firm bites of potato.

American Potato Salad with Hard-Cooked Eggs and Sweet Pickles

SERVES 4 TO 6

Use sweet pickles, not relish, for the best results. For potatoes that cook through at the same rate, buy potatoes that are roughly the same size.

- 2 pounds red potatoes (about 6 medium), scrubbed (see note)
- ¼ cup red wine vinegar
    Table salt and ground black pepper
- ½ cup mayonnaise
- ¼ cup sweet pickles, chopped fine (see note)
- 3 hard-cooked eggs (see page 23), peeled and cut into ½-inch pieces

1 celery rib, chopped fine
2 tablespoons minced red onion
2 tablespoons minced fresh parsley leaves
2 teaspoons Dijon mustard

1. Place the potatoes in a large saucepan, cover with 1 inch of water, and bring to a boil over medium-high heat. Reduce the heat to medium and simmer, stirring occasionally, until the potatoes are tender (a paring knife can be slipped in and out of the potatoes with little resistance), 25 to 30 minutes.

2. Drain the potatoes and cool slightly; peel if desired. Cut the potatoes into ¾-inch pieces, using a serrated knife, while still warm, rinsing the knife occasionally in warm water to remove starch.

3. Combine the potatoes, vinegar, ½ teaspoon salt, and ¼ teaspoon pepper in a large bowl and toss gently. Cover and refrigerate until cool, about 20 minutes.

4. Meanwhile, combine the remaining ingredients and salt and pepper to taste. Add the potatoes, stir gently to combine, and serve. (The salad can be refrigerated for up to 1 day.)

AUSTRIAN POTATO SALAD

WHY THIS RECIPE WORKS: Austrian-style potato salad, seasoned with vinegar and mustard for a tart-and-tangy flavor, can be a welcome change of pace from traditional creamy potato salad. The ingredients might be different, but the goals are the same: keeping the salad saucy and the potatoes tender but not so tender they fall apart.

This style of potato salad calls on the starch from the potatoes along with an unexpected ingredient, chicken broth, to create the lush, flavor-packed dressing. After cooking the sliced potatoes in broth, which we cut with

an equal amount of water, we reduced the cooking liquid and mixed it with vinegar, mustard, chives, and cornichons for best flavor. To give the dressing more body, and impart a rustic, country-style texture, we mashed in a small amount of our cooked potatoes. After mixing the rest of the sliced potatoes (which retained their shape but were soft and tender) with the thick vinaigrette, we had a luxurious, rich, and very different kind of potato salad.

Austrian-Style Potato Salad

SERVES 4 TO 6

If you can't find cornichons, chopped kosher dill pickles can be used in their place. To maintain its consistency, don't refrigerate the salad; it should be served within a few hours of preparation.

2 pounds Yukon Gold potatoes (about 4 medium), peeled, quartered, and sliced ½ inch thick
1 cup low-sodium chicken broth
2 tablespoons white wine vinegar
1 tablespoon sugar
   Table salt
¼ cup vegetable oil
1 small red onion, minced
6 cornichons, minced (about 2 tablespoons) (see note)
2 tablespoons minced fresh chives
1 tablespoon Dijon mustard
   Ground black pepper

1. Bring 1 cup water, the potatoes, broth, 1 tablespoon of the vinegar, the sugar, and 1 teaspoon salt to a boil in a 12-inch skillet over high heat. Reduce the heat to medium-low, cover, and cook until the potatoes are tender (a paring knife can be slipped in and out of the potatoes with little resistance), 15 to 17 minutes. Remove the cover, increase the heat to high, and cook until the liquid has reduced, about 2 minutes.

2. Drain the potatoes in a colander set over a large bowl, reserving the cooking liquid. Set the potatoes aside. Pour off all but ½ cup cooking liquid (if ½ cup liquid does not remain, add water to make this amount). Whisk the cooking liquid, the remaining 1 tablespoon vinegar, the oil, onion, cornichons, chives, and mustard together in a large bowl.

3. Add ½ cup of the cooked potatoes to the bowl with the cooking liquid mixture and mash with a potato masher until a thick vinaigrette forms (the mixture will be slightly chunky). Add the remaining potatoes, stirring gently to combine. Season with salt and pepper to taste. Serve warm or at room temperature.

CHAPTER 3

EASY SKILLET SUPPERS

Skillet Baked Ziti 38

Skillet Chicken, Broccoli, and Ziti 39

Skillet Lasagna 40

Skillet Chicken Pot Pie with Biscuit Topping 41

Skillet Tamale Pie 42

Skillet Beef Stroganoff 43

Skillet-Roasted Chicken Breasts with Potatoes 44

Skillet Chicken and Rice with Peas and Scallions 45

Skillet Chicken and Rice with Broccoli and Cheddar 46

Skillet Curried Chicken and Rice 46

Skillet Jambalaya 47

SKILLET BAKED ZITI

WHY THIS RECIPE WORKS: Baked ziti, a hearty combination of pasta, tomato sauce, and gooey cheese, can be time-consuming and fussy, between making the sauce, boiling the pasta, and then assembling and baking the dish. We were looking for a method that would give us the same delicious results but in less time and without watching over, or dirtying, a multitude of pots.

Instead of preparing the components of the dish separately, we found we could get all our cooking done in a skillet—including the pasta. How did we do it? We thinned the sauce with water so that the pasta cooked through in the sauce without drying out. (And the thin sauce reduced to a nicely thick consistency.) To start building the sauce, we sautéed lots of garlic with red pepper flakes, then added crushed tomatoes, water, and the ziti. When the pasta was almost tender (it would finish cooking in the oven), we added some heavy cream, for richness and body, and shredded mozzarella cheese. A little grated Parmesan boosted the cheesy flavor, and minced fresh basil and pepper were all the seasonings we needed to finish our skillet version of this family favorite.

Skillet Baked Ziti

SERVES 4

To complete this recipe in 30 minutes, preheat your oven before assembling the ingredients. If your skillet is not ovensafe, transfer the pasta mixture to a shallow 2-quart casserole dish before sprinkling with the cheese and baking. Packaged preshredded mozzarella is a real time-saver here. Penne can be used in place of the ziti.

- 1 tablespoon olive oil
- 6 medium garlic cloves, minced or pressed through a garlic press (about 2 tablespoons)
- ¼ teaspoon red pepper flakes
  Table salt
- 1 (28-ounce) can crushed tomatoes
- 3 cups water
- 12 ounces ziti (3¾ cups) (see note)
- ½ cup heavy cream
- 1 ounce Parmesan cheese, grated (about ½ cup)
- ¼ cup minced fresh basil leaves
  Ground black pepper
- 4 ounces whole milk mozzarella cheese, shredded (about 1 cup) (see note)

1. Adjust an oven rack to the middle position and heat the oven to 475 degrees.

2. Heat the oil in a 12-inch ovensafe nonstick skillet over medium-high heat until hot. Add the garlic, red pepper flakes, and ½ teaspoon salt and sauté until fragrant, about 1 minute. Add the crushed tomatoes, water, ziti, and ½ teaspoon salt. Cover and cook, stirring often and adjusting the heat as needed to maintain a vigorous simmer, until the ziti is almost tender, 15 to 18 minutes.

3. Stir in the cream, Parmesan, and basil. Season with salt and pepper to taste. Sprinkle the mozzarella evenly over the ziti. Transfer the skillet to the oven and bake until the cheese has melted and browned, about 10 minutes. Using potholders (the skillet handle will be hot), remove the skillet from the oven. Serve.

SKILLET CHICKEN, BROCCOLI, AND ZITI

WHY THIS RECIPE WORKS: This classic restaurant dish rarely lives up to its promise. The flavors are mediocre, the texture suffers from overcooking (bone-dry chicken), or the sauce is oily and contains an overpowering amount of garlic. Our challenge would lie in getting the flavors and textures just right: well-seasoned, tender chunks of chicken, crisp broccoli, and pasta in a light, fresh-flavored sauce. At the same time, we wanted to streamline its preparation for an easy weeknight dinner.

To start, we turned to our skillet to make short work of this dish. First we browned pieces of skinless, boneless chicken breasts in the skillet, then we removed the chicken to build our sauce. (Briefly cooking the chicken, then reheating it later in the sauce would keep it from overcooking.) We started with a base of sautéed onion, a modest amount of garlic, oregano, and red pepper flakes. And to keep all our work limited to the skillet, we cooked the pasta right in the sauce. The broccoli went in next, along with chopped sun-dried tomatoes for depth of flavor. We then covered the skillet and simmered everything just until the broccoli turned bright green. At this point, we returned the chicken to the pan to finish cooking.

A few final touches: a little heavy cream made the sauce silky without obscuring the flavor of the broccoli and chicken. Grated Asiago cheese enriched the sauce and gave it a pleasantly tangy flavor. And a little lemon juice added a bright note. Our chicken, broccoli, and ziti not only boasted a great balance of flavors and textures, but it was quick and easy to prepare as well.

Skillet Chicken, Broccoli, and Ziti

SERVES 4

This recipe also works well with 8 ounces of penne. Parmesan cheese can be substituted for the Asiago.

- 1 **pound boneless, skinless chicken breasts, cut into 1-inch pieces**
  Table salt and ground black pepper
- 2 **tablespoons vegetable or olive oil**
- 1 **medium onion, minced**
- 3 **medium garlic cloves, minced or pressed through a garlic press (about 1 tablespoon)**
- ¼ **teaspoon dried oregano**
- ⅛ **teaspoon red pepper flakes**
- 8 **ounces ziti (2½ cups) (see note)**
- 2¾ **cups water**
- 1⅔ **cups low-sodium chicken broth**
- 12 **ounces broccoli florets (4 cups)**
- ¼ **cup oil-packed sun-dried tomatoes, rinsed and chopped coarse**
- ½ **cup heavy cream**
- 1 **ounce Asiago cheese, grated (about ½ cup), plus extra for serving (see note)**
- 1 **tablespoon juice from 1 lemon**

1. Season the chicken with salt and pepper. Heat 1 tablespoon of the oil in a 12-inch nonstick skillet over medium-high heat until just smoking. Add the chicken in a single layer and cook for 1 minute without stirring. Stir the chicken and continue to cook until most, but not all, of the pink color has disappeared and the chicken is lightly browned around the edges, 1 to 2 minutes longer. Transfer the chicken to a clean bowl and set aside.

2. Add the remaining 1 tablespoon oil, the onion, and ½ teaspoon salt to the skillet. Return the skillet to medium-high heat and cook, stirring often, until the onion is softened, 2 to 5 minutes. Stir in the garlic, oregano, and red pepper flakes and cook until fragrant, about 30 seconds.

3. Add the ziti, 2 cups of the water, and the broth. Bring to a boil over high heat and cook until the liquid is very thick and syrupy and almost completely absorbed, 12 to 15 minutes.

4. Add the broccoli, sun-dried tomatoes, and the remaining ¾ cup water. Cover, reduce the heat to medium, and cook until the broccoli turns bright green and is almost tender, 3 to 5 minutes.

5. Uncover and return the heat to high. Stir in the cream, Asiago, and reserved chicken with any accumulated juices and continue to simmer, uncovered, until the sauce is thickened and the chicken is cooked and heated through, 1 to 2 minutes. Off the heat, stir in the lemon juice and season with salt and pepper to taste. Serve, passing more grated Asiago at the table, if desired.

SKILLET LASAGNA

WHY THIS RECIPE WORKS: Lasagna isn't usually a dish you can throw together at the last minute. Even with no-boil noodles, it takes a good amount of time to get the components just right. Our goal was to transform traditional baked lasagna into a stovetop skillet dish without losing any of its flavor or appeal.

We built a hearty, flavorful meat sauce with onions, garlic, red pepper flakes, and meatloaf mix (a more flavorful alternative to plain ground beef). A large can of diced tomatoes along with tomato sauce provided juicy tomato flavor and a nicely chunky texture. We scattered regular curly-edged lasagna noodles, broken into pieces, over the top of the sauce (smaller pieces are easier to eat and serve). We then diluted the sauce with a little water so that the noodles would cook through. After a 20-minute simmer with the lid on, the pasta was tender, the sauce was properly thickened, and it was time for the cheese. Stirring Parmesan into the dish worked well, but we discovered that the sweet creaminess of ricotta was lost unless we placed it in heaping tablespoonfuls on top of the lasagna. Replacing the lid and letting the cheese warm through for several minutes was the final step for this super-easy one-pan dish.

Skillet Lasagna

SERVES 4 TO 6

Meatloaf mix is a combination of ground beef, pork, and veal, sold prepackaged in many supermarkets. If it's unavailable, use ground beef. A skillet with a tight-fitting lid works best for this recipe.

- 1 (28-ounce) can diced tomatoes
  Water
- 1 tablespoon olive oil
- 1 medium onion, minced
  Table salt
- 3 medium garlic cloves, minced or pressed through a garlic press (about 1 tablespoon)
- ⅛ teaspoon red pepper flakes
- 1 pound meatloaf mix (see note)
- 10 curly-edged lasagna noodles, broken into 2-inch lengths
- 1 (8-ounce) can tomato sauce
- 1 ounce Parmesan cheese, grated (½ cup), plus extra for serving
  Ground black pepper
- 1 cup ricotta cheese
- 3 tablespoons chopped fresh basil leaves

1. Pour the tomatoes with their juice into a 4-cup liquid measuring cup. Add water until the mixture measures 4 cups.

2. Heat the oil in a 12-inch nonstick skillet over medium heat until shimmering. Add the onion and ½ teaspoon salt and cook until the onion begins to brown, 6 to 8 minutes. Stir in the garlic and red pepper flakes and cook until fragrant, about 30 seconds. Add the ground meat and cook, breaking apart the meat, until no longer pink, about 4 minutes.

3. Scatter the pasta over the meat but do not stir. Pour the diced tomatoes with their juice and the tomato sauce over the pasta. Cover and bring to a simmer. Reduce the heat to medium-low and simmer, stirring occasionally, until the pasta is tender, about 20 minutes.

4. Remove the skillet from the heat and stir in all but 2 tablespoons of the Parmesan. Season with salt and pepper to taste. Dot with heaping tablespoons of the ricotta, cover, and let stand off the heat for 5 minutes. Sprinkle with the basil and the remaining 2 tablespoons Parmesan. Serve.

SKILLET CHICKEN POT PIE

WHY THIS RECIPE WORKS: Quick versions of chicken pot pie are often plagued by dried-out leftover chicken, bland sauce made with canned soup, and biscuits popped out of a tube. We saw no reason why pot pie couldn't be a whole lot better. We wanted moist chicken, a richly flavored sauce, and a homemade biscuit crust.

Instead of the refrigerated biscuit dough used in most recipes, we turned to homemade biscuits, and it was easy enough to put together a simple dough for baking powder biscuits. We just whisked the dry ingredients together and stirred in heavy cream, kneaded the dough briefly, and cut it into rounds (wedges would also work fine). We then popped the biscuits into the oven to bake, while we turned to the filling.

Next, we decided to contain all our cooking to a skillet for ease of preparation. We first sautéed skinless, boneless breasts in butter, keeping the heat at medium so the exterior wouldn't toughen. We set the chicken aside after it was browned and started the sauce in the skillet with onion, celery, thyme, vermouth, and chicken broth—ingredients that contributed lots of flavor. Flour thickened the liquid, and heavy cream gave it richness and a lush texture. Gently simmering the browned chicken in this sauce not only enhanced the flavor of the sauce but also kept the chicken juicy. Using frozen peas and carrots made quick work of the vegetables. All that was left to do was to assemble our pie by placing the hot biscuits over the filling in the skillet. Our flavorful, meaty stew with tender biscuits on top was not only delicious but also fast and easy.

Skillet Chicken Pot Pie with Biscuit Topping

SERVES 4

If you don't have time to make your own biscuits for the topping, use packaged refrigerated biscuits and bake them according to the package instructions. We prefer the flavor of Pillsbury Golden Homestyle Biscuits but you can use your favorite brand (you will need anywhere from four to eight biscuits depending on their size). This pot pie can be served in a large pie plate with the biscuits arranged on top, or served directly from the skillet.

BISCUITS

- 2 cups (10 ounces) unbleached all-purpose flour, plus extra for the work surface
- 2 teaspoons sugar
- 2 teaspoons baking powder
- ½ teaspoon table salt
- 1½ cups heavy cream

FILLING

- 1½ pounds boneless, skinless chicken breasts
  Table salt and ground black pepper
- 4 tablespoons (½ stick) unsalted butter
- 1 medium onion, minced
- 1 celery rib, sliced thin
- ¼ cup unbleached all-purpose flour
- ¼ cup dry vermouth or dry white wine
- 2 cups low-sodium chicken broth
- ½ cup heavy cream
- 1½ teaspoons minced fresh thyme leaves
- 2 cups frozen pea-carrot medley, thawed

1. FOR THE BISCUITS: Adjust an oven rack to the upper-middle position and heat the oven to 450 degrees. Line a baking sheet with parchment paper and set aside.

2. Whisk the flour, sugar, baking powder, and salt together in a large bowl. Stir in the cream with a wooden spoon until a dough forms, about 30 seconds. Turn the dough out onto a lightly floured work surface and gather into a ball. Knead the dough briefly until smooth, about 30 seconds.

3. Pat the dough into a ¾-inch-thick circle. Cut the biscuits into rounds using a 2½-inch biscuit cutter or cut into eight wedges using a knife.

4. Place the biscuits on the prepared baking sheet. Bake until golden brown, about 15 minutes. Set aside on a wire rack.

5. FOR THE FILLING: While the biscuits bake, pat the chicken dry with paper towels and season with salt and pepper. Melt 2 tablespoons of the butter in a 12-inch skillet over medium heat until the foam subsides. Brown the

Take a walk through our test kitchen and you'll see stacks of skillets—small, medium, large, traditional and nonstick—all of them ovensafe. They're undoubtedly the most useful pans in the test kitchen. We use a skillet to cook everything from burgers, steaks, and chicken to eggs, stir-fries, and sauces. But that's not all. We use skillets to cook a host of other dishes that are started on the stovetop and finished in the oven, turning typically long-cooking dishes like roast chicken and baked ziti into weeknight meals. How do we do it? We brown chicken parts on the stovetop and then slide the chicken into the oven to finish cooking through. And for baked ziti? We cook the pasta right in sauce on the stovetop, add the cheese, then pop it into the oven to brown. Both dishes take only about 30 minutes from start to finish.

For most recipes the test kitchen prefers a 12-inch skillet. This large size is the most versatile because it can accommodate a big steak or all of the pieces of a cut-up 3-pound chicken. Look for a skillet that weighs about 3 or 4 pounds. Lighter weight pans performed poorly in the test kitchen and cooked food unevenly. Pans in the 3-to-4-pound range browned foods beautifully and have enough heft for heat retention and structural integrity, but not so much that they are difficult to lift or manipulate. A word of caution: when moving a skillet from the oven to the stovetop, remember that the skillet (and handle) will be hot for some time. To remind ourselves of this (after more than a few burns), we wrap a dry towel around the handle right after we pull it from the oven or slide an oven mitt over it. For more information on skillets and recommended brands of both traditional and nonstick skillets, see page 586.

chicken lightly on both sides, about 5 minutes total. Transfer the chicken to a clean plate.

6. Add the remaining 2 tablespoons butter to the skillet and return to medium heat until melted. Add the onion, celery, and ½ teaspoon salt and cook until the onion is softened, about 5 minutes. Stir in the flour and cook, stirring constantly, until incorporated, about 1 minute.

7. Stir in the vermouth and cook until evaporated, about 30 seconds. Slowly whisk in the broth, cream, and thyme, and bring to a simmer. Nestle the chicken into the sauce, cover, and cook over medium-low heat until the thickest part of the breasts registers 160 to 165 degrees on an instant-read thermometer, 8 to 10 minutes.

8. Transfer the chicken to a plate. Stir the peas and carrots into the sauce and simmer until heated through, about 2 minutes. When the chicken is cool enough to handle, cut or shred it into bite-sized pieces and return it to the skillet. Season the filling with salt and pepper to taste.

9. FOR SERVING: Transfer the filling to a large pie plate and arrange the biscuits over the top, or serve directly from the skillet, topping individual portions with the biscuits.

SKILLET TAMALE PIE

WHY THIS RECIPE WORKS: Tamale pie—lightly seasoned, tomatoey ground beef with cornbread topping—is easy to make and makes a satisfying supper. But in many recipes, the filling either tastes bland and one-dimensional or turns heavy. As for the cornbread topping, it's usually from a mix and tastes like it. We wanted a skillet tamale pie with a rich, well-seasoned filling and a cornbread topping with real corn flavor.

For the beef, we found 90 percent lean ground sirloin gave us a good balance of richness and flavor. We started by sautéing minced onion and garlic. For seasoning, we used a generous amount of chili powder, which we added to the aromatics in the skillet to "bloom," or intensify, its flavor. The addition of canned black beans made our pie heartier, and canned diced tomatoes contributed additional flavor and texture. Cheddar cheese stirred into the mixture enriched the filling and also helped thicken it, and some minced fresh cilantro contributed a bright, fresh note. And to finish our pie, we skipped the cornbread mix and instead devised an easy homemade version. We spread the cornbread batter over the filling in the skillet, put the skillet in the oven to bake through, and the result was crunchy, corny topping that perfectly complemented the spicy tamale filling.

Skillet Tamale Pie
SERVES 4

Parsley can be substituted for the cilantro, if desired.

TAMALE FILLING
- 2 tablespoons vegetable oil
- 1 medium onion, minced
- 2 tablespoons chili powder
  Table salt
- 2 medium garlic cloves, minced or pressed through a garlic press (about 2 teaspoons)
- 1 pound 90 percent lean ground sirloin
- 1 (15-ounce) can black beans, drained and rinsed
- 1 (14.5-ounce) can diced tomatoes, drained
- 4 ounces cheddar cheese, shredded (about 1 cup)
- 2 tablespoons minced fresh cilantro leaves (see note)
  Ground black pepper

CORNBREAD TOPPING
- ¾ cup (3¾ ounces) unbleached all-purpose flour
- ¾ cup (3¾ ounces) yellow cornmeal
- 3 tablespoons sugar
- ¾ teaspoon table salt
- ¾ teaspoon baking powder
- ¼ teaspoon baking soda
- ¾ cup buttermilk
- 1 large egg
- 3 tablespoons unsalted butter, melted and cooled

1. Adjust an oven rack to the middle position and heat the oven to 450 degrees.

2. FOR THE TAMALE FILLING: Heat the oil in a 12-inch ovensafe skillet over medium heat until shimmering. Add the onion, chili powder, and ½ teaspoon salt and cook until the onion is softened, about 5 minutes. Stir in the garlic and cook until fragrant, about 30 seconds.

3. Stir in the ground sirloin, beans, and tomatoes and bring to a simmer, breaking up the meat with a wooden spoon, about 5 minutes. Stir the cheddar and cilantro into the filling and season with salt and pepper to taste.

4. FOR THE CORNBREAD TOPPING: Whisk the flour, cornmeal, sugar, salt, baking powder, and baking soda together in a large bowl. In a separate bowl, whisk the buttermilk and egg together. Stir the buttermilk mixture into the flour mixture until uniform. Stir in the butter until just combined.

5. Dollop the cornbread batter evenly over the filling and spread into an even layer. Bake until the cornbread is cooked through in the center, 10 to 15 minutes. Using potholders (the skillet handle will be hot), remove the skillet from the oven. Serve.

SKILLET BEEF STROGANOFF

WHY THIS RECIPE WORKS: Beef stroganoff is more often associated with bad banquet fare than with a hearty, satisfying dinner. But originally, this dish was quite elegant and was even made with filet mignon. Our goal was twofold: find a less expensive option for the beef to turn it into a within-reach weeknight supper, and bring the too-rich, often gloppy sauce back to its refined roots.

We started with the beef. Blade steaks shrank too much during cooking; sirloin tips became tender and held their shape well, but the pieces of meat crinkled up oddly. We solved that problem by pounding the meat before cutting it into strips. We first seared the meat and removed it from the pan, then sautéed mushrooms and onion in the same pan. To finish cooking the beef, we built a braising liquid with equal amounts of chicken and beef broth (beef broth alone tasted flat) and a little flour to thicken the sauce. We didn't want to overload the dish with seasonings—they would mask the flavor of the beef and mushrooms—but we found that some brandy was essential. We then returned the meat to the sauce to cook through.

To avoid cooking the noodles separately, we borrowed our method of cooking pasta directly in sauce and added the egg noodles to the braising liquid. When the noodles were tender and the beef was cooked through, we added the final touches, sour cream and lemon juice—but off the heat so that it wouldn't curdle.

Skillet Beef Stroganoff
SERVES 4

To prepare the beef, pound it with a meat pounder to an even ½-inch thickness. Slice the meat, with the grain, into 2-inch strips, then slice each piece against the grain into ½-inch strips. Brandy can ignite if added to a hot, empty skillet. Be sure to add the brandy to the skillet after stirring in the broth.

1½ pounds sirloin tips, pounded and cut into ½-inch strips (see note)
   Table salt and ground black pepper
4 tablespoons vegetable oil
10 ounces white mushrooms, wiped clean and sliced thin
1 medium onion, minced
2 tablespoons unbleached all-purpose flour
1½ cups low-sodium chicken broth
1½ cups beef broth
⅓ cup brandy (see note)
6 ounces wide egg noodles (4 cups)
⅔ cup sour cream
2 teaspoons juice from 1 lemon

1. Pat the beef dry with paper towels and season with salt and pepper. Heat 1 tablespoon of the oil in a 12-inch skillet over medium-high heat until just smoking. Cook half of the beef until well browned, 3 to 4 minutes per side. Transfer to a medium bowl and repeat with 1 tablespoon more oil and the remaining beef.

2. Heat the remaining 2 tablespoons oil in the now-empty skillet until shimmering. Cook the mushrooms, onion, and ½ teaspoon salt until the liquid from the mushrooms has evaporated, about 8 minutes. (If the pan becomes too brown, pour the accumulated beef juices into the skillet.) Stir in the flour and cook for 30 seconds. Gradually stir in the broths, then the brandy, and return the beef and accumulated juices to the skillet. Bring to a simmer, cover, and cook over low heat until the beef is tender, 30 to 35 minutes.

3. Stir the noodles into the beef mixture, cover, and cook, stirring occasionally, until the noodles are tender, 10 to 12 minutes. Off the heat, stir in the sour cream and lemon juice. Season with salt and pepper to taste and serve.

SKILLET-ROASTED CHICKEN DINNER

WHY THIS RECIPE WORKS: Roasted chicken and potatoes are a favorite combination for Sunday dinner. But on a busy weeknight, who has time to prepare a meal that requires at least an hour in the oven? We wanted to come up with a skillet preparation that would give us juicy, tender chicken and crispy potatoes in about half an hour.

To start, we borrowed the restaurant method of browning meat on the stovetop and finishing it in the oven. We swapped in bone-in split breasts for the whole chicken and seared the chicken in a skillet. This turned the skin nicely brown and crisp. Next, we transferred the chicken to a baking dish in the oven to finish cooking through.

Meanwhile, we turned to the potatoes. We chose red potatoes because their skins are tender and don't require peeling. This saved some prep time, but we couldn't get them to cook in the same amount of time as the chicken. The microwave turned out to be the solution; while the chicken was browning, we tossed the potatoes with a little olive oil, salt, pepper and microwaved them for a few minutes to jump-start the cooking process. Placing the potatoes in a single layer in the skillet—the same one in which we'd browned

the chicken—helped them cook up creamy and moist inside while their exteriors became crispy and caramelized, just when it was time to take the chicken out of the oven. Before serving, we drizzled a mixture of olive oil, lemon juice, garlic, red pepper flakes, and thyme over our chicken and potatoes for an extra hit of moisture and flavor. In about half an hour, we had re-created the great flavors of a Sunday roast chicken dinner.

Skillet-Roasted Chicken Breasts with Potatoes
SERVES 4

To complete this recipe in 30 minutes, preheat your oven before assembling the ingredients. If the split breasts are different sizes, check the smaller ones a few minutes early and remove them from the oven if they are done.

    4   (10 to 12-ounce) bone-in, split chicken breasts
        Table salt and ground black pepper
    6   tablespoons olive oil
    1½ pounds red potatoes (4 to 5 medium), cut into
        1-inch wedges
    2   tablespoons juice from 1 lemon
    1   medium garlic clove, minced or pressed through a garlic
        press (about 1 teaspoon)
    1   teaspoon minced fresh thyme leaves
        Pinch red pepper flakes

1. Adjust an oven rack to the lowest position and heat the oven to 450 degrees.

2. Pat the chicken dry with paper towels and season with salt and pepper. Heat 1 tablespoon of the oil in a 12-inch nonstick skillet over medium-high heat until just smoking. Add the chicken, skin side down, and cook until deep golden, about 5 minutes.

3. Meanwhile, toss the potatoes with 1 more tablespoon of the oil, ½ teaspoon salt, and ¼ teaspoon pepper in a microwave-safe bowl. Cover tightly with plastic wrap. Microwave on high power until the potatoes begin to soften, 5 to 10 minutes, shaking the bowl (without removing the plastic) to toss the potatoes halfway through.

4. Transfer the chicken, skin side up, to a baking dish and bake until the thickest part of the breasts registers 160 to 165 degrees on an instant-read thermometer, 15 to 20 minutes.

5. While the chicken bakes, pour off any fat in the skillet, add 1 tablespoon more oil, and return to medium heat until shimmering. Drain the microwaved potatoes, then

add to the skillet and cook, stirring occasionally, until golden brown and tender, about 10 minutes.

6. Whisk the remaining 3 tablespoons oil, the lemon juice, garlic, thyme, and red pepper flakes together. Drizzle the oil mixture over the chicken and potatoes before serving.

SKILLET CHICKEN AND RICE

WHY THIS RECIPE WORKS: There are lots of bad recipes out there for quick chicken and rice. Most contain leftover chicken, instant rice, and canned cream-of-something soup. We aimed to improve this dish all around and still deliver it to the table on time.

Boneless, skinless chicken breasts are definitely convenient, but we needed to prevent them from drying out. Dredging them in flour not only gave the chicken a nice brown crust but also kept the meat juicy inside. After browning the breasts on one side in a nonstick skillet, we removed them to deal with the rice. We first sautéed minced onion, garlic, and red pepper flakes in butter, then added the rice and stirred to coat the grains. Coating and toasting the rice this way before adding liquid is a technique that imparts deeper flavor and keeps the rice grains distinct and firm. We added a little white wine to the skillet for brightness. We then added chicken broth and returned the chicken to the skillet to cook through. When the chicken was done, we removed it from the skillet and finished cooking the rice. Off the heat, we added frozen peas, which cooked in a just couple of minutes, and stirred in lemon juice and sliced scallions for a fresh, bright flavor. In about 30 minutes, this dish was perfectly cooked, flavorful, and ready to serve. In addition, we developed two variations: one with cheddar and broccoli and the other with the spicy flavors of curry.

Skillet Chicken and Rice with Peas and Scallions

SERVES 4

Be sure to use chicken breasts that are roughly the same size to ensure even cooking.

- 4 (6 to 8-ounce) boneless, skinless chicken breasts, trimmed (see note)
  Table salt and ground black pepper
- ½ cup unbleached all-purpose flour
- 2 tablespoons vegetable oil
- 2 tablespoons unsalted butter
- 1 medium onion, minced
- 3 medium garlic cloves, minced or pressed through a garlic press (about 1 tablespoon)
  Pinch red pepper flakes
- 1½ cups long-grain white rice
- ½ cup dry white wine
- 4½ cups low-sodium chicken broth
- 1 cup frozen peas
- 5 scallions, sliced thin
- 2 tablespoons juice from 1 lemon
  Lemon wedges, for serving

1. Pat the chicken dry with paper towels and season with salt and pepper. Dredge the chicken in the flour to coat and shake off any excess. Heat the oil in a 12-inch nonstick skillet over medium-high heat just until smoking. Brown the chicken well on one side, about 5 minutes. Transfer the chicken to a plate and set aside.

2. Off the heat, add the butter to the skillet, and swirl to melt. Add the onion and ½ teaspoon salt and return to medium-high heat until softened, 2 to 5 minutes. Stir in the garlic and red pepper flakes and cook until fragrant, about 30 seconds. Stir in the rice thoroughly and let toast for about 30 seconds.

3. Stir in the wine and let the rice absorb it completely, about 1 minute. Stir in the broth, scraping up any browned bits. Nestle the chicken into the rice, browned side up, and add any accumulated juices. Cover and cook over medium heat until the thickest part of the chicken registers 160 to 165 degrees on an instant-read thermometer, about 10 minutes.

4. Transfer the chicken to a clean plate. Gently brush off and discard any rice clinging to the chicken, then tent the chicken with foil and set aside. Return the skillet of rice to medium-low heat, cover, and continue to cook, stirring occasionally, until the liquid is absorbed and the rice is tender, 8 to 12 minutes longer.

5. Off the heat, sprinkle the peas over the rice, cover, and let warm through, about 2 minutes. Add the scallions and lemon juice to the rice. Season with salt and pepper to taste and serve with the chicken and lemon wedges.

Skillet Chicken and Rice with Broccoli and Cheddar

SERVES 4

Be sure to use chicken breasts that are roughly the same size to ensure even cooking.

    4   (6 to 8-ounce) boneless, skinless chicken breasts,
        trimmed (see note)
        Table salt and ground black pepper
    ½   cup unbleached all-purpose flour
    3   tablespoons vegetable oil
    1   onion, minced
    1½ cups long-grain white rice
    3   garlic cloves, minced or pressed through a garlic press
        (about 1 tablespoon)
    1½ cups low-sodium chicken broth
    1   (10-ounce) package frozen broccoli florets, thawed
    4   ounces cheddar cheese, shredded (about 1 cup)
    1   teaspoon hot sauce

1. Pat the chicken dry with paper towels and season with salt and pepper. Dredge the chicken in the flour to coat and shake off any excess. Heat 2 tablespoons of the oil in a 12-inch nonstick skillet over medium-high heat until just smoking. Brown the chicken well on one side, about 5 minutes. Transfer the chicken to a plate and set aside.

2. Add the remaining 1 tablespoon oil to the skillet and return to medium-high heat until shimmering. Add the onion and ½ teaspoon salt and cook until softened, about 5 minutes. Stir in the rice and garlic and cook until fragrant, about 30 seconds.

3. Stir in the broth, scraping up any browned bits. Nestle the chicken and any accumulated juices into the rice, browned side up. Cover and cook over medium heat until the liquid is absorbed and the thickest part of the chicken registers 160 to 165 degrees on an instant-read thermometer, about 10 minutes.

4. Transfer the chicken to a clean plate. Gently brush off and discard any rice clinging to the chicken, then tent the chicken with foil and set aside. Return the skillet of rice to medium-low heat, cover, and continue to cook, stirring occasionally, until the liquid is absorbed and the rice is tender, 8 to 12 minutes longer.

5. Off the heat, gently fold the broccoli, ½ cup of the cheddar, and the hot sauce into the rice and season with salt and pepper to taste. Sprinkle the remaining ½ cup cheddar over the top, cover, and let sit until the cheese melts, about 2 minutes. Serve with the chicken.

Skillet Curried Chicken and Rice

SERVES 4

Be sure to use chicken breasts that are roughly the same size to ensure even cooking. The heat level of curry varies from brand to brand. If your curry powder is very spicy, you may need to reduce the amount.

    4   (6 to 8-ounce) boneless, skinless chicken breasts,
        trimmed (see note)
        Table salt and ground black pepper
    ½   cup unbleached all-purpose flour
    3   tablespoons vegetable oil
    1   onion, minced
    1   tablespoon curry powder (see note)
    1½ cups long-grain white rice
    3   garlic cloves, minced or pressed through a garlic press
        (about 1 tablespoon)
    1½ cups low-sodium chicken broth
    1   cup frozen peas, thawed
    ¼   cup raisins
    ¼   cup minced fresh cilantro leaves

1. Pat the chicken dry with paper towels and season with salt and pepper. Dredge the chicken in the flour to coat and shake off any excess. Heat 2 tablespoons of the oil in a 12-inch nonstick skillet over medium-high heat until just smoking. Brown the chicken well on one side, about 5 minutes. Transfer the chicken to a plate and set aside.

2. Add the remaining 1 tablespoon oil to the skillet and return to medium-high heat until shimmering. Add the onion, curry powder, and ½ teaspoon salt and cook until softened, about 5 minutes. Stir in the rice and garlic and cook until fragrant, about 30 seconds.

3. Stir in the broth, scraping up any browned bits. Nestle the chicken and any accumulated juices into the rice, browned side up. Cover and cook over medium heat until the liquid is absorbed and the thickest part of the chicken registers 160 to 165 degrees on an instant-read thermometer, about 10 minutes.

4. Transfer the chicken to a clean plate. Gently brush off and discard any rice clinging to the chicken, then tent the chicken with foil and set aside. Return the skillet of rice to medium-low heat, cover, and continue to cook, stirring occasionally, until the liquid is absorbed and the rice is tender, 8 to 12 minutes longer.

5. Off the heat, sprinkle the peas and raisins over the rice, cover, and let warm through, about 2 minutes. Add the cilantro and gently fold into the rice. Season with salt and pepper to taste and serve with the chicken.

SKILLET JAMBALAYA

WHY THIS RECIPE WORKS: Jambalaya, a hearty mix of chicken, andouille sausage, shrimp, and rice, is typically made in a Dutch oven and can take at least an hour to prepare. We wanted a quicker, easier version without sacrificing any of the complex flavors of this Creole classic.

Bone-in, skin-on chicken thighs rather than the typical whole cut-up chicken called for in many recipes saved us time and fuss. To mimic long-simmered flavor, we browned the sausage in the skillet, added the chicken, then cooked the vegetables in some of the rendered fat. We then stirred the rice in to coat it with the fat for deep flavor. For our cooking liquid, we relied on chicken broth and clam juice (to complement the shrimp). To prevent the shrimp from overcooking, we cooked it for only a few minutes, then allowed it to finish cooking through off the heat (the residual heat is hot enough to cook it through). Entirely made in a skillet, this jambalaya makes a fast and satisfying supper.

Skillet Jambalaya

SERVES 4 TO 6

If you cannot find andouille sausage, either chorizo or linguiça can be substituted. For a spicier jambalaya, you can add ¼ teaspoon of cayenne pepper along with the vegetables, and/or serve it with hot sauce.

- 4 bone-in, skin-on chicken thighs (about 1½ pounds), trimmed
  Table salt and ground black pepper
- 5 teaspoons vegetable oil
- ½ pound andouille sausage, halved lengthwise and sliced into ¼-inch pieces (see note)
- 1 medium onion, chopped medium
- 1 medium red bell pepper, stemmed, seeded, and chopped medium
- 5 medium garlic cloves, minced or pressed through a garlic press (about 1½ tablespoons)
- 1½ cups long-grain white rice
- 1 (14.5-ounce) can diced tomatoes, drained
- 1 (8-ounce) bottle clam juice
- 2½ cups low-sodium chicken broth
- 1 pound large shrimp (31 to 40 per pound), peeled and deveined (see page 160)
- 2 tablespoons chopped fresh parsley leaves

1. Dry the chicken thoroughly with paper towels, then season generously with salt and pepper. Heat 2 teaspoons of the oil in a 12-inch nonstick skillet over medium-high heat until just smoking. Carefully lay the chicken thighs in the skillet, skin-side down, and cook until golden, 4 to 6 minutes. Flip the chicken over and continue to cook until the second side is golden, about 3 minutes. Remove the pan from the heat and transfer the chicken to a plate. Using paper towels, remove and discard the browned chicken skin.

2. Pour off all but 2 teaspoons of the fat left in the skillet and return to medium-high heat until shimmering. Add the andouille and cook until lightly browned, about 3 minutes; transfer the sausage to a small bowl and set aside.

3. Add the remaining 3 teaspoons oil to the skillet and return to medium heat until shimmering. Add the onion, bell pepper, garlic, and ½ teaspoon salt; cook, scraping the browned bits off the bottom of the skillet, until the onion is softened, about 5 minutes. Add the rice and cook until the edges turn translucent, about 3 minutes. Stir in the tomatoes, clam juice, and chicken broth; bring to a simmer. Gently nestle the chicken and any accumulated juices into the rice. Cover, reduce the heat to low, and cook until the chicken is tender and cooked through, 30 to 35 minutes.

4. Transfer the chicken to a plate and cover with foil to keep warm. Stir the shrimp and sausage into the rice and continue to cook, covered, over low heat for 2 more minutes. Remove the skillet from the heat and let stand, covered, until the shrimp are fully cooked and the rice is tender, about 5 minutes. Meanwhile, shred the chicken into into bite-sized pieces. Stir the parsley and shredded chicken into the rice, season with salt and pepper to taste, and serve.

CHAPTER 4

ONE POT DINNERS

Simple Pot Roast   50

Carbonnade à la Flamande
(Belgian Beef, Beer, and
Onion Stew)   51

Hungarian Beef Stew   52

Braised Beef Short Ribs   54

Slow-Cooker Beer-Braised
Short Ribs   55

Chicken and
Dumplings   56

Latino-Style Chicken
and Rice   57

Latino-Style Chicken
and Rice with Bacon and
Roasted Red Peppers   58

Latino-Style Chicken
and Rice with Ham,
Peas, and Orange   58

Paella   59

Creole-Style Shrimp
and Sausage Gumbo   60

POT ROAST

WHY THIS RECIPE WORKS: The long braise that a pot roast needs can result in either a succulent roast or a dry, bland disappointment. We wanted our pot roast to be fall-apart tender with a savory sauce—a meal that would be worth the wait.

We first determined that chuck-eye is the best choice for pot roast; its fat and connective tissue break down and keep the meat moist during the long oven stay. Browning the meat first was important for flavor as well as color. Caramelizing the vegetables with a little sugar added another layer of flavor. For the braising liquid, equal amounts of beef and chicken broth tasted best; and we added just enough water for the liquid to come about halfway up the sides of the roast and prevent it from drying out. Before we moved the roast into the oven, we covered the pot with foil and then covered with the lid for a tight seal, so no steam (or flavor) escaped. The secret to tenderness is in the cooking time. Cook the meat in the oven until it reaches 210 degrees internally, then cook it for an hour longer. The reward is moist, flavorful meat that is also remarkably tender.

Simple Pot Roast

SERVES 6 TO 8

Our favorite cut for pot roast is a chuck-eye roast. Most markets sell this roast with twine tied around the center; if necessary, do this yourself. Seven-bone and top-blade roasts are also good choices for this recipe. Remember to add only enough water to come halfway up the sides of these thinner roasts, and begin checking for doneness after 2 hours. If using a top-blade roast, tie it before cooking to keep it from falling apart. Mashed or boiled potatoes are a good accompaniment to pot roast.

1 (3½-pound) boneless chuck-eye roast (see note)
  Table salt and ground black pepper
2 tablespoons vegetable oil
1 medium onion, chopped medium
1 small carrot, chopped medium
1 small rib celery, chopped medium
2 medium garlic cloves, minced or pressed through a garlic press (about 2 teaspoons)
2 teaspoons sugar
1 cup low-sodium chicken broth
1 cup beef broth
1 sprig fresh thyme
1–1½ cups water
¼ cup dry red wine

1. Adjust an oven rack to the middle position and heat the oven to 300 degrees. Thoroughly pat the roast dry with paper towels; sprinkle generously with salt and pepper.

2. Heat the oil in a large Dutch oven over medium-high heat until shimmering but not smoking. Brown the roast thoroughly on all sides, reducing the heat if the fat begins to smoke, 8 to 10 minutes. Transfer the roast to a large plate; set aside. Reduce the heat to medium; add the onion, carrot, and celery to the pot and cook, stirring occasionally, until beginning to brown, 6 to 8 minutes. Add the garlic and sugar; cook until fragrant, about 30 seconds. Add the chicken and beef broths and thyme, scraping the bottom of the pan with a wooden spoon to loosen the browned bits. Return the roast and any accumulated juices to the pot; add enough water to come halfway up the sides of the roast. Place a large piece of foil over the pot and cover tightly with the lid; bring the liquid to a simmer over medium heat, then transfer the pot to the oven. Cook, turning the roast every 30 minutes, until fully tender and a meat fork or sharp knife easily slips in and out of the meat, 3½ to 4 hours.

3. Transfer the roast to a carving board; tent with foil to keep warm. Allow the liquid in the pot to settle about 5 minutes, then use a wide spoon to skim the fat off the surface; discard the thyme sprig. Boil over high heat until reduced to about 1½ cups, about 8 minutes. Add the red wine and reduce again to 1½ cups, about 2 minutes. Season with salt and pepper to taste.

4. Using a chef's or carving knife, cut the meat into ½-inch-thick slices, or pull apart into large pieces; transfer the meat to a warmed serving platter and pour about ½ cup sauce over the meat. Serve, passing the remaining sauce separately.

BEEF CARBONNADE

WHY THIS RECIPE WORKS: Most recipes for this Belgian beef, onion, and beer stew go in one of two directions: In one version, the recipe masks its genuine flavors and, in others, the recipes rigidly adhere to the "three ingredients only" rule, so the stew is stripped down to a pale, tasteless version of itself. We wanted hearty chunks of beef and sliced sweet onion in a lightly thickened broth, laced with the malty flavor of beer.

Most recipes suggest using chuck-eye roast for the beef, but we tried several other cuts and found that top blade steak, which has a fair amount of marbling, provided the best texture and a "buttery" flavor that worked well alongside the onions and beer. White and red onions were too sweet in our stew; yellow onions worked better. The onions should be browned only lightly; overcaramelization caused them to disintegrate. An untraditional ingredient—tomato paste—gave the stew depth, as did garlic. Fresh thyme and bay leaves provided seasoning, and a splash of cider vinegar added the right level of acidity. Beer is a staple of Belgian cooking, and we found that it's less forgiving than wine when used in a stew. The light lagers we tried resulted in pale, watery stews; better were dark ales and stouts. But beer alone often made for bitter-tasting stew, so we included some broth; a combination of chicken and beef broth gave us more solid and complex flavor.

Carbonnade à la Flamande (Belgian Beef, Beer, and Onion Stew)

SERVES 6

Top blade steaks (also called blade or flatiron steaks) are our first choice, but any boneless roast from the chuck will work. If you end up using a chuck roast, look for the chuck-eye roast, an especially flavorful cut that can easily be trimmed and cut into 1-inch pieces. Buttered egg noodles or mashed potatoes make excellent accompaniments to carbonnade.

3½ pounds top blade steaks, 1 inch thick, trimmed of gristle and fat and cut into 1-inch pieces (see photo) (see note)
    Table salt and ground black pepper
 3 tablespoons vegetable oil
 2 pounds yellow onions (about 4 medium), halved and sliced ¼ inch thick
 1 tablespoon tomato paste
 2 medium garlic cloves, minced or pressed through a garlic press (about 2 teaspoons)
 3 tablespoons unbleached all-purpose flour
 ¾ cup low-sodium chicken broth
 ¾ cup beef broth
1½ cups (12-ounce bottle or can) dark beer or stout
 4 sprigs fresh thyme, tied with kitchen twine
 2 bay leaves
 1 tablespoon cider vinegar

1. Adjust an oven rack to the lower-middle position and heat the oven to 300 degrees. Dry the beef thoroughly with paper towels, then season generously with salt and pepper. Heat 2 teaspoons of the oil in a large Dutch oven over medium-high heat until beginning to smoke; add about one third of the beef to the pot. Cook without

---

NOTES FROM THE TEST KITCHEN

TRIMMING BLADE STEAKS

To trim blade steaks, halve each steak lengthwise, leaving the gristle on one half. Then simply cut the gristle away.

moving the pieces until well browned, 2 to 3 minutes; using tongs, turn each piece and continue cooking until the second side is well browned, about 5 minutes longer. Transfer the browned beef to a medium bowl. Repeat with 2 teaspoons more oil and half of the remaining beef. (If the drippings in the bottom of the pot are very dark, add ½ cup of the chicken or beef broth and scrape the pan bottom with a wooden spoon to loosen the browned bits; pour the liquid into the bowl with the browned beef, then proceed.) Repeat once more with 2 teaspoons more oil and the remaining beef.

2. Add the remaining 1 tablespoon oil to the now-empty Dutch oven; reduce the heat to medium-low. Add the onions, ½ teaspoon salt, and the tomato paste; cook, scraping the bottom of the pot with a wooden spoon to loosen the browned bits, until the onions have released some moisture, about 5 minutes. Increase the heat to medium and continue to cook, stirring occasionally, until the onions are lightly browned, 12 to 14 minutes. Stir in the garlic and cook until fragrant, about 30 seconds. Add the flour and stir until the onions are evenly coated and the flour is lightly browned, about 2 minutes. Stir in the broths, scraping the pan bottom to loosen any browned bits; stir in the beer, thyme, bay leaves, vinegar, browned beef with any accumulated juices, and salt and pepper to taste. Increase the heat to medium-high and bring to a full simmer, stirring occasionally; cover partially, then place the pot in the oven. Cook until a fork inserted into the beef meets little resistance, 2 to 2½ hours.

3. Discard the thyme and bay leaves. Season with salt and pepper to taste and serve. (The stew can be cooled and refrigerated in an airtight container for up to 4 days; reheat over medium-low heat.)

HUNGARIAN BEEF STEW

WHY THIS RECIPE WORKS: The Americanized versions of Hungarian goulash served in the United States bear little resemblance to the authentic dish. Sour cream has no place in the pot, nor do mushrooms, green peppers, or most herbs. We wanted the real deal—a simple dish of tender braised beef packed with paprika flavor.

To achieve the desired level of spicy intensity, some recipes call for as much as half a cup of paprika per three pounds of meat, but with that much fine spice, the dish took on a gritty, dusty texture. After consulting chefs

at a few Hungarian restaurants, we were introduced to paprika cream, a condiment that's as common in Hungarian cooking as the dried spice—but hard to find in the U.S. Instead, we created our own quick version by pureeing dried paprika with roasted red peppers and a little tomato paste and vinegar. This mixture imparted vibrant paprika flavor without any offensive grittiness.

As for the meat, after settling on chuck-eye roast, we bought a whole roast and cut it ourselves into uniform, large pieces to ensure even cooking. Since searing the meat first—normally standard stew protocol—competed with the paprika's brightness, we referred back to a trend we noticed in the goulash recipes gathered during research: skipping the sear. We tried this, softening the onions in the pot first, adding paprika paste, carrots, and then meat before placing the covered pot in the oven. Sure enough, the onions and meat provided enough liquid to stew the meat, and the bits of beef that cooked above the liquid line browned in the hot air. A bit of broth added near the end of cooking thinned out the stewing liquid to just the right consistency.

Hungarian Beef Stew

SERVES 6

Do not substitute hot, half-sharp, or smoked Spanish paprika for the sweet paprika in the stew, as they will compromise the flavor of the dish. Since paprika is vital to this recipe, it is best to use a fresh container. We prefer chuck-eye roast, but any boneless roast from the chuck will work. Cook the stew in a Dutch oven with a tight-fitting lid. (Alternatively, to ensure a tight seal, place a sheet of foil over the pot before adding the lid.) Serve the stew over boiled potatoes or egg noodles.

1 boneless chuck-eye roast (about 3½ pounds), trimmed of excess fat and cut into 1½-inch cubes (see note)
   Table salt
1 (12-ounce) jar roasted red peppers, drained and rinsed (about 1 cup)
⅓ cup sweet paprika (see note)
2 tablespoons tomato paste
3 teaspoons white vinegar
2 tablespoons vegetable oil
6 medium onions, minced (about 6 cups)
4 large carrots, peeled and cut into 1-inch-thick rounds (about 2 cups)
1 bay leaf

1 cup beef broth, warmed
¼ cup sour cream (optional)
Ground black pepper

1. Adjust an oven rack to the lower-middle position and heat the oven to 325 degrees. Sprinkle the meat evenly with 1 teaspoon salt and let stand for 15 minutes. Process the roasted peppers, paprika, tomato paste, and 2 teaspoons of the vinegar in a food processor until smooth, 1 to 2 minutes, scraping down the sides as needed.

2. Combine the oil, onions, and 1 teaspoon salt in a large Dutch oven; cover and set over medium heat. Cook, stirring occasionally, until the onions have softened but have not yet begun to brown, 8 to 10 minutes. (If the onions begin to brown, reduce the heat to medium-low and stir in 1 tablespoon water.)

3. Stir in the paprika mixture; cook, stirring occasionally, until the onions stick to the bottom of the pan, about 2 minutes. Add the beef, carrots, and bay leaf; stir until the beef is well coated. Using a rubber spatula, scrape down the sides of the pot. Cover the pot and transfer to the oven. Cook until the meat is almost tender and the surface of the liquid is ½ inch below the top of the meat, 2 to 2½ hours, stirring every 30 minutes. Remove the pot from the oven and add enough beef broth that the surface of the liquid is ¼ inch from the top of the meat (the beef should not

be fully submerged). Return the covered pot to the oven and continue to cook until a fork slips easily in and out of the beef, about 30 minutes longer.

4. Skim the fat off the surface using a wide spoon; stir in the remaining teaspoon vinegar and sour cream (if using). Remove the bay leaf, season with salt and pepper to taste, and serve. (The stew can be cooled, covered tightly, and refrigerated for up to 2 days; wait to add the optional sour cream until after reheating. Before reheating, skim the hardened fat from the surface and add enough water to the stew to thin it slightly.)

BRAISED SHORT RIBS

WHY THIS RECIPE WORKS: Short ribs have great flavor and luscious texture, but their excess fat can be a problem since so much fat is rendered during the ribs' stint in the oven. Most recipes call for resting them in the braising liquid overnight, so that the fat solidifies into an easy-to-remove layer. However, most people don't plan their dinners days in advance and skimming such a large amount of fat off with a spoon doesn't work well enough. The meat and sauce come out greasy, no matter how diligent one's spoon-wielding. We wanted a silky, grease-free sauce and fork-tender short rib meat, all in a few hours.

The first task was to choose the right rib. Instead of traditional bone-in short ribs, we used boneless short ribs, which rendered significantly less fat than bone-in. While we didn't miss much flavor from the bones, we did want the body that the bones' connective tissue added. To solve this, we sprinkled a bit of gelatin into the sauce to restore suppleness. We also wanted to ramp up the richness of the sauce. We jump-started flavor by reducing wine with browned aromatics (onions, garlic, and carrots) before using the liquid to cook the meat. This added the right intensity, but we needed another cup of liquid to keep the meat half-submerged—the right level for braises. More wine yielded too much wine flavor; we used beef broth instead. As for the excess fat, the level was low enough that we could strain and defat the liquid in a fat separator. Reducing the liquid concentrated the flavors and made for a rich, luxurious sauce for our fork-tender boneless short ribs.

Braised Beef Short Ribs

SERVES 6

Make sure that the ribs are at least 4 inches long and 1 inch thick. If boneless ribs are unavailable, substitute 7 pounds of bone-in beef short ribs at least 4 inches long with 1 inch of meat above the bone and bone them yourself (see photos).

3½ **pounds boneless beef short ribs, trimmed of excess fat (see note)**
   Table salt and ground black pepper
2 **tablespoons vegetable oil**
2 **large onions, sliced thin from pole to pole (about 4 cups)**
1 **tablespoon tomato paste**
6 **medium garlic cloves, peeled**
2 **cups red wine, such as Cabernet Sauvignon or Côtes du Rhône**
1 **cup beef broth**
4 **large carrots, peeled and cut crosswise into 2-inch pieces**
4 **sprigs fresh thyme**
1 **bay leaf**
¼ **cup cold water**
½ **teaspoon powdered gelatin**

1. Adjust an oven rack to the lower-middle position and heat the oven to 300 degrees. Pat the beef dry with paper towels and season with 2 teaspoons salt and 1 teaspoon pepper. Heat 1 tablespoon of the oil in a large Dutch oven over medium-high heat until smoking. Add half of the beef and cook, without stirring, until well browned, 4 to 6 minutes. Turn the beef and continue to cook on the second side until well browned, 4 to 6 minutes longer, reducing the heat if the fat begins to smoke. Transfer the beef to a medium bowl. Repeat with the remaining 1 tablespoon oil and the remaining meat.

2. Reduce the heat to medium, add the onions, and cook, stirring occasionally, until softened and beginning to brown, 12 to 15 minutes. (If the onions begin to darken too quickly, add 1 to 2 tablespoons water to the pan.) Add the tomato paste and cook, stirring constantly, until it browns on the sides and bottom of the pan, about 2 minutes. Add the garlic and cook until aromatic, about 30 seconds. Increase the heat to medium-high, add the wine, and simmer, scraping the bottom of the pan with a wooden spoon to loosen the browned bits, until reduced by half, 8 to 10 minutes. Add the broth, carrots, thyme, and bay leaf. Add the beef and any accumulated juices to the pot; cover and bring to a simmer. Transfer the pot to the oven and cook, using tongs to turn the meat twice during cooking, until a fork slips easily in and out of the meat, 2 to 2½ hours.

3. Place the water in a small bowl and sprinkle the gelatin on top; let stand at least 5 minutes. Using tongs, transfer the meat and carrots to a serving platter and tent with foil. Strain the cooking liquid through a fine-mesh strainer into a fat separator or bowl, pressing on the solids to extract as much liquid as possible; discard the solids. Allow the liquid to settle for about 5 minutes and strain off the fat. Return the cooking liquid to the Dutch oven and cook over medium heat until reduced to 1 cup, 5 to 10 minutes. Remove from the heat and stir in the gelatin mixture; season with salt and pepper to taste. Pour the sauce over the meat and carrots and serve.

NOTES FROM THE TEST KITCHEN

BONING SHORT RIBS

1. With a chef's knife as close as possible to the bone, carefully remove the meat.

2. Trim the excess hard fat and silver skin from both sides of the meat.

SLOW-COOKER BRAISED SHORT RIBS

WHY THIS RECIPE WORKS: Beef short ribs, which contain lots of fat and connective tissue, are ideal for long, slow cooking. We wanted to develop a recipe for the slow cooker that would produce meaty ribs in a rich, oniony sauce.

Thoroughly browning the ribs first gave us a good start. Next we browned lots of onions. Instead of stock or broth, we chose beer as the braising liquid, and dark beer worked best. Tomato paste and soy sauce intensified the taste and color of the sauce (flavors tend to become muted after hours in a slow cooker). But we thought the dish lacked balance. We found our solution in an unusual source: prunes. They melted into the sauce and were unidentifiable, but their sweetness balanced the other flavors nicely. Livened up just before serving with some Dijon mustard and fresh thyme, these slow-cooker short ribs had the rich, complex flavor we were looking for.

Slow-Cooker Beer-Braised Short Ribs

SERVES 4 TO 6

The only way to remove fat from the braising liquid is to prepare this recipe a day or two before you want to serve it. Luckily, the short ribs actually taste better if cooked in advance and then reheated in the defatted braising liquid.

- 5 pounds English-style beef short ribs (6 to 8 ribs), trimmed of excess fat
  Table salt and ground black pepper
- 2 tablespoons vegetable oil
- 2 tablespoons unsalted butter
- 3 pounds yellow onions (about 6 medium), halved and sliced thin
- 2 tablespoons tomato paste
- 2 (12-ounce) bottles dark beer
- 12 pitted prunes
- 2 tablespoons soy sauce
- 2 tablespoons Minute tapioca
- 2 bay leaves
- 2 teaspoons minced fresh thyme leaves
- 3 tablespoons Dijon mustard
- 2 tablespoons minced fresh parsley leaves

1. Season the ribs with salt and pepper. Heat the oil in a 12-inch skillet over medium-high heat until just smoking. Add half of the ribs, meaty side down, and cook until well browned, about 5 minutes. Turn each rib on one side and cook until well browned, about 1 minute. Repeat with the remaining sides. Transfer the ribs to a slow-cooker insert, arranging them meaty side down. Repeat with the remaining ribs.

2. Pour off all but 1 teaspoon fat from the skillet. Add the butter and reduce the heat to medium. When the butter has melted, add the onions and cook, stirring occasionally, until well browned, 25 to 30 minutes. Stir in the tomato paste and cook, coating the onions with the tomato paste, until the paste begins to brown, about 5 minutes. Stir in the beer, bring to a simmer, and cook, scraping the browned bits from the pan bottom with a wooden spoon, until the foaming subsides, about 5 minutes. Remove the skillet from the heat and stir in the prunes, soy sauce, tapioca, bay leaves, and 1 teaspoon of the thyme. Transfer to the slow-cooker insert.

3. Set the slow cooker on low, cover, and cook until the ribs are fork-tender, 10 to 11 hours. (Alternately, cook on high for 4 to 5 hours.) Transfer the ribs to a baking dish and strain the liquid through a fine-mesh strainer into a bowl. Cover and refrigerate for at least 8 hours or up to 2 days.

4. When ready to serve, use a spoon to skim off the hardened fat from the liquid; discard the bay leaves. Place the short ribs, meaty side down, and the liquid in a Dutch oven and reheat over medium heat until warmed through, about 20 minutes. Transfer the ribs to a serving platter. Whisk the mustard and remaining 1 teaspoon thyme into the sauce and season with salt and pepper to taste. Pour 1 cup of the sauce over the ribs. Sprinkle with the parsley and serve, passing the remaining sauce separately.

CHICKEN AND DUMPLINGS

WHY THIS RECIPE WORKS: Chicken and dumplings make chicken pot pie look easy. There's no disguising a leaden dumpling. One goal was to develop a dumpling that was light yet substantial, and tender yet durable. The other was to develop a well-rounded recipe that, like chicken pot pie, included vegetables, therein supplying the cook with a complete meal in one dish.

Dumplings can contain myriad ingredients, and there are just as many different ways to mix them. We tried them all—with disastrous results. But when we stumbled on a unique method of adding warm liquid rather than cold to the flour and fat, our dumplings were great—firm but light and fluffy. The reason? The heat expands and sets the flour so that the dumplings don't absorb liquid in the stew. The best-tasting dumplings were made with all-purpose flour, whole milk, and the chicken fat left from browning the chicken.

For the filling, we chose bone-in, skin-on chicken thighs for their deep flavor and added enough vegetables to make this dish into a meal. After browning the chicken and vegetables separately, we simmered them in the sauce until the chicken was done and the sauce thickened. We added some peas and parsley, then steamed the dumplings on top of everything until the dumplings turned light and tender.

Chicken and Dumplings

SERVES 6 TO 8

Don't use low-fat or fat-free milk in this recipe. Be sure to reserve 3 tablespoons of chicken fat for the dumplings in step 4; however, if you prefer not to use chicken fat, unsalted butter can be substituted. Start the dumpling dough only when you're ready to top the stew with the dumplings.

STEW

- 5 pounds bone-in, skin-on chicken thighs (about 12 thighs)
  Table salt and ground black pepper
- 4 teaspoons vegetable oil
- 4 tablespoons (½ stick) unsalted butter
- 4 carrots, peeled and sliced ¼ inch thick
- 2 celery ribs, sliced ¼ inch thick
- 1 medium onion, minced
- 6 tablespoons unbleached all-purpose flour
- ¼ cup dry sherry
- 4½ cups low-sodium chicken broth
- ¼ cup whole milk (see note)
- 1 teaspoon minced fresh thyme leaves
- 2 bay leaves
- 1 cup frozen green peas
- 3 tablespoons minced fresh parsley leaves

DUMPLINGS

- 2 cups unbleached all-purpose flour
- 1 tablespoon baking powder
- 1 teaspoon table salt
- 1 cup whole milk (see note)
- 3 tablespoons reserved chicken fat (see note)

1. FOR THE STEW: Pat the chicken dry with paper towels, then season with salt and pepper. Heat 2 teaspoons of the oil in a large Dutch oven over medium-high heat until just smoking. Add half of the chicken and cook until golden on both sides, about 10 minutes. Transfer the chicken to a plate and remove the browned skin. Pour off the chicken fat and reserve. Return the pot to medium-high heat and repeat with the remaining 2 teaspoons oil and the remaining chicken. Pour off and reserve any chicken fat.

2. Add the butter to the Dutch oven and melt over medium-high heat. Add the carrots, celery, onion, and ¼ teaspoon salt and cook until softened, about 7 minutes. Stir in the flour. Whisk in the sherry, scraping up any browned bits. Stir in the broth, milk, thyme, and bay leaves. Nestle the chicken, with any accumulated juices, into the pot. Cover and simmer until the chicken is fully cooked and tender, about 1 hour.

3. Transfer the chicken to a carving board. Discard the bay leaves. Allow the sauce to settle for a few minutes, then skim the fat from the surface using a wide spoon. Shred the chicken, discarding the bones, then return it to the stew.

4. FOR THE DUMPLINGS: Stir the flour, baking powder, and salt together. Microwave the milk and chicken fat in a microwave-safe bowl on high power until just warm (do not overheat), about 1 minute. Stir the warmed milk mixture into the flour mixture with a wooden spoon until incorporated and smooth.

5. Return the stew to a simmer, stir in the peas and parsley, and season with salt and pepper to taste. Drop golf-ball-sized dumplings over the top of the stew, about ¼ inch apart (you should have about 18 dumplings). Reduce the heat to low, cover, and cook until the dumplings have doubled in size, 15 to 18 minutes. Serve.

LATINO-STYLE CHICKEN AND RICE (ARROZ CON POLLO)

WHY THIS RECIPE WORKS: The traditional way of cooking this bold-flavored cousin of American chicken and rice is time-consuming, requiring an overnight marinade of the chicken and then a long, slow stewing with rice and vegetables. Could we find a way to achieve the same results in a lot less time?

We began by choosing chicken thighs, not only for shopping convenience but also to ensure that all of the pieces would cook at the same rate—a problem when using a combination of white and dark meat. We poached the thighs in a broth preseasoned with a *sofrito*, a classic Latin American mixture of chopped onions and green peppers. About half an hour before the chicken finished cooking, we added medium-grain rice (which we preferred over long-grain for its creamy texture), stirring it a few times to ensure even cooking. And for maximum flavor, we devised two marinades. Before cooking, we marinated the chicken quickly in garlic, oregano, and distilled white vinegar; after cooking we tossed the cooked chicken with olive oil, vinegar, and cilantro.

We had one final dilemma: how to give the dish its traditional orange hue that comes from infusing oil with achiote, a tropical seed not readily available in local grocery stores. Adding canned tomato sauce solved the problem.

Latino-Style Chicken and Rice

SERVES 4 TO 6

To keep the dish from becoming greasy, remove any visible pockets of waxy yellow fat from the chicken and most of the skin, leaving just enough to protect the meat. To use long-grain rice instead of medium-grain, increase the amount of water added in step 2 from ¼ to ¾ cup and add the additional ¼ cup water in step 3 as needed. When removing the chicken from the bone in step 4, we found it better to use two spoons rather than two forks; forks tend to shred the meat, while spoons pull it apart in chunks.

- 6 medium garlic cloves, minced or pressed through a garlic press (about 2 tablespoons)
  Table salt
- 1 tablespoon plus 2 teaspoons distilled white vinegar
- ½ teaspoon dried oregano
  Ground black pepper
- 4 pounds bone-in, skin-on chicken thighs (about 10 thighs), trimmed (see note)
- 2 tablespoons olive oil
- 1 medium onion, minced
- 1 small green pepper, stemmed, seeded, and chopped fine
- ¼ teaspoon red pepper flakes
- ¼ cup minced fresh cilantro leaves
- 1¾ cups low-sodium chicken broth
- 1 (8-ounce) can tomato sauce
- ¼ cup water, plus more if needed (see note)
- 3 cups medium-grain rice (see note)
- ½ cup green manzanilla olives, pitted and halved
- 1 tablespoon capers
- ½ cup jarred pimientos, cut into 2 by ¼-inch strips
  Lemon wedges, for serving

1. Adjust an oven rack to the middle position and heat the oven to 350 degrees. Place the garlic and 1 teaspoon salt in a large bowl; using a rubber spatula, mix to make a smooth paste. Add 1 tablespoon of the vinegar, the oregano, and ½ teaspoon black pepper to the garlic-salt mixture; stir to combine. Place the chicken in the bowl with the marinade. Coat the chicken pieces evenly with the marinade; set aside for 15 minutes.

2. Heat 1 tablespoon of the oil in a Dutch oven over medium heat until shimmering. Add the onion, green pepper, and red pepper flakes; cook, stirring occasionally, until the vegetables begin to soften, 4 to 8 minutes. Add 2 tablespoons of the cilantro; stir to combine. Push the vegetables to the sides of the pot and increase the heat to medium-high. Add the chicken to the clearing in the center of the pot, skin side down, in an even layer. Cook, without moving the chicken, until the outer layer of the meat becomes opaque, 2 to 4 minutes. (If the chicken begins to brown, reduce the heat to medium.) Using tongs, flip the chicken and cook on the second side until opaque, 2 to 4 minutes more. Add the broth, tomato sauce, and water; stir to combine. Bring to a simmer; cover, reduce the heat to medium-low, and simmer for 20 minutes.

3. Add the rice, olives, capers, and ¾ teaspoon salt; stir well. Bring to a simmer, cover, and place the pot in the oven. After 10 minutes, remove the pot from the oven and stir the chicken and rice once from the bottom up. Cover and return the pot to the oven. After another 10 minutes, stir once more, adding another ¼ cup water if the rice appears dry and the bottom of the pot is beginning to burn. Cover and return the pot to the oven; cook until the rice has absorbed all the liquid and is tender but still holds its shape and the thickest part of the thighs registers 175 degrees on an instant-read thermometer, about 10 minutes longer.

4. Using tongs, remove the chicken from the pot; replace the lid and set the pot aside. Remove and discard the chicken skin; using two spoons, pull the meat off the bones into large chunks. Using your fingers, remove the remaining fat and any dark veins from the chicken pieces. Place the chicken in a large bowl and toss with the remaining 1 tablespoon oil, remaining 2 teaspoons vinegar, remaining 2 tablespoons cilantro, and the pimientos; season with salt and pepper to taste. Place the chicken on top of the rice, cover, and let stand until warmed through, about 5 minutes. Serve, passing the lemon wedges separately.

Latino-Style Chicken and Rice with Bacon and Roasted Red Peppers

Bacon adds a welcome layer of richness, and red peppers bring subtle sweet flavor and color to this variation. To use long-grain rice, increase the amount of water to ¾ cup in step 2 and the salt added in step 3 to 1 teaspoon.

1. Follow the recipe for Latino-Style Chicken and Rice through step 1, substituting 2 teaspoons sweet paprika for the oregano and sherry vinegar for the white vinegar.

2. Fry 4 ounces (about 4 strips) bacon, cut into ½-inch pieces, in a Dutch oven over medium heat until crisp, 6 to 8 minutes. Using a slotted spoon, transfer the bacon to a paper towel–lined plate; pour off all but 1 tablespoon bacon fat. Continue with step 2, substituting 1 small red pepper, chopped fine, and 1 medium carrot, chopped fine, for the green pepper and sautéing the vegetables in the bacon fat.

3. Continue with the recipe, substituting ¼ cup minced fresh parsley leaves for the cilantro, omitting the olives and capers, and substituting ½ cup roasted red peppers, cut into 2 by ¼-inch strips, for the pimientos. Garnish the chicken and rice with the reserved bacon before serving.

Latino-Style Chicken and Rice with Ham, Peas, and Orange

Ham gives this variation further richness, and orange zest and juice provide a bright accent. To use long-grain rice, increase the amount of water to ¾ cup in step 2 and the salt added in step 3 to 1 teaspoon.

1. Follow the recipe for Latino-Style Chicken and Rice through step 1, substituting 1 tablespoon ground cumin for the oregano.

2. Continue with step 2, adding 8 ounces ham steak or Canadian bacon, cut into ½-inch pieces (about 1½ cups), with the onion, green pepper, and red pepper flakes.

3. With a vegetable peeler, remove three 3-inch strips of zest from 1 orange. Continue with step 3, adding the orange zest with the rice, olives, capers, and salt. Add 1 cup frozen peas to the pot with ¼ cup water, if necessary, after stirring the contents of the pot the second time.

4. In step 4, add 3 tablespoons juice from 1 orange to the bowl with the olive oil, vinegar, cilantro, and pimientos and proceed with the recipe.

PAELLA

WHY THIS RECIPE WORKS: Paella can be a big hit at restaurants but an unwieldy production at home. Could we re-create this Spanish classic in two hours without using any fancy equipment?

The key to our paella was finding equipment and ingredients that stayed true to the dish's heritage. First, we substituted a Dutch oven for a single-purpose paella pan. Then we pared down our ingredients, dismissing lobster (too much work), diced pork (sausage would be enough), fish (flakes too easily), rabbit and snails (too unconventional). We were left with chorizo, chicken (boneless, skinless thighs), shrimp (marinated in a garlic–olive oil mixture), and mussels (favored over scallops, clams, and calamari). We next simplified our *sofrito*—in this Spanish version, a combination of onions, garlic, and tomatoes—by mincing a can of drained diced tomatoes rather than seeding and grating a fresh tomato.

When we focused on the rice, we found we preferred short-grain varieties. Valencia was our favorite, with Italian Arborio a close second. Sautéing the rice in the same pot used to brown the chicken and sausage and make the sofrito boosts its flavor. For the cooking liquid and seasonings, we chose chicken broth, white wine, saffron, and a bay leaf. Once the rice had absorbed almost all the liquid, we added the mussels, shrimp, and peas to the mix. The result? A colorful, streamlined, yet flavorful rendition of the Spanish classic.

Paella

SERVES 6

Use a Dutch oven that is 11 to 12 inches in diameter with at least a 6-quart capacity. Dry-cured Spanish chorizo is the sausage of choice for paella, but fresh chorizo or linguiça is an acceptable substitute.

Soccarat, a layer of crusty browned rice that forms on the bottom of the pan, is a traditional part of paella. In our version, soccarat does not develop because most of the cooking is done in the oven. We have provided instructions to develop soccarat in step 5; if you prefer, skip this step and go directly from step 4 to step 6.

- 1 pound extra-large shrimp (21 to 25 per pound), peeled and deveined (see page 160)
  Table salt and ground black pepper
- 2 tablespoons olive oil, plus extra as needed
- 8–9 medium garlic cloves, minced or pressed through a garlic press (2 generous tablespoons)
- 1 pound boneless, skinless chicken thighs (about 4 thighs) trimmed and halved crosswise
- 1 red bell pepper, stemmed, seeded, and cut pole to pole into ½-inch-wide strips
- 8 ounces Spanish chorizo, sliced ½ inch thick on the bias (see note)
- 1 medium onion, minced
- 1 (14.5-ounce) can diced tomatoes, drained, minced, and drained again
- 2 cups Valencia or Arborio rice
- 3 cups low-sodium chicken broth
- ⅓ cup dry white wine
- ½ teaspoon saffron threads, crumbled
- 1 bay leaf
- 1 dozen mussels, scrubbed and debearded
- ½ cup frozen peas, thawed
- 2 tablespoons chopped fresh parsley leaves
- 1 lemon, cut into wedges, for serving

1. Adjust an oven rack to the lower-middle position and heat the oven to 350 degrees. Toss the shrimp, ¼ teaspoon salt, ¼ teaspoon pepper, 1 tablespoon oil, and 1 teaspoon of the garlic in a medium bowl; cover with plastic wrap and refrigerate until needed. Season the chicken thighs with salt and pepper; set aside.

2. Heat 2 teaspoons oil in a large Dutch oven over medium-high heat until shimmering but not smoking. Add the pepper strips and cook, stirring occasionally, until the skin begins to blister and turn spotty black, 3 to 4 minutes. Transfer the pepper to a small plate and set aside.

3. Add 1 teaspoon oil to the now-empty Dutch oven; heat the oil until shimmering but not smoking. Add the chicken pieces in a single layer; cook, without moving the pieces, until browned, about 3 minutes. Turn the pieces and brown on the second side, about 3 minutes longer; transfer the chicken to a medium bowl. Reduce the heat to medium and add the chorizo to the pot; cook, stirring frequently, until deeply browned and the fat begins to render, 4 to 5 minutes. Transfer the chorizo to the bowl with the chicken and set aside.

4. Add enough oil to the fat in the Dutch oven to equal 2 tablespoons; heat over medium heat until shimmering but not smoking. Add the onion and cook, stirring frequently, until softened, about 3 minutes; stir in the remaining garlic and cook until fragrant, about 1 minute. Stir in the tomatoes; cook until the mixture begins to darken and thicken slightly, about 3 minutes. Stir in the rice and cook until the grains are well coated with the tomato mixture, 1 to 2 minutes. Stir in the chicken broth, wine, saffron, bay leaf, and ½ teaspoon salt. Return the chicken and chorizo to the pot, increase the heat to medium-high, and bring to a boil, uncovered, stirring occasionally. Cover the pot and transfer it to the oven; cook until the rice absorbs almost all of the liquid, about 15 minutes. Remove the pot from the oven (close the oven door to retain heat). Uncover the pot; scatter the shrimp over the rice, insert the mussels, hinged side down, into the rice (so they stand upright), arrange the bell pepper strips in a pinwheel pattern, and scatter the peas over the top. Cover and return to the oven; cook until the shrimp are opaque and the mussels have opened, 10 to 12 minutes.

5. Optional: If soccarat is desired (see note), set the Dutch oven, uncovered, over medium-high heat for about 5 minutes, rotating the pot 180 degrees after about 2 minutes for even browning.

6. Let the paella stand, covered, about 5 minutes. Discard any mussels that have not opened and the bay leaf, if it can be easily removed. Sprinkle with the parsley and serve, passing the lemon wedges separately.

GUMBO

WHY THIS RECIPE WORKS: With shrimp, sausage, and vegetables in a deeply flavored, rich brown sauce with a touch of heat, gumbo is a unique one-pot meal. We wanted a foolproof, streamlined technique for gumbo that featured a thick, smooth sauce with lots of well-seasoned vegetables, meat, and fish.

The basis of gumbo is the roux, which is flour cooked in fat. For a deep, dark roux in half the time, we heated the oil before adding the flour. We also added the roux to room-temperature shrimp stock (supplemented with clam juice) to prevent separating. Although tomatoes are traditional in gumbo, our tasters didn't think they were necessary—but garlic was, and lots of it. Some cayenne pepper added the requisite heat. We added spicy andouille sausage and simmered everything for half an hour, tossing in the shrimp only during the last few minutes of cooking. You can add filé powder if you like, but our gumbo is delicious even without it.

Creole-Style Shrimp and Sausage Gumbo
SERVES 6 TO 8

Making a dark roux can be dangerous, as the mixture reaches temperatures in excess of 400 degrees. Therefore, use a deep pot for cooking the roux and long-handled utensils for stirring it, and be careful not to splash it on yourself. One secret to smooth gumbo is adding shrimp stock that is neither too hot nor too cold to the roux. For a stock that is at the right temperature when the roux is done, start preparing it before you tend to the vegetables and other ingredients, strain it, and then give it a head start on cooling by immediately adding the ice water and clam juice. So that your constant stirring of the roux will not be interrupted, start the roux only after you've made the stock. Alternatively, you can make the stock well ahead of time and bring it back to room temperature before using it. Spicy andouille sausage is a Louisiana specialty that may not be available everywhere; kielbasa or any fully cooked smoked sausage makes a fine substitute. Gumbo is traditionally served over white rice.

1½ pounds small shrimp (51 to 60 per pound),
shells removed and reserved
3½ cups ice water
1 (8-ounce) bottle clam juice
½ cup vegetable oil
½ cup all-purpose flour, preferably bleached
2 medium onions, minced
1 medium red bell pepper, stemmed, seeded,
and chopped fine
1 medium celery rib, chopped fine
6 medium garlic cloves, minced or pressed through
a garlic press (about 2 tablespoons)
1 teaspoon dried thyme
Table salt
Cayenne pepper
2 bay leaves
1 pound smoked sausage, such as andouille or kielbasa
(see note), sliced ¼ inch thick
½ cup minced fresh parsley leaves
4 medium scallions, white and green parts, sliced thin
Ground black pepper

1. Bring the reserved shrimp shells and 4½ cups water to a boil in a stockpot or large saucepan over medium-high heat. Reduce the heat to medium-low and simmer for 20 minutes. Strain the stock and add the ice water and clam juice (you should have about 2 quarts of tepid stock, 100 to 110 degrees); discard the shells. Set the stock aside.

2. Heat the oil in a Dutch oven or large, heavy-bottomed saucepan over medium-high heat until it registers 200 degrees on an instant-read thermometer, 1½ to 2 minutes. Reduce the heat to medium and gradually stir in the flour with a wooden spatula or spoon, making sure to work out any lumps that may form. Continue stirring constantly, reaching into the corners of the pan, until the mixture has a toasty aroma and is deep reddish brown, about 20 minutes. (The roux will thin as it cooks; if it begins to smoke, remove the pan from the heat and stir the roux constantly to cool slightly.)

3. Add the onions, bell pepper, celery, garlic, thyme, 1 teaspoon salt, and ¼ teaspoon cayenne to the roux and cook, stirring frequently, until the vegetables soften, 8 to 10 minutes. Add 4 cups of the reserved stock in a slow, steady stream while stirring vigorously. Stir in the remaining 4 cups of stock. Increase the heat to high and bring to a boil. Reduce the heat to medium-low, skim the foam from the surface with a wide spoon, add the bay leaves, and simmer, uncovered, skimming the foam as it rises to the surface, about 30 minutes. (The mixture can be covered and set aside for several hours. Reheat when ready to proceed.)

BEHIND THE SCENES

A PEEK INSIDE THE TEST KITCHEN FREEZER

Curious as to what we keep in our freezer? A whole lot more than you might think. In fact, we've found that some pantry staples are better preserved in the freezer. Here's a list of the more unusual items the test kitchen keeps on ice.

RIPE OR OVERRIPE BANANAS: Great to have for making banana bread or muffins, or drop them into a blender while still frozen for fruit smoothies. Peel bananas before freezing.

NUTS: Sealed in a zipper-lock freezer bag, nuts stay fresh tasting for months. And there's no need to defrost; frozen nuts chop just as easily as fresh.

HERBS: Dried bay leaves retain their potency much longer when stored in the freezer. Chopped fresh herbs such as parsley, sage, rosemary, and thyme can be covered with water in an ice cube tray and then frozen indefinitely. Keep the frozen cubes in a zipper-lock freezer bag until needed for sauces, soups, or stews. Homemade pesto can also be frozen in ice cube trays, and there's no need to add water.

BUTTER: When stored in the refrigerator, butter picks up off-odors and eventually turns rancid. You can prolong its life by storing it in the freezer. Transfer it to the refrigerator one stick at a time, as you need it.

DRY GOODS: Stored in the freezer, flour, bread crumbs, cornmeal, oats, and other grains are protected from humidity, bugs, and rancidity.

4. Stir in the sausage and continue simmering to blend the flavors, about 30 minutes. Stir in the shrimp and simmer until cooked through, about 5 minutes. Off the heat, stir in the parsley and scallions and season with salt, ground black pepper, and cayenne to taste. Discard the bay leaves and serve immediately.

CHAPTER 5

SIMPLY CHICKEN

Sautéed Chicken
Cutlets with Mustard-
Cider Sauce   64

Breaded Chicken
Cutlets   65

Stuffed Chicken Cutlets
with Ham and
Cheddar   66

Chicken Kiev   67

Sweet and Tangy
Oven-Barbecued
Chicken   69

Spice-Rubbed Picnic
Chicken   70

Pan-Roasted Chicken
Breasts with Sage-Vermouth
Sauce   71

Simple Roast Chicken   72

Classic Roast
Lemon Chicken   73

Crisp-Skinned
Roast Chicken   74

Glazed Roast Chicken   75

Stovetop Roast
Chicken with Lemon-
Herb Sauce   77

High-Roast Butterflied
Chicken with
Potatoes   78

Mustard-Garlic Butter
with Thyme

"Stuffed" Roast
Butterflied Chicken   79

Mushroom-Leek Bread
Stuffing with Herbs

Crispy Fried Chicken   80

Oven-Fried Chicken   82

Buffalo Wings   83

SAUTÉED CHICKEN CUTLETS

WHY THIS RECIPE WORKS: Sautéed super-thin cutlets are satisfying midweek fare, except when they are tough and dry. We wanted juicy, ultrathin sautéed chicken cutlets, paired with a sauce that complements, rather than over-powers, the meat.

For evenly sized cutlets, we took a two-step approach. We halved the chicken breasts horizontally before pounding them to an even thickness under plastic wrap. Halving and pounding the breasts ensures that they cook at the same rate, and turn out moist, tender, and juicy. To further ensure the cutlets turned out juicy, we browned them on only one side. And for the sauce, we kept the flavors simple, relying on the sweet, tangy combination of apple cider and cider vinegar complemented with the kick of whole grain mustard.

Sautéed Chicken Cutlets with Mustard-Cider Sauce
SERVES 4

To make slicing the chicken easier, freeze it for 15 minutes.

CHICKEN

- **4 (6 to 8-ounce) boneless, skinless chicken breasts, tenderloins removed and breasts trimmed**
  Table salt and ground black pepper
- **2 tablespoons vegetable oil**

MUSTARD-CIDER SAUCE

- **2 teaspoons vegetable oil**
- **1 medium shallot, minced (about 3 tablespoons)**
- **1¼ cups apple cider**
- **2 tablespoons cider vinegar**
- **2 teaspoons whole grain mustard**
- **2 teaspoons minced fresh parsley leaves**
- **2 tablespoons unsalted butter**
  Table salt and ground black pepper

1. FOR THE CHICKEN: Adjust an oven rack to the middle position and heat the oven to 200 degrees. Halve the chicken horizontally, then cover the chicken halves with plastic wrap and use a meat pounder to pound the cutlets to an even ¼-inch thickness. Season both sides of each cutlet with salt and pepper. Heat 1 tablespoon of the oil in a 12-inch skillet over medium-high heat until just smoking. Place four cutlets in the skillet and cook without moving them until browned, about 2 minutes. Using a

spatula, flip the cutlets and continue to cook until the second sides are opaque, 15 to 20 seconds. Transfer to a large heatproof plate. Add the remaining 1 tablespoon oil to the now-empty skillet and repeat to cook the remaining cutlets. Cover the plate loosely with foil and transfer it to the oven to keep warm while making the sauce.

2. FOR THE SAUCE: Off the heat, add the oil and shallot to the hot skillet. Using residual heat, cook, stirring constantly, until softened, about 30 seconds. Set the skillet over medium-high heat and add the cider and vinegar. Bring to a simmer, scraping the pan bottom with a wooden spoon to loosen any browned bits. Simmer until reduced to ½ cup, 6 to 7 minutes. Off the heat, stir in the mustard and parsley; whisk in the butter 1 tablespoon at a time. Season with salt and pepper to taste and serve immediately with the cutlets.

BREADED CHICKEN CUTLETS

WHY THIS RECIPE WORKS: Breaded chicken cutlets, for all their apparent simplicity, can be problematic. Too often, they emerge from the frying pan with either an underdone or burnt coating, which falls off the tasteless, rubbery chicken underneath. We wanted chicken cutlets with flavorful meat and a crisp, crunchy crust that would adhere nicely to the meat.

To ensure even cooking, we flattened the chicken breasts to ½ inch; thin enough to cook evenly, but thick enough to make a hearty, crisp cutlet. To prevent crust separation, we coated the chicken with flour, an egg and oil mixture, and flavorful, fresh bread crumbs. We then let them sit for five minutes to help set the crust. For the crispiest coating, we fried the cutlets in batches in vegetable oil.

Breaded Chicken Cutlets

SERVES 4

If you'd rather not prepare fresh bread crumbs, use panko, the extra-crisp Japanese bread crumbs. The chicken is cooked in batches of two because the crust is noticeably more crisp if the pan is not overcrowded. Note that these cutlets are a bit thicker than others in the chapter and should not be halved horizontally.

- **4 (5 to 6-ounce) boneless, skinless chicken breasts, tenderloins removed and breasts trimmed**
   Table salt and ground black pepper
- **3 slices high-quality white sandwich bread, torn into quarters**
- **¾ cup unbleached all-purpose flour**
- **2 large eggs**
- **1 tablespoon plus ¾ cup vegetable oil**
   Lemon wedges for serving

1. Use a meat pounder to pound the chicken breasts to an even ½-inch thickness. Sprinkle the cutlets with salt and pepper and set aside. Set a large wire rack over a large baking sheet and set aside.

2. Adjust an oven rack to the lower-middle position, set a heatproof plate on the rack, and heat the oven to 200 degrees. Process the bread in a food processor until evenly fine-textured, 20 to 30 seconds. Transfer the crumbs to a pie plate or shallow dish. Spread the flour in a second plate. Beat the eggs with 1 tablespoon of the oil in a third plate.

3. Working with one cutlet at a time, dredge each cutlet in the flour, shaking off the excess. Using tongs, dip both sides of the cutlets in the egg mixture, allowing the excess to drip off. Dip both sides of the cutlets in the bread crumbs, pressing the crumbs with your fingers to form an even, cohesive coat. Place the breaded cutlets on the wire rack and allow the coating to dry about 5 minutes.

4. Meanwhile, heat 6 tablespoons more oil in a 12-inch nonstick skillet over medium-high heat until shimmering but not smoking, about 2 minutes. Lay 2 cutlets gently in the skillet; cook until deep golden brown and crisp on the first side, gently pressing down on the cutlets with a metal spatula, about 2½ minutes. Using tongs, flip the cutlets, reduce the heat to medium, and continue to cook until the meat feels firm when pressed gently and the second side is deep golden brown and crisp, 2½ to

3 minutes longer. Line the warmed plate with a double layer of paper towels and set the cutlets on top; return the plate to the oven.

5. Discard the oil in the skillet and wipe the skillet clean with paper towels. Repeat step 4 using the remaining 6 tablespoons oil and remaining cutlets; serve with lemon wedges.

STUFFED CHICKEN CUTLETS

WHY THIS RECIPE WORKS: Cutlets that are stuffed and breaded are special-occasion food. The filling moistens the chicken from the inside with a creamy, tasty sauce, while the crust makes a crunchy counterpoint. The problem is that these bundles can leak and getting the right proportion of filling to cutlet can be tricky. We wanted stuffed chicken cutlets with a creamy filling that wouldn't turn runny and flavors that would complement, not overpower, the chicken. And we wanted the crust to be crisp all over and completely seal in the filling so that none leaked out.

We pounded the chicken breasts thin so they rolled easily and cooked evenly. A combination of cream cheese and cheddar mixed with onion, garlic, and fresh thyme gave us a creamy, well-flavored filling. Thin-sliced ham added another layer of flavor to our cutlets. Before we breaded the cutlets, we chilled them in the refrigerator to help the filling set—this step prevented leaks during cooking. For perfectly cooked stuffed cutlets, we sautéed them just until brown, then moved them into the oven to finish cooking through.

Stuffed Chicken Cutlets with Ham and Cheddar

SERVES 4

To make slicing the chicken easier, freeze it for 15 minutes. The cutlets can be filled and rolled in advance, then refrigerated for up to 24 hours. To dry fresh bread crumbs, spread them out on a baking sheet and bake in a 200-degree oven, stirring occasionally, for 30 minutes. Removing some moisture from the crumbs cuts down on splattering when the breaded cutlets are pan-fried.

FILLING

- 1 tablespoon unsalted butter
- 1 small onion, minced
- 1 small garlic clove, minced or pressed through a garlic press (½ teaspoon)
- 4 ounces cream cheese, softened
- 1 teaspoon minced fresh thyme leaves
- 2 ounces cheddar cheese, shredded (about ½ cup)
  Table salt and ground black pepper
- 4 slices (about 4 ounces) thin-sliced cooked deli ham

CHICKEN

- 4 (5 to 6-ounce) boneless, skinless chicken breasts, tenderloins removed and breasts trimmed
  Table salt and ground black pepper
- ¾ cup unbleached all-purpose flour
- 2 large eggs
- 1 tablespoon plus ¾ cup vegetable oil
- 4 slices high-quality white sandwich bread, pulsed in a food processor to coarse crumbs and dried (see note)

1. FOR THE FILLING: Melt the butter in a medium skillet over low heat; add the onion and cook, stirring occasionally, until deep golden brown, 15 to 20 minutes. Stir in the garlic and cook until fragrant, about 30 seconds longer; set aside.

2. In a medium bowl and using an electric mixer, beat the cream cheese on medium speed until light and fluffy, about 1 minute. Stir in the onion mixture, thyme, and cheddar; season with salt and pepper to taste and set aside.

3. Following the photos, butterfly each chicken breast and pound between two sheets of plastic wrap to a uniform ¼-inch thickness. Pound the outer perimeter to ⅛ inch. Place the chicken cutlets, smooth side down, on a work surface and season with salt and pepper. Spread each cutlet with one-quarter of the cheese mixture, then place 1 slice of ham on top of the cheese, folding the ham as necessary to fit onto the surface of the cutlet. Roll up each cutlet from the tapered end, folding in the edges to form a neat cylinder. Refrigerate until the filling is firm, at least 1 hour.

4. FOR THE CHICKEN: Adjust an oven rack to the lower-middle position and heat the oven to 450 degrees. Set a large wire rack over a large baking sheet and set aside. Place the flour in a pie plate or shallow dish. Beat the eggs with 1 tablespoon of the oil in a second plate. Spread the bread crumbs in a third plate. Dredge 1 chicken roll in the flour, shaking off the excess, then coat with the egg mixture, allowing the excess to drip off. Coat all sides of the chicken roll with the bread crumbs, pressing gently so that the crumbs adhere. Place on the wire rack and repeat the flouring and breading with the remaining chicken. Allow the coating to dry about 5 minutes. Transfer the chicken to a plate. Wipe the wire rack and baking sheet clean and set aside.

5. Heat the remaining ¾ cup oil in a 10-inch nonstick skillet over medium-high heat until shimmering, but not smoking. Using tongs, carefully add the chicken, seam side down, to the pan, and cook until medium golden brown, about 2 minutes. Turn each roll and cook until medium golden brown on all sides, 2 to 3 minutes longer. Transfer the chicken rolls, seam side down, to the now-clean wire rack on the baking sheet; bake until deep golden brown and an instant-read thermometer inserted into the center of a roll registers 160 to 165 degrees, about 15 minutes. Let stand 5 minutes before slicing each roll crosswise on the diagonal with a serrated knife into five pieces; arrange on individual dinner plates and serve.

CHICKEN KIEV

WHY THIS RECIPE WORKS: Chicken Kiev is a recipe that elevates the humdrum boneless, skinless chicken breast to star status. Traditionally, the dish is a crisp fried chicken breast encasing a buttery herb sauce that dramatically oozes out when knife meets fork. But today, the dish has sunk to the level of bad banquet food—a greasy, bread crumb–coated chicken breast whose meat is dry and chalky despite the butter filling. This was a dish that truly needed its greatness restored.

We found that butterflying the chicken breasts, then pounding them thin—and even thinner at the edges—helped created chicken bundles that wouldn't leak the butter filling. Instead of deep-frying the chicken as is traditionally done, we chose to oven-fry the chicken. This made for a crisp, rather than greasy, Kiev. Toasting the bread crumbs prior to breading the chicken helped mimic the flavorful, golden brown crust of the original. All we had left to do was to perk up the plain filling. Traditional recipes stuff the Kievs with butter spiked with nothing more than parsley and chives, but we found that minced shallots were more flavorful than chives and a small amount of minced tarragon added a pleasant hint of sweetness. A squeeze of lemon juice tamed the rich butter with a bit of acidity and Dijon mustard, whisked into the egg wash (for coating the chicken), provided another layer of flavor for a chicken Kiev that was anything but bland.

NOTES FROM THE TEST KITCHEN

ASSEMBLING CHICKEN KIEV

1. Cut the butter into four rectangular pieces. Place one butter piece near the tapered end of the cutlet.

2. Roll up the tapered end of the chicken over the butter, then fold in the sides and continue rolling, pressing on the seam to seal. Repeat with the remaining butter pieces and cutlets. The chicken is now ready to be breaded.

Chicken Kiev

SERVES 4

To make slicing the chicken easier, freeze it for 15 minutes. Unbaked, breaded chicken Kievs can be refrigerated overnight and baked the next day or frozen for up to one month. To cook frozen chicken Kievs, increase the baking time to 50 to 55 minutes (do not thaw the chicken).

HERB BUTTER

- 8 tablespoons (1 stick) unsalted butter, softened
- 1 tablespoon juice from 1 lemon
- 1 small shallot, minced (about 1 tablespoon)
- 1 tablespoon minced fresh parsley leaves
- ½ teaspoon minced fresh tarragon leaves
- ⅜ teaspoon table salt
- ⅛ teaspoon ground black pepper

CHICKEN

- 4 slices high-quality white sandwich bread, torn into quarters
  Table salt and ground black pepper
- 2 tablespoons vegetable oil
- 4 (7 to 8-ounce) boneless, skinless chicken breasts, tenderloins removed and breasts trimmed
- 1 cup unbleached all-purpose flour
- 3 large eggs, beaten
- 1 teaspoon Dijon mustard

1. FOR THE HERB BUTTER: Mix the ingredients in a medium bowl with a rubber spatula until thoroughly combined. Form into a 3-inch square on a sheet of plastic wrap; wrap tightly and refrigerate until firm, about 1 hour.

2. FOR THE CHICKEN: Adjust an oven rack to the lower-middle position and heat the oven to 300 degrees. Add half of the bread to a food processor and pulse until the bread is coarsely ground, about 16 pulses. Transfer the crumbs to a large bowl and repeat with the remaining

SHOPPING FOR CHICKEN—WHAT YOU NEED TO KNOW

Every good chicken dish starts with high-quality, fresh chicken. But there are an overwhelming number of choices at the supermarket—so how do you recognize superior poultry? Here are a few tips the test kitchen has learned over time. If you're buying boneless, skinless chicken breasts, you should be aware that breasts of different sizes are often packaged together, and it's usually impossible to tell what you've bought until you've opened the package. If possible, buy chicken breasts individually. If that isn't an option, pound the thicker ends of the larger pieces of chicken to match those of the smaller pieces. Some breasts will still be larger than others, but pounding will help make their thickness the same and ensure even cooking. As for chicken parts—say for making a dish such as fried chicken or stew—we prefer to butcher our own birds rather than buy packaged parts. Not only is this a less expensive option, but the parts will be consistently sized. (We also use this approach with stew meat—there's no guarantee that packaged stew meat is going to be cut into even-sized pieces or be from the same cut or even the same cow!) And what about ground chicken? Prepackaged ground chicken is made from either dark or white meat or a mix of the two. Higher-end markets often grind their chicken to order, so the choice is yours. In most of our testing, we found ground white meat chicken to be exceedingly dry and almost void of flavor. The dark meat was more flavorful and juicy due to its higher fat content. For our recommended brands of chicken, see pages 606–607.

bread. Add ⅛ teaspoon salt and ⅛ teaspoon pepper to the bread crumbs. Add the oil and toss until the crumbs are evenly coated. Spread the crumbs on a rimmed baking sheet and bake until golden brown and dry, about 25 minutes, stirring twice during the baking time. Cool to room temperature.

3. Following the photos on page 66, butterfly each chicken breast and pound between two sheets of plastic wrap to a uniform ¼-inch thickness. Pound the outer perimeter to ⅛ inch. Unwrap the herb butter and cut it into four rectangular pieces. Following the photos on page 67, place a chicken breast, cut side up, on a work surface; season both sides with salt and pepper. Place one piece of butter in the center of the bottom half of the breast. Roll the bottom edge of the chicken over the butter, then fold in the sides and continue rolling to form a neat, tight package, pressing on the seam to seal. Repeat with the remaining butter and chicken. Refrigerate the chicken, uncovered, to allow the edges to seal, about 1 hour.

4. Adjust an oven rack to the middle position and heat the oven to 350 degrees. Set a large wire rack over a large baking sheet and set aside. Place the flour, eggs, and bread crumbs in separate pie plates or shallow dishes. Season the flour with ¼ teaspoon salt and ⅛ teaspoon pepper; season the bread crumbs with ½ teaspoon salt and ¼ teaspoon pepper. Add the mustard to the eggs and whisk to combine. Dredge 1 chicken roll in the flour, shaking off the excess, then coat with the egg mixture, allowing the excess to drip off. Coat all sides of the chicken roll with the bread crumbs, pressing gently so that the crumbs adhere. Place on the wire rack set over a rimmed baking sheet. Repeat the flouring and breading with the remaining chicken rolls.

5. Bake until the center of the chicken registers 160 to 165 degrees on an instant-read thermometer, 40 to 45 minutes. Let rest for 5 minutes on the wire rack before serving.

OVEN-BARBECUED CHICKEN

WHY THIS RECIPE WORKS: Smoky, tender, and tangy, barbecued chicken is a real crowd pleaser. What do you do when a craving for this summertime favorite strikes in midwinter? Oven-barbecued chicken is the obvious solution. But while recipes for this dish abound, so do the disappointments: tough, rubbery, or unevenly cooked chicken in sauces ranging from pasty and candy-sweet to greasy, stale, thin, or commercial-tasting.

We started with boneless, skinless chicken breasts; the mild white meat is a perfect backdrop for the sauce. (Skinless breasts also meant that we wouldn't have to deal with the problem of flabby skin.) We lightly seared the chicken breasts in a skillet, then removed them from the pan to make a simple but flavorful barbecue sauce with pantry ingredients like grated onion, ketchup, Worcestershire sauce, mustard, molasses, and maple syrup. When we returned the chicken to the pan, the sauce clung nicely to the meat, thanks to the light searing we had given the chicken. We slid the chicken and sauce, still in the skillet, into the oven to cook through. Finally, for a nicely caramelized coating on the sauce, we finished the chicken under the high heat of the broiler. The result? Juicy chicken, thickly coated with a pleasantly tangy barbecue sauce.

Sweet and Tangy Oven-Barbecued Chicken

SERVES 4

Real maple syrup is preferable to imitation syrup, and "mild" or "original" molasses is preferable to darker, more bitter types. Use a rasp-style grater or the fine holes of a box grater to grate the onion. Make this recipe only in an in-oven broiler; do not use a drawer-type broiler. Broiling times may differ from one oven to another, so we urge you to check the chicken for doneness after only 3 minutes of broiling. You may also have to lower the oven rack if your broiler runs very hot. It is important to remove the chicken from the oven before switching to the broiler setting to allow the broiler element to come up to temperature.

- 1 **cup ketchup**
- 3 **tablespoons molasses (see note)**
- 3 **tablespoons cider vinegar**
- 2 **tablespoons finely grated onion (see note)**
- 2 **tablespoons Worcestershire sauce**
- 2 **tablespoons Dijon mustard**
- 2 **tablespoons maple syrup (see note)**
- 1 **teaspoon chili powder**
- ¼ **teaspoon cayenne pepper**
- 4 **(5 to 6-ounce) boneless, skinless chicken breasts, tenderloins removed and breasts trimmed**
  Table salt and ground black pepper
- 1 **tablespoon vegetable oil**

1. Adjust an oven rack to the upper-middle position, about 5 inches from the heating element, and heat the oven to 325 degrees. Whisk the ketchup, molasses, vinegar, onion, Worcestershire sauce, mustard, maple syrup, chili powder, and cayenne together in a small bowl; set aside. Pat the chicken dry with paper towels and season with salt and pepper.

2. Heat the oil in a 12-inch ovensafe skillet over high heat until just smoking. Add the chicken, smooth side down, and cook until very light golden, 1 to 2 minutes;

using tongs, turn the chicken and cook until very light golden on the second side, 1 to 2 minutes longer. Transfer the chicken to a plate and set aside.

3. Discard the fat in the skillet; off the heat, add the sauce mixture and, using a wooden spoon, scrape up the browned bits on the bottom of the skillet. Simmer the sauce over medium heat, stirring frequently with a heatproof spatula, until the sauce is thick and glossy and a spatula leaves a clear trail in the sauce, about 4 minutes. Off the heat, return the chicken to the skillet and turn to coat thickly with the sauce; set the chicken pieces smooth side up and spoon extra sauce over each piece to create a thick coating.

4. Place the skillet in the oven and cook until the thickest part of the breasts registers 130 degrees on an instant-read thermometer, 8 to 12 minutes. Remove the skillet from the oven, turn the oven to broil, and heat for 5 minutes. Once the broiler is heated, place the skillet back in the oven and broil the chicken until the thickest part of the breasts registers 160 to 165 degrees, 3 to 8 minutes longer. Transfer the chicken to a platter and let rest for 5 minutes. Meanwhile, whisk the sauce in the skillet to recombine and transfer to a small bowl. Serve the chicken, passing the extra sauce separately.

5   pounds bone-in, skin-on chicken parts (split breasts, thighs, drumsticks, or a mix, with breasts cut into 3 pieces or halved if small), trimmed of excess fat and skin
3   tablespoons brown sugar
2   tablespoons chili powder
2   tablespoons sweet paprika
2   tablespoons kosher salt
2   teaspoons ground black pepper
¼–½ teaspoon cayenne pepper

1. Use a sharp knife to make two or three short slashes in the skin of each piece of chicken, taking care not to cut into the meat. Combine the sugar, chili powder, paprika, salt, and pepper in a small bowl and mix thoroughly. Coat the chicken pieces with the spices, gently lifting the skin to distribute the spice rub underneath but leaving it attached to the chicken. Transfer the chicken, skin side up, to a wire rack set over a large, rimmed baking sheet, lightly tent it with foil, and refrigerate 6 to 24 hours.

2. If desired, secure the skin of each breast piece with two or three toothpicks placed near the edges of the skin (see note).

3. Adjust an oven rack to the middle position and heat the oven to 425 degrees. Roast the chicken until the thickest part of the smallest piece registers 140 degrees on an instant-read thermometer, 15 to 20 minutes. Increase the oven temperature to 500 degrees and continue roasting until the chicken is browned and crisp and the thickest part of the breasts registers 160 to 165 degrees, 5 to 8 minutes longer, removing the pieces from the oven and transferring them to a clean wire rack as they finish cooking. Continue to roast the thighs and/or drumsticks, if using, until the thickest part of the meat registers 175 degrees, about 5 minutes longer. Remove from the oven, transfer the chicken to a rack, and cool completely before refrigerating or serving.

PICNIC CHICKEN

WHY THIS RECIPE WORKS: Cold barbecued picnic chicken presents numerous challenges: the meat may be dry, the skin flabby, and the chicken covered with a sticky, messy sauce. We wanted a recipe for chicken that would be easy to pack (and eat) for a picnic, chicken with moist, tender meat flavored with robust spicy and slightly sweet barbecue flavors.

We first threw out the idea of a sticky sauce, substituting a robust dry rub (brown sugar, chili powder, paprika, and pepper) that reproduced the flavors of a good barbecue sauce. We partly solved the flabby skin problem by diligently trimming the chicken pieces as well as by slitting the skin before cooking (which allowed the excess fat to render). But the skin was still flabby from the moisture contributed by our traditional brine (we brine most poultry for better flavor and moister meat). We tried eliminating the brine, adding salt to the rub, and applying it the night before. Sure enough, when we oven-roasted the chicken the next day, we found the meat well seasoned throughout and very moist. Best of all, the skin was flavorful, delicate, and definitely not flabby.

Spice-Rubbed Picnic Chicken

SERVES 8

If you plan to serve the chicken later on the same day that you cook it, refrigerate it immediately after it has cooled, then let it come back to room temperature before serving. On the breast pieces, we use toothpicks to secure the skin, which otherwise shrinks considerably in the oven, leaving the meat exposed and prone to drying out. We think the extra effort is justified, but you can omit this step. This recipe halves easily.

PAN-ROASTED CHICKEN BREASTS

WHY THIS RECIPE WORKS: Cooking bone-in, skin-on chicken breasts can be a challenge. They are difficult to sauté or cook through on the stovetop because of their uneven shape. We wanted to find a method that would produce crisp skin, moist meat, and a quick, flavorful pan sauce.

We chose whole breasts, then split them ourselves to control their size. We brined the breasts for maximum moistness and then seared them on the stovetop before

letting them cook through in a 450-degree oven. For the pan sauce, we sautéed minced shallot in the same skillet used to cook the chicken, so we could take advantage of the flavorful browned bits left in the pan. We deglazed the pan with chicken broth and vermouth, then added fresh sage for a sauce with deep herbal flavor. Butter whisked into the sauce after it had reduced lent the sauce body and richness—a perfect partner to our moist, juicy chicken.

Pan-Roasted Chicken Breasts with Sage-Vermouth Sauce
SERVES 4

We prefer to split whole chicken breasts ourselves because store-bought split chicken breasts are often sloppily butchered. However, if you prefer to purchase split chicken breasts, try to choose 10 to 12-ounce pieces with skin intact. If split breasts are of different sizes, check the smaller ones a few minutes early to see if they are cooking more quickly, and remove them from the skillet when they are done.

CHICKEN
- ½ cup table salt
- 2 (1½-pound) whole bone-in, skin-on chicken breasts, split in half along breast bone and trimmed of rib sections
   Ground black pepper
- 1 teaspoon vegetable oil

SAGE-VERMOUTH SAUCE
- 1 large shallot, minced (about 4 tablespoons)
- ¾ cup low-sodium chicken broth
- ½ cup dry vermouth
- 4 medium fresh sage leaves, each leaf torn in half
- 3 tablespoons unsalted butter, cut into 3 pieces
   Table salt and ground black pepper

1. FOR THE CHICKEN: Dissolve the salt in 2 quarts cold water in a large container; submerge the chicken in the brine, cover, and refrigerate about 30 minutes. Rinse the chicken well and pat dry with paper towels. Season the chicken with pepper.

2. Adjust an oven rack to the lowest position and heat the oven to 450 degrees.

3. Heat the oil in a 12-inch ovenproof skillet over medium-high heat until beginning to smoke. Brown the chicken, skin side down, until deep golden, about 5 minutes; turn the chicken and brown until golden on the second side, about 3 minutes longer. Turn the chicken skin side down and place the skillet in the oven. Roast until the thickest part of the breasts registers 160 to 165 degrees on an instant-read thermometer, 15 to 18 minutes. Transfer the chicken to a platter, and let it rest while making the sauce. (If you're not making the sauce, let the chicken rest 5 minutes before serving.)

4. FOR THE SAUCE: Using a potholder to protect your hands from the hot skillet handle, pour off all but 1 teaspoon of the fat from the skillet; add the shallot, then set the skillet over medium-high heat and cook, stirring frequently, until the shallot is softened, about 1½ minutes. Add the chicken broth, vermouth, and sage; increase the heat to high and simmer rapidly, scraping the skillet bottom with a wooden spoon to loosen the browned bits, until slightly thickened and reduced to about ¾ cup, about 5 minutes. Pour the accumulated chicken juices into the skillet, reduce the heat to medium, and whisk in the butter 1 piece at a time; season with salt and pepper to taste and discard the sage. Spoon the sauce around the chicken breasts and serve immediately.

NOTES FROM THE TEST KITCHEN

TRIMMING SPLIT CHICKEN BREASTS

Using kitchen shears, trim off the rib sections from each breast, following the vertical line of fat from the tapered end of the breast up to the socket where the wing was attached.

SIMPLE ROAST CHICKEN

WHY THIS RECIPE WORKS: Most home-cooked chickens are either grossly overcooked or so underdone that they resemble an avian version of steak tartare. We wanted a simple method for producing perfectly roasted chicken, where the white meat cooks up juicy and tender, but with a hint of chew, and the dark meat is fully cooked, all the way to the bone.

For maximum juiciness and well-seasoned meat, we brined the chicken. And for further flavor and a moisture boost to the delicate breast, we rubbed butter under the skin and over the breast. Trussing and continuous basting both proved unnecessary for this ideal chicken. In fact, basting turned its skin greasy and chewy. We had hoped that the bird wouldn't have to be turned while cooking, but even cooking is crucial for successful chicken roasting. In the end, we found that roasting the bird for 15 minutes on each side and then putting it on its back rendered perfectly cooked white and dark meat as well as golden, crunchy skin.

Simple Roast Chicken

SERVES 2 TO 3

If using a kosher chicken, skip the brining process and begin with step 2. We recommend using a V-rack to roast the chicken. If you don't have a V-rack, set the bird on a regular roasting rack and use balls of aluminum foil to keep the roasting chicken propped up on its side.

- ½ **cup table salt**
- ½ **cup sugar**
- 1 **(3½ to 4-pound) whole chicken, giblets discarded (see note)**
- 2 **tablespoons unsalted butter, softened**
- 1 **tablespoon olive oil**
  Ground black pepper

1. Dissolve the salt and sugar in 2 quarts cold water in a large container. Submerge the chicken in the brine, cover, and refrigerate for 1 hour.

2. Adjust an oven rack to the lower-middle position, place a roasting pan on the rack, and heat the oven to 400 degrees. Coat a V-rack with vegetable oil spray and set aside (see note). Remove the chicken from the brine, rinse well, and pat dry with paper towels.

3. Following the photo, use your fingers to gently loosen the center portion of the skin covering each

breast; place the butter under the skin, directly on the meat in the center of each breast. Gently press on the skin to distribute the butter over the meat. Tuck the wings behind the back. Rub the skin with the oil, season with pepper, and place the chicken, wing side up, on the prepared V-rack. Place the V-rack in the preheated roasting pan and roast for 15 minutes.

4. Remove the roasting pan from the oven and, using two large wads of paper towels, rotate the chicken so that the opposite wing side is facing up. Return the roasting pan to the oven and roast for another 15 minutes.

5. Using two large wads of paper towels, rotate the chicken again so that the breast side is facing up and continue to roast until the thickest part of the breast registers 160 to 165 degrees and the thickest part of the thigh registers 175 degrees on an instant-read thermometer, about 20 to 25 minutes longer. Transfer the chicken to a carving board and let rest for 10 minutes. Carve the chicken and serve.

CLASSIC ROAST LEMON CHICKEN

WHY THIS RECIPE WORKS: Roast lemon chicken can be disappointing. The chicken itself can be dry and uninteresting, tasting nothing like lemon, or, even worse, bursting with bitter citric acidity. The accompanying pan sauce (if any) usually suffers a similar fate: bland and lemon-less or pucker-up harsh. We wanted to find a way to bring out the full potential of the two main ingredients. The chicken should be evenly roasted and moist, with crispy skin, and the lemon flavor should be bright and pure, with not a trace of bitterness.

We brined the chicken for extra juiciness. Then we filled the chicken cavity with a cut-up lemon and garlic cloves. To further ensure a juicy bird, we found that the roasting technique was key. We started the chicken breast side down in a moderately hot oven, then flipped it breast side up, added some broth to prevent the drippings from burning, and raised the oven temperature for the remainder of the cooking time. Once the chicken was cooked, we cut it into four pieces and broiled the pieces to get an evenly crisped skin. For the truest lemon flavor, we added a squirt of fresh lemon juice to a simple pan sauce of chicken broth, butter, and fresh herbs.

Classic Roast Lemon Chicken

SERVES 3 TO 4

If using a kosher chicken, skip the brining process and begin with step 2. Broiling the fully roasted and quartered chicken skin side up as it sits in a shallow pool of sauce crisps and browns the skin while keeping the meat succulent. If you decide to skip the broiling step, go directly from quartering the chicken to finishing the sauce with lemon juice, butter, and herbs.

½ cup table salt
1 (3½ to 4-pound) whole chicken, giblets discarded
2 lemons
6 medium garlic cloves, crushed and peeled
4 tablespoons (½ stick) unsalted butter, 2 tablespoons melted and 2 tablespoons chilled and cut into 2 pieces
Ground black pepper
1¾ cups low-sodium chicken broth
1 tablespoon minced fresh parsley leaves
1 teaspoon minced fresh thyme leaves

1. Dissolve the salt in 2 quarts cold water in a large container. Submerge the chicken in the brine, cover, and refrigerate for 1 hour. Remove the chicken from the brine, rinse well, and pat dry with paper towels.

2. Adjust an oven rack to the lower-middle position; heat the oven to 375 degrees. Spray a V-rack with vegetable oil spray and set in a roasting pan.

3. Cut 1 of the lemons lengthwise into quarters. Place the lemon quarters and garlic in the cavity of the chicken. Brush the breast side of the chicken with 1 tablespoon of the melted butter and season generously with pepper. Place the chicken, breast side down, in the V-rack, then brush the back with the remaining 1 tablespoon melted butter and season generously with pepper.

4. Roast the chicken 40 minutes. Remove the roasting pan from the oven; increase the oven temperature to 450 degrees. Using two large wads of paper towels, rotate the chicken breast side up; add 1 cup of the chicken broth to the roasting pan. Return the roasting pan to the oven and continue roasting until the thickest part of the breast registers 160 to 165 degrees and the thickest part of the thigh registers 175 degrees on an instant-read thermometer, about 35 to 40 minutes longer. Remove the roasting pan from the oven; tip the V-rack to let the juices from the chicken cavity run into the roasting pan. Transfer the chicken to a carving board and let rest, uncovered, while making the sauce. Remove the V-rack from the roasting pan.

5. Adjust the oven rack to the upper-middle position and heat the broiler. Skim the fat from the drippings in the roasting pan, add the remaining ¾ cup chicken broth, and set the roasting pan on a burner over high heat. Simmer the liquid, scraping the pan bottom with a wooden spoon to loosen the browned bits, until reduced to ½ cup, about 4 minutes; set aside off the heat.

6. Discard the lemons and garlic from the chicken cavity. Following photos 1 and 3 on page 76, cut the chicken into quarters. Pour the accumulated chicken juices into the roasting pan, then place the chicken quarters, skin side up, into the sauce in the roasting pan; broil the chicken until the skin is crisp and deep golden brown, 3 to 5 minutes. Transfer the chicken to a serving platter.

7. Halve the remaining lemon lengthwise; squeeze the juice of one half into the roasting pan; cut the remaining half into four wedges and set aside. Whisk the remaining 2 tablespoons butter into the sauce until combined; stir in the parsley and thyme. Season with salt and pepper to taste. Serve the chicken with the pan sauce and lemon wedges.

CRISP-SKINNED ROAST CHICKEN

WHY THIS RECIPE WORKS: During roasting, juices and rendered fat can accumulate beneath the chicken skin and turn it wet and flabby. We wanted a juicy roasted chicken with skin that would crackle against your teeth with every bite.

A five-step process was the solution. We first cut an incision down the chicken's back to allow fat to escape and then loosened the skin from the thighs and breasts, poking holes in the fat deposits to allow multiple channels for excess fat and juices to escape. And since skin can't brown until all the surface moisture evaporates, we added baking powder to our salt rub. This helped dehydrate the skin and enhanced the effects of our fourth step: overnight air-drying. Finally, we roasted the bird at high heat to speed the browning. To prevent our kitchen from filling with smoke from the pan drippings, we placed a sheet of foil with holes punched into it under the chicken to shield the rendered fat from direct oven heat. The final result? Roast chicken with tender, juicy meat and the crispest skin ever.

Crisp-Skinned Roast Chicken

SERVES 2 TO 3

Do not brine the bird; it will prevent the skin from becoming crisp. The sheet of foil between the roasting pan and V-rack will keep the drippings from burning and smoking.

- 1 (3½ to 4-pound) whole chicken, giblets discarded (see note)
- 1 tablespoon kosher salt or 1½ teaspoons table salt
- 1 teaspoon baking powder
- ½ teaspoon ground black pepper

1. Place the chicken, breast side down, on a work surface. Following the photos, use the tip of a sharp knife to make four 1-inch incisions along the back of the chicken. Using your fingers or the handle of a wooden spoon, separate the skin from the thighs and breast, being careful not to break the skin. Using a metal skewer, poke 15 to 20 holes in the fat deposits on top of the breast halves and thighs. Tuck the wings behind the back.

2. Combine the salt, baking powder, and pepper in a small bowl. Pat the chicken dry with paper towels and sprinkle all over with the salt mixture. Rub in the mixture with your hands, coating the entire surface evenly. Set the chicken, breast side up, in a V-rack set on a rimmed baking sheet and refrigerate, uncovered, for 12 to 24 hours.

3. Adjust an oven rack to the lowest position and heat the oven to 450 degrees. Using a paring knife, poke 20 holes about 1½ inches apart in a 16 by 12-inch piece of foil. Place the foil loosely in a large roasting pan. Flip the chicken so the breast side faces down, and set the V-rack in the roasting pan on top of the foil. Roast the chicken for 25 minutes.

4. Remove the roasting pan from the oven. Using two large wads of paper towels, rotate the chicken breast side

---

NOTES FROM THE TEST KITCHEN

PREPARING CRISP ROAST CHICKEN

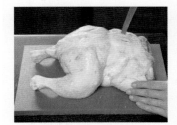

1. Cut incisions in the skin along the chicken's back for the fat to escape.

2. Loosen the skin from the thighs and breast to allow rendering fat to trickle out the openings.

3. Poke holes in the skin of the breast and thighs to create additional channels for fat and juices to escape.

4. Rub a mixture of baking powder and salt into the skin and air-dry the chicken in the refrigerator to help the skin crisp and brown.

up. Continue to roast until the thickest part of the breast registers 135 degrees on an instant-read thermometer, 15 to 25 minutes.

5. Increase the oven temperature to 500 degrees. Continue to roast until the skin is golden brown and crisp and the thickest part of the breast registers 160 to 165 degrees and the thickest part of the thigh registers 175 degrees, 10 to 20 minutes.

6. Transfer the chicken to a carving board and let rest, uncovered, for 20 minutes. Carve the chicken following the illustrations on page 76 and serve immediately.

GLAZED ROAST CHICKEN

WHY THIS RECIPE WORKS: Glazed chicken might sound simple but actually turns up a host of troubles, as the problems inherent in roasting chicken (dry breast meat, flabby skin, big deposits of fat under the skin) are compounded by the glaze (won't stick to the meat, burns in patches, introduces moisture to already flabby skin). We wanted evenly glazed roast chicken with crisp skin and moist, tender meat.

We started with a large roaster chicken. We separated the skin from the meat and pricked holes in the fat deposits to allow rendered fat to escape, then rubbed it with salt and baking powder—to dehydrate the skin and help it to crisp—and we roasted the chicken straddled on top of a beer can set in a roasting pan (a popular grilling technique). The technique seemed like a winner—no awkward flipping, glazing every nook and cranny was easy, and fat dripped freely out of the bird. But cutting into the chicken revealed that the breast, now exposed to the high oven heat for the entire cooking time, was dry and tough. Two techniques solved these problems. First, we rested the chicken before putting it in the oven for a final blast of heat—the skin came out crisper than before and the breast meat was perfectly cooked. Second, we thickened our glaze with a little cornstarch and reduced it to a syrupy consistency, then applied it before the final five minutes of roasting. The result? Moist, tender chicken with deeply flavorful crisp, glazed skin.

Glazed Roast Chicken

SERVES 4 TO 6

For best results, use a 16-ounce can of beer. A larger can will work, but avoid using a 12-ounce can, as it will not support the weight of the chicken. A vertical roaster can be used in place of the beer can, but we recommend only using a model that can be placed in a roasting pan. Taste your marmalade before using it; if it is overly sweet, reduce the amount of maple syrup in the glaze by 2 tablespoons. Trappist Seville Orange Marmalade is the test kitchen's preferred brand.

CHICKEN
- 1 (6 to 7-pound) whole chicken, giblets discarded
- 2½ teaspoons table salt
- 1 teaspoon baking powder
- 1 teaspoon ground black pepper
- 1 (16-ounce) can beer (see note)

GLAZE
- 1 tablespoon water
- 1 teaspoon cornstarch
- ½ cup maple syrup
- ½ cup orange marmalade (see note)
- ¼ cup cider vinegar
- 2 tablespoons unsalted butter
- 2 tablespoons Dijon mustard
- 1 teaspoon ground black pepper

1. FOR THE CHICKEN: Place the chicken, breast side down, on a work surface. Following the photos on page 74, use the tip of a sharp knife to make four 1-inch incisions along the back of the chicken. Using your fingers or the handle of a wooden spoon, separate the skin from the thighs and breast, being careful not to break the skin. Using a metal skewer, poke 15 to 20 holes in the fat deposits on top of the breast halves and thighs. Tuck the wings behind the back.

2. Combine the salt, baking powder, and pepper in a small bowl. Pat the chicken dry with paper towels and sprinkle evenly all over with the salt mixture. Rub in the mixture with your hands, coating the entire surface evenly.

Set the chicken, breast side up, on a rimmed baking sheet and refrigerate, uncovered, 30 to 60 minutes. Meanwhile, adjust an oven rack to the lowest position and heat the oven to 325 degrees.

3. Open the beer can and pour out (or drink) about half of the liquid. Spray the can lightly with vegetable oil spray and place in the middle of a roasting pan. Slide the chicken over the can so the drumsticks reach down to the bottom of the can, the chicken stands upright, and the breast is perpendicular to the bottom of the pan. Roast until the skin starts to turn golden and the thickest part of the breast registers 140 degrees on an instant-read thermometer, 75 to 90 minutes. Carefully remove the chicken and pan from the oven and increase the oven temperature to 500 degrees.

4. FOR THE GLAZE: While the chicken cooks, stir the water and cornstarch together in a small bowl until no lumps remain; set aside. Bring the remaining glaze ingredients to a simmer in a medium saucepan over medium-high heat. Cook, stirring occasionally, until reduced to ¾ cup, 6 to 8 minutes. Slowly whisk the cornstarch mixture into the glaze. Return to a simmer and cook 1 minute. Remove the pan from the heat.

5. When the oven is heated to 500 degrees, place 1½ cups water in the bottom of the roasting pan and return to the oven. Roast until the entire chicken skin is browned and crisp, the thickest part of the breast registers 160 to 165 degrees and the thickest part of the thigh registers 175 degrees on an instant-read thermometer, 24 to 30 minutes. Check the chicken halfway through roasting; if the top is becoming too dark, place a 7-inch square piece of foil over the neck and wingtips of the chicken and continue to roast (if the pan begins to smoke and sizzle, add ½ cup water to the roasting pan).

6. Brush the chicken with ¼ cup of the glaze and continue to roast until browned and sticky, about 5 minutes. (If the glaze has become stiff, return to low heat to soften.) Carefully remove the chicken from the oven, transfer the chicken, still on the can, to a carving board, and brush with ¼ cup more glaze. Let rest 20 minutes.

7. While the chicken rests, strain the juices from the pan through a fine-mesh strainer into a fat separator; allow the liquid to settle 5 minutes. Whisk ½ cup juices into the remaining ¼ cup glaze in a saucepan and set over low heat. Using a kitchen towel, carefully lift the chicken off the can and onto a platter or carving board. Following the photos, carve the chicken, adding any accumulated juices to the sauce. Serve, passing the sauce separately.

NOTES FROM THE TEST KITCHEN

CARVING A WHOLE CHICKEN

1. Cut the chicken where the leg meets the breast, then pull the leg quarter away. Push up on the joint, then carefully cut through it to remove the leg quarter.

2. Cut through the joint that connects the drumstick to the thigh. Repeat on the second side to remove the other leg.

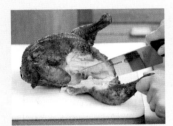

3. Cut down along one side of the breastbone, pulling the breast meat away from the bone.

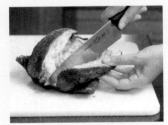

4. Remove the wing from the breast by cutting through the wing joint. Slice the breast into attractive slices.

STOVETOP ROAST CHICKEN

WHY THIS RECIPES WORKS: Roasting chicken in the oven is the usual route to crisp skin and moist meat, but sometimes you want your oven for something else. Cooking chicken pieces in a skillet easily yields a flavorful pan sauce, but the skin on the chicken is often flabby and the meat unevenly cooked. We wanted to combine the best aspects of both roasted and skillet-cooked chicken. Our goals were ambitious: crisp, golden skin; evenly cooked, juicy meat; and a flavorful sauce—all produced in a single large skillet that would never go into the oven.

We started with a standard set of mixed chicken parts: four breast halves, two drumsticks, and two thighs. We tested a variety of approaches to achieve moist meat and crisp skin, but ran into numerous problems. One method—steaming the raw chicken in broth and then searing it in a hot pan, skin side down—crisped the skin but caused it to shrink dramatically. To avoid this, we found that searing the chicken first and then steaming was the answer. After steaming, we poured off all the liquid from the pan (reserving it to use for the pan sauce) and returned the chicken to sear again skin side down. This second searing produced the deep, russet-hued crisp skin we had hoped for. After removing the finished chicken, we set out to make our pan sauce with shallot, lemon, and fresh herbs. This quick pan sauce was the perfect complement to our tender roast chicken with crisp skin.

Stovetop Roast Chicken with Lemon-Herb Sauce

SERVES 4

Use a splatter screen when browning the chicken.

CHICKEN
- 3½ **pounds bone-in, skin-on chicken pieces (split breasts cut in half, drumsticks, and/or thighs), trimmed**
  Table salt and ground black pepper
- 1 **tablespoon vegetable oil**
- ¾–1¼ **cups low-sodium chicken broth**

LEMON-HERB SAUCE
- 1 **teaspoon vegetable oil**
- 1 **medium shallot, minced (about 3 tablespoons)**
- 1 **teaspoon unbleached all-purpose flour**
- 1½ **tablespoons minced fresh parsley leaves**
- 1½ **tablespoons minced fresh chives**
- 1 **tablespoon juice from 1 lemon**
- 1 **tablespoon unsalted butter, chilled**
  Table salt and ground black pepper

1. FOR THE CHICKEN: Pat the chicken dry with paper towels and season with salt and pepper. Heat 2 teaspoons of the oil in a 12-inch nonstick skillet over medium-high heat until just smoking. Add the chicken pieces skin side down and cook without moving until golden brown, 5 to 8 minutes.

2. Using tongs, flip the chicken pieces skin side up. Reduce the heat to medium-low, add ¾ cup of the broth to the skillet, cover, and cook until the thickest part of the breasts registers 155 degrees and the thickest part of the thighs/drumsticks registers 170 degrees on an instant-read thermometer, 10 to 16 minutes. Transfer the chicken to a plate, skin side up.

3. Pour off the liquid from the skillet into a 2-cup measuring cup and reserve. Wipe out the skillet with paper towels. Add the remaining 1 teaspoon oil to the skillet and heat over medium-high heat until shimmering. Return the chicken pieces skin side down and cook undisturbed until the skin is deep golden brown and crisp, the thickest part of the breast registers 160 to 165 degrees, and the thickest part of the thigh/drumstick registers 175 degrees, 4 to 7 minutes. Transfer to a serving platter and tent loosely with foil. Using a spoon, skim any fat from the reserved cooking liquid and add enough broth to measure ¾ cup.

4. FOR THE SAUCE: Heat the oil in the now-empty skillet over low heat. Add the shallot and cook, stirring frequently, until softened, about 2 minutes. Add the flour and cook, stirring constantly, 30 seconds. Increase the heat to medium-high, add the reserved cooking liquid, and bring to a simmer, scraping the skillet bottom with a wooden spoon to loosen any browned bits. Simmer rapidly until reduced to ½ cup, 2 to 3 minutes. Stir in any accumulated juices from the resting chicken; return to a simmer and cook for 30 seconds. Off the heat, whisk in the parsley, chives, lemon juice, and butter; season with salt and pepper to taste. Pour the sauce around the chicken and serve immediately.

HIGH-ROAST CHICKEN

WHY THIS RECIPES WORKS: "High roasting"—cooking a bird at temperatures in excess of 450 degrees—is supposed to produce tastier chicken with crisper skin in record time. But recipes we've tried overcook the bird while producing enough smoke to be mistaken for a five-alarm fire. We wanted to improve upon this method for a quick roasted chicken with skin that is crisp and tanned to a deep golden hue and meat that is irresistibly tender and moist. And while we were at it, we wanted roasted potatoes too.

We began by brining the chicken for moist, well-seasoned meat. Then we butterflied the chicken, which allowed for more even and faster roasting. We found that we were able to add moisture and flavor to the chicken by rubbing flavored herb butter under the skin. (Some recipes instruct rubbing the butter over the skin, but the herbs burn and the butter doesn't season the meat.) We cooked the chicken on top of a broiler pan with a bottom attached. In the bottom of the pan under the chicken, we placed a layer of potatoes. To ensure that the potatoes cooked through, we sliced them thin—⅛ to ¼ inch thick. As the chicken cooked, the potatoes absorbed the juices from the chicken and became well seasoned. In just one hour we had roast chicken with spectacularly crisp skin and moist meat—and potatoes too.

High-Roast Butterflied Chicken with Potatoes

SERVES 2 TO 3

If using a kosher bird, skip the brining process and begin with step 2. Because you'll be cooking the chicken under high heat, it's important that you rinse it thoroughly before proceeding—otherwise, the sugar remaining on the skin from the brine will caramelize and ultimately burn. For this cooking technique, russet potatoes offer the best potato flavor, but Yukon Golds develop a beautiful color and retain their shape better after cooking. Either works well in this recipe. A food processor makes quick and easy work of slicing the potatoes.

CHICKEN AND BRINE
- ½   cup table salt
- ½   cup sugar
- 1   (3½ to 4-pound) whole chicken, giblets discarded (see note)
- 1   recipe Mustard-Garlic Butter with Thyme (recipe follows)
- 1   tablespoon olive oil
     Ground black pepper

POTATOES
- 2½ pounds russet or Yukon Gold potatoes (4 or 5 medium), peeled and sliced ⅛ to ¼ inch thick (see note)
- 1   tablespoon olive oil
- ½   teaspoon table salt
- ⅛   teaspoon ground black pepper

1. FOR THE CHICKEN AND BRINE: Dissolve the salt and sugar in 2 quarts cold water in a large container. Submerge the chicken in the brine, cover, and refrigerate for 1 hour.

2. Adjust an oven rack to the lower-middle position and heat the oven to 500 degrees. Line a broiler-pan bottom with foil. Remove the chicken from the brine, rinse well, and pat dry with paper towels. Following the photos, remove the backbone from the chicken, pound the chicken to a fairly even thickness, and tuck the wings behind the back.

3. Use your fingers to gently loosen the center portion of skin covering each side of the breast. Place the butter mixture under the skin, directly on the meat in the center

---

NOTES FROM THE TEST KITCHEN

BUTTERFLYING A CHICKEN

1. With the breast side down, cut along each side of the backbone and remove it.

2. Turn the chicken breast side up. Open the chicken on the work surface. Use the heel of your hand to flatten the breastbone.

3. Cover the chicken with plastic wrap, then pound it with a meat pounder to a fairly even thickness.

of each side. Gently press on the skin to distribute the butter over the meat. Rub the skin with the oil and season with pepper. Place the chicken on the broiler-pan top and push each leg up to rest between the thigh and breast.

4. FOR THE POTATOES: Toss the potatoes with the oil, salt, and pepper. Spread the potatoes in an even layer in the prepared broiler-pan bottom. Place the broiler-pan top with the chicken on top.

5. Roast the chicken until just beginning to brown, about 20 minutes. Rotate the pan and continue to roast until the skin is crisped and deep brown and the thickest part of the breast registers 160 to 165 degrees and the thickest part of the thigh registers 175 degrees on an instant-read thermometer, 20 to 25 minutes longer. Transfer the chicken to a carving board and let rest for 10 minutes.

6. While the chicken rests, remove the broiler-pan top and, using paper towels, soak up any excess grease from the potatoes. Transfer the potatoes to a serving platter. Carve the chicken, transfer to the platter with the potatoes, and serve.

Mustard-Garlic Butter with Thyme

MAKES ABOUT 3 TABLESPOONS

- 2 tablespoons unsalted butter, softened
- 1 tablespoon Dijon mustard
- 1 medium garlic clove, minced or pressed through a garlic press (about 1 teaspoon)
- 1 teaspoon minced fresh thyme leaves
   Pinch ground black pepper

Mash all the ingredients together in a small bowl.

"STUFFED" ROAST CHICKEN

WHY THIS RECIPE WORKS: Stuffed roast chicken can be a conundrum—it's either a perfectly cooked bird filled with lukewarm stuffing (risking salmonella) or safe-to-eat stuffing packed in parched poultry. And given the small cavity of a roasting chicken, there's often no more than a few tablespoons of stuffing per person. We wanted our stuffed roast chicken to produce both flavorful white and dark chicken meat along with an ample amount of intensely flavored stuffing. And we wanted to solve the problem of cooking the stuffing to a safe temperature without drying out the delicate breast meat of the chicken.

We ensured moist, savory meat by brining the bird before we stuffed and roasted it. While the chicken was brining, we jazzed up the stuffing mix by replacing the customary onion with a thinly sliced leek, adding it along with celery, mushrooms, minced garlic, fresh sage, thyme, and parsley, and chicken broth. Our most creative solution, however, was to make an aluminum foil bowl, mound the stuffing into it, and place the chicken—after butterflying it—on top. This improvised cooking vessel allowed the stuffing to become moist and flavorful throughout from the chicken juices, while also becoming brown and chewy on the bottom. And cleanup was a snap.

"Stuffed" Roast Butterflied Chicken

SERVES 4 TO 6

If using a kosher bird, skip the brining process. Use a traditional (not nonstick) roasting pan to prepare this recipe. When arranging the chicken over the stuffing, it should extend past the edges of the bowl so that most of the fat renders into the roasting pan.

- ½ cup table salt
- ½ cup sugar
- 1 (5 to 6-pound) whole chicken, giblets discarded (see note)
- 1 tablespoon olive oil
   Ground black pepper
- 1 recipe Mushroom-Leek Bread Stuffing with Herbs (recipe follows)

1. Dissolve the salt and sugar in 2 quarts cold water in a large container. Submerge the chicken in the brine, cover, and refrigerate for 1½ hours.

2. Adjust an oven rack to the lower-middle position and heat the oven to 450 degrees. Remove the chicken from the brine, rinse well, and pat dry with paper towels.

Following the photos on page 78, remove the backbone from the chicken, pound the chicken to a fairly even thickness, and tuck the wings behind the back. Rub the skin with the oil and season with pepper.

3. To make the foil bowl, place two 12-inch squares of foil on top of each other. Fold the edges to construct an 8 by 6-inch bowl. Coat the inside of the bowl with vegetable oil spray, and place the bowl in a roasting pan. Gently mound and pack the stuffing into the foil bowl and position the chicken over the stuffing. Roast the chicken until just beginning to brown, about 30 minutes. Rotate the pan and continue to roast until the skin is crisped and deep golden brown, the thickest part of the breast registers 160 to 165 degrees, and the thickest part of the thigh registers 175 degrees on an instant-read thermometer, 25 to 35 minutes longer. Transfer the chicken to a carving board and let rest for 10 minutes.

4. While the chicken rests, transfer the stuffing to a serving bowl and fluff. Cover the stuffing with foil to keep warm. Carve the chicken and serve with the stuffing.

Mushroom-Leek Bread Stuffing with Herbs
MAKES ABOUT 6 CUPS

The dried bread cubes for this stuffing can be stored in an airtight container for up to 1 week.

- 6   slices high-quality white sandwich bread, cut into ¼-inch cubes
- 2   tablespoons unsalted butter
- 1   leek, white and light green parts only, halved lengthwise, sliced ⅛ inch thick, and rinsed thoroughly
- 1   celery rib, chopped fine
- 8   ounces white mushrooms, wiped clean and chopped medium
- ¼   cup minced fresh parsley leaves
- 2   medium garlic cloves, minced or pressed through a garlic press (about 2 teaspoons)
- ½   teaspoon minced fresh sage leaves or ¼ teaspoon dried sage
- ½   teaspoon minced fresh thyme leaves or ¼ teaspoon dried thyme
- ½   cup plus 2 tablespoons low-sodium chicken broth
- 1   large egg
- ½   teaspoon table salt
- ½   teaspoon ground black pepper

1. Adjust an oven rack to the middle position and heat the oven to 250 degrees. Spread the bread cubes in a single layer on a rimmed baking sheet. Bake until thoroughly dried but not browned, about 30 minutes, stirring halfway through the baking time.

2. Meanwhile, melt the butter in a 12-inch skillet over medium-high heat. Add the leek, celery, and mushrooms and cook, stirring occasionally, until the vegetables begin to brown, 6 to 8 minutes. Stir in the parsley, garlic, sage, and thyme and cook until fragrant, about 30 seconds.

3. Whisk the broth, egg, salt, and pepper together in a large bowl. Add the bread cubes and leek-mushroom mixture and toss gently until evenly moistened and combined. Use as directed.

FRIED CHICKEN

WHY THIS RECIPE WORKS: Frying chicken at home is a daunting task, with its messy preparation and spattering hot fat. In the end, the chicken often ends up disappointingly greasy, with a peeling crust and dry, tasteless meat. We wanted fried chicken worthy of the mess and splatter: moist, seasoned meat coated with a delicious, crispy mahogany crust.

We soaked chicken parts in a seasoned buttermilk brine for ultimate flavor and juiciness. Then we air-dried the brined chicken parts to help ensure a crisp skin. Flour made the crispest coating. We found that peanut oil can withstand the demands of frying and has the most neutral flavor of all the oils tested. Vegetable oil was a close runner-up. As for frying the chicken, we found that a Dutch oven worked best. With its high sides and lid, a Dutch oven minimizes splatters and retains heat that helps the chicken cook through.

Crispy Fried Chicken
SERVES 4 TO 6

Avoid using kosher chicken in this recipe or it will be too salty. Maintaining an even oil temperature is key. After the chicken is added to the pot, the temperature will drop dramatically, and most of the frying will be done at about 325 degrees. Use an instant-read thermometer with a high upper range; a clip-on candy/deep-fry thermometer is fine, too, though it can be clipped to the pot only for the uncovered portion of frying.

CHICKEN

½ cup table salt

¼ cup sugar

2 tablespoons paprika

7 cups buttermilk

3 medium garlic heads, cloves separated and smashed

3 bay leaves, crumbled

4 pounds bone-in, skin-on chicken pieces (split breasts cut in half, drumsticks, and/or thighs), trimmed (see note)

3–4 quarts peanut oil or vegetable oil, for frying

COATING

4 cups (20 ounces) unbleached all-purpose flour

1 large egg

1 teaspoon baking powder

½ teaspoon baking soda

1 cup buttermilk

1. FOR THE CHICKEN: Dissolve the salt, sugar, and paprika in the buttermilk in a large container. Add the garlic and bay leaves, submerge the chicken in the brine, cover, and refrigerate for 2 to 3 hours.

2. Rinse the chicken well and place in a single layer on a wire rack set over a rimmed baking sheet. Refrigerate uncovered for 2 hours. (At this point, the chicken can be covered with plastic wrap and refrigerated for up to 6 more hours.)

3. Adjust an oven rack to the middle position and heat the oven to 200 degrees. In a large Dutch oven, heat 2 inches of oil over medium-high heat to 375 degrees (see note).

4. FOR THE COATING: Place the flour in a shallow dish. Whisk the egg, baking powder, and baking soda together in a medium bowl, then whisk in the buttermilk (the mixture will bubble and foam). Working with 3 chicken pieces at a time, dredge in the flour, shaking off the excess, then coat with the egg mixture, allowing the excess to drip off. Finally, coat with flour again, shake off the excess, and return to the wire rack.

5. When the oil is hot, add half of the chicken pieces to the pot, skin side down, cover, and fry until deep golden brown, 7 to 11 minutes, adjusting the heat as necessary to maintain an oil temperature of about 325 degrees. (After 4 minutes, check the chicken pieces for even browning and rearrange if some pieces are browning faster than others.) Turn the chicken pieces over and continue to cook until the thickest part of the breast registers 160 to 165 degrees and the thickest part of the thigh or drumstick registers 175 degrees on an instant-read thermometer, 6 to 8 minutes. Drain the chicken briefly on a paper towel–lined plate, then transfer to a clean wire rack set over a rimmed baking sheet and keep warm in the oven.

6. Return the oil to 375 degrees (if necessary) over medium-high heat and repeat with the remaining chicken pieces. Serve.

OVEN-FRIED CHICKEN

WHY THIS RECIPE WORKS: Oven-fried chicken never seems to taste as good as the real thing. The coating, often plain bread crumbs or cornflakes, just never gets as crunchy or as flavorful as a deep-fried coating does. We wanted a good alternative to regular fried chicken—one that would have real crunch and good flavor, and wouldn't taste like diet food.

We soaked bone-in chicken legs and thighs in a buttermilk brine to achieve maximum juiciness and flavor in the meat. And we removed the skin from the chicken before brining because it simply didn't render in the oven and turned flabby. A mixture of eggs and mustard helped the crumbs stick to the chicken and encouraged the formation of a crunchy crust. Melba toast crumbs made the crispest coating. We baked the chicken on a wire rack set over a baking sheet that we had lined with foil. This method allowed heat to circulate around the chicken during baking, resulting in crisp chicken all over without turning. As a bonus, the foil protected the pan, which made cleanup quick and easy.

Oven-Fried Chicken

SERVES 4

Avoid using kosher chicken in this recipe or it will be too salty. If you don't want to buy whole chicken legs and cut them into drumsticks and thighs, simply buy four drumsticks and four thighs. To make Melba toast crumbs, place the toasts in a heavy-duty plastic freezer bag, seal, and pound with a meat pounder or other heavy blunt object. Leave some crumbs in the mixture the size of pebbles, but most should resemble coarse sand.

CHICKEN

- ½ cup plus 2 tablespoons table salt
- ¼ cup sugar
- 2 tablespoons paprika
- 3 medium heads garlic, cloves separated
- 3 bay leaves, crumbled
- 7 cups buttermilk
- 4 whole chicken legs, separated into drumsticks and thighs and skin removed (see note)

COATING

- ¼ cup vegetable oil
- 1 box (about 5 ounces) plain Melba toast, crushed (see note)
- 2 large eggs
- 1 tablespoon Dijon mustard
- 1 teaspoon dried thyme
- ¾ teaspoon table salt
- ½ teaspoon ground black pepper
- ½ teaspoon dried oregano
- ¼ teaspoon garlic powder
- ¼ teaspoon cayenne pepper (optional)

1. FOR THE CHICKEN: In a large zipper-lock plastic bag, combine the salt, sugar, paprika, garlic cloves, and bay leaves. With a flat meat pounder, smash the garlic into the salt and spice mixture thoroughly. Pour the mixture into a large container. Add the buttermilk and stir until the salt and sugar are completely dissolved. Submerge the chicken in the brine and refrigerate, 2 to 3 hours. Rinse the chicken well and place on a large wire rack set over a rimmed baking sheet. Refrigerate uncovered for 2 hours. (After 2 hours, the chicken can be covered with plastic wrap and refrigerated up to 6 hours longer.)

2. Adjust an oven rack to the upper-middle position and heat the oven to 400 degrees. Line a large, rimmed baking sheet with foil and set a large wire rack over the pan.

3. FOR THE COATING: Drizzle the oil over the Melba toast crumbs in a pie plate or shallow dish; toss well to coat. Mix the eggs, mustard, thyme, salt, pepper, oregano, garlic powder, and cayenne (if using) with a fork in a second plate.

4. Working with one piece at a time, coat the chicken on both sides with the egg mixture. Set the chicken in the Melba crumbs, sprinkle the crumbs over the chicken, and press to coat. Turn the chicken over and repeat on the other side. Gently shake off the excess and place on the rack. Bake until the chicken is deep nutty brown and the thickest part of a piece registers 175 degrees on an instant-read thermometer, about 40 minutes. Serve.

BUFFALO WINGS

WHY THIS RECIPE WORKS: Buffalo wings are the ultimate bar snack. Great wings boast juicy meat, a crisp coating, and a spicy, slightly sweet, and vinegary sauce. But dry, flabby wings are often the norm and the sauce can be scorchingly hot. We wanted perfectly cooked wings, coated in a well-seasoned sauce—good enough to serve with our homemade creamy blue cheese dressing.

We coated the wings with cornstarch for a supercrisp exterior and deep-fried (rather than roasting, sautéing, or pan-frying) the wings for the best texture. Then we deepened the flavor of the traditional hot sauce by adding brown sugar and cider vinegar. And for heat, we chose Frank's RedHot Original Sauce, which is traditional, but not very spicy, so we added a little Tabasco for even more kick.

Buffalo Wings

SERVES 6 TO 8

Frank's RedHot Original Sauce is not terribly spicy. We like to combine it with a more potent hot sauce, such as Tabasco, to bring up the heat.

SAUCE

- **4** tablespoons (½ stick) unsalted butter
- **½** cup Frank's RedHot Original Sauce (see note above)
- **2** tablespoons Tabasco or other hot sauce, plus more to taste (see note above)
- **1** tablespoon packed dark brown sugar
- **2** teaspoons cider vinegar

WINGS

- **1–2** quarts peanut oil, for frying
- **3** tablespoons cornstarch
- **1** teaspoon table salt
- **1** teaspoon ground black pepper
- **1** teaspoon cayenne pepper
- **18** chicken wings (about 3 pounds), wings separated into 2 parts at joint and wingtips removed (see photos)

VEGETABLES AND DRESSING

- **2** medium carrots, peeled and cut into thin sticks
- **4** medium celery ribs, cut into thin sticks
- **1** recipe Rich and Creamy Blue Cheese Dressing (see page 21)

1. FOR THE SAUCE: Melt the butter in a small saucepan over low heat. Whisk in the hot sauces, brown sugar, and vinegar until combined. Remove from the heat and set aside.

2. FOR THE WINGS: Heat the oven to 200 degrees. Line a baking sheet with paper towels. In a large Dutch oven fitted with a clip-on candy thermometer, heat 2½ inches of oil over medium-high heat to 360 degrees. While the oil heats, combine the cornstarch, salt, black pepper, and cayenne in a small bowl. Dry the chicken with paper towels and place the pieces in a large mixing bowl. Sprinkle the spice mixture over the wings and toss with a rubber spatula until evenly coated. Fry half of the chicken wings until golden and crisp, 10 to 12 minutes. With a slotted spoon, transfer the fried chicken wings to

the prepared baking sheet. Keep the first batch of chicken warm in the oven while frying the remaining wings.

3. TO SERVE: Pour the sauce mixture into a large bowl, add the chicken wings, and toss until the wings are uniformly coated. Serve immediately with the carrot and celery sticks and blue cheese dressing on the side.

NOTES FROM THE TEST KITCHEN

CUTTING UP CHICKEN WINGS

1. Cut into the skin between the larger sections of the wing until you hit the joint.

2. Bend back the two sections to pop and break the joint.

3. Cut through the skin and flesh to completely separate the two meaty portions.

4. Hack off the wingtip and discard.

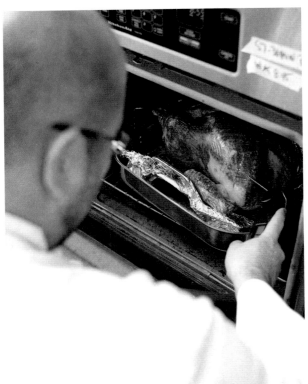

CHAPTER 6

TALKING TURKEY AND ALL THE TRIMMINGS

Classic Roast Turkey 86

    Giblet Pan Gravy

Roast Turkey for a Crowd 88

    Giblet Pan Gravy for a Crowd

Classic Roast Stuffed Turkey 89

    Bread Stuffing with Bacon, Apples, Sage, and Caramelized Onions

Slow-Roasted Turkey with Gravy 91

Roast Salted Turkey 92

Crisp-Skin High-Roast Butterflied Turkey with Sausage Dressing 94

    Golden Corn Bread

    Turkey Gravy

Herbed Roast Turkey 97

    All-Purpose Turkey Gravy

Grill-Roasted Turkey on a Charcoal Grill 100

Grill-Roasted Turkey on a Gas Grill 101

Charcoal Grill–Roasted Boneless Turkey Breast 102

Gas Grill–Roasted Boneless Turkey Breast 102

Classic Cranberry Sauce 103

Classic Green Bean Casserole 103

Quick Green Bean "Casserole" 104

Candied Sweet Potato Casserole 105

MORE RECIPES FOR ROUNDING OUT YOUR HOLIDAY MEAL

    Cream Biscuits 444

    Rustic Dinner Rolls 445

    Classic Mashed Potatoes 397

    Creamy Mashed Potatoes 398

    Fluffy Mashed Potatoes 400

    Classic Apple Pie 563

    Deep Dish Apple Pie 564

    Pumpkin Pie 569

    Spiced Pumpkin Cheesecake 521

CLASSIC ROAST TURKEY

WHY THIS RECIPE WORKS: Few of us want to take chances when cooking the holiday bird. We wanted to find a way that guaranteed moist, flavorful meat and bronzed skin— a true holiday table centerpiece.

First we brined our turkey, which helped prevent the meat from drying out and also seasoned it right to the bone. After brining, we rinsed the bird of excess salt and let it rest on a wire rack in the refrigerator so that the skin dried out. This step helped ensure the skin would cook up crisp, not flabby. Placing the turkey on a V-rack allowed for air circulation all around so that the bird cooked evenly. And turning the turkey three times also helped to ensure even cooking. Finally, once the turkey was cooked, we waited 30 minutes before carving it. That might seem like a long time, but it allowed the juices in the turkey to redistribute so that, once carved, each slice was moist and full of flavor.

Classic Roast Turkey

SERVES 10 TO 12

Resist the temptation to tent the roasted turkey with foil while it rests on the carving board. Covering the bird will make the skin soggy.

- 2 **cups table salt**
- 1 **(12 to 14-pound) turkey; giblets, neck, and tailpiece removed and reserved for gravy**
- 2 **medium onions, chopped coarse**
- 2 **medium carrots, chopped coarse**
- 2 **celery ribs, chopped coarse**
- 6 **sprigs fresh thyme**
- 3 **tablespoons unsalted butter, melted**
- 1 **cup water, plus more as needed**
- 1 **recipe Giblet Pan Gravy (recipe follows)**

1. Dissolve the salt in 2 gallons cold water in a large container. Submerge the turkey in the brine, cover, and refrigerate or store in a very cool spot (40 degrees or less) for 4 to 6 hours.

2. Set a wire rack over a large rimmed baking sheet. Remove the turkey from the brine and rinse it well. Pat the turkey dry, inside and out, with paper towels. Place the turkey on the prepared baking sheet. Refrigerate, uncovered, for at least 8 hours or overnight.

3. Adjust an oven rack to the lowest position and heat the oven to 400 degrees. Line a V-rack with heavy duty foil and poke several holes in the foil. Set the V-rack in a roasting pan and spray the foil with vegetable oil spray.

4. Toss half of the onions, carrots, celery, and thyme with 1 tablespoon of the melted butter in a medium bowl and place inside the turkey. Tie the legs together with kitchen twine and tuck the wings under the bird. Scatter the remaining vegetables into the roasting pan.

5. Pour 1 cup water over the vegetable mixture. Brush the turkey breast with 1 tablespoon more melted butter, then place the turkey, breast side down, on the V-rack. Brush with the remaining 1 tablespoon butter.

6. Roast the turkey for 45 minutes. Remove the pan from the oven; baste with juices from the pan. With a dish towel in each hand, turn the turkey leg/thigh side up. If the liquid in the pan has totally evaporated, add another ½ cup water. Return the turkey to the oven and roast for 15 minutes. Remove the turkey from the oven again, baste, and turn the other leg/thigh side up; roast for another 15 minutes. Remove the turkey from the oven for a final time, baste, and turn it breast side up; roast until the thickest part of the breast registers 160 to 165 degrees and the thickest part of the thigh registers 175 degrees on an instant-read thermometer, 30 to 45 minutes.

7. Remove the turkey from the oven. Gently tip the turkey so that any accumulated juices in the cavity run into the roasting pan. Transfer the turkey to a carving board and let rest, uncovered, for 30 minutes. Carve the turkey and serve with the gravy.

Giblet Pan Gravy

MAKES ABOUT 6 CUPS

Complete step 1 up to a day ahead, if desired. Begin step 3 once the bird has been removed from the oven and is resting on a carving board.

- 1 tablespoon vegetable oil
  Reserved turkey giblets, neck, and tailpiece
- 1 medium onion, chopped
- 4 cups low-sodium chicken broth
- 2 cups water
- 2 sprigs fresh thyme
- 8 sprigs fresh parsley
- 3 tablespoons unsalted butter
- ¼ cup unbleached all-purpose flour
- 1 cup dry white wine
  Table salt and ground black pepper

1. Heat the oil in a large Dutch oven over medium heat until shimmering; add the giblets, neck, and tailpiece, and cook until golden and fragrant, about 5 minutes. Add the onion and continue to cook until softened, 3 to 4 minutes longer. Reduce the heat to low, cover, and cook until the turkey parts and onion release their juices, about 15 minutes. Add the broth, water, and herbs, bring to a boil, and adjust the heat to low. Simmer, uncovered, skimming any impurities that may rise to the surface, until the broth is rich and flavorful, about 30 minutes longer. Strain the broth into a large container and reserve the giblets. When cool enough to handle, chop the giblets. Refrigerate the giblets and broth until ready to use. (The broth can be stored in the refrigerator up to 1 day ahead.)

2. While the turkey is roasting, return the reserved turkey broth to a simmer. Heat the butter in a large saucepan over medium-low heat. Vigorously whisk in the flour (the mixture will froth and then thin out again). Cook slowly, stirring constantly, until nutty brown and fragrant, 10 to 15 minutes. Vigorously whisk all but 1 cup of the hot broth into the flour mixture. Bring to a boil, then continue to simmer, stirring occasionally, until the gravy is lightly thickened and very flavorful, about 30 minutes longer. Set aside until the turkey is done.

3. When the turkey has been transferred to a carving board to rest, spoon out and discard as much fat as possible from the roasting pan, leaving the caramelized herbs and vegetables. Place the roasting pan over two burners set on

BEHIND THE SCENES

HOW BRINING SAVED THANKSGIVING

Once upon a time, the only thing the Thanksgiving turkey had going for it was tradition—and even that was tenuous, as many of us sometimes dreamed of cheating with a big buttery beef tenderloin. The problem was a familiar one. Sometimes the bird turned out juicy and flavorful, but most often, it was a dry disappointment. Passing the gravy didn't help much either. Then, 15 years ago, the test kitchen came upon an obscure technique called brining. Brining turkey involves soaking the turkey in a saltwater solution (which sometimes includes sugar) before cooking—this protects it from the ravages of heat and guarantees tender, flavorful meat from the surface all the way to the bone. (Brining does the same for other delicate white meat like chicken and pork.) How does brining work?

Simply put, the brining solution flows into the meat, distributing moisture and seasoning. In our testing, we found that while a turkey roasted straight out of its package will retain about 82 percent of its total weight after cooking, a brined turkey will retain about 93 percent of its total weight after cooking—and thus be moister and more flavorful. Once a little-known technique, brining has now become mainstream—and Thanksgiving dinners everywhere are all the better for it.

medium-high heat. Return the gravy to a simmer. Add the wine to the roasting pan of caramelized vegetables, scraping up any browned bits with a wooden spoon, and boil until reduced by half, about 5 minutes. Add the remaining 1 cup turkey broth and continue to simmer for 15 minutes; strain the pan juices into the gravy, pressing as much juice as possible out of the vegetables. Stir the reserved giblets into the gravy and return to a boil. Season with salt and pepper to taste and serve.

ROAST TURKEY FOR A CROWD

WHY THIS RECIPE WORKS: Unless you have access to multiple ovens, only a very large turkey will do when you've got a crowd coming to dinner. But finding a container large enough to brine a gargantuan bird can be tricky. And turning the bird in the oven, our usual method for evenly cooked meat, can be hot, heavy, and dangerous. We wanted the Norman Rockwell picture of perfection: a crisp, mahogany skin wrapped around tender, moist meat. And it had to be easy to prepare in a real home kitchen.

We chose a Butterball turkey, which has already been brined for juicy flavor (a kosher bird, which has been salted, works well too). A combination of high and low heat resulted in a tender, juicy bird with deeply browned skin. We made the meat and pan drippings more flavorful with the addition of onion, carrot, and celery. A quartered lemon added bright, clean flavor. After roasting, we allowed the turkey to rest so the juices would redistribute, but didn't tent it with foil so the skin wouldn't become soggy. Serve with Giblet Pan Gravy for a Crowd (recipe follows).

Roast Turkey for a Crowd
SERVES ABOUT 20

Rotating the bird helps produce moist, evenly cooked meat, but for the sake of ease, you may opt not to rotate it. In that case, skip the step of lining the V-rack with foil and roast the bird breast side up for the entire cooking time. Because we do not brine the bird, we had the best results with a frozen Butterball (injected with salt and water) or a kosher bird (soaked in salt water during processing).

- 3 medium onions, chopped coarse
- 3 medium carrots, chopped coarse
- 3 celery ribs, chopped coarse
- 1 lemon, quartered
- 2 sprigs fresh thyme
- 5 tablespoons unsalted butter, melted
- 1 (18 to 22-pound) frozen Butterball or kosher turkey (see note); giblets, neck, and tailpiece removed and reserved for gravy (recipe follows)
- 1 cup water, plus more as needed
- 1 teaspoon table salt
- 1 teaspoon ground black pepper
- 1 recipe Giblet Pan Gravy for a Crowd (recipe follows)

1. Adjust an oven rack to the lowest position. Heat the oven to 425 degrees. Line a large V-rack with heavy-duty foil and poke several holes in the foil. Set the V-rack in a large roasting pan and spray the foil with vegetable oil spray.

2. Toss half of the onions, carrots, celery, lemon, and thyme with 1 tablespoon of the melted butter in a medium bowl and place inside the turkey. Tie the legs together with kitchen twine and tuck the wings under the bird. Scatter the remaining vegetables into the roasting pan.

3. Pour 1 cup water over the vegetable mixture. Brush the turkey breast with 2 tablespoons more of the melted butter, then sprinkle with half of the salt and half of the pepper. Place the turkey, breast side down, on the V-rack. Brush with the remaining 2 tablespoons melted butter and sprinkle with the remaining salt and pepper.

4. Roast the turkey for 1 hour. Remove the pan from the oven; baste with juices from the pan. With a dish towel in each hand, turn the turkey breast side up. If the liquid in the pan has totally evaporated, add another ½ cup water. Lower the oven temperature to 325 degrees. Return the turkey to the oven and continue to roast until the thickest part of the breast registers 160 to 165 degrees and the thickest part of the thigh registers 175 degrees on an instant-read thermometer, about 2 hours longer.

5. Remove the turkey from the oven. Gently tip the turkey up so that any accumulated juices in the cavity run into the roasting pan. Transfer the turkey to a carving board. Let rest, uncovered, for 35 to 40 minutes. Carve the turkey and serve with the gravy.

Giblet Pan Gravy for a Crowd
MAKES ABOUT 8 CUPS

Complete step 1 up to a day ahead, if desired. Begin step 3 once the bird has been removed from the oven and is resting on a carving board.

- 1 tablespoon vegetable oil
  Reserved turkey giblets, neck, and tailpiece
- 1 medium onion, unpeeled and chopped
- 6 cups low-sodium chicken broth
- 3 cups water
- 2 sprigs fresh thyme
- 8 sprigs fresh parsley
- 5 tablespoons unsalted butter
- ¼ cup plus 2 tablespoons unbleached all-purpose flour
- 1½ cups dry white wine
  Table salt and ground black pepper

1. Heat the oil in a large Dutch oven over medium heat until shimmering; add the giblets, neck, and tailpiece, and cook until golden and fragrant, about 5 minutes. Add the onion and continue to cook until softened, 3 to 4 minutes longer. Reduce the heat to low, cover, and cook until the turkey parts and onion release their juices, about 15 minutes. Add the broth, water, and herbs, bring to a boil, and adjust the heat to low. Simmer, uncovered, skimming any impurities that may rise to the surface, until the broth is rich and flavorful, about 30 minutes longer. Strain the broth into a large container and reserve the giblets. When cool enough to handle, chop the giblets. Refrigerate the giblets and broth until ready to use. (The broth can be stored in the refrigerator up to 1 day ahead.)

2. While the turkey is roasting, return the reserved turkey broth to a simmer. Heat the butter in a large saucepan over medium-low heat. Vigorously whisk in the flour (the mixture will froth and then thin out again). Cook slowly, stirring constantly, until nutty brown and fragrant, 10 to 15 minutes. Vigorously whisk all but 2 cups of the hot broth into the flour mixture. Bring to a boil, then continue to simmer, stirring occasionally, until the gravy is lightly thickened and very flavorful, about 35 minutes longer. Set aside until the turkey is done.

3. When the turkey has been transferred to a carving board to rest, spoon out and discard as much fat as possible from the roasting pan, leaving the caramelized herbs and vegetables. Place the roasting pan over two burners set on medium-high heat. Return the gravy to a simmer. Add the wine to the roasting pan of caramelized vegetables, scraping up any browned bits with a wooden spoon, and boil until reduced by half, about 7 minutes. Add the remaining 2 cups turkey broth and continue to simmer for 15 minutes; strain the pan juices into the gravy, pressing as much juice as possible out of the vegetables. Stir the reserved giblets into the gravy and return to a boil. Season with salt and pepper to taste and serve.

CLASSIC ROAST STUFFED TURKEY

WHY THIS RECIPE WORKS: There is something undeniably festive about a stuffed roasted turkey. Every year, though, we are warned that for health and safety reasons, turkeys are best roasted unstuffed. Despite these warnings, many cooks continue to stuff their holiday bird. For the sake of flavorful, moist, turkey-infused stuffing, these cooks sacrifice perfectly cooked breast meat and risk food-borne illness from underdone stuffing. We wanted to find a way to safely and successfully roast a stuffed turkey, making sure that the breast meat would be succulent and the stuffing fully cooked.

At the outset, we decided to limit our turkey to a maximum of 14 pounds, because it is just too difficult to safely stuff and roast a larger bird. We heated the stuffing in the microwave before placing half of it in the bird to give it a head start on cooking. We baked the remaining stuffing separately in a casserole dish. This ensured that there would be enough stuffing to go around. We also brined the bird to add flavor and moisture (brining will not, as we feared, make the stuffing soggy or overly salty).

Classic Roast Stuffed Turkey

SERVES 10 TO 12

A 12 to 14-pound turkey will accommodate approximately half of the stuffing. Bake the remainder in a casserole dish while the bird rests before carving. If serving with Giblet Pan Gravy (page 87), note that you can complete step 1 up to a day ahead, if desired. Begin step 3 once the bird has been removed from the oven and is resting on a carving board.

- 2 **cups table salt**
- 1 **(12 to 14-pound) turkey; giblets, neck, and tailpiece removed and reserved for gravy (see page 87)**
- 2 **medium onions, chopped coarse**
- 1 **medium carrot, chopped coarse**
- 1 **celery rib, chopped coarse**
- 4 **sprigs fresh thyme**
- 1 **cup water, plus more as needed**
- 12 **cups prepared stuffing (recipe follows)**
- 3 **tablespoons unsalted butter, plus extra for the casserole dish and foil**
- ¼ **cup low-sodium chicken broth**
- 1 **recipe Giblet Pan Gravy (page 87)**

1. Dissolve the salt in 2 gallons cold water in a large container. Submerge the turkey in the brine, cover, and

STUFFING A TURKEY

1. After placing 4 to 5 cups of the preheated stuffing into the turkey, use metal skewers (or cut bamboo skewers) and thread them through the skin on both sides of the cavity to seal the cavity shut.

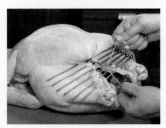

2. Center a 2-foot piece of kitchen twine on the top skewer and then cross the twine as you wrap each end of it around and under the skewers. Loosely tie the legs together with another short piece of twine.

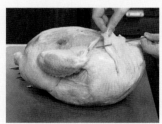

3. Flip the turkey over onto its breast. Stuff the neck cavity loosely with approximately 1 cup of stuffing. Pull the skin flap over and use a skewer to pin the flap to the turkey.

4 to 5 cups of stuffing into the turkey cavity until very loosely packed. Following the photos, secure the skin flap over the cavity opening with skewers. Melt the remaining 2 tablespoons butter. Tuck the wings under the bird, brush the turkey breast with half of the melted butter, then turn the turkey breast side down. Fill the neck cavity with the remaining heated stuffing and secure the skin flap over the opening. Place the turkey, breast side down, on the V-rack. Brush with the remaining butter.

5. Roast the turkey for 1 hour, then reduce the temperature to 250 degrees and roast for 2 hours longer, adding water if the pan becomes dry. Remove the pan from the oven (close the oven door) and, with a dish towel in each hand, turn the bird breast side up, and baste (the temperature of the thickest part of the breast should be 145 to 150 degrees). Increase the oven temperature to 400 degrees; continue to roast until the thickest part of the breast registers 160 to 165 degrees, the thickest part of the thigh registers 175 degrees, and the center of the stuffing registers 165 degrees on an instant-read thermometer, 1 to 1½ hours longer. Remove the turkey from the oven, transfer to a carving board, and let rest for 30 minutes.

6. Add the broth to the dish of reserved stuffing, replace the foil, and bake until hot throughout, about 20 minutes. Remove the foil; continue to bake until the stuffing forms a golden brown crust, about 15 minutes longer.

7. Carve the turkey and serve with the stuffing and the gravy.

refrigerate or store in a very cool spot (40 degrees or less) for 4 to 6 hours.

2. Set a wire rack over a large rimmed baking sheet. Remove the turkey from the brine and rinse it well. Pat the turkey dry inside and out with paper towels. Place the turkey on the prepared baking sheet. Refrigerate, uncovered, and air-dry for at least 8 hours or overnight.

3. Adjust an oven rack to the lowest position and heat the oven to 400 degrees. Line a V-rack with heavy-duty foil and poke several holes in the foil. Set the V-rack inside a roasting pan and spray the foil with vegetable oil spray. Scatter the onions, carrot, celery, and thyme into the roasting pan. Pour 1 cup water over the vegetable mixture.

4. Place half of the stuffing in a buttered medium casserole dish, dot the surface with 1 tablespoon of the butter, cover with foil, and refrigerate until ready to use. Microwave the remaining stuffing on high power, stirring two or three times, until very hot (120 to 130 degrees on an instant-read thermometer), 6 to 8 minutes. Spoon

Bread Stuffing with Bacon, Apples, Sage, and Caramelized Onions

MAKES ABOUT 12 CUPS

To dry the bread, spread the cubes out onto 2 large baking sheets and dry in a 300-degree oven for 30 to 60 minutes. Let the bread cool before using in the stuffing.

- 1 **pound bacon, cut crosswise into ¼-inch strips**
- 6 **medium onions, sliced thin (about 7 cups)**
- 1 **teaspoon table salt**
- 2 **Granny Smith apples, peeled, cored, and cut into ½-inch cubes (about 2 cups)**
- ½ **cup fresh parsley leaves, chopped fine**
- 3 **tablespoons minced fresh sage leaves**
- ½ **teaspoon ground black pepper**
- 3 **pounds high-quality white sandwich bread, cut into ¾-inch cubes (about 12 cups)**
- 1 **cup low-sodium chicken broth**
- 3 **large eggs, lightly beaten**

1. Cook the bacon in a large skillet or Dutch oven over medium heat until crisp and browned, about 12 minutes. Remove the bacon from the pan with a slotted spoon and drain on paper towels. Discard all but 3 tablespoons of the rendered bacon fat.

2. Increase the heat to medium-high and add the onions and ¼ teaspoon of the salt. Cook the onions until golden in color, making sure to stir occasionally and scrape the sides and bottom of the pan, about 20 minutes. Reduce the heat to medium and continue to cook, stirring more often to prevent burning, until the onions are deep golden brown, another 5 minutes. Add the apples and continue to cook another 5 minutes. Transfer the contents of the pan to a large bowl.

3. Add the parsley, sage, remaining ¾ teaspoon salt, and the pepper to the bowl and mix to combine. Add the bread cubes.

4. Whisk the broth and eggs together in a small bowl. Pour the mixture over the bread cubes. Gently toss to evenly distribute the ingredients.

SLOW-ROASTED TURKEY WITH GRAVY

WHY THIS RECIPE WORKS: Roasting a whole turkey is a race to keep the white meat from drying out while the dark meat cooks through. We wanted no less than the perfect turkey recipe—an approach that would get our fowl from supermarket to table in just a few hours. We required meat as moist as prime rib and with crisp, crackling skin, and it all needed to be accompanied by rich gravy. For a greater challenge, we wanted to do it without salting the turkey or brining it, both of which take the better part of a day.

First, we roasted two nonbrined turkeys, one using our standard high-heat method and the other at 275 degrees the entire time. The outer layers of the high-heat breast dried out, but the slow-roasted breast cooked through moist, even without a brine. Coordinating the cooking between the breast and legs and thighs, however, was a problem. Instead we discovered that swapping in turkey parts for a whole turkey would help ensure the breast and thighs cooked through at about the same time. We roasted a breast and two leg quarters (thighs and drumsticks) on a rack over a baking sheet to promote air circulation. The results? Tender, juicy meat.

We next had to tackle crisping the skin. Most recipes achieve crisp skin by starting the bird in a hot oven to brown it, then lowering the heat. But that meant a higher oven temperature, which meant dried-out meat. Instead, we let the turkey cool before popping it back in the oven to crisp the skin. This turned out a perfect turkey from center to edge surrounded by flawless, crisp skin.

Slow-Roasted Turkey with Gravy

SERVES 10 TO 12

Instead of drumsticks and thighs, you may use 2 whole leg quarters, 1½ to 2 pounds each. The recipe will also work with turkey breast alone; in step 2, reduce the butter to 1½ tablespoons, the salt to 1½ teaspoons, and the pepper to 1 teaspoon. If you are roasting kosher or self-basting turkey parts, season the turkey with only 1½ teaspoons salt.

TURKEY

- 3 medium onions, chopped medium
- 3 medium celery ribs, chopped medium
- 2 medium carrots, peeled and chopped medium
- 5 sprigs fresh thyme
- 5 medium garlic cloves, peeled and halved
- 1 cup low-sodium chicken broth
- 1 (5 to 7-pound) whole bone-in, skin-on turkey breast, trimmed (see note)
- 4 pounds turkey drumsticks and thighs, trimmed (see note)
- 3 tablespoons unsalted butter, melted
- 1 tablespoon table salt
- 2 teaspoons ground black pepper

GRAVY

- 2 cups low-sodium chicken broth
- 3 tablespoons unsalted butter
- 3 tablespoons unbleached all-purpose flour
- 2 bay leaves
  Table salt and ground black pepper

1. FOR THE TURKEY: Adjust an oven rack to the lower-middle position and heat the oven to 275 degrees. Arrange the onions, celery, carrots, thyme, and garlic in an even layer on a large rimmed baking sheet. Pour the broth into the baking sheet. Place a wire rack on top of the vegetables.

2. Pat the turkey pieces dry with paper towels. Brush the turkey pieces on all sides with the melted butter. Sprinkle the salt and pepper evenly over the turkey. Place the breast, skin side down, and the drumsticks and thighs, skin side up, on the rack on the vegetable-filled baking sheet, leaving at least ¼ inch between the pieces.

3. Roast the turkey pieces for 1 hour. With a dish towel in each hand, turn the turkey breast skin side up. Continue roasting until the thickest part of the breast registers 160 to 165 degrees the thickest part of the thigh registers 175 degrees on an instant-read thermometer, 1 to 2 hours longer. Remove the baking sheet from the oven and transfer the rack with the turkey to a second baking sheet. Allow the pieces to rest for at least 30 minutes or up to 1½ hours.

4. FOR THE GRAVY: Strain the vegetables and liquid from the baking sheet through a colander set in a large bowl. Press the solids with the back of a spatula to extract as much liquid as possible. Discard the vegetables. Transfer the liquid in the bowl to a 4-cup liquid measuring cup. Add the chicken broth to the measuring cup (you should have about 3 cups liquid).

5. In a medium saucepan, heat the butter over medium-high heat; add the flour and cook, stirring constantly, until the flour is dark golden brown and fragrant, about 5 minutes. Whisk in the broth mixture and bay leaves and gradually bring to a boil. Reduce the heat to medium-low and simmer, stirring occasionally, until the gravy is thick and reduced to 2 cups, 15 to 20 minutes. Discard the bay leaves. Remove the gravy from the heat and season with salt and pepper to taste. Keep the gravy warm.

6. TO SERVE: Heat the oven to 500 degrees. Place the baking sheet with the turkey in the oven. Roast until the skin is golden brown and crisp, about 15 minutes. Transfer the turkey to a carving board and let rest, uncovered, for 20 minutes. Carve and serve with the gravy.

ROAST SALTED TURKEY

WHY THIS RECIPE WORKS: Brining is the best way to guarantee a moist turkey, but it isn't always the most practical way, especially if you have limited refrigerator space. We wanted to develop an alternative method to brining that would both season the meat and keep it moist.

Instead of brining, we turned to salting—it seasons the meat, but no bucket is required. We wanted to make sure the salt penetrated the meat, but we didn't want to tear the skin. We found that either chopsticks or the handle of a wooden spoon worked well to help us gently separate the skin from the meat. To ensure moist breast meat, we chilled the breast by placing a small bag of ice inside the cavity against the breast and setting the turkey, breast side down, on ice. This trick brought down the temperature of the breast, thus allowing it to cook through over a longer period in the oven (more in line with the cooking time of the dark meat) without drying out.

Roast Salted Turkey

SERVES 10 TO 12

This recipe was developed and tested using Diamond Crystal Kosher Salt. If you have Morton's Kosher Salt, which is denser than Diamond Crystal, use only 4½ teaspoons of salt in the cavity, 2¼ teaspoons of salt per each half of the breast, and 1 teaspoon of salt per leg. Table salt is too fine and is not recommended for this recipe. If you are roasting a kosher or self-basting turkey (such as a frozen Butterball), do not salt it; it already contains a good amount of sodium. If serving with Giblet Pan Gravy (page 87), note that you can complete step 1 of the gravy recipe up to a day ahead, if desired. Begin step 3 once the bird has been removed from the oven and is resting on a carving board.

1 **(12 to 14-pound) turkey; giblets, neck, and tailpiece removed and reserved for gravy (see page 87)**

5 **tablespoons kosher salt (see note)**

1 **(5-pound) bag ice cubes**

4 **tablespoons (½ stick) unsalted butter, melted**

3 **medium onions, chopped coarse**

2 **medium carrots, chopped coarse**

2 **celery ribs, chopped coarse**

6 **sprigs fresh thyme**

1 **cup water, plus more as needed**

1. Following the photos, carefully separate the turkey skin from the meat on the breast, legs, thighs, and back; avoid breaking the skin. Then rub 2 tablespoons of the salt evenly inside the cavity of the turkey, 1 tablespoon more salt under the skin of each breast half, and 1½ teaspoons more salt under the skin of each leg. Wrap the turkey tightly with plastic wrap; refrigerate 24 to 48 hours.

2. Remove the turkey from the refrigerator. Rinse off any excess salt between the meat and skin and in the cavity, then pat dry inside and out with paper towels. Add ice to two 1-gallon zipper-lock bags until each is half full. Place the bags in a large roasting pan and lay the turkey, breast side down, on top of the ice. Add ice to two 1-quart zipper-lock bags until each is one-third full; place one bag of ice in the large cavity of the turkey and the other bag in the neck cavity. (Make sure that the ice touches the breast only, not the thighs or legs; see the photo.) Keep the turkey on ice for 1 hour (the roasting pan should remain on the counter).

3. Meanwhile, adjust an oven rack to the lowest position and heat the oven to 425 degrees. Line a large V-rack with heavy-duty foil and poke several holes in the foil. Set the V-rack in a roasting pan and spray the foil with vegetable oil spray.

4. Remove the turkey from the ice and pat dry with paper towels (discard the ice). Tuck the tips of the drumsticks into the skin at the tail to secure and tuck the wings under the bird. Brush the turkey breast with 2 tablespoons of the melted butter. Scatter the vegetables into the roasting pan and pour 1 cup water over the vegetable mixture. Place the turkey, breast side down, on the V-rack. Brush the turkey with the remaining 2 tablespoons melted butter.

5. Roast the turkey for 45 minutes. Remove the pan from the oven (close the oven door to retain the oven heat) and reduce the oven temperature to 325 degrees. With a dish towel in each hand, rotate the turkey breast side up;

NOTES FROM THE TEST KITCHEN

ICING THE TURKEY BREAST

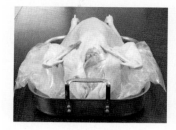

Cooling the breast down with ice ensures that it will cook more slowly than the legs and thighs, preventing the meat from drying out. Place bags of ice underneath the breast and inside both the large cavity and the neck area.

HOW TO SALT A TURKEY

1. Use a chopstick or a thin wooden spoon handle to separate the skin from the meat over the breast, legs, thighs, and back.

2. Rub 2 tablespoons kosher salt inside the main cavity.

3. Lift the skin and apply 1 tablespoon kosher salt over each breast half, placing half of the salt on each end of each breast, then massaging the salt evenly over the meat.

4. Apply 1½ teaspoons kosher salt over the top and bottom of each leg.

continue to roast until the thickest part of the breast registers 160 to 165 degrees and the thickest part of the thigh registers 175 degrees on an instant-read thermometer, 1 to 1½ hours longer. Transfer the turkey to a carving board and let rest, uncovered, for 30 minutes. Carve the turkey and serve with the gravy (see note).

CRISP-SKIN HIGH-ROAST TURKEY

WHY THIS RECIPE WORKS: High-roasting (oven-roasting at very high temperatures for the sake of speed and flavor) a turkey presents the home cook with two potential problems: billowing smoke from incinerated pan drippings and torched breast meat. We wanted to find a way to prepare a high-roast turkey with crisp, picture-perfect skin and moist, evenly cooked meat in less than two hours—without setting off the smoke alarm.

We butterflied the turkey for crisp skin and evenly cooked meat, and then roasted it on a broiler pan set over the stuffing—which absorbed the drippings. This step helped season the stuffing and kept the kitchen from filling with smoke. These techniques let us crank up the heat to get the bird done in record time. To complement our moist, crisp-skinned turkey, we made a corn bread and sausage stuffing that was both rich and easy to prepare.

Crisp-Skin High-Roast Butterflied Turkey with Sausage Dressing

SERVES 10 TO 12

The dressing can be made with corn bread or white bread, but note that they are not used in equal amounts. The turkey is roasted in a broiler pan top, or a sturdy wire rack, set in a 16 by 12-inch disposable roasting pan. If using a wire rack, choose one that measures about 17 by 11 inches so that it will span the roasting pan and sit above the dressing in the pan.

TURKEY
- 1 cup table salt
- 1 cup sugar
- 1 (12 to 14-pound) turkey; giblets, neck, and tailpiece removed and reserved for gravy; turkey butterflied (see page 95) and backbone and rib bones reserved for gravy
- 1 tablespoon unsalted butter, melted

SAUSAGE DRESSING
- 12 cups corn bread (recipe follows) broken into 1-inch pieces (include crumbs), or 18 cups 1-inch challah or Italian bread cubes (from about 1½ loaves)
- 1¾ cups low-sodium chicken broth
- 1 cup half-and-half
- 2 large eggs, beaten lightly
- 12 ounces bulk pork sausage, broken into 1-inch pieces
- 3 medium onions, minced (about 3 cups)
- 3 celery ribs, chopped fine (about 1½ cups)
- 2 tablespoons unsalted butter
- 2 tablespoons minced fresh thyme leaves
- 2 tablespoons minced fresh sage leaves
- 3 medium garlic cloves, minced or pressed through a garlic press (about 1 tablespoon)
- 1½ teaspoons table salt
- 2 teaspoons ground black pepper
- 1 recipe Turkey Gravy (see page 96)

1. TO BRINE THE TURKEY: Dissolve the salt and sugar in 2 gallons cold water in a large container. Submerge the turkey in the brine and refrigerate or store in a very cool spot (40 degrees or less) for 4 to 6 hours.

2. TO PREPARE THE DRESSING: While the turkey brines, adjust the oven racks to the upper-middle and lower-middle positions and heat the oven to 250 degrees. Spread the bread in an even layer on two rimmed baking sheets and dry in the oven 50 to 60 minutes for corn bread or 40 to 50 minutes for challah or Italian bread.

3. Place the bread in a large bowl. Whisk the broth, half-and-half, and eggs together in a medium bowl; pour over the bread and toss very gently to coat so that the bread does not break into smaller pieces. Set aside.

4. Heat a 12-inch skillet over medium-high heat until hot, about 1½ minutes. Add the sausage and cook, stirring occasionally, until the sausage loses its raw color, 5 to 7 minutes. With a slotted spoon, transfer the sausage to a medium bowl. Add half the onions and celery to the fat in the skillet; sauté, stirring occasionally, over medium-high heat until softened, about 5 minutes. Transfer the onion mixture to the bowl with the sausage. Return the skillet to the heat and add the butter; when melted add the remaining onions and celery and sauté, stirring occasionally, until softened, about 5 minutes. Stir in the thyme, sage, and garlic; cook until fragrant, about 30 seconds; add the salt and pepper. Add this mixture along with the sausage and onion mixture to the bread and stir gently to combine (try not to break the bread into smaller pieces).

5. Spray a disposable aluminum 16 by 12-inch roasting pan with vegetable oil spray. Transfer the dressing to the roasting pan and spread in an even layer. Cover the pan with foil and refrigerate while preparing the turkey.

6. TO PREPARE THE TURKEY FOR ROASTING: Remove the turkey from the brine and rinse it well. Position the turkey on a broiler pan top or wire rack (see note); thoroughly pat the surface of the turkey dry with paper towels. Place the broiler pan top with the turkey on top of the roasting pan with the dressing; refrigerate, uncovered, 8 to 24 hours.

7. TO ROAST THE TURKEY WITH THE DRESSING: Adjust an oven rack to the lower-middle position and heat the oven to 450 degrees. Remove the broiler pan top with the turkey and remove the foil from the dressing; place the broiler pan top with the turkey on the dressing in the roasting pan. Brush the turkey with the melted butter. Roast the turkey until the turkey skin is crisp and deep brown and the thickest part of the breast registers 160 to 165 degrees and the thickest part of the thigh registers 175 degrees on an instant-read thermometer, 1 hour 20 minutes to 1 hour 40 minutes, rotating the pan from front to back after 40 minutes.

8. Transfer the broiler pan top with the turkey to a carving board, tent loosely with foil, and let rest for 20 minutes. Meanwhile, adjust an oven rack to the upper-middle position, place the roasting pan with the dressing back in the oven, and bake until golden brown, about 10 minutes. Carve the turkey and serve with the dressing and gravy.

PREPARING THE BUTTERFLIED TURKEY

1. Holding the turkey upright with the backbone facing front, use a hacking motion to cut through the turkey directly to one side of the backbone with a chef's knife.

2. Holding the backbone with one hand, hack through the turkey directly to the other side of the backbone; the backbone will fall away.

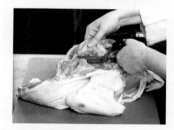

3. Using kitchen scissors, cut out the rib plate and remove any small pieces of bone.

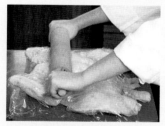

4. Place the turkey, breast side up, on a cutting board and cover with plastic wrap. With a large rolling pin, whack the breastbone until it cracks and the turkey flattens.

5. After brining and rinsing, place the turkey, breast side up, on a wire rack set over a rimmed baking sheet. Tuck the wings under the turkey. Push the legs up to rest between the thigh and breast. Tie the legs together.

Golden Corn Bread

MAKES ABOUT 16 CUPS CRUMBLED CORN BREAD

You need about three-quarters of this recipe for the dressing; the rest is for nibbling.

- 4 tablespoons (½ stick) unsalted butter, melted, plus extra for the baking dish
- 4 large eggs
- 1⅓ cups buttermilk
- 1⅓ cups milk
- 2 cups yellow cornmeal
- 2 cups (10 ounces) unbleached all-purpose flour
- 2 tablespoons sugar
- 4 teaspoons baking powder
- 1 teaspoon baking soda
- 1 teaspoon salt

1. Adjust an oven rack to the middle position and heat the oven to 375 degrees. Grease a 13 by 9-inch baking dish with butter.

2. Beat the eggs in medium bowl; whisk in the buttermilk and milk.

3. Whisk the cornmeal, flour, sugar, baking powder, baking soda, and salt together in a large bowl. Push the dry ingredients up the sides of the bowl to make a well, then pour the egg and milk mixture into the well and stir with a whisk until just combined; stir in the melted butter.

4. Pour the batter into the prepared baking dish. Bake until the top is golden brown and the edges have pulled away from the sides of the pan, 30 to 40 minutes.

5. Transfer the baking dish to a wire rack and cool to room temperature before using, about 1 hour.

Turkey Gravy

MAKES ABOUT 4 CUPS

Because this gravy doesn't use drippings from the roasted turkey but instead uses the trimmings from butterflying the bird, the gravy can conveniently be made a day in advance (while the turkey brines and air-dries in the refrigerator) and then reheated before serving.

Reserved giblets, neck, tailpiece, and backbone and rib bones from the turkey (see note)
- 2 small onions, chopped coarse
- 1 medium carrot, cut into 1-inch pieces
- 1 celery rib, cut into 1-inch pieces
- 6 garlic cloves, unpeeled
- 3½ cups low-sodium chicken broth
- 3 cups water
- 2 cups dry white wine
- 6 sprigs fresh thyme
- ¼ cup unbleached all-purpose flour
  Table salt and ground black pepper

1. Heat the oven to 450 degrees. Adjust an oven rack to the middle position. Place the turkey trimmings, onions, carrot, celery, and garlic in a large roasting pan or broiler pan bottom. Spray lightly with vegetable oil spray and toss to combine. Roast, stirring every 10 minutes, until well browned, 40 to 50 minutes.

2. Remove the pan from the oven and place over two burners set at high heat; add the chicken broth and bring to a boil, scraping up the browned bits on the bottom of the pan with a wooden spoon.

3. Transfer the contents of the pan to a large saucepan. Add the water, wine, and thyme; bring to a boil over high heat. Reduce the heat to low and simmer until reduced by half, about 1½ hours. Strain the stock into a large measuring cup or container. Cool to room temperature; cover with plastic wrap, and refrigerate until the fat congeals on the surface, about 2 hours.

4. Skim the fat from the stock using a soup spoon; reserve the fat. Pour the stock through a fine-mesh strainer to remove remaining bits of fat. Bring the stock to a simmer in a medium saucepan over medium-high heat.

5. In a second medium saucepan, heat ¼ cup reserved turkey fat over medium-high heat until bubbling; whisk in the flour and cook, whisking constantly, until combined and honey-colored, about 2 minutes. Continuing to whisk constantly, gradually add the hot stock; bring to a boil, then reduce the heat to medium-low and simmer, stirring occasionally, until slightly thickened, about 5 minutes. Season with salt and pepper to taste. (The gravy can be stored in an airtight container in the refrigerator for up to 1 day. While the turkey is resting, heat the gravy in a medium saucepan over medium heat until hot, about 8 minutes.)

HERBED ROAST TURKEY

WHY THIS RECIPE WORKS: Throwing a bunch of herbs into the cavity of a turkey or rubbing the outside of the bird with a savory paste only flirts with great herb flavor—it doesn't infuse that flavor into each and every bite. We wanted an intensely herby turkey, one with a powerful, aromatic flavor that permeated well beyond the meat's surface.

First we tried an intense brine, but it made the bird taste more pickled than infused with herbs. Next, we pumped the paste into the bird with a syringe, which created nothing but ugly blobs of overwhelmingly strong, raw-tasting herbs. Then we tried a technique we had developed for stuffing a thick-cut pork chop. We made a vertical slit in the breast meat and, using a paring knife, created an expansive pocket by sweeping the blade back and forth. This created a void into which we could rub a small amount of herb paste. This along with three other herbal applications—underneath the skin, inside the cavity, and over the skin—made for a successful four-pronged approach that gave every bite of turkey herb flavor. The herb paste itself, balanced with small amounts of pungent herbs (sage and rosemary) and greater amounts of softer flavors (thyme and parsley), also included lemon zest for a fresh, bright note and olive oil and Dijon mustard to make it spreadable. This was a moist roast turkey packed with bright herb flavor—a fresh alternative to the usual holiday bird.

Herbed Roast Turkey

SERVES 10 TO 12

If you have the time and the refrigerator space, air-drying produces extremely crisp skin and is worth the effort. After brining, rinsing, and patting the turkey dry, place the turkey, breast side up, on a wire rack set over a rimmed baking sheet and refrigerate, uncovered, 8 to 24 hours. Proceed with the recipe. Serve with All-Purpose Turkey Gravy (recipe follows).

TURKEY AND BRINE
- **2** cups table salt
- **1** (12 to 14-pound) turkey; giblets, neck, and tailpiece removed and discarded

HERB PASTE
- **1¼** cups roughly chopped fresh parsley leaves
- **4** teaspoons minced fresh thyme leaves
- **2** teaspoons roughly chopped fresh sage leaves
- **1½** teaspoons minced fresh rosemary leaves
- **1** medium shallot, minced (about 3 tablespoons)
- **2** medium garlic cloves, minced or pressed through a garlic press (about 2 teaspoons)
- **¾** teaspoon grated zest from 1 lemon
- **¾** teaspoon table salt
- **1** teaspoon ground black pepper
- **¼** cup olive oil
- **1** teaspoon Dijon mustard

1. FOR THE TURKEY AND BRINE: Dissolve the salt in 2 gallons cold water in a large container. Submerge the turkey in the brine, cover, and refrigerate or store in a very cool spot (40 degrees or less) for 4 to 6 hours.

2. Remove the turkey from the brine and rinse it well. Pat dry inside and out with paper towels. Place the turkey, breast side up, on a wire rack set over a rimmed baking sheet or roasting pan and refrigerate, uncovered, for

APPLYING HERB PASTE TO THE TURKEY

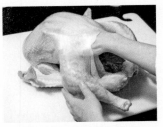

1. Carefully separate the skin from the meat on the breast, thigh, and drumstick areas.

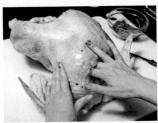

2. Rub the herb paste under the skin and directly onto the flesh, distributing it evenly.

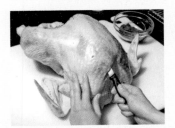

3. Make a 1½-inch slit in each breast. Swing a knife tip through the breast to create a large pocket.

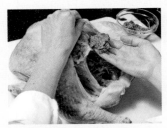

4. Place a thin layer of paste inside each pocket.

5. Rub the remaining paste inside the turkey cavity and on the skin.

30 minutes. (Alternatively, air-dry the turkey; see note.)

3. FOR THE HERB PASTE: Pulse the parsley, thyme, sage, rosemary, shallot, garlic, lemon zest, salt, and pepper together in a food processor until a coarse paste is formed, ten pulses. Add the olive oil and mustard; continue to pulse until the mixture forms a smooth paste, ten to twelve 2-second pulses; scrape the sides of the processor bowl with a rubber spatula after 5 pulses. Transfer the mixture to a small bowl.

4. TO PREPARE THE TURKEY: Adjust an oven rack to the lowest position and heat the oven to 400 degrees. Line a large V-rack with heavy-duty foil and poke several holes in the foil. Set the V-rack in a large roasting pan and spray the foil with vegetable oil spray. Remove the turkey from the refrigerator and wipe away any water collected in the baking sheet; set the turkey, breast side up, on the baking sheet.

5. Following the photos, use your hands to carefully loosen the skin from the meat of the breast, thighs, and drumsticks. Using your fingers or a spoon, slip 1½ table-spoons of the paste under the breast skin on each side of the turkey. Using your fingers, distribute the paste under the skin over the breast, thigh, and drumstick meat.

6. Using a sharp paring knife, cut a 1½-inch vertical slit into the thickest part of each side of the breast. Starting from the top of the incision, swing the knife tip down to create a 4 to 5-inch pocket within the flesh. Place 1 table-spoon more paste in the pocket of each side of the breast; using your fingers, rub the paste in a thin, even layer.

7. Rub 1 tablespoon more paste inside the turkey cavity. Rotate the turkey breast side down; apply half the remaining herb paste to the turkey skin; flip the turkey breast side up and apply the remaining herb paste to the skin, pressing and patting to make the paste adhere; reapply the herb paste that falls onto the baking sheet. Tuck the tips of the drumsticks into the skin at the tail to secure, and tuck the wings under the bird.

8. TO ROAST THE TURKEY: Place the turkey, breast side down, on the V-rack. Roast the turkey for 45 minutes.

9. Remove the pan from the oven (close the oven door to retain the oven heat). With a dish towel in each hand, rotate the turkey breast side up. Continue to roast until the thickest part of the breast registers 160 to 165 degrees and the thickest part of the thigh registers 175 degrees on an instant-read thermometer, 50 to 60 minutes longer. Transfer the turkey to a carving board and let rest, uncovered, for 30 minutes. Carve the turkey and serve.

All-Purpose Turkey Gravy

MAKES ABOUT 2 CUPS

Adding drippings from the roasted turkey will enhance the flavor of the gravy.

- 1 small carrot, peeled and chopped coarse
- 1 small celery rib, chopped coarse
- 1 small onion, chopped coarse
- 3 tablespoons unsalted butter
- ¼ cup unbleached all-purpose flour
- 2 cups low-sodium chicken broth
- 2 cups beef broth
- 1 bay leaf
- 2 sprigs fresh thyme
- 5 whole black peppercorns
  Defatted pan drippings from Herbed Roast Turkey (optional; see note)
  Table salt and ground black pepper

1. Pulse the carrot into ¼-inch pieces in a food processor, about 5 pulses. Add the celery and onion and continue to pulse until all of the vegetables are chopped fine, 5 pulses.

2. Melt the butter in a large saucepan over medium-high heat. Add the vegetables and cook, stirring often, until softened and well browned, about 7 minutes. Reduce the heat to medium, stir in the flour, and cook, stirring constantly, until well browned, about 5 minutes.

3. Gradually whisk in the broths until smooth. Bring to a boil, skimming any foam that rises to the surface. Add the bay leaf, thyme, and peppercorns. Reduce the heat to medium–low and simmer, stirring occasionally, until the gravy is thickened and measures about 3 cups, 20 to 25 minutes. Stir in any juices from the roasted meat (if using) and continue to simmer the gravy as needed to re-thicken.

NOTES FROM THE TEST KITCHEN

CARVING THE BREAST

The wings and legs on our Herbed Roast Turkey can be carved just as they would be on any other turkey, but the breast, which is stuffed with herb paste, needs some special attention. Here's how to ensure that every slice has a nice swirl of herbs.

1. With the wings facing toward you, cut along both sides of the breastbone, slicing from the tip of the breastbone to the cutting board.

2. Gently pull each breast half away to expose the wishbone. Then pull and remove the wishbone.

3. Using the knife tip, cut along the rib cage to remove the breast completely.

4. Place the entire breast half on a carving board and cut on the bias into thin slices. Repeat step 3 on the other side.

4. Strain the gravy through a fine-mesh strainer into a serving pitcher, pressing on the solids to extract as much liquid as possible; discard the solids. Season the gravy with salt and pepper to taste and cover to keep warm until needed.

GRILL-ROASTED TURKEY

WHY THIS RECIPE WORKS: Grill-roasting a turkey can be hard to manage. Cooking times can vary depending on the weather, and it's much easier to burn the bird's skin on a grill. There also remain the usual problems inherent to roasting a turkey: dry, overcooked breast meat and undercooked thighs.

But grill-roasting can produce the best-tasting, best-looking turkey ever, with crispy skin and moist meat wonderfully perfumed with smoke. We wanted to take the guesswork out of preparing the holiday bird on the grill.

Because the skin on larger birds will burn before the meat is done, we chose a small turkey (less than 14 pounds). We ditched stuffing the turkey or trussing it—both can lead to burnt skin and undercooked meat. To season the meat and help it from drying out on the grill, we brined the turkey. To protect the skin and promote slow cooking, we placed the turkey on the opposite side of the glowing coals or lit gas burner. Using a V-rack also helped, as it improved air circulation. And we turned the turkey three times instead of twice; this way, all four sides received equal exposure to the hot side of the grill for evenly bronzed skin.

Grill-Roasted Turkey on a Charcoal Grill

SERVES 10 TO 12

The total cooking time is 2 to 2½ hours, depending on the size of the bird, the ambient conditions (the bird will require more time on a cool, windy day), and the intensity of the fire. Check the internal temperature in the thigh when rotating the bird at the 1-hour-and-45-minute mark. If the thigh is nearly up to temperature (the final temperature should be 175 degrees), check the temperature again after about 15 minutes. If the thigh is still well below temperature (145 degrees or cooler), don't bother checking the bird again for at least another 30 minutes.

- 1 **cup table salt**
- 1 **(12 to 14-pound) turkey; giblets, neck, and tailpiece removed and wings tucked under the bird**
- 6 **(3-inch) wood chunks**
- 2 **tablespoons unsalted butter, melted**

1. Dissolve the salt in 2 gallons cold water in a large container. Submerge the turkey in the brine, cover, and refrigerate or store in a very cool spot (40 degrees or less) for 12 hours, or overnight.

2. Toward the end of brining, soak the wood chunks in cold water to cover for 1 hour; drain.

3. Light a large chimney starter filled three-quarters with charcoal (about 4½ quarts) and allow to burn until the coals are partially covered with a layer of ash, about 20 minutes. Open the bottom grill vents completely.

4. Meanwhile, spray a V-rack with vegetable oil spray. Remove the turkey from the brine and rinse inside and out under cool running water to remove all traces of salt. Pat the turkey dry with paper towels; brush both sides with melted butter. Set the turkey, breast side down, in the V-rack.

5. Build a single-banked fire by banking the coals over half of the grill, piling them up two or three coals high, leaving the other half empty. Place three wood chunks on top of the charcoal. Set the cooking grate in place,

open the lid vents halfway, and cover the grill. Heat the grate until hot, about 5 minutes, turning the lid so that the vents are opposite the wood chunks to draw smoke through the grill.

6. Position the V-rack with the turkey on the side of the grill opposite the fire. Cover and cook for 1 hour.

7. Remove the lid from the grill. Using thick potholders, transfer the V-rack with the turkey to a large rimmed baking sheet or roasting pan. Remove the cooking grate and place 12 new pieces of charcoal and three remaining wood chunks on top of the coals; replace the grate. With a dish towel in each hand, flip the turkey breast side up in the rack. Return the V-rack with the turkey to the cool part of the grill so that the leg and wing that were facing the coals are now facing away. Cover and cook for 45 minutes.

8. Using thick potholders, carefully turn the V-rack with the turkey (the breast remains up) so that the leg and wing that were facing the coals are now facing away from the coals. Insert an instant-read thermometer into each thigh to check the temperature and gauge how much longer the turkey must cook (see note).

9. Cover and continue to cook until the thickest part of the thigh registers 175 degrees on an instant-read thermometer, 15 to 45 minutes longer.

10. Remove the turkey from the grill, cover loosely with foil, and let rest for 30 minutes. Carve and serve.

Grill-Roasted Turkey on a Gas Grill

The total cooking time is 2 to 2½ hours, depending on the size of the bird, the ambient conditions (the bird will require more time on a cool, windy day), and the intensity of the fire. Check the internal temperature in the thigh when rotating the bird at the 1-hour-and-45-minute mark. If the thigh is nearly up to temperature (the final temperature should be 175 degrees), check the temperature again after about 15 minutes. If the thigh is still well below temperature (145 degrees or cooler), don't bother checking the bird again for at least another 30 minutes.

Follow the recipe for Grill-Roasted Turkey on a Charcoal Grill through step 4, making the following changes: Cover 3 cups wood chips with water and soak 30 minutes, then drain. Place the soaked wood chips in a small disposable aluminum pan; set the pan on the burner that will remain on. Turn all the burners to high, close the lid, and heat the grill until the chips smoke heavily, about 20 minutes. Turn off the burner(s) without the wood chips. Place the turkey over the cool part of the grill and proceed as directed in step 6.

GRILL-ROASTED TURKEY BREAST

WHY THIS RECIPE WORKS: Grill-roasting a turkey breast makes a nice change from the same old oven-roasted holiday bird. And unleashing the smoky fire of the grill on mild-mannered turkey breast is bound to add great flavor. The problem is that unlike fatty pork butt or brisket, which turns moist and tender after a stint on the grill, ultra-lean turkey breast easily dries out. Plus its irregular shape can lead to uneven cooking. We wanted to develop a recipe that would deliver a grill-roasted breast with all the richness and juiciness we associate with the thighs and legs, along with crisp, well-rendered skin, and meat that was moist all the way through.

We began by salting our turkey breast. Salting, much like brining, imparts flavor and moisture to the meat. When meat is salted, its juices are initially drawn out of the flesh and beads of liquid pool on its surface. Eventually, the salty liquid slowly migrates back into the meat, keeping it moist as it cooks. We grill-roasted the turkey breast over a modified two-level fire, starting the meat over the cool side of the grill and later moving it to the hot side to finish cooking. Although most of the meat turned out moist and flavorful, there were still desiccated spots on the tapered ends of the breast and in places where the skin didn't completely cover the meat. Inspired by a restaurant technique, we reshaped our turkey breast like a roulade so that it would cook through evenly. After carefully removing the skin, we rolled the boneless turkey breast into a tight cylinder. Then we rewrapped the skin around the roulade of meat to completely cover and protect it. Our roast held its shape beautifully on the grill and, once carved, the roulade revealed moist, evenly cooked meat and crisp skin.

Charcoal Grill–Roasted Boneless Turkey Breast

SERVES 6 TO 8

We prefer either a natural (unbrined) or kosher turkey breast for this recipe. Using a kosher turkey breast (rubbed with salt and rinsed during processing) or self-basting turkey breast (injected with salt and water) eliminates the need for salting in step 2. If the breast has a pop-up timer, remove it before cooking.

- 1 (5 to 7-pound) whole bone-in, skin-on turkey breast (see note)
- 2 teaspoons table salt (see note)
- ½ cup wood chips (optional)
- 1 teaspoon vegetable oil, plus extra for the cooking grate
  Ground black pepper

1. Set a wire rack over a large rimmed baking sheet and set aside. Following photos 1 and 2, remove the skin from the breast meat and then remove the breasts from the bone structure (discard the bones or save for stock).

2. Sprinkle the entire surface of each breast half with 1 teaspoon of the salt. Following photos 3 and 4, assemble and tie the turkey roast. Place the roast on the prepared baking sheet and refrigerate, uncovered, for 1 hour.

3. Meanwhile, if using, soak the wood chips in cold water to cover for 30 minutes; drain. Light a large chimney starter filled with charcoal (about 6 quarts) and allow to burn until the coals are partially covered with a layer of ash, about 20 minutes. Build a modified two-level fire by arranging all the coals over one half of the grill, leaving the other half empty. Sprinkle the wood chips (if using) over the coals. Set the cooking grate in place, cover, and heat the grate until hot, about 5 minutes. Use a grill brush to scrape the grate clean. Dip a wad of paper towels in the oil; holding the wad with tongs, oil the cooking grate.

4. Rub the surface of the roast with 1 teaspoon oil and season with pepper. Place the roast on the cooler side of the grill. Cover the grill and cook until an instant-read thermometer inserted into the thickest part of the roast registers 150 degrees, 40 to 60 minutes, turning the roast 180 degrees halfway through the cooking time.

5. Slide the roast to the hot side of the grill and cook, uncovered, until the roast is browned and the skin is crisp on all sides, 2 to 2½ minutes per side (8 to 10 minutes total). Transfer the roast to a carving board and let rest, uncovered, for 20 minutes. Cut into ½-inch-thick slices, removing the twine as you cut. Serve.

Gas Grill–Roasted Boneless Turkey Breast

Follow the recipe for Charcoal Grill–Roasted Boneless Turkey Breast through step 2. If using wood chips, place them in a disposable aluminum pie plate and place the pie plate on the primary burner and reposition the cooking grate(s). Turn all the burners to high, close the lid, and heat the grill until hot, about 15 minutes. Scrape the cooking grate clean with a grill brush. Dip a wad of

NOTES FROM THE TEST KITCHEN

TURNING A BONE-IN TURKEY BREAST INTO A BONELESS TURKEY ROAST

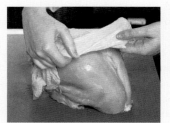

1. Starting at one side of the breast and using your fingers to separate the skin from the meat, peel the skin off the breast meat and reserve.

2. Using the tip of a knife, cut along the rib cage to remove each breast half completely.

3. Arrange one breast, cut side up; top with the second breast, cut side down, the thick end over the tapered end. Drape the skin over the breasts and tuck the ends under.

4. Tie a 3-foot piece of twine lengthwise around the roast. Then, tie five to seven pieces of twine at 1-inch intervals crosswise along the roast, starting at its center, then at either end, and then filling in the rest.

paper towels in the oil; holding the wad with tongs, wipe the cooking grate. Leave the primary burner on high and turn off the other burner(s). Continue with the recipe from step 4, placing the roast seam-side up on the side opposite the primary burner and cooking with the lid down in step 5.

CRANBERRY SAUCE

WHY THIS RECIPE WORKS: The best cranberry sauce has a clean, pure cranberry flavor, with enough sweetness to temper the assertively tart fruit but not so much that the sauce is cloying or candylike. The texture should be that of a soft gel, neither too liquidy nor too stiff, cushioning some softened but still intact berries.

For the most part, it turned out that simpler was better. We used white table sugar, which, unlike brown sugar, honey, or syrup, balanced the tartness of the cranberries without adding a flavor profile of its own. Simpler was also better when it came to liquid: water proved the best choice. We also discovered that adding just a pinch of salt brought out an unexpected sweetness in the berries, heightening the flavor of the sauce overall.

Classic Cranberry Sauce

MAKES 2¼ CUPS

If you've got frozen cranberries, do not defrost them before use; just pick through them and add about 2 minutes to the simmering time.

- 1 **cup (7 ounces) sugar**
- ¾ **cup water**
- ¼ **teaspoon table salt**
- 1 **(12-ounce) bag cranberries, picked through (see note)**

Bring the sugar, water, and salt to a boil in a medium saucepan over high heat, stirring occasionally to dissolve the sugar. Stir in the cranberries; return to a boil. Reduce the heat to medium; simmer until saucy and slightly thickened, and about two-thirds of the berries have popped open, about 5 minutes. Transfer to a medium bowl, cool to room temperature, and serve. (The cranberry sauce can be covered and refrigerated up to 7 days; let stand at room temperature 30 minutes before serving.)

GREEN BEAN CASSEROLE

WHY THIS RECIPE WORKS: The classic combination of green beans, condensed soup, and canned onions isn't bad. But for a holiday centered on homemade food, shouldn't every dish be great? We wanted to upgrade green bean casserole to give it fresh, homemade flavor.

Our first tasting determined that we definitely needed to use fresh green beans rather than frozen or canned beans. A preliminary blanching and shocking prepared the beans to finish cooking perfectly in the casserole, enabling them to keep a consistent texture and retain their beautiful green color. For our sauce, we made a mushroom variation of the classic French velouté sauce (chicken broth thickened with a roux made from butter and flour, then finished with heavy cream). Our biggest challenge was the onion topping. Ultimately we found that the canned onions couldn't be entirely replaced without sacrificing the level of convenience we thought appropriate to the dish, but we masked their "commercial" flavor with freshly made buttered bread crumbs.

Classic Green Bean Casserole

SERVES 8 TO 10

All the components of this dish can be cooked ahead of time. The assembled casserole needs only 15 minutes in a 375-degree oven to warm through and brown.

TOPPING
- 4 **slices high-quality white sandwich bread, torn into quarters**
- 2 **tablespoons unsalted butter, softened**
- ¼ **teaspoon table salt**
- ⅛ **teaspoon ground black pepper**
- 3 **cups canned fried onions (about 6 ounces)**

BEANS

    Table salt
 2 pounds green beans, ends trimmed, cut on the diagonal
    into 2-inch pieces
 ½ ounce dried porcini mushrooms
 6 tablespoons (¾ stick) unsalted butter
 1 medium onion, minced
 3 medium garlic cloves, minced or pressed through a
    garlic press (about 1 tablespoon)
12 ounces white button mushrooms, wiped clean and sliced
    ¼ inch thick
12 ounces cremini mushrooms, wiped clean and sliced
    ¼ inch thick
 2 tablespoons minced fresh thyme leaves
 ¼ teaspoon ground black pepper
 2 tablespoons unbleached all-purpose flour
 1 cup low-sodium chicken broth
 2 cups heavy cream

1. FOR THE TOPPING: Pulse the bread, butter, salt, and pepper in a food processor until the mixture resembles coarse crumbs, about 10 to 15 pulses. Transfer to a large bowl and toss with the onions; set aside.

2. FOR THE BEANS: Heat the oven to 375 degrees. Bring 4 quarts water to a boil in a large pot. Add 2 tablespoons salt and the beans. Cook until bright green and slightly crunchy, 4 to 5 minutes. Drain the beans and plunge immediately into a large bowl filled with ice water to stop cooking. Spread the beans out onto a paper towel–lined baking sheet to drain.

3. Meanwhile, cover the dried porcini with ½ cup hot tap water in a small microwave-safe bowl; cover with plastic wrap, cut several steam vents with a paring knife, and microwave on high power for 30 seconds. Let stand until the mushrooms soften, about 5 minutes. Lift the mushrooms from the liquid with a fork and mince using a chef's knife (you should have about 2 tablespoons). Pour the liquid through a paper towel–lined sieve and reserve.

4. Melt the butter in a large nonstick skillet over medium-high heat. Add the onion, garlic, button mushrooms, and cremini mushrooms and cook until the mushrooms release their moisture, about 2 minutes. Add the porcini mushrooms along with their strained soaking liquid, thyme, 1 teaspoon salt, and the pepper and cook until all the mushrooms are tender and the liquid has reduced to 2 tablespoons, about 5 minutes. Add the flour and cook for 1 minute. Stir in the chicken broth and reduce the heat to medium. Stir in the cream and simmer gently until the

sauce has the consistency of dense soup, about 15 minutes.

5. Arrange the beans in a 3-quart gratin dish. Pour the mushroom mixture over the beans and mix to coat the beans evenly. Sprinkle with the bread-crumb mixture and bake until the top is golden brown and the sauce is bubbling around the edges, about 15 minutes. Serve immediately.

QUICK GREEN BEAN CASSEROLE

WHY THIS RECIPE WORKS: We love traditional green bean casserole, but we wanted a streamlined technique for preparing the dish—one with tender beans in a tasty sauce worthy of a holiday spread and yet speedy enough for a last-minute supper.

Rather than using two pots—one for the beans and one for the sauce—we cooked both in just one pot, a skillet. First, we built a sauce in the skillet with onion, garlic, chicken broth, cream, and a little flour; then we added the beans along with thyme and bay leaves, covered them, and allowed them to steam until the beans were almost done. We then stirred in meaty browned cremini mushrooms and thickened the sauce by uncovering the skillet during the final phase of cooking. And instead of canned fried onions, we sprinkled crunchy fried sliced shallots over our easy, tasty skillet casserole.

Quick Green Bean "Casserole"
SERVES 8

 3 large shallots, sliced thin (about 1 cup)
    Table salt and ground black pepper
 3 tablespoons unbleached all-purpose flour
 5 tablespoons vegetable oil
10 ounces cremini mushrooms, wiped clean and sliced
    ¼ inch thick
 2 tablespoons unsalted butter
 1 medium onion, minced
 2 medium garlic cloves, minced or pressed through
    a garlic press (about 2 teaspoons)
1½ pounds green beans, trimmed
 3 sprigs fresh thyme
 2 bay leaves
 ¾ cup heavy cream
 ¾ cup low-sodium chicken broth

1. Toss the shallots with ¼ teaspoon salt, ⅛ teaspoon pepper, and 2 tablespoons of the flour in a bowl. Heat 3 tablespoons of the oil in a 12-inch nonstick skillet over medium-high heat until smoking; add the shallots and cook, stirring frequently, until golden and crisp, about 5 minutes. Transfer the shallots with the oil to a baking sheet lined with paper towels.

2. Wipe out the skillet and return to medium-high heat. Add the remaining 2 tablespoons oil, the mushrooms, and ¼ teaspoon salt; cook, stirring occasionally, until the mushrooms are well browned, about 8 minutes. Transfer to a plate and set aside.

3. Wipe out the skillet. Melt the butter in the skillet over medium heat, then add the onion and cook, stirring occasionally, until the edges begin to brown, about 2 minutes. Stir in the garlic and remaining 1 tablespoon flour; toss in the green beans, thyme, and bay leaves. Add the cream and chicken broth, increase the heat to medium-high, cover, and cook until the beans are partly tender but still crisp at the center, about 4 minutes. Add the mushrooms and continue to cook, uncovered, until the green beans are tender, about 4 minutes. Off the heat, discard the bay leaves and thyme; season with salt and pepper to taste. Transfer to a serving dish, sprinkle evenly with the shallots, and serve.

CANDIED SWEET POTATO CASSEROLE

WHY THIS RECIPE WORKS: Sweet potato casserole is often claimed as a must-have at the Thanksgiving table. Kids love this sweet, sticky dish, but adults long for a side dish with more restrained sweetness, rather than one that could double as dessert. We set out to develop a sweet potato casserole with a bit of a savory accent to please everyone.

For the best texture and flavor, we steamed the sweet potatoes on the stovetop with a little water, butter, and brown sugar. We kept the other flavorings simple—just salt and pepper. In the topping, we used whole pecans instead of chopped; this gave the casserole a better texture and appearance. And a little cayenne and cumin lent a hit of spice to the topping that offset the sweetness of the potato.

Candied Sweet Potato Casserole

SERVES 10 TO 12

For a more intense molasses flavor, use dark brown sugar in place of light brown sugar.

SWEET POTATOES

8 tablespoons (1 stick) unsalted butter, cut into 1-inch chunks

5 pounds sweet potatoes (about 8 medium), peeled and cut into 1-inch cubes

1 cup (7 ounces) packed light brown sugar (see note)

½ cup water

1½ teaspoons table salt

½ teaspoon ground black pepper

PECAN TOPPING

2 cups pecan halves

½ cup packed (3½ ounces) light brown sugar (see note)

1 egg white, lightly beaten

⅛ teaspoon table salt

Pinch cayenne pepper

Pinch ground cumin

1. FOR THE SWEET POTATOES: Melt the butter in a large Dutch oven over medium-high heat. Add the sweet potatoes, brown sugar, water, salt, and black pepper; bring to a simmer. Reduce the heat to medium-low, cover, and cook, stirring often, until the sweet potatoes are tender (a paring knife can be slipped into and out of the center of the potatoes with very little resistance), 45 to 60 minutes.

2. When the sweet potatoes are tender, remove the lid and bring the sauce to a rapid simmer over medium-high heat. Continue to simmer until the sauce has reduced to a glaze, 7 to 10 minutes.

3. FOR THE TOPPING: Meanwhile, mix all the ingredients for the topping together in a medium bowl; set aside.

4. Adjust an oven rack to the middle position and heat the oven to 450 degrees. Pour the potato mixture into a 13 by 9-inch baking dish (or a shallow casserole dish of similar size). Spread the topping over the potatoes. Bake until the pecans are toasted and crisp, 10 to 15 minutes. Serve immediately.

CHAPTER 7

WE'LL HAVE THE STEAK

Pan-Seared Steaks 108

    Red Wine Pan Sauce

    Shallot Butter Sauce

Pan-Seared Thick-Cut Steaks 109

    Red Wine–Mushroom Pan Sauce

    Thai Chili Butter

Pan-Seared Inexpensive Steaks 111

    Tomato-Caper Pan Sauce

    Mustard-Cream Pan Sauce

Pan-Seared Filet Mignon 112

    Madeira Pan Sauce with Mustard and Anchovies

    Argentinian-Style Fresh Parsley and Garlic Sauce (Chimichurri)

Pepper-Crusted Filet Mignon 114

    Port-Cherry Reduction

    Blue Cheese–Chive Butter

Flank Steak and Arugula Sandwiches with Red Onion 115

    Garlic-Soy Mayonnaise

PAN-SEARED STEAKS

WHY THIS RECIPE WORKS: The flavor of a juicy, grilled steak is hard to beat. We wanted to produce outstanding steaks—indoors—that were every bit as good as those cooked on the grill, with a flavorful crust and perfectly cooked, rosy meat.

We found that heating a heavy-bottomed skillet until very hot is essential for a good sear and, thus, a good crust. Thoroughly drying the steaks is also key—soggy steaks will steam, not sear. For best flavor, we seasoned the steaks with salt and pepper prior to cooking. And we reduced the heat before adding the steaks—the skillet was still hot, but not so hot that it burned the fond (the brown bits left in the pan), which we used to make a pan sauce. After removing the steaks from the pan, we let them rest for five minutes, enough time to prepare the pan sauce and allow the juices in the meat to redistribute.

Pan-Seared Steaks

SERVES 4

Serve these steaks with either Red Wine Pan Sauce or Shallot Butter Sauce (recipes follow). Prepare all the sauce ingredients before starting the steaks and don't wash the skillet after cooking the steaks; the fat left in the pan will be used for the sauce. Note that the wine reduction used in the red wine sauce should be started before the steaks are cooked.

  1 tablespoon vegetable oil
  4 (8-ounce) boneless strip or rib-eye steaks, each 1 to
     1¼ inches thick, thoroughly dried with paper towels
     Table salt and ground black pepper

1. Heat the oil in a 12-inch skillet over high heat until just smoking. Meanwhile, season both sides of the steaks with salt and pepper.

2. Lay the steaks in the pan, leaving ¼ inch of space between them; reduce the heat to medium-high and cook, not moving the steaks until well browned, about 4 minutes. Using tongs, flip the steaks; cook until the center of the steaks registers 120 degrees on an instant-read thermometer for rare (4 minutes), 125 degrees for medium-rare (5 minutes), or 130 degrees for medium (6 minutes). Transfer the steaks to a large plate, tent with foil, and let rest 5 minutes while preparing one of the pan sauces.

Red Wine Pan Sauce

MAKES ABOUT ½ CUP

Start cooking the steaks when the wine has almost finished reducing. Use a smooth, medium-bodied, fruity wine, such as a Côtes du Rhône.

WINE REDUCTION
  1 cup red wine (see note)
  1 medium shallot, minced (about 3 tablespoons)
  2 white mushrooms, wiped clean and chopped fine
     (about 3 tablespoons)
  1 small carrot, chopped fine (about 2 tablespoons)
  1 bay leaf
  3 sprigs fresh parsley

SAUCE
  1 medium shallot, minced (about 3 tablespoons)
  ½ cup low-sodium chicken broth
  ½ cup low-sodium beef broth
  3 tablespoons cold unsalted butter, cut into 6 pieces
  ½ teaspoon fresh thyme leaves
     Table salt and ground black pepper

1. FOR THE WINE REDUCTION: Heat the wine, shallot, mushrooms, carrot, bay leaf, and parsley in a 12-inch skillet over low heat; cook, without simmering (the liquid should be steaming but not bubbling), until the entire mixture reduces to 1 cup, 15 to 20 minutes. Strain through a fine-mesh strainer and return the liquid (about ½ cup) to the clean skillet. Continue to cook over low heat, without simmering, until the liquid is reduced to 2 tablespoons, 15 to 20 minutes. Transfer the reduction to a bowl.

2. FOR THE SAUCE: Follow the recipe for Pan-Seared Steaks. After removing the steaks from the skillet, add the shallot and cook over low heat until softened, about 1 minute. Turn the heat to high; add the chicken and beef broths. Bring to a boil, scraping up the browned bits on the pan bottom with a wooden spoon, until the liquid is reduced to 2 tablespoons, about 6 minutes. Turn the heat to medium-low, gently whisk in the reserved wine reduction and any accumulated juices from the plate with the steaks. Whisk in the butter, one piece at a time, until melted and the sauce is thickened and glossy; add the thyme and season with salt and pepper to taste. Spoon the sauce over the steaks and serve immediately.

Shallot Butter Sauce

MAKES ABOUT ½ CUP

2 medium shallots, minced (about ⅓ cup)
4 tablespoons (½ stick) cold unsalted butter,
  cut into 4 pieces
1 teaspoon juice from 1 lemon
1 teaspoon minced fresh parsley leaves
  Table salt and ground black pepper

Follow the recipe for Pan-Seared Steaks. After removing the steaks from the skillet, add the shallots and cook over low heat until softened, about 1 minute. Turn the heat to medium-low; stir in the butter, scraping up the browned bits on the pan bottom with a wooden spoon. When the butter is just melted, stir in the lemon juice and parsley; season with salt and pepper to taste. Spoon the sauce over the steaks and serve immediately.

PAN-SEARED THICK-CUT STEAKS

WHY THIS RECIPE WORKS: A nicely charred thick-cut steak certainly looks appealing. But cutting into the steak to find that the rosy meat is confined to a measly spot in the center—with the rest a thick band of overcooked gray—is a great disappointment. We wanted to find a surefire method for pan-searing thick-cut steaks that could deliver both a flavorful crust and juicy, perfectly pink meat throughout.

We found it was essential to sear the steaks quickly to keep the meat directly under the crust from turning gray. But we'd need to take an untraditional approach for these thick-cut steaks and sear them at the end of cooking, rather than at the beginning. We began by moving the steaks straight from the fridge into a 275-degree oven, which not only warmed them to 95 degrees but also dried the meat thoroughly—dry meat is essential for a well-browned crust. At this temperature, when the steak met the hot skillet, our steaks developed a beautiful brown crust in less than four minutes, while the rest of the meat stayed pink, juicy, and tender.

Pan-Seared Thick-Cut Steaks

SERVES 4

Rib-eye or filet mignon of similar thickness can be substituted for strip steaks. If using filet mignon, buying a 2-pound center-cut tenderloin roast and portioning it into four 8-ounce steaks yourself will produce more consistent results. If using filet mignon, increase the oven time by about 5 minutes. When cooking lean strip steaks (without an external fat cap) or filet mignon, add an extra tablespoon of oil to the pan. To serve the steaks with the Red Wine–Mushroom Pan Sauce (recipe follows), prepare all the sauce ingredients while the steaks are in the oven, and don't wash the skillet after cooking the steaks.

2 (1-pound) boneless strip steaks, each 1½ to 1¾ inches
  thick (see note)
  Table salt and ground black pepper
1 tablespoon vegetable oil

1. Adjust an oven rack to the middle position and heat the oven to 275 degrees. Pat the steaks dry with paper towels. Cut each steak in half vertically to create four 8-ounce steaks. Season the steaks liberally with salt and pepper; using your hands, gently shape into a uniform thickness. Place the steaks on a wire rack set over a rimmed baking sheet; transfer the baking sheet to the oven. Cook until an instant-read thermometer inserted horizontally into the center of the steaks registers 90 to 95 degrees for rare to medium-rare (20 to 25 minutes), or 100 to 105 degrees for medium (25 to 30 minutes).

2. Heat the oil in a 12-inch skillet over high heat until smoking. Place the steaks in the skillet and sear until well browned and crusty, 1½ to 2 minutes, lifting once halfway through to redistribute the fat underneath each steak. (Reduce the heat if the fond begins to burn.) Using tongs, turn the steaks and cook until well browned on the second side, 2 to 2½ minutes. Transfer the steaks to a clean rack and reduce the heat under the pan to medium. Use tongs to stand 2 steaks on their sides. Holding the steaks together, return to the skillet and sear on all edges until browned, about 1½ minutes (see photo). Repeat with the remaining 2 steaks.

3. Return the steaks to the wire rack and let rest, loosely tented with foil, for about 10 minutes. If desired, cook the sauce in the now-empty skillet. Serve immediately.

Red Wine–Mushroom Pan Sauce

MAKES ABOUT 1 CUP

Prepare all the ingredients for the pan sauce while the steaks are in the oven.

- 1 tablespoon vegetable oil
- 8 ounces white mushrooms, wiped clean and sliced thin (about 3 cups)
- 1 small shallot, minced (about 1 tablespoon)
- 1 cup dry red wine
- ½ cup low-sodium chicken broth
- 1 tablespoon balsamic vinegar
- 1 teaspoon Dijon mustard
- 2 tablespoons cold unsalted butter, cut into 4 pieces
- 1 teaspoon minced fresh thyme leaves
  Table salt and ground black pepper

Follow the recipe for Pan-Seared Thick-Cut Steaks. After removing the steaks from the skillet, pour off the fat from the skillet. Heat the oil over medium-high heat until just smoking. Add the mushrooms and cook, stirring occasionally, until beginning to brown and the liquid has evaporated, about 5 minutes. Add the shallot and cook, stirring frequently, until beginning to soften, about 1 minute. Increase the heat to high; add the red wine and broth, scraping the bottom of the skillet with a wooden spoon to loosen any browned bits. Simmer rapidly until the liquid and mushrooms are reduced to 1 cup, about

6 minutes. Add the vinegar, mustard, and any juices from the resting steaks; cook until thickened, about 1 minute. Off the heat, whisk in the butter and thyme; season with salt and pepper to taste. Spoon the sauce over the steaks and serve immediately.

Thai Chili Butter

MAKES ABOUT ⅓ CUP

Prepare all the ingredients for the butter while the steaks are in the oven. If red curry paste isn't available, increase the chili-garlic sauce to 2½ teaspoons.

- 4 tablespoons (½ stick) unsalted butter, softened
- 1 tablespoon chopped fresh cilantro leaves
- 2 teaspoons Asian chili-garlic sauce (preferably Thai)
- 1½ teaspoons thinly sliced scallion, green part only (from 1 scallion)
- 1 small garlic clove, minced or pressed through a garlic press (about ½ teaspoon)
- ½ teaspoon red curry paste (preferably Thai) (see note)
- 2 teaspoons fresh lime juice from 1 lime
  Table salt

Beat the butter vigorously with a spoon until soft and fluffy. Add the cilantro, chili-garlic sauce, scallion, garlic, and red curry paste; beat to incorporate. Add the lime juice a little at a time, beating vigorously between each addition until fully incorporated. Add salt to taste. Spoon a dollop over each steak, giving it time to melt before serving.

NOTES FROM THE TEST KITCHEN

SEARING TWO STEAKS AT ONCE

Use tongs to sear the sides of two steaks at the same time.

PAN-SEARED INEXPENSIVE STEAKS

WHY THIS RECIPE WORKS: Buying cheap steak can be a gamble and a lesson in confusion. Names differ from region to region, some cuts are wonderfully tender while others are hopelessly tough, and some recipes recommend cuts that are almost impossible to find, leaving the consumer to make a blind substitution. We wanted inexpensive steak with the flavor and texture to rival its pricey counterparts.

We first visited meat purveyors to learn what makes some steaks more expensive than others as well as to decipher all the different names. After sorting through the confusion, we were left with a list of 12 candidates. We cooked them as we would any steak, creating a nice sear on both sides without overcooking or allowing the browned bits in the pan to burn. Tasters judged most to be too tough and/or lacking beefy flavor, while others were livery or gamy. We tried a variety of preparation methods—salting, aging, tenderizing, marinating—but none really improved flavor and texture. In the end, only two cuts earned favored status: boneless shell sirloin steak (aka top butt) and flap meat steak (aka sirloin tips). To prepare the steak, season the steaks simply with salt and pepper and start with a very hot skillet. Allow the meat to rest before slicing. Slice the steak thin, against the grain and on the bias, to ensure the tenderest meat.

Pan-Seared Inexpensive Steaks

SERVES 4

Serve these steaks with Tomato-Caper Pan Sauce or Mustard-Cream Pan Sauce (recipes follow). Prepare all of the sauce ingredients before cooking the steaks, and don't wash the skillet after removing the steaks; the sauce will use some of the fat left in the pan. To serve two instead of four, use a 10-inch skillet to cook a 1-pound steak and halve the sauce ingredients. Bear in mind that even those tasters who usually prefer rare beef preferred these steaks cooked medium-rare or medium because the texture is firmer and not quite so chewy. The times in the recipe are for 1¼-inch-thick steaks.

- 2 tablespoons vegetable oil
- 2 1-pound whole boneless shell sirloin steaks (top butt) or whole flap meat steaks, each about 1¼ inches thick
  Table salt and ground black pepper

1. Heat the oil in a heavy-bottomed 12-inch skillet over medium-high heat until smoking. Meanwhile, season both sides of the steaks with salt and pepper. Place the steaks in the skillet; cook, without moving the steaks, until well browned, about 2 minutes. Using tongs, flip the steaks; reduce the heat to medium. Cook until well browned on the second side and the center of the steaks registers 125 degrees on an instant-read thermometer for medium-rare (about 5 minutes) or 130 degrees for medium (about 6 minutes).

2. Transfer the steaks to a large plate and tent loosely with foil; let rest about 10 minutes. Meanwhile, prepare the pan sauce, if making.

3. Using a sharp chef's knife or carving knife, slice the steak about ¼ inch thick against the grain on the bias, arrange on a platter or on individual plates, and spoon some sauce (if using) over each steak; serve immediately.

Tomato-Caper Pan Sauce

MAKES ABOUT ¾ CUP

If ripe fresh tomatoes are not available, substitute 2 to 3 canned whole tomatoes, seeded and cut into ¼-inch pieces.

- 1 medium shallot, minced (about 3 tablespoons)
- 1 teaspoon unbleached all-purpose flour
- 2 tablespoons dry white wine
- 1 cup low-sodium chicken broth
- 2 tablespoons capers, drained
- 1 medium ripe tomato, seeded and cut into ¼-inch dice (about ¼ cup) (see note)
- ¼ cup minced fresh parsley leaves
  Table salt and ground black pepper

BEHIND THE SCENES

REDUCTION DEDUCTION

We've all seen recipe instructions such as "Reduce sauce to ½ cup" or "Simmer until broth is reduced to 2 cups." Those directions are clear, but when you look into a pan of sauce, can you really discern volume? Unless you have wizard-like abilities, the answer is probably "No."

Here in the test kitchen, we know that getting the right amount of sauce can make or break a dish, and to be sure of success we keep a heatproof liquid measuring cup next to the stove. As the sauce appears to be getting near the targeted amount, we pour it into the cup to get an exact measure. If it needs more time on the stove, back into the pan it goes until just the right amount is obtained. No guessing, no problem.

Follow the recipe for Pan-Seared Inexpensive Steaks. After removing the steaks from the skillet, pour off all but 1 tablespoon of the fat. Return the skillet to low heat and add the shallot; cook, stirring frequently, until beginning to brown, 2 to 3 minutes. Sprinkle the flour over the shallot; cook, stirring constantly, until combined, about 1 minute. Add the wine and increase the heat to medium–high; simmer rapidly, scraping up the browned bits on the pan bottom with a wooden spoon. Simmer until the liquid is reduced to a glaze, about 30 seconds; add the broth and simmer until reduced to ⅔ cup, about 4 minutes. Reduce the heat to medium; add the capers, tomato, and any meat juices that have accumulated on the plate and cook until the flavors are blended, about 1 minute. Stir in the parsley and season with salt and pepper to taste; spoon the sauce over the sliced steak and serve immediately.

Mustard-Cream Pan Sauce

MAKES ABOUT ¾ CUP

- 1 medium shallot, minced (about 3 tablespoons)
- 2 tablespoons dry white wine
- ½ cup low-sodium chicken broth
- 6 tablespoons heavy cream
- 3 tablespoons grainy Dijon mustard
- Table salt and ground black pepper

Follow the recipe for Pan-Seared Inexpensive Steaks. After removing the steaks from the skillet, pour off all but 1 tablespoon of the fat. Return the skillet to low heat and add the shallot; cook, stirring frequently, until beginning to brown, 2 to 3 minutes. Add the wine and increase the heat to medium–high; simmer rapidly, scraping up the browned bits on the pan bottom with a wooden spoon. Simmer until the liquid is reduced to a glaze, about 30 seconds; add the broth and simmer until reduced to ¼ cup, about 3 minutes. Add the cream and any meat juices that have accumulated on the plate; cook until heated through, about 1 minute. Stir in the mustard; season with salt and pepper to taste. Spoon over the sliced steak and serve immediately.

PAN-SEARED FILET MIGNON

WHY THIS RECIPE WORKS: Many cooks feel that filet mignon should be reserved for a celebratory restaurant meal rather than a less-expensive home-cooked meal. We wanted to replicate the best restaurant filet at home, with a rich, brown crust and a tender interior, topped with a quick but luscious pan sauce.

For a great crust, we patted the steaks dry before searing them in a very hot skillet. Then we transferred the meat to a hot oven to cook through. Finishing the steak in the oven prevents the richly flavored brown bits in the bottom of the pan from burning and gives the cook time to start the sauce, which can be made in minutes while the steaks rest.

Pan-Seared Filet Mignon

SERVES 4

If you choose to serve the steaks with one of the sauces that follow, have all the sauce ingredients ready before searing the steaks, and don't wash the skillet after removing the steaks. Begin the sauce while the steaks are in the oven. To cook six steaks instead of four, switch to a 12-inch pan and use 6 teaspoons of olive oil.

4 (7 to 8-ounce) center-cut filets mignons, 1½ inches thick, each dried thoroughly with paper towels

4 teaspoons olive oil

Table salt and ground black pepper

1. Adjust an oven rack to the lower-middle position, place a large rimmed baking sheet on the oven rack, and heat the oven to 450 degrees. When the oven reaches 450 degrees, heat a large skillet over high heat on the stovetop until very hot.

2. Meanwhile, rub each side of the steaks with ½ teaspoon oil and sprinkle generously with salt and pepper. Place the steaks in the hot skillet and cook, without moving the steaks, until well browned and a nice crust has formed, about 3 minutes. Turn the steaks with tongs and cook until well browned and a nice crust has formed on the second side, about 3 minutes longer. Remove the pan from the heat and use tongs to transfer the steaks to the hot baking sheet in the oven.

3. Roast until the center of the steaks registers 120 degrees on an instant-read thermometer for rare (4 to 5 minutes), 125 degrees for medium-rare (6 to 8 minutes), or 130 degrees for medium (8 to 10 minutes). Transfer the steaks to a large plate; loosely tent with foil and let rest about 10 minutes before serving.

Madeira Pan Sauce with Mustard and Anchovies

MAKES ABOUT ⅔ CUP

If you do not have Madeira on hand, sherry makes a fine substitute. The accumulated pan juices from the steaks in the oven are incorporated into the reduction. If the steaks haven't finished cooking once the sauce has reduced, simply set the sauce aside until the steaks (and accumulated juices) are ready.

1 medium shallot, minced (about 3 tablespoons)

1 cup Madeira (see note)

2 anchovy fillets, minced to a paste (about 1 teaspoon)

1 tablespoon minced fresh parsley leaves

1 tablespoon minced fresh thyme leaves

1 tablespoon Dijon mustard

1 tablespoon juice from 1 lemon

3 tablespoons unsalted butter, softened

Table salt and ground black pepper

Follow the recipe for Pan-Seared Filet Mignon. While the steaks are in the oven, set the skillet over medium-low heat; add the shallot and cook, stirring constantly, until

softened, about 1 minute. Add the Madeira, increase the heat to high, and scrape the pan bottom with a wooden spoon to loosen the browned bits. Simmer until the liquid is reduced to about ⅓ cup, 6 to 8 minutes. Add the accumulated juices from the baking sheet and reduce the liquid 1 minute longer. Off the heat, whisk in the anchovies, parsley, thyme, mustard, lemon juice, and butter until the butter has melted and the sauce is slightly thickened. Season with salt and pepper to taste, spoon the sauce over the steaks, and serve immediately.

Argentinian-Style Fresh Parsley and Garlic Sauce (Chimichurri)

MAKES ABOUT 1 CUP

For best results use flat-leaf parsley.

1 cup packed fresh parsley leaves from one large bunch, washed and dried (see note)

5 medium garlic cloves, peeled

½ cup extra-virgin olive oil

¼ cup red wine vinegar

2 tablespoons water

1 small red onion, finely minced

1 teaspoon table salt

¼ teaspoon red pepper flakes

Pulse the parsley and garlic in a food processor, stopping as necessary to scrape down the sides of the bowl with a rubber spatula, until the garlic and parsley are chopped fine, about 20 pulses; transfer to a medium bowl. Whisk in the oil, vinegar, water, onion, salt, and red pepper flakes until thoroughly blended. Spoon about 2 tablespoons over each steak and serve. (This sauce tastes best when used fresh but can be refrigerated, with plastic wrap pressed directly on the surface, up to 3 days.)

PEPPER-CRUSTED FILET MIGNON

WHY THIS RECIPE WORKS: Filet mignon is ultra-tender, but it has only mild beefy flavor. Chefs often compensate by wrapping the delicate meat in bacon or puff pastry, serving it with rich wine sauces or flavored butter, or giving it a crust of cracked black peppercorns. We decided to pursue the peppercorn approach and found several problems to solve: The peppercorns tend to fall off in the pan, interfere with the meat's browning, and—when used in sufficient quantity to create a real crust—deliver punishing pungency.

Our first step was to mellow the peppercorns' heat by gently simmering them in olive oil. We then created a well-browned and attractive pepper crust using a two-step process: First, we rubbed the raw steaks with a paste of the cooked cracked peppercorns, salt, and oil, then we pressed the paste into each steak through a sheet of plastic wrap. We let the steaks sit, covered, for an hour before cooking. The paste not only added flavor to the meat but drew out the meat's own beefy flavor. While the steaks sat wrapped and covered in paste, we had plenty of time to simmer a rich reduction sauce—though a flavored butter also made an excellent accompaniment.

Pepper-Crusted Filet Mignon

SERVES 4

If you prefer a very mild pepper flavor, drain the cooled peppercorns in a fine-mesh strainer in step 1, toss them with 5 tablespoons of fresh oil, add the salt, and proceed. Serve with Port-Cherry Reduction or Blue Cheese–Chive Butter (recipes follow).

- 5 tablespoons black peppercorns, cracked
- 5 tablespoons plus 2 teaspoons olive oil
- 1½ teaspoons table salt
- 4 (7 to 8-ounce) center-cut filets mignons, 1½ to 2 inches thick, each dried thoroughly with paper towels

1. Heat the peppercorns and 5 tablespoons of the oil in a small saucepan over low heat until faint bubbles appear. Continue to cook at a bare simmer, swirling the pan occasionally, until the pepper is fragrant, 7 to 10 minutes. Remove from the heat and set aside to cool. When the mixture is at room temperature, add the salt and stir to combine. Rub the steaks with the pepper mixture, thoroughly coating the top and bottom of each steak with the peppercorns. Cover the steaks with plastic wrap and press gently to make sure the peppercorns adhere; let stand at room temperature for 1 hour.

2. Meanwhile, adjust an oven rack to the middle position, place a rimmed baking sheet on the oven rack, and heat the oven to 450 degrees. Heat the remaining 2 teaspoons oil in a 12-inch heavy-bottomed skillet over medium-high heat until faint smoke appears. Place the steaks in the skillet and cook, without moving the steaks, until a dark brown crust has formed, 3 to 4 minutes. Using tongs, turn the steaks and cook until well browned on the second side, about 3 minutes. Remove the pan from the heat and transfer the steaks to the hot baking sheet. Roast until the center of the steaks registers 120 degrees on an instant-read thermometer for rare (3 to 5 minutes), 125 degrees for medium-rare (5 to 7 minutes), and 130 degrees for medium (7 to 9 minutes). Transfer the steaks to a wire rack and let rest, loosely tented with foil, for about 10 minutes before serving.

Port-Cherry Reduction

MAKES ABOUT 1 CUP

- 1½ cups port
- ½ cup balsamic vinegar
- ½ cup dried tart cherries
- 1 large shallot, minced (about 4 tablespoons)
- 2 sprigs fresh thyme
- 1 tablespoon unsalted butter
  Table salt

1. Combine the port, balsamic vinegar, cherries, shallot, and thyme in a medium saucepan; simmer over medium-low heat until the liquid is reduced to ⅓ cup, about 30 minutes. Set aside, covered.

2. While the steaks are resting, reheat the sauce. Off the heat, remove the thyme, then whisk in the butter until melted. Season with salt to taste. Serve, passing the sauce at the table with the steak.

Blue Cheese–Chive Butter

MAKES ABOUT ½ CUP

- 3 tablespoons unsalted butter, softened
- ⅓ cup crumbled mild blue cheese, at room temperature
- ⅛ teaspoon table salt
- 2 tablespoons minced fresh chives

Combine the butter, cheese, and salt in a medium bowl and mix with a stiff rubber spatula until smooth. Fold in the chives. While the steaks are resting, spoon 1 to 2 tablespoons of the butter on each one.

STEAK SANDWICHES

WHY THIS RECIPE WORKS: Steak sandwiches run the gamut from oversized "bombs" with greasy, gristly meat (break out the napkins) to precious restaurant concoctions (hold the truffle butter, please) with a price tag to match. We wanted to find a satisfying steak sandwich with some middle ground—easy to eat and gussied up with flavorful, but not costly, ingredients.

We started with the choice of steak, and flank steak won out over all other cuts. It's relatively inexpensive, lean, and tender, as long as the meat is cooked correctly. For a flavorful browned crust, we generously seasoned the steak with salt and pepper and then pan-seared it in a very hot skillet on both sides until browned. To keep the steak tender and juicy, we allowed the meat to rest and then sliced it thin across the grain. Soft, squishy bread needn't apply here—only a crusty French baguette or similar artisan-style bread would do. We slathered the bread with mayonnaise doctored with soy sauce, honey, garlic, and ginger. And to finish, thinly sliced onion and arugula scattered on top of the steak provided a little spicy bite.

Flank Steak and Arugula Sandwiches with Red Onion

SERVES 4

For juicy, tender meat, be sure to let the steak rest for 10 minutes after cooking and slice the steak thin across the grain.

- 1½ pounds flank steak, trimmed of excess fat and patted dry with paper towels
  Table salt and ground black pepper
- 1 tablespoon vegetable oil
- 1 baguette, cut into four 5-inch lengths, each piece split into top and bottom pieces
- ½ cup Garlic-Soy Mayonnaise (recipe follows)
- ½ small red onion, sliced thin
- 3 ounces arugula, stemmed, washed, and dried (about 3 cups)

1. Heat a 12-inch skillet over high heat until very hot, about 4 minutes. While the skillet is heating, season the steak generously with salt and pepper. Add the oil to the pan and swirl to coat the bottom. Lay the steak in the pan and cook without moving it until well browned, about 5 minutes. Using tongs, flip the steak; cook until well browned on the second side, about 5 minutes longer. Transfer the steak to a carving board, tent with foil, and let rest 10 minutes. Cut the steak into ¼-inch slices on the bias against the grain.

2. Spread each baguette piece with 1 tablespoon mayonnaise; portion the steak over the bottom pieces of the bread and sprinkle with salt and pepper to taste. Evenly divide the onion and arugula over the steak; top each with a baguette piece and serve.

Garlic-Soy Mayonnaise

MAKES ABOUT ½ CUP

Hellmann's is the test kitchen's favorite brand of mayonnaise—read why on page 610.

- ½ cup mayonnaise
- 1 tablespoon soy sauce
- 1 teaspoon minced or grated fresh ginger
- ½ teaspoon honey
- 1 small garlic clove, minced or pressed through a garlic press (about ½ teaspoon)
- ½ teaspoon toasted sesame oil

Mix all the ingredients together in a small bowl. (The mayonnaise can be covered and refrigerated for up to 1 day.)

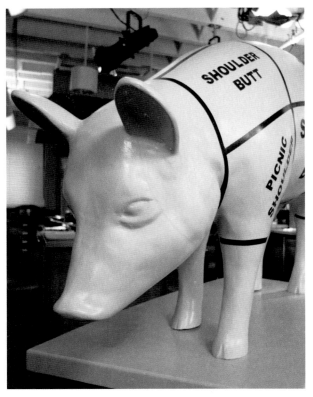

CHAPTER 8

PORK CHOPS EVERYDAY

**Oven-Roasted
Pork Chops** 118

    Lemon-Caper Sauce

**Pan-Seared Thick-Cut
Pork Chops** 119

    Garlic and Thyme Sauce

**Skillet-Barbecued
Pork Chops** 120

**Cider-Glazed
Pork Chops** 122

**Smothered
Pork Chops** 123

**Crunchy Baked
Pork Chops** 125

Stuffed Pork Chops 126

    Ginger-Apple Chutney

    Quick All-Purpose Gravy

OVEN-ROASTED PORK CHOPS

WHY THIS RECIPE WORKS: Tender, juicy, double-thick pork chops make for a satisfying dinner, but most home cooks pass up thick chops at the market because they mistakenly assume the cooking time will be lengthy. However, roasting these chops in a blazing hot oven (their thickness prevents them from drying out) cuts down on cooking time and frees up stovetop real estate so you can make an easy pan sauce at the same time.

We chose extra-thick rib loin pork chops, which are cut from the rib section of the loin, and flavored them with a brown sugar and salt brine. We found that our thick chops couldn't go straight into the oven—they had to be cooked in three stages. First, we seared them in a hot pan to give them a nicely browned crust, then we transferred them to a preheated pan in the oven to cook most of the way through, and finally we moved them to a platter and covered them with foil to gently come up to serving temperature (while the meat stayed moist and tender). This last step also gave us time to make a speedy lemon-caper sauce right in the pan using the fond (browned bits) left behind from searing the chops.

Oven-Roasted Pork Chops
SERVES 4

We prefer natural to enhanced pork (pork that has been injected with a salt solution to increase moistness and flavor) for this recipe, though enhanced pork can be used. If using enhanced pork, skip the brining in step 1. To serve the pork chops with the Lemon-Caper Sauce (recipe follows), have all the sauce ingredients ready to go and don't wash the skillet after browning the chops; begin the sauce, using the fat left behind from browning the chops, after the pork chops come out of the oven and are resting.

- ¾ cup (5¼ ounces) dark brown sugar
- ¼ cup table salt
- 10 medium garlic cloves, crushed
- 4 bay leaves, crumbled
- 8 whole cloves
- 3 tablespoons whole black peppercorns, crushed
- 4 (12-ounce) bone-in rib loin pork chops, about 1½ inches thick, trimmed of excess fat (see note)
- 2 tablespoons vegetable oil

1. Dissolve the sugar and salt in 6 cups cold water in a large bowl or container. Add the garlic, bay leaves, cloves, and peppercorns. Submerge the chops in the brine, cover with plastic wrap, and refrigerate for 1 hour. Remove the chops from the brine, rinse, and pat dry with paper towels. Following the photo on page 122, use a sharp knife to cut two slits, about 2 inches apart, through the outer layer of fat and silver skin of each chop (do not cut into the meat of the chops).

2. Adjust an oven rack to the lower-middle position, place a rimmed baking sheet on the rack, and heat the oven to 450 degrees. When the oven reaches 450 degrees, heat the oil in a 12-inch skillet over high heat until shimmering. Place the chops in the skillet and cook until well browned, about 2 minutes. Flip the chops and continue to cook until the second side is well browned, about 2 minutes longer.

3. Transfer the chops to the baking sheet in the oven. Roast until the center of the chops registers 140 to 145 degrees on an instant-read thermometer, about 15 minutes, turning the chops over once halfway through the cooking time. Transfer the chops to a platter, cover loosely with foil, and let rest until the internal temperature registers 150 degrees on an instant-read thermometer, 5 to 10 minutes, or while preparing the pan sauce.

Lemon-Caper Sauce
MAKES ABOUT ½ CUP

- 1 medium shallot, minced (about 3 tablespoons)
- 1 cup low-sodium chicken broth
- ¼ cup juice from 2 lemons
- 2 tablespoons capers, drained
- 3 tablespoons unsalted butter, softened

Follow the recipe for Oven-Roasted Pork Chops. After removing the chops from the pan, add the shallot and cook over medium heat until softened, about 30 seconds. Increase the heat to high and stir in the broth, scraping up any browned bits. Add the lemon juice and capers, bring to a simmer, and cook until the sauce measures ⅓ cup, 3 to 4 minutes. Off the heat, whisk in the butter; serve with the pork chops.

PAN-SEARED THICK-CUT PORK CHOPS

WHY THIS RECIPE WORKS: Pan-seared thick-cut pork chops boast a juicy interior and crisp, browned exterior. Usually, though, they aren't prepared well and fall flat on both fronts. We wanted a simple skillet-roasting recipe that would give us plump, juicy meat and a well-formed crust every time.

Instead of brining our chops, we salted the meat and let it rest for almost an hour. This helped to draw out additional moisture, which would be pulled back in later to produce juicy, well-seasoned meat. Instead of cooking our chops on the stovetop, we turned to the oven. Slow-roasting the chops at a gentle temperature broke down connective tissue and tenderized the meat. This step also dried the exterior of the chops, creating a thin outer layer that, when seared, caramelized and turned into the crisp crust that we were after. For a completely browned crust, we seared the sides of the chops as well, using tongs to hold them up on their edges. While the cooked chops rested, we created a simple wine and garlic sauce using the browned bits left behind in the pan; now, we had the perfect rich, tangy accompaniment to our chops' tender meat and crisp surface.

Pan-Seared Thick-Cut Pork Chops
SERVES 4

We prefer natural to enhanced pork (pork that has been injected with a salt solution to increase moistness and flavor) for this recipe, though enhanced pork can be used. If using enhanced pork, skip the salting in step 1. To serve the pork chops with the Garlic and Thyme Sauce (recipe follows), have all the sauce ingredients ready to go and don't wash the skillet after browning the chops; begin the sauce, using the fat left behind from browning the chops, when you set them aside to rest.

- 4 (12-ounce) bone-in rib loin pork chops, about 1½ inches thick, trimmed of excess fat (see note)
  Table salt and ground black pepper (see note)
- 1–2 tablespoons vegetable oil

1. Adjust an oven rack to the middle position and heat the oven to 275 degrees. Pat the chops dry with paper towels. Following the photo on page 122, use a sharp knife to cut two slits, about 2 inches apart, through the outer layer of fat and silver skin of each chop (do not cut into the meat of the chops). Sprinkle each chop with ½ teaspoon salt.

KOSHER? YES. ENHANCED? NO.

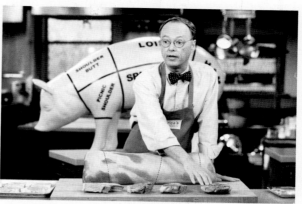

In the test kitchen we often brine chicken and pork to ensure moist, well-seasoned meat. But there are options at the store that allow you to skip this step. For chicken, that means buying a kosher bird. Koshering is a process similar to brining; it involves coating the chicken with salt to draw out any impurities. Kosher birds are also all-natural and contain no hormones or antibiotics. In a side-by-side taste test of all kinds of chicken, Empire brand kosher birds rated highest.

Some people are surprised that pork is lean and prone to drying out. In fact, today's pork is 50 percent leaner than its 1950s counterpart, and less fat means less flavor and moisture. The industry has addressed this issue by introducing enhanced pork, which is meat injected with a solution of water, salt, and sodium phosphate. The idea is to both season the pork and prevent it from drying out. We've conducted countless tests comparing "enhanced" pork to natural pork and unequivocally prefer the latter. Natural pork has a better flavor and, if it's cooked correctly, moisture isn't an issue. We also strongly recommend brining most cuts of pork, which lends both moisture and seasoning to the meat. Manufacturers don't use the terms "enhanced" or "natural" on package labels, but if the pork has been enhanced it will have an ingredient list. Natural pork contains just pork and won't have an ingredient list. While natural pork benefits from brining, enhanced pork should not be brined because it's already pretty salty.

Place the chops on a wire rack set over a rimmed baking sheet and let stand at room temperature for 45 minutes.

2. Season the chops with pepper; transfer the baking sheet to the oven. Cook until the center of the chops registers 120 to 125 degrees on an instant-read thermometer, 30 to 45 minutes.

3. Heat 1 tablespoon oil in a 12-inch skillet over high heat until smoking. Place 2 chops in the skillet and sear until well browned, 2 to 3 minutes, lifting once halfway through to redistribute the fat underneath each chop.

(Reduce the heat if the browned bits on the pan bottom start to burn.) Flip the chops and cook until the second side is well browned, 2 to 3 minutes longer. Transfer the chops to a plate and repeat with the remaining 2 chops, adding 1 tablespoon more oil if the pan is dry.

4. Reduce the heat to medium. Using tongs, stand 2 pork chops on their sides. Hold them together with the tongs, return them to the skillet, and sear the sides (do not sear the bone side) until browned and the center of the chops registers 140 to 145 degrees on an instant-read thermometer, about 1½ minutes. Repeat with the remaining 2 chops. Transfer the chops to a platter, cover loosely with foil, and let rest until the internal temperature reaches 150 degrees, about 5 minutes, or while preparing the pan sauce.

Garlic and Thyme Sauce
MAKES ABOUT ½ CUP

- 1 large shallot, minced (about 4 tablespoons)
- 2 medium garlic cloves, minced or pressed through a garlic press (about 2 teaspoons)
- ¾ cup low-sodium chicken broth
- ½ cup dry white wine
- 1 teaspoon minced fresh thyme leaves
- ¼ teaspoon white wine vinegar
- 3 tablespoons unsalted butter, chilled and cut into 3 pieces
- Table salt and ground black pepper

Follow the recipe for Pan-Seared Thick-Cut Pork Chops. Pour off all but 1 teaspoon oil from the pan used to cook the chops and return the pan to medium heat. Add the shallot and garlic and cook, stirring constantly, until softened, about 1 minute. Add the broth and wine, scraping up any browned bits. Bring to a simmer and cook until the sauce measures ½ cup, 6 to 7 minutes. Off the heat, stir in the thyme and vinegar; whisk in the butter, 1 tablespoon at a time. Season with salt and pepper to taste and serve with the pork chops.

SKILLET-BARBECUED PORK CHOPS

WHY THIS RECIPE WORKS: One of our favorite summer flavors is that of charred, salty-sweet grilled pork chops coated with spicy barbecue sauce. But because winter sometimes seems endless, we wanted to come up with an indoor method for replicating the tangy, sweet burnished crust and juicy meat of grilled chops.

Brining the chops first ensured that our meat would be juicy and well seasoned. We quickly learned that searing the chops in a blazing hot skillet and then turning the heat down once they had developed a nice crust only made the test kitchen smoky. Instead, we coated the chops with a dry spice rub—the rub charred rather than the pork chops and gave the meat the flavor and appearance of real barbecue. To prevent the rub from blackening, we cooked the chops over medium heat and used a nonstick skillet. Homemade barbecue sauce, made with ketchup, molasses, onion, and just a few other ingredients, provided a tangy flavor that contrasted nicely with the tender meat, and some reserved spice rub gave the sauce a spicy kick. A touch of liquid smoke gave our barbecue sauce more grill flavor. Finally, we brushed our chops with a small amount of sauce for a second sear so the sauce would caramelize and intensify in flavor—just as it would on the grill.

Skillet-Barbecued Pork Chops
SERVES 4

We prefer natural to enhanced pork (pork that has been injected with a salt solution to increase moistness and flavor) for this recipe, though enhanced pork can be used. If using enhanced pork, skip the brining in step 1 and add ½ teaspoon salt to the spice rub. Grate the onion on the

large holes of a box grater. In step 5, check your chops after 3 minutes. If you don't hear a definite sizzle and the chops have not started to brown on the underside, increase the heat to medium-high and continue cooking as directed (follow the indicated temperatures for the remainder of the recipe).

PORK CHOPS

- ½ cup table salt
- 4 (8 to 10-ounce) bone-in rib loin pork chops, ¾ to 1 inch thick, trimmed of excess fat (see note)
- 4 teaspoons vegetable oil

SPICE RUB

- 1 tablespoon paprika
- 1 tablespoon brown sugar
- 2 teaspoons ground coriander
- 1 teaspoon ground cumin
- 1 teaspoon ground black pepper

SAUCE

- ½ cup ketchup
- 3 tablespoons light or mild molasses
- 2 tablespoons grated onion (see note)
- 2 tablespoons Worcestershire sauce
- 2 tablespoons Dijon mustard
- 1 tablespoon cider vinegar
- 1 tablespoon brown sugar
- 1 teaspoon liquid smoke

1. FOR THE PORK CHOPS: Dissolve the salt in 2 quarts cold water in a large bowl or container. Submerge the chops in the brine, cover with plastic wrap, and refrigerate for 30 minutes.

2. FOR THE SPICE RUB: Combine the ingredients in a small bowl. Measure 2 teaspoons of the mixture into a medium bowl and set aside for the sauce. Transfer the remaining spice rub to a large plate.

3. FOR THE SAUCE: Whisk the ingredients in the bowl with the reserved spice mixture until thoroughly combined; set aside.

4. Remove the chops from the brine, rinse, and pat dry with paper towels. Following the photo on page 122, use a sharp knife to cut two slits, about 2 inches apart, through the outer layer of fat and silver skin of each chop (do not cut into the meat of the chops). Coat both sides

of the chops with the spice rub, pressing gently so the rub adheres. Shake off the excess rub.

5. Heat 1 tablespoon of the oil in a 12-inch nonstick skillet over medium heat until just smoking. Place the chops in the skillet in a pinwheel pattern, with the ribs pointing toward the center, and cook until browned and charred in spots, 5 to 8 minutes. Flip the chops and continue to cook until the second side is browned and the center of the chops registers 130 degrees on an instant-read thermometer, 4 to 8 minutes. Remove the skillet from the heat and transfer the chops to a plate. Lightly brush the top of each chop with 2 teaspoons of the sauce.

6. Wipe out the pan with paper towels and return to medium heat. Add the remaining 1 teaspoon oil and heat until just smoking. Add the chops to the pan, sauce side down, and cook without moving them until the sauce has caramelized and charred in spots, about 1 minute. While cooking, lightly brush the top of each chop with 2 more teaspoons sauce. Flip the chops and cook until the second side is charred and caramelized and the center of the chops registers 140 to 145 degrees on an instant-read thermometer, 1 to 2 minutes.

7. Transfer the chops back to the plate, cover loosely with foil, and let rest until the center of the chops registers 150 degrees on an instant-read thermometer, about 5 minutes.

8. Meanwhile, add the remaining sauce to the pan and cook over medium heat, scraping up any browned bits, until thickened and it measures ⅔ cup, about 3 minutes. Brush each chop with 1 tablespoon of the sauce and serve, passing the remaining sauce separately.

GLAZED PORK CHOPS

WHY THIS RECIPE WORKS: Thin boneless pork chops are readily available straight from the meat case—no butcher required. Plus they cook fast and are a bargain compared to other meats. But because they do cook quickly, they're prone to overcooking. We wanted to combine the convenience and speed of thin boneless pork chops with the flavor and moist, juicy interior of their thicker, bone-in counterparts.

To cook pork chops on the stove, it's best to stick with thin chops. Before searing the chops, it's important to cut through the fat and silver skin, which create a bowing effect (especially pronounced with thin chops) as it contracts. We found the chops needed an initial quick sear—we didn't want them to cook all the way through just yet but we still wanted a nicely browned side. A sweet and sticky glaze of cider, brown sugar, soy sauce, vinegar, and mustard went into the pan to finish cooking the chops. Not only did the sauce give the chops rich flavor, but it also reduced down to a nice, thick glaze, which perfectly coated the juicy, tender chops.

Cider-Glazed Pork Chops

SERVES 4

We prefer natural to enhanced pork (pork that has been injected with a salt solution to increase moistness and flavor) for this recipe, though either will work here. If your chops are on the thinner side, check their internal temperature after the initial sear. If they are already at the

140-degree mark, remove them from the skillet and allow them to rest, covered loosely with foil, for 5 minutes, then add the accumulated juices and glaze ingredients to the skillet and proceed with step 4. If your chops are a little thicker than we specify, you may need to increase the simmering time in step 3.

GLAZE
- ½ cup distilled white vinegar or cider vinegar
- ⅓ cup (2⅓ ounces) light brown sugar
- ⅓ cup apple cider or apple juice
- 2 tablespoons Dijon mustard
- 1 tablespoon soy sauce
  Pinch cayenne pepper

PORK CHOPS
- 4 (5 to 7-ounce) boneless center-cut or loin pork chops, ½ to ¾ inch thick, trimmed of excess fat (see note)
  Table salt and ground black pepper
- 1 tablespoon vegetable oil

1. FOR THE GLAZE: Combine the ingredients in a medium bowl and set aside.

2. FOR THE PORK CHOPS: Following the photo, use a sharp knife to cut two slits, about 2 inches apart, through the outer layer of fat and silver skin of each chop (do not cut into the meat of the chops). Pat the chops dry with paper towels and season with salt and pepper. Heat the oil in a 12-inch skillet over medium-high heat until smoking. Add the chops to the skillet and cook until well browned, 4 to 6 minutes. Flip the chops and cook 1 minute longer; transfer the chops to a platter and pour

---

NOTES FROM THE TEST KITCHEN

HOW TO PREVENT CURLED PORK CHOPS

Whether your pork chops are boneless or bone-in, you can use the same technique to prevent them from buckling in a hot pan or oven. Simply cut two slits, about 2 inches apart, through one side of each chop.

off any oil in the skillet. (Check the internal temperature of the thinner chops; see the note.)

3. Return the chops to the skillet, browned side up, and add the glaze mixture; cook over medium heat until the center of the chops registers 140 to 145 degrees on an instant-read thermometer, 5 to 8 minutes. Remove the skillet from the heat; transfer the chops to a clean platter, cover loosely with foil, and let rest until the center of the chops registers 150 degrees on an instant-read thermometer, about 5 minutes.

4. Stir any accumulated meat juices from the plate into the glaze in the skillet and simmer, whisking constantly, until the glaze has thickened, 2 to 6 minutes. Return the chops to the skillet and turn to coat both sides with the glaze. Transfer the chops back to the plate, browned side up, spread the remaining glaze over the top, and serve.

SMOTHERED PORK CHOPS

WHY THIS RECIPE WORKS: Tender, flavorful chops stand up very well to rich, hearty gravy. But most of the time, the gravy misses the mark—it's either so thick you can't find the pork chop, or so thin and watery that the meat seems to be floating on the plate. We wanted a foolproof recipe for juicy chops smothered in rich gravy with a satiny, thick texture.

For a nice balance with the gravy and to allow for the best absorption of the gravy's flavors, we used thin, not thick, rib chops. Browning them well left meaty browned bits in the pan, essential for making a flavorful gravy. To build further flavor, we made a nut-brown, bacony roux. Thinly sliced yellow onions contributed a significant amount of moisture to the gravy. Garlic, thyme, and bay leaves rounded out the flavorful gravy; we skipped the salt because we had already salted the onions to encourage their browning and so they would give up liquid. For the tenderest chops, we combined the sauce and browned chops in the pan and braised them for half an hour. Not only did the lengthy braise result in moist, tender chops, it also allowed the gravy to thicken and its flavors to meld, so the chops had a rich, velvety coating when served.

Smothered Pork Chops

SERVES 4

We prefer natural to enhanced pork (pork that has been injected with a salt solution to increase moistness and flavor) for this recipe, though either will work here. Serve smothered chops with egg noodles or mashed potatoes to soak up the rich gravy.

- 3   ounces bacon (about 3 slices), cut into ¼-inch pieces
- 2   tablespoons unbleached all-purpose flour
- 1¾ cups low-sodium chicken broth
- 2   tablespoons vegetable oil, plus more as needed
- 4   (7-ounce) bone-in rib loin pork chops, ½ to ¾ inch thick, trimmed of excess fat (see note)
-     Ground black pepper
- 2   medium yellow onions, halved and sliced thin (about 3½ cups)
-     Table salt
- 2   tablespoons water
- 2   medium garlic cloves, minced or pressed through a garlic press (about 2 teaspoons)
- 1   teaspoon minced fresh thyme leaves
- 2   bay leaves
- 1   tablespoon minced fresh parsley leaves

WHY IS THAT PORK STILL PINK?

In the test kitchen, we steer clear of dishes like Parchingly Dry Pork Chops and No-Pink Pork Loin. But there's a reason that older recipes recommend cooking pork to startlingly high internal temperatures. Years ago, when pork quality was inconsistent and trichinosis concerns ran high, pink pork was considered a safety risk, thus most recipes recommended cooking pork to 190 degrees. Today, however, the risk of trichinosis is nearly nonexistent in the United States. What's more, even when the trichinosis parasite is present, it is killed when the temperature of the meat rises to 137 degrees.

Both the U.S. Department of Agriculture and the National Pork Board recommend cooking pork to a final internal temperature of 160 degrees. If you are concerned about contamination with salmonella (which is possible in any type of meat), you must cook the pork to 160 degrees to be certain that all potential pathogens are eliminated. Unfortunately, given the leanness of today's pork, these recommendations result in dry, tough meat. (In fact, today's pork has 50 percent less fat than it did 50 years ago, which explains why older recipes that called for cooking pork to 190 degrees weren't a total disaster—all that fat kept even overcooked pork moist.)

In the test kitchen, we have found cooking modern pork beyond 150 degrees to be a waste of time and money. We cook pork to an internal temperature of 140 to 145 degrees—the meat will still be slightly rosy in the center and juicy. As the meat rests and juices are redistributed throughout the meat, the internal temperature will continue to climb to the final serving temperature of 150. Of course, if safety is your top concern, cook all meat (including pork) until it is well-done; that is, when the internal temperature reaches 160 degrees.

1. Fry the bacon in a small saucepan over medium heat, stirring occasionally, until crisp, 8 to 10 minutes. Using a slotted spoon, transfer the bacon to a paper towel–lined plate, leaving the fat in the saucepan (you should have 2 tablespoons bacon fat; if not, add oil to make this amount). Whisk in the flour and cook over medium-low

heat until golden, about 5 minutes. Whisk in the broth and bring to a boil, stirring occasionally, over medium-high heat; cover and set aside off the heat.

2. Heat 1 tablespoon of the oil in a 12-inch skillet over high heat until smoking. Pat the chops dry with paper towels. Following the photo on page 122, use a sharp knife to cut two slits, about 2 inches apart, through the outer layer of fat and silver skin of each chop (do not cut into the meat of the chops). Sprinkle each chop with ½ teaspoon pepper. Brown the chops in a single layer until browned on the first side, about 3 minutes. Flip the chops and cook until the second side is browned, about 3 minutes longer. Transfer the chops to a plate and set aside.

3. Add the remaining 1 tablespoon oil to the skillet and return to medium heat until shimmering. Add the onions, ¼ teaspoon salt, and the water, scraping up any browned bits, and cook until lightly browned, about 5 minutes. Stir in the garlic and thyme and cook until fragrant, about 30 seconds longer. Return the chops to the skillet and cover with the onions. Add the reserved sauce, the bay leaves, and any accumulated meat juices from the plate to the skillet. Cover and simmer over low heat until the chops are tender and a paring knife inserted into the chops meets little resistance, about 30 minutes.

4. Transfer the chops to a platter and cover loosely with foil. Simmer the sauce over medium-high heat, stirring frequently, until thickened, about 5 minutes. Discard the bay leaves, stir in the parsley, and season with salt and pepper to taste. Cover the chops with the sauce, sprinkle with the reserved bacon, and serve.

CRUNCHY BAKED PORK CHOPS

WHY THIS RECIPE WORKS: When done right, baked, breaded pork chops are the ultimate comfort food— juicy, tender chops covered with a well-seasoned, crunchy crust. We were on a mission to perfect these chops and avoid the common missteps of a soggy, flavorless crust, flabby meat, and a coating that just won't stay on.

We used center-cut boneless loin chops—which are easy to find and affordable—and brined them so the meat would stay moist and juicy. For the coating, only fresh bread crumbs would do; we toasted them first for crispness, then doctored them with garlic, shallots, Parmesan cheese, and minced herbs for flavor. To form a strong adhering agent for the crumbs, and prevent the chops from ending up bald in patches, we made a quick batterlike mixture by whisking flour and mustard into egg whites; whole eggs were a no-go because their higher amount of fat made for a soft, puffy layer under the bread crumbs. Baking the breaded chops on a wire rack set over a baking sheet allowed air to circulate completely around the chops, keeping the bottom crumbs crisp. Out of the oven, these chops were tender and moist, with a crisp coating that stayed put, even through some heavy knife-and-fork action.

Crunchy Baked Pork Chops

SERVES 4

We prefer natural to enhanced pork (pork that has been injected with a salt solution to increase moistness and flavor) for this recipe, though enhanced pork can be used. If using enhanced pork, skip the brining in step 1. The breaded chops can be frozen for up to 1 week. They don't need to be thawed before baking; simply increase the cooking time in step 5 to 35 to 40 minutes.

Table salt
4 (6 to 8-ounce) boneless center-cut or loin pork chops, ¾ to 1 inch thick, trimmed of excess fat (see note)
4 slices high-quality white sandwich bread, torn into 1-inch pieces
2 tablespoons vegetable oil
1 small shallot, minced (about 1 tablespoon)
3 medium garlic cloves, minced or pressed through a garlic press (about 1 tablespoon)
Ground black pepper
2 tablespoons grated Parmesan cheese
2 tablespoons minced fresh parsley leaves
½ teaspoon minced fresh thyme leaves
¼ cup plus 6 tablespoons unbleached all-purpose flour
3 large egg whites
3 tablespoons Dijon mustard
Lemon wedges, for serving

1. Adjust an oven rack to the middle position and heat the oven to 350 degrees. Dissolve ¼ cup salt in 4 cups cold water in a medium bowl or gallon-sized zipper-lock bag. Submerge the chops in the brine, cover the container with plastic wrap or seal the bag, and refrigerate for 30 minutes. Remove the chops from the brine, rinse, and pat dry with paper towels.

2. Meanwhile, pulse the bread in a food processor to coarse crumbs, about 8 pulses (you should have about 3½ cups crumbs). Transfer the crumbs to a rimmed baking sheet, add the oil, shallot, garlic, ¼ teaspoon salt, and ¼ teaspoon pepper, and toss until the crumbs are evenly coated with the oil. Bake until golden brown and dry,

about 15 minutes, stirring twice during the baking time. (Do not turn off the oven.) Cool to room temperature. Toss the crumbs with the Parmesan, parsley, and thyme. (The bread-crumb mixture can be stored in an airtight container for up to 3 days.)

3. Place ¼ cup of the flour in a pie plate. In a second pie plate, whisk the egg whites and mustard together; add the remaining 6 tablespoons flour and whisk until almost smooth, with pea-sized lumps remaining.

4. Increase the oven temperature to 425 degrees. Spray a wire rack with vegetable oil spray and place over a rimmed baking sheet. Season the chops with pepper. Dredge 1 pork chop in the flour; shake off the excess. Using tongs, coat with the egg mixture; let the excess drip off. Coat all sides of the chop with the bread-crumb mixture, pressing gently so that a thick layer of crumbs adheres to the chop. Transfer the breaded chop to the wire rack. Repeat with the remaining 3 chops.

5. Bake until the center of the chops registers 140 to 145 degrees on an instant-read thermometer, about 20 minutes. Let rest on the rack 5 minutes; serve with the lemon wedges.

STUFFED PORK CHOPS

WHY THIS RECIPE WORKS: Thick-cut pork chops make the perfect home for a simple stuffing. Unfortunately, most stuffed pork chops are extremely dry and bland, with a filling that looks like it's trying to escape. We wanted the stuffing to be especially flavorful and rich to offset the mildness of the pork, and we wanted the chops to be moist and juicy.

Our stuffing was easy enough to make—we used a simple combination of aromatic vegetables, herbs, and fresh bread. But the stuffing was so loose, it crumbled and

STUFFING PORK CHOPS

1. Using a paring knife, trim away the excess fat and connective tissue around the edge of the meat.

2. With the knife positioned as shown, insert the blade through the center of the side of the chop until the tip touches the bone.

3. Swing the tip of the blade through the middle of the chop to create a pocket (the opening should be about 1 inch wide).

4. With your fingers, gently press the stuffing mixture into the pocket, without enlarging the opening.

skillet to develop a nice brown crust but finished cooking them through on a baking sheet in a hot oven. A sweet chutney of ginger, apples, and apple cider provided a nice contrast to the savory filling.

For an alternative to chutney, flavorful gravy (sans big roast) is ideal for draping over the stuffed chops. Thoroughly browning both the aromatic vegetables and the flour added significant flavor, as did the inclusion of two kinds of broth: beef and chicken.

Stuffed Pork Chops
SERVES 4

We prefer natural to enhanced pork (pork that has been injected with a salt solution to increase moistness and flavor) for this recipe, though either will work here. Serve these pork chops with Ginger-Apple Chutney or Quick All-Purpose Gravy (recipes follow). The gravy is best made before you start the chops and reheated as needed. If you choose to serve the chops with the chutney instead, prepare it in the skillet used to cook the chops while the chops are in the oven.

CHOPS
- 4 (12-ounce) bone-in rib loin pork chops, about 1½ inches thick, trimmed of excess fat (see note)
- ¾ cup packed light brown sugar
- ¼ cup table salt
   Ground black pepper
- 1 tablespoon vegetable oil

STUFFING
- 3 tablespoons unsalted butter
- 1 small onion, minced
- 1 celery rib, chopped fine
- ½ teaspoon table salt
- 2 medium garlic cloves, minced or pressed through a garlic press (about 2 teaspoons)
- 2 teaspoons minced fresh thyme leaves
- 1 tablespoon minced fresh parsley leaves
- 2 slices high-quality white sandwich bread, cut into ¼-inch cubes (about 2 cups)
- 2 tablespoons heavy cream
   Ground black pepper

spilled out over the plate when the chops were served. Clearly, we needed a binder. Instead of eggs, we chose cream, which added richness and enough moisture to bring the stuffing together. Because the stuffing didn't contain eggs, the chops could be cooked to a lower (and more palatable) internal temperature, making for tender and juicy meat. After brining the chops and creating a small "pocket" to hold the stuffing, we started them in a

1. FOR THE CHOPS: Following the photos, cut a small pocket through the side of each chop. Dissolve the sugar and salt in 6 cups cold water in a large bowl or container.

Submerge the chops in the brine, cover with plastic wrap, and refrigerate for 1 hour.

2. FOR THE STUFFING: Melt the butter in a 12-inch skillet over medium heat. Add the onion, celery, and salt and cook until the vegetables are softened, 6 to 8 minutes. Add the garlic, thyme, and parsley and cook until fragrant, about 30 seconds. Transfer to a medium bowl and toss with the bread cubes, cream, and ⅛ teaspoon pepper. Mix, lightly pressing the mixture against the sides of the bowl, until it comes together.

3. Adjust an oven rack to the lower-middle position, place a rimmed baking sheet on the rack, and heat the oven to 450 degrees. Remove the chops from the brine, rinse, and pat dry with paper towels. Place one-quarter of the stuffing (about ⅓ cup) in the pocket of each pork chop. Season the chops with pepper.

4. Heat the oil in a 12-inch skillet over high heat until shimmering. Place the chops in the skillet and cook until well browned, about 3 minutes. Flip the chops and cook until the second side is well browned, about 2 minutes longer.

5. Transfer the chops to the baking sheet in the oven. Roast until the center of the chops registers 140 degrees on an instant-read thermometer, about 15 minutes, turning the chops over halfway through the cooking time. Transfer the chops to a plate, cover loosely with foil, and let rest for 5 to 10 minutes. Serve.

Ginger-Apple Chutney

MAKES ABOUT 3½ CUPS

If you want more heat, add a little more cayenne pepper.

- 1 tablespoon vegetable oil
- 1 small onion, chopped medium
- 2 Granny Smith apples, peeled, cored, and cut into ½-inch pieces
- 1 tablespoon minced ginger
- ¼ teaspoon ground allspice
- ⅛ teaspoon cayenne pepper (see note)
- 1 cup apple cider
- ¼ cup (1¾ ounces) packed light brown sugar
  Table salt and ground black pepper

Follow the recipe for Stuffed Pork Chops. After removing the chops from the pan, pour off any fat left in the skillet. Heat the oil over medium-high heat until shimmering.

Add the onion and apples and cook, stirring occasionally, until softened, about 10 minutes. Add the ginger, allspice, and cayenne and cook until fragrant, about 30 seconds. Add the cider and sugar and bring to a boil, scraping up any browned bits, until the cider is slightly thickened, about 4 minutes. Season with salt and pepper to taste and serve with the pork chops.

Quick All-Purpose Gravy

MAKES 2 CUPS

This gravy can be served with almost any type of meat and with mashed potatoes as well. The recipe can be doubled. If doubling it, use a Dutch oven so that the vegetables brown properly and increase the cooking times by roughly half. The finished gravy can be frozen. To thaw it, place the gravy and 1 tablespoon of water in a saucepan over low heat and slowly bring it to a simmer. It may appear broken or curdled as it thaws, but a vigorous whisking will recombine it.

- 3 tablespoons unsalted butter
- 1 onion, minced
- 1 small carrot, peeled and chopped fine
- 1 celery rib, chopped fine
- ¼ cup unbleached all-purpose flour
- 2 cups low-sodium chicken broth
- 2 cups beef broth
- 1 bay leaf
- ¼ teaspoon dried thyme
- 5 whole black peppercorns
  Table salt and ground black pepper

1. Melt the butter in a large saucepan over medium-high heat. Add the onion, carrot, and celery and cook, stirring frequently, until softened, about 7 minutes. Reduce the heat to medium, add the flour, and cook, stirring constantly, until thoroughly browned, about 5 minutes. Gradually whisk in the broths and bring to a boil, skimming off any foam that forms on the surface. Add the bay leaf, thyme, and peppercorns and simmer, stirring occasionally, until thickened and reduced to 3 cups, 20 to 25 minutes.

2. Strain the gravy through a fine-mesh strainer into a clean saucepan, pressing on the solids to extract as much liquid as possible; discard the solids. Season with salt and pepper to taste and serve with the pork chops.

CHAPTER 9

ROASTS, MEATLOAF, AND MORE

Slow-Roasted Beef 130

    Horseradish Cream Sauce

Roast Beef Tenderloin 131

    Shallot and Parsley Butter

    Chipotle and Garlic Butter with Lime and Cilantro

Roast Beef Tenderloin with Caramelized Onion and Mushroom Stuffing 132

Prime Rib 135

Onion-Braised Beef Brisket 135

Thick-Cut Pork Tenderloin Medallions 137

    Maple-Mustard Sauce

    Apple Cider Sauce

Breaded Pork Cutlets (Pork Schnitzel) 139

Maple-Glazed Pork Tenderloin 140

Pan-Seared Oven-Roasted Pork Tenderloins 141

    Dried Cherry–Port Sauce with Onions and Marmalade

    Garlicky Lime Sauce with Cilantro

Maple-Glazed Pork Roast 143

Maple-Glazed Pork Roast with Rosemary 143

Maple-Glazed Pork Roast with Orange Essence 143

Maple-Glazed Pork Roast with Star Anise 143

Maple-Glazed Pork Roast with Smoked Paprika 143

Garlic-Studded Roast Pork Loin 144

    Mustard–Shallot Sauce with Thyme

Roast Fresh Ham 145

    Cider and Brown Sugar Glaze

    Spicy Pineapple-Ginger Glaze

    Orange, Cinnamon, and Star Anise Glaze

    Coca-Cola Glaze with Lime and Jalapeño

Glazed Spiral-Sliced Ham 147

    Maple-Orange Glaze

    Cherry-Port Glaze

SLOW-ROASTED BEEF

WHY THIS RECIPE WORKS: Roasting inexpensive beef usually yields tough meat best suited for sandwiches. We wanted to take an inexpensive cut and turn it into a tender, rosy, beefy-tasting roast worthy of Sunday dinner.

First, we selected the best cut for our roast. Our favorite, the eye round, has good flavor and tenderness and a uniform shape that guarantees even cooking. Next, we chose between the two classic methods for roasting meat—high and fast or low and slow. Low temperature was the way to go. Keeping the meat's internal temperature below 122 degrees as long as possible allowed the meat's enzymes to act as natural tenderizers, breaking down its tough connective tissue (this action stops at 122 degrees). Since most ovens don't heat below 200 degrees, we needed to devise a special method to lengthen this tenderizing period. We roasted the meat at 225 degrees (after searing it to give the meat a crusty exterior) and shut off the oven when the roast reached 115 degrees. The meat stayed below 122 degrees an extra 30 minutes, allowing the enzymes to continue their work before the temperature reached 130 degrees for medium-rare. As for seasoning, we found that salting the meat a full 24 hours before roasting made it even more tender and seasoned the roast throughout.

Slow-Roasted Beef

SERVES 6 TO 8

We don't recommend cooking this roast past medium. Open the oven door as little as possible and remove the roast from the oven while taking its temperature. If the roast has not reached the desired temperature in the time specified in step 3, heat the oven to 225 degrees for 5 minutes, shut it off, and continue to cook the roast to the desired temperature. For a smaller (2½ to 3½-pound) roast, reduce the amount of pepper to 1½ teaspoons. For a 4½ to 6-pound roast, cut in half crosswise before cooking to create two smaller roasts. Slice the roast as thin as possible and serve with Horseradish Cream Sauce, if desired (recipe follows).

- 1 (3½ to 4½-pound) boneless eye-round roast (see note)
- 2 teaspoons table salt
- 1 tablespoon plus 2 teaspoons vegetable oil
- 2 teaspoons ground black pepper (see note)

SALTING—THE SECRET TO JUICY ROASTS

We're big advocates of brining in the test kitchen (see "How Brining Saved Thanksgiving" on page 87). But brining works best for lean types of meat like poultry and pork. Is there an alternative to brining for fattier meats like beef? There is—salting. Salting is a kind of "dry brine" in which meat is rubbed with salt and then refrigerated for several hours. How does salting do its work? Initially, the salt draws out moisture from the meat, and this moisture mixes with the salt to form a shallow brine. Over time, the salt migrates from the shallow brine into the meat, just as it does in our usual brining technique. Once inside the meat, the salt changes the structure of the muscle fibers, allowing the meat to hold on to more water, so that it turns out juicy and well-seasoned.

We tried salting in developing our Slow-Roasted Beef and found that salting for 24 hours worked best—the results were remarkable. In addition to the slow-cooking technique we use in this recipe, salting helped transform our bargain eye round into a tender, juicy roast that rivals beef tenderloin. (Note that smaller cuts of meat, like steak, do not need to be salted nearly as long—about 40 minutes is sufficient.)

1. Sprinkle all sides of the roast evenly with the salt. Wrap with plastic wrap and refrigerate for 18 to 24 hours.

2. Adjust an oven rack to the middle position and heat the oven to 225 degrees. Pat the roast dry with paper towels; rub with 2 teaspoons of the oil and sprinkle all sides evenly with the pepper. Heat the remaining 1 tablespoon oil in a 12-inch skillet over medium-high heat until starting to smoke. Sear the roast until browned on all sides, 3 to 4 minutes per side. Transfer the roast to a wire rack set over a rimmed baking sheet. Roast until the center of the roast registers 115 degrees on an instant-read thermometer for medium-rare (1¼ to 1¾ hours), or 125 degrees for medium (1¾ to 2¼ hours).

3. Turn the oven off; leave the roast in the oven, without opening the door, until the center of the roast registers 130 degrees for medium-rare or 140 degrees for medium, 30 to 50 minutes longer. Transfer the roast to a carving board and let rest for 15 minutes. Slice the meat crosswise as thin as possible and serve with the sauce, if using.

Horseradish Cream Sauce

MAKES ABOUT 1 CUP

- ½ cup heavy cream, chilled
- ½ cup prepared horseradish
- 1 teaspoon table salt
- ⅛ teaspoon ground black pepper

Whisk the cream in a medium bowl until thickened but not yet holding soft peaks, 1 to 2 minutes. Gently fold in the horseradish, salt, and pepper. Transfer to a serving bowl and refrigerate at least 30 minutes or up to 1 hour before serving.

ROAST BEEF TENDERLOIN

WHY THIS RECIPE WORKS: There's nothing like the buttery texture of a roasted beef tenderloin. Ideally, it has rosy meat all the way through and a deep brown crust; too often, though, this roast has only one or the other. We wanted a technique that produced perfectly cooked and deeply flavored meat—without too much fuss.

Tenderloins come whole or center-cut, and the obvious choice was the latter; it's already trimmed, and it lacks the narrow "tail" of the whole cut. We first tried searing the meat in the oven as many recipes recommend, but it never browned evenly and came out with a gray band of overcooked meat around the edge. Stovetop browning was better for producing a crust, but the roast still came out of the oven with that same gray band. The trick was to reverse the process, first roasting the meat in the oven, then searing at the end. The warmer surface of the meat browned in less time and so didn't overcook. Lowering the oven temperature eliminated the ring of overcooked meat altogether. To add flavor to this mild cut of beef, a simple technique of salting it before roasting worked wonders; rubbing the roast with a little softened butter added richness. A flavored butter served alongside was the final touch. With its uniformly rosy meat, deep brown crust, and beefy flavor, this beef tenderloin was worthy of its price tag.

Roast Beef Tenderloin

SERVES 4 TO 6

Ask your butcher to prepare a trimmed, center-cut Châteaubriand from the whole tenderloin, as this cut is not usually available without special ordering. If you are cooking for a crowd, this recipe can be doubled to make two roasts. Sear the roasts one after the other, wiping out the pan and adding new oil after searing the first roast. Both pieces of meat can be roasted on the same rack.

- 1 (2-pound) beef tenderloin center-cut Châteaubriand, trimmed (see note)
- 1 teaspoon table salt
- 1 teaspoon coarsely ground black pepper
- 2 tablespoons unsalted butter, softened
- 1 tablespoon vegetable oil
- 1 recipe flavored butter (recipes follow)

1. Using 12-inch lengths of kitchen twine, tie the roast crosswise at 1½-inch intervals. Sprinkle the roast evenly with the salt, cover loosely with plastic wrap, and let stand at room temperature for 1 hour. Meanwhile, adjust an oven rack to the middle position and heat the oven to 300 degrees.

2. Pat the roast dry with paper towels. Sprinkle the roast evenly with the pepper and spread the butter evenly over the surface. Transfer the roast to a wire rack set over a rimmed baking sheet. Roast until the center of the roast registers 125 degrees on an instant-read thermometer for medium-rare (40 to 55 minutes), or 135 degrees for medium (55 to 70 minutes), flipping the roast halfway through cooking.

3. Heat the oil in a 12-inch heavy-bottomed skillet over medium-high heat until just smoking. Place the roast in the skillet and sear until well browned on four sides, 1 to 2 minutes per side (a total of 4 to 8 minutes). Transfer the roast to a carving board and spread 2 tablespoons of the

flavored butter evenly over the top of the roast; let rest for 15 minutes. Remove the twine and cut the meat crosswise into ½-inch-thick slices. Serve, passing the remaining flavored butter separately.

Shallot and Parsley Butter

MAKES ABOUT ½ CUP

    4 tablespoons (½ stick) unsalted butter, softened
    1 small shallot, minced (about 1 tablespoon)
    1 medium garlic clove, minced or pressed through a
       garlic press (about 1 teaspoon)
    1 tablespoon finely chopped fresh parsley leaves
    ¼ teaspoon table salt
    ¼ teaspoon ground black pepper

Combine all the ingredients in a medium bowl.

Chipotle and Garlic Butter with Lime and Cilantro

MAKES ABOUT ½ CUP

    5 tablespoons unsalted butter, softened
    1 medium chipotle chile in adobo sauce, seeded and
       minced, with 1 teaspoon adobo sauce
    1 medium garlic clove, minced or pressed through a
       garlic press (about 1 teaspoon)
    1 teaspoon honey
    1 teaspoon grated zest from 1 lime
    1 tablespoon minced fresh cilantro leaves
    ½ teaspoon table salt

Combine all the ingredients in a medium bowl.

ULTIMATE BEEF TENDERLOIN

WHY THIS RECIPE WORKS: Beef tenderloin is perfect holiday fare. Add a rich stuffing and you've got the ultimate main course—at least in theory. We found three problems with stuffed tenderloin. The tenderloin's thin, tapered shape made for uneven cooking; in the time it took to develop a nice crust, the meat overcooked; and "deluxe" fillings such as lobster and chanterelles were so chunky they fell out of the meat when sliced. We wanted a stuffed beef tenderloin with a deeply charred crust, a tender, rosy-pink interior, and an intensely flavored stuffing that stayed neatly rolled in the meat.

We had determined for our Roast Beef Tenderloin recipe (see page 109) that a center-cut tenderloin cooks more evenly than a whole one, and its cylindrical shape had an added advantage here as it made the roast easier to stuff. But making a slit in the roast didn't give us much room for stuffing; double-butterflying the meat, to open it up like a book, gave us more space. After we stuffed, rolled, and tied it, we rubbed the roast with salt, pepper, and olive oil, which added flavor and helped develop a good crust when we seared the meat. We could fit just a cupful of stuffing in the meat, so we knew the flavors had to be intense. Chunky stuffings fell out when the roast was sliced, and anything with bread in it became a sponge that soaked up the meat juice. We finally decided on woodsy cremini mushrooms and caramelized onions, seasoned with Madeira and garlic; this combination made a savory-sweet jamlike filling that spread easily on the meat and held together well. Baby spinach added color and freshness. This roast was juicy and flavorful, and the filling was the ultimate touch of luxury.

Roast Beef Tenderloin with Caramelized Onion and Mushroom Stuffing

SERVES 4 TO 6

The roast can be stuffed, rolled, and tied a day ahead, but don't season the exterior until you are ready to cook it. This recipe can be doubled to make two roasts. Sear the roasts one after the other, cleaning the pan and adding new oil after searing the first roast. Both pieces of meat can be roasted on the same rack.

STUFFING

- 8 ounces cremini mushrooms, cleaned, stems trimmed, and broken into rough pieces
- 1½ teaspoons unsalted butter
- 1½ teaspoons olive oil
- 1 medium onion, halved and sliced ¼ inch thick
- ¼ teaspoon table salt
- ⅛ teaspoon ground black pepper
- 1 medium garlic clove, minced or pressed through a garlic press (about 1 teaspoon)
- ½ cup Madeira or sweet Marsala wine

BEEF ROAST

- 1 (2 to 3-pound) beef tenderloin center-cut Châteaubriand, trimmed and butterflied (see photos)
  Table salt and ground black pepper
- ½ cup lightly packed baby spinach
- 3 tablespoons olive oil

HERB BUTTER

- 4 tablespoons (½ stick) unsalted butter, softened
- 1 tablespoon chopped fresh parsley leaves
- ¾ teaspoon chopped fresh thyme leaves
- 1 medium garlic clove, minced or pressed through a garlic press (about 1 teaspoon)
- 1 tablespoon whole grain mustard
- ⅛ teaspoon table salt
- ⅛ teaspoon ground black pepper

1. FOR THE STUFFING: Pulse the mushrooms in a food processor until coarsely chopped, about 6 pulses. Heat the butter and oil in a 12-inch nonstick skillet over medium-high heat. Add the onion, salt, and pepper; cook, stirring occasionally, until the onion begins to soften, about 5 minutes. Add the mushrooms and cook, stirring occasionally, until all the moisture has evaporated, 5 to 7 minutes. Reduce the heat to medium and continue to cook, stirring frequently, until the vegetables are deeply browned and sticky, about 10 minutes. Stir in the garlic and cook until fragrant, about 30 seconds. Slowly stir in the Madeira and cook, scraping the bottom of the skillet to loosen any browned bits, until the liquid has evaporated, 2 to 3 minutes. Transfer the onion-mushroom mixture to a plate and cool to room temperature.

2. FOR THE ROAST: Pat the tenderloin dry and season the cut side of the tenderloin liberally with salt and pepper. Following the photos, spread the cooled stuffing mixture

STUFFING AND TYING A TENDERLOIN

1. Insert a chef's knife about 1 inch from the bottom of the roast and cut horizontally, stopping just before the edge. Open the meat like a book.

2. Make another cut diagonally into the thicker portion of the roast. Open up this flap, smoothing out the butterflied rectangle of meat.

3. Spread the filling evenly over the entire surface, leaving a ½-inch border on all sides. Press the spinach leaves evenly on top of the filling.

4. Using both hands, gently but firmly roll up the stuffed tenderloin, making it as compact as possible without squeezing out the filling.

5. Evenly space eight pieces of kitchen twine (each about 14 inches) beneath the roast. Tie each strand tightly around the roast, starting with the ends.

GIVE THAT MEAT A REST

You'll never see anyone in the test kitchen cut into a roast, or any meat, straight from the oven. They always let it rest before slicing. Exposed to heat during cooking, proteins, which resemble coiled springs, undergo a radical transformation in which they uncoil and then reconnect to each other in haphazard structures. This process, called coagulation, is the reason that proteins become firm and lose moisture during the cooking process. The longer that proteins are exposed to heat, the tighter they coagulate and the more liquid they drive toward both the surface and the center of the meat, much like wringing a wet kitchen towel.

If you were to cut the meat immediately after removing it from the heat source, the liquid suspended between the interior proteins is driven toward the surface and would simply pool (or what many chefs call bleed) on the cutting board or plate because the proteins have not had time to relax. The best way to prevent this pooling of juices and a dry hunk of meat is to rest the roast. Although the process of coagulation is not reversible, allowing the protein molecules to relax after cooking slows the rate which they continue to squeeze the liquid between their tight coils and increases their capacity to retain moisture. A short rest on the cutting board will decrease the amount of liquid lost during carving by about 40 percent. There's another good reason to have some patience and let your meat rest—it allows you some time to finish the other components of dinner, which is especially useful around the holidays when there are typically loads of sides to get to the table too.

over the interior of the beef, leaving a ½-inch border on all sides; press the spinach leaves on top of the stuffing. Roll the roast lengthwise, making it as compact as possible without squeezing out any filling. Evenly space eight pieces of kitchen twine (each about 14 inches) beneath the roast. Tie each strand tightly around the roast, starting with the ends.

3. In a small bowl, stir together 1 tablespoon of the olive oil, 1½ teaspoons salt, and 1½ teaspoons pepper. Rub the roast with the oil mixture and let stand at room temperature for 1 hour.

4. Adjust an oven rack to the middle position and heat the oven to 450 degrees. Heat the remaining 2 tablespoons olive oil in a 12-inch skillet over medium-high heat until smoking. Add the beef to the pan and cook until well browned on all sides, 8 to 10 minutes total. Transfer the beef to a wire rack set over a rimmed baking sheet and place in the oven. Roast until the thickest part of the roast registers 120 degrees on an instant-read thermometer for rare (16 to 18 minutes), or 125 degrees for medium-rare (20 to 22 minutes).

5. FOR THE BUTTER: While the meat roasts, combine all the ingredients in a small bowl. Transfer the tenderloin to a carving board; spread half of the butter evenly over the top of the roast. Loosely tent the roast with foil; let rest for 15 minutes. Cut the roast between the pieces of twine into thick slices. Remove the twine and serve, passing the remaining butter separately.

PRIME RIB

WHY THIS RECIPE WORKS: Most of us cook prime rib only once a year, if that, and don't want to risk experimenting with the cooking method—especially when the results are no better than mediocre. We thought that a special-occasion roast deserved better and wanted to find the best way to get the juicy, tender, rosy meat that prime rib should have.

The principal question for roasting prime rib was oven temperature, and our research turned up a wide range of recommendations. Most delivered meat that was well-done on the outside but increasingly rare toward the center—not too bad, but not exactly great. Surprisingly, the roast we cooked at a temperature of only 250 degrees was rosy from the center all the way out. Additionally, it retained more juice than a roast cooked at a higher temperature, and the internal temperature rose less during resting, so we had more control over the final degree of doneness. Searing before roasting gave us a crusty brown exterior. For seasoning, prime rib needs nothing more than salt and pepper. Now that we'd found a dependable cooking method, we could serve this once-a-year roast with confidence.

SERVES 6 TO 8

With two pieces of kitchen twine running parallel to the bone, tie the roast at both ends to prevent the outer layer of meat from pulling away from the rib-eye muscle and overcooking.

1 (7-pound; 3-rib) standing rib roast, trimmed and tied (see note)

Table salt and ground black pepper

1. Pat the roast dry with paper towels and season with salt and pepper. Cover the roast loosely with plastic wrap and let sit at room temperature for 1 to 2 hours.

2. Adjust an oven rack to the lowest position and heat the oven to 250 degrees. Heat a large roasting pan over two burners set at medium-high heat until hot, about 4 minutes. Place the roast in the hot pan and cook on all sides until nicely browned and about ½ cup fat has rendered, 6 to 8 minutes.

3. Remove the roast from the pan. Set a wire rack in the pan, then set the roast on the rack.

4. Place the roast in the oven and roast until the meat registers 125 degrees on an instant-read thermometer for rare, 130 degrees for medium-rare, and 140 degrees for medium, 3 to 3½ hours. Remove the roast from the oven and tent with foil. Let stand for 20 to 30 minutes to allow

NOTES FROM THE TEST KITCHEN

CARVING PRIME RIB

1. Using a carving fork to hold the roast in place, cut along the rib bones to sever the meat from the bones.

2. Set the roast cut side down; carve the meat across the grain into thick slices.

the juices to redistribute evenly throughout the roast.

5. Remove the twine and set the roast on a carving board, with the rib bones at a 90-degree angle to the board. Carve and serve immediately.

BRAISED BRISKET

WHY THIS RECIPE WORKS: Brisket is naturally flavorful, but because it is so lean, it requires long, slow braising to become tender—and the result is almost always stringy, dry meat. We wanted a better way to cook brisket so that it would remain moist, and we wanted to serve it with a flavorful sauce that would complement the beef, not disguise it.

The fat in a piece of brisket is all on the surface; there's no marbling to keep the interior moist. We needed to find a way to get the moisture inside. We tried many different types and amounts of liquids and a variety of cooking vessels and techniques, but no matter what we did, the meat was still dry. Could the answer lie in adding moisture after the long braise? We left the meat in the sauce after cooking it, and after about an hour there was a noticeable difference. Taking this discovery further, we refrigerated the cooked meat and sauce overnight. The meat reabsorbed some of the liquid, becoming more moist and easier to carve without shredding. The sauce—based on red wine, chicken broth, and lots of onions—had improved as well; the fat had risen to the surface and congealed, making it easier to remove. All we had to do was reheat the sliced meat in the sauce, and this hearty dish was ready.

Onion-Braised Beef Brisket

SERVES 6

This recipe requires a few hours of unattended cooking. It also requires advance preparation. After cooking, the brisket must stand overnight in the braising liquid that later becomes the sauce; this helps to keep the brisket moist and flavorful. Defatting the sauce is essential. If the fat has congealed into a layer on top of the sauce, it can be easily removed while cold. Sometimes, however, fragments of solid fat are dispersed throughout the sauce; in this case, the sauce should be skimmed of fat after reheating. If you prefer a spicy sauce, increase the amount of cayenne to ¼ teaspoon. You will need 18-inch-wide heavy-duty foil for this recipe. If you own an electric knife, it will make easy work of slicing the cold brisket.

If you would like to make and serve the brisket on the same day, after removing the brisket from the oven in step 4, reseal the foil and let the brisket stand at room temperature for an hour. Then transfer the brisket to a carving board and continue with the recipe to strain, defat, and reheat the sauce and slice the meat; because the brisket will still be hot, there will be no need to put it back into the oven once the reheated sauce is poured over it.

1 (4 to 5-pound) beef brisket, preferably flat cut
   Table salt and ground black pepper
1 teaspoon vegetable oil, plus more as needed
3 large onions (about 2½ pounds), halved and
   sliced ½ inch thick
1 tablespoon brown sugar
3 medium garlic cloves, minced or pressed through a
   garlic press (about 1 tablespoon)
1 tablespoon tomato paste
1 tablespoon paprika
⅛ teaspoon cayenne pepper (see note)
2 tablespoons unbleached all-purpose flour
1 cup low-sodium chicken broth
1 cup dry red wine
3 bay leaves
3 sprigs fresh thyme
2 teaspoons cider vinegar (to season the sauce
   before serving)

1. Adjust an oven rack to the lower-middle position and heat the oven to 300 degrees. Line a 13 by 9-inch baking dish with two 24-inch-long sheets of 18-inch-wide heavy-duty foil, positioning the sheets perpendicular to each other and allowing the excess foil to extend beyond the edges of the pan. Pat the brisket dry with paper towels. Place the brisket, fat side up, on a cutting board; using a dinner fork, poke holes in the meat through the fat layer

about 1 inch apart. Season both sides of the brisket liberally with salt and pepper.

2. Heat 1 teaspoon oil in a 12-inch skillet over medium-high heat until the oil just begins to smoke. Place the brisket, fat side up, in the skillet (the brisket may climb up the sides of the skillet); weight the brisket with a heavy Dutch oven or cast-iron skillet and cook until well browned, about 7 minutes. Remove the Dutch oven; using tongs, flip the brisket and cook on the second side without the weight until well browned, about 7 minutes longer. Transfer the brisket to a platter.

3. Pour off all but 1 tablespoon fat from the pan (or, if the brisket is lean, add enough oil to the fat in the skillet to equal 1 tablespoon); stir in the onions, brown sugar, and ¼ teaspoon salt and cook over medium-high heat, stirring occasionally, until the onions are softened and golden, 10 to 12 minutes. Add the garlic and cook, stirring frequently, until fragrant, about 1 minute; add the tomato paste and cook, stirring to combine, until the paste darkens, about 2 minutes. Add the paprika and cayenne and cook, stirring constantly, until fragrant, about 1 minute. Sprinkle the flour over the onions and cook, stirring constantly, until well combined, about 2 minutes. Add the broth, wine, bay leaves, and thyme, stirring to scrape up the browned bits from the pan; bring to a simmer and simmer about 5 minutes to fully thicken.

4. Pour the sauce and onions into the foil-lined baking dish. Nestle the brisket, fat side up, in the sauce and onions. Fold the foil extensions over and seal (do not tightly crimp the foil because it must later be opened to test for doneness). Place in the oven and cook until a fork can be inserted into and removed from the center of the brisket with no resistance, 3½ to 4 hours (when testing for doneness, open the foil with caution as the contents will be steaming). Carefully open the foil and let the brisket cool at room temperature for 20 to 30 minutes.

5. Transfer the brisket to a large bowl; set a mesh strainer over the bowl and strain the sauce over the brisket. Discard the bay leaves and thyme from the onions and transfer the onions to a small bowl. Cover both bowls with plastic wrap, cut vents in the plastic with a paring knife, and refrigerate overnight.

6. About 45 minutes before serving, adjust an oven rack to the lower-middle position and heat the oven to 350 degrees. While the oven heats, transfer the cold brisket to a carving board. Scrape off and discard any congealed fat from the sauce, then transfer the sauce to a medium saucepan and heat over medium heat until warm, skimming any fat on the surface with a wide shallow spoon (you should have about 2 cups of sauce without onions; if necessary, simmer the sauce over medium-high heat until

reduced to 2 cups). While the sauce heats, use an electric knife, chef's knife, or carving knife to slice the brisket against the grain into ¼-inch-thick slices, trimming and discarding any excess fat, if desired; place the slices in a 13 by 9-inch baking dish. Stir the reserved onions and the vinegar into the warmed sauce and season with salt and pepper to taste. Pour the sauce over the brisket slices, cover the baking dish with foil, and bake until heated through, 25 to 30 minutes. Serve immediately.

SAUTÉED PORK TENDERLOIN

WHY THIS RECIPE WORKS: When cooked properly, ultra-lean pork tenderloin has a tenderness rivaling that of beef tenderloin; unfortunately it also has ultra-mild flavor. Long marinades and hybrid searing and roasting techniques help remedy the flavor deficiency, but they take the home cook a long way from the realm of the no-fuss meal. We wanted a recipe for a fast weeknight dinner that still offered maximum flavor.

Packaging and shape presented the first challenge: we needed to deal with the tenderloin's oblong, tapered shape as well as the fact that the tenderloins (which are usually sold in a pair in a vacuum pack) were almost guaranteed to be substantially different in weight and length. The solution was to cut them into 1½-inch-thick medallions (the end pieces were scored, creating a small flap of meat that folded underneath the larger half to yield the right-sized medallion). To preserve their tidy cylindrical shape, we developed two approaches: tying the medallions or wrapping blanched bacon around them, fastened with toothpicks. We found we could create a beautiful sear on all sides of these neat packages in the time it took to reach an internal temperature of 140 to 145 degrees, and the searing process had the extra benefit of producing enough fond (flavorful browned bits) to create a few easy, flavorful pan sauces.

Thick-Cut Pork Tenderloin Medallions

SERVES 4 TO 6

We prefer natural to enhanced pork (pork that has been injected with a salt solution to increase moistness and flavor), though both will work in this recipe. Begin checking the doneness of smaller medallions 1 or 2 minutes early; they may need to be taken out of the pan a little sooner. Be sure not to rinse out the skillet if serving with a pan sauce (recipes follow).

2 (1 to 1¼-pound) pork tenderloins, trimmed, cut crosswise into 1½-inch pieces, and tied; thinner end pieces removed and tied together (see photos) Table salt and ground black pepper
2 tablespoons vegetable oil

1. Pat the pork medallions dry and season with salt and pepper.

2. Heat the oil in a 12-inch skillet over medium-high heat until shimmering. Add the pork and cook, without moving the pieces, until well browned, 3 to 5 minutes. Turn the pork and brown on the second side, 3 to 5 minutes more. Reduce the heat to medium. Using tongs, stand each piece on its side and cook, turning the pieces as necessary, until the sides are well browned and the internal temperature registers 140 to 145 degrees on an instant-read thermometer, 8 to 12 minutes. Transfer the pork to a platter, tent loosely with foil, and let rest until the temperature registers 150 degrees on an instant-read thermometer, while making a pan sauce (recipes follow). Serve with the sauce.

NOTES FROM THE TEST KITCHEN

TURNING THE TAILPIECE INTO A MEDALLION

1. Score the tenderloin's tapered tail end.

2. Fold in half at the incision.

3. Tie the medallion with kitchen twine, making sure the outer surfaces are flat.

the skillet with a wooden spoon to loosen any browned bits. Simmer until the liquid is reduced to ½ cup, 3 to 4 minutes. Add the maple syrup, vinegar, mustard, and any juices from the resting meat and cook until thickened and reduced to 1 cup, 3 to 4 minutes longer. Season with salt and pepper to taste, pour the sauce over the pork, and serve immediately.

Apple Cider Sauce

MAKES ABOUT 1¼ CUPS

Complete step 1 of this recipe either before or during the cooking of the pork, then finish the sauce while the pork rests.

1½	cups apple cider
1	cup low-sodium chicken broth
2	teaspoons cider vinegar
1	cinnamon stick
4	tablespoons (½ stick) unsalted butter, cut into 4 pieces
2	large shallots, minced (about ½ cup)
1	tart apple, such as Granny Smith, peeled, cored, and diced small
¼	cup Calvados or apple-flavored brandy
1	teaspoon minced fresh thyme leaves
	Table salt and ground black pepper

1. Combine the cider, broth, vinegar, and cinnamon stick in a medium saucepan; simmer over medium-high heat until the liquid is reduced to 1 cup, 10 to 12 minutes. Remove the cinnamon stick and discard. Set the sauce aside until the pork is cooked.

2. Pour off any fat from the skillet in which the pork was cooked. Add 1 tablespoon of the butter and heat over medium heat until melted. Add the shallots and apple and cook, stirring occasionally, until softened and beginning to brown, 1 to 2 minutes. Remove the skillet from the heat and add the Calvados. Return the skillet to the heat and cook about 1 minute, scraping the bottom of the skillet with a wooden spoon to loosen any browned bits. Add the reduced cider mixture, any juices from the resting meat, and the thyme; increase the heat to medium-high and simmer until thickened and reduced to 1¼ cups, 3 to 4 minutes. Off the heat, whisk in the remaining 3 tablespoons butter and season with salt and pepper to taste. Pour the sauce over the pork and serve immediately.

Maple-Mustard Sauce

MAKES ABOUT 1 CUP

2	teaspoons vegetable oil
1	medium onion, halved and sliced thin
1	cup low-sodium chicken broth
⅓	cup maple syrup
3	tablespoons balsamic vinegar
3	tablespoons whole grain mustard
	Table salt and ground black pepper

Pour off any fat from the skillet in which the pork was cooked. Add the oil and heat the skillet over medium heat until shimmering. Add the onion and cook, stirring occasionally, until softened and beginning to brown, 3 to 4 minutes. Increase the heat to medium-high and add the broth; bring to a simmer, scraping the bottom of

NOTES FROM THE TEST KITCHEN

TYING THICK MEDALLIONS

Thick medallions allow for more browning, but they can flop over in the pan. To prevent this, tie each piece with kitchen twine.

BREADED PORK CUTLETS

WHY THIS RECIPE WORKS: While classic Wiener schnitzel features a thin, tender veal cutlet coated in ultrafine bread crumbs and then fried until puffy and golden brown, many recipes—to avoid the toughness and high price of veal—substitute pork. But too often these recipes yield dry, tough pork cutlets with greasy coatings. We wanted tender pork cutlets with the crisp, wrinkled, puffy coating that is Wiener schnitzel's signature.

Dismissing pork chops and prepackaged cutlets, we chose tenderloin, which has a mild flavor similar to veal and isn't tough. We cut the tenderloin crosswise on an angle into four pieces, which when pounded thin gave us long, narrow cutlets that would fit two at a time in the pan. Schnitzel is breaded with the usual flour, egg, and bread-crumb sequence of coatings, but we had to figure out how to get the characteristic puffiness and "rumpled" appearance of the finished cutlets; with good schnitzel you should be able to slide a knife between the meat and the coating. Drying bread in the microwave produced extra-dry crumbs that helped with the crispness, and a little vegetable oil whisked into the egg helped separate the coating from the meat.

But the real breakthrough was in the frying method: Instead of sautéing the cutlets, we cooked them in a Dutch oven in an inch of oil, shaking the pot to get some of the oil over the top of the meat. The extra heat quickly solidified the egg in the coating, so that the steam from the meat couldn't escape and puffed the coating instead. With the traditional schnitzel garnishes of lemon, parsley, capers, and a sieved hard-cooked egg, these cutlets, with their tender meat and crisp coating, delivered on all fronts.

Breaded Pork Cutlets (Pork Schnitzel)
SERVES 4

To make cutlets, cut the tenderloin in half on a 20-degree angle, then cut each piece in half again at the same angle. Cut the tapered tail pieces slightly thicker than the middle ones. Using 2 cups of oil for cooking may seem like a lot, but it is necessary to get an authentic, wrinkled texture on the finished cutlets. When properly cooked, the cutlets absorb very little oil. To ensure ample room for the cutlets as they fry, it is essential to use a Dutch oven with a large surface area. Although spaetzle is the traditional side dish, boiled potatoes or egg noodles also make terrific accompaniments.

- 7 slices high-quality white sandwich bread, crusts removed, cut into ¾-inch cubes (about 4 cups)
- ½ cup unbleached all-purpose flour
- 2 large eggs
- 2 cups plus 1 tablespoon vegetable oil (see note)
- 1 (1¼-pound) pork tenderloin, trimmed of fat and silver skin and tenderloin cut on an angle into 4 equal pieces (see note)
  Table salt and ground black pepper

GARNISHES
- 1 lemon, cut into wedges
- 2 tablespoons chopped fresh parsley leaves
- 2 tablespoons capers, rinsed
- 1 large hard-cooked egg (page 23), yolk and white separated and passed separately through a fine-mesh strainer (optional)

1. Place the bread cubes on a large microwave-safe plate. Microwave on high power for 4 minutes, stirring well halfway through the cooking time. Microwave on medium power until the bread is dry and a few pieces start to lightly brown, 3 to 5 minutes longer, stirring every minute. Process the dry bread in a food processor to very fine crumbs, about 45 seconds. Transfer the bread crumbs to a shallow dish (you should have about 1¼ cups crumbs). Spread the flour in a second shallow dish. Beat the eggs with 1 tablespoon of the oil in a third shallow dish.

2. Place the pork, with one cut side down, between two sheets of plastic wrap and pound to an even thickness of between ⅛ and ¼ inch. Season the cutlets with salt and pepper. Working with one cutlet at a time, dredge the cutlets thoroughly in flour, shaking off the excess, then coat with the egg, allowing the excess to drip back into the dish to ensure a very thin coating, and coat evenly with the bread crumbs, pressing on the crumbs to adhere. Place the breaded cutlets in a single layer on a wire rack set over a baking sheet; let the coating dry for 5 minutes.

3. Heat the remaining 2 cups oil in a large Dutch oven over medium-high heat until it registers 375 degrees on an instant-read thermometer. Lay two cutlets, without overlapping, in the pan and cook, shaking the pan continuously and gently, until wrinkled and light golden brown on both sides, 1 to 2 minutes per side. Transfer the cutlets to a paper towel–lined plate and flip the cutlets several times to blot the excess oil. Repeat with the remaining cutlets. Serve immediately with the garnishes.

MAPLE-GLAZED PORK TENDERLOIN

WHY THIS RECIPE WORKS: When done right, nothing can quite match pork tenderloin's fine-grained, buttery-smooth texture, but even when perfectly cooked, too often it's still sorely lacking in flavor. We thought a thick, sweet, fragrant glaze would be just the solution and decided it should feature New England's signature ingredient, maple syrup.

Getting the glaze right was comparatively easy: To temper the sweetness of the maple syrup, we added molasses, mustard, and a shot of bourbon; with a little cinnamon, cloves, and cayenne, the glaze was ready. To give the glaze something to hold on to, we rolled the tenderloins in a mixture of cornstarch and sugar before searing them. When we'd built a good crust in the skillet, we painted on some glaze and transferred the pork to the oven. It occurred to us that the painting analogy was a good one—why not put multiple coats on the tenderloins to get the best coverage? When the meat was nearly done, we put on more glaze, and we added yet another coat when the tenderloins were completely done. Finally, after letting the tenderloins rest, we glazed them one last time. Slicing into this roast revealed success: A thick maple glaze coated the meat.

Maple-Glazed Pork Tenderloin

SERVES 6

We prefer natural to enhanced pork (pork that has been injected with a salt solution to increase moistness and flavor) for this recipe, though enhanced pork can be used.

If your tenderloins are smaller than 1¼ pounds, reduce the cooking time in step 3 (and use an instant-read thermometer for best results). If the tenderloins don't fit in the skillet initially, let their ends curve toward each other; the meat will eventually shrink as it cooks. Make sure to cook the tenderloins until they turn deep golden brown in step 2 or they will appear pale after glazing. Be sure to pat off the cornstarch mixture thoroughly in step 1, as any excess will leave gummy spots on the tenderloins.

¾ cup maple syrup, preferably grade B
¼ cup light or mild molasses
2 tablespoons bourbon or brandy
⅛ teaspoon ground cinnamon
Pinch ground cloves
Pinch cayenne pepper
¼ cup cornstarch
2 tablespoons sugar
1 tablespoon table salt
2 teaspoons ground black pepper
2 (1¼ to 1½-pound) pork tenderloins (see note), trimmed of fat and silver skin
2 tablespoons vegetable oil
1 tablespoon whole grain mustard

1. Adjust an oven rack to the middle position and heat the oven to 375 degrees. Stir ½ cup of the maple syrup, the molasses, bourbon, cinnamon, cloves, and cayenne together in a 2-cup liquid measure; set aside. Whisk the cornstarch, sugar, salt, and black pepper in a small bowl until combined. Transfer the cornstarch mixture to a rimmed baking sheet. Pat the tenderloins dry with paper towels, then roll them in the cornstarch mixture until evenly coated on all sides. Thoroughly pat off the excess cornstarch mixture.

2. Heat the oil in a 12-inch heavy-bottomed nonstick skillet over medium-high heat until just beginning to smoke. Reduce the heat to medium and place both tenderloins in the skillet, leaving at least 1 inch between them. Cook until well browned on all sides, 8 to 12 minutes. Transfer the tenderloins to a wire rack set over a rimmed baking sheet.

3. Pour off the fat from the skillet and return to medium heat. Add the syrup mixture to the skillet, scraping up the browned bits with a wooden spoon, and cook until reduced to ½ cup, about 2 minutes. Transfer 2 tablespoons of the glaze to a small bowl and set aside. Using the remaining glaze, brush each tenderloin with approximately 1 tablespoon glaze. Roast the pork until the thickest part of the tenderloins registers 130 degrees on an instant-read thermometer, 12 to 20 minutes. Brush each tenderloin with another tablespoon of the glaze and continue to roast until the thickest part of the tenderloins registers 140 degrees, 2 to 4 minutes longer. Remove the tenderloins from the oven and brush each with the remaining glaze; let rest, uncovered, until the temperature reaches 150 degrees, about 10 minutes.

4. While the tenderloins rest, stir the remaining ¼ cup maple syrup and mustard into the reserved 2 tablespoons glaze. Brush each tenderloin with 1 tablespoon mustard glaze. Transfer the meat to a carving board and slice into ¼-inch-thick pieces. Serve, passing the extra mustard glaze at the table.

PAN-SEARED PORK TENDERLOIN

WHY THIS RECIPE WORKS: Because pork tenderloins are so lean, they cook relatively quickly and are therefore a good choice for an easy-to-prepare meal. But that same leanness means there's also less flavor. Grilling is often used to add more flavor, but we wanted an indoor preparation for pork tenderloins that would deliver a flavor boost to this quick-cooking roast.

Simply roasted in the oven, the pork tended to dry out and never achieved the dark brown crust we wanted. We got that crust when we seared the tenderloins on the stovetop—but then the pork wasn't cooked through. A combination of searing the meat in a skillet, then transferring the pork to the oven to finish cooking, produced a flavorful crust and well-cooked meat. The browned crust added some flavor, but we wanted more. A dry rub of just salt and pepper, left on for half an hour before searing, provided enough seasoning and further encouraged a

browned crust, and a pan sauce made with the browned bits left from sautéing was an additional flavor boost. Not only were these pork tenderloins delicious; they were also on the dinner table in about half an hour.

Pan-Seared Oven-Roasted Pork Tenderloins
SERVES 4

We prefer natural to enhanced pork (pork that has been injected with a salt solution to increase moisture and flavor) for this recipe. Enhanced pork can be used, but the meat won't brown as well. Because two are cooked at once, tenderloins larger than 1 pound apiece will not fit comfortably in a 12-inch skillet. If time permits, season the tenderloins up to 30 minutes before cooking; the seasonings will better penetrate the meat. The recipe will work in a nonstick or a traditional skillet. A pan sauce can be made while the tenderloins are in the oven (recipes follow); if you intend to make a sauce, make sure to prepare all of the sauce ingredients before cooking the pork.

- **2** (12 to 16-ounce) pork tenderloins, trimmed of fat and silver skin (see note)
- **1¼** teaspoons table salt
- **¾** teaspoon ground black pepper
- **2** teaspoons vegetable oil
- **1** recipe pan sauce (optional; recipes follow)

1. Adjust an oven rack to the middle position and heat the oven to 400 degrees. Sprinkle the tenderloins evenly with the salt and pepper; rub the seasoning into the meat. Heat the oil in a 12-inch skillet over medium-high heat until smoking. Place both tenderloins in the skillet; cook until well browned, about 3 minutes. Using tongs, rotate the tenderloins a quarter-turn; cook until well browned, 45 to 60 seconds. Repeat until all sides are browned, about 1 minute longer. Transfer the tenderloins to a rimmed baking sheet and place in the oven (reserve the skillet if making a pan sauce); roast until the internal temperature registers 140 to 145 degrees on an instant-read thermometer, 10 to 16 minutes. (Begin the pan sauce, if making, while the meat roasts.)

2. Transfer the tenderloins to a carving board and tent loosely with foil (continue with the pan sauce, if making); let rest until the internal temperature registers 150 degrees, 8 to 10 minutes. Cut the tenderloins crosswise into ½-inch-thick slices, arrange on a platter or individual plates, and spoon the sauce (if using) over; serve immediately.

Dried Cherry–Port Sauce with Onions and Marmalade

MAKES ABOUT ½ CUP

The flavors in this sauce are especially suited to the winter holiday season.

- 1 teaspoon vegetable oil
- 1 large onion, halved and sliced ½ inch thick (about 1½ cups)
- ¾ cup port
- ¾ cup dried cherries
- 2 tablespoons orange marmalade
- 3 tablespoons unsalted butter, cut into 3 pieces
  Table salt and ground black pepper

1. Immediately after placing the pork in the oven, add the oil to the still-hot skillet, swirl to coat, and set the skillet over medium-high heat; add the onion and cook, stirring frequently, until softened and browned around the edges, 5 to 7 minutes. (If the drippings are browning too quickly, add 2 tablespoons water and scrape up the browned bits with a wooden spoon.) Set the skillet aside off the heat.

2. While the pork is resting, set the skillet over medium-high heat and add the port and cherries; simmer, scraping up the browned bits with a wooden spoon, until the mixture is slightly thickened, 4 to 6 minutes. Add any accumulated pork juices and continue to simmer until thickened and reduced to about ⅓ cup, 2 to 4 minutes longer. Off the heat, whisk in the orange marmalade and butter, one piece at a time. Season with salt and pepper to taste.

Garlicky Lime Sauce with Cilantro

MAKES ABOUT ½ CUP

This assertive sauce is based on a Mexican sauce called *mojo de ajo*. A rasp grater is the best way to break down the garlic to a fine paste. Another option is to put the garlic through a press and then finish mincing it to a paste with a knife. If your garlic cloves contain green sprouts or shoots, remove the sprouts before grating—their flavor is bitter and hot. The initial cooking of the garlic off the heat will prevent scorching.

- 10 garlic cloves, peeled and grated to a fine paste on a rasp grater (about 2 tablespoons) (see note)
- 2 tablespoons water
- 1 tablespoon vegetable oil
- ¼ teaspoon red pepper flakes
- 2 teaspoons light brown sugar
- ¼ cup chopped fresh cilantro leaves
- 3 tablespoons juice from 2 limes
- 1 tablespoon chopped fresh chives
- 4 tablespoons (½ stick) unsalted butter, cut into 4 pieces
  Table salt and ground black pepper

1. Immediately after placing the pork in the oven, mix the garlic paste with the water in a small bowl. Add the oil to the still-hot skillet and swirl to coat; add the garlic paste and cook with the skillet's residual heat, scraping up the browned bits with a wooden spoon, until the sizzling subsides, about 2 minutes. Set the skillet over low heat and continue cooking, stirring frequently, until the garlic is sticky, 8 to 10 minutes; set the skillet aside off the heat.

2. While the pork is resting, set the skillet over medium heat; add the pepper flakes and brown sugar to the skillet and cook until sticky and the sugar is dissolved, about 1 minute. Add the cilantro, lime juice, and chives; simmer to blend the flavors, 1 to 2 minutes. Add any accumulated pork juices and simmer 1 minute longer. Off the heat, whisk in the butter, one piece at a time. Season with salt and pepper to taste.

MAPLE-GLAZED PORK ROAST

WHY THIS RECIPE WORKS: Maple-glazed pork roast often falls short of its savory-sweet promise. Many roasts turn out dry (a constant concern when cooking today's lean pork), but the glazes often present even bigger problems. Most are too thin to coat the pork properly, some are so sweet that they require a hotline to the dentist's office, and few have a pronounced maple flavor. We wanted a glistening roast, which, when sliced, would combine the juices from tender, well-seasoned pork with a rich maple glaze to create complex flavor in every bite.

For this dish we chose a blade-end loin roast, which has a deposit of fat that helps keep the meat moist. We tied it at intervals to make a neat bundle. Searing the roast first on the stovetop was a must for a brown, flavorful exterior. We then removed the pork so that we could use the browned bits in the skillet to build the glaze. Maple syrup, with complementary spices and a touch of cayenne pepper for heat, made a thick, clingy glaze. Instead of brushing the glaze onto the pork, however, we decided to keep things simple: Rather than hauling out our roasting pan, we returned the pork to the skillet, rolled it in the glaze to coat it, and put the whole thing into the oven. The

smaller area of the skillet kept the glaze from spreading out and burning, and the glaze reduced nicely while the roast cooked. Rolling the roast in the glaze periodically ensured even coverage and resulted in a tender, juicy roast packed with maple flavor.

Maple-Glazed Pork Roast
SERVES 4 TO 6

We prefer natural to enhanced pork (pork that has been injected with a salt solution to increase moisture and flavor) for this recipe, though enhanced pork can be used. We prefer a nonstick ovenproof skillet because it is much easier to clean than a traditional one. Whichever you use, remember that the handle will be blistering hot when you take it out of the oven, so be sure to use a potholder or oven mitt. Note that you should not trim the pork of its thin layer of fat. This dish is unapologetically sweet, so we recommend side dishes that take well to the sweetness. Garlicky sautéed greens, braised cabbage, and soft polenta are good choices.

⅓ cup maple syrup, preferably grade B
⅛ teaspoon ground cinnamon
   Pinch ground cloves
   Pinch cayenne pepper
1 (2½-pound) boneless blade-end pork loin roast, tied at 1½-inch intervals (see note)
¾ teaspoon table salt
½ teaspoon ground black pepper
2 teaspoons vegetable oil

1. Adjust an oven rack to the middle position and heat the oven to 325 degrees. Stir the maple syrup, cinnamon, cloves, and cayenne together in a measuring cup or small

bowl and set aside. Pat the roast dry with paper towels, then sprinkle evenly with the salt and pepper.

2. Heat the oil in a heavy-bottomed ovenproof 10-inch nonstick skillet over medium-high heat until just beginning to smoke, about 3 minutes. Place the roast, fat side down, in the skillet and cook until well browned, about 3 minutes. Using tongs, rotate the roast a quarter-turn and cook until well browned, about 2½ minutes; repeat until the roast is well browned on all sides. Transfer the roast to a large plate. Reduce the heat to medium and pour off the fat from the skillet; add the maple syrup mixture and cook until fragrant, about 30 seconds (the syrup will bubble immediately). Turn off the heat and return the roast to the skillet; using tongs, roll the roast to coat with the glaze on all sides.

3. Place the skillet in the oven and roast until the center of the pork registers 140 to 145 degrees on an instant-read thermometer, 35 to 45 minutes, using tongs to roll and spin the roast to coat with the glaze twice during the roasting time. Transfer the roast to a carving board; set the skillet aside to cool slightly to thicken the glaze, about 5 minutes. Pour the glaze over the roast and let rest 15 minutes longer (the center of the loin should register 150 degrees on an instant-read thermometer). Remove the twine, cut the meat into ¼-inch slices, and serve immediately.

Maple-Glazed Pork Roast with Rosemary

Follow the recipe for Maple-Glazed Pork Roast, substituting 2 teaspoons minced fresh rosemary for the cinnamon, cloves, and cayenne.

Maple-Glazed Pork Roast with Orange Essence

Follow the recipe for Maple-Glazed Pork Roast, adding 1 tablespoon fresh grated orange zest to the maple syrup along with the spices.

Maple-Glazed Pork Roast with Star Anise

Follow the recipe for Maple-Glazed Pork Roast, adding 4 star anise pods to the maple syrup along with the spices.

Maple-Glazed Pork Roast with Smoked Paprika

Follow the recipe for Maple-Glazed Pork Roast, adding 2 teaspoons smoked hot paprika to the maple syrup along with the spices.

GARLIC-STUDDED ROAST PORK LOIN

WHY THIS RECIPE WORKS: Although it has a little more fat than pork tenderloin, a center loin pork roast is still quite lean and requires special handling to roast without drying out. We sought the best way to roast this cut so that the juices would remain inside the meat, not wind up on the carving board.

It turns out that a two-step roasting process is the key to juicy pork loin. After poking slivers of garlic into the meat and rubbing the surface with a mixture of thyme, cloves, salt, and pepper for extra flavor, we refrigerated the roast overnight. The next day we cranked up the oven to 475 degrees and added the pork directly from the fridge, leaving it for just half an hour before removing it. After we rested the roast, we returned it to the oven, this time at a lower temperature, to finish cooking. The texture of the meat was remarkably tender, and it had lost very little juice. It turns out the reason this method works is that during the rest, the middle of the roast heats by conduction from the heat absorbed by the outside of the roast. When the meat goes back into the oven, the center cooks through but the outside doesn't overcook. A mustard-shallot sauce provides additional moisture and flavor, although the roast is so juicy and flavorful on its own, it can be omitted.

Garlic-Studded Roast Pork Loin

SERVES 4 TO 6

We prefer natural to enhanced pork (pork that has been injected with a salt solution to increase moisture and flavor) for this recipe, though enhanced pork can be used. For extra flavor and moisture, serve the sliced roast with the mustard-shallot sauce.

- 2 teaspoons dried thyme
- 2 teaspoons table salt
- 1 teaspoon ground black pepper
- ¼ teaspoon ground cloves or allspice
- 2 large garlic cloves, peeled and cut into slivers
- 1 (2¼-pound) boneless center loin pork roast, fat trimmed to about ⅛ inch thick and roast tied at 1½-inch intervals (see note)
- 1 recipe Mustard-Shallot Sauce with Thyme (recipe follows)

1. Mix together the thyme, salt, pepper, and cloves. Coat the garlic slivers in the spice mixture. Poke slits in the roast with the point of a paring knife; insert the garlic slivers. Rub the remaining spice mixture onto the meat. Tie the roast with kitchen twine into a tight cylinder. Wrap the roast in plastic wrap and refrigerate for at least 2 hours and up to 24 hours.

2. Adjust an oven rack to the middle position and heat the oven to 475 degrees. Take the meat directly from the refrigerator, remove the plastic, and place it on a wire rack set in a shallow roasting pan. Roast exactly 30 minutes.

3. Remove the meat from the oven; immediately reduce the oven temperature to 325 degrees. Insert an instant-read thermometer at one end of the roast, going into the thickest part at the center (the temperature will range from 80 to 110 degrees); let the roast rest at room temperature, uncovered, for exactly 30 minutes. (At this point the roast's internal temperature will range from 115 to 140 degrees.) After this 30-minute rest, remove the thermometer, return the meat to the oven, and roast until the thickest part of the roast reaches an internal temperature of 140 to 145 degrees, 15 to 30 minutes longer, depending on the roast's internal temperature at the end of the resting period. Since the roast may cook unevenly, take temperature readings from a couple of locations, each time plunging the thermometer into the center of the meat and waiting 15 seconds.

4. Let the roast stand at room temperature, uncovered, for 15 to 20 minutes to finish cooking. (The temperature should register 150 degrees.) Remove the twine, slice the meat thin, and serve with the sauce, if using.

Mustard-Shallot Sauce with Thyme

MAKES ABOUT 1 CUP

Start making the sauce as soon as the roast comes out of the oven for the second time. Use a grainy, or country-style, mustard in this recipe. For extra body and richness, swirl another tablespoon or two of softened butter into the finished sauce.

- 2 tablespoons unsalted butter (see note)
- 4 medium shallots, minced (about ¾ cup)
- ¾ cup dry white wine or dry vermouth
- 1 cup low-sodium chicken broth
- ¾ teaspoon minced fresh thyme leaves or ¼ teaspoon dried thyme, crumbled
- ¼ cup whole grain mustard (see note)

Melt the butter in a medium skillet over medium-high heat. Add the shallots and sauté until softened, 3 to 4 minutes. Add the wine and boil until nearly evaporated, 8 to 10 minutes. Add the broth and thyme; boil until reduced by one third, about 5 minutes. Remove the pan from the heat and stir in the mustard. Serve immediately.

HAM

WHY THIS RECIPE WORKS: Fresh ham is not cured like a Smithfield ham or salted and air-dried like prosciutto. It's not pressed or molded like a canned ham, and it's not smoked like a country ham. In fact, some people think there's no such thing as "fresh" ham. There is—and we wanted to figure out the best way to cook it so we'd end up with a roasted ham that boasted rich, moist meat and crackling crisp skin

Fresh hams are large, so they're usually cut in half and sold as either the sirloin or the shank end; we chose the latter for its ease of carving. But even cut into these smaller roasts, fresh ham needs a long time in the oven, so the danger is drying out the meat. To prevent this, we brined our ham overnight. A garlic and herb rub added further flavor. We positioned the ham face down on a rack in a roasting pan; the rack allowed the heat to circulate all around the ham for more even cooking. A brief roasting at a high temperature followed by longer cooking at a lower temperature produced crunchy skin and succulent meat. The crowning touch was a sweet glaze, which we brushed on periodically while the meat roasted.

Roast Fresh Ham

SERVES 8 TO 10

Fresh ham comes from the pig's hind leg. Because a whole leg is quite large, it is usually cut into two sections. The sirloin, or butt, end is harder to carve than our favorite, the shank end. If you don't have room in your refrigerator, brine the ham in an insulated cooler or a small plastic garbage can; add five or six freezer packs to the brine to keep it well cooled.

ROAST

- 1 (6 to 8-pound) bone-in fresh half ham with skin, preferably shank end, rinsed (see note)

BRINE

- 3 cups packed brown sugar
- 2 cups table salt
- 2 heads garlic, cloves separated, lightly crushed and peeled
- 10 bay leaves
- ½ cup black peppercorns, crushed

GARLIC AND HERB RUB

- 1 cup lightly packed fresh sage leaves
- ½ cup parsley leaves
- ¼ cup olive oil
- 8 medium garlic cloves, peeled
- ½ tablespoon ground black pepper
- 1½ teaspoons table salt

GLAZE

- 1 recipe glaze (recipes follow)

1. FOR THE ROAST: Carefully slice through the skin and fat with a serrated knife, making a 1-inch diamond pattern. Be careful not to cut into the meat.

2. FOR THE BRINE: In a large container, dissolve the brown sugar and salt in 2 gallons cold water. Add the garlic, bay leaves, and crushed peppercorns. Submerge the ham in the brine and refrigerate for 8 to 24 hours.

3. Set a large disposable roasting pan on a baking sheet for extra support; place a flat wire rack in the roasting pan. Remove the ham from the brine; rinse under cold water and dry thoroughly with paper towels. Place the ham, wide cut side down, on the rack. (If using the sirloin end, place the ham skin side up.) Let the ham stand, uncovered, at room temperature for 1 hour.

4. FOR THE RUB: Meanwhile, adjust an oven rack to the lowest position and heat the oven to 500 degrees. Process the sage, parsley, oil, garlic, pepper, and salt in a food processor until the mixture forms a smooth paste, about 30 seconds. Rub all sides of the ham with the paste.

5. Roast the ham at 500 degrees for 20 minutes. Reduce the oven temperature to 350 degrees and continue to roast, brushing the ham with the glaze every 45 minutes, until the center of the ham registers 145 to 150 degrees on an instant-read thermometer, about 2½ hours longer. Remove from the oven and tent the ham loosely with foil and let stand until the center of the ham registers 155 to 160 degrees, 30 to 40 minutes. Carve and serve.

Cider and Brown Sugar Glaze
MAKES ABOUT 1⅓ CUPS

- 1 cup apple cider
- 2 cups packed brown sugar
- 5 whole cloves

Bring the cider, brown sugar, and cloves to a boil in a small saucepan over high heat; reduce the heat to medium-low and simmer until syrupy and reduced to about 1⅓ cups, 5 to 7 minutes. (The glaze will thicken as it cools between bastings; cook over medium heat about 1 minute, stirring once or twice, before using.)

Spicy Pineapple-Ginger Glaze
MAKES ABOUT 1⅓ CUPS

- 1 cup pineapple juice
- 2 cups packed brown sugar
- 1 (1-inch) piece fresh ginger, grated (about 1 tablespoon)
- 1 tablespoon red pepper flakes

Bring the pineapple juice, brown sugar, ginger, and red pepper flakes to a boil in a small saucepan over high heat; reduce the heat to medium-low and simmer until syrupy and reduced to about 1⅓ cups, 5 to 7 minutes. (The glaze will thicken as it cools between bastings; cook over medium heat about 1 minute, stirring once or twice, before using.)

Orange, Cinnamon, and Star Anise Glaze
MAKES ABOUT 1⅓ CUPS

- 1 cup fresh orange juice plus 1 tablespoon grated zest from 2 large oranges
- 2 cups packed brown sugar
- 4 pods star anise
- 1 (3-inch) cinnamon stick

Bring the orange juice, zest, brown sugar, star anise, and cinnamon stick to a boil in a small nonreactive saucepan over high heat; reduce the heat to medium-low and simmer until syrupy and reduced to about 1⅓ cups, 5 to 7 minutes. (The glaze will thicken as it cools between bastings; cook over medium heat about 1 minute, stirring once or twice, before using.)

Coca-Cola Glaze with Lime and Jalapeño
MAKES ABOUT 1⅓ CUPS

- 1 cup Coca-Cola
- ¼ cup fresh lime juice from 2 limes
- 2 cups packed brown sugar
- 2 medium jalapeño chiles, cut crosswise into ¼-inch-thick slices

Bring the Coca-Cola, lime juice, brown sugar, and jalapeños to a boil in a small nonreactive saucepan over high heat; reduce the heat to medium-low and simmer until syrupy and reduced to about 1⅓ cups, 5 to 7 minutes. (The glaze will thicken as it cools between bastings; heat over medium heat about 1 minute, stirring once or twice, before using.)

GLAZED HOLIDAY HAM

WHY THIS RECIPE WORKS: Nothing could be easier than heating up a cured ham, right? Well, we've made enough of them to know that as easy as it may be, the results are often leathery meat with an overly sweet glaze. We wanted to revisit the way to cook this roast to get moist meat accompanied by a glaze that didn't overwhelm it.

We have found that bone-in hams, labeled "with natural juices," have the best flavor, and spiral-sliced ones make carving a cinch. We knew that the longer the ham spent in the oven, the greater the chances we'd end up with dried-out meat, so we focused on reducing the cooking time. First we soaked the ham in hot water so that it wouldn't be ice-cold when it went into the oven; this step saved a full hour. Roasting the ham in an oven bag further reduced the cooking time, and using the bag had the added advantage of holding in moisture. For the glaze, we threw out the packet that came with our ham and made a fruit-based glaze with just a touch of

sweetness to complement the moist, tender meat. This foolproof method will make the perfect holiday ham every time.

Glazed Spiral-Sliced Ham

SERVES 12 TO 14

You can bypass the 90-minute soaking time, but the heating time will increase to 18 to 20 minutes per pound for a cold ham. If there is a tear or hole in the ham's inner covering, wrap the ham in several layers of plastic wrap before soaking it in hot water. Instead of using the plastic oven bag, the ham may be placed cut side down in the roasting pan and covered tightly with foil, but you will need to add 3 to 4 minutes per pound to the heating time. If using an oven bag, be sure to cut slits in the bag so it does not burst.

- 1 (7 to 10-pound) spiral-sliced bone-in half ham
- 1 large plastic oven bag (see note)
- 1 recipe glaze (recipes follow)

1. Leaving the ham's inner plastic or foil covering intact, place the ham in a large container and cover with hot tap water; set aside for 45 minutes. Drain and cover again with hot tap water; set aside for another 45 minutes.

2. Adjust an oven rack to the lowest position and heat the oven to 250 degrees. Unwrap the ham; remove and discard the plastic disk covering the bone. Place the ham in the oven bag. Gather the top of the bag tightly so the bag fits snugly around the ham, tie the bag, and trim the excess plastic. Set the ham, cut side down, in a large roasting pan and cut four slits in the top of the bag with a paring knife.

3. Bake the ham until the center registers 100 degrees on an instant-read thermometer, 1 to 1½ hours (about 10 minutes per pound).

4. Remove the ham from the oven and increase the oven temperature to 350 degrees. Cut open the oven bag and roll back the sides to expose the ham. Brush the ham with one-third of the glaze and return to the oven until the glaze becomes sticky, about 10 minutes (if the glaze is too thick to brush, return it to the heat to loosen).

5. Remove the ham from the oven, transfer it to a carving board, and brush the entire ham with another third of the glaze. Let the ham rest, loosely tented with foil, for 15 minutes. While the ham rests, heat the remaining third of the glaze with 4 to 6 tablespoons of the ham juices until it forms a thick but fluid sauce. Carve and serve the ham, passing the sauce at the table.

Maple-Orange Glaze

MAKES 1 CUP

- ¾ cup maple syrup
- ½ cup orange marmalade
- 2 tablespoons unsalted butter
- 1 tablespoon Dijon mustard
- 1 teaspoon ground black pepper
- ¼ teaspoon ground cinnamon

Combine all the ingredients in a small saucepan. Cook over medium heat, stirring occasionally, until the mixture is thick, syrupy, and reduced to 1 cup, 5 to 10 minutes; set aside.

Cherry-Port Glaze

MAKES 1 CUP

- ½ cup ruby port
- ½ cup cherry preserves
- 1 cup packed dark brown sugar
- 1 teaspoon ground black pepper

Simmer the port in a small saucepan over medium heat until reduced to 2 tablespoons, about 5 minutes. Add the remaining ingredients and cook, stirring occasionally, until the sugar dissolves and the mixture is thick, syrupy, and reduced to 1 cup, 5 to 10 minutes; set aside.

CHAPTER 10

FAVORITE WAYS
WITH FISH

Crunchy Oven-Fried Fish 150

   Sweet and Tangy Tartar Sauce

Fish and Chips 151

Pan-Seared Salmon 152

   Sweet-and-Sour Chutney

Broiled Salmon with Mustard and Crisp Dilled Crust 153

Poached Salmon with Herb and Caper Vinaigrette 154

Oven-Roasted Salmon 155

   Tangerine and Ginger Relish

   Fresh Tomato Relish

   Spicy Cucumber Relish

Pan-Roasted Halibut Steaks 157

   Chipotle-Garlic Butter with Lime and Cilantro

   Chunky Cherry Tomato–Basil Vinaigrette

Pan-Seared Sesame-Crusted Tuna Steaks 158

   Ginger-Soy Sauce with Scallions

   Avocado-Orange Salsa

Pan-Seared Shrimp 160

Pan-Seared Shrimp with Garlic-Lemon Butter 160

Pan-Seared Shrimp with Ginger-Hoisin Glaze 160

Pan-Seared Shrimp with Chipotle-Lime Glaze 160

Garlicky Shrimp with Buttered Bread Crumbs 161

Spanish-Style Garlic Shrimp 162

Shrimp Cocktail 163

Shrimp Salad 164

Shrimp Salad with Roasted Red Pepper and Basil 164

Shrimp Salad with Avocado and Orange 164

Flambéed Pan-Roasted Lobster 165

Maryland Crab Cakes 166

   Creamy Chipotle Chile Sauce

Crab Towers with Avocado and Gazpacho Salsas 168

Indoor Clambake 169

SUPER-CRISPY OVEN-FRIED FISH

WHY THIS RECIPE WORKS: The golden brown coating and moist, flaky flesh of batter-fried fish come at a price: the oil. Cooks have turned to the oven to avoid the bother of deep-fat frying, but oven-frying often falls short. The coating never gets very crisp and the fish usually ends up overcooked. We aimed to put the crunch back into oven-frying.

We used thick fillets so that the fish and coating would finish cooking at the same time. Flaky cod and haddock provided the best contrast to the crunchy exterior we envisioned. A conventional bound breading—flour, egg, and fresh bread crumbs—wasn't as crisp as we wanted, so we toasted the bread crumbs with a little butter. (Precooking the crumbs also ensured we wouldn't have to overcook the fish to get really crunchy crumbs.) Placing the coated fish on a wire rack while baking allowed air to circulate all around the fish, crisping all sides. We boosted flavor in two ways, adding shallots and parsley to the breading and horseradish, cayenne, and paprika to the egg wash. As a final touch, we whipped up a creamy tartar sauce with mayonnaise, capers, and sweet relish.

Crunchy Oven-Fried Fish

SERVES 4

To prevent overcooking, buy fish fillets that are at least 1 inch thick. The bread crumbs can be made up to 3 days in advance and stored at room temperature in a tightly sealed container (allow to cool fully before storing). Serve the dish with Sweet and Tangy Tartar Sauce (recipe follows).

- 4 slices high-quality white sandwich bread, torn into quarters
- 2 tablespoons unsalted butter, melted
  Table salt and ground black pepper
- 2 tablespoons minced fresh parsley leaves
- 1 small shallot, minced (about 1 tablespoon)
- ¼ cup plus 5 tablespoons unbleached all-purpose flour
- 2 large eggs
- 3 tablespoons mayonnaise
- 2 teaspoons prepared horseradish (optional)
- ½ teaspoon paprika
- ¼ teaspoon cayenne pepper (optional)
- 1¼ pounds cod, haddock, or other thick whitefish fillets (1 to 1½ inches thick), cut into 4 pieces (see note)
  Lemon wedges, for serving

1. Adjust an oven rack to the middle position and heat the oven to 350 degrees. Pulse the bread, butter, ¼ teaspoon salt, and ¼ teaspoon black pepper in a food processor until the bread is coarsely ground, about 8 pulses. Transfer to a rimmed baking sheet and bake until deep golden brown and dry, about 15 minutes, stirring twice during the baking time. Cool the crumbs to room temperature, about 10 minutes. Transfer the crumbs to a pie plate and toss with the parsley and shallot. Increase the oven temperature to 425 degrees.

2. Place ¼ cup of the flour in a second pie plate. In a third pie plate, whisk together the eggs, mayonnaise, horseradish (if using), paprika, cayenne (if using), and ¼ teaspoon black pepper until combined; whisk in the remaining 5 tablespoons flour until smooth.

3. Spray a wire rack with vegetable oil spray and place over a rimmed baking sheet. Dry the fish thoroughly with paper towels and season with salt and black pepper. Dredge 1 fillet in the flour; shake off the excess. Using tongs, coat the fillet with the egg mixture. Coat all sides of the fillet with the bread-crumb mixture, pressing gently so that a thick layer of crumbs adheres to the fish. Transfer the breaded fish to the wire rack. Repeat with the remaining 3 fillets.

4. Bake the fish until the center of the fillets registers 140 degrees on an instant-read thermometer, 18 to 25 minutes. Using a thin spatula, transfer the fillets to individual plates and serve immediately with the lemon wedges.

Sweet and Tangy Tartar Sauce
MAKES ABOUT 1 CUP

This sauce can be refrigerated, tightly covered, for up to 1 week.

- ¾ cup mayonnaise
- 2 tablespoons drained capers, minced
- 2 tablespoons sweet pickle relish
- 1 small shallot, minced (about 1 tablespoon)
- 1½ teaspoons distilled white vinegar
- ½ teaspoon Worcestershire sauce
- ½ teaspoon ground black pepper

Mix all the ingredients together in a small bowl. Cover the bowl with plastic wrap and let sit until the flavors meld, about 15 minutes. Stir again before serving.

FISH AND CHIPS

WHY THIS RECIPE WORKS: The fish and chips served at most American pubs are mediocre at best. But the alternative—deep-frying fish at home—can be a hassle and a mess. Plus, by the time the fries finish frying, the fish is cold. We wanted fish with a light, crisp crust and moist interior, and we wanted to serve both the fish and the fries at their prime.

Our first challenge was to come up with a batter that not only would protect the fish as it cooked (allowing it to steam gently) but would also provide the fish with a nicely crisp contrast. We discovered that a wet batter was the most effective way to coat and protect the fish. We liked beer—the traditional choice—as the liquid component. What was the best way to keep the coating crisp? The answer was a 3-1 ratio of flour to cornstarch, along with a teaspoon of baking powder. Still, the coating was so tender it puffed away from the fish as it cooked. A final coating of flour on top of the battered fish solved the problem.

To solve the second challenge—delivering the fish and fries while both are still hot—we cooked them alternately. First, we precooked the fries in the microwave, which not only lessened cooking time but removed excess moisture that could dilute the oil and diminish crisping. Then we gave the fries their first, quick fry in hot oil. While the potatoes were draining, we battered and fried the fish. Then, as the fish drained, we gave the fries a quick final fry.

Fish and Chips
SERVES 4

For safety, use a Dutch oven with at least a 7-quart capacity. Serve with traditional malt vinegar or with Sweet and Tangy Tartar Sauce (at left).

- 3 pounds russet potatoes (about 4 large potatoes), peeled, ends and sides squared off, and cut lengthwise into ½-inch by ½-inch fries
- 3 quarts plus ¼ cup peanut oil or canola oil
- 1½ cups unbleached all-purpose flour
- ½ cup cornstarch
- ½ teaspoon cayenne pepper
- ½ teaspoon paprika
- ⅛ teaspoon ground black pepper
   Table salt
- 1 teaspoon baking powder
- 1½ pounds cod or other thick whitefish fillets, such as hake or haddock, cut into eight 3-ounce pieces about 1 inch thick
- 1½ cups (12 ounces) cold beer

1. Place the cut fries in a large microwave-safe bowl, toss with ¼ cup of the oil, and cover with plastic wrap. Microwave on high power until the potatoes are partially translucent and pliable but still offer some resistance when pierced with the tip of a paring knife, 6 to 8 minutes, tossing them with a rubber spatula halfway through the cooking time. Carefully pull back the plastic wrap from the side farthest from you and drain the potatoes into a large mesh strainer set over a sink. Rinse well under cold running water. Spread the potatoes on a few clean kitchen towels and pat dry. Let rest until the fries have reached room temperature, at least 10 minutes or up to 1 hour.

2. While the fries cool, whisk the flour, cornstarch, cayenne, paprika, black pepper, and 2 teaspoons salt in a large mixing bowl; transfer ¾ cup of the mixture to a rimmed baking sheet. Add the baking powder to the bowl and whisk to combine.

3. In a large Dutch oven fitted with a clip-on candy thermometer, heat 2 quarts more oil over medium heat to 350 degrees. Add the fries to the hot oil and increase the heat to high. Fry, stirring with a mesh spider or slotted metal spoon, until the potatoes turn light golden and just begin to brown at the corners, 6 to 8 minutes. Transfer the fries to a thick paper bag or paper towels to drain.

4. Reduce the heat to medium-high, add the remaining 1 quart oil, and heat the oil to 375 degrees. Meanwhile,

thoroughly dry the fish with paper towels and dredge each piece in the flour mixture on the baking sheet; transfer the pieces to a wire rack, shaking off any excess flour. Add 1¼ cups of the beer to the flour mixture in the mixing bowl and stir until the mixture is just combined (the batter will be lumpy). Add the remaining ¼ cup beer as needed, 1 tablespoon at a time, whisking after each addition, until the batter falls from the whisk in a thin, steady stream and leaves a faint trail across the surface of the batter. Using tongs, dip 1 piece of fish in the batter and let the excess run off, shaking gently. Place the battered fish back on the baking sheet with the flour mixture and turn to coat both sides. Repeat with the remaining fish, keeping the pieces in a single layer on the baking sheet.

5. When the oil reaches 375 degrees, increase the heat to high and add the battered fish to the oil with the tongs, gently shaking off any excess flour. Fry, stirring occasionally, until golden brown, 7 to 8 minutes. Transfer the fish to a thick paper bag or paper towels to drain. Allow the oil to return to 375 degrees.

6. Add all of the fries back to the oil and fry until golden brown and crisp, 3 to 5 minutes. Transfer to a fresh paper bag or paper towels to drain. Season the fries with salt to taste and serve immediately with the fish.

PAN-SEARED SALMON

WHY THIS RECIPE WORKS: We love salmon cooked on the grill, but when the weather makes grilling unpleasant or impossible, we don't want to forgo serving this flavorful fish. We wanted a great recipe for pan-seared salmon with a crisp, even, golden brown crust.

Preheating the skillet over high heat and using just a teaspoon of neutral canola or vegetable oil (butter tended to burn and was too rich) produced the brown crust we wanted—no flour or other coating was necessary. To prevent burning, we turned the heat down just after adding the fillets. Allowing plenty of space around the fillets kept them from merely steaming. We flipped the fillets when they turned opaque from the bottom to about halfway up; there was no need to shake the pan or move the fish until then. We found that removing the salmon just before it was done prevented overcooking; residual heat brought it up to serving temperature. Simply seasoned and perfectly cooked, these salmon fillets were easy to make and just as good as any cooked on the grill.

Pan-Seared Salmon

SERVES 4

To ensure uniform pieces of fish that cook at the same rate, buy a whole center-cut fillet and cut it into four pieces. With the addition of the fish fillets, the pan temperature drops; compensate for the heat loss by keeping the heat on high for 30 seconds after adding them. If cooking two or three fillets instead of the full recipe of four, use a 10-inch skillet and medium-high heat for both preheating the pan and cooking the salmon. A splatter screen helps reduce the mess of pan-searing.

    1   (1¾ to 2-pound) skinless salmon fillet, about 1½ inches
        at the thickest part (see note)
    1   teaspoon canola or vegetable oil
        Table salt and ground black pepper
        Sweet-and-Sour Chutney (recipe follows) or lemon
        wedges, for serving

1. Use a sharp knife to trim any whitish fat from the belly of the fillet and cut it into four equal pieces. Heat the oil in a 12-inch skillet over high heat until shimmering but not smoking. Sprinkle the salmon with salt and pepper.

2. Add the fillets, skin-side down, and cook, without moving the fillets, until the pan regains lost heat, about 30 seconds. Reduce the heat to medium-high; continue to cook until the skin side is well browned and the bottom half of the fillets turns opaque, 4½ minutes. Turn the fillets and cook, without moving them, until they are no longer translucent on the exterior and are firm, but not hard, when gently squeezed, 3 minutes for medium-rare and 3½ minutes for medium. Remove the fillets from the pan; let stand for 1 minute. Pat the fillets with a paper towel to absorb excess fat on the surface, if desired. Serve immediately with the chutney or the lemon wedges.

Sweet-and-Sour Chutney

MAKES ABOUT ⅓ CUP

A little of this intensely flavored condiment goes a long way.

- 1 teaspoon fennel seeds
- ½ teaspoon ground cumin
- ½ teaspoon ground coriander
- ¼ teaspoon ground cardamom
- ¼ teaspoon paprika
- ¼ teaspoon table salt
- 2 teaspoons olive oil
- ½ medium onion, minced (about ½ cup)
- ¼ cup red wine vinegar
- 1 tablespoon sugar
- 1 tablespoon minced fresh parsley leaves

Mix the fennel, cumin, coriander, cardamom, paprika, and salt in a small bowl; set aside. Heat the oil in a medium skillet over medium heat; sauté the onion until soft, 3 to 4 minutes. Add the reserved spice mixture; sauté until fragrant, about 1 minute more. Increase the heat to medium-high and add the vinegar, sugar, and 2 tablespoons water; cook until the mixture reduces by about one third and reaches a syrupy consistency, about 1½ minutes. Stir in the parsley. Serve with the salmon.

BROILED SALMON

WHY THIS RECIPE WORKS: Cooking an entire side of salmon in the oven often results in fish that is either soggy or chalky. We wanted to pull off a crowd-pleasing side of salmon that is moist and firm, with a golden crumb crust that contrasts with the flavorful fish.

Most of the time, we achieve a crisp crust on salmon through pan-searing in a skillet on the stovetop. With a crumb crust, it made sense to use the broiler. A plain bread crumb-topping seemed bland, but when we toasted the crumbs and mixed in crushed potato chips and chopped dill, the result was a crisp and flavorful coating. To get the

crumb mixture to adhere to the fish, we relied on a thin layer of mustard. One problem: the crust burned by the time the fish was cooking through. We switched gears and broiled the fish almost unadorned (save for salt, pepper, and a bit of olive oil) until it was nearly done, then spread on the mustard and crumbs for a second run under the broiler to crisp the crust. To get the fish onto a platter in one piece, we lined a baking sheet with heavy-duty foil before adding the fish, creating a sling with which we could move it. Our two-step broiling method resulted in firm, moist fish and a flavorful crunchy topping.

Broiled Salmon with Mustard and Crisp Dilled Crust

SERVES 8 TO 10

If you prefer to cook a smaller 2-pound fillet, ask to have it cut from the thick center of the fillet, not the thin tail end, and begin checking doneness a minute earlier.

- 3 slices high-quality white sandwich bread, torn into quarters
- 4 ounces plain high-quality potato chips, crushed into rough ⅛-inch pieces (about 1 cup)
- 6 tablespoons chopped fresh dill
- 1 whole side salmon fillet, about 3½ pounds, white belly fat trimmed
- 1 teaspoon olive oil
  Table salt and ground black pepper
- 3 tablespoons Dijon mustard

1. Adjust one oven rack to the top position (about 3 inches from the heat source) and the second rack to the upper-middle position; heat the oven to 400 degrees.

2. Pulse the bread in a food processor to fairly even ¼-inch pieces about the size of Grape-Nuts cereal (you should have about 1 cup), about 10 pulses. Spread the

crumbs evenly on a rimmed baking sheet; toast on the lower oven rack, shaking the pan once or twice, until golden brown and crisp, 4 to 5 minutes. Toss the bread crumbs, crushed potato chips, and dill together in a small bowl; set aside.

3. Change the oven setting to broil. Cut a piece of heavy-duty foil 6 inches longer than the fillet. Fold the foil lengthwise in thirds and place lengthwise on a rimmed baking sheet; position the salmon lengthwise on the foil, allowing the excess foil to overhang the baking sheet. Rub the fillet evenly with the oil; sprinkle with salt and pepper. Broil the salmon on the upper rack until the surface is spotty brown and the outer ½ inch of the thick end is opaque when gently flaked with a paring knife, 9 to 11 minutes. Remove the baking sheet from the oven, spread the fish evenly with the mustard, and press the bread-crumb mixture onto the fish. Return the baking sheet to the lower oven rack and continue broiling until the crust is deep golden brown, about 1 minute longer.

4. Grasping the ends of the foil sling, lift the salmon, sling and all, onto a platter. Slide an offset spatula under the thick end. Grasp the foil, press the spatula against the foil, and slide it under the fish down to the thin end, loosening the entire side of fish. Grasp the foil again, hold the spatula perpendicular to the fish to stabilize it, and pull the foil out from under the fish. Wipe the platter clean with a damp paper towel. Serve the salmon immediately.

FLAVORFUL POACHED SALMON

WHY THIS RECIPE WORKS: When salmon is poached incorrectly, not only is it dry, but the flavor is so washed out that not even the richest sauce can redeem it. We wanted irresistibly supple salmon accented by the delicate flavor of the poaching liquid, accompanied by a simple pan sauce—all in under half an hour.

We started our tests with a classic court-bouillon, which is made by boiling water, wine, herbs, vegetables, and aromatics and then straining out the solids. But discarding all those vegetables seemed wasteful for a simple weeknight supper. Using less liquid—poaching the salmon in just enough liquid to come half an inch up the side of the fillets—allowed us to cut back on the quantity of vegetables and aromatics; in fact, a couple of shallots, a few herbs, and some wine were all we needed to solve the flavor issue. However, the part of the salmon that wasn't submerged in liquid needed to be steamed for thorough cooking, and the low cooking temperature required to poach the salmon evenly didn't create enough steam. The solution was to increase the ratio of wine to water. The additional alcohol lowered the liquid's boiling point, producing more vapor even at the lower temperature. Meanwhile, the bottom of the fillets had the opposite problem, overcooking due to direct contact with the pan. Resting the salmon fillets on top of lemon slices provided sufficient insulation. For a finishing touch, after removing the salmon, we reduced the liquid and added a few tablespoons of olive oil to create an easy vinaigrette-style sauce.

Poached Salmon with Herb and Caper Vinaigrette

SERVES 4

To ensure uniform pieces of fish that cook at the same rate, buy a whole center-cut fillet and cut it into four pieces. If a skinless whole fillet is unavailable, remove the skin yourself or follow the recipe as directed with a skin-on fillet, adding 3 to 4 minutes to the cooking time in step 2.

  2 **lemons**
  1 **large shallot, minced (about 4 tablespoons)**
  2 **tablespoons minced fresh parsley leaves, stems reserved**
  2 **tablespoons minced fresh tarragon leaves, stems reserved**
  ½ **cup dry white wine**
  ½ **cup water**
  1 **(1¾ to 2-pound) skinless salmon fillet, about 1½ inches at the thickest part (see note)**
  2 **tablespoons capers, rinsed and roughly chopped**
  2 **tablespoons extra-virgin olive oil**
  1 **tablespoon honey**
    Table salt and ground black pepper

1. Cut the top and bottom off 1 lemon; cut the lemon into eight to ten ¼-inch-thick slices. Cut the remaining lemon into eight wedges and set aside. Arrange the lemon slices in a single layer across the bottom of a 12-inch skillet. Scatter 2 tablespoons of the shallot and herb stems evenly over the lemon slices. Add the wine and water.

2. Use a sharp knife to trim any whitish fat from the belly of the fillet and cut it into four equal pieces. Place the salmon fillets in the skillet, skinned side down, on top of the lemon slices. Set the pan over high heat and bring the liquid to a simmer. Reduce the heat to low, cover, and cook until the sides of the fillets are opaque but the center of the thickest part of the fillets is still translucent (or until the thickest part of the fillets registers 125 degrees on an instant-read thermometer), 11 to 16 minutes. Remove the pan from the heat and, using a spatula, carefully transfer the salmon and lemon slices to a paper towel–lined plate. Tent loosely with foil.

3. Return the pan to high heat and simmer the cooking liquid until slightly thickened and reduced to 2 tablespoons, 4 to 5 minutes. Meanwhile, combine the remaining 2 tablespoons shallot, the minced herbs, capers, olive oil, and honey in a medium bowl. Strain the reduced cooking liquid through a fine-mesh strainer into the bowl with the herb-caper mixture, pressing on the solids to extract as much liquid as possible. Whisk to combine

and season with salt and pepper to taste.

4. Season the salmon lightly with salt and pepper. Using a spatula, carefully lift and tilt the salmon fillets to remove the lemon slices. Place the salmon on a serving platter or individual plates and spoon the vinaigrette over the top. Serve, passing the reserved lemon wedges separately.

OVEN-ROASTED SALMON

WHY THIS RECIPE WORKS: Roasting a salmon fillet can create a brown exterior, but often at the risk of a dry, overcooked interior. The best roasted salmon should have moist, flavorful flesh inside, with a contrasting crisp texture on the outside.

In order to ensure that the salmon fillets would cook evenly, we cut a whole center-cut fillet into four pieces. We roasted the fish at a low temperature and achieved the buttery flesh we were after, but no browning—and the fillets were a little mushy from the rendered fat. Taking the opposite approach, we put the fish on a preheated baking sheet and started the oven at a high temperature to firm up and brown the exterior. This gave us a crust, but we still needed to get rid of the fat; cutting slits in the skin released the fat rendered by the high heat. Lowering the temperature as soon as we put the fish in the oven enabled it to cook through gradually after the initial blast of heat, so it didn't dry out. Now we had the contrast between moist interior and crisp brown exterior that we wanted. Salmon is rich and flavorful all on its own, but we devised a couple of easy no-cook relishes that can be served alongside for even more flavor.

Oven-Roasted Salmon

SERVES 4

To ensure uniform pieces of fish that cook at the same rate, buy a whole center-cut fillet and cut it into four pieces. If your knife is not sharp enough to easily cut through the skin, try a serrated knife. It is important to keep the skin on during cooking; remove it afterward if you choose not to serve it.

- 1 (1¾ to 2-pound) skin-on salmon fillet, about 1½ inches at the thickest part (see note)
- 2 teaspoons olive oil
  Table salt and ground black pepper
- 1 recipe relish (recipes follow)

1. Adjust an oven rack to the lowest position, place a rimmed baking sheet on the rack, and heat the oven to 500 degrees. Remove any whitish fat from the belly of the fillet and cut it into four equal pieces. Make four or five shallow slashes about an inch apart along the skin side of each piece, being careful not to cut into the flesh.

2. Pat the salmon dry with paper towels. Rub the fillets evenly with the oil and season liberally with salt and pepper. Reduce the oven temperature to 275 degrees and remove the baking sheet. Carefully place the salmon, skin-side down, on the baking sheet. Roast until the thickest part of the fillets is still translucent when cut into with a paring knife (or the thickest part of the fillets registers 125 degrees on an instant-read thermometer), 9 to 13 minutes. Transfer the fillets to individual plates or a platter. Top with relish and serve.

Tangerine and Ginger Relish
MAKES ABOUT 1¼ CUPS

- 4 tangerines, rind and pith removed and segments cut into ½-inch pieces (about 1 cup)
- 1 scallion, sliced thin (about ¼ cup)
- 1½ teaspoons minced or grated fresh ginger
- 2 teaspoons juice from 1 lemon
- 2 teaspoons extra-virgin olive oil
  Table salt and ground black pepper

1. Place the tangerines in a fine-mesh strainer set over a medium bowl and drain for 15 minutes.

2. Pour off all but 1 tablespoon tangerine juice from the bowl; whisk in the scallion, ginger, lemon juice, and oil. Stir in the tangerines and season with salt and pepper to taste.

Fresh Tomato Relish
MAKES ABOUT 1½ CUPS

- ¾ pound ripe tomatoes, cored, seeded, and cut into ¼-inch dice (about 1½ cups)
- 2 tablespoons chopped fresh basil leaves
- 1 small shallot, minced (about 1 tablespoon)
- 1 tablespoon extra-virgin olive oil
- 1 teaspoon red wine vinegar
- 1 small garlic clove, minced or pressed through a garlic press (about ½ teaspoon)
  Table salt and ground black pepper

Combine the tomatoes, basil, shallot, oil, vinegar, and garlic in a medium bowl. Season with salt and pepper to taste.

Spicy Cucumber Relish
MAKES ABOUT 2 CUPS

- 1 medium cucumber, peeled, seeded, and cut into ¼-inch dice (about 2 cups)
- 2 tablespoons minced fresh mint leaves
- 1 small shallot, minced (about 1 tablespoon)
- 1 serrano chile, seeds and ribs removed, chile minced (about 1 tablespoon)
- 1–2 tablespoons juice from 1 lime
  Table salt

Combine the cucumber, mint, shallot, chile, 1 tablespoon of the lime juice, and ¼ teaspoon salt in a medium bowl. Let sit at room temperature until the flavors meld, about 15 minutes. Season with additional lime juice and salt to taste.

PAN-ROASTED HALIBUT

WHY THIS RECIPE WORKS: Chefs often choose to braise halibut instead of pan-roasting or sautéing because this moist-heat cooking technique keeps the fish from drying out. The problem is that braising doesn't allow for browning, therefore producing a fish that the test kitchen considers bland-tasting. We didn't want to make any compromises on either texture or flavor, so we set out to develop a technique for pan-roasting halibut that would produce perfectly cooked, moist, and tender fish.

Halibut is most frequently sold as steaks, but there is quite a bit of range in size; to ensure that they cooked at the same rate, we chose steaks that were as close in size to each other as possible. We knew we could get a crust on the fish by pan-searing or oven-roasting, but neither technique proved satisfactory. A combination of the two proved best: browning on the stovetop and roasting in the oven. To be sure the steaks wouldn't overcook, we seared them on one side in a piping-hot skillet, then turned them over before placing them into the oven to finish cooking through. When they were done, the steaks were browned but still moist inside. To complement the lean fish, we paired the halibut with a rich flavored butter.

Pan-Roasted Halibut Steaks

SERVES 4 TO 6

If you plan to serve the fish with the flavored butter or vinaigrette (recipes follow), prepare it before cooking the fish. Even well-dried fish can cause the hot oil in the pan to splatter. You can minimize splattering by laying the halibut steaks in the pan gently and putting the edge closest to you in the pan first so that the far edge falls away from you.

2 tablespoons olive oil
2 (full) halibut steaks, about 1¼ inches thick and 10 to 12 inches long (about 2½ pounds total), gently rinsed, dried well with paper towels, and trimmed of cartilage at both ends (see photo)
  Table salt and ground black pepper
1 recipe flavored butter or vinaigrette (recipes follow)

NOTES FROM THE TEST KITCHEN

TRIMMING AND SERVING FULL HALIBUT STEAKS

BEFORE COOKING: Cut off the cartilage at each end of the steaks to ensure that they will fit neatly in the pan and diminish the likelihood that the small bones located there will wind up on your dinner plate.

BEFORE SERVING: Remove the skin from the cooked steaks and separate the quadrants of meat from the bone by slipping a spatula gently between them.

1. Adjust an oven rack to the middle position and heat the oven to 425 degrees. When the oven reaches 425 degrees, heat the oil in a 12-inch ovenproof skillet over high heat until the oil just begins to smoke.

2. Meanwhile, sprinkle both sides of the halibut steaks generously with salt and pepper. Reduce the heat to medium-high and swirl the oil in the pan to distribute; carefully lay the steaks in the pan and sear, without moving them, until spotty brown, about 4 minutes. (If the steaks are thinner than 1¼ inches, check browning at 3½ minutes; thicker steaks of 1½ inches may require extra time, so check at 4½ minutes.) Off the heat, flip the steaks over in the pan using two thin-bladed metal spatulas.

3. Transfer the skillet to the oven and roast until an instant-read thermometer inserted into the steaks reads 140 degrees and the fish flakes loosen and the flesh is opaque when checked with the tip of a paring knife, about 9 minutes (thicker steaks may take up to 10 minutes). Remove the skillet from the oven. Remove the skin from the cooked steaks and separate each quadrant of meat from the bones by slipping a spatula or knife gently between them (see photo). Transfer the fish to a warm platter and serve with the flavored butter or vinaigrette.

IS THAT PAN HOT YET? SHIMMER AND SMOKE

Pan-searing and sautéing both require you to heat the oil in the skillet to a certain heat level. But how do you know when the pan is hot enough? We find visual cues helpful and offer them in our recipes, as follows: When searing thick cuts of meat like a roast, steak, bone-in chop, or thick fish fillet, you want the pan *very* hot. Searing over high heat will give your food a well-browned crust. Look for wisps of smoke rising from the oil—this means the pan is ripping hot and ready. By contrast, when sautéing thin, delicate cuts of meat like cutlets, thin fish fillets, or vegetables such as onions, you want the oil to be just moderately hot. You'll know the pan is ready when the oil shimmers. Why does it make a difference? If you put a thin fillet into a smoking hot pan, the food will do more than sear—it will cook through before you've had time to flip it.

Chipotle-Garlic Butter with Lime and Cilantro

MAKES ABOUT ¼ CUP

- 4 tablespoons (½ stick) unsalted butter, softened
- 1 medium chipotle chile in adobo sauce, seeded and minced, plus 1 teaspoon adobo sauce
- 2 teaspoons minced fresh cilantro leaves
- 1 medium garlic clove, minced or pressed through a garlic press (about 1 teaspoon)
- 1 teaspoon honey
- 1 teaspoon grated zest from 1 lime
- ½ teaspoon table salt

Beat the butter with a fork until light and fluffy. Stir in the remaining ingredients until thoroughly combined. Dollop a portion of the butter over the pieces of hot cooked fish and allow the butter to melt. Serve immediately.

Chunky Cherry Tomato–Basil Vinaigrette

MAKES ABOUT 1½ CUPS

- ½ pint cherry or grape tomatoes, each tomato quartered (about 1 cup)
- ¼ teaspoon salt
- ¼ teaspoon ground black pepper
- 2 medium shallots, minced (about 6 tablespoons)
- 6 tablespoons extra-virgin olive oil
- 3 tablespoons juice from 1 lemon
- 2 tablespoons minced fresh basil leaves

Mix the tomatoes with the salt and pepper in a medium bowl; let stand until juicy and seasoned, about 10 minutes. Whisk the shallots, oil, lemon juice, and basil together in a small mixing bowl, pour the vinaigrette over the tomatoes, and toss to combine. Pour over the pieces of hot cooked fish and serve immediately.

PAN-SEARED TUNA STEAKS

WHY THIS RECIPE WORKS: Moist and rare in the middle with a seared crust, pan-seared tuna is a popular entrée in restaurants. This dish is so simple that we thought it would be easy to make at home, and set out to determine the best method.

Starting with high-quality tuna—sushi grade if possible—is paramount; we prefer the flavor of yellowfin. A thickness of at least an inch is necessary for the center of the tuna to be rare while the exterior browns. Before searing the tuna in a nonstick skillet, we rubbed the steaks with oil, then coated them with sesame seeds; the oil helped the seeds stick to the fish. The sesame seeds browned in the skillet and formed a beautiful, nutty-tasting crust. We learned that tuna, like beef, will continue to cook from residual heat when removed from the stove, so when the interior of the tuna was near the desired degree of doneness (about 110 degrees on an instant-read thermometer), we transferred it to a platter.

Pan-Seared Sesame-Crusted Tuna Steaks

SERVES 4

If you plan to serve the fish with the sauce or salsa (recipes follow), prepare it before cooking the fish. Most members of the test kitchen staff prefer their tuna steaks rare to medium-rare; the cooking times given in this recipe are for tuna steaks cooked to these two degrees of doneness. For tuna steaks cooked medium, observe the timing for

medium-rare, then tent the steaks loosely with foil for 5 minutes before slicing. If you prefer tuna steaks cooked so rare that they are still cold in the center, try to purchase steaks that are 1½ inches thick and cook them according to the timing below for rare steaks. Bear in mind, though, that the cooking times below are estimates; check for doneness by nicking the fish with a paring knife. To cook only two steaks, use half as many sesame seeds, reduce the amount of oil to 2 teaspoons both on the fish and in the pan, use a 10-inch nonstick skillet, and follow the same cooking times.

¾ cup sesame seeds

4 (8-ounce) tuna steaks, preferably yellowfin, about 1 inch thick (see note)

2 tablespoons vegetable oil

Table salt and ground black pepper

1 recipe sauce or salsa (recipes follow)

1. Spread the sesame seeds in a shallow baking dish or pie plate. Pat the tuna steaks dry with a paper towel; use 1 tablespoon of the oil to rub both sides of the steaks, then sprinkle them with salt and pepper. Press both sides of each steak in the sesame seeds to coat.

2. Heat the remaining 1 tablespoon oil in a 12-inch non-stick skillet over high heat until just beginning to smoke and swirl to coat the pan. Add the tuna steaks and cook 30 seconds without moving the steaks. Reduce the heat to medium-high and continue to cook until the seeds are golden brown, about 1½ minutes. Using tongs, flip the tuna steaks carefully and cook, without moving them, until golden brown on the second side and the centers register 110 degrees on an instant-read thermometer for rare (about 1½ minutes), or 120 degrees for medium-rare (about 3 minutes). Serve with the sauce or salsa.

Ginger-Soy Sauce with Scallions

MAKES ABOUT 1 CUP

If available, serve pickled ginger and wasabi, passed separately, with the tuna and this sauce.

¼ cup soy sauce

¼ cup rice vinegar

¼ cup water

1 medium scallion, sliced thin

2½ teaspoons sugar

2 teaspoons minced or grated fresh ginger

1½ teaspoons toasted sesame oil

½ teaspoon red pepper flakes

Combine all the ingredients in a small bowl, stirring to dissolve the sugar.

Avocado-Orange Salsa

MAKES ABOUT 1 CUP

To keep the avocado from discoloring, prepare this salsa just before you cook the tuna steaks.

1 large orange, cut into segments (see page 167)

1 ripe avocado, pitted, peeled, and diced medium (see page 280)

2 tablespoons minced red onion

2 tablespoons minced fresh cilantro leaves

4 teaspoons juice from 1 to 2 limes

1 small jalapeño chile, stemmed, seeded, and minced

Table salt

Combine all the ingredients, including salt to taste, in a small nonreactive bowl.

PAN-SEARED SHRIMP

WHY THIS RECIPE WORKS: A good recipe for pan-seared shrimp is hard to find. Of the handful of recipes we uncovered, the majority resulted in shrimp that were either dry and flavorless or pale, tough, and gummy. We wanted shrimp that were well caramelized but still moist, briny, and tender.

We peeled the shrimp first and tried using a brine to add moisture, but found that it inhibited browning. Instead, we seasoned the shrimp with salt, pepper, and sugar, which brought out their natural sweetness and aided in browning. We cooked the shrimp in batches in a large, piping-hot skillet and then paired them with thick, glazelike sauces with assertive ingredients and plenty of acidity as a foil for the shrimp's richness.

Pan-Seared Shrimp

SERVES 4

This recipe can also be prepared with large shrimp (31 to 40 per pound); the cooking time will be slightly shorter. Either a nonstick or a traditional skillet will work for this recipe, but a nonstick simplifies cleanup.

> 2 tablespoons vegetable oil
> 1½ pounds extra-large shrimp (21 to 25 per pound), peeled and deveined (see photos) (see note)
> ¼ teaspoon table salt
> ¼ teaspoon ground black pepper
> ⅛ teaspoon sugar

Heat 1 tablespoon of the oil in a 12-inch skillet over high heat until smoking. Meanwhile, toss the shrimp, salt, pepper, and sugar in a medium bowl. Add half of the shrimp to the pan in a single layer and cook until spotty brown and the edges turn pink, about 1 minute. Remove the pan from the heat. Using tongs, flip each shrimp and let stand until all but the very center is opaque, about 30 seconds. Transfer the shrimp to a large plate. Repeat with the remaining tablespoon oil and the remaining shrimp. After the second batch has stood off the heat, return the first batch to the skillet and toss to combine. Cover the skillet and let stand until the shrimp are cooked through, 1 to 2 minutes. Serve immediately.

Pan-Seared Shrimp with Garlic-Lemon Butter

Beat 3 tablespoons softened unsalted butter with a fork in a small bowl until light and fluffy. Stir in 1 medium garlic clove, minced or pressed through a garlic press, 1 tablespoon juice from 1 lemon, 2 tablespoons chopped fresh parsley leaves, and ⅛ teaspoon salt until combined. Follow the recipe for Pan-Seared Shrimp, adding the flavored butter when returning the first batch of shrimp to the skillet. Serve with lemon wedges, if desired.

Pan-Seared Shrimp with Ginger-Hoisin Glaze

Stir 2 tablespoons hoisin sauce, 1 tablespoon rice vinegar, 1½ teaspoons soy sauce, 2 teaspoons minced or grated fresh ginger, 2 teaspoons water, and 2 scallions, sliced thin, together in a small bowl. Follow the recipe for Pan-Seared Shrimp, substituting an equal amount of red pepper flakes for the black pepper and adding the hoisin mixture when returning the first batch of shrimp to the skillet.

Pan-Seared Shrimp with Chipotle-Lime Glaze

Stir 1 chipotle chile in adobo, minced, 2 teaspoons adobo sauce, 4 teaspoons brown sugar, 2 tablespoons lime juice from 1 lime, and 2 tablespoons chopped fresh cilantro leaves together in a small bowl. Follow the recipe for Pan-Seared Shrimp, adding the chipotle mixture when returning the first batch of shrimp to the skillet.

NOTES FROM THE TEST KITCHEN

DEVEINING SHRIMP

1. After removing the shell, use a paring knife to make a shallow cut along the back of the shrimp so that the vein is exposed.

2. Use the tip of the knife to lift the vein out of the shrimp. Discard the vein by wiping the blade against a paper towel.

GARLICKY SHRIMP WITH BREAD CRUMBS

WHY THIS RECIPE WORKS: Just about every all-purpose cookbook includes a recipe for a casserole of shrimp in a sherry-garlic sauce topped with bread crumbs, but the ones we tried produced rubbery shrimp and gluey toppings. We wanted all the potent flavors and contrasting textures that the name of this dish promises—tender, moist shrimp infused with garlic and blanketed with crisp, buttery bread crumbs.

Most recipes call for cooking the shrimp twice, first poaching them on the stovetop and then baking them in the casserole dish. No wonder they're usually overdone! Our experiments with skipping the poaching weren't very successful—the shrimp were just plain bland—so we abandoned the oven altogether and decided to make the entire dish in a skillet on top of the stove. After searing the shrimp on one side, sprinkled with a pinch of sugar to promote browning, we removed them to build the sauce; we would add the shrimp back at the end to heat through and finish cooking. For the sauce, we started with garlic. Sherry alone tasted too boozy, so we cut it with clam juice, which underscored the briny flavor of the shrimp. A pinch of flour and some butter thickened the sauce, and lemon juice brightened everything up. A chewy supermarket baguette made the perfect buttery bread crumbs; sprinkled on at the last minute, they were sturdy enough to stay crisp on the saucy shrimp. Our modernized skillet "casserole" was definitely an improvement on the tired old version.

Garlicky Shrimp with Buttered Bread Crumbs

SERVES 4

Vermouth can be substituted for the sherry. If using vermouth, increase the amount to ½ cup and reduce the amount of clam juice to ½ cup. To prepare this recipe in a 10-inch skillet, brown the shrimp in three batches for about 2 minutes each, using 2 teaspoons oil per batch. Serve the shrimp with rice and either broccoli or asparagus.

1 (3-inch) piece baguette, cut into small pieces
5 tablespoons unsalted butter, cut into 5 pieces
1 small shallot, minced (about 1 tablespoon)
  Table salt and ground black pepper
2 tablespoons minced fresh parsley leaves
2 pounds extra-large shrimp (21 to 25 per pound), peeled and deveined (see page 160)
¼ teaspoon sugar
4 teaspoons vegetable oil
4 medium garlic cloves, minced or pressed through a garlic press (about 4 teaspoons)
⅛ teaspoon red pepper flakes
2 teaspoons unbleached all-purpose flour
⅔ cup bottled clam juice
⅓ cup dry sherry (see note)
2 teaspoons juice from 1 lemon, plus lemon wedges for serving

1. Pulse the bread in a food processor until coarsely ground, about 8 pulses; you should have about 1 cup crumbs. Melt 1 tablespoon of the butter in a 12-inch nonstick skillet over medium heat. Add the crumbs, shallot, ⅛ teaspoon salt, and ⅛ teaspoon pepper. Cook, stirring occasionally, until the bread crumbs are golden brown, 7 to 10 minutes. Stir in 1 tablespoon of the parsley and transfer to a plate to cool. Wipe out the skillet with paper towels.

2. Pat the shrimp dry with paper towels and toss with the sugar, ¼ teaspoon salt, and ¼ teaspoon pepper in a bowl. Return the skillet to high heat, add 2 teaspoons of the oil, and heat until shimmering. Add half of the shrimp in a single layer and cook until spotty brown and the edges turn pink, about 3 minutes (do not flip the shrimp). Remove the pan from heat and transfer the shrimp to a large plate. Wipe out the skillet with paper towels. Repeat with the remaining 2 teaspoons oil and remaining shrimp; transfer the shrimp to the plate.

3. Return the skillet to medium heat and add 1 tablespoon more butter. When melted, add the garlic and red pepper flakes; cook, stirring frequently, until the garlic just begins to color, about 1 minute. Add the flour and

cook, stirring frequently, for 1 minute. Increase the heat to medium-high and slowly whisk in the clam juice and sherry. Bring to a simmer and cook until the mixture reduces to ¾ cup, 3 to 4 minutes. Whisk in the remaining 3 tablespoons butter, 1 tablespoon at a time. Stir in the lemon juice and remaining 1 tablespoon parsley.

4. Reduce the heat to medium-low, return the shrimp to the pan, and toss to combine. Cook, covered, until the shrimp are pink and cooked through, 2 to 3 minutes. Uncover and sprinkle with the toasted bread crumbs. Serve with the lemon wedges.

SIZZLING GARLIC SHRIMP

WHY THIS RECIPE WORKS: Sizzling *gambas al ajillo* is a tempting dish served in tapas bars. We knew we would have to make some adjustments to re-create this dish as an appetizer to serve at home, but our work would pay off when we could savor the juicy shrimp in spicy, garlic-infused oil.

The shrimp in the Spanish original are completely submerged in oil and cooked slowly. We didn't want to use that much oil, so we added just enough to a skillet to come halfway up the sides of the shrimp. We cooked them over very low heat and turned them halfway through; these shrimp cooked as evenly as they would have if completely covered with oil. We built heady garlic flavor in three ways: We added raw minced garlic to a marinade, we browned smashed cloves in the oil in which the shrimp would be cooked, and we cooked slices of garlic along with the shrimp. We included the traditional bay leaf and red chile, and added sherry vinegar (rather than sherry) and parsley, all of which brightened the richness of the oil. Served with plenty of bread to soak up the extra juices and flavorful oil, these garlicky shrimp rival the best restaurant versions.

Spanish-Style Garlic Shrimp
SERVES 6

Serve the shrimp with crusty bread for dipping in the richly flavored olive oil. This dish can be served directly from the skillet (make sure to use a trivet) or, for a sizzling effect, transferred to an 8-inch cast-iron skillet that's been heated for 2 minutes over medium-high heat. We prefer the slightly sweet flavor of dried chiles in this recipe, but ¼ teaspoon sweet paprika can be substituted. If sherry vinegar is unavailable, use 2 teaspoons dry sherry and 1 teaspoon white vinegar.

14 medium garlic cloves, peeled
 1 pound large shrimp (31 to 40 per pound), peeled, deveined (see page 160), and tails removed
 8 tablespoons olive oil
 ½ teaspoon table salt
 1 bay leaf
 1 (2-inch) piece mild dried chile, such as New Mexico, roughly broken, seeds included (see note)
1½ teaspoons sherry vinegar (see note)
 1 tablespoon minced fresh parsley leaves

1. Mince 2 of the garlic cloves with a chef's knife or garlic press. Toss the minced garlic with the shrimp, 2 tablespoons of the olive oil, and salt in a medium bowl. Let the shrimp marinate at room temperature for 30 minutes.

2. Meanwhile, using the flat side of a chef's knife, smash 4 more garlic cloves. Heat the smashed garlic with the remaining 6 tablespoons olive oil in a 12-inch skillet over medium-low heat, stirring occasionally, until the garlic is light golden brown, 4 to 7 minutes. Remove the pan from the heat and allow the oil to cool to room temperature. Using a slotted spoon, remove the smashed garlic from the skillet and discard.

3. Slice the remaining 8 garlic cloves thin. Return the skillet to low heat and add the sliced garlic, bay leaf, and chile. Cook, stirring occasionally, until the garlic is tender but not browned, 4 to 7 minutes. (If the garlic has not begun to sizzle after 3 minutes, increase the heat to medium-low.) Increase the heat to medium-low and add the shrimp with the marinade to the pan in a single layer. Cook the shrimp, undisturbed, until the oil starts to gently bubble, about 2 minutes. Using tongs, flip the shrimp and continue to cook until almost cooked through, about 2 minutes longer. Increase the heat to high and add the sherry vinegar and parsley. Cook, stirring constantly, until the shrimp are cooked through and the oil is bubbling vigorously, 15 to 20 seconds. Serve immediately, discarding the bay leaf.

SHRIMP COCKTAIL

WHY THIS RECIPE WORKS: Nothing is more basic than shrimp cocktail and, given its simplicity, few dishes are more difficult to improve. Yet we set out to do just that, seeing three ways in which we might challenge tradition: work on the flavor of the shrimp, work on the cooking method for the shrimp, and produce a great cocktail sauce.

Shrimp cook very quickly, so there's little time to add flavor to them in the pan. We based our cooking liquid on shrimp stock, easily made by boiling the shells, and added wine, lemon juice, and herbs and spices. In order to keep the shrimp in contact with this flavorful liquid as long as possible without overcooking them, we brought the mixture to a boil, turned off the heat, and only then added the shrimp; the hot liquid cooked the shrimp slowly while they absorbed flavor from the stock. Turning to the sauce, we determined that the classic base, ketchup, is the best. We added horseradish, which is the usual ingredient for spicing up the sauce, but we also included chili powder, cayenne, and lemon juice for extra spiciness.

Shrimp Cocktail
SERVES 4

When using larger or smaller shrimp, increase or decrease the cooking times for the shrimp by one to two minutes, respectively. When using such large shrimp, we find it wise to remove the large black vein. Use horseradish from a freshly opened bottle and mild chili powder for the best flavor in the sauce.

SHRIMP
- 1 pound jumbo shrimp (16 to 20 per pound; see note), peeled, deveined (see page 160), and shells reserved
- 1 teaspoon table salt
- 1 cup dry white wine
- 4 peppercorns
- 5 coriander seeds
- ½ bay leaf
- 5 sprigs fresh parsley
- 1 sprig fresh tarragon
- 1 teaspoon juice from 1 lemon

COCKTAIL SAUCE
- 1 cup ketchup
- 2½ teaspoons prepared horseradish (see note)
- Table salt

- Ground black pepper
- 1 teaspoon ancho or other mild chili powder (see note)
- Pinch cayenne pepper
- 1 tablespoon juice from 1 small lemon

1. FOR THE SHRIMP: Bring the reserved shells, 3 cups water, and salt to a boil in a medium saucepan over medium-high heat; reduce the heat to low, cover, and simmer until fragrant, about 20 minutes. Strain the stock through a fine-mesh strainer, pressing on the shells to extract all the liquid.

2. Bring the stock and remaining ingredients except the shrimp to a boil in a 3- or 4-quart saucepan over high heat; boil for 2 minutes. Turn off the heat and stir in the shrimp; cover and let stand until the shrimp are firm and pink, 8 to 10 minutes. Meanwhile, fill a large bowl with ice water. Drain the shrimp, reserving the stock for another use. Immediately transfer the shrimp to the ice water to stop cooking and chill thoroughly, about 3 minutes. Remove the shrimp from the ice water and pat dry with paper towels.

3. FOR THE SAUCE: Stir all the ingredients together in a small bowl; season with salt and pepper to taste. Serve the chilled shrimp with the cocktail sauce.

BETTER SHRIMP SALAD

WHY THIS RECIPE WORKS: Most shrimp salads drown in a sea of mayonnaise, in part to hide the rubbery, flavorless boiled shrimp. We wanted perfectly cooked shrimp without the extra work of grilling, roasting, or sautéing. And we needed to coat them with the perfect deli-style dressing—something creamy that wouldn't mask the shrimp flavor or drown out the other ingredients.

Overcooking is the culprit when shrimp turn out rubbery. We found that starting the shrimp in cold water combined with lemon, parsley, tarragon, pepper, sugar, and salt, then cooking them over very gentle heat, resulted in tender shrimp. The longer cooking time enabled the poaching liquid to add more flavor to the shrimp. Because the shrimp were now flavorful on their own, we didn't want to mask them with dressing, so we scaled back the mayonnaise to a modest amount. Celery added a nice crunch, and shallot, herbs, and lemon juice perked up and rounded out the flavors.

Shrimp Salad

SERVES 4

This recipe can also be prepared with large shrimp (31 to 40 per pound); the cooking time will be 1 to 2 minutes shorter. The shrimp can be cooked up to 24 hours in advance, but hold off on dressing the salad until ready to serve. The recipe can be easily doubled; cook the shrimp in a 7-quart Dutch oven and increase the cooking time to 12 to 14 minutes. Serve the salad spooned over salad greens or on buttered and grilled buns.

- 1 pound extra-large shrimp (21 to 25 per pound; see note), peeled and deveined (see page 160)
- ¼ cup plus 1 tablespoon juice from 2 to 3 lemons, spent halves reserved
- 5 sprigs fresh parsley plus 1 teaspoon minced fresh parsley leaves
- 3 sprigs fresh tarragon plus 1 teaspoon minced fresh tarragon leaves
- 1 teaspoon whole black peppercorns plus ground black pepper
- 1 tablespoon sugar
  Table salt
- ¼ cup mayonnaise
- 1 small celery rib, minced (about ⅓ cup)
- 1 small shallot, minced (about 1 tablespoon)

1. Combine the shrimp, ¼ cup of the lemon juice, the reserved lemon halves, parsley sprigs, tarragon sprigs, whole peppercorns, sugar, and 1 teaspoon salt with 2 cups cold water in a medium saucepan. Place the saucepan over medium heat and cook the shrimp, stirring several times, until pink, firm to the touch, and the centers are no longer translucent, 8 to 10 minutes (the water should be just bubbling around the edge of the pan and register 165 degrees on an instant-read thermometer). Remove the pan from the heat, cover, and let the shrimp sit in the broth for 2 minutes.

2. Meanwhile, fill a medium bowl with ice water. Drain the shrimp into a colander and discard the lemon halves, herbs, and spices. Immediately transfer the shrimp to the ice water to stop the cooking and chill thoroughly, about 3 minutes. Remove the shrimp from the ice water and pat dry with paper towels.

3. Whisk together the mayonnaise, celery, shallot, remaining tablespoon lemon juice, minced parsley, and minced tarragon in a medium bowl. Cut the shrimp in half lengthwise and then each half into thirds; add the shrimp to the mayonnaise mixture and toss to combine. Season with salt and pepper to taste and serve.

Shrimp Salad with Roasted Red Pepper and Basil

This Italian-style variation is especially good served over bitter greens.

Follow the recipe for Shrimp Salad, omitting the tarragon sprigs from the cooking liquid. Replace the celery, minced parsley, and minced tarragon with ⅓ cup thinly sliced jarred roasted red peppers, 2 teaspoons rinsed capers, and 3 tablespoons chopped fresh basil leaves.

Shrimp Salad with Avocado and Orange

Avocado and orange are a refreshing addition to this salad.

Follow the recipe for Shrimp Salad, omitting the tarragon sprigs from the cooking liquid. Replace the celery, minced parsley, and minced tarragon with 4 halved and thinly sliced radishes; 1 large orange, peeled and cut into ½-inch pieces; ½ ripe avocado, cut into ½-inch pieces; and 2 teaspoons minced fresh mint leaves.

FLAMBÉED PAN-ROASTED LOBSTER

WHY THIS RECIPE WORKS: Boiling and steaming are the usual ways of preparing lobster, and they're just fine. But we wanted an alternative cooking method that would be even tastier, and we didn't want to spend a whole lot more time in the kitchen. Our solution was a restaurant dish adapted for home cooking.

The New England restaurant chef Jasper White created a pan-roasted lobster dish that we took as our starting point. We quartered the lobsters and tossed them into a very hot skillet—shells down, so the meat wouldn't overcook—to pan-roast. The heat roasted the shells and permeated the lobster meat with intense flavor. To cook the exposed meat, we put the skillet under the broiler, returning it to the stovetop when the meat was cooked through. Now came the fun part: We flambéed the lobster with bourbon (carefully, of course!). A quick pan sauce, made in the skillet after we removed the lobsters, was the final touch; we used shallots, white wine, herbs, and, for unusual and intense flavor, the lobster tomalley. This way of cooking lobsters is a little more trouble than dunking them in a pot of boiling water, but we think the results are well worth it.

Flambéed Pan-Roasted Lobster

SERVES 2

If you want to prepare more than two lobsters, we suggest that you engage some help. This dish requires close attention, and managing multiple extremely hot pans can be tricky. Before flambéing, make sure to roll up long shirtsleeves, tie back long hair, turn off the exhaust fan (otherwise the fan may pull up the flames), and turn off any lit burners (this is critical if you have a gas stove). For equipment, you will need a large ovensafe skillet, oven mitts, a pair of tongs, and long fireplace or grill matches.

2   (1½ to 2-pound) live lobsters
2   tablespoons peanut or canola oil
¼   cup bourbon or cognac
6   tablespoons (¾ stick) unsalted butter, cut into 6 pieces
2   medium shallots, minced (about 6 tablespoons)
3   tablespoons dry white wine
1   teaspoon minced fresh tarragon leaves
1   tablespoon minced fresh chives
    Table salt and ground black pepper
    Lemon wedges, for serving (optional)

1. Following the photos at right, use a large heavy-duty chef's knife to quarter the lobsters. (Don't be put off if the lobsters continue to twitch a little after quartering; it's a reflexive movement.)

PREPARING LOBSTER FOR PAN-ROASTING

1. Plunge a chef's knife into the body at the point where the shell forms a "T" to kill the lobster. Move the blade straight down through the head. (Freezing the lobster for 5 to 10 minutes first will sedate it.)

2. Turn the lobster around and, while holding the upper body with one hand, cut through the body toward the tail.

3. Remove and discard the stomach and intestinal tract. Reserve the green tomalley for the sauce, if desired.

4. Cut the tail from the body.

5. Twist off the claws from the body. Remove the rubber bands from the claws. (Don't be put off if the lobster continues to twitch a little; it's a reflexive movement.)

2. Adjust an oven rack so it is 6 inches from the broiler element and heat the broiler. Heat the peanut oil in a large ovensafe skillet over high heat until smoking. Add the lobster pieces, shell-side down, in a single layer and cook, without disturbing, until the shells are bright red and lightly browned, 2 to 3 minutes. Transfer the skillet to the broiler and cook until the tail meat is just opaque, about 2 minutes.

3. Carefully remove the pan from the oven and return it to the stovetop. Off the heat, pour the bourbon over the lobsters. Wait for 10 seconds, then light a long match and wave it over the skillet until the bourbon ignites. Return the pan to medium-high heat and shake it until the flames subside. Transfer the lobster pieces to a warmed serving bowl and tent with foil to keep warm.

4. Using tongs, remove any congealed albumen (white substance) from the skillet and add 2 tablespoons of the butter and shallots. Cook, stirring constantly, until the shallots are softened and lightly browned, 1 to 2 minutes. Add the tomalley (if using) and white wine and stir until completely combined. Remove the skillet from the heat and add the tarragon and chives. Stirring constantly, add the remaining 4 tablespoons butter, 1 piece at a time, until fully emulsified. Season with salt and pepper to taste. Pour the sauce over the lobster pieces. Serve immediately, accompanied by the lemon wedges, if desired.

MARYLAND CRAB CAKES

WHY THIS RECIPE WORKS: Making crab cakes at home is the only way to avoid the pricey crab-flecked dough balls that pass for crab cakes in many restaurants. We wanted cakes with a crisp brown exterior and creamy, well-seasoned filling that tasted of sweet crab, not filler.

Fresh crabmeat provided the best taste and texture; we think jumbo lump crabmeat is worth the high price tag. Pasteurized crabmeat is not quite as good, but it is less expensive. At all costs, avoid the canned crabmeat sold near canned tuna. After experimenting with different binders, we settled on fine dry bread crumbs; their flavor is mild, they held the cakes together well, and they mixed easily with the crab. We used just a few tablespoons of crumbs so that the crab's flavor and texture would shine. An egg and some mayonnaise bound the cakes together. Old Bay is the traditional seasoning for crab, and there was no reason to leave it out; some herbs and white pepper were the only additions we found necessary. Carefully folding the ingredients together rather than stirring them kept the texture chunky rather than pasty,

and a short chilling in the refrigerator ensured that the cakes wouldn't fall apart. Pan-frying in vegetable oil gave our crab cakes the crisp exterior we wanted, and the interior tasted intensely of crab.

Maryland Crab Cakes
SERVES 4

The amount of bread crumbs you add will depend on the crabmeat's juiciness. Start with the smallest amount, adjust the seasonings, then add the egg. If the cakes won't bind at this point, add more bread crumbs, 1 tablespoon at a time. If you can't find fresh jumbo lump crabmeat, pasteurized crabmeat, though not as good, is a decent substitute. Either a nonstick or a traditional skillet will work for this recipe, but a nonstick simplifies cleanup.

- 1 pound fresh jumbo lump crabmeat, carefully picked over to remove cartilage and shell fragments (see note)
- 4 scallions, green parts only, minced (about ½ cup)
- 1 tablespoon chopped fresh herb, such as cilantro, dill, basil, or parsley
- 1½ teaspoons Old Bay seasoning
- 2–4 tablespoons plain dry bread crumbs (see note)
- ¼ cup mayonnaise
  Table salt and ground white pepper
- 1 large egg
- ¼ cup unbleached all-purpose flour
- ¼ cup vegetable oil
  Sweet and Tangy Tartar Sauce (page 151), Creamy Chipotle Chile Sauce (recipe follows), or lemon wedges

1. Gently mix the crabmeat, scallions, herb, Old Bay, 2 tablespoons of the bread crumbs, and mayonnaise in a medium bowl, being careful not to break up the lumps of crab. Season with salt and white pepper to taste. Carefully fold in the egg with a rubber spatula until the mixture just clings together. Add more bread crumbs if necessary.

2. Divide the crab mixture into four portions and shape each into a fat, round cake, about 3 inches across and 1½ inches high. Arrange the cakes on a baking sheet lined with waxed or parchment paper; cover with plastic wrap and chill at least 30 minutes. (The crab cakes can be refrigerated for up to 24 hours.)

3. Place the flour in a pie plate. Lightly dredge the crab cakes in the flour. Heat the oil in a large skillet over medium-high heat until hot but not smoking. Gently place the chilled crab cakes in the skillet; pan-fry until the outsides are crisp and browned, 4 to 5 minutes per side. Serve immediately with a sauce or lemon wedges.

Creamy Chipotle Chile Sauce

MAKES ABOUT ½ CUP

The addition of sour cream makes this sauce richer than traditional tartar sauce. The chipotles add smoky and spicy flavors.

- ¼ cup mayonnaise
- ¼ cup sour cream
- 2 teaspoons canned minced chipotle chiles in adobo sauce
- 1 small garlic clove, minced or pressed through a garlic press (about ½ teaspoon)
- 2 teaspoons minced fresh cilantro leaves
- 1 teaspoon juice from 1 lime

Mix all of the ingredients in a small bowl. Cover and refrigerate until the flavors blend, about 30 minutes. (The sauce can be refrigerated for 2 days.)

CRAB TOWERS WITH AVOCADO AND GAZPACHO SALSA

WHY THIS RECIPE WORKS: Sometimes a dish served in a restaurant is so delicious and impressive-looking that we just have to try to make it ourselves. A crab salad molded into towers, from the Mayflower Park Hotel in Seattle, is one such dish, but a hotel restaurant can easily handle the recipe's 35 ingredients. Was there a way to re-create the flavors and presentation at home, with fewer ingredients and a lot less effort?

By breaking down the recipe for this appetizer into its components—crab salad, avocado–hearts of palm salsa, and gazpacho salsa—we were able to address each one separately. For the crab salad, we used lump crabmeat mixed with a little mayonnaise and champagne vinaigrette. We eliminated the hearts of palm from the salsa; it was impossible to find any that tasted decent, and tasters felt the avocado alone worked quite well. For the gazpacho salsa, we used only one kind of bell pepper rather than two and omitted the diced lime and orange segments that were in the original recipe; we also cut back on some of the seasonings, limiting ourselves to sherry vinegar and olive oil. Garnishes were simplified to frisée and orange segments. Now that we'd streamlined the components, we had to assemble the dish. The restaurant uses timbale rings, but we found our workaday biscuit cutter did the job just fine.

NOTES FROM THE TEST KITCHEN

SEGMENTING ORANGES

1. Start by slicing a ½-inch piece from the top and bottom of the orange. With the fruit resting flat against a work surface, use a very sharp paring knife to slice off the rind, including the white pith.

2. Slip the knife blade between a membrane and one section of the fruit and slice to the center. Turn the blade so that it is facing out and slide the blade from the center out along the membrane to completely free the section.

ASSEMBLING CRAB TOWERS

1. Place the biscuit cutter in the center of the plate and, using the back of a soup spoon, press ⅓ cup of the Avocado Salsa evenly into the cutter. Lift the cutter off the plate slightly to reveal some but not all of the avocado.

2. Holding the cutter aloft, press ⅓ cup of the Crabmeat Salad evenly into the cutter, on top of the avocado. Lift the cutter farther off the plate and press ⅓ cup of the Gazpacho Salsa evenly into the cutter, on top of the crab.

3. Gently lift the cutter up and away from the plate to reveal the crab tower. Repeat with the remaining salsas and crabmeat salad.

Crab Towers with Avocado and Gazpacho Salsas

SERVES 6

You can prepare the crabmeat salad and gazpacho salsa several hours ahead of serving, but the avocado salsa should be prepared just before assembly.

CRABMEAT SALAD

- 3 tablespoons extra-virgin olive oil
- 1 tablespoon champagne vinegar
- 1 teaspoon minced or grated lemon zest
- ½ teaspoon Dijon mustard
- ½ teaspoon table salt
- ⅛ teaspoon ground black pepper
- 2 tablespoons mayonnaise
- 12 ounces lump or backfin Atlantic blue crabmeat, carefully picked over to remove cartilage and shell fragments

GAZPACHO SALSA

- 1 small yellow bell pepper, cored, seeded, and cut into ⅛-inch pieces (about ½ cup)
- ½ small cucumber, peeled if desired, seeded, and cut into ⅛-inch pieces (about ½ cup)
- 1 medium plum tomato, cored, seeded, and cut into ⅛-inch pieces (about ½ cup)
- 1 small celery rib, cut into ⅛-inch pieces (about ½ cup)
- ½ small red onion, minced (about ¼ cup)
- ½ small jalapeño chile, stemmed, seeded, and minced
- 1 tablespoon minced fresh cilantro leaves
- 2 tablespoons extra-virgin olive oil
- 1 tablespoon sherry vinegar
- ¾ teaspoon table salt
- ¼ teaspoon ground black pepper

AVOCADO SALSA

- 3 ripe avocados, cut into ¼-inch dice
- 2 tablespoons juice from 1 lime
- ¼ teaspoon ground coriander
- ½ teaspoon table salt
- ⅛ teaspoon ground black pepper

GARNISH

- 1 cup frisée
- 2 oranges, peeled using a paring knife and segmented (see page 167; optional)

1. FOR THE CRABMEAT SALAD: Whisk the olive oil, champagne vinegar, lemon zest, mustard, salt, and pepper together in a small bowl. Measure 3 tablespoons of the vinaigrette into a medium bowl and mix with the mayonnaise. Add the crabmeat to the mayonnaise mixture and toss to coat. Cover with plastic wrap and refrigerate until needed. Set the remaining vinaigrette aside.

2. FOR THE GAZPACHO SALSA: Toss the bell pepper, cucumber, tomato, celery, red onion, jalapeño, cilantro, olive oil, sherry vinegar, salt, and pepper in a medium bowl and set aside.

3. FOR THE AVOCADO SALSA: Toss the avocados, lime juice, coriander, salt, and pepper in a medium bowl and set aside.

4. TO ASSEMBLE: Place a 3-inch-wide round biscuit cutter in the center of an individual plate. Following the photos on page 167, press ⅓ cup of the Avocado Salsa into the bottom of the cutter using the back of a soup spoon. Lift the cutter off the plate slightly to reveal some but not all of the avocado. Holding the cutter aloft, press ⅓ cup of the Crabmeat Salad evenly into the cutter on top of the avocado. Lift the cutter farther to reveal some but not all of the crab salad. Holding the cutter aloft, use a soup spoon to press ⅓ cup of the Gazpacho Salsa evenly into the cutter on top of the crab. Gently lift the cutter up and away from the plate to reveal the crab tower. Repeat the procedure five more times with the remaining ingredients.

5. Dress the frisée with the remaining champagne vinaigrette. Place a few sprigs of the dressed frisée on top of each crab tower and arrange the orange segments (if using) around the towers. Serve immediately.

INDOOR CLAMBAKE

WHY THIS RECIPE WORKS: A clambake is perhaps the ultimate seafood meal: clams, mussels, and lobster, nestled with sausage, corn, and potatoes, all steamed together with hot stones in a sand pit by the sea. A genuine clambake is an all-day affair and, of course, requires a beach. But we wanted to re-create the great flavors of the clambake indoors, so we could enjoy this flavorful feast without hours of preparation.

A large stockpot was the cooking vessel of choice. Many recipes suggest cooking the ingredients separately before adding them to the pot, but we found that with careful layering, we could cook everything in the same pot and have it all finish at the same time. And we didn't need to add water, because the shellfish released enough liquid to steam everything else. Sliced sausage went into the pot first (we liked kielbasa), so that it could sear before the steam was generated. Clams and mussels were next, wrapped in cheesecloth for easy removal. Then in went the potatoes, which would take the longest to cook; they were best placed near the heat source, and we cut them into 1-inch pieces to cook more quickly. Corn, with the husks left on to protect it from seafood flavors and lobster foam, was next, followed by the lobsters. It took less than half an hour for everything to cook—and we had all the elements of a clambake (minus the sand and surf) without having spent all day preparing them.

Indoor Clambake

SERVES 4 TO 6

Choose a large, narrow stockpot in which you can easily layer the ingredients. The recipe can be cut in half and layered in an 8-quart Dutch oven, but it should cook for the same amount of time. We prefer small littlenecks for this recipe. If your market carries larger clams, use 4 pounds. Mussels often contain a weedy beard protruding from the crack between the two shells. It's fairly small and can be difficult to tug out of place. To remove it easily, trap the beard between the side of a small paring knife and your thumb and pull to remove it. The flat surface of the knife gives you some leverage to remove the beard.

2 pounds small littleneck or cherrystone clams, scrubbed (see note)

2 pounds mussels, shells scrubbed and beards removed (see note)

1 pound kielbasa, sliced into ⅓-inch-thick rounds

1 pound small new or red potatoes, scrubbed and cut into 1-inch pieces

6 medium ears corn, silk and all but the last layer of husk removed

2 (1½-pound) live lobsters

8 tablespoons (1 stick) salted butter, melted

1. Place the clams and mussels on a large piece of cheesecloth and tie the ends together to secure; set aside. In a heavy-bottomed 12-quart stockpot, layer the sliced kielbasa, the sack of clams and mussels, the potatoes, the corn, and the lobsters on top of one another. Cover with the lid and place over high heat. Cook until the potatoes are tender (a paring knife can be slipped into and out of the center of a potato with little resistance), and the lobsters are bright red, 17 to 20 minutes.

2. Remove the pot from the heat and remove the lid (watch out for scalding steam). Remove the lobsters and set aside until cool enough to handle. Remove the corn from the pot and peel off the husks; arrange the ears on a large platter. Using a slotted spoon, remove the potatoes and arrange them on the platter with the corn. Transfer the clams and mussels to a large bowl and cut open the cheesecloth with scissors. Using a slotted spoon, remove the kielbasa from the pot and arrange it on the platter with the potatoes and corn. Pour the remaining steaming liquid in the pot over the clams and mussels. Using a kitchen towel to protect your hand, twist and remove the lobster tails, claws, and legs (if desired). Arrange the lobster parts on the platter. Serve immediately with the melted butter and napkins.

CHAPTER 11

DINNER AT THE DINER

Classic Tuna Salad   172

Tuna Salad with Balsamic
Vinegar and Grapes   172

Curried Tuna Salad with
Apples and Currants   172

Tuna Salad with Lime and
Horseradish   172

Classic Grilled Cheese
Sandwiches   173

Classic Macaroni and
Cheese   174

Stovetop Macaroni
and Cheese   175

Light Macaroni
and Cheese   176

Turkey Tetrazzini   176

Cincinnati Chili   178

Chicken-Fried Steaks   179

Glazed All-Beef
Meat Loaf   180

Meat Loaf with Brown
Sugar–Ketchup Glaze   181

Classic Stuffed Bell
Peppers   182

Best Old-Fashioned
Burgers   183

   Classic Burger Sauce

Oven-Fried Onion
Rings   184

Steak Fries   185

Classic French Fries   186

Easier French Fries   187

   Chive and Black Pepper
   Dipping Sauce

   Belgian-Style
   Dipping Sauce

TUNA SALAD SANDWICHES

WHY THIS RECIPE WORKS: Tuna salads have been given a bad name by their typically mushy, watery, and bland condition. We wanted a tuna salad that was evenly textured, moist, and well seasoned.

We learned that there are three keys to a great tuna salad. The first is to drain the tuna thoroughly in a colander; don't just tip the water out of the can. Next, instead of using a fork, break up the tuna with your fingers for a finer, more even texture. Finally, season the tuna before adding the mayonnaise for maximum flavor. Some additions to tuna salad are a matter of taste, but we thought that small amounts of garlic and mustard added another dimension, and minced pickle was a piquant touch. In addition to classic tuna salad, we developed a few variations that include tuna with balsamic vinegar with grapes, another with curry and apples, and a third with lime and horseradish.

Classic Tuna Salad

MAKES ABOUT 2 CUPS, ENOUGH FOR 4 SANDWICHES

Our favorite canned tuna is Chicken of the Sea Solid White Albacore. For more information on why we like this brand, see page 616.

- 2 (6-ounce) cans solid white tuna in water (see note)
- 1 small celery rib, minced (about ¼ cup)
- 2 tablespoons juice from 1 lemon
- 2 tablespoons minced red onion
- 2 tablespoons minced dill or sweet pickles
- 2 tablespoons minced fresh parsley leaves
- ½ small garlic clove, minced or pressed through a garlic press (about ½ teaspoon)
- ½ teaspoon table salt
- ¼ teaspoon ground black pepper
- ½ cup mayonnaise
- ¼ teaspoon Dijon mustard

Drain the tuna in a colander and shred with your fingers until no clumps remain and the texture is fine and even. Transfer the tuna to a medium bowl and mix in the celery, lemon juice, onion, pickles, parsley, garlic, salt, and pepper until evenly blended. Fold in the mayonnaise and mustard until the tuna is evenly moistened. (The tuna salad can be covered and refrigerated for up to 3 days.)

Tuna Salad with Balsamic Vinegar and Grapes

Follow the recipe for Classic Tuna Salad, omitting the lemon juice, pickles, garlic, and parsley and adding 2 tablespoons balsamic vinegar, 6 ounces halved red seedless grapes (about 1 cup), ¼ cup lightly toasted slivered almonds, and 2 teaspoons minced thyme leaves to the tuna along with the salt and pepper.

Curried Tuna Salad with Apples and Currants

Follow the recipe for Classic Tuna Salad, omitting the pickles, garlic, and parsley and adding 1 medium firm, juicy apple, cut into ¼-inch dice (about 1 cup), ¼ cup currants, and 2 tablespoons minced fresh basil leaves to the tuna along with the lemon juice, salt, and pepper; mix 1 tablespoon curry powder into the mayonnaise before folding into the tuna.

Tuna Salad with Lime and Horseradish

Follow the recipe for Classic Tuna Salad, omitting the lemon juice, pickles, and garlic and adding 2 tablespoons juice and ½ teaspoon grated zest from 1 lime and 3 tablespoons prepared horseradish to the tuna along with the salt and pepper.

GRILLED CHEESE SANDWICHES

WHY THIS RECIPE WORKS: The perfect grilled cheese sandwich consists of evenly melted cheese between slices of lacy-crisp, buttery bread, but most don't turn out that way. We set out to find the keys to getting that ideal sandwich every time.

Cutting slices from a block of cheese often produces uneven, scraggly pieces. We found that grating the cheese on a box grater enabled us to get an even layer of cheese onto the bread. Butter melted in the pan sometimes burned and didn't always coat the bread evenly, so we opted to butter the bread rather than the pan. And to coat the bread evenly and prevent it from tearing, we melted the butter first. Finally, we learned that the secret of a crisp exterior is low heat; the longer it takes for the bread to become golden, the crispier the bread will become—these are grilled cheese sandwiches worth the wait.

Classic Grilled Cheese Sandwiches

SERVES 2

The traditional grilled cheese sandwich usually uses a mild cheddar cheese, but our technique for this sandwich works with most any cheese. Grilled cheese sandwiches are best served hot out of the pan, though in a pinch they can be held, unsliced, for up to 20 minutes in a warm oven. If you want to make more than two sandwiches at once, get two skillets going or use an electric griddle set at medium-low (about 250 degrees), grilling 10 minutes per side. The possible variations on the basic grilled cheese sandwich are endless, but the extras are best sandwiched between the cheese. Try a few very thin slices of baked ham, prosciutto, turkey breast, or ripe, in-season tomato. Condiments such as Dijon mustard, pickle relish, or chutney can be spread on the bread instead of sandwiched in the cheese.

- **3 ounces cheese (preferably mild cheddar) or a combination of cheeses, shredded on the large holes of a box grater (about ¾ cup) (see note)**
- **4 slices high-quality white sandwich bread**
- **2 tablespoons unsalted butter, melted**

BEHIND THE SCENES

COOKS WHO CAN MAKE THE CUT

Our recipes are created by a team of test cooks—more than three dozen cooks in total—who spend their day mincing, roasting, tasting, and talking about food. So what does it take to join our army of test cooks? It goes without saying that you must love to cook. Everyone in the test kitchen has professional cooking experience (this usually includes work in a restaurant kitchen as well as a degree from one of the top cooking schools in the country). But in-depth food knowledge and cooking skills are just a start.

To get hired, you must have a passion for understanding how things work in the kitchen. A curious mind is essential, as are attention to detail and a scientific approach to problem solving. Our test cooks are continually developing hypotheses to explain how a recipe works and then devising a testing protocol to prove (or disprove) their theory. Finally, we look for cooks who understand the realities of cooking at home—with imperfect equipment, the usual distractions (kids, pets, and phone calls), and no one to wash the dishes.

So how do we find test cooks? Our test kitchen director, Erin McMurrer, has developed a bench test for potential hires—it's like an audition, with knives. Erin gives potential hires two of our published recipes and watches them as they set to work preparing them. Chop those onions when the recipe says to mince them, and you're in trouble. Use a dry measuring cup to measure milk, and you're in serious trouble. Shape cookie dough into ½-inch balls when the recipe says 1-inch balls, and you're in very serious trouble. But job candidates can save the day when the cooking is done and Erin asks them to analyze their success and failures during the bench test. A candidate who can thoughtfully examine his or her work (and figure out how to remedy problems) might just make the cut.

1. Heat a heavy 12-inch skillet over low to medium-low heat. Meanwhile, sprinkle the cheese evenly over two bread slices. Top each with a remaining bread slice, pressing down gently to set.

2. Brush the sandwich tops completely with half of the melted butter; place each sandwich, buttered side down, in the skillet. Brush the remaining side of each sandwich completely with the remaining butter. Cook until crisp and deep golden brown, 5 to 10 minutes per side, flipping the sandwiches back to the first side to reheat and crisp, about 15 seconds. Serve immediately.

CLASSIC MACARONI AND CHEESE

WHY THIS RECIPE WORKS: Old-fashioned macaroni and cheese takes no shortcuts. This family favorite should boast tender pasta in a smooth, creamy sauce with great cheese flavor. Too often, the dish, which is baked in the oven, dries out or curdles. We aimed to create a foolproof version.

We cooked the pasta until just past al dente and then combined it with a béchamel-based cheese sauce. For best flavor and a creamy texture, we used a combination of sharp cheddar and Monterey Jack. We combined the cooked pasta with the sauce and heated it through on the stovetop, rather than in the oven. This step helped ensure the dish didn't dry out, but remained smooth and creamy. And to give the dish a browned topping, we sprinkled it with bread crumbs and ran it briefly under the broiler.

Classic Macaroni and Cheese

SERVES 6 TO 8

It's crucial to cook the pasta until tender—that is, just past the al dente stage. Whole, low-fat, and skim milk all work well in this recipe. The recipe may be halved and baked in an 8-inch square, broiler-safe baking dish. If desired, offer celery salt or hot sauce for sprinkling at the table.

BREAD-CRUMB TOPPING
- 6 **slices high-quality white sandwich bread, torn into quarters**
- 3 **tablespoons cold unsalted butter, cut into 6 pieces**

PASTA AND CHEESE
- 1 **tablespoon plus 1 teaspoon table salt**
- 1 **pound elbow macaroni**
- 5 **tablespoons unsalted butter**
- 6 **tablespoons unbleached all-purpose flour**
- 1½ **teaspoons dry mustard**
- ¼ **teaspoon cayenne pepper (optional)**
- 5 **cups milk (see note)**
- 8 **ounces Monterey Jack cheese, shredded (2 cups)**
- 8 **ounces sharp cheddar cheese, shredded (2 cups)**

1. **FOR THE BREAD CRUMBS:** Pulse the bread and butter in a food processor until coarsely ground, 10 to 15 pulses. Set aside.

2. **FOR THE PASTA AND CHEESE:** Adjust an oven rack to the lower-middle position and heat the broiler. Bring 4 quarts water to a rolling boil in a large pot. Add 1 tablespoon of the salt and the macaroni and stir to separate the noodles. Cook until tender, drain, and set aside.

3. In the now-empty pot, melt the butter over medium-high heat. Add the flour, mustard, cayenne (if using), and remaining 1 teaspoon salt and whisk well to combine. Continue whisking until the mixture becomes fragrant and deepens in color, about 1 minute. Whisking constantly, gradually add the milk; bring the mixture to a boil, whisking constantly (the mixture must reach a full boil to fully thicken), then reduce the heat to medium and simmer, whisking occasionally, until thickened to the consistency of heavy cream, about 5 minutes. Off the heat, whisk in the cheeses until fully melted. Add the pasta and cook over medium-low heat, stirring constantly, until the mixture is steaming and heated through, about 6 minutes.

4. Transfer the mixture to a broiler-safe 13 by 9-inch baking dish and sprinkle with the bread crumbs. Broil until deep golden brown, 3 to 5 minutes. Cool 5 minutes, then serve.

STOVETOP MACARONI AND CHEESE

WHY THIS RECIPE WORKS: Just about the only thing boxed macaroni and cheese has going for it is its fast prep—and the fact that kids will almost always gobble it up. We wanted a quick stovetop macaroni and cheese with an ultra-creamy texture and authentic cheese flavor—so good that it would satisfy everyone at the table.

We cooked the macaroni to just shy of al dente, then drained and combined it with butter and an egg custard mixture that included evaporated milk, eggs, hot sauce, and dry mustard. For the cheese we chose cheddar, American, or Monterey Jack—and plenty of it. We stirred the cheese into the macaroni mixture until thick and creamy and then topped the mixture with toasted homemade bread crumbs—the final touch to this easy-to-prepare family favorite.

Stovetop Macaroni and Cheese

SERVES 4

If you're in a hurry or prefer to sprinkle the dish with crumbled crackers (saltines aren't bad), you can skip the bread-crumb step.

BREAD CRUMBS

- 3 slices high-quality white sandwich bread, torn into quarters
- 2 tablespoons unsalted butter
  Table salt

MACARONI AND CHEESE

- 2 large eggs
- 1 (12-ounce) can evaporated milk
- 2 teaspoons table salt
- ¼ teaspoon ground black pepper
- 1 teaspoon dry mustard, dissolved in 1 teaspoon water
- ¼ teaspoon hot sauce
- 8 ounces elbow macaroni (about 2 cups)
- 4 tablespoons (½ stick) unsalted butter
- 12 ounces sharp cheddar, American, or Monterey Jack cheese, shredded (about 3 cups)

1. FOR THE BREAD CRUMBS: Pulse the bread in a food processor until coarsely ground, 10 to 15 pulses. Melt the butter in a large skillet over medium heat. Add the bread crumbs and cook, tossing to coat with the butter, until the crumbs just begin to color, about 10 minutes. Season with salt to taste; set aside.

During the tasting lab segments, Jack asks Chris to pick out the test kitchen's winning brands from the losers. It doesn't look hard on television, but what viewers don't know is that we film as many as eleven tasting segments in a single day. That's because it takes the production team a few hours to light the tasting lab and position the cameras. Once the crew is in place, it makes sense to keep shooting one segment after another. That means Chris has to do at least one—often two—tasting segments every hour, starting as early as 8 a.m. and ending around 6 p.m. So what's on the menu? Here's the lineup from Chris's toughest-ever day in the tasting lab, May 5, 2006: Mail-order filet mignon, cider vinegar, alternative (non-wheat) pasta, mayonnaise, vanilla ice cream, sandwich bread, dark chocolate, French roast coffee, white wine for cooking, ketchup, and hot sauce. How does Chris end a day like this, after tasting 49 different samples in 11 separate segments? Antacid to settle his stomach followed by a few beers to erase the memory of the day.

2. FOR THE MACARONI AND CHEESE: Mix the eggs, 1 cup of the evaporated milk, ½ teaspoon of the salt, pepper, mustard mixture, and hot sauce in a small bowl; set aside.

3. Meanwhile, bring 2 quarts water to a boil in a large heavy-bottomed saucepan or Dutch oven. Add the remaining 1½ teaspoons salt and the macaroni; cook until almost tender but still a little firm to the bite. Drain and return to the pan over low heat. Add the butter; toss to melt.

4. Pour the egg mixture over the buttered noodles along with three-quarters of the cheese; stir until thoroughly combined and the cheese starts to melt. Gradually add the remaining ½ cup milk and the remaining cheese, stirring constantly, until the mixture is hot and creamy, about 5 minutes. Serve immediately, topped with the toasted bread crumbs.

LIGHT MACARONI AND CHEESE

WHY THIS RECIPE WORKS: Weighing in at about 650 calories and 40 grams of fat per serving, a bowl of homemade mac and cheese should really be a treat every once in a while, like a slice of cheesecake. But the truth is, most of us like to enjoy this family favorite a little more often. We aimed to develop a lighter version of mac and cheese—macaroni in a creamy (not rubbery or grainy), cheesy sauce—with a fraction of the calories.

We slashed both fat and calories by replacing full-fat cheddar with low-fat—its flavor and texture are vastly superior to nonfat cheddar. We also swapped in 2 percent milk for the whole milk and added 2 percent evaporated milk to ensure a creamy consistency. And we found that we could eliminate butter entirely by thickening the sauce with cornstarch instead of a classic roux. In the end, we cut the calories by almost half and the fat grams by 75 percent, turning full-fat macaroni and cheese into a dish you could eat every day.

Light Macaroni and Cheese

SERVES 4 TO 6

Don't be tempted to use either preshredded or nonfat cheddar cheese in this dish—the texture and flavor of the macaroni and cheese will suffer substantially. For best results, choose a low-fat cheddar cheese that is sold in block form and has roughly 50 percent of the fat and calories of regular cheese (we like Cabot brand).

> Table salt
> 8 ounces elbow macaroni (about 2 cups)
> 1 (12-ounce) can 2 percent reduced-fat evaporated milk
> ¾ cup 2 percent milk
> ¼ teaspoon dry mustard
> ⅛ teaspoon garlic powder or celery salt (optional)
> Pinch cayenne pepper
> 2 teaspoons cornstarch
> 8 ounces 50 percent light cheddar cheese, shredded (about 2 cups) (see note)

1. Bring 2½ quarts water to a boil in a large saucepan. Stir in 2 teaspoons salt and the macaroni; cook until the pasta is completely cooked and tender, about 5 minutes. Drain the pasta and leave it in the colander; set aside.

2. Add the evaporated milk, ½ cup of the 2 percent milk, the mustard, garlic powder (if using), cayenne, and ½ teaspoon salt to the now-empty saucepan. Bring the mixture to a boil, then reduce to a simmer. Whisk the cornstarch and remaining ¼ cup milk together, then whisk it into the simmering mixture. Continue to simmer, whisking constantly, until the sauce has thickened and is smooth, about 2 minutes.

3. Off the heat, gradually whisk in the cheddar until melted and smooth. Stir in the macaroni and let the macaroni and cheese sit off the heat until the sauce has thickened slightly, 2 to 5 minutes, before serving.

TURKEY TETRAZZINI

WHY THIS RECIPE WORKS: Overcooking is the inevitable fate of many casseroles, as the contents are usually cooked twice: once on their own and once again when joined with the other casserole ingredients. We wanted a casserole with a silky sauce, a generous portion of turkey meat, and noodles cooked just till done.

We found we could cut the second cooking down to just 15 minutes by baking the recipe in a shallow dish that would allow it to heat through quickly. Most recipes for turkey Tetrazzini call for a béchamel sauce, in which milk is added to a roux (a paste made from fat and flour that is then cooked on the stovetop). In switching to a velouté, which is based on chicken stock rather than milk, we brightened up the texture and the flavor. We also used less sauce than most recipes call for, giving the other ingredients a chance to express themselves. Still looking for brighter flavor, we spruced things up with a shot of sherry and a little lemon juice and nutmeg. Parmesan cheese provided tang and bite, and a full 2 teaspoons of fresh thyme helped to freshen the overall impression of the dish.

Turkey Tetrazzini

SERVES 8

Don't skimp on the salt and pepper; this dish needs aggressive seasoning.

BREAD-CRUMB TOPPING
> 6 slices high-quality white sandwich bread, torn into quarters
> 4 tablespoons (½ stick) unsalted butter, melted
> Pinch table salt
> ½ ounce Parmesan cheese, grated (about ¼ cup)

FILLING
> 8 tablespoons (1 stick) unsalted butter, plus extra for the baking dish

8 ounces white mushrooms, wiped cleaned and sliced thin (about 3 cups)

2 medium onions, minced
   Table salt and ground black pepper (see note)

12 ounces spaghetti or other long-strand pasta, strands snapped in half

6 tablespoons unbleached all-purpose flour

3 cups low-sodium chicken broth

1½ ounces Parmesan cheese, grated (¾ cup)

¼ cup dry sherry

1 tablespoon juice from 1 lemon

2 teaspoons minced fresh thyme leaves

¼ teaspoon grated nutmeg

2 cups frozen peas

4 cups leftover cooked boneless turkey or chicken meat, cut into ¼-inch pieces

1. FOR THE TOPPING: Adjust an oven rack to the middle position and heat the oven to 350 degrees. Pulse the bread in a food processor until coarsely ground, 10 to 15 pulses. Mix the bread crumbs, butter, and salt in a small baking dish; bake until golden brown and crisp, 15 to 20 minutes. Cool to room temperature and mix with the Parmesan in a small bowl. Set aside.

2. FOR THE FILLING: Increase the oven temperature to 450 degrees. Melt 2 tablespoons of the butter in a large skillet over medium heat; add the mushrooms and onions and sauté, stirring frequently, until the liquid from the mushrooms evaporates, 12 to 15 minutes. Season with salt and pepper to taste; transfer the vegetables to a medium bowl and set aside. Clean the skillet.

3. Meanwhile, bring 4 quarts water to a boil in a large pot. Add 1 tablespoon salt and the pasta and cook until al dente. Reserve ¼ cup cooking water, drain the spaghetti, and return to the pot with the reserved liquid.

4. Melt the remaining 6 tablespoons butter in the cleaned skillet over medium heat. Whisk in the flour and cook, whisking constantly, until the flour turns golden, 1 to 2 minutes. Whisking constantly, gradually add the chicken broth. Turn the heat to medium-high and simmer until the mixture thickens, 3 to 4 minutes. Off the heat, whisk in the Parmesan, sherry, lemon juice, thyme, nutmeg, and ½ teaspoon salt. Add the sauce, sautéed vegetables, peas, and turkey to the spaghetti and mix well; season with salt and pepper to taste.

5. Turn the mixture into a buttered 13 by 9-inch gratin dish (or other shallow ovenproof baking dish of similar size), sprinkle evenly with the reserved bread crumbs, and bake until the bread crumbs brown and the mixture is bubbly, 13 to 15 minutes. Serve immediately.

CINCINNATI CHILI

WHY THIS RECIPE WORKS: This Midwestern diner specialty is an unusual marriage of American chili and Middle Eastern spices. For an easy weeknight meal, we wanted to pare the list of ingredients down to the essentials without compromising the distinctive character of the dish.

The beef in Cincinnati Chili isn't sautéed like the beef in other chilis, so there is no way to remove the fat. To avoid greasiness, we blanched ground chuck for half a minute, which got rid of most of the fat but still left plenty of flavor. The spices used in this chili vary from recipe to recipe. We settled on a limited palette starring chile powder, oregano, cinnamon, and cocoa powder, which we bloomed in hot oil for more depth of flavor. Water and tomato sauce are the traditional base for the sauce; we added chicken broth for balance. Vinegar and brown sugar livened things up. After a long simmer, the chili was ready to be served, and we couldn't think of a better way to do it than "five-way"—over spaghetti, topped with cheddar cheese, chopped onions, and kidney beans.

Cincinnati Chili

SERVES 6 TO 8

CHILI

- **2 teaspoons table salt, plus more to taste**
- **1½ pounds 80 percent lean ground chuck**
- **2 tablespoons vegetable oil**
- **2 medium onions, minced**
- **2 medium garlic cloves, minced or pressed through a garlic press (about 2 teaspoons)**
- **2 tablespoons chili powder**
- **2 teaspoons dried oregano**
- **2 teaspoons cocoa powder**
- **1½ teaspoons ground cinnamon**
- **½ teaspoon cayenne pepper**
- **½ teaspoon ground allspice**
- **¼ teaspoon ground black pepper**
- **2 cups tomato sauce**
- **2 cups low-sodium chicken broth**
- **2 cups water**
- **2 tablespoons cider vinegar**
- **2 teaspoons dark brown sugar**
   Hot sauce

ACCOMPANIMENTS

- **1 pound spaghetti, cooked, drained, and tossed with 2 tablespoons unsalted butter**
- **3 cups sharp cheddar cheese, shredded (12 ounces)**
- **1 (15-ounce) can red kidney beans, drained, rinsed, and warmed**
- **1 medium onion, chopped**

1. FOR THE CHILI: Bring 2 quarts water and 1 teaspoon of the salt to a boil in a large saucepan. Add the ground chuck, stirring vigorously to separate the meat into individual strands. As soon as the foam from the meat rises to the top (this takes about 30 seconds) and before the water returns to a boil, drain the meat into a strainer and set it aside.

2. Rinse and dry the empty saucepan. Set the pan over medium heat and add the oil. When the oil is warm, add the onions and cook, stirring frequently, until the onions are soft and browned around the edges, about 8 minutes. Add the garlic and cook until fragrant, about 1 minute. Stir in the chili powder, oregano, cocoa, cinnamon, cayenne, allspice, black pepper, and the remaining 1 teaspoon salt. Cook, stirring constantly, until the spices are fragrant, about 30 seconds. Stir in the tomato sauce, broth, water, vinegar, and sugar, scraping the pan bottom to remove any browned bits.

3. Add the blanched ground beef and increase the heat to high. As soon as the liquid boils, reduce the heat to medium-low and simmer, stirring occasionally, until the chili is deep red and has thickened slightly, about 1 hour. Season with salt and hot sauce to taste. (The chili can be refrigerated in an airtight container for up to 3 days. Bring to a simmer over medium-low heat before serving.)

4. TO SERVE: Divide the buttered spaghetti among individual bowls. Spoon the chili over the spaghetti and top with the cheese, beans, and onion. Serve immediately.

CHICKEN-FRIED STEAK

WHY THIS RECIPE WORKS: Although this truck-stop favorite often gets a bad rap, chicken-fried steak can be delicious when cooked just right. Poorly prepared versions feature dry, rubbery steaks that snap back with each bite, coated in damp, pale breading and topped with a bland, pasty white sauce. When cooked well, thin cutlets of beef are breaded and fried until a crisp, golden brown. The creamy gravy that accompanies the steak is well seasoned and not too thick. This was our goal.

A thin steak works best here, so we turned to cube steak and pounded the meat to an even thickness. What makes this steak special is the crisp coating. After trying a variety of coatings—Melba toast, corn flakes, panko, and the like—we determined simple was best. We dredged the steaks in heavily seasoned flour, dipped them in a thick buttermilk and egg mixture aerated with baking power and baking soda, and then returned them to the seasoned flour for a second coat. This coating fried up to an impressive dark mahogany color with a resilient texture to stand up to the gravy. For the gravy, we built in flavor by using the fried bits left in the pan after cooking the steaks and by making a roux. Onions and cayenne are traditional for the gravy, but we found that small additions of thyme and garlic also improved its flavor.

Chicken-Fried Steaks

SERVES 6

Getting the initial oil temperature to 375 degrees is key to the success of this recipe. Use an instant-read thermometer with a high upper range to check the temperature; a clip-on candy/deep-fry thermometer is also fine. If your Dutch oven measures 11 inches across (as ours does), you will need to fry the steaks in two batches.

STEAKS

- 3 cups unbleached all-purpose flour
  Table salt and ground black pepper
- ⅛ teaspoon cayenne pepper
- 1 large egg
- 1 teaspoon baking powder
- ½ teaspoon baking soda
- 1 cup buttermilk
- 6 (5-ounce) cube steaks, pounded ⅓ inch thick
- 4–5 cups peanut oil

CREAM GRAVY

- 1 medium onion, minced
- ⅛ teaspoon dried thyme
- 2 medium garlic cloves, minced or pressed through a garlic press (about 2 teaspoons)
- 3 tablespoons unbleached all-purpose flour
- ½ cup low-sodium chicken broth
- 2 cups whole milk
- ¾ teaspoon table salt
- ¼ teaspoon ground black pepper
  Pinch cayenne pepper

1. FOR THE STEAKS: Mix the flour, 5 teaspoons salt, 1 teaspoon black pepper, and the cayenne together in a large shallow dish. In a second large shallow dish, beat the egg, baking powder, and baking soda; stir in the buttermilk.

2. Set a wire rack over a large rimmed baking sheet. Pat the steaks dry with paper towels and sprinkle each side with salt and pepper. One at a time, drop the steaks into the flour and shake the dish to coat. Shake excess flour from each steak, then, using tongs, dip each steak into the egg mixture, turning to coat well and allowing the excess to drip off. Coat the steaks with flour again, shake off the excess, and place them on the wire rack.

3. Adjust an oven rack to the middle position, set a second wire rack over a second rimmed baking sheet, and place the sheet on the oven rack; heat the oven to 200 degrees. Line a large plate with a double layer of paper towels. Meanwhile, heat 1 inch of oil in a large (11-inch diameter) Dutch oven over medium-high heat to 375 degrees. Place 3 steaks in the oil and fry, turning once, until deep golden brown on each side, about 5 minutes (the oil temperature will drop to around 335 degrees). Transfer the steaks to the paper towel–lined plate to drain, then transfer them to the wire rack in the oven. Bring the oil back to 375 degrees and repeat the cooking and draining process (use fresh paper towels) with the 3 remaining steaks.

4. FOR THE GRAVY: Carefully pour the hot oil through a fine-mesh strainer into a clean pot. Return the browned bits from the strainer along with 2 tablespoons of the frying oil to the Dutch oven. Turn the heat to medium, add the onion and thyme, and cook until the onion has softened and is beginning to brown, 4 to 5 minutes. Add the garlic and cook until aromatic, about 30 seconds. Add the flour to the pan and stir until well combined and starting to dissolve, about 1 minute. Whisk in the broth, scraping any browned bits off the bottom of the pan. Whisk in the milk, salt, black pepper, and cayenne; bring to a simmer over medium-high heat. Cook until thickened (the gravy should have a loose consistency—it will thicken as it cools), about 5 minutes.

5. Transfer the chicken-fried steaks to individual plates. Spoon a generous amount of gravy over each steak. Serve immediately, passing any remaining gravy separately.

ALL-BEEF MEAT LOAF

WHY THIS RECIPE WORKS: Every all-beef meat loaf we've tasted has had the same problems—chewy texture and uninteresting flavor, making it more of a hamburger in the shape of a log than bonafide meat loaf. In the past, when we wanted a great meat loaf, we turned to a traditional meat-loaf mix consisting of beef, pork, and veal. Could we create an all-beef meat loaf to compete with this classic?

Supermarkets offer a wide selection of "ground beef," and after testing them alone and in combination we determined that equal parts of chuck (for moisture) and sirloin (for beefy flavor) were best. Beef has a livery taste that we wanted to subdue, and the usual dairy additions to meat loaf didn't work. Chicken broth, oddly enough, neutralized this off-flavor and provided moisture. For additional moisture and richness, we included mild-tasting Monterey Jack cheese, which also helped bind the mixture. To avoid pockets of oozing hot cheese in the meat loaf, we shredded the cheese and froze it briefly. Crushed saltines, our choice for the starchy filler, provided texture, but we felt our meat loaf needed more "sliceability." Surprisingly, gelatin gave us just the smooth, luxurious texture we sought. We seasoned the mixture with onions, celery, garlic (all sautéed), thyme, paprika, soy sauce, and mustard. A traditional ketchup glaze crowned our flavorful all-beef meat loaf.

Glazed All-Beef Meat Loaf

SERVES 6 TO 8

If you can't find chuck and/or sirloin, substitute 85 percent lean ground beef.

MEAT LOAF

- 3 ounces Monterey Jack cheese, shredded on the small holes of a box grater (about 1 cup)
- 1 tablespoon unsalted butter
- 1 medium onion, minced
- 1 medium celery rib, minced
- 2 teaspoons minced fresh thyme leaves
- 1 teaspoon paprika
- 1 medium garlic clove, minced or pressed through a garlic press (about 1 teaspoon)
- ¼ cup tomato juice
- ½ cup low-sodium chicken broth
- 2 large eggs
- ½ teaspoon unflavored powdered gelatin
- ⅔ cup crushed saltines
- 2 tablespoons minced fresh parsley leaves
- 1 tablespoon soy sauce
- 1 teaspoon Dijon mustard
- ¾ teaspoon table salt
- ½ teaspoon ground black pepper
- 1 pound 90 percent lean ground sirloin (see note)
- 1 pound 80 percent lean ground chuck (see note)

GLAZE

- ½ cup ketchup
- ¼ cup cider vinegar
- 3 tablespoons light brown sugar
- 1 teaspoon hot sauce
- ½ teaspoon ground coriander

1. FOR THE MEAT LOAF: Adjust an oven rack to the middle position and heat the oven to 375 degrees. Spread the cheese on a plate and place in the freezer until ready to use. To prepare the baking sheet, set a wire rack over a rimmed baking sheet. Fold a sheet of heavy-duty aluminum foil to form a 10 by 6-inch rectangle. Center the foil on the rack and poke holes in the foil with a skewer (about half an inch apart). Spray the foil with vegetable oil spray or use nonstick foil.

2. Melt the butter in a 10-inch skillet over medium-high heat; add the onion and celery and cook, stirring occasionally, until beginning to brown, 6 to 8 minutes. Add the thyme, paprika, and garlic and cook, stirring, until fragrant, about 1 minute. Reduce the heat to low and add the tomato juice. Cook, stirring to scrape up the browned bits from the pan, until thickened, about 1 minute. Transfer the mixture to a small bowl and set aside to cool.

3. Whisk the broth and eggs together in a large bowl until combined. Sprinkle the gelatin over the liquid and let stand for 5 minutes. Stir in the saltines, parsley, soy sauce, mustard, salt, pepper, and onion mixture. Crumble the frozen cheese into a coarse powder and sprinkle over the mixture. Add the sirloin and chuck; mix gently with your hands until thoroughly combined, about 1 minute. Transfer the meat to the foil rectangle and shape into a 10 by 6-inch oval about 2 inches high. Smooth the top and edges of the meat loaf with a moistened spatula. Bake until the center of the loaf registers 135 to 140 degrees on an instant-read thermometer, 55 to 65 minutes. Remove the meat loaf from the oven and turn on the broiler.

4. FOR THE GLAZE: While the meat loaf cooks, combine the glaze ingredients in a small saucepan; bring to a simmer over medium heat and cook, stirring, until thick and syrupy, about 5 minutes. Spread half of the glaze evenly over the cooked meat loaf with a rubber spatula; place under the broiler and cook until the glaze bubbles and begins to brown at the edges, about 5 minutes. Remove the meat loaf from the oven and spread evenly with the remaining glaze; place back under the broiler and cook until the glaze is again bubbling and beginning to brown, about 5 minutes more. Let the meat loaf cool about 20 minutes before slicing.

CLASSIC MEAT LOAF

WHY THIS RECIPE WORKS: Not all meat loaves resemble Mom's. Some recipes go the canned soup route and, frankly, taste like it. Others become gussied up with ingredients that have no place in this humble family dish—canned pineapple, sun-dried tomatoes, and the like. Our goal was not to develop the ultimate meat loaf but to bring it back to its classic roots—a tender, well-seasoned loaf smothered with tangy sweet glaze.

We started, of course, with the meat. We determined that supermarkets haven't been selling "meat loaf mix" for no reason—a mixture of ground beef chuck, ground pork, and ground veal produced the best balance of flavors and textures. A starch turned out to be a necessity for binding the meat and giving it that classic meat loaf texture; cracker crumbs, quick-cooking oatmeal, and fresh bread crumbs all worked well. To prevent the filler from drying out the meat loaf, we knew we needed to

add some moisture. After trying a host of options, we determined that whole milk and plain yogurt are equally acceptable. Finally, we realized that the pan in which the meat loaf baked made a big difference. A standard loaf pan traps the fat and stews the meat, and the juice bubbles up and destroys the glaze. Baking the meat loaf free-form in a shallow baking pan gave the loaf a good crust, preserved our sweet-tart glaze, and helped the bacon topping crisp nicely.

Meat Loaf with Brown Sugar–Ketchup Glaze
SERVES 6 TO 8

If you like, you can omit the bacon topping from the loaf. In this case, brush on half of the glaze before baking and the other half during the last 15 minutes of baking. If you choose not to special-order the mix of meat below, we recommend the standard meat loaf mix of equal parts beef, pork, and veal, available at most grocery stores. Lining the baking pan with foil makes for easier cleanup.

BROWN SUGAR–KETCHUP GLAZE
- ½ **cup ketchup or chili sauce**
- ¼ **cup brown sugar**
- 4 **teaspoons cider or white vinegar**

MEAT LOAF
- 2 **teaspoons vegetable oil**
- 1 **medium onion, chopped**
- 2 **medium garlic cloves, minced or pressed through a garlic press (about 2 teaspoons)**
- 2 **large eggs**
- ½ **cup whole milk or plain yogurt, plus more as needed**
- 2 **teaspoons Dijon mustard**
- 2 **teaspoons Worcestershire sauce**
- 1 **teaspoon table salt**
- ½ **teaspoon ground black pepper**
- ½ **teaspoon dried thyme**
- ¼ **teaspoon hot sauce**
- 2 **pounds meat loaf mix (50 percent ground chuck, 25 percent ground pork, 25 percent ground veal) (see note)**
- ⅔ **cup crushed saltine crackers (about 16) or quick oatmeal or 1⅓ cups fresh bread crumbs**
- ⅓ **cup minced fresh parsley leaves**
- 6–8 **ounces bacon (8 to 12 slices, depending on loaf shape) (see note)**

1. FOR THE GLAZE: Mix all the ingredients together in a small saucepan; set aside.

2. FOR THE MEAT LOAF: Line a 13 by 9-inch baking pan with foil; set aside. Heat the oven to 350 degrees. Heat the oil in a medium skillet. Add the onion and garlic; sauté until softened, about 5 minutes. Set aside to cool while preparing the remaining ingredients.

3. Mix the eggs with the milk, mustard, Worcestershire sauce, salt, pepper, thyme, and hot sauce. Add the egg mixture to the meat in a large bowl along with the crackers, parsley, and cooked onion and garlic; mix with a fork until evenly blended and the meat mixture does not stick to the bowl. (If necessary, add more milk, a couple of tablespoons at a time, until the mixture no longer sticks.)

4. Turn the meat mixture onto a work surface. With wet hands, pat the mixture into approximately a 9 by 5-inch loaf shape. Place on the prepared baking pan. Brush with half the glaze, then arrange the bacon slices, crosswise, over the loaf, overlapping them slightly and tucking only the bacon tip ends under the loaf.

5. Bake the loaf until the bacon is crisp and the center of the loaf registers 160 degrees on an instant-read thermometer, about 1 hour. Cool at least 20 minutes. Simmer the remaining glaze over medium heat until thickened slightly. Slice the meat loaf and serve with the extra glaze passed separately.

STUFFED PEPPERS

WHY THIS RECIPE WORKS: A vegetable can be more than just a side dish, and stuffed peppers are a perfect case in point. But slimy or too-crunchy peppers and tasteless fillings can ruin the show. We wanted to revamp this dish to be a flavorful option for a weeknight dinner.

Cooking the peppers correctly is critical; they need to be sturdy enough to hold the filling but not crunchy and bitter. We found that blanching them before adding the filling resulted in peppers that held their shape, had good color, and were sweeter. Rice is the classic stuffing for peppers, but rice alone didn't have much flavor. Tastings of various fillings showed us that simpler is better for this dish; a mixture of rice and ground beef was the favorite. To save time, we cooked the rice in the water we'd used to blanch the peppers. For additional flavor, we included sautéed onion and garlic, tomatoes, cheddar cheese, and ketchup. We'd taken this recipe back to its 1950s version, but made it into a simple preparation suitable for today's busy cooks.

Classic Stuffed Bell Peppers
SERVES 4

When shopping for bell peppers to stuff, it's best to choose those with broad bases that will allow the peppers to stand up on their own. It's easier to fill the peppers after they have been placed in the baking dish because the sides of the dish will hold the peppers steady.

Table salt
4 medium red, yellow, or orange bell peppers (about 6 ounces each), ½ inch trimmed off tops, cores and seeds discarded (see note)
½ cup long-grain white rice
1½ tablespoons olive oil
1 medium onion, minced
12 ounces ground beef, preferably 80 percent lean ground chuck
3 medium garlic cloves, minced or pressed through a garlic press (about 1 tablespoon)
1 (14.5-ounce) can diced tomatoes, drained, ¼ cup juice reserved
5 ounces Monterey Jack cheese, shredded (1¼ cups)
2 tablespoons chopped fresh parsley leaves
Ground black pepper
¼ cup ketchup

1. Bring 4 quarts water to a boil in a large stockpot or Dutch oven over high heat. Add 1 tablespoon salt and the bell peppers. Cook until the peppers just begin to soften, about 3 minutes. Using a slotted spoon, remove the peppers from the pot, drain off the excess water, and place the peppers, cut side up, on paper towels. Return the water to a boil; add the rice and boil until tender, about 13 minutes. Drain the rice and transfer it to a large bowl; set aside.

2. Adjust an oven rack to the middle position and heat the oven to 350 degrees.

3. Meanwhile, heat the oil in a heavy-bottomed 12-inch skillet over medium-high heat until shimmering. Add the onion and cook, stirring occasionally, until softened and beginning to brown, about 5 minutes. Add the ground beef and cook, breaking the beef into small pieces with a spoon, until no longer pink, about 4 minutes. Stir in the garlic and cook until fragrant, about 30 seconds. Transfer the mixture to the bowl with the rice; stir in the tomatoes, 1 cup of the cheese, the parsley, and salt and pepper to taste.

4. Stir together the ketchup and the reserved tomato juice in a small bowl.

5. Place the peppers, cut side up, in a 9-inch square baking dish. Using a soup spoon, divide the filling evenly among the peppers. Spoon 2 tablespoons of the ketchup mixture over each filled pepper and sprinkle each with 1 tablespoon of the remaining ¼ cup cheese. Bake until the cheese is browned and the filling is heated through, 25 to 30 minutes. Serve immediately.

OLD-FASHIONED BURGERS

WHY THIS RECIPE WORKS: The burger you find at most drive-ins is a rubbery, thin, gray patty with little beef flavor. We wanted to create, at home, the classic drive-in burger. Made from freshly ground beef, cooked on a flat griddle, this style of burger is ultracrisp, ultrabrowned, and ultrabeefy. Topped with melted cheese and tangy sauce, it's the burger fast food restaurants wish they could produce.

We learned right off the bat that the thin patty typical of this burger style requires freshly ground meat. Prepackaged hamburger is ground very fine and packaged tightly, which produces dense, rubbery, and dry patties. For the meat, we settled on short ribs ground up with sirloin steak tips. Numerous grinding tests revealed that while beefiness depends on cut, juiciness corresponds to fat. Well-marbled short ribs added the perfect amount of

fat to complement the beefy flavor from the sirloin tips. And if you don't have a meat grinder? The food processor works just fine as long as the meat is first chilled in the freezer until firm but still pliable. We still had to deal with a rubbery texture caused by meat collagen proteins shrinking and tightening when exposed to heat. To fight this, the meat needed to be as loosely packed as possible— not pressed but rather gently shaped into loose patties. To top our burgers, we went back to the tried-and-true flavors of a tangy and sweet Thousand Island–style dressing, American cheese, and thinly sliced onion.

Best Old-Fashioned Burgers

MAKES 4 BURGERS

Sirloin steak tips are also labeled "flap meat" by some butchers. Flank steak can be used in its place. This recipe yields juicy medium to medium-well burgers. If doubling the recipe, process the meat in three batches in step 2. Because the cooked burgers do not hold well, fry four burgers and serve them immediately before frying more. Or cook them in two pans. Extra patties can be frozen for up to 2 weeks. Stack the patties, separated by parchment paper, and wrap them in three layers of plastic wrap. Thaw burgers in a single layer on a baking sheet at room temperature for 30 minutes before cooking.

- 10 ounces sirloin steak tips, cut into 1-inch chunks (see note)
- 6 ounces boneless beef short ribs, cut into 1-inch chunks
  Table salt and ground black pepper
- 1 tablespoon unsalted butter
- 4 soft hamburger buns
- ½ teaspoon vegetable oil
- 4 slices American cheese
  Thinly sliced onion
- 1 recipe Classic Burger Sauce (recipe follows)

1. Place the beef chunks on a baking sheet in a single layer, leaving ½ inch of space around each chunk. Freeze the meat until very firm and starting to harden around the edges but still pliable, 15 to 25 minutes.

2. Place half of the meat in a food processor and pulse until the meat is coarsely ground, 10 to 15 pulses, stopping and redistributing the meat around the bowl as necessary to ensure the beef is evenly ground. Transfer the meat to a baking sheet by overturning the bowl, without touching the meat. Repeat the grinding with the remaining meat. Spread the meat over the sheet and inspect carefully,

discarding any long strands of gristle or large chunks of hard meat or fat.

3. Gently separate the ground meat into four equal mounds. Without picking the meat up, with your fingers gently shape each mound into a loose patty ½ inch thick and 4 inches in diameter, leaving the edges and surface ragged. Season the top of each patty with salt and pepper. Using a spatula, flip the patties and season the other side. Refrigerate while toasting the buns.

4. Melt ½ tablespoon of the butter in a heavy-bottomed 12-inch skillet over medium heat. Add the bun tops, cut side down, and toast until light golden brown, about 2 minutes. Repeat with the remaining ½ tablespoon butter and the bun bottoms. Set the buns aside and wipe out the skillet with paper towels.

5. Return the skillet to high heat; add the oil and heat until just smoking. Using a spatula, transfer the burgers to the skillet and cook without moving them for 3 minutes. Using the spatula, flip the burgers over and cook for 1 minute. Top each patty with a slice of the cheese and continue to cook until the cheese is melted, about 1 minute longer.

6. Transfer the patties to the bun bottoms and top with the onion. Spread 2 teaspoons of the burger sauce on each bun top. Cover the burgers with the bun tops and serve immediately.

Classic Burger Sauce
MAKES ABOUT ¼ CUP

- 2 **tablespoons mayonnaise**
- 1 **tablespoon ketchup**
- ½ **teaspoon sweet pickle relish**
- ½ **teaspoon sugar**
- ½ **teaspoon white vinegar**
- ¼ **teaspoon ground black pepper**

Whisk all the ingredients together in a small bowl.

OVEN-FRIED ONION RINGS

WHY THIS RECIPE WORKS: Fried onion rings are the perfect accompaniment to burgers, barbecue, and other casual fare. But who wants the mess and smell of deep-frying? We wanted an oven method that produced tender, sweet onions with a super-crunchy coating.

We made a batter with buttermilk, egg, and flour, but when we put the baking sheet in the oven the batter slid right off the onions. Coating the onion rings with flour first gave the batter something to cling to. But we wanted even more crunch. For an extra layer of coating, we turned to crushed saltines and crushed potato chips. We preheated the oil in the baking sheet before adding the coated onions so they'd start crisping right away. The result: crispy, crunchy oven-fried onion rings with deep-fried flavor.

Oven-Fried Onion Rings
SERVES 4 TO 6

Slice the onions into ½-inch-thick rounds, separate the rings, and discard any rings smaller than 2 inches in diameter.

- ½ **cup unbleached all-purpose flour**
- 1 **large egg, at room temperature**
- ½ **cup buttermilk, at room temperature**
- ½ **teaspoon table salt**
- ¼ **teaspoon ground black pepper**
- ¼ **teaspoon cayenne pepper**
- 30 **saltine crackers**
- 4 **cups kettle-cooked potato chips**
- 2 **large yellow onions, cut into 24 large rings (see note)**
- 6 **tablespoons vegetable oil**

1. Adjust the oven racks to the lower-middle and upper-middle positions and heat the oven to 450 degrees. Place ¼ cup of the flour in a shallow baking dish. Beat the egg and buttermilk in a medium bowl. Whisk the remaining flour, the salt, black pepper, and cayenne into the buttermilk mixture. Pulse the saltines and chips together in a food processor until finely ground; place in a separate shallow baking dish.

2. Working one at a time, dredge each onion ring in the flour, shaking off the excess. Dip in the buttermilk mixture, allowing the excess to drip back into the bowl, then drop into the crumb coating, turning the ring over to coat evenly. Transfer to a large plate. (At this point, the onion rings can be refrigerated for up to 1 hour. Let them sit at room temperature for 30 minutes before baking.)

3. Pour 3 tablespoons of the oil onto each of two rimmed baking sheets. Place in the oven and heat until just smoking, about 8 minutes. Carefully tilt the heated sheets to coat evenly with the oil, then arrange the onion rings on the sheets. Bake, flipping the onion rings over and switching and rotating the position of the baking sheets halfway through baking, until golden brown on both sides, about 15 minutes. Briefly drain the onion rings on paper towels. Serve immediately.

STEAK FRIES

WHY THIS RECIPE WORKS: Thick spears of skin-on potato, steak fries are the heartier, more rustic cousins of the crisp, skinny french fry. But getting steak fries crisp on the outside and tender inside can be tricky—soggy steak fries are too often the norm. We wanted to find a way to achieve a steak fry with hearty potato flavor and great crunch.

We found that the dense starchiness of russet potatoes makes them the best variety for frying. We got the proper ratio of crisp exterior to tender interior when we cut them into ¾-inch wedges. As for the frying oil, peanut oil was our top choice. Chilling the potatoes in cold water before frying proved to be an essential step. Prepared this way, they cooked more slowly and evenly, without burning. Even after chilling, though, our fries were overcooked when we simply fried them in oil. A two-step process worked wonders. After chilling and drying the potatoes, we par-fried them at a lower temperature to cook the interiors without browning them.

Following a brief rest, we fried them again at a higher temperature to brown and crisp the exteriors. Neither greasy nor soggy, these fries boasted great flavor and crunch.

Steak Fries

SERVES 4

The potatoes must be soaked in cold water, fried once, cooled, and then fried a second time—so start this recipe at least one hour before dinner.

- 2½ pounds russet potatoes (about 4 large), scrubbed and cut lengthwise into ¾-inch-thick wedges (about 12 wedges per potato)
- 2 quarts peanut oil
- Table salt and ground black pepper

1. Place the cut potatoes in a large bowl, cover with cold water by at least 1 inch, and then cover with ice cubes. Refrigerate at least 30 minutes or up to 3 days.

2. In a large Dutch oven fitted with a clip-on candy thermometer, heat the oil over medium-low heat to 325 degrees. (The oil will bubble up when you add the potatoes, so be sure you have at least 3 inches of room at the top of the pot.)

3. Pour off the ice and water, quickly wrap the potatoes in a clean kitchen towel, and thoroughly pat them dry. Increase the heat to medium-high and add the potatoes, one handful at a time, to the hot oil. Fry, stirring with a Chinese skimmer or large-holed slotted spoon, until the potatoes are limp and soft and have turned from white to gold, about 10 minutes. (The oil temperature will drop 50 to 60 degrees during this frying.) Use the skimmer or slotted spoon to transfer the fries to a triple thickness of paper towels to drain; let rest at least 10 minutes. (The fries can stand at room temperature for up to 2 hours.)

4. When ready to serve the fries, reheat the oil to 350 degrees. Using the paper towels as a funnel, pour the potatoes into the hot oil. Discard the paper towels and line a wire rack with another triple thickness of paper towels. Fry the potatoes, stirring fairly constantly, until medium brown and puffed, 8 to 10 minutes. Transfer to the paper towel–lined rack to drain. Season with salt and pepper to taste. Serve immediately.

CLASSIC FRENCH FRIES

WHY THIS RECIPE WORKS: Efforts to re-create restaurant-style fries at home have always disappointed, with fries that were greasy or droopy or burnt on the outside and raw on the inside. We wanted to find a recipe and method for the home cook that would rival those cooked by professionals—crunchy fries with deep potato flavor.

As we found in developing our recipe for Steak Fries (page 185), russet potatoes were preferred for their dense texture and hearty flavor. Because these are starchy potatoes, it was important to rinse the starch off the surface after cutting the potatoes into fries. To achieve evenly cooked fries, we first refrigerated the cut potatoes in a bowl of ice water for at least 30 minutes and then took a double-fry approach. During the first fry, because the potatoes are nearly frozen, the potatoes can cook long and slow, which ensures a soft, rich-tasting interior. A quick second fry at a higher temperature crisped and colored the exterior. We used peanut oil for frying but felt our fries lacked the flavor imparted by lard. A little strained bacon grease gave our fries a touch of meaty flavor just like those found in our favorite restaurant fries.

Classic French Fries

SERVES 4

We prefer to peel the potatoes. Leaving the skin on keeps the potato from forming those little airy blisters that we like. Peeling the potato also allows the removal of any imperfections and greenish coloring. Once the potatoes are peeled and cut, plan on at least an hour before the fries are ready to eat.

- 2½ **pounds russet potatoes (about 4 large), peeled and cut into ¼-inch by ¼-inch lengths**
- 2 **quarts peanut oil**
- ¼ **cup bacon fat, strained (optional)**
  Table salt and ground black pepper

1. Place the cut potatoes in a large bowl, cover with at least 1 inch of water, then cover with ice cubes. Refrigerate at least 30 minutes or up to 3 days.

2. In a large Dutch oven fitted with a clip-on candy thermometer, heat the oil over medium-low heat to 325 degrees. (The oil will bubble up when you add the potatoes, so be sure you have at least 3 inches of room at the top of the pot.) Add the bacon grease (if using).

3. Pour off the ice and water, quickly wrap the potatoes in a clean kitchen towel, and thoroughly pat them dry. Increase the heat to medium-high and add the potatoes, one handful at a time, to the hot oil. Fry, stirring with a Chinese skimmer or large-holed slotted spoon, until the potatoes are limp and soft and have turned from white to gold, about 10 minutes. (The oil temperature will drop 50 to 60 degrees during this frying.) Use the skimmer or slotted spoon to transfer the fries to a triple thickness of paper towels to drain; let rest at least 10 minutes. (The fries can stand at room temperature for up to 2 hours.)

4. When ready to serve the fries, reheat the oil to 350 degrees. Using the paper towels as a funnel, pour the potatoes into the hot oil. Discard the paper towels and line a wire rack with another triple thickness of paper towels. Fry the potatoes, stirring fairly constantly, until medium brown and puffed, about 1 minute. Transfer to the paper towel–lined rack to drain. Season with salt and pepper to taste. Serve immediately.

EASIER FRENCH FRIES

WHY THIS RECIPE WORKS: Our recipe for Classic French Fries works beautifully, but we'll admit that it sometimes seems like a lot of trouble. We challenged ourselves to devise a shortcut that would give us crisp, golden fries with less work.

Oven-frying is the usual "quick" method, but we wanted real french fries. We started with an unorthodox procedure of starting the cut potatoes in a few cups of cold oil. To our surprise, the fries were pretty good, if a little dry. Because russets are fairly dry potatoes, we wondered if a different type of potato would work better. Sure enough, Yukon Golds, which have more water and less starch, came out creamy and smooth inside and crisp outside. A bonus was their thin skin—we could save time by not having to peel the potatoes. We were almost there, but the fries tended to stick to the bottom of the pot and they also tended to clump. Stirring seemed like the obvious solution, but this tended to break the potatoes. After some experimentation, we found that leaving the fries undisturbed for 15 minutes, then stirring them, kept them from sticking and from breaking apart. Thinner batons were also less likely to stick. These fries had all the qualities of classic french fries, without all the bother.

Easier French Fries

SERVES 4

For those who like it, flavoring the oil with bacon fat gives the fries a mild meaty flavor. We prefer peanut oil for frying, but vegetable oil can be substituted. This recipe will not work with sweet potatoes or russets. Serve with dipping sauces (recipes follow), if desired.

- 2½   **pounds Yukon Gold potatoes (about 6 medium), scrubbed, dried, sides squared off, and cut lengthwise into ¼-inch by ¼-inch batons (see note)**
- 6   **cups peanut oil (see note)**
- ¼   **cup bacon fat, strained (optional; see note)**
    Table salt

1. Combine the potatoes, oil, and bacon fat (if using) in a large Dutch oven. Cook over high heat until the oil has reached a rolling boil, about 5 minutes. Continue to cook, without stirring, until the potatoes are pale golden and the exteriors are beginning to crisp, about 15 minutes.

2. Using tongs, stir the potatoes, gently scraping up any that stick, and continue to cook, stirring occasionally, until golden and crisp, 5 to 10 minutes longer. Using a skimmer or slotted spoon, transfer the fries to a thick paper bag or paper towels. Season with salt to taste and serve immediately.

Chive and Black Pepper Dipping Sauce

MAKES ABOUT ½ CUP

- 5   **tablespoons mayonnaise**
- 3   **tablespoons sour cream**
- 2   **tablespoons chopped fresh chives**
- 1½   **teaspoons juice from 1 lemon**
- ¼   **teaspoon table salt**
- ¼   **teaspoon ground black pepper**

Whisk all the ingredients together in a small bowl.

Belgian-Style Dipping Sauce

MAKES ABOUT ½ CUP

- 5   **tablespoons mayonnaise**
- 3   **tablespoons ketchup**
- 1   **medium garlic clove, minced or pressed through a garlic press (about 1 teaspoon)**
- ½   **teaspoon hot sauce or more to taste**
- ¼   **teaspoon table salt**

Whisk all the ingredients together in a small bowl.

CHAPTER 12

WHO WANTS PASTA?

Pasta with Garlic and Oil   190

Pasta with Fresh Tomatoes and Herbs   191

Pasta and Fresh Tomato Sauce with Garlic and Basil   191

Pasta with Creamy Tomato Sauce   192

Pasta Caprese   193

Farfalle with Tomatoes, Olives, and Feta   194

Quick Tomato Sauce   194

Marinara Sauce   195

Spaghetti Puttanesca   196

Pasta with Tomato, Bacon, and Onion (Pasta all'Amatriciana)   197

Farfalle with Pesto   198

Pasta with Tomato and Almond Pesto (Pesto alla Trapanese)   198

Campanelle with Arugula, Goat Cheese, and Sun-Dried Tomato Pesto   199

Penne with Toasted Nut and Parsley Pesto

Spaghetti with Olive Pesto

Campanelle with Asparagus, Basil, and Balsamic Glaze   201

Cavatappi with Asparagus, Arugula, Walnuts, and Blue Cheese

Pasta with Sautéed Mushrooms and Thyme   202

Orecchiette with Broccoli Rabe and Sausage   203

Garlicky Shrimp Pasta   204

Shrimp fra Diavolo   205

Pasta with Hearty Italian Meat Sauce (Sunday Gravy)   206

Simple Italian-Style Meat Sauce   207

Fettuccine with Slow-Simmered Bolognese Sauce   208

Pasta with Weeknight Bolognese Sauce   209

Pasta and Slow-Simmered Tomato Sauce with Meat   210

Spaghetti and Meatballs   211

Penne with Vodka Sauce (Penne alla Vodka)   212

Spaghetti alla Carbonara   213

Fettuccine Alfredo   213

Creamy Baked Four-Cheese Pasta   214

Baked Ziti   215

Baked Manicotti   216

Four-Cheese Lasagna   217

Lasagna with Hearty Tomato-Meat Sauce   219

PASTA WITH GARLIC AND OIL

WHY THIS RECIPE WORKS: Nothing sounds easier than pasta with olive oil and garlic, but too often this dish turns out oily or rife with burnt garlic. We were after a flawless version of this quick classic, with bright, deep garlic flavor and no trace of bitterness or harshness.

For a mellow flavor, we cooked most of the garlic over low heat until sticky and straw-colored; a modest amount of raw garlic added at the end brought in some potent fresh garlic flavor. Extra-virgin olive oil and reserved pasta cooking water helped to keep our garlic and pasta saucy. A splash of lemon juice and sprinkling of red pepper flakes added some spice and brightness to this simple, yet complex-flavored recipe.

Pasta with Garlic and Oil

SERVES 4 TO 6

For a twist on pasta with garlic and oil, try sprinkling toasted fresh bread crumbs over individual bowls, but prepare them in advance. Simply pulse two slices of high-quality white sandwich bread, torn into quarters, in a food processor to coarse crumbs. Combine with 2 tablespoons extra-virgin olive oil, season with salt and pepper, and bake on a rimmed baking sheet at 375 degrees until golden brown, 8 to 10 minutes.

Table salt
1 pound spaghetti
6 tablespoons extra-virgin olive oil
12 medium garlic cloves, minced or pressed through a garlic press (about 4 tablespoons)
¾ teaspoon red pepper flakes
3 tablespoons chopped fresh parsley leaves
2 teaspoons juice from 1 lemon
½ cup grated Parmesan cheese (optional)

1. Bring 4 quarts water to a boil in a large pot. Add 1 tablespoon salt and the pasta to the boiling water and cook, stirring often, until al dente; reserve ⅓ cup of the cooking water then drain the pasta and return it to the pot.

2. Meanwhile, heat 3 tablespoons of the oil, 3 tablespoons of the garlic, and ½ teaspoon salt over low heat in a 10-inch nonstick skillet. Cook, stirring constantly, until the garlic is sticky and straw-colored, 10 to 12 minutes. Off the heat, stir in the remaining 1 tablespoon garlic, the red pepper flakes, parsley, lemon juice, and 2 tablespoons of the reserved pasta cooking water.

3. Transfer the drained pasta to a warm serving bowl; add the remaining 3 tablespoons oil and remaining reserved pasta cooking water and toss to combine. Add the garlic mixture and ¾ teaspoon salt; toss to combine. Serve, sprinkling individual bowls with Parmesan cheese, if desired.

PASTA WITH FRESH TOMATOES

WHY THIS RECIPE WORKS: Fully ripe tomatoes need little else besides high-quality olive oil and a smattering of fresh herbs to become a bright, summery dressing for pasta. We set out to create the perfect raw tomato sauce—ideal for a quick yet flavorful dinner.

Selecting the ripest tomatoes guarantees fresh flavor in the sauce, but to prevent their sweetness and acidity from taking over, we mixed in a generous amount of extra-virgin olive oil and a hefty amount of fresh herbs—you can use basil, parsley, cilantro, mint, oregano, or tarragon. We let the flavors of the tomatoes, olive oil, herbs, and some minced garlic blend while we cooked the pasta. Short, tubular pasta shapes work best, as they hold on to the chunky sauce.

Pasta with Fresh Tomatoes and Herbs

SERVES 4 TO 6

This chunky sauce works best with tubular pasta shapes, such as penne or fusilli. The success of this dish depends on using ripe, flavorful tomatoes.

- 1½ **pounds ripe tomatoes (about 3 large), cored and cut into ½-inch pieces (see note)**
- ¼ **cup minced fresh herbs, such as basil, parsley, cilantro, mint, oregano, or tarragon**
- 1 **medium garlic clove, minced or pressed through a garlic press (about 1 teaspoon)**
- ¼ **cup extra-virgin olive oil**
  Table salt and ground black pepper
- 1 **pound penne, fusilli, or other short tubular pasta (see note)**

1. Combine the tomatoes, herbs, garlic, oil, and salt and pepper to taste in a medium bowl. Set aside.

2. Bring 4 quarts water to a boil in a large pot. Add 1 tablespoon salt and the pasta to the boiling water and cook, stirring often, until al dente. Reserve ½ cup of the cooking water then drain the pasta and return it to the pot. Add the tomatoes and toss to combine; adjust the consistency of the sauce with the reserved pasta cooking water. Serve.

PASTA AND FRESH TOMATO SAUCE

WHY THIS RECIPE WORKS: The best fresh tomato sauces capture the contrasting sweet and tart flavors of ripe tomatoes. But often, these sauces get waterlogged from the tomato juice. We wanted a cooked sauce that allowed the flavors of the traditional players—tomatoes, basil, garlic, and oil—to meld, but not become watered down.

Quick cooking was the key to preserving fresh tomato flavor and creating a sauce that is both hearty and brightly flavored. To prevent unattractive pieces of curled-up tomato skin floating in our finished sauce, we simply peeled the tomatoes by boiling them and pulling off their skins. Seeded tomatoes made for a less watery start to the sauce, and cooking them down for a brief period facilitated the evaporation of any remaining liquid. Chopped fresh basil rounded out the flavors of the sauce, and a last-minute drizzle of olive oil brought a richness that complemented the sweetness of the tomatoes.

BEHIND THE SCENES

TOMATOES—SKIP THE FRIDGE, PLEASE

We never store tomatoes in the refrigerator. Cold damages tomatoes in two ways: It destroys an enzyme that produces flavorful compounds, and it makes water in the tomato expand, rupturing cells and turning the flesh mealy. But what about storing a partially used tomato? We cut a dozen ripe tomatoes in two, stored half of each in the fridge, and kept the other half at room temperature (both were wrapped tightly in plastic). After a few days, the halves at room temperature had begun to soften, while the refrigerated halves were still as firm as the day they were cut. Upon tasting, however, we found the refrigerated halves were bland and mealy compared with the never-refrigerated halves. Our advice? Keep cut tomatoes tightly wrapped at room temperature and consume them within a few days. The shelf life gained by refrigeration doesn't make up for the loss in flavor and texture.

Pasta and Fresh Tomato Sauce with Garlic and Basil

SERVES 4 TO 6

To peel the tomatoes, dunk the cored tomatoes in a pot of boiling water until the skins split and begin to curl around the cored area, about 15 to 30 seconds; transfer the tomatoes to a bowl of ice water, then peel off the skins with your fingers. This chunky sauce works best with tubular pasta shapes, such as penne or fusilli. If you'd like to serve it with spaghetti or linguine, puree the sauce in a blender or food processor before adding the basil. This recipe can be doubled and prepared in a 12-inch skillet.

- 3 **tablespoons extra-virgin olive oil**
- 2 **medium garlic cloves, minced or pressed through a garlic press (about 2 teaspoons)**
- 2 **pounds ripe tomatoes (about 4 large), cored, peeled, seeded, and cut into ½-inch pieces (see note)**
- 2 **tablespoons chopped fresh basil leaves**
  Table salt
- 1 **pound penne, fusilli, or other short tubular pasta (see note)**

1. Cook 2 tablespoons of the oil and the garlic in a 10-inch skillet over medium heat until fragrant, about 30 seconds. Stir in the tomatoes and cook over medium-high heat until the liquid released by the tomatoes evaporates and the tomato pieces form a chunky sauce, about 10 minutes. Stir in the basil and salt to taste; cover.

2. Meanwhile, bring 4 quarts water to a boil in a large pot. Add 1 tablespoon salt and the pasta to the boiling water and cook, stirring often, until al dente. Reserve ½ cup of the cooking water then drain the pasta and return it to the pot. Add ¼ cup of the reserved cooking water, the sauce, and remaining 1 tablespoon oil and toss to combine. Adjust the consistency of the sauce with the remaining reserved pasta cooking water. Serve.

PASTA WITH CREAMY TOMATO SAUCE

WHY THIS RECIPE WORKS: In the best examples of creamy tomato sauce, the acidity of fruity tomatoes is balanced with the richness of dairy; the worst deliver instant heartburn and make you wish the two elements had never met. We wanted a smooth, full-flavored tomato sauce enriched with, but not overwhelmed by, cream.

Readily available, canned crushed tomatoes trumped canned whole and diced tomatoes—they're bright in flavor, easy to puree in the food processor, and contain

just the right amount of juice. Before adding the tomatoes to the pot, we cooked a few tablespoons of tomato paste with some onion and garlic, and added sun-dried tomatoes, to deepen the flavor of the sauce. A pinch of red pepper flakes, a splash of wine, and a little minced prosciutto added depth and tamed some of the sauce's sweetness; a bit of reserved uncooked crushed tomatoes and another splash of wine stirred in before serving brought the sauce's ingredients together. As for the cream, traditional heavy cream can't be beat; we added it to the just-finished sauce to enrich it without subduing the bright tomato flavor.

Pasta with Creamy Tomato Sauce

SERVES 4 TO 6

Use high-quality crushed tomatoes; our favorite brands are Tuttorosso and Muir Glen.

- 3 tablespoons unsalted butter
- 1 small onion, minced
- 1 ounce prosciutto, minced (about 2 tablespoons)
- 1 bay leaf
  Pinch red pepper flakes
  Table salt
- 3 medium garlic cloves, minced or pressed through a garlic press (about 1 tablespoon)
- 2 ounces oil-packed sun-dried tomatoes, drained, rinsed, patted dry, and chopped coarse (about 3 tablespoons)
- 2 tablespoons tomato paste
- ¼ cup plus 2 tablespoons dry white wine
- 2 cups plus 2 tablespoons crushed tomatoes (from one 28-ounce can) (see note)
- 1 pound ziti, penne, or other short tubular pasta
- ½ cup heavy cream
  Ground black pepper
- ¼ cup chopped fresh basil leaves
  Grated Parmesan cheese, for serving

1. Melt the butter in a medium saucepan over medium heat. Add the onion, prosciutto, bay leaf, red pepper flakes, and ¼ teaspoon salt; cook, stirring occasionally, until the onion is very soft and beginning to turn light gold, 8 to 12 minutes. Increase the heat to medium-high, add the garlic, and cook until fragrant, about 30 seconds. Stir in the sun-dried tomatoes and tomato paste and cook, stirring constantly, until slightly darkened, 1 to 2 minutes. Add ¼ cup of the wine and cook, stirring frequently, until the liquid has evaporated, 1 to 2 minutes.

2. Add 2 cups of the crushed tomatoes and bring to a simmer. Reduce the heat to low, partially cover, and cook, stirring occasionally, until the sauce is thickened, 25 to 30 minutes.

3. Meanwhile, bring 4 quarts water to a boil in a large pot. Add 1 tablespoon salt and the pasta to the boiling water and cook, stirring often, until al dente. Reserve ½ cup of the cooking water then drain the pasta and return it to the pot.

4. Remove the bay leaf from the sauce and discard. Stir the cream, remaining 2 tablespoons crushed tomatoes, and remaining 2 tablespoons wine into the sauce; season with salt and pepper to taste. Add the sauce to the pasta and adjust the consistency of the sauce with the reserved pasta cooking water. Stir in the basil and serve, passing the Parmesan separately.

PASTA CAPRESE

WHY THIS RECIPE WORKS: The summer salad composed of creamy mozzarella, fresh basil, and sweet tomatoes has become so popular that we wanted to translate it to a simple-yet-elegant pasta dish, one in which the primary ingredients work in harmony with the pasta. Specifically, we wanted creamy pockets of milky mozzarella throughout the dish, rather than the chewy wads that can occur when cheese hits hot pasta. And we wanted to find a way to guarantee sweet tomato flavor, even when we were working with substandard tomatoes.

Supermarket mozzarella works well in this dish; the trick is to dice and freeze it for just 10 minutes before tossing it with the hot pasta. This extra step helps to keep the cheese soft and creamy (instead of dry and clumpy). Otherwise, handmade buffalo- or cow's-milk mozzarella (minus the freezing step) works well. To boost the flavor of less-than-stellar tomatoes, we added a little sugar for sweetness and fresh lemon juice for brightness. Marinating the tomatoes and mozzarella with olive oil, minced shallot, a sprinkle of salt, and a few twists of black pepper while the pasta was cooking added even more flavor. We decided not to cut corners with a substandard olive oil—because there are few flavors in this dish, the fruity nuances of a good extra-virgin olive oil definitely make a difference.

Pasta Caprese
SERVES 4 TO 6

This dish will be very warm, not hot. The success of this recipe depends on high-quality ingredients, including ripe, in-season tomatoes and a fruity olive oil (the test kitchen prefers Columela extra-virgin). Don't skip the step of freezing the mozzarella, as freezing prevents it from turning chewy when it comes in contact with the hot pasta. If handmade buffalo- or cow's-milk mozzarella is available (it's commonly found, packed in water, in gourmet and cheese shops), we highly recommend using it, but do not freeze it. Additional lemon juice or up to 1 teaspoon sugar can be added at the end to taste, depending on the ripeness of the tomatoes.

¼ cup extra-virgin olive oil (see note)
2-4 teaspoons juice from 1 lemon (see note)
1 small garlic clove, minced or pressed through a garlic press (about ½ teaspoon)
1 small shallot, minced (about 1 tablespoon)
Table salt and ground black pepper
1½ pounds ripe tomatoes (about 3 large), cored, seeded, and cut into ½-inch dice (see note)
12 ounces fresh mozzarella cheese, cut into ½-inch cubes (see note)
1 pound penne, fusilli, or campanelle
¼ cup chopped fresh basil leaves
1 teaspoon sugar (optional; see note)

1. Whisk the oil, 2 teaspoons of the lemon juice, the garlic, shallot, ½ teaspoon salt, and ¼ teaspoon pepper together in a large bowl. Add the tomatoes and gently toss to combine; set aside. Do not marinate the tomatoes for longer than 45 minutes.

2. While the tomatoes are marinating, place the mozzarella on a plate and freeze until slightly firm, about 10 minutes. Bring 4 quarts water to a boil in a large pot. Add 1 tablespoon salt and the pasta to the boiling water and cook, stirring often, until al dente. Drain well.

3. Add the pasta and mozzarella to the tomato mixture and gently toss to combine. Let stand 5 minutes. Stir in the basil, season with salt and pepper to taste, and add additional lemon juice or sugar, if desired. Serve immediately.

PASTA WITH TOMATOES AND OLIVES

WHY THIS RECIPE WORKS: When tomatoes are in season, there's no better time to make a simple, fresh tomato sauce. We like the classic pairing of tomatoes and olives, so we set out to make an easy, not too watery, sauce with Mediterranean flavors.

Seeding the tomatoes rid them of excess moisture and prevented a watery sauce. Instead of peeling the tomato skins, we decided to leave them on so the chopped tomatoes would have some structural integrity and not disintegrate. By making a no-cook sauce—the other components were fresh mint, chopped kalamata olives, and feta—we were able to prepare it quickly while the drained pasta waited on the sidelines. The potent olives and feta added a bright zestiness to our pasta, and the mint amplified the sauce's freshness.

Farfalle with Tomatoes, Olives, and Feta

SERVES 4 TO 6

To prevent the feta from melting into the pasta, add it only after the tomatoes have been tossed with the pasta, which gives the mixture the opportunity to cool slightly.

    Table salt
1   pound farfalle
1½ pounds ripe tomatoes (about 3 large), cored, seeded, and cut into ½-inch pieces
½   cup pitted kalamata olives, chopped coarse
¼   cup extra-virgin olive oil
1   tablespoon chopped fresh mint leaves
    Ground black pepper
6   ounces feta cheese, crumbled (about 1½ cups) (see note)

1. Bring 4 quarts water to a boil in a large pot. Add 1 tablespoon salt and the pasta to the boiling water and cook, stirring often, until al dente. Reserve ½ cup of the cooking water then drain the pasta and return it to the pot.

2. Meanwhile, combine the tomatoes, olives, oil, mint, ½ teaspoon salt, and ¼ teaspoon pepper in a medium bowl. Add the sauce to the pasta and adjust the consistency of the sauce with the reserved pasta cooking water. Add the feta and toss to combine. Season with salt and pepper to taste and serve.

QUICK TOMATO SAUCE

WHY THIS RECIPE WORKS: In a perfect world, garden-ripe tomatoes make the best quick tomato sauce. But that isn't a realistic option for most of the year. We wanted to create a complex, brightly flavored sauce with the next best alternative—canned tomatoes—that tasted of full, fruity tomatoes, in the time it took to boil pasta.

Choosing the right can of tomatoes was a critical first step. Crushed tomatoes were the best choice because they would save us the step of pureeing. We also shredded a small amount of onion on a box grater before sautéing; the shredded pieces cooked faster and became sweeter more quickly. We sautéed the onion in butter, which caramelizes when heated, and added garlic, sugar, and the crushed tomatoes, then simmered the sauce briefly. To make up for the lost fragrance of fresh tomatoes, we added chopped fresh basil and extra-virgin olive oil. Swirled in just before serving, these ingredients infused the sauce with fresh herbal flavor and a hit of richness.

Quick Tomato Sauce

MAKES ABOUT 3 CUPS

This recipe makes enough to sauce a pound of pasta. High-quality canned tomatoes will make a big difference in this sauce; our preferred brands of crushed tomatoes are Tuttorosso and Muir Glen. Grate the onion on the large holes of a box grater.

2 tablespoons unsalted butter

¼ cup grated onion (see note)

¼ teaspoon dried oregano

   Table salt

2 medium garlic cloves, minced or pressed through a garlic press (about 2 teaspoons)

1 (28-ounce) can crushed tomatoes (see note)

¼ teaspoon sugar

2 tablespoons chopped fresh basil leaves

1 tablespoon extra-virgin olive oil

   Ground black pepper

Melt the butter in a medium saucepan over medium heat. Add the onion, oregano, and ½ teaspoon salt; cook, stirring occasionally, until the liquid has evaporated and the onion is golden brown, about 5 minutes. Add the garlic and cook until fragrant, about 30 seconds. Stir in the tomatoes and sugar; bring to a simmer over high heat. Lower the heat to medium-low and simmer until slightly thickened, about 10 minutes. Off the heat, stir in the basil and oil; season with salt and pepper to taste.

MARINARA SAUCE

WHY THIS RECIPE WORKS: Usually, developing a tomato sauce with deep, complex flavor requires hours of slow simmering. But we wanted to produce a multidimensional marinara sauce in less than an hour—perfect for any night of the week.

Our first challenge was picking the right tomatoes. We found canned whole tomatoes, which we hand-crushed to remove the hard core, to be the best choice in terms of both flavor and texture. We boosted tomato flavor by sautéing the tomato pieces until they glazed the bottom of the pan, after which we added their liquid. We shortened the simmering time by using a skillet instead of a saucepan (the greater surface area of a skillet encourages faster evaporation and flavor concentration). Finally, we added just the right amount of sugar, red wine (we especially liked Chianti and Merlot), and, just before serving, a few uncooked canned tomatoes for texture, fresh basil for fresh herbal flavor, and olive oil for richness.

Marinara Sauce

MAKES 4 CUPS

You can figure on about 3 cups of sauce per pound of pasta. Chianti or Merlot work well for the dry red wine. Because canned tomatoes vary in acidity and saltiness, it's best to add salt, pepper, and sugar to taste just before serving. If you prefer a chunkier sauce, give it just three or four pulses in the food processor in step 4.

2 (28-ounce) cans whole tomatoes packed in juice

3 tablespoons extra-virgin olive oil

1 medium onion, minced

2 medium garlic cloves, minced or pressed through a garlic press (about 2 teaspoons)

½ teaspoon dried oregano

⅓ cup dry red wine (see note)

3 tablespoons chopped fresh basil leaves

   Table salt and ground black pepper

1–2 teaspoons sugar, as needed (see note)

1. Pour the tomatoes into a strainer set over a large bowl. Open the tomatoes with your hands and remove and discard the fibrous cores; let the tomatoes drain excess liquid, about 5 minutes. Remove ¾ cup tomatoes from the strainer and set aside. Reserve 2½ cups tomato juice and discard the remainder.

2. Heat 2 tablespoons of the olive oil in a 12-inch skillet over medium heat until shimmering. Add the onion and cook, stirring occasionally, until softened and golden around the edges, 6 to 8 minutes. Add the garlic and oregano and cook, stirring constantly, until the garlic is fragrant, about 30 seconds.

3. Add the tomatoes from the strainer and increase the heat to medium-high. Cook, stirring every minute, until the liquid has evaporated and the tomatoes begin to stick to the bottom of the pan and browned bits form around the pan edges, 10 to 12 minutes. Add the wine and cook until thick and syrupy, about 1 minute. Add the reserved tomato juice and bring to a simmer; reduce the heat to medium and cook, stirring occasionally and loosening any browned bits, until the sauce is thickened, 8 to 10 minutes.

4. Transfer the sauce to a food processor and add the reserved tomatoes; process until slightly chunky, about 8 pulses. Return the sauce to the skillet, add the basil and remaining 1 tablespoon olive oil, and season with salt, pepper, and sugar to taste. (The sauce can be refrigerated in an airtight container for up to 3 days or frozen for 1 month.)

PASTA PUTTANESCA

WHY THIS RECIPE WORKS: Puttanesca is a gutsy tomato sauce punctuated by the brash, zesty flavors of garlic, anchovies, olives, and capers. But too often, the sauce comes off as too fishy, too garlicky, too briny, or just plain too salty. We wanted to harmonize the bold flavors in this Neapolitan dish and not let any one preside over the others.

For a sauce with the best tomato flavor and a slightly clingy consistency, we used canned diced tomatoes and kept the cooking time to a minimum to retain their fresh flavor and their meaty texture. To tame the garlic and prevent it from burning, we soaked minced garlic in a bit of water before sautéing it. Cooking the garlic and anchovies with red pepper flakes (before adding the tomatoes) helped their flavors bloom and added a subtle heat. We chose to add the olives and capers when the sauce was finished—this prevented them from disintegrating in the sauce. Reserved tomato juice from the canned tomatoes moistened the pasta, and a last-minute addition of minced parsley preserved the fresh flavors of the sauce.

Spaghetti Puttanesca

SERVES 4 TO 6

The pasta and sauce cook in about the same amount of time, so begin the sauce just after you add the pasta to the boiling water in step 1.

- 3   **medium garlic cloves, minced or pressed through a garlic press (about 1 tablespoon)**
     Table salt
- 1   **pound spaghetti**
- 1   **(28-ounce) can diced tomatoes, drained and ½ cup juice reserved**
- 2   **tablespoons extra-virgin olive oil, plus extra for drizzling**
- 4   **teaspoons minced anchovy fillets (about 8 fillets)**
- 1   **teaspoon red pepper flakes**
- ½   **cup pitted kalamata olives, chopped coarse**
- ¼   **cup minced fresh parsley leaves**
- 3   **tablespoons capers, rinsed**

1. Combine the garlic with 1 tablespoon water in a small bowl; set aside. Bring 4 quarts water to a boil in a large pot. Add 1 tablespoon salt and the pasta to the boiling water and cook, stirring often, until al dente. Reserve ½ cup of the cooking water then drain the pasta and return it to the pot. Add ¼ cup of the reserved tomato juice and toss to combine.

2. Meanwhile, heat the oil, anchovies, garlic mixture, and red pepper flakes in a 12-inch skillet over medium heat. Cook, stirring frequently, until the garlic is fragrant, 2 to 3 minutes. Add the tomatoes and simmer until slightly thickened, about 8 minutes.

3. Stir the olives, parsley, and capers into the sauce. Pour the sauce over the pasta and toss to combine; adjust the consistency of the sauce with the remaining reserved tomato juice or reserved pasta cooking water. Season with salt to taste, drizzle with 1 tablespoon oil, if desired, and serve immediately.

PASTA ALL'AMATRICIANA

WHY THIS RECIPE WORKS: Pasta all'Amatriciana is a classic Roman pasta dish that boasts a rich sauce containing tomato, bacon, onion, and Pecorino Romano cheese. Unfortunately, for a truly authentic dish, you need a specific type of bacon, *guanciale* (made from pork jowls), which is easy to find in central Italy but not so easy to locate in the States. We wanted to create a recipe that would do this classic sauce justice using ingredients found locally.

Thickly sliced pancetta (unsmoked Italian bacon) is the best substitute for guanciale but if you can't find pancetta, bacon works too. We cut the pancetta into strips and cooked them in a skillet until crisp, then built the sauce in the remaining fat. Canned diced tomatoes, onion, and red pepper flakes made up the sauce; we kept the pancetta separate until the end so it stayed crisp in the finished dish. For the last steps, we tossed the crisp pancetta in with the tomato sauce and pasta (long-strand pasta, like bucatinior linguine, works best) and sprinkled grated Pecorino Romano cheese on top.

Pasta with Tomato, Bacon, and Onion (Pasta all'Amatriciana)

SERVES 4 TO 6

This dish is traditionally made with bucatini, also called perciatelli, which appear to be thick, round strands but are actually thin, extralong tubes. Linguine works fine, too. When buying pancetta, ask the butcher to slice it ¼ inch thick; if using bacon, buy slab bacon and cut it into ¼-inch-thick slices yourself. If the pancetta that you're using is very lean, it's unlikely that you will need to drain off any fat before adding the onion.

- 2 tablespoons extra-virgin olive oil
- 6 ounces pancetta or bacon, sliced ¼ inch thick and cut into strips 1 inch long and ¼ inch wide (see note)
- 1 medium onion, minced
- ½ teaspoon red pepper flakes, or to taste
- 1 (28-ounce) can diced tomatoes, drained and juice reserved
- Table salt
- 1 pound bucatini, perciatelli, or linguine (see note)
- ⅓ cup grated Pecorino Romano cheese

1. Bring 4 quarts water to a boil in a large pot.

2. Meanwhile, heat the oil in a 12-inch skillet over medium heat until shimmering. Add the pancetta and cook, stirring occasionally, until lightly browned and crisp,

about 8 minutes. Using a slotted spoon, transfer the pancetta to a paper towel–lined plate; set aside. Pour off all but 2 tablespoons of fat from the skillet. Add the onion and cook over medium heat until softened, about 5 minutes. Add the red pepper flakes and cook, about 30 seconds. Stir in the tomatoes and reserved juice and simmer until slightly thickened, about 10 minutes.

3. While the sauce is simmering, add 1 tablespoon salt and the pasta to the boiling water and cook, stirring often, until al dente. Reserve ½ cup of the cooking water then drain the pasta and return it to the pot.

4. Add the pancetta to the sauce and season with salt to taste. Add the sauce to the pasta and toss over low heat to combine, about 30 seconds. Add the Pecorino and toss again. Adjust the consistency of the sauce with the reserved pasta cooking water and serve immediately.

PASTA WITH PESTO

WHY THIS RECIPE WORKS: Pasta with pesto makes for a satisfying, summery meal. But getting pesto right isn't always so easy; the sauce can be anywhere from too thin and watery to too thick and overpoweringly garlicky. Our goal was to heighten the basil and subdue the garlic flavors in pesto so that each major element balanced the next.

We started by briefly blanching whole unpeeled garlic cloves to tame their flavor and prevent them from taking over the sauce. Then we bruised the basil in a plastic bag with a meat pounder (you could also use a rolling pin) to unlock its flavor; we found that this method released the most herbal flavors from the basil. With the basil flavor boosted and the garlic toned down, it was time to process the ingredients with toasted nuts and stir in the Parmesan. Finally, we reserved some of the pasta cooking water, which was essential to thin out the pesto once it had been added to the pasta. The water also softened and blended the flavors a bit, and highlighted the creaminess of the cheese and nuts.

Farfalle with Pesto

SERVES 4 TO 6

Basil usually darkens in homemade pesto, but you can preserve the green color by adding the optional parsley. For sharper flavor, substitute 1 tablespoon finely grated Pecorino Romano cheese for 1 tablespoon of the Parmesan. For a change from farfalle, try curly shapes, such as fusilli, which can trap bits of the pesto.

- 3 **medium garlic cloves, threaded on a skewer**
- 2 **cups packed fresh basil leaves**
- 2 **tablespoons fresh flat-leaf parsley leaves (optional; see note)**
- ¼ **cup pine nuts, walnuts, or almonds, toasted**
- 7 **tablespoons extra-virgin olive oil**
  Table salt
- ¼ **cup finely grated Parmesan (see note)**
- 1 **pound farfalle (see note)**

1. Bring 4 quarts water to a boil in a large pot. Lower the skewered garlic into the water and boil for 45 seconds. Immediately run the garlic under cold water. Remove the garlic from the skewer, peel, and mince.

2. Place the basil and parsley (if using) in a zipper-lock bag and pound with the flat side of a meat pounder or a rolling pin until all the leaves are bruised.

3. Process the nuts, garlic, basil, oil, and ½ teaspoon salt in a food processor until smooth, scraping down the sides of the workbowl as necessary. Transfer the mixture to a small bowl, stir in the cheese, and season with salt to taste. (The pesto can be covered with a sheet of plastic wrap pressed against the surface and refrigerated for up to 5 days.)

4. Add 1 tablespoon salt and the pasta to the boiling water and cook, stirring often, until al dente. Reserve ½ cup of the cooking water then drain the pasta and return it to the pot. Stir in ¼ cup reserved cooking water and the pesto; adjust the consistency of the sauce with the remaining reserved pasta cooking water. Serve immediately.

PASTA WITH TOMATO AND ALMOND PESTO

WHY THIS RECIPE WORKS: In the Sicilian village of Trapani, there's a very different kind of pesto—it's basically pesto crossed with tomato sauce. Almonds replace pine nuts, but the big difference is the appearance of fresh tomatoes—not as the main ingredient, but as a fruity, sweet accent. We wanted a recipe for a clean, bright version of this sauce, not a chunky tomato salsa or thin, watery slush.

For an uncooked sauce, fresh tomatoes were best. Cherry and grape tomatoes proved equal contenders, sharing a similar brightness and juiciness that was far more reliable than that of their larger cousins. We processed the tomatoes with a handful of basil, garlic, and toasted almonds. The almonds contributed body and thickened the sauce while retaining just enough crunch to offset the tomatoes' pulpiness; using blanched, slivered almonds avoided the muddy flavor often contributed by papery skins. We added a scant amount of hot vinegar peppers for zing, then drizzled in olive oil in a slow, steady stream to emulsify the pesto. Parmesan was stirred in for the finishing touch to this light, bright, and texturally satisfying pesto.

Pasta with Tomato and Almond Pesto (Pesto alla Trapanese)

SERVES 4 TO 6

While we prefer linguine or spaghetti, any pasta shape will work here. You may substitute ½ teaspoon of red wine vinegar and ¼ teaspoon of red pepper flakes for the pepperoncini.

Table salt

1 pound linguine or spaghetti (see note)

¼ cup slivered almonds, toasted

12 ounces cherry or grape tomatoes (about 2½ cups)

½ cup packed fresh basil leaves

1 medium garlic clove, minced or pressed through a garlic press (about 1 teaspoon)

1 small pepperoncini (hot peppers in vinegar), stemmed, seeded, and minced (about ½ teaspoon) (see note)

Pinch red pepper flakes (optional)

⅓ cup extra-virgin olive oil

1 ounce Parmesan cheese, grated (about ½ cup), plus extra for serving

1. Bring 4 quarts water to a boil in a large pot. Add 1 tablespoon salt and the pasta to the boiling water and cook, stirring often, until al dente. Reserve ½ cup of the cooking water then drain the pasta and return it to the pot.

2. Meanwhile, process the almonds, tomatoes, basil, garlic, pepperoncini, 1 teaspoon salt, and red pepper flakes (if using) in a food processor until smooth, about 1 minute. Scrape down the sides of the workbowl with a rubber spatula. With the machine running, slowly drizzle in the oil, about 30 seconds.

3. Add the pesto and ½ cup Parmesan to the cooked pasta and adjust the consistency of the sauce with the reserved pasta cooking water. Serve immediately, passing extra Parmesan separately.

NONTRADITIONAL PESTOS

WHY THIS RECIPE WORKS: Pesto doesn't always mean basil, pine nuts, and Parmesan. We wanted to make quick pestos with a variety of other potent ingredients, like sun-dried tomatoes, goat cheese, and kalamata olives.

For pestos that were flavorful but not harsh, we tamed the garlic by toasting unpeeled cloves in a hot skillet or replaced most of it with sun-dried tomatoes. Then we processed the garlic or sun-dried tomatoes with olive oil, nuts, cheese, and olives, among other ingredients, to create smooth sauces that cling well to pasta. And to keep the pasta moist, we made sure to reserve some of the pasta cooking water to thin the pesto.

Campanelle with Arugula, Goat Cheese, and Sun-Dried Tomato Pesto

SERVES 4 TO 6

Make sure to rinse the herbs and seasonings from the sun-dried tomatoes. Farfalle can be substituted for the campanelle.

1 cup oil-packed sun-dried tomatoes (one 8½-ounce jar), drained, rinsed, patted dry, and chopped coarse (see note)

1 ounce Parmesan cheese, grated (about ½ cup)

6 tablespoons extra-virgin olive oil

¼ cup walnuts, toasted

1 small garlic clove, minced or pressed through a garlic press (about ½ teaspoon)

Table salt and ground black pepper

1 pound campanelle (see note)

1 medium bunch arugula, washed, dried, stemmed, and torn into bite-sized pieces (about 6 cups)

3 ounces goat cheese, crumbled (about ¾ cup)

1. Process the sun-dried tomatoes, Parmesan, oil, walnuts, garlic, ½ teaspoon salt, and ⅛ teaspoon pepper in a food processor until smooth, scraping down the workbowl as necessary. Transfer the mixture to a small bowl and set aside.

2. Bring 4 quarts water to a boil in a large pot. Add 1 tablespoon salt and the pasta to the boiling water and cook, stirring often, until al dente. Reserve ¾ cup of the cooking water then drain the pasta and return it to the pot. Immediately stir in the arugula until wilted. Stir ½ cup of the reserved pasta cooking water into the pesto and add the pesto to the pasta. Toss to combine, adjusting the consistency of the sauce with the remaining reserved pasta cooking water. Serve immediately, sprinkling the cheese over individual bowls.

Penne with Toasted Nut and Parsley Pesto

SERVES 4 TO 6

Toasting the unpeeled garlic in a skillet reduces its harshness and gives it a mellow flavor that works well in pesto.

3 medium garlic cloves, unpeeled

1 cup pecans, walnuts, whole blanched almonds, skinned hazelnuts, unsalted pistachios, or pine nuts, or any combination thereof, toasted

½ cup packed fresh parsley leaves

7 tablespoons extra-virgin olive oil

1 ounce Parmesan cheese, grated (about ½ cup)

Table salt and ground black pepper

1 pound penne

1. Toast the garlic in a small skillet over medium heat, shaking the pan occasionally, until softened and spotty brown, about 8 minutes; when cool, remove and discard the skins.

2. Process the garlic, nuts, parsley, and oil in a food processor until smooth, scraping down the side of the workbowl as necessary. Transfer the mixture to a small bowl and stir in the Parmesan; season with salt and pepper to taste.

3. Bring 4 quarts water to a boil in a large pot. Add 1 tablespoon salt and the pasta to the boiling water and cook, stirring often, until al dente. Reserve ½ cup of the cooking water then drain the pasta and return it to the pot. Stir ¼ cup of the reserved pasta cooking water into the pesto and add the pesto to the pasta. Toss to combine, adjusting the consistency of the sauce with the remaining reserved pasta cooking water. Serve immediately.

Spaghetti with Olive Pesto

SERVES 4 TO 6

This black pesto is called olivada in Italy. Make sure to use high-quality olives in this recipe. The anchovy adds flavor but not fishiness to the pesto and we recommend its inclusion.

- 3 **medium garlic cloves, unpeeled**
- 1½ **cups pitted kalamata olives (see note)**
- 1 **ounce Parmesan cheese, grated (about ½ cup), plus extra for serving**
- 6 **tablespoons extra-virgin olive oil**
- ¼ **cup packed fresh parsley leaves**
- 1 **medium shallot, chopped coarse (about 3 tablespoons)**
- 8 **large basil leaves**
- 1 **tablespoon juice from 1 lemon**
- 1 **anchovy fillet, rinsed (optional; see note)**
  Table salt and ground black pepper
- 1 **pound spaghetti**
  Lemon wedges, for serving

1. Toast the garlic in a small skillet over medium heat, shaking the pan occasionally, until the garlic is softened and spotty brown, about 8 minutes; when cool, remove and discard the skins.

2. Process the garlic, olives, ½ cup Parmesan, oil, parsley, shallot, basil, lemon juice, and anchovy in a food processor, scraping down the sides of the workbowl as necessary. Transfer the mixture to a small bowl and season with salt and pepper to taste.

3. Bring 4 quarts water to a boil in a large pot. Add 1 tablespoon salt and the pasta to the boiling water and cook, stirring often, until al dente. Reserve ½ cup of the cooking water then drain the pasta and return it to the pot. Stir ¼ cup of the reserved pasta cooking water into the pesto and add the pesto to the pasta. Toss to combine, adjusting the consistency of the sauce with the remaining reserved pasta cooking water. Serve immediately, passing the lemon wedges and extra Parmesan separately.

PASTA WITH ASPARAGUS

WHY THIS RECIPE WORKS: Asparagus is a natural starting point when trying to make a tomato-free vegetarian pasta sauce. Its sweet, vegetable flavor and quick-cooking nature is a terrific match to pasta. But more often than not, asparagus sauces are bland and boring. We wanted to keep it simple but make this dish livelier.

First, we focused on how to cook the asparagus. Boiling and steaming dilute the vegetable's grassy flavor, so they were out. Instead, we browned the asparagus in a hot skillet, after cutting it into bite-size pieces, for a sauce that's both quick and flavorful. The asparagus caramelized just a bit, and the heat brought out the flavors of the other ingredients, such as onions, walnuts, and garlic. To finish off the dish, we paired the asparagus with a balance of salty, sweet, and sour ingredients. In one dish, we teamed asparagus with balsamic vinegar, basil, and pecorino and in another, arugula, blue cheese, and apple worked well.

NOTES FROM THE TEST KITCHEN

TRIMMING ASPARAGUS SPEARS

1. Before cooking asparagus, it's important to remove the tough ends. Remove one asparagus spear from the bunch and snap off the end.

2. Using the broken asparagus as a guide, trim off the ends of the remaining spears using a chef's knife

then stir and continue to cook, stirring occasionally, until the asparagus is crisp-tender, about 4 minutes longer.

4. Add the asparagus mixture, basil, ½ cup of the Pecorino, the lemon juice, and the remaining 3 tablespoons oil to the pasta and toss to combine. Adjust the consistency of the sauce with the reserved pasta cooking water. Serve immediately, drizzling 1 to 2 teaspoons balsamic glaze over individual servings and passing the remaining Pecorino separately.

Cavatappi with Asparagus, Arugula, Walnuts, and Blue Cheese
SERVES 4 TO 6

Cavatappi is a short, tubular corkscrew-shaped pasta; penne is a fine substitute. The grated apple balances the other flavors in this dish.

Table salt
- 1 **pound cavatappi (see note)**
- 5 **tablespoons extra-virgin olive oil**
- 1 **pound asparagus, tough ends trimmed (see the photos on page 200), thick spears halved lengthwise, and cut into 1-inch lengths**
- ½ **teaspoon ground black pepper**
- 1 **cup walnuts, chopped**
- 4 **cups lightly packed arugula leaves from 1 large bunch, washed and dried**
- 6 **ounces strong blue cheese, such as Roquefort, crumbled (about 1½ cups)**
- 2 **tablespoons cider vinegar**
- 1 **Granny Smith apple, peeled, for garnish**

1. Bring 4 quarts water to a boil in a large pot. Add 1 tablespoon salt and the pasta to the boiling water and cook, stirring often, until al dente. Reserve ½ cup of the cooking water then drain the pasta and return it to the pot.

2. While the pasta is cooking, heat 2 tablespoons of the oil in a 12-inch nonstick skillet over high heat until smoking. Add the asparagus, pepper, and ½ teaspoon salt and cook, without stirring, until the asparagus begins to brown, about 1 minute. Add the walnuts and continue to cook, stirring frequently, until the asparagus is crisp-tender and the nuts are toasted, about 4 minutes longer. Add the arugula and toss to wilt.

3. Add the asparagus mixture, blue cheese, vinegar, and the remaining 3 tablespoons oil to the pasta and toss to combine. Adjust the consistency of the sauce with the reserved pasta cooking water. Serve immediately, grating the apple over individual servings.

Campanelle with Asparagus, Basil, and Balsamic Glaze
SERVES 4 TO 6

Campanelle is a frilly trumpet-shaped pasta that pairs nicely with this sauce. If you cannot find it, fusilli works well, too. Use a vegetable peeler to shave the cheese.

Table salt
- 1 **pound campanelle (see note)**
- ¾ **cup balsamic vinegar**
- 5 **tablespoons extra-virgin olive oil**
- 1 **pound asparagus, tough ends trimmed (see the photos on page 200), thick spears halved lengthwise, and cut into 1-inch lengths**
- 1 **medium red onion, halved and sliced thin (about 1½ cups)**
- ½ **teaspoon ground black pepper**
- ¼ **teaspoon red pepper flakes**
- 1 **cup chopped fresh basil leaves**
- 2 **ounces Pecorino Romano cheese, shaved (about 1 cup) (see note)**
- 1 **tablespoon juice from 1 lemon**

1. Bring 4 quarts water to a boil in a large pot. Add 1 tablespoon salt and the pasta to the boiling water and cook, stirring often, until al dente. Reserve ½ cup of the cooking water then drain the pasta and return it to the pot.

2. While the pasta is cooking, bring the balsamic vinegar to a boil in an 8-inch skillet over medium-high heat; reduce the heat to medium and simmer gently until reduced to ¼ cup, 15 to 20 minutes.

3. Meanwhile, heat 2 tablespoons of the oil in a 12-inch nonstick skillet over high heat until smoking. Add the asparagus, onion, black pepper, red pepper flakes, and ½ teaspoon salt and stir to combine. Cook, without stirring, until the asparagus begins to brown, about 1 minute,

PASTA WITH MUSHROOMS

WHY THIS RECIPE WORKS: Pasta with mushrooms can be watery and tasteless. But when done right, this dish transforms an ordinary box of pasta and a package of mushrooms into something special. We wanted to combine the intense flavor of sautéed mushrooms with a light cream sauce to create a woodsy, full-flavored pasta dish.

For optimum flavor and texture, we used a combination of shiitake and cremini mushrooms; cremini mushrooms provided richness and meatiness, and the shiitakes contributed hearty flavor and a pleasant, chewy texture. Cooking the mushrooms in a skillet (not in the sauce) improved their flavor; adding salt to the pan helped the mushrooms release their juices and enhanced browning. We then added chicken broth and cream to the browned bits left in the skillet after the mushrooms were removed. Garlic, shallots, and thyme rounded out the flavors of our simple sauce, and lemon juice added brightness. We added the browned mushrooms back in for a chunky sauce that paired nicely with short pasta with lots of crevices—we liked either campanelle or farfalle.

Pasta with Sautéed Mushrooms and Thyme

SERVES 4 TO 6

Vegetable broth can be substituted for the chicken broth to make this dish vegetarian. If you add the pasta to the boiling water at the same time the cremini go into the skillet, the pasta and sauce will finish at the same time.

> Table salt
> 1 pound campanelle or farfalle
> 2 tablespoons unsalted butter
> 2 tablespoons extra-virgin olive oil
> 4 large shallots, minced (about 1 cup)
> 3 medium garlic cloves, minced or pressed through a garlic press (about 1 tablespoon)
> 10 ounces shiitake mushrooms, stems discarded, caps wiped clean and sliced ¼ inch thick
> 10 ounces cremini mushrooms, wiped clean and sliced ¼ inch thick
> 1 tablespoon plus 1 teaspoon minced fresh thyme leaves
> 1¼ cups low-sodium chicken broth (see note)
> ½ cup heavy cream
> 1 tablespoon juice from 1 lemon
>   Ground black pepper
> 2 ounces grated Parmesan cheese (about 1 cup)
> 2 tablespoons minced fresh parsley leaves

1. Bring 4 quarts water to a boil in a large pot. Add 1 tablespoon salt and the pasta to the boiling water and cook, stirring often, until al dente. Reserve ½ cup of the cooking water then drain the pasta and return it to the pot.

2. Meanwhile, melt the butter with the oil over medium heat in a 12-inch skillet. Add the shallots and cook, stirring occasionally, until softened and translucent, about 4 minutes. Add the garlic and cook until fragrant, about 30 seconds. Increase the heat to medium-high; add the shiitakes and cook, stirring occasionally, for 2 minutes. Add the cremini and ½ teaspoon salt; cook, stirring occasionally, until the moisture released by the mushrooms has evaporated and the mushrooms are golden brown, about 8 minutes. Add the thyme and cook until fragrant, about 30 seconds. Transfer the mushrooms to a bowl and set aside.

3. Add the chicken broth to the skillet and bring to a boil, scraping up the browned bits. Off the heat, stir in the cream and lemon juice and season with salt and pepper to taste.

4. Add the mushrooms, chicken broth mixture, cheese, and parsley to the pasta. Toss over medium-low heat until the cheese melts and the pasta absorbs most of the liquid, about 2 minutes. Adjust the consistency of the sauce with the reserved pasta cooking water and serve immediately.

PASTA WITH BROCCOLI RABE AND SAUSAGE

WHY THIS RECIPE WORKS: In southern Italy, broccoli rabe and orecchiette, which translates loosely as "little ears," is a popular combination. The trick to this pasta dish is cooking the broccoli rabe just right and limiting the number of ingredients so that at the end, you have a moist and flavorful (but not oily) pasta dish.

For a hearty, filling dish, we decided to include some

Italian sausage. Tasters preferred spicy Italian sausage to the sweet variety, but if you like less heat, the sweet sausage still makes for a satisfying dish. We started by browning the sausage in a skillet, then adding the broccoli rabe and chicken broth to absorb the rich, meaty flavors in the pan; covering the pan allowed us to steam the rabe with the other sauce ingredients. Besides eliminating the need for a separate pot to blanch the rabe, this cooking method doesn't wash away the pleasantly bitter flavor of this Italian vegetable. Some red pepper flakes amplified the heat from the sausage, and a drizzle of olive oil and fresh grated Parmesan cheese brought the whole dish together.

Orecchiette with Broccoli Rabe and Sausage
SERVES 4 TO 6

If you prefer to use broccoli instead of broccoli rabe in this recipe, use 2 pounds broccoli cut into 1-inch florets and increase the cooking time by several minutes. If you prefer a less spicy dish, use sweet Italian sausage.

    Table salt
 1 pound orecchiette
 8 ounces hot Italian sausage, casings removed (see note)
 6 medium garlic cloves, minced or pressed through a
    garlic press (about 2 tablespoons)
 ½ teaspoon red pepper flakes
 1 bunch broccoli rabe (about 1 pound), washed, trimmed,
    and cut into 1½-inch pieces (see note)
 ½ cup low-sodium chicken broth
 1 tablespoon extra-virgin olive oil
 1 ounce Parmesan cheese, grated (about ½ cup)

1. Bring 4 quarts water to a boil in a large pot. Add 1 tablespoon salt and the pasta to the boiling water and cook, stirring often, until al dente. Reserve ½ cup of the cooking water then drain the pasta and return it to the pot.

2. While the pasta is cooking, cook the sausage until browned in a 12-inch nonstick skillet over medium-high heat, breaking it into ½-inch pieces with a wooden spoon, about 3 minutes. Stir in the garlic, red pepper flakes, and ½ teaspoon salt. Cook, stirring constantly, until the garlic is fragrant, about 1½ minutes. Add the broccoli rabe and chicken broth, cover, and cook until the broccoli rabe turns bright green, about 2 minutes. Uncover and cook, stirring frequently, until most of the broth has evaporated and the broccoli rabe is tender, 2 to 3 minutes.

3. Add the sausage mixture, oil, and cheese to the pasta and toss to combine. Adjust the consistency of the sauce with the reserved pasta cooking water and serve immediately.

BEHIND THE SCENES

PASTA PARAPHERNALIA

What's our opinion on pasta gadgets? For the most part, *fuggedaboutit*. Pasta pots with perforated inserts tend to boil over if filled with the necessary amount of water. A pot with a strainer lid might look promising, but we found that if your grip isn't secure, the lid pops off and pasta can end up all over your sink. Ditto for crescent-shaped strainer plates that fit to the edge of the pot. The only pasta tool we've come across through the years that we've actually liked is a pasta fork, which is a long-handled spoon with ridged teeth. But no need to rush out and buy one, basic tongs work just fine.

SHRIMP AND GARLIC WITH PASTA

WHY THIS RECIPE WORKS: In theory, garlic shrimp pasta has all the makings of an ideal weeknight meal—just toss a few quick-cooking ingredients with boiled pasta. In reality, delicate shrimp cooks fast, which translates to overcooked in a matter of seconds. Meanwhile, garlic can become overbearing or bitter, depending on how it's treated. Add to that the challenge of getting a brothy sauce to coat the pasta, and this simple recipe turns into a precarious balancing act. We wanted it all: al dente pasta and moist shrimp bound by a supple sauce infused with a deep garlic flavor.

For the best flavor and texture, we prefer to buy individually quick-frozen shrimp and thaw them ourselves. We settled on extra-large shrimp and marinated them with minced garlic before a quick sauté in garlic oil (olive oil we simmered with smashed garlic cloves). We also cut each shrimp into thirds before cooking to ensure that every bite of pasta had a tasty morsel of shrimp. With sweet low notes from the infused oil and brasher high notes from the minced garlic, we finally had a balanced, deeply layered garlic flavor. As for the sauce, to deglaze the pan, tasters preferred the clean taste of vermouth or white wine; bottled clam broth added complexity to the sauce. Using a chunky tubular pasta instead of traditional linguine made it easy to find the shrimp. To get the sauce to cling to the pasta, we simply stirred flour into the oil as a thickener just before adding the vermouth and clam juice and tossed in some cold butter to finish.

Garlicky Shrimp Pasta

SERVES 4 TO 6

Marinate the shrimp while you prepare the remaining ingredients. Any short tubular or curly pasta works well here. If you prefer more heat, use the greater amount of red pepper flakes given.

- **1 pound extra-large shrimp (21 to 25 per pound), peeled, deveined (see page 160), and each shrimp cut into 3 pieces**
- **3 tablespoons olive oil**
- **5 medium garlic cloves, minced or pressed through a garlic press (about 5 teaspoons), plus 4 medium garlic cloves, smashed**
- **Table salt**
- **1 pound mezze rigatoni, fusilli, or campanelle (see note)**
- **¼–½ teaspoon red pepper flakes (see note)**
- **2 teaspoons unbleached all-purpose flour**
- **½ cup dry vermouth or white wine**
- **¾ cup clam juice**
- **½ cup chopped fresh parsley leaves**
- **3 tablespoons unsalted butter, cut into 3 pieces**
- **1 teaspoon lemon juice, plus lemon wedges for serving**
- **Ground black pepper**

1. Toss the shrimp, 1 tablespoon of the oil, 2 teaspoons of the minced garlic, and ¼ teaspoon salt in a medium bowl. Let the shrimp marinate at room temperature 20 minutes.

2. Heat the 4 smashed garlic cloves and the remaining 2 tablespoons oil in a 12-inch skillet over medium-low heat, stirring occasionally, until the garlic is light golden brown, 4 to 7 minutes. Remove the skillet from the heat and use a slotted spoon to remove the garlic from the skillet; discard the garlic. Set the skillet aside.

3. Bring 4 quarts water to a boil in a large pot. Add 1 tablespoon salt and the pasta to the boiling water and cook, stirring often, until al dente. Reserve ½ cup of the cooking water then drain the pasta and return it to the pot.

4. While the pasta cooks, return the skillet with the oil to medium heat; add the shrimp with the marinade to the skillet in a single layer. Cook the shrimp, undisturbed, until the oil starts to bubble gently, 1 to 2 minutes. Stir the shrimp and continue to cook until almost cooked through, about 1 minute longer. Using a slotted spoon, transfer the shrimp to a medium bowl. Add the remaining 3 teaspoons minced garlic and the red pepper flakes to the skillet and cook until fragrant, about 1 minute. Add the flour and

cook, stirring constantly, for 1 minute; stir in the vermouth and cook for 1 minute. Add the clam juice and parsley; cook until the mixture starts to thicken, 1 to 2 minutes. Off the heat, whisk in the butter and lemon juice. Add the shrimp and sauce to the pasta and adjust the consistency of the sauce with the reserved pasta cooking water. Season with black pepper to taste. Serve immediately, passing the lemon wedges separately.

SHRIMP FRA DIAVOLO

WHY THIS RECIPE WORKS: Most shrimp *fra diavolo* recipes ("brother devil" in Italian) lack depth of flavor, with the star ingredients, shrimp and garlic, contributing little to an acidic, unbalanced tomato sauce. We wanted a shrimp fra diavolo with a seriously garlicky, spicy tomato sauce studded with sweet, firm shrimp.

Most fra diavolo recipes add raw shrimp to the finished sauce, but this doesn't infuse the shrimp with any flavor whatsoever. We seared the shrimp first to help them caramelize and enrich their sweetness. Following a brief sear with olive oil, salt, and red pepper flakes—the pepper flakes also benefited from the sear, as they took on a toasty, earthy note—we flambéed the shrimp with cognac. The combined forces of cognac and flame brought out the shrimp's sweet, tender notes and imbued our fra diavolo with the cognac's richness and complexity. We then sautéed the garlic slowly for a mellow nutty flavor, and reserved some raw garlic for a last-minute punch of heat and spice. Simmered diced tomatoes and a splash of white wine (balanced by a bit of sugar) completed our perfect fra diavolo in less than 30 minutes.

Shrimp fra Diavolo

SERVES 4 TO 6

One teaspoon of red pepper flakes will give the sauce a little kick, but you may want to add more depending on your taste. For safety notes on flambéing, see page 274.

Table salt

1 pound linguine or spaghetti

1 pound large shrimp (31 to 40 per pound), peeled and deveined (see page 160)

6 tablespoons extra-virgin olive oil

1 teaspoon red pepper flakes, plus more to taste (see note)

¼ cup cognac or brandy

12 medium garlic cloves, minced or pressed through a garlic press (about ¼ cup)

1 (28-ounce) can diced tomatoes, drained

1 cup dry white wine

½ teaspoon sugar

¼ cup minced fresh parsley leaves

1. Bring 4 quarts water to a boil in a large pot. Add 1 tablespoon salt and the pasta to the boiling water and cook, stirring often, until al dente. Reserve ½ cup of the cooking water then drain the pasta and return it to the pot.

2. Meanwhile, toss the shrimp with 2 tablespoons of the oil, ½ teaspoon of the red pepper flakes, and ¾ teaspoon salt. Heat a 12-inch skillet over high heat. Add the shrimp to the skillet in a single layer and cook, without stirring, until the bottoms of the shrimp turn spotty brown, about 30 seconds. Remove the skillet from the heat, flip the shrimp, and add the cognac; wait until the cognac has warmed slightly, about 5 seconds, and return the skillet to high heat. Wave a lit match over the skillet until the cognac ignites, shaking the pan to distribute the flame over the entire pan. When the flames subside (this will take 15 to 30 seconds), transfer the shrimp to a medium bowl and set aside. Let the skillet cool, off the heat, about 2 minutes.

3. Add 3 tablespoons more oil and 3 tablespoons of the garlic to the cooled skillet and cook over low heat, stirring constantly, until the garlic becomes sticky and straw colored, 7 to 10 minutes. Add the remaining red pepper flakes, ¾ teaspoon salt, the tomatoes, wine, and sugar, increase the heat to medium-high, and simmer until thickened, about 8 minutes.

4. Stir the shrimp with accumulated juices, the remaining 1 tablespoon garlic, and parsley into the tomato sauce. Simmer until the shrimp have heated through, about 1 minute. Off the heat, stir in the remaining 1 tablespoon oil. Add ½ cup of the tomato sauce (no shrimp) to the pasta; toss to coat and adjust the consistency of the sauce with the reserved pasta cooking water. Serve immediately, topping individual bowls with the sauce and shrimp.

HEARTY ITALIAN MEAT SAUCE

WHY THIS RECIPE WORKS: Traditional "Sunday gravy" is more than just meat sauce—it's a labor of love, an all-day kitchen affair, involving several types of meat, a bunch of tomatoes, and at least one Italian grandmother. We wanted to honor this meaty extravaganza but shortcut the cooking so we could get this traditional dish on the table in a reasonable amount of time.

When you're using six or seven types of meat, the browning alone can take up to 40 minutes. Our first step was to limit the dish to just one kind of sausage and one pork cut—plus meatballs. Hot Italian links gave the sauce a mild kick; baby back ribs were our favorite cut of pork because they weren't too fatty and turned moist and tender in just a few hours. Meat loaf mix, a combination of ground beef, pork, and veal, produced juicy, tender meatballs, especially when mixed with a panade of bread and buttermilk. To further bump up flavor, we mixed in minced garlic, parsley, and red pepper flakes, plus an egg yolk for richness. To help the meatballs retain their shape we browned them first in a skillet before adding them to the sauce.

For the tomato sauce, canned crushed tomatoes were a winner, leading to a sauce with nice thickness and bright tomato flavor. Instead of merely browning the tomato paste for 30 seconds, we cooked it until it nearly blackened, which concentrated its sweetness. The sauce was still lacking some beefy undercurrents; the best booster turned out to be the simple, straightforward addition of an ingredient rarely found in tomato sauce: beef broth.

Pasta with Hearty Italian Meat Sauce (Sunday Gravy)

SERVES 8 TO 10

We prefer meat loaf mix (a combination of ground beef, pork, and veal) for the meatballs in this recipe. Ground beef may be substituted, but the meatballs won't be as flavorful. Six tablespoons of plain yogurt thinned with 2 tablespoons of milk can be substituted for the buttermilk. Our preferred brands of crushed tomatoes are Tuttorosso and Muir Glen. This recipe can be prepared through step 4 and then cooled and refrigerated in the Dutch oven for up to 2 days. To reheat, drizzle ½ cup water over the sauce (do not stir in) and warm on the lower-middle rack of a preheated 325-degree oven for 1 hour before proceeding with the recipe.

SAUCE

- 2 tablespoons olive oil
- 1 (2¼-pound) rack baby back ribs, cut into 2-rib sections
  Table salt and ground black pepper
- 1 pound hot Italian sausage links
- 2 medium onions, minced
- 1¼ teaspoons dried oregano
- 3 tablespoons tomato paste
- 4 medium garlic cloves, minced or pressed through a garlic press (about 4 teaspoons)
- 2 (28-ounce) cans crushed tomatoes (see note)
- ⅔ cup low-sodium beef broth

MEATBALLS AND PASTA

- 2 slices high-quality white sandwich bread, crusts removed and bread cut into ½-inch cubes
- ½ cup buttermilk (see note)
- ¼ cup chopped fresh parsley leaves
- 2 medium garlic cloves, minced or pressed through a garlic press (about 2 teaspoons)
- 1 large egg yolk
  Table salt
- ¼ teaspoon red pepper flakes
- 1 pound meat loaf mix (see note)
- 2 ounces thinly sliced prosciutto, minced
- 1 ounce Pecorino Romano cheese, grated (about ½ cup)
- ½ cup olive oil
- 1½ pounds spaghetti or linguine
- ¼ cup chopped fresh basil leaves
  Grated Parmesan cheese, for serving

1. FOR THE SAUCE: Adjust an oven rack to the lower-middle position and heat the oven to 325 degrees. Heat the oil in a large Dutch oven over medium-high heat until just smoking. Pat the ribs dry with paper towels and season with salt and pepper. Add half of the ribs to the pot and brown on both sides, 5 to 7 minutes total. Transfer the ribs to a large plate and repeat with the remaining ribs. After transferring the second batch of ribs to the plate, brown the sausages on all four sides, 5 to 7 minutes total. Transfer the sausages to the plate with the ribs.

2. Reduce the heat to medium, add the onions and oregano; cook, stirring occasionally, until beginning to brown, about 5 minutes. Add the tomato paste and cook, stirring constantly, until very dark, about 3 minutes. Stir in the garlic and cook until fragrant, about 30 seconds. Add the crushed tomatoes and broth, scraping up any browned bits. Return the ribs and sausage to the pot; bring to a simmer, cover, and transfer to the oven. Cook until the ribs are tender, about 2½ hours.

3. FOR THE MEATBALLS: Meanwhile, combine the bread cubes, buttermilk, parsley, garlic, egg yolk, ½ teaspoon salt, and red pepper flakes in a medium bowl and mash with a fork until no bread chunks remain. Add the meat loaf mix, prosciutto, and Pecorino Romano to the bread mixture; mix with your hands until thoroughly combined. Divide the mixture into 12 pieces; roll into balls, transfer to a plate, cover with plastic, and refrigerate until ready to use.

4. When the sauce is 30 minutes from being done, heat the oil in a large nonstick skillet over medium-high heat until shimmering. Add the meatballs and cook until well browned all over, 5 to 7 minutes. Transfer the meatballs to a paper towel–lined plate to drain briefly. Remove the sauce from the oven and skim the fat from the top with a large spoon. Transfer the browned meatballs to the sauce and gently submerge. Return the pot to the oven and continue cooking until the meatballs are just cooked through, about 15 minutes.

5. Meanwhile, bring 6 quarts water to a boil in a large pot. Add 2 tablespoons salt and the pasta to the boiling water and cook, stirring often, until al dente. Reserve ½ cup of the cooking water then drain the pasta and return it to the pot.

6. Using tongs, transfer the meatballs, ribs, and sausage to a serving platter and cut the sausages in half. Stir the basil into the sauce and season with salt and pepper to taste. Add 1 cup of the sauce and the reserved pasta cooking water to the pasta; toss to coat. Serve, passing the remaining sauce, meat platter, and Parmesan separately.

SIMPLE ITALIAN-STYLE MEAT SAUCE

WHY THIS RECIPE WORKS: Old-fashioned Italian-style meat sauces are on an old-fashioned time line—they require hours of simmering. But just giving browned ground beef, onions, garlic, and canned tomatoes a quick simmer produces lackluster flavor and meat with the texture of a rubber band. We wanted a quick, weeknight meat sauce with long-simmered flavor.

Our goal required concentrated flavor and tender meat. Browned chopped onions and mushrooms gave the sauce a rich base of flavor, and browning the mushrooms made them so soft and supple they practically disappeared into the finished sauce. Deglazing the pan with tomato paste and tomato juice further boosted flavor. To tenderize the meat, we incorporated a panade—a paste of bread and milk—into the meat before cooking; we combined the panade and the meat in a food processor to avoid chili-like chunks. We cooked the meat mixture just until it lost its raw color; any longer, and the meat would have turned dry and mealy. Finishing the meat in a combination of canned diced and crushed tomatoes gave us the best mix of textures. A handful of grated Parmesan, added just before serving, lent the sauce a tangy, complex character.

Simple Italian-Style Meat Sauce

MAKES ABOUT 6 CUPS

You can figure on about 3 cups of sauce per pound of pasta. Except for ground round (which tasters found spongy and bland), this recipe will work with most types of ground beef, as long as it is 85 percent lean. Use high-quality crushed tomatoes; our favorite brands are Tuttorosso and Muir Glen. If using dried oregano, add the entire amount with the canned tomato liquid in step 2.

4 ounces white mushrooms, wiped clean and broken into rough pieces
1 large slice high-quality white sandwich bread, torn into quarters
2 tablespoons whole milk
 Table salt and ground black pepper
1 pound 85 percent lean ground beef (see note)
1 tablespoon olive oil
1 medium onion, minced
6 medium garlic cloves, minced or pressed through a garlic press (about 2 tablespoons)
1 tablespoon tomato paste
¼ teaspoon red pepper flakes
1 (14.5-ounce) can diced tomatoes, drained, ¼ cup juice reserved
1 tablespoon minced fresh oregano leaves or 1 teaspoon dried oregano (see note)
1 (28-ounce) can crushed tomatoes (see note)
¼ cup grated Parmesan cheese

1. Pulse the mushrooms in a food processor until finely chopped, about 8 pulses, scraping down the sides of the workbowl as needed; transfer to a medium bowl. Add the bread, milk, ½ teaspoon salt, and ½ teaspoon pepper to the food processor and pulse until a paste forms, about 8 pulses. Add the beef and pulse until the mixture is well combined, about 6 pulses.

2. Heat the oil in a large saucepan over medium-high heat until just smoking. Add the onion and mushrooms; cook, stirring frequently, until the vegetables are browned and dark bits form on the pan bottom, 6 to 12 minutes. Stir in the garlic, tomato paste, and red pepper flakes; cook until fragrant and the tomato paste starts to brown, about 1 minute. Add the ¼ cup reserved tomato juice and 2 teaspoons of the fresh oregano (if using dried, add the full amount), scraping the bottom of the pan with a wooden spoon to loosen the browned bits. Add the meat mixture and cook, breaking the meat into small pieces with a wooden spoon, until no longer pink, 2 to 4 minutes, making sure that the meat does not brown.

3. Stir in the diced and crushed tomatoes and bring to a simmer; reduce the heat to low and gently simmer until the sauce has thickened and the flavors have blended, about 30 minutes. Stir in the cheese and the remaining 1 teaspoon fresh oregano; season with salt and pepper to taste. (The sauce can be refrigerated in an airtight container for up to 3 days or frozen for up to 1 month.)

PASTA WITH CLASSIC BOLOGNESE SAUCE

WHY THIS RECIPE WORKS: Unlike meat sauces in which tomatoes dominate, Bolognese sauce is about the meat, with the tomatoes in a supporting role. We wanted a traditional recipe for this complexly flavored sauce, with rich meatiness up front and a good balance of sweet, salty, and acidic flavors.

We started simple—with just onions, carrots, and celery, sautéed in butter. A combination of meats, in the form of meat loaf mix, provided the right amount of meatiness. For the most tender texture, we cooked the meat just until it lost its pink color and didn't let it brown. For dairy, which is used to tenderize the meat and give the sauce a sweet, appealing flavor, we used milk. Once the milk had reduced, we added white wine, which gave the sauce a delicate brightness. For the tomato element, diced canned tomatoes imparted sweet, acidic notes. Finally, we simmered the sauce at the lowest possible heat for about three hours and served it with rich, eggy fettuccine.

Fettuccine with Slow-Simmered Bolognese Sauce

SERVES 4

Don't drain the pasta of its cooking water too meticulously when using this sauce; a little water left clinging to the noodles will help distribute the very thick sauce evenly over the noodles, as will the addition of 2 tablespoons of butter along with the sauce. If doubling this recipe, increase the simmering times for the milk and the wine to 30 minutes each, and increase the simmering time once the tomatoes are added to 4 hours. You can substitute equal amounts of 80 percent lean ground beef, ground veal, and ground pork for the meat loaf mix (the total amount of meat should be ¾ pound).

5 tablespoons unsalted butter
2 tablespoons minced onion
2 tablespoons minced carrot
2 tablespoons minced celery
¾ pound meat loaf mix (see note)
 Table salt
1 cup whole milk
1 cup dry white wine
1 (28-ounce) can diced tomatoes
1 pound fresh or dried fettuccine
 Grated Parmesan cheese, for serving

1. Melt 3 tablespoons of the butter in a large Dutch oven over medium heat. Add the onion, carrot, and celery and cook until softened but not browned, about 6 minutes. Add the meat and ½ teaspoon salt; crumble the meat into tiny pieces with a wooden spoon. Cook, continuing to crumble the meat, just until it loses its raw color but has not yet browned, about 3 minutes.

2. Add the milk and simmer until the milk evaporates and only rendered fat remains, 10 to 15 minutes. Add the wine and simmer until the wine evaporates, 10 to 15 minutes longer. Add the tomatoes with their juice and bring to a simmer. Reduce the heat to low so that the sauce continues to simmer just barely, with an occasional bubble or two at the surface, until the liquid has evaporated, about 3 hours. Season with salt to taste. (The sauce can be refrigerated in an airtight container for up to 3 days or frozen for up to 1 month.)

3. Bring 4 quarts water to a boil in a large pot. Add 1 tablespoon salt and the pasta to the boiling water and cook, stirring often, until al dente. Reserve ½ cup of the cooking water then drain the pasta and return it to the pot. Add the sauce and remaining 2 tablespoons butter; toss to combine. Adjust the consistency of the sauce with the reserved pasta cooking water. Serve, passing the Parmesan separately.

PASTA WITH STREAMLINED BOLOGNESE SAUCE

WHY THIS RECIPE WORKS: Bolognese, including our own recipe, gets its big flavor from braising ground meat and softened vegetables in slowly reducing milk, wine, and tomatoes. The process typically takes about three hours. But on a busy weeknight, we rarely have that much time to spend making dinner. We wanted to streamline Bolognese into a weeknight-friendly dinner—but keep all the lush, decadent flavor.

Using a food processor to chop the vegetables, including a big can of whole tomatoes with their juice, cut down on preparation time. To develop sweetness in the sauce without the day-long simmering, we reduced white wine in a separate pan and added it to the sauce at the end; a little bit of sugar, stirred in with the garlic to help it caramelize, amplified the sweetness. Instead of browning the ground meat, we cooked it with milk, which helped to break down and soften the meat in a short amount of time. To beef up the meaty flavor of the sauce, we added chopped pancetta, dried porcini mushrooms, and the flavorful liquid left behind from rehydrating the mushrooms. In about an hour, our sauce was ready, with all the rich meatiness of a long-simmered Bolognese.

Pasta with Weeknight Bolognese Sauce

SERVES 4 TO 6

Sweet white wines such as Gewürztraminer, Riesling, and even white Zinfandel work especially well in this sauce. To obtain the best texture, be careful not to break up the meat too much when cooking it with the milk in step 4; with additional cooking and stirring, it will continue to break up. Just about any pasta shape complements this meaty sauce, but spaghetti and linguine are the test kitchen favorites. If using pancetta that has been sliced thin rather than cut into 1-inch chunks, reduce the processing time in step 3 from 30 seconds to about 5 seconds. You can substitute equal amounts of 80 percent lean ground beef, ground veal, and ground pork for the meat loaf mix (the total amount of meat should be 1¼ pounds).

- ½ ounce dried porcini mushrooms
- 1¼ cups sweet white wine (see note)
- ½ small carrot, peeled and chopped coarse (about ½ cup)
- ½ small onion, chopped coarse (about ¼ cup)
- 3 ounces pancetta, cut into 1-inch chunks (see note)
- 1 (28-ounce) can whole tomatoes
- 1½ tablespoons unsalted butter
- 1 teaspoon sugar
- 1 small garlic clove, minced or pressed through a garlic press (about ½ teaspoon)
- 1¼ pounds meat loaf mix (see note)
- 1½ cups whole milk
- 2 tablespoons tomato paste
   Table salt
- ⅛ teaspoon ground black pepper
- 1 pound pasta (see note)
   Grated Parmesan cheese, for serving

1. Combine the porcini and ½ cup water in a small microwave-safe bowl; cover the bowl with plastic wrap, cut three vents for steam with a knife, and microwave on high power for 30 seconds. Let stand until the mushrooms have softened, about 5 minutes. Transfer the mushrooms to a second small bowl and reserve the liquid; pour the liquid through a paper towel–lined mesh strainer. Set the mushrooms and the strained liquid aside.

2. Bring the wine to a simmer in a 10-inch nonstick skillet over medium heat; reduce the heat to low and continue to simmer until the wine is reduced to 2 tablespoons, about 20 minutes. Set aside.

3. Meanwhile, pulse the carrot in a food processor until broken down into ¼-inch pieces, about 10 pulses. Add the onion and pulse until the vegetables are broken down into ⅛-inch pieces, about 10 pulses. Transfer the vegetables to a small bowl. Process the reserved mushrooms until well ground, about 15 seconds, scraping down the side of the workbowl as needed. Transfer the mushrooms to the bowl with the vegetables. Process the pancetta until the pieces are no larger than ¼ inch, 30 to 35 seconds, scraping down the side of the workbowl as needed; transfer to a small bowl. Pulse the tomatoes with their juice until chopped fine, about 8 pulses.

4. Melt the butter in a 12-inch skillet over medium-high heat. Cook the pancetta, stirring frequently, until well browned, about 2 minutes. Add the carrot, onion, and mushrooms and cook, stirring frequently, until the vegetables are softened but not browned, about 4 minutes. Add the sugar and garlic and cook until fragrant, about 30 seconds. Add the meat, breaking it into 1-inch pieces with a wooden spoon, and cook about 1 minute. Add the milk and stir to break the meat into ½-inch pieces; bring to a simmer, reduce the heat to medium, and cook, stirring to break the meat into smaller pieces, until most of the liquid has evaporated and the meat begins to sizzle, 18 to 20 minutes. Stir in the tomato paste and cook until combined, about 1 minute. Add the tomatoes, reserved mushroom soaking liquid, ¼ teaspoon salt, and pepper; bring to a simmer over medium-high heat, then reduce the heat to medium and simmer until the liquid is reduced and the sauce is thickened, 12 to 15 minutes. Stir in the reduced wine and simmer to blend the flavors, about 5 minutes.

5. Meanwhile, bring 4 quarts water to a boil in a large pot. Add 1 tablespoon salt and the pasta to the boiling water and cook, stirring often, until al dente. Reserve ½ cup of the cooking water then drain the pasta and return it to the pot. Add 2 cups of the sauce and 2 tablespoons of the reserved pasta cooking water to the pasta; toss to combine and adjust the consistency of the sauce with the remaining reserved pasta cooking water. Serve immediately, topping individual bowls with ¼ cup sauce and passing the Parmesan separately.

PASTA AND SLOW-SIMMERED TOMATO SAUCE WITH MEAT

WHY THIS RECIPE WORKS: Slow-simmered Italian meat sauce—the kind without meatballs—relies on pork for rich flavor. But the pork found in supermarkets is so lean, we weren't convinced that any of the options could provide enough fat and flavor. So we set out to make a rich, flavorful meat sauce with fall-off-the-bone tender meat that was made from readily available supermarket products.

Today's pork chops turn dry and leathery when cooked for long periods, so instead we used a fattier cut. Country-style pork ribs turn meltingly tender when cooked for a long time and gave our tomato sauce a truly meaty flavor. Beef short ribs can also be used, but since they tend to be thicker than pork ribs, it's important to remember to let them cook a little longer. Red wine accentuated the meatiness of the sauce, which was built on a simple combination of sautéed onion and canned diced tomatoes.

Pasta and Slow-Simmered Tomato Sauce with Meat (Sunday Gravy)

SERVES 4 TO 6

This sauce can be made with either beef or pork ribs. Depending on their size, you will need 4 or 5 ribs.

- 1 tablespoon olive oil
- 1½ pounds pork spareribs or country-style ribs or beef short ribs, trimmed of fat (see note)
  Table salt and ground black pepper
- 1 medium onion, minced
- ½ cup red wine
- 1 (28-ounce) can diced tomatoes
- 1 pound ziti, rigatoni, or other short tubular pasta
  Grated Parmesan cheese, for serving

1. Heat the oil in a 12-inch skillet over medium-high heat until shimmering. Season the ribs with salt and pepper and brown on all sides, turning occasionally, 8 to 10 minutes. Transfer the ribs to a plate; pour off all but 1 teaspoon fat from the skillet. Add the onion and cook until softened, 2 to 3 minutes. Add the wine and simmer, scraping up any browned bits, until the wine reduces to a glaze, about 2 minutes.

2. Return the ribs and accumulated juices to the skillet; add the tomatoes with their juice. Bring to a boil, then reduce the heat to low, cover, and simmer gently, turning the ribs several times, until the meat is very tender and falling off the bones, 1½ hours (for pork spareribs or country-style ribs) to 2 hours (for beef short ribs).

3. Transfer the ribs to a clean plate. When cool enough to handle, remove the meat from the bones and shred, discarding the fat and bones. Return the shredded meat to the sauce. Bring the sauce to a simmer over medium heat and cook, uncovered, until heated through and slightly thickened, about 5 minutes. Season with salt and pepper to taste. (The sauce can be refrigerated for up to 4 days or frozen for up to 2 months.)

4. Meanwhile, bring 4 quarts water to a boil in a large pot. Add 1 tablespoon salt and the pasta to the boiling water and cook, stirring often, until al dente. Reserve ½ cup of the cooking water then drain the pasta and return it to the pot. Add the sauce to the pasta and toss to combine. Adjust the consistency of the sauce with the reserved pasta cooking water. Serve immediately, passing the Parmesan separately.

SPAGHETTI AND MEATBALLS

WHY THIS RECIPE WORKS: One of the problems with meatballs is that they're thought of as smaller, rounder versions of hamburgers. This would be fine if meatballs were generally cooked to rare or medium-rare, as most hamburgers are, but meatballs are often cooked through till well-done. This can leave them flavorless, dry, and dense. As a result, they need some help to lighten their texture. What we were after was nothing short of great meatballs: crusty and dark brown on the outside, soft and moist on the inside.

White bread soaked in buttermilk is the best binder for meatballs, giving them a creamy texture and an appealing tang. Eggs are also important for texture and flavor; their fats and emulsifiers add moistness and richness. Egg yolks alone work best and keep meatballs moist and light; the whites just make the mixture sticky and hard to handle, with no other added benefits. Adding some ground pork to the usual ground beef enhanced the flavor; we found 1 part pork to 3 parts beef to be about right. Pan-frying (as opposed to broiling, which dried out the meatballs) was the best way to brown the meatballs and kept the interior moist. Finally, building the tomato sauce on top of the browned bits left in the pan after frying the meatballs made for a hearty, robust-tasting sauce.

Spaghetti and Meatballs

SERVES 4 TO 6

The shaped meatballs can be covered with plastic wrap and refrigerated for several hours ahead of serving time; fry the meatballs and make the sauce at the last minute. If you don't have buttermilk, you can substitute 6 tablespoons of plain yogurt thinned with 2 tablespoons of milk.

MEATBALLS

- **2 slices high-quality white sandwich bread, crusts removed and bread torn into small pieces**
- **½ cup buttermilk (see note)**
- **¾ pound 85 percent lean ground beef**
- **¼ pound ground pork**
- **¼ cup grated Parmesan cheese**
- **2 tablespoons minced fresh parsley leaves**
- **1 large egg yolk**
- **1 medium garlic clove, minced or pressed through a garlic press (about 1 teaspoon)**
- **¾ teaspoon table salt**
- **⅛ teaspoon ground black pepper**
  Vegetable oil, for pan-frying

TOMATO SAUCE AND PASTA

- **2 tablespoons extra-virgin olive oil**
- **1 medium garlic clove, minced or pressed through a garlic press (about 1 teaspoon)**
- **1 (28-ounce) can crushed tomatoes**
- **1 tablespoon minced fresh basil leaves**
  Table salt and ground black pepper
- **1 pound spaghetti**
  Grated Parmesan cheese, for serving

1. FOR THE MEATBALLS: Mash the bread and buttermilk to a smooth paste in a large bowl. Let stand 10 minutes.

2. Add the beef, pork, cheese, parsley, egg yolk, garlic, salt, and pepper to the mashed bread; stir gently until uniform. Gently form into 1½-inch round meatballs (about 14 meatballs). (When forming the meatballs use a light touch; if you compact the meatballs too much, they can become dense and hard.)

3. Pour the vegetable oil into a 12-inch skillet until it measures a depth of ¼ inch. Heat over medium-high heat until shimmering. Add the meatballs in a single layer and cook until nicely browned on all sides, about 10 minutes. Transfer the meatballs to a paper towel–lined plate and discard the oil left in the skillet.

4. FOR THE SAUCE: Add the olive oil and garlic to the skillet and cook over medium heat, scraping up any browned bits, until fragrant, about 30 seconds. Add the tomatoes with their juice, bring to a simmer, and cook until the sauce thickens, about 10 minutes. Stir in the basil and season with salt and pepper to taste. Add the meatballs and simmer, turning them occasionally, until heated through, about 5 minutes.

5. Meanwhile, bring 4 quarts water to a boil in a large pot for the pasta. Add 1 tablespoon salt and the pasta to the boiling water and cook, stirring often, until al dente. Reserve ½ cup of the cooking water then drain the pasta and return it to the pot. Stir in several large spoonfuls of the tomato sauce (without meatballs) over the pasta and toss to coat. Adjust the consistency of the sauce with the reserved pasta cooking water. Serve immediately, topping individual bowls with more tomato sauce and several meatballs and passing the Parmesan separately.

PENNE WITH VODKA SAUCE

WHY THIS RECIPE WORKS: Splashes of vodka and cream can turn run-of-the-mill tomato sauce into luxurious restaurant fare—or a heavy, boozy mistake. Despite the limited number of ingredients—vodka, cream, red pepper flakes, and tomatoes—we found recipes for *penne alla vodka* with results that varied widely. Many were absurdly rich (with more cream than tomatoes) and others were too harsh from a heavy hand with the vodka. We wanted to fine-tune this modern classic to strike the right balance of sweet, tangy, spicy, and creamy.

To achieve a sauce with the right consistency, we pureed half the tomatoes (which helped the sauce cling nicely to the pasta) and cut the rest into chunks. For sweetness, we added sautéed minced onions; for depth of flavor, we used a bit of tomato paste. We found we needed a liberal amount of vodka to cut through the richness and add "zinginess" to the sauce, but we needed to add it to the tomatoes early on to allow the alcohol to mostly (but not completely) cook off and prevent a boozy flavor. Adding a little heavy cream to the sauce gave it a nice consistency, and we finished cooking the penne in the sauce to encourage cohesiveness.

Penne with Vodka Sauce (Penne alla Vodka)

SERVES 4 TO 6

So that the sauce and pasta finish cooking at the same time, drop the pasta into the boiling water just after adding the vodka to the sauce.

- 1 (28-ounce) can whole tomatoes, drained, juice reserved
- 2 tablespoons olive oil
- ½ small onion, minced
- 1 tablespoon tomato paste
- 2 medium garlic cloves, minced or pressed through a garlic press (about 2 teaspoons)
- ¼ teaspoon red pepper flakes
  Table salt
- ⅓ cup vodka
- ½ cup heavy cream
- 1 pound penne
- 2 tablespoons minced fresh basil leaves
  Grated Parmesan cheese, for serving

1. Puree half of the tomatoes in a food processor until smooth. Dice the remaining tomatoes into ½-inch pieces, discarding the cores. Combine the pureed and diced tomatoes in a liquid measuring cup (you should have about 1⅔ cups). Add the reserved juice to equal 2 cups.

2. Heat the oil in a large saucepan over medium heat until shimmering. Add the onion and tomato paste and cook, stirring occasionally, until the onion is light golden around the edges, about 3 minutes. Add the garlic and red pepper flakes; cook, stirring constantly, until fragrant, about 30 seconds.

3. Stir in the tomatoes and ½ teaspoon salt. Remove the pan from the heat and add the vodka. Return the pan to medium-high heat and simmer briskly until the alcohol flavor is cooked off, 8 to 10 minutes; stir frequently and lower the heat to medium if the simmering becomes too vigorous. Stir in the cream and cook until hot, about 1 minute.

4. Meanwhile, bring 4 quarts water to a boil in a large pot. Add 1 tablespoon salt and the pasta to the boiling water. Cook, stirring often, until just shy of al dente. Reserve ½ cup of the cooking water then drain the pasta and return it to the pot. Add the sauce to the pasta and toss over medium heat until the pasta absorbs some of the sauce, 1 to 2 minutes. Adjust the consistency of the sauce with the reserved pasta cooking water. Stir in the basil and season with salt to taste. Serve immediately, passing the Parmesan separately.

SPAGHETTI ALLA CARBONARA

WHY THIS RECIPE WORKS: Standard carbonara is often a lackluster spaghetti dish; it's either covered in a leaden sauce or riddled with dry bits of cheese. To add to the problems, if the dish gets to the table a few minutes too late, the sauce congeals and the pasta turns rubbery. We set out to make the sauce silky and smooth.

Eggs form the base of the lush, silky sauce, so we

used three whole eggs to guarantee superior texture and richness. A combination of Pecorino Romano, with its distinctly sharp flavor, and Parmesan, with its sweet, nutty flavor, provided the most bite and creaminess. Raw garlic balanced the richness of the eggs and cheese. In place of the traditional *guanciale* (salt-cured pork jowl), we used American bacon, which gave our dish the perfect crunch and a hint of sweetness and smoke. Skipping over the heavy cream—which deadened the flavor of the cheeses—we added white wine to achieve a rich, translucent sauce. Pouring the cheese and egg mixture right over the hot pasta in a warmed serving bowl helped ensure that everyone at the table could enjoy a perfectly coated portion of pasta and sauce.

Spaghetti alla Carbonara

SERVES 4 TO 6

Although we call for spaghetti in this recipe, you can substitute linguine or fettuccine.

- ¼ **cup extra-virgin olive oil**
- 8 **ounces (about 8 slices) bacon, halved lengthwise and cut into ¼-inch pieces**
- ½ **cup dry white wine**
- 3 **large eggs**
- 1½ **ounces Parmesan cheese, grated (about ¾ cup)**
- ¼ **cup grated Pecorino Romano cheese**
- 1 **large garlic clove, minced or pressed through a garlic press (about 1½ teaspoons)**
- 1 **pound spaghetti (see note)**
  Table salt and ground black pepper

1. Adjust an oven rack to the lower-middle position, set an ovensafe serving bowl on the rack, and heat the oven to 200 degrees. Bring 4 quarts water to a boil in a large pot.

2. While the water is heating, heat the oil in a large skillet over medium heat until shimmering. Add the bacon and cook, stirring occasionally, until crisp, about 8 minutes. Add the wine and simmer until it is slightly reduced, 6 to 8 minutes. Remove from the heat and cover. Whisk the eggs, cheeses, and garlic together in a small bowl; set aside.

3. When the water comes to a boil, add 1 tablespoon salt and the pasta. Cook, stirring often, until al dente. Reserve ½ cup of the cooking water; drain the pasta. Remove the warm bowl from the oven and add the pasta. Immediately pour the egg and bacon mixtures over the pasta, season with salt and pepper to taste, and toss to coat; adjust the consistency of the sauce with the reserved pasta cooking water. Serve immediately.

FETTUCCINE ALFREDO

WHY THIS RECIPE WORKS: Fettuccine Alfredo—tender pasta bathed in a silky, creamy cheese sauce—always sounds so tempting. But too often, restaurant-style fettuccine Alfredo means gargantuan portions, overcooked pasta, and a sauce that quickly congeals in the bowl (or your stomach). We were after a better Alfredo, with a luxurious sauce that remained supple and velvety from the first bite of pasta to the last.

We first discovered that fresh pasta was essential as a base—dried noodles didn't hold on to the sauce, and the delicate nature of fresh pasta brought a more sophisticated tone to the dish. Turning our attention to the sauce, we found that a light hand was necessary when adding two of the richer ingredients: the cheese and the butter. Smaller amounts were sufficient to add distinctive flavor without being overwhelming. To manage the heavy cream, we reduced a portion of it, then added the remaining amount uncooked. This technique produced not only a luxurious texture but also a fresher flavor. A pinch of freshly grated nutmeg added a spicy, sweet undertone to this elegant dish.

Fettuccine Alfredo

SERVES 4 TO 6

Fresh pasta is the best choice for this dish; supermarkets sell 9-ounce containers of fresh pasta in the refrigerated section. When boiling the pasta, undercook it slightly (just shy of al dente) because the pasta cooks an additional minute or two in the sauce just before serving. Note that fettuccine Alfredo must be served immediately; it does not hold or reheat well.

- 1½ cups heavy cream
- 2 tablespoons unsalted butter
- Table salt
- ¼ teaspoon ground black pepper
- 9 ounces fresh fettuccine (see note)
- 1½ ounces Parmesan cheese, grated (about ¾ cup)
- ⅛ teaspoon grated nutmeg

1. Bring 1 cup of the heavy cream and the butter to a simmer in a medium saucepan over medium heat; reduce the heat to low and simmer gently until the mixture reduces to ⅔ cup, 12 to 15 minutes. Off the heat, stir in the remaining ½ cup cream, ½ teaspoon salt, and the pepper.

2. While the cream reduces, bring 4 quarts water to a boil in a large pot. Add 1 tablespoon salt and the pasta to the boiling water and cook, stirring often, until just shy of al dente. Reserve ¼ cup of the cooking water then drain the pasta and return it to the pot.

3. Meanwhile, return the cream mixture to a simmer over medium-high heat; reduce the heat to low and add the pasta, cheese, and nutmeg to the cream mixture. Cook over low heat, tossing the pasta to combine, until the cheese is melted, the sauce coats the pasta, and the pasta is just al dente, 1 to 2 minutes. Stir in the reserved pasta cooking water and toss to coat; the sauce may look thin but will gradually thicken as the pasta is served. Serve immediately.

BAKED CHEESY PASTA CASSEROLE

WHY THIS RECIPE WORKS: We love macaroni and cheese (who doesn't?), but sometimes we want a more adult version than the typical neon orange mac and cheese. Enter the classic Italian iteration of macaroni and cheese, *pasta ai quattro formaggi,* made with four cheeses and heavy cream. We set out to make a four-cheese creamy pasta casserole with great flavor, properly cooked pasta, and a crisp bread-crumb topping.

The cheese was first up for consideration; for the best flavor and texture, we used Italian fontina, Gorgonzola, Pecorino Romano, and Parmesan cheeses. Heating the cheese and cream together made a greasy, curdled mess, so instead we built a basic white sauce (a béchamel) by cooking butter with flour and then adding cream. Combining the hot sauce and pasta with the cheese—and not cooking the cheese in the sauce—preserved the fresh flavor of the different cheeses. Knowing the pasta would spend some time in the oven, we drained it before it was al dente so it wouldn't turn to mush when

baked. Topped with bread crumbs and more Parmesan, and baked briefly in a very hot oven, our pasta dinner was silky smooth and rich but not heavy—a grown-up, sophisticated version of macaroni and cheese with Italian flavors.

Creamy Baked Four-Cheese Pasta

SERVES 4 TO 6

To streamline the process, prepare the bread-crumb topping and shred, crumble, and grate the cheeses while you wait for the pasta water to boil.

- 2 slices high-quality white sandwich bread, torn into quarters
- 1 ounce Parmesan cheese, grated (about ½ cup)
  Table salt and ground black pepper
- 4 ounces Italian fontina cheese, rind removed, shredded (about 1 cup)
- 3 ounces Gorgonzola cheese, crumbled (about ¾ cup)
- 1 ounce Pecorino Romano cheese, grated (about ½ cup)
- 1 pound penne
- 2 teaspoons unsalted butter
- 2 teaspoons unbleached all-purpose flour
- 1½ cups heavy cream

1. Pulse the bread in a food processor to coarse crumbs, about 10 to 15 pulses. Transfer to a small bowl. Stir in ¼ cup of the Parmesan, ¼ teaspoon salt, and ⅛ teaspoon pepper; set aside.

2. Adjust an oven rack to the middle position and heat the oven to 500 degrees.

3. Bring 4 quarts water to a boil in a large pot. Combine the remaining Parmesan and the fontina, Gorgonzola, and Pecorino Romano cheeses in a large bowl; set aside. Add 1 tablespoon salt and the pasta to the boiling water and cook, stirring often.

4. While the pasta is cooking, melt the butter in a small saucepan over medium-low heat. Whisk in the flour until no lumps remain, about 30 seconds. Gradually whisk in the cream, increase the heat to medium, and bring to a boil, stirring occasionally; reduce the heat to medium-low and simmer, 1 minute longer. Stir in ¼ teaspoon salt and ¼ teaspoon pepper; cover and set aside.

5. When the pasta is just shy of al dente, drain it, leaving it slightly wet. Add the pasta to the bowl with the cheeses; immediately pour the cream mixture over, then cover the bowl and let stand 3 minutes. Uncover the bowl and stir with a rubber spatula, scraping the bottom of the bowl, until the cheeses are melted and the mixture is thoroughly combined.

6. Transfer the pasta to a 13 by 9-inch baking dish, then sprinkle evenly with the reserved bread crumbs, pressing down lightly. Bake until the topping is golden brown, about 7 minutes. Serve immediately.

BAKED ZITI

WHY THIS RECIPE WORKS: Most versions of baked ziti seem like they went directly from the pantry into the oven, calling for little more than cooked pasta, jarred tomato sauce, a container of ricotta, and some preshredded cheese. The results: overcooked ziti in a dull, grainy sauce topped with a rubbery mass of mozzarella. We wanted to rescue baked ziti so we could have perfectly al dente pasta, a rich and flavorful sauce, and melted cheese in every bite.

For a sauce that's big on flavor and light on prep, we cooked sautéed garlic with two canned products—diced tomatoes and tomato sauce. Fresh basil and dried oregano added aromatic flavor. Just when the tomato sauce seemed perfect, we added ricotta, and a familiar problem reared its head: Rather than baking up creamy and rich, the ricotta was grainy and dulled the sauce. Cottage cheese was the best choice for a replacement—its curds have a texture similar to ricotta, but are creamier and tangier. For more flavor, we combined the cottage cheese with eggs, Parmesan, and heavy cream thickened with cornstarch. Adding this milky, tangy mixture to the tomato sauce produced a sauce that was bright, rich, and creamy.

When it came to the pasta, we undercooked it and then baked it with a generous amount of sauce for perfectly al dente pasta and plenty of sauce left to keep our baked ziti moist. As for the mozzarella, we cut it into small cubes instead of shredding it, which dotted the finished casserole with gooey bits of cheese.

Baked Ziti
SERVES 8 TO 10

We prefer baked ziti made with heavy cream, but whole milk can be substituted by increasing the amount of cornstarch to 2 teaspoons and increasing the cooking time in step 3 by 1 to 2 minutes. Our preferred brand of mozzarella is Dragone Whole Milk Mozzarella. Part-skim mozzarella can also be used.

- 1 **pound whole milk or 1 percent cottage cheese**
- 2 **large eggs, lightly beaten**
- 3 **ounces Parmesan cheese, grated (about 1½ cups)**
   Table salt
- 1 **pound ziti or other short tubular pasta**
- 2 **tablespoons extra-virgin olive oil**
- 5 **medium garlic cloves, minced or pressed through a garlic press (about 5 teaspoons)**
- 1 **(28-ounce) can tomato sauce**
- 1 **(14.5-ounce) can diced tomatoes**
- 1 **teaspoon dried oregano**
- ½ **cup plus 2 tablespoons chopped fresh basil leaves**
- 1 **teaspoon sugar**
   Ground black pepper
- ¾ **teaspoon cornstarch**
- 1 **cup heavy cream (see note)**
- 8 **ounces whole milk mozzarella cheese, cut into ¼-inch pieces (about 1½ cups) (see note)**

1. Adjust an oven rack to the middle position and heat the oven to 350 degrees. Whisk the cottage cheese, eggs, and 1 cup of the Parmesan together in a medium bowl; set aside. Bring 4 quarts water to a boil in a large pot. Add 1 tablespoon salt and the pasta; cook, stirring occasionally, until the pasta begins to soften but is not yet cooked through, 5 to 7 minutes. Drain the pasta and leave in the colander (do not wash the pot).

2. Meanwhile, heat the oil and garlic in a 12-inch skillet over medium heat until the garlic is fragrant but not brown, about 2 minutes. Stir in the tomato sauce, diced tomatoes, and oregano; simmer until thickened, about 10 minutes. Off the heat, stir in ½ cup of the basil and the sugar; season with salt and pepper to taste.

3. Stir the cornstarch and heavy cream together in a small bowl; transfer the mixture to the now-empty pot set over medium heat. Bring to a simmer and cook until thickened, 3 to 4 minutes. Remove the pot from the heat and add the cottage cheese mixture, 1 cup of the tomato sauce, and ¾ cup of the mozzarella; stir to combine. Add the pasta and stir to coat thoroughly with the sauce.

4. Transfer the pasta to a 13 by 9-inch baking dish and spread the remaining tomato sauce evenly over the pasta. Sprinkle the remaining ¾ cup mozzarella and remaining ½ cup Parmesan over the top. Cover the baking dish tightly with foil and bake for 30 minutes.

5. Remove the foil and continue to cook until the cheese is bubbling and beginning to brown, about 30 minutes longer. Cool for 20 minutes. Sprinkle with the remaining 2 tablespoons basil and serve.

MANICOTTI

WHY THIS RECIPE WORKS: Despite being composed of a straightforward collection of ingredients (pasta, cheese, and tomato sauce), manicotti is surprisingly fussy to prepare. Blanching, shocking, draining, and stuffing slippery pasta requires a lot of patience and time. We wanted an easy-to-prepare recipe that still produced great-tasting manicotti.

Our biggest challenge was filling the slippery manicotti tubes. We solved the problem by discarding the tubes completely and spreading the filling onto a lasagna noodle, which we then rolled up. For the lasagna noodles, we found that the no-boil variety were ideal. We soaked the noodles in boiling water for 5 minutes until pliable, then used the tip of a knife to separate them and prevent sticking. For the cheese filling, we needed only to taste-test several ricottas (part-skim proved to have an ideal level of richness). Eggs, Parmesan, and an ample amount of mozzarella added richness, flavor, and structure to the ricotta filling. For a quick but brightly flavored tomato sauce, we pureed canned diced tomatoes and simmered them until slightly thickened with sautéed garlic and red pepper flakes, then finished the sauce with fresh basil.

Baked Manicotti

SERVES 6 TO 8

We prefer Barilla no-boil lasagna noodles for their delicate texture resembling fresh pasta. Note that Pasta Defino and Ronzoni brands contain only 12 no-boil noodles per package; the recipe requires 16 noodles. The manicotti can be prepared through step 5, covered with a sheet of parchment paper, wrapped in aluminum foil, and refrigerated for up to 3 days or frozen for up to 1 month. (If frozen, thaw the manicotti in the refrigerator for 1 to 2 days.) To bake, remove the parchment, replace the aluminum foil, and increase the baking time to 1 to 1¼ hours.

TOMATO SAUCE
- **2** (28-ounce) cans diced tomatoes
- **2** tablespoons extra-virgin olive oil
- **3** medium garlic cloves, minced or pressed through a garlic press (about 1 tablespoon)
- **½** teaspoon red pepper flakes (optional) Table salt
- **2** tablespoons chopped fresh basil leaves

CHEESE FILLING AND PASTA

- **3** cups part-skim ricotta cheese
- **4** ounces Parmesan cheese, grated (about 2 cups)
- **8** ounces whole milk mozzarella cheese, shredded (about 2 cups)
- **2** large eggs, lightly beaten
- **2** tablespoons chopped fresh parsley leaves
- **2** tablespoons chopped fresh basil leaves
- **¾** teaspoon table salt
- **½** teaspoon ground black pepper
- **16** no-boil lasagna noodles (see note)

1. FOR THE SAUCE: Adjust an oven rack to the middle position and heat the oven to 375 degrees. Pulse 1 can of the tomatoes with their juice in a food processor until coarsely chopped, 3 or 4 pulses. Transfer to a bowl. Repeat with the remaining tomatoes.

2. Heat the oil, garlic, and red pepper flakes (if using) in a large saucepan over medium heat until fragrant but not brown, 1 to 2 minutes. Stir in the tomatoes and ½ teaspoon salt and simmer until thickened slightly, about 15 minutes. Stir in the basil; season with salt to taste.

3. FOR THE CHEESE FILLING: Combine the ricotta, 1 cup of the Parmesan, the mozzarella, eggs, parsley basil, salt, and pepper in a medium bowl; set aside.

4. Pour 2 inches boiling water into a 13 by 9-inch broiler-safe baking dish. Slip the noodles into the water, one at a time, and let them soak until pliable, about 5 minutes, separating them with the tip of a knife to prevent sticking. Remove the noodles from the water and place in a single layer on clean kitchen towels. Discard the water and dry the baking dish.

5. Spread the bottom of the baking dish evenly with 1½ cups of the sauce. Using a spoon, spread ¼ cup of the cheese mixture evenly onto the bottom three-quarters of each noodle (with the short side facing you), leaving the top quarter of the noodle exposed. Roll into a tube shape and arrange in the baking dish, seam side down. Top evenly with the remaining sauce, making certain that the pasta is completely covered.

6. Cover the baking dish tightly with foil and bake until bubbling, about 40 minutes. Remove the baking dish from the oven and remove the foil. Adjust the oven rack to the uppermost position (about 6 inches from the heating element) and heat the broiler. Sprinkle the manicotti evenly with the remaining cup Parmesan. Broil until the cheese is spotty brown, 4 to 6 minutes. Cool 15 minutes; cut into pieces and serve.

FOUR-CHEESE LASAGNA

WHY THIS RECIPE WORKS: Cheese lasagna offers an elegant alternative to meat-laden, red sauce lasagna. But some cheese lasagna is just heavy and bland, due to the use of plain-tasting cheeses. And even those with good cheese flavor can have soupy, dry, or greasy textures. We wanted a robust cheese lasagna with great structure, creamy texture, and maximum flavor.

For the best cheese flavor, we settled on a combination of fontina, Parmesan, Gorgonzola, and Gruyère cheeses. We found that making the white sauce (a béchamel) with a high ratio of flour to butter created a thick binder that provided enough heft to keep the lasagna layers together. And replacing some of the milk with chicken broth was the key to balancing the richness of the sauce and bringing the cheese flavor forward. But the real secret of a great four-cheese lasagna proved to be a fifth cheese. While ricotta didn't add much flavor, it gave the lasagna body without making the dish heavy and starchy. Our final challenge was to keep the baking time short enough to avoid harming this delicate pasta dish. Both presoaking the no-boil noodles and using a low-heat/high-heat baking method—baking at a moderate temperature and then briefly broiling to brown the top—kept the lasagna from overbaking.

Four-Cheese Lasagna

SERVES 10

It's important to not overbake the lasagna. Once the sauce starts bubbling around the edges, uncover the lasagna and turn the oven to broil. If your lasagna pan is not broiler-safe, brown the lasagna at 500 degrees for about 10 minutes. Whole milk is best in the sauce, but skim and low-fat milk also work. Supermarket-brand cheeses work fine in this recipe. The Gorgonzola may be omitted, but the flavor of the lasagna won't be as complex. We prefer Barilla no-boil lasagna noodles for their delicate texture resembling fresh pasta. Note that Pasta Defino and Ronzoni brands contain only 12 no-boil noodles per package; this recipe requires 15 noodles. This lasagna is very rich; serve small portions with a green salad.

- 6 ounces Gruyère cheese, shredded (about 1½ cups)
- 2 ounces Parmesan cheese, grated (about 1 cup)
- 1½ cups part-skim ricotta cheese
- 1 large egg, lightly beaten
- 2 tablespoons plus 2 teaspoons minced fresh parsley leaves
- ¼ teaspoon ground black pepper
- 3 tablespoons unsalted butter
- 1 medium shallot, minced (about 2 tablespoons)
- 1 medium garlic clove, minced or pressed through a garlic press (about 1 teaspoon)
- ⅓ cup unbleached all-purpose flour
- 2½ cups whole milk (see note)
- 1½ cups low-sodium chicken broth
- ½ teaspoon table salt
- 1 bay leaf
  Pinch cayenne pepper
- 15 no-boil lasagna noodles (see note)
- 8 ounces fontina cheese, rind removed, shredded (about 2 cups)
- 3 ounces Gorgonzola cheese, crumbled fine (about ¾ cup) (see note)

1. Place the Gruyère and ½ cup of the Parmesan in a large ovensafe bowl. Combine the ricotta, egg, 2 tablespoons of the parsley, and the black pepper in a medium bowl. Set both bowls aside.

2. Melt the butter in a medium saucepan over medium heat; add the shallot and garlic and cook, stirring frequently, until beginning to soften, about 2 minutes. Add the flour and cook, stirring constantly, until thoroughly combined, about 1½ minutes; the mixture should not brown. Gradually whisk in the milk and broth; increase the heat to medium-high and bring to a full boil, whisking frequently. Add the salt, bay leaf, and cayenne; reduce the heat to medium-low and simmer until the sauce thickens and coats the back of a spoon, about 10 minutes, stirring occasionally with a heatproof rubber spatula or wooden spoon and making sure to scrape the bottom and corners of the saucepan.

3. Remove the saucepan from the heat and discard the bay leaf. Gradually whisk ¼ cup of the sauce into the ricotta mixture. Pour the remaining sauce over the Gruyère mixture and stir until smooth; set aside.

4. Adjust an oven rack to the upper-middle position and heat the oven to 350 degrees. Pour 2 inches boiling water into a 13 by 9-inch broiler-safe baking dish. Slip the noodles into the water, one at a time, and let them soak until pliable, about 5 minutes, separating them with the tip of a knife to prevent sticking. Remove the noodles from the water and place in a single layer on clean kitchen towels. Discard the water, dry the baking dish, and spray lightly with vegetable oil spray.

5. Spread the bottom of the baking dish evenly with ½ cup of the sauce. Place 3 noodles in a single layer on top of the sauce. Spread ½ cup of the ricotta mixture evenly over the noodles and sprinkle evenly with ½ cup of the fontina and 3 tablespoons of the Gorgonzola. Drizzle ½ cup of the sauce evenly over the cheese. Repeat the layering of noodles, ricotta, fontina, Gorgonzola, and sauce three more times. Place the final 3 noodles on top and cover completely with the remaining sauce, spreading with a rubber spatula and allowing it to spill over the noodles. Sprinkle evenly with the remaining ½ cup Parmesan.

6. Spray a large sheet of foil with vegetable oil spray and cover the lasagna; bake until the edges are just bubbling, 25 to 30 minutes, rotating the pan halfway through the baking time. Remove the foil and turn the oven to broil. Broil until the surface is spotty brown, 3 to 5 minutes. Cool 15 minutes. Sprinkle with the remaining 2 teaspoons parsley; cut into pieces and serve.

LASAGNA WITH MEAT SAUCE

WHY THIS RECIPE WORKS: Traditional meaty lasagna is one of the best comfort foods out there. Unfortunately, this hearty dish takes the better part of a day to make (not very comforting, if you ask us). The noodles must be boiled and the sauce slow-cooked. Then, once the cheese filling is mixed, the ingredients must be carefully layered before the whole thing is baked off. We wanted a really good meat lasagna, with all of the rich, hearty meatiness of an all-day lasagna, but ready in a lot less time.

We made a speedy meaty tomato sauce by simmering onion, garlic, and meat loaf mixture (ground beef, pork, and veal) together for about 15 minutes. Adding some heavy cream created a richer, creamier, more cohesive sauce; we stirred in pureed and diced tomatoes for a luxurious, soft sauce with chunks of tomatoes. Using no-boil lasagna noodles eliminated the tedious process of boiling and draining the pasta. For a classic cheese layer, we combined ricotta cheese, Parmesan cheese, fresh basil, and an egg, which helped thicken and bind the mixture; a layer of shredded mozzarella upped the creaminess and cheesiness of the filling. Covering the lasagna with foil before baking helped to soften the noodles; removing it during the last half-hour of baking ensured that the cheeses were properly browned.

Lasagna with Hearty Tomato-Meat Sauce

SERVES 6 TO 8

You can substitute equal amounts of 80 percent lean ground beef, ground veal, and ground pork for the meat-loaf mix (the total amount of meat should be 1 pound). The assembled, unbaked lasagna will keep in the freezer for up to 2 months; wrap it tightly with plastic wrap, then foil, before freezing. To bake, defrost it in the refrigerator for up to 2 days and bake as directed, extending the covered baking time by 5 to 10 minutes.

TOMATO-MEAT SAUCE

- 1 tablespoon olive oil
- 1 medium onion, minced
- 6 medium garlic cloves, minced or pressed through a garlic press (about 2 tablespoons)
- 1 pound meat loaf mix (see note)
- ½ teaspoon table salt
- ½ teaspoon ground black pepper
- ¼ cup heavy cream
- 1 (28-ounce) can tomato puree
- 1 (28-ounce) can diced tomatoes, drained

CHEESE FILLING AND PASTA

- 1¾ cups whole milk or part-skim ricotta cheese
- 2½ ounces Parmesan cheese, grated (about 1¼ cups)
- ½ cup chopped fresh basil leaves
- 1 large egg, lightly beaten
- ½ teaspoon table salt
- ½ teaspoon ground black pepper
- 12 no-boil lasagna noodles
- 16 ounces whole milk mozzarella cheese, shredded (about 4 cups)

1. Adjust an oven rack to the middle position and heat the oven to 375 degrees.

2. FOR THE SAUCE: Heat the oil in a large Dutch oven over medium heat until shimmering. Add the onion and cook, stirring occasionally, until softened but not browned, about 2 minutes. Add the garlic and cook until fragrant, about 2 minutes. Increase the heat to medium-high and add the meatloaf mix, salt, and pepper; cook, breaking the meat into small pieces with a wooden spoon, until the meat loses its raw color but has not browned, about 4 minutes. Add the cream and simmer, stirring occasionally, until the liquid evaporates and only rendered fat remains, about 4 minutes. Add the tomato puree and diced tomatoes and bring to a simmer; reduce the heat to low and simmer until the flavors have blended, about 3 minutes. Set aside. (The cooled sauce

A FRESH CRUSH IS BEST

We're always looking for ways to make our kitchen work more efficient and will often prep recipes in advance if we know we've got a lot of recipes to get through on a given day. But noticing that garlic can develop a particularly strong odor if minced too far in advance, we decided to run a quick test. We used garlic in three different applications: lightly cooked in Pasta with Garlic and Oil (page 190), raw, when stirred into mayonnaise, and as a more subtle flavoring in a vinaigrette. For each recipe, we used freshly minced garlic, garlic that had been minced six hours in advance, and garlic that had been minced the day before. Both the six-hour and one-day-old minced garlic were so powerful they overwhelmed the other flavors in the dish.

Turns out, garlic flavor comes from a compound called allicin, which is not formed until after the garlic's cells are ruptured. As soon as you cut into garlic, the allicin will start to build and build until its flavor becomes overwhelmingly strong. So if you're going to prep a recipe in advance, make sure to leave the garlic cloves whole until the last minute.

can be refrigerated in an airtight container for up to 2 days; reheat before assembling the lasagna.)

3. FOR THE CHEESE FILLING: Combine the ricotta, 1 cup of the Parmesan, the basil, egg, salt, and pepper in a medium bowl; set aside.

4. Spread the bottom of a 13 by 9-inch baking dish evenly with ¼ cup of the meat sauce (avoiding large chunks of meat). Place 3 noodles in a single layer on top of the sauce. Spread each noodle evenly with 3 tablespoons of the ricotta mixture and sprinkle the entire layer evenly with 1 cup of the mozzarella cheese. Spread the cheese evenly with 1½ cups of the meat sauce. Repeat the layering of noodles, ricotta, mozzarella, and sauce two more times. Place the 3 remaining noodles on top of the sauce, spread evenly with the remaining sauce, sprinkle with the remaining cup mozzarella, then sprinkle with the remaining ¼ cup Parmesan. Spray a large sheet of foil with vegetable oil spray and cover the lasagna.

5. Bake 15 minutes, then remove the foil. Continue to bake until the cheese is spotty brown and the sauce is bubbling, about 25 minutes longer. Cool the lasagna 10 minutes; cut into pieces and serve.

CHAPTER 13

BRINGING HOME ITALIAN FAVORITES

Crisp Thin-Crust Pizza 222

Quick Tomato Sauce for Pizza

Deep-Dish Pizza with Tomatoes, Mozzarella, and Basil 223

Pizza Bianca 224

Grilled Tomato and Cheese Pizzas 225

Spicy Garlic Oil

Tomato and Mozzarella Tart 227

Classic Garlic Bread 228

Cheesy Garlic Bread 229

Frico 230

Italian Pasta and Bean Soup (Pasta e Fagioli) 231

Hearty Tuscan Bean Stew 232

Eggplant Parmesan 233

Basic Polenta 234

Mushroom Risotto 235

Butternut Squash Risotto 236

Chicken Marsala 237

Lighter Chicken Parmesan 238

Simple Tomato Sauce

Chicken Piccata 239

Parmesan-Crusted Chicken Cutlets 240

Chicken Francese 241

Chicken Saltimbocca 242

Italian-Style Grilled Chicken 243

Pork Chops with Vinegar and Sweet Peppers 244

Osso Buco 245

Beef Braised in Barolo 246

Shrimp Scampi 247

THIN-CRUST PIZZA

WHY THIS RECIPE WORKS: Few dishes say "Italian" better than a slice of pizza. At one end of the pizza spectrum is crisp-crust Neapolitan-style pizza. We aimed to develop the ultimate version, one with a shatteringly crisp, wafer-thin crust with a deeply caramelized flavor that bears no trace of raw yeast or flour.

For a pizza dough that comes together quickly and easily, we turned to the food processor. Letting the dough rise slowly in the refrigerator overnight made it easier to handle the next day, and it developed good flavor from the slow fermentation. For the thinnest crust possible, we used a rolling pin. A sheet of plastic wrap on top of the dough made rolling easier; we didn't need to add more flour to prevent sticking. This slim crust can't handle heavy toppings, nor should it. A thin layer of tomato sauce and mozzarella packs lots of flavor.

Crisp Thin-Crust Pizza

SERVES 6 TO 8

Note that the pizza dough needs to be started at least 1 day before serving. Keep in mind that it is more important for the rolled dough to be of even thinness than to be a perfect circle. For topping the pizzas, we recommend buying shrink-wrapped mozzarella from the supermarket; do not use fresh because it is too moist and will make the crust soggy. If you don't have a pizza stone, bake the pizza on a rimless or overturned baking sheet that has been preheated just like the pizza stone.

DOUGH

- 1¾–2 cups (8¾ to 10 ounces) unbleached all-purpose flour, plus extra for the work surface
- ½ teaspoon instant or rapid-rise yeast
- ½ teaspoon honey
- ½ teaspoon table salt
- ¼ cup olive oil
- ¾ cup warm water (110 degrees)

TOPPINGS

- 1 cup Quick Tomato Sauce for Pizza (recipe follows)
- 8 ounces whole milk mozzarella cheese, shredded (about 2 cups) (see note)

1. FOR THE DOUGH: Pulse 1¾ cups of the flour, the yeast, honey, and salt in a food processor (fitted with the dough blade, if possible) until combined, about 5 seconds. With the machine running, pour the oil and then the water

through the feed tube and process until the dough forms a ball, about 30 seconds. If after 30 seconds the dough is sticky and clings to the blade, add the remaining ¼ cup flour 1 tablespoon at a time. Turn the dough out onto a work surface.

2. Divide the dough in half and place each piece in a gallon-sized, heavy-duty zipper-lock bag and seal. Refrigerate overnight or up to 48 hours.

3. TO MAKE THE PIZZA: One hour before baking the pizza, adjust an oven rack to the lowest position, set a pizza stone on the rack, and heat the oven to 500 degrees.

4. Remove the dough from the plastic bags. Set each piece in the center of a lightly floured large sheet of parchment paper. Cover each with two 18-inch lengths of plastic wrap, overlapping them in the center; let the dough rest for 10 minutes.

5. Setting one piece of dough aside, roll the other into a 14-inch round with an even thickness, using the tackiness of the dough against the parchment to help roll it. If the parchment wrinkles, flip the dough sandwich over and smooth the wrinkles with a metal bench scraper.

6. Peel the plastic wrap off the top of the rolled dough. Spread ½ cup of the tomato sauce to the edges of the dough. Sprinkle with 1 cup of the cheese.

7. Slip the dough with the parchment onto a pizza peel or rimless baking sheet. Slide the pizza, parchment and all, onto the hot pizza stone. Bake until a deep golden brown, about 10 minutes. Remove the pizza from the oven with a pizza peel or pull the parchment with the pizza onto a baking sheet. Transfer the pizza to a cutting board, slide the parchment out from under the pizza, and slide it onto a wire rack. Cool 2 minutes until crisp; slide to a cutting board, cut into wedges, and serve.

8. While the first pizza is baking, repeat steps 5 and 6 to roll and top the second pizza; allow the baking stone to reheat for 15 minutes after baking the first pizza, then repeat step 7 to bake the second pizza.

Quick Tomato Sauce for Pizza

MAKES ABOUT 1½ CUPS

For pizza, you want the smoothest possible sauce. Start with crushed tomatoes and puree them in a food processor before cooking them with the garlic and oil. This recipe makes a bit more sauce than needed to sauce two thin-crust pizzas.

- 1 (14.5-ounce) can crushed tomatoes
- 1 tablespoon olive oil
- 1 medium garlic clove, minced or pressed through a garlic press (about 1 teaspoon)
  Table salt and ground black pepper

1. Process the tomatoes in a food processor until smooth, about 5 pulses.

2. Heat the oil and garlic in a medium saucepan over medium heat until the garlic is fragrant, about 30 seconds. Stir in the tomatoes; bring to a simmer and cook, uncovered, until the sauce thickens, about 15 minutes. Season with salt and pepper to taste.

DEEP-DISH PIZZA

WHY THIS RECIPE WORKS: Unlike its thin-crust cousin, deep-dish pizza has a soft, chewy, thick crust and can stand up to substantial toppings. We wanted to try our hand at this restaurant-style pizza at home, without a lot of fuss, and it had to taste better than takeout.

Most of the allure of deep-dish pizza is in the crust, so it was important to get it right. After trying numerous ingredients and techniques, we discovered that a boiled potato gave the crust exactly the right qualities: It was soft and moist, yet with a bit of chew and good structure. The potato even made the unbaked dough easier to handle. To keep the outside of the crust from toughening during baking, we added a generous amount of olive oil to the pan before putting in the dough. Toppings put onto the crust before it went into the oven weighed it down so that it didn't rise much and became dense, so we baked the crust untopped for a few minutes first. Our deep-dish crust wasn't just a platform for the topping; it had great flavor and texture of its own.

Deep-Dish Pizza with Tomatoes, Mozzarella, and Basil

SERVES 4

Prepare the topping while the dough is rising so the two will be ready at the same time. Baking the pizza in a deep-dish pan on a hot pizza stone will help produce a crisp, well-browned bottom crust. If you don't have a pizza stone, use a heavy rimless baking sheet. The amount of oil used to grease the pan may seem excessive, but it helps brown the crust while also preventing sticking. If you don't have a 14-inch deep-dish pizza pan, use two 10-inch cake pans. Grease them with 2 tablespoons oil each; divide the pizza dough in half and pat each half into a 9-inch round. Use shrink-wrapped supermarket cheese rather than fresh mozzarella.

DOUGH

- 1 medium russet potato (about 9 ounces), peeled and quartered
- 3¼–3½ cups (16¼ to 17½ ounces) unbleached all-purpose flour
- 1½ teaspoons instant or rapid-rise yeast
- 1¾ teaspoons table salt
- 6 tablespoons olive oil, plus extra for oiling the bowl (see note)
- 1 cup warm water (110 degrees)

TOPPING

- 1½ pounds plum tomatoes (5 to 6 medium), cored, seeded, and cut into 1-inch pieces
- 2 medium garlic cloves, minced or pressed through a garlic press (about 2 teaspoons)
  Table salt and ground black pepper
- 6 ounces whole milk mozzarella cheese, shredded (about 1½ cups) (see note)
- 1¼ ounces Parmesan cheese, grated (about ⅔ cup)
- 3 tablespoons shredded fresh basil leaves

1. FOR THE DOUGH: Bring 4 cups water and the potato to a boil in a small saucepan over medium-high heat; cook until tender, 10 to 15 minutes. Drain and cool until the potato can be handled; press the potato through the fine disk of a potato ricer or grate it on the large holes of a box grater. Measure 1⅓ cups lightly packed potato; discard the remaining potato.

2. Process 3¼ cups of the flour, the potato, yeast, and salt in a food processor (fitted with the dough blade, if possible) until combined, about 5 seconds. With the motor running, pour 2 tablespoons of the oil and then the water through the feed tube and process until the dough comes together in a ball, about 30 seconds. If after 30 seconds the dough is sticky and clings to the blade, add the remaining ¼ cup flour 1 tablespoon at a time. Lightly coat a medium bowl with oil. Transfer the dough to the bowl; cover tightly with plastic wrap and set in a warm spot until doubled in volume, 1½ to 2 hours.

3. Meanwhile, mix the tomatoes and garlic together in a medium bowl; season with salt and pepper to taste and set aside.

4. Oil the bottom of a 14-inch deep-dish pizza pan with the remaining 4 tablespoons olive oil. Remove the dough from the oven and gently punch it down; turn the dough onto a clean, dry work surface and pat it into a 12-inch round. Transfer the round to the oiled pan, cover with plastic wrap, and let rest until the dough no longer resists shaping, about 10 minutes.

5. Adjust the oven racks to the lowest and top positions, set a pizza stone on the lower rack, and heat the oven to 500 degrees. Uncover the dough and pull it into the edges and up the sides of the pan to form a 1-inch-high lip. Cover with plastic wrap; let rise in a warm, draft-free spot until doubled in size, about 30 minutes. Uncover the dough and prick it generously with a fork. Reduce the oven temperature to 425, place the pan with the pizza on the hot pizza stone, and bake until dry and lightly browned, about 15 minutes. Add the tomato mixture, followed by the mozzarella, then the Parmesan. Bake the pizza on the stone or baking sheet until the cheese melts, 10 to 15 minutes (5 to 10 minutes for 10-inch pizzas). Move the pizza to the top rack and bake until the cheese is spotty golden brown, about 5 minutes longer. Cool for 5 minutes, then, holding the pizza pan at an angle with a potholder, use a wide spatula to slide the pizza from the pan to a cutting board, cut into wedges, and serve.

PIZZA BIANCA

WHY THIS RECIPE WORKS: The Roman version of pizza has a crust like no other we've ever tasted: crisp but extraordinarily chewy. It's so good on its own that it is usually topped with just olive oil, rosemary, and kosher salt. We wanted to figure out how we could enjoy this marvel without taking a trip to Italy.

This pizza dough contains significantly more water than other styles, which is the secret to its chewy texture. But extra-wet doughs require more kneading, and we wanted to make this dish at home in a reasonable amount of time. Instead of a long knead, we let the dough rest for 20 minutes, which let us get away with just 10 minutes of kneading. After an initial rise, the dough was still sticky; we couldn't roll it out, but it was easy to pour out then press onto a baking sheet. After letting the dough rest briefly, we baked the crust, adding just kosher salt, oil, and rosemary to remain true to the authentic version.

Pizza Bianca

SERVES 6 TO 8

Serve the pizza by itself as a snack, or with soup or salad as a light entrée. Once the dough has been placed in the oiled bowl, it can be transferred to the refrigerator and kept for up to 24 hours. Bring the dough to room temperature, 2 to 2½ hours, before proceeding with step 4 of the recipe. While kneading the dough on high speed, the mixer tends to wobble and walk on the countertop. Place a towel or shelf liner under the mixer and watch it at all times while mixing. Handle the dough with lightly oiled hands. Resist flouring your fingers or the dough might stick further. This recipe was developed using an 18 by 13-inch baking sheet. Smaller baking sheets can be used, but because the pizza will be thicker, baking times will be longer. If you don't have a pizza stone, bake the pizza on a rimless or overturned baking sheet that has been preheated just like the pizza stone.

- 3 **cups (15 ounces) unbleached all-purpose flour**
- 1⅔ **cups water, room temperature**
- 1¼ **teaspoons table salt**
- 1½ **teaspoons instant or rapid-rise yeast**
- 1¼ **teaspoons sugar**
- 5 **tablespoons extra-virgin olive oil**
- 1 **teaspoon kosher salt**
- 2 **tablespoons whole fresh rosemary leaves**

surface of the dough 30 to 40 times and sprinkle with the kosher salt.

6. Bake until golden brown, 20 to 30 minutes, sprinkling the rosemary over the top and rotating the baking sheet halfway through baking. Using a metal spatula, transfer the pizza to a cutting board. Brush the dough lightly with the remaining 1 tablespoon oil. Slice and serve immediately.

GRILLED PIZZA

WHY THIS RECIPE WORKS: Most homemade versions of this restaurant classic disappoint with charred crusts and sauce and cheese that drip onto the coals. We set out to find the secret to great grilled pizza at home.

Regular pizza dough stuck to the cooking grate and burned easily. We found that the dough has to be both thinner and sturdier to work on the grill. We used high-protein bread flour to strengthen the dough, and a greater proportion of water made it easier to stretch. The crust also needed more flavor to stand up to the heat of the fire, so we added extra salt, a little whole wheat flour, and some olive oil. The oil in the dough also kept the crust from sticking to the cooking grate. Salted chopped tomatoes rather than sauce and a mixture of soft fontina (which has more flavor than mozzarella) and nutty Parmesan made a flavorful but light topping that didn't weigh down the crust or make it soggy. Spicy garlic oil and a scattering of fresh basil added complexity without heaviness. Full of flavor and with a cracker-crisp crust, these grilled pizzas are as good as any we've had in a restaurant.

1. Mix the flour, water, and table salt in the bowl of a standing mixer fitted with the dough hook on low speed until no areas of dry flour remain, 3 to 4 minutes, occasionally scraping down the sides of the bowl. Turn off the mixer and let the dough rest for 20 minutes.

2. Sprinkle the yeast and sugar over the dough. Knead on low speed until fully combined, 1 to 2 minutes, occasionally scraping down the sides of the bowl. Increase the mixer speed to high and knead until the dough is glossy and smooth and pulls away from the sides of the bowl, 6 to 10 minutes. (The dough will pull away from the sides only while the mixer is on. When the mixer is off, the dough will fall back to the sides.)

3. Using your fingers, coat a large bowl with 1 tablespoon of the oil, rubbing the excess oil from your fingers onto the blade of a rubber spatula. Using the oiled spatula, transfer the dough to the bowl and pour 1 tablespoon more oil over the top. Flip the dough over once so that it is well coated with the oil; cover tightly with plastic wrap. Let the dough rise at room temperature until nearly tripled in volume and large bubbles have formed, 2 to 2½ hours.

4. One hour before baking the pizza, adjust an oven rack to the middle position, place a pizza stone on the rack, and heat the oven to 450 degrees.

5. Coat a rimmed baking sheet with 2 tablespoons more oil. Using a rubber spatula, turn the dough out onto the baking sheet along with any oil in the bowl. Using your fingertips, press the dough out toward the edges of the baking sheet, taking care not to tear it. (The dough will not fit snugly into corners. If the dough resists stretching, let it relax for 5 to 10 minutes before trying to stretch it again.) Let the dough rest until slightly bubbly, 5 to 10 minutes. Using a dinner fork, poke the

Grilled Tomato and Cheese Pizzas for a Charcoal Grill

SERVES 4

The pizzas cook very quickly on the grill, so before you begin, be sure to have all the equipment and ingredients you need at hand. Equipment includes a pizza peel (or a rimless baking sheet), a pair of tongs, a paring knife, a large cutting board, and a pastry brush; ingredients include all the toppings and a small bowl of flour for dusting. The pizzas are best served hot off the grill but can be kept warm for 20 to 30 minutes on a wire rack in a 200-degree oven.

DOUGH

- 1 cup water, room temperature
- 2 tablespoons olive oil, plus extra for oiling the bowl
- 2 cups (11 ounces) bread flour, plus extra for the work surface
- 1 tablespoon whole wheat flour (optional)
- 2 teaspoons sugar
- 1¼ teaspoons table salt
- 1 teaspoon instant or rapid-rise yeast

TOPPING

- 1½ pounds plum tomatoes (5 to 6 medium), cored, seeded, and cut into ½-inch pieces
- ¾ teaspoon table salt
- 6 ounces fontina cheese, shredded (about 1½ cups)
- 1½ ounces Parmesan cheese, grated fine (about ¾ cup)
  Vegetable oil for the cooking grate
- 1 recipe Spicy Garlic Oil (recipe follows)
- ½ cup chopped fresh basil leaves
  Kosher salt

1. FOR THE DOUGH: Combine the water and 2 tablespoons olive oil in a liquid measuring cup. Process 1¾ cup of the bread flour, whole wheat flour (if using), sugar, salt, and yeast in a food processor (fitted with the dough blade, if possible) until combined, about 5 seconds. With the machine running, pour the oil and water mixture through the feed tube and process until the dough forms a ball, about 1½ minutes. If after 1½ minutes the dough is sticky and clings to the blade, add the remaining ¼ cup flour 1 tablespoon at a time. Lightly coat a medium bowl with oil. Transfer the dough to the bowl; cover tightly with plastic wrap and set in a warm spot until doubled in volume, 1½ to 2 hours.

2. When the dough has doubled, press down gently to deflate; turn the dough out onto a work surface and divide into four equal pieces. With cupped palms, form each piece into a smooth, tight ball. Set the dough balls on a well-floured work surface. Press the dough rounds by hand to flatten; cover loosely with plastic wrap and let rest about 15 minutes.

3. FOR THE TOPPING: Meanwhile, toss the tomatoes and salt in a medium bowl; transfer to a colander and drain for 30 minutes (wipe out and reserve the bowl). Shake the colander to drain off the excess liquid; transfer the tomatoes to the now-empty bowl and set aside. Combine the cheeses in a second medium bowl and set aside.

4. Gently stretch the dough rounds into disks about ½ inch thick and 5 to 6 inches in diameter. Working with one piece at a time and keeping the rest covered, roll out each disk to ⅛-inch thickness, 9 to 10 inches in diameter, on a well-floured sheet of parchment paper, dusting with additional flour as needed to prevent sticking. (If the dough shrinks when rolled out, cover with plastic wrap and let rest until relaxed, 10 to 15 minutes.) Dust the surface of the rolled dough with flour and set aside. Repeat with the remaining dough, stacking the sheets of rolled dough on top of each other (with parchment in between) and covering the stack with plastic wrap; set aside until the grill is ready.

5. TO GRILL: Light a large chimney starter filled with charcoal (about 6 quarts) and allow to burn until the coals are partially covered with a layer of ash, about 20 minutes. Open the bottom vent on the grill. Arrange the coals evenly over three-quarters of the bottom of the grill, leaving one quadrant free of coals. Set the cooking grate in place, cover the grill with the lid, and heat the grill, about 5 minutes. Use a grill brush to scrape the cooking grate clean. Dip a wad of paper towels in vegetable oil; holding the wad with tongs, oil the cooking grate.

6. Lightly flour a pizza peel; invert one dough round onto the peel, gently stretching it as needed to retain its shape (do not stretch the dough too thin; thin spots will burn quickly). Peel off and discard the parchment; carefully slide the round onto the hotter side of the grill. Immediately repeat with another dough round. Cook until the tops are covered with bubbles (pierce larger bubbles with a paring knife) and the bottoms are grill-marked and charred in spots, 1 to 2 minutes; while the rounds cook, check the undersides and slide to a cooler area of the grill if browning too quickly. Transfer the crusts to a cutting board, browned-sides up. Repeat with the two remaining dough rounds.

7. Brush two crusts generously with the garlic oil; top each evenly with one-quarter of the cheese mixture and one-quarter of the tomatoes. Return the pizzas to the grill and cover the grill with the lid; cook until the bottoms are well browned and the cheese is melted, 2 to 4 minutes, checking the bottoms frequently to prevent burning. Transfer the pizzas to a cutting board; repeat with the remaining two crusts. Sprinkle the pizzas with the basil and kosher salt to taste; cut into wedges and serve.

Grilled Tomato and Cheese Pizzas for a Gas Grill

Follow the recipe for Grilled Tomato and Cheese Pizzas for a Charcoal Grill through step 4. Turn all the burners to high, cover, and heat the grill with the lid down until very hot, about 15 minutes. Use a grill brush to scrape the cooking grate clean. Dip a wad of paper towels in vegetable oil; holding the wad with tongs, oil the cooking grate. Continue with the recipe from step 6, cooking the pizzas with the lid down in both steps 6 and 7 and increasing the cooking times in steps 6 and 7 by 1 to 2 minutes, if needed.

Spicy Garlic Oil
MAKES ENOUGH FOR 4 PIZZAS

- ⅓ cup extra-virgin olive oil
- 4 medium garlic cloves, minced or pressed through a garlic press (about 4 teaspoons)
- ½–¾ teaspoon red pepper flakes

Cook all the ingredients in a small saucepan over medium heat, stirring occasionally, until the garlic begins to sizzle, 2 to 3 minutes. Transfer to a small bowl.

TOMATO TART

WHY THIS RECIPE WORKS: Falling somewhere in between pizza and quiche, tomato and mozzarella tart shares the flavors of both but features unique problems. For starters, this is not fast food, as some sort of pastry crust is required. Second, the moisture in the tomatoes almost guarantees a soggy crust. Third, tomato tarts are often tasteless, despite their good looks, falling short on flavor. We wanted a recipe that could easily be made at home with a solid bottom crust and great vine-ripened flavor.

Frozen puff pastry was the solution to an easy crust, and prebaking it was a start—but only a start—to solving the problem of sogginess. Sealing the puff pastry shell with an egg wash helped. Yet even with these preventive measures, the tomato juice still found its way into the crust. To extract more moisture from the tomatoes before baking the tart, we sliced and salted them, then pressed them lightly between paper towels. This removed much of the moisture. But even with a layer of grated mozzarella cheese (whole milk worked best) between tomatoes and crust, the tart shell still came out a bit soggy. Our breakthrough came when we added a layer of grated Parmesan cheese, which sealed the crust fully and repelled moisture. After a short stay in the oven, our tart had a crisp and sturdy crust, nutty flavor from the Parmesan, and rich flavors from the cheese and tomatoes.

Tomato and Mozzarella Tart
SERVES 4 TO 6

To keep the frozen dough from cracking, it's best to let it thaw slowly in the refrigerator overnight. For the best flavor, use authentic Parmesan cheese and very ripe, flavorful tomatoes. Fresh mozzarella will make the crust soggy, so be sure to use low-moisture, shrink-wrapped mozzarella.

- 1 (9 by 9½-inch) sheet frozen puff pastry, thawed (see note)
- 1 large egg, lightly beaten
- 1 ounce Parmesan cheese, grated (about ½ cup) (see note)
- ½ pound plum tomatoes (2 medium), cored and sliced ¼ inch thick (see note)
- ½ teaspoon table salt
- 4 ounces whole milk mozzarella cheese, shredded (1 cup) (see note)
- 2 tablespoons extra-virgin olive oil
- 1 medium garlic clove, minced or pressed through a garlic press (about 1 teaspoon)
- 2 tablespoons minced fresh basil

1. Adjust an oven rack to the lowest position and heat the oven to 425 degrees. Line a large baking sheet with parchment paper. Lay the pastry in the center of the prepared baking sheet. Brush the pastry with the beaten egg.

To form a rimmed crust, fold the long edges of the pastry over by ½ inch, then brush with the egg. Fold the short edges of the pastry over by ½ inch and brush with the egg. Use a paring knife to cut through the folded edges and corner of the pastry. Sprinkle the Parmesan evenly over the crust bottom. Poke the dough uniformly with a fork. Bake until golden brown and crisp, 15 to 20 minutes. Transfer to a wire rack to cool.

2. Meanwhile, spread the tomatoes over several layers of paper towels. Sprinkle with the salt and let drain for 30 minutes.

3. Sprinkle the mozzarella evenly over the crust bottom. Press excess moisture from the tomatoes, using additional paper towels. Following the photo, shingle the tomatoes evenly over the mozzarella. Whisk the olive oil and garlic together and drizzle over the tomatoes. Bake until the shell is deep golden, 10 to 15 minutes.

4. Cool on a wire rack for 5 minutes and then sprinkle with the basil. Slide the tart onto a cutting board and slice into pieces.

NOTES FROM THE TEST KITCHEN

PREPARING THE TART

1. Fold the short edges of the pastry over by ½ inch and brush with egg. Then fold the long edges of the pastry over by ½ inch, making sure to keep the edges flush and square. Brush with egg.

2. Using a paring knife, cut through the folded edges and corners of the tart shell.

3. After sprinkling the bottom of the tart with the Parmesan, poke the dough repeatedly with a fork. Bake the pastry shell.

4. Sprinkle the mozzarella evenly over the crust and shingle the tomatoes attractively over the mozzarella.

GARLIC BREAD

WHY THIS RECIPE WORKS: Garlic bread is a classic accompaniment to spaghetti and meatballs, baked ziti, and countless other Italian favorites. It seems so simple, yet it often goes so wrong. We wanted to banish greasy, bland, and bitter-tasting garlic bread forever in favor of crisp toasted bread imbued with sweet, nutty garlic flavor.

Starting with the bread, we chose a substantial loaf of football-shaped Italian bread, the best quality we could find, to give us generous slices. We cut it in half horizontally, so that the surfaces would crisp up in the oven. We tamed the garlic's harshness by toasting whole cloves, which turned them rich and mellow. We cut out the step of melting butter and simply spread it, after softening and mixing in the garlic, on the bread—not too much, so the bread wouldn't be greasy or soggy. The addition of some grated Parmesan cheese was nearly undetectable, but it added a deep and complex flavor. For baking, we found that leaving the bread unwrapped on a baking sheet gave us the crispy crust we wanted, and exposure to the oven's heat further mellowed the garlic.

Classic Garlic Bread

SERVES 6 TO 8

Plan to pull the garlic bread from the oven when you are ready to serve the other dishes—it is best served piping hot.

9-10 medium garlic cloves, unpeeled
 6 tablespoons (¾ stick) unsalted butter, softened
 2 tablespoons grated Parmesan cheese
 ½ teaspoon table salt
 1 (1-pound) loaf high-quality Italian bread (preferably football-shaped), halved horizontally
  Ground black pepper

1. Adjust an oven rack to the middle position and heat the oven to 500 degrees. Meanwhile, toast the garlic cloves in a small skillet over medium heat, shaking the pan occasionally, until fragrant and the color of the cloves deepens slightly, about 8 minutes. When cool enough to handle, peel and mince the cloves (you should have about 3 tablespoons). Using a dinner fork, mash the garlic, butter, cheese, and salt in a small bowl until thoroughly combined.

2. Spread the cut sides of the loaf evenly with the butter mixture; season with pepper to taste. Transfer the loaf halves, buttered side up, onto a rimmed baking sheet; bake, reversing the position of the baking sheet in the oven from front to back halfway through the baking time, until the surface of the bread is golden brown and toasted, 5 to 10 minutes. Cut each half into 2-inch slices; serve immediately.

CHEESY GARLIC BREAD

WHY THIS RECIPE WORKS: Garlic bread is a balancing act between the butter, garlic, and bread. Add cheese to the mix and things get complicated. We wanted cheese-topped garlic bread that was crisp on the outside but chewy within, buttery all the way through, and with no bitter garlic aftertaste.

Supermarket baguettes already have a chewy interior and crisp crust, so we started there. Grating the garlic cloves made for a smoother butter, and to tone down the garlic's harshness we sautéed it in butter with a little water (to prevent burning). We mixed the garlic into more softened butter, spread it on our split baguette, and wrapped the bread in foil. Baking it this way "steams" the bread and infuses it with garlic-butter flavor. To crisp the crust, we took the bread out of the foil and baked it a little longer. The final adornment was the cheese; rather than shredding several different kinds ourselves, we took a shortcut and used a prepackaged mixture of shredded Italian cheeses. The last step was to run it under the broiler, which gave us both melted cheese and an extra-crisp crust.

Cheesy Garlic Bread
SERVES 6 TO 8

The serrated edges on a bread knife can pull off the cheesy crust. To prevent this, place the finished garlic bread cheese side down on a cutting board. Slicing through the crust first (rather than the cheese) will keep the cheese in place. Shredded Italian cheese blend is sold in bags in the supermarket case near other packaged cheeses.

- 5 medium garlic cloves, peeled and grated
- 8 tablespoons (1 stick) unsalted butter, softened
- ½ teaspoon water
- ¼ teaspoon table salt
- ¼ teaspoon ground black pepper
- 1 (18 to 20-inch) baguette, sliced in half horizontally
- 1½ cups shredded Italian cheese blend (see note)

1. Adjust an oven rack to the lower-middle position and heat the oven to 400 degrees. Cook the garlic, 1 tablespoon of the butter, and the water in a small nonstick skillet over low heat, stirring occasionally, until straw-colored, 7 to 10 minutes.

2. Mix the hot garlic, remaining 7 tablespoons butter, the salt, and pepper in a bowl and spread on the cut sides of the bread. Sandwich the bread back together and wrap the loaf in foil. Place on a baking sheet and bake for 15 minutes.

3. Carefully unwrap the bread and place the halves, buttered sides up, on a baking sheet. Bake until just beginning to color, about 10 minutes. Remove from the oven and set the oven to broil.

4. Sprinkle the bread with the cheese. Broil until the cheese has melted and the bread is crisp, 1 to 2 minutes. Transfer the bread to a cutting board with the cheese side facing down. Cut into pieces and serve.

FRICO

WHY THIS RECIPE WORKS: As an accompaniment to cocktails or eaten just as a snack, frico is a simple, crisp wafer of flavorful cheese, usually Montasio, that has been melted and browned. We wanted to find the secret behind great frico, and then determine the best substitute for Montasio cheese, which can be difficult to find.

Cheese simply grated into a hot pan could turn into a sticky mess, but we found that using a nonstick skillet allowed us to cook the frico without adding butter or oil. We discovered that it was easy to turn the frico to the other side once the first side was browned if we first took the skillet off the heat; the slightly cooled cheese didn't stretch or tear when we flipped it. Turning the heat down

THE TEST KITCHEN'S TOP FIVE ESSENTIAL KITCHEN TOOLS

Face it: Americans are crazy about gadgets. Since the time of Benjamin Franklin, we have valued the ingenuity of the inventor who designs a simple tool that makes the execution of an everyday task easier. But as anyone who watches late-night television knows, America's love of the gadget can—and does—go too far at times. No one needs a syringe to inject marinades into meat.

So how do you know which gadgets work and which ones don't? That's where we can help. Here's our list of five gadgets you might not own, but really should. (See pages 585–593 for recommended brands.)

1. DIGITAL INSTANT-READ THERMOMETER: How else do you know when food is done? And, because it's digital, it works in seconds so your hands don't tarry in hot spots like the oven or grill.

2. LOCKING TONGS: Don't use a fork. Sturdy, long-handled tongs (with scalloped edges that won't pierce food) can turn, flip, rotate, stir, and more.

3. GARLIC PRESS: Stop kidding yourself. You're never going to mince garlic finely and evenly enough. A garlic press ensures consistent (and perfect) results every time.

4. OVEN THERMOMETER: News flash—your oven probably isn't properly calibrated. How do we know? We tested 20 home ovens and only a handful came close. You could pay big bucks to get your oven serviced by a professional or spend a few dollars on an oven thermometer so cookies don't burn and roasts are perfectly cooked.

5. KNIFE SHARPENER: Cooking with dull knives is slow and unsafe. You wouldn't drive a car with nearly flat tires, would you? A fancy electric sharpener is nice, but even a good (and cheap) manual sharpener is far better than nothing.

to cook the second side gave the best results; a pan that was too hot turns the cheese bitter. Many recipes suggest Parmesan as a substitute for Montasio, but we found Asiago cheese to be a better stand-in—though the real thing is even better.

Frico

MAKES 8 LARGE WAFERS

Serve frico with drinks and a bowl of marinated olives or marinated sun-dried tomatoes. Frico is also good crumbled into a salad, crouton-style.

1 pound Montasio or aged Asiago cheese, grated fine (about 8 cups)

1. Sprinkle 2 ounces (about 1 cup) grated cheese over the bottom of a 10-inch nonstick skillet set over medium-high heat. Use a heat-resistant rubber spatula or a wooden spoon to tidy the lacy outer edges of the cheese. Cook, shaking the pan occasionally to ensure an even distribution of the cheese over the pan bottom, until the edges are lacy and toasted, about 4 minutes. Remove the pan from the heat and allow the cheese to set for about 30 seconds.

2. Using a fork on top and a heatproof spatula underneath, carefully flip the cheese wafer and return the pan to medium heat. Cook until the second side is golden brown, about 2 minutes. Slide the cheese wafer out of the pan and transfer to a plate. Repeat with the remaining cheese. Serve the frico within 1 hour.

PASTA E FAGIOLI

WHY THIS RECIPE WORKS: The American version of this hearty Italian bean-and-vegetable stew—sometimes called pasta fazool—often turns out bland, with mushy beans and pasta and too much tomato. And it can take hours to prepare. We wanted rich broth, perfectly cooked beans and pasta, and complex flavors—and we wanted to prepare it in a reasonable amount of time.

Substituting canned beans for dried would save the most preparation time, and we found cannellini beans to be the closest to the dried cranberry beans used in authentic recipes. We started to build deep flavor by sautéing pancetta (though bacon also works) and, for aromatics, onion, garlic, and celery. Tomatoes (diced worked better than crushed or sauce) went in next. A small amount of minced anchovies was unidentifiable but added complexity. Chicken broth diluted with water was our cooking liquid; chicken broth alone made the dish taste too much like chicken soup. A Parmesan rind added another layer of flavor. Last into the pot went the pasta. The flavors of our thick, hearty soup harmonized perfectly and, best of all, we had spent less than an hour at the stove.

Italian Pasta and Bean Soup (Pasta e Fagioli)

SERVES 8 TO 10

This soup does not hold well because the pasta absorbs the liquid, becomes mushy, and leaves the soup dry. You can, however, make the soup in two stages. Once the beans are simmered with the tomatoes, before the broth and water are added, the mixture can be cooled and refrigerated for up to 3 days. When ready to complete the soup, discard the Parmesan rind (otherwise it will become stringy), add the liquid, bring the soup to a boil, and proceed with the recipe.

- 1 tablespoon extra-virgin olive oil, plus extra for drizzling
- 3 ounces pancetta or bacon (about 3 slices), chopped fine
- 1 medium onion, minced
- 1 celery rib, chopped fine
- 4 medium garlic cloves, minced or pressed through a garlic press (about 4 teaspoons)
- 1 teaspoon dried oregano
- ¼ teaspoon red pepper flakes
- 3 anchovy fillets, minced to a paste (about 1½ teaspoons)
- 1 (28-ounce) can diced tomatoes
- 1 piece Parmesan cheese rind, about 5 inches by 2 inches
- 2 (15.5-ounce) cans cannellini beans, drained and rinsed
- 3½ cups low-sodium chicken broth
- 2½ cups water
  Table salt
- 8 ounces small pasta such as ditalini, tubetini, conchiglietti, or orzo
- 4 tablespoons chopped fresh parsley leaves
  Ground black pepper
  Grated Parmesan cheese, for serving

1. Heat the oil in a large Dutch oven over medium-high heat until shimmering. Add the pancetta and cook, stirring occasionally, until it begins to brown, 3 to 5 min-

utes. Add the onion and celery and cook, stirring occasionally, until the vegetables are softened, 5 to 7 minutes. Add the garlic, oregano, red pepper flakes, and anchovies and cook, stirring constantly, until fragrant, about 30 seconds. Add the tomatoes with their juice, scraping up any browned bits. Add the cheese rind and beans; bring to a boil, then reduce the heat to low and simmer to blend the flavors, 10 minutes. Add the chicken broth, water, and 1 teaspoon salt; increase the heat to high and bring to a boil. Add the pasta and cook until tender, about 10 minutes.

2. Discard the cheese rind. Off the heat, stir in 3 tablespoons of the parsley; season with salt and pepper to taste. Ladle the soup into individual bowls; drizzle each serving with olive oil and sprinkle with a portion of the remaining 1 tablespoon parsley. Serve immediately, passing the grated Parmesan separately.

HEARTY TUSCAN BEAN STEW

WHY THIS RECIPE WORKS: Unlike *Pasta e Fagioli*, where beans and pasta share the spotlight, Tuscan bean soup boasts creamy, buttery cannellini beans in the starring role. Ideally, the beans should have a uniformly tender texture, but too often the skins are tough and the insides mealy—or the beans turn mushy. We wanted to fix the bean problem and convert this Italian classic into a hearty, rustic stew for a deeply flavorful one-pot meal.

Since the beans are the centerpiece of this stew, we concentrated on cooking them perfectly. After testing a variety of soaking times, we settled on soaking the beans overnight, a method that consistently produced the most tender and evenly cooked beans. But none of the methods we tested properly softened the skins. The answer was to soak the beans in salted water. Brining the beans, rather than the conventional approach of soaking them in plain water and then cooking them in saltwater, allowed the salt to soften the skins but kept it from penetrating inside, where it could make the beans mealy. Tests showed that gently cooking the beans in a 250-degree oven produced perfectly cooked beans that stayed intact. The final trick was to add the tomatoes toward the end of cooking, since their acid interfered with the softening process. To complete our stew, we looked for other traditional Tuscan flavors, including pancetta, kale, lots of garlic, and a sprig of rosemary. And to make it even more substantial, we served the stew on a slab of toasted country bread, drizzled with fruity extra-virgin olive oil.

Hearty Tuscan Bean Stew

SERVES 8

We prefer the creamier texture of beans soaked overnight for this recipe. If you're short on time, quick-soak them: Place the rinsed beans in a large heat-resistant bowl. Bring 2 quarts water and 3 tablespoons salt to a boil. Pour the water over the beans and let them sit for 1 hour. Drain and rinse the beans well before proceeding with step 2. If pancetta is unavailable, substitute 4 ounces bacon (about 4 slices).

Table salt
- 1 **pound (about 2 cups) dried cannellini beans, picked over and rinsed**
- 1 **tablespoon extra-virgin olive oil, plus extra for drizzling**
- 6 **ounces pancetta or bacon, cut into ¼-inch pieces**
- 1 **large onion, chopped medium (about 1½ cups)**
- 2 **medium celery ribs, cut into ½-inch pieces (about ¾ cup)**
- 2 **medium carrots, peeled and cut into ½-inch pieces (about 1 cup)**
- 8 **medium garlic cloves, peeled and crushed**
- 4 **cups low-sodium chicken broth**
- 3 **cups water**
- 2 **bay leaves**
- 1 **bunch kale or collard greens (about 1 pound), stems trimmed and leaves chopped into 1-inch pieces (about 8 cups loosely packed)**
- 1 **(14.5-ounce) can diced tomatoes, drained**
- 1 **sprig fresh rosemary**
  Ground black pepper
- 8 **slices country white bread, each 1¼ inches thick, broiled until golden brown on both sides and rubbed with a garlic clove (optional)**

1. Dissolve 3 tablespoons salt in 4 quarts cold water in a large bowl or container. Add the beans and soak at room temperature for at least 8 hours or up to 24 hours. Drain the beans and rinse well.

2. Adjust an oven rack to the lower-middle position and heat the oven to 250 degrees. Heat the oil and pancetta in a large Dutch oven over medium heat. Cook, stirring occasionally, until the pancetta is lightly browned and the fat has rendered, 6 to 10 minutes. Add the onion, celery, and carrots. Cook, stirring occasionally, until the vegetables are softened and lightly browned, 10 to 16 minutes. Stir in the garlic and cook until fragrant, about 1 minute. Stir in the broth, water, bay leaves, and soaked beans. Increase the heat to high and bring the mixture to a simmer. Cover the pot, transfer it to the oven, and cook until the beans are almost tender (the very center of the beans will still be firm), 45 minutes to 1 hour.

3. Remove the pot from the oven and stir in the kale and tomatoes. Return the pot to the oven and continue to cook until the beans and greens are fully tender, 30 to 40 minutes longer.

4. Remove the pot from the oven and submerge the rosemary sprig in the stew. Cover and let stand 15 minutes. Discard the bay leaves and rosemary sprig and season the stew with salt and pepper to taste. If desired, use the back of a spoon to press some beans against the side of the pot to thicken the stew. Serve over the toasted bread (if using) and drizzle with olive oil.

EGGPLANT PARMESAN

WHY THIS RECIPE WORKS: Frying the eggplant for this classic Italian dish not only is time-consuming but also can make the dish heavy and dull. In hopes of eliminating the grease as well as some of the prep time, we decided to cook the eggplant in the oven and see what other measures we could take to freshen up this Italian classic.

We salted and drained the eggplant slices to remove bitterness and improve the texture. A traditional bound breading—flour, egg, and fresh bread crumbs—worked best for giving the eggplant a crisp coating. Baking the eggplant on preheated and oiled baking sheets resulted in crisp, golden brown slices. While the eggplant was in the oven, we made a quick tomato sauce using garlic, red pepper flakes, basil, and canned diced tomatoes. We layered the sauce, eggplant, and mozzarella in a baking dish and left the top layer of eggplant mostly unsauced, so that it would crisp up in the oven. Our re-engineered eggplant Parmesan was lighter and fresher tasting, and a lot less work.

Eggplant Parmesan

SERVES 6 TO 8

Use kosher salt when salting the eggplant. The coarse grains don't dissolve as readily as the fine grains of regular table salt, so any excess can be easily wiped away. It's necessary to divide the eggplant into two batches when tossing it with the salt. To be time-efficient, use the 30 to 45 minutes during which the salted eggplant sits to prepare the breading.

EGGPLANT

- 2 pounds globe eggplant (2 medium eggplants), cut crosswise into ¼-inch-thick rounds
- 1 tablespoon kosher salt (see note)
- 8 slices high-quality white sandwich bread, torn into quarters
- 2 ounces Parmesan cheese, grated (about 1 cup)
  Table salt and ground black pepper
- 1 cup unbleached all-purpose flour
- 4 large eggs
- 6 tablespoons vegetable oil

TOMATO SAUCE

- 3 (14.5-ounce) cans diced tomatoes
- 2 tablespoons extra-virgin olive oil
- 4 medium garlic cloves, minced or pressed through a garlic press (about 4 teaspoons)
- ¼ teaspoon red pepper flakes
- ½ cup coarsely chopped fresh basil leaves
  Table salt and ground black pepper

- 8 ounces whole milk or part-skim mozzarella cheese, shredded (about 2 cups)
- 1 ounce Parmesan cheese, grated (about ½ cup)
- 10 fresh basil leaves, torn, for garnish

1. FOR THE EGGPLANT: Toss half of the eggplant slices and 1½ teaspoons of the kosher salt in a large bowl until combined; transfer the salted eggplant to a large colander set over a bowl. Repeat with the remaining eggplant and kosher salt, placing the second batch on top of the first. Let stand until the eggplant releases about 2 tablespoons liquid, 30 to 45 minutes. Spread the eggplant slices on a triple thickness of paper towels; cover with another triple thickness of paper towels. Press firmly on each slice to remove as much liquid as possible, then wipe off the excess salt.

2. While the eggplant is draining, adjust the oven racks to the upper-middle and lower-middle positions, place a rimmed baking sheet on each rack, and heat the oven to 425 degrees. Process the bread in a food processor to fine, even crumbs, about 20 to 30 seconds. Transfer the crumbs to a pie plate and stir in the Parmesan, ¼ teaspoon table salt, and ½ teaspoon pepper; set aside. Wipe out the workbowl (do not wash) and set aside.

3. Combine the flour and 1 teaspoon pepper in a large zipper-lock bag; shake to combine. Beat the eggs in a second pie plate. Place 8 to 10 eggplant slices in the bag with the flour; seal the bag and shake to coat the slices. Remove the slices, shaking off the excess flour, dip into the eggs, let the excess egg run off, then coat evenly with the breadcrumb mixture; set the breaded slices on a wire rack set over a baking sheet. Repeat with the remaining eggplant.

4. Remove the preheated baking sheets from the oven; add 3 tablespoons of the oil to each sheet, tilting to coat evenly with the oil. Place half of the breaded eggplant slices on each sheet in a single layer; bake until the eggplant is well browned and crisp, about 30 minutes, switching and rotating the baking sheets after 10 minutes, and flipping the eggplant slices with a wide spatula after 20 minutes. Do not turn off the oven.

5. FOR THE SAUCE: While the eggplant bakes, process 2 cans of the diced tomatoes in the food processor until almost smooth, about 5 seconds. Heat the olive oil, garlic, and red pepper flakes in a large heavy-bottomed saucepan over medium-high heat, stirring occasionally, until fragrant and the garlic is light golden, about 3 minutes; stir in the processed tomatoes and remaining can of diced tomatoes. Bring the sauce to a boil, then reduce the heat to medium-low and simmer, stirring occasionally, until slightly thickened and reduced, about 15 minutes (you should have about 4 cups). Stir in the basil and season with table salt and pepper to taste.

6. TO ASSEMBLE: Spread 1 cup of the tomato sauce in the bottom of a 13 by 9-inch baking dish. Layer in half of the eggplant slices, overlapping the slices to fit; distribute 1 more cup of the sauce over the eggplant; sprinkle with half of the mozzarella. Layer in the remaining eggplant and dot with 1 more cup of the sauce, leaving the majority of eggplant exposed so it will remain crisp; sprinkle with the Parmesan and the remaining mozzarella. Bake until bubbling and the cheese is browned, 13 to 15 minutes. Cool 10 minutes, scatter the basil over the top, and serve, passing the remaining tomato sauce separately.

POLENTA

WHY THIS RECIPE WORKS: A creamy mound of hot polenta can be a comforting dish, especially when served with a stew or saucy braise. Composed of little more than cornmeal and water, it should be easy to prepare. But often it's lumpy or gummy, and getting it right requires constant stirring. We wanted the smooth, creamy texture and great corn flavor of real polenta, but without the hassle.

It turns out that the type of cornmeal makes a difference in the end result, and we found that a medium-grind meal worked best. The traditional method of making polenta requires half an hour or more of constant stirring after the cornmeal is added to boiling salted water. Experimentation revealed that the way to avoid this continuous attention is very low heat. We added the cornmeal (very gradually, so it wouldn't seize up) to barely simmering water with the flame set as low as possible. With the cover on the pot to keep in moisture, the cornmeal had time to release its starches gradually and develop flavor, and we needed to stir it only every five minutes or so. Our polenta was smooth and creamy with lots of corn flavor, and we were able to serve it in half an hour without standing at the stove the whole time.

Basic Polenta

SERVES 4 TO 6

If you do not have a heavy-bottomed saucepan, you may want to use a flame tamer to manage the heat. A flame tamer can be purchased at most kitchen supply stores. Use this polenta as the base for any stew or braise, especially osso buco (see page 245), or serve with a chunk of Gorgonzola cheese. Cooked leafy greens also make an excellent topping for soft polenta.

- 6 cups water
  Table salt
- 1½ cups medium-grind cornmeal, preferably stone-ground
- 3 tablespoons unsalted butter, cut into large chunks
  Ground black pepper

1. Bring the water to a rolling boil in a 4-quart heavy-bottomed saucepan over medium-high heat. Reduce the heat to the lowest possible setting, add 1½ teaspoons salt, and pour the cornmeal into the water in a very slow stream from a measuring cup, all the while whisking in a circular motion to prevent lumps.

2. Cover and cook, vigorously stirring the polenta with a wooden spoon for about 10 seconds once every 5 minutes and making sure to scrape clean the bottom and corners of the pot, until the polenta has lost its raw cornmeal taste and becomes soft and smooth, about 30 minutes. Stir in the butter, season with salt and pepper to taste, and serve immediately.

MUSHROOM RISOTTO

WHY THIS RECIPE WORKS: Earthy wild mushrooms added to a basic Italian risotto make a great main course. But the difficulty, not to mention the expense, of finding exotic fungi prompted us to try our hand at reproducing these flavors with supermarket mushrooms.

Cultivated mushrooms just don't have enough flavor for a dish like this, so we turned to aromatic dried porcini, which pack quite a flavor punch. But they need to be chopped, so for visual appeal and substantive texture we added fresh cremini. Because simmering the cremini in the rice-broth mixture would make them rubbery, we browned them in a separate skillet with some onion and garlic for added flavor, folding this mixture into the risotto only when the rice was done. We added extra wine to our basic risotto so that its acidity would balance the richness of the mushrooms, and used a decidedly un-Italian ingredient, soy sauce, to intensify the earthiness of the mushrooms and round out the flavors. Without relying on pricey fungi, we had created a risotto with the same exotic earthiness.

Mushroom Risotto

SERVES 4 TO 6

Cremini mushrooms are sometimes sold as baby bella mushrooms. If they're not available, button mushrooms make a fine, though somewhat less flavorful, substitute. Tie the thyme and parsley sprigs together with kitchen twine so they will be easy to retrieve from the pan.

- 2 bay leaves
- 6 sprigs fresh thyme (see note)
- 4 sprigs fresh parsley, plus 2 tablespoons minced parsley leaves (see note)
- 3½ cups low-sodium chicken broth
- 3½ cups water
- 1 ounce dried porcini mushrooms, rinsed in a mesh strainer under running water
- 2 teaspoons soy sauce
- 6 tablespoons (¾ stick) unsalted butter
- 1¼ pounds cremini mushrooms, wiped clean and cut into quarters if small or sixths if medium or large (see note)
- 2 medium onions, minced (about 2 cups)
  Table salt
- 3 medium garlic cloves, minced or pressed through a garlic press (about 1 tablespoon)
- 2⅛ cups Arborio rice
- 1 cup dry white wine or dry vermouth
- 2 ounces Parmesan cheese, grated fine (about 1 cup)
  Ground black pepper

1. Tie the bay leaves, thyme sprigs, and parsley sprigs together with kitchen twine. Bring the bundled herbs, chicken broth, water, porcini mushrooms, and soy sauce to a boil in a medium saucepan over medium-high heat; reduce the heat to medium-low and simmer until the dried mushrooms are softened and fully hydrated, about 15 minutes. Remove and discard the herb bundle and strain the broth through a fine-mesh strainer set over a medium bowl (you should have about 6½ cups strained liquid); return the liquid to the saucepan and keep warm over low heat. Finely mince the porcini and set aside.

2. Adjust an oven rack to the middle position and heat the oven to 200 degrees. Heat 2 tablespoons of the butter in a 12-inch nonstick skillet over medium-high heat. Add the cremini mushrooms, 1 cup of the onions, and ½ teaspoon salt; cook, stirring occasionally, until the moisture released by the mushrooms evaporates and the mushrooms are well browned, about 7 minutes. Stir in the garlic until fragrant, about 1 minute, then transfer the mushroom mixture to an ovensafe bowl and keep warm in the oven. Off the heat, add ¼ cup water to the now-empty skillet and scrape with a wooden spoon to loosen any browned bits on the pan bottom; pour the liquid from the skillet into the saucepan with the broth.

3. Melt 3 tablespoons more butter in a large saucepan over medium heat. Add the remaining 1 cup onions and ¼ teaspoon salt; cook, stirring occasionally, until the onions are softened and translucent, about 9 minutes. Add the rice and cook, stirring frequently, until the edges of the grains are transparent, about 4 minutes. Add the wine and cook, stirring frequently, until the rice absorbs the wine. Add the minced porcini and 3½ cups of the broth and cook, stirring every 2 to 3 minutes, until the liquid is absorbed, 9 to 11 minutes. Stir in ½ cup more broth every 2 to 3 minutes until the rice is cooked through but the grains are still somewhat firm at the center, 10 to 12 minutes (the rice may not require all of the broth). Stir in the remaining 1 tablespoon butter, then stir in the mushroom mixture (and any accumulated juice), cheese, and reserved chopped parsley. Season with salt and pepper to taste; serve immediately in warmed bowls.

BUTTERNUT SQUASH RISOTTO

WHY THIS RECIPE WORKS: Butternut squash and risotto should make a perfect culinary couple, but too often the squash and rice never become properly intertwined. The squash is reduced to overly sweet orange blobs or the whole dish becomes a gluey squash paste. We wanted to find a way to integrate the flavor of the squash with the risotto but still preserve their individual personalities— to create a creamy, orange-tinged rice fully infused with deep (but not overly sweet) squash flavor.

We started with our basic risotto recipe, then addressed the squash. When added to the rice at the beginning, the squash ended up as squash paste; if we waited until the end, it never integrated properly with the rice. We decided to brown the diced squash in a skillet (oven-roasting made it too sweet) and set it aside while we sautéed the aromatics and toasted the rice. We added only half of the squash with the first addition of liquid. This squash broke down somewhat during cooking and infused the rice with its flavor; the remaining squash, added when the rice was finished, retained its shape and texture. Chicken broth cut with water was the basis of the liquid, but we simmered the squash seeds and fibers in it to intensify the squash flavor. And white wine balanced the squash's sweetness. This creamy risotto had deep squash flavor and pleasing textures.

Butternut Squash Risotto

SERVES 4 TO 6

Infusing the chicken broth with the squash's seeds and fibers helps to reinforce the earthy squash flavor without adding more squash. We found that a 2-pound squash often yields more than the 3½ cups in step 1; this can be added to the skillet along with the squash scrapings in step 2. To make this dish vegetarian, vegetable broth can be used instead of chicken broth, but the resulting risotto will have more pronounced sweetness.

- 2 **tablespoons olive oil**
- 1 **medium butternut squash (about 2 pounds), peeled, seeded (reserve fibers and seeds), and cut into ½-inch cubes (about 3½ cups) (see note)**
- ¾ **teaspoon table salt**
- ¾ **teaspoon ground black pepper**
- 4 **cups low-sodium chicken broth (see note)**
- 1 **cup water**
- 4 **tablespoons (½ stick) unsalted butter**
- 2 **small onions, minced (about 1½ cups)**
- 2 **medium garlic cloves, minced or pressed through a garlic press (about 2 teaspoons)**
- 2 **cups Arborio rice**
- 1½ **cups dry white wine**
- 1½ **ounces Parmesan cheese, grated fine (about ¾ cup)**
- 2 **tablespoons minced fresh sage leaves**
- ¼ **teaspoon grated nutmeg**

1. Heat the oil in a 12-inch nonstick skillet over medium-high heat until shimmering but not smoking. Add the squash in an even layer and cook without stirring until golden brown, 4 to 5 minutes; stir in ¼ teaspoon of the salt and ¼ teaspoon of the pepper. Continue to cook, stirring occasionally, until the squash is tender and browned, about 5 minutes longer. Transfer the squash to a bowl and set aside.

2. Return the skillet to medium heat; add the reserved squash fibers and seeds and any leftover diced squash. Cook, stirring frequently to break up the fibers, until lightly browned, about 4 minutes. Transfer to a large saucepan and add the chicken broth and water; cover the saucepan and bring the mixture to a simmer over high heat, then reduce the heat to medium-low to maintain a bare simmer.

3. Melt 3 tablespoons of the butter in the now-empty skillet over medium heat; add the onions, garlic, remaining ½ teaspoon salt, and remaining ½ teaspoon pepper. Cook, stirring occasionally, until the onions are softened, 4 to 5 minutes. Add the rice to the skillet and cook, stirring frequently, until the grains are translucent around the edges, about 3 minutes. (To prevent the rice from spilling out of the pan, stir inward, from the edges of the pan toward the center, not in a circular motion.) Add the wine and cook, stirring frequently, until the liquid is fully absorbed, 4 to 5 minutes. Meanwhile, strain the hot broth through a fine-mesh strainer into a medium bowl, pressing on the solids to extract as much liquid as possible. Return the strained broth to the saucepan and discard the solids in the strainer; cover the saucepan and set over low heat to keep the broth hot.

4. When the wine is fully absorbed, add 3 cups of the hot broth and half of the reserved squash to the rice. Simmer, stirring every 3 to 4 minutes, until the liquid is absorbed and the bottom of the pan is almost dry, about 12 minutes.

5. Stir in ½ cup of the hot broth and cook, stirring constantly, until absorbed, about 3 minutes; repeat with additional broth until the rice is cooked through but the grains are still somewhat firm at the center. Off the heat, stir in the remaining 1 tablespoon butter, the Parmesan, sage, and nutmeg; gently fold in the remaining cooked squash. If desired, add up to ¼ cup more broth to loosen the texture of the risotto. Serve immediately in warmed bowls.

CHICKEN MARSALA

WHY THIS RECIPE WORKS: Developed in Italy after a successful 19th-century marketing campaign to promote Marsala wine from Sicily, this combination of chicken and mushrooms in wine sauce has become an Italian restaurant staple. Too often, however, the chicken is dry, the mushrooms flabby, and the sauce nondescript. We felt a rescue was in order.

We browned chicken breasts in a skillet to start and kept them warm while we prepared the mushrooms and sauce. The mushrooms went into the skillet next, but the chicken drippings burned. Our solution was to sauté some pancetta before browning the mushrooms, which rendered additional fat as well as added meaty flavor. We preferred sweet (as opposed to dry) Marsala for its depth of flavor and smooth finish. Some lemon juice tempered the Marsala's sweetness, while a little garlic and tomato paste rounded out the flavors. Finally, butter, whisked into the sauce at the end, added a rich finish and beautiful sheen.

Chicken Marsala

SERVES 4

Our wine of choice for this dish is Sweet Marsala Fine, an imported wine that gives the sauce body, soft edges, and a smooth finish. To make slicing the chicken easier, freeze it for 15 minutes.

- 2 **tablespoons vegetable oil**
- 1 **cup unbleached all-purpose flour**
- 4 **(5 to 6-ounce) boneless, skinless chicken breasts, tenderloins removed and breasts trimmed (see note) Table salt and ground black pepper**
- 2½ **ounces pancetta (about 3 slices), cut into pieces 1 inch long and ⅛ inch wide**
- 8 **ounces white mushrooms, wiped clean and sliced (about 2 cups)**
- 1 **medium garlic clove, minced or pressed through a garlic press (about 1 teaspoon)**
- 1 **teaspoon tomato paste**
- 1½ **cups sweet Marsala (see note)**
- 1½ **tablespoons juice from 1 lemon**
- 4 **tablespoons (½ stick) unsalted butter, cut into 4 pieces**
- 2 **tablespoons minced fresh parsley leaves**

1. Adjust an oven rack to the lower-middle position, place a large ovensafe dinner plate on the oven rack, and heat the oven to 200 degrees. Heat the oil in a 12-inch skillet over medium-high heat until shimmering. Meanwhile, place the flour in a shallow baking dish or pie plate. Halve the chicken horizontally, then cover the chicken halves with plastic wrap and pound the cutlets to an even ¼-inch thickness. Pat the chicken breasts dry. Season both sides of the breasts with salt and pepper; working with one piece at a time, coat both sides with flour. Cooking the cutlets in two batches, place 4 floured cutlets in a single layer in the skillet and cook until golden brown, about 3 minutes. Using tongs, flip the cutlets and cook on the second side until golden brown and the meat feels firm when pressed with a finger, about 3 minutes longer. Transfer the chicken to the heated plate and return the plate to the oven, while you cook the remaining cutlets.

2. Return the skillet to low heat and add the pancetta; sauté, stirring occasionally and scraping the pan bottom to loosen the browned bits, until the pancetta is brown and crisp, about 4 minutes. With a slotted spoon, transfer the pancetta to a paper towel–lined plate. Add the mushrooms and increase the heat to medium-high; sauté, stirring occasionally and scraping the pan bottom, until the liquid released by the mushrooms evaporates and the mushrooms begin to brown, about 8 minutes. Add the garlic, tomato paste, and cooked pancetta; sauté while stirring until the tomato paste begins to brown, about 1 minute. Off the heat, add the Marsala; return the pan to high heat and simmer vigorously, scraping the browned bits from the pan bottom, until the sauce is slightly syrupy and reduced to about 1¼ cups, about 5 minutes. Off the heat, add the lemon juice and any accumulated juices from the chicken; whisk in the butter 1 piece at a time. Season with salt and pepper to taste and stir in the parsley. Pour the sauce over the chicken and serve immediately.

LIGHTER CHICKEN PARMESAN

WHY THIS RECIPE WORKS: Crunchy fried chicken cutlets topped with cheese and tomato sauce, chicken Parmesan isn't exactly a dish for dieters. Not wanting to eliminate it as an option for healthy eating, we looked for a way to get the crispy coating without using all the oil.

Baking seemed to be the best alternative to frying. We toasted panko (ultracrisp Japanese-style bread crumbs) with a little oil for color and to give them "fried" flavor without the fat. Adopting the conventional breading technique of dipping the cutlets in flour (with garlic powder for flavor), then egg, then bread crumbs, we cut more calories by using only the egg whites. We baked the breasts on a wire rack until they were almost done,

then topped them with tomato sauce and shredded low-fat mozzarella to finish. Leaving the breasts on the rack rather than putting them in a casserole dish ensured that they would stay crisp as they baked. Served with a little extra sauce and grated Parmesan on the side, these oven-baked chicken Parmesan cutlets were crisp and full of flavor. And with 310 calories and 8 grams of fat, they have one-third less calories and two-thirds less fat grams than traditional versions.

Lighter Chicken Parmesan

SERVES 6

If you are tight on time, you can substitute 2 cups of your favorite plain tomato sauce for the Simple Tomato Sauce. To make slicing the chicken easier, freeze it for 15 minutes.

- 1½ cups panko (Japanese-style bread crumbs)
- 1 tablespoon olive oil
- 1 ounce Parmesan cheese, grated (about ½ cup), plus extra for serving
- ½ cup unbleached all-purpose flour
- 1½ teaspoons garlic powder
  Table salt and ground black pepper
- 3 large egg whites
- 1 tablespoon water
- 3 (7 to 8-ounce) boneless, skinless chicken breasts, tenderloins removed and breasts trimmed (see note)
- 1 recipe Simple Tomato Sauce (recipe follows), warmed (see note)
- 3 ounces low-fat mozzarella cheese, shredded (about ¾ cup)
- 1 tablespoon minced fresh basil leaves

1. Adjust an oven rack to the middle position and heat the oven to 475 degrees. Combine the bread crumbs and oil in a 12-inch skillet and toast over medium heat, stirring often, until golden, about 10 minutes. Spread the bread crumbs in a shallow dish and cool slightly; when cool, stir in the Parmesan.

2. In a second shallow dish, combine the flour, garlic powder, 1 tablespoon salt, and ½ teaspoon pepper. In a third shallow dish, whisk the egg whites and water together.

3. Line a rimmed baking sheet with foil, place a wire rack over the sheet, and spray the rack with vegetable oil spray. Halve the chicken horizontally, then cover the chicken halves with plastic wrap and pound the cutlets to an even ¼-inch thickness. Pat the chicken dry with paper towels, then season with salt and pepper. Lightly dredge the cutlets in the flour, shaking off the excess. Using tongs, dip both sides of the cutlets into the egg whites and allow

the excess egg to drip back into the dish. Finally, coat both sides of the chicken with the bread crumbs. Press on the bread crumbs to make sure they adhere. Lay the chicken on the wire rack.

4. Spray the tops of the chicken with vegetable oil spray. Bake until the meat is no longer pink in the center and feels firm when pressed with a finger, about 15 minutes.

5. Remove the chicken from the oven. Spoon 2 tablespoons of the sauce onto the center of each cutlet and top the sauce with 2 tablespoons of the mozzarella. Return the chicken to the oven and continue to bake until the cheese has melted, about 5 minutes. Sprinkle with the basil and serve, passing the remaining sauce and Parmesan separately.

Simple Tomato Sauce

MAKES ABOUT 2 CUPS

This easy sauce also works well with pasta.

- 1 (28-ounce) can diced tomatoes
- 4 medium garlic cloves, minced or pressed through a garlic press (about 4 teaspoons)
- 1 tablespoon tomato paste
- 1 teaspoon olive oil
- ⅛ teaspoon red pepper flakes
- 1 tablespoon minced fresh basil leaves
  Table salt and ground black pepper

Pulse the tomatoes in a food processor until mostly smooth, about 10 pulses; set aside. Cook the garlic, tomato paste, oil, and red pepper flakes in a medium saucepan over medium heat until the tomato paste begins to brown, about 2 minutes. Stir in the pureed tomatoes and cook until the sauce is thickened and measures 2 cups, about 20 minutes. Off the heat, stir in the basil and season with salt and pepper to taste. Cover and set aside until needed.

CHICKEN PICCATA

WHY THIS RECIPE WORKS: Many recipes for chicken piccata are either bland or overcomplicated, with extra ingredients that ruin the dish's simplicity. Many recipes contain just a tablespoon of lemon juice and a teaspoon of capers, neither of which provides much flavor. But chicken piccata is one of those appealing Italian recipes that taste complex but are actually easy to prepare. Our goal was properly cooked chicken with a streamlined sauce that really tastes of lemons and capers.

Many recipes suggest breading cutlets for chicken piccata, but we found that flour alone was sufficient; there was no point building a crisp crust that would end up drenched in sauce. After browning the chicken and sautéing aromatics, we deglazed the pan with chicken broth alone; although wine is sometimes suggested, we found it to be too acidic for this dish. We simmered slices from half a lemon in the broth for a few minutes; this was easier than grating the zest. For maximum lemon flavor in the sauce, we used a full quarter-cup of lemon juice, added when the sauce was nearly done so as not to blunt its impact. Butter gave the sauce body and was preferable to flour, which made it overly thick. Plenty of capers and a bit of parsley finished our ultra-lemony piccata.

Chicken Piccata

SERVES 4

Because this sauce is so light, we find that each person should be served 1½ small cutlets. To make slicing the chicken easier, freeze it for 15 minutes.

- 2 large lemons
- 6 (5 to 6-ounce) boneless, skinless chicken breasts, tenderloins removed and breasts trimmed (see note)
  Table salt and ground black pepper
- ½ cup unbleached all-purpose flour
- 4 tablespoons vegetable oil
- 1 small shallot, minced (about 1 tablespoon), or 1 medium garlic clove, minced or pressed through a garlic press (about 1 teaspoon)
- 1 cup low-sodium chicken broth
- 2 tablespoons drained small capers
- 3 tablespoons cold unsalted butter
- 2 tablespoons minced fresh parsley leaves

1. Adjust an oven rack to the lower-middle position, set a large ovensafe plate on the rack, and heat the oven to 200 degrees.

2. Halve 1 lemon pole to pole. Trim the ends from one half and cut it crosswise into slices ⅛ to ¼ inch thick; set aside. Juice the remaining half and whole lemon to obtain ¼ cup juice; reserve.

3. Halve the chicken horizontally, then cover the chicken halves with plastic wrap and pound the cutlets to an even ¼-inch thickness. Sprinkle both sides of the cutlets generously with salt and pepper. Place the flour in a shallow baking dish or pie plate. Working with 1 cutlet at a time, coat with flour and shake to remove the excess.

4. Heat 2 tablespoons of the oil in a heavy-bottomed 12-inch skillet over medium-high heat until shimmering. Lay 3 chicken cutlets in the skillet. Cook the cutlets until lightly browned on the first side, 2 to 3 minutes. Flip the cutlets and cook until the second side is lightly browned, 2 to 3 minutes longer. Remove the pan from the heat and transfer the cutlets to the plate in the warm oven. Add the remaining 2 tablespoons oil to the now-empty skillet and heat until shimmering. Add the remaining 3 chicken cutlets and repeat.

5. Add the shallot or garlic to the now-empty skillet and return the skillet to medium heat. Sauté until fragrant, about 30 seconds for the shallot or 10 seconds for the garlic. Add the broth and lemon slices, increase the heat to high, and scrape the pan bottom with a wooden spoon or spatula to loosen the browned bits. Simmer until the liquid reduces to about ⅓ cup, about 4 minutes. Add the lemon juice and capers and simmer until the sauce reduces again to ⅓ cup, about 1 minute. Remove the pan from the heat and swirl in the butter until it melts and thickens the sauce. Stir in the parsley and season with salt and pepper to taste. Spoon the sauce over the chicken and serve immediately.

PARMESAN-CRUSTED CHICKEN BREASTS

WHY THIS RECIPE WORKS: With a short ingredient list of only chicken breasts and Parmesan cheese plus one or two binders such as eggs or flour, Parmesan-crusted chicken breasts should be straightforward. But we found pale, wet, and gummy baked versions as well as bitter and burnt pan-fried versions. We wanted moist and tender chicken coated with a thin, crispy-yet-chewy, waferlike sheath of Parmesan cheese.

A standard breading in which we merely substituted cheese for the bread crumbs and flour was disappointing; the cheese didn't provide the dry base to which the rest of the coating would stick. So we went back to flour, with a bit of Parmesan for flavor, and we left out the egg yolks to eliminate the eggy taste. For the outermost layer, shredding the cheese on the large holes of a box grater made a sturdier, more even crust, and a little flour added to this cheese helped the coating turn crisp. Pan-frying in a nonstick skillet prevented sticking, and keeping the heat no higher than medium browned the cheese without making it bitter. These cutlets were pale golden rather than deep golden brown, but the nutty, crisp Parmesan crust was everything we hoped it would be.

Parmesan-Crusted Chicken Cutlets

SERVES 4

To make slicing the chicken easier, freeze it for 15 minutes. Note that part of the Parmesan is grated on the smallest holes of a box grater (or rasp grater) and the remaining Parmesan is shredded on the largest holes of the box grater. We like the flavor that authentic Parmigiano-Reggiano lends to this recipe. A less-expensive cheese, such as Boar's Head Parmesan cheese, can also be used, but the resulting cheese crust will be slightly saltier and chewier. Although the portion size (one cutlet per person) might seem small, these cutlets are rather rich due to the cheese content. To make eight cutlets, double the ingredients and cook the chicken in four batches, transferring the cooked cutlets to a warm oven and wiping out the skillet after each batch.

- 2 (7 to 8-ounce) boneless, skinless chicken breasts, tenderloins removed and breasts trimmed (see note)
  Table salt and ground black pepper
- 5 tablespoons unbleached all-purpose flour
- ¼ cup grated Parmesan cheese plus 6 ounces, shredded (about 2 cups) (see note)
- 3 large egg whites
- 2 tablespoons minced fresh chives (optional)
- 4 teaspoons olive oil
  Lemon wedges, for serving

1. Adjust an oven rack to the middle position and heat the oven to 200 degrees. Halve the chicken horizontally, then cover the chicken halves with plastic wrap and pound the cutlets to an even ¼-inch thickness. Pat the chicken dry with paper towels and season with salt and pepper.

2. Whisk ¼ cup of the flour and the ¼ cup grated Parmesan together in a shallow dish. Whisk the egg whites

and chives (if using) in a medium bowl until slightly foamy. Combine the 2 cups shredded Parmesan and remaining 1 tablespoon flour in a second shallow dish. Working with 1 chicken cutlet at a time, dredge in the flour mixture, shaking off the excess, then coat with the egg white mixture, allowing the excess to drip off. Finally, coat with the shredded Parmesan mixture, pressing gently so that the cheese adheres. Place the coated cutlets in a single layer on a wire rack set over a rimmed baking sheet.

3. Heat 2 teaspoons of the oil in a 12-inch nonstick skillet over medium heat until shimmering. Add 2 of the cutlets and cook until pale golden brown on both sides, 4 to 6 minutes in total. (While the chicken is cooking, use a thin nonstick spatula to gently separate any cheesy edges that have melted together.) Transfer to a clean wire rack set over a rimmed baking sheet and keep warm in the oven. Wipe out the skillet with paper towels. Repeat with the remaining 2 teaspoons oil and chicken. Serve with the lemon wedges.

CHICKEN FRANCESE

WHY THIS RECIPE WORKS: This fast-fading star of red-sauce Italian restaurants often features a rubbery coating and a puckery lemon sauce. Yet this quick dinner still holds promise for the home cook. We wanted our chicken to have a rich, eggy coating that would remain soft and tender yet be sturdy enough to stand up to a silky, well-balanced lemon sauce.

We found that a first coating of flour was essential for getting the egg to stick, and a little milk added to the egg prevented it from turning rubbery. A final dip into flour made a soft, delicate veneer. We sautéed the cutlets in butter for its flavor, adding a little oil to keep the butter from burning, and kept them warm in the oven while we made our sauce. Fresh lemon juice with some vermouth and chicken broth gave us the bright, fresh citrus flavor we wanted; a little sautéed shallot balanced the lemon but didn't overpower it. To get the sauce to cling to the chicken without making it soggy, we made a roux with butter and flour. Our sauce was just right, but the chicken had dried out while waiting in the oven. Our solution was to make the sauce first, then cook the chicken and finish the sauce. We think this revitalized dish deserves a place in today's home kitchens.

Chicken Francese

SERVES 4

To make slicing the chicken easier, freeze it for 15 minutes. The sauce is very lemony—for less tartness, reduce the amount of lemon juice by about 1 tablespoon.

SAUCE

- 3 tablespoons unsalted butter
- 1 large shallot, minced (about 4 tablespoons)
- 1 tablespoon unbleached all-purpose flour
- 2¼ cups low-sodium chicken broth
- ½ cup dry vermouth or white wine
- ⅓ cup juice from 2 lemons (see note)
  Table salt and ground black pepper

CHICKEN

- 4 (5 to 6-ounce) boneless, skinless chicken breasts, tenderloins removed and breasts trimmed (see note)
  Table salt and ground black pepper
- 1 cup unbleached all-purpose flour
- 2 large eggs
- 2 tablespoons milk
- 2 tablespoons unsalted butter
- 2 tablespoons olive oil
- 2 tablespoons minced fresh parsley leaves

1. Adjust an oven rack to the middle position and heat the oven to 200 degrees.

2. FOR THE SAUCE: Melt 1 tablespoon of the butter in a medium saucepan over medium heat. Add the shallot and cook, stirring occasionally, until softened, about 2 minutes. Stir in the flour and cook until light golden brown, about 1 minute. Whisk in the broth, vermouth, and lemon juice and bring to a simmer. Cook, whisking occasionally, until the sauce measures 1½ cups, about 15 minutes. Strain the sauce through a fine-mesh strainer. Return the sauce to the saucepan and set aside, discarding the solids.

3. FOR THE CHICKEN: Halve the chicken horizontally, then cover the chicken halves with plastic wrap and pound the cutlets to an even ¼-inch thickness. Pat the chicken dry with paper towels and season with salt and pepper.

4. Combine the flour, 1 teaspoon salt, and ¼ teaspoon pepper in a shallow dish and whisk the eggs and milk together in a medium bowl. Working with 1 chicken cutlet at a time, dredge in the flour, shaking off the excess, then coat with the egg mixture, allowing the excess to drip off.

Finally, coat with the flour again, shaking off the excess. Place the coated chicken in a single layer on a wire rack set over a rimmed baking sheet.

5. Heat 1 tablespoon each of the butter and oil in a 12-inch nonstick skillet over medium-high heat. Add 4 of the cutlets and cook until lightly browned on one side, 2 to 3 minutes. Flip the chicken over and continue to cook until no longer pink and lightly browned on the second side, about 1 minute. Transfer the chicken to a clean wire rack set over a rimmed baking sheet and keep warm in the oven. Wipe out the skillet with paper towels. Add the remaining 1 tablespoon each of the butter and oil to the skillet and repeat with the remaining cutlets, then transfer to the oven. Wipe out the skillet with paper towels.

6. TO FINISH THE SAUCE AND SERVE: Transfer the sauce to the now-empty skillet and cook over medium-low heat until warmed, about 2 minutes. Whisk in the remaining 2 tablespoons butter, 1 tablespoon at a time, and season with salt and pepper to taste. Transfer 4 of the chicken cutlets to the skillet, turn to coat with the sauce, then transfer each serving (2 cutlets) to individual plates. Repeat with the remaining cutlets. Spoon 2 tablespoons of the sauce over each serving and sprinkle with the parsley. Serve, passing the remaining sauce separately.

CHICKEN SALTIMBOCCA

WHY THIS RECIPE WORKS: In its classic Italian form, saltimbocca is made with veal, prosciutto, and sage, but chicken is frequently substituted for the veal. The combination of flavors is meant to "jump in the mouth," as the name suggests. Preparing this dish can be complicated, but we wanted to streamline it and ensure that the flavors were well balanced.

Flouring only the chicken, rather than the chicken-prosciutto package, avoided gummy spots. The prosciutto is usually secured to the chicken with a toothpick, but we found that we could do without the toothpick if we seared the prosciutto side of the chicken first; once browned, the two stuck together just fine. Prosciutto can overwhelm the other flavors in this dish, so it's important to use thin slices, but not so thin that they disintegrate during cooking. A single sage leaf is the usual garnish, but we wanted more sage flavor, so we sprinkled some minced fresh sage over the floured chicken before adding the prosciutto. (A single fried sage leaf is a pretty but optional garnish.) With a simple pan sauce of vermouth, lemon juice, butter, and parsley, our chicken saltimbocca was ready to serve and full of flavor.

Chicken Saltimbocca
SERVES 4

To make slicing the chicken easier, freeze it for 15 minutes. Although whole sage leaves make a beautiful presentation, they are optional and can be left out of step 3. Make sure to buy prosciutto that is thinly sliced, not shaved; also avoid slices that are too thick, as they won't stick to the chicken. The prosciutto slices should be large enough to fully cover one side of each cutlet.

- 4 **(5 to 6-ounce) boneless, skinless chicken breasts, tenderloins removed and breasts trimmed (see note)**
- ½ **cup unbleached all-purpose flour**
  Ground black pepper
- 1 **tablespoon minced fresh sage leaves, plus 8 large leaves (optional; see note)**
- 8 **thin prosciutto slices (about 3 ounces) (see note)**
- 4 **tablespoons olive oil**
- 1¼ **cups dry vermouth or white wine**
- 2 **teaspoons juice from 1 lemon**
- 4 **tablespoons (½ stick) unsalted butter, cut into 4 pieces and chilled**
- 1 **tablespoon minced fresh parsley leaves**
  Table salt

1. Halve the chicken horizontally, then cover the chicken halves with plastic wrap and pound the cutlets to an even ¼-inch thickness.

2. Combine the flour and 1 teaspoon pepper in a shallow dish. Pat the chicken dry with paper towels. Dredge the chicken in the flour, shaking off any excess. Lay the cutlets flat and sprinkle evenly with the minced sage. Place 1 prosciutto slice on top of each cutlet, pressing lightly to adhere; set aside.

3. Heat 2 tablespoons of the oil in a 12-inch skillet over medium-high heat until shimmering. Add the sage leaves (if using) and cook until the leaves begin to change color and are fragrant, 15 to 20 seconds. Using a slotted spoon, transfer the sage to a paper towel–lined plate and set aside. Add 4 of the cutlets to the pan, prosciutto side down, and cook until lightly browned on one side, about 2 minutes. Flip the chicken over and continue to cook until no longer pink, 30 seconds to 1 minute. Transfer the chicken to a plate and tent loosely with foil. Add the remaining 2 tablespoons oil to the skillet and repeat with the remaining 4 cutlets. Transfer to the plate and tent loosely with foil while making the sauce.

4. Pour off the excess fat from the skillet. Stir in the vermouth, scraping up any browned bits, and simmer until reduced to about ⅓ cup, 5 to 7 minutes. Stir in the lemon juice. Turn the heat to low and whisk in the butter, 1 tablespoon at time. Off the heat, stir in the parsley and season with salt and pepper to taste. Spoon the sauce over the chicken, place a sage leaf (if using) on each cutlet, and serve.

ITALIAN GRILLED CHICKEN

WHY THIS RECIPE WORKS: Anyone who has tried to grill a whole chicken knows that it's challenging at best, and the results are often inedible. Many cuisines have developed methods to overcome the problems of chicken cooked over a fire; the Italian way is to cook the chicken under bricks. This was one method we had to try.

One attempt to grill a butterflied chicken the Italian way was enough to let us know that we needed more than just bricks to make this recipe work. We thought of brining to keep the meat moist, but it produced burned chicken when the liquid dripped into the fire. An alternate way to retain moisture in meat is salting; we rubbed the flesh under the skin with salt, mixed with garlic, pepper flakes, and herbs for Italian flavor. With a modified two-level fire in the grill, we cooked the chicken under preheated bricks on the cooler side, skin side down, to firm up the flesh

and release fat and liquid where the fire wouldn't cause flare-ups. We flipped the chicken and finished cooking it on the hot side; another flip and a few minutes without the bricks crisped up the skin. The combination of flipping and moving the chicken from the cool side to the hot side guaranteed even cooking, and the salting had kept the meat juicy. With a finishing embellishment of a quick vinaigrette, we had perfectly cooked chicken with zesty Italian flavor, and not a burnt piece in sight.

Italian-Style Charcoal-Grilled Chicken

SERVES 4

Use an oven mitt or dish towel to safely grip and maneuver the hot bricks. You will need two standard-sized bricks for this recipe. Placing the bricks on the chicken while it cooks ensures that the skin will be evenly browned and well rendered—don't skip this step. A cast-iron skillet or other heavy pan can be used in place of the bricks.

⅓   **cup extra-virgin olive oil**
8   **medium garlic cloves, minced or pressed through a garlic press (about 2½ tablespoons)**
1   **teaspoon finely grated zest plus 2 tablespoons juice from 1 lemon**
    Pinch crushed red pepper flakes
4   **teaspoons chopped fresh thyme leaves**
3   **teaspoons chopped fresh rosemary leaves**
1   **(3¾ to 4¼-pound) whole chicken**
    Kosher salt
    Ground black pepper
    Vegetable oil for the cooking grate

1. Combine the olive oil, garlic, lemon zest, and red pepper flakes in a small saucepan. Bring to a simmer, stirring frequently, over medium-low heat, about 3 minutes. Once the mixture is simmering, add 3 teaspoons of the thyme and 2 teaspoons of the rosemary and cook 30 seconds longer. Strain the mixture through a fine-mesh strainer set over a small bowl, pushing on the solids to extract the oil. Transfer the solids to a small bowl and cool; set the oil and solids aside.

2. Butterfly the chicken by cutting through the bones on either side of the backbone; discard the backbone. Flatten the breastbone and tuck the wings behind the back. Using your hands or the handle of a wooden spoon, loosen the skin over the breast and thighs and remove any excess fat. Combine 1 tablespoon salt and 1 teaspoon pepper in a small bowl. Mix 3 teaspoons of the salt mixture with the cooled garlic solids. Spread the salt-garlic mixture evenly under the skin over the chicken breast and thighs. Sprinkle the remaining teaspoon salt mixture on the exposed meat of the bone side. Place the chicken, skin side up, on a wire rack set over a rimmed baking sheet and refrigerate for 1 to 2 hours.

3. Wrap two bricks tightly in aluminum foil. Light a large chimney starter filled three-quarters with charcoal (4½ quarts) and allow to burn until the coals are partially covered with a layer of gray ash, about 20 minutes. Build a modified two-level fire by arranging all the coals over one half of the grill, leaving the other half empty. Set the cooking grate in place, cover, and heat the grate until hot, about 5 minutes. Use a grill brush to scrape the cooking grate clean. Dip a wad of paper towels in oil; holding the wad with tongs, oil the cooking grate.

4. Place the chicken, skin side down, over the cooler side of the grill with the legs facing the fire, place the hot bricks lengthwise over each breast half, cover the grill, and cook until the skin is lightly browned and faint grill marks appear, 22 to 25 minutes. Remove the bricks from the chicken. Using tongs or a dish towel, grip the legs and flip the chicken (the chicken should release freely from the grill; use a thin metal spatula to loosen it if it sticks); transfer the chicken to the hot side of the grill, skin side up, with the breast facing the center of the grill. Place the bricks over the breast, cover the grill, and cook until the chicken is well browned, 12 to 15 minutes.

5. Remove the bricks, flip the chicken skin side down over the hot coals, and cook until the chicken skin is well crisped and the thickest part of the breast registers 160 to 165 degrees and the thickest part of the thigh registers 175 degrees on an instant-read thermometer, 5 to 10 minutes, moving the chicken as necessary to prevent flare-ups. Transfer the chicken to a carving board and let rest for 10 minutes. Whisk the lemon juice, the remaining teaspoon thyme, and the remaining teaspoon rosemary into the reserved oil; season with salt and pepper to taste. Carve the chicken and serve, passing the sauce separately.

Italian-Style Gas-Grilled Chicken

Follow the instructions for Italian-Style Charcoal-Grilled Chicken through step 2 and wrap two bricks tightly with aluminum foil. Turn all the burners to high, place the bricks on the cooking grate, and heat the grill with the lid down until very hot, about 15 minutes. Use a grill brush to scrape the cooking grate clean. Dip a wad of paper towels in oil; holding the wad with tongs, oil the cooking grate. Leave the primary burner on high and turn off the other burner(s). Proceed with the recipe from step 4, cooking with the lid down.

PORK CHOPS WITH VINEGAR AND PEPPERS

WHY THIS RECIPE WORKS: This Italian-American dish was devised when pork chops had plenty of fat to keep them juicy; the leaner pork we have today tends to dry out and ruin it. But the thought of succulent pork with a tangy vinegar and pepper sauce spurred us to search for a way to make this dish taste the way it should.

The first step was choosing the right chop to use. Bone-in rib chops of medium thickness had the best flavor, and the bone helped keep the meat juicy. Brining the chops in a solution of salt and sugar added moisture and flavor, and the sugar enhanced browning. Cooking the chops and then assembling a pan sauce of vinegar and peppers didn't give us the marriage of flavors the dish should have, but braising the chops in a vinegar sauce produced chalky meat. We discovered that browning the chops, removing them from the pan to build the sauce, then finishing everything together in the oven worked best to get the flavors of the sauce into the meat. We also ditched the jarred vinegar peppers, which are traditional, and made our own; they were far superior to any we'd found at the supermarket.

Pork Chops with Vinegar and Sweet Peppers
SERVES 4

We prefer natural to enhanced pork (pork that has been injected with a salt solution to increase moistness and flavor) for this recipe, though enhanced pork can be used. If using enhanced pork, skip the brining in step 1. To keep the chops from overcooking and becoming tough and dry, remove them from the oven when they are just shy of fully cooked; as they sit in the hot skillet, they will continue to cook with residual heat.

1 cup sugar
½ cup table salt, plus more to taste
4 (8 to 10-ounce) bone-in rib loin pork chops, ¾ to 1 inch thick, trimmed of excess fat (see note)
  Ground black pepper
2 tablespoons olive oil
1 medium onion, minced
1 medium red bell pepper, stemmed, seeded, and cut into ¼-inch-wide strips
1 medium yellow bell pepper, stemmed, seeded, and cut into ¼-inch-wide strips
2 anchovy fillets, minced (about 1 teaspoon)
1 medium sprig fresh rosemary
2 medium garlic cloves, minced or pressed through a garlic press (about 2 teaspoons)
¾ cup water
½ cup white wine vinegar, plus 2 tablespoons to finish the sauce (optional)
2 tablespoons cold unsalted butter
2 tablespoons chopped fresh parsley leaves

1. Dissolve the sugar and ½ cup salt in 2 quarts water in a large container; add the pork chops and refrigerate for 30 minutes. Remove the chops from the brine, rinse, and pat dry with paper towels. Using a sharp knife, cut two slits, about 2 inches apart, through the outer layer of fat and silver skin of each chop (do not cut into the meat of the chops). Season the chops with ¾ teaspoon pepper and set aside.

2. Adjust an oven rack to the middle position and heat the oven to 400 degrees. Heat the oil in an oven-safe 12-inch skillet over medium-high heat until the oil begins to smoke; swirl the skillet to coat with the oil. Place the chops in the skillet; cook until well browned, 3 to 4 minutes, using a spoon or spatula to press down on the center of the chops to aid in browning. Using tongs, flip the chops and brown lightly on the second side, about 1 minute. Transfer the chops to a large plate; set aside.

3. Set the skillet over medium-high heat. Add the onion and cook, stirring occasionally, until just beginning to soften, about 2 minutes. Add the peppers, anchovies, and rosemary; cook, stirring frequently, until the peppers just begin to soften, about 4 minutes. Add the garlic; cook, stirring constantly, until fragrant, about 30 seconds. Add the water and ½ cup of the vinegar and bring to a boil, scraping up the browned bits with a wooden spoon. Reduce the heat to medium; simmer until the liquid is reduced to about ⅓ cup, 6 to 8 minutes. Off the heat, discard the rosemary.

4. Return the pork chops, browner side up, to the skillet; nestle the chops in the peppers, but do not cover them. Add any accumulated juices to the skillet; set the skillet in the oven and cook until the center of the chops registers 140 to 145 degrees on an instant-read thermometer, 8 to 12 minutes (begin checking the temperature after 6 minutes). Using potholders, carefully remove the skillet from the oven (the handle will be very hot) and cover the skillet with a lid or foil; let stand until the center of the chops registers 150 degrees, 5 to 7 minutes. Transfer the chops to a platter or individual plates. Swirl the butter into the sauce and the peppers in the skillet; taste and stir in the remaining 2 tablespoons vinegar (if using) and the parsley. Season with salt and pepper to taste, then pour or spoon the sauce and peppers over the chops. Serve immediately.

OSSO BUCO

WHY THIS RECIPE WORKS: Osso buco, veal shanks braised in a rich sauce until tender, is incredibly rich and hearty. We felt that this time-honored recipe shouldn't be altered much, but we hoped to identify the keys to flavor so that we could perfect it.

To serve one shank per person, we searched for medium-sized shanks, and tied them around the equator to keep the meat attached to the bone for an attractive presentation. Most recipes suggest flouring the veal before browning it, but we got better flavor when we seared the meat, liberally seasoned with just salt and pepper. Browning in two batches enabled us to deglaze the pan twice, thus enriching the sauce. Celery, onion, and carrots formed the basis of the sauce; for the liquid we used a combination

of chicken broth, white wine, and canned tomatoes. The traditional garnish of gremolata—minced garlic, lemon, and parsley—required no changes; we stirred half into the sauce and sprinkled the rest over individual servings for a fresh burst of citrus flavor.

Osso Buco

SERVES 6

To keep the meat attached to the bone during the long simmering process, tie a piece of kitchen twine around the thickest portion of each shank before it is browned. Just before serving, taste the liquid and, if it seems too thin, simmer it on the stovetop as you remove the strings from the osso buco and arrange them in individual bowls. Serve with Polenta (page 234).

OSSO BUCO

- 4 tablespoons vegetable oil
- 6 (8 to 10-ounce) veal shanks, 1½ inches thick, patted dry with paper towels and tied with kitchen twine at 1½-inch intervals
  Table salt and ground black pepper
- 2½ cups dry white wine
- 2 medium onions, cut into ½-inch pieces
- 2 medium carrots, cut into ½-inch pieces
- 2 medium celery ribs, cut into ½-inch pieces
- 6 medium garlic cloves, minced or pressed through a garlic press (about 2 tablespoons)
- 2 cups low-sodium chicken broth
- 2 small bay leaves
- 1 (14.5-ounce) can diced tomatoes, drained

GREMOLATA

- ¼ cup minced fresh parsley leaves
- 3 medium garlic cloves, minced or pressed through a garlic press (about 1 tablespoon)
- 2 teaspoons grated minced zest from 1 lemon

1. FOR THE OSSO BUCO: Adjust an oven rack to the lower-middle position and heat the oven to 325 degrees. Heat 1 tablespoon of the oil in a large Dutch oven over medium-high heat until shimmering. Meanwhile, sprinkle both sides of the shanks generously with salt and pepper. Place 3 shanks in the pan and cook until they are golden brown on one side, about 5 minutes. Using tongs, flip the shanks and cook on the second side until golden brown, about 5 minutes longer. Transfer the shanks to a bowl and set aside. Off the heat, add ½ cup of the wine to the Dutch oven, scraping the pan bottom with a wooden spoon to loosen any browned bits. Pour the liquid into the bowl with the browned shanks. Return the pot to medium-high heat, add 1 tablespoon more oil, and heat until shimmering. Brown the remaining shanks, about 5 minutes for each side. Transfer the shanks to the bowl. Off the heat, add 1 cup more wine to the pot, scraping the bottom to loosen the browned bits. Pour the liquid into the bowl with the shanks.

2. Set the pot over medium heat. Add the remaining 2 tablespoons oil and heat until shimmering. Add the onions, carrots, celery, ¼ teaspoon salt, and ⅛ teaspoon pepper and cook, stirring occasionally, until soft and lightly browned, about 9 minutes. Stir in the garlic and cook until fragrant, about 30 seconds. Increase the heat to high and stir in the broth, remaining 1 cup wine, and bay leaves. Add the tomatoes; return the veal shanks to the pot along with any accumulated juices (the liquid should just cover the shanks). Bring the liquid to a simmer. Cover the pot and transfer the pot to the oven. Cook the shanks until the meat is easily pierced with a fork but not falling off the bone, about 2 hours. (At this point the osso buco can be refrigerated for up to 2 days. Bring to a simmer over medium-low heat.)

3. FOR THE GREMOLATA: Combine the parsley, garlic, and lemon zest in a small bowl. Stir half of the gremolata into the pot, reserving the rest for garnish. Season with salt and pepper to taste. Let the osso buco stand, uncovered, for 5 minutes.

4. Using tongs, remove the shanks from the pot, cut off and discard the twine, and place 1 veal shank in each of six bowls. Ladle some of the braising liquid over each shank and sprinkle each serving with the remaining gremolata. Serve immediately.

BEEF IN BAROLO

WHY THIS RECIPE WORKS: The Italian version of pot roast is an inexpensive cut of beef braised in wine. But what a difference that wine makes. Full-bodied Barolo has been called the "wine of kings"—and can be somewhat expensive, so this pot roast has to be special. We wanted moist, tender meat in a rich, savory sauce that would do justice to the regal wine.

A chuck-eye roast won't dry out after a long braise, but it has a line of fat in the middle that we felt was out of place in this refined dish. Separating one roast into two smaller ones enabled us to discard most of this fat before cooking the meat, and the two roasts cooked more quickly than one larger one. We tied the roasts to hold them together, then browned them in the fat rendered from pancetta,

which added rich flavor. Aromatics were browned next; then we poured a whole bottle of the wine into the pot. Barolo is so bold-flavored that we needed something in the braising liquid to temper it, and that proved to be a can of diced tomatoes. When the meat was done, we removed it from the pot, reduced the sauce, and strained out the vegetables. Dark, full-flavored, and lustrous, this sauce bestowed nobility on our humble cut of meat.

Beef Braised in Barolo

SERVES 6

Don't skip tying the roasts—it keeps them intact during the long cooking time. Purchase pancetta that is cut to order, about ¼ inch thick. If pancetta is not available, substitute an equal amount of salt pork (find the meatiest piece possible), cut it into ¼-inch cubes, and boil it in 3 cups of water for about 2 minutes to remove excess salt. After draining, use it as you would pancetta.

- 1 (3½-pound) boneless chuck-eye roast
  Table salt and ground black pepper
- 4 ounces pancetta (about 4 slices), cut into ¼-inch cubes (see note)
- 2 medium onions, chopped medium
- 2 medium carrots, chopped medium
- 2 medium celery ribs, chopped medium
- 1 tablespoon tomato paste
- 3 medium garlic cloves, minced or pressed through a garlic press (about 1 tablespoon)
- 1 tablespoon unbleached all-purpose flour
- ½ teaspoon sugar
- 1 (750-milliliter) bottle Barolo wine
- 1 (14.5-ounce) can diced tomatoes, drained
- 1 sprig fresh thyme plus 1 teaspoon minced thyme leaves
- 1 sprig fresh rosemary
- 10 sprigs fresh parsley

1. Adjust an oven rack to the middle position and heat the oven to 300 degrees. Pull the roast apart at its major seams (delineated by lines of fat) into two halves. Use a knife as necessary. With the knife, remove the large knobs of fat from each piece, leaving a thin layer of fat on the meat. Tie three pieces of kitchen twine around each piece of meat. Thoroughly pat the beef dry with paper towels; sprinkle generously with salt and pepper. Place the pancetta in a large Dutch oven; cook over medium heat, stirring occasionally, until browned and crisp, about 8 minutes. Using a slotted spoon, transfer the pancetta to a paper towel–lined plate and reserve. Pour off all but 2 tablespoons of fat; set the Dutch oven over medium-high heat and heat the fat until beginning to smoke. Add the beef to the pot and cook until well browned on all sides, about 8 minutes total. Transfer the beef to a large plate; set aside.

2. Reduce the heat to medium; add the onions, carrots, celery, and tomato paste to the pot and cook, stirring occasionally, until the vegetables begin to soften and brown, about 6 minutes. Add the garlic, flour, sugar, and reserved pancetta; cook, stirring constantly, until combined and fragrant, about 30 seconds. Add the wine and tomatoes, scraping the bottom of the pan with a wooden spoon to loosen the browned bits; add the thyme sprig, rosemary, and parsley. Return the roast and any accumulated juice to the pot; increase the heat to high and bring the liquid to a boil, then place a large sheet of foil over the pot and cover tightly with the lid. Set the pot in the oven and cook, using tongs to turn the beef every 45 minutes, until a dinner fork easily slips in and out of the meat, about 3 hours.

3. Transfer the beef to a carving board and tent with foil to keep warm. Allow the braising liquid to settle about 5 minutes, then, using a wide shallow spoon, skim the fat off the surface. Add the minced thyme, bring the liquid to a boil over high heat, and cook, whisking vigorously to help the vegetables break down, until the mixture is thickened and reduced to about 3½ cups, about 18 minutes. Strain the liquid through a large fine-mesh strainer, pressing on the solids with a spatula to extract as much liquid as possible; you should have 1½ cups strained sauce (if necessary, return the strained sauce to the Dutch oven and reduce to 1½ cups). Discard the solids in the strainer. Season the sauce with salt and pepper to taste.

4. Remove the kitchen twine from the meat and discard. Using a chef's knife or carving knife, cut the meat against the grain into ½-inch-thick slices. Divide the meat among warmed bowls or plates; pour about ¼ cup sauce over each portion and serve immediately.

SHRIMP SCAMPI

WHY THIS RECIPE WORKS: Restaurant versions of shrimp scampi often run the gamut from boiled shrimp and tomato sauce on a bed of pasta to rubbery shrimp overloaded in butter or olive oil. We wanted lightly cooked, moist shrimp in a light garlic and lemon sauce.

A quick sauté in batches was all the shrimp needed to cook fully without becoming rubbery; we then set them aside to build the sauce. We cooked minced garlic briefly in butter, so as not to scorch it, then added lemon juice and vermouth for depth of flavor; the liquids also protected the garlic from burning. Additional butter thickened the sauce, and parsley and cayenne provided the finishing touches to this light, flavorful Italian favorite.

Shrimp Scampi

SERVES 4 TO 6

Serve scampi with plenty of chewy bread to soak up extra juices.

> 2 **tablespoons olive oil**
> 2 **pounds extra-large shrimp (21 to 25 per pound), peeled and deveined (see page 160)**
> 3 **tablespoons unsalted butter**
> 4 **medium garlic cloves, minced or pressed through a garlic press (about 4 teaspoons)**
> 2 **tablespoons juice from 1 lemon**
> 1 **tablespoon dry vermouth**
> 2 **tablespoons minced fresh parsley leaves**
> **Pinch cayenne pepper**
> **Table salt and ground black pepper**

1. Heat one tablespoon of the oil in a 12-inch skillet over high heat until shimmering. Add 1 pound of the shrimp and cook, stirring occasionally, until just opaque, about 1 minute; transfer to a medium bowl. Return the pan to high heat and repeat with the remaining 1 tablespoon oil and 1 pound shrimp.

2. Return the skillet to medium-low heat; melt 1 tablespoon of the butter. Add the garlic and cook, stirring constantly, until fragrant, about 30 seconds. Off the heat, add the lemon juice and vermouth. Whisk in the remaining 2 tablespoons butter; add the parsley and cayenne, and season with salt and black pepper to taste. Return the shrimp and any accumulated juices to the skillet. Toss to combine; serve immediately.

CHAPTER 14

THE FLAIR OF THE FRENCH

Classic French
Onion Soup   250

Streamlined French
Onion Soup   251

French Potato Salad   252

French Onion and
Bacon Tart   253

Pissaladière   254

Summer Vegetable
Gratin   256

Pommes Anna   257

French Mashed
Potatoes with Cheese
and Garlic (Aligot)   258

Potatoes Lyonnaise   259

French-Style Stuffed
Chicken Breasts   260

French Chicken
in a Pot   262

Coq au Vin   263

Chicken with 40 Cloves
of Garlic   264

Chicken Provençal   265

Daube Provençal   266

Beef Burgundy   268

Slow-Cooker Beef
Burgundy   269

Simplified Cassoulet with
Pork and Kielbasa   271

Steak au Poivre with
Brandied Cream
Sauce   272

Steak Diane   273

  Sauce Base for
  Steak Diane

Fish Meunière with Browned
Butter and Lemon   275

CLASSIC FRENCH ONION SOUP

WHY THIS RECIPE WORKS: With too many onion soups, digging through a layer of congealed cheese unearths a disappointing broth that just doesn't taste like onions. The ideal French onion soup combines a satisfying broth redolent of sweet caramelized onions with a slice of toasted baguette and melted cheese. We wanted a foolproof method for achieving extraordinarily deep flavor from the humble onion—the star of this classic soup.

The secret to a rich broth was to caramelize the onions fully. The good news is that caramelizing the onions, deglazing the pot, and then repeating this process dozens of times will keep ratcheting up the flavor. The bad news is what a laborious, hands-on process this proved to be. Fortunately, we found that if we first cooked the onions covered in a hot oven for two and a half hours, we only needed to deglaze the onions on the stovetop three or four times. Just one type of onion (yellow) was sufficient, but a combination of three different liquids (water, chicken broth, and beef broth) added maximum flavor. For the topping, we toasted the bread before floating it on the soup to ward off sogginess and added only a modest sprinkling of nutty Gruyère so the broth wasn't overpowered.

Classic French Onion Soup

SERVES 6

Sweet onions, such as Vidalia or Walla Walla, will make this dish overly sweet. Be patient when caramelizing the onions in step 2; the entire process takes 45 to 60 minutes. Use broiler-safe crocks and keep the rims of the bowls 4 to 5 inches from the heating element to obtain a proper gratinée of melted, bubbly cheese. If using ordinary soup bowls, sprinkle the toasted bread slices with Gruyère and return them to the broiler until the cheese melts, then float them on top of the soup. For the best flavor, make the soup a day or two in advance. Alternatively, the onions can be prepared through step 1, cooled in the pot, and refrigerated for up to 3 days before proceeding with the recipe.

SOUP
- 3 tablespoons unsalted butter, cut into 3 pieces
- 4 pounds onions (about 6 large), halved pole to pole and sliced lengthwise ¼ inch thick (see note)
  Table salt
- 2 cups water, plus extra for deglazing
- ½ cup dry sherry
- 4 cups low-sodium chicken broth
- 2 cups beef broth
- 6 sprigs fresh thyme, tied together with kitchen twine
- 1 bay leaf
  Ground black pepper

CHEESE CROUTONS
- 1 small baguette, cut on the bias into ½-inch slices
- 8 ounces Gruyère cheese, shredded (about 2 cups)

1. FOR THE SOUP: Adjust an oven rack to the lower-middle position and heat the oven to 400 degrees. Generously spray the inside of a large (at least 7-quart) Dutch oven with vegetable oil spray. Add the butter, onions, and 1 teaspoon salt to the pot. Cook, covered, for 1 hour (the onions will be moist and slightly reduced in volume). Remove the pot from the oven and stir the onions, scraping the bottom and sides of the pot. Return the pot to the oven with the lid slightly ajar and continue to cook until the onions are very soft and golden brown, 1½ to 1¾ hours longer, stirring the onions and scraping the bottom and sides of the pot after 1 hour.

2. Carefully remove the pot from the oven and place over medium-high heat. Cook the onions, stirring frequently and scraping the bottom and sides of the pot, until the liquid evaporates and the onions brown, 15 to 20 minutes, reducing the heat to medium if the onions are browning too quickly. Continue to cook, stirring frequently, until the pot bottom is coated with a dark crust, 6 to 8 minutes, adjusting the heat as necessary. (Scrape any browned bits that collect on the spoon back into the onions.) Stir in ¼ cup water, scraping the pot bottom to loosen the crust, and cook until the water evaporates and the pot bottom has formed another dark crust, 6 to 8 minutes. Repeat the process of deglazing

2 or 3 more times, until the onions are very dark brown. Stir in the sherry and cook, stirring frequently, until the sherry evaporates, about 5 minutes.

3. Stir in 2 cups water, the chicken broth, beef broth, thyme, bay leaf, and ½ teaspoon salt, scraping up any final bits of browned crust on the bottom and sides of the pot. Increase the heat to high and bring to a simmer. Reduce the heat to low, cover, and simmer 30 minutes. Remove and discard the thyme and bay leaf, then season with salt and pepper to taste.

4. FOR THE CROUTONS: While the soup simmers, heat the oven to 400 degrees. Arrange the baguette slices in a single layer on a rimmed baking sheet and bake until dry, crisp, and golden at the edges, about 10 minutes. Set aside.

5. Adjust an oven rack 6 inches from the broiler element and heat the broiler. Set individual broiler-safe crocks on the baking sheet and fill each with about 1¾ cups of the soup. Top each bowl with one or two baguette slices (do not overlap the slices) and sprinkle evenly with the Gruyère. Broil until the cheese is melted and bubbly around the edges, 3 to 5 minutes. Cool 5 minutes; serve.

STREAMLINED FRENCH ONION SOUP

WHY THIS RECIPE WORKS: Streamlined versions of onion soup often amount to a sad crock of flavorless onions floating in super-salty beef bouillon topped with an oily blob of cheese. Or it might be just the opposite: a weak and watery affair. We wanted to make a better onion soup—a dark, rich broth, intensely flavored by an abundance of seriously cooked onions, covered by a broth-soaked crouton with a cheesy, crusty top—and we wanted to make it in record time.

We cheated from the get-go and created a simple broth with store-bought beef and chicken broths and wine. Red onions were chosen for their subtle complexity and nuance, and for the maximum flavor they offered when caramelized. Parsley, thyme, and a bay leaf rounded out the flavors and imparted freshness. To prevent the croutons from getting too soggy, we placed them atop the soup, so only the bottom was submerged. For the cheese, we liked a combination of pungent Swiss cheese topped with subdued Asiago; their flavors added some punch to our speedy but still irresistible soup.

BEHIND THE SCENES

SHEDDING TEARS IN THE TEST KITCHEN

We can't tell you how many onions we've chopped over the years. Let's just say a lot. As a result, we've shed more than a few tears. What causes cut onions to be so pesky? When an onion is cut, the cells that are damaged in the process release sulfuric compounds as well as various enzymes, notably one called sulfoxide lyase. Those compounds and enzymes, which are separated when the onion's cell structure is intact, activate and mix to form the real culprit behind crying, a volatile new compound called thiopropanal sulfoxide. When thiopropanal sulfoxide evaporates in the air, it irritates the eyes, causing redness and tears.

Through the years we've collected dozens of ideas from readers, books, and conversations with colleagues, all aimed at reducing tears while cutting onions. We finally decided to put those ideas to the test. They ranged from common sense (work underneath an exhaust fan or freeze onions for 30 minutes before slicing) to the comical (wear ski goggles or hold a toothpick in your teeth). Overall, the methods that worked best were to protect our eyes by covering them with goggles or contact lenses or to introduce a flame near the cut onions. The flame, which can be produced by either a candle or a gas burner, changes the activity of the thiopropanal sulfoxide (the volatile compound that causes tearing) by completing its oxidization. Contact lenses and goggles form a physical barrier that the vapors cannot penetrate. So if you want to keep tears at bay when handling onions, light a candle or gas burner—or put on some ski goggles, even if it does look a bit silly.

Streamlined French Onion Soup
SERVES 6

Tie the parsley and thyme sprigs together with kitchen twine so they will be easy to retrieve from the soup pot. Use broiler-safe crocks and keep the rims of the bowls 4 to 5 inches from the heating element to obtain a proper gratinée of melted, bubbly cheese. If using ordinary soup bowls, top the toasted bread slices with the cheeses as directed in step 3 and return them to the broiler until the cheese melts, then float them on top of the soup.

SOUP

- 2 tablespoons unsalted butter
- 3 pounds red onions (about 6 medium), halved pole to pole and sliced crosswise ⅛ inch thick
  Table salt
- 6 cups low-sodium chicken broth
- 1¾ cups beef broth
- ¼ cup dry red wine
- 2 sprigs fresh parsley (see note)
- 1 sprig fresh thyme (see note)
- 1 bay leaf
- 1 tablespoon balsamic vinegar
  Ground black pepper

CHEESE CROUTONS

- 1 small baguette, cut on the bias into ½-inch slices
- 4½ ounces thinly sliced Swiss cheese
- 1½ ounces Asiago cheese, grated (about ¾ cup)

1. FOR THE SOUP: Melt the butter in a large Dutch oven over medium-high heat. Add the onions and ½ teaspoon salt and cook, stirring frequently, until the onions are reduced and syrupy and the inside of the pot is coated with a deep brown crust, 30 to 35 minutes. Add the chicken and beef broths, red wine, parsley, thyme, and bay leaf, scraping the pot bottom with a wooden spoon to loosen the browned bits, and bring to a simmer. Simmer to blend the flavors, about 20 minutes; discard the herbs. Stir in the balsamic vinegar and season with salt and pepper to taste. (The cooled soup can be refrigerated in an airtight container for up to 2 days; return to a simmer before finishing the soup with the croutons and cheese.)

2. FOR THE CROUTONS: Adjust an oven rack to the upper-middle position and heat the oven to 350 degrees. Arrange the baguette slices on a rimmed baking sheet and bake, turning once, until lightly browned, about 15 minutes. Remove the bread from the oven, carefully adjust an oven rack 6 inches from the broiler element, and heat the broiler.

3. Set individual broiler-safe crocks on the baking sheet and fill each with about 1½ cups of the soup. Top each bowl with two baguette slices and divide the Swiss cheese slices, placing them in a single layer, if possible, on the bread; sprinkle with 2 tablespoons of the grated Asiago and broil until the cheese is browned and bubbly around the edges, 7 to 10 minutes. Cool 5 minutes; serve.

FRENCH POTATO SALAD

WHY THIS RECIPE WORKS: French potato salad is served warm or at room temperature and is composed of sliced potatoes glistening with olive oil, white wine vinegar, and plenty of fresh herbs. We wanted a potato salad that was not only pleasing to the eye but to the palate as well. The potatoes should be tender but not mushy, and the flavor of the vinaigrette should penetrate the relatively bland potatoes but not be oily or dull.

We learned the hard way that to prevent torn skins and broken slices, we had to slice the potatoes before boiling them. To tone down the flavor of harsh garlic, we blanched it before mixing the vinaigrette. A little extra vinegar—more than we would normally call for in a vinaigrette—added a pleasing sharpness, while some reserved potato water added just the right amount of moisture and saltiness to the salad. Dijon mustard combined with strong herbs also perked things up. Tossing the vinaigrette with the cooked potatoes led to mangled, shabby slices, but pouring the vinaigrette over the warm potatoes on a sheet pan, then folding in the other ingredients, kept the potato slices intact.

French Potato Salad

SERVES 4 TO 6

If fresh chervil isn't available, substitute an additional ½ tablespoon minced parsley and an additional ½ teaspoon minced tarragon. For best flavor, serve the salad warm, but to make ahead, follow the recipe through step 2, cover with plastic wrap, and refrigerate. Before serving, bring the salad to room temperature, then add the shallot and herbs.

- 2 pounds red potatoes (about 6 medium or 18 small), scrubbed and sliced ¼ inch thick
- 2 tablespoons table salt
- 1 medium garlic clove, peeled and threaded on a skewer
- ¼ cup olive oil
- 1½ tablespoons champagne vinegar or white wine vinegar
- 2 teaspoons Dijon mustard
- ½ teaspoon ground black pepper
- 1 small shallot, minced (about 1 tablespoon)
- 1 tablespoon minced fresh chervil leaves (see note)
- 1 tablespoon minced fresh parsley leaves
- 1 tablespoon minced fresh chives
- 1 teaspoon minced fresh tarragon leaves

1. Place the potatoes, 6 cups cold water, and the salt in a large saucepan. Bring to a boil over high heat, then

their pure onion flavor, and cooking more evenly. We liked bacon, which acted as a crisp foil to the creamy filling, but we found a traditional custard with the bacon to be simply too rich. To resolve the issue, we reduced the number of eggs and switched out the cream for half-and-half. And to ensure the bacon stayed crisp, we sprinkled it on top of the custard. We tried several classic crust recipes, looking for one that had the intense butteriness of traditional tart dough but could still be easily patted into a tart pan. We found that using a food processor to cut cold butter completely into the flour mixture required less ice water than a conventional crust, which kept the dough firm enough to press into the pan.

reduce the heat to medium. Lower the skewered garlic into the simmering water and blanch, about 45 seconds. Immediately run the garlic under cold tap water to stop the cooking process; remove the garlic from the skewer and set aside. Simmer the potatoes, uncovered, until tender but still firm (a paring knife can be slipped into and out of the center of a potato slice with no resistance), about 5 minutes. Drain the potatoes, reserving ¼ cup cooking water. Arrange the hot potatoes close together in a single layer on a rimmed baking sheet.

2. Press the garlic through a garlic press or mince by hand. Whisk the garlic, reserved potato cooking water, oil, vinegar, mustard, and pepper together in a small bowl until combined. Drizzle the dressing evenly over the warm potato slices; let stand 10 minutes.

3. Meanwhile, toss the shallot and herbs gently together in a small bowl. Transfer the potatoes to a large serving bowl. Add the shallot-herb mixture and mix lightly with a rubber spatula to combine. Serve immediately.

FRENCH ONION TART

WHY THIS RECIPE WORKS: French onion tart is similar to quiche but delivers a more refined slice of pie, with more onions than custard. But re-creating this tart at home can produce a tough and crackery crust, which is doubly disappointing after spending long hours delicately cooking the onions, making the custard, and baking the whole thing together. We wanted to simplify the crust and shorten the overall preparation time.

We found that our onions would cook in half the usual time if we left the lid on the skillet throughout cooking. And covering the onions allowed them to cook entirely in their own juices, thereby becoming tender, retaining

French Onion and Bacon Tart

SERVES 6 TO 8

Either yellow or white onions work well in this recipe, but stay away from sweet onions, such as Vidalias, which will make the tart watery. Use a 9-inch tinned-steel tart pan; see page 594 for our recommended brand. This tart can be served hot or at room temperature and pairs well with a green salad as a main course.

CRUST

- 1¼ cups (6¼ ounces) unbleached all-purpose flour
- 1 tablespoon sugar
- ½ teaspoon table salt
- 8 tablespoons (1 stick) unsalted butter, cut into ½-inch cubes and chilled
- 2-3 tablespoons ice water

FILLING

- 4 ounces bacon (about 4 slices), halved lengthwise and cut crosswise into ¼-inch pieces
  Vegetable oil, as needed
- 1½ pounds onions (about 3 medium), halved pole to pole and cut crosswise into ¼-inch slices (about 6 cups) (see note)
- ¾ teaspoon table salt
- 1 sprig fresh thyme
- 2 large eggs
- ½ cup half-and-half
- ¼ teaspoon ground black pepper

1. FOR THE CRUST: Spray a 9-inch tart pan with a removable bottom with vegetable oil spray; set aside. Pulse the flour, sugar, and salt together in a food processor until combined, about 4 pulses. Scatter the butter pieces over the flour mixture and pulse until the mixture resembles coarse sand, about 15 pulses. Add 2 tablespoons of the ice water and continue to process until large clumps of dough form and no powdery bits remain, about 5 seconds. If the dough doesn't clump, add the remaining 1 tablespoon water and pulse to incorporate, about 4 pulses. Transfer the dough to the greased tart pan and, working outward from the center, pat the dough into an even layer, sealing any cracks. Working around the edge, press the dough firmly into the corners of the pan and up the sides, using your thumb to level off the top edge. Lay plastic wrap over the dough and smooth out any bumps or shallow areas. Place the tart shell on a plate and freeze for 30 minutes.

2. Adjust an oven rack to the middle position and heat the oven to 375 degrees. Place the frozen tart shell (still in the tart pan) on a rimmed baking sheet. Gently press a piece of extra-wide heavy-duty foil that has been sprayed with vegetable oil spray against the dough and over the edges of the tart pan. Fill the shell with pie weights and bake until the top edge of the dough just starts to color and the surface of dough under the foil no longer looks wet, about 30 minutes. Remove the tart shell from the oven and carefully remove the foil and weights. Return the baking sheet with the tart shell to the oven and continue to bake, uncovered, until golden brown, 5 to 10 minutes. Set the baking sheet with the tart shell on a wire rack to cool while making the filling. (Do not turn off the oven.)

3. FOR THE FILLING: While the crust is baking, cook the bacon in a 12-inch nonstick skillet over medium heat until browned and crisp, 8 to 10 minutes. Using a slotted spoon, transfer the bacon to a paper towel–lined plate; set aside. Pour off all but 2 tablespoons bacon fat from the skillet (or add vegetable oil if needed to make this amount).

4. Add the onions, salt, and thyme to the skillet. Cover and cook until the onions release their liquid and start to wilt, about 10 minutes. Reduce the heat to low and continue to cook, covered, until the onions are very soft, about 20 minutes, stirring once or twice (if after 15 minutes the onions look wet, remove the lid and continue to cook another 5 minutes). Remove the pan from the heat and cool 5 minutes.

5. Whisk the eggs, half-and-half, and pepper together in a large bowl. Remove the thyme from the onions; discard. Stir the onions into the egg mixture until just incorporated. Spread the onion mixture over the bottom of the baked crust and sprinkle the reserved bacon evenly on top.

6. Bake the tart on the baking sheet until the center of the tart feels firm to the touch, 20 to 25 minutes. Set the baking sheet with the tart on a wire rack and cool at least 10 minutes. Remove the tart pan ring, gently slide a thin-bladed spatula between the pan bottom and crust to loosen, and slide the tart onto a serving plate. Cut into wedges and serve.

PISSALADIÈRE

WHY THIS RECIPE WORKS: *Pissaladière,* the classic olive, anchovy, and onion tart from Provence, is easy enough to prepare, but each ingredient must be handled carefully. We wanted to harmonize the onions, olives, and anchovies with a crisp crust to produce a tart worthy of the finest bakery in Nice.

We made the dough in a food processor and kneaded it as little as possible to create a pizza-like dough with a cracker-like exterior and a decently chewy crumb, a dough with the structure to stand up to the heavy toppings. Bread flour was our flour of choice as it has more protein than all-purpose flour, and that translates to a more substantial chew. Using a combination of high and low heat to cook the onions—starting the onions on high to release their juices and soften them, then turning the heat to medium-low to caramelize them—gave us perfectly browned and caramelized, but not burnt, onions. Adding a bit of water before spreading them on the crust kept them from clumping. We placed the onions on top of the chopped black olives, anchovies (also chopped; whole anchovies were too overpowering), and fresh thyme leaves to protect them from burning in the oven. Diehard fish lovers can add more anchovies as a garnish if desired.

Pissaladière

MAKES 2 TARTS, SERVING 6

For the best flavor, use high-quality oil-packed anchovies; in a tasting, Ortiz was our favorite brand (see page 602). If desired, you can slow down the dough's rising time by letting it rise in the refrigerator for 8 to 16 hours in step 1; let the refrigerated dough soften at room temperature for 30 minutes before using. The caramelized onions can also be made a day ahead and refrigerated.

DOUGH

- 2 **cups (11 ounces) bread flour, plus extra for dusting the work surface**
- 1 **teaspoon instant or rapid-rise yeast**
- 1 **teaspoon table salt**
- 1 **tablespoon olive oil, plus extra for brushing the dough and greasing hands**
- 1 **cup warm water (110 degrees)**

CARAMELIZED ONIONS

- 2 **tablespoons olive oil**
- 2 **pounds onions (about 4 medium), halved and sliced ¼ inch thick**
- 1 **teaspoon brown sugar**
- ½ **teaspoon table salt**
- 1 **tablespoon water**

OLIVES, ANCHOVIES, AND GARNISHES

- **Olive oil**
- ½ **teaspoon ground black pepper**
- ½ **cup niçoise olives, pitted and chopped coarse**
- 8 **anchovy fillets, rinsed, patted dry, and chopped coarse (about 2 tablespoons), plus 12 fillets, rinsed and patted dry for garnish (optional) (see note)**
- 2 **teaspoons minced fresh thyme leaves**
- 1 **teaspoon fennel seeds (optional)**
- 1 **tablespoon minced fresh parsley leaves (optional)**

1. FOR THE DOUGH: Pulse the flour, yeast, and salt in a food processor (fitted with a dough blade if possible) until combined, about 5 pulses. With the machine running, slowly add the oil, then the water, through the feed tube; continue to process until the dough forms a ball, about 15 seconds. Turn the dough out onto a lightly floured work surface and form it into a smooth, round ball. Place the dough in a large lightly oiled bowl and cover tightly with greased plastic wrap. Let rise in a warm place until doubled in volume, 1 to 1½ hours.

2. FOR THE CARAMELIZED ONIONS: While the dough is rising, heat the oil in a 12-inch nonstick skillet over medium-low heat until shimmering. Stir in the onions, sugar, and salt. Cover and cook, stirring occasionally, until the onions are softened and have released their juice, about 10 minutes. Remove the lid, increase the heat to medium-high, and continue to cook, stirring often, until the onions are deeply browned, 10 to 15 minutes. Off the heat, stir in the water, then transfer the onions to a bowl and set aside. Adjust the oven rack to the lowest position, set a baking stone on the rack, and heat the oven to 500 degrees. (Let the baking stone heat for at least 30 minutes but no longer than 1 hour.)

3. To shape, top, and bake the dough: Turn the dough out onto a lightly floured work surface, divide it into two equal pieces, and cover with greased plastic wrap. Working with one piece at a time (keep the other piece covered), form each piece into a rough ball by gently pulling the edges of the dough together and pinching to seal. With floured hands, turn the dough ball seam-side down. Cupping the dough with both hands, gently push the dough in a circular motion to form a taut ball. Repeat with the second piece. Brush each piece lightly with oil, cover with plastic wrap, and let rest 10 minutes. Meanwhile, cut two 20-inch lengths of parchment paper and set aside.

4. Coat your fingers and palms generously with oil. Working with one piece of dough at a time, hold the dough up and gently stretch it to a 12-inch length. Place the dough on the parchment sheet and gently dimple the surface of the dough with your fingertips. Using your oiled palms, push and flatten the dough into a 14 by 8-inch oval. Brush the dough with oil and sprinkle with ¼ teaspoon of the pepper. Leaving a ½-inch border around the edge, sprinkle ¼ cup of the olives, 1 tablespoon of the chopped anchovies, and 1 teaspoon of the thyme evenly over the dough, then evenly scatter with half of the onions. Arrange 6 whole anchovy fillets, if using, on the tart and sprinkle with ½ teaspoon of the fennel seeds, if using. Slip the parchment with the tart onto a pizza peel (or inverted baking sheet), then slide it onto the hot baking stone. Bake until deep golden brown, 13 to 15 minutes. While the first tart bakes, shape and top the second tart.

5. Remove the first tart from the oven with a peel (or pull the parchment onto a baking sheet). Transfer the tart to a cutting board and slide the parchment out from under the tart; cool for 5 minutes. While the first tart cools, bake the second tart. Sprinkle with the parsley (if using) and cut each tart into 8 pieces before serving.

SUMMER VEGETABLE GRATIN

WHY THIS RECIPE WORKS: Layering summer's best vegetables into a gratin can lead to a memorable side dish—or a soggy mess. Juicy summer vegetables like zucchini and tomatoes can exude a torrent of liquid that washes away flavors and turns the dish squishy and soggy. We wanted a simple, Provençal-style vegetable gratin, where a golden brown, cheesy topping provides a rich contrast to the fresh, bright flavor of the vegetables.

To start, we chose our vegetables. The typical combination of tomatoes, zucchini, and summer squash won out (eggplant was too mushy and bell peppers took on a steamed flavor). To eliminate excess moisture, we baked the casserole uncovered, after salting the vegetables. Salting worked like a charm to both season and dry out the zucchini and summer squash, but proved insufficient to deal with all the tomato juice. While we could remove the watery jelly and seeds from the tomatoes, the jelly was crucial for full tomato flavor. We moved the tomatoes to the top gratin layer, which allowed them to roast and caramelize. The roasting not only eliminated moisture but also added flavor, especially when drizzled with an aromatic garlic-thyme oil. Finally, for more complexity, we added a layer of caramelized onions between the zucchini/squash and tomato layers and sprinkled the dish with Parmesan bread crumbs before baking.

Summer Vegetable Gratin
SERVES 6 TO 8

The success of this recipe depends on good-quality produce. Buy zucchini and summer squash of roughly the same diameter. We like the visual contrast zucchini and summer squash bring to the dish, but you can also use just one or the other. A similarly sized ovensafe gratin dish can be substituted for the 13 by 9-inch baking dish. Serve the gratin alongside grilled fish or meat, accompanied by bread to soak up any flavorful juices.

- 6 tablespoons extra-virgin olive oil
- 1 pound zucchini, ends trimmed and cut crosswise into ¼-inch-thick slices (see note)
- 1 pound yellow summer squash, ends trimmed and cut crosswise into ¼-inch-thick slices (see note)
- 2 teaspoons table salt
- 1½ pounds ripe tomatoes (3 to 4 large), cut into ¼-inch-thick slices
- 2 medium onions, halved pole to pole and sliced thin (about 3 cups)
- ¾ teaspoon ground black pepper
- 2 medium garlic cloves, minced or pressed through a garlic press (about 2 teaspoons)
- 1 tablespoon minced fresh thyme leaves
- 1 slice high-quality white sandwich bread, torn into quarters
- 2 ounces grated Parmesan cheese (about 1 cup)
- 2 medium shallots, minced (about 6 tablespoons)
- ¼ cup chopped fresh basil leaves

1. Adjust an oven rack to the upper-middle position and heat the oven to 400 degrees. Brush a 13 by 9-inch baking dish with 1 tablespoon of the oil; set aside.

2. Toss the zucchini and summer squash slices with 1 teaspoon of the salt in a large bowl; transfer to a colander set over a bowl. Let stand until the zucchini and squash release at least 3 tablespoons of liquid, about 45 minutes. Arrange the slices on a triple layer of paper towels; cover with another triple layer of paper towels. Firmly press each slice to remove as much liquid as possible.

3. Place the tomato slices in a single layer on a double layer of paper towels and sprinkle evenly with ½ teaspoon more salt; let stand 30 minutes. Place a second double layer of paper towels on top of the tomatoes and press firmly to dry the tomatoes.

4. Meanwhile, heat 1 tablespoon more oil in a 12-inch nonstick skillet over medium heat until shimmering. Add the onions, the remaining ½ teaspoon salt, and ¼ teaspoon of the pepper; cook, stirring occasionally, until the onions are softened and dark golden brown, 20 to 25 minutes. Set the onions aside.

5. Combine the garlic, 3 tablespoons more oil, the remaining ½ teaspoon pepper, and the thyme in a small bowl. In a large bowl, toss the zucchini and summer squash in half of the oil mixture, then arrange in the greased baking dish. Arrange the caramelized onions in an even layer over the squash. Slightly overlap the tomato slices in a single layer on top of the onions. Spoon the remaining garlic-oil mixture evenly over the tomatoes. Bake until the vegetables are tender and the tomatoes are starting to brown on the edges, 40 to 45 minutes.

6. Meanwhile, process the bread in a food processor until finely ground, about 10 seconds. (You should have about 1 cup crumbs.) Combine the bread crumbs, remaining 1 tablespoon oil, the Parmesan, and shallots in a medium bowl. Remove the baking dish from the oven and increase the heat to 450 degrees. Sprinkle the bread-crumb mixture evenly on top of the tomatoes. Bake the gratin until bubbling and the cheese is lightly browned, 5 to 10 minutes. Sprinkle with the basil and cool 10 minutes before serving.

POMMES ANNA

WHY THIS RECIPE WORKS: Traditional *pommes Anna* is rarely seen on home or restaurant menus these days because it takes an inordinately long time to compose, and it is hard to remove cleanly from the pan, resulting in an unsatisfactory time-consuming and messy dish. We wanted a foolproof, elegant potato cake with a crisp, deep brown crust covering the soft, creamy potato layers within.

We used a nonstick skillet to ensure easy release of our potatoes. Most recipes for pommes Anna call for clarified butter, but we decided to cut down on time and waste (a good portion of the butter is lost with clarifying) and instead tossed the sliced potatoes with melted butter. To accelerate cooking, we arranged the potatoes in the skillet as it was heating on the stovetop; when we were done layering the slices, we pressed the potatoes with the bottom of a cake pan to compact them into a cohesive cake. To unmold, we simply inverted the potato cake onto a baking sheet and then slid it onto a serving dish.

Pommes Anna

SERVES 6 TO 8

Use a food processor fitted with a fine slicing disk or a mandoline to slice the potatoes, but do not slice them until you are ready to start assembling; see page 585 for our recommended mandoline. Remember to start timing when you begin arranging the potatoes in the skillet; they will need 30 minutes on the stovetop to brown properly no matter how quickly you arrange them.

3 pounds russet or Yukon Gold potatoes (about 6 medium), peeled and sliced ⅛ inch thick (see note)
5 tablespoons unsalted butter, melted
¼ cup vegetable oil or peanut oil
Table salt and ground black pepper

1. Adjust an oven rack to the lower-middle position and heat the oven to 450 degrees. Toss the potatoes with the butter to coat.

2. Heat the oil in an ovensafe 10-inch nonstick skillet over medium-low heat. Begin timing, and arrange the potato slices in the skillet, using the most attractive slices to form the bottom layer, by placing one slice in the center of the skillet and overlapping more slices in a circle around the center slice; form another circle of overlapping slices to cover the pan bottom. Season with ¼ teaspoon salt and black pepper to taste. Arrange the second layer of potatoes, working in the opposite direction of the first layer; season with ¼ teaspoon salt and black pepper to taste. Repeat, layering the potatoes in opposite directions and seasoning with ¼ teaspoon salt and black pepper to taste, until no slices remain (broken or uneven slices can be pieced together to form a single slice; potatoes will mound in the center of the skillet). Continue to cook until 30 minutes elapse from when you began arranging the potatoes in the skillet.

3. Using the bottom of a 9-inch cake pan, press on the potatoes firmly to compact. Cover the skillet and place in the oven; bake until the potatoes begin to soften, about 15 minutes. Uncover and continue to bake until

the potatoes are tender when pierced with the tip of a paring knife and the edge of the potatoes near the skillet is browned, about 10 minutes longer. Meanwhile, line a rimless baking sheet or an upside-down rimmed baking sheet with foil and spray lightly with vegetable oil spray. Carefully drain off the excess fat from the potatoes by pressing the bottom of the cake pan against the potatoes while tilting the skillet. (Be sure to use heavy potholders.)

4. Set the baking sheet, foil side down, on top of the skillet. Using potholders, hold the baking sheet in place with one hand and carefully invert the skillet and baking sheet together. Lift the skillet off the potatoes; slide the potatoes from the baking sheet onto a platter. Cut into wedges and serve immediately.

FRENCH-STYLE MASHED POTATOES

WHY THIS RECIPE WORKS: *Aligot* is French cookery's intensely rich, cheesy take on mashed potatoes. These potatoes get their elastic, satiny texture through prolonged, vigorous stirring—which can easily go awry and lead to a gluey, sticky mess. We wanted to create cheesy, garlicky mashed potatoes with a smooth, elastic texture and the same signature stretch as the French original.

After making aligot with different potatoes, we found medium-starch Yukon Golds to be the clear winner, yielding a puree with a mild, buttery flavor and a light, creamy consistency. We boiled the potatoes, then used a food processor to "mash" them. Traditional aligot uses butter and crème fraîche to add flavor and creaminess and loosen the texture before mixing in the cheese. But crème fraîche isn't always easy to find, so we substituted whole milk, which provided depth without going overboard. For the cheese, a combination of mild mozzarella and nutty Gruyère proved just right. As for the stirring, we needed to monitor the consistency closely: too much stirring and the aligot turned rubbery, too little and the cheese didn't marry with the potatoes for that essential elasticity.

French Mashed Potatoes with Cheese and Garlic (Aligot)

SERVES 6

The finished potatoes should have a smooth and slightly elastic texture. White cheddar can be substituted for the Gruyère. For richer, stretchier aligot, double the mozzarella.

- **2 pounds Yukon Gold potatoes (about 4 medium), peeled, cut into ½-inch-thick slices, rinsed well, and drained**
  Table salt
- **6 tablespoons (¾ stick) unsalted butter**
- **2 medium garlic cloves, minced or pressed through a garlic press (about 2 teaspoons)**
- **1–1½ cups whole milk**
- **4 ounces mozzarella cheese, shredded (about 1 cup; see note)**
- **4 ounces Gruyère cheese, shredded (about 1 cup) (see note)**
  Ground black pepper

1. Place the potatoes and 1 tablespoon salt in a large saucepan; add water to cover by 1 inch. Partially cover the saucepan with a lid and bring to a boil over high heat. Reduce the heat to medium-low and simmer until the potatoes are tender and just break apart when poked with a fork, 12 to 17 minutes. Drain the potatoes and dry the saucepan.

2. Add the potatoes, butter, garlic, and 1½ teaspoons salt to a food processor. Pulse until the butter is melted and incorporated, about 10 pulses. Add 1 cup milk and continue to process until the potatoes are smooth and creamy, about 20 seconds, scraping down the sides of the workbowl halfway through.

3. Return the potato mixture to the saucepan and set over medium heat. Stir in the cheeses, 1 cup at a time, until incorporated. Continue to cook the potatoes, stirring vigorously, until the cheese is fully melted and the mixture is smooth and elastic, 3 to 5 minutes. If the mixture is difficult to stir and seems thick, stir in 2 tablespoons milk at a time (up to ½ cup) until the potatoes are loose and creamy. Season with salt and pepper to taste. Serve immediately.

POTATOES LYONNAISE

WHY THIS RECIPE WORKS: Originally conceived as a way to use up leftover boiled potatoes, *potatoes Lyonnaise* came to represent the best of classic French bistro cuisine: buttery, browned potato slices with strands of sweet, caramelized onion and fresh parsley—a simple yet complex skillet potato dish. Sadly, many versions are greasy and heavy rather than rich and complex. We wanted a return to the original elegant, buttery potato and onion dish—but one that didn't require leftover potatoes to make.

First, we had to choose the right potato. Yukon Golds beat out high-starch russets and low-starch Red Bliss. We precooked the potatoes in the microwave so that, once added to the skillet, they would cook through in the time they took to brown (without the microwave, the potatoes charred on the outside before cooking through). While the potatoes were in the microwave, we cooked the onions just long enough to release moisture and cook in their own juices. To finish the dish, we united the onions and potatoes in a brief sauté for the perfect melding of flavors. A sprinkling of minced parsley gave the dish a fresh taste and bright color.

1. Melt 1 tablespoon of the butter in a 12-inch heavy nonstick skillet over medium-high heat. Add the onion and ¼ teaspoon of the salt and stir to coat; cook, stirring occasionally, until the onion begins to soften, about 3 minutes. Reduce the heat to medium and cook, covered, stirring occasionally, until the onion is light brown and soft, about 12 minutes longer, deglazing with the water when the pan gets dry, about halfway through the cooking time. Transfer to a bowl and cover. Do not wash the skillet.

2. While the onion cooks, microwave 1 tablespoon more butter on high power in a large microwave-safe bowl until melted, about 15 seconds. Add the potatoes to the bowl and toss to coat with the melted butter. Microwave on high power until the potatoes just start to turn tender, about 6 minutes, tossing halfway through the cooking time. Toss the potatoes again and set aside.

3. Melt the remaining 1 tablespoon butter in the now-empty skillet over medium-high heat. Add the potatoes and shake the skillet to distribute evenly. Cook, without stirring, until browned on the bottom, about 3 minutes. Using a spatula, stir the potatoes carefully and continue to cook, stirring every 2 to 3 minutes, until the potatoes are well browned and tender when pierced with the tip of a paring knife, 8 to 10 minutes more. Season with the remaining salt and the pepper.

4. Add the onion back to the skillet and stir to combine. Cook until the onion is heated through and the flavors have melded, 1 to 2 minutes. Transfer to a large plate, sprinkle with the parsley, and serve.

Potatoes Lyonnaise

SERVES 4

Toss the potatoes halfway through the microwave session to prevent uneven cooking. If using a lightweight skillet, you will need to stir the potatoes more frequently to prevent burning.

- **3 tablespoons unsalted butter**
- **1 large onion, halved pole to pole
    and sliced ¼ inch thick (about 3 cups)**
- **½ teaspoon table salt**
- **2 tablespoons water**
- **1½ pounds Yukon Gold potatoes (about 3 medium),
    peeled and sliced crosswise into ¼-inch rounds**
- **¼ teaspoon ground black pepper**
- **1 tablespoon minced fresh parsley leaves**

STUFFED CHICKEN BREASTS

WHY THIS RECIPE WORKS: Most American cooks stuff chicken breasts with cheesy, bready fillings. French chefs, on the other hand, use a forcemeat stuffing to transform ordinary chicken breasts into a four-star affair. The French technique requires some serious labor, and includes skinning and boning a whole chicken, stuffing the breasts with the leg meat, and wrapping them up in the skin. We wanted to achieve the same flavorful package of chicken and filling—using a much simpler procedure.

Starting with boneless, skinless chicken breasts eliminated the need to bone a whole chicken. We mimicked a forcemeat stuffing by trimming a bit of meat from each chicken breast, and combining the meat with mushrooms, herbs, and leeks. (And pureeing the meat trimmings created a cohesive filling that stayed put inside the chicken breasts.)

Turning to the mechanics, we needed to create easy-to-roll rectangles of chicken breast to encase the stuffing. After butterflying the chicken breasts, we pounded them thin and trimmed them into a rectangular shape. The stuffing was easy to spread on the breasts, which we simply rolled up and tied with twine. Finally, we browned the chicken in a hot skillet and then added chicken broth and wine to braise the meat in the pan. Not only did the chicken stay tender when simmered, but the liquid served as a base for a simple yet intensely flavored pan sauce.

French-Style Stuffed Chicken Breasts

SERVES 4

To make slicing the chicken easier, freeze it for 15 minutes. If your chicken breasts come with the tenderloins attached, pull them off and reserve them to make the puree (along with the breast meat you will trim in step 1). Because the stuffing contains raw chicken, it is important to check its temperature in step 5.

CHICKEN AND STUFFING

- 4 (7 to 8-ounce) boneless, skinless chicken breasts, tenderloins removed and breasts trimmed (see note)
- 3 tablespoons vegetable oil
- 10 ounces white mushrooms, wiped clean and sliced thin
- 1 small leek, white part only, chopped and rinsed thoroughly (about 1 cup)
- 2 medium garlic cloves, minced or pressed through a garlic press (about 2 teaspoons)
- ½ teaspoon minced fresh thyme leaves
- 1 tablespoon juice from 1 lemon
- ½ cup dry white wine
- 1 tablespoon minced fresh parsley leaves
  Table salt and ground black pepper
- 1 cup low-sodium chicken broth

SAUCE

- 1 teaspoon Dijon mustard
- 2 tablespoons unsalted butter
  Table salt and ground black pepper

1. FOR THE CHICKEN AND STUFFING: Following the photos on page 261, butterfly the chicken horizontally, stopping ½ inch from the edges so the halves remain attached, then open up each breast, cover with plastic wrap, and pound the cutlets to an even ¼-inch thickness (each cutlet should measure about 8 by 6 inches). Trim about ½ inch from the long sides of the cutlets (1½ to 2 ounces of meat per cutlet, or a total of ½ cup from all 4 cutlets) to form rectangles that measure about 8 by 5 inches. Process all the trimmings in a food processor until smooth, about 20 seconds. Transfer the puree to a medium bowl and set aside. (Do not wash the food processor bowl.)

2. Heat 1 tablespoon of the oil in a 12-inch skillet over medium-high heat until shimmering. Add the mushrooms and cook, stirring occasionally, until all the moisture has evaporated and the mushrooms are golden brown, 8 to 11 minutes. Add 1 tablespoon more oil and the leek; continue to cook, stirring frequently, until softened, 2 to 4 minutes. Add the garlic and thyme and cook until fragrant, about 30 seconds. Add 1½ teaspoons of the lemon juice and cook until all the moisture has evaporated, about 30 seconds. Transfer the mixture to the bowl of the food processor. Return the pan to the heat, add the wine, and scrape the pan bottom to loosen any browned bits. Transfer the wine to a small bowl and set aside. Rinse and dry the skillet.

3. Pulse the mushroom mixture in the food processor until roughly chopped, about 5 pulses. Transfer the mushroom mixture to the bowl with the pureed chicken. Add 1½ teaspoons of the parsley, ¾ teaspoon salt, and ½ teaspoon pepper. Using a rubber spatula, fold together the stuffing ingredients until well combined (you should have about 1½ cups stuffing).

4. Spread one-quarter of the stuffing evenly over each cutlet with a rubber spatula, leaving a ¾-inch border along the short sides of the cutlet and a ¼-inch border along the long sides. Roll each breast up as tightly as possible without squeezing out the filling and place seam-side down. Evenly space three pieces of twine (each about 12 inches long) beneath each breast and tie, trimming any excess.

5. Season the chicken with salt and pepper. Heat the remaining 1 tablespoon oil in the skillet over medium-high heat until just smoking. Add the chicken bundles and brown on all four sides, about 2 minutes per side. Add the broth and reserved wine to the pan and bring to a boil. Reduce the heat to low, cover the pan, and cook until the center of the chicken registers 160 to 165 degrees on an instant-read thermometer, 12 to 18 minutes. Transfer the chicken to a carving board and tent loosely with foil.

6. FOR THE SAUCE: While the chicken rests, whisk the mustard into the cooking liquid. Increase the heat to high and simmer, scraping the pan bottom to loosen the browned bits, until dark brown and reduced to ½ cup, 7 to 10 minutes. Off the heat, whisk in the butter and the remaining 1½ teaspoons parsley and 1½ teaspoons lemon juice; season with salt and pepper to taste. Remove the twine and cut each chicken bundle on the bias into six medallions. Spoon the sauce over the chicken and serve.

NOTES FROM THE TEST KITCHEN

STUFFING CHICKEN BREASTS

1. Slice each breast horizontally, stopping ½ inch from the edges so the halves remain attached.

2. Open up each breast, cover it with plastic wrap, and pound it to an even ¼-inch thickness.

3. Trim about ½ inch from the long side of each cutlet to form an 8 by 5-inch rectangle. Reserve the trimmings for the stuffing.

4. Spread the stuffing evenly over each cutlet, leaving a ¾-inch border along the short sides and a ¼-inch border along the long sides.

5. With the short side facing you, roll up each cutlet and secure it snugly with twine.

FRENCH CHICKEN IN A POT

WHY THIS RECIPE WORKS: *Poulet en cocotte* (chicken in a pot) is a classic French specialty—at its best, it's a whole chicken baked with root vegetables in a covered pot that delivers incredibly tender and juicy meat. Sounds simple, but it's actually more challenging than throwing chicken in a pot with vegetables. One potential problem is too much moisture in the pot, which washes out the flavor; another pitfall is overcooking. We wanted chicken in a pot that delivered moist meat and satisfying flavor.

We removed the vegetables—the liquid they released made the pot too steamy—and cooked the chicken by itself (after browning it in a little oil to prevent it from sticking). We also tightly sealed the pot with foil before adding the lid. To keep the breast meat from drying out and becoming tough, we cooked the chicken very slowly. After developing the basic technique, we revisited the idea of vegetables, and found that a small amount of potently flavored aromatic vegetables could be added if they were lightly browned with the chicken to erase most of their moisture. Finally, defatting the liquid in the pot rewarded us with a richly flavored sauce.

French Chicken in a Pot

SERVES 4

The cooking times in the recipe are for a 4½ to 5-pound bird. A 3½ to 4½-pound chicken will take about an hour to cook, and a 5 to 6-pound bird will take close to 2 hours. We developed this recipe to work with a 5 to 8-quart Dutch oven with a tight-fitting lid. If using a 5-quart pot, do not cook a chicken larger than 5 pounds. If using a kosher chicken, reduce the amount of table salt to ½ teaspoon. If you choose not to serve the skin with the chicken, simply remove it before carving. The amount of sauce will vary depending on the size of the chicken; season it with about ¼ teaspoon lemon juice for every ¼ cup.

- 1 (4½ to 5-pound) whole chicken, giblets discarded, wings tucked under back (see note)
- 1 teaspoon table salt (see note)
- ¼ teaspoon ground black pepper
- 1 tablespoon olive oil
- 1 small onion, chopped medium
- 1 small celery rib, chopped medium
- 6 medium garlic cloves, peeled and trimmed
- 1 bay leaf
- 1 medium sprig fresh rosemary (optional)
- ½–1 teaspoon juice from 1 lemon (see note)

1. Adjust an oven rack to the lowest position and heat the oven to 250 degrees. Pat the chicken dry with paper towels and season with the salt and pepper.

2. Heat the oil in a large Dutch oven over medium heat until just smoking. Add the chicken, breast side down, and scatter the onion, celery, garlic cloves, bay leaf, and rosemary (if using) around the chicken. Cook until the breast is lightly browned, about 5 minutes. Flip the chicken breast side up and continue to cook until the chicken and vegetables are well browned, 6 to 8 minutes.

3. Off the heat, place a large sheet of foil over the pot and cover tightly with the lid. Transfer the pot to the oven and cook until the thickest part of the breast registers 160 to 165 degrees and the thickest part of the thighs registers 175 degrees on an instant-read thermometer, 1 hour and 20 minutes to 1 hour and 50 minutes.

4. Remove the pot from the oven. Transfer the chicken to a cutting board, tent loosely with foil, and let rest 20 minutes. Strain the chicken juices from the pot into a fat separator, pressing on the solids to extract the liquid; discard the solids (you should have about ¾ cup juices). Let the liquid settle 5 minutes, then pour into a saucepan and cook over low heat until hot. Carve the chicken, adding any accumulated juices to the saucepan. Season the sauce with lemon juice to taste (see note). Serve the chicken, passing the sauce separately.

COQ AU VIN

WHY THIS RECIPE WORKS: Although conventional recipes for *coq au vin* take upwards of three hours to prepare, we felt that this rustic dish shouldn't be so time-consuming. After all, it's basically a chicken fricassee. We wanted to create a dish with tender, juicy chicken infused with the flavors of red wine, onions, mushrooms, and bacon in under two hours.

We decided to use chicken parts; this way, we could pick the parts we liked best. If using a mix of dark and white meat, we found it's essential to start the dark before the white, so that all the meat finishes cooking at the same time and nothing is overcooked or undercooked. To thicken the stewing liquid, we sprinkled flour over the sautéed vegetables and whisked in butter toward the end of cooking; the butter also provided a nice richness in the sauce. Chicken broth added a savory note to the sauce and gave it some body; an entire bottle of red wine provided a great base of flavor. Tomato paste was a fuss-free way to add extra depth and body to the sauce, while a sprinkling of crisp, salty bacon rounded out the acidity of the wine.

Coq au Vin

SERVES 4

Use any $10 bottle of fruity, medium-bodied red wine such a Pinot Noir, Côtes du Rhône, or Zinfandel. If using both chicken breasts and thighs/drumsticks, we recommend cutting the breast pieces in half so that each person can have some white meat and dark meat. The breasts and thighs/drumsticks do not cook at the same rate; if using both, note that the breast pieces are added partway through the cooking time. Serve with egg noodles.

- 6 **ounces thick-cut bacon (about 5 slices), chopped medium**
  Vegetable oil, as needed
- 4 **pounds bone-in, skin-on chicken pieces (split breasts cut in half, drumsticks, and/or thighs; see note)**
  Table salt and ground black pepper
- 8 **ounces (about 2 cups) frozen pearl onions**
- 10 **ounces white mushrooms, wiped clean and quartered**
- 2 **medium garlic cloves, minced or pressed through a garlic press (about 2 teaspoons)**
- 1 **tablespoon tomato paste**
- 3 **tablespoons unbleached all-purpose flour**
- 1 **(750-milliliter) bottle medium-bodied red wine (see note)**
- 2½ **cups low-sodium chicken broth**
- 1 **teaspoon minced fresh thyme leaves or ¼ teaspoon dried**
- 2 **bay leaves**
- 2 **tablespoons unsalted butter, cut into 2 pieces, chilled**
- 2 **tablespoons minced fresh parsley leaves**

1. Fry the bacon in a large Dutch oven over medium heat until crisp, 5 to 7 minutes. Transfer the bacon to a paper towel–lined plate, leaving the fat in the pot (you should have about 2 tablespoons; if necessary, add vegetable oil to make this amount). Set aside.

2. Pat the chicken dry with paper towels and season with salt and pepper. Return the pot with the bacon fat to medium-high heat until shimmering. Brown half of the chicken on both sides, 5 to 8 minutes per side, reducing the heat if the pan begins to scorch. Transfer the chicken to a plate, leaving the fat in the pot. Return the pot to medium-high heat and repeat with the remaining chicken; transfer the chicken to the plate.

3. Pour off all but 1 tablespoon of the fat in the pot (or add vegetable oil if needed to make this amount). Add the onions and mushrooms and cook over medium heat, stirring occasionally, until lightly browned, about 10 minutes. Stir in the garlic and tomato paste and cook until fragrant, about 30 seconds. Stir in the flour and cook for 1 minute. Stir in the wine, broth, thyme, and bay leaves, scraping up any browned bits.

4. Nestle the chicken, along with any accumulated juices, into the pot and bring to a simmer. Cover, turn the heat to medium-low, and simmer until the chicken is tender and the thickest part of the breasts registers 160 to 165 degrees on an instant-read thermometer, about 20 minutes, or the thickest part of the thighs and drumsticks registers 175 degrees on an instant-read thermometer, about 1 hour. (If using both types of chicken, simmer the thighs and drumsticks for 40 minutes before adding the breasts.)

5. Transfer the chicken to a serving dish, tent loosely with foil, and let rest while finishing the sauce. Skim as much fat as possible off the surface of the sauce and return to a simmer until the sauce is thickened and measures about 2 cups, about 20 minutes. Off the heat, remove the bay leaves, whisk in the butter, and season with salt and pepper to taste. Pour the sauce over the chicken, sprinkle with the reserved bacon and the parsley, and serve.

CHICKEN WITH 40 CLOVES OF GARLIC

WHY THIS RECIPE WORKS: In most versions of chicken with 40 cloves of garlic, the garlic is soft and spreadable, but its flavor is spiritless. The chicken is tender, but the breast meat takes on a dry, chalky quality, and its flavor is washed out. We wanted to revisit this classic French dish to make it faster and better, so it would boast well-browned, full-flavored chicken, sweet and nutty garlic, and a savory sauce.

Using a cut-up chicken rather than a whole bird ensures that the meat cooks quickly and evenly. We roasted the garlic cloves first to caramelize them and develop their flavor, then added them to the braising liquid with the

CUTTING UP A WHOLE CHICKEN

Buying chicken parts is convenient, but packages often contain pieces of varying sizes. Cutting up a whole chicken yourself isn't difficult and it will guarantee evenly sized pieces of meat.

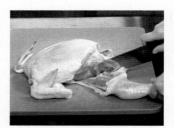

1. Using a chef's knife, cut off the legs, one at a time, by severing the joint between the leg and the body.

2. Cut each leg into two pieces—the drumstick and thigh—by slicing through the joint that connects them (marked by a thick white line of fat).

3. Flip the chicken over and remove the wings by slicing through each wing joint.

4. Turn the chicken (now without its legs and wings) on its side and, using scissors, remove the back from the chicken breast.

5. Flip the breast skin side down and, using a chef's knife, cut it in half through the breast plate (marked by a thin white line of cartilage), then cut each piece in half again.

chicken. Cooking it all with a two-part pan-roasting/braising technique kept the chicken moist, and finishing the chicken under the broiler made the chicken skin crispy. Some shallots and herbs added flavor to the sauce, and several roasted garlic cloves, smashed into a paste, thickened and flavored the sauce. A few tablespoons of butter, swirled in before serving, added richness.

Chicken with 40 Cloves of Garlic

SERVES 4

If using a kosher chicken, skip the brining process and begin with step 2. Avoid heads of garlic that have begun to sprout (the green shoots will make the sauce taste bitter). Tie the rosemary and thyme sprigs together with kitchen twine so they will be easy to retrieve from the pan. Serve the dish with slices of crusty baguette; you can spread them with the roasted garlic cloves.

> Table salt
> 1 (3½ to 4-pound) chicken, cut into 8 pieces (4 breast pieces, 2 thighs, 2 drumsticks) and trimmed
> Ground black pepper
> 3 medium heads garlic (about 8 ounces), outer papery skins removed, cloves separated and unpeeled (see note)
> 2 medium shallots, peeled and quartered
> 1 tablespoon olive oil
> ¾ cup dry vermouth or dry white wine
> ¾ cup low-sodium chicken broth
> 2 sprigs fresh thyme (see note)
> 1 sprig fresh rosemary (see note)
> 1 bay leaf
> 2 tablespoons unsalted butter

1. Adjust an oven rack to the middle position and heat the oven to 400 degrees. Dissolve ¼ cup salt in 2 quarts cold water in a large container; submerge the chicken in the brine, cover with plastic wrap, and refrigerate for 30 minutes. Remove the chicken from the brine, rinse, and pat dry with paper towels. Season both sides of the chicken pieces with pepper.

2. Meanwhile, combine the garlic, shallots, 2 teaspoons of the olive oil, and ½ teaspoon salt and ¼ teaspoon pepper to taste in a 9-inch pie plate; cover tightly with foil and roast until softened and beginning to brown, about 30 minutes, shaking the pan once halfway through cooking. Uncover, stir, and continue to roast, uncovered, until browned and fully tender, about 10 minutes longer, stirring once or twice. Remove from the oven and increase the oven temperature to 450 degrees.

3. Heat the remaining teaspoon oil in a 12-inch oven-safe skillet over medium-high heat until smoking. Brown the chicken, skin side down, until golden, about 5 minutes; flip the chicken pieces and brown until golden on the second side, about 4 minutes longer. Transfer the chicken to a large plate and pour off the fat from the skillet. Off the heat, add the vermouth, chicken broth, thyme, rosemary, and bay leaf to the pan, scraping up any browned bits. Set the skillet over medium heat, add the garlic mixture, and return the chicken, skin side up, to the pan, nestling the pieces on top of and between the garlic cloves. Place the skillet in the oven and roast until the thickest part of the breasts registers 160 to 165 degrees on an instant-read thermometer; remove the skillet from the oven.

4. Adjust an oven rack 6 inches from the broiler element and heat the broiler. Broil the chicken to crisp the skin, 3 to 5 minutes. Remove the skillet from the oven and transfer the chicken to a serving dish. Transfer 10 to 12 garlic cloves to a fine-mesh sieve and reserve. Using a slotted spoon, scatter the remaining garlic cloves and shallots around the chicken; discard the herbs. With a rubber spatula, push the reserved garlic cloves through the sieve and into a bowl; discard the skins. Add the garlic paste to the skillet and bring the liquid to a simmer over medium-high heat, whisking to incorporate the garlic. Whisk in the butter and season with salt and pepper to taste. Serve the chicken, passing the sauce separately.

CHICKEN PROVENÇAL

WHY THIS RECIPE WORKS: Chicken Provençal represents the best of rustic, peasant food—bone-in chicken is simmered all day in a tomatoey, garlicky herb broth. But all too often, this formula results in dry, rubbery chicken, watery or overly thick sauce, and dulled or muddied flavors. We wanted to rejuvenate this dish, and create a chicken dish that was meltingly tender, moist, and flavorful, napped in an aromatic, garlicky tomato sauce that we could mop up with a good loaf of crusty bread.

For the best flavor and most tender texture, we used bone-in chicken thighs and browned them in a sheer film of olive oil. Skinless thighs stuck to the pan, and skin-on thighs developed a flabby texture when braised later on. So we settled on a compromise—browning the thighs with the skin on (to develop rich flavor and leave browned bits in the pan), then ditching the skins prior to the braising (to avoid flab central). To keep the

sauce from becoming greasy, we spooned off the excess fat left behind from browning the chicken, but kept enough to sauté our garlic and onion. Diced tomatoes, white wine, and chicken broth also went into the sauce. We then braised the chicken until it was meltingly tender. As for flavor enhancers, a small amount of niçoise olives added an essential brininess to the dish, and some minced anchovy made the sauce taste richer and fuller.

Chicken Provençal

SERVES 4

This dish is often served with rice or slices of crusty bread, but soft polenta is also a good accompaniment. Niçoise olives are the preferred olives here; the flavor of kalamatas and other types of brined or oil-cured olives is too potent.

- 8 (5 to 6-ounce) bone-in, skin-on chicken thighs, trimmed
  Table salt
- 1 tablespoon extra-virgin olive oil
- 1 small onion, minced
- 6 medium garlic cloves, minced or pressed through a garlic press (about 2 tablespoons)
- 1 anchovy fillet, minced (about ½ teaspoon)
- ⅛ teaspoon cayenne pepper
- 1 cup dry white wine
- 1 cup low-sodium chicken broth
- 1 (14.5-ounce) can diced tomatoes, drained
- 2½ tablespoons tomato paste
- 1½ tablespoons chopped fresh thyme leaves
- 1 teaspoon chopped fresh oregano leaves
- 1 teaspoon herbes de Provence (optional)
- 1 bay leaf
- 1½ teaspoons grated zest from 1 lemon
- ½ cup pitted niçoise olives (see note)
- 1 tablespoon chopped fresh parsley leaves

1. Adjust an oven rack to the lower-middle position and heat the oven to 300 degrees. Season both sides of the chicken thighs with salt. Heat 1 teaspoon of the oil in a large Dutch oven over medium-high heat until shimmering. Add 4 chicken thighs, skin side down, and cook, without moving, until the skin is crisp and well browned, about 5 minutes. Flip the chicken pieces and brown on the second side, about 5 minutes longer; transfer to a large plate. Repeat with the remaining 4 chicken thighs, then transfer them to the plate and set aside. Discard all but 1 tablespoon of fat from the pot.

2. Add the onion to the pot and cook, stirring occasionally, over medium heat until softened and browned, about 4 minutes. Add the garlic, anchovy, and cayenne; cook, stirring constantly, until fragrant, about 1 minute. Add the wine, scraping up any browned bits. Stir in the chicken broth, tomatoes, tomato paste, thyme, oregano, herbes de Provence (if using), and bay leaf. Remove and discard the skin from the chicken thighs, then submerge the chicken pieces in the liquid and add the accumulated chicken juices to the pot. Increase the heat to high, bring to a simmer, cover, and set the pot in the oven; cook until the chicken offers no resistance when poked with a knife but is still clinging to the bones, about 1¼ hours.

3. Using a slotted spoon, transfer the chicken to a serving platter and tent loosely with foil. Discard the bay leaf. Set the pot over high heat, stir in 1 teaspoon of the lemon zest, bring to a boil, and cook, stirring occasionally, until slightly thickened and reduced to 2 cups, about 5 minutes. Stir in the olives and cook until heated through, about 1 minute. Combine the remaining ½ teaspoon zest and the parsley. Spoon the sauce over the chicken, drizzle the chicken with the remaining 2 teaspoons oil, sprinkle with the parsley mixture, and serve.

DAUBE PROVENÇAL

WHY THIS RECIPE WORKS: *Daube Provençal,* also known as daube Niçoise, has all the elements of the best French fare: tender beef, a luxurious sauce, and complex flavors. So why does it usually end up as beef stew with a few misplaced ingredients instead of being its own, coherent dish? We wanted to translate the flavors of Provence—olive oil, olives, garlic, wine, herbs, oranges, tomatoes, mushrooms, and anchovies—to an American home kitchen, and create a bold, brash, and full-flavored beef stew, with ingredients that married into a robust but unified dish.

We started with the test kitchen's reliable set of techniques to turn tough but flavorful beef into a tender stew: Brown the beef; add the aromatics; sprinkle some flour in the pan to thicken the braising liquid; deglaze with more cooking liquid; add the meat back to the pot; and finally, cover and cook slowly in the oven until tender. Technique established, we concentrated on selecting and managing the complex blend of ingredients that defines this dish. We chose briny niçoise olives, bright tomatoes, floral orange peel, and the regional flavors of thyme and bay. A few anchovies added complexity without a fishy taste, and salt pork contributed rich body. A whole bottle of wine added bold flavor and needed just a little cooking to tame its raw bite. Finally, to keep the meat from drying out during the long braising time required to create a complex-tasting sauce, we cut it into relatively large 2-inch pieces.

Daube Provençal

SERVES 4 TO 6

Serve this French beef stew with egg noodles or boiled potatoes. If niçoise olives are not available, kalamata olives, though not authentic, can be substituted. Cabernet Sauvignon is our favorite wine for this recipe, but Côtes du Rhône and Zinfandel also work. Our favorite cut of beef for this recipe is chuck-eye roast, but any boneless roast from the chuck will work. Because the tomatoes are added just before serving, it is preferable to use canned whole tomatoes and dice them yourself—uncooked, they are more tender than canned diced tomatoes. Once the salt pork, thyme, and bay leaves are removed in step 4, the daube can be cooled and refrigerated in an airtight container for up to 4 days. Before reheating, skim the hardened fat from the surface, then continue with the recipe.

¾ ounce dried porcini mushrooms, rinsed

1 (3½-pound) boneless beef chuck-eye roast, trimmed and cut into 2-inch chunks (see note)

1½ teaspoons table salt

1 teaspoon ground black pepper

4 tablespoons olive oil

5 ounces salt pork, rind removed

2 medium onions, halved and cut into ⅛-inch-thick slices (about 4 cups)

4 large carrots, peeled and cut into 1-inch-thick rounds (about 2 cups)

2 tablespoons tomato paste

4 medium garlic cloves, peeled and sliced thin

⅓ cup unbleached all-purpose flour

1 (750-milliliter) bottle bold red wine (see note)

1 cup low-sodium chicken broth

1 cup water

1 cup pitted niçoise olives, drained well (see note)

4 strips zest from 1 orange, each strip about 3 inches long, removed with a vegetable peeler, cleaned of white pith, and cut lengthwise into thin strips

2 anchovy fillets, minced (about 1 teaspoon)

5 sprigs fresh thyme, tied together with kitchen twine

2 bay leaves

1 (14.5-ounce) can whole tomatoes, drained and cut into ½-inch cubes (see note)

2 tablespoons minced fresh parsley leaves

1. Combine the mushrooms and 1 cup water in a small microwave-safe bowl; cover with plastic wrap, cut three vents for steam with a knife, and microwave on high power for 30 seconds. Let stand until the mushrooms soften, about 5 minutes. Lift the mushrooms from the liquid with a fork and chop into ½-inch pieces (you should have about 4 tablespoons). Strain the liquid through a fine-mesh strainer lined with a paper towel into a medium bowl. Set the mushrooms and liquid aside.

2. Adjust an oven rack to the lower-middle position and heat the oven to 325 degrees. Dry the beef thoroughly with paper towels, then season with the salt and pepper. Heat 2 tablespoons of the oil in a large heavy-bottomed Dutch oven over medium-high heat until just smoking; add half of the beef. Cook without moving the pieces until well browned, about 2 minutes on each side, for a total of 8 to 10 minutes, reducing the heat if the fat begins to smoke. Transfer the meat to a medium bowl. Repeat with the remaining 2 tablespoons oil and the remaining meat.

3. Reduce the heat to medium and add the salt pork, onions, carrots, tomato paste, and garlic to the now-empty pot; cook, stirring occasionally, until light brown, about 2 minutes. Stir in the flour and cook, stirring constantly, about 1 minute. Slowly add the wine, gently scraping up any browned bits. Add the broth, water, and beef with any juices. Increase the heat to medium-high and bring to a simmer. Add the mushrooms and their liquid, ½ cup of the olives, the orange zest, anchovies, thyme, and bay leaves, distributing evenly and arranging the beef so it is completely covered by the liquid; partially cover the pot and place in the oven. Cook until a fork inserted in the beef meets little resistance (the meat should not be falling apart), 2½ to 3 hours.

4. Discard the salt pork, thyme, and bay leaves. Add the tomatoes and the remaining ½ cup olives; warm over medium-high heat until heated through, about 1 minute. Cover the pot and allow the stew to settle, about 5 minutes. Using a spoon, skim the excess fat from the surface of the stew. Stir in the parsley and serve.

BEEF BURGUNDY

WHY THIS RECIPE WORKS: Leave it to the French to make beef stew into an elegant affair. Unfortunately, when translated to the home kitchen, classic, intensely flavorful beef burgundy, also known as *boeuf bourguignon*, tends to lose its appeal. We've seen too many versions of this rustic French dish with tough meat or a dull sauce and no flavor complexity. We wanted to bring this dish to its earthy, robust, warm potential: satisfyingly large chunks of tender meat draped with a velvety sauce brimming with the flavor of good Burgundy wine and studded with caramelized mushrooms and pearl onions.

We started by rendering salt pork until crisp, then browned large chunks of beef chuck roast in the rendered fat. For the braising liquid, a combination of chicken broth and water, enhanced with a small amount of dried porcini mushrooms and tomato paste, provided balanced, well-rounded flavor. Using anything less than a full bottle of red wine (preferably a Burgundy, but a good Pinot Noir will suffice) left the sauce lacking and unremarkable. We deglazed the pan twice, used a roux to thicken the sauce, and then added the wine. Wrapping the aromatic vegetables in cheesecloth made it easy to remove them from the braising liquid. While the liquid reduced to a velvety sauce, we simmered pearl onions then sautéed them briefly with mushrooms to create the perfect garnish for our rich, tender beef.

Beef Burgundy

SERVES 6

Thick-cut bacon can be substituted for the salt pork; cut the bacon crosswise into ¼-inch pieces and treat it just as you would the salt pork, but note that you will have no rind to include in the vegetable and herb pouch. Boiled potatoes are the traditional accompaniment, but mashed potatoes or buttered noodles are nice as well.

STEW

- 6 ounces salt pork, trimmed of rind and rind reserved, salt pork cut into ¼-inch pieces (see note)
- 2 medium onions, chopped coarse
- 2 medium carrots, chopped coarse
- 1 medium head garlic, cloves separated and crushed but unpeeled
- 10 sprigs fresh parsley, torn into pieces
- 6 sprigs fresh thyme
- 2 bay leaves, crumbled
- ½ teaspoon black peppercorns
- ½ ounce dried porcini mushrooms, rinsed (optional)
- 1 (4 to 4½-pound) boneless beef chuck-eye roast, trimmed and cut into 2-inch chunks

  Table salt and ground black pepper
- 2½ cups water
- 4 tablespoons (½ stick) unsalted butter, cut into 4 pieces
- ⅓ cup unbleached all-purpose flour
- 1¾ cups low-sodium chicken broth
- 1 (750-milliliter) bottle red Burgundy or Pinot Noir
- 1 teaspoon tomato paste
- 2 tablespoons brandy
- 3 tablespoons minced fresh parsley leaves

ONION AND MUSHROOM GARNISH

- 7 ounces (about 1¾ cups) frozen pearl onions
- ¾ cup water
- 1 tablespoon unsalted butter
- 1 tablespoon sugar
- ½ teaspoon table salt
- 10 ounces medium white mushrooms, wiped clean and halved

1. FOR THE STEW: Bring the salt pork, reserved salt pork rind, and 3 cups water to a boil in a medium saucepan over high heat. Boil 2 minutes, then drain well.

2. Lay a double layer of cheesecloth (each piece should measure 22 by 8 inches) in a medium bowl, placing the sheets perpendicular to each other. Place the onions, carrots, garlic, parsley pieces, thyme, bay leaves, peppercorns, porcini mushrooms (if using), and salt pork rind in the cheesecloth-lined bowl. Gather together the edges of the cheesecloth and fasten them securely with kitchen twine; trim the excess cheesecloth with scissors if necessary. Set the pouch in a large ovensafe Dutch oven. Adjust the oven rack to the lower-middle position and heat oven to 300 degrees.

3. Cook the salt pork in a 12-inch skillet over medium heat until lightly browned and crisp, about 12 minutes. With a slotted spoon, transfer the salt pork to the pot. Pour off and reserve all but 2 teaspoons of the fat from the skillet. Pat the beef dry with paper towels and season with salt and pepper. Add half of the beef to the skillet, increase the heat to high, and brown in a single layer, turning once or twice, until deep brown, about 7 minutes; transfer the browned beef to the pot. Add ½ cup of the water to the skillet and scrape the pan with a wooden spoon to loosen the browned bits; add the liquid to the pot.

4. Heat 2 teaspoons of the reserved pork fat in the skillet over high heat until smoking. Add the remaining beef in a single layer, turning once or twice, until deep brown, about 7 minutes; transfer the browned beef to the pot. Add ½ cup more water to the skillet and scrape the pan with a wooden spoon to loosen the browned bits; add the liquid to the pot.

5. Melt the butter in the skillet over medium heat. Whisk in the flour and cook, stirring constantly, until light brown, about 5 minutes. Gradually whisk in the chicken broth and the remaining 1½ cups water. Increase the heat to medium-high and bring to a simmer, stirring frequently, until thickened; add the mixture to the pot. Add 3 cups of the wine and the tomato paste to the pot and season with salt and pepper to taste; stir to combine. Set the pot over high heat and bring to a boil; cover and place in the oven. Cook until the meat is tender, 2½ to 3 hours.

6. Remove the pot from the oven and transfer the vegetable and herb pouch to a mesh strainer; set the strainer over the pot. Using the back of a spoon, press the liquid from the pouch into the pot; discard the pouch. With a slotted spoon, transfer the beef to a medium bowl; set aside. Let the pot contents settle about 15 minutes, then skim off and discard the fat.

7. Bring the liquid in the pot to a boil over medium-high heat. Simmer, stirring occasionally, until thickened and reduced to about 3 cups, 15 to 25 minutes.

8. FOR THE ONION AND MUSHROOM GARNISH: Meanwhile, bring the pearl onions, ½ cup of the water, the butter, sugar, and ¼ teaspoon of the salt to a boil in a 10-inch skillet over high heat. Cover, reduce the heat to medium-low, and simmer, shaking the pan occasionally, until the onions are tender, about 5 minutes. Uncover, increase the heat to high, and simmer until all the liquid evaporates, about 3 minutes. Add the mushrooms and the remaining ¼ teaspoon salt. Cook, stirring occasionally, until the liquid released by the mushrooms evaporates and the vegetables are browned, about 5 minutes. Transfer the vegetables to a bowl and set aside. Add the remaining ¼ cup water to the skillet and scrape the pan with a wooden spoon to loosen the browned bits; add the liquid to the reducing sauce.

9. When the sauce has reduced, reduce the heat to medium-low and stir in the beef, the remaining 2 tablespoons wine, the brandy, and mushrooms and onions (and any accumulated juices). Cover the pot and cook until heated through, 5 to 8 minutes. Season with salt and pepper to taste and serve, sprinkling individual servings with the parsley.

SLOW-COOKER BEEF BURGUNDY

WHY THIS RECIPE WORKS: Given the amount of simmering time required for classic Beef Burgundy (page 268), we thought this stew could be easily morphed into a slow-cooker adaptation that would have the same tender beef chunks and rich, earthy sauce as the original.

For a long braise, chuck roast cut into pieces is the best choice. The usual first step in making a stew is to brown the meat, but we found that we could get the same meaty flavor base from browning only half the beef. We used rendered bacon fat instead of oil; the bacon would go back into the stew at the end, lending a smoky note. Sautéed carrots and onions went into the slow-cooker insert next, with plenty of garlic, thyme, and tomato paste to withstand the long cooking time. As our braising liquid, beef broth tasted tinny but chicken broth worked well. We mixed it with red wine and a surprising ingredient, soy sauce, which intensified the savory flavors in the stew as well as deepened its color. To enrich the sauce, we stirred in a small amount of tapioca, a common thickening agent, in place of flour. We prepared the traditional onion and mushroom garnish separately, when the stew was almost finished cooking, and folded it in. The final touch was more red wine, which we reduced first so that it wouldn't impart a sour

alcoholic taste. This slow-cooker beef burgundy had everything we would expect from the refined French original.

Slow-Cooker Beef Burgundy
SERVES 6 TO 8

Make sure to use the low setting on your slow cooker; the stew will burn on the high setting. Don't spend a lot of money for the wine in this recipe—in our testing, we found that California Pinot Noir wines in the $6 to $20 price range worked just fine. Boiled potatoes are the traditional accompaniment, but mashed potatoes or buttered noodles are nice as well.

STEW

- 8 ounces (about 8 slices) bacon, cut into ¼-inch pieces
- 1 (4-pound) boneless beef chuck-eye roast, trimmed and cut into 1½-inch chunks
  Table salt and ground black pepper
- 1 large onion, minced
- 2 carrots, peeled and minced
- 8 medium garlic cloves, minced or pressed through a garlic press (about 2 tablespoons plus 2 teaspoons)
- 2 teaspoons chopped fresh thyme leaves
- 4 tablespoons tomato paste
- 2½ cups Pinot Noir (see note)
- 1½ cups low-sodium chicken broth
- ⅓ cup soy sauce
- 3 bay leaves
- 3 tablespoons Minute tapioca
- 3 tablespoons minced fresh parsley leaves

ONION AND MUSHROOM GARNISH

- 8 ounces (about 2 cups) frozen pearl onions
- ½ cup water
- 5 tablespoons unsalted butter
- 1 tablespoon sugar
- 10 ounces white mushrooms, wiped clean and quartered
  Table salt

1. FOR THE STEW: Cook the bacon in a 12-inch skillet over medium-high heat until crisp. Using a slotted spoon, transfer the bacon to a paper towel–lined plate and refrigerate. Pour half of the bacon fat into a small bowl; set the skillet with the remaining bacon fat aside.

2. Pat the beef dry with paper towels and season with salt and pepper; place half of the beef in a slow-cooker insert. Heat the skillet with the remaining bacon fat over medium-high heat until smoking. Cook the remaining beef in a single layer until deep brown on all sides, about 8 minutes. Transfer the browned beef to the slow-cooker insert.

3. Add the reserved bacon fat to the now-empty skillet and heat over medium-high heat until shimmering. Add the onion, carrots, and ¼ teaspoon salt and cook until the vegetables begin to brown, about 5 minutes. Add the garlic and thyme and cook until fragrant, about 30 seconds. Add the tomato paste and stir until beginning to brown, about 45 seconds. Transfer the mixture to the slow-cooker insert.

4. Return the now-empty skillet to high heat and add 1½ cups of the wine, the chicken broth, and soy sauce. Simmer, scraping up any browned bits, about 1 minute. Transfer the wine mixture to the slow-cooker insert.

5. Stir the bay leaves and tapioca into the slow-cooker insert. Set the slow cooker on low, cover, and cook until the meat is fork-tender, about 9 hours.

6. FOR THE ONION AND MUSHROOM GARNISH: Bring the pearl onions, water, butter, and sugar to a boil in a 12-inch skillet over high heat. Cover and simmer over medium-low heat until the onions are tender, about 5 minutes. Uncover, increase the heat to high, and cook until the liquid evaporates, about 3 minutes. Add the mushrooms and ¼ teaspoon salt and cook until the vegetables are browned and glazed, about 5 minutes.

7. When ready to serve, discard the bay leaves and stir in the onion and mushroom garnish and the reserved bacon. Bring the remaining 1 cup wine to a boil in a 12-inch skillet over high heat and simmer until reduced by half, about 5 minutes. Stir the reduced wine and parsley into the stew and season with salt and pepper to taste. Serve.

CASSOULET

WHY THIS RECIPE WORKS: Comforting and delectable as it is, cassoulet is just too much trouble for most cooks. It can take three days to make, and the ingredients can be both hard to find and difficult to prepare. We wanted to see if there was a way to streamline the preparation of this dish without compromising its essential character.

Instead of duck confit, which is difficult to find and time-consuming to prepare, we brined chicken thighs and cooked them in bacon fat to simulate the smoky flavor and moist texture of the confit. With our mock confit lined up, the other elements fell into place. We decided on the flavorful, fatty blade-end pork roast for stewing, dried beans instead of canned beans (canned beans were out because they fell apart during cooking), and smoky kielbasa for the sausage component (the classically correct French sausage was too hard to find). We cooked the beans with onion and garlic to season them, then added some crisp bacon to infuse them with a salty smokiness. Cooking the dish entirely on the stove at a slow simmer, with a quick finish to brown our homemade croutons, gave us a quick and easy cassoulet that was worthy of the name.

Simplified Cassoulet with Pork and Kielbasa

SERVES 8

This dish can be made without brining the chicken, but we recommend that you do so. To ensure the most time-efficient preparation of the cassoulet, while the chicken is brining and the beans are simmering, prepare the remaining ingredients. Look for dried flageolet beans in specialty food stores. You can substitute a boneless Boston butt for the boneless blade-end pork loin roast. Additional salt is not necessary because the brined chicken adds a good deal of it, but if you skip the brining step, add salt to taste before serving.

CHICKEN

- 1 cup sugar
- ½ cup table salt
- 10 (5 to 6-ounce) bone-in, skin-on chicken thighs, trimmed and skin removed (see note)

BEANS

- 1 pound dried flageolet or great Northern beans, picked over and rinsed (see note)
- 1 medium onion, peeled plus 1 small onion, minced
- 1 medium head garlic, outer papery skin removed and top ½ inch sliced off plus 2 medium garlic cloves, minced or pressed through a garlic press (about 2 teaspoons)
- 1 teaspoon table salt
    Ground black pepper
- 6 ounces (about 6 slices) bacon, cut into ¼-inch pieces
- 1 (1-pound) boneless blade-end pork loin roast, trimmed and cut into 1-inch pieces (see note)
- 1 (14.5-ounce) can diced tomatoes, drained
- 1 tablespoon tomato paste
- 1 large sprig fresh thyme
- 1 bay leaf
- ¼ teaspoon ground cloves
- 3½ cups low-sodium chicken broth
- 1½ cups dry white wine
- ½ pound kielbasa, halved lengthwise and cut into ¼-inch slices

CROUTONS

- 6 slices high-quality white sandwich bread, cut into ½-inch cubes
- 3 tablespoons unsalted butter, melted

1. FOR THE CHICKEN: Dissolve the sugar and salt in 1 quart cold water in a gallon-size zipper-lock bag. Add the chicken, pressing out as much air as possible, seal the bag, and refrigerate for 1 hour. Remove the chicken from the brine, rinse, and pat dry with paper towels. Refrigerate until ready to use.

2. FOR THE BEANS: Bring the beans, the peeled onion, head of garlic, salt, ¼ teaspoon pepper, and 8 cups water to a boil in a large Dutch oven over high heat. Cover, reduce the heat to medium-low, and simmer until the beans are almost tender, 1¼ to 1½ hours. Drain the beans; discard the onion and garlic.

3. While the beans are cooking, fry the bacon in a large Dutch oven over medium heat until just beginning to crisp and most of the fat has rendered, 5 to 6 minutes. Using a slotted spoon, add half of the bacon to the pot with the beans; transfer the remaining bacon to a paper towel–lined plate and set aside. Increase the heat to medium-high and add half of the chicken, skinned side down; cook until lightly browned, 4 to 5 minutes. Flip the chicken thighs and cook until lightly browned on the second side, 3 to 4 minutes longer. Transfer the chicken to a large plate; repeat with the remaining thighs and set aside. Pour off all but 2 tablespoons fat from the pot. Return the pot to medium heat; add the pork pieces and cook, stirring occasionally, until lightly browned, about 5 minutes. Add the minced onion and cook, stirring occasionally, until softened, 3 to 4 minutes. Add the minced garlic, tomatoes, tomato paste, thyme, bay leaf, cloves, and pepper to taste and cook until fragrant, about 1 minute. Stir in the chicken broth and wine, scraping up any browned bits. Submerge the chicken in the pot, adding any accumulated juices, increase the heat to high, and bring to a boil. Reduce the heat to low, cover, and simmer, for 40 minutes. Uncover and continue to simmer until the chicken and pork are fully tender, 20 to 30 minutes more.

4. FOR THE CROUTONS: While the chicken is simmering, adjust an oven rack to the lower-middle position and heat the oven to 400 degrees. Toss the bread cubes with the butter and spread out over a rimmed baking sheet. Bake until light golden brown and crisp, 8 to 12 minutes. Cool to room temperature; set aside (do not turn off the oven).

5. Gently stir the kielbasa, drained beans, and reserved bacon into the pot with the chicken and pork; remove and discard the thyme and bay leaf and season with pepper to taste (see note). Sprinkle the croutons evenly over the surface and bake, uncovered, until the croutons are deep golden brown, about 15 minutes. Let stand 10 minutes; serve.

WHY THE TEST KITCHEN IS FOND OF FOND AND WHY YOU SHOULD BE, TOO

Ever wonder how restaurants make rich sauces to accompany sautéed cutlets and steaks? Chances are it's a pan sauce, made with the delicious caramelized browned bits (called fond) that sit on the bottom of the pan after the meat has been sautéed or pan-seared.

Pan sauces are usually made by adding liquid (broth, wine, or juice) to the pan once the cooked cutlets or steaks have been transferred to a plate to rest. The liquid dissolves the fond (a process known as deglazing) and incorporates it into the sauce.

So what makes those browned bits so flavorful and so valuable? When meat or chicken browns, a process called the Maillard reaction occurs. This process is named after the French chemist who first described this reaction about 100 years ago. When the amino acids (or protein components) and natural sugars in meat are subjected to intense heat, like that found in a skillet, they begin to combine and form new compounds. These compounds in turn break down and form yet more new flavor compounds, and so on and so on, like rabbits multiplying. The browned bits left in the pan once the meat has been cooked are packed with complex flavors, which in turn are carried over to the pan sauce once the fond has been dissolved. And fond isn't limited to just pan sauces—we also rely on fond to flavor braises, as well as other dishes where meat is browned, such as soups and stews.

STEAK AU POIVRE

WHY THIS RECIPE WORKS: Steak au poivre is often nothing more than uninspired skillet steak. We were after the real thing—a perfectly cooked steak with a well-seared crust of pungent, cracked peppercorns and a silky sauce.

The trick to successful steak au poivre is coating just one side of the steaks with peppercorns and cooking the steaks on the uncoated side as long as possible to promote browning and prevent scorching of the peppercorns. With the first side browned, the steaks can be flipped and cooked for less time on the peppered side. Pressing the steaks with a cake pan once they have been placed in the hot skillet ensures that the peppercorns stick. After the steaks were done to our liking, we made a simple pan sauce with a mixture of beef broth and chicken broth that we first reduced, then flavored with brandy and lemon

juice. Cream made the sauce luxurious and gave it some substance; butter whisked in at the end brought silkiness.

Steak au Poivre with Brandied Cream Sauce

SERVES 4

To save time, crush the peppercorns and trim the steaks while the broth mixture simmers. Many pepper mills do not have a sufficiently coarse setting. In that case, crush peppercorns with the back of a heavy pan. See page 589 for information on our top-rated pepper mill.

- 4 tablespoons (½ stick) unsalted butter
- 1 medium shallot, minced (about 3 tablespoons)
- 1 cup beef broth
- ¾ cup low-sodium chicken broth
- 4 (8 to 10-ounce) strip steaks, ¾ to 1 inch thick, trimmed
  Table salt
- 4 teaspoons black peppercorns, crushed (see note)
- 1 tablespoon vegetable oil
- ¼ cup plus 1 tablespoon brandy
- ¼ cup heavy cream
- 1 teaspoon juice from 1 lemon or 1 teaspoon champagne vinegar

1. Melt 1 tablespoon of the butter in a 12-inch skillet over medium heat. Add the shallot and cook, stirring occasionally, until softened, about 2 minutes. Add the beef and chicken broths and bring to a boil over high heat; cook until reduced to ½ cup, about 8 minutes. Transfer the broth mixture to a small bowl; wipe out the skillet with paper towels.

2. Meanwhile, pat the steaks dry with paper towels and season with salt. Sprinkle one side of each steak with 1 teaspoon of the crushed peppercorns and press them into the steaks with your fingers to adhere.

3. Heat the oil in the skillet over medium-high heat until just smoking. Carefully lay the steaks in the skillet, peppered side up. Press on the steaks with the bottom of a cake pan and cook until well-browned on the first side, 3 to 5 minutes. Flip the steaks over and continue to cook, pressing again with the cake pan, until the center of the steaks registers 120 degrees on an instant-read thermometer for rare (3 minutes), 125 degrees for medium-rare (4 minutes), or 130 degrees for medium (5 minutes). Transfer the steaks to a plate, tent loosely with foil, and let rest while making the sauce.

4. Pour off any fat left in the pan and remove any stray peppercorns. Add the broth mixture, ¼ cup of the brandy, and the cream to the skillet and bring to a boil over high heat, scraping up any browned bits. Simmer until golden brown and thickened, about 5 minutes. Off the heat, whisk in the remaining 3 tablespoons butter, the remaining 1 tablespoon brandy, the lemon juice, and any accumulated meat juices from the plate; season with salt to taste. Spoon the sauce over the steaks and serve immediately.

STEAK DIANE

WHY THIS RECIPE WORKS: For a different spin on the usual pan-seared steaks, we turn to the French classic, steak Diane. But the demanding rich sauce is based on an all-day veal stock reduction—then the steaks still have to be cooked (if you have the energy, that is), and the sauce completed. We aimed to determine the right cut of steak, create a lighter, less labor-intensive sauce, and find a fool-proof method for cooking the meat.

For a rich sauce base that mimics the complexity of labor-intensive veal stock in a fraction of the time, we used a flavorful combination of sautéed tomato paste, aromatics such as garlic, onion, and carrots, both beef broth and chicken broth, red wine, peppercorns, and herbs. Omitting the traditional cream allowed the sauce to fully develop in intensity, and the inclusion of cognac gave the sauce a slightly sweet, complex flavor. For the meat, we selected strip steaks for great beefy flavor and ease of preparation. To brown the steaks evenly and develop enough fond (the flavorful browned meaty bits that cling to the pan and give pan sauces their rich, meaty flavor), we weighted the steaks with a heavy-bottomed skillet when cooking the second side.

Steak Diane

SERVES 4

If you prefer not to make the sauce base (recipe follows), mix ½ cup glace de viande with ¾ cup water and ¼ cup red wine and use this mixture in place of the base in step 2. Glace de viande is meat stock, in this case veal stock, that's been reduced to a thick syrup; we recommend Provimi Glace de Veau and CulinArte' Bonewerks Glace de Veau. Before preparing the sauce, read "Tips for Fearless Flambé" on page 274, or, if you do not wish to flambé, simmer the cognac in step 2 for 10 to 15 seconds for a slightly less sweet flavor profile.

STEAKS

- **4 (12-ounce) strip steaks, 1 to 1¼ inch thick, trimmed**
  Table salt and ground black pepper
- **2 tablespoons vegetable oil**

SAUCE

- **1 tablespoon vegetable oil**
- **1 small shallot, minced (about 1 tablespoon)**
- **¼ cup cognac**
- **1 recipe Sauce Base for Steak Diane (recipe follows; see note)**
- **2 teaspoons Dijon mustard**
- **2 tablespoons unsalted butter, chilled**
- **1 teaspoon Worcestershire sauce**
- **2 tablespoons minced fresh chives**
  Table salt and ground black pepper

1. FOR THE STEAKS: Cover the steaks with plastic wrap and use a meat pounder to pound them to an even ½-inch thickness; season them with salt and pepper. Heat 1 tablespoon of the oil in a 12-inch skillet over medium-high heat until smoking. Place 2 steaks in the skillet and cook until well browned, about 1½ minutes. Flip the steaks and weight with a heavy-bottomed pan; continue to cook until well browned on the second side, about 1½ minutes longer. Transfer the steaks to a plate and tent with foil. Add the remaining tablespoon oil to the skillet and repeat with the remaining steaks; transfer the second batch of steaks to the plate.

2. FOR THE SAUCE: Off the heat, add the oil and shallot to the skillet. Using the skillet's residual heat, cook, stirring frequently, until the shallot is slightly softened and browned, about 45 seconds. Add the cognac and let stand until the cognac warms slightly, about 10 seconds, then set

TIPS FOR FEARLESS FLAMBÉ

Flambéing is more than just tableside theatrics: As dramatic as it looks, igniting alcohol actually helps develop a deeper, more complex flavor in sauces—thanks to flavor-boosting chemical reactions that occur only at the high temperatures reached in flambéing. But accomplishing this feat at home can be daunting. Here are some tips for successful—and safe—flambéing at home.

BE PREPARED: Turn off the exhaust fan, tie back long hair, and have a lid at the ready to smother flare-ups.

USE THE PROPER EQUIPMENT: A pan with flared sides (such as a skillet) rather than straight sides will allow more oxygen to mingle with the alcohol vapors, increasing the chance that you'll spark the desired flame. If possible, use long chimney matches, and light the alcohol with your arm extended to full length.

IGNITE WARM ALCOHOL: If the alcohol becomes too hot, the vapors can rise to dangerous heights, causing large flare-ups once lit. Inversely, if the alcohol is too cold, there won't be enough vapors to light at all. We found that heating alcohol to 100 degrees Fahrenheit (best achieved by adding alcohol to a hot pan off heat and letting it sit for five to 10 seconds) produced the most moderate, yet long-burning, flames.

IF A FLARE-UP SHOULD OCCUR: Simply slide the lid over the top of the skillet (coming in from the side of, rather than over, the flames) to put out the fire quickly. Let the alcohol cool down and start again.

IF THE ALCOHOL WON'T LIGHT: If the pan is full of other ingredients (as is the case in Crêpes Suzette, page 551), the potency of the alcohol can be diminished as it becomes incorporated. For a more foolproof flame, ignite the alcohol in a separate small skillet or saucepan; once the flame has burned off, add the reduced alcohol to the remaining ingredients.

the skillet over high heat. Wave a lit match over the skillet until the cognac ignites, shaking the skillet until the flames subside, then simmer the cognac until reduced to about 1 tablespoon, about 10 seconds. Add the sauce base and mustard and simmer until slightly thickened and reduced to 1 cup, 2 to 3 minutes. Whisk in the butter. Off the heat, add the Worcestershire sauce, any accumulated juices from the steaks, and 1 tablespoon of the chives. Season with salt and pepper to taste.

3. Serve immediately, spooning 2 tablespoons sauce and sprinkling a portion of the remaining chives over each steak, and passing the remaining sauce separately.

Sauce Base for Steak Diane

MAKES 1¼ CUPS

This recipe yields a sauce base that is an excellent facsimile of a demi-glace, a very labor-intensive and time-consuming classic French sauce base. Because the sauce base is very concentrated, make sure to use low-sodium chicken and beef broths; otherwise, the base may be unpalatably salty.

    2 tablespoons vegetable oil
    4 teaspoons tomato paste
    2 small onions, chopped medium
    1 medium carrot, chopped medium
    4 medium garlic cloves, peeled
    ¼ cup water
    4 teaspoons unbleached all-purpose flour
  1½ cups dry red wine
  3½ cups low-sodium beef broth (see note)
  1¾ cups low-sodium chicken broth (see note)
    2 teaspoons black peppercorns
    8 sprigs fresh thyme
    2 bay leaves

1. Heat the oil and tomato paste in a Dutch oven over medium-high heat and cook, stirring constantly, until the paste begins to brown, about 3 minutes. Add the onions, carrot, and garlic and cook, stirring frequently, until the mixture is reddish brown, about 2 minutes. Add 2 tablespoons of the water and continue to cook, stirring constantly, until the mixture is well browned, about 3 minutes, adding the remaining 2 tablespoons water as needed to prevent scorching. Add the flour and cook, stirring constantly, about 1 minute. Add the wine, scraping up the browned bits on the bottom and sides of the pot; bring to a boil, stirring occasionally (the mixture will thicken slightly). Add the beef and chicken broths, peppercorns, thyme, and bay leaves; bring to a boil and cook, uncovered, occasionally scraping the bottom and sides of the pot with a spatula, until reduced to 2½ cups, 35 to 40 minutes.

2. Strain the mixture through a fine-mesh strainer, pressing on the solids to extract as much liquid as possible; you should have about 1¼ cups. (The sauce base can be refrigerated in an airtight container for up to 3 days.)

FISH MEUNIÈRE

WHY THIS RECIPE WORKS: Fish meunière typically features pale, soggy fillets in pools of greasy sauce—that is, if the fish doesn't stick to the pan or fall apart as it is plated. We wanted perfectly cooked fillets that were delicately crisp and golden brown on the outside and moist and flavorful on the inside, napped in a buttery yet light sauce.

Whole Dover sole is the most authentic choice, but it's also hard to come by and prohibitively expensive; either sole or flounder fillets are good stand-ins. To prevent the likelihood of overcooking the fish, the fillets need to be no less than ⅜ inch thick. The fillets must be patted dry before being seasoned with salt and pepper and dredged in flour (no need for eggs and bread crumbs). Using a nonstick skillet for pan-frying meant there was less chance for our fillets to fall apart; lubricating the pan with a mixture of oil and butter added extra insurance. Removing the pan from the heat just before the fish was cooked prevented the fish from being dry (the fish will continue to cook off the heat). Butter browned in a traditional skillet (so the changing color is easy to monitor) and brightened with lemon juice made the ideal accompaniment to our crispy, golden fillets.

Fish Meunière with Browned Butter and Lemon
SERVES 4

Try to purchase fillets that are of similar size, and avoid those that weigh less than 5 ounces because they will cook too quickly. When placing the fillets in the skillet, be sure to place them skinned-side up so that the opposite side, which had bones, will brown first. To flip the fillets while cooking, use two spatulas; gently lift one side of the fillet with one spatula, then support the fillet with the other spatula and gently flip it so that the browned side faces up. A nonstick skillet ensures that the fillets will release from the pan, but for the sauce a traditional skillet is preferable because its light-colored surface will allow you to monitor the color of the butter as it browns.

FISH
- ½ cup unbleached all-purpose flour
- 4 (5 to 6-ounce) sole or flounder fillets, ⅜ inch thick (see note)
- Table salt and ground black pepper
- 2 tablespoons vegetable oil
- 2 tablespoons unsalted butter, cut into 2 pieces

BROWNED BUTTER
- 4 tablespoons (½ stick) unsalted butter, cut into 4 pieces
- 1 tablespoon chopped fresh parsley leaves
- 1½ tablespoons juice from 1 lemon
- Table salt
- Lemon wedges, for serving

1. FOR THE FISH: Adjust an oven rack to the lower-middle position, set four heatproof dinner plates on the rack, and heat the oven to 200 degrees. Place the flour in a large baking dish. Pat the fillets dry with paper towels and season with salt and pepper; let stand until the fillets are glistening with moisture, about 5 minutes. Coat both sides of the fillets with flour, shake off the excess, and place in a single layer on a rimmed baking sheet.

2. Heat 1 tablespoon of the oil in a 12-inch nonstick skillet over high heat until shimmering; add 1 tablespoon of the butter and swirl to coat the pan bottom. Carefully place 2 fillets, skinned side up, in the skillet. Immediately reduce the heat to medium-high and cook, without moving the fish, until the edges of the fillets are opaque and the bottoms are golden brown, about 3 minutes. Using two spatulas, gently flip the fillets and cook on the second side until the thickest part of the fillet easily separates into flakes when a toothpick is inserted, about 2 minutes longer. Transfer the fillets to two of the heated dinner plates, keeping them boned side up, and return the plates to the oven. Wipe out the skillet and repeat with the remaining tablespoon oil, remaining tablespoon butter, and the remaining fish fillets.

3. FOR THE BROWNED BUTTER: Melt the butter in a 10-inch traditional skillet over medium-high heat. Continue to cook, swirling the pan constantly, until the butter is golden brown and has a nutty aroma, 1 to 1½ minutes; remove the skillet from the heat. Remove the plates from the oven and sprinkle the fillets with the parsley. Add the lemon juice to the browned butter and season with salt to taste. Spoon the sauce over the fish and serve immediately, garnished with the lemon wedges.

SCOVILLE SCALE

Cherry   New Mexico Green   Anaheim   Poblano   Jalapeño   Banana   Serrano

CHAPTER 15

TEX-MEX TONIGHT

Fresh Margaritas   278

Sangria   278

Cheesy Nachos with
Guacamole and Salsa   279

   One-Minute Salsa

Chunky Guacamole   280

Quesadillas   281

Tortilla Soup   281

Black Bean Soup   283

Beef Tacos   284

   Home-Fried Taco Shells

Steak Tacos   285

   Sweet and Spicy
   Pickled Onions

Chicken Fajitas   287

Steak Fajitas   288

Chicken Enchiladas with
Red Chili Sauce   289

Enchiladas Verdes   290

Mexican Pulled Pork
(Carnitas)   292

Mexican Rice   292

Beef Chili with Kidney
Beans   293

Chili Con Carne   294

White Chicken Chili   295

Huevos Rancheros   297

   Refried Beans

MARGARITAS

WHY THIS RECIPE WORKS: The typical margarita tends to be a slushy, headache-inducing concoction made with little more than ice, tequila, and artificially flavored corn syrup. We wanted a margarita with a balanced blend of fresh citrus flavors and tequila.

We found that the key was using the right proportions of alcohol and citrus juice—equal parts of each one. For a mellow, delicate flavor, we preferred reposado tequila, made from 100 percent blue agave, which is aged about 12 months. Unaged tequilas gave our margaritas a raw, harsh flavor. And those made with superpremium tequilas, which are aged up to 6 years, tasted smooth, but their distinct tannic taste dominated the cocktail. As for orange-flavored liqueurs, a lower-alcohol liqueur, such as triple sec, worked best. Mixes and bottled citrus juice had no place in our cocktail—instead we steeped lemon and lime zest in their own juice for a deep, refreshing citrus flavor. And with a bit of easy-to-dissolve superfine sugar and crushed ice, our margaritas were complete.

Fresh Margaritas

SERVES 4 TO 6

The longer the zest and juice mixture is allowed to steep, the more developed the citrus flavors will be in the finished margaritas. We recommend steeping for the full 24 hours, although the margaritas will still be great if the mixture is steeped for only the minimum 4 hours. If you're in a rush and want to serve margaritas immediately, omit the zest and skip the steeping process altogether. If you can't find superfine sugar, process an equal amount of regular sugar in a food processor for 30 seconds.

- 4 teaspoons grated zest plus ½ cup juice from 4 limes (see note)
- 4 teaspoons grated zest plus ½ cup juice from 3 lemons (see note)
- ¼ cup superfine sugar (see note)
  Pinch table salt
- 2 cups crushed ice
- 1 cup 100 percent agave tequila, preferably reposado
- 1 cup triple sec

1. Combine the lime zest and juice, lemon zest and juice, sugar, and salt in a large liquid measuring cup; cover with plastic wrap and refrigerate until the flavors meld, 4 to 24 hours.

2. Divide 1 cup of the crushed ice among 4 or 6 margarita or double old-fashioned glasses. Strain the juice mixture into a 1-quart pitcher or cocktail shaker. Add the tequila, triple sec, and the remaining 1 cup crushed ice; stir or shake until thoroughly combined and chilled, 20 to 60 seconds. Strain into the ice-filled glasses and serve immediately.

SANGRIA

WHY THIS RECIPE WORKS: Many people mistake sangria for an unruly collection of fruit awash in a sea of overly sweetened red wine. We wanted a robust, sweet-tart wine punch.

After trying a variety of red wines, we found that inexpensive wine works best. (Experts told us that the sugar and fruit called for in sangria throw off the balance of any wine used, so why spend a lot on something that was carefully crafted?) We experimented with untold varieties of fruit to put in our sangria and finally concluded that simpler is better. We preferred the straightforward tang of citrus in the form of oranges and lemons. And we discovered that the zest and pith as well as the fruit itself make an important contribution to flavor. Orange liqueur is standard in recipes for sangria, and after experimenting we found that here, as with the wine, cheaper was just fine, this time in the form of triple sec. Fortification with any other alcoholic beverage, from gin to port to brandy, simply gave the punch too much punch. What we wanted, and what we now had, was a light, refreshing drink.

Sangria

SERVES 4

Although this punch hails from Spain, it has become a mainstay on Mexican restaurant menus and pairs well with the country's spicy dishes. The longer sangria sits before drinking, the more smooth and mellow it will taste. A full day is best, but if that's impossible, give it an absolute minimum of two hours to sit. Use large, heavy, juicy oranges and lemons for the best flavor. If you can't find superfine sugar, process an equal amount of regular sugar in a food processor for 30 seconds. Doubling or tripling the recipe is fine, but you'll have to switch to a large punch bowl in place of the pitcher. An inexpensive Merlot is the best choice for this recipe.

2 large juice oranges, washed; one orange sliced,
    remaining orange juiced (see note)
1 large lemon, washed and sliced (see note)
¼ cup superfine sugar (see note)
1 (750-milliliter) bottle inexpensive, fruity,
    medium-bodied red wine, chilled (see note)
¼ cup triple sec

1. Add the sliced orange and lemon and the sugar to a large pitcher. Mash the fruit gently with a wooden spoon until the fruit releases some juice, but is not totally crushed, and the sugar dissolves, about 1 minute. Stir in the orange juice, wine, and triple sec; refrigerate for at least 2 hours or up to 8 hours.

2. Before serving, add 6 to 8 ice cubes and stir briskly to distribute the settled fruit and pulp; serve immediately.

NACHOS

WHY THIS RECIPE WORKS: The availability of prepackaged shredded cheese and jars or tubs of premade salsa and guacamole has transformed nachos from something delicious into bland, stale-tasting fast food. We wanted nachos with hot, crisp tortilla chips, plentiful cheese and toppings, and the right amount of spicy heat.

To ensure that all of the chips would be cheesy and spicy, we layered tortilla chips with a full pound of shredded cheddar cheese and sliced jalapeños. Layering the jalapeños with the cheese also helped the chiles stick to the chips. We prepared a quick homemade salsa and chunky guacamole to spoon around the edges of the hot nachos after they came out of the oven. Spoonfuls of sour cream and a sprinkling of chopped fresh scallions provided final touches. Served with lime wedges, this fresh take on nachos is light-years beyond any fast-food version of the dish.

Cheesy Nachos with Guacamole and Salsa

SERVES 4 TO 6

8 ounces tortilla chips
1 pound cheddar cheese, shredded (about 4 cups)
2 large jalapeño chiles, sliced thin (about ¼ cup)
2 scallions, sliced thin
½ cup sour cream
1 recipe One-Minute Salsa (recipe follows)
1 recipe Chunky Guacamole (page 280)
    Lime wedges, for serving

Adjust an oven rack to the middle position and heat the oven to 400 degrees. Spread half of the chips in an even layer in a 13 by 9-inch baking dish. Sprinkle the chips evenly with 2 cups of the cheese and half of the jalapeño slices. Repeat with the remaining chips, cheese, and jalapeños. Bake until the cheese is melted, 7 to 10 minutes. Remove the nachos from the oven and sprinkle with the scallions. Along the edge of the baking dish, drop scoops of the sour cream, salsa, and guacamole. Serve immediately, passing the lime wedges separately.

One-Minute Salsa

MAKES ABOUT 1 CUP

This quick salsa can be made with either fresh or canned tomatoes. If you like, replace the jalapeño with ½ chipotle chile in adobo sauce, minced.

2 tablespoons chopped red onion
2 tablespoons fresh cilantro leaves
2 teaspoons juice from 1 lime
½ small jalapeño chile, stemmed and seeded (about
    1½ teaspoons) (see note)
1 small garlic clove, minced or pressed through
    a garlic press (about ½ teaspoon)
¼ teaspoon table salt
    Pinch ground black pepper
2 small ripe tomatoes, each cored and cut into eighths,
    or one (14.5-ounce) can diced tomatoes, drained

Pulse all the ingredients except the tomatoes in a food processor until minced, about 5 pulses, scraping down the sides of the workbowl as necessary. Add the tomatoes and pulse until roughly chopped, about 2 pulses.

GUACAMOLE

WHY THIS RECIPE WORKS: Not only eaten as a party dip, guacamole is also the traditional accompaniment to several Mexican dishes. Unfortunately, it often has so many ingredients that the primary one—the avocado—becomes overshadowed by secondary ingredients. We wanted to get back to the basics of this dish, emphasizing the avocado.

Hass avocados, the dark, pebbly-skinned type, work best, and they must be ripe; they should yield slightly to a gentle squeeze. We wanted a chunky texture in our guacamole, so instead of mashing or pureeing the avocados we diced two of them and mashed one lightly. Combining the avocados gave the guacamole a chunky, cohesive texture. As for flavorings, just a bit of finely minced onion provided some bite but not overwhelming onion flavor. Lime juice was essential for its bright citrus flavor. Cumin, a jalapeño, and fresh cilantro rounded out the dip's flavors. Cool and creamy, our guacamole makes a perfect partner to a bowl of tortilla chips or a garnish to a variety of Mexican dishes.

Chunky Guacamole

MAKES 2½ TO 3 CUPS

To minimize the risk of discoloration, prepare the minced ingredients first so they are ready to mix with the avocados as soon as they are cut. Ripe avocados are essential here. To test for ripeness, try to flick the small stem off the end of the avocado. If it comes off easily and you can see green underneath it, the avocado is ripe. If it does not come off or if you see brown underneath after prying it off, the avocado is not ripe. If you like, garnish the guacamole with diced tomatoes and chopped cilantro just before serving.

- 3   medium, ripe avocados (see note)
- ¼   cup minced fresh cilantro leaves
- 2   tablespoons minced onion
- 1   small jalapeño chile, stemmed, seeded, and minced
- 1   medium garlic clove, minced or pressed through a garlic press (about 1 teaspoon)
- ½   teaspoon ground cumin (optional)
     Table salt
- 2   tablespoons juice from 1 lime

1. Halve 1 avocado, remove the pit, and scoop the flesh into a medium bowl. Mash the flesh lightly with the cilantro, onion, jalapeño, garlic, cumin (if using), and ¼ teaspoon salt with the tines of a fork until just combined.

DICING AN AVOCADO

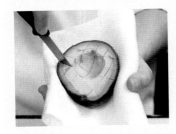

1. After halving and pitting the avocado, make ½-inch crosshatch incisions in the flesh of each half with a dinner knife, cutting down to but not through the skin.

2. Separate the diced flesh from the skin with a soup spoon, gently scooping out the avocado cubes.

2. Halve, pit, and cube the remaining 2 avocados. Add the cubes to the bowl with the mashed avocado mixture.

3. Sprinkle the lime juice over the diced avocado and mix the entire contents of the bowl lightly with a fork until combined but still chunky. Season with salt, if necessary, and serve. (The guacamole can be covered with plastic wrap, pressed directly onto the surface of the mixture, and refrigerated for up to 1 day. Return the guacamole to room temperature, removing the plastic wrap at the last moment, before serving.)

QUICK AND EASY QUESADILLAS

WHY THIS RECIPE WORKS: An authentic quesadilla is meant to be a quick snack, not an overstuffed tortilla with complicated fillings. We wanted a simple toasted tortilla, crisp and hot, filled with just the right amount of cheese.

We kept the tortillas crisp by lightly toasting them in a dry skillet. We then filled them with cheese and pickled jalapeños, lightly coated the tortillas with oil, and returned them to the skillet until they were well browned and the cheese was fully melted. Not yet satisfied that our recipe was speedy enough, we made the process even more convenient by switching to small 8-inch tortillas and folding them in half around the

filling. This allowed us to cook two at one time in the same skillet, and the fold also kept our generous cheese filling from oozing out.

Quesadillas

MAKES 2 FOLDED 8-INCH QUESADILLAS

Cooling the quesadillas before cutting and serving them is important; straight from the skillet, the melted cheese will ooze out. Finished quesadillas can be held on a baking sheet in a 200-degree oven for up to 20 minutes.

- 2 (8-inch) flour tortillas
- 2 ounces Monterey Jack or cheddar cheese, shredded (about ½ cup)
- 1 tablespoon minced pickled jalapeños (optional)
  Vegetable oil for brushing the tortillas
  Kosher salt

1. Heat a 10-inch nonstick skillet over medium heat until hot, about 2 minutes. Place 1 tortilla in the skillet and toast until soft and puffed slightly at the edges, about 2 minutes. Flip the tortilla and toast until puffed and slightly browned, 1 to 2 minutes longer. Slip the tortilla onto a cutting board. Repeat to toast the second tortilla while assembling the first quesadilla. Sprinkle ¼ cup of the cheese and half of the jalapeños (if using) over half of the tortilla, leaving a ½-inch border around the edge. Fold the tortilla in half and press to flatten. Brush the top generously with oil, sprinkle lightly with salt, and set aside. Repeat to form the second quesadilla.

2. Place both quesadillas in the skillet, oiled sides down; cook over medium heat until crisp and well browned, 1 to 2 minutes. Brush the tops with oil and sprinkle lightly with salt. Flip the quesadillas and cook until the second sides are crisp, 1 to 2 minutes. Transfer the quesadillas to a cutting board; cool about 3 minutes, halve each quesadilla, and serve.

NOTES FROM THE TEST KITCHEN

COOKING QUESADILLAS

To cook two quesadillas at the same time, arrange the folded edges at the center of a 10-inch nonstick skillet.

TORTILLA SOUP

WHY THIS RECIPE WORKS: The classic method of making this flavorful Mexican soup is not only arduous, but it relies on a long list of ingredients, many of which are difficult, if not impossible, to find outside of specialty markets. We wanted to make an intensely and authentically flavored tortilla soup in less than one hour, using supermarket ingredients.

By breaking the soup down to its three classic components—the flavor base (tomatoes, garlic, onion, and chiles), the chicken stock, and the garnishes (including fried tortilla chips)—we found we could devise techniques and substitute ingredients that together make a compelling version of tortilla soup. We began achieving maximum flavor by composing a puree made from chipotle chiles, tomatoes, onions, garlic, jalapeños, and a cilantro/oregano substitute for the Mexican ingredient epazote, and then frying the puree in oil over high heat. We then added the puree to low-sodium canned chicken broth that we strained after poaching chicken in it and infusing it with onions, garlic, cilantro, and oregano. Addressing the garnish issue, we oven-toasted our lightly oiled tortilla strips instead of frying them and substituted sour cream and Monterey Jack cheese for the harder-to-find Mexican crema and cotija.

Tortilla Soup

SERVES 6

Despite its somewhat lengthy ingredient list, this recipe is very easy to prepare. If desired, the soup can be completed short of adding the shredded chicken to the pot at the end of step 3. Return the soup to a simmer over medium-high heat before proceeding. The tortilla strips and the garnishes are best prepared the day of serving.

TORTILLA STRIPS

- **8** (6-inch) corn tortillas, cut into ½-inch-wide strips
- **1** tablespoon vegetable oil
  Table salt

SOUP

- **2** bone-in, skin-on split chicken breasts (about 1½ pounds) or 4 bone-in, skin-on chicken thighs (about 1¼ pounds), skin removed and trimmed
- **8** cups low-sodium chicken broth
- **1** very large white onion (about 1 pound), peeled and quartered
- **4** medium garlic cloves, peeled
- **2** sprigs fresh epazote or 8 to 10 sprigs fresh cilantro plus 1 sprig fresh oregano
  Table salt
- **2** medium tomatoes, cored and quartered
- **½** medium jalapeño chile
- **1** chipotle chile in adobo sauce, plus up to 1 tablespoon adobo sauce
- **1** tablespoon vegetable oil

GARNISHES

  Lime wedges
  Avocado, peeled, pitted, and diced fine (see page 280)
  Cotija cheese, crumbled, or Monterey Jack cheese, diced fine
  Fresh cilantro leaves
  Jalapeño chile, minced
  Crema Mexicana or sour cream

1. FOR THE TORTILLA STRIPS: Adjust an oven rack to the middle position and heat the oven to 425 degrees. Spread the tortilla strips on a rimmed baking sheet; drizzle with the oil and toss until evenly coated. Bake until the strips are deep golden brown and crisped, about 14 minutes, rotating the pan and shaking the strips (to redistribute) halfway through baking. Season the strips lightly with salt; transfer to a plate lined with several layers of paper towels.

2. FOR THE SOUP: While the tortilla strips bake, bring the chicken, broth, 2 of the onion quarters, 2 of the garlic cloves, the epazote, and ½ teaspoon salt to a boil over medium-high heat in a large saucepan; reduce the heat to low, cover, and simmer until the chicken is just cooked through, about 20 minutes. Using tongs, transfer the chicken to a large plate. Pour the broth through a fine-mesh strainer; discard the solids in the strainer. When cool enough to handle, shred the chicken into bite-sized pieces; discard the bones.

3. Puree the tomatoes, remaining 2 onion quarters, remaining 2 garlic cloves, the jalapeño, chipotle chile, and 1 teaspoon of the adobo sauce in a food processor until smooth, about 20 seconds. Heat the oil in a Dutch oven over high heat until shimmering; add the tomato-onion puree and ⅛ teaspoon salt and cook, stirring frequently, until the mixture has darkened in color, about 10 minutes. Stir the strained broth into the tomato mixture, bring to a boil, then reduce the heat to low and simmer to blend the flavors, about 15 minutes. Taste the soup; if desired, add up to 2 teaspoons more adobo sauce. Add the shredded chicken and simmer until heated through, about 5 minutes. To serve, place portions of tortilla strips in the bottom of individual bowls and ladle the soup into the bowls; pass the garnishes separately.

BLACK BEAN SOUP

WHY THIS RECIPE WORKS: Making traditional black bean soup used to be an all-day affair. Generating full flavor required hours of simmering soaked beans with numerous ingredients, including parsnips, carrots, beef bones, and smoked ham hocks. But quicker versions developed for modern kitchens often produce watery, bland, and unattractive soups. We wanted a simplified procedure that would result in an attractive, dark-colored soup full of sweet, spicy, smoky flavors and brightened with fresh garnishes.

Though convenient, canned beans couldn't compare in flavor to dried, which imparted good flavor to the broth as they simmered, and we discovered that we didn't have to soak them. A touch of baking soda in the cooking water kept the beans from turning gray. Homemade stock would be time-consuming to prepare, so we focused on adding flavor to prepared broth. Ham steak provided the smoky pork flavor of the more conventional ham hock and more meat as well. We spiced up our aromatics—carrot, celery, onion, and garlic—with lots of cumin and some red pepper flakes. We wanted a chunky texture in our soup, so we pureed it only partially, thickening it further with a slurry of cornstarch and water. Some lime juice added brightness. The customary garnishes of sour cream, avocado, red onion, cilantro, and lime wedges topped our richly flavored but easy-to-make black bean soup.

Black Bean Soup

SERVES 6

Dried beans tend to cook unevenly, so be sure to taste several beans to determine their doneness in step 1. For efficiency, you can prepare the soup ingredients while the beans simmer and the garnishes while the soup simmers. Though you do not need to offer all of the garnishes listed below, do choose at least a couple; garnishes are essential for this soup, as they add not only flavor but texture and color as well. Leftover soup can be refrigerated in an airtight container for 3 days; reheat it in a saucepan over medium heat until hot, stirring in additional chicken broth if it has thickened beyond your liking.

BEANS

- 1 pound (2 cups) dried black beans, rinsed and picked over
- 4 ounces ham steak, trimmed of rind
- 2 bay leaves
- 5 cups water
- ⅛ teaspoon baking soda
- 1 teaspoon table salt

SOUP

- 3 tablespoons olive oil
- 2 large onions, minced
- 3 celery ribs, chopped fine
- 1 large carrot, chopped
- ½ teaspoon table salt
- 5–6 medium garlic cloves, minced or pressed through a garlic press (about 1½ tablespoons)
- 1½ tablespoons ground cumin
- ½ teaspoon red pepper flakes
- 6 cups low-sodium chicken broth
- 2 tablespoons cornstarch
- 2 tablespoons water
- 2 tablespoons juice from 1 lime

GARNISHES

- Lime wedges
- Minced fresh cilantro leaves
- Red onion, diced fine
- Avocado, peeled, pitted, and diced medium (see page 280)
- Sour cream

1. FOR THE BEANS: Place the beans, ham, bay leaves, water, and baking soda in a large saucepan with a tight-fitting lid. Bring to a boil over medium-high heat; using a large spoon, skim the foam as it rises to the surface. Stir in the salt, reduce the heat to low, cover, and simmer briskly until the beans are tender, 1¼ to 1½ hours (if necessary, add 1 cup more water and continue to simmer until the beans are tender); do not drain the beans. Discard the bay leaves. Remove the ham steak (ham steak darkens to the color of the beans), cut it into ¼-inch cubes, and set aside.

2. FOR THE SOUP: Heat the oil in a large Dutch oven over medium-high heat until shimmering but not smoking; add the onions, celery, carrot, and salt and cook, stirring occasionally, until the vegetables are soft and lightly browned, 12 to 15 minutes. Reduce the heat to medium-low and add the garlic, cumin, and red pepper flakes; cook, stirring constantly, until fragrant, about 3 minutes. Stir in the beans, bean cooking liquid, and chicken broth. Increase the heat to medium-high and bring to a boil, then reduce the heat to low and simmer, uncovered, stirring occasionally, to blend the flavors, about 30 minutes.

3. TO FINISH THE SOUP: Ladle 1½ cups of the beans and 2 cups of the liquid into a food processor or blender, process until smooth, and return to the pot. Stir together the cornstarch and water in a small bowl until combined, then gradually stir half of the cornstarch mixture into the soup; bring to a boil over medium-high heat, stirring occasionally, to fully thicken. If the soup is still thinner than desired once boiling, stir the remaining cornstarch mixture to recombine and gradually stir the mixture into the soup; return to a boil to fully thicken. Off the heat, stir in the lime juice and reserved ham; ladle the soup into bowls and serve immediately, passing the garnishes separately.

BEEF TACOS

WHY THIS RECIPE WORKS: Tacos made from supermarket kits are disappointing substitutes for the real thing. Easy as they may be to prepare, taco fillings made with store-bought spice mixes taste flat and stale, and the shells don't taste much different than the cardboard they're packaged in. We set out to develop a recipe for toasty, not greasy, taco shells filled with a boldly spiced beef mixture and fresh toppings.

Home-fried corn tortillas made superior homemade taco shells. For the filling, we seasoned lean ground beef with onions, garlic, and spices (chili powder, cumin, coriander, and oregano). To moisten and further flavor the beef filling, we added chicken broth, brown sugar, and vinegar. Spooned into our fresh, crisp taco shells and topped with tomatoes, lettuce, avocado, Monterey Jack, onion, and cilantro, these tacos have far better flavor than taco-kit versions.

Beef Tacos

SERVES 4

Taco toppings are highly individual. We consider the ones listed below essential, but you might also want to consider diced avocado, sour cream, and chopped onion.

BEEF FILLING

- 2 teaspoons vegetable oil
- 1 small onion, minced
- 3 medium garlic cloves, minced or pressed through a garlic press (about 1 tablespoon)
- 2 tablespoons chili powder
- 1 teaspoon ground cumin
- 1 teaspoon ground coriander
- ½ teaspoon dried oregano
- ¼ teaspoon cayenne pepper
  Table salt
- 1 pound 90 percent lean ground beef
- ½ cup canned tomato sauce
- ½ cup low-sodium chicken broth
- 2 teaspoons vinegar, preferably cider vinegar
- 1 teaspoon brown sugar
  Ground black pepper

SHELLS AND TOPPINGS

- 8 Home-Fried Taco Shells (recipe follows)
  Shredded Monterey Jack cheese
  Shredded iceberg lettuce
  Diced tomatoes
  Chopped fresh cilantro leaves

1. FOR THE FILLING: Heat the oil in a medium skillet over medium heat until shimmering. Add the onion and cook, stirring occasionally, until softened, about 4 minutes. Add the garlic, spices, and ½ teaspoon salt; cook, stirring constantly, until fragrant, about 30 seconds. Add the ground beef and cook, breaking up the meat with a wooden spoon and scraping the pan bottom to prevent scorching, until the beef is no longer pink, about 5 minutes. Add the tomato sauce, broth, vinegar, and brown sugar; bring to a simmer. Reduce the heat to medium-low and simmer uncovered, stirring frequently and breaking up the meat so that no chunks remain, until the liquid has reduced and thickened (the mixture should not be completely dry), about 10 minutes. Season with salt and pepper to taste.

2. Using a wide, shallow spoon, divide the mixture evenly among the taco shells; place two tacos on each plate. Serve immediately, passing the toppings separately.

Home-Fried Taco Shells

MAKES 8 SHELLS

Fry the taco shells before you make the filling, then rewarm them in a 200-degree oven for about 10 minutes before serving.

- ¾ cup corn oil, vegetable oil, or canola oil
- 8 (6-inch) corn tortillas

1. Line a rimmed baking sheet with a double thickness of paper towels and set aside. Heat the oil in an 8-inch skillet over medium heat to 350 degrees, about 5 minutes (the oil should bubble when a small piece of tortilla is dropped in; the piece should rise to the surface in 2 seconds and be light golden brown in about 1 minute).

2. Following the photos on page 285, fry the tortillas. One at a time, place each fried taco shell on the prepared baking sheet (see note).

MAKING YOUR OWN TACO SHELLS

1. Using tongs to hold the tortilla, slip half of it into the hot oil. With a metal spatula in the other hand, submerge the half in the oil. Fry until just set, but not brown, about 30 seconds.

2. Flip the tortilla and, using tongs, hold the tortilla open about 2 inches while keeping the bottom submerged in the oil. Fry until golden brown, about 1½ minutes. Flip again and fry the other side until golden brown, about 30 seconds.

3. Transfer the shell, upside down, to the paper towel-lined baking sheet to drain. Repeat with the remaining tortillas, adjusting the heat as necessary to keep the oil between 350 and 375 degrees.

STEAK TACOS

WHY THIS RECIPE WORKS: Upscale steak tacos usually get their rich, beefy flavor from the grill, but cooking outdoors isn't always possible. We wanted an indoor cooking method that would always yield steak taco meat as tender, juicy, and rich-tasting as the grilled method.

We didn't want to wrap a pricey cut of beef in a taco, so we explored inexpensive cuts and chose flank steak for its good flavor and ready availability; when sliced against the grain, it can be just as tender as pricier cuts. To add flavor, we poked holes in the meat with a fork and rubbed it with a paste of oil, cilantro, jalapeño, garlic, and scallions; salt helped draw all the flavors into the steak and ensured juiciness. Pan-searing, with a sprinkling of sugar to enhance browning, gave us a crust that mimicked the char of the grill. To maximize this effect, we cut the steak into four long pieces, which gave us more sides to brown and turn crispy. For additional flavor, we tossed the

cooked steak with some marinade that we had reserved and garnished the tacos simply with onion, cilantro, and lime wedges. In Mexico, steak tacos are often served with *curtido,* a relish of pickled vegetables; we devised a quick recipe for pickled onions to accompany our good-as-grilled steak tacos.

Steak Tacos

SERVES 4 TO 6

Our preferred method for warming tortillas is to place each one over the medium flame of a gas burner until slightly charred, about 30 seconds per side. We also like toasting them in a dry skillet over medium-high heat until softened and speckled with brown spots, 20 to 30 seconds per side. For a less spicy dish, remove some or all of the ribs and seeds from the jalapeños before chopping them for the marinade. In addition to the toppings suggested below, try serving the tacos with Sweet and Spicy Pickled Onions (recipe follows), thinly sliced radish or cucumber, or salsa.

MARINADE

- ½ cup packed fresh cilantro leaves
- 3 medium scallions, roughly chopped
- 1 medium jalapeño chile, stemmed and roughly chopped (see note)
- 3 medium garlic cloves, roughly chopped
- ½ teaspoon ground cumin
- ¼ cup vegetable oil
- 1 tablespoon juice from 1 lime

STEAK

- 1 (1½ to 1¾-pound) flank steak, trimmed and cut lengthwise (with the grain) into 4 equal pieces
- 1 tablespoon kosher salt or 1½ teaspoons table salt
- ½ teaspoon sugar
- ½ teaspoon ground black pepper
- 2 tablespoons vegetable oil

TACOS

- 12 (6-inch) corn tortillas, warmed (see note)
- Fresh cilantro leaves
- Minced white onion
- Lime wedges

1. FOR THE MARINADE: Pulse the cilantro, scallions, jalapeño, garlic, and cumin in a food processor until finely chopped, 10 to 12 pulses, scraping down the sides of the workbowl as necessary. Add the oil and process until the mixture is smooth and resembles pesto, about 15 seconds, scraping down the sides as necessary. Transfer 2 tablespoons of the herb paste to a medium bowl; whisk in the lime juice and set aside.

2. FOR THE STEAK: Using a dinner fork, poke each piece of steak 10 to 12 times on each side. Place in a large baking dish; rub all sides of the steak pieces evenly with the salt and then coat with the remaining herb paste. Cover with plastic wrap and refrigerate at least 30 minutes or up to 1 hour.

3. Scrape the herb paste off the steak and sprinkle all sides of the pieces evenly with the sugar and black pepper. Heat the oil in a 12-inch nonstick skillet over medium-high heat until smoking. Place the steak in the skillet and cook until well browned, about 3 minutes. Flip the steak and sear until the second side is well browned, 2 to 3 minutes. Using tongs, stand each piece on a cut side and cook, turning as necessary, until all cut sides are well browned and the internal steak temperature registers 125 to 130 degrees on an instant-read thermometer, 2 to 7 minutes. Transfer the steak to a cutting board and let rest for 5 minutes.

4. FOR THE TACOS: Slice the steak against the grain into ⅛-inch-thick pieces. Transfer the sliced steak to the bowl with the herb paste–lime juice mixture and toss to coat. Season with salt to taste. Spoon a small amount of the sliced steak into the center of each warm tortilla and serve immediately, passing the toppings separately.

Sweet and Spicy Pickled Onions
MAKES ABOUT 2 CUPS

The onions can be refrigerated, tightly covered, for up to 1 week.

- 1 **medium red onion, halved and sliced thin (about 1½ cups)**
- 1 **cup red wine vinegar**
- ⅓ **cup sugar**
- 2 **jalapeño chiles, stemmed, seeded, and cut into thin rings**
- ¼ **teaspoon table salt**

Place the onions in a medium heat-resistant bowl. Bring the vinegar, sugar, jalapeños, and salt to a simmer in a small saucepan over medium-high heat, stirring occasionally, until the sugar dissolves. Pour the vinegar mixture over the onions, cover loosely, and let cool to room temperature, about 30 minutes. Once cool, drain and discard the liquid.

CHICKEN FAJITAS

WHY THIS RECIPE WORKS: Too often, chicken fajitas need to be slathered with guacamole, sour cream, and salsa to compensate for the bland flavor of the soggy underlying ingredients. We wanted to go back to the basics, creating a simple combination of smoky grilled vegetables and strips of chicken wrapped up in warm flour tortillas. The chicken and vegetables should be flavorful enough to make condiments unnecessary.

Chicken has such a mild flavor that we wanted to add more; a marinade of lime juice and oil worked here. We added jalapeño and cilantro for some bright spice and herbal flavor, and a surprising addition—Worcestershire sauce—lent a subtle but complex savory note. We marinated the chicken only briefly, so the acid wouldn't turn the delicate chicken to mush. Bell peppers and onions are the customary vegetables, and we found that their sweet-bitter flavors contrasted well with the chicken. To prepare the vegetables for grilling, we quartered the peppers, so they'd lie flat on the grill, and cut the onion into thick rounds that would hold together during cooking. A two-level fire enabled us to grill the chicken and vegetables at the same time, the latter on the cooler part so they wouldn't burn. We saved some of the marinade to toss with everything at the end for a bright flavor burst; nestled in a warm tortilla, the smoky vegetables and well-seasoned chicken were so good on their own that we forgot all about toppings.

Chicken Fajitas for a Charcoal Grill

SERVES 4 TO 6

The chicken and vegetables in these fajitas are only mildly spicy. For more heat, include the jalapeño seeds and ribs when mincing. When you head outside to grill, bring along a clean kitchen towel or a large piece of foil in which to wrap the tortillas and keep them warm as they come off the grill. Although the chicken and vegetables have enough flavor to stand on their own, accompaniments (guacamole, salsa, sour cream, shredded cheddar or Monterey Jack cheese, and lime wedges) can be offered at the table. The chicken tenderloins can be reserved for another use or marinated and grilled along with the breasts.

6	tablespoons vegetable oil, plus extra for the cooking grate
⅓	cup juice from 3 to 4 limes
3	medium garlic cloves, minced or pressed through a garlic press (about 1 tablespoon)
1	tablespoon Worcestershire sauce
1½	teaspoons brown sugar
1	jalapeño chile, stemmed, seeded, and minced (see note)
1½	tablespoons minced fresh cilantro leaves
	Table salt and ground black pepper
3	(7 to 8-ounce) boneless, skinless chicken breasts, tenderloins removed (see note), and breasts trimmed and pounded to ½-inch thickness
1	large red onion, peeled and cut into ½-inch-thick rounds (do not separate the rings)
1	large red bell pepper, stemmed, seeded, and quartered
1	large green bell pepper, stemmed, seeded, and quartered
8–12	(6-inch) flour tortillas

1. In a medium bowl, whisk together 4 tablespoons of the oil, the lime juice, garlic, Worcestershire sauce, brown sugar, jalapeño, cilantro, 1 teaspoon salt, and ¾ teaspoon pepper. Reserve ¼ cup of the marinade in a small bowl; set aside. Add 1 teaspoon salt to the remaining marinade. Place the chicken in the marinade; cover with plastic wrap and refrigerate for 15 minutes. Brush both sides of the onion rounds and peppers with the remaining 2 tablespoons oil and season with salt and pepper.

2. Meanwhile, light a large chimney starter filled with charcoal (about 6 quarts) and allow to burn until the coals are partially covered with a layer of ash, about 20 minutes. Build a two-level fire by arranging two-thirds of the coals evenly over half of the grill and arranging the remaining coals over the other half. Set the cooking grate in place, cover the grill, and heat the grate until hot, about

5 minutes. Use a grill brush to scrape the cooking grate clean. Dip a wad of paper towels in oil; holding the wad with tongs, oil the cooking grate.

3. Remove the chicken from the marinade and place the chicken, smooth side down, on the hotter side of the grill; discard the remaining marinade. Place the onion rounds and peppers (skin side down) on the cooler side of the grill. Cook the chicken until well browned, 4 to 5 minutes; using tongs, flip the chicken and continue grilling until the thickest part of the chicken registers 160 to 165 degrees on an instant-read thermometer, 4 to 5 minutes longer. Meanwhile, cook the peppers until spottily charred and crisp-tender, 8 to 10 minutes, turning once or twice as needed; cook the onions until tender and charred on both sides, 10 to 12 minutes, turning every 3 to 4 minutes. When the chicken and vegetables are done, transfer them to a large plate and tent with foil to keep warm.

4. Working in two or three batches, place the tortillas in a single layer on the cooler side of the now-empty grill and cook until warm and lightly browned, about 20 seconds per side (do not grill too long or the tortillas will become brittle). As the tortillas are done, wrap them in a kitchen towel or large sheet of foil.

5. Separate the onions into rings and place in a medium bowl; slice the bell peppers lengthwise into thin strips and place in the bowl with the onions. Add 2 tablespoons of the reserved unused marinade to the vegetables and toss well to combine. Slice the chicken into ¼-inch strips and toss with the remaining 2 tablespoons reserved marinade in another bowl; arrange the chicken and vegetables on a large platter and serve with the warmed tortillas.

Chicken Fajitas for a Gas Grill

1. Follow the recipe for Chicken Fajitas for a Charcoal Grill through step 1.

2. Turn all the burners to high and heat the grill, with the lid down, until very hot, about 15 minutes. Use a grill brush to scrape the cooking grate clean. Dip a wad of paper towels in the oil; holding the wad with tongs, oil the cooking grate. Leave one burner on high heat and turn the remaining burner(s) down to medium. Continue with the recipe from step 3, cooking the chicken and vegetables covered.

3. When the grill is empty, set all the burners to medium. Working in batches, if necessary, place the tortillas in a single layer on the cooking grate and grill until warm and lightly browned, about 20 seconds per side. As they are done, wrap the tortillas in a kitchen towel or large sheet of foil. Proceed as directed in step 5 of Chicken Fajitas for a Charcoal Grill.

STEAK FAJITAS

WHY THIS RECIPE WORKS: Steak fajitas were originally made with skirt steak, but the wider availability of flank steak has made it the cut of choice for this dish. Recipes for fajitas are fairly straightforward—grill the meat and vegetables and serve them in a warm tortilla. But too often, fajitas are lackluster or ruined by unnecessary complexity. We want fajitas that boasted flawless, flavorful meat with a rosy interior and browned crust.

Marinating is often recommended as a way to tenderize flank steak, but we learned that it's plenty tender without a marinade if sliced thin against the grain after being cooked. But we did want to add flavor. A long soak turned the meat mushy, but a squeeze of lime juice and a generous dose of salt and pepper just before grilling added all the extra flavor we wanted. The tried-and-true way of cooking flank steak—over high heat for a short period of time—required no changes. We found that the meat is juicier when allowed to rest after grilling, and that gave us time to grill the vegetables. Served in tortillas with freshly made guacamole, these fajitas delivered on all fronts.

Steak Fajitas for a Charcoal Grill

SERVES 8

The ingredients go on the grill in order as the fire dies down: steak over a medium-hot fire, vegetables over a medium fire, and tortillas around the edge of a medium to low fire just to warm them. Make sure to cover the grilled but unsliced flank steak with foil; it will take you at least 10 minutes to get the vegetables and tortillas ready.

> Vegetable oil for the cooking grate
> 1 (2½-pound) flank steak, trimmed
> ¼ cup juice from 2 limes
> Table salt and ground black pepper
> 1 very large onion, peeled and cut into ½-inch-thick rounds (do not separate the rings)
> 2 very large red or green bell peppers, stemmed, seeded, and quartered
> 16 (10 to 12-inch) flour tortillas
> 1 recipe Chunky Guacamole (page 280)

1. Light a large chimney starter filled with charcoal (about 6 quarts) and allow to burn until the coals are partially covered with a layer of ash, about 20 minutes. Build a single-level file by arranging the coals evenly over the bottom of the grill. Set the cooking grate in place, cover the grill, and heat the grate until hot, about 5 minutes. Use a grill brush to scrape the cooking grate clean. Dip a wad of paper towels in oil; holding the wad with tongs, oil the cooking grate.

2. Generously sprinkle both sides of the steak with the lime juice and season with salt and pepper. Grill the steak over the coals until well seared and dark brown on one side, 5 to 7 minutes. Flip the steak using tongs; continue grilling on the other side until the interior of the meat is slightly less done than you want it to be when you eat it, 2 to 5 minutes more for medium-rare (depending on the heat of the fire and the thickness of the steak). Transfer the meat to a cutting board; cover loosely with foil, and let rest for 10 minutes.

3. While the meat rests, grill the onions and peppers, turning them occasionally, until the onions are lightly charred, about 6 minutes, and the peppers are streaked with grill marks, about 10 minutes. Remove the vegetables from the grill. Separate the onions into rings and slice the bell peppers lengthwise into thin strips; set aside. Arrange the tortillas around the edge of the grill; heat until just warmed, about 20 seconds per side. Wrap the tortillas in a towel to keep warm and place in a basket.

4. Slice the steak very thin on the bias against the grain; season with salt and pepper to taste. Arrange the sliced meat and the vegetables on a large platter; serve immediately with the tortillas and guacamole passed separately.

Steak Fajitas for a Gas Grill

Follow the recipe for Steak Fajitas for a Charcoal Grill. In step 1, turn all the burners to high and heat the grill, covered, until very hot, about 15 minutes. Scrape the cooking grate clean with a wire brush. Dip a wad of paper towels in oil; holding the wad with tongs, oil the cooking grate. Cook the steak in step 2 with the lid down for 4 to 6 minutes on the first side and 2 to 5 minutes on the second side. In step 3, adjust the burners to medium before grilling the vegetables.

CHICKEN ENCHILADAS

WHY THIS RECIPE WORKS: Chicken enchiladas are a complete meal that offers a rich and complex combination of flavors, textures, and ingredients. The problem with preparing enchiladas at home is that traditional cooking methods require a whole day of preparation. We wanted a recipe for an Americanized version of chicken enchiladas that could be made in 90 minutes from start to finish.

To save time preparing the tortillas, we sprayed them with vegetable oil spray and warmed them on a baking sheet in the oven. We created a quick chili sauce with onions, garlic, spices, and tomato sauce, and to further enhance the sauce's flavor, we poached the chicken right in the sauce. This step also made for moist, flavorful meat. And cheddar cheese spiked with canned jalapeños and fresh cilantro made a rich, flavorful filling.

Chicken Enchiladas with Red Chili Sauce

SERVES 4 TO 5

Monterey Jack can be used instead of cheddar, or for a mellower flavor and creamier texture, try farmer's cheese. Be sure to cool the chicken before filling the tortillas; otherwise the hot filling will make the enchiladas soggy.

SAUCE AND FILLING

- 1½ tablespoons vegetable oil
- 1 medium onion, chopped fine
- 3 medium garlic cloves, minced or pressed through a garlic press (about 1 tablespoon)
- 3 tablespoons chili powder
- 2 teaspoons ground coriander
- 2 teaspoons ground cumin
- 2 teaspoons sugar
- ½ teaspoon table salt
- 12 ounces boneless, skinless chicken thighs (about 4 thighs), trimmed and cut into ¼-inch-wide strips
- 2 (8-ounce) cans tomato sauce
- ¾ cup water
- 8 ounces sharp cheddar cheese (see note), shredded (about 2 cups)
- ½ cup coarsely chopped fresh cilantro leaves
- 1 (4-ounce) can pickled jalapeño chiles, drained and chopped (about ¼ cup)

TORTILLAS AND TOPPINGS

- 10 (6-inch) corn tortillas
  Vegetable oil spray
- 3 ounces sharp cheddar cheese (see note), shredded (about ¾ cup)
- ¾ cup sour cream
- 1 medium, ripe avocado, diced medium (see page 280)
- 5 romaine lettuce leaves, shredded
  Lime wedges

1. FOR THE SAUCE AND FILLING: Heat the oil in a medium saucepan over medium-high heat until shimmering. Add the onion and cook, stirring occasionally, until softened and beginning to brown, about 5 minutes. Add the garlic, chili powder, coriander, cumin, sugar, and salt and cook, stirring constantly, until fragrant, about 30 seconds. Add the chicken and cook, stirring constantly, until coated with the spices, about 30 seconds. Add the tomato sauce and water, stir to separate the chicken pieces, and bring to a simmer. Reduce the heat to medium-low and simmer, uncovered, stirring occasionally, until the chicken is cooked through and the flavors have melded, about 8 minutes. Pour the mixture through a medium-mesh strainer into a medium bowl, pressing on the chicken and onions to extract as much sauce as possible; set the sauce aside. Transfer the chicken mixture to a large plate; place in the freezer for 10 minutes to cool, then combine with the cheddar, cilantro, and jalapeños in a medium bowl.

2. Adjust the oven racks to the upper-middle and lower-middle positions and heat the oven to 300 degrees.

3. TO ASSEMBLE: Smear the bottom of a 13 by 9-inch baking dish with ¾ cup of the chili sauce. Place the tortillas in a single layer on two baking sheets. Spray both sides of the tortillas lightly with vegetable oil spray. Bake until the tortillas are soft and pliable, about 4 minutes. Transfer the warm tortillas to a work surface. Increase the oven temperature to 400 degrees. Spread ⅓ cup of the filling down the center of each tortilla. Roll each tortilla tightly by hand and place, seam side down, side by side on the sauce in the baking dish. Pour the remaining chili sauce over the top of the enchiladas. Use the back of a spoon to spread the sauce so it coats the top of each tortilla. Sprinkle the cheese down the center of the enchiladas.

4. TO BAKE: Cover the baking dish with foil. Bake the enchiladas on the lower-middle rack until heated through and the cheese is melted, 20 to 25 minutes. Uncover and serve immediately, passing the sour cream, avocado, lettuce, and lime wedges separately.

ENCHILADAS VERDES

WHY THIS RECIPE WORKS: We love the bright taste of enchiladas verdes. But too often the green chili sauce is watery and lacks good green chile flavor. We wanted to re-create the memorable enchiladas verdes found in good Mexican restaurants: moist, tender chicken and fresh, citrusy flavors wrapped in soft corn tortillas and topped with just the right amount of melted cheese.

The chicken was easy; we poached it in chicken broth enhanced with sautéed onion, garlic, and cumin. The green sauce is based on tomatillos and chiles. Jalapeños and serranos are good for adding heat to a dish, but we wanted a more complex herbal flavor and opted for poblanos. To get the characteristic char, which Mexican cooks achieve by roasting on a comal, we tossed the chiles and fresh tomatillos with a little oil and ran them under the broiler. Pulsed in a food processor and thinned with a bit of the broth left from poaching the chicken, the tomatillos and chiles formed a well-seasoned, chunky sauce. To enrich the filling, we liked pepper Jack cheese—and sprinkled more on top of the dish. To make the tortillas pliable and easy to roll, we picked up the same technique from our Chicken Enchiladas with Red Chili Sauce (page 289): We sprayed them with vegetable oil spray and baked them for a few minutes. The enchiladas required

just a brief stint in the oven to heat through and melt the cheese. Garnished with sour cream, scallions, and radishes, these enchiladas may have the authentic restaurant version beat.

Enchiladas Verdes

SERVES 4 TO 6

You can substitute 3 (11-ounce) cans tomatillos, drained and rinsed, for the fresh ones in this recipe. Halve large tomatillos (more than 2 inches in diameter) and place them skin side up for broiling in step 2 to ensure even cooking and charring. If you can't find poblanos, substitute 4 large jalapeño chiles (with seeds and ribs removed). To increase the spiciness of the sauce, reserve some of the chiles' ribs and seeds and add them to the food processor in step 3.

ENCHILADAS

- 4 teaspoons vegetable oil
- 1 medium onion, chopped medium
- 3 medium garlic cloves, minced or pressed through a garlic press (about 1 tablespoon)
- ½ teaspoon ground cumin
- 1½ cups low-sodium chicken broth
- 1 pound boneless, skinless chicken breasts (2 to 3 breasts), trimmed
- 1½ pounds tomatillos (16 to 20 medium), husks and stems removed, rinsed well and dried (see note)
- 3 medium poblano chiles, halved lengthwise, stemmed, and seeded (see note)
- 1–2 teaspoons sugar
  Table salt and ground black pepper
- ½ cup coarsely chopped fresh cilantro leaves
- 8 ounces pepper Jack or Monterey Jack cheese, grated (about 2 cups)
- 12 (6-inch) corn tortillas

GARNISHES

- 2 medium scallions, sliced thin
  Thinly sliced radishes
  Sour cream

1. Adjust the oven racks to the middle and highest positions and heat the broiler. Heat 2 teaspoons of the oil in a medium saucepan over medium heat until shimmering; add the onion and cook, stirring frequently, until golden, 6 to 8 minutes. Add 2 teaspoons of the garlic and the cumin; cook, stirring frequently, until fragrant, about 30 seconds. Decrease the heat to low and stir in the broth. Add the chicken, cover, and simmer until the thickest part of the chicken registers 160 to 165 degrees on an instant-read thermometer, 15 to 20 minutes, flipping the chicken halfway through cooking. Transfer the chicken to a large bowl; place in the refrigerator to cool, about 20 minutes. Remove ¼ cup liquid from the saucepan and set aside; discard the remaining liquid.

2. Meanwhile, toss the tomatillos and poblanos with the remaining 2 teaspoons oil; arrange on a rimmed baking sheet lined with foil, with the poblanos skin side up. Broil until the vegetables blacken and start to soften, 5 to 10 minutes, rotating the pan halfway through cooking. Cool 10 minutes, then remove the skin from the poblanos (leave the tomatillo skins intact). Transfer the tomatillos and chiles to a food processor. Decrease the oven temperature to 350 degrees. Discard the foil from the baking sheet and set the baking sheet aside for warming the tortillas.

3. Add 1 teaspoon of the sugar, 1 teaspoon salt, the remaining teaspoon garlic, and the reserved ¼ cup cooking liquid to the food processor; pulse until the sauce is somewhat chunky, about 8 pulses. Taste the sauce; season with salt and pepper and adjust tartness by stirring in the remaining sugar, ½ teaspoon at a time. Set the sauce aside (you should have about 3 cups).

4. When the chicken is cool, pull into shreds using your hands or two forks, then chop into small bite-sized pieces. Combine the chicken with the cilantro and 1½ cups of the cheese; season with salt to taste.

5. Smear the bottom of a 13 by 9-inch baking dish with ¾ cup of the tomatillo sauce. Place the tortillas in a single layer on two baking sheets. Spray both sides of the tortillas lightly with vegetable oil spray. Bake until the tortillas are soft and pliable, 2 to 4 minutes. Increase the oven temperature to 450 degrees. Place the warm tortillas on the work surface and spread ⅓ cup of the filling down the center of each tortilla. Roll each tortilla tightly by hand and place in the baking dish, seam side down. Pour the remaining tomatillo sauce over the top of the enchiladas. Use the back of a spoon to spread the sauce so that it coats the top of each tortilla. Sprinkle with the remaining ½ cup cheese and cover the baking dish with foil.

6. Bake the enchiladas on the middle oven rack until heated through and the cheese is melted, 15 to 20 minutes. Uncover, sprinkle with the scallions, and serve immediately, passing the radishes and sour cream separately.

MEXICAN PULLED PORK

WHY THIS RECIPE WORKS: Traditional *carnitas*, Mexico's version of pulled pork, is fried in gallons of lard or oil. The results are tasty, but who wants to deal with all that hot fat? We wanted to create restaurant-style carnitas—tender chunks of lightly crisped, caramelized pork, subtly accented with oregano and citrus—without the hassle of frying.

Our initial recipe for carnitas started by simmering the meat (taste tests proved boneless pork butt had the best flavor) in a seasoned broth in the oven and then sautéing it in some of the rendered fat. The flavor was OK, but too much of the pork flavor went down the drain when we discarded the cooking liquid. So we kept the liquid and reduced it on the stovetop (after the meat had been removed) until it developed the consistency of a thick, syrupy glaze that was perfect for coating the meat. Broiled on a rack set over a baking sheet, the glazed meat developed a wonderfully rich flavor and the rack allowed the excess fat to drip off. We emulated the flavor of the Mexican sour oranges used in authentic carnitas with a mixture of fresh lime and orange juices. Bay leaves and oregano provided aromatic notes, and cumin brought an earthy dimension that complemented the other flavors.

Mexican Pulled Pork (Carnitas)

SERVES 6

We like serving carnitas spooned into tacos, but you can also use it as a filling for tamales, enchiladas, and burritos.

PORK

1 (3½ to 4-pound) boneless pork butt, fat cap trimmed to ⅛ inch thick, cut into 2-inch chunks

1 small onion, peeled and halved

2 bay leaves

1 teaspoon dried oregano

1 teaspoon ground cumin

Table salt and ground black pepper

2 cups water

2 tablespoons juice from 1 lime

1 medium orange, halved

TORTILLAS AND GARNISHES

18 (6-inch) corn tortillas, warmed (see note on page 285)

Lime wedges

Minced white or red onion

Fresh cilantro leaves

Thinly sliced radishes

Sour cream

1. Adjust an oven rack to the lower-middle position and heat the oven to 300 degrees. Combine the pork, onion, bay leaves, oregano, cumin, 1 teaspoon salt, ½ teaspoon pepper, water, and lime juice in a large Dutch oven (the liquid should just barely cover the meat). Juice the orange into a medium bowl and remove any seeds (you should have about ⅓ cup juice). Add the juice and spent orange halves to the pot. Bring the mixture to a simmer over medium-high heat, stirring occasionally. Cover the pot and transfer it to the oven; cook until the meat is soft and falls apart when prodded with a fork, about 2 hours, flipping the pieces of meat once during cooking.

2. Remove the pot from the oven and turn the oven to broil. Using a slotted spoon, transfer the pork to a bowl; remove the orange halves, onion, and bay leaves from the cooking liquid and discard (do not skim the fat from the liquid). Place the pot over high heat (use caution, as the handles will be very hot) and simmer the liquid, stirring frequently, until thick and syrupy (a heatproof spatula should leave a wide trail when dragged through the glaze), 8 to 12 minutes. You should have about 1 cup reduced liquid.

3. Using two forks, pull each piece of pork in half. Fold in the reduced liquid; season with salt and pepper to taste. Spread the pork in an even layer on a wire rack set over a rimmed baking sheet or on a broiler pan (the meat should cover almost the entire surface of the rack or broiler pan). Place the baking sheet on the lower-middle oven rack and broil until the top of the meat is well browned (but not charred) and the edges are slightly crisp, 5 to 8 minutes. Using a wide metal spatula, flip the pieces of meat and continue to broil until the top is well browned and the edges are slightly crisp, 5 to 8 minutes longer. Serve immediately with the warm tortillas and garnishes.

MEXICAN RICE

WHY THIS RECIPE WORKS: Rice cooked the Mexican way is a flavorful pilaf-style dish, but we've had our share of soupy or greasy versions. We wanted tender rice infused with well-balanced fresh flavor.

Texture is the backbone of this dish. To keep the rice grains distinct, we found it important to rinse the rice of excess starch before cooking it. And sautéing the rice in vegetable oil before adding the cooking liquid produced superior grains. The best texture for the rice was achieved by properly balancing the grain-to-liquid ratio. We found that equal portions of chicken broth and fresh tomatoes were ideal for a flavorful liquid base, which we combined in a 2:1 ratio with the rice. To further guarantee the right flavor, color, and texture, we added a little tomato paste and stirred the rice midway through cooking to reincorporate the tomato mixture. The garlic and jalapeños, meanwhile, fared best sautéed and then combined with a raw puree of tomato and onion. More than a garnish, fresh cilantro, minced jalapeño, and squirt of fresh lime juice complemented the richer tones of the cooked tomatoes, garlic, and onions. Our rice was neither greasy nor soggy, and the fresh flavors and easy preparation made it a unique side dish for a weeknight dinner.

Mexican Rice

SERVES 6 TO 8

Because the spiciness of jalapeños varies from chile to chile, we try to control the heat by removing the ribs and seeds (the source of most of the heat) from those chiles that are cooked into the rice. It is important to use an ovensafe pot about 12 inches in diameter so that the rice cooks evenly and in the time indicated. The pot's depth is less important than its diameter; we've successfully

used both a straight-sided sauté pan and a Dutch oven. Whichever type of pot you use, it should have a tight-fitting, ovensafe lid. Vegetable broth can be substituted for the chicken broth.

2 medium ripe tomatoes (about 12 ounces), cored and quartered

1 medium onion, preferably white, peeled and quartered

3 medium jalapeño chiles (see note)

2 cups long-grain white rice

⅓ cup vegetable oil

4 medium garlic cloves, minced or pressed through a garlic press (about 4 teaspoons)

2 cups low-sodium chicken broth (see note)

1 tablespoon tomato paste

1½ teaspoons table salt

½ cup minced fresh cilantro leaves

Lime wedges, for serving

1. Adjust an oven rack to the middle position and heat the oven to 350 degrees. Process the tomatoes and onion in a food processor until smooth and thoroughly pureed, about 15 seconds, scraping down the bowl if necessary. Transfer the mixture to a liquid measuring cup; you should have 2 cups (if necessary, spoon off the excess so that the volume equals 2 cups). Remove the ribs and seeds from 2 of the jalapeños and discard; mince the flesh and set aside. Mince the remaining jalapeño, including the ribs and seeds; set aside.

2. Place the rice in a large fine-mesh strainer and rinse under cold running water until the water runs clear, about 1½ minutes. Shake the rice vigorously in the strainer to remove all excess water.

3. Heat the oil in a heavy-bottomed straight-sided 12-inch ovenproof sauté pan or Dutch oven with a tight-fitting lid over medium-high heat for 1 to 2 minutes. Drop 3 or 4 grains of rice into the oil; if the grains sizzle, the oil is ready. Add the rice and fry, stirring frequently, until the rice is light golden and translucent, 6 to 8 minutes. Reduce the heat to medium, add the garlic and seeded minced jalapeños, and cook, stirring constantly, until fragrant, about 1½ minutes. Stir in the pureed tomato mixture, chicken broth, tomato paste, and salt. Increase the heat to medium-high and bring to a boil. Cover the pan and transfer to the oven. Bake until the liquid is absorbed and the rice is tender, 30 to 35 minutes, stirring well after 15 minutes.

4. Stir in the cilantro and reserved minced jalapeño with seeds to taste. Serve immediately, passing the lime wedges separately.

BASIC CHILI

WHY THIS RECIPE WORKS: Many basic chili recipes yield a pot of underspiced, underflavored chili reminiscent of sloppy Joes. We wanted an easy recipe for a basic chili, made with supermarket staples, that would have some heat and great flavors—chili that would please almost everyone.

To start, we added the spices to the pan with the aromatics (bell peppers, onion, and lots of garlic) to get the most flavor, and used commercial chili powder with a boost from more cumin, oregano, cayenne, and coriander. For the meat, we found that 85 percent lean beef gave us full flavor. A combination of diced tomato and tomato puree gave our chili a well-balanced saucy backbone. We added quick-cooking canned red kidney beans with the tomatoes so that they heated through and absorbed flavor. For a rich, thick consistency, we cooked the chili with the lid on for half of the cooking time.

Beef Chili with Kidney Beans

SERVES 8 TO 10

Good choices for condiments include diced fresh tomatoes, diced avocado, sliced scallions, chopped red onion, chopped cilantro leaves, sour cream, and shredded Monterey Jack or cheddar cheese. If you are a fan of spicy food, consider using a little more of the red pepper flakes or cayenne—or both. The flavor of the chili improves with age; if possible, make it a day or up to 3 days in advance and reheat before serving. Leftovers can be frozen for up to 1 month.

2 tablespoons vegetable oil

2 medium onions, minced (about 2 cups)

1 medium red bell pepper, stemmed, seeded, and cut into ½-inch dice

6 medium garlic cloves, minced or pressed through a garlic press (about 2 tablespoons)

¼ cup chili powder

1 tablespoon ground cumin

2 teaspoons ground coriander

1 teaspoon red pepper flakes (see note)

1 teaspoon dried oregano

½ teaspoon cayenne pepper (see note)

2 pounds 85 percent lean ground beef

2 (15-ounce) cans dark red kidney beans, drained and rinsed

1 (28-ounce) can diced tomatoes

1 (28-ounce) can tomato puree

Table salt

Lime wedges, for serving

1. Heat the oil in a large heavy-bottomed nonreactive Dutch oven over medium heat until shimmering but not smoking. Add the onions, bell pepper, garlic, chili powder, cumin, coriander, red pepper flakes, oregano, and cayenne and cook, stirring occasionally, until the vegetables are softened and beginning to brown, about 10 minutes. Increase the heat to medium-high and add half of the beef. Cook, breaking up the pieces with a wooden spoon, until no longer pink and just beginning to brown, 3 to 4 minutes. Add the remaining beef and cook, breaking up the pieces with a wooden spoon, until no longer pink, 3 to 4 minutes.

2. Add the beans, tomatoes with juice, tomato puree, and ½ teaspoon salt. Bring to a boil, then reduce the heat to low and simmer, covered, stirring occasionally, for 1 hour. Remove the lid and continue to simmer for 1 hour longer, stirring occasionally (if the chili begins to stick to the bottom of the pot, stir in ½ cup water and continue to simmer), until the beef is tender and the chili is dark, rich, and slightly thickened. Season with salt to taste. Serve with the lime wedges and condiments (see note), if desired.

CHILI CON CARNE

WHY THIS RECIPE WORKS: Real Texas chili, made with dried chiles rather than chili powder, should have exceptional chile flavor but not overpowering heat, a smooth, rich sauce, and hearty chunks of meat. We wanted to develop the ultimate version.

There are many types of dried chiles, and we chose a combination of ancho and New Mexican for a combination of earthy, fruity sweetness and crisp acidity. While chili powder works fine, we got the best flavor by toasting and grinding chiles ourselves. Chuck-eye is our favored cut of beef for stews and it seemed right for our chili. We cut the meat into 1-inch chunks, which gave the chili a hearty texture. Then, we browned the meat in fat rendered from bacon, which added a smoky depth to the dish. From among the many recommended liquids to use in chili con carne, we chose plain old water—everything else diluted or competed with the flavor of the chiles. Although many "authentic" recipes include neither tomatoes nor onions, we found both to be valuable additions. To thicken the chili, we mixed in some masa harina, which also imparted a subtle corn flavor.

Chili Con Carne

SERVES 6

To ensure the best chile flavor, we recommend toasting whole dried chiles and grinding them in a minichopper or spice-dedicated coffee grinder, all of which takes only 10 (very well-spent) minutes. Select dried chiles that are moist and pliant, like dried fruit. To toast and grind dried chiles: Place the chiles on a baking sheet in a 350-degree oven until fragrant and puffed, about 6 minutes. Cool, stem, and seed the pods, and tear them into pieces. Place pieces of the pods in a spice grinder and process until powdery, 30 to 45 seconds. For hotter chili, boost the heat with a pinch of cayenne pepper or a dash of hot sauce. Top with any of the following garnishes: chopped fresh cilantro leaves, minced white onion, diced avocado, shredded cheddar or Jack cheese, or sour cream.

3 medium ancho pods (about ½ ounce), toasted and ground (see note), or 3 tablespoons ancho chile powder

3 medium New Mexico pods (about ¾ ounce), toasted and ground (see note), or 3 tablespoons New Mexico chile powder

2 tablespoons cumin seeds, toasted in a dry skillet over medium heat until fragrant, about 4 minutes, and ground

2 teaspoons dried oregano, preferably Mexican

7½ cups water, plus extra for the masa harina or cornstarch

4. Mix the masa harina with ⅔ cup water (or corn-starch with 3 tablespoons water) in a small bowl to form a smooth paste. Increase the heat to medium, stir in the paste, and simmer until thickened, 5 to 10 minutes. Season generously with salt and ground black pepper to taste. Serve immediately or, for best flavor, cool slightly, cover, and refrigerate overnight or for up to 5 days. Reheat before serving.

WHITE CHICKEN CHILI

WHY THIS RECIPE WORKS: Chili made with chicken has become popular as a lighter, fresher alternative to the red kind. Though many recipes produce something more akin to chicken and bean soup, we thought there was potential to develop a rich stewlike chili with moist chicken, tender beans, and a complex flavor profile.

Ground chicken had a spongy texture and crumbly appearance, so we chose bone-in, skin-on breasts, later shredding the meat and discarding the skin and bones, and used the fat rendered from searing them to cook the aromatics. A single type of chile was one-dimensional; we used a combination of jalapeño, Anaheim, and poblano chiles, which have distinct characteristics that complement one another. Simply sautéing the chiles with the other aromatics left them flat-tasting and too crisp, so we covered the pot and cooked them longer to soften them and deepen their flavors. Canned cannellini beans circumvented the hassle of dried beans and tasted just as good. We tried thickening the chili with masa harina, which we had used for chili con carne, but the texture and flavor didn't work well here. Instead, we pureed some of the chili mixture, beans, and broth, which made the chili thicker without compromising its flavor. To finish, a minced raw jalapeño stirred in before serving provided a shot of fresh chile flavor.

---

4   **pounds beef chuck-eye roast, trimmed of excess fat and cut into 1-inch cubes**
    Table salt
8   **ounces bacon (about 8 slices), cut into ¼-inch pieces**
1   **medium onion, minced**
5   **medium garlic cloves, minced or pressed through a garlic press (about 5 teaspoons)**
4–5 **small jalapeño chiles, stemmed, seeded, and minced**
1   **cup canned crushed tomatoes or plain tomato sauce**
2   **tablespoons juice from 1 lime**
5   **tablespoons masa harina or 3 tablespoons cornstarch**
    Ground black pepper

1. Mix the chili powders, cumin, and oregano in a small bowl and stir in ½ cup of the water to form a thick paste; set aside. Toss the beef cubes with 2 teaspoons salt in a large bowl; set aside.

2. Fry the bacon in a large Dutch oven over medium-low heat until the fat renders and the bacon crisps, about 10 minutes. Remove the bacon with a slotted spoon to a paper towel–lined plate; pour all but 2 teaspoons fat from the pot into a small bowl; set aside. Increase the heat to medium-high; sauté the meat in four batches until well browned on all sides, about 5 minutes per batch, adding 2 teaspoons more bacon fat to the pot each time as necessary. Set the browned meat aside in a large bowl.

3. Reduce the heat to medium and add 3 tablespoons more bacon fat to the now-empty pan. Add the onion and sauté until softened, 5 to 6 minutes. Add the garlic and jalapeños and sauté until fragrant, about 1 minute. Add the chili powder mixture and sauté until fragrant, 2 to 3 minutes. Add the reserved bacon and browned beef, the remaining 7 cups water, the crushed tomatoes, and lime juice. Bring to a simmer. Continue to cook at a steady simmer (lowering the heat as necessary) until the meat is tender and the juices are dark and rich and starting to thicken, about 2 hours.

White Chicken Chili

SERVES 6 TO 8

Adjust the heat in this dish by adding the minced ribs and seeds from the jalapeño as directed in step 6. If Anaheim chiles cannot be found, add an additional poblano and jalapeño to the chili. This dish can also be successfully made by substituting chicken thighs for the chicken breasts. If using thighs, increase the cooking time in step 4 to about 40 minutes or until the chicken registers 175 degrees on an instant-read thermometer. Serve the chili with sour cream, tortilla chips, and lime wedges.

3 pounds bone-in, skin-on chicken breast halves, trimmed
Table salt and ground black pepper
1 tablespoon vegetable oil
3 medium jalapeño chiles (see note)
3 medium poblano chiles (see note), stemmed, seeded, and cut into large pieces
3 medium Anaheim chiles (see note), stemmed, seeded, and cut into large pieces
2 medium onions, cut into large pieces (about 2 cups)
6 medium garlic cloves, minced or pressed through a garlic press (about 2 tablespoons)
1 tablespoon ground cumin
1½ teaspoons ground coriander
2 (15-ounce) cans cannellini beans, drained and rinsed
3 cups low-sodium chicken broth
¼ cup minced fresh cilantro leaves
3 tablespoons juice from 2 limes
4 scallions, white and light green parts sliced thin

1. Season the chicken liberally with salt and pepper. Heat the oil in a large Dutch oven over medium-high heat until just smoking. Add the chicken, skin-side down, and cook without moving until the skin is golden brown, about 4 minutes. Using tongs, turn the chicken and lightly brown the other side, about 2 minutes. Transfer the chicken to a plate; remove and discard the skin.

2. While the chicken is browning, remove and discard the ribs and seeds from 2 of the jalapeños; mince the flesh. In a food processor, pulse half of the poblanos, Anaheims, and onions until the consistency of chunky salsa, 10 to 12 pulses, scraping down the sides of the workbowl halfway through. Transfer the mixture to a medium bowl. Repeat with the remaining poblanos, Anaheims, and onions; combine with the first batch (do not wash the food processor blade or workbowl).

3. Pour off all but 1 tablespoon of the fat from the Dutch oven (adding more vegetable oil if necessary) and reduce the heat to medium. Add the minced jalapeños, chile-onion mixture, garlic, cumin, coriander, and ¼ teaspoon salt. Cover and cook, stirring occasionally, until the vegetables soften, about 10 minutes. Remove the pot from the heat.

4. Transfer 1 cup of the cooked vegetable mixture to the now-empty food processor workbowl. Add 1 cup of the beans and 1 cup of the broth and process until smooth, about 20 seconds. Add the vegetable-bean mixture, remaining 2 cups broth, and chicken breasts to the Dutch oven and bring to a boil over medium-high heat. Reduce the heat to medium-low and simmer, covered, stirring occasionally, until the chicken registers 160 degrees (175 degrees if using thighs) on an instant-read thermometer, 15 to 20 minutes (40 minutes if using thighs).

5. Using tongs, transfer the chicken to a large plate. Stir in the remaining beans and continue to simmer, uncovered, until the beans are heated through and the chili has thickened slightly, about 10 minutes.

6. Mince the remaining jalapeño, reserving and mincing the ribs and seeds (see note), and set aside. When cool enough to handle, shred the chicken into bite-sized pieces, discarding the bones. Stir the shredded chicken, cilantro, lime juice, scallions, and minced jalapeño (with seeds if desired) into the chili and return to a simmer. Season with salt and pepper to taste and serve.

HUEVOS RANCHEROS

WHY THIS RECIPE WORKS: This Mexican egg dish was devised to use up leftover salsa and tortillas for a quick but filling "rancher-style" breakfast. What you get on this side of the border, however, is often spoiled with unnecessary ingredients and muddy flavors. We wanted to use readily available ingredients to produce as authentic a version of this dish as we could.

The salsa is a crucial element, and we know from experience that jarred salsa can't compare to freshly made, so we looked for ways to maximize the flavor of our supermarket tomatoes. We found that roasting plum tomatoes turned them more flavorful, and we thought roasting the onion and jalapeños improved their flavor as well. It was difficult to get fried eggs from the skillet onto the tortillas neatly (and without breaking the yolks), so we turned to poaching the eggs for a tidier presentation. We made things even easier by poaching them right in the simmering salsa, saving ourselves a pot to clean in the bargain. To pep up the supermarket tortillas, we brushed them with a little oil, sprinkled them with salt, and toasted them in the oven. Crisp tortillas, creamy eggs, and fiery salsa combined for a great American version of this Mexican classic.

Huevos Rancheros

SERVES 2 TO 4

To save time, make the salsa the day before and store it in the refrigerator. If you like, serve with Refried Beans (recipe follows).

- 3 jalapeño chiles, halved, seeds and ribs removed
- 1½ pounds ripe plum tomatoes (about 6 medium), cored and halved
- ½ medium onion, cut into ½-inch wedges
- 3 tablespoons vegetable oil
- 1 tablespoon tomato paste
- 2 medium garlic cloves, peeled
   Table salt
- ½ teaspoon ground cumin
- ⅛ teaspoon cayenne pepper
- 3 tablespoons minced fresh cilantro leaves
   Ground black pepper
- 1–2 tablespoons juice from 1 lime, plus an additional lime cut into wedges, for serving
- 4 (6-inch) corn tortillas
- 4 large eggs

1. FOR THE SALSA: Adjust an oven rack to the middle position and heat the oven to 375 degrees. Mince 1 jalapeño and set aside. In a medium bowl, combine the tomatoes, remaining 2 jalapeños, onion, 2 tablespoons of the oil, the tomato paste, garlic, 1 teaspoon salt, cumin, and cayenne; toss to mix thoroughly. Place the vegetables, cut side down, on a rimmed baking sheet. Roast until the tomatoes are tender and the skins begin to shrivel and brown, 35 to 45 minutes; cool on the baking sheet for 10 minutes. Increase the oven heat to 450 degrees. Using tongs, transfer the roasted onion, garlic, and jalapeños to a food processor. Process until almost completely broken down, about 10 seconds, pausing halfway through to scrape down the sides of the workbowl with a rubber spatula. Add the tomatoes and process until the salsa is slightly chunky, about 15 seconds more. Add 2 tablespoons of the cilantro, and the reserved minced jalapeño, salt, pepper, and lime juice to taste.

2. FOR THE TORTILLAS: Brush both sides of each tortilla lightly with the remaining tablespoon oil, sprinkle both sides with salt, and place on a clean baking sheet. Bake until the tops just begin to color, 5 to 7 minutes; flip the tortillas and continue to bake until golden brown, 2 to 3 minutes more.

3. FOR THE EGGS: Meanwhile, bring the salsa to a gentle simmer in a 12-inch nonstick skillet over medium heat.

Remove from the heat and make four shallow wells in the salsa with the back of a large spoon. Break 1 egg into a cup, then carefully pour the egg into a well in the salsa; repeat with the remaining 3 eggs. Season each egg with salt and pepper, then cover the skillet and place over medium–low heat. Cook to the desired doneness: 4 to 5 minutes for runny yolks, 6 to 7 minutes for set yolks.

4. TO SERVE: Place the tortillas on serving plates; gently scoop one egg onto each tortilla. Spoon the salsa around each egg, covering the tortillas but leaving a portion of the eggs exposed. Sprinkle with the remaining cilantro and serve with the lime wedges.

Refried Beans

MAKES ABOUT 3 CUPS

- 2 (15-ounce) cans pinto beans, drained and rinsed
- ¾ cup low-sodium chicken broth
- ½ teaspoon table salt
- 3 slices (about 3 ounces) bacon, minced
- 1 small onion, minced (about ¾ cup)
- 1 large jalapeño chile, stemmed, seeded, and minced (about 2 tablespoons)
- ½ teaspoon ground cumin
- 2 medium garlic cloves, minced or pressed through a garlic press (about 2 teaspoons)
- 2 tablespoons minced fresh cilantro leaves
- 2 teaspoons juice from 1 lime

1. Process all but 1 cup of the beans, the broth, and salt in a food processor until smooth, about 15 seconds, scraping down the sides of the workbowl with a rubber spatula if necessary. Add the remaining beans and pulse until slightly chunky, about 10 pulses.

2. Cook the bacon in a 12-inch nonstick skillet over medium heat until the bacon just begins to brown and most of the fat has rendered, about 4 minutes; transfer to a small bowl lined with a strainer; discard the bacon and add 1 tablespoon bacon fat back to the skillet. Increase the heat to medium-high, add the onion, jalapeño, and cumin, and cook until softened and just starting to brown, 3 to 5 minutes. Stir in the garlic and cook until fragrant, about 30 seconds. Reduce the heat to medium, stir in the pureed beans, and cook until thick and creamy, about 4 to 6 minutes. Off the heat, stir in the cilantro and lime juice and serve.

CHAPTER 16

LET'S DO TAKEOUT

Potstickers with Scallion Dipping Sauce   300

Shrimp Tempura   301

Thai Pork Lettuce Wraps   302

Beef Satay   303

Spicy Peanut Dipping Sauce

Thai-Style Chicken Soup   304

Hot and Sour Soup   305

Sesame Noodles with Shredded Chicken   306

Fried Rice with Shrimp, Pork, and Shiitakes   307

Fried Rice with Peas and Bean Sprouts   308

Basic White Rice

Chicken Teriyaki   309

Orange-Flavored Chicken   309

Stir-Fried Chicken with Bok Choy and Crispy Noodle Cake   310

Stir-Fried Chicken and Zucchini with Ginger Sauce   312

Stir-Fried Shrimp, Asparagus, and Yellow Pepper with Lemon Sauce   312

Stir-Fried Tofu, Snow Peas, and Red Onion with Hot and Sour Sauce   313

Stir-Fried Beef and Broccoli with Oyster Sauce   314

Teriyaki Stir-Fried Beef with Green Beans and Shiitakes   315

Tangerine Stir-Fried Beef with Onion and Snow Peas   316

Stir-Fried Pork, Eggplant, and Onion with Garlic and Black Pepper   317

Stir-Fried Pork, Green Beans, and Red Bell Pepper with Gingery Oyster Sauce   318

Pork Lo Mein   319

Kung Pao Shrimp   320

Stir-Fried Portobellos with Ginger-Oyster Sauce   321

Stir-Fried Portobellos with Sweet Chili-Garlic Sauce   322

Thai Green Curry with Chicken, Broccoli, and Mushrooms   322

Green Curry Paste

Thai Red Curry with Shrimp, Pineapple, and Peanuts   323

Red Curry Paste

Stir-Fried Thai-Style Beef with Chiles and Shallots   324

Pad Thai   326

Thai Grilled Chicken with Spicy, Sweet, and Sour Dipping Sauce   327

Chicken Biryani   328

Chicken Tikka Masala   329

Indian Curry   330

Indian-Style Curry with Potatoes, Cauliflower, Peas, and Chickpeas   331

Indian-Style Curry with Sweet Potatoes, Eggplant, Green Beans, and Chickpeas   332

Onion Relish

Cilantro-Mint Chutney

Tandoori Chicken   333

PERFECT POTSTICKERS

WHY THIS RECIPE WORKS: Too often, potstickers are dense, flavorless meatballs wrapped in a doughy blanket. We wanted soft, savory pillows filled with tender ground meat and crunchy cabbage and spiked with a pleasing hit of garlic, ginger, and soy. And we weren't willing to make wrappers from scratch.

To lighten up the filling a bit, we increased the amount of cabbage, after first salting and draining it to get rid of excess moisture, and then added lightly beaten egg whites. For the wrappers, we found that store-bought gyoza-style wrappers and wonton wrappers both made terrific potstickers, although tasters preferred the slightly chewy texture of the gyoza-style. To keep the filling in place and the wrapper from puffing up and away from the meat during cooking, we found it best to fold each meat-filled wrapper into a half-moon, pinch the middle closed, then carefully press out any air while sealing the edges. Our final challenge was the cooking method. A sequence of browning, steaming, then cranking up the heat produced potstickers with a perfect balance of soft and crispy textures.

Potstickers with Scallion Dipping Sauce

MAKES 24 DUMPLINGS

We prefer to use gyoza wrappers. You can substitute wonton wrappers, but the cooking time and recipe yield will vary. Potstickers are best served hot from the skillet; we recommend that you serve the first batch immediately, then cook the second batch.

SCALLION DIPPING SAUCE

- ¼ cup soy sauce
- 2 tablespoons rice vinegar
- 2 tablespoons mirin or sweet sherry
- 2 tablespoons water
- 1 teaspoon chili oil (optional)
- ½ teaspoon toasted sesame oil
- 1 scallion, minced

POTSTICKERS

- 12 ounces napa cabbage (½ medium head), cored and minced
- ¾ teaspoon table salt
- 12 ounces ground pork
- 4 scallions, minced
- 2 large egg whites, lightly beaten
- 4 teaspoons soy sauce
- 1½ teaspoons minced or grated fresh ginger
- 1 medium garlic clove, minced or pressed through a garlic press (about 1 teaspoon)
- ⅛ teaspoon ground black pepper
- 24 round gyoza wrappers (see note)
- 4 teaspoons peanut or vegetable oil

1. FOR THE SAUCE: Combine all the ingredients in a small bowl and set aside. (The sauce can be refrigerated in an airtight container for up to 24 hours.)

2. FOR THE FILLING: Toss the cabbage and salt together in a colander set over a bowl and let sit until the cabbage begins to wilt, about 20 minutes. Press the cabbage gently with a rubber spatula to squeeze out excess moisture, then transfer to a medium bowl. Stir the pork, scallions, egg whites, soy sauce, ginger, garlic, and pepper into the cabbage until combined. Cover and refrigerate until the mixture is cold, at least 30 minutes and up to 24 hours.

3. Working with 4 wrappers at a time (keep the remaining wrappers covered with plastic wrap), follow the photos on page 301 to fill, seal, and shape the dumplings using a generous 1 tablespoon of the chilled filling per dumpling. Transfer the dumplings to a baking sheet. (The filled dumplings can be refrigerated for up to 24 hours in a single layer on a baking sheet wrapped tightly with plastic wrap or frozen for up to 1 month. Once frozen, the dumplings can be transferred to a zipper-lock bag to save space in the freezer; do not thaw before cooking.)

4. Brush 2 teaspoons of the peanut oil over the bottom of a 12-inch nonstick skillet and arrange half of the dumplings in the skillet, with a flat side facing down (overlapping just slightly, if necessary). Place the skillet over medium-high heat and cook the dumplings, without moving, until golden brown on the bottom, about 5 minutes.

5. Reduce the heat to low, add ½ cup water, and cover immediately. Cook until most of the water is absorbed and the wrappers are slightly translucent, about 10 minutes. Uncover, increase the heat to medium-high, and cook, without stirring, until the dumpling bottoms are well browned and crisp, 3 to 4 minutes. Slide the dumplings from the skillet onto a paper towel–lined plate, browned side down, and let drain briefly.

6. Transfer the dumplings to a platter and serve with the sauce. Let the skillet cool until just warm, then wipe out the skillet with a wad of paper towels and repeat with the remaining peanut oil and dumplings.

NOTES FROM THE TEST KITCHEN

WRAPPING POTSTICKERS

The instructions below are for round wrappers, our preferred shape. If using square wrappers, fold diagonally into a triangle (step 2) and proceed with the recipe. For rectangular wrappers, fold in half lengthwise.

1. Place a rounded tablespoon of the filling in the center of each gyoza wrapper.

2. After moistening the edge of the wrapper, fold it in half to make a half-moon shape.

3. With your forefinger and thumb, pinch the dumpling closed, pressing out any air pockets.

4. Place the dumpling on its side and press gently to flatten the bottom.

SHRIMP TEMPURA

WHY THIS RECIPE WORKS: A few preliminary attempts at making tempura made us see why some Japanese chefs devote their entire careers to this one technique. Success hinges almost entirely on the batter—which is maddeningly hard to get right. We wanted a recipe for perfectly cooked shrimp tempura—light, crisp, and so fresh-tasting that it barely seemed fried.

We settled on using the largest shrimp available, since it's easy to overcook small shrimp. Instead of a wok, we substituted a large Dutch oven, the test kitchen's preferred deep-frying vessel. Cooking the tempura in 400-degree oil also helped limit grease absorption. To prevent the batter from clumping on the inside curl of the shrimp, we made two shallow cuts on the underside of its flesh. For the batter, we replaced a bit of the flour with cornstarch to improve the structure and lightness. For a super tender coating, we used a combination of seltzer and vodka instead of the traditional tap water. Seltzer is a little more acidic than tap water and therefore slows down gluten development, while the vodka prevents the formation of gluten. Our tempura was now light and crisp with the essence of sweet, tender shrimp.

Shrimp Tempura

SERVES 8

Do not omit the vodka; it is critical for a crisp coating. For safety, use a Dutch oven with a capacity of at least 7 quarts. Be sure to begin mixing the batter when the oil reaches 385 degrees (the final temperature should reach 400 degrees). It is important to maintain a high oil temperature throughout cooking. If you are unable to find colossal shrimp (8 to 12 per pound), jumbo (16 to 20 per pound) or extra-large (21 to 25 per pound) may be substituted. Fry smaller shrimp in three batches, reducing the cooking time to 1½ to 2 minutes per batch.

3 quarts peanut or vegetable oil

1½ pounds colossal shrimp (8 to 12 per pound), peeled and deveined (see page 160), tails left on (see note)

1½ cups (7½ ounces) unbleached all-purpose flour

½ cup cornstarch

1 cup vodka (see note)

1 large egg

1 cup seltzer water

Table salt

1 recipe Scallion Dipping Sauce (page 300)

1. Adjust an oven rack to the upper-middle position and heat the oven to 200 degrees. In a large, heavy Dutch oven fitted with a clip-on candy thermometer, heat the oil over high heat to 385 degrees, 18 to 22 minutes.

2. While the oil heats, make two shallow cuts about ¼ inch deep and 1 inch apart on the underside of each shrimp. Whisk the flour and cornstarch together in a large bowl. Whisk the vodka and egg together in a second large bowl, then whisk in the seltzer water.

3. When the oil reaches 385 degrees, whisk the vodka mixture into the bowl with the flour mixture until just combined (it is OK if small lumps remain). Submerge half of the shrimp in the batter. Using tongs, remove the shrimp from the batter one at a time, allowing the excess batter to drip off, and carefully place in the oil (the temperature should now be at 400 degrees). Fry, stirring with a chopstick or wooden skewer to prevent sticking, until light brown, 2 to 3 minutes. Using a slotted spoon, transfer the shrimp to a paper towel–lined plate and sprinkle with salt. Once the paper towels absorb the excess oil, transfer the shrimp to a wire rack set over a rimmed baking sheet and place in the oven to keep warm.

4. Return the oil to 400 degrees, about 4 minutes, then repeat with the remaining shrimp. Serve with the dipping sauce.

THAI PORK LETTUCE WRAPS

WHY THIS RECIPE WORKS: The classic Thai salad, *larb*, is made with finely chopped meat and nutty rice powder tossed with fresh herbs and a light dressing that embodies the cuisine's signature balance of sweet, sour, hot, and salty flavors. We aimed to develop a home-cook-friendly recipe.

Americanized recipes typically call for ground pork, but inconsistent results with supermarket ground pork inspired us to grind our own, using pork tenderloin and a food processor. To impart flavor and moisture to this lean cut, we marinated the meat in fish sauce. Toasted

rice powder, which adds a nutty flavor and texture to the pork, can be found in Asian markets, but we found it was easier to just make our own by toasting rice until golden brown and grinding it in a mini food processor or mortar and pestle. As for the aromatic components, we found that the pungency of sliced shallots and the bright flavor of chopped mint and cilantro yielded a very flavorful salad without a trip to a specialty store. For serving, the pork is spooned into lettuce leaves and wrapped. We preferred the crisp spine, tender leaf, and mild taste of Bibb lettuce.

Thai Pork Lettuce Wraps

SERVES 6

We prefer natural pork in this recipe. If using enhanced pork, skip the marinating in step 2 and reduce the amount of fish sauce to 2 tablespoons, adding it all in step 4.

1 (1-pound) pork tenderloin, trimmed of silver skin and fat, cut into 1-inch chunks, and frozen for 20 minutes (see note)

2½ tablespoons fish sauce

1 tablespoon white rice

¼ cup low-sodium chicken broth

3 medium shallots, peeled and sliced into thin rings (about ½ cup)

3 tablespoons roughly chopped fresh mint leaves

3 tablespoons roughly chopped fresh cilantro leaves

3 tablespoons juice from 2 limes

2 teaspoons sugar

¼ teaspoon red pepper flakes

1 head Bibb lettuce, washed and dried, leaves separated and left whole

1. Pulse half of the pork in a food processor until coarsely chopped, about 6 pulses. Transfer the ground pork to a medium bowl and repeat with the remaining chunks. Stir 1 tablespoon of the fish sauce into the ground pork, cover, refrigerate, and let marinate for 15 minutes.

2. Toast the rice in a small skillet over medium-high heat, stirring constantly, until deep golden brown, about 5 minutes. Transfer to a small bowl and cool for 5 minutes. Grind the rice with a spice grinder, mini food processor, or mortar and pestle until it resembles fine meal, 10 to 30 seconds (you should have about 1 tablespoon rice powder).

3. Bring the broth to a simmer in a 12-inch nonstick skillet over medium-high heat. Add the pork and cook, stirring frequently, until about half of the pork is no longer pink, about 2 minutes. Sprinkle 1 teaspoon of the rice powder over the pork and continue to cook, stirring constantly, until the remaining pork is no longer pink, 1 to 1½ minutes longer. Transfer the pork to a large bowl and cool for 10 minutes.

4. Add the remaining 1½ tablespoons fish sauce, remaining 2 teaspoons rice powder, the shallots, mint, cilantro, lime juice, sugar, and red pepper flakes to the pork and toss to combine. Serve with the lettuce leaves, spooning the meat into the leaves at the table.

BEEF SATAY

WHY THIS RECIPE WORKS: This Southeast Asian street food should be simple enough, but more often than not it is tough, bland, and boring. We wanted tender meat that could easily be pulled apart into small bites right off the skewer, with great Southeast Asian flavors like garlic, chiles, and cilantro.

Choosing the right cut of meat proved to be more about texture than flavor. Flank steak was the winner. We used two special techniques to slice it, first freezing the meat to firm it up enough to slice cleanly, then cutting the beef across the grain to keep it tender. Since the meat is so thin, cooking it was a breeze. Placing the skewered meat on a wire rack set over a baking sheet and cooking it 6 inches from the heating element proved just right. We found our marinade ingredients in the supermarket (Asian chile sauce is now commonly available) and added generous amounts of cilantro and garlic.

Beef Satay

SERVES 8 TO 10

Asian chili sauce, also called sriracha, is available in most supermarkets. Use 6-inch-long skewers for this recipe; you'll need about 24.

- ¼ **cup soy sauce**
- ¼ **cup peanut or vegetable oil**
- ¼ **cup packed dark brown sugar**
- ¼ **cup minced fresh cilantro leaves**
- 4 **scallions, sliced thin**
- 2 **tablespoons Asian chili sauce, or more to taste (see note)**
- 2 **medium garlic cloves, minced or pressed through a garlic press (about 2 teaspoons)**
- 1 **(1½-pound) flank steak, trimmed, halved lengthwise, frozen for 30 minutes, and sliced across the grain into ¼-inch-thick strips**
- 1 **recipe Spicy Peanut Dipping Sauce (recipe follows)**

1. Combine the soy sauce, oil, sugar, cilantro, scallions, chili sauce, and garlic in a large bowl. Stir in the beef, cover, and refrigerate for 1 hour.

2. Adjust an oven rack 6 inches from the heating element and heat the broiler.

3. Weave the meat onto 6-inch bamboo skewers (one piece per skewer). Lay the skewers on a wire rack set over a rimmed baking sheet and cover the skewer ends with foil. Broil the skewers until the meat is browned, 6 to 9 minutes, flipping the skewers over halfway through. Transfer the skewers to a serving platter and serve with the peanut sauce.

Spicy Peanut Dipping Sauce

MAKES ABOUT 1½ CUPS

This sauce can be refrigerated in an airtight container for up to 24 hours; bring to room temperature before serving.

- ½ **cup creamy peanut butter**
- ¼ **cup hot water**
- 2 **tablespoons juice from 1 lime**
- 2 **tablespoons Asian chili sauce**
- 1 **tablespoon soy sauce**
- 1 **tablespoon dark brown sugar**
- 1 **tablespoon chopped fresh cilantro leaves**
- 2 **scallions, sliced thin**
- 1 **medium garlic clove, minced or pressed through a garlic press (about 1 teaspoon)**

Whisk the peanut butter and hot water together in a small bowl until smooth. Stir in the remaining ingredients.

THAI-STYLE CHICKEN SOUP

WHY THIS RECIPE WORKS: Replicating the complex flavors of Thai chicken soup at home can be difficult, since it relies on such exotica as galangal, kaffir lime leaves, lemon grass, and bird's eye chiles. We wanted a plausibly authentic version of Thai chicken soup that could be prepared with more readily available (i.e., supermarket) substitutions.

We started by making a classic version of the soup, then substituting one ingredient at a time. We developed an acceptably rich and definitely chicken-flavored broth by using equal parts chicken broth and coconut milk (adding the coconut milk in two stages: at the beginning and just before serving). We couldn't fake the flavor of lemon

grass, but it proved to be easy enough to find. Our most exciting find was a "magic bullet" substitution: jarred red curry paste includes all the other exotic ingredients we were missing. Just adding a dollop at the very end of cooking and whisking it with pungent fish sauce and tart lime juice allowed all the classic flavors to come through loud and clear.

Thai-Style Chicken Soup

SERVES 6 TO 8

To make slicing the chicken easier, freeze it for 15 minutes. Although we prefer the richer, more complex flavor of regular coconut milk, light coconut milk can be substituted for one or both cans. For a spicier soup, add additional red curry paste to taste.

SOUP

- 1 teaspoon peanut or vegetable oil
- 3 stalks lemon grass, bottom 5 inches only, trimmed and sliced thin (see page 323)
- 3 large shallots, chopped coarse (about ¾ cup)
- 8 sprigs fresh cilantro, chopped coarse
- 3 tablespoons fish sauce
- 4 cups low-sodium chicken broth
- 2 (14-ounce) cans coconut milk (see note)
- 1 tablespoon sugar
- 8 ounces white mushrooms, wiped clean and sliced ¼ inch thick
- 1 pound boneless, skinless chicken breasts, trimmed, halved lengthwise, and cut on the bias into ⅛-inch pieces (see note)
- 3 tablespoons juice from 2 limes
- 2 teaspoons Thai red curry paste (see note)

GARNISH

- ½ cup loosely packed fresh cilantro leaves
- 2 Thai, serrano, or jalapeño chiles, seeds and ribs removed, chiles sliced thin
- 2 scallions, sliced thin on the bias
  Lime wedges, for serving

1. Heat the oil in a large saucepan over medium heat until just shimmering. Add the lemon grass, shallots, cilantro sprigs, and 1 tablespoon of the fish sauce and cook, stirring frequently, until just softened but not browned, 2 to 5 minutes.

2. Stir in the broth and 1 can of the coconut milk and bring to a simmer over high heat. Cover, reduce the heat to low, and simmer until the flavors have blended, about 10 minutes. Pour the broth through a fine-mesh strainer, discarding the solids in the strainer. (At this point, the soup can be refrigerated in an airtight container for up to 1 day.)

3. Return the strained soup to a clean saucepan and bring to a simmer over medium-high heat. Stir in the remaining can of coconut milk and the sugar and bring to a simmer. Reduce the heat to medium, add the mushrooms, and cook until just tender, 2 to 3 minutes. Add the chicken and cook, stirring constantly, until no longer pink, 1 to 3 minutes. Remove the soup from the heat.

4. Whisk the remaining 2 tablespoons fish sauce, the lime juice, and curry paste together, then stir into the soup. Ladle the soup into individual bowls and garnish with the cilantro, chiles, and scallions. Serve with the lime wedges.

HOT AND SOUR SOUP

WHY THIS RECIPE WORKS: Authentic versions of this soup have some hard-to-find ingredients such as mustard pickle, pig's-foot tendon, and dried sea cucumber—ingredients we couldn't find in the local grocery store. Using inventory only from our local supermarket, we wanted an authentic take on hot and sour soup, including spicy, bracing, pungent elements.

We created the "hot" side of the soup with two heat sources—distinctive, penetrating white pepper and a little chili oil. For the "sour" component, we preferred the traditional Chinese black vinegar, but found that a tablespoon each of balsamic and red wine vinegar made a suitable substitution. Cornstarch turned out to be a key ingredient: A cornstarch-based slurry thickened the soup; adding cornstarch to the pork marinade gave the pork a protective sheath that kept it tender; and beating the egg with cornstarch before drizzling it into the thickened soup kept the egg light, wispy, and cohesive. Pork and tofu are the usual, easy-to-find additions to the broth, but we had to come up with substitutes for a few other classic ingredients, settling on fresh shiitakes in lieu of wood ear mushrooms and canned bamboo shoots instead of lily buds. Spicy, bracing, rich, and complex, this soup has all the flavor of the classic version.

Hot and Sour Soup

SERVES 6 TO 8

To make slicing the pork chop easier, freeze it for 15 minutes. We prefer the distinctive flavor of Chinese black vinegar; look for it in Asian supermarkets. If you can't find it, use 1 tablespoon red wine vinegar and 1 tablespoon balsamic vinegar. This soup is very spicy. For a less spicy soup, omit the chili oil altogether or add only 1 teaspoon.

- **7** ounces (½ block) extra-firm tofu
- **¼** cup soy sauce
- **3** tablespoons plus 1½ teaspoons cornstarch
- **1** teaspoon toasted sesame oil
- **1** (6-ounce) boneless center-cut pork chop (about ½ inch thick), trimmed and cut into 1-inch-long matchsticks (see note)
- **3** tablespoons plus 1 teaspoon water
- **1** large egg
- **6** cups low-sodium chicken broth
- **1** (5-ounce) can bamboo shoots, sliced into matchsticks (about 1 cup)
- **4** ounces shiitake mushrooms, stemmed, wiped clean, caps sliced ¼ inch thick
- **5** tablespoons Chinese black vinegar (see note)
- **2** teaspoons chili oil (see note)
- **1** teaspoon ground white pepper
- **3** scallions, sliced thin

1. Place the tofu in a pie plate, top with a heavy plate, and weigh down with two heavy cans. Set the tofu aside until it has released about ½ cup liquid, about 15 minutes. When drained, cut the tofu into ½-inch cubes and set aside.

2. Meanwhile, whisk 1 tablespoon of the soy sauce, 1 teaspoon of the cornstarch, and the sesame oil together in a medium bowl. Stir in the pork, cover, and let marinate for

at least 10 minutes or up to 30 minutes.

3. Combine 3 tablespoons more cornstarch with 3 tablespoons of the water in a small bowl. Mix the remaining ½ teaspoon cornstarch with the remaining 1 teaspoon water in a second small bowl, then add the egg and beat with a fork until combined.

4. Bring the broth to a simmer in a large saucepan over medium-low heat. Add the bamboo shoots and mushrooms and simmer until the mushrooms are just tender, 2 to 3 minutes. Stir in the diced tofu and pork with its marinade and continue to simmer, stirring to separate any pieces of pork that stick together, until the pork is no longer pink, about 2 minutes.

5. Stir the cornstarch mixture to recombine, then add it to the soup, increase the heat to medium-high, and cook, stirring occasionally, until the soup thickens and turns translucent, about 1 minute. Stir in the remaining 3 tablespoons soy sauce, vinegar, chili oil, and pepper and turn off the heat.

6. Without stirring the soup, use a soupspoon to slowly drizzle very thin streams of the egg mixture into the pot in a circular motion. Let the soup sit off the heat for 1 minute. Briefly return the soup to simmer over medium-high heat, then remove from the heat immediately. Gently stir the soup once to evenly distribute the egg; ladle into individual bowls, sprinkle with the scallions, and serve.

COLD SESAME NOODLES

WHY THIS RECIPE WORKS: Cold noodles are underrated. Not as humble as they appear, these toothsome noodles tossed with shreds of tender chicken and fresh sesame sauce can be addicting if made properly. For this recipe, we set out to eliminate sticky noodles, gloppy sauce, and lackluster flavors.

We found that rinsing and tossing the noodles (either fresh Chinese noodles or dried spaghetti) with a little sesame oil after cooking prevents a rubbery texture and washes away much of their sticky starch. Boneless, skinless chicken breasts were the obvious choice for easy cooking and shredding, and broiling the meat helped retain the chicken's moisture and flavor. And for an authentic sauce, a combination of chunky peanut butter and freshly ground toasted sesame seeds was the best substitute for Asian sesame paste. After adding fresh garlic and ginger, as well as soy sauce, rice vinegar, hot sauce, and brown sugar, we achieved the perfect texture by thinning out the sauce with hot water.

Sesame Noodles with Shredded Chicken

SERVES 4 TO 6

Although our preference is for fresh Chinese noodles, we found that dried spaghetti works well, too. Because dried pasta swells so much more than fresh pasta during cooking, 12 ounces of dried spaghetti can replace 1 pound of fresh noodles.

> 5   tablespoons soy sauce
> ¼   cup sesame seeds, toasted
> ¼   cup chunky peanut butter
> 2   tablespoons rice vinegar
> 2   tablespoons light brown sugar
> 1   tablespoon minced or grated fresh ginger
> 2   medium garlic cloves, minced or pressed through a garlic press (about 2 teaspoons)
> 1   teaspoon hot sauce
>   Hot water
> 1   pound fresh Chinese noodles or 12 ounces dried spaghetti (see note)
> 1   tablespoon table salt
> 2   tablespoons toasted sesame oil
> 1½ pounds boneless, skinless chicken breasts, trimmed
> 4   scallions, sliced thin on the bias
> 1   carrot, peeled and shredded

1. Process the soy sauce, 3 tablespoons of the sesame seeds, the peanut butter, vinegar, brown sugar, ginger, garlic, and hot sauce together in a blender or food processor until smooth, about 30 seconds. With the machine running, add hot water, 1 tablespoon at a time, until the sauce has the consistency of heavy cream (you should need about 5 tablespoons); set aside.

2. Position an oven rack 6 inches from the heating element and heat the broiler.

3. Bring 6 quarts water to a boil in a large pot. Add the noodles and salt and cook, stirring often, until tender, about 4 minutes for fresh and 10 minutes for dried. Drain the noodles, rinse them under cold running water until cold, then toss them with the sesame oil.

4. Set a wire rack over a foil-lined rimmed baking sheet and lightly coat the rack with vegetable oil spray. Lay the chicken on the rack and broil until lightly browned, 4 to 8 minutes. Flip the chicken over and continue to broil until the thickest part of the breast registers 160 to 165 degrees on an instant-read thermometer, 6 to 8 minutes longer. Transfer the chicken to a carving board and let rest for 5 minutes. Using two forks, shred the chicken into bite-sized pieces and set aside.

5. Transfer the noodles to a large bowl, add the shredded chicken, sauce, scallions, and carrot and toss to combine. Divide the mixture among individual bowls, sprinkle with the remaining 1 tablespoon sesame seeds, and serve.

FRIED RICE

WHY THIS RECIPE WORKS: Fried rice is the perfect solution for leftover rice, but it often arrives in the bowl as a soggy mess of greasy rice doused in so much flavor-disguising soy sauce that you can hardly tell the vegetables from the chicken. We wanted fried rice with firm, separate grains, and we wanted a finished dish so clean and light that we could distinguish its many different flavors in every bite.

For fried rice that is light and flavorful rather than sodden and greasy, we found it essential to start with cold, dry rice (like leftover rice). Instead of gallons of soy sauce, we added a small amount in conjunction with complex oyster-flavored sauce to yield well-seasoned but not soggy rice. Cooking the vegetables and shrimp separately ensured that everything was cooked to perfection—no rubbery shrimp or mushy peas. And frying in just a couple tablespoons of oil kept the rice from being greasy. Lastly, we finished the dish with tender vegetables including bean sprouts and a sprinkling of scallions.

Fried Rice with Shrimp, Pork, and Shiitakes
SERVES 4 TO 6
See the Basic White Rice recipe on page 308 for tips on preparing and cooling rice.

- ½ ounce (5 to 6 medium) dried shiitake mushrooms
- ¼ cup oyster-flavored sauce
- 1 tablespoon soy sauce
- 3 tablespoons plus 1½ teaspoons peanut or vegetable oil
- 2 large eggs, lightly beaten
- 8 ounces small shrimp (51 to 60 per pound), peeled and deveined (see page 160)
- 1 cup frozen peas, thawed
- 8 ounces sliced smoked ham, cut into ½-inch pieces
- 2 medium garlic cloves, minced or pressed through a garlic press (about 2 teaspoons)
- 5 cups cold cooked white rice, large clumps broken up with fingers (see note)
- 1 cup bean sprouts
- 5 scallions, sliced thin

1. Cover the dried shiitakes with 1 cup hot tap water in a small microwave-safe bowl. Cover the bowl with plastic wrap and microwave on high power for 30 seconds. Let sit until the mushrooms soften, about 5 minutes. Lift the mushrooms from the liquid with a fork. Trim the stems, slice into ¼-inch strips, and set aside.

2. Combine the oyster-flavored sauce and soy sauce in a small bowl and set aside.

3. Heat 1½ teaspoons of the oil in a 12-inch nonstick skillet over medium heat until shimmering. Add the eggs and cook, without stirring, until they just begin to set, about 20 seconds. Scramble and break into small pieces with a wooden spoon and continue to cook, stirring constantly, until the eggs are cooked through but not browned, about 1 minute longer. Transfer the eggs to a small bowl and set aside.

4. Add 1½ teaspoons more oil to the skillet and heat over medium heat until shimmering. Add the shrimp and cook, stirring constantly, until opaque and just cooked through, about 30 seconds. Transfer the shrimp to the bowl with the eggs and set aside.

5. Add the remaining 2½ tablespoons oil to the skillet and heat over medium heat until shimmering. Add the mushrooms, peas, and ham and cook, stirring constantly, for 1 minute. Stir in the garlic and cook until fragrant, about 30 seconds. Add the rice and oyster-flavored sauce mixture and cook, stirring constantly and breaking up any rice clumps, until the mixture is heated through, about 3 minutes. Stir in the eggs, shrimp, bean sprouts, and scallions and cook until heated through, about 1 minute. Serve.

Fried Rice with Peas and Bean Sprouts

SERVES 4 TO 6

See the Basic White Rice recipe below for tips on preparing and cooling rice.

- ¼ **cup oyster-flavored sauce**
- 1 **tablespoon soy sauce**
- 3 **tablespoons peanut or vegetable oil**
- 2 **large eggs, lightly beaten**
- 1 **cup frozen peas, thawed**
- 2 **medium garlic cloves, minced or pressed through a garlic press (about 2 teaspoons)**
- 5 **cups cold cooked white rice, large clumps broken up with fingers (see note)**
- 1 **cup bean sprouts**
- 5 **scallions, sliced thin**

1. Combine the oyster-flavored sauce and soy sauce in a small bowl and set aside.

2. Heat 1½ teaspoons of the oil in a 12-inch nonstick skillet over medium heat until shimmering. Add the eggs and cook, without stirring, until they just begin to set, about 20 seconds. Scramble and break into small pieces with a wooden spoon and continue to cook, stirring constantly, until the eggs are cooked through but not browned, about 1 minute longer. Transfer the eggs to a small bowl and set aside.

3. Add the remaining 2½ tablespoons oil to the skillet and heat over medium heat until shimmering. Add the peas and cook, stirring constantly, for 1 minute. Stir in the garlic and cook until fragrant, about 30 seconds. Add the rice and oyster-flavored sauce mixture and cook, stirring constantly and breaking up any rice clumps, until the mixture is heated through, about 3 minutes. Stir in the eggs, bean sprouts, and scallions and cook until heated through, about 1 minute. Serve.

Basic White Rice

MAKES ABOUT 5 CUPS

To rinse the rice, you can either place it in a fine-mesh strainer and rinse it under cool water or place it in a medium bowl and repeatedly fill the bowl with water while swishing the rice around, then drain off the water. In either case, you must rinse the rice until the water runs clear.

- 3 **cups water**
- 2 **cups long-grain white rice, rinsed (see note)**

1. Bring the water and rice to a boil in a large saucepan over high heat. Reduce the heat to low, cover, and cook until all the water has been absorbed, about 10 minutes. Remove the pot from the heat and let sit, covered, until the rice is tender, about 15 minutes.

2. Serve, or to make fried rice, spread the cooked rice out over a baking sheet and let cool to room temperature, about 30 minutes. (The rice can be refrigerated in an airtight container for up to 24 hours.)

CHICKEN TERIYAKI

WHY THIS RECIPE WORKS: Too many chicken teriyaki recipes are lackluster—they can include everything from skewered chicken chunks shellacked in a corn-syrupy sauce to overmarinated, preformed chicken breast patties. They're a long way away from the simple recipe promised in the name "teriyaki"—meaning "to shine" (referring to the sauce) and meaning "to broil." We wanted a straightforward recipe that delivered the simple and authentic result of crisp and moist, sweet and salty, glazed chicken.

First, we decided against using breast meat. Bone-in, skin-on thighs stood up best to the salty profile of the teriyaki sauce. We set a weight on top of the chicken as it cooked (we used a heavy Dutch oven), which helped to

brown a greater surface area of the chicken evenly, as well as to aid in pressing out most of the fat. We also found that a quick mixture of soy sauce, sugar, mirin, and a few other flavorings made an incredible teriyaki sauce that far surpassed any we could buy in a bottle.

Chicken Teriyaki

SERVES 4

A splatter screen (or an inverted large strainer or colander) is helpful for controlling the splatter that occurs when the second side of the chicken browns. There is a fair amount of soy sauce in this dish, so there is no need to salt it before serving. Serve with Basic White Rice (page 308).

- 8 (5 to 6-ounce) bone-in, skin-on chicken thighs, trimmed
  Ground black pepper
- 2 teaspoons peanut or vegetable oil
- ½ cup soy sauce
- ½ cup sugar
- 2 tablespoons mirin or sweet sherry
- 2 teaspoons minced or grated fresh ginger
- 1 medium garlic clove, minced or pressed through a garlic press (about 1 teaspoon)
- ½ teaspoon cornstarch
- ⅛ teaspoon red pepper flakes

1. Pat the chicken thighs dry with paper towels and season with pepper. Heat the oil in a 12-inch nonstick skillet over medium-high heat until just smoking. Carefully lay the chicken in the skillet, skin side down. Weigh down the chicken with a heavy pot and cook until the skin is a deep mahogany brown and very crisp, 15 to 20 minutes. (The chicken should be moderately brown after 10 minutes. If it is very brown, reduce the heat; if it is still pale, increase the heat.)

2. Remove the weight and flip the chicken over. Reduce the heat to medium and continue to cook, without the weight, until the second side is brown and the thickest part of the thighs registers 175 degrees on an instant-read thermometer, about 10 minutes longer.

3. Meanwhile, whisk the soy sauce, sugar, mirin, ginger, garlic, cornstarch, and pepper flakes together in a small bowl; set aside.

4. Transfer the chicken to a plate. Pour off all of the fat from the skillet. Whisk the soy mixture to recombine, then add to the skillet and return to medium heat. Return the chicken to the skillet, skin side up, and spoon the sauce over the top. Continue to simmer until the sauce is thick and glossy, about 2 minutes longer. Serve.

ORANGE-FLAVORED CHICKEN

WHY THIS RECIPE WORKS: Chinese takeout orange-flavored chicken is never as good as its name promises—too often the dish delivers ultrathick breading wrapped around scraps of greasy, gristly, tasteless chicken bathed in an "orange" sauce that tastes likes a mixture of corn syrup and orange food coloring. We wanted substantial, well-seasoned chicken chunks with a crisp, golden brown crust, and a sauce that offered a clear hit of fresh orange flavor with balanced sweet, sour, and spicy background notes.

We chose thigh meat over breast meat for its rich flavor and tendency to remain moist when deep-fried. We marinated the chicken in a mixture of soy sauce, garlic, ginger, sugar, vinegar, fresh orange juice, and chicken broth, reserving some marinade to become the base for the final sauce. Then, we created a tender/crisp coating by dunking the marinated chicken first in egg white, then cornstarch. The egg white created a thin sheath of protein beneath the cornstarch that kept it dry, helping it to brown more readily than a wet, gluey coating would. A touch of baking soda helped the chicken pieces develop golden color during frying.

Orange-Flavored Chicken

SERVES 4

We prefer the flavor and texture of thigh meat for this recipe, though an equal amount of boneless, skinless chicken breasts can be used. Unless you have a taste for the incendiary, do not eat the whole chiles in the finished dish. Serve with Basic White Rice (page 308).

MARINADE AND SAUCE
- ¾ cup low-sodium chicken broth
- ¾ cup juice, 1½ teaspoons grated zest, and 8 strips peel (each about 2 inches long by ½ inch wide) from 2 oranges
- ½ cup packed dark brown sugar
- 6 tablespoons distilled white vinegar
- ¼ cup soy sauce
- 3 medium garlic cloves, minced or pressed through a garlic press (about 1 tablespoon)
- 1 tablespoon minced or grated fresh ginger
- ¼ teaspoon cayenne pepper
- 1½ pounds boneless, skinless chicken thighs, trimmed and cut into 1½-inch pieces (see note)
- 2 tablespoons cold water
- 1 tablespoon plus 2 teaspoons cornstarch
- 8 small whole dried red chiles (optional)

Transfer the chicken pieces to a paper towel–lined plate. Return the oil to 350 degrees and repeat with the remaining chicken.

5. TO SERVE: Reheat the sauce over medium heat until simmering, about 2 minutes. Add the chicken and gently toss until evenly coated and heated through. Serve.

CHICKEN STIR-FRY WITH CRISPY NOODLE CAKE

WHY THIS RECIPE WORKS: Stir-fries are the quintessential weeknight dinner. And while a stir-fry served on top of rice is great, a pan-fried noodle cake—crispy and crunchy on the outside and tender and chewy in the middle—offers a welcome change of pace.

For the noodle cake, we had the most success with fresh Chinese egg noodles—they made for a cohesive cake with a crunchy exterior. A nonstick skillet was crucial—it kept the cake from sticking and falling apart and allowed us to use less oil so the cake wasn't greasy. We found the best way to flip the cake in the skillet was to slide it onto a plate, invert it onto another plate, and then slide it back in the pan to finish cooking. We kept the stir-fry simple; chicken and bok choy are a classic combination. A quick marinade gave our chicken welcome flavor, and a modified version of the Chinese technique called velveting prevented the chicken from drying out over high heat.

COATING AND FRYING OIL

3 large egg whites
1 cup cornstarch
½ teaspoon baking soda
¼ teaspoon cayenne pepper
3 cups peanut or vegetable oil

1. FOR THE MARINADE AND SAUCE: Whisk the broth, orange juice, grated zest, sugar, vinegar, soy sauce, garlic, ginger, and cayenne together in a large saucepan until the sugar is fully dissolved. Transfer ¾ cup of the mixture to a medium bowl and add the chicken. Let marinate for at least 10 minutes or up to 1 hour.

2. In a small bowl, stir the cold water and cornstarch together. Bring the remaining mixture in the saucepan to a simmer over high heat. Whisk the cornstarch mixture into the sauce, bring to a simmer, and cook, stirring occasionally, until thick and translucent, about 1 minute. Off the heat, stir in the orange peel and chiles (if using) and set aside. (The sauce should measure 1½ cups.)

3. FOR THE COATING: Using a fork, lightly beat the egg whites in a shallow dish until frothy. In a second shallow dish, whisk the cornstarch, baking soda, and cayenne together until combined. Drain the chicken and pat dry with paper towels. Place half of the chicken pieces in the egg whites and turn to coat. Transfer the chicken pieces to the cornstarch mixture and coat thoroughly. Place the dredged chicken pieces on a wire rack set over a baking sheet. Repeat with the remaining chicken pieces.

4. TO FRY THE CHICKEN: Heat the oil in a Dutch oven over high heat until the oil registers 350 degrees on an instant-read or deep-fry thermometer. Carefully place half of the chicken in the oil and fry until golden brown, about 5 minutes, turning each piece with tongs halfway through.

Stir-Fried Chicken with Bok Choy and Crispy Noodle Cake

SERVES 4

To make slicing the chicken easier, freeze it for 15 minutes. Fresh Chinese noodles are often kept in the produce section of the grocery store. If you can't find them, substitute an equal amount of fresh spaghetti.

SAUCE

¼ cup low-sodium chicken broth
2 tablespoons soy sauce
1 tablespoon dry sherry
1 tablespoon oyster-flavored sauce
1 teaspoon sugar
1 teaspoon cornstarch
¼ teaspoon red pepper flakes

NOODLE CAKE

- 1 (9-ounce) package fresh Chinese noodles (see note)
- 1 teaspoon table salt
- 2 scallions, sliced thin
- ¼ cup peanut or vegetable oil

CHICKEN AND VEGETABLES

- 1 pound boneless, skinless chicken breasts, trimmed and sliced thin (see note)
- 1 tablespoon soy sauce
- 1 tablespoon dry sherry
- 2 tablespoons toasted sesame oil
- 1 tablespoon cornstarch
- 1 tablespoon unbleached all-purpose flour
- 2 tablespoons plus 2 teaspoons peanut or vegetable oil
- 1 tablespoon minced or grated fresh ginger
- 1 medium garlic clove, minced or pressed through a garlic press (about 1 teaspoon)
- 1 small head bok choy, stalks cut on the bias into ¼-inch pieces and greens cut into ½-inch strips
- 1 small red bell pepper, stemmed, seeded, and cut into ¼-inch strips

1. FOR THE SAUCE: Combine all the ingredients in a small bowl and set aside.

2. FOR THE NOODLE CAKE: Bring 6 quarts water to a boil in a large pot. Add the noodles and salt and cook, stirring often, until almost tender, 2 to 3 minutes. Drain the noodles, then toss them with the scallions.

3. Heat 2 tablespoons of the peanut oil in a 12-inch non-stick skillet over medium heat until shimmering. Spread the noodles evenly across the bottom of the skillet and press with a spatula to flatten into a cake. Cook until crisp and golden brown, 5 to 8 minutes.

4. Slide the noodle cake onto a large plate. Add the remaining 2 tablespoons peanut oil to the skillet and swirl to coat. Invert the noodle cake onto a second plate and slide it, browned side up, back into the skillet. Cook until golden brown on the second side, 5 to 8 minutes.

5. Slide the noodle cake onto a cutting board and let sit for at least 5 minutes before slicing into wedges and serving. (The noodle cake can be transferred to a wire rack set over a baking sheet and kept warm in a 200-degree oven for up to 20 minutes.) Wipe out the skillet with a wad of paper towels.

6. FOR THE CHICKEN AND VEGETABLES: While the noodles boil, toss the chicken with the soy sauce and sherry in a medium bowl and let marinate for at least 10 minutes or up to 1 hour. In a large bowl, whisk the sesame oil, cornstarch, and flour together. In a small bowl, mix 1 teaspoon of the peanut oil, the ginger, and garlic together.

7. Stir the marinated chicken into the sesame oil–cornstarch mixture. Heat 2 teaspoons more peanut oil in the skillet over high heat until just smoking. Add half of the chicken, break up any clumps, then cook without stirring until the meat is browned at the edges, about 1 minute. Stir the chicken and continue to cook until cooked through, about 1 minute longer. Transfer the chicken to a clean bowl and cover with foil to keep warm. Repeat with 2 teaspoons more peanut oil and the remaining chicken.

8. Add the remaining 1 tablespoon peanut oil to the skillet and return to high heat until just smoking. Add the bok choy stalks and bell pepper and cook until lightly browned, 2 to 3 minutes.

9. Clear the center of the skillet, add the ginger mixture, and cook, mashing the mixture into the pan, until fragrant, 15 to 20 seconds. Stir the ginger mixture into the vegetables, then stir in the bok choy greens and cook until beginning to wilt, about 30 seconds.

10. Stir in the chicken with any accumulated juices. Whisk the sauce to recombine, then add to the skillet and cook, tossing constantly, until the sauce is thickened, about 30 seconds. Transfer to a serving platter and serve with the noodle cake.

STIR-FRIES MADE SIMPLE

WHY THIS RECIPE WORKS: A good stir-fry made with chicken, shrimp, or tofu is more difficult to prepare than a beef or pork stir-fry because these proteins, which have less fat, are often bland. Worse, they inevitably become dry and stringy or rubbery when cooked over high heat. We aimed to create stir-fry recipes that harmonized the flavors and textures of these lighter proteins with complementary vegetables and sauces.

These leaner proteins inspired us to create light, fresh-tasting stir-fries. We paired the chicken with zucchini, red bell pepper, and a zesty ginger sauce. And asparagus, yellow bell pepper, and a brightly flavored lemon sauce were a natural fit for the shrimp. Lastly, we selected a slightly more assertive hot and sour sauce, along with red onion and snow peas, to enhance the mild-flavored tofu. As with most of our stir-fries, we marinated the thinly sliced chicken and shrimp, and cubes of tofu in a combination of soy sauce and dry sherry to add flavor and moisture. After cooking the chicken, shrimp, or tofu and removing it from the pan, we stir-fried the vegetables in batches, quickly cooked the garlic and ginger (the classic stir-fry combination) in the center of the pan, and returned the protein to the pan along with the sauce. This final mixture needed less than a minute over medium heat to finish.

Stir-Fried Chicken and Zucchini with Ginger Sauce

SERVES 4

To make slicing the chicken easier, freeze it for 15 minutes. Serve with Basic White Rice (page 308).

SAUCE

- ¼ cup soy sauce
- 3 tablespoons minced or grated fresh ginger
- 2 tablespoons low-sodium chicken broth
- 1 tablespoon dry sherry
- ½ teaspoon sugar

CHICKEN AND VEGETABLES

- 12 ounces boneless, skinless chicken breasts, trimmed and sliced thin (see note)
- 1 tablespoon soy sauce
- 1 tablespoon dry sherry
- 2 tablespoons toasted sesame oil
- 1 tablespoon cornstarch
- 1 tablespoon unbleached all-purpose flour
- 2 tablespoons peanut or vegetable oil
- 1 tablespoon minced or grated fresh ginger

- 3 medium garlic cloves, minced or pressed through a garlic press (about 1 tablespoon)
- 2 scallions, white parts only, minced
- 2 carrots, peeled and cut into 2-inch-long matchsticks
- 1 red bell pepper, stemmed, seeded, and cut into ½-inch strips
- 1 medium zucchini, halved lengthwise and sliced ½ inch thick

1. FOR THE SAUCE: Combine all the ingredients in a small bowl and set aside.

2. FOR THE CHICKEN AND VEGETABLES: Toss the chicken with the soy sauce and sherry in a medium bowl and let marinate for at least 10 minutes or up to 1 hour. In a large bowl, whisk the sesame oil, cornstarch, and flour together. In a small bowl, mix 1 teaspoon of the peanut oil, the ginger, garlic, and scallions together.

3. Stir the marinated chicken into the sesame oil–cornstarch mixture. Heat 2 teaspoons more peanut oil in a 12-inch nonstick skillet over high heat until just smoking. Add the chicken, break up any clumps, then cook without stirring until the meat is browned at the edges, about 1 minute. Stir the chicken and continue to cook until cooked through, about 1 minute longer. Transfer the chicken to a clean bowl and cover with foil to keep warm.

4. Add the remaining 1 tablespoon peanut oil to the skillet and return to high heat until just smoking. Add the carrots and cook until beginning to soften, about 1 minute. Add the bell pepper and cook until spotty brown, about 1 minute. Add the zucchini and cook for 15 to 30 seconds, until just tender.

5. Clear the center of the skillet, add the ginger mixture, and cook, mashing the mixture into the pan, until fragrant, 15 to 20 seconds. Stir the ginger mixture into the vegetables.

6. Stir in the chicken with any accumulated juices. Whisk the sauce to recombine, then add to the skillet and cook, tossing constantly, until the sauce is thickened, about 30 seconds. Transfer to a serving platter and serve.

Stir-Fried Shrimp, Asparagus, and Yellow Pepper with Lemon Sauce

SERVES 4

One large lemon yields enough juice and zest for this sauce. Serve with Basic White Rice (page 308).

SAUCE

- 3 tablespoons juice plus ½ teaspoon zest from 1 lemon
- 2 tablespoons low-sodium chicken broth
- 1 tablespoon soy sauce
- 2 teaspoons sugar

SHRIMP AND VEGETABLES

- 1 **pound medium shrimp (41 to 50 per pound), peeled and deveined (see page 160)**
- 1 **tablespoon soy sauce**
- 1 **tablespoon dry sherry**
- 2 **tablespoons plus 2 teaspoons peanut or vegetable oil**
- 1 **tablespoon minced or grated fresh ginger**
- 3 **garlic cloves, minced or pressed through a garlic press (about 1 tablespoon)**
- 2 **scallions, white parts only, minced**
- 1 **pound asparagus (1 bunch), tough ends trimmed, cut on the bias into 1-inch lengths**
- ¼ **cup water**
- 1 **yellow bell pepper, stemmed, seeded, and cut into ½-inch strips**
- **Table salt and ground black pepper**
- ¼ **cup chopped fresh cilantro leaves**

1. FOR THE SAUCE: Combine all the ingredients in a small bowl and set aside.

2. FOR THE SHRIMP AND VEGETABLES: Toss the shrimp with the soy sauce and sherry in a medium bowl and let marinate for at least 10 minutes or up to 1 hour. In a small bowl, mix 1 teaspoon of the oil, the ginger, garlic, and scallions together.

3. Heat 2 teaspoons more oil in a 12-inch nonstick skillet over high heat until just smoking. Add the shrimp and cook without stirring until bright pink, about 1 minute. Stir the shrimp and continue to cook until cooked through, 15 to 30 seconds longer. Transfer the shrimp to a clean bowl and cover with foil to keep warm.

4. Add 1 tablespoon more oil to the skillet and return to high heat until just smoking. Add the asparagus and cook, stirring frequently, until spotty brown, about 2 minutes. Add the water, cover the pan, and lower the heat to medium. Cook the asparagus until crisp-tender, about 2 minutes. Transfer the asparagus to the bowl with the shrimp. Add the remaining 2 teaspoons oil to the skillet and return to high heat until just smoking. Add the bell pepper and cook, stirring frequently, until spotty brown, about 1½ minutes.

5. Clear the center of the skillet, add the ginger mixture, and cook, mashing the mixture into the pan, until fragrant, 15 to 20 seconds. Stir the ginger mixture into the bell pepper.

6. Stir in the asparagus and shrimp with any accumulated juices. Whisk the sauce to recombine, then add to the skillet and cook, tossing constantly, until the sauce is thickened, about 30 seconds. Season with salt and pepper to taste. Transfer to a serving platter, sprinkle with the cilantro, and serve.

BEHIND THE SCENES

STIR-FRIES AT HOME? THROW OUT YOUR WOK!

We love the theatrics of the kitchen. And few pans seem as fun to use as a wok—watching a Chinese cook stir-fry with a wok can be as exciting as catching a great drum solo at a rock concert. So imagine our disappointment when we realized woks simply don't perform as well as we thought. A wok's shape is the culprit. A wok's conical bottom is designed for a pit-style stove; the flames lick and engulf the pan, making most of the surface area hot even when food is added. But when you set a wok over a conventional stovetop, the heat becomes concentrated in the pan's bottom—and the larger surface area—the sides—simply don't heat as well. And when food is added to the wok, the pan's temperature drops. The results? Meat that steams instead of sears and vegetables that turn soggy, rather than crisp-tender.

What *does* work on a conventional stovetop? A large nonstick skillet. Its flat-bottom design allows more of surface area to come in direct contact with the flat burner, delivering more heat over more parts than a wok—and enabling it to remain hot even after food is added.

To quantify their differences, we heated oil in a wok and a heavy 12-inch skillet over high heat on gas burners. Once the oil was smoking (at around 415 degrees), we added stir-fry ingredients to each pan. The wok's temperature plummeted dramatically, to 220 degrees at its center, rising only another 50 degrees over the course of cooking. The skillet's temperature dipped to 345 degrees, then recovered quickly, continuing to rise to almost 500 degrees. This higher heat translated to better browning and more flavor. The bottom line? Don't invest in a wok—use what you probably already have: a skillet. And if you want theatrics order some concert tickets.

Stir-Fried Tofu, Snow Peas, and Red Onion with Hot and Sour Sauce

SERVES 4

Make sure to buy firm or extra-firm tofu; silken or soft tofu will crumble if stir-fried. To promote caramelization on the exterior of the tofu, turn the cubes as little as possible so that they have time to brown on several sides. For more heat, include the jalapeño seeds and ribs when mincing.

SAUCE

- 3 tablespoons cider vinegar
- 1 tablespoon low-sodium chicken broth
- 1 tablespoon soy sauce
- 2 teaspoons sugar

TOFU AND VEGETABLES

- 1 (14-ounce) block firm or extra-firm tofu, drained and cut into 1-inch cubes (see note)
- 1 tablespoon soy sauce
- 1 tablespoon dry sherry
- 2 tablespoons plus 1 teaspoon peanut or vegetable oil
- 1 tablespoon minced or grated fresh ginger
- 3 garlic cloves, minced or pressed through a garlic press (about 1 tablespoon)
- 2 scallions, white parts only, minced
- 1 jalapeño chile, seeds and ribs removed, chile minced (see note)
- 1 medium red onion, halved and sliced thin
- 1 pound snow peas, tips and strings removed
- 2 tablespoons water

1. FOR THE SAUCE: Combine all the ingredients in a small bowl and set aside.

2. FOR THE TOFU AND VEGETABLES: Toss the tofu with the soy sauce and sherry in a medium bowl and let marinate for at least 10 minutes or up to 1 hour. In a small bowl, mix 1 teaspoon of the oil, the ginger, garlic, scallions, and jalapeño together.

3. Heat 1 tablespoon more oil in a 12-inch nonstick skillet over high heat until just smoking. Add the tofu and cook until golden brown on several sides, 2 to 3 minutes, turning as needed. Transfer the tofu to a clean bowl and cover with foil to keep warm.

4. Add the remaining 1 tablespoon oil to the skillet and return to high heat until just smoking. Add the onion and cook, stirring frequently, until beginning to brown, about 2 minutes. Add the snow peas and cook until spotty brown, about 2 minutes. Add the water, cover the pan, and lower the heat to medium. Cook the snow peas until crisp-tender, about 1 minute.

5. Clear the center of the skillet, add the ginger mixture, and cook, mashing the mixture into the pan, until fragrant, 15 to 20 seconds. Stir the ginger mixture into the vegetables.

6. Stir in the tofu. Whisk the sauce to recombine, then add to the skillet and cook, tossing constantly, until the sauce is thickened, about 30 seconds. Transfer to a serving platter and serve.

STIR-FRIED BEEF AND BROCCOLI

WHY THIS RECIPE WORKS: Order beef and broccoli in most Chinese restaurants, and you are served a pile of tough meat and overcooked army-issue broccoli. Worst of all is the thick-as-pudding brown sauce, which, aside from being flavored with burnt garlic, is otherwise tasteless. We set out to rescue this dish from the tyranny of third-rate Chinese restaurants.

For the meat, we found that flank steak offered the biggest beefy taste and slicing it thin made it tender. We cooked the beef in two batches over high heat to make sure it browned and didn't steam. Then we cooked the broccoli until crisp-tender using a combination of methods—sautéing and steaming—and added some red bell pepper for sweetness and color. For the sauce, we made a simple mixture of oyster-flavored sauce, chicken broth, dry sherry, sugar, and sesame oil, which we lightly thickened with cornstarch so it clung beautifully to the beef and vegetables, but was in no way gloppy. Now we had it: Every component of the dish—the beef, the broccoli, and sauce—was distinct and cooked to the best of its ability.

Stir-Fried Beef and Broccoli with Oyster Sauce

SERVES 4

To make slicing the flank steak easier, freeze it for 15 minutes. Serve with Basic White Rice (page 308).

SAUCE

- 5 tablespoons oyster-flavored sauce
- 2 tablespoons low-sodium chicken broth
- 1 tablespoon dry sherry
- 1 tablespoon light brown sugar
- 1 teaspoon toasted sesame oil
- 1 teaspoon cornstarch

BEEF AND BROCCOLI

1 (1-pound) flank steak, trimmed and cut into 2-inch-wide strips with the grain, then sliced across the grain into ⅛-inch-thick slices (see note)

3 tablespoons soy sauce

3 tablespoons peanut or vegetable oil

6 medium garlic cloves, minced or pressed through a garlic press (about 2 tablespoons)

1 tablespoon minced or grated fresh ginger

1¼ pounds broccoli, florets cut into 1-inch pieces, stems trimmed and sliced thin

⅓ cup water

1 small red bell pepper, stemmed, seeded, and cut into ½-inch pieces

3 scallions, sliced ½ inch thick on the bias

1. FOR THE SAUCE: Combine all the ingredients in a small bowl and set aside.

2. FOR THE BEEF AND BROCCOLI: Toss the beef with the soy sauce in a medium bowl and let marinate for at least 10 minutes or up to 1 hour. In a small bowl, mix 1 teaspoon of the peanut oil, the garlic, and ginger together.

3. Heat 2 teaspoons more peanut oil in a 12-inch non-stick skillet over high heat until just smoking. Add half of the beef, break up any clumps, then cook without stirring until the meat is browned at the edges, about 1 minute. Stir the beef and continue to cook until cooked through, about 1 minute longer. Transfer the beef to a clean bowl and cover with foil to keep warm. Repeat with 2 tea-spoons more peanut oil and the remaining beef.

4. Add 1 tablespoon more peanut oil to the skillet and return to high heat until just smoking. Add the broccoli and cook for 30 seconds. Add the water, cover the pan, and lower the heat to medium. Cook the broccoli until crisp-tender, about 2 minutes. Transfer the broccoli to a paper towel–lined plate.

5. Add the remaining 1 teaspoon peanut oil to the skillet and return to high heat until just smoking. Add the bell pepper and cook, stirring frequently, until spotty brown, about 1½ minutes. Clear the center of the skillet, add the garlic mixture, and cook, mashing the mixture into the pan, until fragrant, 15 to 20 seconds. Stir the garlic mixture into the bell pepper.

6. Stir in the broccoli and beef with any accumulated juices. Whisk the sauce to recombine, then add to the skillet and cook, tossing constantly, until the sauce is thickened, about 30 seconds. Transfer to a serving platter, sprinkle with the scallions, and serve.

BEEF AND VEGETABLE STIR-FRIES

WHY THIS RECIPE WORKS: More often than not, beef and vegetable stir-fries consist of chewy, gray beef, surrounded by unevenly cooked vegetables, smothered in a gloppy sauce. We wanted browned, tender beef and crisp-tender vegetables coated in deep-flavored, silky sauces.

We chose flank steak for the best texture and flavor. We thinly sliced and marinated the steak in soy sauce and sugar and cooked it over high heat to achieve a good sear. We cooked the vegetables in batches for best texture. For one stir-fry, we paired the beef with green beans, shiitakes, and a teriyaki sauce. Next, we combined the beef with a tangerine sauce, snow peas, and onion. The sauces were lightly thickened with just 1 teaspoon of cornstarch, so they clung to the beef and vegetables but were not overly thick.

Teriyaki Stir-Fried Beef with Green Beans and Shiitakes

SERVES 4

To make slicing the flank steak easier, freeze it for 15 minutes. Serve with Basic White Rice (page 308).

SAUCE

½ cup low-sodium chicken broth

2 tablespoons soy sauce

2 tablespoons sugar

1 tablespoon mirin or sweet sherry

1 teaspoon cornstarch

¼ teaspoon red pepper flakes

BEEF AND VEGETABLES

12 ounces flank steak, trimmed and cut into 2-inch-wide strips with the grain, then sliced across the grain into ⅛-inch-thick slices (see note)

2 tablespoons soy sauce

1 teaspoon sugar

2 tablespoons peanut or vegetable oil

1 tablespoon minced or grated fresh ginger

3 medium garlic cloves, minced or pressed through a garlic press (about 1 tablespoon)

8 ounces shiitake mushrooms, stemmed, wiped clean, caps cut into 1-inch pieces

12 ounces green beans, ends trimmed, cut into 2-inch lengths

¼ cup water

3 scallions, quartered lengthwise and cut into 1½-inch pieces

1. FOR THE SAUCE: Combine all the ingredients in a small bowl and set aside.

2. FOR THE BEEF AND VEGETABLES: Toss the beef with the soy sauce and sugar in a medium bowl and let marinate for at least 10 minutes or up to 1 hour. In a small bowl, mix 1 teaspoon of the oil, the ginger, and garlic together.

3. Heat 2 teaspoons more oil in a 12-inch nonstick skillet over high heat until just smoking. Add the beef, break up any clumps, then cook without stirring until the meat is browned at the edges, about 1 minute. Stir the beef and continue to cook until cooked through, about 1 minute longer. Transfer the beef to a clean bowl and cover with foil to keep warm.

4. Add the remaining 1 tablespoon oil to the skillet and return to high heat until just smoking. Add the mushrooms and cook until beginning to brown, about 2 minutes. Add the green beans and cook, stirring frequently, until spotty brown, 3 to 4 minutes. Add the water, cover the pan, and lower the heat to medium. Cook the green beans until crisp-tender, about 2 minutes.

5. Clear the center of the skillet, add the ginger mixture, and cook, mashing the mixture into the pan, until fragrant, 15 to 20 seconds. Stir the ginger mixture into the vegetables.

6. Stir in the beef with any accumulated juices. Whisk the sauce to recombine, then add to the skillet and cook, tossing constantly, until the sauce is thickened, about 30 seconds. Stir in the scallions. Transfer to a serving platter and serve.

NOTES FROM THE TEST KITCHEN

TRIMMING GREEN BEANS QUICKLY

Line up several green beans in a row on a cutting board. Trim about ½ inch from each end, then cut the beans as directed in the recipe.

Tangerine Stir-Fried Beef with Onion and Snow Peas

SERVES 4

To make slicing the flank steak easier, freeze it for 15 minutes. Two to 3 oranges can be substituted for the tangerines. Note that you should zest the tangerines before juicing them. Use the larger amount of red pepper flakes if you desire a spicier dish. If available, substitute 1 teaspoon toasted and ground Sichuan peppercorns for the red pepper flakes. Serve with Basic White Rice (page 308).

SAUCE

- ¾ cup juice from 3 to 4 tangerines (see note)
- 2 tablespoons soy sauce
- 1 tablespoon light brown sugar
- 1 teaspoon toasted sesame oil
- 1 teaspoon cornstarch

BEEF AND VEGETABLES

- 12 ounces flank steak, trimmed and cut into 2-inch-wide strips with the grain, then sliced across the grain into ⅛-inch-thick slices (see note)
- 2 tablespoons soy sauce
- 1 teaspoon light brown sugar
- 2 tablespoons peanut or vegetable oil
- 1 tablespoon minced or grated fresh ginger
- 3 medium garlic cloves, minced or pressed through a garlic press (about 1 tablespoon)
- 1 tablespoon Chinese black bean sauce
- 1 teaspoon grated zest from 1 tangerine (see note)
- ¼–½ teaspoon red pepper flakes (see note)
- 1 large onion, halved and cut into ½-inch wedges
- 10 ounces snow peas, tips and strings removed
- 2 tablespoons water

1. FOR THE SAUCE: Combine all the ingredients in a small bowl and set aside.

2. FOR THE BEEF AND VEGETABLES: Toss the beef with the soy sauce and sugar in a medium bowl and let marinate for at least 10 minutes or up to 1 hour. In a small bowl, mix 1 teaspoon of the peanut oil, the ginger, garlic, black bean sauce, tangerine zest, and red pepper flakes together.

3. Heat 2 teaspoons more peanut oil in a 12-inch nonstick skillet over high heat until just smoking. Add the beef, break up any clumps, then cook without stirring until the meat is browned at the edges, about 1 minute. Stir the beef and continue to cook until cooked through, about 1 minute longer. Transfer the beef to a clean bowl and cover with foil to keep warm.

4. Add the remaining 1 tablespoon peanut oil to the skillet and return to high heat until just smoking. Add the onion and cook, stirring frequently, until beginning to brown, about 2 minutes. Add the snow peas and cook until spotty brown, about 2 minutes. Add the water, cover the pan, and lower the heat to medium. Cook the snow peas until crisp-tender, about 1 minute.

5. Clear the center of the skillet, add the ginger mixture, and cook, mashing the mixture into the pan, until fragrant, 15 to 20 seconds. Stir the ginger mixture into the vegetables.

6. Stir in the beef with any accumulated juices. Whisk the sauce to recombine, then add to the skillet and cook, tossing constantly, until the sauce is thickened, about 30 seconds. Transfer to a serving platter and serve.

PORK AND VEGETABLE STIR-FRIES

WHY THIS RECIPE WORKS: Pork and vegetable stir-fries, homemade or ordered out, are usually nothing more than tough, tasteless pork and barely cooked vegetables in a thick, slithery sauce. We wanted to make pork and vegetable stir-fries that had tender, flavorful pork and perfectly cooked vegetables—dishes that would taste authentic but would not have epic ingredient lists.

We chose pork tenderloin for our stir-fry because it is so tender. Marinating improved the pork's flavor. As with most stir-fries, cooking quickly over high heat ensured browning. Because different vegetables cook at different rates, we batch-cooked the vegetables and added aromatics (like ginger and garlic) at the end so they would cook long enough to develop their flavors but not burn. For the sauce, we used chicken broth as the backbone and added an acid to brighten the flavors. As with our other stir-fries, cornstarch created a slightly thickened sauce that lightly cloaked the pork and vegetables.

Stir-Fried Pork, Eggplant, and Onion with Garlic and Black Pepper

SERVES 4

To make slicing the pork easier, freeze it for 15 minutes. This classic Thai stir-fry is not for those with timid palates. Serve with Basic White Rice (page 308).

SAUCE

- 2½ tablespoons soy sauce
- 2½ tablespoons fish sauce
- 2½ tablespoons light brown sugar
- 2 tablespoons low-sodium chicken broth
- 2 teaspoons juice from 1 lime
- 1 teaspoon cornstarch

PORK AND VEGETABLES

- 1 (12-ounce) pork tenderloin, trimmed of fat and silver skin and cut into ¼-inch strips (see note)
- 1 teaspoon soy sauce
- 1 teaspoon fish sauce
- 3 tablespoons peanut or vegetable oil
- 12 medium garlic cloves, minced or pressed through a garlic press (about ¼ cup)
- 2 teaspoons ground black pepper
- 1 medium eggplant (1 pound), cut into ¾-inch cubes
- 1 large onion, halved and cut into ¼-inch wedges
- ½ cup chopped fresh cilantro leaves

1. FOR THE SAUCE: Combine all the ingredients in a small bowl and set aside.

2. FOR THE PORK AND VEGETABLES: Toss the pork with the soy sauce and fish sauce in a medium bowl and let marinate for at least 10 minutes or up to 1 hour. In a small bowl, mix 2 teaspoons of the oil, the garlic, and pepper together.

3. Heat 2 teaspoons more oil in a 12-inch nonstick skillet over high heat until just smoking. Add the pork, break up any clumps, then cook without stirring until the meat is browned at the edges, about 1 minute. Stir the pork and continue to cook until cooked through, about 1 minute longer. Transfer the pork to a clean bowl and cover with foil to keep warm.

4. Add 1 tablespoon more oil to the skillet and return to high heat until just smoking. Add the eggplant and cook, stirring frequently, until browned and no longer spongy, about 5 minutes. Transfer the eggplant to the bowl with the pork. Add the remaining 2 teaspoons peanut oil to the skillet and return to high heat until just smoking. Add the onion and cook until beginning to brown and soften, about 2 minutes.

5. Clear the center of the skillet, add the garlic mixture, and cook, mashing the mixture into the pan, until fragrant, 15 to 20 seconds. Stir the garlic mixture into the onion.

6. Stir in the eggplant and pork with any accumulated juices. Whisk the sauce to recombine, then add to the skillet and cook, tossing constantly, until the sauce is thickened, about 30 seconds. Transfer to a serving platter, sprinkle with the cilantro, and serve.

Stir-Fried Pork, Green Beans, and Red Bell Pepper with Gingery Oyster Sauce

SERVES 4

To make slicing the pork easier, freeze it for 15 minutes. Serve with Basic White Rice (page 308).

SAUCE

- ⅓ **cup low-sodium chicken broth**
- 2½ **tablespoons oyster-flavored sauce**
- 1 **tablespoon dry sherry**
- 2 **teaspoons toasted sesame oil**
- 1 **teaspoon rice vinegar**
- 1 **teaspoon cornstarch**
- ¼ **teaspoon ground white pepper**

PORK AND VEGETABLES

- 1 **(12-ounce) pork tenderloin, trimmed of fat and silver skin and cut into ¼-inch strips (see note)**
- 2 **teaspoons soy sauce**
- 2 **teaspoons dry sherry**
- 3 **tablespoons peanut or vegetable oil**
- 2 **tablespoons minced or grated fresh ginger**
- 2 **garlic cloves, minced or pressed through a garlic press (about 2 teaspoons)**
- 12 **ounces green beans, trimmed and cut on the bias into 2-inch lengths**
- ¼ **cup water**
- 1 **large red bell pepper, stemmed, seeded, and cut into ¾-inch squares**
- 3 **scallions, sliced thin on the bias**

1. FOR THE SAUCE: Combine all the ingredients in a small bowl and set aside.

2. FOR THE PORK AND VEGETABLES: Toss the pork with the soy sauce and sherry in a medium bowl and let marinate for at least 10 minutes or up to 1 hour. In a small bowl, mix 2 teaspoons of the peanut oil, the ginger, and garlic together.

3. Heat 2 teaspoons more peanut oil in a 12-inch nonstick skillet over high heat until just smoking. Add the pork, break up any clumps, then cook without stirring until the meat is browned at the edges, about 1 minute. Stir the pork and continue to cook until cooked through, about 1 minute longer. Transfer the pork to a clean bowl and cover with foil to keep warm.

4. Add 1 tablespoon more peanut oil to the skillet and return to high heat until just smoking. Add the green beans and cook, stirring frequently, until spotty brown, 3 to 4 minutes. Add the water, cover the pan, and lower the heat to medium. Cook the green beans until crisp-tender, about 2 minutes. Transfer the green beans to the bowl with the pork. Add the remaining 2 teaspoons peanut oil to the skillet and return to high heat until just smoking. Add the bell pepper and cook until spotty brown, about 1½ minutes.

5. Clear the center of the skillet, add the ginger mixture, and cook, mashing the mixture into the pan, until fragrant, 15 to 20 seconds. Stir the ginger mixture into the bell pepper.

6. Stir in the green beans and pork with any accumulated juices. Whisk the sauce to recombine, then add to the skillet and cook, tossing constantly, until the sauce is thickened, about 30 seconds. Transfer to a serving platter, sprinkle with the scallions, and serve.

PORK LO MEIN

WHY THIS RECIPE WORKS: Ordinary takeout pork lo mein invariably disappoints, with greasy flavors and sodden vegetables. We wanted a dish representative of the best that a good Chinese home cook could turn out: chewy noodles tossed in a salty-sweet sauce and accented with bits of smoky, barbecued pork and still-crisp cabbage.

First we needed to tackle the char siu, preferably perfecting a stir-fried version since we were already stir-frying the vegetables. Country-style pork ribs won for best cut. Though fatty, these meaty ribs have the same rich flavor of pork shoulder—but don't need to be cooked for hours since they're naturally tender. To avoid an overly greasy dish, we trimmed the fat and cut the meat into thin strips that would allow our classic Chinese marinade to penetrate effectively. A few drops of liquid smoke mimicked char siu's characteristic smoky flavor. Turning to the noodles, only ones labeled "lo mein" at the Asian market won raves. Fortunately, dried linguine, cooked to al dente, worked beautifully. For the vegetables, we opted for traditional choices—cabbage, scallions, and shiitake mushrooms—stir-frying them with garlic and fresh ginger. We used our meat marinade as a sauce base, with a little chicken broth and a teaspoon of cornstarch added for body. A splash of Asian chili-garlic sauce added a little kick.

Pork Lo Mein

SERVES 4

Use a cast-iron skillet for this recipe if you have one—it will help create the best sear on the pork. If boneless pork ribs are unavailable, substitute 1½ pounds bone-in country-style ribs, followed by the next-best option, pork tenderloin. Liquid smoke provides a flavor reminiscent of the Chinese barbecued pork traditional to this dish. It is important to cook the noodles at the last minute to avoid clumping.

- **3** tablespoons soy sauce
- **2** tablespoons oyster-flavored sauce
- **2** tablespoons hoisin sauce
- **1** tablespoon toasted sesame oil
- **¼** teaspoon Chinese five-spice powder
- **1** pound boneless country-style pork ribs, trimmed of fat and gristle, sliced crosswise into ⅛-inch pieces (see note)
- **¼** teaspoon liquid smoke (optional; see note)
- **½** cup low-sodium chicken broth
- **1** teaspoon cornstarch
- **2** tablespoons plus 1 teaspoon peanut or vegetable oil
- **2** teaspoons minced or grated fresh ginger
- **2** medium garlic cloves, minced or pressed through a garlic press (about 2 teaspoons)
- **¼** cup Chinese rice cooking wine (Shao-Xing) or dry sherry
- **8** ounces shiitake mushrooms, stemmed, wiped clean, caps sliced ¼ inch thick
- **2** bunches scallions, whites sliced thin, greens cut into 1-inch pieces
- **1** pound napa cabbage (1 small head), cored and cut into ½-inch strips
- **12** ounces fresh Chinese noodles or 8 ounces dried linguine
- **1** tablespoon Asian chili-garlic sauce

1. Whisk the soy sauce, oyster-flavored sauce, hoisin sauce, sesame oil, and five-spice powder together in a small bowl. Transfer 3 tablespoons of the mixture to a medium bowl and add the pork and liquid smoke (if using). Let marinate for at least 10 minutes or up to 1 hour. Whisk the broth and cornstarch into the remaining soy sauce mixture and set aside. In a small bowl, mix 1 teaspoon of the peanut oil, the ginger, and garlic together and set aside.

2. Heat 2 teaspoons more peanut oil in a 12-inch nonstick or cast-iron skillet over high heat until just smoking. Add half of the pork, break up any clumps, then cook without stirring until the meat is browned at the edges, about 1 minute. Stir the pork and continue to cook until cooked through, about 1 minute longer. Add 2 tablespoons of the wine to the skillet and cook, stirring constantly, until the liquid is reduced and the pork is well coated, 30 to 60 seconds. Transfer the pork to a clean bowl and cover with foil to keep warm. Repeat with 2 teaspoons more peanut oil, the remaining pork, and the remaining 2 tablespoons wine. Wipe out the skillet with a wad of paper towels.

3. Add 1 teaspoon more peanut oil to the skillet and return to high heat until just smoking. Add the mushrooms and cook, stirring occasionally, until light golden brown, 4 to 6 minutes. Add the scallion whites and greens and cook, stirring occasionally, until wilted, 2 to 3 minutes. Transfer the vegetables to the bowl with the pork.

4. Add the remaining 1 teaspoon peanut oil to the skillet and heat over high heat until just smoking. Add the cabbage and cook, stirring occasionally, until spotty brown, 3 to 5 minutes. Clear the center of the skillet, add the ginger mixture, and cook, mashing the mixture into the pan, until fragrant, 15 to 20 seconds. Stir the ginger mixture into the cabbage.

5. Stir in the vegetables and pork with any accumulated juices. Whisk the sauce to recombine, then add to the skillet and cook, tossing constantly, until the sauce is thickened, about 30 seconds.

6. Bring 6 quarts water to a boil in a large pot. Add the noodles and cook, stirring often, until tender, about 4 minutes for fresh and 10 minutes for dried. Drain the noodles and return them to the pot. Add the cooked stir-fry mixture and the chili-garlic sauce to the noodles and toss to combine. Transfer to a serving platter and serve.

KUNG PAO SHRIMP

WHY THIS RECIPE WORKS: Kung pao is meant to have a fiery personality, but many restaurant versions are dismal, featuring tiny, tough shrimp drenched in a quart of pale, greasy, bland sauce. We wanted to make this classic Sichuan stir-fry at home, with large, tender shrimp, crunchy peanuts, and an assertive, well-balanced brown sauce.

For tender, flavorful shrimp, we stir-fried marinated extra-large shrimp for just a few seconds, then added small whole red chiles and whole unsalted roasted peanuts. For vegetables, we kept things simple and added just one diced red bell pepper (tasters found other vegetables to be superfluous) and the usual aromatics, garlic and ginger. We made a potently flavored, syrupy sauce using a mixture of chicken broth, rice vinegar, toasted sesame oil, oyster-flavored sauce, hoisin sauce, and cornstarch. Stirring in sliced scallions just before serving put the final touch on our dish. We no longer need to rely on dull, gloppy restaurant renditions of this Sichuan classic.

Kung Pao Shrimp

SERVES 4

Roasted unsalted cashews can be substituted for the peanuts. Unless you have a taste for the incendiary, do not eat the whole chiles in the finished dish. Serve with Basic White Rice (page 308).

SAUCE
- ¾ cup low-sodium chicken broth
- 1 tablespoon oyster-flavored sauce
- 1 tablespoon hoisin sauce
- 2 teaspoons rice vinegar
- 2 teaspoons toasted sesame oil
- 1½ teaspoons cornstarch

SHRIMP AND VEGETABLES
- 1 pound extra-large shrimp (21 to 25 per pound), peeled and deveined (see page 160)
- 1 tablespoon Chinese rice cooking wine (Shao-Xing) or dry sherry
- 2 teaspoons soy sauce
- 2 tablespoons plus 1 teaspoon peanut or vegetable oil
- 3 medium garlic cloves, minced or pressed through a garlic press (about 1 tablespoon)
- 2 teaspoons minced or grated fresh ginger
- ½ cup unsalted roasted peanuts (see note)
- 6 small whole dried red chiles
- 1 red bell pepper, stemmed, seeded, and cut into ½-inch pieces
- 3 scallions, sliced thin

1. FOR THE SAUCE: Combine all the ingredients in a small bowl and set aside.

2. FOR THE SHRIMP AND VEGETABLES: Toss the shrimp with the rice cooking wine and soy sauce in a medium bowl and let marinate for at least 10 minutes or up to 1 hour. In a small bowl, mix 1 teaspoon of the peanut oil, the garlic, and ginger together.

3. Heat 1 tablespoon more peanut oil in a 12-inch non-stick skillet over high heat until just smoking. Add the shrimp and cook until barely opaque, 30 to 40 seconds, stirring halfway through. Add the peanuts and chiles and continue to cook until the shrimp are bright pink and the peanuts have darkened slightly, 30 to 40 seconds longer. Transfer the shrimp, peanuts, and chiles to a clean bowl and cover with foil to keep warm.

4. Add the remaining 1 tablespoon peanut oil to the skillet and return to high heat until just smoking. Add the bell pepper and cook, stirring frequently, until spotty brown, about 1½ minutes. Clear the center of the skillet, add the garlic mixture, and cook, mashing the mixture into the pan, until fragrant, 15 to 20 seconds. Stir the garlic mixture into the bell pepper.

5. Stir in the peanuts, chiles, and shrimp with any accumulated juices. Whisk the sauce to recombine, then add to the skillet and cook, tossing constantly, until the sauce is thickened, about 30 seconds. Stir in the scallions, transfer to a serving platter, and serve.

VEGETABLE STIR-FRIES

WHY THIS RECIPE WORKS: Without meat, vegetable stir-fries can devolve from a one-dish meal into a side dish. We wanted to make a satisfying, filling meal out of stir-fried vegetables—without meat.

We chose hefty, meaty portobello mushrooms as the main vegetable. We found that removing the gills kept them from tasting leathery and raw. We tried cutting them in a variety of shapes, but settled on 2-inch wedges, which were so hearty we didn't miss the meat. We cooked the mushrooms over medium-high heat until browned and tender, then added a mixture of broth, soy sauce, and sugar and reduced it to a glaze—this provided an intense flavor boost to the mushrooms. For this stir-fry, we bulked up the amount of vegetables in our traditional stir-fries, settling on carrots, snow peas, and napa cabbage. Finally, the sauce: A simple mixture of broth, oyster-flavored sauce, soy sauce, cornstarch, and sesame oil, and a heavy dose of ginger tied the dish together, giving the vegetables great flavor—and nobody missed the meat!

Stir-Fried Portobellos with Ginger-Oyster Sauce
SERVES 4

Serve with Basic White Rice (see page 308).

GLAZE

- ¼ **cup low-sodium chicken or vegetable broth**
- 2 **tablespoons soy sauce**
- 2 **tablespoons sugar**

SAUCE

- 1 **cup low-sodium chicken or vegetable broth**
- 3 **tablespoons oyster-flavored sauce**
- 1 **tablespoon soy sauce**
- 1 **tablespoon cornstarch**
- 2 **teaspoons toasted sesame oil**

VEGETABLES

- ¼ **cup peanut or vegetable oil**
- 4 **teaspoons minced or grated fresh ginger**
- 2 **medium garlic cloves, minced or pressed through a garlic press (about 2 teaspoons)**
- 6–8 **portobello mushrooms (each 4 to 6 inches), stemmed, wiped clean, gills removed, and cut into 2-inch wedges**
- 4 **carrots, peeled and sliced ¼ inch thick on the bias**
- ½ **cup low-sodium chicken or vegetable broth**
- 3 **ounces snow peas, tips and strings removed**
- 1 **pound napa cabbage (1 small head), cored and cut into ¾-inch strips**
- 1 **tablespoon sesame seeds, toasted (optional)**

1. FOR THE GLAZE: Combine all the ingredients in a small bowl and set aside.

2. FOR THE SAUCE: Combine all the ingredients in a small bowl and set aside.

3. FOR THE VEGETABLES: In a small bowl, mix 1 teaspoon of the peanut oil, the ginger, and garlic together.

4. Heat 3 tablespoons more peanut oil in a 12-inch nonstick skillet over medium-high heat until shimmering. Add the mushrooms and cook without stirring until browned on one side, 2 to 3 minutes. Using tongs, flip the mushrooms, reduce the heat to medium, and cook until the second sides are browned and the mushrooms are tender, about 5 minutes. Increase the heat to medium-high, add the glaze, and cook, stirring frequently, until the glaze is thick and the mushrooms are coated, 1 to 2 minutes. Transfer the mushrooms to a plate. Rinse the skillet clean and dry with a wad of paper towels.

5. Add 1 teaspoon more peanut oil to the skillet and return to high heat until just smoking. Add the carrots and cook, stirring frequently, until beginning to brown, 1 to 2 minutes. Add the broth, cover the pan, and lower the heat to medium. Cook the carrots until just tender, 2 to 3 minutes. Uncover and cook until the liquid evaporates, about 30 seconds. Transfer the carrots to the plate with the mushrooms.

6. Add the remaining 1 teaspoon peanut oil to the skillet and return to high heat until just smoking. Add the snow peas and cook until spotty brown, about 2 minutes. Add the cabbage and cook, stirring frequently, until wilted, about 2 minutes.

7. Clear the center of the skillet, add the ginger mixture, and cook, mashing the mixture into the pan, until fragrant, 15 to 20 seconds. Stir the ginger mixture into the vegetables.

8. Stir in the mushrooms and carrots. Whisk the sauce to recombine, then add to the skillet and cook, tossing constantly, until the sauce is thickened, 2 to 3 minutes. Transfer to a serving platter, sprinkle with the sesame seeds (if using), and serve.

Stir-Fried Portobellos with Sweet Chili-Garlic Sauce

Follow the recipe for Stir-Fried Portobellos with Ginger-Oyster Sauce, replacing the sugar in the glaze with 2 tablespoons honey. For the sauce, increase the soy sauce to 3 tablespoons, reduce the broth to ¾ cup, and replace the oyster-flavored sauce and toasted sesame oil with 2 tablespoons honey, 1 tablespoon rice vinegar, and 1 teaspoon Asian chili sauce. Increase the garlic to 4 cloves.

THAI CURRY

WHY THIS RECIPE WORKS: Like most Thai food, Thai curries embrace a delicate balance of tastes, textures, temperatures, and colors that come together to create a harmonious whole. Unlike Indian curries, Thai curries almost always contain coconut milk. Also, they tilt the spice balance towards fresh aromatics, which are added in the form of a paste. We wanted an authentic Thai red curry and green curry, perfumed with lemon grass, hot chiles, and coconut milk, both of which could be made easily by the home cook.

A food processor made quick work of blending together the curry pastes. For the green curry, we favored Thai green chiles (although serrano or jalapeño chiles make great substitutes), while the red curry was best with small dried red chiles and a fresh red jalapeño. Shallots, lemon grass, cilantro stems, garlic, ginger, coriander, and cumin rounded out the flavors of the pastes. And to approximate the flavor of kaffir lime leaves, we added grated lime zest. To make the curries, we skimmed the coconut cream off the coconut milk and cooked it with the curry paste—this gave our curries silky body and intense, rich flavor. We paired the green curry with chicken, broccoli, mushrooms, and bell pepper, and the red curry with shrimp, pineapple, and peanuts. All that we needed now was rice to soak up the flavorful sauce.

Thai Green Curry with Chicken, Broccoli, and Mushrooms

SERVES 4

To make slicing the chicken easier, freeze it for 15 minutes. Serve with Basic White Rice (page 308).

- 2 (14-ounce) cans unsweetened coconut milk, not shaken
- ½ cup Green Curry Paste (recipe follows) or 2 tablespoons store-bought green curry paste
- 2 tablespoons fish sauce
- 2 tablespoons brown sugar
- 1½ pounds boneless, skinless chicken breasts, trimmed and sliced thin (see note)
  Table salt
- 8 ounces broccoli (½ small bunch), florets cut into 1-inch pieces
- 4 ounces white mushrooms, wiped clean and quartered
- 1 red bell pepper, stemmed, seeded, and cut into ¼-inch strips
- 1 Thai chile, stemmed, seeded, and quartered lengthwise (optional)
- ½ cup loosely packed fresh basil leaves
- ½ cup loosely packed fresh mint leaves
- 1 tablespoon juice from 1 lime

1. Carefully spoon off about 1 cup of the top layer of cream from one can of the coconut milk. Whisk the coconut cream and curry paste together in a large Dutch oven, bring to a simmer over high heat, and cook until almost all of the liquid evaporates, 5 to 7 minutes. Reduce the heat to medium-high and continue to cook, whisking constantly, until the cream separates into a puddle of colored oil and coconut solids, 3 to 8 minutes. Continue cooking until the curry paste is very aromatic, 1 to 2 minutes.

2. Whisk in the remaining coconut milk, the fish sauce, and sugar, bring to a simmer, and cook until the flavors meld and the sauce thickens, about 5 minutes. Season the chicken with salt, stir into the sauce, and cook until evenly coated, about 1 minute. Stir in the broccoli and mushrooms and cook until the vegetables are almost tender, about 5 minutes. Stir in the bell pepper and chile (if using) and cook until the bell pepper is crisp-tender, about 2 minutes. Off the heat, stir in the basil, mint, and lime juice. Serve.

Green Curry Paste

MAKES ABOUT ½ CUP

We strongly prefer the flavor of Thai chiles here; however, serrano and jalapeño chiles are decent substitutes. For more heat, include the chile seeds and ribs when chopping.

- ⅓ **cup water**
- 12 **fresh green Thai, serrano, or jalapeño chiles, seeds and ribs removed, chile chopped coarse (see note)**
- 8 **medium garlic cloves, peeled**
- 3 **medium shallots, peeled and quartered**
- 2 **stalks lemon grass, bottom 5 inches only, trimmed and sliced thin (see photos)**
- 2 **tablespoons grated zest from 2 limes**
- 2 **tablespoons vegetable oil**
- 2 **tablespoons minced fresh cilantro stems**
- 1 **tablespoon minced or grated fresh ginger**
- 2 **teaspoons ground coriander**
- 1 **teaspoon ground cumin**
- 1 **teaspoon table salt**

Process all the ingredients in a food processor to a fine paste, about 3 minutes, scraping down the sides of the workbowl as needed.

Thai Red Curry with Shrimp, Pineapple, and Peanuts

SERVES 4

Roasted unsalted cashews can be substituted for the peanuts. For a more authentic appearance, leave the shells on the shrimp tails. Serve with Basic White Rice (page 308).

- 2 **(14-ounce) cans unsweetened coconut milk, not shaken**
- ½ **cup Red Curry Paste (recipe follows) or 2 tablespoons store-bought red curry paste**
- 2 **tablespoons fish sauce**
- 2 **tablespoons brown sugar**

NOTES FROM THE TEST KITCHEN

CUTTING LEMON GRASS

Because of its tough outer leaves, lemon grass can be difficult to slice or mince. We like this method, which relies on a sharp knife.

1. Trim all but the bottom 5 inches of the lemon grass stalk.

2. Remove the tough outer sheath from the trimmed lemon grass. If the lemon grass is particularly thick or tough, you may need to remove several layers to reveal the tender inner portion of the stalk.

3. TO SLICE: Thinly slice the trimmed and peeled lemon grass on a slight bias. **TO MINCE:** Cut the trimmed and peeled lemon grass in half lengthwise, then mince.

- 1½ **pounds medium shrimp (41 to 50 per pound), peeled and deveined (see page 160; see note)**
  Table salt
- 1 **pound peeled and cored pineapple, cut into 1-inch pieces**
- 4 **ounces snow peas, tips and strings removed**
- 1 **red bell pepper, stemmed, seeded, and cut into ¼-inch strips**
- 1 **Thai chile, stemmed, seeded, and quartered lengthwise (optional)**
- ½ **cup loosely packed fresh basil leaves**
- ½ **cup loosely packed fresh mint leaves**
- 1 **tablespoon juice from 1 lime**
- ½ **cup unsalted roasted peanuts, chopped coarse (see note)**

1. Carefully spoon off about 1 cup of the top layer of cream from one can of the coconut milk. Whisk the coconut cream and curry paste together in a large Dutch oven, bring to a simmer over high heat, and cook until almost all of the liquid evaporates, 5 to 7 minutes. Reduce the heat to medium-high and continue to cook, whisking constantly, until the cream separates into a puddle of colored oil and coconut solids, 3 to 8 minutes. Continue cooking until the curry paste is very aromatic, 1 to 2 minutes.

2. Whisk in the remaining coconut milk, the fish sauce, and sugar, bring to a simmer, and cook until the flavors meld and the sauce thickens, about 5 minutes. Season the shrimp with salt, add them to the sauce with the pineapple, and cook, stirring occasionally, until the shrimp are almost opaque, about 4 minutes. Stir in the snow peas, bell pepper, and chile (if using) and cook until the vegetables are crisp-tender, about 2 minutes. Off the heat, stir in the basil, mint, and lime juice. Sprinkle with the peanuts and serve.

Red Curry Paste
MAKES ABOUT ½ CUP

If you can't find a red jalapeño chile, you can substitute a green jalapeño. For more heat, include the jalapeño seeds and ribs when chopping.

8	**dried small red chiles, such as Thai, japonés, or de árbol**
⅓	**cup water**
4	**medium shallots, peeled and quartered**
2	**stalks lemon grass, bottom 5 inches only, trimmed and sliced thin (see page 323)**
6	**medium garlic cloves, peeled**
1	**medium fresh red jalapeño chile, seeds and ribs removed, chile chopped coarse (see note)**
2	**tablespoons minced cilantro stems**
2	**tablespoons vegetable oil**
1	**tablespoon grated zest from 1 lime**
2	**teaspoons ground coriander**
1	**teaspoon ground cumin**
1	**teaspoon minced or grated fresh ginger**
1	**teaspoon tomato paste**
1	**teaspoon table salt**

1. Adjust an oven rack to the middle position and heat the oven to 350 degrees. Place the dried red chiles on a baking sheet and toast in the oven until fragrant and puffed, about 5 minutes. Remove the chiles from the oven and set aside to cool. When cool enough to handle, seed and stem the chiles, then break them into small pieces.

2. Process the chile pieces with the remaining ingredients in a food processor to a fine paste, about 3 minutes, scraping down the sides of the workbowl as needed.

THAI CHILE BEEF

WHY THIS RECIPE WORKS: Most recipes for Thai chile beef require exotic ingredients and three hours of preparation—definitely not suitable for making midweek supper in an average American home kitchen. We wanted to create a sophisticated Thai chile beef recipe built around the traditional Thai flavors—spicy, sweet, sour, and salty—using readily available ingredients and requiring minimal cooking time.

A cheap and readily available cut—blade steak—won our taste test for its tenderness and very beefy flavor. We added the beef to our transformed stir-fry marinade—made with fish sauce for its briny flavor, white pepper for its spicy and almost gamy flavor, citrusy coriander, and a little light brown sugar for both sweetness and help in developing caramelization. With these elements, the beef only needed to marinate for 10 minutes to develop full flavor. We also wanted some heat and decided to use both a jalapeño and Asian chili-garlic paste (which added toasty garlicky flavors along with heat). More fish sauce, brown sugar, rice vinegar, fresh mint and cilantro, a few crunchy chopped peanuts, and a bright squirt of lime juice finished the dish.

Stir-Fried Thai-Style Beef with Chiles and Shallots
SERVES 4

To make slicing the blade steaks easier, freeze them for 15 minutes. If you cannot find blade steak, use flank steak; because flank steak requires less trimming, you will need only about 1¾ pounds. To cut a flank steak into the proper-sized slices for stir-frying, first cut the steak with the grain into 2-inch strips, then cut the strips against the grain into ⅛-inch-thick slices. Serve with Basic White Rice (page 308).

SAUCE

- 2 tablespoons fish sauce
- 2 tablespoons rice vinegar
- 2 tablespoons water
- 1 tablespoon light brown sugar
- 1 tablespoon Asian chili-garlic paste

BEEF AND VEGETABLES

- 2 pounds blade steaks, halved lengthwise, trimmed, and sliced into ⅛-inch-thick slices (see note)
- 1 tablespoon fish sauce
- 1 teaspoon light brown sugar
- ¾ teaspoon ground coriander
- ⅛ teaspoon ground white pepper
- 3 tablespoons peanut or vegetable oil
- 3 medium garlic cloves, minced or pressed through a garlic press (about 1 tablespoon)
- 3 serrano or jalapeño chiles, halved, seeds and ribs removed, chiles sliced thin
- 3 medium shallots, ends trimmed, peeled, quartered lengthwise, and layers separated
- ½ cup fresh mint leaves, large leaves torn into bite-sized pieces
- ½ cup fresh cilantro leaves
- ⅓ cup unsalted roasted peanuts, chopped coarse
  Lime wedges, for serving

1. FOR THE SAUCE: Combine all the ingredients in a small bowl and set aside.

2. FOR THE BEEF AND VEGETABLES: Toss the beef with the fish sauce, sugar, coriander, and white pepper in a medium bowl and let marinate for at least 10 minutes or up to 1 hour. In a small bowl, mix 1 teaspoon of the oil and the garlic together.

3. Heat 2 teaspoons more oil in a 12-inch nonstick skillet over high heat until just smoking. Add one-third of the beef, break up any clumps, then cook without stirring until the meat is browned at the edges, about 1 minute. Stir the beef and continue to cook until cooked through, about 1 minute longer. Transfer the beef to a clean bowl and cover with foil to keep warm. Repeat with 4 teaspoons more oil and the remaining beef in two batches.

4. Add the remaining 2 teaspoons oil to the skillet and return to medium heat until shimmering. Add the chiles and shallots and cook until beginning to soften, 3 to 4 minutes. Clear the center of the skillet, add the garlic mixture, and cook, mashing the mixture into the pan, until fragrant, 15 to 20 seconds. Stir the garlic mixture into the shallots and chiles.

5. Stir in the beef with any accumulated juices. Whisk

the sauce to recombine, then add to the skillet and cook, tossing constantly, until the sauce is thickened, about 30 seconds. Stir in the half of the mint and half of the cilantro. Transfer to a serving platter, sprinkle with the remaining mint, remaining cilantro, and peanuts, and serve with the lime wedges.

PAD THAI

WHY THIS RECIPE WORKS: Ordered out, pad thai suffers from indiscriminate amounts of sugar; slick, greasy noodles; or bloated, sticky, lifeless strands that clump together. We hoped to develop a pad thai with clean, fresh, not-too-sweet flavors, perfectly cooked noodles, and plenty of plump, juicy shrimp with tender bits of scrambled egg.

Soaking the rice sticks in boiling water for 10 minutes before stir-frying made for tender but not sticky noodles. We created the salty, sweet, sour, and spicy flavor profile of pad thai by combining fish sauce, sugar, ground chiles, and vinegar. For the fresh, bright, fruity taste that is essential to the dish, we used tamarind paste, which we soaked in hot water and passed through a fine-mesh strainer to make a smooth puree. Tossed with fresh and dried shrimp and eggs, and garnished with scallions, peanuts, and cilantro, this dish is an excellent rendition of the Thai classic.

Pad Thai

SERVES 4

Although pad thai cooks very quickly, the ingredient list is long, and everything must be prepared and within easy reach at the stovetop when you begin cooking. For maximum efficiency, use the time during which the tamarind and noodles soak to prepare the other ingredients. If tamarind paste is unavailable, substitute ⅓ cup lime juice and ⅓ cup water and use light brown sugar instead of granulated sugar.

SAUCE

- ¾ cup boiling water
- 2 tablespoons tamarind paste (see note)
- 3 tablespoons fish sauce
- 3 tablespoons sugar
- 2 tablespoons peanut or vegetable oil
- 1 tablespoon rice vinegar
- ¾ teaspoon cayenne pepper

NOODLES, SHRIMP, AND GARNISH

- 8 ounces dried rice stick noodles, ⅛ to ¼ inch wide
- 2 tablespoons peanut or vegetable oil
- 12 ounces medium shrimp (41 to 50 per pound), peeled and deveined (see page 160)
  Table salt
- 1 medium shallot, minced (about 2 tablespoons)
- 3 garlic cloves, minced or pressed through a garlic press (about 1 tablespoon)
- 2 large eggs, lightly beaten
- 2 tablespoons chopped Thai salted preserved radish (optional)
- 1 tablespoon dried shrimp, chopped fine (optional)
- 3 cups bean sprouts
- ½ cup unsalted roasted peanuts, chopped coarse
- 5 scallions, green parts only, sliced thin on the bias
- ¼ cup loosely packed cilantro leaves (optional)
  Lime wedges, for serving

1. FOR THE SAUCE: Combine the water and tamarind paste in a small bowl and let sit until the tamarind is softened and mushy, 10 to 30 minutes. Mash the tamarind to break it up, then push it through a mesh strainer into a medium bowl to remove the seeds and fibers and extract as much pulp as possible. Stir in the remaining sauce ingredients and set aside.

2. FOR THE NOODLES, SHRIMP, AND GARNISH: Bring 4 quarts water to a boil in a large pot. Remove the boiling water from the heat, add the rice noodles, and let sit, stirring occasionally, until almost tender, about 10 minutes. Drain the noodles and set aside.

3. Heat 1 tablespoon of the oil in a 12-inch nonstick skillet over high heat until just smoking. Add the shrimp, sprinkle with ⅛ teaspoon salt, and cook without stirring until bright pink, about 1 minute. Stir the shrimp and continue to cook until cooked through, 15 to 30 seconds longer. Transfer the shrimp to a clean bowl and cover with foil to keep warm.

4. Add the remaining 1 tablespoon oil to the skillet and return to medium heat until shimmering. Add the shallot and garlic and cook, stirring constantly, until light golden brown, about 1½ minutes. Stir in the eggs and cook, stirring constantly, until scrambled and barely moist, about 20 seconds.

5. Add the noodles and the salted radish and dried shrimp (if using) to the eggs and toss to combine. Add the sauce, increase the heat to high, and cook, tossing constantly, until the noodles are evenly coated, about 1 minute.

6. Add the cooked shrimp, bean sprouts, ¼ cup of the peanuts, and all but ¼ cup of the scallions and continue to cook, tossing constantly, until the noodles are tender, about 2½ minutes. (If not yet tender add 2 tablespoons water to the skillet and continue to cook until tender.) Transfer the noodles to a serving platter, sprinkle with the remaining ¼ cup peanuts, remaining ¼ cup scallions, and cilantro (if using) and serve with the lime wedges.

THAI GRILLED CHICKEN

WHY THIS RECIPE WORKS: This herb- and spice-rubbed chicken is served in small pieces and eaten as finger food, along with a sweet and spicy dipping sauce. We wanted to develop a recipe for Thai grilled chicken to offer a refreshing change of pace from typical barbecue fare.

After testing numerous rub combinations, we liked the simplest version, made only with cilantro, black pepper, lime juice, and garlic, accented with the earthy flavor of coriander and fresh ginger. To flavor the meat as well as the skin, we took some of the rub and placed it in a thick layer under the skin as well as on top of it. For perfectly cooked chicken, we made a modified two-level fire (one side of the grill holds all of the coals; the other side is empty), first browning the chicken directly over the coals and then moving it to the cool side of the grill to finish cooking. The true Thai flavors of this dish come through in the sauce, a classic combination of sweet and spicy. We found balance in a blend of sugar, lime juice, white vinegar, hot red pepper flakes, fish sauce, and garlic.

Thai Grilled Chicken with Spicy, Sweet, and Sour Dipping Sauce

SERVES 4

To help ensure that each breast finishes cooking at approximately the same time, buy pieces of similar size. Some of the rub is inevitably lost to the grill, but the chicken will still be flavorful.

CHICKEN AND BRINE

- ½ cup sugar
- ½ cup table salt
- 2 (1½-pound) bone-in, skin-on chicken breasts, split in half along the breast bone and trimmed of rib sections (see page 71)

SAUCE

- ⅓ cup sugar
- ¼ cup distilled white vinegar
- ¼ cup juice from 2 to 3 limes
- 2 tablespoons fish sauce
- 2 medium garlic cloves, minced or pressed through a garlic press (about 2 teaspoons)
- 1 teaspoon red pepper flakes

RUB

- ⅔ cup chopped fresh cilantro leaves
- 12 medium garlic cloves, minced or pressed through a garlic press (about ¼ cup)
- ¼ cup juice from 2 to 3 limes
- 2 tablespoons minced or grated fresh ginger
- 2 tablespoons ground black pepper
- 2 tablespoons ground coriander
- 2 tablespoons vegetable oil, plus extra for the cooking grate

1. FOR THE CHICKEN AND BRINE: Dissolve the sugar and salt in 2 quarts cold water in a large container. Submerge the chicken, cover with plastic wrap, and refrigerate for 1 hour. Rinse the chicken and pat dry with paper towels.

2. FOR THE SAUCE: Whisk all the ingredients together in a small bowl until the sugar dissolves and set aside.

3. FOR THE RUB: Combine all the ingredients in a small bowl.

4. Working with one chicken breast at a time, slide your fingers between the skin and meat to loosen the skin, taking care not to detach the skin. Rub about 2 tablespoons of the mixture under the skin, then rub an even layer of the mixture onto all exterior surfaces, including the bottom and sides.

5. TO GRILL THE CHICKEN: Light a large chimney starter filled with charcoal (about 6 quarts) and allow to burn until the coals are partially covered with a layer of ash, about 20 minutes. Build a modified two-level fire by arranging all the coals over one-half of the grill, leaving the other half empty. Set the cooking grate in place, cover, and heat the grate until hot, about 5 minutes. Use a grill brush to scrape the cooking grate clean. Dip a wad of paper towels in oil; holding the wad with tongs, oil the cooking grate.

6. Cook the chicken on all sides over the hotter part of the grill until the skin is lightly browned and faint grill marks appear, 6 to 8 minutes. (If constant flare-ups occur, slide the chicken to the cooler side of the grill and mist the fire with water from a spray bottle.) Move the chicken, skin side down, to the cooler side of the grill, with the thicker sides of the breasts facing the coals. Cover the chicken loosely with foil, cover the grill, and continue to cook until the thickest part of the breasts registers 160 to 165 degrees on an instant-read thermometer, 20 to 30 minutes longer.

7. Transfer the chicken to a platter and let rest for 5 minutes. Serve, passing the sauce separately.

Thai Grilled Chicken on a Gas Grill

Follow the recipe for Thai Grilled Chicken with Spicy, Sweet, and Sour Dipping Sauce through step 4. Turn all the burners to high and heat the grill, with the lid down, until very hot, about 15 minutes. Use a grill brush to scrape the cooking grate clean. Dip a wad of paper towels in oil; holding the wad with tongs, oil the cooking grate. Leave the primary burner on high and turn off the other burner(s). Proceed with the recipe from step 6, increasing the browning time to 10 to 14 minutes.

INDIAN-STYLE CHICKEN AND RICE

WHY THIS RECIPE WORKS: Chicken biryani is a complicated (and often greasy) "gourmet" Indian dish. Chicken and rice is a simple, but unremarkable, American one-pot meal. We wanted to find a happy medium between the two.

In biryani, long-grain basmati rice takes center stage, enriched with butter, saffron, and a variety of fresh herbs and pungent spices. Pieces of tender chicken and browned onions are layered with the rice and baked until the flavors have mingled. For our recipe, we browned bone-in, skin-on chicken thighs, then removed the skin and layered them with basmati rice, lots of caramelized onions, and just the right blend of spices. To get the most flavor out of the spices, we tied them into a cheesecloth bundle and simmered them in the rice cooking water—then we added some of that water to the biryani. For a finishing touch, we added saffron, currants, and plenty of ginger and chiles.

Chicken Biryani

SERVES 4

This recipe requires a 3½ to 4-quart saucepan about 8 inches in diameter. Do not use a large, wide Dutch oven, as it will adversely affect both the layering of the dish and the final cooking times. For more heat, add the jalapeño seeds and ribs when mincing.

YOGURT SAUCE

- 1 **cup whole milk or low-fat plain yogurt**
- 2 **tablespoons minced fresh cilantro leaves**
- 2 **tablespoons minced fresh mint leaves**
- 1 **medium garlic clove, minced or pressed through a garlic press (about 1 teaspoon)**
  Table salt and ground black pepper

CHICKEN AND RICE

- 10 **cardamom pods, preferably green, smashed with a chef's knife**
- 1 **cinnamon stick**
- 1 **(2-inch) piece fresh ginger, peeled, cut into ½-inch-thick coins, and smashed**
- ½ **teaspoon cumin seeds**
- 3 **quarts water**
  Table salt
- 4 **(5 to 6-ounce) bone-in, skin-on chicken thighs, trimmed**
  Ground black pepper
- 3 **tablespoons unsalted butter**
- 2 **medium onions, halved and sliced thin**
- 2 **jalapeño chiles, seeds and ribs removed, chiles minced (see note)**
- 4 **medium garlic cloves, minced or pressed through a garlic press (about 4 teaspoons)**
- 1¼ **cups basmati rice**
- ½ **teaspoon saffron threads, lightly crumbled**
- ¼ **cup dried currants or raisins**
- 2 **tablespoons chopped fresh cilantro leaves**
- 2 **tablespoons chopped fresh mint leaves**

1. FOR THE YOGURT SAUCE: Combine all the ingredients in a small bowl, season with salt and pepper to taste, and set aside. (The sauce can be refrigerated in an airtight container for up to 2 days.)

2. FOR THE CHICKEN AND RICE: Wrap the cardamom pods, cinnamon stick, ginger, and cumin in a small piece of cheesecloth and secure with kitchen twine. In a 3½ to 4-quart heavy-bottomed saucepan about 8 inches in diameter, bring the spice bundle, water, and 1½ teaspoons salt to a boil over medium-high heat. Reduce the heat to medium and simmer, partially covered, until the spices have infused the water, at least 15 minutes (but no longer than 30 minutes).

3. Meanwhile, pat the chicken thighs dry with paper towels and season with salt and pepper. Melt the butter in a 12-inch nonstick skillet over medium-high heat. Add the onions and cook, stirring frequently, until soft and dark brown around the edges, 10 to 12 minutes. Stir in the jalapeños and garlic and cook, stirring frequently, until fragrant, about 2 minutes. Transfer the onion mixture to a bowl, season with salt, and set aside. Wipe out the skillet with a wad of paper towels.

4. Place the chicken, skin side down, in the skillet, return the skillet to medium-high heat, and cook until well browned on both sides, 8 to 10 minutes, flipping halfway through. Transfer the chicken to a plate and remove and discard the skin. Tent loosely with foil to keep warm.

5. If necessary, return the spice-infused water to a boil over high heat. Add the rice and cook, stirring occasionally, for 5 minutes. Drain the rice through a fine-mesh strainer, reserving ¾ cup of the cooking liquid; discard the spice bundle. Transfer the rice to a medium bowl and stir in the saffron and currants (the rice will turn splotchy yellow).

6. Spread half of the rice evenly in the bottom of the saucepan using a rubber spatula. Scatter half of the onion mixture over the rice, then place the chicken thighs, skinned side up, on top of the onions; add any accumulated chicken juices. Sprinkle evenly with the cilantro and mint, scatter the remaining onions over the herbs, then cover with the remaining rice. Pour the reserved ¾ cup cooking liquid evenly over the rice.

7. Cover the saucepan and cook over medium-low heat until the rice is tender and the chicken registers 175 degrees on an instant-read thermometer, about 30 minutes (if a large amount of steam is escaping from the pot, reduce the heat to low).

8. Run a heatproof rubber spatula around the inside rim of the saucepan to loosen any affixed rice. Using a large serving spoon, spoon the biryani into individual bowls, scooping from the bottom of the pot. Serve, passing the yogurt sauce separately.

CHICKEN TIKKA MASALA

WHY THIS RECIPE WORKS: Chicken tikka masala is arguably the single most popular Indian restaurant dish in the world. Turns out, it's not an authentic Indian dish—it was invented in a London curry house. Without historical roots, there is no definitive recipe. The variations we found had mushy or dry chicken and sauces that were unbearably rich and/or overspiced. We wanted an approachable method for producing moist, tender chunks of chicken in a rich, lightly spiced tomato sauce.

To season the chicken, we rubbed it with salt, coriander, cumin, and cayenne and refrigerated it for 30 to 60 minutes. Then we dipped it in yogurt mixed with oil, garlic, and ginger and broiled it. And since large pieces don't dry out as quickly as smaller ones under the broiler, we cooked the chicken breasts whole, cutting them into pieces only after cooking. While the chicken was cooking, we made the masala sauce. Masala means "hot spice," and the ingredients in a masala sauce depend on the whim of the cook, although tomatoes and cream are always present. We added onions, ginger, garlic, chile, and a readily available commercial garam masala spice mixture. A little tomato paste and sugar gave our sauce color and sweetness.

Chicken Tikka Masala

SERVES 4 TO 6

This dish is best when prepared with whole milk yogurt, but low-fat yogurt can be substituted. For more heat, include the chile seeds and ribs when mincing. Serve with Rice Pilaf (see page 406).

CHICKEN

- 1 teaspoon table salt
- ½ teaspoon ground cumin
- ½ teaspoon ground coriander
- ¼ teaspoon cayenne pepper
- 2 pounds boneless, skinless chicken breasts, trimmed
- 1 cup plain whole milk yogurt (see note)
- 2 tablespoons vegetable oil
- 1 tablespoon minced or grated fresh ginger
- 2 medium garlic cloves, minced or pressed through a garlic press (about 2 teaspoons)

SAUCE

- 3 tablespoons vegetable oil
- 1 medium onion, minced (about 1 cup)
- 1 tablespoon garam masala
- 1 tablespoon tomato paste
- 2 medium garlic cloves, minced or pressed through a garlic press (about 2 teaspoons)
- 2 teaspoons minced or grated fresh ginger
- 1 serrano chile, seeds and ribs removed, chile minced (see note)
- 1 (28-ounce) can crushed tomatoes
- 2 teaspoons sugar
  Table salt
- ⅔ cup heavy cream
- ¼ cup chopped fresh cilantro leaves

1. FOR THE CHICKEN: Combine ½ teaspoon salt, cumin, coriander, and cayenne in a small bowl. Pat the chicken dry with paper towels and sprinkle with the spice mixture, pressing gently so the mixture adheres. Place the chicken on a plate, cover with plastic wrap, and refrigerate for 30 minutes or up to 1 hour. In a large bowl, whisk the yogurt, oil, ginger, and garlic together and set aside.

2. FOR THE SAUCE: Heat the oil in a large Dutch oven over medium heat until shimmering. Add the onion and cook, stirring frequently, until softened and light golden, 8 to 10 minutes. Stir in the garam masala, tomato paste, garlic, ginger, and serrano and cook, stirring frequently, until fragrant, about 3 minutes. Add the crushed tomatoes, sugar, and salt and bring to a boil. Reduce the heat to medium-low, cover, and simmer for 15 minutes, stirring occasionally. Stir in the cream and return to a simmer. Remove the pan from the heat and cover to keep warm. (The sauce can be refrigerated in an airtight container for up to 4 days and gently reheated before adding the hot chicken.)

3. TO COOK THE CHICKEN: While the sauce simmers, position an oven rack 6 inches from the heating element and heat the broiler. Line a rimmed baking sheet or broiler pan with foil and place a wire rack over the sheet.

4. Using tongs, dip the chicken into the yogurt mixture (the chicken should be coated with a thick layer of yogurt) and arrange on the wire rack. Discard the excess yogurt mixture. Broil the chicken until lightly charred and the thickest part of the breasts registers 160 to 165 degrees on an instant-read thermometer, 10 to 18 minutes, flipping the chicken halfway through.

5. Let the chicken rest for 5 minutes, then cut into 1-inch chunks and stir into the warm sauce (do not simmer the chicken in the sauce). Stir in the cilantro, season with salt to taste, and serve.

INDIAN CURRY

WHY THIS RECIPE WORKS: For many home cooks Indian cooking is a mystery, full of exotic spices and unfamiliar, laborious cooking techniques. We hoped to create a complex but not heavy-flavored curry that wouldn't take all day to prepare.

Allowing the spices to cook completely provided the authentic, intense flavor we were after in our curry. We used a combination of whole spices—cinnamon sticks, cloves, green cardamom pods, black peppercorns, and a bay leaf—and toasted them in the oil before adding the aromatics, jalapeño, and ground spices. Instead of browning the meat (we chose lamb, but chicken thighs can also be used) like we normally do, we simply stirred it into

the pot along with crushed tomatoes and cooked the mixture until the liquid evaporated and the oil separated. This is a classic Indian technique that allows the spices to further release and develop their flavors in the oil, flavors which are then cooked into the meat (because it's not browned, it doesn't have a crust to inhibit its ability to absorb the flavors). We then added water and simmered the mixture until the meat was tender, then we stirred in the spinach and channa dal (yellow split peas) and cooked the dish until all the ingredients were melded and tender.

Indian Curry

SERVES 4 TO 6

If desired, 1½ pounds boneless, skinless chicken thighs, trimmed and cut into ¾-inch chunks, can be substituted for the lamb. For more heat, add the jalapeño seeds and ribs when mincing. For a creamier curry, choose yogurt over the crushed tomatoes. Serve with Yogurt Sauce (page 328), Onion Relish (page 332), Cilantro-Mint Chutney (page 332), and Rice Pilaf (page 406).

SPICE BLEND
1½ cinnamon sticks
4 whole cloves
4 green cardamom pods
8 whole black peppercorns
1 bay leaf

CURRY
¼ cup vegetable oil
1 medium onion, halved and sliced thin
5 medium garlic cloves, minced or pressed through a garlic press (about 5 teaspoons)
1 tablespoon minced or grated fresh ginger
1 jalapeño chile, stemmed and halved lengthwise, seeds and ribs removed (see note)
2 teaspoons ground cumin
2 teaspoons ground coriander
1 teaspoon ground turmeric
Table salt
1½ pounds boneless leg of lamb, trimmed and cut into ¾-inch cubes (see note)
⅔ cup crushed tomatoes or ½ cup plain low-fat yogurt (see note)
2 cups water
1½ pounds spinach, stemmed, washed, and chopped coarse (optional)
½ cup channa dal (yellow split peas)
¼ cup chopped fresh cilantro leaves

1. **FOR THE SPICE BLEND:** Combine all the ingredients in a small bowl and set aside.

2. **FOR THE CURRY:** Heat the oil in a Dutch oven over medium heat until shimmering. Add the spice blend and cook, stirring frequently, until the cinnamon stick unfurls and the cloves pop, about 5 seconds. Add the onion and cook, stirring occasionally, until softened, 5 to 7 minutes. Stir in the garlic, ginger, jalapeño, cumin, coriander, turmeric, and ½ teaspoon salt and cook until fragrant, about 30 seconds.

3. Stir in the lamb and the tomatoes. Bring to a simmer and cook, stirring frequently, until the liquid evaporates and the oil separates and turns orange, 5 to 7 minutes. Continue to cook until the spices are sizzling, about 30 seconds longer.

4. Stir in the water and bring to a simmer over medium heat. Reduce the heat to medium-low, cover, and cook until the lamb is almost tender, about 40 minutes.

5. Stir in the spinach (if using) and channa dal and cook until the channa dal are tender, about 15 minutes. Season with salt to taste, stir in the cilantro, and serve.

VEGETABLE CURRY

WHY THIS RECIPE WORKS: Vegetable curries can be complicated affairs, with lengthy ingredient lists and fussy techniques meant to compensate for the lack of meat. We wanted a curry we could make on a weeknight in less than an hour—without sacrificing flavor or overloading the dish with spices.

Although initially reluctant to use store-bought curry powder, we found that toasting the curry powder in a skillet turned it into a flavor powerhouse. Further experimentation proved that adding a few pinches of garam masala added even more spice flavor. To build the rest of our flavor base we started with a generous amount of sautéed onion, vegetable oil, garlic, ginger, fresh chile, and tomato paste for sweetness. When we chose our vegetables (chickpeas and potatoes for heartiness and cauliflower and peas for texture and color), we found that sautéing the spices and main ingredients together enhanced and melded the flavors. Finally, we rounded out our sauce with a combination of water, pureed canned tomatoes, and a splash of cream or coconut milk.

Indian-Style Curry with Potatoes, Cauliflower, Peas, and Chickpeas

SERVES 4 TO 6

This curry is moderately spicy when made with one chile. For more heat, include the chile seeds and ribs when mincing. Serve with Yogurt Sauce (page 328), Onion Relish (page 332), Cilantro-Mint Chutney (page 332), and Rice Pilaf (page 406).

- 2 tablespoons sweet or mild curry powder
- 1½ teaspoons garam masala
- 4 tablespoons vegetable oil
- 3 medium garlic cloves, minced or pressed through a garlic press (about 1 tablespoon)
- 1 tablespoon minced or grated fresh ginger
- 1 serrano chile, seeds and ribs removed, chile minced (see note)
- 1 tablespoon tomato paste
- 1 (14.5-ounce) can diced tomatoes
- 2 medium onions, minced (about 2 cups)
- 12 ounces red potatoes (about 2 medium), scrubbed and cut into ½-inch pieces
- 1¼ pounds cauliflower (½ medium head), trimmed, cored, and cut into 1-inch florets
- 1¼ cups water
- 1 (15-ounce) can chickpeas, drained and rinsed
  Table salt
- 1½ cups frozen peas
- ¼ cup heavy cream or coconut milk

CONDIMENTS
  Onion Relish (recipe follows)
  Cilantro-Mint Chutney (recipe follows) or mango chutney

1. Toast the curry powder and garam masala in a small skillet over medium-high heat, stirring constantly, until the spices darken slightly and become fragrant, about 1 minute. Transfer the spices to a small bowl and set aside. In a separate small bowl, stir 1 tablespoon of the oil, the garlic, ginger, serrano, and tomato paste together. Pulse the tomatoes with their juice in a food processor until coarsely chopped, 3 to 4 pulses.

2. Heat the remaining 3 tablespoons oil in a large Dutch oven over medium-high heat until shimmering. Add the onions and potatoes and cook, stirring occasionally, until the onions are caramelized and the potatoes are golden brown around the edges, about 10 minutes. (Reduce the heat to medium if the onions darken too quickly.)

3. Reduce the heat to medium. Clear the center of the pot, add the garlic mixture, and cook, mashing the mixture into the pan, until fragrant, 15 to 20 seconds. Stir the garlic mixture into the vegetables. Add the toasted spices and cook, stirring constantly, for 1 minute longer. Add the cauliflower and cook, stirring constantly, until the spices coat the florets, about 2 minutes longer.

4. Add the tomatoes, water, chickpeas, and 1 teaspoon salt, scraping up any browned bits. Bring to a boil over medium-high heat. Cover, reduce the heat to medium, and cook, stirring occasionally, until the vegetables are tender, 10 to 15 minutes. Stir in the peas and cream and continue to cook until heated through, about 2 minutes longer. Season with salt to taste and serve, passing the condiments separately.

Indian-Style Curry with Sweet Potatoes, Eggplant, Green Beans, and Chickpeas

Follow the recipe for Indian-Style Curry with Potatoes, Cauliflower, Peas, and Chickpeas, substituting 12 ounces sweet potato (1 medium), peeled and cut into ½-inch pieces, for the red potatoes. Substitute 8 ounces green beans, trimmed and cut into 1-inch pieces, and 1 medium eggplant (1 pound), cut into ½-inch pieces, for the cauliflower. Omit the peas.

Onion Relish

MAKES ABOUT 1 CUP

If using a regular yellow onion, increase the sugar to 1 teaspoon. This relish can be refrigerated in an airtight container for up to 24 hours.

- 1 medium Vidalia onion, minced (about 1 cup) (see note)
- 1 tablespoon juice from 1 lime
- ½ teaspoon sweet paprika
- ½ teaspoon sugar
- ⅛ teaspoon table salt
  Pinch cayenne pepper

Combine all the ingredients in a small bowl.

Cilantro-Mint Chutney

MAKES ABOUT 1 CUP

This chutney can be refrigerated in an airtight container for up to 24 hours.

- 2 cups packed fresh cilantro leaves
- 1 cup packed fresh mint leaves
- ⅓ cup plain yogurt
- ¼ cup minced onion
- 1 tablespoon juice from 1 lime
- 1½ teaspoons sugar
- ½ teaspoon ground cumin
- ¼ teaspoon table salt

Process all the ingredients together in a food processor until smooth, about 20 seconds, scraping down the sides of the workbowl as needed.

TANDOORI CHICKEN

WHY THIS RECIPE WORKS: We weren't going to let a 24-hour marinade or the lack of a 900-degree oven keep us from turning this great Indian classic into an easy weeknight dinner. We set out to reinvent this traditional dish as a recipe that could be made year-round in the oven.

Traditional tandoors produce moist, smoky meat because the fierce heat allows protein molecules on the meat's surface to cross-link and contract, trapping moisture inside. Juices fall on the coals along with rendered fat, creating smoke that flavors the food. Trying to mimic the tandoor by cooking chicken in a very hot oven gave us disappointing results. Instead we turned to a technique we use to preserve the juiciness of thick-cut steaks. We baked the chicken in a low-temperature oven until almost done, then gave it a quick broil to char the exterior. To get flavor into the meat, we turned to a salt-spice rub made with garam masala, cumin, and chili powder bloomed in oil with ginger and garlic. We massaged the rub into chicken pieces to lock in juices and infuse flavor, then left them to sit. Following a dunk in yogurt flavored with the same spice mix, the chicken was ready for the oven. The results? Juicy, lightly charred, well-seasoned meat with just the right degree of tenderness.

Tandoori Chicken

SERVES 4

We prefer this dish with whole milk yogurt, but low-fat yogurt can be substituted. It is important to remove the chicken from the oven before switching to the broiler setting to allow the heating element to come up to temperature. Serve with Yogurt Sauce (page 328), Onion Relish (page 332), Cilantro-Mint Chutney (page 332), and Rice Pilaf (page 406).

- 2 tablespoons vegetable oil
- 6 medium garlic cloves, minced or pressed through a garlic press (about 2 tablespoons)
- 2 tablespoons minced or grated fresh ginger
- 1 tablespoon garam masala
- 2 teaspoons ground cumin
- 2 teaspoons chili powder
- 1 cup plain whole milk yogurt (see note)
- ¼ cup juice from 2 limes, plus 1 lime, cut into wedges (for serving)
- 2 teaspoons table salt
- 3 pounds bone-in, skin-on chicken pieces (split breasts cut in half, drumsticks, and/or thighs), trimmed and skin removed

1. Heat the oil in an 8-inch skillet over medium heat until shimmering. Add the garlic and ginger and cook until fragrant, about 1 minute. Stir in the garam masala, cumin, and chili powder and cook until fragrant, about 30 seconds. Transfer half of the garlic-spice mixture to a medium bowl, stir in the yogurt and 2 tablespoons of the lime juice, and set aside.

2. In a large bowl, combine the remaining garlic-spice mixture, remaining 2 tablespoons lime juice, and salt. Using a sharp knife, lightly score the skinned side of each piece of chicken, making two or three shallow cuts about 1 inch apart and about ⅛ inch deep. Transfer the chicken to the bowl and gently rub with the salt-spice mixture until evenly coated. Let sit at room temperature for 30 minutes.

3. Adjust an oven rack to the upper-middle position (about 6 inches from the heating element) and heat the oven to 325 degrees. Set a wire rack over a foil-lined rimmed baking sheet or broiler pan bottom.

4. Pour the yogurt mixture over the chicken and toss until the chicken is evenly coated with a thick layer. Arrange the chicken pieces, scored side down, on the prepared wire rack. Discard the excess yogurt mixture. Bake the chicken until an instant-read thermometer inserted into the thickest part of the chicken registers 125 degrees for breasts and 130 degrees for legs and thighs, 15 to 25 minutes. (Smaller pieces may cook faster than larger pieces.) Transfer the chicken to a plate.

5. Turn the oven to broil and heat for 10 minutes. Flip the chicken pieces scored side up and broil until lightly charred in spots and the thickest part of the breasts registers 165 degrees and the thickest part of the legs and thighs register 175 degrees, 8 to 15 minutes.

6. Transfer the chicken to a serving platter, tent loosely with foil, and let rest for 5 minutes. Serve with the lime wedges.

CHAPTER 17

IT'S GRILL TIME!

Grilled Bone-In
Chicken Breasts 336

Orange-Chipotle Glaze

Soy-Ginger Glaze

Barbecued Pulled
Chicken 338

Barbecued Pulled Chicken
for a Crowd 339

Grill-Roasted Beer
Can Chicken 340

Spice Rub

Grill-Roasted Cornish
Game Hens 341

Grilled Hamburgers 343

Grilled Cheeseburgers 344

Well-Done Grilled
Hamburgers 344

Well-Done Grilled
Bacon Cheeseburgers 345

Grilled Marinated
Flank Steak 346

Garlic-Shallot-Rosemary
Wet Paste Marinade

Garlic-Ginger-Sesame
Wet Paste Marinade

Garlic-Chile Wet
Paste Marinade

Grilled Stuffed
Flank Steak 347

Grilled Stuffed Flank
Steak with Spinach and
Pine Nuts 349

Grilled Steak Tips 349

Southwestern
Marinade

Garlic, Ginger, and
Soy Marinade

Grilled Steaks 350

Roasted Red Pepper
and Smoked Paprika
Butter

Lemon, Garlic, and
Parsley Butter

Grill-Roasted Beef
Tenderloin 352

Salsa Verde

Barbecued Beef
Brisket 354

Spicy Chili Rub

Grilled Pork Chops 356

Basic Spice Rub for
Pork Chops

Grill-Roasted Pork
Loin 357

Chili-Mustard Spice Rub

Grilled Pork Loin with
Apple-Cranberry
Filling 359

Barbecued
Pulled Pork 360

Dry Rub for Barbecue

Eastern North Carolina
Barbecue Sauce

Mid–South Carolina
Mustard Sauce

Kansas City Sticky
Ribs 362

Kansas City
Barbecue Sauce

Smoky Kansas City
Barbecue Beans

Oven-Barbecued
Spareribs 365

Quick Barbecue Sauce

Barbecued Baby
Back Ribs 367

Texas-Style Barbecued
Beef Ribs 368

Barbecue Sauce for
Texas-Style Beef Ribs

Grilled Shish Kebabs 370

Warm-Spiced Parsley
Marinade with Ginger

Garlic and Cilantro
Marinade with
Garam Masala

Grilled Rack of Lamb 371

Grilled Salmon Fillets 372

Olive Vinaigrette

Almond Vinaigrette

Grilled Glazed Salmon 374

Orange-Sesame Glaze

Spicy Apple Glaze

Barbecued Salmon 375

Horseradish Cream Sauce
with Chives

Mustard-Dill Sauce

Grilled Blackened
Red Snapper 377

Rémoulade

Pineapple and Cucumber
Salsa with Mint

Grilled Shrimp
Skewers 379

Spicy Lemon-Garlic
Sauce

Fresh Tomato Sauce with
Feta and Olives

Grilled Baba
Ghanoush 380

Grilled Potatoes with
Garlic and Rosemary 382

Mexican-Style Grilled
Corn 383

GRILLED BONE-IN CHICKEN

WHY THIS RECIPE WORKS: Grilled chicken breasts aren't all that easy to get right. Burnt, limp skin and sooty, parched meat are too often the reality. The perfectly grilled chicken breast should boast tender and succulent meat and crisp skin.

Brining the chicken breasts for an hour or so before grilling helped ensure juicy, seasoned meat throughout, but consistency was an issue. We needed to focus on developing a precise grilling technique to minimize temperature fluctuation, thereby ensuring perfect meat every time. To do so, we created a sort of oven within an oven by covering the chicken with a piece of foil before closing the lid. This approach, combined with cooking the breasts skin side down on the cooler half of a modified two-level fire, finished cooking all six of the chicken breasts simultaneously. But we had one remaining problem: flabby skin. To solve it, we revised our plan and developed a three-step dance: We cooked the chicken on all sides over the hotter part of the grill until lightly browned; moved it to the cooler half and covered it with foil; and finished the breasts on the hotter side, cooking on both sides until the skin was brown and crisp.

Charcoal-Grilled Bone-In Chicken Breasts
SERVES 6

To help ensure that each breast finishes cooking at approximately the same time, buy pieces of similar size. Barbecue sauce can replace the optional glaze in step 4.

- ⅓ cup table salt
- 3 (1½-pound) bone-in, skin-on chicken breasts, split in half along breast bone and trimmed of rib sections (see page 71) (see note)
- Ground black pepper
- Vegetable oil for the cooking grate
- 1 recipe glaze (recipes follow; optional; see note)

1. Dissolve the salt in 2 quarts cold water in a large container. Submerge the chicken in the brine, cover with plastic wrap, and refrigerate 1 hour. Rinse the chicken under running water and pat dry with paper towels. Season the chicken with pepper.

2. Meanwhile, light a large chimney starter filled with charcoal (about 6 quarts) and allow to burn until the coals are partially covered with a layer of ash, about 20 minutes. Build a modified two-level fire by arranging all the coals over one half of the grill, leaving the other half empty. Set the cooking grate in place, cover, and heat the grate until

hot, about 5 minutes. Use a grill brush to scrape the cooking grate clean. Dip a wad of paper towels in oil; holding the wad with tongs, oil the cooking grate.

3. Cook the chicken on all sides over the hotter part of the grill until the skin is lightly browned and faint grill marks appear, 6 to 8 minutes. (If constant flare-ups occur, slide the chicken to the cooler side of the grill and mist the fire with water from a spray bottle.) Move the chicken, skin side down, to the cooler side of the grill, with the thicker sides of the breasts facing the coals. Cover loosely with foil, cover the grill, and continue to cook until the thickest part of the breast registers 150 degrees an instant-read thermometer, 15 to 25 minutes longer.

4. Brush the bone side of the chicken with glaze (if using). Move the chicken, bone side down, to the hotter side of the grill and cook until browned, 4 to 6 minutes. Brush the skin side of the chicken with glaze, turn the chicken over, and continue to cook until browned and the thickest part of the breast registers 160 to 165 degrees, 2 to 3 minutes longer. Transfer the chicken to a plate and let rest, tented with foil, 5 minutes. Serve, passing the remaining glaze separately.

Gas-Grilled Bone-In Chicken Breasts

Follow the recipe for Charcoal-Grilled Bone-In Chicken Breasts through step 1. Turn all the burners to high and heat the grill, with the lid down, until very hot, about 15 minutes. Use a grill brush to scrape the cooking grate

clean. Dip a wad of paper towels in oil; holding the wad with tongs, oil the cooking grate. Leave the primary burner on high and turn off the other burner(s). Proceed with the recipe from step 3, increasing the browning time in step 3 to 10 to 14 minutes.

Orange-Chipotle Glaze

MAKES ABOUT ¾ CUP

If you prefer more heat in this glaze, use the greater amount of chipotle chiles given.

- ⅔ cup juice plus 1 teaspoon grated zest from 2 oranges
- 1 small shallot, minced (about 1 tablespoon)
- 1-2 tablespoons minced chipotle chiles in adobo sauce (see note)
- 2 teaspoons minced fresh thyme leaves
- 1 tablespoon light molasses
- ¾ teaspoon cornstarch
  Table salt

Combine the juice, zest, shallot, chipotles, and thyme in a small saucepan; whisk in the molasses and cornstarch. Simmer the mixture over medium heat until thickened, about 5 minutes. Season with salt to taste. Reserve half of the glaze for serving and use the other half for brushing on the chicken in step 4.

Soy-Ginger Glaze

MAKES ABOUT 1 CUP

Reduce the amount of salt in the brine to ¼ cup when using this glaze.

- ⅓ cup water
- ¼ cup soy sauce
- 2 tablespoons mirin
- 1 tablespoon minced or grated fresh ginger
- 2 medium garlic cloves, minced or pressed through a garlic press (about 2 teaspoons)
- 3 tablespoons sugar
- ¾ teaspoon cornstarch
- 2 scallions, minced

Combine the water, soy sauce, mirin, ginger, and garlic in a small saucepan; whisk in the sugar and cornstarch. Simmer the mixture over medium heat until thickened, about 5 minutes; stir in the scallions. Reserve half of the glaze for serving and use the other half for brushing on the chicken in step 4.

BARBECUED PULLED CHICKEN

WHY THIS RECIPE WORKS: Made-from-scratch barbecued pulled chicken sandwiches often rely on boneless chicken breasts and bottled barbecue sauce. The result is a sandwich with no smoke, tough meat, and artificial flavor. We wanted to take pulled chicken sandwiches seriously—using tender, smoky meat pulled off the bone in moist, soft shreds and then tossed with a tangy, sweet sauce—but we didn't want to take all day to make them.

We chose whole chicken legs for great flavor, low cost, and resistance to overcooking. The legs cooked gently but thoroughly over indirect heat, absorbing plenty of smoke flavor along the way. Cooking the chicken to a higher-than-usual temperature also dissolves connective tissue and renders more fat, making the meat tender and less greasy. Once the chicken finished cooking, we hand-shredded half and machine-processed the other half to produce the perfect texture—one similar to pulled pork. The chicken then just had to be combined with a thin but tangy barbecue sauce to become truly bun-worthy.

**NAKED ROAST CHICKEN AND
OTHER WACKY RECIPE TESTS**

Our test cooks will do almost anything in pursuit of the perfect recipe. No idea is too silly or odd to try—not if it will make a recipe better. Here are some notable recipe tests performed over the years. Each one was deemed promising but ultimately never worked.

• Removing the skin from a chicken before it goes into the oven, pulling the skin taut with toothpicks, and then roasting the skin separately from the chicken pieces to maximize crispness. Too Hannibal Lechter.

• Cooking a roast beef in a 130-degree oven for 24 hours to maximize juiciness. Most ovens don't operate at such a low temperature, and it's probably just as well; this is a perfect recipe for food-borne illness.

• Rubbing the skin off every single chickpea to make extra-smooth hummus. Peeling chickpeas? What were we thinking?!

• Flipping a steak every 4 seconds—for a total of 176 flips over the course of the 11-minute cooking time—to ensure absolutely even heat distribution. Only cooks with Olympic aspirations need to try this.

• Attaching a still (yes, like you might devise to make moonshine) to a covered grill to make our own liquid smoke. The cost for 1 teaspoon of liquid smoke? Fifty bucks. And it didn't taste very good. Plus, this odd setup looked just a little suspicious (read: illegal) to our neighbors.

Barbecued Pulled Chicken for a Charcoal Grill
SERVES 6 TO 8

Chicken leg quarters consist of drumsticks attached to thighs; often also attached are backbone sections that must be trimmed away. To do this, carefully grasp the leg and bend the backbone section to pop out the joint; using a sharp boning knife, cut the backbone section from the leg. When trimming the fat from the chicken legs, try to leave the excess skin intact, as it will keep the meat moist on the grill. You will need a 16 by 12-inch disposable aluminum pan for this recipe. We prefer to use hickory or mesquite wood chunks with this dish.

If you would like to hold the dish once the chicken and sauce are combined and heated through, transfer the mixture to a 13 by 9-inch glass baking dish, cover with foil, and place in a 250-degree oven for up to an hour. Serve the pulled chicken on hamburger rolls or sandwich bread, and with pickles and coleslaw.

2 (3-inch) wood chunks (see note)
1 tablespoon vegetable oil, plus extra for the cooking grate
8 bone-in, skin-on chicken leg quarters (about 7 pounds), trimmed (see note)
  Table salt and ground black pepper
1 large onion, peeled and quartered
¼ cup water
1½ cups ketchup
1½ cups apple cider
¼ cup molasses
3 tablespoons Worcestershire sauce
3 tablespoons Dijon mustard
4 tablespoons apple cider vinegar
2 medium garlic cloves, minced or pressed through a garlic press (about 2 teaspoons)
1½ tablespoons chili powder
½ teaspoon cayenne pepper
  Hot sauce

1. Soak the wood chunks in cold water to cover for 1 hour; drain.

2. Light a large chimney starter filled three-quarters with charcoal (about 4½ quarts) and allow to burn until the coals are partially covered with a layer of ash, about 20 minutes. Open the bottom grill vents completely. Place a 16 by 12-inch disposable aluminum pan in the center of the grill. Build a double-banked fire by banking half the coals into a pile on each side of the pan. Place one wood chunk on top of one of the coal piles. Set the cooking grate in place, cover, and heat the grate until hot, about 5 minutes. Use a grill brush to scrape the cooking grate clean. Dip a wad of paper towels in oil; holding the wad with tongs, oil the cooking grate.

3. Pat the chicken dry with paper towels and season with salt and black pepper. Place the chicken, skin side up, in a single layer in the center of the grill over the pan. Cover and cook, rotating the chicken pieces halfway through (do not flip the chicken over) and adding the remaining wood chunk to either pile of coals, until the thickest part of the thigh registers about 185 degrees on an instant-read thermometer, 1 to 1¼ hours. Transfer the chicken to a carving board, tent loosely with foil, and let rest until cool enough to handle.

4. While the chicken is cooking or cooling, puree the onion and water in a food processor until the mixture resembles slush, about 30 seconds. Pass the mixture through a fine-mesh strainer into a liquid measuring cup, pressing on the solids with a rubber spatula (you should have ¾ cup strained onion juice). Discard the solids in the strainer.

5. Whisk the onion juice, ketchup, cider, molasses, Worcestershire sauce, mustard, ½ teaspoon black pepper, and 3 tablespoons of the cider vinegar together in a medium bowl. Heat 1 tablespoon oil in a large saucepan over medium heat until shimmering; add the garlic, chili powder, and cayenne and cook until fragrant, about 30 seconds. Stir in the ketchup mixture and bring to a boil over medium-high heat; reduce the heat to medium-low and simmer, uncovered, until the sauce is slightly thickened, about 15 minutes (you should have about 4 cups of sauce). Transfer 2 cups of the sauce to a serving bowl; leave the remaining sauce in the saucepan.

6. Remove and discard the skin from the chicken legs. Using your fingers, pull the meat off the bones, separating the larger pieces (which should fall off the bones easily) from the smaller, drier pieces into two equal piles.

7. Pulse the smaller chicken pieces in a food processor until just coarsely chopped, 3 to 4 pulses, stirring the chicken with a rubber spatula after each pulse. Add the chicken to the sauce in the saucepan. Using your fingers or two forks, pull the larger chicken pieces into long shreds and add to the saucepan. Stir in the remaining 1 tablespoon cider vinegar; cover the saucepan and heat the chicken over medium-low heat, stirring occasionally, until heated through, about 10 minutes. Add hot sauce to taste and serve, passing the remaining sauce separately.

Barbecued Pulled Chicken for a Gas Grill

You will need a disposable aluminum pie plate for this recipe.

1. Substitute 2 cups wood chips for the wood chunks and soak them in cold water to cover for 30 minutes; drain. Place the chips in a small disposable aluminum pie plate; place the pan on top of the primary burner. Turn all the burners to high and heat the grill, with the lid down, until very hot and the chips are smoking, about 15 minutes. (If the chips ignite, use a water-filled spray bottle to extinguish them.) Use a grill brush to scrape the cooking grate clean. Dip a wad of paper towels in the oil; holding the wad with tongs, oil the cooking grate. Leave the primary burner on high and turn off the other burner(s).

2. Follow the recipe for Barbecued Pulled Chicken for a Charcoal Grill from step 3, placing the chicken, skin side up, in a single layer on the cooler side of the grill. Proceed as directed, omitting the wood chunks and disposable aluminum pan and extending the cooking time in step 3 to 1¼ to 1½ hours.

BARBECUED PULLED CHICKEN FOR A CROWD

To make barbecued pulled chicken for a crowd, we found that a roasting rack, with six slots, was the perfect tool for the job. By sliding two legs into each slot, a total of 12 legs fit (and finish cooking) at once—plenty to feed a hungry crowd.

Barbecued Pulled Chicken for a Crowd

This technique works well on a charcoal grill but not so well on a gas grill. If your gas grill is large and can accommodate more than 8 legs, follow the recipe above, adding as many legs as will comfortably fit in a single layer. You may need to increase the cooking time.

Follow the recipe for Barbecued Pulled Chicken for a Charcoal Grill, lighting a large chimney starter filled with charcoal (about 6 quarts), using 12 chicken legs, and slotting them into a V-shaped roasting rack set on top of the cooking grate over a 16 by 12-inch disposable aluminum pan (see photo). Increase the cooking time in step 3 to 1½ to 1¾ hours. In step 5, remove only 1 cup of sauce from the saucepan. In step 7, pulse the chicken in a food processor in two batches.

BEER CAN CHICKEN

WHY THIS RECIPE WORKS: We wanted to know if the curious cooking method of grill-roasting chicken over a can of beer really worked. To earn our approval, this technique would have to produce a tender, juicy, and deeply seasoned bird.

We found that beer can chicken is the real deal—why? The beer in the open can simmers and turns to steam as the chicken roasts, which makes the meat remarkably juicy and rich-textured, similar to braised chicken. As an added bonus, the dry heat of the grill crisps the skin and renders the fat away. To perfect the technique, we added a few hardwood chunks to the fire for smoky flavor. The best grilling setup (for a charcoal grill) proved to be banking the lit coals on either side of the grill and propping the chicken up on an open can of beer on the grill in the center, using the bird's drumsticks to form a tripod. Finally, we found we didn't have to spend money on an expensive beer—the beer flavor wasn't really detectable in the chicken, so a cheap brew worked just fine (so does lemonade, which proved an acceptable substitute for the beer).

Grill-Roasted Beer Can Chicken for a Charcoal Grill

SERVES 4

Using the right amount of charcoal is crucial here; using too much charcoal will burn the chicken, while using too little will extend the cooking time substantially. The temperature inside the grill should be about 375 degrees at the outset and will fall to about 300 by the time the chicken is done. For added accuracy, place a grill thermometer in the lid vents as the chicken cooks. If you prefer, use lemonade instead of beer; fill an empty 12-ounce soda or beer can with 10 ounces (1¼ cups) of lemonade and proceed as directed. You will need a 13 by 9-inch disposable aluminum pan for this recipe.

- 2 (3-inch) wood chunks or 2 cups wood chips
- 1 (12-ounce) can beer (see note)
- 2 bay leaves
- 1 (3½-pound) whole chicken
- 3 tablespoons Spice Rub (recipe follows)
  Vegetable oil for the cooking grate

1. Soak the wood chunks or chips in cold water to cover for 1 hour and drain. If using wood chips, divide them between two 18-inch squares of foil, fold in the sides of each piece of foil and seal to make two packets, and use a fork to poke about six holes in each packet to allow smoke to escape.

2. Open the beer can and pour out (or drink) about ¼ cup. With a church key can opener, punch two more large holes in the top of the can (for a total of three holes). Crumble the bay leaves into the beer. Pat the chicken dry with paper towels and massage the spice rub all over the chicken, inside and out. Gently lift up the skin over the breast and rub the spice rub directly onto the meat. Using a skewer, poke the skin all over. Slide the chicken over the beer can so that the drumsticks reach down to the bottom of the can and the chicken stands upright; set aside at room temperature.

3. Light a large chimney starter filled two-thirds with charcoal (about 4 quarts) and allow to burn until the coals are partially covered with a layer of ash, about 20 minutes.

4. Place a 13 by 9-inch disposable aluminum pan in the center of the grill. Build a double-banked fire by banking half the coals into a pile on each side of the pan. Place one soaked wood chunk (or one foil packet) on top of each coal pile. Set the cooking grate in place, cover, and heat the grate until hot, about 5 minutes. Use a grill brush to scrape the cooking grate clean. Dip a wad of paper towels in oil; holding the wad with tongs, oil the cooking grate.

5. Place the chicken (with the can) in the center of the cooking grate with the wings facing the coals (the ends of the drumsticks will help steady the bird). Cover and cook until the thickest part of the breast registers 160 to 165 degrees and the thickest part of the thigh registers 175 degrees on an instant-read thermometer, 65 to 85 minutes.

6. With a large wad of paper towels in each hand, transfer the chicken to a platter or tray, making sure to keep the can upright; let rest for 15 minutes. Carefully lift the chicken off the can and onto a cutting board. Discard the remaining beer and can. Carve the chicken and serve.

Grill-Roasted Beer Can Chicken for a Gas Grill

Be sure not to open the lid of the gas grill too often during cooking; the temperature of the grill will drop significantly each time you open it. You will need a disposable aluminum pie plate for this recipe.

1. Soak 2 cups wood chips in cold water to cover for 30 minutes and drain. Place the wood chips in a disposable aluminum pie plate; place the pie plate on top of the primary burner (the burner that will remain on during cooking). Turn all the burners to high and heat the grill with the lid down until very hot and the chips are smoking heavily, about 15 minutes.

2. Meanwhile, follow the recipe for Grill-Roasted Beer Can Chicken for a Charcoal Grill from step 2. Carefully open the grill (there may be some smoke) and use a grill brush to scrape the cooking grate clean. Dip a wad of paper towels in the oil; holding the wad with tongs, oil the cooking grate. Turn the primary burner down to medium and turn off the other burner(s). Position the chicken over the cool part of the grill with a wing side facing the primary burner. Cover and cook for 35 minutes. (The temperature inside the grill should be 325 to 350 degrees; adjust the lit burner as necessary.) Rotate the chicken so that the drumstick and wing that were facing away from the lit burner are now facing toward it. Cover and continue to cook until the thickest part of the breast registers 160 to 165 degrees and the thickest part of the thigh registers 175 degrees on an instant-read thermometer, 25 to 40 minutes longer; proceed as directed in step 6.

Spice Rub
MAKES 1 CUP

½ cup sweet paprika
2 tablespoons kosher salt
2 tablespoons garlic powder
1 tablespoon dried thyme
2 teaspoons ground celery seed
2 teaspoons ground black pepper
2 teaspoons cayenne pepper

Combine all the ingredients in a small bowl. (Extra rub can be stored in an airtight container for 2 months.)

GRILLED CORNISH GAME HENS

WHY THIS RECIPE WORKS: Grilled Cornish game hens provide an attractive, elegant alternative to grilled chicken. We wanted to develop a foolproof technique that would deliver smoky notes, really crisp skin, and juicy meat infused with great grilled flavor.

We found that by butterflying the birds we could keep all of the skin on one side, which meant it crisped more quickly when placed facing the coals. Butterflying also produced a uniformly thick bird, which promoted even cooking. We needed to secure the legs to the body to keep the skin from tearing, so we developed a special skewering procedure that stabilized the legs, made it easier to fit the birds on the cooking grate, and created a restaurant-worthy presentation. A seven-ingredient rub gave the hens a sweet and savory complexity and helped crisp the skin even further, giving it a rich mahogany hue. Our quick glaze of ketchup, brown sugar, and soy sauce provided the crowning touch.

Grill-Roasted Cornish Game Hens for a Charcoal Grill
SERVES 4

Butterflying a Cornish game hen is similar to butterflying a chicken or turkey (see page 78 and page 95). Use poultry shears to cut out and remove the backbone, then make a ¼-inch cut in the breastbone to separate the breast halves and lightly press down to flatten the bird. Finally, with the skin facing up, fold the wingtips behind the bird to secure them.

If your hens weigh 1½ to 2 pounds, cook three instead of four, brine them for an extra 15 minutes, and extend the cooking time in step 5 by 10 to 15 minutes. Thaw frozen game hens in the refrigerator for 24 to 36 hours before brining. To add smoke flavor to the hens, use the optional wood chunks. Note that you will need a 16 by 12-inch disposable aluminum pan and four 8 to 10-inch flat metal skewers to secure the hens.

HENS

1 cup table salt
4 (1¼ to 1½-pound) Cornish game hens, butterflied (see note)
2 tablespoons brown sugar
1 tablespoon paprika
2 teaspoons garlic powder
2 teaspoons chili powder
1 teaspoon ground black pepper
1 teaspoon ground coriander
⅛ teaspoon cayenne pepper
4 (3-inch) wood chunks (optional; see note)
Vegetable oil for the cooking grate

BARBECUE GLAZE

½ cup ketchup
2 tablespoons brown sugar
1 tablespoon soy sauce
1 tablespoon distilled white vinegar
1 tablespoon yellow mustard
1 medium garlic clove, minced or pressed through a garlic press (about 1 teaspoon)

SKEWERING GAME HENS

1. Insert a flat metal skewer ½ inch from the end of a drumstick through the skin and meat and out the other side.

2. Turn the leg so that the end of the drumstick faces the wing, then insert the tip of the skewer into the meaty section of the thigh under the bone.

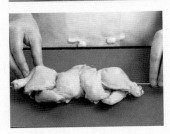

3. Press the skewer all the way through the breast and second thigh. Fold the end of the drumstick toward the wing and insert the skewer ½ inch from the end.

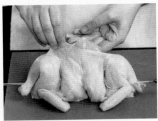

4. Press the skewer so that the blunt end rests against the bird and stretch the skin tight over the legs, thighs, and breast halves.

1. FOR THE HENS: Dissolve the salt in 4 quarts cold water in a large container. Submerge the hens in the brine, cover with plastic wrap, and refrigerate 1 hour.

2. While the hens brine, combine the sugar and spices in a small bowl. If using the wood chunks, soak them in cold water to cover for 1 hour; drain. Remove the birds from the brine and rinse inside and out under running water; pat dry with paper towels. Following the photos, use an 8 to 10-inch flat metal skewer to secure each hen. Rub the hens evenly with the spice mixture and refrigerate while preparing the grill.

3. FOR THE GLAZE: Cook all the ingredients in a small saucepan over medium heat, stirring occasionally, until thick and slightly reduced, about 5 minutes. Set aside.

4. Light a large chimney starter filled with charcoal (about 6 quarts) and allow to burn until the coals are partially covered with a layer of ash, about 20 minutes. Place a 16 by 12-inch disposable aluminum pan in the center of the grill. Build a double-banked fire by banking half of the coals into a pile on each side of the pan. Place two soaked wood chunks on each pile of coals, if using. Set the cooking grate in place, cover, and heat the grate until hot, about 5 minutes. Use a grill brush to scrape the cooking grate clean. Dip a wad of paper towels in oil; holding the wad with tongs, oil the cooking grate.

5. Place the hens, skin side down, on the center of the grill over the pan. Open the grill lid vents completely and cover, positioning the vents over the hens. Cook the hens until the thickest part of the thigh registers 160 to 165 degrees on an instant-read thermometer, 20 to 30 minutes.

6. Using tongs, move the birds to the hot sides of the grill (2 hens per side). Cover and continue to cook until browned, about 5 minutes. Brush the birds with half of the glaze; flip and cook for 2 minutes. Brush the remaining glaze over the hens; flip and continue to cook until the thickest part of the breast registers 160 to 165 degrees and the thickest part of the thigh registers 175 degrees, 1 to 3 minutes longer.

7. Transfer the hens to a cutting board and let rest 10 minutes. Cut in half through the breastbone and serve immediately.

Grill-Roasted Cornish Game Hens for a Gas Grill

If using the optional wood chips for a smoky flavor, you will need a disposable aluminum pie plate for this recipe.

1. Follow the recipe for Grill-Roasted Cornish Game Hens for a Charcoal Grill through step 3, substituting 1 cup wood chips for the wood chunks and soaking them in cold water to cover for 30 minutes. Drain the chips and place in a disposable aluminum pie plate; set the pie plate on one burner. Turn all the burners to high and heat the grill, with the lid down, until very hot and the chips are smoking, about 15 minutes (if the chips ignite, use a water-filled spray bottle to extinguish). Use a grill brush to scrape the cooking grate clean. Dip a wad of paper towels in vegetable oil; holding the wad with tongs, oil the cooking grate. Turn all the burners to medium.

2. Place the hens, skin side down, on the cooking grate. Cover and cook until the skin is deeply browned and has grill marks, 10 to 15 minutes. (If the grill has hot spots, you might have to move the hens on the grill.) Using tongs, flip the birds; cover and continue to cook until the thickest part of the thigh registers 160 to 165 degrees on an instant-read thermometer, 10 to 15 minutes more.

3. Brush the birds with half of the glaze. Using tongs, flip the birds and cook until deeply browned, 2 to 3 minutes. Brush the remaining glaze over the hens; flip and continue to cook until deeply browned and the thickest part of the breast registers 160 to 165 degrees and the thickest part of the thigh registers 175 degrees, 2 to 3 minutes more.

4. Transfer the hens to a carving board and let rest 10 minutes. Cut in half through the breastbone and serve immediately.

GRILLED HAMBURGERS

WHY THIS RECIPE WORKS: Burgers often come off the grill tough, dry, and bulging in the middle. We wanted a moist and juicy burger, with a texture that is tender and cohesive, not dense and heavy. Just as important, we wanted a flavorful, deeply caramelized reddish brown crust with an even surface capable of holding as many condiments as we could pile on.

Ground chuck gave us the most robustly flavored burgers when pitted head to head against burgers made from other cuts of ground beef. We selected meat with a ratio of

20 percent fat to 80 percent lean; more fat than that, and the burgers were too greasy. Burgers made with less fat lacked in juiciness and moisture. We formed the meat into 6-ounce patties that were fairly thick, with a depression in the middle. Rounds of testing taught us that indenting the center of each burger ensured that the patties would come off the grill with an even thickness instead of puffed up like a tennis ball. Cooking the burgers over the fire for just a few minutes kept them tender, and lightly oiling the cooking grate prevented them from sticking.

Charcoal-Grilled Hamburgers

SERVES 4

For those who like their burgers well-done, we found that poking a small hole in the center of the patty before cooking helped the center to cook through before the edges dried out.

     Vegetable oil for the cooking grate
1½ **pounds 80 percent lean ground chuck**
 1 **teaspoon table salt**
 ½ **teaspoon ground black pepper**
 4 **buns or rolls**

1. Light a large chimney starter filled with charcoal (about 6 quarts) and allow to burn until the coals are partially covered with a layer of ash, about 20 minutes. Build a single-level fire by arranging the coals evenly over the bottom of the grill. Set the cooking grate in place, cover, and heat the grate until hot, about 5 minutes. Use a grill brush to scrape the cooking grate clean. Dip a wad of paper towels in oil; holding the wad with tongs, oil the cooking grate.

2. Meanwhile, using your hands, gently break up the meat, season with the salt and pepper, and toss lightly to distribute. Divide the meat into four equal portions. Gently toss one portion of meat back and forth between your hands to form a loose ball. Gently flatten into a ¾-inch-thick patty that measures about 4½ inches in diameter. Press the center of the patty down with your fingertips until it is about ½ inch thick, creating a slight depression in each patty. Repeat with the remaining portions of meat.

3. Grill the burgers, uncovered, until well seared on the first side, about 2½ minutes. Using a wide metal spatula, flip the burgers and continue grilling, about 2 minutes for rare, 2½ minutes for medium-rare, 3 minutes for medium, or 4 minutes for well-done. While the burgers grill, toast the buns on the cooler side of the grill. Serve on buns with desired toppings.

Gas-Grilled Hamburgers

Turn all the burners to high and heat the grill, with the lid down, until very hot, about 15 minutes. Use a grill brush to scrape the cooking grate clean. Dip a wad of paper towels in oil; holding the wad with tongs, oil the cooking grate. Follow the recipe for Charcoal-Grilled Hamburgers, proceeding with step 2. In step 3, grill the burgers on the first side for 3 minutes and increase the cooking times on the second side by 1 minute.

Grilled Cheeseburgers

Since the cheese is evenly distributed in these burgers, just a little goes a long way.

Follow the recipe for Charcoal- or Gas-Grilled Hamburgers, sprinkling 3 ounces cheddar, Swiss, or Monterey Jack cheese, shredded (about ¾ cup), or 3 ounces blue cheese, crumbled (about ¾ cup), over the meat with the salt and pepper in step 2.

WELL-DONE BURGERS

WHY THIS RECIPE WORKS: We know that many backyard cooks grill their burgers to medium-well and beyond, but we aren't willing to accept the usual outcome of tough, desiccated hockey pucks with no beefy flavor. We wanted to work with supermarket ground beef to produce a tender and moist-as-can-be burger, with perfect grill marks and all, even when well-done.

Taste tests proved that well-done burgers made with 80 percent lean chuck were noticeably moister than burgers made from leaner beef, but they still weren't juicy enough. Because we couldn't force the meat to retain moisture, we opted to pack the patties with a panade, a paste made from bread and milk that's often used to keep meat loaf and meatballs moist. To punch up the flavor, we also added minced garlic and tangy steak sauce. To keep our burgers from puffing up the way most burgers do, we made use of a previous test kitchen discovery: If you make a slight depression in the center of the patty, it will puff slightly as it cooks and level out to form a flat top.

Well-Done Charcoal-Grilled Hamburgers

SERVES 4

Adding bread and milk to the beef creates burgers that are juicy and tender even when well-done. For cheeseburgers, follow the optional instructions below.

  Vegetable oil for the cooking grate
1 large slice high-quality white sandwich bread, crust removed and discarded, bread cut into ¼-inch pieces (about ½ cup)
2 tablespoons whole milk
2 teaspoons steak sauce, such as A-1
1 medium garlic clove, minced or pressed through a garlic press (about 1 teaspoon)
¾ teaspoon table salt
¾ teaspoon ground black pepper
1½ pounds 80 percent lean ground chuck
6 ounces sliced cheese (optional)
4 buns or rolls

1. Light a large chimney starter filled with charcoal (about 6 quarts) and allow to burn until the coals are partially covered with a layer of ash, about 20 minutes.

Open the bottom grill vents. Build a modified two-level fire by arranging the coals over half of the grill, leaving the other half empty. Set the cooking grate in place, cover the grill, and heat the grate until hot, about 5 minutes. Use a grill brush to scrape the cooking grate clean. Dip a wad of paper towels in oil; holding the wad with tongs, oil the cooking grate.

2. Meanwhile, mash the bread and milk in a large bowl with a fork until homogeneous (you should have about ¼ cup). Stir in the steak sauce, garlic, salt, and pepper.

3. Break up the beef into small pieces over the bread mixture. Using a fork or your hands, lightly mix together until the mixture forms a cohesive mass. Divide the meat into four equal portions. Gently toss one portion of meat back and forth between your hands to form a loose ball. Gently flatten into a ¾-inch-thick patty that measures about 4½ inches in diameter. Press the center of the patty down with your fingertips until it is about ½ inch thick, creating a slight depression in each patty. Repeat with the remaining portions of meat.

4. Grill the burgers on the hot side of the grill, uncovered, until well seared on the first side, 2 to 4 minutes. Using a wide metal spatula, flip the burgers and continue grilling, about 3 minutes for medium-well or 4 minutes for well-done. (Add the cheese, if using, about 2 minutes before reaching the desired doneness, covering the burgers with a disposable aluminum pan to melt the cheese.) While the burgers grill, toast the buns on the cooler side of the grill. Serve the burgers on the buns with desired toppings.

Well-Done Gas-Grilled Hamburgers

Turn all the burners to high and heat the grill, with the lid down, until very hot, about 15 minutes. Use a grill brush to scrape the cooking grate clean. Dip a wad of paper towels in oil; holding the wad with tongs, oil the cooking grate. Leave the primary burner on high and turn the other burner(s) to low. Follow the recipe for Well-Done Charcoal-Grilled Hamburgers from step 2, grilling the patties with the lid down.

Well-Done Grilled Bacon Cheeseburgers

Most bacon burgers simply top the burgers with bacon. The test kitchen goes a step further, adding bacon fat to the ground beef, which adds juiciness and unmistakable bacon flavor throughout the burger.

Cook 8 slices bacon (about 8 ounces) in a medium skillet over medium heat until crisp, 7 to 9 minutes. Transfer the bacon to a paper towel–lined plate; set aside. Measure 2 tablespoons bacon fat into a heatproof bowl; refrigerate until just warm. Follow the recipe for Well-Done Charcoal- or Gas-Grilled Hamburgers, including the optional cheese, adding the reserved bacon fat to the beef mixture in step 3, and topping each finished burger with 2 strips of bacon just before serving.

GRILLED FLANK STEAK

WHY THIS RECIPE WORKS: A common way to prepare flank steak is to marinate it in a bottle of Italian-style salad dressing. But while the resulting flavor can be interesting, the acid in the vinegar can ruin the texture, making the exterior mushy and gray. We wanted to develop a fresh, Mediterranean-style marinade without acid—a marinade that would really boost flavor without over-tenderizing the meat.

We turned to the optimal method for cooking a flank steak—use a two-level fire (which lets you move the thin part of the steak to the cooler side of the grill once it is done), cook the steak only to medium-rare to keep it from getting tough, and let the steak rest before slicing to reduce the loss of juices. Now we could concentrate on developing and applying an acid-free marinade.

Because fat carries flavor so well, we knew oil would be a key ingredient—the challenge was to infuse Mediterranean flavors (garlic, shallots, and rosemary) into the oil and then into the steak. We developed two key steps. First, we minced the aromatics and combined them with the oil in a blender to create a marinade paste. Next, we invented a novel "marinating" technique—prick the steak all over with a fork, rub it first with salt and then with the marinade paste, then let it sit for up to 24 hours. After marinating, the paste is wiped off to prevent burning, and the steak is ready for the grill. Our technique was so successful, we were free to create two more marinades—one with Asian flavors, and the other with a smoky-spicy kick.

browned but the meat is not yet cooked through, move the steak to the cooler side of the grill and continue to grill to the desired doneness. Transfer the steak to a carving board.

4. Tent the steak loosely with foil; let rest 5 to 10 minutes. Using a sharp chef's knife or carving knife, slice the steak about ¼ inch thick against the grain and on the bias. Serve immediately.

Gas-Grilled Marinated Flank Steak

Follow the recipe for Charcoal-Grilled Marinated Flank Steak through step 1. Turn all the burners to high and heat the grill, with the lid down, until very hot, about 15 minutes. Use a grill brush to scrape the cooking grate clean. Dip a wad of paper towels in the oil; holding the wad with tongs, oil the cooking grate. Leave all the burners on high. Proceed with the recipe from step 3, cooking with the lid down. If the meat is significantly underdone when tested with a paring knife, turn off one burner and position the steak so that the thinner side is over the cool part of the grill and the thicker side is over the hot part of the grill.

Garlic-Shallot-Rosemary Wet Paste Marinade
MAKES ENOUGH FOR 1 FLANK STEAK

- 6 tablespoons olive oil
- 1 medium shallot, minced (about 3 tablespoons)
- 6 medium garlic cloves, minced or pressed through a garlic press (about 2 tablespoons)
- 2 tablespoons minced fresh rosemary leaves

Puree all of the ingredients in a blender until smooth, scraping down the sides of the blender jar as needed.

Garlic-Ginger-Sesame Wet Paste Marinade
MAKES ENOUGH FOR 1 FLANK STEAK

- ¼ cup toasted sesame oil
- 3 tablespoons minced or grated fresh ginger
- 2 tablespoons vegetable oil
- 2 scallions, minced
- 3 medium garlic cloves, minced or pressed through a garlic press (about 1 tablespoon)

Puree all of the ingredients in a blender until smooth, scraping down the sides of the blender jar as needed.

Charcoal-Grilled Marinated Flank Steak
SERVES 4 TO 6

Flank steaks smaller or larger than 2 pounds can be used, but adjust the amount of salt and pepper accordingly. We prefer flank steak cooked medium-rare or medium. To keep the steak juicy, allow it to rest before slicing it.

- 1 (2-pound) whole flank steak, trimmed (see note)
- 1 teaspoon table salt (see note)
- 1 recipe wet paste marinade (recipes follow)
  Vegetable oil for the cooking grate
- ¼ teaspoon ground black pepper (see note)

1. Pat the steak dry with paper towels and plate it on a rimmed baking sheet or in a large baking dish. Using a dinner fork, prick the steak about 20 times on each side. Rub both sides of the steak evenly with the salt, and then with the paste. Cover with plastic wrap and refrigerate at least 1 hour or up to 24 hours.

2. Light a large chimney starter filled with charcoal (about 6 quarts) and allow to burn until the coals are partially covered with a layer of ash, about 20 minutes. Open the bottom grill vents. Build a two-level fire by arranging two-thirds of the coals evenly over half of the grill and arranging the remaining coals over the other half. Set the cooking grate in place, cover the grill, and heat the grate until hot, about 5 minutes. Use a grill brush to scrape the cooking grate clean. Dip a wad of paper towels in oil; holding the wad with tongs, oil the cooking grate.

3. Using paper towels, wipe the paste off the steak; season both sides with the pepper. Grill the steak directly over the coals until well browned, 4 to 6 minutes. Using tongs, flip the steak; grill until the second side is well browned and an instant-read thermometer inserted into the steak reads 125 degrees for medium-rare and 135 degrees for medium, 3 to 6 minutes; if the exterior of the meat is

Garlic-Chile Wet Paste Marinade

MAKES ENOUGH FOR 1 FLANK STEAK

- 6 tablespoons vegetable oil
- 6 medium garlic cloves, minced or pressed through a garlic press (about 2 tablespoons)
- 2 scallions, minced
- 1 tablespoon minced chipotle chiles in adobo sauce
- 1 medium jalapeño chile, minced

Puree all of the ingredients in a blender until smooth, scraping down the sides of the blender jar as needed.

GRILLED STUFFED FLANK STEAK

WHY THIS RECIPE WORKS: Stuffed steak originated with Italian-American cooking as a way transform an inexpensive steak into something more exciting and colorful. But when we tried a few of the premade stuffed "pinwheels" from our local grocery store, both the stuffing and the cheese tried to make a run for it, with the cheese oozing out all over the grill, and the stuffing—which can include prosciutto, nuts, or spinach, among other things—falling out onto the grill in big clumps. We were sure we could turn this dish into an easy dinner, with tender beef and a juicy, flavorful filling that stayed in place.

Thanks to its uniform shape and good beefy taste, flank steak was clearly the best bet. To guarantee the filling stayed in place, we butterflied and pounded the steak, so we were starting with the flattest and widest surface possible. As for the filling, we eliminated bread crumbs from consideration—after grilling, they contributed a taste of burnt toast. The classic Italian-American combo of prosciutto and provolone won raves for its salty savor and the way the dry cheese melted inside the pinwheel yet turned crisp where exposed to the grill. To prevent the meat from shrinking on the grill, and squeezing the centers of the pinwheels, we rolled up our flank steak, tied it with twine, and skewered it at 1-inch intervals before slicing and grilling. The twine kept the steak from unraveling, while the skewers prevented the meat from shrinking. Finally, we had stuffing that stayed stuffed and rich, smoky beef.

Grilled Stuffed Flank Steak for a Charcoal Grill

SERVES 4 TO 6

Look for a flank steak measuring approximately 8 by 6 inches, with the grain running the long way. Depending on the steak's size, you may have more or less than eight slices of meat at the end of step 2. You will need both wooden skewers and twine for this recipe.

- 2 tablespoons olive oil, plus extra for the cooking grate
- 1 small shallot, minced (about 1 tablespoon)
- 2 tablespoons finely minced fresh parsley leaves
- 2 medium garlic cloves, minced or pressed through a garlic press (about 2 teaspoons)
- 1 teaspoon finely minced fresh sage leaves
- 1 (2 to 2½-pound) flank steak, trimmed (see note)
- 4 ounces thinly sliced prosciutto
- 4 ounces thinly sliced provolone cheese
  Table salt and ground black pepper

1. Combine the oil, shallot, parsley, garlic, and sage in a small bowl. Following the photos on page 348, butterfly and pound the flank steak into a rough rectangle. Spread the herb mixture evenly over the opened side of the steak. Lay the prosciutto evenly over the steak,

HOW TO BUTTERFLY AND STUFF FLANK STEAK

1. Lay the flank steak on the edge of a cutting board. Slice the steak horizontally, making sure to leave a ½-inch "hinge" along the top edge.

2. Open up the steak, cover with plastic wrap, and pound it to a 12 by 8-inch rectangle of even thickness.

3. Leaving the steak in place with the grain still running perpendicular to the edge of the cutting board, rub the steak evenly with the herb mixture, and layer it with the prosciutto and cheese, leaving a 2-inch border along the top edge.

4. Roll the steak away from you into a tight log, then tie it at even 1-inch intervals. Skewer the meat directly through each string, making sure to insert the skewer through the seam in the roll to prevent the beef from unraveling during cooking.

5. Slice the beef into 1-inch-thick pinwheels. Each spiral should be held together with a skewer and a piece of twine.

leaving a 2-inch border along the top edge. Cover the prosciutto with an even layer of cheese, leaving a 2-inch border along the top edge. Starting from the short edge, roll the beef into a tight log and place on the cutting board seam side down.

2. Soak eight to 12 wooden skewers in warm water to cover (you will need one skewer per inch of rolled steak length) for 30 minutes; set aside. Starting ½ inch from the end of the rolled steak, evenly space eight to twelve 14-inch pieces of kitchen twine at 1-inch intervals underneath the steak. Tie the middle string first, then, working from the outer strings toward the center, tightly tie the roll and turn the tied steak 90 degrees so the seam is facing you. Dry the skewers and skewer the beef directly through the outer flap of steak near the seam through each piece of string, allowing the skewers to extend ½ inch on the other side. Using a chef's knife, slice the roll between each piece of twine into 1-inch-thick pinwheels. Season the pinwheels with salt and pepper.

3. Light a large chimney starter three-quarters full with charcoal (about 4½ quarts) and allow to burn until the coals are partially covered with a layer of ash, about 20 minutes. Build a modified two-level fire by arranging all the coals over half of the grill, leaving the other half empty. Set the cooking grate in place, cover, and heat the grate until hot, about 5 minutes. Use a grill brush to scrape the cooking grate clean. Dip a wad of paper towels in oil; holding the wad with tongs, oil the cooking grate.

4. Grill the pinwheels directly over the hot side of the grill until well browned, 3 to 6 minutes. Using tongs, flip the pinwheels; grill until the second side is well browned, 3 to 5 minutes longer. Transfer the pinwheels to the cooler side of the grill, cover, and continue to cook until the center of the pinwheels registers 125 degrees on an instant-read thermometer, 1 to 4 minutes (slightly thinner pinwheels may not need time on the cooler side of the grill). Transfer the pinwheels to a large plate, tent loosely with foil, and let rest 5 minutes. Remove and discard the skewers and string and serve immediately.

Grilled Stuffed Flank Steak for a Gas Grill

Follow the recipe for Grilled Stuffed Flank Steak for a Charcoal Grill through step 2. Turn all the burners to high and heat the grill, with the lid down, until very hot, about 15 minutes. Use a grill brush to scrape the cooking grate clean. Dip a wad of paper towels in oil; holding the wad with tongs, oil the cooking grate. Leave the primary burner on high and turn the other burner(s) off. Proceed as directed in step 4.

Grilled Stuffed Flank Steak with Spinach and Pine Nuts

Combine 4 ounces washed, chopped spinach, ½ teaspoon ground black pepper, ½ teaspoon table salt, and 1 tablespoon water in a medium microwave-safe bowl. Cover and microwave on high power until the spinach is wilted and decreased in volume by half, 3 to 4 minutes. Allow to cool completely, then stir in ¼ cup toasted pine nuts. Follow the recipe for Grilled Stuffed Flank Steak for a Charcoal or Gas Grill, replacing the prosciutto with the spinach mixture in step 1.

STEAK TIPS

WHY THIS RECIPE WORKS: Steak tips have long been the darling of all-you-can-eat restaurant chains where quantity takes precedence over quality. If they're not mushy, they land on the table tough and dry. We wanted to improve this classic bar food and instill it with deep flavor and a tender texture.

To stay true to the inexpensive nature of this dish, we set our sights on finding the best affordable (read: cheap) cut of meat that would stay tender and moist during a brief stint on the grill. The best cut, we found, is what butchers call flap meat. To tenderize and flavor the meat, we used a soy sauce–based marinade and let the meat marinate for at least an hour—just the right amount of time to allow the thicker parts of the meat to become tender while preventing the thinner sections from becoming too salty. Grilling the tips over a two-level fire, which has hotter and cooler areas, helps to cook this often unevenly shaped cut evenly. We let the meat rest for five minutes after grilling to ensure juicy meat, then sliced it thin so the meat would be tender and flavorful. Lime or orange wedges provided a bright acidic counterpoint to the steak tips.

Charcoal-Grilled Steak Tips

SERVES 4 TO 6

A two-level fire allows you to brown the steak over the hot side of the grill, then move it to the cooler side if it is not yet cooked through. If your steak is thin, however, you may not need to use the cooler side of the grill. The times in the recipe below are for relatively even, 1-inch-thick steak tips. When grilling, bear in mind that even those tasters who usually prefer rare beef preferred steak tips cooked medium-rare to medium because the texture

is firmer and not quite so chewy. Serve lime wedges with the Southwestern-marinated tips and orange wedges with the tips marinated in garlic, ginger, and soy sauce.

- 1 recipe marinade (recipes follow)
- 2 pounds flap meat sirloin steak tips, trimmed
  Vegetable oil for the cooking grate
  Lime or orange wedges, for serving (see note)

1. Combine the marinade and meat in a gallon-sized zipper-lock bag, seal the bag, and refrigerate for 1 hour, flipping the bag once halfway through the marinating time.

2. About halfway through the marinating time, light a large chimney starter filled with charcoal (about 6 quarts) and allow to burn until the coals are partially covered with a layer of ash, about 20 minutes. Build a two-level fire by arranging two-thirds of the coals evenly over half of the grill and arranging the remaining coals over the other half. Set the cooking grate in place, cover the grill, and heat the grate until hot, about 5 minutes. Use a grill brush to scrape the cooking grate clean. Dip a wad of paper towels in vegetable oil; holding the wad with tongs, oil the cooking grate.

3. Remove the steak tips from the marinade and pat dry with paper towels. Grill, uncovered, until well seared and dark brown on the first side, about 4 minutes. Using tongs, flip the steak tips and grill until the second side is well seared and an instant-read thermometer inserted into the center of the steak reads 130 degrees for medium-rare (4 to 5 minutes) or 135 degrees for medium (6 to 8 minutes); if the exterior of the meat is browned but the steak is not yet cooked through, move the steak tips to the cooler side of the grill and continue to grill to the desired doneness.

4. Transfer the steak tips to a cutting board, tent loosely with foil, and let rest 5 minutes. Slice the steak tips very thin on the bias; serve immediately with the lime or orange wedges.

Gas-Grilled Steak Tips

Follow the recipe for Charcoal-Grilled Steak Tips through step 1. When about 15 minutes of marinating time remain, turn all the burners to high and heat the grill, with the lid down, until very hot, about 15 minutes. Use a grill brush to scrape the cooking grate clean. Dip a wad of paper towels in oil; holding the wad with tongs, oil the cooking grate. Leave all the burners on high. Proceed with the recipe from step 3, grilling the steak tips covered.

Southwestern Marinade

MAKES ABOUT ¾ CUP

- ⅓ cup soy sauce
- ⅓ cup vegetable oil
- 3 medium garlic cloves, minced or pressed through a garlic press (about 1 tablespoon)
- 1 tablespoon dark brown sugar
- 1 tablespoon tomato paste
- 1 tablespoon chili powder
- 2 teaspoons ground cumin
- ¼ teaspoon cayenne pepper

Mix all the ingredients together in a small bowl.

Garlic, Ginger, and Soy Marinade

MAKES ABOUT ⅔ CUP

- ⅓ cup soy sauce
- 3 tablespoons vegetable oil
- 3 tablespoons toasted sesame oil
- 3 medium garlic cloves, minced or pressed through a garlic press (about 1 tablespoon)
- 2 tablespoons dark brown sugar
- 1 tablespoon minced or grated fresh ginger
- 2 teaspoons grated zest from 1 orange
- ½ teaspoon red pepper flakes
- 1 scallion, sliced thin

Mix all the ingredients together in a small bowl.

GRILLED STEAKS

WHY THIS RECIPE WORKS: Grilled steaks have many tempting qualities—rich, beefy flavor, a thick, caramelized crust, and almost zero cleanup or prep for the cook. But the occasional small bonfire caused by the rendered fat can leave pricey cuts of meat charred and tasting like the inside of a smokestack. We wanted to develop a surefire technique for grilling the three most popular premium steaks—strip, rib eye, and filet mignon—so they would turn out juicy and tender every time.

To get the crust we wanted, a very hot fire was essential. But we quickly learned we couldn't cook a thick steak over consistently high heat without either burning the steak or causing the fat to drip down onto the charcoal and ignite. The solution was to cook these premium steaks over a two-level fire, searing them first over high heat and then moving them to the cooler part of the grill to cook through. For the strip and rib-eye steaks, lightly oiling the cooking grate was enough to get them going and keep them from sticking, but the lean filets mignons required a bit of olive oil to encourage browning. Otherwise, we didn't fuss with our steaks before cooking them—a light seasoning with salt and pepper was sufficient.

To add a little richness to the filets mignons, we made two compound butters, one with smoked paprika and roasted red peppers, the other with lemon, parsley, and garlic—perfect for melting down the sides of the still-warm steaks.

Charcoal-Grilled Strip or Rib Steaks

SERVES 4

If your guests are more likely to eat only an 8-ounce steak, grill two 1-pound steaks, slice them, and serve half-steak portions. The most accurate way to judge doneness is to stick an instant-read thermometer through the side of the steak deep into the meat, so that most of the shaft is embedded in the steak.

- Vegetable oil for the cooking grate
- 4 (12 to 16-ounce) strip or rib steaks, 1¼ to 1½ inches thick (see note)
- Table salt and ground black pepper

1. Light a large chimney starter filled with charcoal (about 6 quarts) and allow to burn until the coals are partially covered with a layer of ash, about 20 minutes. Build a two-level fire by arranging two-thirds of the coals evenly over half of the grill and arranging the remaining coals over the other half. Set the cooking grate in place, cover the grill, and heat the grate until hot, about 5 minutes. Use a grill brush to scrape the cooking grate clean. Dip a wad of paper towels in vegetable oil; holding the wad with tongs, oil the cooking grate.

2. Meanwhile, pat the steaks dry with paper towels and season both sides of the steaks with salt and pepper. Grill the steaks, uncovered, over the hotter part of the grill until well browned on one side, 2 to 3 minutes. Flip the steaks and cook until well browned on the other side, 2 to

3 minutes. (Small flare-ups may occur; if flames become constant, slide the steaks to the cooler side of the grill and mist the fire with water from a spray bottle.)

3. Move the steaks to the cooler side of the grill. Continue cooking, uncovered, until an instant-read thermometer inserted into the center of the steaks registers 120 degrees for rare (5 to 6 minutes), 125 degrees for medium-rare (6 to 7 minutes), or 135 degrees for medium (7 to 8 minutes).

4. Remove the steaks from the grill and let rest 5 minutes. Serve immediately.

Gas-Grilled Strip or Rib Steaks

Depending on the heat output of your gas grill, you may need to cook the steaks on the cooler side of the grill for an extra minute or two.

Turn all the burners to high and heat the grill, with the lid down, until very hot, about 15 minutes. Use a grill brush to scrape the cooking grate clean. Dip a wad of paper towels in oil; holding the wad with tongs, oil the cooking grate. Leave the primary burner on high and turn the other burner(s) to medium. Follow the recipe for Charcoal-Grilled Strip or Rib Steaks from step 2.

Charcoal-Grilled Filets Mignons

SERVES 4

Filet mignon steaks are cut from the tenderloin, which is, as the name indicates, an extremely tender portion of meat. Though tender, the steaks are not very rich. To prevent the steaks from drying out on the grill and to encourage browning, we found it helpful to lightly rub each steak with a little oil before grilling. We suggest drizzling the grilled steaks with olive oil and serving them with lemon wedges, or serving the steaks with one of our flavored butters (recipes follow).

Vegetable oil for the cooking grate
4 **(7 to 8-ounce) center-cut filets mignons, 1½ to 2 inches thick**
4 **teaspoons olive oil**
Table salt and ground black pepper

1. Light a large chimney starter filled with charcoal (about 6 quarts) and allow to burn until the coals are partially covered with a layer of ash, about 20 minutes. Build a two-level fire by arranging two-thirds of the coals evenly over half of the grill and arranging the remaining coals over the other half. Set the cooking grate in place, cover the grill, and heat the grate until hot, about 5 minutes. Use a grill brush to scrape the cooking grate clean. Dip a wad of paper towels in vegetable oil; holding the wad with tongs, oil the cooking grate.

2. Meanwhile, pat the steaks dry with paper towels and lightly rub them with the olive oil; season both sides of the steaks with salt and pepper. Grill the steaks, uncovered, on the hotter side of the grill until well browned on one side, 2 to 3 minutes. Flip the steaks and cook until well browned on the second side, 2 to 3 minutes.

3. Move the steaks to the cooler side of the grill. Continue cooking, uncovered, until the center of the steaks registers 120 degrees for rare (about 6 minutes), 125 degrees for medium-rare (7 to 8 minutes), or 135 degrees for medium (about 9 minutes) on an instant-read thermometer.

4. Remove the steaks from the grill and let rest 5 minutes. Serve immediately.

Gas-Grilled Filets Mignons

Depending on the heat output of your gas grill, you may need to cook the steaks on the cooler side of the grill for an extra minute or two.

Turn all the burners to high and heat the grill, with the lid down, until very hot, about 15 minutes. Use a grill brush to scrape the cooking grate clean. Dip a wad of paper towels in vegetable oil; holding the wad with tongs, oil the cooking grate. Leave the primary burner on high and turn the other burner(s) to medium. Follow the recipe for Charcoal-Grilled Filets Mignons from step 2.

Roasted Red Pepper and Smoked Paprika Butter

MAKES ¼ CUP

- 4 tablespoons (½ stick) unsalted butter, softened
- 2 tablespoons finely minced jarred roasted red peppers
- 1 tablespoon minced fresh thyme leaves
- ¾ teaspoon smoked paprika
- ½ teaspoon table salt
  Ground black pepper

Combine all the ingredients and pepper to taste in a small bowl and mix until smooth. While the steaks are resting, spoon 1 tablespoon of the butter on each one.

Lemon, Garlic, and Parsley Butter

MAKES ¼ CUP

- 4 tablespoons (½ stick) unsalted butter, softened
- 1 tablespoon minced fresh parsley leaves
- 1 medium garlic clove, minced or pressed through a garlic press (about 1 teaspoon)
- ½ teaspoon grated zest from 1 lemon
- ½ teaspoon table salt
  Ground black pepper

Combine all the ingredients and pepper to taste in a small bowl and mix until smooth. While the steaks are resting, spoon 1 tablespoon of the butter on each one.

GRILL-ROASTED BEEF TENDERLOIN

WHY THIS RECIPE WORKS: Grilled tenderloin sounds appealing, but with a whole tenderloin going for as much as $100, uneven cooking, bland flavor, and a tough outer crust just don't cut it. We wanted it cheaper and better. At its peak, tenderloin should be an even, rosy pink throughout, have a browned, crusty exterior, and boast a well-seasoned, grilled flavor.

In need of an affordable alternative to butcher prices, we found that beef at wholesale clubs was far more wallet-friendly. Though these tenderloins needed some home butchering, they were well worth the modest time and effort it took to trim them. Flavor-enhancement came next through just an hour of salting the meat, wrapping it in plastic, and letting it rest on the countertop before hitting the hot coals. Tucking the narrow tip end of the tenderloin under and tying it securely gave the tenderloin a more consistent thickness that allowed it to cook through more evenly on the grill. Direct fire was too hot for the roast to endure throughout the cooking stages, so after briefly searing the meat over the coals, we moved it away from the coals (and soaked wood chips that had been added to amplify the smoky flavor) for grill-roasting via indirect heat. Removing it from the grill while still rare, we let the meat rest before slicing to ensure the meat stayed juicy.

Grill-Roasted Beef Tenderloin for a Charcoal Grill

SERVES 10 TO 12

Beef tenderloins purchased from wholesale clubs require a good amount of trimming before cooking. At the grocery store, however, you may have the option of having the butcher trim it for you. Once trimmed, and with the butt tenderloin still attached (the butt tenderloin is the lobe attached to the large end of the roast), the roast should weigh 4½ to 5 pounds. If you purchase an already-trimmed tenderloin without the butt tenderloin attached, begin checking for doneness about 5 minutes early. If you prefer your tenderloin without a smoky flavor, you may opt not to use wood chips or chunks. Serve as is or with Salsa Verde (recipe follows).

- 1 (6-pound) beef tenderloin, trimmed of fat and silver skin, tail end tucked and tied with kitchen twine at 2-inch intervals (see note)
- ¾ tablespoon table salt
- 2 (2-inch) wood chunks (optional; see note)
  Vegetable oil for the cooking grate
- 2 tablespoons olive oil
- 1 tablespoon ground black pepper

1. About 1 hour prior to grilling, set the tenderloin on a cutting board and rub with the salt. Cover loosely with plastic wrap and let stand at room temperature. If using, soak the wood chunks in cold water to cover for 1 hour; drain.

2. About 30 minutes prior to grilling, light a large chimney starter filled with charcoal (about 6 quarts) and allow to burn until the coals are partially covered with a layer of ash, about 20 minutes. Build a modified two-level fire by arranging all the coals over half of the grill, leaving the other half empty; set the wood chunks (if using) on the coals and open the bottom grill vents. Set the cooking grate in place, cover, and heat the grate until hot, about 5 minutes. Use a grill brush to scrape the cooking grate clean. Dip a wad of paper towels in vegetable oil; holding the wad with tongs, oil the cooking grate.

3. Uncover the tenderloin, coat with the olive oil, and season with the pepper. Place the tenderloin on the hot side of the grill directly over the coals. Cook until well browned, about 2 minutes, then rotate one quarter-turn and repeat until all sides are well browned, a total of 8 minutes. Move the tenderloin to the cooler side of the grill and cover, positioning the lid vents over the tenderloin. Cook until the thickest part of the tenderloin registers 120 degrees for rare (16 to 20 minutes) or 125 degrees for medium-rare (20 to 25 minutes) on an instant-read thermometer.

4. Transfer the tenderloin to a cutting board, tent loosely with foil, and let rest 10 to 15 minutes. Cut into ½-inch-thick slices and serve.

Grill-Roasted Beef Tenderloin for a Gas Grill

You will need a disposable aluminum pie plate for this recipe.

1. Follow step 1 of the recipe for Grill-Roasted Beef Tenderloin for a Charcoal Grill, substituting 2 cups wood chips for the wood chunks and soaking them for 30 minutes. Drain the chips, place in a disposable aluminum pie plate, and cover with heavy-duty foil; poke six holes in the foil and set aside.

2. About 20 minutes prior to grilling, place the pie plate on top of the primary burner (the burner that will remain on during cooking). Turn all the burners to high and heat the grill, with the lid down, until very hot and the chips are smoking heavily, about 20 minutes (if the chips ignite, extinguish the flames with water from a spray bottle). Use a grill brush to scrape the cooking grate clean. Dip a wad of paper towels in the oil; holding the wad with tongs, oil the cooking grate.

3. Uncover the tenderloin, coat with the olive oil, and season all sides with the pepper. Place the tenderloin on

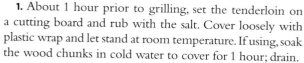

ABUSE TESTS: ADAM GETS TOUGH

Adam and our team of equipment experts spend weeks—often months—testing leading brands to see which are worth buying. We start by answering basic performance questions—such as "Does this skillet heat evenly?" or "Is this knife sharp?"—with controlled kitchen tests. We sauté onions in every skillet in the line-up or we slice tomatoes with each knife. Once we've evaluated each brand in terms of performance (and design), it's time to assess durability. Here's where Adam and our equipment testers can get pretty creative. They devise abuse tests—the kinds of things you might do at home, even though you shouldn't—to see how products will fare.

Some abuse tests are pretty straightforward. We cut and serve lasagna baked in nonstick baking dishes with a metal spatula to see how the nonstick coating will hold up. Other tests are downright wacky. Here are some favorites over the years:

• Trying to melt rubber spatulas by leaving them in a cast-iron skillet heated to 674 degrees, then simmering the spatulas in a pot of curry for an hour to see if they would stain and absorb odors.

• Dropping sealed food storage bags filled with spaghetti sauce from a height of 3 feet onto a plastic tarp to see which bags would survive without sending sauce all over the kitchen.

• Holding our mitt-covered hands in the gas flame on a cooktop for 5 seconds to see which mitts are truly flame-resistant.

Why are Adam and his team willing to abuse kitchen equipment (and their hands) to see how products will perform during worst-case scenarios? Simple. Because we want to know which items really work, and which ones don't.

the side of the grate opposite the primary burner. Grill the tenderloin over the burner(s) without wood chips until well browned, 2 to 3 minutes, then rotate one quarter-turn and repeat until all sides are well browned, for a total of 8 to 12 minutes. Turn off all burner(s) except the primary burner (the tenderloin should be positioned over the extinguished burner[s]). Cover and cook until the thickest part of the tenderloin registers 120 degrees for rare (16 to 20 minutes) or 125 degrees for medium-rare (20 to 25 minutes) on an instant-read thermometer.

4. Transfer the tenderloin to a cutting board, tent loosely with foil, and let rest 10 to 15 minutes. Cut into ½-inch-thick slices and serve.

Salsa Verde

MAKES 1½ CUPS

Toasting the bread rids it of excess moisture that might otherwise make a gummy sauce. Salsa verde is excellent with our Grill-Roasted Beef Tenderloin (page 352) and other roasted meats, but it can also be used as a garnish for fish or poultry or as a condiment on sandwiches. It can be refrigerated in an airtight container for up to 2 days; before serving, bring the sauce to room temperature and stir it to recombine.

- 2 slices high-quality white sandwich bread, lightly toasted and cut into ½-inch pieces (about 1½ cups) (see note)
- 1 cup extra-virgin olive oil
- ¼ cup juice from 2 lemons
- 4 cups lightly packed flat-leaf parsley leaves, washed and dried thoroughly
- ¼ cup capers, drained
- 4 anchovy fillets
- 1 medium garlic clove, minced or pressed through a garlic press (about 1 teaspoon)
- ¼ teaspoon table salt

Process the bread, oil, and lemon juice in a food processor until smooth, about 10 seconds. Add the parsley, capers, anchovies, garlic, and salt. Pulse until the mixture is finely chopped (the mixture should not be smooth), about 5 pulses, scraping down the sides of the workbowl with a rubber spatula once. Transfer the mixture to a small bowl and serve.

BARBECUED BRISKET

WHY THIS RECIPE WORKS: The main reason it's so hard to cook brisket is that it starts out as a very tough cut of meat. It's also big, sometimes weighing upward of 13 pounds, which is why most butchers separate it into two cuts: the "point" (the fattier of the two pieces) and the "flat" (which is leaner and also a little tougher). Slow-cooking for as many as six to 12 hours at a low temperature tends to be the norm for cooking brisket, but we wanted to jump-start the cooking on the grill, to give us tender, smoky meat.

We didn't get the total cooking time below six hours, but we did make the job easier using the grill. First, we cooked the meat over the grill for two hours to let in those all-important smoky flavors; barbecuing the brisket fat side up allowed the fat to melt slowly over the meat. Then we moved it to the oven to cook for a few more hours unattended. For flavor, we turned to a dry rub; typical barbecuing methods like basting the meat or setting a pan of liquid on the cooking grate to create a moist environment just didn't work. Our grill-to-oven approach, although unconventional, gave us fork-tender meat with real barbecue flavor in about half the time it would take to cook the meat entirely on the grill.

Charcoal-Grilled Barbecued Beef Brisket

SERVES 18 TO 24

Cooking a whole brisket, which weighs about 10 pounds, may seem like overkill. However, the process is easy, and the leftovers keep well in the refrigerator for up to 4 days. (Leave leftover brisket unsliced, and reheat the foil-wrapped meat in a 300-degree oven until warm.) Still, if you don't want to bother with a big piece of meat or if your grill has fewer than 400 square inches of cooking space, barbecuing brisket for less than a crowd is easy to do. Simply ask your butcher for either the point or flat portion of the brisket, each of which weighs about half as much as a whole brisket. Then follow this recipe, reducing the spice rub by half and barbecuing for just one hour and 30 minutes. Wrap the meat tightly in foil and reduce the time in the oven to two hours. No matter how large or small a piece you cook, it's a good idea to save the juices the meat gives off while in the oven to enrich the barbecue sauce. Hickory and mesquite are both traditional wood choices with brisket.

- 1 recipe Spicy Chili Rub (recipe follows)
- 1 (9 to 11-pound) whole beef brisket, fat trimmed to ¼-inch thickness (see note)
- 2 (3-inch) wood chunks (see note)
  Vegetable oil for the cooking grate
- 3 cups store-bought barbecue sauce

1. Apply the dry rub liberally to all sides of the meat, patting it on firmly to make sure the spices adhere and completely cover the meat. Wrap the brisket tightly in plastic wrap and refrigerate for 2 hours. (For stronger flavor, refrigerate for up to 2 days.)

2. About 1 hour prior to cooking, remove the brisket from the refrigerator, unwrap, and let it come up to room temperature. Soak the wood chunks in cold water to cover for 1 hour and drain.

3. Meanwhile, light a large chimney starter filled halfway with charcoal (about 3 quarts) and allow to burn until the coals are partially covered with a layer of ash, about

20 minutes. Build a single-banked fire by banking the coals over half of the grill, piling them up two or three coals high, leaving the other half empty. Open the bottom grill vents. Place the wood chunks on top of the charcoal. Set the cooking grate in place, open the grill lid vents completely, and cover the grill, turning the lid so that the vents are opposite the wood chunks to draw smoke through the grill. Heat the grate until hot, about 5 minutes. Use a grill brush to scrape the cooking grate clean. Dip a wad of paper towels in oil; holding the wad with tongs, oil the cooking grate.

4. Position the brisket, fat side up, on the side of the grill opposite the fire. Cook, without removing the lid, for 2 hours. (The temperature inside the grill should be about 350 degrees and will fall to 250 degrees after 2 hours.)

5. Adjust an oven rack to the middle position and heat the oven to 300 degrees. Attach two pieces of heavy-duty foil, 4 feet long, by folding the long edges together two or three times, crimping tightly to seal well, to form an approximately 4 by 3-foot rectangle. Position the brisket lengthwise in the center of the foil. Bring the short edges over the brisket and fold down, crimping tightly to seal. Repeat with the long sides of the foil to seal the brisket completely. Place the brisket on a rimmed baking sheet. Bake until the meat is fork-tender, 3 to 3½ hours.

6. Remove the brisket from the oven, loosen the foil at one end to release steam, and let rest for 30 minutes. If you like, drain the juices into a bowl and defat in a gravy skimmer.

7. Unwrap the brisket and place it on a carving board. Separate the meat into two sections and carve it on the bias across the grain into long, thin slices. Serve with plain barbecue sauce or with barbecue sauce that has been flavored with up to 1 cup of the defatted brisket juices.

Gas-Grilled Barbecued Beef Brisket

You will need a pretty large grill to cook a whole brisket. If your grill has fewer than 400 square inches of cooking space, barbecue either the point or flat end, each of which weighs about half as much as a whole brisket. Follow the directions in the note on page 354 for cooking a smaller piece of brisket. You will need a disposable aluminum pie plate for this recipe.

Follow the recipe for Charcoal-Grilled Barbecued Beef Brisket through step 2, substituting 2 cups wood chips for the wood chunks and soaking them for 30 minutes in cold water to cover. Drain the chips and place them in a disposable aluminum pie plate. Place the pie plate on top of the primary burner (the burner that will remain on during cooking). Turn all the burners to high and heat the grill with the lid down, until very hot and the chips are smoking heavily, about 20 minutes. Use a grill brush to scrape the cooking grate clean. Dip a wad of paper towels in the oil; holding the wad with tongs, oil the cooking grate. Turn the primary burner to medium and turn off the other burner(s). Position the brisket, fat side up, over the cooler part of the grill. Cover and cook for 2 hours. (The temperature inside the grill should be 275 degrees; adjust the lit burner as necessary.) Proceed as directed from step 5.

Spicy Chili Rub

MAKES ABOUT 1 CUP

If you cannot abide spicy hot food, reduce or eliminate the cayenne.

- 4 **tablespoons paprika**
- 2 **tablespoons chili powder**
- 2 **tablespoons ground cumin**
- 2 **tablespoons dark brown sugar**
- 2 **tablespoons table salt**
- 1 **tablespoon ground oregano**
- 1 **tablespoon granulated sugar**
- 1 **tablespoon ground black pepper**
- 1 **tablespoon ground white pepper**
- 2 **teaspoons cayenne pepper (see note)**

Combine all the ingredients in a small bowl. (The rub can be stored in an airtight container at room temperature for up to a month.)

GRILLED PORK CHOPS

WHY THIS RECIPE WORKS: Too many grilled pork chops are burnt on the outside and raw on the inside. And even if they are cooked evenly, they can still be tough and bland. We wanted great-looking and great-tasting chops with a perfectly grilled, crisp crust and juicy, flavorful meat. What's more, we wanted our chops plump and meaty, not thin and tough.

We started with the right chops—tender and flavorful bone-in rib loin or center-cut loin chops worked best—and brined them to pump up their flavor and lock in moisture. To brown the pork chops, only a really hot fire would do. But keeping them over high heat long enough to cook through dried them out. So we grilled the chops over a two-level fire, with one side of the grill intensely hot to sear the chops, and the other only moderately hot to allow the chops to cook through without burning the exterior. So they wouldn't overcook, we pulled the chops from the grill when they were just underdone, then we covered them with a foil pan, and let the chops rest until the temperature rose to serving temperature and the juices were redistributed in the meat. A spice rub, made with potent spices and applied before grilling, added big flavor and gave our chops a nice crust.

Charcoal-Grilled Pork Chops

SERVES 4

We prefer natural to enhanced pork (pork that has been injected with a salt solution to increase moistness and flavor) for this recipe, though enhanced pork can be used. If using enhanced pork, skip the brining in step 1. Rib loin chops are our top choice for their big flavor and juiciness. Spice rubs add a lot of flavor for very little effort, but the chops can also be seasoned with pepper alone just before grilling. You will need a 13 by 9-inch disposable aluminum pan to cover the chops and help them finish cooking through.

- 6 tablespoons table salt
- 6 tablespoons sugar
- 4 (12-ounce) bone-in rib loin pork chops or center-cut loin pork chops, about 1½ inches thick (see note)
- 1 recipe Basic Spice Rub for Pork Chops (recipe follows) or ground black pepper (see note)
  Vegetable oil for the cooking grate

1. Dissolve the salt and sugar in 3 quarts cold water in a large bowl or container. Submerge the chops in the brine, cover with plastic wrap, and refrigerate for 1 hour. Remove the chops from the brine, rinse under running water, and pat dry with paper towels. Coat the chops with the spice rub or season generously with pepper.

2. Light a large chimney starter filled with charcoal (about 6 quarts) and allow to burn until the coals are partially covered with a layer of ash, about 20 minutes. Build a two-level fire by arranging two-thirds of the coals evenly over half of the grill and arranging the remaining coals over the other half. Set the cooking grate in place, cover the grill, and heat the grate until hot, about 5 minutes. Use a grill brush to scrape the cooking grate clean. Dip a wad of paper towels in oil; holding the wad with tongs, oil the cooking grate.

3. Grill the chops, uncovered, on the hotter side of the grill until browned on each side, 2½ to 3 minutes per side. Move the chops to the cooler side of the grill and cover with a large disposable aluminum pan. Continue to cook, turning once, until the center of the chops registers 140 to 145 degrees on an instant-read thermometer, 7 to 9 minutes longer. Transfer the chops to a platter, tent loosely with foil, and let rest until the temperature registers 150 degrees, about 5 minutes. Serve immediately.

Gas-Grilled Pork Chops

We prefer natural to enhanced pork (pork that has been injected with a salt solution to increase moistness and flavor) for this recipe, though enhanced pork can be used. If using enhanced pork, skip the brining in step 1.

Follow the recipe for Charcoal-Grilled Pork Chops through step 1. Turn all the burners to high and heat the grill, with the lid down, until very hot, about 15 minutes. Use a grill brush to scrape the cooking grate clean. Dip a wad of paper towels in oil; holding the wad with tongs, oil the cooking grate. Leave the primary burner on high and turn the other burner(s) off. Place the chops on the hotter side of the grill, cover, and cook until browned on each side, 3 to 4 minutes per side. Move the chops to the cooler side of the grill. Cover and continue to cook, turning once, until the center of the chops registers 140 to 145 degrees on an instant-read thermometer, 7 to 9 minutes longer. Transfer the chops to a platter, tent loosely with foil, and let rest until the temperature registers 150 degrees, about 5 minutes. Serve immediately.

Basic Spice Rub for Pork Chops
MAKES ¼ CUP

- 1 tablespoon ground cumin
- 1 tablespoon chili powder
- 1 tablespoon curry powder
- 1 teaspoon ground black pepper
- 2 teaspoons brown sugar

Combine all the ingredients in a small bowl.

GRILL-ROASTED PORK LOIN

WHY THIS RECIPE WORKS: When we're looking to dress up an outdoor dinner—and offer guests more than burgers or grilled chicken—we like to serve a juicy, crisp-crusted pork loin. But because the roasts available at the supermarket nowadays are so incredibly lean, this cut of meat can dry out considerably when cooked with the dry heat of the grill. We planned to bring back the juiciness and produce a succulent roast with a deep brown crust and aromatic, smoke-flavored meat.

First, we chose the best cut. Our top choice—the blade-end roast—was moist and flavorful and was the hands-down winner over center-cut, sirloin, and tenderloin roasts. Brining ensured that our finished roast met with rave reviews from testers and stayed juicy and moist, and a generous coating of black pepper—or our own spicy rub—provided ample flavoring. We then used a two-step grilling process, searing the roast directly over hot coals for a nice crust and finishing it over indirect heat, so as not to overcook it. The final step was removing the roast from the grill when the internal temperature was just shy of done, then allowing it to rest until the temperature rose and the meat was juicy and tender.

Grill-Roasted Pork Loin for a Charcoal Grill
SERVES 4 TO 6

We prefer natural to enhanced pork (pork that has been injected with a salt solution to increase moistness and flavor) for this recipe, though enhanced pork can be used. If using enhanced pork, skip the brining in step 1. Instead, simply add 1 tablespoon table salt to the black pepper seasoning.

With minor recipe adjustments, a roast larger than the one called for can be cooked using the same method. For each additional pound of meat over 3 pounds (do not use a roast larger than 6 pounds), increase the salt in the brine by ¼ cup and the water by 1 quart; also increase the olive oil and pepper by 1 teaspoon each (if using a spice rub, increase the recipe by one third). Because the cooking time depends more on the diameter of the loin than on its length, the cooking time for a larger roast will not increase significantly. After rotating the roast in step 5, begin checking the internal temperature after 30 minutes of cooking.

- ¾ cup table salt (see note)
- 1 (2½ to 3-pound) boneless blade-end pork loin roast, tied with kitchen twine at 1½-inch intervals (see note)
- 2 tablespoons olive oil
- 1 tablespoon ground black pepper or 1 recipe Chili-Mustard Spice Rub (recipe follows)
- 2 (3-inch) wood chunks
  Vegetable oil for the cooking grate

1. Dissolve the salt in 3 quarts water in a large container; submerge the roast, cover with plastic wrap, and refrigerate 3 to 4 hours. Remove the roast from the brine, rinse under running water, and pat dry with paper towels.

2. Rub the roast with the olive oil, season with the pepper, and press the pepper into the meat. Let stand at room temperature 1 hour.

3. Meanwhile, soak the wood chunks in cold water to cover for 1 hour; drain. About 25 minutes prior to grilling, open the bottom grill vents. Light a large chimney starter filled three-quarters with charcoal (about 4½ quarts) and allow to burn until the coals are partially covered with a layer of ash, about 20 minutes. Build a modified two-level fire by arranging all the coals over half of the grill, leaving the other half empty. Place the wood chunks on top of the coals. Set the cooking grate in place, cover, and heat the grate until hot, about 5 minutes. Use a grill brush to scrape the cooking grate clean. Dip a wad of paper towels in vegetable oil; holding the wad with tongs, oil the cooking grate.

4. Grill the pork on the hot side of the grill until browned, about 2 minutes; using tongs, rotate one quarter-turn and repeat until all the sides are well browned, about 8 minutes total. Move the loin to the cooler side of the grill, positioning the roast parallel with and as close as possible to the fire. Open the grill lid vents halfway; cover the grill, turning the lid so that the vents are opposite the fire and draw smoke through the grill, and cook 20 minutes. (The temperature inside the grill should be about 425 degrees.)

5. Uncover and rotate the roast 180 degrees so that the side facing the fire now faces away. Cover and continue to cook until the thickest part of the roast registers 140 to 145 degrees on an instant-read thermometer, 10 to 30 minutes longer, depending on the thickness.

6. Transfer the roast to a carving board, tent loosely with foil, and let rest until the temperature registers 150 degrees, about 15 minutes. Remove the twine, cut the roast into ½-inch-thick slices, and serve.

Grill-Roasted Pork Loin for a Gas Grill

1. Follow the recipe for Grill-Roasted Pork Loin for a Charcoal Grill through step 2. Substitute 2 cups wood chips for the wood chunks and soak them in cold water to cover for 30 minutes; drain. Place the chips in a disposable aluminum pie plate.

2. About 20 minutes prior to grilling, place the pie plate on top of the primary burner (the burner that will remain on during cooking). Turn all the burners to high and heat the grill with the lid down, until very hot and the chips are smoking, about 15 minutes (if the chips ignite, extinguish the flames with water from a spray bottle). Use a grill brush to scrape the cooking grate clean. Dip a wad of paper towels in the vegetable oil; holding the wad with tongs, oil the cooking grate.

3. Continue with the recipe from step 4, turning off all the burner(s) except the primary burner after browning the pork.

Chili-Mustard Spice Rub

MAKES ABOUT 2 TABLESPOONS

This rub packs some heat, so use the lesser amount of cayenne if you want a milder rub.

- **2 teaspoons chili powder**
- **2 teaspoons dry mustard**
- **1 teaspoon ground cumin**
- **½–1 teaspoon cayenne pepper (see note)**

Combine all the ingredients in a small bowl.

GRILLED STUFFED PORK LOIN

WHY THIS RECIPE WORKS: Center-cut pork loin is an especially lean cut, making it difficult to cook without drying out. We wanted to cook our pork loin on the grill but keep it moist using an approach other than traditional brines or sauces. We decided to use a moist, well-seasoned stuffing (and careful cooking) so our grilled pork loin would be juicy and flavorful.

We bought a short and wide roast, more square than cylindrical. This shape only required four straight, short cuts to open to a long, flat sheet that was easy to fill and roll up. The best stuffing required both a deep flavor to counter the pork's rather bland taste and a texture thick enough to stay put. Poaching apples and cranberries in a blend of apple cider, apple cider vinegar, and spices developed a filling with the dense, chewy consistency we wanted. And this process had an added bonus—we had ample poaching liquid left, which could be reduced to a glaze. We had already decided not to give the loin a preliminary sear, which can create a tough exterior, but found we missed the brown color that searing produces. Rolling the loin in our glaze gave it a beautifully burnished finish.

Charcoal-Grilled Pork Loin with Apple-Cranberry Filling

SERVES 6

This recipe is best prepared with a loin that is 7 to 8 inches long and 4 to 5 inches wide. To make cutting the pork easier, freeze it for 30 minutes. If mustard seeds are unavailable, stir an equal amount of whole grain mustard into the filling after the apples have been processed. Use more or less cayenne, depending on how spicy you'd like the stuffing. The pork loin can be stuffed and tied a day ahead of time, but don't season the exterior until you are ready to grill.

FILLING

- 1½ cups packed dried apples
- 1 cup apple cider
- ¾ cup packed light brown sugar
- ½ cup cider vinegar
- ½ cup packed dried cranberries
- 1 large shallot, halved lengthwise and sliced thin crosswise (about ¼ cup)
- 1 tablespoon minced or grated fresh ginger
- 1 tablespoon yellow mustard seeds (see note)
- ½ teaspoon ground allspice
- ⅛–¼ teaspoon cayenne pepper (see note)

PORK

- 2 (3-inch) wood chunks
- 1 (2½-pound) boneless center-cut pork loin roast (see note)
- Table salt and ground black pepper
- Vegetable oil for the cooking grate

1. FOR THE FILLING: Bring all of the ingredients to a simmer in a medium saucepan over medium-high heat. Cover, reduce the heat to low, and cook until the apples

are very soft, about 20 minutes. Pour the mixture through a fine-mesh strainer set over a bowl, pressing with the back of a spoon to extract as much liquid as possible. Return the liquid to the saucepan and simmer over medium-high heat until reduced to ⅓ cup, about 5 minutes; reserve the glaze. Meanwhile, pulse the apple mixture in a food processor until uniformly coarsely chopped, about 15 pulses. Transfer the filling to a bowl and refrigerate while preparing the pork.

2. FOR THE PORK: Soak the wood chunks in cold water to cover for 1 hour. Meanwhile, following the photos on page 360, cut the meat to an even ½-inch thickness. Season with salt and spread the apple filling in an even layer, leaving a ½-inch border. Roll tightly and tie with kitchen twine at 1-inch intervals. Season with salt and pepper.

3. Light a large chimney starter filled three-quarters with charcoal (about 4½ quarts) and allow to burn until the coals are partially covered with a layer of ash, about 20 minutes. Build a modified two-level fire by arranging all the coals over half of the grill, leaving the other half empty. Drain the wood chunks and place on the coals. Open the bottom grill vents completely. Set the cooking grate in place, cover, and heat the grate until hot, about 5 minutes. Use a grill brush to scrape the cooking grate clean. Dip a wad of paper towels in oil; holding the wad with tongs, oil the cooking grate.

4. Place the roast, fat side up, on the cool side of the grill. Cover the grill and position the vent, halfway open, over the roast to draw the smoke through the grill. Cook until the thickest part of the roast registers 130 to 135 degrees on an instant-read thermometer, 55 to 70 minutes, flipping the roast once halfway through the cooking time. Brush the roast with half of the reserved glaze; flip and brush with the remaining glaze. (You may need to reheat the glaze briefly to make it spreadable.) Continue to cook until the glaze is glossy and sticky, about 5 minutes longer.

5. Transfer the roast to a carving board, tent loosely with foil, and let rest until the center registers 150 degrees, about 15 minutes. Cut into ½-inch-thick slices, removing the twine as you cut. Serve immediately.

Gas-Grilled Pork Loin with Apple-Cranberry Filling

You will need a disposable aluminum pie plate for this recipe.

Follow the recipe for Charcoal-Grilled Pork Loin with Apple-Cranberry Filling through step 2, substituting 2 cups wood chips for the wood chunks and soaking

HOW TO STUFF A PORK LOIN

1. Position the roast fat side up. Insert a knife ½ inch from the bottom of the roast and cut horizontally, stopping ½ inch before the edge. Open up this flap.

2. Cut through the thicker half of the roast about ½ inch from the bottom, stopping about ½ inch before the edge. Open up this flap.

3. Repeat until the pork loin is an even ½-inch thickness throughout. If uneven, cover with plastic wrap and use a meat pounder to even out.

4. With the long side of the meat facing you, season the meat and spread the filling, leaving a ½-inch border on all sides.

5. Starting from the short side, roll the pork loin tightly then tie the roast with twine at 1-inch intervals.

them in cold water to cover for 30 minutes. Drain the chips and place in a disposable aluminum pie plate. About 20 minutes prior to grilling, place the pie plate on top of the primary burner (the burner that will remain on during cooking). Turn all the burners to high and heat the grill with the lid down, until very hot and the chips are smoking, about 15 minutes. Use a grill brush to scrape the cooking grate clean. Dip a wad of paper towels in the oil; holding the wad with tongs, oil the cooking grate. Turn off all the burner(s) except the primary burner. Place the roast, fat side up, on the side opposite the primary burner and proceed with the recipe from step 4.

PULLED PORK

WHY THIS RECIPE WORKS: Pulled pork is classic summertime party food: slow-cooked pork roast, shredded and seasoned, served on the most basic of hamburger buns (or sliced white bread), with just enough of your favorite barbecue sauce, a couple of dill pickle chips, and a topping of coleslaw. However, many barbecue procedures demand the regular attention of the cook for eight hours or more. We wanted to find a way to make moist, fork-tender pulled pork without the marathon cooking time and constant attention to the grill.

After testing shoulder roasts (also called Boston butt), fresh ham, and picnic roasts, we determined that the shoulder roast, which has the most fat, also retains the most moisture and flavor during a long, slow cook. We massaged a spicy chili rub into the meat, then wrapped the roast in plastic and refrigerated it for at least three hours to "marinate." The roast is first cooked on the grill to absorb smoky flavor (from wood chips—no smoker required), then finished in the oven (largely unattended). Finally, we let the pork rest in a paper bag so the meat would steam and any remaining collagen would break down, allowing the flavorful juices to be reabsorbed. We also engineered a pair of sauce recipes to please barbecue fans with different tastes.

Barbecued Pulled Pork for a Charcoal Grill
SERVES 8

Pulled pork can be made with a fresh ham or picnic roast, although our preference is for Boston butt. If using a fresh ham or picnic roast, remove the skin by cutting through it with the tip of a chef's knife; slide the blade just under the skin and work around to loosen it while pulling it off

with your other hand. Boston butt, or shoulder roast, does not need to be trimmed. Preparing pulled pork requires little effort but lots of time. Plan on 10 hours from start to finish: three hours with the spice rub, one hour to come to room temperature, three hours on the grill, two hours in the oven, and one hour to rest. Wood chunks help flavor the meat; hickory is the traditional choice with pork, although mesquite can be used if desired. Serve the pulled pork on plain white bread or warmed buns with the classic accompaniments of dill pickle chips and coleslaw. You will need a 13 by 9-inch disposable aluminum pan as well as heavy-duty aluminum foil and a brown paper grocery bag.

¾ cup Dry Rub for Barbecue (recipe follows)
1 (6 to 8-pound) bone-in pork roast, preferably Boston butt (see note)
4 (3-inch) wood chunks (see note)
Vegetable oil for the cooking grate
2 cups barbecue sauce (recipes follow)

1. Massage the dry rub into the meat. Wrap the meat tightly in a double layer of plastic wrap and refrigerate for at least 3 hours. (For stronger flavor, the roast can be refrigerated for up to 3 days.)

2. At least 1 hour prior to cooking, remove the roast from the refrigerator, unwrap, and let it come to room temperature. Soak the wood chunks in cold water to cover for 1 hour and drain.

3. Meanwhile, light a large chimney starter filled halfway with charcoal (about 3 quarts) and allow to burn until the coals are partially covered with a layer of ash. Build a modified two-level fire by arranging all the coals over half of the grill, leaving the other half empty. Open the bottom grill vents completely. Place the wood chunks on the coals. Set the cooking grate in place, cover, and heat the grate until hot, about 5 minutes. Use a grill brush to scrape the cooking grate clean. Dip a wad of paper towels in oil; holding the wad with tongs, oil the cooking grate.

4. Set the unwrapped roast in a 13 by 9-inch disposable aluminum pan and place it on the grate opposite the coals. Open the grill lid vents three-quarters of the way and cover, turning the lid so that the vents are opposite the wood chunks to draw smoke through the grill. Cook, adding about eight briquettes every hour or so to maintain an average temperature of 275 degrees, for 3 hours.

5. Adjust an oven rack to the middle position and heat the oven to 325 degrees. Wrap the pan holding the roast with heavy-duty foil to cover completely. Place the pan in the oven and cook until the meat is fork-tender, about 2 hours.

6. Carefully slide the foil-wrapped pan with the roast into a brown paper bag. Crimp the end shut. Let rest for 1 hour.

7. Transfer the roast to a carving board and unwrap. When cool enough to handle, separate the roast into muscle sections, removing the fat, if desired, and tearing the meat into shreds with your fingers. Place the shredded meat in a large bowl. Toss with 1 cup of the barbecue sauce, adding more to taste. Serve, passing the remaining sauce separately.

Barbecued Pulled Pork for a Gas Grill

You will need a disposable aluminum pie plate as well as a 10 by 8-inch disposable aluminum pan for this recipe.

1. Follow the recipe for Barbecued Pulled Pork for a Charcoal Grill through step 2, substituting 4 cups wood chips for the wood chunks and soaking them in cold water to cover for 30 minutes. Drain the chips and place in a disposable aluminum pie plate.

2. Place the pie plate on the primary burner (the burner that will remain on during cooking). Turn all the burners to high and heat the grill with the lid down, until very hot and the chips are smoking heavily, about 20 minutes (if the chips ignite, use a water-filled spray bottle to extinguish). Use a grill brush to scrape the cooking grate clean. Dip a wad of paper towels in oil; holding the wad with tongs, oil the cooking grate. Turn the primary burner down to medium and turn off the other burner(s). Set the unwrapped roast in a 10 by 8-inch disposable aluminum pan, position the pan over the cooler side of the grill, close the lid, and cook for 3 hours. (The temperature inside the grill should be 275 degrees; adjust the lit burner as necessary.) Proceed as directed from step 5 of the recipe.

Dry Rub for Barbecue

MAKES ABOUT 1 CUP

You can adjust the proportions of spices in this all-purpose rub or add or subtract a spice, as you wish. For instance, if you don't like spicy foods, reduce the cayenne. Or, if you are using hot chili powder, eliminate the cayenne entirely.

- 4 tablespoons sweet paprika
- 2 tablespoons chili powder
- 2 tablespoons ground cumin
- 2 tablespoons dark brown sugar
- 2 tablespoons table salt
- 1 tablespoon dried oregano
- 1 tablespoon granulated sugar
- 1 tablespoon ground black pepper
- 1 tablespoon ground white pepper
- 1–2 teaspoons cayenne pepper

Combine all the ingredients in a small bowl.

Eastern North Carolina Barbecue Sauce

MAKES ABOUT 2 CUPS

- 1 cup distilled white vinegar
- 1 cup cider vinegar
- 1 tablespoon sugar
- 1 tablespoon red pepper flakes
- 1 tablespoon hot sauce
  Table salt and ground black pepper

Mix all the ingredients and salt and pepper to taste together in a medium bowl. (The sauce can be refrigerated in an airtight container for up to 4 days.)

Mid-South Carolina Mustard Sauce

MAKES ABOUT 2½ CUPS

- 1 cup cider vinegar
- 1 cup vegetable oil
- 6 tablespoons Dijon mustard
- 2 tablespoons maple syrup or honey
- 4 teaspoons Worcestershire sauce
- 2 teaspoons table salt
- 1 teaspoon hot sauce
  Ground black pepper

Mix all the ingredients and pepper to taste together in a medium bowl. (The sauce can be refrigerated in an airtight container for up to 4 days.)

KANSAS CITY RIBS

WHY THIS RECIPE WORKS: Kansas City ribs are slow-smoked pork ribs slathered in a sauce so thick, sweet, and sticky that you need a case of wet naps to get your hands clean after eating them. But authentic ribs can take all day to prepare. We knew we could come up with a faster method for Kansas City ribs—one that would produce the same fall-off-the-bone, tender smoky meat of the long-cooked original recipe.

We quickly learned that spareribs, which are well marbled with fat, produce moist, tender ribs, but some racks are so big they barely fit on the grill. We turned to a more manageable cut, referred to as "St. Louis" ribs, which is a narrower, rectangular rack that offers all the taste of whole spareribs without any of the trouble. A spice rub added flavor and encouraged a savory crust on the meat. We barbecued the ribs, covered with foil, over indirect heat for four hours—the foil traps some of the steam over the meat, so that it cooks up tender, not dry. Using wood chips on the grill imparts the meat with great smoky flavor. For sticky, saucy ribs, we brushed the ribs all over with barbecue sauce during the last hour of cooking, then wrapped them in foil and cooked them until they were tender and falling off the bone.

Kansas City Sticky Ribs for a Charcoal Grill

SERVES 4 TO 6

Buy St. Louis–style racks, which are more manageable than untrimmed pork ribs. If you can find only whole spareribs, use the biggest grill possible and be prepared to increase the cooking time significantly. We prefer our sauce recipe but store-bought works, too. You will need a 13 by 9-inch disposable aluminum pan for this recipe.

- 3 tablespoons paprika
- 2 tablespoons light brown sugar
- 1 tablespoon ground black pepper
- 1 tablespoon table salt
- ¼ teaspoon cayenne pepper
- 2 full racks pork spareribs, preferably St. Louis cut, trimmed of large pieces of excess fat and membrane removed (see note and step 1 on page 365)
- 2 cups wood chips
  Vegetable oil for the cooking grate
- 2 cups Kansas City Barbecue Sauce (see note; recipe follows)

1. Combine the paprika, sugar, black pepper, salt, and cayenne in a small bowl. Pat the rib racks dry with paper towels and massage the spice rub into both sides.

2. Soak the wood chips in cold water to cover for 30 minutes; drain. Open the bottom grill vents. Light a large chimney starter filled three-quarters with charcoal (about 4½ quarts) and allow to burn until the coals are partially covered with a layer of ash, about 20 minutes. Arrange a 13 by 9-inch disposable aluminum pan on one side of the grill and build a single-banked fire by steeply banking all the coals on the opposite side. Sprinkle 1 cup of the wood chips over the coals. Set the cooking grate in place, cover, and heat the grate until hot, about 5 minutes. Use a grill brush to scrape the cooking grate clean. Dip a wad of paper towels in oil; holding the wad with tongs, oil the cooking grate. Place the ribs over the pan.

3. Place a sheet of foil on top of the ribs and cover the grill, positioning the lid vents, three-quarters open, directly over the ribs. Cook until the coals are almost spent, about 2 hours, turning and rotating the ribs once halfway through the cooking time.

4. About 20 minutes before the coals are spent, light the chimney starter filled again three-quarters with charcoal (about 4½ quarts) and allow to burn until the coals are partially covered with a layer of ash, about 20 minutes. Place the hot coals from the chimney on top of the spent coals and sprinkle the remaining 1 cup of wood chips over the coals. Turn and rotate the ribs and cook, covered, about 1 hour. Brush the ribs on both sides with the sauce, wrap tightly with foil, and cook until tender, about 1 hour.

5. Transfer the ribs (still in the foil) to a cutting board and let rest 30 minutes. Unwrap the ribs and brush with additional barbecue sauce. Slice the ribs between the bones and serve with the remaining sauce.

Kansas City Sticky Ribs for a Gas Grill

You will need a disposable aluminum pie plate for this recipe.

Follow step 1 of Kansas City Sticky Ribs for a Charcoal Grill. Soak the wood chips in cold water to cover for 30 minutes; drain. Place the wood chips in a disposable aluminum pie plate. Place the pie plate on top of the primary burner (the burner that will remain on during cooking). Turn all the burners to high and heat the grill, with the lid down, until very hot and the chips are smoking heavily, about 20 minutes. Use a grill brush to scrape the cooking grate clean. Dip a wad of paper towels in oil; holding the wad with tongs, oil the cooking grate. Turn the primary burner to medium and turn off the other burner(s). (The temperature inside the grill should

be about 275 degrees; adjust the lit burner as necessary.) Place the ribs on the cooler part of the grill and cook as directed, omitting the disposable aluminum pan, through step 3. Brush the ribs and wrap in foil as directed in step 4, then continue as directed.

Easiest Kansas City Sticky Ribs

Not keen on tending a grill for four hours? Our ribs will taste good even if they spend the last two hours of cooking in your oven.

Follow the recipe for Kansas City Sticky Ribs for a Gas or Charcoal Grill through step 3. Wrap the ribs tightly in foil, place on a rimmed baking sheet, and bake in a 250-degree oven for 1 hour. Remove from the oven, brush both sides with the barbecue sauce, rewrap with foil, and bake until tender, about 1 hour. Proceed as directed in step 5.

Kansas City Barbecue Sauce

MAKES ABOUT 4 CUPS

Kansas City barbecue sauce is a sweet, smoky, sticky, and thick tomato-based sauce. This style of sauce is the model for most bottled brands, including KC Masterpiece. We like our barbecue sauce extra-thick. If you like a thinner, smoother texture, the sauce can be strained after it has finished cooking.

2 teaspoons vegetable oil
1 medium onion, minced
4 cups low-sodium chicken broth
1 cup root beer
1 cup cider vinegar
1 cup dark corn syrup
½ cup molasses
½ cup tomato paste
½ cup ketchup
2 tablespoons brown mustard
1 tablespoon hot sauce
½ teaspoon garlic powder
¼ teaspoon liquid smoke (optional)

Heat the oil in a saucepan over medium-high heat until shimmering. Add the onion and cook until softened, about 5 minutes. Whisk in the remaining ingredients, except for the liquid smoke, and bring to a boil. Reduce the heat to medium and simmer until the mixture is thick and has reduced to 4 cups, about 1 hour. Stir in the liquid smoke, if using. (The sauce can be refrigerated in an airtight container for up to 1 week.)

NOTES FROM THE TEST KITCHEN

MAKING BEANS ON THE GRILL
Our barbecue beans finish cooking on the grill, where they pick up smoke and pork flavors. Here's how to let the flavors in and keep the grease out.

1. Transfer the precooked beans to a 13 by 9-inch disposable aluminum pan. Wrap tightly in foil and poke several holes in the foil so that the juices from the ribs can flavor the beans.

2. When you're ready to add more coals, nestle the beans in the pan already on the bottom of the grill. Replace the cooking grate, making sure to position the ribs directly above the beans.

Smoky Kansas City Barbecue Beans
SERVES 4 TO 6

This recipe is meant for a charcoal grill. If you're cooking on a gas grill, omit step 3 and finish cooking the beans in a 300-degree oven for 2 to 2½ hours. We prefer our sauce recipe but store-bought works, too. You will need a 13 by 9-inch disposable aluminum pan for this recipe.

4 ounces (about 4 slices) bacon, chopped fine
1 medium onion, minced
4 medium garlic cloves, minced or pressed through a garlic press (about 4 teaspoons)
1 pound dried pinto beans, picked over, rinsed, and soaked overnight
6 cups water
1 cup Kansas City Barbecue Sauce (see note; see page 363)
⅓ cup packed light brown sugar
2 tablespoons brown mustard
1 teaspoon hot sauce
Table salt

1. Cook the bacon in a Dutch oven over medium heat until beginning to crisp, about 5 minutes. Add the onion and cook until softened, about 5 minutes. Add the garlic and cook until fragrant, about 30 seconds. Add the beans and water and bring to a simmer. Reduce the heat to medium-low, cover, and cook until the beans are just softened, about 1 hour.

2. Stir in ½ cup of the barbecue sauce, the brown sugar, mustard, hot sauce, and 2 teaspoons salt and simmer, uncovered, over medium-low heat until the beans are tender and the sauce is slightly thickened, about 1 hour. (If the mixture becomes too thick, add water.) Transfer the beans to a 13 by 9-inch disposable aluminum pan and wrap tightly with aluminum foil. Using a paring knife or skewer, poke holes in the foil.

3. In step 4 of Kansas City Sticky Ribs for a Charcoal Grill on page 362, when new coals are added, nestle the pan with the beans inside the disposable pan already in the grill. Replace the cooking grate and position the ribs directly above the beans. Cover the grill and cook until the beans are smoky and completely tender, about 2 hours. Discard the foil, stir in the remaining ½ cup barbecue sauce, and season with salt to taste. Serve.

RAINY DAY BARBECUED RIBS

WHY THIS RECIPE WORKS: When the craving for barbecued ribs strikes in the dead of winter, you're out of luck unless you visit the local rib joint. There are recipes for oven barbecuing, but the smoke-flavored sauce they use is no substitute for actual smoke. We wanted the real thing, but prepared indoors.

St. Louis–style ribs, which have been trimmed of skirt meat and excess cartilage, work best here. We started with a spice rub as we would for grilling, but found that a thin coating of mustard, ketchup, and garlic helped the rub adhere. We tried wood chips in a stovetop smoker, but we had difficulty fitting the ribs in the pan, it's hard to find wood chips in wintertime—and the smoke-filled kitchen was the clincher. We gave up on wood chips and instead borrowed a Chinese cooking method of smoking over tea leaves. Lapsang Souchong tea, which itself has a smoky flavor, worked perfectly when we ground it fine. Chilling the ribs first helped prevent toughening in the oven's initial high heat. Apple juice, a common ingredient in barbecue "mops," added moisture and more flavor. And running the ribs under the broiler at the end browned and crisped them. These tender, smoky, and spicy ribs taste amazingly like those barbecued on the grill, but can be made any time of the year.

Oven-Barbecued Spareribs

SERVES 4

To make this recipe, you will need a baking stone, a sturdy baking sheet with a 1-inch rim, and a wire rack that fits inside it. It's fine if the ribs overlap slightly on the rack. In step 1, removing the surface fat keeps the ribs from being too greasy. And removing the membrane from the ribs allows the smoke to penetrate both sides of the racks and also makes the ribs easier to eat. Note that the ribs must be coated with the rub and refrigerated at least 8 hours or up to 24 hours ahead of cooking. Be careful when opening the crimped foil to add the juice, as hot steam and smoke will billow out. If desired, serve the ribs with Quick Barbecue Sauce (recipe follows) or your favorite store-bought brand (and for information on the test kitchen favorite, Bull's-Eye Original, see page 602).

RIBS

- 2 (2½ to 3-pound) racks St. Louis–style spareribs
- ¼ cup finely ground Lapsang Souchong tea (from about 10 tea bags, or ½ cup loose tea leaves ground to a powder in a spice grinder)
- ½ cup apple juice

RUB

- 6 tablespoons yellow mustard
- 2 tablespoons ketchup
- 3 medium garlic cloves, minced or pressed through a garlic press (about 1 tablespoon)
- 3 tablespoons brown sugar
- 1 tablespoon sweet paprika
- 1 tablespoon chili powder
- 2 teaspoons ground black pepper
- ¾ teaspoon table salt
- ½ teaspoon cayenne pepper

1. FOR THE RIBS: Using a sharp knife, trim any surface fat from both racks. To remove the membrane (the thin white sheath that lines the concave side of the rack), insert a spoon handle between the membrane and the ribs of one rack to loosen slightly. Using a paper towel, grasp the loosened membrane and pull away gently to remove. Repeat with the second rack.

2. FOR THE RUB: Combine the mustard, ketchup, and garlic in a small bowl; combine the sugar, paprika, chili powder, black pepper, salt, and cayenne in a separate small bowl. Spread the mustard mixture in a thin, even layer over both sides of the ribs and coat both sides with the spice mixture, then wrap the ribs in plastic wrap and refrigerate for at least 8 hours or up to 24 hours.

3. Transfer the ribs from the refrigerator to the freezer for 45 minutes. Adjust one oven rack to the lowest position and the second rack to the upper-middle position (at least 5 inches below the broiler). Place the baking stone on the lower rack and heat the oven to 500 degrees. Sprinkle the ground tea evenly over the bottom of the rimmed baking sheet and set the wire rack on the sheet. Place the ribs, meat side up, on the rack and cover with heavy-duty foil, crimping the edges tightly to seal. Set the baking sheet with the ribs directly on the stone and roast for 30 minutes, then reduce the oven temperature to 250 degrees, leaving the oven door open for 1 minute to cool. While the oven is open, carefully open one corner of the foil and pour the apple juice into the bottom of the baking sheet; reseal the foil. Continue to roast until the meat is very tender and begins to pull away from the bones, about 1½ hours. (Begin to check the ribs after 1 hour; leave loosely covered with foil for the remaining cooking time.)

4. Remove the foil, carefully flip the racks bone side up, and place the baking sheet on the upper-middle oven rack. Turn on the broiler and cook the ribs until well browned and crispy in spots, 5 to 10 minutes. Flip the ribs meat side up and cook until well browned and crispy, 5 to 7 minutes more. Cool for at least 10 minutes before cutting into individual ribs. Serve with barbecue sauce, if desired.

Quick Barbecue Sauce

MAKES ABOUT 1½ CUPS

Classic barbecue sauce must simmer for a long time for the whole tomatoes in it to break down. However, we found that starting with ketchup can shorten the process.

    1   medium onion, peeled and quartered
    ¼   cup water
    1   cup ketchup
    5   tablespoons molasses
    2   tablespoons cider vinegar
    2   tablespoons Worcestershire sauce
    2   tablespoons Dijon mustard
    1½ teaspoons liquid smoke (optional)
    1   teaspoon hot sauce
    ¼   teaspoon ground black pepper
    2   tablespoons vegetable oil
    1   medium garlic clove, minced or pressed through a
        garlic press (about 1 teaspoon)
    1   teaspoon chili powder
    ¼   teaspoon cayenne pepper

1. Process the onion with the water in a food processor until pureed and the mixture resembles slush, about 30 seconds. Strain the mixture through a fine-mesh strainer into a liquid measuring cup, pressing on the solids with a rubber spatula to obtain ½ cup juice. Discard the solids.

2. Whisk the onion juice, ketchup, molasses, vinegar, Worcestershire sauce, mustard, liquid smoke (if using), hot sauce, and black pepper together in a medium bowl.

3. Heat the oil in a large nonreactive saucepan over medium heat until shimmering but not smoking. Add the garlic, chili powder, and cayenne and cook until fragrant, about 30 seconds. Whisk in the ketchup mixture and bring to a boil; reduce the heat to medium-low and simmer gently, uncovered, until the flavors meld and the sauce is thickened, about 25 minutes. Cool the sauce to room temperature before using. (The sauce can be refrigerated in an airtight container for up to 1 week.)

BARBECUED BABY BACK RIBS

WHY THIS RECIPE WORKS: Dry, flavorless ribs are a true culinary disaster. More often than not, baby back ribs cooked at home come out tasting like dry shoe leather on a bone. We wanted ribs that were juicy, tender, and fully seasoned, with an intense smokiness, ribs that would be well worth the time, money, and effort.

Meaty ribs—racks as close to 2 pounds as possible—provided substantial, satisfying portions. For ribs that are so good and moist they don't even need barbecue sauce, they must be brined first—we used a salt, sugar, and water solution—then rubbed with a spice mix before barbecuing. Chili powder, cayenne pepper, cumin, and dark brown sugar formed a nice, crisp crust on the ribs and provided the best balance of sweet and spicy. For even more flavor, we piled wood chunks on top of the coals before barbecuing and used the "low and slow" cooking method: barbecue the ribs for a few hours on the cool side of the grill, then add fresh briquettes to the coals and continue to cook for another hour or two. This extended amount of time on the grill made for tender baby back ribs with an intensely smoky flavor.

Barbecued Baby Back Ribs for a Charcoal Grill

SERVES 4

For a more potent spice flavor, you can brine and dry the ribs as directed, then coat them with the spice rub and refrigerate them overnight, wrapped tightly in plastic, before grilling.

    Table salt
½ **cup sugar**
2 **(2-pound) racks baby back or loin back ribs, membrane removed**
2 **(3-inch) wood chunks**
1 **tablespoon plus ½ teaspoon sweet paprika**
1½ **teaspoons chili powder**
1¾ **teaspoons ground cumin**
1½ **teaspoons dark brown sugar**
¾ **teaspoon dried oregano**
¾ **teaspoon ground black pepper**
1 **teaspoon ground white pepper**
½ **teaspoon cayenne pepper**
    Vegetable oil for the cooking grate

1. Dissolve ½ cup salt and the sugar in 4 quarts cold water in a large bowl or container. Submerge the ribs in the brine, cover with plastic wrap, and refrigerate for 1 hour. Remove the ribs from the brine, rinse under running water, and pat dry with paper towels. Soak the wood chunks in cold water to cover for 1 hour; drain.

2. Combine the paprika, chili powder, cumin, brown sugar, ¾ teaspoon salt, oregano, black pepper, white pepper, and cayenne in a small bowl. Rub each rack with 1 tablespoon of the spice rub and refrigerate for 30 minutes.

3. Light a large chimney starter filled three-quarters with charcoal (about 4½ quarts) and allow to burn until the coals are partially covered with a layer of ash, about

20 minutes. Build a modified two-level fire by arranging all the coals over half of the grill, leaving the other half empty. Place the wood chunks on top of the coals. Open the bottom grill vents. Set the cooking grate in place, cover, and heat the grate until hot, about 5 minutes. Use a grill brush to scrape the cooking grate clean. Dip a wad of paper towels in oil; holding the wad with tongs, oil the cooking grate.

4. Place the ribs on the cooler side of the grill parallel to the fire. Cover the grill so that the vents are opposite the fire and draw smoke through the grill (the temperature inside the grill should be about 350 degrees, but will start to fall). Cook, flipping the rib racks, switching their position so the rack that was nearest the fire is on the outside, and turning the racks 180 degrees every 30 minutes, about 2 hours (the temperature inside the grill should be about 250 degrees); add 10 fresh briquettes to the coals. Continue to cook (the temperature inside the grill should be 275 to 300 degrees), flipping, switching, and rotating the ribs every 30 minutes, until the meat easily pulls away from the bone, 1½ to 2 hours longer. Transfer the ribs to a carving board, slice between the bones, and serve.

Barbecued Baby Back Ribs for a Gas Grill

You will need a disposable aluminum pie plate for this recipe.

1. Follow the recipe for Barbecued Baby Back Ribs for a Charcoal Grill through step 2, substituting 2 cups wood chips for the wood chunks. Soak the wood chips in cold water to cover for 30 minutes; drain. Place the chips in a disposable aluminum pie plate and place the pie plate on top of the primary burner (the burner that will remain on during cooking). Turn all the burners to high and heat the grill with the lid down, until very hot and the chips are smoking heavily, about 20 minutes (if the chips ignite, extinguish the flames with water from a spray bottle). Use a grill brush to scrape the cooking grate clean. Dip a wad of paper towels in the oil; holding the wad with tongs, oil the cooking grate. Turn off all the burner(s) except the primary burner.

2. Place the ribs on the cooler side of the grill and cover (the temperature inside the grill should be about 275 degrees; adjust the lit burner as necessary). Cook, until the meat easily pulls away from bone, flipping the racks, switching their position so that the rack that was nearest the fire is on the outside, and turning the racks 180 degrees every 30 minutes, about 4 hours. Transfer the ribs to a carving board, slice between the bones, and serve.

single pile of coals on one side of the grill and kept the temperature in the range of 250 to 300 degrees. A couple hours of slow cooking were enough to render some of the fat and make the ribs juicy, tender, and slightly toothy. When cooked any longer, as is the case with pork ribs, the meat disintegrates into messy shreds, taking on a sticky, pot-roasted sort of texture that any real Texan would immediately reject.

For real Texas-style barbecue sauce to pair with our ribs, we pulled together the usual ingredients—vinegar, onion, molasses, to name a few—with dry mustard and chipotle chiles for spiciness. Savory Worcestershire sauce added depth while tomato juice (in place of ketchup) provided tangy flavor and helped thin the sauce out.

TEXAS BEEF RIBS

WHY THIS RECIPE WORKS: In Texas, good beef ribs are all about intense meat flavor—not just smoke and spice. The barbecue chefs we've met get this flavor just right, thanks to the assistance of massive electric smokers with automated temperature controls. But can a backyard cook replicate this Lone Star classic without the help of special equipment? We were looking for a recipe that would yield potent meat flavor with a bit of honest Texas chew—on our conventional-size grill.

We began by debating whether to trim the fatty membrane that runs along the back side of the ribs. Surprisingly, the juiciest meat with the most flavor was accomplished by the path of least resistance: simply leaving the membrane in place. The fat not only bastes the ribs as they cook but also renders to a crisp, bacon-like texture. A simple mixture of salt, pepper, cayenne, and chili powder rubbed into each rack was all that it took to bring out the flavor of the meat. To turn our grill into a backyard smoker, we made a slow, even fire with a

Texas-Style Barbecued Beef Ribs for a Charcoal Grill

SERVES 4

It is important to use beef ribs with a decent amount of meat, not bony scraps; otherwise, the rewards of making this recipe are few. For the wood chunks, use any type of wood but mesquite, which can have an overpowering smokiness. Except when adding coals, do not lift the grill lid, which will allow both smoke and heat to escape.

- 4 teaspoons chili powder
- 2 teaspoons table salt
- 1½ teaspoons ground black pepper
- ½ teaspoon cayenne pepper
- 3-4 beef rib slabs (3 to 4 ribs per slab, about 5 pounds total) (see note)
- 2 (3-inch) wood chunks (see note)
  Vegetable oil for the cooking grate
- 1 recipe Barbecue Sauce for Texas-Style Beef Ribs (recipe follows)

1. Combine the chili powder, salt, black pepper, and cayenne in a small bowl; rub the ribs evenly with the spice mixture and let stand at room temperature for 1 hour.

2. Meanwhile, soak the wood chunks in cold water to cover for 1 hour; drain. About 20 minutes prior to grilling, open the bottom grill vents. Light a large chimney starter filled one-third with charcoal (about 2 quarts) and allow to burn until the coals are partially covered with a layer of ash, about 10 minutes. Build a single-banked fire by steeply banking all the coals on one side of the grill. Place one wood chunk on top of the coals. Set the cooking grate in place, cover, opening the lid vents so they are two-thirds open, and heat the grate until hot, about 5 minutes. Use a grill brush to scrape the cooking grate clean. Dip a wad of paper towels in oil; holding the wad with tongs, oil the cooking grate.

3. Place the ribs, meat side down, on the cooler side of the grill (they may overlap slightly); cover, positioning the lid so that the vents are directly above the ribs. (The temperature inside the grill should be about 300 degrees.) Cook until the grill temperature drops to about 250 degrees, about 1 hour. (If necessary, add five additional briquettes to maintain the temperature above 250 degrees during the first hour of cooking.)

4. After 1 hour, add 20 more briquettes and the remaining wood chunk to the coals. Using tongs, flip the ribs meat side up and rotate the racks. Cover the grill, positioning the lid so that the vents are opposite the wood chunk. Continue to cook until a fork can be inserted into and removed from the meat with some resistance and the meat begins to pull away from the bone and shrinks ½ to 1 inch up the bone, 1¼ to 1¾ hours longer. Transfer the ribs to a carving board and let rest 5 minutes. Slice between the bones and serve, passing the sauce separately.

Texas-Style Barbecued Beef Ribs for a Gas Grill

You will need a disposable aluminum pie plate for this recipe. Try to maintain a 250 to 300-degree grill temperature by adjusting the lit burner.

1. Follow the recipe for Texas-Style Barbecued Beef Ribs for a Charcoal Grill through step 1.

2. Substitute 3 cups wood chips for the wood chunks. Soak the chips in cold water to cover for 30 minutes; drain. Place the chips in a disposable aluminum pie plate; set the pie plate on top of the primary burner (the burner that will remain on during cooking). Turn all the burners to high and heat the grill with the lid down, until very hot and the chips are smoking heavily, about

20 minutes (if the chips ignite, extinguish the flames with water from a spray bottle). Use a grill brush to scrape the cooking grate clean. Dip a wad of paper towels in oil; holding the wad with tongs, oil the cooking grate. Turn off all the burner(s) except the primary burner. Place the ribs, meat side down, on the cooler side of the grill. Cover and cook 1¼ hours (the temperature inside the grill should be 250 to 300 degrees; adjust the lit burner as necessary).

3. Using tongs, flip the ribs meat side up and rotate the racks. Cover and continue to cook until a fork can be inserted into and removed from the meat with little resistance and the meat shrinks ½ to 1 inch up the bone, 1 to 1½ hours longer. Transfer the ribs to a carving board and let rest 5 minutes. Slice between the bones and serve, passing the sauce separately.

Barbecue Sauce for Texas-Style Beef Ribs

MAKES 1¾ CUPS

This is a simple, vinegary dipping sauce quite unlike the sweet, thick barbecue sauces found in the supermarket.

- 2 tablespoons unsalted butter
- ¼ cup minced onion
- 1½ teaspoons chili powder
- 1 medium garlic clove, minced or pressed through a garlic press (about 1 teaspoon)
- 2 cups tomato juice
- ¾ cup distilled white vinegar
- 2 tablespoons Worcestershire sauce
- 2 tablespoons mild or dark (not blackstrap) molasses
- ½ teaspoon dry mustard mixed with 1 tablespoon water
- 1½ teaspoons table salt
- 1 teaspoon minced chipotle chiles in adobo sauce
- ¼ teaspoon ground black pepper

Melt the butter in a small saucepan over medium heat. Add the onion and cook, stirring occasionally, until softened, 2 to 3 minutes. Add the chili powder and garlic and cook, stirring constantly, until fragrant, about 20 seconds. Add the tomato juice, ½ cup of the vinegar, the Worcestershire sauce, molasses, mustard, salt, and chipotles. Bring to a simmer over high heat, then reduce the heat to medium and continue to simmer, stirring occasionally, until the sauce is slightly thickened and reduced to 1½ cups, 30 to 40 minutes. Off the heat, stir in the pepper and remaining ¼ cup vinegar. Cool to room temperature before serving. (The sauce can be refrigerated in an airtight container for up to 4 days; bring to room temperature before serving.)

SHISH KEBABS

WHY THIS RECIPE WORKS: Kebabs, for all their popularity and convenience, are usually over- or undercooked, with vegetables and meat that are either burnt or raw and falling off the skewer. But kebabs are so simple, they should be a go-to grilling recipe for most home cooks; they're easy to put together and take little time on the grill, thanks to the vegetables and meat already being in bite-sized pieces. We decided to revisit the kebab, grabbed some metal skewers, and headed to our grill, in search of perfectly cooked lamb and crisp, slightly charred vegetables.

To avoid the raw lamb and charred vegetables that cooking on skewers often delivers, we cut the meat (boneless leg of lamb, trimmed of fat and silver skin) into 1-inch cubes and narrowed the vegetable field. Onions and peppers were the vegetable combination most preferred by tasters; they aren't incredibly watery like tomatoes, which were out from the beginning, and they cooked at the same rate as the meat. Marinating the meat for 2 hours added extra flavor; for the marinades, we used fruity, sweet, and spicy ingredients that stood up well to the hearty lamb.

Charcoal-Grilled Shish Kebabs

SERVES 6

Cutting up the onion so the pieces will stay together on skewers is a little tricky; we recommend the following method: Trim away the stem and root end and cut the onion into quarters. Peel the three outer layers of the onion away from the inner core. Working with the outer layers only, cut each quarter—from pole to pole—into three strips of equal width. Cut each of the 12 strips crosswise into three pieces, for 36 small stacks of three layers each. You will need 12 metal skewers for this recipe.

- 1 recipe marinade (recipes follow)
- 1 (2¼-pound) shank end boneless leg of lamb, trimmed of fat and silver skin, cut into 1-inch pieces
  Vegetable oil for the cooking grate
- 1 large red onion, cut into 36 stacks of three ¾-inch pieces (see note)
- 3 medium bell peppers, 1 red, 1 yellow, and 1 orange, cut into twenty-four 1-inch pieces
  Lemon or lime wedges (optional)

1. Toss the marinade and lamb in a gallon-sized zipper-lock bag or a large bowl; seal the bag, or cover the bowl with plastic wrap, and refrigerate for at least 2 hours or up to 24 hours.

2. Light a large chimney starter filled with charcoal (about 6 quarts) and allow to burn until the coals are partially covered with a layer of ash, about 20 minutes. Build a single-level fire by spreading all the coals evenly over the bottom of the grill. Set the cooking grate in place, cover the grill, and heat the grate until hot, about 5 minutes. Use a grill brush to scrape the cooking grate clean. Dip a wad of paper towels in oil; holding the wad with tongs, oil the cooking grate.

3. Meanwhile, starting and ending with the meat, thread 4 pieces of meat, 3 pieces of onion (three 3-layer stacks), and 6 pieces of pepper in mixed order on 12 metal skewers.

4. Grill the kebabs, uncovered, until the meat is well browned and grill marks appear, about 7 minutes for medium-rare or about 8 minutes for medium, turning each kebab one-quarter turn every 1¾ minutes to brown all sides. Transfer the kebabs to a serving platter, tent loosely with foil, and let rest 5 minutes. Squeeze the lemon or lime wedges over the kebabs, if desired, and serve.

Gas-Grilled Shish Kebabs

Follow the recipe for Charcoal-Grilled Shish Kebabs through step 1. Turn all the burners to high and heat the grill, with the lid down, until very hot, about 15 minutes. Use a grill brush to scrape the cooking grate clean. Dip a wad of paper towels in oil; holding the wad with tongs, oil the cooking grate. Starting and ending with the meat, thread 4 pieces of meat, 3 pieces of onion (three 3-layer stacks), and 6 pieces of pepper in mixed order on 12 metal skewers. Grill the kebabs, covered, until the meat is well browned and grill marks appear, about 8 minutes for medium-rare or about 9 minutes for medium, turning each kebab one-quarter turn every 2 minutes to brown all sides. Transfer the kebabs to a serving platter, tent loosely with foil, and let rest 5 minutes. Squeeze the lemon or lime wedges over the kebabs, if desired, and serve.

Warm-Spiced Parsley Marinade with Ginger

MAKES ABOUT ¾ CUP

- ½ cup olive oil
- ½ cup packed fresh parsley leaves
- 1 jalapeño chile, seeded and chopped coarse
- 2 tablespoons minced or grated fresh ginger
- 3 medium garlic cloves, peeled

1 teaspoon ground cumin
1 teaspoon ground cardamom
1 teaspoon ground cinnamon
1 teaspoon table salt
⅛ teaspoon ground black pepper

Process all the ingredients in a food processor until smooth, about 1 minute, scraping down the sides of the workbowl as necessary.

Garlic and Cilantro Marinade with Garam Masala

MAKES ABOUT ¾ CUP

½ cup olive oil
½ cup packed fresh cilantro leaves
¼ cup raisins
1½ tablespoons juice from 1 lemon
3 medium garlic cloves, peeled
1 teaspoon table salt
½ teaspoon garam masala
⅛ teaspoon ground black pepper

Process all the ingredients in a food processor until smooth, about 1 minute, scraping down the sides of the workbowl as necessary.

GRILLED RACK OF LAMB

WHY THIS RECIPE WORKS: With its juicy, pink meat, rich crust, and classic stand-up-straight presentation, rack of lamb is a bona fide showstopper—and it has the price tag to prove it. But grill this piece of meat improperly and you've made a very costly mistake. That's why we wanted to come up with a foolproof technique for grilling rack of lamb—one that would deliver a great crust and flavorful, tender meat, every time.

Our first challenge was choosing just the right cut. While the racks from butcher shops and high-end specialty stores cost more than those from the supermarket, they come already trimmed. And once we trimmed all the excess fat from our supermarket samples, we found this meat wasn't actually much cheaper. However, even the trimmed lamb needed additional butchering, both to remove the "cap" of fat that creates meat-scorching flare-ups and to trim away any excess meat and fat. (For perfect grilling results, we needed fairly lean racks of uniform thickness.)

To cook the lamb evenly as well as to effectively render its fat, we placed a disposable aluminum pan in the middle of the grill and heaped a small pile of coals on either side of the pan. Placing the lamb in the middle of the grill, over the pan, ensured the pan would catch the rendering fat, preventing flare-ups. A wet rub (garlic, rosemary, thyme, and olive oil) was the best way to flavor the meat—marinades turned the lamb mushy and dry rubs simply didn't work with our grilling method. For a rich crust that wasn't charred, we applied the wet rub during the last few minutes of grilling, keeping the surface crisp.

Charcoal-Grilled Rack of Lamb

SERVES 4

We prefer the milder taste and bigger size of domestic lamb, but you may substitute imported lamb from New Zealand or Australia. Since imported racks are generally smaller, follow the shorter cooking times given in the recipe. Most lamb is sold frenched (meaning part of each rib bone is exposed), but chances are there will still be some extra fat between the bones. Remove the majority of this fat, leaving an inch at the top of the small eye of meat. Also, make sure that the chine bone (along the bottom of the rack) has been removed to ensure that it will be easy to cut between the ribs after cooking. Ask the butcher to do it; it's very hard to cut off at home. You will need a 13 by 9-inch disposable aluminum pan for this recipe.

Vegetable oil for the cooking grate
4 teaspoons olive oil
4 teaspoons chopped fresh rosemary leaves
2 teaspoons chopped fresh thyme leaves
2 medium garlic cloves, minced or pressed through a garlic press (about 2 teaspoons)
2 (1½-pound) racks of lamb, rib bones frenched, meat trimmed of all excess fat (see note; see page 372)
Table salt and ground black pepper

1. Light a large chimney starter filled with charcoal (about 6 quarts) and allow to burn until the coals are partially covered with a layer of ash, about 20 minutes. Place a 13 by 9-inch disposable aluminum pan in the center of the grill. Build a double-banked fire by banking half of the coals into a pile on each side of the pan. Set the cooking grate in place, cover, and heat the grate until hot, about 5 minutes. Use a grill brush to scrape the cooking grate clean. Dip a wad of paper towels in vegetable oil; holding the wad with tongs, oil the cooking grate.

TRIMMING FAT FROM RACK OF LAMB

Use a boning or paring knife to cut away any thick portions of fat until a thin layer remains.

2. Combine 3 teaspoons of the olive oil, the rosemary, thyme, and garlic in a small bowl; set aside. Rub the lamb with the remaining 1 teaspoon oil and season generously with salt and pepper. Place the racks, bone-side up, on the center of the grill over the pan, with the meaty side of the racks very close to, but not quite over, the coals. Cover and grill until the meat is lightly browned, faint grill marks appear, and the fat has begun to render, 8 to 10 minutes.

3. Flip the racks over, bone side down, and move to the hotter sides of the grill. Grill, without moving, until well browned, 3 to 4 minutes. Brush the racks with the rosemary mixture. Flip the racks bone side up and continue to grill over the hotter parts of the grill until well browned, 3 to 4 minutes. Stand the racks up and lean them against each other; continue to grill over one side of the hotter part of the grill until the bottoms are well browned and the center of the racks registers 120 degrees for medium-rare or 125 degrees for medium on an instant-read thermometer inserted from the side of a rack into the center, but away from any bones, 3 to 8 minutes longer.

4. Transfer the lamb to a carving board, tent loosely with foil, and let rest for 15 minutes. Cut between each rib to separate the chops and serve immediately.

Gas-Grilled Rack of Lamb

Follow the recipe for Charcoal-Grilled Rack of Lamb, turning all the burners to high and heating the grill, with the lid down, until very hot, about 15 minutes. Use a grill brush to scrape the cooking grate clean. Dip a wad of paper towels in vegetable oil; holding the wad with tongs, oil the cooking grate. Proceed with the recipe from step 2, leaving the primary burner on high and turning off the other burner(s). Grill the lamb, on the cooler side of the grill, omitting the disposable pan, with the lid down and proceed as directed.

GRILLED SALMON FILLETS

WHY THIS RECIPE WORKS: Cooking delicate salmon can be tricky. Even using a nonstick skillet, it's still easy to break the occasional fillet. Introduce that same fillet to a grill, and you've got a real challenge. We wanted grilled salmon with a tender interior and crisp skin, and with each fillet perfectly intact.

Part of the solution lay in a procedure we developed to clean the grill thoroughly: Place an overturned disposable aluminum pan over the grate as the grill warms up, trapping hot air and superheating the grate. Just like in a self-cleaning oven, the high heat causes grease and debris to disintegrate. By replacing the disposable pan with foil pressed against the grate, we bumped the temperature up higher, making the technique even more effective. We chose thicker salmon fillets, which could stand the heat of the grill for a little while longer before the first turn. To prevent the fish from sticking, we dried the fish's exterior by wrapping it in kitchen towels and "seasoned" our cooking grate by brushing it over and over with multiple layers of oil until it developed a dark, shiny coating. After laying the fillets on the grate, we easily flipped each fillet without even the tiniest bit of sticking.

Charcoal-Grilled Salmon Fillets

SERVES 4

This recipe works best with salmon fillets but can be used with any thick, firm-fleshed white fish, including red snapper, grouper, halibut, and sea bass (cook white fish to 140 degrees, up to two minutes longer per side). If you are using skinless fillets, treat the skinned side of each as if it were the skin side. If your fillets are thicker than 1 inch, increase the cooking time on the second side in step 3 until the center of the fillet registers 125 degrees (or 140 degrees for white fish). If desired, serve with Olive Vinaigrette or Almond Vinaigrette (recipes follow).

> 1 (1½ to 2-pound) skin-on salmon fillet, about 1 inch thick at the thickest part (see note)
> Vegetable oil for the fish and cooking grate
> Table salt and ground black pepper
> Lemon wedges, for serving

1. Remove any whitish fat from the belly of the fillet and cut it into four equal pieces. Place the fillets, skin side up, on a rimmed baking sheet, or large plate, lined with a clean kitchen towel. Place a second clean kitchen towel

on top of the fillets and press down to blot the liquid. Refrigerate the fish, wrapped in towels, while preparing the grill, at least 20 minutes.

2. Meanwhile, light a large chimney starter filled three-quarters with charcoal (about 4½ quarts) and allow to burn until the coals are partially covered with a layer of ash, about 20 minutes. Open the bottom grill vents. Build a modified two-level fire by arranging the coals over half of the grill, leaving the other half empty. Loosely cover the cooking grate with a large piece of heavy-duty aluminum foil and set the cooking grate in place, cover the grill, and heat the grate until hot, about 5 minutes. Remove the foil with tongs and discard. Use a grill brush to scrape the cooking grate clean. Dip a wad of paper towels in oil; holding the wad with tongs, oil the cooking grate. Continue to wipe the grate with oiled paper towels, re-dipping towels in the oil between applications, until the cooking grate is black and glossy, 5 to 10 times.

3. Brush both sides of the fish with a thin coat of oil and season with salt and pepper. Place the fish, skin side down, on the grill diagonal to the grate and directly over the coals, and cook, covered, without moving until the skin side is brown, well marked, and crisp, 3 to 5 minutes. (Try lifting the fish gently with a spatula after 3 minutes; if it doesn't cleanly lift off the grill, continue to cook, checking at 30-second intervals until it releases.) Flip the fish to the second side and cook, covered, until the center of fillet is opaque and registers 125 degrees on an instant-read thermometer, 2 to 6 minutes longer. Serve immediately with lemon wedges.

Gas-Grilled Salmon Fillets

Follow the recipe for Charcoal-Grilled Salmon Fillets through step 1. While the fish dries, loosely cover the cooking grate with a large piece of heavy-duty aluminum foil. Turn all the burners to high and heat the grill, with the lid down, until very hot, about 15 minutes. Remove the foil with tongs and discard. Use a grill brush to scrape the cooking grate clean. Dip a wad of paper towels in oil; holding the wad with tongs, oil the cooking grate. Continue to wipe the grate with oiled paper towels, re-dipping towels in the oil between applications, until the cooking grate is black and glossy, 5 to 10 times. Proceed with the recipe from step 3. Immediately reduce the heat to medium after placing the fish on the grill and continue with the recipe, grilling the fish with the lid down.

Olive Vinaigrette

MAKES ABOUT ½ CUP, ENOUGH FOR 4 PIECES OF GRILLED SALMON

- ½ cup pitted green or kalamata olives, coarsely chopped
- ¼ cup extra-virgin olive oil
- 2 tablespoons chopped fresh parsley leaves
- 1 small shallot, minced (about 1 tablespoon)
- 2 teaspoons juice from 1 lemon
  Table salt and ground black pepper

Combine all the ingredients in a medium bowl and season with salt and pepper to taste. Rewhisk before serving with the grilled salmon.

Almond Vinaigrette

MAKES ABOUT ½ CUP, ENOUGH FOR 4 PIECES OF GRILLED SALMON

- ⅓ cup almonds, toasted
- 1 small shallot, minced (about 1 tablespoon)
- 4 teaspoons white wine vinegar
- 2 teaspoons honey
- 1 teaspoon Dijon mustard
- ⅓ cup extra-virgin olive oil
- 1 tablespoon cold water
- 1 tablespoon chopped fresh tarragon leaves
  Table salt and ground black pepper

Place the almonds in a zipper-lock bag and, using a rolling pin or the bottom of a skillet, pound until pieces no larger than ½ inch remain. Combine the pounded almonds, shallot, vinegar, honey, and mustard in a medium bowl. Whisking constantly, slowly drizzle in the oil until a smooth emulsion forms. Add the water and tarragon and whisk to combine, then season with salt and pepper to taste. Rewhisk before serving with the salmon.

BEHIND THE SCENES

HOW TO AVOID A STICKY SITUATION—PREVENTING FISH (AND MORE) FROM STICKING TO THE GRILL

To prevent food from sticking, the grill grate should be oiled once it is hot, after being scraped clean. (Or superheat your grill by placing aluminum foil directly on the grate before heating it. The foil traps hot air and heats the grill to nearly 900 degrees F, which disintegrates stuck-on gunk—much like a self-cleaning oven.) Debris is more readily removed from a hot grate than a cool one, and once these stuck-on bits are gone, the grate can be more effectively slicked down with an oil-dipped wad of paper towels.

Oiling the grill grate once it's hot also helps the oil to bond quickly to the metal and prevent proteins from sticking to the grill grate. When oil is added to a cold grill grate, the oil slowly vaporizes as the grill reaches the desired cooking temperature. The more the oil vaporizes, the less oil will be left on the grill grate, making sticking more likely.

And for foods that are especially prone to sticking to the grill, like fish, multiple applications of oil work wonders. Simply apply the oil to the grate five to 10 times, re-dipping the towels in the oil between applications, until the grate is black and glossy.

One more point: Never try to take a shortcut by spraying a hot cooking grate with vegetable oil spray. You might save about 10 seconds, but you risk having a flare-up on your hands.

GRILLED GLAZED SALMON

WHY THIS RECIPE WORKS: A burnt, stuck-to-the-grill crust and flavorless interior are too often the reality of glazed salmon. But truly great glazed salmon right off the grill is a thing of beauty—the sweet glaze not only forms a glossy, deeply caramelized crust, but it also permeates the flesh, making the last bite of fish every bit as good as the first. This was the salmon that we wanted to re-create—sweet, crisp, moist, and flavorful.

Our recipe coup came early on in development—we realized that the best way to prevent the glazed salmon from sticking to the cooking grate was by not letting it touch the grate at all. We grilled the salmon fillets in individual aluminum trays set over the grill. There was no need for special equipment—we simply folded heavy-duty foil into 7 by 5-inch trays. This way, the fish still picked up great smoky flavor, but didn't stick to the cooking grate. Jelly was the best base ingredient for a sweet and sticky glaze. For the deepest flavor, we brushed some glaze over the fish toward the end of grilling, so it caramelized, and spooned the remaining glaze, enriched with butter, over the fish just before serving.

Charcoal-Grilled Glazed Salmon

SERVES 4

Use any brand of heavy-duty aluminum foil to make the grill trays, but be sure to spray the foil with nonstick cooking spray. Alternatively, you can use Reynolds Wrap nonstick aluminum foil and skip the cooking spray.

- ½ cup jalapeño jelly
- ½ cup packed fresh cilantro leaves and stems
- 1 teaspoon grated zest and 2 tablespoons juice from 1 large lime
- 2 medium garlic cloves, minced or pressed through a garlic press (about 2 teaspoons)
- 2 scallions, chopped coarse
- 2 tablespoons unsalted butter
    Vegetable oil for the cooking grate
- 1 (1½ to 2-pound) skin-on salmon fillet, about 1½ inches thick at the thickest part, skin removed (see page 155)
    Table salt and ground black pepper

1. Process the jelly, cilantro, lime zest and juice, garlic, and scallions in a food processor or blender until smooth. Heat the glaze in a small saucepan over medium heat until just bubbling, 2 to 3 minutes. Remove from the heat and transfer ¼ cup of the glaze to a small bowl to cool slightly. Stir the butter into the glaze remaining in the saucepan, cover, and set aside.

2. Light a large chimney starter filled with charcoal (about 6 quarts) and allow to burn until the coals are partially covered with a layer of ash, about 20 minutes. Build a three-quarter fire by evenly arranging the coals over three-quarters of the grill. Set the cooking grate in place, cover, and heat the grill until hot, about 5 minutes. Use a grill brush to scrape the cooking grate clean.

3. Following the photo on page 375, use heavy-duty foil to make four 7 by 5-inch trays. Coat the trays with vegetable oil spray. Remove any whitish fat from the belly of the fillet and cut it into four equal pieces. Season the salmon with salt and pepper, brush each side of each fillet with ½ tablespoon reserved glaze (without the butter), and place skinned-side up on the trays.

4. Place the trays with the salmon over the hot side of the grill and grill until the glaze forms a golden brown crust, 6 to 8 minutes. (Move the fillets to the cooler part of the grill if they darken too soon.) Using tongs, flip the salmon and cook 1 minute. Spoon half of the buttered glaze on the salmon and cook until the center of each fillet is just translucent, about 1 minute. Transfer the salmon to a platter, spoon the remaining buttered glaze over the top, and serve.

Gas-Grilled Glazed Salmon

Follow the recipe for Charcoal-Grilled Glazed Salmon through step 1. Turn all the burners to high and heat the grill, with the lid down, until very hot, about 15 minutes. Use a grill brush to scrape the cooking grate clean. Proceed with the recipe from step 3, leaving the burners on high and cooking with the lid down.

NOTES FROM THE TEST KITCHEN

MAKING A FOIL TRAY

Cut out four rectangles of heavy-duty aluminum foil and crimp the edges until each tray measures 7 by 5 inches.

Grilled Salmon with Orange-Sesame Glaze

Follow the recipe for Charcoal- or Gas-Grilled Glazed Salmon, replacing the lime zest and juice with lemon zest and juice, and replacing the jalapeño jelly with orange marmalade. Puree 2 tablespoons oyster-flavored sauce and 1 teaspoon toasted sesame oil with the other glaze ingredients. Add 1 teaspoon toasted sesame seeds along with the butter.

Grilled Salmon with Spicy Apple Glaze

Follow the recipe for Charcoal- or Gas-Grilled Glazed Salmon, replacing the lime zest and juice with 2 tablespoons cider vinegar and replacing the jalapeño jelly with apple jelly. Puree ½ teaspoon red pepper flakes with the other glaze ingredients.

BARBECUED SALMON

WHY THIS RECIPE WORKS: Store-bought smoked salmon is inconsistent in quality and also incredibly expensive—up to $8 for just 4 ounces. We wanted to create our own easy recipe for this dish that's often reserved for weekend brunch, and make moist (but not too moist), nicely crusted salmon with a hint of smoked flavor in any covered grill—in just two hours.

Surprisingly, impatience turned out to be the key to our success. Instead of the traditional cold-smoking technique, which keeps the salmon moist but lacks flavor, we developed a "hot-smoked" method, and kept the salmon moist by brining. We achieved full smoked salmon flavor on the grill using a whole side of salmon. To get a firm but not overly dry texture, complemented by a strong hit of smoke and wood, we slow-cooked the salmon for more than an hour over a modified two-level fire, with wood chunks on the coals, but kept the fish on the cooler part of the grill the whole time. Using two spatulas to transfer the cooked fish from the grill prevented it from falling apart, and cutting through the pink flesh, not the skin, to divide individual portions kept the meat intact while leaving the skin behind.

Barbecued Salmon for a Charcoal Grill

SERVES 4 TO 6

The cooking grate must be hot and thoroughly clean before you place the salmon on it; otherwise the fish might stick. Use foil or the back of a large rimmed baking sheet to get the fish onto the grill. Alder wood is our first choice for this recipe, but hickory works fine, too. If desired, serve the salmon with one of the sauces that follow.

- 1 cup sugar
- ½ cup table salt
- 1 (2½-pound) skin-on salmon fillet
- 2 (3-inch) wood chunks (see note)
- 2 tablespoons vegetable oil, plus extra for the cooking grate
- 1½ teaspoons sweet paprika
- 1 teaspoon ground white pepper

1. Dissolve the sugar and salt in 7 cups cold water in a gallon-sized zipper-lock bag. Add the salmon, seal the bag, and refrigerate for 3 hours.

2. Meanwhile, soak the wood chunks in cold water to cover for 1 hour; drain and set aside.

3. Remove the salmon from the brine and pat dry with paper towels. Place the fillet, skin side down, on a 30-inch sheet of heavy-duty foil. Rub both sides of the fillet with the oil. Season the flesh side of the fillet with the paprika and pepper.

4. Meanwhile, light a large chimney starter filled halfway with charcoal (about 3 quarts) and allow to burn until the coals are partially covered with a layer of ash, about 10 minutes. Build a modified two-level fire by arranging all the coals over half of the grill, leaving the other half empty; set the wood chunks on the coals and open the bottom grill vents. Set the cooking grate in place, cover, and heat the grate until hot, about 5 minutes. Use a grill brush to scrape the cooking grate clean. Dip a wad of paper towels in oil; holding the wad with tongs, oil the cooking grate.

5. Slide the salmon onto the grill opposite the fire so that the long side of the fillet is perpendicular to the grill grate. Cover, turning the lid so that the vents are opposite the wood chunks to draw smoke through the grill. Cook until heavily flavored with smoke, about 1½ hours. (The temperature inside the grill should be about 350 degrees and will fall to 250 degrees.)

6. Use two spatulas to remove the salmon from the grill. Serve hot or at room temperature, cutting through the flesh but not the skin to divide the salmon into individual portions, leaving the skin behind.

Barbecued Salmon for a Gas Grill

You will need a disposable aluminum pie plate for this recipe. Keep a close eye on the temperature of the grill; it should remain around 275 degrees.

Follow the recipe for Barbecued Salmon for a Charcoal Grill through step 3, substituting 2 cups wood chips for the wood chunks. Soak the wood chips in cold water to cover for 30 minutes, then drain. Place the wood chips in a disposable aluminum pie plate; set the pie plate on the primary burner (the burner that will remain on during cooking). Turn all the burners to high and heat the grill with the lid down until very hot and the chips are smoking heavily, about 20 minutes. (If the chips ignite, extinguish the flames with water from a spray bottle.) Use a grill brush to scrape the cooking grate clean. Dip a wad of paper towels in oil; holding the wad with tongs, oil the cooking grate. Leave the primary burner on high and turn the other burner(s) off. Slide the salmon onto the grill as directed in step 5 and proceed with the recipe.

Horseradish Cream Sauce with Chives

MAKES ABOUT 1 CUP

Horseradish and crème fraîche are natural partners to the smoky salmon.

- 1 cup crème fraîche or sour cream
- 2 tablespoons prepared horseradish
- 2 tablespoons minced fresh chives
  Pinch table salt

Combine the ingredients in a small bowl. (The sauce can be refrigerated in an airtight container for up to 1 day.)

Mustard-Dill Sauce

MAKES ABOUT 1 CUP

Use Dijon, honey, or grainy mustard, as desired. Depending on your choice of mustard, this sauce can be fairly hot.

- 1 cup mustard (see note)
- ¼ cup minced fresh dill

Combine the ingredients in a small bowl. (The sauce can be refrigerated in an airtight container for up to 1 day.)

BLACKENED SNAPPER

WHY THIS RECIPE WORKS: Blackened fish is usually prepared in a cast-iron skillet, but it can lead to one smoky kitchen. We thought we'd solve this issue by throwing our fish on the barbie (it works for more than just shrimp, right?). Unfortunately, this move created a host of other problems, including fish stuck to the grate, the outside of the fish being way overdone by the time the flesh had cooked through, and the skin-on fillets curling midway through cooking. We were done with the smoke—and were ready for our fillets to have a dark brown, crusty, sweet-smoky, toasted spice exterior, providing a rich contrast to the moist, mild-flavored fish inside.

The curling problem was easy to fix. We simply needed to score the skin. The sticking solution proved more difficult, but the answer turned out to be a trick that we'd used before to grill salmon fillets (see page 372)—setting a big piece of heavy-duty foil on the grill. By placing a large piece of foil over the grate while it preheated, we made the grill superhot. This heat incinerated all the nasty gunk on the grate and gave us a really clean surface on which to cook the fish; oiling the grate with a heavy

hand didn't hurt, either. Finally, to give the fish its flavorful "blackened but not burned" coating, we bloomed our spice mixture in melted butter, allowed it to cool, and then applied the coating to the fish. Once on the grill, the spice crust acquired the proper depth and richness while the fish cooked through.

Charcoal-Grilled Blackened Red Snapper
SERVES 4

If using fillets that are ½ inch or thinner, reduce the cooking time to 3 minutes per side. If using fillets that are 1 inch or thicker, increase the cooking time on the second side by 2 minutes, moving the fish to the cooler side of the grill after the second side has browned. If you cannot find red snapper, substitute striped bass, halibut, or catfish. Making the slashes in the skin requires a sharp knife. If your knife isn't sharp enough, try cutting through the skin with a serrated knife. However, cut in one direction (don't saw) and be careful to not cut into the flesh. If you choose not to eat the skin, be sure to remove it after cooking rather than beforehand. Serve the fish with lemon wedges, Rémoulade, or Pineapple and Cucumber Salsa with Mint (recipes follow).

- 2 tablespoons sweet paprika
- 2 teaspoons onion powder
- 2 teaspoons garlic powder
- ¾ teaspoon ground coriander
- ¾ teaspoon table salt
- ¼ teaspoon cayenne pepper
- ¼ teaspoon ground black pepper
- ¼ teaspoon ground white pepper
- 3 tablespoons unsalted butter
  Vegetable oil for the cooking grate
- 4 (6 to 8-ounce) red snapper fillets, ¾ inch thick (see note)

1. Combine the paprika, onion powder, garlic powder, coriander, salt, cayenne, and peppers in a small bowl. Melt the butter in a 10-inch skillet over medium heat. Stir in the spice mixture and cook, stirring frequently, until fragrant and the spices turn a dark rust color, 2 to 3 minutes. Transfer the mixture to a pie plate and cool, stirring occasionally, to room temperature, about 10 minutes. Once cooled, use a fork to break up any large clumps.

2. Light a large chimney starter filled three-quarters with charcoal (about 4½ quarts) and allow to burn until the coals are partially covered with a layer of ash, about 20 minutes. Build a modified two-level fire by arranging the coals over half of the grill, leaving the other half empty. Loosely cover the cooking grate with a large piece of heavy-duty aluminum foil and set the cooking grate in place, cover the grill, and heat the grate until hot, about 5 minutes. Remove the foil with tongs and discard. Use a grill brush to scrape the cooking grate clean. Dip a wad of paper towels in oil; holding the wad with tongs, oil the cooking grate. Continue to wipe the grate with oiled paper towels, re-dipping towels in the oil between applications, until the cooking grate is black and glossy, 5 to 10 times.

3. Meanwhile, pat the fillets dry on both sides with paper towels. Using a sharp knife, make shallow diagonal slashes every inch along the skin side of the fish, being careful not to cut into the flesh. Place the fillets, skin side up, on a rimmed baking sheet or a large plate. Using your fingers, rub the spice mixture in a thin, even layer on the top and sides of the fish. Flip the fillets over and repeat on the other side (you should use all of the spice mixture).

4. Place the fish lengthwise so it is perpendicular to the grill grate, skin side down, on the hot side of the grill. Grill, uncovered, until the skin is very dark brown and crisp, 3 to 4 minutes. Using a thin metal spatula, carefully flip the fish and continue to grill until dark brown and beginning to flake and the center is opaque but still moist, about 5 minutes longer. Serve immediately.

Gas-Grilled Blackened Red Snapper

Follow the recipe for Charcoal-Grilled Blackened Red Snapper, skipping step 2. Loosely cover the cooking grate with a large piece of heavy-duty aluminum foil. Turn all the burners to high and heat the grill, with the lid down, until very hot, about 15 minutes. Remove the foil with tongs and discard. Use a grill brush to scrape the cooking grate clean. Dip a wad of paper towels in oil; holding the wad with tongs, oil the cooking grate. Continue to wipe the grate with oiled paper towels, re-dipping towels in the oil between applications, until the cooking grate is black and glossy, 5 to 10 times. Proceed with the recipe from step 3, leaving the burners on high and cooking with the lid up.

Rémoulade

MAKES ABOUT ½ CUP

The rémoulade can be refrigerated for up to three days.

- ½ cup mayonnaise
- 1½ teaspoons sweet pickle relish
- 1 teaspoon hot sauce
- 1 teaspoon juice from 1 lemon
- 1 teaspoon minced fresh parsley leaves
- ½ teaspoon capers, drained and rinsed
- ½ teaspoon Dijon mustard
- 1 small garlic clove, minced or pressed through a garlic press (about ½ teaspoon)
  Table salt and ground black pepper

Pulse the mayonnaise, relish, hot sauce, lemon juice, parsley, capers, mustard, and garlic in a food processor until well combined but not smooth, about 10 pulses. Season with salt and pepper to taste. Transfer to a serving bowl.

Pineapple and Cucumber Salsa with Mint

MAKES ABOUT 3 CUPS

This salsa can be made spicier by mincing and adding the seeds and ribs from the chile.

- ½ large pineapple, peeled, cored, and cut into ¼-inch pieces (about 2 cups)
- ½ medium cucumber, peeled, seeded, and cut into ¼-inch pieces (about 1 cup)
- 1 small shallot, minced (about 1 tablespoon)
- 1 medium serrano chile, seeds and ribs removed, chile minced (about 2 tablespoons) (see note)
- 2 tablespoons chopped fresh mint leaves
- 1-2 tablespoons juice from 1 lime
- ½ teaspoon minced or grated fresh ginger
  Table salt
  Sugar

Combine the pineapple, cucumber, shallot, chile, mint, 1 tablespoon lime juice, ginger, and ½ teaspoon salt in a medium bowl; let stand at room temperature 15 to 30 minutes. Season with additional lime juice and salt to taste, and add sugar as needed if the pineapple is tart; transfer to a serving bowl.

GRILLED SHRIMP

WHY THIS RECIPE WORKS: Great grilled shrimp—tender, moist, and flavorful—are hard to come by. Usually, they're overcooked and rubbery, giving the jaws a workout, thanks to their quick cooking time and the high temperature of the grill. Grilling shrimp in their shells can guarantee juiciness, but the seasoning tends to be lost when the shells are pulled off. We wanted tender, juicy, boldly seasoned grilled shrimp, with the flavor in the shrimp and not on our fingers.

Our decision to go with peeled shrimp for this recipe meant we had to revisit how we traditionally grilled shrimp. First we eliminated brining, which created waterlogged shrimp and hindered caramelization. Then we set the shrimp over a screaming-hot fire. This worked well with jumbo shrimp, but smaller shrimp overcooked before charring. With jumbo shrimp costing as much as $25 per pound, we decided against them. They did give us an idea, though. For our next step, we created faux jumbo shrimp by cramming a skewer with several normal-sized shrimp pressed tightly together. Our final revision was to take the shrimp off the fire before they were completely cooked (but after they had picked up attractive grill marks). We finished cooking them in a heated sauce waiting on the cool side of the grill; this final simmer gave them tons of flavor.

Charcoal-Grilled Shrimp Skewers

SERVES 4

The shrimp and sauce (recipes follow) finish cooking together on the grill, so prepare the sauce ingredients while the coals are heating. To fit all of the shrimp on the cooking grate at once, you'll need three 14-inch metal skewers. Serve with grilled bread.

- 1½ **pounds extra-large shrimp (21 to 25 per pound), peeled and deveined (see page 160)**
- 2–3 **tablespoons olive oil for brushing the shrimp**
  Table salt and ground black pepper
- ¼ **teaspoon sugar**
  Vegetable oil for the cooking grate
- 1 **recipe Spicy Lemon-Garlic Sauce or Fresh Tomato Sauce with Feta and Olives (recipes follow)**
  Lemon wedges, for serving

1. Pat the shrimp dry with paper towels. Thread the shrimp onto three skewers, alternating direction of heads and tails. Brush both sides of the shrimp with the olive oil and season lightly with salt and pepper. Sprinkle one side of each skewer evenly with the sugar.

2. Light a large chimney starter filled with charcoal (about 6 quarts) and allow to burn until the coals are partially covered with a layer of ash, about 20 minutes. Open the bottom vent on the grill. Build a modified two-level fire by arranging the coals over half of the grill, leaving the other half empty. Set the cooking grate in place, cover the grill, and heat the grate until hot, about 5 minutes. Use a grill brush to scrape the cooking grate clean. Dip a wad of paper towels in vegetable oil; holding the wad with tongs, oil the cooking grate.

3. Set the disposable pan with the sauce ingredients on the hot side of the grill and cook, stirring occasionally, until hot, about 1½ minutes; transfer the pan to the cooler side of the grill. Place the shrimp skewers, sugared sides down, on the hot side of the grate and use tongs to push the shrimp together on the skewers if they have separated. Grill the shrimp, uncovered, until lightly charred, 4 to 5 minutes. Using tongs, flip and grill until the second side is pink and slightly translucent, 1 to 2 minutes longer.

4. Using a potholder or oven mitt, carefully lift each skewer from the grill and use tongs to slide the shrimp off the skewers into the pan with the sauce. Toss the shrimp and sauce to combine and transfer the pan to the hot side of the grill; cook, stirring, until the shrimp are opaque and fully cooked, about 30 seconds. Remove from the grill, add the remaining sauce ingredients, and toss to combine. Transfer to a serving platter and serve immediately with the lemon wedges.

Gas-Grilled Shrimp Skewers

Follow step 1 of the recipe for Charcoal-Grilled Shrimp Skewers. Turn all the burners to high and heat the grill, with the lid down, until very hot, about 15 minutes. Use a grill brush to scrape the cooking grate clean. Dip a wad of paper towels in vegetable oil; holding the wad with

ARRANGING SHRIMP ON A SKEWER

Pass the skewer through the center of each shrimp. As you add shrimp to the skewer, alternate the directions of the heads and tails for a compact arrangement of shrimp. The shrimp should fit snugly against one another.

tongs, oil the cooking grate. Proceed with step 3 of the recipe, setting the sauce aside off the heat once hot and grilling the shrimp with the lid down, checking occasionally to make sure they're not burning (the timing may be a few minutes longer than in the charcoal grill recipe).

Spicy Lemon-Garlic Sauce

MAKES ABOUT ½ CUP

You will need a 10-inch disposable aluminum pan or pie plate for this recipe.

    4 tablespoons (½ stick) unsalted butter, cut into 4 pieces
    4 tablespoons juice from 2 lemons
    3 medium garlic cloves, minced or pressed through a garlic press (about 1 tablespoon)
    ½ teaspoon red pepper flakes
    ⅛ teaspoon table salt
    ⅓ cup minced fresh parsley leaves

Combine the butter, lemon juice, garlic, pepper flakes, and salt in a 10-inch disposable aluminum pan or pie plate. Cook over the hot side of the grill, stirring occasionally, until the butter melts, about 1½ minutes; transfer to the cooler side of the grill (if using a charcoal grill) or set aside off the heat (if using a gas grill). Proceed to grill the shrimp, adding the parsley just before serving.

Fresh Tomato Sauce with Feta and Olives

MAKES ABOUT ½ CUP

You will need a 10-inch disposable aluminum pan or pie plate for this recipe.

    4 tablespoons extra-virgin olive oil
    1 large ripe tomato, cored, seeded, and minced

    1 tablespoon minced fresh oregano leaves
    ⅛ teaspoon salt
    4 ounces feta cheese, crumbled into ¼-inch pieces (about 1 cup)
    ⅓ cup pitted kalamata olives, chopped fine
    2 tablespoons juice from 1 lemon
    3 scallions, sliced very thin

Combine the oil, tomato, oregano, and salt in a 10-inch disposable aluminum pan or pie plate. Cook over the hot side of the grill, stirring occasionally, until hot, about 1½ minutes; transfer to the cooler side of the grill (if using a charcoal grill) or set aside off the heat (if using a gas grill). Proceed to grill the shrimp, adding the feta, olives, lemon juice, and scallions just before serving.

BABA GHANOUSH

WHY THIS RECIPE WORKS: Baba ghanoush often appears on the appetizer table as a gray, bitter, watery mass of eggplant puree. We were after a dip that had realized its potential—full of smoky eggplant flavor and brightened with garlic and lemon juice. And one certain way to produce this creation was to start off by grilling our eggplant.

For the best flavor, it's imperative to start out with firm, shiny, and unblemished eggplants. To achieve a deep smoky flavor, we grilled the eggplants until they had completely collapsed—directly over a hot fire until wrinkled and soft. So the eggplant wouldn't burst over the heat, we had to poke the entire surface with a fork. To avoid a watery texture and any bitterness, we drained the pulp of excess fluid, but didn't bother spending time deseeding the eggplants. We processed the pulp with a modest amount of garlic, tahini paste, and lemon juice for the creaminess and bright flavor that traditional baba ghanoush is known for.

Charcoal-Grilled Baba Ghanoush

MAKES ABOUT 2 CUPS

We prefer to serve baba ghanoush only lightly chilled. If yours is cold, let it stand at room temperature for about 20 minutes before serving. Baba ghanoush does not keep well, so plan to make it the day you want to serve it. Pita bread, black olives, tomato wedges, and cucumber slices are nice accompaniments.

       Vegetable oil for the cooking grate
    2 pounds eggplant (about 2 large globe eggplants,

5 medium Italian eggplants, or 12 medium Japanese eggplants), each eggplant poked uniformly over the entire surface with a fork
2 tablespoons tahini paste
1 tablespoon juice from 1 lemon
1 small garlic clove, minced or pressed through a garlic press (about ½ teaspoon)
  Table salt and ground black pepper
1 tablespoon extra-virgin olive oil
2 teaspoons chopped fresh parsley leaves

1. Light a large chimney starter filled with charcoal (about 6 quarts) and allow to burn until the coals are partially covered with a layer of ash, about 20 minutes. Build a single-level fire by arranging the coals evenly over the bottom of the grill; arrange an additional chimney starter of unlit charcoal (about 6 quarts) over the lit coals. Set the cooking grate in place, cover, and heat the grate until hot, about 5 minutes. Use a grill brush to scrape the cooking grate clean. Dip a wad of paper towels in vegetable oil; holding the wad with tongs, oil the cooking grate.

2. Place the eggplants on the grill and cook until the skins darken and wrinkle on all sides and the eggplants are uniformly soft when pressed with tongs, about 25 minutes for large globe eggplants, 20 minutes for Italian eggplants, and 15 minutes for Japanese eggplants, turning every 5 minutes and reversing the direction of the eggplants on the grill with each turn. Transfer the eggplants to a rimmed baking sheet and cool 5 minutes.

3. Set a small colander over a bowl. Trim the top and bottom off each eggplant. Slice the eggplants lengthwise and use a spoon to scoop the hot pulp from the skins and place the pulp in the colander (you should have about 2 cups packed pulp); discard the skins. Let the pulp drain 3 minutes.

4. Pulse the pulp, tahini, lemon juice, garlic, ¼ teaspoon salt, and ¼ teaspoon pepper in a food processor until coarse, about eight pulses. Season with salt and pepper to taste; transfer to a serving bowl, cover with plastic wrap pressed against the surface of the dip, and refrigerate 1 hour. Use a spoon to make a trough in the center of the dip and spoon the olive oil into it; sprinkle with the parsley and serve.

Gas-Grilled Baba Ghanoush

Turn all the burners to high and heat the grill, with the lid down, until very hot, about 15 minutes. Use a grill brush to scrape the cooking grate clean. Dip a wad of paper towels in vegetable oil; holding the wad with tongs, oil the cooking grate. Follow the recipe for Charcoal-Grilled Baba Ghanoush from step 2.

GRILLED POTATOES

WHY THIS RECIPE WORKS: Grilled potatoes are a summer classic, but we wanted to put a new spin on our grilled potatoes by adding rosemary and garlic for a heartier, more savory side. Unfortunately, we found it harder than it sounded to add garlic and rosemary flavors to plain grilled potatoes. Coating the potatoes with oil, garlic, and rosemary produced burnt, bitter garlic and charred rosemary. If we tossed the potatoes in garlic oil after cooking, the raw garlic was too harsh. We wanted potent garlic and rosemary flavors in our potatoes, without bitterness and charring.

We learned that we needed to introduce the potatoes to the garlic-oil mixture not once, but three times. Before cooking, we pierced the potatoes, skewered them, seasoned them with salt, brushed on a garlic-rosemary oil, and precooked them in the microwave. Then, before grilling, we brushed them again with the infused oil. After grilling, we tossed them with the garlic and rosemary oil yet again. We finally had it—tender grilled potatoes infused with the smoky flavor of the grill and enlivened with the bold flavors of garlic and rosemary.

SKEWERING POTATOES FOR THE GRILL

Place a potato half, cut side down, on the work surface and pierce through the center with a skewer. Repeat, holding the already-skewered potatoes for better leverage.

Charcoal-Grilled Potatoes with Garlic and Rosemary

SERVES 4

This recipe allows you to grill an entrée while the hot coals burn down in step 1. Once that item is done, start grilling the potatoes. This recipe works best with small potatoes that are about 1½ inches in diameter. If using medium potatoes, 2 to 3 inches in diameter, cut them into quarters. If the potatoes are larger than 3 inches in diameter, cut each potato into eighths. Since the potatoes are cooked in the microwave, use wooden skewers. You will need a 13 by 9-inch disposable aluminum pan for this recipe.

  Vegetable oil for cooking grate
¼ cup olive oil
9 medium garlic cloves, minced or pressed through a garlic press (about 3 tablespoons)
1 teaspoon chopped fresh rosemary leaves
  Table salt
2 pounds small red potatoes (about 18), scrubbed, halved, and skewered (see note)
  Ground black pepper
2 tablespoons chopped fresh chives

1. Light a large chimney starter filled with charcoal (about 6 quarts) and allow to burn until the coals are partially covered with a layer of ash, about 20 minutes. Open the bottom vent on the grill. Build a two-level fire by arranging two-thirds of the coals evenly over half of the grill and arranging the remaining coals over the other half. Set the cooking grate in place, cover the grill, and heat the grate until hot, about 5 minutes. Remove the lid and let the coals burn until the fire on the hotter part of the grill is medium (you can hold your hand 5 inches above the grate for 5 to 6 seconds), about 10 minutes. Use a grill brush to scrape the cooking grate clean. Dip a wad of paper towels in vegetable oil; holding the wad with tongs, oil the cooking grate.

2. Meanwhile, heat the olive oil, garlic, rosemary, and ½ teaspoon salt in a small skillet over medium heat until sizzling, about 3 minutes. Reduce the heat to medium-low and continue to cook until the garlic is light blond, about 3 minutes. Pour the mixture through a fine-mesh strainer into a small bowl; press on the solids. Measure 1 tablespoon of the solids and 1 tablespoon of the oil into a large bowl and set aside. Discard the remaining solids but reserve the remaining oil.

3. Following the photo, place the skewered potatoes in a single layer on a large microwave-safe plate and poke each potato several times with a skewer. Brush with 1 tablespoon of the strained oil and season liberally with salt. Microwave on high power until the potatoes offer slight resistance when pierced with the tip of a paring knife, about 8 minutes, turning them halfway through the cooking time. Transfer the potatoes to a baking sheet coated with 1 tablespoon of the strained oil. Brush with the remaining 1 tablespoon strained oil; season with salt and pepper to taste.

4. Place the potatoes on the hotter side of the grill. Cook, turning once, until grill marks appear, about 4 minutes. Move the potatoes to the cooler side of the grill; cover with the disposable pan and continue to cook until a paring knife slips in and out of the potatoes easily, 5 to 8 minutes longer. Remove the potatoes from the skewers and transfer to the bowl with the reserved garlic-oil mixture; add the chives and toss until thoroughly coated. Serve immediately.

Gas-Grilled Potatoes with Garlic and Rosemary

Turn all the burners to high and heat the grill, with the lid down, until very hot, about 15 minutes. Use a grill brush to scrape the cooking grate clean. Dip a wad of paper towels in vegetable oil; holding the wad with tongs, oil the cooking grate. Leave the primary burner on high and reduce the other burner(s) to medium. Follow the recipe for Charcoal-Grilled Potatoes with Garlic and Rosemary from step 2, grilling the potatoes with the lid down and omitting the disposable pan.

GRILLED CORN

WHY THIS RECIPE WORKS: In Mexico, street vendors add kick to grilled corn by slathering it with a creamy, spicy sauce. The corn takes on an irresistibly sweet, smoky, charred flavor, which is heightened by the lime juice and chili powder in the cheesy sauce. We wanted to develop our own rendition of this south-of-the-border street fare.

To cook the corn, we ditched the husks, coated the ears with oil to prevent sticking, and grilled them directly on the grate. Over a single-level fire, the corn emerged nicely smoky but insufficiently charred, so we pushed all the coals to one side to create a modified two-level fire, allowing the ears to cook closer to the coals.

The traditional base for the sauce is *crema*, a thick, soured Mexican cream. But given its spotty availability in supermarkets, we replaced the crema with a combination of mayonnaise (for richness) and sour cream (for tanginess). Most recipes call for *queso fresco* or *Cotija*, but these cheeses can be hard to find. Pecorino Romano made a good substitute. We included the usual seasonings of chopped cilantro, lime juice, minced garlic, and chili powder. To provide more depth, we added some chili powder to the oil used for coating the corn; once heated on the grill, the chili powder bloomed with a full flavor that penetrated the corn kernels.

Mexican-Style Charcoal-Grilled Corn

SERVES 6

If you can find queso fresco or Cotija, use either in place of the Pecorino Romano. If you prefer the corn spicy, add the optional cayenne pepper.

- 4 teaspoons vegetable oil plus extra for the cooking grate
- 1½ ounces Pecorino Romano, grated (about ½ cup)
- ¼ cup mayonnaise
- 3 tablespoons sour cream
- 3 tablespoons minced fresh cilantro leaves
- 4 teaspoons juice from 1 lime
- 1 medium garlic clove, minced or pressed through a garlic press (about 1 teaspoon)
- ¾ teaspoon chili powder
- ¼ teaspoon ground black pepper
- ¼ teaspoon cayenne pepper (optional; see note)
- ¼ teaspoon table salt
- 6 large ears corn, husks and silk removed

1. Light a large chimney starter filled with charcoal (about 6 quarts) and allow to burn until the coals are partially covered with a layer of ash, about 20 minutes. Build a modified two-level fire by arranging all the coals over half of the grill, leaving the other half empty. Set the cooking grate in place, cover, and heat the grate until hot, about 5 minutes. Use a grill brush to scrape the cooking grate clean. Dip a wad of paper towels in vegetable oil; holding the wad with tongs, oil the cooking grate.

2. Meanwhile, combine the cheese, mayonnaise, sour cream, cilantro, lime juice, garlic, ¼ teaspoon of the chili powder, the black pepper, and cayenne (if using) in a large bowl; set aside. In a second large bowl, combine the olive oil, salt, and remaining ½ teaspoon chili powder; add the corn and toss to coat evenly.

3. Grill the corn until lightly charred on all sides, 7 to 12 minutes total. Place the corn in the bowl with the cheese mixture; toss to coat evenly. Serve immediately.

Mexican-Style Gas-Grilled Corn

Turn all the burners to high and heat the grill, with the lid down, until very hot, about 15 minutes. Use a grill brush to scrape the cooking grate clean. Dip a wad of paper towels in vegetable oil; holding the wad with tongs, oil the cooking grate. Follow the recipe for Mexican-Style Charcoal-Grilled Corn from step 2, leaving the burners on high and cooking the corn with the lid down.

CHAPTER 18

SIDES OF PLENTY

Simple Applesauce   386

Broiled Asparagus   386

Pan-Roasted Asparagus   387

Roasted Broccoli   387

Roasted Broccoli with Garlic   388

Roasted Carrots   388

Glazed Carrots   389

Corn Fritters   389

Boston Baked Beans   390

Blanched Green Beans   391

Green Beans with Sautéed Shallots and Vermouth   391

Green Beans with Toasted Hazelnuts and Brown Butter   391

Roasted Green Beans   392

Green Beans Amandine   392

Sautéed Garlic-Lemon Spinach   393

Sautéed Baby Spinach with Almonds and Golden Raisins   394

Creamy Herbed Spinach Dip   394

Quick-Cooked Tough Greens   395

Simple Sautéed Swiss Chard   396

Smashed Potatoes   396

Classic Mashed Potatoes   397

Creamy Mashed Potatoes   398

Garlic and Olive Oil Mashed Potatoes   398

Mashed Potatoes and Root Vegetables   399

Fluffy Mashed Potatoes   400

Buttermilk Mashed Potatoes   401

Crispy Roasted Potatoes   401

Skillet-Roasted Potatoes   402

Scalloped Potatoes   403

Twice-Baked Potatoes   404

Quick Roasted Acorn Squash with Brown Sugar   405

Mashed Sweet Potatoes   405

Rice Pilaf   406

Wild Rice Pilaf with Pecans and Dried Cranberries   406

Spiced Pecans with Rum Glaze   407

SIMPLE APPLESAUCE

WHY THIS RECIPE WORKS: Applesauce should taste like apples, but all too often the tart, sweet, and fruity nuances of fresh apple flavor are overpowered by sweeteners and spices, and the sauce ends up tasting like bad pie filling. The texture, too, can vary from dry and chunky to loose and thin. We wanted a smooth, thick sauce that showcases fresh apple flavor without too much sweetness or spice—the perfect partner to pork chops or as a snack.

The first step was to find the right variety of apple. We began by gathering 18 varieties and making each into applesauce. We found that Jonagold, Jonathan, Pink Lady, and Macoun varieties all produce a sauce with a pleasing balance of tart and sweet. We tried blending varieties in combination with each other, but concluded that single-variety sauces had purer, stronger character. Cooking the apples with their skins on saved us the step of peeling and enhanced the flavor of the sauce. Processing the cooked apples through a food mill, not a food processor or blender, removed the skins and produced a sauce with the silky-smooth, thick texture we were after. Adding a little water, sugar, and a pinch of salt—and no spices—resulted in a perfectly sweetened sauce that tasted first and foremost of apples.

Simple Applesauce

MAKES ABOUT 3½ CUPS

If you do not own a food mill or prefer applesauce with a coarse texture, peel the apples before coring and cutting them and, after cooking, mash them against the side of the pot with a wooden spoon or against the bottom of the pot with a potato masher. Applesauce made with out-of-season apples may be somewhat drier than sauce made with peak-season apples, so it's likely that in step 2 of the recipe you will need to add more water to adjust the texture. If you double the recipe, the apples will need 10 to 15 minutes of extra cooking time.

- 4 pounds apples (about 10 medium), preferably Jonagold, Pink Lady, Jonathan, or Macoun, unpeeled, cored, and cut into rough 1½-inch pieces (see note)
- 1 cup water, plus more as needed
- ¼ cup sugar, plus more to taste
  Pinch table salt

1. Toss the apples, water, sugar, and salt in a large Dutch oven. Cover the pot and cook the apples over medium-high heat until they begin to break down, 15 to 20 minutes, checking and stirring occasionally with a wooden spoon to break up any large chunks.

2. Process the cooked apples through a food mill fitted with the medium disk. Season with extra sugar to taste or add water to adjust the consistency as desired. Serve hot, warm, at room temperature, or chilled.

BROILED ASPARAGUS

WHY THIS RECIPE WORKS: Broiling can intensify the flavor of asparagus, turning it sweet and nutty. But getting the asparagus to cook through evenly can be tricky. We wanted a foolproof broiling method for turning out browned, tender spears every time.

To start, we found that with thicker asparagus, the exterior began to char before the interior of the spears became fully tender. When we used thinner spears, however, the interior was tender by the time the exterior was browned. Keeping the spears about four inches away from the broiling element allowed them to caramelize properly without charring. To encourage browning, we tossed the asparagus with olive oil before broiling. Shaking the pan with the asparagus as it cooked ensured that the spears cooked evenly. The intense dry heat of the broiler concentrated the flavor of the asparagus, and the exterior caramelization made the spears especially sweet.

Broiled Asparagus

SERVES 6

Broilers vary significantly in intensity, thus the wide range of cooking times in this recipe. Choose asparagus no thicker than ½ inch for this recipe.

- 2 pounds thin asparagus (about 2 bunches), tough ends trimmed (see page 200) (see note)
- 1 tablespoon olive oil
  Table salt and ground black pepper

Adjust an oven rack to the highest position (about 4 inches from the heating element) and heat the broiler. Toss the asparagus with the oil and salt and pepper to taste, then lay the spears in a single layer on a rimmed baking sheet. Broil, shaking the pan halfway through cooking to turn the spears, until the asparagus is tender and lightly browned, 6 to 10 minutes. Serve hot or warm.

PAN-ROASTED ASPARAGUS

WHY THIS RECIPE WORKS: Recipes for pan-roasted asparagus promise ease and flavor, but the results are usually disappointing: limp, greasy, and shriveled spears. We wanted a simple stovetop method that would deliver crisp, nicely browned spears.

We quickly learned to choose thick spears because thinner spears overcooked too quickly. Taking a cue from restaurant chefs who blanch asparagus first, we developed a method to lightly steam and then brown the asparagus in the same skillet. For optimal flavor and browning, we used both olive oil and butter. Positioning half the spears in one direction and the other half in the opposite direction ensured a better fit in the pan. Browning just one side of the asparagus provided a contrast in texture and guaranteed that the asparagus remained firm and tender, but never limp.

Pan-Roasted Asparagus

SERVES 3 TO 4

This recipe works best with asparagus that is at least ½ inch thick near the base. If using thinner spears, reduce the covered cooking time to 3 minutes and the uncovered cooking time to 5 minutes. Do not use pencil-thin asparagus; it cannot withstand the heat and overcooks too easily.

- 1 tablespoon olive oil
- 1 tablespoon unsalted butter
- 2 pounds thick asparagus (about 2 bunches), tough ends trimmed (see page 200) (see note)
  Table salt and ground black pepper
- ½ lemon (optional)

1. Heat the oil and butter in a 12-inch skillet over medium-high heat. When the butter has melted, add half of the asparagus to the skillet with the tips pointed in one direction; add the remaining asparagus with the tips pointed in the opposite direction. Using tongs, distribute the spears in an even layer (the spears will not quite fit into a single layer); cover and cook until the asparagus is bright green and still crisp, about 5 minutes.

2. Uncover and increase the heat to high; season the asparagus with salt and pepper to taste. Cook until the spears are tender and well browned along one side, 5 to 7 minutes, using the tongs to occasionally move the spears from the center of the pan to the edge of the pan to ensure all are browned. Transfer the asparagus to a dish, season with salt and pepper to taste, and squeeze the lemon half (if using) over the spears. Serve.

ROASTED BROCCOLI

WHY THIS RECIPE WORKS: Roasting can concentrate flavor to turn dull vegetables into something great, but roasting broccoli usually makes for spotty browning and charred, bitter florets. We wanted to figure out how to roast broccoli so that it turned out perfectly browned and deeply flavorful every time.

To ensure that the broccoli would brown evenly, we cut the crown into uniform wedges that lay flat on the baking sheet, increasing contact with the pan. To promote even cooking of the stem, we sliced away the exterior and cut the stalk into rectangular pieces slightly smaller than the more delicate wedges. After trial and error, we discovered that preheating the baking sheet helped the broccoli cook faster, crisping but not charring the florets, while a very hot oven delivered the best browning. Sprinkling a little sugar over the broccoli along with the salt and pepper helped it brown even more deeply. We finally had roasted broccoli with crispy-tipped florets and sweet, browned stems.

Roasted Broccoli

SERVES 4

It is important to trim away the outer peel from the broccoli stalks; otherwise they will turn tough when cooked.

1¾ **pounds broccoli (about 1 large bunch)**

3 **tablespoons extra-virgin olive oil**

½ **teaspoon table salt**

½ **teaspoon sugar**

Ground black pepper

Lemon wedges, for serving

1. Adjust an oven rack to the lowest position, place a large rimmed baking sheet on the rack, and heat the oven to 500 degrees. Cut the broccoli at the juncture of the florets and stems; remove the outer peel from the stalk. Cut the stalk into 2 to 3-inch lengths and each length into ½-inch-thick pieces. Cut the crowns into four wedges (if 3 to 4 inches in diameter) or six wedges (if 4 to 5 inches in diameter). Place the broccoli in a large bowl; drizzle with the oil and toss well until evenly coated. Season with the salt, sugar, and pepper to taste and toss to combine.

2. Carefully remove the baking sheet from the oven. Working quickly, transfer the broccoli to the baking sheet and spread into an even layer, placing the flat sides down. Return the baking sheet to the oven and roast until the stalks are well browned and tender and the florets are lightly browned, 9 to 11 minutes. Transfer to a dish and serve with the lemon wedges.

Roasted Broccoli with Garlic

Follow the recipe for Roasted Broccoli, adding 1 garlic clove, minced or pressed through a garlic press, to the oil before drizzling it over the broccoli in step 1.

ROASTED CARROTS

WHY THIS RECIPE WORKS: Roasted carrots frequently end up either undercooked, with a bitter, hard center or, at the other end of the spectrum, are subjected to such intense heat that they become wan, limp, and utterly unpalatable. We wanted to release the sweetness from the carrots, yielding a caramelized exterior and a creamy, tender interior.

First we settled on prepared baby carrots for our dish, because they require no cleaning or cutting. The flavor of the carrots needed a little help; plain olive oil with a little salt worked best—it neither masked the carrots' flavor nor changed their texture. Roasting the carrots

uncovered at a high temperature created the caramelized exterior we were after and using the bottom of a broiler pan prevented them from burning. We were now able to produce perfectly cooked, deeply flavorful roasted carrots in just 20 minutes.

Roasted Carrots

SERVES 8

When buying carrots, inspect the bag carefully for pockets of water. Bags taken from the top of the super-market's pile are often waterlogged. This not only makes carrots mealy, it also prevents them from caramelizing properly.

2 **pounds baby carrots (two 16-ounce bags; see note)**

2 **tablespoons olive oil**

½ **teaspoon table salt**

Adjust an oven rack to the middle position and heat the oven to 475 degrees. Toss the carrots, oil, and salt in a broiler pan bottom. Spread into a single layer and roast for 12 minutes. Shake the pan to toss the carrots; continue roasting about 8 minutes longer, shaking the pan twice more, until the carrots are browned and tender. Serve.

GLAZED CARROTS

WHY THIS RECIPE WORKS: Glazing is probably the most popular way to prepare carrots, but they often turn out saccharine, with a limp and soggy or undercooked and fibrous texture. We wanted fully tender, well-seasoned carrots with a glossy and clingy—yet modest—glaze.

Peeling regular bagged carrots and cutting them on the bias yielded uniform ovals that cooked evenly. We cooked and glazed the carrots in one single operation, starting by cooking the sliced carrots in a covered skillet with chicken broth, salt, and sugar. After the carrots were cooked until almost tender, we removed the lid and turned up the heat to reduce the liquid. Finally, a little butter and a bit more sugar added to the skillet resulted in a pale amber glaze with light caramel flavor. A sprinkle of fresh lemon juice gave the dish sparkle, and a pinch of freshly ground black pepper provided depth.

Glazed Carrots

SERVES 4

We like to use a nonstick skillet here for easy cleanup, but any 12-inch skillet with a cover will work.

- 1 **pound carrots (about 6 medium), peeled and sliced ¼ inch thick on the bias**
- ½ **cup low-sodium chicken broth**
- 3 **tablespoons sugar**
- ½ **teaspoon table salt**
- 1 **tablespoon unsalted butter, cut into 4 pieces**
- 2 **teaspoons juice from 1 lemon**
  Ground black pepper

1. Bring the carrots, broth, 1 tablespoon of the sugar, and the salt to a boil in a 12-inch nonstick skillet, covered, over medium-high heat. Reduce the heat to medium and simmer, stirring occasionally, until the carrots are almost tender when poked with the tip of a paring knife, about 5 minutes. Uncover, increase the heat to high, and simmer rapidly, stirring occasionally, until the liquid is reduced to about 2 tablespoons, 1 to 2 minutes.

2. Add the butter and remaining 2 tablespoons sugar to the skillet. Toss the carrots to coat and cook, stirring frequently, until the carrots are completely tender and the glaze is light gold, about 3 minutes. Off the heat, add the lemon juice and toss to coat. Transfer the carrots to a dish, scraping the glaze from the pan into the dish. Season with pepper to taste and serve.

CORN FRITTERS

WHY THIS RECIPE WORKS: Good corn fritters should be light—creamy in the middle and crisp on the outside. This is rarely the case, however; most corn fritters have little corn flavor and cook up dense and greasy. We wanted to make perfect corn fritters—light, crisp, and packed with fresh corn flavor.

We found that combining whole corn kernels and grated kernels worked best for visual appeal, textural contrast, and fullest corn flavor. Running the back of a knife over the cobs from which the corn had been grated helped us extract the flavorful pulp. Equal amounts of flour and cornmeal bound the mixture together without making the fritters heavy and kept the corn flavor strong. A bit of heavy cream added welcome richness. For pan-frying the cakes, vegetable oil was the cooking medium of choice for its high smoke point and neutral flavor, which didn't overpower the corn. Keeping the oil hot helped the fritters brown quickly.

Corn Fritters

MAKES TWELVE 2-INCH FRITTERS

Serve these fritters with hot sauce, salsa, or even maple syrup.

- 4 **ears corn, husks and silk removed**
- 1 **large egg, lightly beaten**
- 3 **tablespoons unbleached all-purpose flour**
- 3 **tablespoons cornmeal**
- 2 **tablespoons heavy cream**
- 1 **small shallot, minced (about 1 tablespoon)**
- ½ **teaspoon table salt**
  Pinch cayenne pepper
- ¼ **cup vegetable oil, plus more as needed**

1. Stand the corn upright inside a large bowl and, using a paring knife, carefully cut the kernels from 2 ears of the corn; you should have about 1 cup. Transfer the kernels to a medium bowl. Use the back of a butter knife to scrape off any pulp remaining on the cobs and transfer it to the bowl. Grate the kernels from the remaining 2 ears of corn on the large holes of a box grater, then firmly scrape off any pulp remaining on the cobs with the back of a butter knife; you should have a generous cup of kernels and pulp. Transfer the grated kernels and pulp to the bowl with the cut kernels.

2. Mix the egg, flour, cornmeal, cream, shallot, salt, and cayenne into the corn mixture to form a thick batter.

3. Heat the oil in a 12-inch skillet over medium-high heat until almost smoking, about 2 minutes. Drop heaping tablespoons of batter into the oil (half the batter, or six fritters, should fit into the pan at once). Fry until golden brown, about 1 minute. Using a thin metal spatula, turn the fritters and fry until the second side is golden brown, about 1 minute longer. Transfer the fritters to a paper towel–lined plate. Repeat with the remaining batter, adding more oil to the skillet if necessary. Serve.

BOSTON BAKED BEANS

WHY THIS RECIPE WORKS: Boston baked beans are both sweet and savory, a unique combination of the simplest ingredients, unified and refined during a long simmer. Unfortunately, recipes with lengthy lists of untraditional ingredients and mushy beans abound. We wanted tender beans in a thick, smoky, slightly sweet sauce.

For depth of flavor, we started by browning a combination of salt pork and bacon in a Dutch oven. Small white beans were preferred for their creamy texture and ability to remain intact during the long simmer. Mild molasses provided just the right amount of sweetness, while brown mustard and cider vinegar added welcome notes of spice and tanginess. We removed the lid for the last hour of cooking to reduce the sauce to a syrupy, intensified consistency that perfectly napped the beans.

Boston Baked Beans

SERVES 4 TO 6

The beans can be made ahead. After cooking, cool them to room temperature and refrigerate in an airtight container for up to 4 days.

- **4** ounces salt pork, trimmed of rind and cut into ½-inch cubes
- **2** ounces (about 2 slices) bacon, cut into ¼-inch pieces
- **1** medium onion, minced
- **9** cups water
- **1** pound (2 cups) dried small white beans, rinsed and picked over
- **½** cup plus 1 tablespoon mild molasses
- **1½** tablespoons prepared brown mustard, such as Gulden's
  Table salt
- **1** teaspoon cider vinegar
  Ground black pepper

1. Adjust an oven rack to the lower-middle position and heat the oven to 300 degrees. Place the salt pork and bacon in a large Dutch oven; cook over medium heat, stirring occasionally, until lightly browned and most of the fat is rendered, about 7 minutes. Add the onion and continue to cook, stirring occasionally, until the onion is softened, 5 to 7 minutes. Add the water, beans, ½ cup of the molasses, the mustard, and 1¼ teaspoons salt; increase the heat to medium-high and bring to a boil. Cover the pot and place in the oven.

2. Bake until the beans are tender, about 4 hours, stirring once after 2 hours. Remove the lid and continue to bake until the liquid has thickened to a syrupy consistency, 1 to 1½ hours longer. Remove the beans from the oven; stir in the remaining 1 tablespoon molasses, the vinegar, and salt and pepper to taste. Serve.

BLANCHED GREEN BEANS

WHY THIS RECIPE WORKS: Most vegetable side dishes require last-minute preparation, but green beans are an ideal side dish that can be prepared largely beforehand without sacrificing texture or flavor. We wanted a foolproof way of cooking beans ahead of time and then simply reheating and seasoning them just before serving.

The easiest way to do this was to blanch the beans in salted water, shock them in ice water to stop the cooking process, and then towel-dry and refrigerate them until needed—a process that could be completed up to three days before serving. To serve, we reheated the beans in a skillet with a little water and flavored them with a butter sauce. The small amount of water came to a boil quickly and evaporated almost completely, helping to heat the beans in just a minute or two for a quick and flavorful side dish.

Blanched Green Beans

SERVES 4

Blanched and cooled beans can be refrigerated in a zipper-lock bag for up to 3 days. To blanch, dress, and serve the beans without holding them first, increase the blanching time to 5 to 6 minutes and don't bother shocking them in ice water. Instead, quickly arrange the warm, drained beans on a serving platter and top them with the sauce you've prepared as the beans blanch (recipes follow).

- 1 teaspoon table salt
- 1 pound green beans, trimmed

Bring 2½ quarts water to a boil in a large saucepan over high heat; add the salt and green beans, return to a boil, and cook until the beans are bright green and crisptender, 3 to 4 minutes. Drain the beans and transfer them immediately to a large bowl filled with ice water. When the beans have cooled to room temperature, drain again and dry thoroughly with paper towels. Set aside (or refrigerate) until needed.

Green Beans with Sautéed Shallots and Vermouth

- 4 tablespoons (½ stick) unsalted butter
- 4 large shallots, sliced thin (about 1 cup)
- 1 recipe Blanched Green Beans
  Table salt and ground black pepper
- 2 tablespoons dry vermouth

1. Melt 2 tablespoons of the butter in a small skillet over medium heat. Add the shallots and cook, stirring frequently, until golden brown, fragrant, and just crisp around the edges, about 10 minutes. Set the skillet aside, off the heat.

2. Heat ¼ cup water and the beans in a 12-inch skillet over high heat; cook, tossing frequently, until warmed through, 1 to 2 minutes. Season with salt and pepper to taste and arrange on a warm platter.

3. Meanwhile, return the skillet with the shallots to high heat, stir in the vermouth, and bring to a simmer. Whisk in the remaining 2 tablespoons butter, 1 tablespoon at a time, and season with salt and pepper to taste. Top the beans with the shallots and sauce and serve.

Green Beans with Toasted Hazelnuts and Brown Butter

Use a light-colored traditional saucepan instead of a darker nonstick saucepan for this recipe to easily monitor the butter's browning.

- 4 tablespoons (½ stick) unsalted butter
- ½ cup hazelnuts, toasted and chopped fine
  Table salt and ground black pepper
- 1 recipe Blanched Green Beans

1. Melt the butter in a small saucepan over medium heat and cook, swirling frequently, until brown and fragrant, 4 to 5 minutes. Add the hazelnuts and cook, stirring constantly, until fragrant, about 1 minute. Season with salt and pepper to taste.

2. Meanwhile, heat ¼ cup water and the beans in a 12-inch skillet over high heat; cook, tossing frequently, until warmed through, 1 to 2 minutes. Season with salt and pepper to taste and arrange on a warm platter. Top the beans with the hazelnuts and butter and serve.

ROASTED GREEN BEANS

WHY THIS RECIPE WORKS: Mature supermarket green beans are often tough and dull, needing special treatment to become tender and flavorful. Braising works, but the stovetop can get awfully crowded as dinnertime approaches. Roasting is a great option for many vegetables, and we wanted to find out if this technique could help transform older green beans, giving them a flavor comparable to sweet, fresh-picked beans.

A remarkably simple test produced outstanding results: Beans roasted in a 450-degree oven with only oil, salt, and pepper transformed aged specimens into deeply caramelized, full-flavored beans. Just 20 minutes of roasting reversed the aging process (converting starch back to sugar) and encouraged flavorful browning. Just 1 tablespoon of oil was enough to lend flavor and moisture without making the beans greasy. Lining the pan with foil prevented scorching and made for easy cleanup.

Roasted Green Beans
SERVES 4

Lining the baking sheet with foil makes for easy cleanup.

- 1 pound green beans, trimmed
- 1 tablespoon olive oil
  Table salt and ground black pepper

1. Adjust an oven rack to the middle position and heat the oven to 450 degrees. Line a large rimmed baking sheet with foil; spread the beans on the baking sheet. Drizzle with the oil; using your hands, toss to coat evenly. Sprinkle with ½ teaspoon salt, toss to coat, and distribute in an even layer. Roast for 10 minutes.

2. Remove the baking sheet from the oven. Using tongs, redistribute the beans. Continue roasting until the beans

are dark golden brown in spots and have started to shrivel, 10 to 12 minutes longer. Season with salt and pepper to taste and serve.

GREEN BEANS AMANDINE

WHY THIS RECIPE WORKS: A simple dish of green beans tossed with toasted almonds and a light lemon-butter sauce, green beans amandine is refined yet not intimidating. Unfortunately, recipes too often yield limp beans swimming in pools of overly acidic sauce, with soft, pale almonds thrown on as an afterthought. We wanted to revive this side dish with tender green beans, crisp almonds, and a balanced sauce.

For maximum flavor, we toasted the almonds then added some butter to the skillet and allowed it to brown for further nuttiness. Adding some lemon juice off the heat brightened our sauce considerably. After steaming the green beans in a little water in a covered skillet until they were crisp-tender, we tossed them with our sauce for a simple, flavorful take on this classic side.

Green Beans Amandine
SERVES 8

Use a light-colored traditional skillet instead of a darker nonstick skillet for this recipe to easily monitor the butter's browning.

- ⅓ cup sliced almonds
- 3 tablespoons unsalted butter, cut into pieces
- 2 teaspoons juice from 1 lemon
- 2 pounds green beans, trimmed
  Table salt

1. Toast the almonds in a large skillet over medium-low heat, stirring often, until just golden, about 6 minutes. Add the butter and cook, stirring constantly, until the butter is golden brown and has a nutty aroma, about 3 minutes. Transfer the almond mixture to a bowl and stir in the lemon juice.

2. Add the beans, ½ cup water, and ½ teaspoon salt to the now-empty skillet. Cover and cook over medium-low heat, stirring occasionally, until the beans are nearly tender, 8 to 10 minutes. Remove the lid and cook over medium-high heat until the liquid evaporates, 3 to 5 minutes. Off the heat, add the reserved almond mixture to the skillet and toss to combine. Season with salt to taste and serve.

SPINACH WITH GARLIC AND LEMON

WHY THIS RECIPE WORKS: Overcooked spinach, bitter burnt garlic, and pallid lemon flavor are all too often the hallmarks of this simple side dish. Instead, we sought tender sautéed spinach, seasoned with a perfect balance of garlic and lemon.

We preferred the hearty flavor and texture of curly-leaf spinach in this classic dish. We cooked the spinach in extra-virgin olive oil with slivered garlic (lightly browned in the pan before the spinach was added), which gave the spinach a sweet nuttiness. Once the spinach was cooked, we used tongs to squeeze the spinach in a colander over the sink to get rid of all the excess moisture. As for seasoning, a squeeze of lemon juice and some grated lemon zest, as well as a pinch of red pepper flakes gave the spinach some gentle heat. And finally, a drizzle of extra-virgin olive oil boosted the fruitiness of the dish.

Sautéed Garlic-Lemon Spinach
SERVES 4

The amount of spinach may seem excessive, but the spinach wilts considerably with cooking. We like to use a salad spinner to wash and dry the spinach.

- 2   tablespoons extra-virgin olive oil, plus 1 teaspoon for drizzling
- 4   medium garlic cloves, sliced thin crosswise (about 4 teaspoons)
- 3   (10-ounce) bags curly-leaf spinach, stems removed, leaves washed and dried
-      Table salt
-      Pinch red pepper flakes
- ½   teaspoon grated zest plus 2 teaspoons juice from 1 lemon

1. Heat 2 tablespoons of the oil and the garlic in a large Dutch oven over medium-high heat until shimmering; cook until the garlic is light golden brown, shaking the pan back and forth when the garlic begins to sizzle, about 3 minutes. Add the spinach by the handful, using tongs to stir and coat the spinach with the oil.

2. Once all the spinach is added, sprinkle ¼ teaspoon salt, the red pepper flakes, and lemon zest over the top and continue stirring with the tongs until the spinach is uniformly wilted and glossy, about 2 minutes. Using the tongs, transfer the spinach to a colander set in a sink and gently squeeze the spinach with the tongs to release excess liquid. Return the spinach to the Dutch oven; sprinkle with the lemon juice and stir to coat. Drizzle with the remaining 1 teaspoon olive oil and season with salt to taste. Serve.

SAUTÉED BABY SPINACH

WHY THIS RECIPE WORKS: Baby spinach is convenient—no stems to remove or grit to rinse out—but cooking often turns this tender green into a watery, mushy mess. We were determined to find a method for cooking baby spinach that would give us a worthwhile side dish.

Wilting, blanching, and steaming proved to be unsuccessful in removing excess water from baby spinach, but parcooking the spinach in the microwave with a little water added to the bowl worked great. After three minutes, the spinach had softened and shrunk to half its size, thanks to the release of a great deal of liquid. But there was still more water to remove. We found that pressing the spinach against the colander before roughly chopping it on a cutting board and then pressing it again removed any remaining excess liquid. The spinach was now tender, sweet, and ready to be combined with complementary ingredients. Pairing almonds and raisins introduced bold flavors and textures that enlivened this quick-cooking green.

Sautéed Baby Spinach with Almonds and Golden Raisins

SERVES 4

If you don't have a microwave-safe bowl large enough to accommodate the entire amount of spinach, cook it in a smaller bowl in two batches. Reduce the amount of water to 2 tablespoons per batch and cook each batch for about 1½ minutes.

- 3 (6-ounce) bags baby spinach (about 18 cups)
- ¼ cup water
- 2 tablespoons extra-virgin olive oil, plus 2 teaspoons for drizzling
- 4 medium garlic cloves, sliced thin crosswise (about 4 teaspoons)
- ¼ teaspoon red pepper flakes
- ½ cup golden raisins
  Table salt
- 2 teaspoons sherry vinegar
- ⅓ cup slivered almonds, toasted

1. Place the spinach and water in a large microwave-safe bowl. Cover the bowl with a large microwave-safe dinner plate (the plate should completely cover the bowl and not rest on the spinach). Microwave on high power until the spinach is wilted and decreased in volume by half, 3 to 4 minutes. Using potholders, remove the bowl from the microwave and keep covered for 1 minute. Carefully remove the plate and transfer the spinach to a colander set in the sink. Using the back of a rubber spatula, gently press the spinach against the colander to release excess liquid. Transfer the spinach to a cutting board and roughly chop. Return to the colander and press a second time.

2. Heat 2 tablespoons of the oil, the garlic, red pepper flakes, and raisins in a 10-inch skillet over medium-high heat. Cook, stirring constantly, until the garlic is light golden brown and beginning to sizzle, 3 to 6 minutes. Add the spinach to the skillet, using tongs to stir and coat with the oil. Sprinkle with ¼ teaspoon salt and continue stirring with the tongs until the spinach is uniformly wilted and glossy, about 2 minutes. Sprinkle with the vinegar and almonds; stir to combine. Drizzle with the remaining 2 teaspoons oil and season with salt to taste. Serve.

CREAMY HERBED SPINACH DIP

WHY THIS RECIPE WORKS: Spinach dip made with sour cream and soup mixes are flat, overly salty, and stale tasting. We wanted to ditch the mix and create a rich, thick, and creamy spinach dip brimming with big, bold flavors.

We were surprised to discover that frozen spinach actually made a better-tasting dip with a vibrant, more intense flavor than one made with fresh spinach. We used a food processor to chop the spinach and then enriched it with sour cream, mayonnaise, and a mixture of fresh herbs and seasonings. The only problem was that our dip, which took just about 15 minutes to make, took almost two hours to chill. Fortunately the solution turned out to be a simple one. Instead of thawing the spinach completely, we only partially thawed it, allowing the chunks of icy spinach to thoroughly cool the dip as they broke down in the food processor. This dip is fresh-tasting, quick to make, and ready to serve immediately.

Creamy Herbed Spinach Dip

MAKES ABOUT 1½ CUPS

Partial thawing of the spinach produces a cold dip that can be served without further chilling. Instead of microwaving, the frozen spinach can also be thawed at room temperature for 1½ hours, then squeezed of excess liquid. The garlic must be minced or pressed before going into the food processor; otherwise, the dip will contain large chunks of garlic.

- 1 (10-ounce) box frozen chopped spinach
- ½ cup sour cream
- ½ cup mayonnaise
- 3 scallions, white parts only, sliced thin
- ½ cup packed fresh parsley leaves
- 1 tablespoon minced fresh dill
- 1 small garlic clove, minced or pressed through a garlic press (about ½ teaspoon) (see note)
- ½ teaspoon table salt
- ¼ teaspoon ground black pepper
- ¼ teaspoon hot sauce
- ½ red bell pepper, chopped fine

1. Thaw the spinach in a microwave for 3 minutes at 40 percent power. (The edges should be thawed but not warm; the center should be soft enough to be broken into icy chunks.) Squeeze the partially frozen spinach to remove excess water.

2. Process the spinach, sour cream, mayonnaise, scallions, parsley, dill, garlic, salt, pepper, and hot sauce in a food processor until smooth and creamy, about 30 seconds. Transfer the mixture to a bowl and stir in the bell pepper; serve. (The dip can be covered with plastic wrap and refrigerated for up to 2 days.)

QUICK-COOKED TOUGH GREENS

WHY THIS RECIPE WORKS: Unlike tender greens, tougher greens such as kale, mustard, turnip, and collard greens don't have enough moisture to be wilted in a hot pan; they'll simply scorch before they wilt. Their flavor is much more assertive, even peppery in some cases, and can be overwhelming. We wanted a technique for cooking Southern-style greens that would mellow their assertive bite and render them tender—while still retaining just the right amount of chew.

Because they are relatively dry, these greens required the addition of some liquid as they cooked. Steaming the greens produced a texture tasters liked, but it didn't help tame their bitter flavor. Shallow blanching removed enough bitterness to make these assertive greens palatable, but didn't rob them of their character. After blanching the greens, we drained and then briefly cooked them with a little garlic and red pepper for a spicy kick. To prevent them from becoming too dry, we added a little chicken broth to the pan for moisture and added flavor.

Quick-Cooked Tough Greens
SERVES 4

Shallow-blanched greens should be shocked in cold water to stop the cooking process, drained, and then braised. Shocked and drained greens can be held for up to an hour before being braised.

Table salt
2 pounds assertive greens, such as kale, collards, or mustard, stemmed, washed in several changes of cold water, and chopped coarse
3 tablespoons extra-virgin olive oil
3 medium garlic cloves, sliced thin crosswise (about 4 teaspoons)
Red pepper flakes
⅓–½ cup low-sodium chicken broth
Lemon wedges, for serving

1. Bring 2 quarts water to a boil in a large pot. Add 1½ teaspoons salt and the greens and stir until wilted, 1 to 2 minutes. Cover and cook until the greens are just tender, about 7 minutes. Drain the greens and pour them into a large bowl filled with ice water. Working with a handful of greens at a time, thoroughly squeeze them dry.

2. Heat the oil, garlic, and ¼ teaspoon red pepper flakes in a large skillet over medium heat until the garlic starts to sizzle, about 1 minute. Add the greens and toss to coat with the oil. Add ⅓ cup of the broth, cover, and cook over medium-high heat, adding more broth if necessary, until the greens are tender and juicy and most of the broth has been absorbed, about 5 minutes. Season with salt and additional red pepper flakes to taste. Serve with the lemon wedges.

SAUTÉED SWISS CHARD

WHY THIS RECIPE WORKS: Swiss chard, like spinach, is delicate and has an earthy flavor that mellows once cooked. A thick stalk runs through the center of each leaf, however, and can make cooking the greens a challenge. We set out to find a simple method for preparing Swiss chard—one that would yield tender, evenly cooked greens (both stalks and leaves) with deep flavor.

After testing blanching, steaming, microwaving, and wilting, the simplest, most straightforward method of cooking proved to be wilting our greens on the stovetop. First, however, we separated the leaves from the stalks and tossed the stalks, wet from washing, into the pan first. We then added garlic for flavor, then added the leaves, covered the pan, and cooked, stirring occasionally, until the greens were wilted by the steam created by their own liquid. We then found that we got even better results when combining this technique with sautéing. To do this, we heated oil in the pan, then proceeded as before, adding the stalks before the leaves. Once the leaves wilted, we removed the lid, seasoned with salt and pepper, and sautéed the greens over high heat until all the liquid evaporated.

Simple Sautéed Swiss Chard

SERVES 4

A thick stalk runs through each Swiss chard leaf, so the leaf must be cut away from it.

- 3 tablespoons extra-virgin olive oil
- 2 pounds Swiss chard, stemmed, washed in several changes of cold water, stalks chopped medium and leaves chopped coarse
- 2 medium garlic cloves, minced or pressed through a garlic press (about 2 teaspoons)
  Table salt and ground black pepper
  Lemon wedges, for serving

1. Heat the oil in a large Dutch oven over medium heat until shimmering. Add the chard stalks and cook, stirring occasionally, until just tender, about 5 minutes. Add the garlic and cook until fragrant, about 30 seconds. Add the chard leaves, cover, increase the heat to medium-high, and cook, stirring occasionally, until the greens completely wilt, 2 to 3 minutes.

2. Uncover and season with salt and pepper to taste. Cook over high heat until the liquid evaporates, about 2 minutes. Serve with the lemon wedges.

SMASHED POTATOES

WHY THIS RECIPE WORKS: Bold flavors and a rustic, chunky texture make smashed potatoes a satisfying side dish, one that pairs well with everything from grilled steak to roast chicken. But good smashed potatoes are hard to find. We were after a good contrast of textures, with chunky potatoes and skins bound by a rich, creamy puree.

Testing revealed that low-starch, high-moisture red potatoes were the best choice for this dish. Their compact structure held up well under pressure, maintaining its integrity. The thin skins were pleasantly tender and paired nicely with the chunky potatoes. Cooked whole in salted water with a bay leaf, the potatoes became lightly

seasoned while also retaining their naturally creamy texture, as the skins protected the potato flesh from the water. For the best chunky texture, we smashed the potatoes with a rubber spatula or the back of a wooden spoon. Cream cheese and butter lent tang, richness, and body to the dish, and stirring in a little of the potato cooking water added enough moisture to the smash to give it a unified and creamy consistency without diluting the potato flavor. Seasoned with salt, freshly ground black pepper, and a sprinkling of chopped chives for bright flavor and color, these potatoes are a quick, no-fuss side dish to complement any casual dinner.

Smashed Potatoes

SERVES 4

Try to get potatoes of equal size; if that's not possible, test the larger potatoes for doneness (use a paring knife). If only large potatoes are available, increase the cooking time by about 10 minutes.

- 2 pounds red potatoes (about 12 small), scrubbed
  Table salt
- 1 bay leaf
- 4 tablespoons (½ stick) unsalted butter, melted
- 4 ounces cream cheese, at room temperature
- 3 tablespoons minced fresh chives (optional)
  Ground black pepper

1. Place the potatoes in a large saucepan and add cold water to cover by 1 inch; add 1 teaspoon salt and the bay leaf. Bring to a boil over high heat, then reduce the heat to medium-low and simmer gently until a paring knife can be inserted into the potatoes with no resistance, 35 to 45 minutes. Reserve ½ cup of the cooking water, then drain the potatoes. Return the potatoes to the pot, discard the bay leaf, and allow the potatoes to stand in the pot, uncovered, until the surfaces are dry, about 5 minutes.

2. While the potatoes dry, whisk the melted butter and softened cream cheese in a medium bowl until smooth and fully incorporated. Add ¼ cup of the reserved cooking water, the chives (if using), ½ teaspoon pepper, and ½ teaspoon salt. Using a rubber spatula or the back of a wooden spoon, smash the potatoes just enough to break the skins. Fold in the butter–cream cheese mixture until most of the liquid has been absorbed and chunks of potatoes remain. Add more cooking water as needed, 1 tablespoon at a time, until the potatoes are slightly looser than desired (the potatoes will thicken slightly with standing). Season with salt and pepper to taste and serve.

CLASSIC MASHED POTATOES

WHY THIS RECIPE WORKS: Many people would never consider consulting a recipe when making mashed potatoes, instead adding chunks of butter and spurts of cream until their conscience tells them to stop. Little wonder then that mashed potatoes made this way are consistent only in their mediocrity. We wanted mashed potatoes that were perfectly smooth and creamy, with great potato flavor and plenty of buttery richness every time.

We began by selecting russet potatoes for their high starch content. Through trial and error, we learned to boil them whole and unpeeled—this method yielded mashed potatoes that were rich, earthy, and sweet. We used a food mill or ricer for the smoothest texture imaginable, but a potato masher can be used if you prefer your potatoes a little chunky. For smooth, velvety potatoes, we added melted butter first and then half-and-half. Melting, rather than merely softening, the butter enables it to coat the starch molecules quickly and easily, so the potatoes turn out creamy and light.

Classic Mashed Potatoes

SERVES 4

Russet potatoes make fluffier mashed potatoes, but Yukon Golds have an appealing buttery flavor and can be used. This recipe yields smooth mashed potatoes. If you don't mind lumps, use a potato masher.

- 2   pounds russet potatoes (about 4 medium), scrubbed (see note)
- 8   tablespoons (1 stick) unsalted butter, melted
- 1   cup half-and-half, warmed
- 1½ teaspoons table salt
      Ground black pepper

1. Place the potatoes in a large saucepan and add cold water to cover by 1 inch. Bring to a boil over high heat, reduce the heat to medium-low, and simmer until the potatoes are just tender when pricked with a fork, 20 to 30 minutes. Drain the potatoes.

2. Set a ricer or food mill over the now-empty saucepan. Using a potholder (to hold the potatoes) and a paring knife, peel the skins from the potatoes. Working in batches, cut the peeled potatoes into large chunks and press or mill into the saucepan.

3. Stir in the butter until incorporated. Gently whisk in the half-and-half, and season with the salt and pepper to taste. Serve.

ULTIMATE CREAMY MASHED POTATOES

WHY THIS RECIPE WORKS: Sometimes we want a luxurious mash, one that is silky smooth and loaded with cream and butter. But there's a fine line between creamy and gluey. We wanted lush, creamy mashed potatoes, with so much richness and flavor they can stand on their own—no gravy necessary.

For a creamier, substantial mash, we found that Yukon Golds were perfect—creamier than russets but not as heavy as red potatoes. Slicing the peeled potatoes into rounds and then rinsing away the surface starch before boiling helped intensify their creamy texture without making them gluey. Setting the boiled and drained potatoes in their pot over a low flame helped further evaporate any excess moisture. Using 1½ sticks of butter and 1½ cups of heavy cream gives these potatoes luxurious flavor and richness without making the mash too thin. We found that melting the butter and warming the cream before adding them to the potatoes ensured that the finished dish arrived at the table piping hot.

Creamy Mashed Potatoes
SERVES 8 TO 10
This recipe can be cut in half, if desired.

- 4 pounds Yukon Gold potatoes (about 8 medium), scrubbed, peeled, and sliced ¾ inch thick
- 1½ cups heavy cream
- 12 tablespoons (1½ sticks) unsalted butter, cut into 6 pieces
- 2 teaspoons table salt

1. Place the potatoes in a colander and rinse under cool running water, tossing with your hands, for 30 seconds. Transfer the potatoes to a large Dutch oven, add cold water to cover by 1 inch, and bring to a boil over high heat. Reduce the heat to medium and boil until the potatoes are tender, 20 to 25 minutes.

2. Meanwhile, heat the heavy cream and butter in a small saucepan over medium heat until the butter is melted, about 5 minutes. Set aside and keep warm.

3. Drain the potatoes and return to the Dutch oven. Stir over low heat until the potatoes are thoroughly dried, 1 to 2 minutes. Set a ricer or food mill over a large bowl and press or mill the potatoes into the bowl. Gently fold in the warm cream mixture and salt with a rubber spatula until the cream is absorbed and the potatoes are thick and creamy. Serve.

GARLIC AND OLIVE OIL MASHED POTATOES

WHY THIS RECIPE WORKS: The Mediterranean approach of flavoring mashed potatoes with olive oil and garlic is an appealing one, but it's not as simple as replacing the dairy with oil: olive oil can turn the texture pasty and garlic can be harsh and overpowering. We wanted to translate these bold flavors into a light and creamy mashed potato side dish that would partner well with simple grilled meats or fish.

We chose to use russets in this dish for their light, fluffy texture. We first simmered the potatoes and then put the drained, peeled, still-hot potatoes through a ricer or food mill for a smooth texture. We created a mild flavor base by slowly cooking minced garlic in oil, then heightened the garlic flavor a bit by adding just a little garlic, mashed to a paste. Fruity extra-virgin olive oil and a splash of fresh lemon juice brightened the final dish.

Garlic and Olive Oil Mashed Potatoes
SERVES 6
As this dish is denser and more intensely flavored than traditional mashed potatoes, our suggested serving size is smaller than you might expect.

- 2 pounds russet potatoes (about 4 medium), scrubbed
- 5 medium garlic cloves, minced or pressed through a garlic press (about 5 teaspoons)
- 2⅛ teaspoons table salt
- ½ cup plus 2 tablespoons extra-virgin olive oil
- ½ teaspoon ground black pepper
- 2 teaspoons juice from 1 lemon

1. Place the potatoes in a large saucepan and add cold water to cover by 1 inch. Bring to a boil over high heat; reduce the heat to medium-low and cook at a bare simmer until just tender (the potatoes will offer very little resistance when poked with a paring knife), 40 to 45 minutes.

2. Meanwhile, place 1 teaspoon of the garlic on a cutting board and sprinkle with ⅛ teaspoon of the salt. Using the flat side of a chef's knife, drag the garlic and salt back and forth across the cutting board in small circular motions until the garlic is ground into a smooth paste. Transfer to a medium bowl and set aside.

3. Place the remaining 4 teaspoons garlic in a small saucepan with ¼ cup of the oil and cook over low heat, stirring constantly, until the garlic begins to sizzle and is soft, fragrant, and golden, about 5 minutes. Transfer the oil and garlic to the bowl with the raw garlic paste.

4. Drain the cooked potatoes; set a ricer or food mill over the now-empty saucepan. Using a potholder (to hold the potatoes) and a paring knife, peel the skins from the potatoes. Working in batches, cut the peeled potatoes into large chunks and press or mill into the saucepan.

5. Add the remaining 2 teaspoons salt, the pepper, lemon juice, and remaining 6 tablespoons oil to the bowl with the cooked garlic and oil and whisk to combine. Fold the mixture into the potatoes and serve.

MASHED POTATOES AND ROOT VEGETABLES

WHY THIS RECIPE WORKS: Root vegetables like carrots, parsnips, turnips, and celery root can add an earthy, intriguing flavor to mashed potatoes, but because root vegetables and potatoes have different starch levels and water content, treating them the same way creates a bad mash. We wanted a potato and root vegetable mash with a creamy consistency and a balanced flavor that highlights the natural earthiness of these humble root cellar favorites.

We found that a 1:3 ratio of root vegetables to potatoes provided an optimal consistency, although the root vegetable flavor was barely recognizable. Caramelizing the root vegetables first in a little butter helped bring out their natural earthy sweetness; this step also boosted the flavor of the overall dish. To use just one pot, we first sautéed the root vegetables in butter until caramelized and then added the potatoes with a little chicken broth. This gave us great flavor, but the mash had a gluey texture. The answer was to remove the starch from the potatoes by rinsing the peeled, sliced potatoes in several changes of water ahead of time.

Mashed Potatoes and Root Vegetables

SERVES 4

Russet potatoes will yield a slightly fluffier, less creamy mash, but they can be used in place of the Yukon Gold potatoes if desired. Rinsing the potatoes in several changes of water reduces the amount of starch and prevents the mashed potatoes from becoming gluey. It is important to cut the potatoes and root vegetables into even-sized pieces so they cook at the same rate. This recipe can be doubled and cooked in a large Dutch oven. If doubling, increase the cooking time in step 2 to 40 minutes.

4 tablespoons (½ stick) unsalted butter
8 ounces carrots, parsnips, turnips, or celery root, peeled; carrots or parsnips cut into ¼-inch-thick half-moons; turnips or celery root cut into ½-inch dice (about 1½ cups)
1½ pounds Yukon Gold potatoes (about 3 medium), peeled, quartered lengthwise, and cut crosswise into ¼-inch-thick slices; rinsed well in 3 or 4 changes of cold water and drained well (see note)
⅓ cup low-sodium chicken broth
Table salt
¾ cup half-and-half, warmed
3 tablespoons minced fresh chives
Ground black pepper

1. Melt the butter in a large saucepan over medium heat. Add the root vegetables and cook, stirring occasionally, until the butter is browned and the vegetables are dark brown and caramelized, 10 to 12 minutes. (If after 4 minutes the vegetables have not started to brown, increase the heat to medium-high.)

2. Add the potatoes, broth, and ¾ teaspoon salt and stir to combine. Cook, covered, over low heat (the broth should simmer gently; do not boil), stirring occasionally, until the potatoes fall apart easily when poked with a fork and all the liquid has been absorbed, 25 to 30 minutes. (If the liquid does not gently simmer after a few minutes, increase the heat to medium-low.) Remove the pan from the heat; remove the lid and allow the steam to escape for 2 minutes.

3. Gently mash the potatoes and root vegetables in the saucepan with a potato masher (do not mash vigorously). Gently fold in the half-and-half and chives. Season with salt and pepper to taste and serve.

FLUFFY MASHED POTATOES

WHY THIS RECIPE WORKS: In Classic Mashed Potatoes (page 397), we boil potatoes in their jackets for earthy potato flavor (and peel them while they're still hot). We don't mind this somewhat inconvenient method when we've got time to spare, but thought an easier alternative was in order.

Cooking potatoes in their skins preserves their earthy flavor and keeps the starch granules from absorbing too much water, thereby preventing gluey mashed potatoes. To give peeled potatoes the same protection, we made two alterations to our usual technique. Steaming rather than boiling the potatoes exposed the potato pieces to less water, reducing the chance of the granules swelling to the point of bursting. When they were cooked partway, we rinsed them under cold water to rid them of free amylose, the substance that results in gluey mashed potatoes, and returned them to the steamer to finish cooking. Because potatoes cooked this way are so full of rich potato flavor, we were able to use less butter and substitute whole milk for cream.

Fluffy Mashed Potatoes

SERVES 4

This recipe works best with either a metal colander that sits easily in a Dutch oven or a large pasta pot with a steamer insert. To prevent excess evaporation, it is important for the lid to fit as snugly as possible over the colander or steamer. For the lightest, fluffiest texture, use a ricer. A food mill is the next best alternative. Russets will also work in this recipe, but avoid red potatoes.

- 2 pounds Yukon Gold potatoes (about 4 medium), peeled, cut into 1-inch chunks, rinsed well, and drained (see note)
- 4 tablespoons (½ stick) unsalted butter, melted
  Table salt
- ⅔ cup whole milk, warmed
  Ground black pepper

1. Place a metal colander or steamer insert in a large pot or Dutch oven. Add enough water to barely reach the bottom of the colander. Bring the water to a boil over high heat. Add the potatoes, cover, and reduce the heat to medium-high. Cook the potatoes for 10 minutes. Transfer the colander to the sink and rinse the potatoes under cold water until no longer hot, 1 to 2 minutes. Return the colander and potatoes to the pot, cover, and continue to cook until the potatoes are soft and the tip of a paring knife inserted into the potatoes meets no resistance, 10 to 15 minutes longer. Drain the potatoes.

2. Set a ricer or food mill over the now-empty pot. Working in batches, transfer the potatoes to the hopper and process or mill, removing any potatoes stuck to the bottom. Using a rubber spatula, stir in the butter and ½ teaspoon salt until incorporated. Stir in the milk until incorporated. Season with salt and pepper to taste and serve.

BUTTERMILK MASHED POTATOES

WHY THIS RECIPE WORKS: Merely replacing butter and cream with buttermilk to create tangy, creamy buttermilk mashed potatoes doesn't work—the finished potatoes are curdled, crumbly, chalky, and dry. We wanted easy mashed potatoes with buttermilk's trademark distinctive tang, but we didn't want to sacrifice texture to get them.

Many recipes for buttermilk mashed potatoes remove so much butter that the potatoes taste lean and lack creaminess. We started by restoring just enough butter to save our mashed potatoes from this fate. We then tackled the curdling problem. Buttermilk curdles at 160 degrees, a temperature reached almost instantly when the cold liquid hits steaming-hot potatoes. By adding the butter, melted, to room-temperature buttermilk, we coated the proteins in the buttermilk and protected them from the heat shock that causes curdling. We also simplified the recipe by choosing peeled and cut Yukon Gold potatoes rather than using unpeeled russets (our usual choice for mashed potatoes). Because Yukon Golds have less starch and are less absorbent than russets, they don't become soggy and thinned out when simmered without their jackets.

Buttermilk Mashed Potatoes

SERVES 4

To achieve the proper texture, it is important to cook the potatoes thoroughly; they are done if they break apart when a knife is inserted and gently wiggled. Buttermilk substitutes like clabbered milk do not produce sufficiently tangy potatoes. To reduce the likelihood of curdling, the buttermilk must be brought to room temperature and mixed with cooled melted butter.

- 2 pounds Yukon Gold potatoes (about 4 medium), peeled and cut into 1-inch chunks
  Table salt
- 6 tablespoons (¾ stick) unsalted butter, melted and cooled (see note)
- ⅔ cup buttermilk, room temperature (see note)
  Ground black pepper

1. Place the potatoes in a large saucepan and add cold water to cover by 1 inch; add 1 tablespoon salt. Bring to a boil over high heat, then reduce the heat to medium and simmer until the potatoes break apart very easily when a paring knife is inserted, about 18 minutes. Drain the potatoes briefly, then immediately return them to the saucepan set on the still-hot (but off) burner.

2. Using a potato masher, mash the potatoes until a few small lumps remain. Gently mix the melted butter and buttermilk in a small bowl until combined. Add the buttermilk mixture to the potatoes; using a rubber spatula, fold gently until just incorporated. Season with salt and pepper to taste and serve.

ULTIMATE ROASTED POTATOES

WHY THIS RECIPE WORKS: The aroma of roasting potatoes draws everyone into the kitchen come meal time. Too often, though, the potatoes turn out brown and leathery with a mealy interior, or worse, soft with no crisp crust at all. We wanted oven-roasted potatoes that had a crisp crust with a silky interior.

We tested using different potatoes and found that we liked Yukon Golds best. Parcooking the potatoes before subjecting them to high oven temperatures helped them develop a somewhat crisper exterior, but the browning was uneven and they still weren't crispy enough. When we switched from cubing the potatoes to slicing them thick, we created more surface area for crisping but enough heft for a creamy interior. As an added bonus, with only two surfaces to cook, we now only had to flip the potatoes once halfway through roasting. We boiled the potatoes very briefly to prevent them from breaking up on the baking sheet, and we tossed the precooked potatoes with some olive oil to rough up the exteriors and increase crispiness.

Crispy Roasted Potatoes

SERVES 4 TO 6

Note that the potatoes should be just undercooked when removed from the boiling water—this helps ensure that they will roast up crispy.

- 2½ pounds Yukon Gold potatoes (about 5 medium), rinsed and cut into ½-inch-thick slices
  Table salt
- 5 tablespoons olive oil
  Ground black pepper

1. Adjust an oven rack to the lowest position, place a rimmed baking sheet on the rack, and heat the oven to 450 degrees. Place the potatoes and 1 tablespoon salt in a Dutch oven; add cold water to cover by 1 inch. Bring to a boil over high heat; reduce the heat and gently simmer until the exterior of a potato has softened, but the center offers resistance when pierced with a paring knife, about 5 minutes. Drain the potatoes well, and transfer to a large bowl. Drizzle with 2 tablespoons of the oil and sprinkle with ½ teaspoon salt; using a rubber spatula, toss to combine. Drizzle with 2 tablespoons more oil and ½ teaspoon salt; continue to toss until the exteriors of the potato slices are coated with a starchy paste.

2. Working quickly, remove the baking sheet from the oven and drizzle the remaining 1 tablespoon oil over the surface. Carefully transfer the potatoes to the baking sheet and spread them into an even layer (skin side up for the end pieces). Bake until the bottoms of the potatoes are golden brown and crisp, 15 to 25 minutes, rotating the baking sheet after 10 minutes.

3. Remove the baking sheet from the oven and, using a metal spatula and tongs, loosen the potatoes from the pan and carefully flip each slice. Continue to roast until the second side is golden and crisp, 10 to 20 minutes longer, rotating the pan as needed to ensure the potatoes brown evenly. Season with salt and pepper to taste and serve.

SKILLET-ROASTED POTATOES

WHY THIS RECIPE WORKS: Skillet-roasted potatoes often cook up unevenly, with a mixture of scorched and pallid potatoes. We wanted to be able to make truly outstanding skillet-roasted potatoes, as good as oven-roasted—extra-crisp on the outside and moist and creamy on the inside, evenly browned, and never greasy. This would be the recipe we'd turn to when we craved roasted potatoes but there was no room in the oven for the conventional kind.

The solution turned out to be choosing the right potato and cutting it uniformly. Red Bliss potatoes, cut in half if small or quartered if medium, offered a great crust and a moist interior, thanks to their high moisture content. We rinsed the cut potatoes to remove surface starch, which otherwise caused the potatoes to stick to the pan and inhibited browning. Olive oil added flavor and richness to the dish. The winning cooking technique was to first brown the potatoes over high heat, then cover and finish cooking over low heat. This allowed the insides to cook through while the outsides stayed crisp.

Skillet-Roasted Potatoes

SERVES 3 TO 4

Small and medium potatoes can be used in this recipe, but they must be cut differently. Small potatoes (1½ to 2 inches in diameter) should be cut in half and medium potatoes (2 to 3 inches in diameter) should be cut into quarters to create ¾ to 1-inch chunks. Large potatoes should not be used because the cut pieces will be uneven and won't cook at the same rate. For even cooking and proper browning, the potatoes must be cooked in a single layer and should not be crowded in the pan.

    1½ pounds small or medium red potatoes (about 9 small
         or 4 to 5 medium), scrubbed, halved if small,
         quartered if medium (see note)
    2   tablespoons olive oil
    ¾   teaspoon table salt
    ¾   teaspoon ground black pepper

1. Rinse the potatoes in cold water and drain well; spread on a clean kitchen towel and thoroughly pat dry.

2. Heat the oil in a 12-inch skillet over medium-high heat until shimmering. Add the potatoes, cut side down, in a single layer. Cook, without stirring, until the potatoes are golden brown (the oil should sizzle but not smoke), 5 to 7 minutes. Using tongs, turn the potatoes skin side down if halved or second cut side down if quartered. Cook, without stirring, until the potatoes are deep golden brown, 5 to 6 minutes longer. Stir the potatoes, then redistribute in a single layer. Reduce the heat to medium-low, cover, and cook until the potatoes are tender (a paring knife can be inserted into the potatoes with no resistance), 6 to 9 minutes.

3. When the potatoes are tender, sprinkle with the salt and pepper and toss gently to combine; serve.

SCALLOPED POTATOES

WHY THIS RECIPE WORKS: Thinly sliced potatoes layered with cream and baked until they are bubbling and browned are a classic accompaniment to baked ham or roast beef. But scalloped potatoes can occupy the oven for over two hours and still produce unevenly cooked potatoes in a heavy, curdled sauce. We wanted to minimize the cooking time while turning out layers of thinly sliced, tender potatoes, a creamy sauce, and a nicely browned, cheesy crust.

We tried using flour to thicken the sauce, but this produced a thick, pasty sauce. Instead we relied on heavy cream lightened with whole milk. To cut the cooking time, we simmered the potatoes briefly in the cream in a covered pot, before transferring the mixture to a baking dish and finishing the potatoes in the oven. We found russet potatoes had the best texture and flavor, and we sliced them thin so they formed neat layers.

Scalloped Potatoes

SERVES 8 TO 10

For the fastest and most consistent results, slice the potatoes in a food processor or on a mandoline or V-slicer.

- 2 **tablespoons unsalted butter**
- 1 **small onion, minced**
- 2 **medium garlic cloves, minced or pressed through a garlic press (about 2 teaspoons)**
- 4 **pounds russet potatoes (about 8 medium), peeled and cut into ⅛-inch-thick slices**
- 3 **cups heavy cream**
- 1 **cup whole milk**
- 4 **sprigs fresh thyme**
- 2 **bay leaves**
- 2 **teaspoons table salt**
- ½ **teaspoon ground black pepper**
- 4 **ounces cheddar cheese, shredded (about 1 cup)**

1. Adjust an oven rack to the middle position and heat the oven to 350 degrees. Melt the butter in a large Dutch oven over medium-high heat. Add the onion and cook until softened and lightly browned, 5 to 7 minutes. Add the garlic and cook until fragrant, about 30 seconds. Add the potatoes, cream, milk, thyme, bay leaves, salt, pepper,

and potatoes and bring to a simmer. Cover, adjusting the heat as necessary to maintain a light simmer, and cook until the potatoes are almost tender (a paring knife can be slipped into and out of the center of a potato slice with some resistance), about 15 minutes.

2. Remove and discard the thyme sprigs and bay leaves. Transfer the potato mixture to a 3-quart gratin dish and sprinkle with the cheese. Bake until the cream has thickened and is bubbling around the sides, and the top is golden brown, about 20 minutes. Cool for 5 minutes before serving.

TWICE-BAKED POTATOES

WHY THIS RECIPE WORKS: Twice-baked potatoes are not difficult to make, but the process can be time-consuming, and too many versions of this dish feature rubbery, chewy skins filled with pasty, bland fillings. We wanted to perfect the process—from baking the potatoes and readying the shells to preparing the filling and finishing the potatoes in the oven—and have twice-baked potatoes with slightly crisp, chewy skins and a rich, creamy filling.

We had a head start, having already perfected a recipe for baked potatoes. Starting there, we oiled the potatoes before baking for a crisp skin, and we let the baked potatoes cool slightly before slicing them open and removing the flesh. We found that we could prevent the hollowed-out shells from turning soggy by keeping them in the oven while making the filling. And for the filling we found it best to combine the potato with tangy dairy ingredients—sour cream and buttermilk were ideal—a small amount of butter, and sharp cheddar cheese for its bold flavor. For a perfect finish, we placed the filled potatoes under the broiler, where they turned brown and crisp.

Twice-Baked Potatoes

SERVES 6 TO 8

Most potatoes have two relatively flat, blunt sides and two curved sides. Halve the baked potatoes lengthwise so the blunt sides are down once the shells are stuffed, making the potatoes much more stable in the pan during final baking. To vary the flavor a bit, try substituting other types of cheese, such as Gruyère, fontina, or feta, for the cheddar. Yukon Gold potatoes can be substituted for the russets.

- 4 medium russet potatoes (about 8 ounces each), scrubbed, dried, and rubbed lightly with vegetable oil (see note)
- 4 ounces sharp cheddar cheese, shredded (about 1 cup) (see note)
- ½ cup sour cream
- ½ cup buttermilk
- 2 tablespoons unsalted butter, softened
- 3 scallions, sliced thin
- ½ teaspoon table salt
  Ground black pepper

1. Adjust an oven rack to the upper-middle position and heat the oven to 400 degrees. Bake the potatoes on a foil-lined baking sheet until the skin is crisp and deep brown and a skewer easily pierces the flesh, about 1 hour. Transfer the potatoes to a wire rack and cool slightly, about 10 minutes. (Leave the oven on.)

2. Using an oven mitt or folded kitchen towel to handle the hot potatoes, cut each potato in half so that the long, blunt sides rest on the work surface. Using a small spoon, scoop the flesh from each half into a medium bowl, leaving a ⅛ to ¼-inch thickness of the flesh in each shell. Arrange the shells on the foil-lined baking sheet and return to the oven until dry and slightly crisp, about 10 minutes. Meanwhile, mash the potato flesh with a fork until smooth. Stir in the remaining ingredients, including pepper to taste, until well combined.

3. Remove the shells from the oven and increase the oven setting to broil. Holding the shells steady on the pan with an oven mitt or towel-protected hand, spoon the mixture into the crisped shells, mounding it slightly at the center, and return the potatoes to the oven. Broil until spotty brown and crisp on top, 10 to 15 minutes. Cool for 10 minutes and serve warm.

ACORN SQUASH

WHY THIS RECIPE WORKS: Cooked properly, acorn squash develops a sweet, almost nutty flavor and moist, smooth flesh—a result that should not take hours. But after what seems like eons in the oven, acorn squash often lands on the table with little flavor and a mealy, stringy texture. We wanted the flavor of better, slow-roasted acorn squash in a fraction of the time.

To our astonishment, microwaving was the ideal cooking method, presenting a squash that was tender and silky smooth, with nary a trace of dryness or stringiness. Microwaved on high power for 20 minutes, the squash was perfectly cooked. It was best to halve and seed the squash before cooking; whole pierced squash cooked unevenly. Last, we learned that when added before cooking, salt seemed to better permeate the squash. Filling in the only remaining gap, equal portions of butter and dark brown sugar gave the squash ample, but not excessive, sweetness. And for a smooth, cohesive filling mixture, combining the butter and sugar with a pinch of salt and briefly broiling the final product eliminated the nagging sticky glaze problem. Finishing the squash under the broiler also gave it a welcome roasted texture and great caramelized flavor.

3. When the squash is cooked, carefully pull back the plastic wrap from the side farthest from you. Using tongs, transfer the cooked squash half, cut side up, to a rimmed baking sheet. Spoon a portion of the butter–sugar mixture onto each squash half. Broil until brown and caramelized, 5 to 8 minutes, rotating the baking sheet halfway through the cooking time and removing the squash halves as they are done. Set the squash halves on individual plates and serve immediately.

MASHED SWEET POTATOES

WHY THIS RECIPE WORKS: Mashed sweet potatoes often turn out overly thick and gluey or, at the other extreme, sloppy and loose. We wanted a recipe that would push sweet potatoes' deep, earthy sweetness to the fore and that would produce a silky puree with enough body to hold its shape on a fork.

We braised the sweet potatoes in a mixture of butter and heavy cream to impart a smooth richness. Adding a little salt brought out the sweet potatoes' delicate flavor and just a teaspoon of sugar bolstered their sweetness. Once the potatoes were tender, we mashed them in the saucepan with a potato masher. We skipped the typical pumpkin pie seasoning and instead let the simple sweet potato flavor shine through.

Quick Roasted Acorn Squash with Brown Sugar

SERVES 4

Squash smaller than 1½ pounds will likely cook a little faster than the recipe indicates, so begin checking for doneness a few minutes early. Likewise, larger squash will take slightly longer to cook. However, keep in mind that the cooking time is largely dependent on the microwave. If microwaving the squash in Pyrex, the manufacturer recommends adding water to the dish (or bowl) prior to cooking. To avoid a steam burn when uncovering the cooked squash, peel back the plastic wrap very carefully, starting from the side that is farthest away from you.

    2 acorn squash (about 1½ pounds each), halved pole to
       pole and seeded
       Table salt
    3 tablespoons unsalted butter
    3 tablespoons dark brown sugar

1. Sprinkle the squash halves with salt and place the halves, cut side down, in a 13 by 9-inch microwave-safe baking dish or arrange the halves in a large (4-quart) microwave-safe bowl so that the cut sides face out. (If using Pyrex, add ¼ cup water to the dish or bowl.) Cover tightly with plastic wrap, using multiple sheets, if necessary; with a paring knife, poke four steam vents in the wrap. Microwave on high power until the squash is very tender and offers no resistance when pierced with a paring knife, 15 to 25 minutes. Using potholders, remove the baking dish or bowl from the microwave and set on a clean, dry surface (avoid damp or cold surfaces).

2. While the squash is cooking, adjust an oven rack to the highest position (about 6 inches from the broiling element) and heat the broiler. Melt the butter, brown sugar, and ⅛ teaspoon salt in a small saucepan over low heat, whisking occasionally, until combined.

Mashed Sweet Potatoes

SERVES 4

Cutting the sweet potatoes into slices of even thickness is important so that they cook at the same rate. The potatoes are best served immediately, but they can be covered tightly with plastic wrap and kept warm for 30 minutes. This recipe can be doubled and prepared in a Dutch oven; the cooking time will need to be doubled as well.

    4 tablespoons (½ stick) unsalted butter, cut into
       4 pieces
    2 tablespoons heavy cream
    1 teaspoon sugar
    ½ teaspoon table salt
    2 pounds sweet potatoes (2 to 3 medium), peeled,
       quartered lengthwise, and cut crosswise into
       ¼-inch-thick slices
       Ground black pepper

1. Melt the butter in a large saucepan over low heat. Stir in the cream, sugar, and salt; add the sweet potatoes and cook, covered, stirring occasionally, until the potatoes fall apart when poked with a fork, 35 to 45 minutes.

2. Off the heat, mash the sweet potatoes in the saucepan with a potato masher or transfer the mixture to a food mill and process into a warmed serving bowl. Season with pepper to taste and serve.

RICE PILAF

WHY THIS RECIPE WORKS: To make rice pilaf, rice is toasted or browned in fat to build flavor before being cooked through in liquid. The result should be rice that is fragrant, fluffy, and tender. Traditional recipes insist that for a truly great pilaf you must soak or at least repeatedly rinse the rice before cooking. We wondered if there was more to making perfect rice pilaf than this.

The variables included the kind of rice to use, the ratio of rice to cooking water, and whether or not to soak the rice before cooking. Testing revealed that using basmati rice was preferable, as was using a lower amount of water than is traditional for cooking rice. The step of rinsing the rice was also important for grains that were more tender, with a slightly shinier, smoother appearance. We also sautéed the rice in plenty of butter before adding the water. After the rice was cooked, we covered it with a kitchen towel and a lid and let it steam off the heat.

Rice Pilaf

SERVES 4

If you like, olive oil can be substituted for the butter depending on what you are serving with the pilaf. For the most evenly cooked rice, use a wide-bottomed saucepan with a tight-fitting lid.

- 1½ **cups basmati or long-grain rice**
- 2½ **cups water**
- 1½ **teaspoons table salt**
  Pinch ground black pepper
- 3 **tablespoons unsalted butter (see note)**
- 1 **small onion, minced (about ½ cup)**

1. Place the rice in a medium bowl and add enough water to cover by 2 inches; using your hands, gently swish the grains to release the excess starch. Carefully pour off the water, leaving the rice in the bowl. Repeat four or five times, until the water runs almost clear. Using a colander

or fine-mesh strainer, drain the rice; place the colander over a bowl and set aside.

2. Bring the water to a boil, covered, in a small saucepan over medium-high heat. Add the salt and pepper; cover to keep hot. Meanwhile, melt the butter in a large saucepan over medium heat; add the onion and cook until softened but not browned, about 4 minutes. Stir in the rice until coated with the butter; cook until the edges of the rice grains begin to turn translucent, about 3 minutes. Stir the hot seasoned water into the rice; return to a boil, then reduce the heat to low, cover, and simmer until all the liquid is absorbed, 16 to 18 minutes. Off the heat, remove the lid and place a clean kitchen towel folded in half over the saucepan; replace the lid. Let stand for 10 minutes; fluff the rice with a fork and serve.

WILD RICE

WHY THIS RECIPE WORKS: Sometimes wild rice turns out undercooked and difficult to chew, other times the rice is overcooked and gluey. We wanted to figure out how to turn out properly cooked wild rice every time.

Through trial and error, we learned to simmer the rice slowly in plenty of liquid, making sure to stop the cooking process at just the right moment by checking it for doneness every couple of minutes past the 35-minute mark. For a simmering liquid, we used chicken broth—its mild yet rich profile tempered the rice's muddy flavor to a pleasant earthiness and affirmed its subdued nuttiness. To further tame the strong flavor of the wild rice, we added some white rice to the mixture, then added onions, carrots, dried cranberries, and toasted pecans for a winning pilaf.

Wild Rice Pilaf with Pecans and Dried Cranberries

SERVES 6 TO 8

Wild rice quickly goes from tough to pasty, so begin testing the rice at the 35-minute mark and drain the rice as soon as it is tender.

- 1¾ **cups low-sodium chicken broth**
- 2½ **cups water**
- 2 **bay leaves**
- 8 **sprigs fresh thyme, divided into 2 bundles, each tied together with kitchen twine**
- 1 **cup wild rice, rinsed well in a strainer**
- 1½ **cups long-grain white rice**

3 tablespoons unsalted butter
1 medium onion, minced
2 carrots, peeled and chopped fine
   Table salt
¾ cup sweetened or unsweetened dried cranberries
¾ cup pecans, toasted and chopped coarse
1½ tablespoons minced fresh parsley leaves
   Ground black pepper

1. Bring the chicken broth, ¼ cup of the water, the bay leaves, and 1 bundle of the thyme to a boil in a medium saucepan over medium-high heat. Add the wild rice, cover, and reduce the heat to low; simmer until the rice is plump and tender and has absorbed most of the liquid, 35 to 45 minutes. Drain the rice in a mesh strainer. Return the rice to the saucepan; cover to keep warm and set aside.

2. While the wild rice is cooking, place the white rice in a medium bowl and add water to cover by 2 inches; gently swish the grains to release excess starch. Carefully pour off the water, leaving the rice in the bowl. Repeat about five times, until the water runs almost clear. Drain the rice in a mesh strainer.

3. Melt the butter in a medium saucepan over medium-high heat. Add the onion, carrots, and 1 teaspoon salt; cook, stirring frequently, until softened but not browned, about 4 minutes. Stir in the rinsed white rice until coated with the butter; cook, stirring frequently, until the grains begin to turn translucent, about 3 minutes. Meanwhile, bring the remaining 2¼ cups water to a boil in a small saucepan or a microwave. Add the boiling water and the second thyme bundle to the rice; return to a boil, then reduce the heat to low, sprinkle the cranberries evenly over the rice, and cover. Simmer until all of the liquid is absorbed, 16 to 18 minutes. Off the heat, fluff the rice with a fork, discard the bay leaves and thyme bundles.

4. Combine the wild rice, white rice mixture, pecans, and parsley in a large bowl; toss with a rubber spatula until the ingredients are evenly mixed. Season with salt and pepper to taste and serve.

SPICED PECANS WITH RUM GLAZE

WHY THIS RECIPE WORKS: Most spiced nuts are made with a heavily sugared syrup that causes the nuts to clump awkwardly and leaves your hands in a sticky mess. We wanted to get maximum flavor and balanced sweetness with minimum mess.

We tried two popular methods—boiling the nuts in syrup and tossing them in butter—and eliminated both straight off. The former made the nuts sticky, and the latter dulled their flavor. A third method, coating the nuts with an egg white mixture, pretty much overwhelmed them with a candy-like coating. What finally worked was a light glaze made from very small amounts of liquid (we like either rum or water), sugar, and butter, which left the nuts just tacky enough to pick up an even, light coating of dry spices.

Spiced Pecans with Rum Glaze
MAKES ABOUT 2 CUPS
The spiced nuts can be stored in an airtight container at room temperature for up to 5 days.

2 cups raw pecan halves

SPICE MIX
2 tablespoons sugar
¾ teaspoon table salt
½ teaspoon ground cinnamon
⅛ teaspoon ground cloves
⅛ teaspoon ground allspice

RUM GLAZE
1 tablespoon rum, preferably dark, or water
1 tablespoon unsalted butter
2 teaspoons vanilla extract
1 teaspoon light or dark brown sugar

1. Adjust an oven rack to the middle position and heat the oven to 350 degrees. Line a rimmed baking sheet with parchment paper and spread the pecans on it in an even layer; toast until fragrant and the color deepens slightly, about 8 minutes, rotating the sheet halfway through the baking time. Transfer the baking sheet with the nuts to a wire rack.

2. FOR THE SPICE MIX: While the nuts are toasting, combine all the spice mix ingredients in a medium bowl; set aside.

3. FOR THE RUM GLAZE: Bring the rum glaze ingredients to a boil in a medium saucepan over medium-high heat, whisking constantly. Stir in the pecans and cook, stirring constantly with a wooden spoon, until almost all the liquid has evaporated, about 1½ minutes.

4. Transfer the glazed pecans to the bowl with the spice mix; toss well to coat. Return the glazed spiced pecans to the parchment-lined baking sheet to cool before serving.

CHAPTER 19

COME FOR BRUNCH

Fluffy Scrambled Eggs 410

Scrambled Eggs with Bacon, Onion, and Pepper Jack Cheese 411

Scrambled Eggs with Sausage, Sweet Pepper, and Cheddar Cheese 411

Fried Eggs 412

Poached Eggs 413

Oven-Fried Bacon 413

Diner-Style Home Fries 414

Denver Omelets 415
    Filling for Denver Omelets

Family-Sized Cheese Omelets 416

French Omelets 417

Spanish Tortilla with Roasted Red Peppers and Peas 418

Spanish Tortilla with Chorizo and Scallions 419
    Garlic Mayonnaise

Asparagus, Ham, and Gruyère Frittata 420

Leek, Prosciutto, and Goat Cheese Frittata 421

Quiche Lorraine 421

Breakfast Strata with Spinach and Gruyère 422

Breakfast Strata with Sausage, Mushrooms, and Monterey Jack 423

Blueberry Pancakes 424

German Apple Pancake 425
    Caramel Sauce

Buttermilk Waffles 426

Banana Bread 427

Cream Scones 427

Blueberry Scones 428

Oatmeal Scones 430

Glazed Maple-Pecan Oatmeal Scones 431

Blueberry Muffins 431

Bran Muffins 432

Corn Muffins 433

Corn and Apricot Muffins with Orange Essence 434

New York–Style Crumb Cake 434

Blueberry Boy Bait 435

Quick Cinnamon Buns with Buttermilk Icing 436

Sticky Buns with Pecans 438

Sour Cream Coffee Cake with Brown Sugar–Pecan Streusel 440

Strawberries and Grapes with Balsamic and Red Wine Reduction 441

Nectarines, Blueberries, and Raspberries with Champagne-Cardamom Reduction 441

Honeydew, Mango, and Blueberries with Lime-Ginger Reduction 441

SCRAMBLED EGGS

WHY THIS RECIPE WORKS: Sometimes the simplest things can be the hardest to get right. Scrambled eggs are a good example. Seemingly easy to make, they can easily go wrong, and overcooking is probably the most common problem. We wanted scrambled eggs that turn out of the pan into a mound of large, soft curds—cooked enough to hold their shape but soft enough to eat with a spoon.

We learned that beating the eggs too much before cooking them can result in toughness, so we whisked our eggs just until they were combined. Milk is better than water as an addition to scrambled eggs; the sugar, proteins, and fat in milk help create large curds, which trap steam for that pillowy texture we were after. A nonstick skillet is a must to prevent sticking, and pan size matters as well; if the skillet is too large, the eggs spread out in too thin a layer and overcook. Getting the pan hot is crucial for moist, puffy curds, and constant gentle stirring—really more like pushing and folding—prevents overcooking. Cooked on the stove until they were almost done, which took only a couple of minutes, these eggs finished cooking on the way to the table, remaining moist and meltingly soft.

Fluffy Scrambled Eggs
SERVES 4

These eggs cook very quickly, so it's important to be ready to eat before you start to cook them.

- 8 **large eggs**
- ½ **cup milk**
- ½ **teaspoon table salt**
  Pinch ground black pepper
- 1 **tablespoon butter**

1. Whisk the eggs, milk, salt, and pepper together in a medium bowl until any streaks are gone and the color is pure yellow.

2. Melt the butter in a 10-inch nonstick skillet over high heat, swirling to coat the pan. Add the eggs and, using a heatproof rubber spatula, cook while gently pushing, lifting, and folding them from one side of the pan to the other as they form curds. Continue until the eggs are nicely clumped into a single mound but remain shiny and wet, 1½ to 2 minutes. Serve.

HEARTY SCRAMBLED EGGS

WHY THIS RECIPE WORKS: Having perfected the technique for cooking scrambled eggs, we figured that we could make a heartier dish by simply adding other ingredients. But even a sprinkling of some sausage or vegetables discolored the eggs and made them watery; clearly, there was more to hearty scrambled eggs than we first thought.

Experiments with the temperature of the ingredients, the addition of binders, and the elimination of the milk demonstrated that none of these was the issue. We had been starting our heartier eggs by sautéing onions in the skillet, then adding the eggs; we tried removing the onions after sautéing and wiping out the skillet, then cooking the eggs. This method of cooking in stages—sautéing the aromatics and removing them, cooking the eggs, then folding in all the other ingredients off the heat—prevented discoloration and helped with the wateriness. Lowering the heat to medium made the texture of the eggs somewhat more substantial, but we were able to get rid of the last bit of wateriness when we substituted a smaller amount of half-and-half—with its higher-fat, lower-water content—for the milk. Breakfast meats, crunchy vegetables, and dry leafy greens were successful additions to these eggs, so long as we avoided any that were moisture-laden. These eggs were not as fluffy as eggs without adornment, but the difference was imperceptible once we added meats and vegetables—and there were no watery puddles on the plate.

Scrambled Eggs with Bacon, Onion, and Pepper Jack Cheese

SERVES 4 TO 6

Note that you'll need to reserve 2 teaspoons of bacon fat to sauté the onion. After removing the cooked bacon from the skillet, be sure to drain it well on paper towels; otherwise, the eggs will be greasy.

12   **large eggs**
6   **tablespoons half-and-half**
¾   **teaspoon table salt**
¼   **teaspoon ground black pepper**
4   **ounces bacon (about 4 slices), halved lengthwise, then cut crosswise into ½-inch pieces**
1   **medium onion, chopped medium**
1   **tablespoon unsalted butter**
1½   **ounces pepper Jack or Monterey Jack cheese, shredded (about ⅓ cup)**
1   **teaspoon minced fresh parsley leaves (optional)**

1. Whisk the eggs, half-and-half, salt, and pepper together in a medium bowl.

2. Cook the bacon in a 12-inch nonstick skillet over medium heat, stirring occasionally, until browned, 4 to 5 minutes. Using a slotted spoon, transfer the bacon to a paper towel–lined plate; discard all but 2 teaspoons bacon fat. Add the onion to the skillet and cook, stirring occasionally, until lightly browned, 2 to 4 minutes; transfer the onion to a second plate.

3. Thoroughly wipe out the skillet with paper towels, add the butter, and melt over medium heat, swirling to coat the pan. Add the eggs and, using a heatproof rubber spatula, cook while gently pushing, lifting, and folding them from one side of the pan to the other as they form curds. Cook until large curds form but the eggs are still very moist, 2 to 3 minutes. Off the heat, gently fold in the onion, pepper Jack, and half of the bacon until evenly distributed; if the eggs are still underdone, return the skillet to medium heat for no longer than 30 seconds. Divide the eggs among individual plates, sprinkle with the remaining bacon and parsley (if using), and serve.

Scrambled Eggs with Sausage, Sweet Pepper, and Cheddar Cheese

SERVES 4 TO 6

We prefer sweet Italian sausage here, especially for breakfast, but you can certainly use spicy sausage, if desired.

12   **large eggs**
6   **tablespoons half-and-half**
¾   **teaspoon table salt**
¼   **teaspoon ground black pepper**
1   **teaspoon vegetable oil**
8   **ounces sweet Italian sausage, casings removed, sausage crumbled into ½-inch pieces (see note)**
1   **red bell pepper, stemmed, seeded, and cut into ½-inch cubes**
3   **scallions, white and green parts separated, both sliced thin on the bias**
1   **tablespoon unsalted butter**
1½   **ounces sharp cheddar cheese, shredded (about ⅓ cup)**

1. Whisk the eggs, half-and-half, salt, and pepper together in a medium bowl.

2. Heat the oil in a 12-inch nonstick skillet over medium heat until shimmering. Add the sausage and cook until beginning to brown but still pink in the center, about 2 minutes. Add the bell pepper and scallion whites; continue to cook, stirring occasionally, until the sausage is cooked through and the pepper is beginning to brown, about 3 minutes. Spread the mixture in a single layer on a medium plate; set aside.

3. Thoroughly wipe out the skillet with paper towels, add the butter, and melt over medium heat, swirling to coat the pan. Add the eggs and, using a heatproof rubber spatula, cook while gently pushing, lifting, and folding them from one side of the pan to the other as they form curds. Cook the eggs until large curds form but the eggs are still very moist, 2 to 3 minutes. Off the heat, gently fold in the sausage mixture and cheddar until evenly distributed; if the eggs are still underdone, return the skillet to medium heat for no longer than 30 seconds. Divide the eggs among individual plates, sprinkle with the scallion greens, and serve.

HELP! MY RECIPE DOESN'T WORK!

It happens—even in America's Test Kitchen. Once in a while, we get a call from a viewer or reader that a recipe isn't working for them. And every time, our hearts sink. What did we do wrong? We not only test our recipes very carefully (as many as 100 times), but we also have our recipes vetted by a professional cook, and THEN we send them out to home cooks to test-drive our recipes. So why do recipes sometimes fail? The answers fall into three broad categories: substitutions, flawed equipment, or ingredient variables.

Substitutions are common (everyone does it), but if you decide to replace a key ingredient or piece of equipment, all bets are off. If you're on a diet, don't try making our crème brûlée with milk rather than cream. And don't sear four steaks in a 10-inch skillet when the recipe calls for a 12-inch pan—that is, unless you want them to taste steamed and bland. Our advice: Make the recipe once as it's written, then improvise.

Flawed equipment is harder to predict and control. Many home ovens are not properly calibrated and an oven that runs hot by 50 degrees (which is fairly common in home kitchens) will ruin many recipes. Always, always pay attention to the visual clues in our recipes, not the clock. And invest in an oven thermometer. It's cheap and will save you much frustration when cooking.

Ingredient variables are the hardest thing for us (or you) to control. Produce varies in sweetness and moisture content. The same cut of meat can have more or less fat. And brands of manufactured products are not all the same. In fact, we had trouble with a chocolate frosting recipe several years ago and realized that our recipe worked with the test kitchen's top-rated bittersweet chocolate (with 60 percent cacao) but failed when readers tried to use gourmet brands with a higher cacao content. We test all of our recipes with the ingredients that have won our blind taste tests (see pages 602 through 617). We suggest you do the same. Not only will your food taste better, but sometimes choosing the right brand can make the difference between a successful recipe and a failed one.

FRIED EGGS

WHY THIS RECIPE WORKS: Anyone can make fried eggs, but few and far between are the cooks who can make them perfectly every time. Eggs can stick to the pan, yolks can break, and over- or undercooked eggs seem to be the norm. We decided to eliminate the guesswork and figure out the best and easiest way to fry the perfect egg every time. For us, this meant a white that is firm and a yolk that sets up high and is thick yet still runny.

We discovered that the first thing to do when about to fry an egg is to reach for a nonstick pan; there is no point in frying eggs in anything else. The initial heat setting is also important. A five-minute preheating of the pan over a very low fire puts it at just the right temperature to receive the eggs. Cover the pan as soon as the eggs are added and cook just a couple of minutes for evenly cooked whites and a yolk that is perfectly set up.

Fried Eggs

MAKES 2

Since burners vary, it may take an egg or two before you determine the ideal heat setting for frying eggs on your stovetop. Adjust the heat as necessary.

> 2 large eggs
> 1½ teaspoons unsalted butter, chilled
> Table salt and ground black pepper

1. Heat an 8-inch nonstick skillet over low heat for 5 minutes. Meanwhile, crack each egg into a cup or small bowl (1 egg per cup). Add the butter to the skillet and melt, swirling to coat the pan.

2. Working quickly, pour 1 egg on one side of the pan and the remaining egg on the other side. Sprinkle the eggs with salt and pepper; cover and cook about 2 minutes for runny yolks, 2½ minutes for soft but set yolks, and 3 minutes for firmly set yolks. Slide the eggs onto a plate and serve.

POACHED EGGS

WHY THIS RECIPE WORKS: A poached egg should be a neat-looking pouch of tender egg, evenly cooked all the way through, with a yolk that is barely runny. But boiling water can agitate the eggs until they are a ragged mess; we needed to figure out how to cook these eggs gently.

Our first thought was to examine the type of pan used. Most recipes require a deep saucepan, but we found that a shallow pan—a skillet—was far better: The water boiled faster, and the egg hit bottom sooner, and thus more gently, so that it could solidify before becoming stringy. A touch of vinegar lowered the boiling point of the water so that we were able to cook the eggs over more gentle heat. Our most important discovery turned out to be the importance of cooking eggs in still, not bubbling, water—as long as it was hot enough. With this in mind, we covered the skillet and turned off the heat after adding the eggs to the boiling water, allowing the residual heat to cook the eggs through. Without bubbling water to tear them apart, our poached eggs came out of the pan perfectly shaped—and cooked—with no feathery whites in sight.

Poached Eggs
MAKES 4

To get four eggs into boiling water at the same time, crack each into a small cup with a handle. Holding two cups in each hand, lower the lip of each cup just into the water and then tip the eggs into the pan.

    Table salt
2 **tablespoons distilled white vinegar**
4 **large eggs, each cracked into a small handled cup (see note)**
    Ground black pepper

1. Fill an 8 to 10-inch nonstick skillet nearly to the rim with water, add 1 teaspoon salt and the vinegar, and bring the mixture to a boil over high heat.

2. Lower the lip of each cup just into the water; tip the eggs into the boiling water, cover, and immediately remove the pan from the heat. Poach the eggs for 4 minutes for medium-firm yolks. (For firmer yolks, poach for 4½ minutes; for looser yolks, poach for 3 minutes.)

3. With a slotted spoon, carefully lift and drain each egg over the skillet. Season with salt and pepper to taste and serve.

BACON

WHY THIS RECIPE WORKS: A couple of strips of crisp bacon are always a welcome accompaniment to a plate of eggs, but bacon requires frequent monitoring when cooked on the stovetop, and the grease can be messy. The microwave produces unevenly cooked and flavorless strips, so we looked to the oven for an easier way to cook bacon.

Bacon renders its fat while cooking, of course, so it was important to choose a pan that would contain it; a rimmed baking sheet worked just fine, and as a bonus it enabled us to cook more strips at the same time. We didn't have to turn the bacon because the heat of the oven cooked it evenly, though rotating the baking sheet front to back halfway through ensured even cooking. In comparison to the results from stovetop frying, bacon cooked in the oven wasn't quite as crisp, but it was certainly crisp enough, and it had the same great meaty flavor. Although preheating the oven and draining the bacon after cooking takes a little extra time, the payoff is that you don't have to stand at the stove while the bacon is in the oven—or deal with grease splattered on your stovetop.

Oven-Fried Bacon
SERVES 4 TO 6

A large rimmed baking sheet is important here to contain the rendered bacon fat. If cooking more than one tray of bacon, switch their oven positions once about halfway through cooking. You can use thin- or thick-cut bacon here, though the cooking times will vary.

12 **slices bacon (see note)**

Adjust an oven rack to the middle position and heat the oven to 400 degrees. Arrange the bacon slices on a rimmed baking sheet. Cook until the fat begins to render, 5 to 6 minutes; rotate the pan. Continue cooking until the bacon is crisp and browned, 5 to 6 minutes longer for thin-cut bacon, 8 to 10 minutes for thick-cut. Transfer the bacon to a paper towel–lined plate, drain, and serve.

HOME FRIES

WHY THIS RECIPE WORKS: Whether made at home or eaten out, home fries frequently suffer from the same problems: greasy or undercooked potatoes, and bland or too-spicy flavors. We wanted to develop a recipe that produced potatoes with a crisp, deep golden brown crust and a tender, moist interior.

We started with the type of potato and determined that medium-starch Yukon Golds beat out russets and reds, remaining moist even when crisped on the outside. Attempts to cook raw diced potato in the skillet ended in failure; precooking was the way to go. But leftover potatoes tasted like—leftovers. We tried baking, boiling, and dicing the potatoes before frying them, but they overcooked, turning to mush and sticking to the pan. What finally worked was parcooking the potatoes—placing them in water and bringing them just to a boil, then immediately draining them before frying. This approach gave the interior of the potatoes a head start in the cooking process, but the potatoes weren't in the water long enough to absorb much liquid. The result: firm cubes of potato with crisp, browned exteriors. A combination of butter (for its rich flavor) and oil (for its higher smoke point) worked best for frying. Onion is the perfect foil for these potatoes; we cooked it in the skillet before adding the potatoes.

Diner-Style Home Fries

SERVES 2 TO 3

If doubling this recipe, cook two batches of home fries separately. While making the second batch, keep the first batch hot and crisp by spreading the fries on a baking sheet placed in a 300-degree oven.

- 2½ tablespoons corn oil or peanut oil
- 1 medium onion, minced
- 1 pound (2 medium) Yukon Gold potatoes, scrubbed and cut into ½-inch cubes
  Table salt
- 1 tablespoon unsalted butter
- 1 teaspoon paprika (optional)
- 1 tablespoon minced fresh parsley leaves (optional)
  Ground black pepper

1. Heat 1 tablespoon of the oil in a 12-inch skillet over medium-high heat until shimmering. Add the onion and cook, stirring frequently, until browned, 8 to 10 minutes. Transfer the onion to a small bowl and set aside.

2. Meanwhile, place the potatoes in a large saucepan, cover with ½ inch of water, add 1 teaspoon salt, and bring to a boil over high heat. As soon as the water begins to boil, drain the potatoes thoroughly in a colander.

3. Heat the butter and the remaining 1½ tablespoons oil in the now-empty skillet over medium-high heat. Add the potatoes and shake the skillet to evenly distribute the potatoes in a single layer, making sure that one side of each piece is touching the surface of the skillet. Cook without stirring until one side of the potatoes is golden brown, about 4 to 5 minutes, then carefully turn the potatoes, making sure the potatoes remain in a single layer. Repeat the process until the potatoes are tender and browned on most sides, turning three or four times, 10 to 15 minutes longer. Add the onions, paprika (if using), parsley (if using), ¼ teaspoon salt, and pepper to taste; serve.

DENVER OMELET

WHY THIS RECIPE WORKS: A substantial Denver omelet has become a breakfast feature in American restaurants and diners. Filled with ham and lots of vegetables in addition to cheese, it's a meal in itself. But it's hard to get the vegetables cooked without overcooking the eggs.

Cooking the filling separately, before the eggs, seemed to be the best way to avoid undercooked vegetables. In addition to the standard onion and green bell pepper, we also included red bell pepper, which made for a more colorful filling. Instead of julienning the vegetables, we finely chopped them; this made our filling easier to eat, and the peppers' skin was less intrusive. Ham steak was the easiest kind of ham to dice: it also imparted a welcome smoky flavor to the rest of the filling. For more complexity of flavor, we included garlic and parsley, which are unusual in a Denver omelet, and a dash of hot sauce livened things up without adding too much spiciness. We cooked the eggs according to our tried-and-true method, with some dairy (we used a little heavy cream, but milk worked as well) to keep the eggs from drying out, and added the warm filling just before folding the omelet onto a plate. Both components—eggs and filling—were perfectly cooked.

Denver Omelets

SERVES 2

You can make one omelet after another in the same pan, although you may need to reduce the heat. Refer to the photos for "How to Make an Oversized Omelet" on page 416—the steps are similar to the ones used here.

- 6 large eggs
- 2 tablespoons heavy cream or milk
- ½ teaspoon table salt
- ¼ teaspoon ground black pepper
- 2 tablespoons unsalted butter
- 4 ounces Monterey Jack cheese, shredded (about 1 cup)
- 1 recipe Filling for Denver Omelets (recipe follows)

1. Whisk together 3 of the eggs, 1 tablespoon of the cream, ¼ teaspoon of the salt, and ⅛ teaspoon of the pepper in a small bowl until thoroughly combined.

2. Melt 1 tablespoon of the butter in a 10-inch nonstick skillet over medium-high heat until it just begins to brown, swirling to coat the pan. Add the eggs to the skillet and cook until the edges begin to set, about 2 to 3 seconds, then, with a rubber spatula, stir in a circular motion until slightly thickened, about 10 seconds. Use the spatula to pull the cooked edges into the center, then tilt the pan to one side so that the uncooked egg runs to the edge of the pan. Repeat until the omelet is just set but still moist on the surface, 1 to 2 minutes.

3. Sprinkle ½ cup of the cheese evenly over the eggs and allow to partially melt, 15 to 20 seconds. With the handle of the pan facing you, spoon half the filling over the left side of the omelet. Following step 4 on page 416, slide the filling-topped half of the omelet onto a warmed plate using the spatula, then tilt the skillet so the remaining omelet folds over the filling in a half-moon shape; set aside. Repeat the instructions for the second omelet. Serve.

Filling for Denver Omelets

MAKES ENOUGH TO FILL 2 OMELETS

A ham steak is our top choice for this recipe, although canned ham and sliced deli ham will work. (If using sliced deli ham, add it with the garlic, parsley, and hot sauce.)

- 1 tablespoon unsalted butter
- ½ red bell pepper, stemmed, seeded, and chopped fine
- ½ green bell pepper, stemmed, seeded, and chopped fine
- 1 small onion, minced
- ¼ teaspoon table salt
- 4 ounces ham steak, diced (about 1 cup) (see note)
- 1 tablespoon minced fresh parsley leaves
- 1 garlic clove, minced or pressed through a garlic press (about 1 teaspoon)
- ½ teaspoon hot sauce

Melt the butter in a 10-inch nonstick skillet over medium-high heat. Add the peppers, onion, and salt and cook, stirring occasionally, until the onion begins to soften, 5 to 7 minutes. Add the ham and cook until the peppers begin to brown, about 2 minutes. Add the parsley, garlic, and hot sauce and cook for 30 seconds. Transfer to a small bowl and cover to keep warm.

FAMILY-SIZED OMELET

WHY THIS RECIPE WORKS: An omelet is a great breakfast or brunch dish, but cooking omelets one at a time for more than a couple of people is just not practical. We wanted to find a way to make an omelet that was big enough to serve four people. We wanted it to have tender, not rubbery, eggs and a rich, cheesy filling.

Flipping a huge eight-egg omelet was clearly not going to work, so we had to find a way to cook the top of the omelet as well as the bottom. Cooking the eggs longer over lower heat resulted in an unpleasant texture. Broiling to cook the top of the eggs worked, but it dried out the omelet, and we wanted it to be creamy. Then we had the idea of covering the pan after the bottom of the eggs was set but the top was still runny, which worked like a charm. The lid trapped the heat and moisture to steam the top of the omelet, and it partially melted the cheese as well. Now we had a perfectly cooked omelet for four, with tender eggs and bits of melted cheese in every bite.

Family-Sized Cheese Omelet

SERVES 4

Monterey Jack, colby, or any other good melting cheese can be substituted for the cheddar.

- 8 large eggs
- ½ teaspoon table salt
- ⅛ teaspoon ground black pepper
- 2 tablespoons unsalted butter
- 3 ounces cheddar cheese, shredded (about ¾ cup) (see note)

1. Whisk the eggs, salt, and pepper together in a medium bowl. Melt the butter in a 12-inch nonstick skillet over medium heat, swirling to coat the pan.

2. Add the eggs and cook, stirring gently in a circular motion, until the mixture is slightly thickened, about 1 minute. Following the photos, use a heatproof rubber spatula to pull the cooked edges of the egg toward the center of the pan, tilting the pan so the uncooked egg runs to the cleared edge of the pan. Repeat until the bottom of the omelet is just set but the top is still runny, about 1 minute. Cover the skillet, reduce the heat to low, and cook until the top of the omelet begins to set but is

still moist, about 5 minutes.

3. Remove the pan from the heat. Sprinkle the cheddar evenly over the eggs, cover, and let sit until the cheese partially melts, about 1 minute. Slide half of the omelet onto a warmed platter using the spatula, then tilt the skillet so the remaining omelet flips over onto itself, forming a half-moon shape. Cut into wedges and serve.

NOTES FROM THE TEST KITCHEN

HOW TO MAKE AN OVERSIZED OMELET

1. Pull the cooked edges of the egg toward the center of the pan and allow the raw egg to run to the edges.

2. When the omelet is set on the bottom but still very runny on the top, cover the skillet and reduce the heat to low.

3. After the top of the omelet begins to set, sprinkle with the cheese and let the omelet rest off the heat, covered, until the cheese has partially melted.

4. After using a heatproof rubber spatula to slide half of the omelet out onto a platter, tilt the skillet so that the omelet folds over onto itself to make the traditional half-moon shape.

FRENCH OMELET

WHY THIS RECIPE WORKS: In contrast to half-moon diner-style omelets, the French omelet is a pristine rolled affair. The temperature of the pan must be just right, the eggs beaten just so, and hand movements must be swift. We decided to ditch the stuffy attitude and come up with a foolproof method for making the ideal French omelet—unblemished golden yellow with an ultra-creamy texture, rolled around minimal filling.

The classic method requires a black carbon steel omelet pan and a fork, but a nonstick skillet worked fine here. Instead of a fork, which scraped our nonstick pans, bamboo skewers and wooden chopsticks gave us small curds with a silky texture. Preheating the pan for 10 minutes over low heat eliminated any hot spots. For creaminess, we added very cold butter, which dispersed evenly and fused with the eggs for a moist, rich omelet. To keep the omelet light, we found the perfect number of strokes; excessive beating unravels egg proteins, leading to dense-ness. We tried different heat levels, but even at medium heat, the omelet cooked so quickly it was hard to judge when it was done, so we turned off the heat when it was still runny and covered it to finish cooking. Finally, for an easy rolling method, we slid the omelet onto a paper towel and used the towel to roll the omelet into the sought-after cylinder.

French Omelet

SERVES 2

Because making these omelets is such a quick process, make sure to have all your ingredients and equipment at the ready. If you don't have skewers or chopsticks to stir the eggs in step 3, use the handle of a wooden spoon. Warm the plates in a 200-degree oven.

- **2 tablespoons unsalted butter, cut into 2 pieces**
- **½ teaspoon vegetable oil**
- **6 large eggs, chilled**
  Table salt and ground black pepper
- **2 tablespoons shredded Gruyère cheese**
- **4 teaspoons minced fresh chives**

1. Cut 1 tablespoon of the butter in half. Cut the remaining 1 tablespoon butter into small pieces, transfer to a small bowl, and place in the freezer while preparing the eggs and the skillet, at least 10 minutes. Meanwhile, heat the oil in an 8-inch nonstick skillet over low heat for 10 minutes.

2. Crack 2 of the eggs into a medium bowl and separate a third egg; reserve the white for another use and add the yolk to the bowl. Add ⅛ teaspoon salt and a pinch of pepper. Break the yolks with a fork, then beat the eggs at a moderate pace, about 80 strokes, until the yolks and whites are well combined. Stir in half of the frozen butter cubes.

3. When the skillet is fully heated, use paper towels to wipe out the oil, leaving a thin film on the bottom and sides of the skillet. Add ½ tablespoon of the reserved butter piece to the skillet and heat until melted. Swirl the butter to coat the skillet, add the egg mixture, and increase the heat to medium-high. Following the photos on page 418, use two chopsticks or wooden skewers to scramble the eggs using a quick circular motion to move around the skillet, scraping the cooked egg from the side of the skillet as you go, until the eggs are almost cooked but still slightly runny, 45 to 90 seconds. Turn off the heat (remove the skillet from the heat if using an electric burner) and smooth the eggs into an even layer using a rubber spatula. Sprinkle the omelet with 1 tablespoon of the Gruyère and 2 teaspoons of the chives. Cover the skillet with a tight-fitting lid and let sit, 1 minute for a runnier omelet and 2 minutes for a firmer omelet.

4. Heat the skillet over low heat for 20 seconds, uncover, and, using a rubber spatula, loosen the edges of the omelet from the skillet. Place a folded square of paper towel onto a warmed plate and slide the omelet out of the skillet onto the paper towel so that the omelet lies flat on the plate and hangs about 1 inch off the paper towel. Roll the omelet into a neat cylinder and set aside. Return the skillet to low heat and heat 2 minutes before repeating instructions for the second omelet starting with step 2. Serve.

NOTES FROM THE TEST KITCHEN

MAKING A FRENCH OMELET

1. Add the beaten egg mixture to the skillet and stir with chopsticks to produce small curds, which result in a silkier texture.

2. Turn off the heat while the eggs are still runny; smooth with a spatula into an even layer.

3. After sprinkling with the cheese and chives, cover so the residual heat gently finishes cooking the omelet.

4. Slide the finished omelet onto a paper towel–lined plate. Use the paper towel to lift the omelet and roll it up.

SPANISH TORTILLA

WHY THIS RECIPE WORKS: This classic Spanish omelet is immensely appealing, but can be greasy, dense, and heavy if prepared incorrectly. Typical recipes call for up to 4 cups of extra-virgin olive oil to cook the potatoes, which can lead to an overly oily—and expensive—tortilla. We wanted an intensely rich, velvety, melt-in-your-mouth egg-and-potato omelet—that didn't require using a quart of oil.

We first stuck with the traditional volume of olive oil until we could determine the proper type and ratio of ingredients. We chose starchy russet potatoes, thinly sliced, and standard yellow onions, which had a sweet, mellow flavor. We also settled on the perfect ratio of eggs to potatoes that allowed the tortilla to set firm and tender, with the eggs and potatoes melding into one another. Next we set out to reduce the amount of oil. Unfortunately, with less oil in the pan, half the potatoes were frying, while the other half were steaming. We started a new tortilla, this time with slightly firmer, less starchy Yukon Golds. With a fraction of the oil in the skillet, they were a winner: starchy enough to become meltingly tender as they cooked, but sturdy enough to stir and flip halfway through cooking with few breaks. Finally, we had to determine the best way to flip the omelet. To do this, we simply slid the tortilla out of the pan and onto one plate. Then, placing another plate upside down over the tortilla, we easily flipped the whole thing and slid the tortilla back in the pan, making a once-messy task easy and foolproof.

Spanish Tortilla with Roasted Red Peppers and Peas

SERVES 4 TO 6

Spanish tortillas are often served warm or at room temperature with olives, pickles, and Garlic Mayonnaise (recipe follows) as an appetizer. They may also be served with a salad as a light entrée. For the most traditional tortilla, omit the roasted red peppers and peas. See page 611 for our top-rated extra-virgin olive oil.

- 6   tablespoons plus 1 teaspoon extra-virgin olive oil (see note)
- 1½ pounds (3 to 4 medium) Yukon Gold potatoes, peeled, quartered, and cut into ⅛-inch-thick slices
- 1   small onion, halved and sliced thin
- 1   teaspoon table salt
- ¼   teaspoon ground black pepper
- 8   large eggs

½ cup jarred roasted red peppers, rinsed, dried, and cut into ½-inch pieces
½ cup frozen peas, thawed
   Garlic Mayonnaise (optional)

1. Toss 4 tablespoons of the oil, the potatoes, onion, ½ teaspoon of the salt, and the pepper in a large bowl until the potato slices are thoroughly separated and coated in oil. Heat 2 tablespoons more oil in a 10-inch nonstick skillet over medium-high heat until shimmering. Reduce the heat to medium-low, add the potato mixture to the skillet, and set the bowl aside (do not rinse). Cover and cook, stirring occasionally with a rubber spatula, until the potatoes offer no resistance when poked with a paring knife, 22 to 28 minutes (some potato slices may break into smaller pieces).

2. Meanwhile, whisk the eggs and remaining ½ teaspoon salt in the reserved bowl until just combined. Using a rubber spatula, fold the hot potato mixture, red peppers, and peas into the eggs until combined, making sure to scrape all the potato mixture out of the skillet. Return the skillet to medium-high heat, add the remaining 1 teaspoon oil, and heat until just beginning to smoke. Add the egg-potato mixture and cook, shaking the pan and folding the mixture constantly for 15 seconds; smooth the top of the mixture with a rubber spatula. Reduce the heat to medium, cover, and cook, gently shaking the pan every 30 seconds, until the bottom is golden brown and the top is lightly set, about 2 minutes.

3. Using a rubber spatula, loosen the tortilla from the pan, shaking it back and forth until the tortilla slides around. Slide the tortilla onto a large plate. Invert the tortilla onto a second large plate and slide it, browned side up, back into the skillet. Tuck the edges of the tortilla into the skillet. Return the pan to medium heat and continue to cook, gently shaking the pan every 30 seconds, until the second side is golden brown, about 2 minutes longer. Slide the tortilla onto a cutting board; cool at least 15 minutes. Cut the tortilla into cubes or wedges and serve with Garlic Mayonnaise, if desired.

Spanish Tortilla with Chorizo and Scallions

Use a cured, Spanish-style chorizo for this recipe. Portuguese linguiça is a suitable substitute.

Follow the recipe for Spanish Tortilla with Roasted Red Peppers and Peas, omitting the roasted red peppers and peas. In step 1, heat 4 ounces Spanish-style chorizo, cut into ¼-inch pieces, with 1 tablespoon oil (reduced from 2 tablespoons) in a 10-inch nonstick skillet over medium-high heat, stirring occasionally, until the chorizo is browned and the fat has rendered, about 5 minutes. Proceed with the recipe as directed, adding the potato mixture to the skillet with the chorizo and rendered fat and folding 4 thinly sliced scallions into the eggs in step 2.

Garlic Mayonnaise
MAKES ABOUT 1¼ CUPS

2 large egg yolks
2 teaspoons Dijon mustard
2 teaspoons juice from 1 lemon
1 medium garlic clove, minced or pressed through a garlic press (about 1 teaspoon)
¾ cup vegetable oil
1 tablespoon water
¼ cup extra-virgin olive oil
½ teaspoon table salt
¼ teaspoon ground black pepper

Process the yolks, mustard, lemon juice, and garlic in a food processor until combined, about 10 seconds. With the machine running, slowly drizzle in the vegetable oil, about 1 minute. Transfer the mixture to a medium bowl and whisk in the water. Whisking constantly, slowly drizzle in the olive oil, about 30 seconds. Whisk in the salt and pepper. (The mayonnaise can be refrigerated in an airtight container for up to 4 days.)

THICK AND HEARTY FRITTATAS

WHY THIS RECIPE WORKS: A frittata loaded with meat and vegetables often ends up dry, overstuffed, and overcooked. We wanted a frittata big enough to make a substantial meal for 6 to 8 people—with a pleasing balance of egg to filling, firm yet moist eggs, and a lightly browned crust.

We started with an even dozen eggs, which we found required 3 cups of cooked vegetables and meat to create the best balance of filling to eggs. When we chose our fillings, we needed to be a little selective about the cheese—Gruyère and goat cheese both had just the right amount of moisture. Most any vegetable or meat can be added to a frittata, with two caveats: The food must be cut into small pieces, and it must be precooked to drive off excess moisture and fat. A little half-and-half added a touch of creaminess. Given the large number of eggs, we discovered we had to shorten the time the frittata spent on the stovetop so the bottom wouldn't scorch by the time the eggs were properly cooked. We solved the problem by starting the eggs on medium heat, and stirring them so they could cook quickly yet evenly. With the eggs still on the wet side, we slid the skillet under the broiler until the top had puffed and browned, but removed it while the eggs in the center were still slightly wet and runny, allowing the residual heat to finish the cooking.

Asparagus, Ham, and Gruyère Frittata

SERVES 6 TO 8

A 12-inch ovensafe nonstick skillet is necessary for this recipe. Because broilers vary so much in intensity, watch the frittata carefully as it cooks.

- 12 large eggs
- 3 tablespoons half-and-half
- ½ teaspoon table salt
- ¼ teaspoon ground black pepper
- 2 teaspoons olive oil
- 8 ounces asparagus, tough ends trimmed, spears cut on the bias into ¼-inch pieces
- 4 ounces ¼-inch-thick deli ham, cut into ½-inch cubes (about ¾ cup)
- 1 medium shallot, minced (about 3 tablespoons)
- 3 ounces Gruyère cheese, cut into ¼-inch cubes (about ¾ cup)

1. Adjust an oven rack about 5 inches from the broiler element and heat the broiler. Whisk the eggs, half-and-half, salt, and pepper together in a medium bowl. Set aside.

2. Heat the oil in a 12-inch ovensafe nonstick skillet over medium heat until shimmering; add the asparagus and cook, stirring occasionally, until lightly browned and almost tender, about 3 minutes. Add the ham and shallot and cook until the shallot softens, about 2 minutes.

3. Stir the Gruyère into the eggs; add the egg mixture to the skillet and cook, using a spatula to stir and scrape the bottom of the skillet, until large curds form and the spatula begins to leave a wake but the eggs are still very wet, about 2 minutes. Shake the skillet to distribute the eggs evenly and cook without stirring to let the bottom set, about 30 seconds.

4. Slide the skillet under the broiler and cook until the surface is puffed and spotty brown, yet the center remains slightly wet and runny when cut into with a paring knife, 3 to 4 minutes. Using a potholder (the skillet handle will be hot), remove the skillet from the oven and let stand for 5 minutes to finish cooking; using the spatula, loosen the frittata from the skillet and slide it onto a platter or cutting board. Cut into wedges and serve.

Leek, Prosciutto, and Goat Cheese Frittata

SERVES 6 TO 8

A 12-inch ovensafe nonstick skillet is necessary for this recipe. The goat cheese will crumble more easily if it is chilled. A 12-inch ovensafe nonstick skillet is necessary for this recipe.

- 12 large eggs
- 3 tablespoons half-and-half
  Table salt and ground black pepper
- 2 tablespoons unsalted butter
- 2 small leeks, white and light green parts only, halved lengthwise, sliced thin, and rinsed thoroughly (about 3 cups)
- 3 ounces very thinly sliced prosciutto, cut into ½-inch-wide strips
- ¼ cup chopped fresh basil leaves
- 4 ounces goat cheese, crumbled (about 1 cup) (see note)

1. Adjust an oven rack about 5 inches from the broiler element and heat the broiler. Whisk the eggs, half-and-half, ½ teaspoon salt, and ¼ teaspoon pepper together in a medium bowl. Set aside.

2. Melt the butter in a 12-inch ovensafe nonstick skillet over medium heat. Add the leeks and ¼ teaspoon salt; reduce the heat to low and cook, covered, stirring occasionally, until softened, 8 to 10 minutes.

3. Stir the prosciutto, basil, and half of the goat cheese into the eggs; add the egg mixture to the skillet and cook, using a spatula to stir and scrape the bottom of the skillet, until large curds form and the spatula begins to leave a wake but the eggs are still very wet, about 2 minutes. Shake the skillet to distribute the eggs evenly and cook without stirring to let the bottom set, about 30 seconds.

4. Distribute the remaining goat cheese evenly over the frittata. Slide the skillet under the broiler and cook until the surface is puffed and spotty brown, yet the center remains slightly wet and runny when cut into with a paring knife, 3 to 4 minutes. Using a potholder (the skillet handle will be hot), remove the skillet from the oven and let stand for 5 minutes to finish cooking; using the spatula, loosen the frittata from the skillet and slide it onto a platter or cutting board. Cut into wedges and serve.

QUICHE

WHY THIS RECIPE WORKS: A really good quiche should have a smooth, creamy custard in a tender pastry crust. The custard should be rich, but not overwhelmingly so, and moist, not dried out. We aimed to find a way to make this perfect pie.

We experimented with multiple combinations of egg and dairy to find the one that would provide just the right balance of richness and lightness. Eggs alone were not rich enough; whole eggs plus yolks provided the degree of richness we wanted. For the dairy component, we found that equal parts of milk and heavy cream worked best. This custard was creamy and smooth. After layering bacon and Gruyère over the bottom of the pie shell—for a classic quiche Lorraine—we poured the custard on top and baked the quiche until it was puffed and set around the edges but still jiggled in the center; the residual heat finished cooking the center without turning the top into a rubbery skin. Before serving the quiche, we let it cool on a wire rack, which is a small but important step; this allows air to circulate under the crust and prevents it from becoming soggy.

Quiche Lorraine

SERVES 8

The center of the quiche will be surprisingly soft when it comes out of the oven, but the filling will continue to set (and sink somewhat) as it cools. If the pie shell has been previously baked and cooled, place it in the heating oven for about five minutes to warm it, making sure that it does not burn.

1 recipe Basic Single-Crust Pie Dough (page 558), fitted into a 9-inch pie plate and chilled

8 ounces bacon (about 8 slices), cut into ½-inch pieces

2 large eggs plus 2 large egg yolks

1 cup whole milk

1 cup heavy cream

½ teaspoon table salt

½ teaspoon ground white pepper

Pinch freshly grated nutmeg

4 ounces Gruyère cheese, shredded (about 1 cup)

1. Adjust an oven rack to the middle position and heat the oven to 375 degrees. Following the photos on page 569, line the chilled crust with a double layer of foil and fill with pie weights. Bake until the pie dough looks dry and is light in color, 25 to 30 minutes. Transfer the pie plate to a wire rack and remove the weights and foil.

2. Cook the bacon in a 12-inch nonstick skillet over medium heat until crisp, about 5 minutes. Using a slotted spoon, transfer the bacon to a paper towel–lined plate. Whisk the remaining ingredients except the Gruyère together in a medium bowl.

3. Spread the Gruyère and bacon evenly over the bottom of the warm pie shell and set the shell on the oven rack. Pour the custard mixture into the pie shell (it should come to about ½ inch below the crust's rim). Bake until light golden brown and a knife blade inserted about 1 inch from the edge comes out clean and the center feels set but still soft, 32 to 35 minutes. Transfer the quiche to a wire rack and cool. Serve warm or at room temperature.

BREAKFAST STRATA

WHY THIS RECIPE WORKS: A classic breakfast dish, strata is easy to prepare, presents a variety of flavors, can feed a crowd, and perhaps best of all, can, and indeed should be made ahead of time. Too often, though, it is overloaded with fillings; we wanted a savory bread pudding with a balanced, well-seasoned filling.

Recipes recommend all kinds of bread to use; we liked supermarket French or Italian loaves, which were neutral in flavor but had a sturdy texture. Rather than cubing the bread, which is often recommended, we sliced it to retain the layered quality of the dish and let the slices dry slightly (stale bread held up better than fresh). We used whole eggs and half-and-half for the custard, with a tad more dairy than eggs, and increased the amount of custard to saturate the bread more fully. A surprisingly

successful addition to the custard was white wine, which we reduced to evaporate the alcohol; it brightened all the flavors. A key to ensuring cohesiveness in the strata was weighting it while it rested for at least one hour; this way, every piece of bread absorbed some custard. We kept our fillings minimal so they wouldn't overwhelm the bread and custard, and we sautéed the filling ingredients before adding them to the casserole to keep the moisture from turning the dish watery.

Breakfast Strata with Spinach and Gruyère

SERVES 6

To weigh down the assembled strata, use two 1-pound boxes of sugar, laid side by side over the plastic-covered surface. To double this recipe, use a 13 by 9-inch baking dish greased with 1½ tablespoons butter and increase the baking time in step 5 to 1 hour and 20 minutes.

8–10 (½-inch-thick) slices supermarket French or Italian bread

5 tablespoons unsalted butter, softened

4 medium shallots, minced (about ½ cup)

1 (10-ounce) package frozen chopped spinach, thawed and squeezed dry

Table salt and ground black pepper

½ cup dry white wine

6 ounces Gruyère cheese, shredded (about 1½ cups)

6 large eggs

1¾ cups half-and-half

1. Adjust an oven rack to the middle position and heat the oven to 225 degrees. Arrange the bread in a single layer on a large baking sheet and bake until dry and crisp, about 40 minutes, turning the slices over halfway through the baking time. (Alternatively, leave the slices out overnight to dry.) Let the bread cool completely, then spread butter evenly over one side of each bread slice, using 2 table-spoons of the butter; set aside.

2. Heat 2 tablespoons more butter in a medium nonstick skillet over medium heat. Add the shallots and cook until softened, about 3 minutes; add the spinach and salt and pepper to taste and cook until the spinach is warm, about 2 minutes. Transfer to a medium bowl and set aside. Add the wine to the skillet, increase the heat to medium-high, and simmer until reduced to ¼ cup, 2 to 3 minutes; set aside.

3. Butter an 8-inch square baking dish with the remaining 1 tablespoon butter; arrange half of the bread slices, buttered-side up, in a single layer in the dish. Sprinkle half of the spinach mixture, then ½ cup of the shredded Gruyère, evenly over the bread slices. Arrange the remaining bread slices in a single layer over the cheese; sprinkle the remaining spinach mixture and ½ cup more Gruyère evenly over the bread. Whisk the eggs in a medium bowl until combined; whisk in the reduced wine, half-and-half, 1 teaspoon salt, and a pinch of pepper. Pour the egg mixture evenly over the bread layers.

4. Wrap the strata tightly with plastic wrap, pressing the wrap against the surface of the strata. Weigh the strata down (see note), and refrigerate for at least 1 hour or up to 24 hours.

5. Remove the dish from the refrigerator and let stand at room temperature for 20 minutes. Meanwhile, adjust an oven rack to the middle position and heat the oven to 325 degrees. Uncover the strata and sprinkle the remaining ½ cup Gruyère evenly over the surface; bake until both edges and center are puffed and the edges have pulled away slightly from the sides of the dish, 50 to 55 minutes. Cool on a wire rack for 5 minutes and serve.

Breakfast Strata with Sausage, Mushrooms, and Monterey Jack

To double this recipe, use a 13 by 9-inch baking dish greased with 1½ tablespoons butter and increase the baking time in step 5 to 1 hour and 20 minutes.

- 8–10 (½-inch-thick) slices supermarket French or Italian bread
- 3 tablespoons unsalted butter, softened
- 8 ounces bulk breakfast sausage, crumbled
- 3 medium shallots, minced (about 6 tablespoons)
- 8 ounces white mushrooms, wiped clean and quartered
  Table salt and ground black pepper
- ½ cup dry white wine
- 6 ounces Monterey Jack cheese, shredded (about 1½ cups)
- 6 large eggs
- 1¾ cups half-and-half
- 2 tablespoons minced fresh parsley leaves

Follow the recipe for Breakfast Strata with Spinach and Gruyère through step 1. Fry the sausage in a medium nonstick skillet over medium heat, breaking the sausage apart with a wooden spoon, until it loses its raw color and begins to brown, about 4 minutes; add the shallots and cook, stirring frequently, until softened, about 3 minutes. Add the mushrooms to the skillet and cook until the mushrooms no longer release liquid, about 6 minutes; transfer to a medium bowl and season with salt and pepper to taste. Reduce the wine as directed in step 2; continue with the recipe from step 3, adding the parsley to the egg mixture along with the salt and pepper and substituting the sausage mixture for the spinach and the Monterey Jack for the Gruyère.

BLUEBERRY PANCAKES

WHY THIS RECIPE WORKS: Blueberry pancakes sound appetizing, but they are often tough and rubbery or dense and soggy. And they inevitably take on an unappealing blue-gray hue. We wanted pancakes that cooked up light and fluffy and were studded with sweet, tangy bursts of summer's best berry.

Starting with the pancakes themselves, we determined that unbleached flour, sugar, a little salt, and both baking powder and baking soda were essential for the dry ingredients. One egg added just enough structure and richness without making the pancakes overly eggy. Buttermilk was the preferred dairy component, but since our ground rules were to use only what most home cooks would be likely to have on hand, we searched for a substitute. Lemon juice thickens milk almost to the consistency of buttermilk and adds a similar tang that tasters actually preferred. Some melted butter added to the mix prevented our pancakes from being dry and bland. Mixing the batter too strenuously leads to tough pancakes; it's time to stop mixing when there are still a few lumps and streaks of flour. Once we had great-tasting pancakes, we turned to the blueberries. Stirring them into the batter would obviously lead to smashing and those blue-gray streaks, so rather than incorporating the berries, we simply dropped some onto the batter after we'd ladled it into the skillet. Smaller wild berries are sweeter than the larger ones, but frozen berries work as well as fresh, which means we can have great blueberry pancakes any time of the year.

Blueberry Pancakes

MAKES ABOUT SIXTEEN 4-INCH PANCAKES, SERVING 4 TO 6

To make sure that frozen berries do not bleed, rinse them under cool water in a mesh strainer until the water runs clear, and then spread them on a paper towel–lined plate to dry. If you have buttermilk on hand, use 2 cups instead of the milk and lemon juice. To keep pancakes warm while cooking the remaining batter, hold them in a 200-degree oven on a greased rack set over a baking sheet.

2	cups milk (see note)
1	tablespoon juice from 1 lemon (see note)
2	cups (10 ounces) unbleached all-purpose flour
2	tablespoons sugar
2	teaspoons baking powder
½	teaspoon baking soda
½	teaspoon table salt
1	large egg
3	tablespoons unsalted butter, melted and cooled slightly
1–2	teaspoons vegetable oil
1	cup fresh or frozen blueberries, preferably wild, rinsed and dried (see note)

1. Whisk the milk and lemon juice together in a medium bowl or large measuring cup; set aside to thicken while preparing the other ingredients. Whisk the flour, sugar, baking powder, baking soda, and salt together in a medium bowl.

2. Whisk the egg and melted butter into the milk until combined. Make a well in the center of the dry ingredients in the bowl; pour in the milk mixture and whisk very gently until just combined (a few lumps should remain). Do not overmix.

3. Heat a 12-inch nonstick skillet over medium heat for 3 to 5 minutes; add 1 teaspoon of the oil and brush to coat the skillet bottom evenly. Pour ¼ cup batter onto three spots on the skillet; sprinkle 1 tablespoon of the blueberries over each pancake. Cook the pancakes until large bubbles begin to appear, 1½ to 2 minutes. Using a thin-bladed spatula, flip the pancakes and cook until golden brown on the second side, 1 to 1½ minutes longer. Serve and repeat with the remaining batter, using the remaining 1 teaspoon vegetable oil if necessary.

GERMAN APPLE PANCAKE

WHY THIS RECIPE WORKS: More akin to popovers than American pancakes, German apple pancakes are golden and puffed outside, custardy inside, with sweet apples baked right in. The dish suffers from many of the same problems as popovers, too: not enough rise, dense texture, and a too-eggy flavor. We wanted to solve these problems and get this pancake just right.

Flour and eggs are the basis of the batter; half-and-half for the dairy component imparted richness and a light texture. Sugar, salt, and vanilla completed the batter. Steam, not leavening, is what puffs the pancake, so to get the maximum rise we needed to find the right oven temperature. A very hot oven burned the exterior of the pancake; preheating the oven to a high temperature as well as preheating the pan, then lowering the temperature when the pancake went in, proved the ideal method. Granny Smith apples were our top pick if you like a little tartness; otherwise Braeburns are a good choice for their sweetness. We cooked apples with brown sugar rather than granulated for a deeper flavor, with butter, cinnamon, and a bright touch of lemon juice. To keep the apples from being pushed out of the pan when the pancake rose, we first poured the batter around the edge of the skillet, then over the apples. Our pancake puffed spectacularly, and when we served it, every bite contained warm, tender apples.

German Apple Pancake

SERVES 4

A 10-inch ovensafe skillet is necessary for this recipe; we highly recommend using a nonstick skillet for the sake of easy cleanup, but a regular skillet will work. If you prefer tart apples, use Granny Smiths; if you prefer sweet ones, use Braeburns.

½   cup (2½ ounces) unbleached all-purpose flour
1   tablespoon granulated sugar
½   teaspoon table salt
2   large eggs
⅔   cup half-and-half
1   teaspoon vanilla extract
2   tablespoons unsalted butter
1¼ pounds Granny Smith or Braeburn apples
    (3 to 4 large apples), peeled, quartered, cored,
    and cut into ½-inch-thick slices (see note)
¼   cup packed (1¾ ounces) light or dark brown sugar
¼   teaspoon ground cinnamon
1   teaspoon juice from 1 lemon
    Confectioners' sugar, for dusting
    Maple syrup or Caramel Sauce (recipe follows),
    for serving

1. Adjust an oven rack to the upper-middle position and heat the oven to 500 degrees.

2. Whisk the flour, granulated sugar, and salt together in a medium bowl. In a second medium bowl, whisk the eggs, half-and-half, and vanilla together until combined. Add the liquid ingredients to the dry ingredients and whisk until no lumps remain, about 20 seconds; set the batter aside.

3. Melt the butter in a 10-inch ovensafe nonstick skillet over medium-high heat. Add the apples, brown sugar, and cinnamon; cook, stirring frequently with a heatproof rubber spatula, until the apples are golden brown, about 10 minutes. Off the heat, stir in the lemon juice.

4. Working quickly, pour the batter around the edge of the pan and then over the apples. Place the skillet in the oven and immediately reduce the oven temperature to 425 degrees. Bake until the pancake edges are brown and puffy and have risen above the edges of the skillet, about 18 minutes.

5. Using a potholder (the skillet handle will be hot), remove the skillet from the oven and loosen the pancake edges with a heatproof rubber spatula; invert the pancake onto a platter. Dust with confectioners' sugar, cut into wedges, and serve with maple syrup or Caramel Sauce.

Caramel Sauce

MAKES ABOUT 1½ CUPS

Cooking the sugar with some water in a covered pot helps trap moisture and ensures that the sugar will dissolve. When the hot cream mixture is added in step 3, the hot sugar syrup will bubble vigorously (and dangerously), so don't use a smaller saucepan. If you make the caramel sauce ahead, reheat it in the microwave or a small saucepan over low heat until warm and fluid.

½   cup water
1   cup (7 ounces) sugar
1   cup heavy cream
⅛   teaspoon table salt
½   teaspoon vanilla extract
½   teaspoon juice from 1 lemon

1. Place the water in a 2-quart saucepan; pour the sugar into the center of the pan, taking care not to let the sugar crystals stick to the sides of the pan. Cover and bring the mixture to a boil over high heat; once the mixture is boiling, uncover the pan and continue to boil until the sugar syrup is thick and straw-colored, and registers 300 degrees on an instant-read thermometer, about 7 minutes. Reduce the heat to medium and continue to cook until the syrup is deep amber and registers 350 degrees, about 1 to 2 minutes.

2. Meanwhile, bring the cream and salt to a simmer in a small saucepan over high heat (if the cream boils before the sugar syrup reaches a deep amber color, remove the cream from the heat and cover to keep warm).

3. Remove the pan with the sugar syrup from the heat; very carefully pour about one-quarter of the hot cream into it (the mixture will bubble vigorously), and let the bubbling subside. Add the remaining cream, the vanilla, and lemon juice; whisk until the sauce is smooth. (The sauce can be cooled and refrigerated in an airtight container for up to 2 weeks.)

WAFFLES

WHY THIS RECIPE WORKS: You cannot simply put pancake batter in a waffle iron and make waffles; waffles should be moist and fluffy inside and crisp and brown outside—more like a soufflé with a crust than a pancake. We wanted to find the way to achieve this archetypal waffle.

Thick batter is the secret of the crisp exterior and custardy interior of a waffle, so we used a higher proportion of flour to liquid than that of standard recipes. With buttermilk (and buttermilk makes the best-tasting waffles) there's no need for baking powder, and we found that eliminating it also helped crisp up the waffles. A small amount of cornmeal added a pleasing crunch.

Separating the egg and folding the whipped white into the batter was a definite improvement; we could see the pockets of air when we cut into a waffle made this way. Like pancakes, waffles turn tough when the batter is overmixed, so we used a light hand, adding the liquid gradually and using more of a folding motion to mix. Cooked to a medium toasty brown, these waffles were everything we wanted them to be.

Buttermilk Waffles

MAKES 3 TO 4, DEPENDING ON THE SIZE OF THE WAFFLE IRON

The secret to great waffles is a thick batter, so don't expect a pourable batter. The optional dash of cornmeal adds a pleasant crunch to the finished waffle. This recipe can be doubled or tripled. Make toaster waffles out of leftover batter—undercook the waffles a bit, cool them on a wire rack, wrap them in plastic wrap, and freeze. Pop them in the toaster for a quick breakfast. The waffles are best served fresh from the iron but can be held in an oven until all of the batter is used. As you make the waffles, place them on a wire rack set in a rimmed baking sheet, cover them with a clean kitchen towel, and place the baking sheet in a 200-degree oven.

1 cup (5 ounces) unbleached all-purpose flour
1 tablespoon cornmeal (optional; see note)
½ teaspoon table salt
¼ teaspoon baking soda
⅞ cup buttermilk
1 large egg, separated
2 tablespoons unsalted butter, melted and cooled

1. Following the manufacturer's instructions, heat a waffle iron. Whisk the flour, cornmeal (if using), salt, and baking soda together in a medium bowl. In a separate medium bowl, whisk the buttermilk, egg yolk, and butter together.

2. Beat the egg white with an electric mixer on medium-low speed until foamy, about 1 minute. Increase the speed to medium-high and whip the whites to stiff peaks, 2 to 4 minutes.

3. Add the liquid ingredients to the dry ingredients in a thin, steady stream while mixing gently with a rubber spatula. (Do not add the liquid faster than you can incorporate it into the batter.) Toward the end of mixing, use a folding motion to incorporate the ingredients. Gently fold the egg white into the batter.

4. Spread an appropriate amount of batter onto the waffle iron. Following the manufacturer's instructions, cook the waffle until golden brown, 2 to 5 minutes. Serve.

BANANA BREAD

WHY THIS RECIPE WORKS: Overripe bananas are a good excuse to make banana bread, but the loaf can be dry, heavy, and bland. We wanted a banana bread with deep banana flavor, plenty of moisture, and a nice, light texture.

Very ripe, darkly speckled bananas contribute moisture as well as flavor to this bread (they're sweeter, too); unripe ones will not work. Pureeing the bananas kept the bread from rising well, so instead we mashed them thoroughly by hand. For additional moisture we included yogurt, which contributed a nice tang without masking the flavor of the bananas. The quick-bread method of mixing—melting the butter and folding the wet ingredients into the dry ones—produced a golden brown loaf and delicate texture; when we tried creaming the butter and sugar first, the bread came out more like butter cake and wasn't as golden brown. However, we found it was important not to over-mix the batter; too-vigorous stirring led to overabundant gluten development that turned the loaf tough and dense.

Banana Bread

MAKES ONE 8-INCH LOAF

For best flavor, use bananas that are very ripe.

- 2 cups (10 ounces) unbleached all-purpose flour
- ¾ cup (5¼ ounces) sugar
- ¾ teaspoon baking soda
- ½ teaspoon table salt
- 3 very ripe bananas, mashed well (about 1½ cups)
- ¼ cup plain yogurt
- 2 large eggs, lightly beaten
- 6 tablespoons (¾ stick) unsalted butter, melted and cooled
- 1 teaspoon vanilla extract
- 1¼ cup walnuts, toasted and chopped coarse

1. Adjust an oven rack to the lower-middle position and heat the oven to 350 degrees. Grease and flour a 9 by 5-inch loaf pan; set aside.

2. Whisk the flour, sugar, baking soda, and salt together in a large bowl; set aside.

3. Mix the mashed bananas, yogurt, eggs, butter, and vanilla together with a wooden spoon in a medium bowl. Lightly fold the banana mixture into the dry ingredients with a rubber spatula until just combined and the batter looks thick and chunky. Fold in the walnuts. Scrape the batter into the prepared loaf pan and smooth the surface with a rubber spatula.

4. Bake until the loaf is golden brown and a toothpick inserted in the center comes out clean, about 55 minutes. Cool in the pan for 5 minutes, then transfer to a wire rack. Serve warm or at room temperature.

CREAM SCONES

WHY THIS RECIPE WORKS: British-style scones, or cream scones, are a far cry from humongous American coffeehouse creations. Cream scones are delicate and light, much like a biscuit. We set out to perfect a technique for making these tea-time (or breakfast) favorites.

Experimentation with different kinds of flour revealed that all-purpose is the best choice for scones, and even better, for maximum tenderness, is a lower-protein brand of flour. Butter was important for flavor, but only a modest amount or the scones would practically melt in the oven. Cream won out over buttermilk and whole milk for the liquid; it made our scones rich and kept them tender. As a nod to American taste, we increased the amount of sugar from that used in traditional recipes, but only slightly to keep them from being too sweet. The discovery that the food processor did a great job of cutting the butter into the flour was a boon, making it even easier to make these treats. Our British-style cream scones were just right served with a bit of jam.

Cream Scones

MAKES 8

Use a low-protein all-purpose flour, such as Gold Medal or Pillsbury. The easiest and most reliable approach to mixing the butter into the dry ingredients is to use a food processor fitted with the metal blade. If you want a light glaze on the scones, brush the tops of the scones with 1 tablespoon heavy cream and then sprinkle them with 1 tablespoon sugar just before you put them in the oven.

Resist the urge to eat the scones hot out of the oven. Letting them cool for at least 10 minutes firms them up and improves their texture.

- 2 **cups (10 ounces) unbleached all-purpose flour (see note)**
- 3 **tablespoons sugar**
- 1 **tablespoon baking powder**
- ½ **teaspoon table salt**
- 5 **tablespoons unsalted butter, chilled and cut into ¼-inch cubes**
- ½ **cup currants**
- 1 **cup heavy cream**

1. Adjust an oven rack to the middle position and heat the oven to 425 degrees.

2. Place the flour, sugar, baking powder, and salt in a food processor and pulse to combine, about 6 pulses.

3. Scatter the butter evenly over the top and continue to pulse until the mixture resembles coarse cornmeal with a few slightly larger butter lumps, about 12 more pulses. Transfer the mixture to a large bowl and stir in the currants. Stir in the heavy cream with a rubber spatula until a dough begins to form, about 30 seconds.

4. Transfer the dough and any dry, floury bits to a work surface and knead the dough by hand just until it comes together into a rough, slightly sticky ball, 5 to 10 seconds. Cut the dough into eight wedges. Place the wedges on an ungreased baking sheet. (The baking sheet can be covered in plastic wrap and refrigerated for up to 2 hours.)

5. Bake until the scone tops are light brown, 12 to 15 minutes. Cool on a wire rack for at least 10 minutes. Serve warm or at room temperature.

BLUEBERRY SCONES

WHY THIS RECIPE WORKS: Berry scones can be a treat—moist, sweet berries throughout a tender, light biscuit, but more often the berries weigh down the scone and impart little flavor. We wanted a rich, flaky scone studded with sweet, juicy blueberries.

Starting with traditional scone recipes, we increased the amounts of sugar and butter to add sweetness and richness to our scones. A combination of sour cream and milk lent both richness and tang. But now our scones were heavier than we wanted. We found two ways to lighten them. First, we borrowed a technique from puff pastry, where the dough is turned, rolled, and folded multiple times to create layers that are forced apart by steam when baked, and added a few quick folds to our scone dough. Then, to ensure that the butter would stay as cold and solid as possible while baking, we froze the butter and grated it into the dry ingredients on a box grater. Both tricks made for lighter, flakier scones. Adding the blueberries was a challenge. If we put them into the dry ingredients, they got mashed when we mixed the dough; when we added them to the already-mixed dough, we ruined our pockets of butter when we worked the berries in. The solution was pressing the berries into the dough, rolling the dough into a log, then pressing the log into a rectangle and cutting the scones. We had successfully transformed the scone into a fruit-filled, rich yet light treat.

Blueberry Scones

MAKES 8

It is important to work the dough as little as possible—work quickly and knead and fold the dough only the number of times called for. The butter should be frozen solid before grating. If your kitchen is hot and humid, chill the flour mixture and bowls before use. The recipe calls for two whole sticks of butter, but only 10 tablespoons are actually used (see step 1). If fresh berries are unavailable, an equal amount of frozen berries, unthawed, can be substituted. An equal amount of raspberries, blackberries, or strawberries can also be used in place of the blueberries. Cut larger berries into ¼ to ½-inch pieces before incorporating. Refrigerate or freeze leftover scones, wrapped in foil, in an airtight container. To serve, remove the foil and place the scones on a baking sheet in a 375-degree oven. Heat until warmed through and recrisped, 8 to 10 minutes if refrigerated, 16 to 20 minutes if frozen.

- 16 **tablespoons (2 sticks) unsalted butter, frozen whole (see note)**
- 1½ **cups (about 7½ ounces) fresh blueberries, picked over (see note)**
- ½ **cup whole milk**
- ½ **cup sour cream**
- 2 **cups (10 ounces) unbleached all-purpose flour, plus extra for the work surface**
- ½ **cup (3½ ounces) sugar, plus 1 tablespoon for sprinkling**
- 2 **teaspoons baking powder**
- ½ **teaspoon table salt**
- ¼ **teaspoon baking soda**
- 1 **teaspoon grated zest from 1 lemon**

1. Adjust an oven rack to the middle position and heat the oven to 425 degrees. Score and remove half of the wrapper from each stick of frozen butter. Grate the unwrapped ends on the large holes of a box grater (you should grate a total of 8 tablespoons). Place the grated butter in the freezer until needed. Melt 2 tablespoons of the remaining ungrated butter and set aside. Save the remaining 6 tablespoons butter for another use. Place the blueberries in the freezer until needed.

2. Whisk the milk and sour cream together in a medium bowl; refrigerate until needed. Whisk the flour, ½ cup of the sugar, the baking powder, salt, baking soda, and lemon zest together in a medium bowl. Add the frozen butter to the flour mixture and toss with your fingers until the butter is thoroughly coated.

3. Add the milk mixture to the flour mixture; fold with a rubber spatula until just combined. Using the spatula, transfer the dough to a liberally floured work surface. Dust the surface of the dough with flour; with floured hands, knead the dough six to eight times, until it just holds together in a ragged ball, adding flour as needed to prevent sticking.

4. Roll the dough into an approximate 12-inch square. Following the photos, fold the dough into thirds like a business letter, using a bench scraper or metal spatula to release the dough if it sticks to the work surface. Lift the short ends of the dough and fold into thirds again to form an approximate 4-inch square. Transfer the dough to a plate lightly dusted with flour and chill in the freezer for 5 minutes.

5. Transfer the dough to a floured work surface and roll into an approximate 12-inch square again. Sprinkle the blueberries evenly over the surface of the dough, then press down so they are slightly embedded in the dough. Using a bench scraper or a thin metal spatula, loosen the

FOLDING AND SHAPING THE SCONES

1. Start by folding the dough into thirds (like a business letter). Then fold in the ends of the dough to form a 4-inch square. Chill the dough.

2. Reroll the dough into a 12-inch square. Press the berries into the dough.

3. Roll the dough into a jellyroll-like log to incorporate the blueberries.

4. Lay the log seam side down and press into an even 12 by 4-inch rectangle.

5. Cut the dough into eight triangular pieces.

dough from the work surface. Roll the dough, pressing to form a tight log. Lay the log seam side down and press it into a 12 by 4-inch rectangle. Using a sharp, floured knife, cut the rectangle crosswise into four equal rectangles. Cut each rectangle diagonally to form two triangles and transfer to a parchment-lined baking sheet.

6. Brush the tops with the melted butter and sprinkle with the remaining 1 tablespoon sugar. Bake until the tops and bottoms are golden brown, 18 to 25 minutes. Transfer to a wire rack and cool for 10 minutes before serving.

OATMEAL SCONES

WHY THIS RECIPE WORKS: The oatmeal scones served in a typical coffeehouse are so dry and leaden that they seem like a ploy to get people to buy more coffee to wash them down. We wanted rich toasted oat flavor in a tender, flaky, not-too-sweet scone.

Whole rolled oats and quick oats performed better than instant and steel-cut oats. The rolled oats had a deeper oat flavor, but the quick-cooking oats made scones with a softer texture; either type will work. Toasting the oats brought out their nutty flavor. We used a minimal amount of sugar and baking powder, but plenty of cold butter. A mixture of milk and heavy cream added richness without making the scones too heavy. An

egg proved to be the ultimate touch of richness. Cutting the cold butter into the flour, instead of using melted butter, resulted in a lighter texture; we were careful not to overmix the dough, which toughened the scones. A very hot oven made the scones rise spectacularly and also gave them a craggy appearance; the high heat meant less time in the oven and therefore less time to dry out. You won't need a gallon of coffee to wash down these light, oaty scones.

Oatmeal Scones

MAKES 8 SCONES

Half-and-half is a suitable substitute for the milk-cream combination.

- 1½ cups (4½ ounces) old-fashioned oats or quick oats
- ¼ cup whole milk (see note)
- ¼ cup heavy cream (see note)
- 1 large egg
- 1½ cups (7½ ounces) unbleached all-purpose flour
- ⅓ cup (2⅓ ounces) sugar, plus 1 tablespoon for sprinkling
- 2 teaspoons baking powder
- ½ teaspoon table salt
- 10 tablespoons unsalted butter, chilled and cut into ½-inch cubes

1. Adjust an oven rack to the middle position and heat the oven to 375 degrees. Spread the oats evenly on a rimmed baking sheet and toast in the oven until fragrant and lightly browned, 7 to 9 minutes; cool the oats on the baking sheet on a wire rack. Increase the oven temperature to 450 degrees. Line a second baking sheet with parchment paper. When the oats are cooled, measure out 2 tablespoons (for dusting the work surface and the dough) and set aside.

2. Whisk the milk, cream, and egg together in a large measuring cup; remove 1 tablespoon of the mixture and reserve for glazing.

3. Pulse the flour, ⅓ cup of the sugar, the baking powder, and salt in a food processor until combined, about 4 pulses. Scatter the cold butter evenly over the dry ingredients and pulse until the mixture resembles coarse cornmeal, about 12 pulses. Transfer the mixture to a medium bowl and stir in the cooled oats. Using a rubber spatula, fold in the liquid ingredients until large clumps form. Mix the dough by hand in the bowl until the dough forms a cohesive mass.

4. Dust a work surface with half of the reserved oats, turn the dough out onto the work surface, and dust the top with the remaining oats. Gently pat into a 7-inch

circle about 1 inch thick. Using a bench scraper or chef's knife, cut the dough into eight wedges and set on the prepared baking sheet, spacing them about 2 inches apart. Brush the surfaces with the reserved egg mixture and sprinkle with the remaining 1 tablespoon sugar. Bake until golden brown, 12 to 14 minutes; cool the scones on the baking sheet on a wire rack for 5 minutes, then transfer the scones to the rack and cool to room temperature, about 30 minutes. Serve.

Glazed Maple-Pecan Oatmeal Scones

Follow the recipe for Oatmeal Scones, toasting ½ cup chopped pecans with the oats, whisking ¼ cup maple syrup into the milk mixture, and omitting the sugar. When the scones are cooled, whisk 3 tablespoons maple syrup and ½ cup confectioners' sugar together in a small bowl until combined; drizzle the glaze over the scones.

BLUEBERRY MUFFINS

WHY THIS RECIPE WORKS: Blueberry muffins should be packed with blueberry flavor and boast a moist crumb. But too often, the blueberry flavor is fleeting, thanks to the fact that the berries in the produce aisle have suffered from long-distance shipping. We wanted blueberry muffins that would taste great with blueberries of any origin, even the watery supermarket kind.

To intensify the blueberry in our muffins, we tried combining blueberry jam with fresh supermarket blueberries. The muffins baked up with a pretty blue filling, but tasters thought the jam made them too sweet. To solve this, we made our own fresh, low-sugar berry jam by simmering fresh blueberries on the stovetop with a bit of sugar. Adding our cooled homemade jam to the batter along with fresh, uncooked berries gave us the best of both worlds: intense blueberry flavor and the liquid burst that only fresh berries could provide.

As for the muffin base, we found that the quick-bread method—whisking together eggs and sugar before adding milk and melted butter, and then gently folding in the dry ingredients—produced a hearty, substantial crumb that could support a generous amount of fruit. We found that an equal amount of butter and oil gave us just the right combination of buttery flavor and moist, tender texture. To make the muffins even richer, we swapped the whole milk for buttermilk. Finally, for a nice crunch, we sprinkled lemon-scented sugar on top of the batter just before baking.

Blueberry Muffins

MAKES 12 MUFFINS

For finely grated lemon zest, use a rasp grater.

LEMON-SUGAR TOPPING
- ⅓ cup (2⅓ ounces) sugar
- 1½ teaspoons finely grated zest from 1 lemon (see note)

MUFFINS
- 2 cups (about 10 ounces) fresh blueberries, picked over
- 1 teaspoon sugar plus 1⅛ cups (8 ounces)
- 2½ cups (12½ ounces) unbleached all-purpose flour
- 2½ teaspoons baking powder
- 1 teaspoon table salt
- 2 large eggs
- 4 tablespoons (½ stick) unsalted butter, melted and cooled slightly
- 4 tablespoons vegetable oil
- 1 cup buttermilk
- 1½ teaspoons vanilla extract

1. FOR THE TOPPING: Stir the sugar and lemon zest together in a small bowl until combined and set aside.

2. FOR THE MUFFINS: Adjust an oven rack to the upper-middle position and heat the oven to 425 degrees. Spray a standard-sized muffin pan with vegetable oil spray. Bring 1 cup of the blueberries and 1 teaspoon of the sugar to

SWIRLING JAM INTO BLUEBERRY MUFFINS

1. Place 1 teaspoon of cooled berry jam in the center of each batter-filled cup, pushing it below the surface.

2. Using a chopstick, swirl the jam into the batter following a figure-eight pattern.

a simmer in a small saucepan over medium heat. Cook, mashing the berries with a spoon several times and stirring frequently, until the berries have broken down and the mixture is thickened and reduced to ¼ cup, about 6 minutes. Transfer to a small bowl and cool to room temperature, 10 to 15 minutes.

3. Whisk the flour, baking powder, and salt together in a large bowl. Whisk the remaining 1⅛ cups sugar and the eggs together in a medium bowl until thick and homogeneous, about 45 seconds. Slowly whisk in the butter and oil until combined. Whisk in the buttermilk and vanilla until combined. Using a rubber spatula, fold the egg mixture and remaining 1 cup blueberries into the flour mixture until just moistened. (The batter will be very lumpy with a few spots of dry flour; do not overmix.)

4. Using a ⅓-cup measure or an ice cream scoop, divide the batter equally among the prepared muffin cups (the batter should completely fill the cups and mound slightly). Following the photos, spoon 1 teaspoon of the cooked berry mixture into the center of each mound of batter. Using a chopstick or skewer, gently swirl the berry filling into the batter using a figure-eight motion. Sprinkle the lemon sugar evenly over the muffins.

5. Bake until the muffin tops are golden and just firm, 17 to 19 minutes, rotating the pan halfway through baking. Cool the muffins in the pan for 5 minutes, then transfer them to a wire rack and cool for 5 minutes before serving.

BRAN MUFFINS

WHY THIS RECIPE WORKS: We've made bran muffins with unprocessed wheat bran, so we know how they're supposed to look and taste. But there are so many bran cereals at the supermarket, just about all of them with a muffin recipe on the box, that we wondered if we could achieve the same thing without a special trip to the natural foods store. Twig-style cereal worked better than flakes, but soaking the twigs in milk, as most recipes recommend, left our muffins dense and heavy—they were soaking up all the moisture, leaving the batter dry. Instead, we stirred together the wet ingredients first and then added the cereal; grinding half of the twigs in the food processor and leaving the rest whole gave us the rustic texture we wanted, and the cereal softened in just a few minutes. Whole milk yogurt added needed moisture to the batter, along with butter. Molasses and brown sugar reinforced the earthy bran flavor. To address the texture of the muffins, we switched to baking soda instead of baking powder and used one egg plus a yolk—two eggs made the muffins too springy. To ensure that they would soften fully, we plumped the raisins in water in the microwave before adding them to the batter and baking the muffins. These muffins were tender and moist, rustic but not dense, with hearty bran flavor—and all the ingredients came from the supermarket.

Bran Muffins

MAKES 12 MUFFINS

The test kitchen prefers Kellogg's All-Bran Original cereal in this recipe. Dried cranberries or dried cherries may be substituted for the raisins. Low-fat or nonfat yogurt can be substituted for whole milk yogurt, though the muffins will be slightly less flavorful.

1	cup raisins (see note)
1	teaspoon water
2¼	cups (5 ounces) All-Bran Original cereal (see note)
1¼	cups (6¼ ounces) unbleached all-purpose flour
½	cup (2½ ounces) whole wheat flour
2	teaspoons baking soda
½	teaspoon table salt
1	large egg plus 1 large egg yolk
⅔	cup packed (4⅔ ounces) light brown sugar
3	tablespoons mild or light molasses
1	teaspoon vanilla extract
6	tablespoons (¾ stick) unsalted butter, melted and cooled
1¾	cups plain whole milk yogurt (see note)

1. Adjust an oven rack to the middle position and heat the oven to 400 degrees. Spray a standard-sized muffin pan with vegetable oil spray. Combine the raisins and water in a small microwave-safe bowl, cover with plastic wrap, cut several steam vents in the plastic with a paring knife, and microwave on high power for 30 seconds. Let stand, covered, until the raisins are softened and plump, about 5 minutes. Transfer the raisins to a paper towel–lined plate to cool.

2. Process half of the bran cereal in a food processor until finely ground, about 1 minute. Whisk the flours, baking soda, and salt in a large bowl to combine; set aside. Whisk the egg and egg yolk together in a medium bowl until well combined and light-colored, about 20 seconds. Add the sugar, molasses, and vanilla; whisk until the mixture is thick, about 30 seconds. Add the melted butter and whisk to combine; add the yogurt and whisk to combine. Stir in the processed cereal and unprocessed cereal; let the mixture sit until the cereal is evenly moistened (there will still be some small lumps), about 5 minutes.

3. Add the wet ingredients to the dry ingredients and gently mix with a rubber spatula until the batter is combined and evenly moistened. Do not overmix. Gently fold the raisins into the batter. Using a ⅓-cup measure or an ice cream scoop, divide the batter evenly among the muffin cups, dropping the batter to form mounds. Do not level or flatten the surfaces of the mounds.

4. Bake until the muffins are dark golden and a toothpick inserted into the center of a muffin comes out with a few crumbs attached, 16 to 20 minutes, rotating the pan halfway through the baking time. Cool the muffins in the pan for 5 minutes, then transfer to a wire rack and cool for 10 minutes before serving.

CORN MUFFINS

WHY THIS RECIPE WORKS: A corn muffin shouldn't be as sweet and fluffy as a cupcake, nor should it be dense and "corny" like corn bread. It should taste like corn, but not overpoweringly, and should be moist with a tender crumb and a crunchy top. Our mission was to come up with a recipe for these seemingly simple muffins that struck just the right balance in both texture and flavor.

The cornmeal itself proved to be an important factor, and degerminated meal just didn't have enough corn flavor. A fine-ground, whole grain meal provided better flavor and texture. Our first batches of muffins were too dry, so we experimented with various ways to add moisture; butter, sour cream, and milk provided the moisture, fat (for richness), and acidity (for its tenderizing effect) that we wanted. We tried mixing the ingredients with both the quick-bread and creaming methods; not only was the former the easier way to go, but it also resulted in less airy, cakey muffins. We got our crunchy top from a 400-degree oven. All in all, we'd resolved all of our issues with corn muffins; these were subtly sweet, rich but not dense, and with a texture that was neither cake nor corn bread.

Corn Muffins

MAKES 12 MUFFINS

Whole grain cornmeal has a fuller flavor than regular cornmeal milled from degerminated corn. To determine what kind of cornmeal a package contains, look closely at the label.

- 2 cups (10 ounces) unbleached all-purpose flour
- 1 cup (5 ounces) fine-ground, whole grain yellow cornmeal (see note)
- 1½ teaspoons baking powder
- 1 teaspoon baking soda
- ½ teaspoon table salt
- 2 large eggs
- ¾ cup (5¼ ounces) sugar
- 8 tablespoons (1 stick) unsalted butter, melted
- ¾ cup sour cream
- ½ cup milk

1. Adjust an oven rack to the middle position and heat the oven to 400 degrees. Spray a standard-sized muffin pan with vegetable oil spray.

2. Whisk the flour, cornmeal, baking powder, baking soda, and salt together in a medium bowl; set aside. Whisk the eggs in a second medium bowl. Add the sugar to the eggs; whisk vigorously until thick and homogeneous, about 30 seconds; add the melted butter in three additions, whisking to combine after each addition. Add half of the sour cream and half of the milk and whisk to combine; whisk in the remaining sour cream and milk until combined. Add the wet ingredients to the dry ingredients; mix gently with a rubber spatula until the batter is just combined and evenly moistened. Do not overmix. Using a ⅓-cup measure or ice cream scoop, divide the batter evenly among the muffin cups, dropping the batter to form mounds. Do not level or flatten the surface of the mounds.

3. Bake until the muffins are light golden brown and a skewer inserted into the center of the muffins comes out clean, about 18 minutes, rotating the pan halfway through the baking time. Cool the muffins in the pan for 5 minutes, then transfer to a wire rack and cool for 10 minutes before serving.

Corn and Apricot Muffins with Orange Essence

1. In a food processor, process ⅔ cup granulated sugar and 1½ teaspoons grated orange zest until pale orange, about 10 seconds. Transfer to a small bowl and set aside.

2. In a food processor, pulse 1½ cups (10 ounces) dried apricots for 10 pulses, until chopped fine. Transfer to a medium microwave-safe bowl; add ⅔ cup orange juice to the apricots, cover the bowl tightly with plastic wrap, and microwave on high power until simmering, about 1 minute. Let the apricots stand, covered, until softened and plump, about 5 minutes. Strain the apricots and discard the juice.

3. Follow the recipe for Corn Muffins, substituting ¼ cup packed dark brown sugar for an equal amount of the granulated sugar and stirring ½ teaspoon grated orange zest and the strained apricots into the wet ingredients before adding them to the dry ingredients. Before baking, sprinkle a portion of the orange sugar over each mound of batter. Cool the muffins in the pan for 5 minutes, then gently lift them out using the tip of a paring knife. Cool on a wire rack for 10 minutes before serving.

CRUMB CAKE

WHY THIS RECIPE WORKS: The original crumb cake was brought to New York by German immigrants; sadly, the bakery-fresh versions have all but disappeared, and most people know only the commercially baked (and preservative-laden) type. We wanted a recipe closer to the original version that could be made at home.

Most modern recipes use butter cake rather than the traditional yeast dough, which made our job that much easier. The essence of this cake is the balance between the tender, buttery cake and the thick, lightly spiced crumb topping. Starting with our favorite yellow cake recipe, we realized we needed to reduce the amount of butter or the richness would be overwhelming. We compensated for the resulting dryness by substituting buttermilk for milk, which also helped make the cake sturdy enough to support the crumbs, and we left out an egg white so the cake wouldn't be rubbery. We wanted our crumb topping to be soft and cookie-like, not a crunchy streusel, so we mixed granulated and brown sugars and melted the butter for a dough-like consistency, flavoring the mixture only with cinnamon. Broken into little pieces and sprinkled over the cake batter, our topping held together during baking and made a thick layer of moist crumbs with golden edges that didn't sink into the cake.

New York–Style Crumb Cake
SERVES 8 TO 10

Don't be tempted to substitute all-purpose flour for the cake flour; doing so will make a dry, tough cake. If you can't find buttermilk, you can use an equal amount of plain low-fat yogurt, but do not substitute powdered buttermilk because it will make a sunken cake. When topping the cake, take care to not push the crumbs into the batter. This recipe can be easily doubled and baked in a 13 by 9-inch baking dish. If doubling, increase the baking time to about 45 minutes.

CRUMB TOPPING
⅓ cup (2⅔ ounces) granulated sugar
⅓ cup packed (2⅓ ounces) dark brown sugar
¾ teaspoon ground cinnamon
⅛ teaspoon table salt
8 tablespoons (1 stick) unsalted butter, melted and still warm
1¾ cups (7 ounces) cake flour (see note)

rolling them between your thumb and forefinger to form crumbs, and spread in an even layer over the batter, beginning with the edges and then working toward the center. Bake until the crumbs are golden and a wooden skewer inserted into the center of the cake comes out clean, 35 to 40 minutes. Cool on a wire rack for at least 30 minutes. Remove the cake from the pan by lifting the parchment overhang. Dust with confectioners' sugar before serving.

BLUEBERRY BOY BAIT

WHY THIS RECIPE WORKS: This coffee cake with the odd name—so called because the girl who created it for the Pillsbury Grand National Baking Contest said that teenage boys found it irresistible—is a moist cake with blueberries and a light streusel topping. We tracked down a version of the contest-winning recipe and decided to see if we could improve it.

The original recipe called for shortening and granulated sugar. We swapped butter for the shortening and brown sugar for some of the granulated sugar. Both exchanges resulted in richer, deeper flavor in the cake. We doubled the amount of blueberries; half went into the cake batter and the other half on top. An extra egg in the cake batter firmed up the structure so that the extra fruit wouldn't make the cake mushy. The topping couldn't be simpler: in addition to the blueberries, just sugar and cinnamon instead of a streusel, which baked into a light, crisp, sweet coating. If the quick disappearance of this cake is any indication, it's not only teenage boys who can't refuse a second piece.

Blueberry Boy Bait

SERVES 12

If using frozen blueberries, do not let them thaw, as they will turn the batter a blue-green color.

CAKE

- 2 cups (10 ounces) plus 1 teaspoon unbleached all-purpose flour
- 1 tablespoon baking powder
- 1 teaspoon table salt
- 16 tablespoons (2 sticks) unsalted butter, softened
- ¾ cup packed (5¼ ounces) light brown sugar
- ½ cup (3½ ounces) granulated sugar
- 3 large eggs
- 1 cup whole milk
- ½ cup blueberries, fresh or frozen (see note)

CAKE

- 1¼ cups (5 ounces) cake flour (see note)
- ½ cup (3½ ounces) granulated sugar
- ¼ teaspoon baking soda
- ¼ teaspoon table salt
- 6 tablespoons (¾ stick) unsalted butter, cut into 6 pieces, softened but still cool
- 1 large egg plus 1 large egg yolk
- ⅓ cup buttermilk (see note)
- 1 teaspoon vanilla extract
  Confectioners' sugar, for dusting

1. FOR THE CRUMB TOPPING: Whisk the sugars, cinnamon, salt, and butter together in a medium bowl to combine. Add the flour and stir with a rubber spatula or wooden spoon until the mixture resembles a thick, cohesive dough; set aside to cool to room temperature, 10 to 15 minutes.

2. FOR THE CAKE: Adjust an oven rack to the upper-middle position and heat the oven to 325 degrees. Cut a 16-inch length of parchment paper or aluminum foil and fold lengthwise to a 7-inch width. Spray an 8-inch square baking dish with vegetable oil spray and fit the parchment into the dish, pushing it into the corners and up the sides; allow the excess to overhang the edges of the dish.

3. In the bowl of a standing mixer fitted with the paddle attachment, mix the flour, sugar, baking soda, and salt on low speed to combine. With the mixer running at low speed, add the butter one piece at a time; continue beating until the mixture resembles moist crumbs, with no visible butter chunks remaining, 1 to 2 minutes. Add the egg, egg yolk, buttermilk, and vanilla; beat on medium-high speed until light and fluffy, about 1 minute, scraping once if necessary.

4. Transfer the batter to the prepared baking pan; using a rubber spatula, spread the batter into an even layer. Break apart the crumb topping into large pea-sized pieces,

½   cup blueberries, fresh or frozen (see note)

¼   cup (1¾ ounces) granulated sugar

½   teaspoon ground cinnamon

1. FOR THE CAKE: Adjust an oven rack to the middle position and heat the oven to 350 degrees. Grease and flour a 13 by 9-inch baking pan.

2. Whisk 2 cups of the flour, the baking powder, and salt together in a medium bowl. With an electric mixer, beat the butter and sugars on medium-high speed until fluffy, about 2 minutes. Add the eggs, one at a time, beating until just incorporated. Reduce the speed to medium and beat in one-third of the flour mixture until incorporated; beat in ½ cup of the milk. Beat in half of the remaining flour mixture, then the remaining ½ cup milk, and finally the remaining flour mixture. Toss the blueberries in a small bowl with the remaining 1 teaspoon flour. Using a rubber spatula, gently fold in the blueberries. Spread the batter into the prepared pan.

3. FOR THE TOPPING: Scatter the blueberries over the top of the batter. Stir the sugar and cinnamon together in a small bowl and sprinkle over the batter. Bake until a toothpick inserted in the center of the cake comes out clean, 45 to 50 minutes. Cool in the pan for 20 minutes, then turn out and place on a serving platter (topping side up). Serve warm or at room temperature. (The cake can be stored in an airtight container at room temperature for up to 3 days.)

CINNAMON BUNS

WHY THIS RECIPE WORKS: A tender, fluffy bun with a sweet cinnamon filling and rich glaze is a brunch treat no one will turn down. Most recipes, though, require yeast, which makes cinnamon buns time-consuming to make. We went into the kitchen to find a shortcut to good-tasting homemade cinnamon buns.

Eliminating the yeast would reduce the prep time substantially, so we started with the assumption that our leavener would be baking powder. A cream biscuit recipe, which could be mixed all in one bowl, was our starting point; buttermilk rather than cream (plus baking soda to balance the acidity of the buttermilk) made the interior of the biscuits light and airy. A small amount of melted butter restored some of the richness we had lost by eliminating the cream. A brief kneading ensured that the rolls would rise in the oven. We patted out the dough rather than rolling it and covered it with the filling of brown and granulated sugar, cinnamon, cloves, and salt, with melted butter to help the mixture adhere to the dough. We rolled up the dough, cut the buns, and put them in a nonstick cake pan to bake. When they were done, we topped the buns with a quick glaze of confectioners' sugar, buttermilk, and cream cheese. These cinnamon buns were on the table in less than a quarter of the time it would have taken for yeast buns—and they were just as tasty.

Quick Cinnamon Buns with Buttermilk Icing

MAKES 8 BUNS

Melted butter is used in both the filling and the dough and to grease the pan; melt the total amount (8 tablespoons) at once and measure it out as you need it. The buns are best eaten warm, but they will hold for up to 2 hours.

1   tablespoon unsalted butter, melted, for the pan (see note)

CINNAMON-SUGAR FILLING

¾   cup packed (5¼ ounces) dark brown sugar

¼   cup (1¾ ounces) granulated sugar

2   teaspoons ground cinnamon

⅛   teaspoon ground cloves

⅛   teaspoon table salt

1   tablespoon unsalted butter, melted (see note)

BISCUIT DOUGH

2½ cups (12½ ounces) unbleached all-purpose flour, plus extra for the work surface

2 tablespoons granulated sugar

1¼ teaspoons baking powder

½ teaspoon baking soda

½ teaspoon table salt

1¼ cups buttermilk

6 tablespoons (¾ stick) unsalted butter, melted (see note)

ICING

2 tablespoons cream cheese, softened

2 tablespoons buttermilk

1 cup (4 ounces) confectioners' sugar

1. Adjust an oven rack to the upper-middle position and heat the oven to 425 degrees. Pour 1 tablespoon of the melted butter into a 9-inch nonstick cake pan; brush to coat the pan. Spray a wire rack with vegetable oil spray and set aside.

2. **FOR THE CINNAMON-SUGAR FILLING:** Combine the sugars, spices, and salt in a small bowl. Add the melted butter and stir with a fork or your fingers until the mixture resembles wet sand; set the filling mixture aside.

3. **FOR THE BISCUIT DOUGH:** Whisk the flour, sugar, baking powder, baking soda, and salt together in a large bowl. Whisk the buttermilk and 2 tablespoons of the melted butter together in a measuring cup or small bowl. Add the liquid to the dry ingredients and stir with a wooden spoon until the liquid is absorbed (the dough will look very shaggy), about 30 seconds. Transfer the dough to a lightly floured work surface and knead until just smooth and no longer shaggy.

4. Pat the dough with your hands into a 12 by 9-inch rectangle. Brush the dough with 2 tablespoons more melted butter. Sprinkle evenly with the filling, leaving a ½-inch border of plain dough around the edges. Press the filling firmly into the dough. Using a bench scraper or metal spatula, loosen the dough from the work surface. Starting at a long side, roll the dough, pressing lightly, to form a tight log. Pinch the seam to seal. Roll the log seam side down and cut it evenly into eight pieces. With your hand, slightly flatten each piece of dough to seal the open edges and keep the filling in place. Place one roll in the center of the prepared pan, then place the remaining seven rolls around the perimeter of the pan. Brush with the remaining 2 tablespoons melted butter.

5. Bake until the edges are golden brown, 23 to 25 minutes. Use an offset metal spatula to loosen the buns from

the pan. Wearing an oven mitt, place a large plate over the pan and invert the buns onto a plate. Place the greased wire rack over the plate and invert the buns onto the rack. Cool for 5 minutes.

6. **FOR THE ICING:** While the buns are cooling, line a rimmed baking sheet with parchment paper; set the rack with the buns over the baking sheet. Whisk the cream cheese and buttermilk together in a large nonreactive bowl until thick and smooth (the mixture will look like cottage cheese at first). Sift the confectioners' sugar over the mixture; whisk until a smooth glaze forms, about 30 seconds. Spoon the glaze evenly over the buns and serve.

STICKY BUNS

WHY THIS RECIPE WORKS: Sticky buns are often too sweet, too big, too rich, and just too much. We wanted a bun that was neither dense nor bready. The crumb should be tender and feathery and the sticky glaze gently chewy and gooey; the flavor should be warm and spicy, buttery and sweet—but just enough so that devouring one isn't a feat.

To keep the sticky bun glaze from hardening into a tooth-shattering, taffy-like shell, we hit on the idea of including cream, which kept the glaze supple. The yeast dough for these buns should be rich. To the basic flour, yeast, and salt we added buttermilk, which gave the buns a complex flavor and a little acidity that balanced the sweetness—though we didn't overload the dough with sugar. Butter and eggs enriched the dough further. After the first rise, we spread the filling—dark brown sugar, cinnamon, cloves, and butter—over the dough, rolled it, cut the individual buns, and laid them in the pan with the caramel to rise once more before being baked. We found that setting the pan (a metal nonstick pan was preferable) on a baking stone in the oven ensured that the bottoms of the buns (which would end up on top) would bake completely. We wanted pecans in our sticky buns, too, but they lost their crunch when we put them into the filling or the topping. To preserve their crispness, we created one more layer: toasted nuts in a lightly sweetened glaze to crown the rolls before serving.

Sticky Buns with Pecans

MAKES 12 BUNS

This recipe has four components: the dough that is shaped into buns, the filling that creates the swirl in the shaped buns, the caramel glaze that bakes in the bottom of the baking dish along with the buns, and the pecan topping that garnishes the buns once they're baked. Although the ingredient list may look long, note that many ingredients are repeated. Leftover sticky buns can be wrapped in foil or plastic wrap and refrigerated for up to 3 days, but they should be warmed through before serving. They reheat quickly in a microwave oven (for two buns, about 2 minutes at 50 percent power works well).

DOUGH
- 3 large eggs, room temperature
- ¾ cup buttermilk, room temperature
- ¼ cup (1¾ ounces) granulated sugar
- 1¼ teaspoons table salt
- 2¼ teaspoons (1 envelope) instant or rapid-rise yeast
- 4¼ cups (21¼ ounces) unbleached all-purpose flour, plus extra for the work surface
- 6 tablespoons (¾ stick) unsalted butter, melted and still warm

CARAMEL GLAZE
- ¾ cup packed (5¼ ounces) light brown sugar
- 6 tablespoons (¾ stick) unsalted butter
- 3 tablespoons light or dark corn syrup
- 2 tablespoons heavy cream
  Pinch table salt

CINNAMON-SUGAR FILLING
- ¾ cup packed (5¼ ounces) light brown sugar
- 2 teaspoons ground cinnamon
- ¼ teaspoon ground cloves
  Pinch table salt
- 1 tablespoon unsalted butter, melted

PECAN TOPPING
- ¼ cup packed (1¾ ounces) light brown sugar
- 3 tablespoons light or dark corn syrup
- 3 tablespoons unsalted butter
  Pinch table salt
- ¾ cup (3 ounces) pecans, toasted in a small, dry skillet over medium heat until fragrant and browned, about 5 minutes, then cooled and chopped coarse
- 1 teaspoon vanilla extract

1. FOR THE DOUGH: In the bowl of a standing mixer, whisk the eggs to combine; add the buttermilk and whisk to combine. Whisk in the granulated sugar, salt, and yeast. Add about 2 cups of the flour and the butter; stir with a wooden spoon or rubber spatula until evenly moistened and combined. Add all but about ¼ cup of the remaining flour and knead with the dough hook at low speed for 5 minutes. Check the consistency of the dough (it should feel soft and moist but should not be wet and sticky; add more flour, if necessary); knead at low speed 5 minutes longer (the dough should clear the sides of the bowl but stick to the bottom). Turn the dough out onto a lightly floured work surface; knead by hand for about 1 minute to ensure that the dough is uniform (the dough should not stick to the work surface during hand kneading; if it does, knead in additional flour 1 tablespoon at a time).

2. Lightly spray a large bowl or plastic container with vegetable oil spray. Transfer the dough to the bowl, spray the dough lightly with vegetable oil spray, then cover the bowl tightly with plastic wrap and set in a warm, draft-free spot until doubled in volume, 2 to 2½ hours.

3. FOR THE CARAMEL GLAZE: Meanwhile, combine all the glaze ingredients in a small saucepan; cook over medium heat, whisking occasionally, until the butter is melted and the mixture is thoroughly combined. Pour the mixture into a nonstick metal 13 by 9-inch baking dish; using a rubber spatula, spread the mixture to cover the surface of the baking dish; set the baking dish aside.

4. TO ASSEMBLE AND BAKE THE BUNS: For the filling, combine the brown sugar, cinnamon, cloves, and salt in a small bowl and mix until thoroughly combined, using your fingers to break up any sugar lumps; set aside. Turn the dough out onto a lightly floured work surface. Gently shape the dough into a rough rectangle with a long side nearest you. Lightly flour the dough and roll to a 16 by 12-inch rectangle. Brush the dough with the melted butter, leaving a ½-inch border along the top edge; brush the sides of the baking dish with the butter remaining on the brush. Sprinkle the filling mixture over the dough, leaving a ¾-inch border along the top edge; smooth the filling in an even layer with your hand, then gently press the mixture into the dough to adhere. Beginning with the long edge nearest you, roll the dough into a taut cylinder. Firmly pinch the seam to seal and roll the cylinder seam side down. Very gently stretch to form a cylinder of even diameter and 18-inch length; push the ends in to create an even thickness. Using a serrated knife and gentle sawing motion, slice the cylinder in half, then slice each half in half again to create evenly sized quarters. Slice each quarter evenly into thirds, yielding 12 buns (the end pieces may be slightly smaller).

5. Arrange the buns cut side down in the prepared baking dish; cover tightly with plastic wrap and set in a warm, draft-free spot until puffy and pressed against one another, about 1½ hours. Meanwhile, adjust an oven rack to the lowest position, place a baking stone on the rack, and heat the oven to 350 degrees.

6. Place the baking pan on the baking stone; bake until golden brown and the center of the dough registers 180 degrees on an instant-read thermometer, 25 to 30 minutes. Cool on a wire rack for 10 minutes; invert onto a rimmed baking sheet, large rectangular platter, or cutting board. With a rubber spatula, scrape any glaze remaining in the baking pan onto the buns; cool while making the pecan topping.

7. FOR THE PECAN TOPPING: Combine the brown sugar, corn syrup, butter, and salt in a small saucepan and bring to a simmer over medium heat, whisking occasionally to thoroughly combine. Off the heat, stir in the pecans and vanilla until the pecans are evenly coated. Using a soup-spoon, spoon a heaping tablespoon of nuts and topping over the center of each sticky bun. Continue to cool until the sticky buns are warm, 15 to 20 minutes. Pull apart or use a serrated knife to cut apart the sticky buns; serve.

SOUR CREAM COFFEE CAKE

WHY THIS RECIPE WORKS: Sour cream coffee cakes should be buttery and rich. But some recipes yield a heavy cake that borders on greasy. We wanted a pleasantly rich cake with lots of streusel on top and throughout.

All-purpose flour gave us a better texture than the cake flour specified in many recipes. For richness, we used plenty of butter, sour cream, and eggs; the eggs contributed to the tight crumb we wanted. A good dose of baking powder, along with baking soda, was necessary to make this hefty batter rise. Rather than creaming the butter and sugar, which made the cake too light and airy, we cut softened butter and some of the sour cream into the dry ingredients, then added the eggs and the rest of the sour cream; the result was a tighter crumb. In addition to the streusel in the middle of the cake, we wanted more on top, so we started with a mixture of brown and granulated sugar and added a big hit of cinnamon and flour (to keep the streusel from congealing). We then divided the mixture—some for the interior streusel layers, which we sweetened further with more brown sugar, and the rest for the topping. To the latter, we added pecans and butter; the nuts toasted as the cake baked, so we didn't have to toast them first. With two layers of streusel in our moist, rich cake and another layer on top with toasty, crunchy nuts, this was a coffee cake worth getting up for.

Sour Cream Coffee Cake with Brown Sugar–Pecan Streusel

SERVES 12 TO 16

A 10-inch tube pan is best for this recipe.

STREUSEL
- ¾ cup (3¾ ounces) unbleached all-purpose flour
- ¾ cup (5¼ ounces) granulated sugar
- ½ cup packed (3½ ounces) dark brown sugar
- 2 tablespoons ground cinnamon
- 1 cup pecans, chopped
- 2 tablespoons unsalted butter, chilled and cut into 2 pieces

CAKE
- 12 tablespoons (1½ sticks) unsalted butter, softened but still cool, cut into ½-inch cubes, plus 2 tablespoons softened butter, for greasing the pan
- 4 large eggs
- 1½ cups sour cream
- 1 tablespoon vanilla extract
- 2¼ cups (11½ ounces) unbleached all-purpose flour
- 1¼ cups (8¾ ounces) granulated sugar
- 1 tablespoon baking powder
- ¾ teaspoon baking soda
- ¾ teaspoon table salt

1. FOR THE STREUSEL: In a food processor, process the flour, granulated sugar, ¼ cup of the brown sugar, and the cinnamon until combined, about 15 seconds. Transfer 1¼ cups of the flour-sugar mixture to a small bowl; stir in the remaining ¼ cup brown sugar and set aside to use for the streusel filling. Add the pecans and butter to the flour-sugar mixture in the food processor; pulse until the nuts and butter resemble small pebbly pieces, about 10 pulses; set aside.

2. FOR THE CAKE: Adjust an oven rack to the lowest position and heat the oven to 350 degrees. Grease a 10-cup tube pan with 2 tablespoons of the softened butter. Whisk the eggs, 1 cup of the sour cream, and the vanilla together in a medium bowl until combined.

3. Mix the flour, granulated sugar, baking powder, baking soda, and salt in the bowl of a standing mixer on low speed until combined, about 30 seconds. Add the remaining 12 tablespoons butter and remaining ½ cup sour cream; mix on low speed until the dry ingredients are moistened and the mixture resembles wet sand, with a few large butter pieces remaining, about 1½ minutes. Increase the speed to medium and beat until the batter comes together, about 10 seconds, scraping down the sides of the bowl with a rubber spatula as necessary. Lower the speed to medium-low and gradually add the egg mixture in three additions, beating for 20 seconds after each addition and scraping down the sides of the bowl as necessary. Increase the speed to medium-high and beat until the batter is light and fluffy, about 1 minute.

4. Using a rubber spatula, spread 2 cups of the batter in the bottom of the prepared pan, smoothing the surface. Sprinkle evenly with ¾ cup of the streusel filling without butter or nuts. Repeat with another 2 cups batter and the remaining ¾ cup streusel filling without butter or nuts. Spread the remaining batter over, then sprinkle with the streusel topping with butter and nuts.

5. Bake until the cake feels firm to the touch and a long toothpick or skewer inserted into the center comes out clean (bits of sugar from the streusel may cling to the tester), 50 to 60 minutes. Cool the cake in the pan on a wire rack for 30 minutes. Invert the cake onto a rimmed baking sheet (the cake will be streusel side down); remove the tube pan, place a wire rack on top of the cake, and reinvert the cake streusel side up. Cool to room temperature, about 2 hours. Cut into wedges and serve. (The cake can be wrapped in foil and stored at room temperature for up to 5 days.)

FRUIT SALAD

WHY THIS RECIPE WORKS: A bowl of cut-up fresh fruit is a nice complement to the sweets and heavier egg dishes at a brunch, but it can be a little boring without additional flavors. Yogurt-based sauces mask the fresh flavors (not to mention the colors) of the fruit, and sweet syrups make the fruit too much like a dessert. We were looking for a lighter, more flavorful alternative.

We adapted a French dressing called a *gastrique*, a reduction of an acidic liquid with sugar that usually accompanies savory dishes made with fruit. It's a simple technique, and our experiments with reducing different types of acid—wine, citrus juice, and balsamic vinegar—were an unqualified success. We were able to use additional flavorings in the basic dressing, such as spices, extracts, and citrus zests, that would complement the flavors of different types of fruit. Served at room temperature or chilled, fresh fruit bathed in a light but sweet-tart dressing is not only delicious but easy to make, too.

Strawberries and Grapes with Balsamic and Red Wine Reduction

MAKES ABOUT 6 CUPS

An inexpensive balsamic vinegar is fine for use in this recipe. Save high-quality vinegar for other preparations in which the vinegar is not cooked.

- ¾ cup balsamic vinegar (see note)
- ¼ cup dry red wine
- ¼ cup sugar
- Pinch table salt
- 1 tablespoon grated zest plus 1 tablespoon juice from 1 lemon
- ¼ teaspoon vanilla extract
- 3 whole cloves
- 1 quart strawberries, hulled and halved lengthwise (about 4 cups)
- 9 ounces large seedless red or black grapes, each grape halved pole to pole (about 2 cups)

1. Simmer the vinegar, wine, sugar, and salt in a small saucepan over high heat until syrupy and reduced to ¼ cup, about 15 minutes. Off the heat, stir in the lemon zest and juice, vanilla, and cloves; steep for 1 minute to blend the flavors and strain.

2. Combine the strawberries and grapes in a medium bowl; pour the warm dressing over the fruit and toss to coat. Serve at room temperature, or cover with plastic wrap, refrigerate for up to 4 hours, and serve chilled.

Nectarines, Blueberries, and Raspberries with Champagne-Cardamom Reduction

MAKES ABOUT 6 CUPS

Dry white wine can be substituted for the champagne.

- 1 cup champagne (see note)
- ¼ cup sugar
- Pinch table salt
- 1 tablespoon grated zest plus 1 tablespoon juice from 1 lemon
- 5 cardamom pods, crushed
- 3 medium nectarines (about 18 ounces), cut into ½-inch wedges (about 3 cups)
- 1 pint blueberries
- ½ pint raspberries

1. Simmer the champagne, sugar, and salt in a small saucepan over high heat until syrupy, honey-colored, and reduced to ¼ cup, about 15 minutes. Off the heat, stir in the lemon zest and juice and cardamom; steep for 1 minute to blend the flavors and strain.

2. Combine the nectarines, blueberries, and raspberries in a medium bowl; pour the warm dressing over the fruit and toss to coat. Serve at room temperature, or cover with plastic wrap, refrigerate for up to 4 hours, and serve chilled.

Honeydew, Mango, and Blueberries with Lime-Ginger Reduction

MAKES ABOUT 6 CUPS

Be sure to zest one of the limes before juicing. Cantaloupe can be used in place of honeydew, although the color contrast with the mango won't be as vivid.

- 1 cup juice plus 1 tablespoon grated zest from 8 limes (see note)
- ¼ cup sugar
- Pinch table salt
- 1 (1-inch) piece fresh ginger, peeled and minced (about 1 tablespoon)
- 1 tablespoon juice from 1 lemon
- ½ small honeydew melon (see note), seeds and rind removed, cut into 1-inch pieces (about 2 cups)
- 1 mango (about 10 ounces), peeled and cut into ½-inch pieces (about 1½ cups)
- 1 pint blueberries

1. Simmer the lime juice, sugar, and salt in a small saucepan over high heat until syrupy, honey-colored, and reduced to ¼ cup, about 15 minutes. Off the heat, stir in the lime zest, ginger, and lemon juice; steep for 1 minute to blend the flavors and strain.

2. Combine the melon, mango, and blueberries in a medium bowl; pour the warm dressing over the fruit and toss to coat. Serve at room temperature, or cover with plastic wrap, refrigerate for up to 4 hours, and serve chilled.

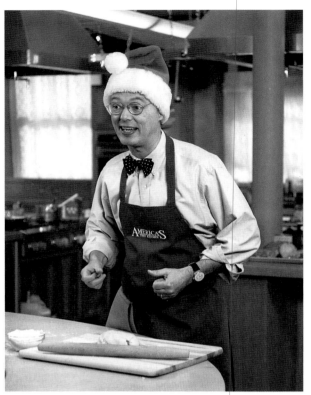

CHAPTER 20

PLEASE PASS THE BREAD

Cream Biscuits 444

Cream Biscuits with
Fresh Herbs 444

Cheddar Biscuits 444

Best Drop Biscuits 445

Rustic Dinner Rolls 445

Irish Soda Bread 447

Whole Wheat Soda
Bread 447

Quick Cheese Bread 447

Quick Cheese Bread
with Bacon, Onion,
and Gruyère 448

All-Purpose Corn
Bread 448

Spicy Jalapeño-Cheddar
Corn Bread 449

Southern Corn Bread 450

Rustic Country Bread 450

Almost No-Knead
Bread 451

Ciabatta 453

Multigrain Bread 455

CREAM BISCUITS

WHY THIS RECIPE WORKS: With a high rise, light texture, and rich flavor, fresh-from-the-oven biscuits tend to disappear quicker than cookies in the test kitchen. So it's a shame that many prospective bakers pass them up, just because the recipe calls for the strenuous step of cutting butter into flour, or the messy move of rolling out dough time and again to get every last piece into a round for the baking sheet. We wanted to make great biscuits that cut out these extra steps and used a basic combination of heavy cream, flour, baking powder, and salt.

Instead of cutting butter into flour, we included a generous amount of heavy cream in our biscuits, which gave them a lighter and more tender texture. Kneading for just 30 seconds was enough to get our dough smooth and uniform. We used an extra bit of cream to soak up all the last bits of flour in the bowl, ensuring that nothing was wasted. To enhance the light flavor of our biscuits, we added a small amount of sugar. All there was left to do was shape them, then pop them into the oven immediately to keep them from spreading. Although it is easy enough to pat out this dough and cut it into rounds with a biscuit cutter, we devised a second strategy of simply pressing the dough into an 8-inch cake pan, turning out the dough, and then slicing it into wedges.

Cream Biscuits

MAKES 8 BISCUITS

Bake the biscuits immediately after cutting them; letting them stand for any length of time can decrease the leavening power and thereby prevent the biscuits from rising properly in the oven.

- 2 cups (10 ounces) unbleached all-purpose flour, plus extra for the work surface
- 2 teaspoons sugar
- 1 teaspoon baking powder
- ½ teaspoon table salt
- 1½ cups heavy cream

1. Adjust an oven rack to the upper-middle position and heat the oven to 425 degrees. Line a large rimmed baking sheet with parchment paper. Whisk the flour, sugar, baking powder, and salt together in a medium bowl.

2. Add 1¼ cups of the cream to the flour mixture and stir with a wooden spoon until a dough forms, about 30 seconds. Transfer the dough to a lightly floured work surface, leaving all dry, floury bits behind in the bowl. Add the remaining ¼ cup of cream, 1 tablespoon at a time, to the

bowl, mixing with a wooden spoon after each addition, until all the loose flour is just moistened; add these moistened bits to the dough. Knead the dough briefly just until smooth, about 30 seconds.

3. Pat the dough into a ¾-inch-thick circle or press it into an 8-inch cake pan and turn it out onto a lightly floured surface. Cut the biscuits into rounds using a 2½-inch biscuit cutter or eight wedges using a knife. Place the rounds or wedges onto the prepared baking sheet and bake until golden brown, about 15 minutes. Serve immediately.

Cream Biscuits with Fresh Herbs

Use the herb of your choice in this variation.

Follow the recipe for Cream Biscuits, adding 2 tablespoons minced fresh herbs to the flour mixture in step 1. Proceed as directed.

Cheddar Biscuits

Follow the recipe for Cream Biscuits, adding 2 ounces sharp cheddar cheese, shredded (about ½ cup), to the flour mixture in step 1. Proceed as directed, increasing the baking time to 18 minutes.

BEST DROP BISCUITS

WHY THIS RECIPE WORKS: Drop biscuits have many things going for them: a crisp outer crust, a tender, flaky interior, and a simple, no-nonsense method. There's only one problem—they're often not very good. Too many are dense, gummy, and doughy or, on the flip side, lean and dry. Drop biscuits should, by nature, be simple to make and tender. We wanted a biscuit that could be easily broken apart and eaten piece by buttery piece.

Identifying the best ingredients was the first task. While oil-based biscuits are easy to work with, they lack flavor, so butter is a must. Replacing the usual milk with buttermilk helped heighten flavor; the biscuits now had a rich, buttery tang and were crisper on the exterior and fluffier on the interior. Choosing the right leavener was also important. We needed a substantial amount, but too much baking powder left a metallic taste. Since we'd added buttermilk, we could replace some of the baking powder with baking soda (buttermilk provides the acid that soda needs to act), which gave us the rise we needed, without the metallic bitterness. Once the ingredients

had been identified, we were left with only one problem. Properly combining the butter and buttermilk requires that both ingredients be at just the right temperature; if they aren't, the melted butter clumps in the buttermilk. But when we had trouble avoiding this, we made a batch with lumpy buttermilk anyway. The result was a surprisingly better biscuit, slightly higher and with better texture. The water in the lumps of butter (butter is 20 percent water) had turned to steam in the oven, helping create additional height.

Best Drop Biscuits

MAKES 12 BISCUITS

A ¼-cup (#16) portion scoop can be used to portion the batter. To refresh day-old biscuits, heat them in a 300-degree oven for 10 minutes.

- 2 cups (10 ounces) unbleached all-purpose flour
- 2 teaspoons baking powder
- 1 teaspoon sugar
- ¾ teaspoon table salt
- ½ teaspoon baking soda
- 1 cup buttermilk, chilled
- 8 tablespoons (1 stick) unsalted butter, melted and cooled slightly, plus 2 tablespoons melted butter for brushing the biscuits

1. Adjust an oven rack to the middle position and heat the oven to 475 degrees. Line a large rimmed baking sheet with parchment paper. Whisk the flour, baking powder, sugar, salt, and baking soda together in a large bowl. Combine the buttermilk and 8 tablespoons of the melted butter in a medium bowl, stirring until the butter forms small clumps.

2. Add the buttermilk mixture to the dry ingredients and stir with a rubber spatula until just incorporated and the batter pulls away from the sides of the bowl. Using a

greased ¼-cup measuring cup, scoop a level amount of batter and drop onto the prepared baking sheet. Repeat with the remaining batter, spacing the biscuits about 1½ inches apart. Bake until the tops are golden brown and crisp, 12 to 14 minutes.

3. Brush the biscuit tops with the remaining 2 tablespoons melted butter. Transfer to a wire rack and cool 5 minutes before serving.

RUSTIC DINNER ROLLS

WHY THIS RECIPE WORKS: The remarkably crisp crust of European-style dinner rolls is what keeps these rolls in the domain of professionals, who typically rely on a steam-injected oven to expose the developing crust to moisture. We wanted to create a reliable recipe for rustic dinner rolls with a crisp crust and chewy crumb that looked—and tasted—like they came from an artisanal bakery.

We baked our first batch using bread flour, but when we broke the rolls open, we found a dense, bland crumb beneath a leathery crust. The flavor was easy to improve—we replaced a few tablespoons of bread flour with whole wheat flour, which contributed earthiness, while honey added sweetness. A little extra yeast improved the crumb slightly, but not enough; making the dough wetter was the fix. Lots of water in the dough created more steam bubbles during baking, which produced an airier crumb. Giving the dough a couple of turns also encouraged the yeast to produce more carbon dioxide, creating more bubbles and a lighter crumb.

As for baking, we came up with a two-step baking process to mimic a steam-injected oven: First, we misted the rolls with water before baking them for an even crisper crust. We then partially baked them in a cake pan at a high temperature to help set their shape. Halfway through baking, we removed the cake pan from the oven, lowered the temperature, pulled the rolls apart, and returned them to the oven spaced out on a baking sheet for uniformly golden rolls with the crust and crumb we were looking for.

Rustic Dinner Rolls

MAKES 16 ROLLS

Because this dough is sticky, keep your hands well floured when handling it. Use a spray bottle to mist the rolls with water. The rolls will keep for up to 2 days at room temperature stored in a zipper-lock bag. To recrisp the crust, place the rolls in a 450-degree oven for 6 to 8 minutes.

The rolls will keep frozen for several months wrapped in foil and placed in a large zipper-lock freezer bag. Thaw the rolls at room temperature and recrisp using the instructions above.

1½ cups plus 1 tablespoon water, room temperature
2 teaspoons honey
1½ teaspoons instant or rapid-rise yeast
3 cups plus 1 tablespoon (16½ ounces) bread flour, plus extra for the dough and work surface
3 tablespoons whole wheat flour
1½ teaspoons table salt

1. Whisk the water, honey, and yeast in the bowl of a standing mixer until well combined, making sure no honey sticks to the bottom of the bowl. Add the flours and mix on low speed with the dough hook until a cohesive dough is formed, about 3 minutes. Cover the bowl with plastic wrap and let sit at room temperature 30 minutes.

2. Remove the plastic wrap and sprinkle the salt evenly over the dough. Knead on low speed 5 minutes. (If the dough creeps up on the attachment, stop the mixer and scrape it down.) Increase the speed to medium and continue to knead until the dough is smooth and slightly tacky, about 1 minute. If the dough is very sticky, add 1 to 2 tablespoons flour and continue mixing for 1 minute. Lightly oil a medium bowl; transfer the dough to the bowl and cover with plastic wrap. Let the dough rise in a warm, draft-free place until doubled in size, about 1 hour.

3. Fold the dough over itself; rotate the bowl a quarter turn and fold again. Rotate the bowl again and fold once more. Cover with plastic wrap and let rise 30 minutes. Repeat folding, replace the plastic wrap, and let the dough rise until doubled in size, about 30 minutes. Spray two 9-inch round cake pans with vegetable oil spray and set aside.

4. Transfer the dough to a floured work surface and sprinkle the top with more flour. Using a bench scraper, cut the dough in half and gently stretch each half into a 16-inch log. Divide each log into quarters, then each quarter into two pieces (you should have 16 pieces total), and dust the top of each piece with more flour. With floured hands, gently pick up each piece and roll in your palms to coat with flour, shaking off the excess, and place in the prepared cake pan. Arrange eight dough pieces in each cake pan, placing one piece in the middle and the others around it, with the long side of each piece running from the center of the pan to the edge and making sure the cut side faces up. Loosely cover the cake pans with plastic wrap and let the rolls rise until doubled in size, about 30 minutes (the dough is ready when it springs back slowly when pressed lightly with a knuckle). Thirty minutes before baking, adjust an oven rack to the middle position and heat the oven to 500 degrees.

5. Remove the plastic wrap from the cake pans, spray the rolls lightly with water, and place in the oven. Bake until the tops of the rolls are brown, 10 minutes, then remove them from the oven. Reduce the oven temperature to 400 degrees; using kitchen towels or oven mitts, invert the rolls from both cake pans onto a rimmed baking sheet. When the rolls are cool enough to handle, turn them right side up, pull apart, and space evenly on the baking sheet. Continue to bake until the rolls develop a deep golden brown crust and sound hollow when tapped on the bottom, 10 to 15 minutes, rotating the baking sheet halfway through baking. Transfer the rolls to a wire rack and cool to room temperature, about 1 hour.

IRISH SODA BREAD

WHY THIS RECIPE WORKS: Authentic Irish soda bread has a tender, dense crumb and a rough-textured, thick crust—definitely a departure from the more common Americanized soda bread, which is closer to a supersized scone. We wanted to try our hand at the authentic version of this bread, which relies on a simple ingredient list of flour, baking soda, salt, and buttermilk.

Our first tests focused on flour. A loaf made with all-purpose flour produced a doughy, heavy bread with an overly thick crust. To soften the crumb, we added some cake flour to the mix, and this made a difference. (It also made historical sense. Because of Ireland's climate, the wheat grown there is a soft, low-protein variety more similar to cake flour than to American all-purpose, which is relatively high in protein.) A version made with all cake flour, however, was heavy and compact. A ratio of 3 parts all-purpose flour to 1 part cake flour proved best. With only the four basic ingredients of flour, buttermilk, baking soda, and salt, our bread was lacking in flavor and still a little tough; we turned to sugar and butter. Traditionally, very small amounts of butter and sugar are sometimes added to Irish soda bread, so we felt justified in using a minuscule amount of each. The sugar added flavor without making the bread sweet, and the butter softened the dough just enough without making it overly rich.

Irish Soda Bread

MAKES 1 LOAF

If you do not have a cast-iron skillet, the bread can be baked on a baking sheet, although the crust won't be quite as crunchy. Soda bread is best eaten on the day it is baked but does keep well covered and stored at room temperature for a couple of days, after which time it will become dry.

- 3 cups (15 ounces) unbleached all-purpose flour
- 1 cup (4 ounces) cake flour
- 2 tablespoons sugar
- 1½ teaspoons baking soda
- 1½ teaspoons cream of tartar
- 1½ teaspoons table salt
- 2 tablespoons unsalted butter, softened, plus 1 tablespoon melted butter for brushing the loaf (optional)
- 1¾ cups buttermilk

1. Adjust an oven rack to the middle position and heat the oven to 400 degrees. Whisk the flours, sugar, baking soda, cream of tartar, and salt together in a large bowl. Add the softened butter and rub it into the flour using your fingers until it is completely incorporated. Make a well in the center of the flour mixture and add 1½ cups of the buttermilk. Work the buttermilk into the flour mixture using a fork until the dough comes together in large clumps and there is no dry flour in the bottom of the bowl, adding up to ¼ cup more buttermilk, 1 tablespoon at a time, until all the loose flour is just moistened. Turn the dough onto a lightly floured work surface and pat together to form a 6-inch round. The dough will be scrappy and uneven.

2. Place the dough in a 12-inch cast-iron skillet. Score a deep cross, about 5 inches long and ¾ inch deep, on the top of the loaf and place in the oven. Bake until nicely browned and a knife inserted in the center of the loaf comes out clean, 40 to 45 minutes. Remove from the oven and brush with the melted butter (if using). Cool at least 30 minutes before slicing.

Whole Wheat Soda Bread

This variation is known as brown bread in Ireland. The dough will be sticky and you may need to add a small amount of flour as you mix it.

Follow the recipe for Irish Soda Bread, reducing the unbleached all-purpose flour to 1½ cups (7½ ounces) and the cake flour to ½ cup (2 ounces) and increasing the sugar to 3 tablespoons. Add 1½ cups (8¼ ounces) whole wheat flour and ½ cup toasted wheat germ with the flours, sugar, baking soda, cream of tartar, and salt in step 1.

QUICK CHEESE BREAD

WHY THIS RECIPE WORKS: Run-of-the-mill cheese bread is at once dry and greasy, with almost no cheese flavor. Unlike pizza, wherein bread dough is merely topped with cheese, a true cheese bread makes equal partners of the two components. We wanted to make the most of this relationship and create a rich, moist loaf topped with a bold, cheesy crust.

We started with all-purpose flour and added whole milk and sour cream for a clean, creamy flavor and rich, moist texture. Just a few tablespoons of butter added enough richness without greasiness, and using less fat made the texture heartier and less cake-like. A single egg gave rise and structure without an overly eggy flavor. As for cheese, small chunks (rather than shreds) of Asiago or cheddar mixed into the dough offered rich, cheesy pockets throughout the bread; a moderate amount added plenty of flavor without weighing down the bread. For added cheesy flavor and a crisp, browned crust, we coated the pan and sprinkled the top of the loaf with shredded Parmesan.

Quick Cheese Bread

MAKES ONE 8-INCH LOAF

If using Asiago, choose a mild supermarket cheese that yields to pressure when pressed. Aged Asiago that is as firm as Parmesan is too sharp and piquant for this bread. If, when testing the bread for doneness, the toothpick comes out with what looks like uncooked batter clinging to it, try again in a different, but still central, spot; if the toothpick hits a pocket of cheese, it may give a false indication.

Quick Cheese Bread with Bacon, Onion, and Gruyère

Cook 5 ounces (about 5 slices) bacon, cut into ½-inch pieces, in a 10-inch nonstick skillet over medium heat, stirring occasionally, until crisp, about 8 minutes. Using a slotted spoon, transfer the bacon to a paper towel–lined plate and pour off all but 3 tablespoons fat from the skillet. Add ½ cup minced onion to the skillet and cook, stirring frequently, until softened, about 3 minutes; set the skillet with the onion aside. Follow the recipe for Quick Cheese Bread, substituting Gruyère for the cheddar, adding the bacon and onion to the flour mixture with the cheese, and omitting the butter.

3 ounces Parmesan cheese, shredded on the large holes of a box grater (about 1 cup)
3 cups (15 ounces) unbleached all-purpose flour
1 tablespoon baking powder
1 teaspoon table salt
¼ teaspoon cayenne pepper
⅛ teaspoon ground black pepper
4 ounces extra-sharp cheddar cheese, cut into ½-inch cubes, or mild Asiago (see note), crumbled into ¼ to ½-inch pieces (about 1 cup)
1¼ cups whole milk
3 tablespoons unsalted butter, melted
1 large egg, lightly beaten
¾ cup sour cream

1. Adjust an oven rack to the middle position and heat the oven to 350 degrees. Spray an 8½ by 4½-inch loaf pan with vegetable oil spray; sprinkle ½ cup of the Parmesan evenly over the bottom of the pan.

2. Whisk the flour, baking powder, salt, cayenne, and black pepper together in a large bowl. Using a rubber spatula, mix in the cheddar, breaking up clumps. Whisk the milk, melted butter, egg, and sour cream together in a medium bowl. Using a rubber spatula, gently fold the wet ingredients into the dry ingredients until just combined (the batter will be heavy and thick); do not overmix. Scrape the batter into the prepared loaf pan; smooth the surface with a rubber spatula. Sprinkle the remaining ½ cup Parmesan evenly over the surface.

3. Bake until deep golden brown and a toothpick inserted in the center comes out clean, 45 to 50 minutes. Cool on a wire rack 5 minutes; invert the loaf onto the wire rack, then turn right side up and continue to cool until warm, about 45 minutes. Cut into slices and serve.

ALL-PURPOSE CORN BREAD

WHY THIS RECIPE WORKS: Corn bread can be sweet and cakey (the Northern version) or savory and light (the Southern version). We wanted a combination of the two. And most important, we wanted our corn bread to be bursting with corn flavor.

The secret to corn bread with real corn flavor was pretty simple: Use corn, not just cornmeal. While fresh corn was best, frozen was nearly as good, and pureeing the kernels in a food processor made them easy to use while eliminating tough, chewy kernels. For flavoring, buttermilk provided a tangy flavor, while light brown sugar enhanced the naturally sweet flavor of the corn. We couldn't assume everyone would own the cast-iron skillet in which Southern corn breads traditionally get their thick crust, so we compensated by baking the bread at a higher than conventional temperature, producing a crunchy crust full of toasted corn flavor.

All-Purpose Corn Bread
MAKES ONE 8-INCH SQUARE

Before preparing the baking dish or any of the other ingredients, measure out the frozen corn kernels and let them stand at room temperature until thawed. When corn is in season, fresh cooked kernels can be substituted for the frozen corn. This recipe was developed with Quaker yellow cornmeal; a stone-ground whole grain cornmeal will work but will yield a drier and less tender corn bread. We prefer a Pyrex glass baking dish because it yields a nice golden brown crust, but a metal baking dish (nonstick or traditional) will also work. The corn bread is best served warm; leftovers can be wrapped in foil and reheated in a 350-degree oven for 10 to 15 minutes.

1½ cups (7½ ounces) unbleached all-purpose flour
1 cup (about 5 ounces) yellow cornmeal (see note)
2 teaspoons baking powder
¾ teaspoon table salt
¼ teaspoon baking soda
1 cup buttermilk
¾ cup frozen corn kernels, thawed (see note)
¼ cup packed (1¾ ounces) light brown sugar
2 large eggs
8 tablespoons (1 stick) unsalted butter, melted and cooled slightly

1. Adjust an oven rack to the middle position and heat the oven to 400 degrees. Spray an 8-inch square baking dish with vegetable oil spray. Whisk the flour, cornmeal, baking powder, salt, and baking soda together in a medium bowl until combined; set aside.

2. Process the buttermilk, thawed corn kernels, and brown sugar in a food processor or blender until combined, about 5 seconds. Add the eggs and process until well combined (corn lumps will remain), about 5 seconds longer.

3. Using a rubber spatula, make a well in the center of the dry ingredients; pour the wet ingredients into the well. Begin folding the dry ingredients into the wet, giving the mixture only a few turns to barely combine; add the melted butter and continue folding until the dry ingredients are just moistened. Pour the batter into the prepared baking dish; smooth the surface with a rubber spatula. Bake until deep golden brown and a toothpick inserted in the center comes out clean, 25 to 35 minutes. Cool on a wire rack 10 minutes; invert the corn bread onto the wire rack, then turn right side up and continue to cool until warm, about 10 minutes longer. Cut into pieces and serve.

Spicy Jalapeño-Cheddar Corn Bread

Follow the recipe for All-Purpose Corn Bread, reducing the table salt to ½ teaspoon; add ⅜ teaspoon cayenne pepper, 1 medium jalapeño chile, seeds and ribs removed, minced, and 2 ounces sharp cheddar cheese, shredded (½ cup), to the flour mixture in step 1 and toss well to combine. Reduce the brown sugar to 2 tablespoons and sprinkle 2 ounces more sharp cheddar, shredded (½ cup), over the batter in the baking dish just before baking.

WEIGHING IN ON WEIGHTS AND MEASURES

Variations in measurement can have a significant effect on baked goods. To prove this point, we asked 10 home cook volunteers to measure out 1 cup of flour and 3 tablespoons of water. The weights of the measured flour and water varied by as much as 20 percent! From these findings, we recommend three things to guarantee more consistent results from your baked goods:

WEIGH FLOUR: Don't rely on cup measurements alone. (One cup all-purpose flour weighs 5 ounces; 1 cup bread or whole wheat flour weighs 5½ ounces; and 1 cup cake flour weighs 4 ounces.)

USE THE RIGHT MEASURING CUP: Liquid measurements should be made in a liquid cup measure (not a dry cup measure). To measure accurately, place the cup on a level surface and bring your eyes down to the level of the measurement markings. Add liquid until the bottom of the curved top surface of the liquid (called the meniscus)—not the edges of the surface, which can cling and ride up the walls of the measuring cup—is level with the measurement marking.

BE PRECISE: When measuring tablespoon or teaspoon amounts of liquid, make sure that the teaspoon is completely filled and that there is no excess liquid clinging to the bottom of the spoon after pouring.

SOUTHERN CORN BREAD

WHY THIS RECIPE WORKS: Classic Southern corn bread is made in a ripping hot skillet greased with bacon fat, which causes it to develop a thin, crispy crust as the bread bakes. The resulting bread is moist and tender, with the aroma of toasted corn and the subtle flavor of dairy. Traditionally, Southern-style corn bread is made from white cornmeal and has only trace amounts of sugar and flour. We wanted to perfect the proportions of ingredients and come up with our own crusty, savory Southern-style corn bread baked in a cast-iron skillet.

Departing from tradition, we chose yellow cornmeal over white—corn breads made with yellow cornmeal consistently had a more potent corn flavor than those made with white cornmeal. We chose a rustic method to incorporate the cornmeal—combining part of the corn-meal with boiling water to create a cornmeal "mush." Corn bread that started with some mush had the most corn flavor, and it also produced a fine, moist crumb. We then stirred the buttermilk and egg into the mush before adding the remaining cornmeal and other dry ingredients. As for sugar, a small amount enhanced the natural sweetness of the corn. Finally, we poured the batter into a hot, greased cast-iron skillet to bake until crusty and fragrant.

Southern Corn Bread

MAKES ONE 8-INCH LOAF

Cornmeal mush of just the right texture is essential to this bread. Make sure that the water is at a rapid boil when it is added to the cornmeal. And for an accurate measurement of boiling water, bring a kettle of water to a boil, then measure out the desired amount. Though we prefer to make corn bread in a preheated cast-iron skillet, a 9-inch round cake pan or 9-inch square baking pan, greased lightly with butter and not preheated, will also produce acceptable results if you double the recipe and bake the bread for 25 minutes. For our top-rated cast-iron skillet, see page 586.

>   4 teaspoons bacon drippings or vegetable oil
>   1 cup (about 5 ounces) yellow cornmeal, preferably stone-ground
>   2 teaspoons sugar
>   1 teaspoon baking powder
>   ½ teaspoon table salt
>   ¼ teaspoon baking soda
>   ⅓ cup boiling water (see note)
>   ¾ cup buttermilk
>   1 large egg, lightly beaten

1. Adjust an oven rack to the lower-middle position and heat the oven to 450 degrees. Add the bacon drippings to an 8-inch cast-iron skillet and place the skillet in the heating oven.

2. Place ⅓ cup of the cornmeal in a medium bowl. Whisk the remaining ⅔ cup cornmeal, the sugar, baking powder, salt, and baking soda together in a small bowl; set aside.

3. Add the boiling water to the ⅓ cup cornmeal and stir to make a stiff mush. Whisk in the buttermilk gradually, breaking up lumps until smooth, then whisk in the egg. When the oven is preheated and the skillet is very hot, add the dry ingredients to the cornmeal mush and stir until just moistened. Carefully remove the skillet from the oven.

Pour the hot bacon fat from the pan into the batter and stir to incorporate, then quickly pour the batter into the heated skillet. Bake until golden brown, about 20 minutes. Remove from the oven and immediately turn the corn bread onto a wire rack. Cool 5 minutes; serve.

RUSTIC COUNTRY BREAD

WHY THIS RECIPE WORKS: Authentic rustic country bread should be made with little more than flour, water, yeast, and salt. We aimed to develop a reliable recipe for a big, crusty, pleasant loaf—one without shortcuts—made the old-fashioned way.

We decided to focus our tests around using a sponge starter—a mixture of flour, water, and yeast, left to ferment and then combined with additional flour, water, and other ingredients. A sponge starter gave our bread a complex flavor that yeast alone could not provide. We soon learned that bread with a high water content produces a chewier texture. So we ended up working with a wet dough, to which we could add more flour if necessary. This wet dough was tricky to work with but resulted in a bread with a texture so rough, chewy, and substantial that it was a meal all by itself. For a finishing touch, we added whole wheat and rye flours to the ingredients to enhance this bread's full flavor.

Rustic Country Bread

MAKES 1 ROUND LOAF

Because of its high water content, the bread will be gummy if pulled from the oven too soon. To ensure the bread's doneness, make sure its internal temperature reads 210 degrees by inserting an instant-read thermometer into the side or bottom of the loaf. Also look at the crust—it should be very dark brown, almost black. Leftover bread can be wrapped in a double layer of plastic wrap and stored at room temperature for 3 days; wrapped with an additional layer of aluminum foil the bread can be frozen for up to one month. To recrisp the crust, place the unwrapped bread in a 450-degree oven for 10 minutes (frozen bread should be thawed at room temperature before recrisping).

SPONGE

>   1 cup water, room temperature
>   ½ teaspoon instant or rapid-rise yeast
>   1 cup (5½ ounces) bread flour
>   1 cup (5½ ounces) whole wheat flour

DOUGH

3–3½ cups (16½ to 19¼ ounces) bread flour, plus extra for the dough and work surface

½ cup (2¾ ounces) rye flour

1⅓ cups water, room temperature

2 tablespoons honey

2 teaspoons table salt

1. FOR THE SPONGE: Combine the water and yeast in a medium bowl and stir until the yeast is dissolved. Add the flours and stir with a rubber spatula to create a stiff, wet dough. Cover the bowl with plastic wrap and let sit at room temperature at least 5 hours or up to 24 hours. (The sponge can be refrigerated up to 24 hours; return to room temperature before continuing with the recipe.)

2. FOR THE DOUGH: Using a rubber spatula, combine 3 cups of the bread flour, the rye flour, water, honey, and sponge in the bowl of a standing mixer. Knead the dough on low speed with the dough hook until smooth, about 15 minutes, adding the salt during the final 3 minutes. If more flour is needed, add the remaining ½ cup bread flour, 1 tablespoon at a time, until the dough clears the sides of the bowl but sticks to the bottom. Lightly oil a large bowl; transfer the dough to the bowl and cover with plastic wrap. Let the dough rise until tripled in size, about 2 hours.

3. Transfer the dough to a lightly floured work surface. Flour the top of the dough. With floured hands, shape the dough into a round by pulling the edges into the middle and gathering it loosely together. Transfer the dough, seam side down, to an inverted baking sheet lined with parchment paper. Cover with plastic wrap and let rise until almost doubled in size, about 45 minutes. (The dough should barely spring back when poked with a knuckle.)

4. Meanwhile, adjust an oven rack to the lower-middle position, place a baking stone on the rack, and heat the oven to 450 degrees at least 30 minutes before baking.

5. Use a razor blade or sharp knife to cut three slashes on the top of the dough. With scissors, trim the excess parchment around the dough. Lightly spray the dough with water.

6. Carefully slide the parchment with the dough onto the baking stone using a jerking motion. Bake until the crust is very dark brown and the center registers 210 degrees on an instant-read thermometer, 35 to 40 minutes, rotating the bread halfway through baking (see note). Turn the oven off, open the oven door, and let the bread remain in the oven 10 minutes longer. Remove from the oven, transfer to a wire rack, and cool to room temperature, about 2 hours.

ALMOST NO-KNEAD BREAD

WHY THIS RECIPE WORKS: The no-knead method of bread making first came to our attention in an article on baker Jim Lahey in the *New York Times.* The article claimed that Lahey's method produces artisanal-style loaves with minimum effort. Lahey uses two approaches to replace kneading (the mechanical process that forms gluten, which gives bread structure): a very high hydration level (85 percent—meaning that for every 10 ounces of flour, there are 8.5 ounces of water) and a 12-hour autolysis period that allows the flour to hydrate and rest before the dough is kneaded. After the dough is briefly kneaded, it is placed in a preheated Dutch oven to bake; the Dutch oven creates a humid environment that gives the loaf a dramatic open crumb structure and crisp crust.

However, as we baked loaf after loaf, we found two big problems: the dough deflated when carried to the pot, causing misshapen loaves, and it lacked flavor. To give the dough more strength, we lowered the hydration and gave the bread the bare minimum of kneading time (under a minute) to compensate. We also figured out a way to transfer the bread without doing any harm to the shape of the loaf—using a parchment paper sling. To solve the lack of flavor, we needed to introduce two elements that a starter adds to artisan breads: an acidic tang with vinegar and a shot of yeasty flavor with beer.

Almost No-Knead Bread

MAKES 1 ROUND LOAF

An enameled cast-iron Dutch oven with a tight-fitting lid yields best results, but the recipe also works in a regular cast-iron Dutch oven or heavy stockpot. Use a mild-flavored lager, such as Budweiser (mild nonalcoholic lager also works). The bread is best eaten the day it is baked but it will keep wrapped in a double layer of plastic wrap and stored at room temperature for up to 2 days. To recrisp the crust, place the unwrapped bread in a 450-degree oven for 6 to 8 minutes.

3 cups (15 ounces) unbleached all-purpose flour, plus extra for the work surface

1½ teaspoons table salt

¼ teaspoon instant or rapid-rise yeast

¾ cup plus 2 tablespoons water, room temperature

6 tablespoons mild-flavored lager, room temperature (see note)

1 tablespoon distilled white vinegar

MAKING ALMOST NO-KNEAD BREAD

1. Mix the dough by stirring the wet ingredients into the dry ingredients with a rubber spatula, then leave the dough to rest for 8 to 18 hours.

2. Turn the dough out onto a lightly floured surface and knead the dough 10 to 15 times.

3. After kneading the dough, shape it into a ball by pulling the edges into the middle.

4. Allow the dough to rise for 2 hours in a parchment paper-lined skillet.

5. Once the dough has risen, use the paper's edges to lift the dough and lower it in the preheated Dutch oven. The bread remains on the parchment as it bakes.

1. Whisk the flour, salt, and yeast together in a large bowl. Add the water, beer, and vinegar. Using a rubber spatula, fold the mixture, scraping up the dry flour from the bottom of the bowl, until a shaggy ball forms. Cover the bowl with plastic wrap and let sit at room temperature for 8 to 18 hours.

2. Lay an 18 by 12-inch sheet of parchment paper inside a 10-inch skillet and spray with vegetable oil spray. Transfer the dough to a lightly floured work surface and knead 10 to 15 times. Shape the dough into a ball by pulling the edges into the middle. Transfer the dough, seam side down, to the parchment-lined skillet and spray the surface of the dough with vegetable oil spray. Cover loosely with plastic wrap and let rise at room temperature until the dough has doubled in size and does not readily spring back when poked with a knuckle, about 2 hours.

3. Thirty minutes before baking, adjust an oven rack to the lowest position, place a 6 to 8-quart heavy-bottomed Dutch oven (with a lid) on the rack, and heat the oven to 500 degrees. Lightly flour the top of the dough and, using a razor blade or sharp knife, make one 6-inch-long, ½-inch-deep slit along the top of the dough. Carefully remove the pot from the oven and remove the lid. Pick up the dough by lifting the parchment overhang and lower into the pot (let any excess parchment hang over the pot edge). Cover the pot and place in the oven. Reduce the oven temperature to 425 degrees and bake, covered, for 30 minutes. Remove the lid and continue to bake until the loaf is deep brown and the center registers 210 degrees on an instant-read thermometer, 20 to 30 minutes longer. Carefully remove the bread from the pot; transfer to a wire rack and cool to room temperature, about 2 hours, before serving.

CIABATTA

WHY THIS RECIPE WORKS: Unless your source is an artisanal bakery, most loaves of ciabatta available just aren't any good. Some lack flavor, others are too flat, and still others have holes so big there's hardly any bread. Ideally, this Italian loaf should boast a crisp, flavorful crust, a full and tangy flavor, and a chewy, open crumb. Uninterested in yet another lackluster loaf from the supermarket, we decided to make our own.

We started with the flour selection—whole wheat, bread, or all-purpose? We preferred all-purpose, which is made from both hard and soft wheat and has less protein than bread flour, producing loaves with a more open, springy texture. The next step was to build flavor through

the sponge (or *biga* in Italian), which we also used in our Rustic Country Bread (page 450). As it ferments, the yeast in the biga produces lactic and acetic acids as by-products, which give the bread its characteristic sourness. Kneading the sponge and remaining dough ingredients in a standing mixer for only a few minutes produced loaves that spread out instead of rising, so we turned to a combination of kneading and folding the dough over itself a few times before letting it rest. This two-step process gives the dough structure but also supports oversized holes. Adding a small amount of milk, which contains a protein that slightly weakens the gluten strands, remedied the problem and took down the size of those big bubbles.

To avoid extra handling of the dough, we formed the loaves, then moved them to parchment paper and slid the parchment onto the baking surface after another rest. We opted to bake the loaves at a cooler temperature than 500 degrees (as most recipes recommend). A final enhancement was to spray the loaves with water in the first minutes of baking for a crisper crust and loaves that rose a bit higher.

Ciabatta

MAKES 2 LOAVES

As you make this bread, keep in mind that the dough is wet and very sticky. The key to manipulating it is working quickly and gently; rough handling will result in flat, tough loaves. When possible, use a large rubber spatula or bowl scraper to move the dough. If you have to use your hands, make sure they are well floured. Because the dough is so sticky, it must be prepared in a standing mixer. If you don't have a baking stone, bake the bread on an overturned and preheated rimmed baking sheet set on the lowest oven rack. Leftover bread can be wrapped in a double layer of plastic wrap and stored at room temperature for 3 days; wrapped with an additional layer of

aluminum foil, the bread can be frozen for up to 1 month. To recrisp the crust, place the unwrapped bread in a 450-degree oven for 6 to 8 minutes (frozen bread should be thawed at room temperature before recrisping).

SPONGE

- 1 cup (5 ounces) unbleached all-purpose flour
- ⅛ teaspoon instant or rapid-rise yeast
- ½ cup water, room temperature

DOUGH

- 2 cups (10 ounces) unbleached all-purpose flour, plus extra for the dough and work surface
- 1½ teaspoons table salt
- ½ teaspoon instant or rapid-rise yeast
- ¾ cup water, room temperature
- ¼ cup milk, room temperature

1. FOR THE SPONGE: Combine the flour, yeast, and water in a medium bowl and stir with a wooden spoon until a uniform mass forms, about 1 minute. Cover the bowl tightly with plastic wrap and let stand at room temperature (about 70 degrees) at least 8 hours or up to 24 hours.

2. FOR THE DOUGH: Place the sponge and dough ingredients in the bowl of a standing mixer fitted with the paddle attachment. Mix on low speed until roughly combined and a shaggy dough forms, about 1 minute; scrape down the sides of the bowl as necessary. Increase the speed to medium-low and continue mixing until the dough becomes a uniform mass that collects on the paddle and pulls away from the sides of the bowl, 4 to 6 minutes. Change to the dough hook and knead the bread on medium speed until smooth and shiny (the dough will be very sticky), about 10 minutes. (If the dough creeps up on the attachment, stop the mixer and scrape it down.) Transfer the dough to a large bowl and cover tightly with plastic wrap. Let the dough rise at room temperature until doubled in size, about 1 hour. (The dough should barely spring back when poked with a knuckle.)

3. Spray a rubber spatula or bowl scraper with vegetable oil spray; fold the partially risen dough over itself by gently lifting and folding the edge of the dough toward the middle. Turn the bowl 90 degrees; fold again. Turn the bowl and fold the dough six more times (for a total of eight turns). Cover with plastic wrap and let rise for 30 minutes. Repeat folding, replace the plastic wrap, and let rise until doubled in size, about 30 minutes longer. Meanwhile, adjust an oven rack to the lower-middle position, place a baking stone on the rack, and heat the oven to 450 degrees at least 30 minutes before baking.

4. Cut two 12 by 6-inch pieces of parchment paper and

MAKING CIABATTA

1. After mixing the dough and allowing it to rest, turn the partially risen dough by folding it in on itself to gently encourage more gluten development. Let it rest again, then repeat this step.

2. Transfer the dough to a lightly floured surface and halve it with a bench scraper.

3. Press each half into a rough 12 by 6-inch rectangle.

4. Fold each dough half like a business letter into a 7 by 4-inch loaf. Transfer each loaf, seam side down, to sheets of parchment, dust with flour, and cover with plastic wrap. Let rest 30 minutes.

5. Use floured fingertips to evenly poke the entire surface of each loaf to form a 10 by 6-inch rectangle; spray the loaves lightly with water. Transfer the loaves, parchment and all, onto the hot baking stone and bake.

liberally dust with flour. Transfer the dough to a floured work surface, being careful not to deflate it completely. Liberally flour the top of the dough and divide in half with a bench scraper. Turn one piece of dough cut side up and dust with flour. Following the photos, with well-floured hands, press the dough into a rough 12 by 6-inch shape. Fold the shorter sides of the dough toward the center, overlapping them like a business letter to form a 7 by 4-inch loaf. Repeat with the second dough piece. Gently transfer each loaf, seam side down, to the parchment sheets, dust with flour, and cover with plastic wrap. Let the loaves sit at room temperature for 30 minutes (the surface of the loaves will develop small bubbles).

5. Slide the parchment with the loaves onto an inverted rimmed baking sheet or pizza peel. Using floured fingertips, evenly poke the entire surface of each loaf to form a 10 by 6-inch rectangle; spray the loaves lightly with water. Carefully slide the parchment with the loaves onto the baking stone using a jerking motion. Bake, spraying the loaves with water twice more during the first 5 minutes of baking time, until the crust is a deep golden brown and the center of the loaves registers 210 degrees on an instant-read thermometer, 22 to 27 minutes. Transfer to a wire rack, discard the parchment, and cool the loaves to room temperature, about 1 hour, before slicing and serving.

MULTIGRAIN BREAD

WHY THIS RECIPE WORKS: Although multigrain bread often has great flavor, the quantity of ingredients weighs it down so much that the loaf becomes as dense and as heavy as a brick. On the other end of the spectrum are loaves with a nice, light sandwich-style texture but so little grain that they're hard to distinguish from plain old white bread. We wanted a multigrain bread with both great flavor and balanced texture.

Our first challenge was to develop more gluten (a protein made when flour and water are mixed and that gives baked goods structure) in the dough, as early tests showed that the whole grains were impeding its development. Because the protein content of any flour is an indicator of how much gluten it will produce, we thought first to switch out all-purpose flour for higher-protein bread flour, but this move only made the bread chewier, not less dense. The solution was twofold: long kneading preceded by an autolyse, a resting period just after the initial mixing of water and flour that gives flour time to hydrate. This combination also made the dough less tacky and therefore easier to work with. The result was a loaf that baked up light yet chewy, without being tough. To incorporate grains into the bread, we hit upon a convenient, one-stop-shopping alternative: packaged seven-grain hot cereal. To soften the grains, we made a thick porridge with the cereal before adding it to the dough. A final step of rolling the shaped loaves in oats yielded a finished, professional look.

Multigrain Bread

MAKES TWO 8-INCH LOAVES

Don't confuse seven-grain hot cereal mix with boxed, cold breakfast cereals that may also be labeled "seven-grain." Our favorite brands of seven-grain mix are Bob's Red Mill and Arrowhead Mills. Leftover bread can be wrapped in a double layer of plastic wrap and stored at room temperature for 3 days; wrapped with an additional layer of aluminum foil, the bread can be frozen for up to 1 month. For an accurate measurement of boiling water, bring a kettle of water to a boil, then measure out the desired amount. See page 594 for information on our top-rated loaf pan.

1¼ cups (6¼ ounces) seven-grain hot cereal mix (see note)
2½ cups boiling water (see note)
3 cups (15 ounces) unbleached all-purpose flour, plus extra for the dough and work surface
1½ cups (8¼ ounces) whole wheat flour
¼ cup honey
4 tablespoons (½ stick) unsalted butter, melted and cooled slightly
1 envelope (2¼ teaspoons) instant or rapid-rise yeast
1 tablespoon table salt
¾ cup unsalted pumpkin seeds or sunflower seeds
½ cup old-fashioned rolled oats or quick oats

1. Place the cereal mix in the bowl of a standing mixer and pour the boiling water over it; let stand, stirring occasionally, until the mixture cools to 100 degrees and resembles thick porridge, about 1 hour. Whisk the flours together in a medium bowl.

2. Once the grain mixture has cooled, add the honey, melted butter, and yeast and stir to combine. Attach the bowl to a standing mixer fitted with the dough hook. With the mixer running on low speed, add the flours, ½ cup at a time, and knead until the dough forms a ball, 1½ to 2 minutes; cover the bowl with plastic wrap and let the dough rest 20 minutes. Add the salt and knead on medium-low speed until the dough clears the sides of the bowl, 3 to 4 minutes (if it does not clear the

sides, add 2 to 3 tablespoons additional all-purpose flour and continue mixing); continue to knead the dough for 5 more minutes. Add the seeds and knead for another 15 seconds. Transfer the dough to a floured work surface and knead by hand until the seeds are dispersed evenly and the dough forms a smooth, taut ball. Place the dough in a greased container with a 4-quart capacity; cover with plastic wrap and allow to rise until doubled in size, 45 to 60 minutes.

3. Adjust an oven rack to the middle position and heat the oven to 375 degrees. Spray two 8½ by 5½-inch loaf pans with vegetable oil spray. Transfer the dough to a lightly floured work surface and pat into a 12 by 9-inch rectangle; cut the dough in half crosswise with a knife or bench scraper. With a short side facing you, starting at the farthest end, roll one dough piece into a log, keeping the roll taut by tucking it under itself as you go. Seal the loaf by pinching the seam together gently with your thumb and forefinger; repeat with the remaining dough. Spray the loaves lightly with water or vegetable oil spray. Roll each dough log in oats to coat evenly and place, seam side down, in the greased loaf pans, pressing gently into the corners; cover lightly with plastic wrap and let rise until almost doubled in size, 30 to 40 minutes. (The dough should barely spring back when poked with a knuckle.) Bake until the center of the loaves registers 200 degrees on an instant-read thermometer, 35 to 40 minutes. Remove the loaves from the pans and cool on a wire rack before slicing, about 3 hours.

CHAPTER 21

COOKIE JAR FAVORITES

Brown Sugar Cookies 458

Molasses Spice
Cookies 459

Molasses Spice Cookies
with Dark Rum Glaze 460

Classic Chocolate Chip
Cookies 461

Thick and Chewy Chocolate
Chip Cookies 462

Thin and Crispy Chocolate
Chip Cookies 462

Chocolate Cookies 463

Thick and Chewy Double-
Chocolate Cookies 464

Thick and Chewy Triple-
Chocolate Cookies 465

Peanut Butter
Cookies 465

Chocolate-Chunk Oatmeal
Cookies with Pecans and
Dried Cherries 466

Big and Chewy Oatmeal-
Raisin Cookies 467

Big and Chewy Oatmeal-
Date Cookies 468

Thin and Crispy Oatmeal
Cookies 468

Salty Thin and Crispy
Oatmeal Cookies 469

Triple-Coconut
Macaroons 469

Chocolate-Dipped Triple-
Coconut Macaroons 470

Spritz Cookies 470

Spritz Cookies with
Lemon Essence 471

Almond Spritz Cookies 471

Sablés (French
Butter Cookies) 472

Chocolate Sablés 473

Black and White Spiral
Cookies 473

Chocolate Sandwich
Cookies 473

Vanilla Pretzel Cookies 473

Glazed Butter Cookies 474

Jam Sandwiches 474

Lime-Glazed Coconut
Snowballs 475

Chocolate-Cherry
Bar Cookies with
Hazelnuts 475

Pecan or Walnut Crescent
Cookies 476

Almond or Hazelnut
Crescent Cookies 476

Meringue Cookies 477

Chocolate Meringue
Cookies 477

Toasted Almond Meringue
Cookies 477

Blondies 478

Congo Bars 478

Classic Brownies 479

Chewy, Fudgy Triple-
Chocolate Brownies 480

Triple-Chocolate
Espresso Brownies 480

Fudgy Low-Fat
Brownies 481

Raspberry Squares 482

Key Lime Bars 483

Triple Citrus Bars 483

BROWN SUGAR COOKIES

WHY THIS RECIPE WORKS: Simple sugar cookies, while classic, can seem too simple—even dull—at times. We wanted to turn up the volume on the sugar cookie by switching out the granulated sugar in favor of brown sugar. We had a clear vision of this cookie. It would be oversized, with a crackling crisp exterior and a chewy interior. And, like Mick Jagger, this cookie would scream "brown sugar."

We wanted butter for optimal flavor, but the traditional creaming method (creaming softened butter with sugar until fluffy, beating in an egg, and then adding the dry ingredients) gave us cakey and tender cookies. Cutting the butter into the flour produced crumbly cookies. What worked was first melting the butter. We then tweaked the amount of eggs, dark brown sugar, flour, and leavener to give us a good cookie, but we wanted even more brown sugar flavor. We made progress by rolling the dough balls in a combination of brown and granulated sugar and adding a healthy amount of vanilla and table salt. But our biggest success came from an unlikely refinement. Browning the melted butter added a complex nuttiness that made a substantial difference.

Brown Sugar Cookies
MAKES ABOUT 24 COOKIES

Avoid using a nonstick skillet to brown the butter. The dark color of the nonstick coating makes it difficult to gauge when the butter is sufficiently browned. Use fresh brown sugar, as hardened brown sugar will make the cookies too dry. Achieving the proper texture—crisp at the edges and chewy in the middle—is critical to this recipe. Because the cookies are so dark, it's hard to judge doneness by color. Instead, gently press halfway between the edge and center of the cookie. When it's done, it will form an indentation with slight resistance. Check early and err on the side of underdone.

- 14 tablespoons (1¾ sticks) unsalted butter
- 2 cups packed (14 ounces) dark brown sugar (see note)
- ¼ cup (1¾ ounces) granulated sugar
- 2 cups plus 2 tablespoons (about 10⅔ ounces) unbleached all-purpose flour
- ½ teaspoon baking soda
- ¼ teaspoon baking powder
- ½ teaspoon table salt
- 1 large egg
- 1 large egg yolk
- 1 tablespoon vanilla extract

1. Melt 10 tablespoons of the butter in a 10-inch skillet over medium-high heat, about 2 minutes. Continue to cook, swirling the pan constantly until the butter is dark golden brown and has a nutty aroma, 1 to 3 minutes. Transfer the browned butter to a large heatproof bowl. Stir the remaining 4 tablespoons butter into the hot butter to melt; set aside for 15 minutes.

2. Meanwhile, adjust an oven rack to the middle position and heat the oven to 350 degrees. Line two large baking sheets with parchment paper. In a shallow baking dish or pie plate, mix ¼ cup of the brown sugar and the granulated sugar, rubbing the mixture between your fingers until well combined; set aside. Whisk the flour, baking soda, and baking powder together in a medium bowl; set aside.

3. Add the remaining 1¾ cups brown sugar and the salt to the bowl with the cooled butter; mix until no sugar lumps remain, about 30 seconds. Scrape down the bowl with a rubber spatula; add the egg, egg yolk, and vanilla and mix until fully incorporated, about 30 seconds. Scrape down the bowl. Add the flour mixture and mix until just combined, about 1 minute. Give the dough a final stir to ensure that no flour pockets remain and the ingredients are evenly distributed.

4. Divide the dough into 24 portions, each about 2 tablespoons, rolling them between your hands into balls about 1½ inches in diameter. Working in batches, drop 12 dough balls into the baking dish with the sugar mixture and toss to coat. Set the dough balls on the prepared baking sheet, spacing them about 2 inches apart; repeat with the second batch of 12.

5. Bake one sheet at a time until the cookies are browned and still puffy and the edges have begun to set but the centers are still soft (the cookies will look raw between the cracks and seem underdone), 12 to 14 minutes, rotating the baking sheet halfway through the baking time. Do not overbake.

6. Cool the cookies on the baking sheet for 5 minutes; using a wide metal spatula, transfer the cookies to a wire rack and cool to room temperature.

MOLASSES SPICE COOKIES

WHY THIS RECIPE WORKS: Molasses spice cookies are often miserable specimens, no more than flat, tasteless cardboard rounds of gingerbread. They can be dry and cakey without the requisite chew; others are timidly flavored with molasses and scantily spiced. We wanted to create the ultimate molasses spice cookie—soft, chewy, and gently spiced with deep, dark molasses flavor. We also wanted it to have the traditional cracks and crinkles so characteristic of these charming cookies.

We started with all-purpose flour and butter for full, rich flavor. Using just the right amount of molasses and brown sugar and flavoring the cookies with a combination of vanilla, ginger, cinnamon, cloves, black pepper, and allspice gave these spiced cookies the warm tingle that we were after. We found that to keep the cookies mild, using a light or mild molasses was imperative; but if it's a stronger flavor you want, dark molasses is in order. We pulled the cookies from the oven when they still looked a bit underdone; residual heat finished the baking and kept the cookies chewy and moist.

Molasses Spice Cookies
MAKES ABOUT 22 COOKIES

For best flavor, make sure that your spices are fresh. Light or mild molasses gives the cookies a milder flavor; for a stronger flavor, use dark molasses. Either way, measure molasses in a liquid measure. If you find that the dough sticks to your palms as you shape the balls, moisten your hands occasionally in a bowl filled with cold tap water and shake off the excess. Bake the cookies one sheet at a time; if baked two sheets at a time, the cookies started on the bottom rack won't develop attractive crackly tops. Remove the cookies from the oven when they still look slightly raw and underbaked.

⅓ cup (2⅓ ounces) granulated sugar, plus ½ cup for coating
2¼ cups (11¼ ounces) unbleached all-purpose flour
1 teaspoon baking soda
1½ teaspoons ground cinnamon
1½ teaspoons ground ginger
½ teaspoon ground cloves
¼ teaspoon ground allspice
¼ teaspoon ground black pepper
¼ teaspoon table salt
12 tablespoons (1½ sticks) unsalted butter, softened
⅓ cup packed (2⅓ ounces) dark brown sugar
1 large egg yolk
1 teaspoon vanilla extract
½ cup light or dark molasses (see note)

1. Adjust an oven rack to the middle position and heat the oven to 375 degrees. Line two large baking sheets with parchment paper. Place ½ cup of the granulated sugar in a shallow baking dish or pie plate; set aside.

2. Whisk the flour, baking soda, spices, and salt together in a medium bowl; set aside.

3. In a standing mixer fitted with the paddle attachment, beat the butter, brown sugar, and remaining ⅓ cup granulated sugar on medium-high speed until light and fluffy, about 3 minutes. Decrease the speed to medium-low and add the egg yolk and vanilla; increase the speed to medium and beat until incorporated, about 20 seconds. Decrease the speed to medium-low and add the molasses; beat until fully incorporated, about 20 seconds, scraping down the bowl once with a rubber spatula. Decrease the speed to low and add the flour mixture; beat until just incorporated,

ERIN KNOWS BEST

Erin McMurrer is our test kitchen director. She oversees all the recipe testing and development in the test kitchen, but one of her most important jobs is to keep an eye on new test cooks to make sure they're keeping up with test kitchen standards. And like the proverbial mother with eyes in the back of her head, Erin doesn't miss much. You'll often hear her issuing gentle admonitions to new test cooks throughout the day. Where do the test cooks sometimes fall short? Cutting vegetables into perfect dice? Filleting fish properly? Efficiently frenching racks of lamb? Not even close. They sometimes neglect to thoroughly scrape out the contents of their measuring cups. Other than the waste factor, there is a second important reason Erin wants to make sure all the ingredients make it into the mixing bowl—it can often make or break a recipe.

To prove this point, we baked two batches of molasses spice cookies. In one batch we used a rubber spatula to scrape every last bit of molasses (an especially viscous ingredient) from the measuring cup and in the other, we simply poured the molasses from the cup, which left some residue behind (nearly 2 tablespoons!). The results were remarkable. The cookies made with less molasses were less flavorful and they were also dry and cakey as opposed to the cookies using the full amount of molasses, which were richly flavored, moist, and chewy.

So whether you're a test cook or home cook, heed Erin's advice and take a few extra minutes to scrape out your measuring cups—it makes a difference.

about 30 seconds, scraping down the bowl once. Give the dough a final stir to ensure that no flour pockets remain. The dough will be soft.

4. Divide the dough into 22 portions, each about 1 tablespoon, and roll them between your hands into balls about 1¼ to 1½ inches in diameter. Working in batches, drop five dough balls into the baking dish with the sugar and toss to coat. Set the dough balls on the prepared baking sheets, spacing them about 2 inches apart. Repeat with the remaining dough.

5. Bake one sheet at a time, rotating the baking sheets halfway through the baking time, until the cookies are browned, still puffy, and the edges have begun to set but the centers are still soft (cookies will look raw between the cracks and seem underdone), about 11 minutes. Do not overbake.

6. Cool the cookies on the baking sheets for 5 minutes; using a wide metal spatula, transfer the cookies to a wire rack and cool to room temperature.

Molasses Spice Cookies with Dark Rum Glaze

If the glaze is too thick to drizzle, whisk in up to an additional ½ tablespoon rum.

Follow the recipe for Molasses Spice Cookies. Whisk 1 cup (4 ounces) confectioners' sugar and 2½ tablespoons dark rum together in a medium bowl until smooth. Drizzle or spread the glaze using the back of a spoon on the cooled cookies. Allow the glazed cookies to dry at least 15 minutes.

CLASSIC CHOCOLATE CHIP COOKIES

WHY THIS RECIPE WORKS: Rich and buttery, with their soft cores and crispy edges, chocolate chip cookies are the American cookie-jar standard. Since Nestlé first began printing the recipe for Toll House cookies on the back of chocolate chip bags in 1939, generations of bakers have packed them into lunches and taken them to potlucks. But after a few samples, we wondered if this was really the best that a chocolate chip cookie could be. We wanted to refine this recipe to create a moist and chewy chocolate chip cookie with crisp edges and deep notes of toffee and butterscotch to balance its sweetness—in short, a more sophisticated cookie than the standard bake sale offering.

Melting a generous amount of butter before combining it with other ingredients gave us the chewy texture we wanted. Since we were melting butter, we browned a portion of it to add nutty flavor. Using a bit more brown sugar than white sugar enhanced chewiness, while a combination of one egg and one egg yolk gave us supremely moist cookies. For the crisp edges and deep toffee flavor, we allowed the sugar to dissolve and rest in the melted butter. We baked the cookies until golden brown and just set, but still soft in the center. The resulting cookies were crisp and chewy and gooey with chocolate, and boasted a complex medley of sweet, buttery, caramel, and toffee flavors.

Classic Chocolate Chip Cookies

MAKES ABOUT 16 LARGE COOKIES

Avoid using a nonstick skillet to brown the butter; the dark color of the nonstick coating makes it difficult to gauge when the butter is browned. Use fresh, moist brown sugar instead of hardened brown sugar, which will make the cookies dry. This recipe works with light brown sugar, but the cookies will be less full-flavored. For our winning brand of chocolate chips, see page 607. If you're using smaller baking sheets, put fewer cookies on each sheet and bake them in batches.

1¾ cups (8¾ ounces) unbleached all-purpose flour
½ teaspoon baking soda
14 tablespoons (1¾ sticks) unsalted butter
¾ cup packed (5¼ ounces) dark brown sugar (see note)
½ cup (3½ ounces) granulated sugar
1 teaspoon table salt
2 teaspoons vanilla extract
1 large egg
1 large egg yolk
1¼ cups (7½ ounces) semisweet chocolate chips or chunks (see note)
¾ cup chopped pecans or walnuts, toasted (optional)

1. Adjust an oven rack to the middle position and heat the oven to 375 degrees. Line two large baking sheets with parchment paper.

2. Whisk the flour and baking soda together in a medium bowl; set aside.

3. Heat 10 tablespoons of the butter in a 10-inch skillet over medium-high heat until melted, about 2 minutes. Continue cooking, swirling the pan constantly until the butter is dark golden brown and has a nutty aroma, 1 to 3 minutes. Transfer the browned butter to a large heatproof bowl. Add the remaining 4 tablespoons butter and stir until completely melted.

4. Add the sugars, salt, and vanilla to the melted butter; whisk until fully incorporated. Add the egg and egg yolk; whisk until the mixture is smooth with no sugar lumps remaining, about 30 seconds. Let the mixture stand 3 minutes, then whisk for 30 seconds. Repeat the process of resting and whisking two more times until the mixture is thick, smooth, and shiny. Using a rubber spatula, stir in the flour mixture until just combined, about 1 minute. Stir in the chocolate chips and nuts (if using), giving the dough a final stir to ensure that no flour pockets remain.

5. Divide the dough into 16 portions, each about 3 tablespoons. Place the cookies on the prepared baking sheets, spacing them about 2 inches apart.

6. Bake one sheet at a time, rotating the sheet halfway through the baking time, until the cookies are golden brown and still puffy, and the edges have begun to set but the centers are still soft, 10 to 14 minutes. Transfer the baking sheet to a wire rack; cool to room temperature.

THICK AND CHEWY CHOCOLATE CHIP COOKIES

WHY THIS RECIPE WORKS: Nowadays, chocolate chip cookies sold in gourmet shops and cafés always come jumbo-sized (think saucer plate). These cookies are incredibly appealing and satisfying—thick and chewy rounds loaded with as many chocolate chips as they can hold. We wanted our own version that retained the soft and tender texture of these café cookies, even after a day or two (not that they'd be hanging around that long).

One key element in achieving this cookie was melting the butter, which creates a product with a chewy texture. But to keep the cookie from becoming tough, we had to add a little extra fat, which we did in the form of an egg yolk; the added fat acts a tenderizer and prevents the cookies from hardening after several hours. The usual suspects of all-purpose flour, baking soda, an egg, brown sugar, and granulated sugar made an appearance in our cookie recipe, and vanilla provided a light flavor. A good amount of chocolate chips guaranteed that every bite was rich and chocolaty. Finally, we formed the dough into balls, then pulled the dough into two pieces and rejoined them with the uneven surface facing up; now our cookies had the rustic, craggy appearance we wanted.

Thick and Chewy Chocolate Chip Cookies

MAKES ABOUT 18 LARGE COOKIES

To ensure the proper texture, cool the cookies on the baking sheets. See page 587 for our top-rated baking sheet.

    2   cups plus 2 tablespoons (about 10⅔ ounces) unbleached all-purpose flour
    ½   teaspoon baking soda
    ½   teaspoon table salt
   12   tablespoons (1½ sticks) unsalted butter, melted and cooled
    1   cup packed (7 ounces) light or dark brown sugar
    ½   cup (3½ ounces) granulated sugar
    1   large egg
    1   large egg yolk
    2   teaspoons vanilla extract
   1½   cups (9 ounces) semisweet chocolate chips

1. Adjust the oven racks to the upper-middle and lower-middle positions and heat the oven to 325 degrees. Line two large baking sheets with parchment paper.

2. Whisk the flour, baking soda, and salt together in a medium bowl; set aside.

3. In a standing mixer fitted with the paddle attachment, beat the butter and sugars at medium speed until smooth, about 1 minute. Add the egg, egg yolk, and vanilla and beat on medium-low speed until fully incorporated, about 30 seconds, scraping down the bowl and beater as needed with a rubber spatula. Add the dry ingredients and mix on low speed until combined, about 30 seconds. Mix in the chocolate chips until just incorporated.

4. Divide the dough into 18 portions, each about ½ cup, and roll them between your hands into balls. Holding one dough ball with your fingers, pull the dough apart into two equal halves. Rotate the halves 90 degrees and, with the jagged surfaces facing up, join the halves together at their base, again forming a single ball, being careful not to smooth the dough's uneven surface. Place the cookies on the prepared baking sheets, spacing them about 2½ inches apart.

5. Bake until the cookies are light golden brown and the edges start to harden but the centers are still soft and puffy, 15 to 18 minutes, switching and rotating the baking sheets halfway through the baking time. Cool the cookies on the baking sheets.

THIN, CRISPY CHOCOLATE CHIP COOKIES

WHY THIS RECIPE WORKS: Too often, thin and crispy chocolate chip cookies are tough and lack flavor. They can be too brittle, too crumbly, too dense, or too greasy. We wanted chocolate chip cookies that were thin, almost like praline cookies, and packed a big crunch without either breaking teeth or shattering into a million pieces when eaten. And they had to have the simple, gratifying flavors of deeply caramelized sugar and rich butter.

For cookies with a notable butterscotch flavor and sufficient crunch, we turned to a combination of light brown sugar and white sugar. Next we focused on the thickness of our cookies. When butter is creamed with sugar, air cells are created in the batter; these cells expand during baking, leading to cookies that rise—and cookies with height were not what we wanted. So we used melted butter and milk to create a batter that would spread (not rise) in the oven, resulting in cookies with the perfect thin crispiness. A bit of baking soda and corn syrup promoted maximum browning and caramelization, and vanilla and salt gave our cookies the best flavor.

Thin and Crispy Chocolate Chip Cookies

MAKES ABOUT 40 COOKIES

The dough, en masse or shaped into balls and wrapped well, can be refrigerated for up to 2 days or frozen for up to 1 month; bring it to room temperature before baking.

   1½   cups (7½ ounces) unbleached all-purpose flour
    ¾   teaspoon baking soda
    ¼   teaspoon table salt
    8   tablespoons (1 stick) unsalted butter, melted and cooled
    ½   cup (3½ ounces) granulated sugar
    ⅓   cup packed (2⅓ ounces) light brown sugar
    2   tablespoons light corn syrup
    1   large egg yolk
    2   tablespoons milk
    1   tablespoon vanilla extract
    ¾   cup (4½ ounces) semisweet chocolate chips

1. Adjust an oven rack to the middle position and heat the oven to 375 degrees. Line two large baking sheets with parchment paper.

2. Whisk the flour, baking soda, and salt together in a medium bowl; set aside.

3. In a standing mixer fitted with the paddle attachment, beat the melted butter, granulated sugar, brown sugar, and corn syrup at low speed until thoroughly blended, about 1 minute. Add the egg yolk, milk, and vanilla; mix until fully incorporated and smooth, about 1 minute, scraping down the bowl and beater as needed. With the mixer still running on low, slowly add the dry ingredients and mix until just combined. Do not overbeat. Add the chocolate chips and mix until evenly distributed throughout the batter, about 5 seconds.

4. Divide the dough into 40 portions, each about 1 tablespoon, and roll them between your hands into balls. Place the cookies on the prepared baking sheets, spacing them about 2 inches apart. Bake, one sheet at a time, until the cookies are deep golden brown and flat, about 12 minutes, switching and rotating the baking sheets halfway through the baking time.

5. Cool the cookies on the baking sheet for 3 minutes. Using a wide metal spatula, transfer the cookies to a wire rack and cool to room temperature.

CHOCOLATE COOKIES

WHY THIS RECIPE WORKS: Cookie recipes that trumpet their extreme chocolate flavor always leave us a bit suspicious. While they provide plenty of intensity, these over-the-top confections also tend to be delicate and crumbly, more like cakey brownies than cookies. We set out to make an exceptionally rich chocolate cookie that we could sink our teeth into—without having it fall apart.

Our first batch, which used modest amounts of cocoa powder and melted chocolate, baked up too cakey and tender—just what we didn't want. The chocolate was the culprit—its fat was softening the dough. We scaled back the chocolate until we eliminated it entirely, which made the cookies less cakey and tender, and thus, more cookie-like. To restore chocolate flavor without adding too much fat, we increased the cocoa powder and reduced the flour. Using an egg white rather than a whole egg (or yolk) gave us the structure we wanted and adding dark corn syrup gave the cookies a nice chewiness and lent a hint of caramel flavor. For more richness, we folded in chopped bittersweet chocolate; the chunks stayed intact and added intense flavor. After rolling the dough into balls, a dip in granulated sugar before baking gave the cookies a sweet crunch and an attractive crackled appearance once they were out of the oven.

Chocolate Cookies

MAKES ABOUT 16 COOKIES

We recommend using the test kitchen's favorite baking chocolates, Ghirardelli Bittersweet Chocolate or Callebaut Intense Dark L-60–40NV, but any high-quality dark, bittersweet, or semisweet chocolate will work. Light brown sugar can be substituted for the dark, as can light corn syrup for the dark, but with some sacrifice in flavor.

- ⅓ cup (2⅓ ounces) granulated sugar, plus ½ cup for coating
- 1½ cups (7½ ounces) unbleached all-purpose flour
- ¾ cup Dutch-processed cocoa powder
- ½ teaspoon baking soda
- ¼ teaspoon plus ⅛ teaspoon table salt
- ½ cup dark corn syrup (see note)
- 1 large egg white
- 1 teaspoon vanilla extract
- 12 tablespoons (1½ sticks) unsalted butter, softened
- ⅓ cup packed (2⅓ ounces) dark brown sugar (see note)
- 4 ounces bittersweet chocolate, chopped into ½-inch pieces (see note)

1. Adjust the oven racks to the upper-middle and lower-middle positions and heat the oven to 375 degrees. Line two large baking sheets with parchment paper. Place ½ cup of the granulated sugar in a shallow baking dish or pie plate. Whisk the flour, cocoa powder, baking soda, and salt together in a medium bowl. Whisk the corn syrup, egg white, and vanilla together in a small bowl.

2. In a standing mixer fitted with the paddle attachment, beat the butter, brown sugar, and remaining ⅓ cup granulated sugar at medium-high speed until light and fluffy, about 2 minutes. Decrease the speed to medium-low, add the corn syrup mixture, and beat until fully incorporated, about 20 seconds, scraping down the bowl and beater as needed with a rubber spatula. Decrease the speed to low, add the flour mixture and chopped chocolate, and mix until just incorporated, about 30 seconds, scraping down the bowl and beater as needed. Give the dough a final stir to ensure that no pockets of flour remain. Chill the dough for 30 minutes to firm slightly (do not chill longer than 30 minutes).

3. Divide the dough into 16 equal portions, each a generous 2 tablespoons, and roll them between your hands into balls about 1½ inches in diameter. Working in batches, drop eight dough balls into the baking dish with the sugar and toss to coat. Place the dough balls on the prepared baking sheet, spacing them about 2 inches apart; repeat with the second batch of eight. Bake, switching and rotating the sheets halfway through the baking time, until the cookies are puffed and cracked and the edges have begun to set but the centers are still soft (the cookies will look raw between the cracks and seem underdone), 10 to 11 minutes. Do not overbake.

4. Cool the cookies on the baking sheets for 5 minutes; using a wide metal spatula, transfer the cookies to a wire rack and cool to room temperature.

DOUBLE-CHOCOLATE COOKIES

WHY THIS RECIPE WORKS: Our goal in creating a traditional double-chocolate cookie recipe seemed more like a fantasy: The first bite of the cookie would reveal a center of hot fudge sauce, the texture would call to mind chocolate bread pudding, and the overall flavor would be of deep and complex chocolate. Was it possible?

In the end, the fulfillment of our fantasy relied on very basic ingredients—chocolate, sugar, eggs, butter, flour, baking powder, and salt. We used a modified creaming method with minimal beating to produce moist cookies that weren't cakey, and we let the batter rest for a half-hour to develop a certain fudginess. Ingredient proportions were all-important—for moist, rich cookies, we had to use more chocolate than flour. The more highly processed semisweet chocolate tasted smoother and richer than unsweetened, and Dutch-processed cocoa—which many bakers find superior in flavor to regular cocoa—and instant coffee further enriched the chocolate flavor. At last, we had a cookie that was both rich and soft, with an intense chocolaty center.

Thick and Chewy Double-Chocolate Cookies

MAKES ABOUT 42 COOKIES

To melt the chocolate using a microwave, heat it at 50 percent power for 2 minutes; stir the chocolate and continue heating until melted, stirring once every additional minute. Resist the urge to bake the cookies longer than indicated; they may appear underbaked at first but will firm up as they cool.

    2   cups (10 ounces) unbleached all-purpose flour
    ½   cup Dutch-processed cocoa powder
    2   teaspoons baking powder
    ½   teaspoon table salt
    16 ounces semisweet chocolate, chopped
    4   large eggs
    2   teaspoons vanilla extract
    2   teaspoons instant coffee or espresso powder
    10 tablespoons (1¼ sticks) unsalted butter, softened
    1½ cups packed (10½ ounces) light brown sugar
    ½   cup (3½ ounces) granulated sugar

1. Whisk the flour, cocoa powder, baking powder, and salt together in a medium bowl; set aside.

2. Melt the chocolate in a medium heatproof bowl set over a saucepan of barely simmering water, stirring occasionally, until smooth; set aside to cool slightly. Whisk the eggs and vanilla together in a medium bowl, sprinkle the coffee powder over the top to dissolve, and set aside.

3. In a standing mixer fitted with the paddle attachment, beat the butter and sugars at medium speed until combined, about 45 seconds; the mixture will look granular. Decrease the speed to low, gradually add the egg mixture, and mix until incorporated, about 45 seconds. Add the melted chocolate in a steady stream and mix until combined, about 40 seconds, scraping down the bowl and beater as needed with a rubber spatula. With the mixer still running on low, add the dry ingredients and mix until just combined. Do not overbeat. Cover the bowl of dough with plastic wrap and let stand at room temperature until the consistency is scoopable and fudge-like, about 30 minutes.

4. Meanwhile, adjust the oven racks to the upper-middle and lower-middle positions and heat the oven to 350 degrees. Line two baking sheets with parchment paper. Divide the dough into 42 equal portions, each about 2 tablespoons, and roll them between your hands into balls about 1¾ inches in diameter. Set the dough balls on the prepared baking sheets, spacing them about 1½ inches apart.

5. Bake two sheets at a time, switching and rotating the baking sheets halfway through the baking time, until the edges have just begun to set but the centers are still very soft, about 10 minutes. Cool the cookies on the baking sheets for 10 minutes; using a wide metal spatula, transfer the cookies to a wire rack and cool to room temperature.

Thick and Chewy Triple-Chocolate Cookies

The addition of chocolate chips will slightly increase the yield of the cookies.

Follow the recipe for Thick and Chewy Double-Chocolate Cookies, adding 2 cups (12 ounces) semisweet chocolate chips to the batter after the dry ingredients are incorporated in step 3.

PEANUT BUTTER COOKIES

WHY THIS RECIPE WORKS: Recipes for peanut butter cookies tend to fall into one of two categories: sweet and chewy with a mild peanut flavor, and sandy and crumbly with a strong peanut flavor. What we wanted, of course, was the best of both worlds—that is, cookies that were crisp on the edges and chewy in the center, with lots of peanut flavor.

First off, we had to determine the amount and type of sugar. Granulated sugar was necessary for crisp edges and chewy centers, while dark brown sugar enriched the peanut flavor. As for flour, too little resulted in an oily cookie, whereas too much made for dry cookies. Baking soda contributed to browning and amplified the peanut flavor and baking powder provided lift, making both leaveners necessary. Extra-crunchy peanut butter also helped the cookie rise and achieve a crisper edge and a softer center. But the best way to get the true peanut flavor we sought was to use peanuts and salt. Adding some roasted, salted peanuts, ground in a food processor, and then adding still more salt (directly to the batter as well in the form of salted rather than unsalted butter) produced a strong roasted nut flavor without sacrificing anything in terms of texture.

Peanut Butter Cookies

MAKES ABOUT 36 COOKIES

These cookies have a strong peanut flavor that comes from extra-crunchy peanut butter as well as from roasted salted peanuts that are ground in a food processor and worked into the dough. In our testing, we found that salted butter brings out the flavor of the nuts. If using unsalted butter, increase the salt to 1 teaspoon.

2½ **cups (12½ ounces) unbleached all-purpose flour**
½ **teaspoon baking soda**
½ **teaspoon baking powder**
½ **teaspoon table salt**
16 **tablespoons (2 sticks) salted butter, softened (see note)**
1 **cup packed (7 ounces) dark brown sugar**
1 **cup (7 ounces) granulated sugar**
1 **cup extra-crunchy peanut butter, room temperature**
2 **large eggs**
2 **teaspoons vanilla extract**
1 **cup (5 ounces) roasted salted peanuts, ground in a food processor to resemble bread crumbs, about 14 pulses**

1. Adjust the oven racks to the upper-middle and lower-middle positions and heat oven to 350 degrees. Line two large baking sheets with parchment paper.

2. Whisk the flour, baking soda, baking powder, and salt together in a medium bowl; set aside.

3. In a standing mixer fitted with the paddle attachment, beat the butter and sugars at medium speed until light and fluffy, about 2 minutes, scraping down the bowl and beater as needed with a rubber spatula. Add the peanut butter and mix until fully incorporated, about 30 seconds; add the eggs, one at a time, and the vanilla and mix until combined, about 30 seconds. Decrease the speed to low and add the dry ingredients; mix until combined, about 30 seconds. Mix in the ground peanuts until just incorporated.

4. Divide the dough into 36 portions, each a generous 2 tablespoons, and roll them between your hands into balls about 2 inches in diameter. Place the dough balls on the prepared baking sheets, spacing them about 2½ inches apart. Press each dough ball twice, at perpendicular angles, with a dinner fork dipped in cold water to make a criss-cross design.

5. Bake, switching and rotating the sheets halfway through the baking time, until the cookies are puffy and slightly brown around the edges but not on top, 10 to 12 minutes; the cookies will not look fully baked. Cool the cookies on the baking sheets for 5 minutes; using a wide metal spatula, transfer the cookies to a wire rack and cool to room temperature.

ULTIMATE OATMEAL COOKIES

WHY THIS RECIPE WORKS: Oatmeal cookies can be great vehicles for additional flavors, but it's easy to get carried away and overload the dough with a crazy jumble of ingredients resulting in a poorly textured cookie monster. Our ultimate oatmeal cookie would have just the right amount of added ingredients and an ideal texture—crisp around the edges and chewy in the middle.

We wanted to add four flavor components—sweet, tangy, nutty, and chocolaty—to the underlying oat flavor. Bittersweet chocolate, dried sour cherries (or cranberries), and toasted pecans gave the right balance of flavors. We also analyzed the cookie dough ingredients and discovered that cookies made with brown sugar were moister and chewier than cookies made with granulated sugar. A combination of baking powder and baking soda (we doubled the usual amount) produced cookies that were light and crisp on the outside, but chewy, dense, and soft in the center. Finally, we focused on appearance to decide when to remove the cookies from the oven—they should be set but still look wet between the fissures; if they look matte rather than shiny, they've been overbaked.

Chocolate-Chunk Oatmeal Cookies with Pecans and Dried Cherries
MAKES ABOUT 16 LARGE COOKIES

We like these cookies made with pecans and dried sour cherries, but walnuts or skinned hazelnuts can be substituted for the pecans, and dried cranberries for the cherries. Quick oats used in place of the old-fashioned oats will yield a cookie with slightly less chewiness. These cookies keep for 4 to 5 days stored in an airtight container or zipper-lock bag, but they will lose their crisp exterior and become uniformly chewy after a day or so. To recrisp the cookies, place them on a baking sheet and in a 425-degree oven for 4 or 5 minutes. Make sure to let the cookies cool on the baking sheet for a few minutes before removing them, and eat them while they're warm.

1¼ cups (6¼ ounces) unbleached all-purpose flour
¾ teaspoon baking powder
½ teaspoon baking soda
½ teaspoon table salt
1¼ cups (3¾ ounces) old-fashioned oats (see note)
1 cup (4 ounces) pecans, toasted and chopped (see note)
1 cup dried sour cherries, chopped coarse (see note)
4 ounces bittersweet chocolate, chopped into chunks about the size of chocolate chips (about ¾ cup)
12 tablespoons (1½ sticks) unsalted butter, softened
1½ cups packed (10½ ounces) brown sugar, preferably dark
1 large egg
1 teaspoon vanilla extract

1. Adjust the oven racks to the upper-middle and lower-middle positions and heat the oven to 350 degrees. Line two large baking sheets with parchment paper.

2. Whisk the flour, baking powder, baking soda, and salt together in a medium bowl. In a second medium bowl, stir together the oats, pecans, cherries, and chocolate.

3. In a standing mixer fitted with the paddle attachment, beat the butter and sugar at medium speed until no sugar lumps remain, about 1 minute, scraping down the bowl and beater as needed with a rubber spatula. Add the egg and vanilla and beat on medium-low until fully incorporated, about 30 seconds, scraping down the bowl and beater as needed. Decrease the speed to low, add the flour mixture, and mix until just combined, about 30 seconds. With the mixer still running on low, gradually add the oat-nut mixture; mix until just incorporated. Give the dough a final stir to ensure that no flour pockets remain and the ingredients are evenly distributed.

4. Divide the dough into 16 portions, each about ¼ cup, and roll them between your hands into balls; stagger eight balls on each prepared baking sheet, spacing them about 2½ inches apart. Using your fingertips, gently press each dough ball to a 1-inch thickness. Bake the cookies for 20 to 22 minutes, switching and rotating the baking sheets halfway through the baking time, until the cookies are medium brown and the edges have begun to set but the centers are still soft (the cookies will seem underdone and will appear raw, wet, and shiny in the cracks).

5. Cool the cookies on the baking sheets for 5 minutes; using a wide metal spatula, transfer the cookies to a wire rack and cool to room temperature.

BIG AND CHEWY OATMEAL-RAISIN COOKIES

WHY THIS RECIPE WORKS: Big, moist, and craggy, oatmeal cookies are so good and so comforting, but also so hard to get just right. Too often, they have textural issues and are dry and brittle; other times, it's the flavor that's off, with cookies that lack any sign of oatiness. We wanted an oversized cookie with buttery oat flavor and the utmost chewiness.

After numerous rounds of testing, we discovered three key changes that made a significant difference in the research recipes we uncovered. First, we substituted baking powder for baking soda. The baking powder gave the dough more lift, which in turn made the cookies less dense and a bit chewier. Second, we eliminated the cinnamon recommended in lots of recipes; by taking away the cinnamon, we revealed more oat flavor. We wanted some spice, however, and chose nutmeg, which has a cleaner, subtler flavor that we like with oats. Finally, we increased the sugar in our cookies, and this made a huge difference in terms of texture and moistness.

A RULE TO COOK BY

Contrary to what you may think, the test kitchen isn't packed with the latest high-tech kitchen gadgets. In fact, one of our favorite gadgets isn't even found in a kitchenware store. Wondering why that cake didn't rise properly? Or why those cookies ran together? Did your expensive steak overcook? Pull out a ruler. It can prove that the 8-inch cake pan you are using is actually 9 inches, that the cookies have been spaced together too closely, and that the supposedly 1-inch-thick steak the butcher sold you is only ½ inch thick. We prefer 18-inch stainless steel rulers, which can be thrown right into the dishwasher. They can be purchased at any office supply store for about $4.

Big and Chewy Oatmeal-Raisin Cookies

MAKES ABOUT 18 LARGE COOKIES

If you prefer a less sweet cookie, you can reduce the granulated sugar to ¾ cup, but you will lose some crispness. Do not overbake these cookies. The edges should be brown, but the rest of the cookie should be very light in color.

- 1½ cups (7½ ounces) unbleached all-purpose flour
- ½ teaspoon table salt
- ½ teaspoon baking powder
- ¼ teaspoon freshly grated nutmeg
- 16 tablespoons (2 sticks) unsalted butter, softened
- 1 cup packed (7 ounces) light brown sugar
- 1 cup (7 ounces) granulated sugar (see note)
- 2 large eggs
- 3 cups (9 ounces) old-fashioned oats
- 1½ cups raisins (optional)

1. Adjust the oven racks to upper-middle and lower-middle positions and heat oven to 350 degrees. Line two large baking sheets with parchment paper. Whisk the flour, salt, baking powder, and nutmeg together in a medium bowl; set aside.

2. In a standing mixer fitted with the paddle attachment, beat the butter and sugars at medium speed until light and fluffy, about 2 minutes. Add the eggs, one at a time, and mix until combined, about 30 seconds.

3. Decrease the speed to low and slowly add the dry ingredients until combined, about 30 seconds. Mix in the oats and raisins (if using) until just incorporated.

4. Divide the dough into 18 portions, each a generous 2 tablespoons, and roll them between your hands into balls about 2 inches in diameter. Place the dough balls on the prepared baking sheets, spacing them about 2 inches apart.

5. Bake, switching and rotating the sheets halfway through the baking time, until the cookies turn golden brown around the edges, 22 to 25 minutes. Cool the cookies on the baking sheets for 2 minutes; using a wide metal spatula, transfer the cookies to a wire rack and cool to room temperature.

Big and Chewy Oatmeal-Date Cookies

Follow the recipe for Big and Chewy Oatmeal-Raisin Cookies, substituting 1½ cups chopped dates for the raisins.

THIN AND CRISPY OATMEAL COOKIES

WHY THIS RECIPE WORKS: Thin and crispy oatmeal cookies can be irresistible—crunchy and delicate, these cookies really let the flavor of the oats take center stage. But the usual ingredients that give thick, chewy oatmeal cookies great texture—generous amounts of sugar and butter, a high ratio of oats to flour, a modest amount of leavener, eggs, raisins, and nuts—won't all fit in a thin, crispy cookie. We wanted to adjust the standard ingredients to create a crispy, delicate cookie in which the simple flavor of buttery oats really stands out.

Given this cookie's simplicity, creating a rich butter flavor was critical, so we kept almost the same amount of butter as in our standard big, chewy oatmeal cookie, but we scaled back the amount of sugar. Fine-tuning the amount and type of leavener led to a surprising result that solved our texture and shape problems. During baking, large carbon dioxide bubbles created by the baking soda and baking powder (upped from our traditional recipe) caused the cookies to puff up, collapse, and spread out, producing the thin, flat cookies we were looking for. Baking the cookies all the way through until they were fully set and evenly browned from center to edge made them crisp throughout but not tough.

Thin and Crispy Oatmeal Cookies

MAKES ABOUT 24 COOKIES

To ensure that the cookies bake evenly and are crisp throughout, bake them one tray at a time. Place them on the baking sheet in three rows, with three cookies in the outer rows and two cookies in the center row. If you reuse a baking sheet, allow the cookies on it to cool at least 15 minutes before transferring them to a wire rack, then reline the sheet with fresh parchment before baking more cookies. We developed this recipe using Quaker Old Fashioned Oats. Other brands of old-fashioned oats can be substituted but may cause the cookies to spread more. Do not use instant or quick oats.

- 1 cup (5 ounces) unbleached all-purpose flour
- ¾ teaspoon baking powder
- ½ teaspoon baking soda
- ½ teaspoon table salt
- 14 tablespoons (1¾ sticks) unsalted butter, softened but still cool
- 1 cup (7 ounces) granulated sugar
- ¼ cup packed (1¾ ounces) light brown sugar
- 1 large egg
- 1 teaspoon vanilla extract
- 2½ cups (7½ ounces) old-fashioned oats (see note)

1. Adjust an oven rack to the middle position and heat the oven to 350 degrees. Line three large baking sheets with parchment paper. Whisk the flour, baking powder, baking soda, and salt in a medium bowl; set aside.

2. In a standing mixer fitted with the paddle attachment, beat the butter and sugars at medium-low speed until just combined, about 20 seconds. Increase the speed to medium and continue to beat until light and fluffy, about 1 minute longer, scraping down the bowl and beater as needed with a rubber spatula. Add the egg and vanilla and beat on medium-low until fully incorporated, about 30 seconds, scraping down the bowl and beater as needed. Decrease the speed to low, add the flour mixture, and mix until just incorporated and smooth, about 10 seconds. With the mixer still running on low, gradually add the oats and mix until well incorporated, about 20 seconds. Give the dough a final stir to ensure that no flour pockets remain and the ingredients are evenly distributed.

3. Divide the dough into 24 portions, each about 2 tablespoons, and roll them between your hands into balls. Place the cookies on the prepared baking sheets, spacing them about 2½ inches apart, eight dough balls per sheet (see note). Using your fingertips, gently press each dough ball to a ¾-inch thickness.

4. Bake one sheet at a time until the cookies are deep golden brown, the edges are crisp, and the centers yield to slight pressure when pressed, 13 to 16 minutes, rotating the sheet halfway through the baking time. Cool the cookies completely on the sheet.

Salty Thin and Crispy Oatmeal Cookies

We prefer the texture and flavor of a coarse-grained sea salt, like Maldon or fleur de sel, but kosher salt can be used. If using kosher salt, reduce the amount sprinkled over the cookies to ¼ teaspoon.

Follow the recipe for Thin and Crispy Oatmeal Cookies, reducing the amount of salt in the dough to ¼ teaspoon. Lightly sprinkle ½ teaspoon coarse sea salt evenly over the flattened dough balls before baking.

COCONUT MACAROONS

WHY THIS RECIPE WORKS: Not that long ago, macaroons (cone-shaped cookies flavored with shredded coconut) were quite elegant and very popular. But today, they have deteriorated into lackluster mounds of beaten egg whites and coconut shreds or, at their worst, nothing more than a baked mixture of condensed milk and sweetened coconut. We set out to create a great coconut macaroon, with a pleasing texture and real, honest coconut flavor.

When we began looking at recipes for modern coconut macaroons, we found that they varied widely, some calling for vanilla or almond extract in addition to different kinds of coconut and sweeteners. We knew that narrowing the field when it came to the coconut and

other flavorings would make a big difference in both taste and texture. After rounds of testing, we determined that unsweetened shredded coconut resulted in a less sticky, more appealing texture. But sweetened shredded coconut packed more flavor than the unsweetened coconut, so we decided to use both; together they worked very well in the cookie. To add one more layer of coconut flavor, we tried cream of coconut and hit the jackpot. As for the structure of our cookie, a few egg whites and some corn syrup ensured that the macaroons held together well and were moist and pleasantly chewy.

Triple-Coconut Macaroons

MAKES ABOUT 48 COOKIES

Cream of coconut, available canned, is a very sweet product commonly used in piña colada cocktails. Be sure to mix the can's contents thoroughly before using, as the mixture separates upon standing. Unsweetened desiccated coconut is commonly sold in natural foods stores and Asian markets. If you are unable to find any, use all sweetened flaked or shredded coconut, but reduce the amount of cream of coconut to ½ cup, omit the corn syrup, and toss 2 tablespoons cake flour with the coconut before adding the liquid ingredients. For larger macaroons, shape haystacks from a generous ¼ cup of batter and increase the baking time to 20 minutes.

1 cup cream of coconut (see note)

2 tablespoons light corn syrup

4 large egg whites

2 teaspoons vanilla extract

½ teaspoon table salt

3 cups unsweetened, shredded, desiccated (dried) coconut (see note)

3 cups sweetened flaked or shredded coconut

1. Adjust the oven racks to the upper-middle and lower-middle positions and heat the oven to 375 degrees. Line two baking sheets with parchment paper and lightly spray the parchment with vegetable oil spray.

2. Whisk the cream of coconut, corn syrup, egg whites, vanilla, and salt together in a small bowl; set aside. Combine the unsweetened and sweetened coconuts in a large bowl; toss together, breaking up clumps with your fingertips. Pour the liquid ingredients over the coconut and mix with a rubber spatula until evenly moistened. Chill for 15 minutes.

3. Drop heaping tablespoons of batter onto the prepared baking sheets, spacing them about 1 inch apart. Using moistened fingertips, form the cookies into loose haystacks. Bake until light golden brown, about 15 minutes, switching and rotating the sheets halfway through the baking time.

4. Cool the cookies on the baking sheets until slightly set, about 2 minutes; using a wide metal spatula, transfer the cookies to a wire rack and cool to room temperature.

Chocolate-Dipped Triple-Coconut Macaroons

Using the two-stage melting process for the chocolate helps ensure that it will be at the proper consistency for dipping the cookies. To melt the 8 ounces of chocolate in a microwave, heat it at 50 percent power for 2 minutes; stir the chocolate and continue heating until melted, stirring once every additional minute.

Follow the recipe for Triple-Coconut Macaroons. Cool the baked macaroons to room temperature; line two large baking sheets with parchment paper. Chop 10 ounces semisweet chocolate; melt 8 ounces of the chocolate in a small heatproof bowl set over a saucepan of barely simmering water, stirring occasionally, until smooth. Off the heat, stir in the remaining 2 ounces of chocolate until smooth. Holding a macaroon by its pointed top, dip the bottom ½ inch up the sides in the chocolate, scrape off the excess, and place the macaroon on the prepared baking sheet. Repeat with the remaining macaroons. Refrigerate until the chocolate sets, about 15 minutes.

HOLIDAY SPRITZ COOKIES

WHY THIS RECIPE WORKS: Spritz cookies, those golden-swirled holiday cookies, often end up bland, gummy, and tasteless. How come they never taste as good as they look? Unfortunately, this Scandinavian treat has fallen victim to many recipe modifications, such as the use of vegetable shortening instead of butter, an overload of eggs, and an excess of starchy confectioners' sugar. We set out to spruce up spritz cookies and make them light, crisp, buttery treats—the life of any holiday party.

The success of these confections rests primarily in the management of a finicky ingredient list. Carefully balancing the butter, sugar, flour, egg (yolk only), heavy cream (just a drop), vanilla, and salt is the only recipe for success—a few simple ingredients gathered in the proper proportions. Creaming the butter and sugar in the traditional fashion worked well and produced a dough light enough to easily press or pipe the cookies. As for shaping, either a cookie press or a pastry bag can be used—it's up to you.

Spritz Cookies

MAKES ABOUT 72 SMALL COOKIES

If using a pastry bag, use a star tip to create the various shapes. For stars, a ½ to ⅝-inch tip (measure the diameter of the tip at the smallest point) works best, but for rosettes and S shapes, use a ⅜-inch tip. To create stars, see the photo on page 471; stars should be about 1 inch in diameter. To create rosettes, pipe the dough while moving the bag in a circular motion, ending at the center of the rosette; rosettes should be about 1¼ inches in diameter. To create S shapes, pipe the dough into compact S's; they should be about 2 inches long and 1 inch wide. If you make an error while piping, the dough can be scraped off the baking sheet and re-piped.

We had the best results baking these cookies one sheet at a time. When reusing a baking sheet, make sure that it has completely cooled before forming more cookies on it. Unbaked dough can be refrigerated in an airtight container for up to 4 days; to use, let it stand at room temperature until softened, about 45 minutes. Baked cookies will keep for more than a week if stored in an airtight container or zipper-lock bag.

- 1 **large egg yolk**
- 1 **tablespoon heavy cream**
- 1 **teaspoon vanilla extract**
- 16 **tablespoons (2 sticks) unsalted butter, softened but still cool**
- ⅔ **cup (4⅔ ounces) granulated sugar**
- ¼ **teaspoon table salt**
- 2 **cups (10 ounces) unbleached all-purpose flour**

1. Adjust an oven rack to the middle position and heat the oven to 375 degrees. Line two large baking sheets with parchment paper. Whisk the egg yolk, cream, and vanilla in a small bowl until combined; set aside.

2. In a standing mixer fitted with the paddle attachment, beat the butter, sugar, and salt at medium-high speed until light and fluffy, about 3 minutes, scraping down the bowl and beater as needed with a rubber spatula. With the mixer running at medium speed, add the yolk-cream mixture and beat until incorporated, about 30 seconds. With the mixer running at low speed, gradually beat in the flour until combined, scraping down the bowl and beater as needed. Give the dough a final stir to ensure that no flour pockets remain.

3. If using a cookie press to form the cookies, follow the manufacturer's instructions to fill the press. If using a pastry bag (see note), fit it with a star tip and fill the bag with half of the dough. Press or pipe cookies onto the prepared baking sheet, spacing them about 1½ inches apart, refilling the cookie press or pastry bag as needed. Bake one sheet at a time, until the cookies are light golden brown, 10 to 12 minutes, rotating the baking sheet halfway through the baking time. Cool the cookies on the baking sheet for 10 to 15 minutes; using a metal spatula, transfer them to a wire rack and cool to room temperature.

Spritz Cookies with Lemon Essence

Follow the recipe for Spritz Cookies, adding 1 teaspoon juice from 1 lemon to the yolk-cream mixture in step 1 and adding 1 teaspoon finely grated zest from 1 lemon to the butter along with the sugar and salt in step 2.

Almond Spritz Cookies

Grind ½ cup sliced almonds and 2 tablespoons of the flour in a food processor until powdery and evenly fine, about 12 pulses; combine the almond mixture with the remaining flour. Follow the recipe for Spritz Cookies, substituting ¾ teaspoon almond extract for the vanilla.

SABLÉ COOKIES

WHY THIS RECIPE WORKS: During the holidays, these French butter cookies offer sophistication and style. That is, if you can capture their elusive sandy texture (*sablé* is French for sandy), which separates them from sturdy American butter cookies. Most of the sablé recipes we came across had only slight differences in ingredient proportions—but they all baked up without the delicate crumbliness that defines this cookie. To create the hallmark sandy texture of sablés—light, with an inviting granular quality similar to shortbread—we would have to do some detective work.

We started with a basic recipe using the typical method of creaming butter and sugar, then adding egg and flour. We then chilled, sliced, and baked the dough—but these cookies were missing the delicate crumbliness that defines sablés. We needed to decrease the liquid in the dough so there would be less moisture to dissolve the sugar particles. Cutting back on butter helped, as did the inclusion of a hard-cooked egg yolk, an addition we came across in our research. Adding the mashed yolk during creaming eliminated moisture and perfected the texture of the cookies. Brushing the cookies with a beaten egg white and sprinkling them with coarse sugar before baking added a delicate crunch and an attractive sparkle.

Sablés (French Butter Cookies)

MAKES ABOUT 40 COOKIES

Turbinado sugar is commonly sold as Sugar in the Raw. Demerara sugar, sanding sugar, or another coarse sugar can be substituted. Make sure the cookie dough is well chilled and firm so that it can be uniformly sliced. After the dough has been wrapped in parchment, it can be double-wrapped in plastic and frozen for up to 2 weeks.

> 1 large egg
> 10 tablespoons (1¼ sticks) unsalted butter, softened
> ⅓ cup plus 1 tablespoon (2¾ ounces) granulated sugar
> ¼ teaspoon salt
> 1 teaspoon vanilla extract
> 1½ cups (7½ ounces) unbleached all-purpose flour
> 1 large egg white, lightly beaten with 1 teaspoon water
> 4 teaspoons turbinado sugar (see note)

1. Place the egg in a small saucepan, cover with water by 1 inch, and bring to a boil over high heat. Remove the pan from the heat, cover, and let sit for 10 minutes. Meanwhile, fill a small bowl with ice water. Using a slotted spoon, transfer the egg to the ice water and let stand for 5 minutes. Crack the egg and peel the shell. Separate the yolk from the white; discard the white. Press the yolk through a fine-mesh strainer into a small bowl.

2. In a standing mixer fitted with the paddle attachment, beat the butter, granulated sugar, salt, and cooked egg yolk on medium speed until light and fluffy, about 4 minutes, scraping down the bowl and beater as needed with a rubber spatula. Decrease the speed to low, add the vanilla, and mix until incorporated. Stop the mixer; add the flour and mix on low speed until just combined, about 30 seconds. Using a rubber spatula, press the dough into a cohesive mass.

3. Divide the dough in half; roll each piece into a log about 6 inches long and 1¾ inches in diameter. Wrap each log in a 12-inch square of parchment paper and twist the ends to seal and firmly compact the dough into a tight cylinder. Chill until firm, about 1 hour.

4. Adjust the oven racks to the upper-middle and lower-middle positions and heat the oven to 350 degrees. Line two large baking sheets with parchment paper. Using a chef's knife, slice the dough into ¼-inch-thick rounds, rotating the dough so that it won't become misshapen from the weight of the knife. Place the cookies 1 inch apart on the baking sheets. Using a pastry brush, gently brush the cookies with the egg white mixture and sprinkle evenly with the turbinado sugar.

NOTES FROM THE TEST KITCHEN

FORMING SPIRAL COOKIES

1. Halve each batch of dough. Roll out each portion on parchment paper into a 8 by 6-inch rectangle, ¼ inch thick. Briefly chill the dough until firm enough to handle.

2. Using a bench scraper, place one plain cookie dough rectangle on top of one chocolate dough rectangle. Repeat to make two double rectangles.

3. Roll out each double rectangle on parchment into a 9 by 6-inch rectangle (if too firm, let rest until malleable). Then, starting at the long end, roll each into a tight log.

4. Twist the ends of the parchment to seal. Chill the logs 1 hour. Slice the logs into ¼-inch-thick rounds.

5. Bake until the centers of the cookies are pale golden brown with edges slightly darker than the centers, about 15 minutes, switching and rotating the baking sheets halfway through the baking time. Cool the cookies on the baking sheets for 5 minutes; using a thin metal spatula, transfer the cookies to a wire rack and cool to room temperature. (The cookies can be stored between sheets of parchment paper in an airtight container for up to 1 week.)

Chocolate Sablés

Follow the recipe for Sablés, reducing the flour to 1⅓ cups (6⅔ ounces) and adding ¼ cup Dutch-processed cocoa powder with the flour in step 2.

Black and White Spiral Cookies

MAKES ABOUT 80 COOKIES

Follow the recipes for Sablés and Chocolate Sablés through step 2. Following the "Forming Spiral Cookies" photos on page 472, form the dough into spiral logs. Proceed with the Sablés recipe from step 4, slicing the logs into ¼-inch-thick rounds, omitting the egg white mixture and turbinado sugar in both recipes, and baking as directed.

Chocolate Sandwich Cookies

MAKES ABOUT 40 COOKIES

Follow the recipe for Sablés through step 3. In step 4, slice one dough log into ⅛-inch-thick rounds, omitting the egg white mixture and turbinado sugar. Bake the cookies as directed in step 5, reducing the baking time to 10 to 13 minutes. Repeat with the second dough log. When all the cookies are completely cool, melt 3½ ounces dark or milk chocolate and cool slightly. Spread the melted chocolate on the bottom of one cookie. Place a second cookie on top, slightly off-center, so some chocolate shows. Repeat with the remaining melted chocolate and cookies.

Vanilla Pretzel Cookies

MAKES ABOUT 40 COOKIES

Follow the recipe for Sablés through step 3, increasing the vanilla extract to 1 tablespoon and reducing the chilling time to 30 minutes (the dough will not be fully hardened). Slice the dough into ¼-inch-thick rounds and roll into balls. Roll each ball into a 6-inch rope, tapering the ends. Following the "Forming Pretzel Cookies" photos, form the ropes into pretzel shapes. Proceed with the recipe, brushing with the egg white mixture, sprinkling with the turbinado sugar, and baking as directed.

NOTES FROM THE TEST KITCHEN

FORMING PRETZEL COOKIES

1. Slice slightly chilled dough into ¼-inch-thick rounds and roll into balls.

2. Roll each ball into a 6-inch rope, tapering the ends.

3. Pick up one end of the rope and cross it over to form half of a pretzel shape.

4. Bring the second end over to complete the pretzel shape.

HOLIDAY ROLLED COOKIES

WHY THIS RECIPE WORKS: Baking holiday cookies should be a fun endeavor but so often it's an exercise in frustration. The dough clings to the rolling pin, it rips and tears as it is rolled out, and the tactic of moving the dough in and out of the fridge to make it easier to work with turns a simple one-hour process into a half-day project. We wanted a simple recipe that would yield a forgiving, workable dough, producing cookies that would be sturdy enough to decorate yet tender enough to be worth eating.

Our first realization was that we had to use enough butter to stay true to the nature of a butter cookie but not so much that the dough became greasy. All-purpose flour had enough gluten to provide structure, while superfine sugar provided a fine, even crumb and a compact, crisp cookie. Cream cheese—a surprise ingredient—gave the cookies flavor and richness without altering their texture.

Glazed Butter Cookies

MAKES ABOUT 38 COOKIES

If you cannot find superfine sugar, process granulated sugar in a food processor for 30 seconds. If desired, the cookies can be finished with sprinkles or other decorations immediately after glazing.

BUTTER COOKIE DOUGH
- 2½ cups (12½ ounces) unbleached all-purpose flour
- ¾ cup (5⅔ ounces) superfine sugar (see note)
- ¼ teaspoon table salt
- 16 tablespoons (2 sticks) unsalted butter, cut into 16 pieces, softened
- 2 tablespoons cream cheese, room temperature
- 2 teaspoons vanilla extract

GLAZE
- 1 tablespoon cream cheese, room temperature
- 3 tablespoons milk
- 1½ cups (6 ounces) confectioners' sugar

1. FOR THE COOKIES: In a standing mixer fitted with the paddle attachment, mix the flour, sugar, and salt at low speed until combined, about 5 seconds. With the mixer running on low, add the butter 1 piece at a time; continue to mix until the mixture looks crumbly and slightly wet, about 1 to 2 minutes longer. Beat in the cream cheese and vanilla until the dough just begins to form large clumps, about 30 seconds.

2. Knead the dough by hand in the bowl, about two to three turns, until it forms a large, cohesive mass. Transfer the dough to a clean work surface and divide it into two even pieces. Press each piece into a 4-inch disk, wrap the disks in plastic, and refrigerate until the dough is firm but malleable, about 30 minutes. (The disks can be refrigerated up to 3 days or frozen up to 2 weeks; defrost in the refrigerator before using.)

3. Adjust an oven rack to the middle position and heat the oven to 375 degrees. Working with one piece of dough at a time, roll out the dough to an even ⅛-inch thickness between two large sheets of parchment paper; slide the rolled dough, still on the parchment, onto a baking sheet and refrigerate until firm, about 10 minutes.

4. Line two large baking sheets with parchment paper. Working with one sheet of dough at a time, cut into desired shapes using cookie cutters and place the cookies on the prepared sheet, spacing them about 1½ inches apart. Bake one sheet at a time, until the cookies are light golden brown, about 10 minutes, rotating the sheet halfway through the baking time. (The dough scraps can be patted together, chilled, and rerolled once.) Cool the cookies on the baking sheet for 3 minutes; using a wide metal spatula, transfer the cookies to a wire rack and cool to room temperature.

5. FOR THE GLAZE: Whisk the cream cheese and 2 tablespoons of the milk together in a medium bowl until combined and no lumps remain. Add the confectioners' sugar and whisk until smooth, adding the remaining 1 tablespoon milk as needed until the glaze is thin enough to spread easily. Using the back of a spoon, drizzle or spread a scant teaspoon of the glaze onto each cooled cookie. Allow the glazed cookies to dry at least 30 minutes.

Jam Sandwiches

MAKES ABOUT 30 COOKIES

See the photos on page 475 to prepare these cookies. Turbinado sugar is commonly sold as Sugar in the Raw. Demerara sugar, sanding sugar, or another coarse sugar can be substituted.

- 1 recipe Butter Cookie Dough, prepared through step 3
- 2 tablespoons turbinado sugar (see note)
- 1¼ cups (12 ounces) raspberry jam, strained, simmered until reduced to 1 cup, and cooled to room temperature

1. Line two large baking sheets with parchment paper. Using a 2-inch round fluted cookie cutter, cut rounds from one piece of rolled dough and bake on a prepared sheet in a 375-degree oven, rotating the baking sheet halfway through the baking time, until the cookies are light golden brown, 8 to 10 minutes.

2. Sprinkle the second piece of rolled dough evenly with the sugar.

3. Using a 2-inch round fluted cookie cutter, cut rounds of sugar-sprinkled dough. Using a ¾-inch round fluted cookie cutter, cut out the centers of the sugared rounds. Place the cookies on a prepared sheet and bake, rotating the baking sheet halfway through the baking time, until the cookies are light golden brown, about 8 minutes.

4. When the cookies have cooled, spread 1 teaspoon jam on the top of each solid cookie, then cover with a cut-out cookie. Let the filled cookies stand until set, about 30 minutes.

Lime-Glazed Coconut Snowballs

MAKES ABOUT 40 COOKIES

> 1 recipe Butter Cookie Dough, with 1 teaspoon grated lime zest added with the dry ingredients, prepared through step 2
>
> 1 recipe Glaze, with 3 tablespoons lime juice substituted for the milk
>
> 1½ cups sweetened shredded coconut, pulsed in a food processor until finely chopped, about 15 pulses

1. Line two baking sheets with parchment paper. Roll the dough between your hands into 1-inch balls. Place the balls on the prepared sheets, spacing them about 1½ inches apart. Bake one sheet at a time in a 375-degree oven until lightly browned, about 12 minutes. Cool to room temperature.

2. Dip the tops of the cookies into the glaze and scrape off the excess, then dip them into the coconut. Place the cookies on a wire rack and let stand until the glaze sets, about 20 minutes.

Chocolate-Cherry Bar Cookies with Hazelnuts

MAKES ABOUT 50 COOKIES

> 1 recipe Butter Cookie Dough, with 1 cup chopped dried cherries added with the dry ingredients, prepared through step 2
>
> 1½ cups (9 ounces) semisweet chocolate chips
>
> 1½ cups (6 ounces) hazelnuts, toasted, skinned, and chopped

1. Adjust an oven rack to the lower-middle position and heat the oven to 375 degrees. Line a 17 by 12-inch rimmed baking sheet with parchment paper. Press the dough evenly into the prepared sheet and bake until

golden brown, about 20 minutes, rotating the sheet halfway through the baking time.

2. Immediately after removing the baking sheet from the oven, sprinkle evenly with the chocolate chips; let stand to melt, about 3 minutes.

3. Using an offset spatula, spread the chocolate into an even layer, then sprinkle the chopped hazelnuts evenly over the chocolate. Cool on a wire rack until just warm, 15 to 20 minutes.

4. Using a pizza wheel, cut on the diagonal into 1½-inch diamonds. Transfer the cookies to a wire rack to cool completely.

NOTES FROM THE TEST KITCHEN

CUTTING AND FILLING JAM SANDWICHES

1. Using a 2-inch round fluted cookie cutter, cut out cookies from one piece of the dough.

2. Sprinkle the second piece of rolled dough evenly with turbinado sugar and cut out 2-inch rounds.

3. Using a ¾-inch round fluted cookie cutter, cut out the centers of the sugared rounds.

4. When the cookies have cooled, spread the reduced jam on the solid cookies, then place the cut-out cookies on top.

NUT CRESCENT COOKIES

WHY THIS RECIPE WORKS: When nut crescent cookies are well made, they can be delicious: buttery, nutty, slightly crisp, slightly crumbly, with a melt-in-your mouth quality. Too often, however, they turn out bland and dry. We wanted to develop a recipe that would put them back in their proper place.

The ratio of 1 cup butter to 2 cups flour in almost all of the recipes we looked at is what worked for us. We tried three kinds of sugar in the batter: granulated, confectioners', and superfine. The last resulted in just what we wanted: cookies that melted in our mouths. In determining the amount, we had to remember that the cookies would be sweetened once more by their traditional coating of confectioners' sugar. Before rolling them, we let the cookies cool to room temperature; coating them with sugar while still warm results in the pasty outer layer we wanted to avoid.

Pecan or Walnut Crescent Cookies

MAKES ABOUT 48 SMALL COOKIES

If you cannot find superfine sugar, you can obtain a close approximation by processing regular granulated sugar in a food processor for about 30 seconds. If you don't have a food processor, you can finely grind the chopped nuts by rolling them between two large sheets of plastic wrap with a rolling pin, applying moderate pressure, until broken down to a coarse cornmeal-like texture.

  2 cups (8 ounces) whole pecans or walnuts, chopped fine
  2 cups (10 ounces) unbleached all-purpose flour
  ½ teaspoon table salt
  16 tablespoons (2 sticks) unsalted butter, softened
  ⅓ cup (2½ ounces) superfine sugar (see note)
  1½ teaspoons vanilla extract
  1½ cups (6 ounces) confectioners' sugar

1. Adjust the oven racks to the upper-middle and lower-middle positions and heat the oven to 325 degrees. Line two large baking sheets with parchment paper.

2. Whisk 1 cup of the chopped nuts, the flour, and salt together in a medium bowl; set aside. Process the remaining 1 cup chopped nuts in a food processor (see note) until they are the texture of coarse cornmeal, 10 to 15 seconds (do not overprocess). Stir the nuts into the flour mixture and set aside.

3. In a standing mixer fitted with the paddle attachment, beat the butter and superfine sugar at medium-low speed until light and fluffy, about 2 minutes; add the

vanilla, scraping down the bowl and beater with a rubber spatula. Add the flour mixture and beat on low speed until the dough just begins to come together but still looks scrappy, about 15 seconds. Scrape down the bowl and beater again with a rubber spatula; continue beating at low speed until the dough is cohesive, 6 to 9 seconds longer. Do not overbeat.

4. Divide the dough into 48 portions, each about 1 tablespoon, and roll them between your hands into 1¼-inch balls. Roll each ball between your palms into a rope that measures 3 inches long. Place the ropes on the prepared baking sheets and turn up the ends to form a crescent shape. Bake until the tops are pale golden and the bottoms are just beginning to brown, 17 to 19 minutes, switching and rotating the baking sheets halfway through the baking time.

5. Cool the cookies on the baking sheets for 2 minutes; using a wide metal spatula, transfer the cookies to a wire rack and cool to room temperature, about 30 minutes. Place the confectioners' sugar in a shallow baking dish or pie plate. Working with three or four cookies at a time, roll the cookies in the sugar to coat them thoroughly; gently shake off the excess. (The cookies can be stored in an airtight container up to 5 days.) Before serving, roll the cookies in the confectioners' sugar again and tap off the excess.

Almond or Hazelnut Crescent Cookies

Almonds can be used raw for cookies that are light in both color and flavor or toasted to enhance the almond flavor and darken the crescents.

Follow the recipe for Pecan or Walnut Crescent Cookies, substituting 1¾ cups (7¾ ounces) whole blanched almonds (toasted, if desired) or 2 cups (8 ounces) toasted, skinned hazelnuts for the pecans or walnuts. If using almonds, add ½ teaspoon almond extract along with the vanilla extract.

MERINGUE COOKIES

WHY THIS RECIPE WORKS: A classic meringue cookie may have only two ingredients—egg whites and sugar—but it requires precise timing. Otherwise, you'll end up with a meringue that's as dense as Styrofoam or weepy, gritty, and cloyingly sweet. A great meringue cookie should emerge from the oven glossy and white, with a shatteringly crisp texture that dissolves instantly in your mouth.

We chose a basic French meringue over a fussier Italian meringue. The French version, in which egg whites are whipped with sugar, is the simpler of the two; the Italian meringue, in which hot sugar syrup is poured into the whites, produces cookies that are dense and candy-like. The key to glossy, evenly textured meringue was adding the sugar at just the right time—when the whites have been whipped enough to gain some volume, but still have enough free water left in them for the sugar to dissolve completely. Surprisingly, we found that cream of tartar wasn't necessary. Without it, the whites formed more slowly, giving a wider time frame in which to add the sugar. It was also important to form the cookies in a uniform shape, so we piped them from either a pastry bag or a zipper-lock bag with a corner cut off.

Meringue Cookies

MAKES ABOUT 48 SMALL COOKIES

Meringues may be a little soft immediately after being removed from the oven but will stiffen as they cool. To minimize stickiness on humid or rainy days, allow the meringues to cool in a turned-off oven for an additional hour (for a total of 2 hours) without opening the door, then transfer them immediately to airtight containers and seal. Cooled cookies can be kept in an airtight container for up to 2 weeks.

- ¾ cup (5¼ ounces) sugar
- 2 teaspoons cornstarch
- 4 large egg whites
- ¾ teaspoon vanilla extract
- ⅛ teaspoon table salt

1. Adjust the oven racks to the upper-middle and lower-middle positions and heat the oven to 225 degrees. Line two large baking sheets with parchment paper. Combine the sugar and cornstarch in a small bowl.

2. In a standing mixer fitted with the whisk attachment, beat the egg whites, vanilla, and salt together at high speed until very soft peaks start to form (the peaks should slowly lose their shape when the whip is removed), 30 to 45 seconds. Decrease the speed to medium and slowly add the sugar mixture in a steady stream down the side of the mixer bowl (the process should take about 30 seconds). Stop the mixer and scrape down the sides and bottom of the bowl with a rubber spatula. Increase the speed to high and beat until glossy and stiff peaks have formed, 30 to 45 seconds.

3. Working quickly, place the meringue in a pastry bag fitted with a ½-inch plain tip or a large zipper-lock bag with ½ inch of the corner cut off. Pipe meringues into 1¼-inch-wide mounds about 1 inch high on the baking sheets, six rows of four meringues on each sheet. Bake for 1 hour, switching and rotating the baking sheets halfway through the baking time. Turn off the oven and allow the meringues to cool in the oven for at least 1 hour. Remove the meringues from the oven and let cool to room temperature before serving, about 10 minutes.

Chocolate Meringue Cookies

Follow the recipe for Meringue Cookies, gently folding 2 ounces finely chopped bittersweet chocolate into the meringue mixture at the end of step 2.

Toasted Almond Meringue Cookies

Follow the recipe for Meringue Cookies, substituting ½ teaspoon almond extract for the vanilla extract. In step 3, sprinkle the meringues with ⅓ cup coarsely chopped toasted almonds and 1 teaspoon coarse sea salt, such as Maldon (optional), before baking.

BLONDIES

WHY THIS RECIPE WORKS: Blondies are first cousins to both brownies and chocolate chip cookies. Although blondies are baked in a pan like brownies, the flavorings are similar to those in chocolate chip cookies—vanilla, butter, and brown sugar. They're sometimes laced with nuts and chocolate chips or butterscotch chips. But even with these extras, blondies can be pretty bland, floury, and dry. We set out to fix the blondie so it would be chewy but not dense, sweet but not cloying, and loaded with nuts and chocolate.

We found that the key to chewy blondies was using melted, not creamed, butter because the creaming process incorporates too much air into the batter. For sweetening, light brown sugar lent the right amount of earthy, molasses flavor. And combined with a substantial amount of vanilla extract and salt (to sharpen the sweetness), the light brown sugar developed a rich butterscotch flavor. To add both texture and flavor to the cookies, we included chocolate chips and pecans. We also tried butterscotch chips, but we found that they did little for this recipe. On a whim, we included white chocolate chips with the semisweet chips, and we were surprised that they produced the best blondie yet.

Blondies

MAKES 36 BARS

If you have trouble finding white chocolate chips, chop a bar of white chocolate into small chunks.

- 1½ cups (7½ ounces) unbleached all-purpose flour
- 1 teaspoon baking powder
- ½ teaspoon table salt
- 1½ cups packed (10½ ounces) light brown sugar
- 12 tablespoons (1½ sticks) unsalted butter, melted and cooled
- 2 large eggs
- 1½ teaspoons vanilla extract
- 1 cup (4 ounces) pecans, toasted and chopped coarse
- ½ cup (3 ounces) semisweet chocolate chips
- ½ cup (3 ounces) white chocolate chips (see note)

1. Adjust an oven rack to the middle position and heat the oven to 350 degrees. Line a 13 by 9-inch baking pan with two pieces of foil (see the photos on page 481) and spray with vegetable oil spray.

2. Whisk the flour, baking powder, and salt together in a medium bowl; set aside.

3. Whisk the brown sugar and melted butter together in a medium bowl until combined. Add the eggs and vanilla and mix well. Using a rubber spatula, fold the dry ingredients into the egg mixture until just combined. Do not overmix. Fold in the nuts and semisweet and white chocolate chips and turn the batter into the prepared pan, smoothing the top with a rubber spatula.

4. Bake until the top is shiny and cracked and feels firm to the touch, 22 to 25 minutes. Transfer the pan to a wire rack and cool completely. Loosen the edges with a paring knife and lift the bars from the pan using the foil extensions. Cut into 2 by 1½-inch bars.

Congo Bars

If you have trouble locating unsweetened shredded coconut, try a natural foods store or an Asian market. Keep a close eye on the coconut when toasting, as it can burn quickly.

Toast 1½ cups unsweetened shredded coconut on a rimmed baking sheet on the middle oven rack at 350 degrees, stirring two or three times, until light golden, about 4 to 5 minutes. Transfer to a small bowl to cool. Follow the recipe for Blondies, adding the toasted coconut with the chocolate chips and nuts in step 3.

CLASSIC BROWNIES

WHY THIS RECIPE WORKS: Chewy and chocolaty, brownies should be a simple and utterly satisfying affair. But too often, brownies are heavy, dense, and remarkably low on chocolate flavor. We wanted old-fashioned brownies that had serious chocolate flavor. They had to be the simple treats we enjoyed in our youth—Mom's brownies—but altered to cater to adult tastes.

To get that tender texture and delicate chew, we shelved the all-purpose flour in favor of cake flour; a bit of baking powder further lightened the crumb. Getting the number of eggs just right prevented our brownies from being cakey or dry. As for chocolatiness, plenty of unsweetened chocolate provided maximum chocolate flavor—not too sweet, with profound chocolate notes. Nailing the baking time was essential—too little time in the oven and the brownies were gummy and underbaked, too much time and they were dry. Finally, for nut-lovers, we toasted pecans and topped the brownies with them just before baking; baked inside the brownies, they steam and get soft.

Classic Brownies

MAKES 24 BROWNIES

Be sure to test for doneness before removing the brownies from the oven. If underbaked (the toothpick has batter clinging to it), the texture of the brownies will be dense and gummy; if overbaked (the toothpick comes out completely clean), the brownies will be dry and cakey. To melt the chocolate using a microwave, heat it with the butter at 50 percent power for 2 minutes; stir the chocolate and continue heating until melted, stirring once every additional minute.

- 1¼ cups (5 ounces) cake flour
- ¾ teaspoon baking powder
- ½ teaspoon table salt
- 6 ounces unsweetened chocolate, chopped fine
- 12 tablespoons (1½ sticks) unsalted butter, cut into 6 pieces
- 2¼ cups (15¾ ounces) sugar
- 4 large eggs
- 1 tablespoon vanilla extract
- 1 cup (4 ounces) pecans or walnuts, toasted and coarsely chopped (optional)

1. Adjust an oven rack to the middle position and heat the oven to 325 degrees. Line a 13 by 9-inch baking pan with two pieces of foil (see the photos on page 481) and spray with vegetable oil spray.

2. Whisk the flour, baking powder, and salt in a medium bowl until combined; set aside.

3. Melt the chocolate and butter in a medium heatproof bowl set over a saucepan of barely simmering water, stirring occasionally, until smooth. Off the heat, gradually whisk in the sugar. Add the eggs, one at a time, whisking after each addition, until thoroughly combined. Whisk in the vanilla. Add the flour mixture in three additions, folding with a rubber spatula until the batter is completely smooth and homogeneous.

4. Transfer the batter to the prepared pan; using a spatula, spread the batter into the corners of the pan and smooth the surface. Sprinkle the toasted nuts (if using) evenly over the batter. Bake until a toothpick or wooden skewer inserted into the center of the brownies comes out with a few moist crumbs attached, 30 to 35 minutes. Cool on a wire rack to room temperature, about 2 hours; loosen the edges with a paring knife and lift the brownies from the pan using the foil extensions. Cut the brownies into 2-inch squares and serve. (The brownies can be stored in an airtight container at room temperature up to 3 days.)

CHEWY, FUDGY BROWNIES

WHY THIS RECIPE WORKS: Classic Brownies (page 479) boast a balance of cakey and chewy. We wanted a brownie that was distinctly chewy—a moist, dark, luscious brownie with a firm, smooth, velvety texture. It must pack an intense chocolate punch and have deep, resonant chocolate flavor, but it must fall just short of overwhelming the palate.

To develop a rich, deep chocolate flavor, we ultimately found it necessary to use three types of chocolate. Unsweetened chocolate laid a solid, intense foundation; semisweet chocolate provided a mellow, even somewhat sweet, flavor; and cocoa powder smoothed out any rough edges introduced by the unsweetened chocolate (which can contribute a sour, acrid flavor) and added complexity to what can be the bland flavor of semisweet chocolate. We focused on flour, butter, and eggs to arrive at the chewy texture we wanted. Too little flour and the batter was goopy; too much made the brownies dry and muted the chocolate flavor. We melted the butter instead of creaming softened butter with the sugar and eggs; as with our Classic Brownies, the melted butter produced a more dense and fudgy texture.

Chewy, Fudgy Triple-Chocolate Brownies

MAKES 64 SMALL BROWNIES

To melt the chocolates in a microwave, heat them with the butter at 50 percent power for 2 minutes; stir the chocolate and continue heating until melted, stirring once every additional minute. Either Dutch-processed or natural cocoa powder works well in this recipe. These brownies are very rich, so we prefer to cut them into very small squares for serving.

- 5 ounces semisweet or bittersweet chocolate, chopped
- 2 ounces unsweetened chocolate, chopped
- 8 tablespoons (1 stick) unsalted butter, cut into quarters
- 3 tablespoons cocoa powder (see note)
- 3 large eggs
- 1¼ cups (8¾ ounces) sugar
- 2 teaspoons vanilla extract
- ½ teaspoon table salt
- 1 cup (5 ounces) unbleached all-purpose flour

1. Adjust an oven rack to the lower-middle position and heat the oven to 350 degrees. Line an 8-inch square baking pan with two pieces of foil (see page 481) and spray with vegetable oil spray.

2. Melt the chocolates and butter in a medium heatproof

bowl set over a saucepan of barely simmering water, stirring occasionally, until smooth. Whisk in the cocoa powder until smooth. Set aside to cool slightly.

3. Whisk the eggs, sugar, vanilla, and salt together in a medium bowl until combined, about 15 seconds. Whisk the warm chocolate mixture into the egg mixture. Using a wooden spoon, stir in the flour until just combined. Transfer the batter to the prepared pan; using a spatula, spread the batter into the corners and smooth the surface. Bake until slightly puffed and a toothpick or wooden skewer inserted into the center of the brownies comes out with a few moist crumbs attached, 35 to 40 minutes. Cool the brownies on a wire rack to room temperature, about 2 hours; loosen the edges with a paring knife and lift the brownies from the pan using the foil extensions. Cut the brownies into 1-inch squares and serve. (Do not cut the brownies until ready to serve; the brownies can be wrapped in plastic wrap and refrigerated up to 5 days.)

Triple-Chocolate Espresso Brownies

Follow the recipe for Chewy, Fudgy Triple-Chocolate Brownies, whisking in 1½ tablespoons instant espresso or coffee powder along with the cocoa powder in step 2.

FUDGY LOW-FAT BROWNIES

WHY THIS RECIPE WORKS: We have tried many recipes for "healthy" brownies, but it usually takes just one bite to regret the effort. Either the texture is incredibly dry or the chocolate flavor is anemic. We wanted a moist, fudgy, chocolaty brownie that had a lower fat and calorie count than a traditional brownie, which can weigh in at over 200 calories and 12 grams of fat.

We knew the richness and flavor would have to come from somewhere if we were cutting back on butter and unsweetened chocolate. We started our tests with "alternative" ingredients, such as prune puree, applesauce, and yogurt, but they resulted in everything from oddly-flavored brownies to flavorless hockey pucks. We had more success replacing some of the butter with low-fat sour cream, which yielded moist, fudgy brownies. A blend of cocoa powder and bittersweet chocolate (which has less fat per ounce than unsweetened chocolate) added deep chocolate flavor. And to boost both the brownies' chocolate flavor and moisture without adding any fat, we used a shot of chocolate syrup. Our brownies were now rich and decadent, but with half the calories (just 110 per serving) and fat (only 4.5 grams) of traditional brownies.

Fudgy Low-Fat Brownies

MAKES 16 BROWNIES

For a truly fudgy consistency, don't overbake the brownies; as soon as a toothpick inserted into the center comes out with moist crumbs attached, the brownies are done. If the toothpick emerges with no crumbs, the brownies will be cakey. To melt the chocolate in a microwave, heat it with the butter at 50 percent power for 2 minutes; stir and continue heating until melted, stirring once every additional minute.

    ¾ cup (3¾ ounces) unbleached all-purpose flour
    ⅓ cup Dutch-processed cocoa powder
    ½ teaspoon baking powder
    ¼ teaspoon table salt
    2 ounces bittersweet chocolate, chopped
    2 tablespoons unsalted butter
    1 cup (7 ounces) sugar
    2 tablespoons low-fat sour cream
    1 tablespoon chocolate syrup
    2 teaspoons vanilla extract
    1 large egg
    1 large egg white

1. Adjust an oven rack to the middle position and heat the oven to 350 degrees. Line an 8-inch square baking pan with two pieces of foil (see photos) and spray with vegetable oil spray.

2. Whisk the flour, cocoa powder, baking powder, and salt together in a medium bowl. Melt the chocolate and butter in a large heatproof bowl set over a saucepan of

barely simmering water, stirring occasionally, until smooth. Set aside to cool slightly, 2 to 3 minutes. Whisk in the sugar, sour cream, chocolate syrup, vanilla, egg, and egg white. Using a rubber spatula, fold the dry ingredients into the chocolate mixture until combined.

3. Transfer the batter to the prepared pan; using a spatula, spread the batter into the corners and smooth the surface. Bake until slightly puffed and a toothpick or wooden skewer inserted into the center of the brownies comes out with a few moist crumbs attached, 20 to 25 minutes. Cool the brownies on a wire rack to room temperature, about 1 hour. Loosen the edges with a paring knife and lift the brownies from the pan using the foil extensions. Cut the brownies into 2-inch squares and serve. (Do not cut the brownies until ready to serve; the brownies can be wrapped in plastic wrap and refrigerated up to 3 days.)

NOTES FROM THE TEST KITCHEN

MAKING A FOIL SLING

1. Place two sheets of aluminum foil perpendicular to each other in the baking pan, with the extra foil hanging over the edges of the pan.

2. Push the foil into the corners and up the sides of the pan, smoothing out any wrinkles in the foil.

3. After the bars or brownies have baked and cooled, use the foil sling to lift and transfer them to a cutting board before cutting into squares.

RASPBERRY SQUARES

WHY THIS RECIPE WORKS: Raspberry squares are one of the best, and easiest, bar cookies to prepare, especially since the filling is ready-made (a jar of raspberry preserves). But sometimes the proportions are uneven, leaving one parched from too much sandy crust, or with a puckered face from an overload of tart filling. We were after a buttery, tender, golden brown crust and crumb topping with just the right amount of sweet and tart raspberry preserves in the middle.

For the tender, almost (but not quite) sandy crumb, we had to get the right combination of ingredients, especially the butter and sugar. Too much butter made the raspberry squares greasy, but too little left them on the dry side. We found that equal amounts of white and light brown sugar made for a deeper flavor than white alone; oats and nuts made a subtle contribution to flavor while also adding some textural interest. For a golden brown bottom crust, we prebaked it before layering it with raspberry preserves and sprinkling on the top crust, which was a small amount of the reserved bottom crust mixture.

Raspberry Squares

MAKES 25 SQUARES

For a nice presentation, trim ¼ inch off the outer rim of the uncut baked block. The outside edges of all cut squares will then be neat.

- 1½ cups (7½ ounces) unbleached all-purpose flour
- 1¼ cups (3¾ ounces) quick oats
- ½ cup pecans or almonds, chopped fine
- ⅓ cup (2⅓ ounces) granulated sugar
- ⅓ cup packed (2⅓ ounces) light brown sugar
- ¼ teaspoon baking soda
- ¼ teaspoon table salt
- 12 tablespoons (1½ sticks) unsalted butter, cut into 12 pieces and softened
- 1 cup raspberry preserves

1. Adjust an oven rack to the lower-middle position and heat the oven to 350 degrees. Line a 9-inch square baking pan with two pieces of foil (see the photos on page 481) and spray with vegetable oil spray.

2. Whisk the flour, oats, nuts, sugars, baking soda, and salt together in a large bowl. In a standing mixer fitted with the paddle attachment, beat the flour mixture and butter at low speed until well blended and the mixture resembles wet sand, about 2 minutes.

3. Transfer two-thirds of the mixture to the prepared pan. Press the crumbs evenly and firmly into the bottom of the pan. Bake until just starting to brown, about 20 minutes. Using a rubber spatula, spread the preserves evenly over the hot crust; sprinkle the remaining flour mixture evenly over the preserves. Bake until bubbling around the edges and the top is golden brown, about 30 minutes, rotating the pan halfway through the baking time. Cool on a wire rack to room temperature, 1 to 1½ hours. Lift the bars from the baking pan using the foil extensions; cut the bars into 25 squares and serve.

KEY LIME BARS

WHY THIS RECIPE WORKS: Key lime pie is a luscious, bright, summery dessert, but like all pies, it's not very portable. Thus, we decided to bring all the essence of Key lime pie to a Key lime bar, creating a cookie that balanced tart and creamy flavors as well as soft and crispy textures.

To support our handheld bars, we needed a thicker, sturdier crust, which required more crumbs and butter than used in traditional pie crust. Tasters found the traditional graham cracker flavor too assertive in such a crust and preferred the more neutral flavor of animal crackers. As for the filling, it also had to be firmer. By adding cream cheese and an egg yolk to the usual sweetened condensed milk, lime juice, and lime zest, we created a firm, rich filling that didn't fall apart when the bars were picked up. Two issues remained: Were Key limes really key? Did we need a topping? While testers preferred Key lime juice to regular lime juice by a narrow margin, regular juice was judged acceptable, especially considering that we needed to squeeze far fewer regular limes (three) than Key limes (20) to get the same amount of juice. For a topping, a heavy streusel was rejected. The favorite was an optional toasted-coconut topping.

Key Lime Bars

MAKES 16 BARS

If you cannot find fresh Key limes, use regular (Persian) limes. Do not use bottled lime juice. Grate the zest from the limes before juicing them, avoiding the bitter white pith that lies just beneath the outermost skin. The optional coconut garnish adds textural interest and tames the lime flavor for those who find it too intense. The recipe can be doubled and baked in a 13 by 9-inch baking pan; you will need a double layer of extra-wide foil for the pan (each sheet about 20 inches in length) and should increase the baking times by a minute or two.

CRUST

- 5 **ounces animal crackers**
- 3 **tablespoons brown sugar**
- **Pinch table salt**
- 4 **tablespoons (½ stick) unsalted butter, melted and cooled slightly**

FILLING

- 2 **ounces cream cheese, room temperature**
- 1 **tablespoon grated zest from 1 lime**
- **Pinch table salt**
- 1 **(14-ounce) can sweetened condensed milk**
- 1 **large egg yolk**
- ½ **cup fresh lime juice, from about 20 Key limes or about 3 Persian limes (see note)**

GARNISH (OPTIONAL)

- ¾ **cup sweetened shredded coconut, toasted until golden and crisp (see note)**

1. Adjust an oven rack to the middle position and heat the oven to 325 degrees. Line an 8-inch square baking pan with two pieces of foil (see the photos on page 481) and spray with vegetable oil spray.

2. FOR THE CRUST: Pulse the animal crackers in a food processor until broken down, about 10 pulses; process the crumbs until evenly fine, about 10 seconds (you should have about 1¼ cups crumbs). Add the brown sugar and salt; process to combine, 10 to 12 pulses (if large sugar lumps remain, break them apart with your fingers). Drizzle the butter over the crumbs and pulse until the crumbs are evenly moistened with the butter, about 10 pulses. Press the crumbs evenly and firmly into the bottom of the prepared pan. Bake until deep golden brown, 18 to

20 minutes. Cool on a wire rack while making the filling. Do not turn off the oven.

3. FOR THE FILLING: While the crust cools, in a medium bowl, stir the cream cheese, zest, and salt with a rubber spatula until softened, creamy, and thoroughly combined. Add the sweetened condensed milk and whisk vigorously until incorporated and no lumps of cream cheese remain; whisk in the egg yolk. Add the lime juice and whisk gently until incorporated (the mixture will thicken slightly).

4. Pour the filling into the crust; spread to the corners and smooth the surface with a rubber spatula. Bake until set and the edges begin to pull away slightly from the sides, 15 to 20 minutes. Cool on a wire rack to room temperature, 1 to 1½ hours. Cover with foil and refrigerate until thoroughly chilled, at least 2 hours.

5. Loosen the edges with a paring knife and lift the bars from the baking pan using the foil extensions; cut the bars into 16 squares. Sprinkle with the toasted coconut (if using) and serve. (Leftovers can be refrigerated up to 2 days; the crust will soften slightly. Let the bars stand at room temperature about 15 minutes before serving.)

Triple Citrus Bars

Using three types of citrus (orange, lemon, and lime) gives these bars a slightly more complex, floral flavor.

Follow the recipe for Key Lime Bars, substituting 1½ teaspoons each grated lime zest, lemon zest, and orange zest for the lime zest, and using 6 tablespoons lime juice, 1 tablespoon lemon juice, and 1 tablespoon orange juice in place of all the lime juice.

CHAPTER 22

A PIECE OF CAKE

Angel Food Cake   486

Rich Chocolate
Bundt Cake   487

Lemon Bundt Cake   488

Lemon Pound Cake   489

Applesauce Snack
Cake   490

Oatmeal Cake with
Broiled Icing   491

Apple Upside-Down
Cake   492

Apple Upside-Down
Cake with Almond   493

Apple Upside-Down
Cake with Lemon
and Thyme   493

Carrot Cake   494

Cream Cheese Frosting

Light Carrot Cake   495

Light Cream Cheese
Frosting

Spice Cake   496

Strawberry Cream
Cake   497

Coconut Layer Cake   498

Lemon Layer Cake with
Fluffy White Icing   500

Classic White Layer Cake
with Butter Frosting
and Raspberry-Almond
Filling   501

Classic Yellow Layer
Cake with Vanilla
Buttercream   502

Fluffy Yellow Layer Cake
with Milk Chocolate
Frosting   504

Old-Fashioned Chocolate
Layer Cake with Chocolate
Frosting   506

Chocolate Sheet Cake
with Easy Chocolate
Frosting   507

German Chocolate
Cake   508

Dark Chocolate
Cupcakes   510

Easy Vanilla Bean
Buttercream

Easy Chocolate
Buttercream

Easy Coffee Buttercream

Flourless Chocolate
Cake   511

Hot Fudge Pudding
Cake   512

Individual Hot Fudge
Pudding Cakes   513

Bittersweet Chocolate
Roulade   513

Espresso-Mascarpone
Cream

Dark Chocolate Ganache

Triple-Chocolate Mousse
Cake   515

Chocolate Volcano
Cakes with Espresso
Ice Cream   517

Tiramisù   518

Tiramisù with Cooked
Eggs   518

New York Cheesecake   519

Strawberry Topping

Light New York
Cheesecake   520

Spiced Pumpkin
Cheesecake   521

Lemon Cheesecake   523

ANGEL FOOD CAKE

WHY THIS RECIPE WORKS: At its heavenly best, an angel food cake should be tall and perfectly shaped, have a snowy-white, tender crumb, and be encased in a thin, delicate golden crust. The difficulty with making a great angel food cake is that it requires a delicate balance of ingredients and proper cooking techniques. In particular, since this cake is only leavened with beaten egg whites, it is critical that you whip them correctly. Overbeaten egg whites produce a flatter cake.

First, we found it key to create a stable egg-white base, starting the whites at medium-low speed just to break them up into a froth and increasing the speed to medium-high speed to form soft, billowy mounds. Next, the sugar should be added, a tablespoon at a time. Once all the sugar is added, the whites become shiny and form soft peaks when the beater is lifted. A delicate touch is required when incorporating the remaining ingredients, such as the flour, which should be sifted over the batter and gently folded in. Angel food cakes are baked in a tube pan. We like to use a tube pan with a removable bottom but a pan without one can be lined with parchment paper. We avoid greasing the sides of the pan so that the cake can climb up and cling to the sides as it bakes—a greased pan will produce a disappointingly short cake. Follow our instructions and you'll be rewarded with the perfect tall, light yet firm angel food cake.

Angel Food Cake

SERVES 10 TO 12

If your tube pan has a removable bottom, you do not need to line it with parchment. Angel food cake can be served plain or dusted with confectioners' sugar.

- 1½ cups (10½ ounces) sugar
- ¾ cup (3 ounces) cake flour
- 12 large egg whites, room temperature
- 1 teaspoon cream of tartar
- ¼ teaspoon table salt
- 1½ teaspoons juice from 1 lemon
- 1½ teaspoons vanilla extract
- ½ teaspoon almond extract

1. Adjust an oven rack to the lower-middle position and heat the oven to 325 degrees. Line the bottom of a 16-cup tube pan with parchment paper but do not grease. Whisk ¾ cup of the sugar and the flour together in a medium bowl.

2. In a standing mixer fitted with the whisk attachment, whip the egg whites and cream of tartar together on medium-low speed until foamy, about 1 minute. Increase the mixer speed to medium-high and whip the whites to soft, billowy mounds, about 1 minute. Gradually whip in the salt and remaining ¾ cup sugar, 1 tablespoon at a time, about 1 minute. Continue to whip the whites until they are shiny and form soft peaks, 1 to 3 minutes.

3. Whisk the lemon juice and extracts into the whipped whites by hand. Sift ¼ cup of the flour mixture over the top of the whites, then gently fold to combine with a large rubber spatula until just a few streaks of flour remain. Repeat with the remaining flour mixture, ¼ cup at a time.

4. Scrape the batter into the prepared pan and smooth the top. Wipe any drops of batter off the sides of the pan and lightly tap the pan against the countertop two or three times to settle the batter. Bake the cake until golden brown and the top springs back when pressed firmly, 50 to 60 minutes.

5. Invert the tube pan over a large metal kitchen funnel or the neck of a sturdy bottle (or, if your pan has "feet" that rise above the top edge of the pan, simply let the cake rest upside down). Cool the cake completely, upside down, 2 to 3 hours.

6. Run a small knife around the edge of the cake to loosen. Gently tap the pan upside down on the countertop to release the cake. Peel off the parchment paper, turn the cake right side up onto a serving platter, and serve.

CHOCOLATE BUNDT CAKE

WHY THIS RECIPE WORKS: A Bundt cake is the pinnacle of cake-baking simplicity. With its decorative shape, this cake doesn't require frosting or fussy finishing techniques. We wanted a cake that would deliver that moment of pure chocolate ecstasy with the first bite—a chocolate Bundt cake that tastes every bit as good as it looks, with a fine crumb, moist texture, and rich chocolate flavor.

We intensified the chocolate flavor by using both bittersweet chocolate and natural cocoa and dissolving them in boiling water, which "bloomed" their flavor. We used sour cream and brown sugar instead of white to add moisture and flavor. Finally, we further enhanced flavor with a little espresso powder and a generous amount of vanilla extract, both of which complemented the floral nuances of the chocolate.

Rich Chocolate Bundt Cake

SERVES 12

We prefer natural cocoa here because Dutch-processed cocoa will result in a compromised rise. For an accurate measurement of boiling water, bring a kettle of water to a boil, then measure out the desired amount. The cake can be served with just a dusting of confectioners' sugar but is easily made more impressive with lightly sweetened whipped cream and raspberries.

- 12 **tablespoons (1½ sticks) unsalted butter, softened, plus 1 tablespoon, melted, for the pan**
- ¾ **cup natural cocoa powder, plus 1 tablespoon for the pan (see note)**
- 6 **ounces bittersweet chocolate, chopped coarse**
- 1 **teaspoon instant espresso powder (optional)**
- ¾ **cup boiling water (see note)**
- 1 **cup sour cream, room temperature**
- 1¾ **cups (8¾ ounces) unbleached all-purpose flour**
- 1 **teaspoon table salt**
- 1 **teaspoon baking soda**
- 2 **cups packed (14 ounces) light brown sugar**
- 1 **tablespoon vanilla extract**
- 5 **large eggs, room temperature**
  Confectioners' sugar, for dusting (see note)

1. Stir together the 1 tablespoon melted butter and 1 tablespoon of the cocoa in a small bowl until a paste forms. Using a pastry brush, coat all the interior surfaces of a standard 12-cup Bundt pan. (If the mixture becomes too thick to brush on, microwave it for 10 to 20 seconds, or until warm and softened.) Adjust an oven rack to the lower-middle position and heat the oven to 350 degrees.

2. Combine the remaining ¾ cup cocoa, the chocolate, and espresso powder (if using) in a medium heatproof bowl. Pour the boiling water over and whisk until smooth. Cool to room temperature; then whisk in the sour cream. Whisk the flour, salt, and baking soda in a second bowl to combine.

3. In a standing mixer fitted with the paddle attachment, beat the remaining 12 tablespoons butter, the brown sugar, and vanilla on medium-high speed until pale and fluffy, about 3 minutes. Reduce the speed to medium and add the eggs one at a time, mixing about 30 seconds after each addition and scraping down the bowl with a rubber spatula after the first two additions. Reduce to medium-low speed (the batter may appear separated); add about one-third of the flour mixture and half of the chocolate mixture and mix until just incorporated, about 20 seconds. Scrape the bowl and repeat using half of the remaining flour mixture and all of the remaining chocolate mixture; add the remaining flour mixture and beat until just incorporated, about 10 seconds. Scrape the bowl and mix on medium-low speed until the batter is thoroughly combined, about 30 seconds.

4. Transfer the batter to the prepared pan, smoothing the top with a rubber spatula. Lightly tap the pan against the countertop two or three times to settle the batter. Bake until a toothpick inserted into the center comes out with a few crumbs attached, 45 to 50 minutes, rotating the pan halfway through the baking time. Cool the cake in the pan on a wire rack for 10 minutes, then invert the cake directly onto the wire rack; cool to room temperature, about 2 hours. Dust with confectioners' sugar, transfer to a serving platter, cut into slices, and serve.

LEMON BUNDT CAKE

WHY THIS RECIPE WORKS: Lemons are tart, brash, and aromatic. Why, then, is it so hard to capture their assertive flavor in a straightforward Bundt cake? The flavor of lemon juice is drastically muted when exposed to the heat of an oven, and its acidity can wreak havoc on the delicate nature of baked goods. We wanted to develop a Bundt cake with potent lemon flavor without ruining its texture.

We developed a battery of tests challenging classic lemon Bundt cake ingredient proportions, finally deciding to increase the butter and to replace the milk with buttermilk. We also found that creaming was necessary to achieve a light and even crumb. But we still needed to maximize the lemon flavor; we couldn't get the flavor we needed from lemon juice alone without using so much that the cake fell apart when sliced. We turned to zest and found that three lemons' worth gave the cake a perfumed lemon flavor, though we needed to give the zest a brief soak in lemon juice to eliminate its fibrous texture. The final challenge was the glaze, and a simple mixture of lemon juice, buttermilk, and confectioners' sugar made the grade.

Lemon Bundt Cake

SERVES 12

The cake has a light, fluffy texture when eaten the day it is baked, but if well wrapped and held at room temperature overnight its texture becomes more dense—like that of pound cake—the following day.

CAKE

- 18 tablespoons (2¼ sticks) unsalted butter, room temperature, plus 1 tablespoon, melted, for the pan
- 3 cups (15 ounces) unbleached all-purpose flour, plus 1 tablespoon for the pan
- 3 tablespoons grated zest plus 3 tablespoons juice from 3 lemons
- 1 teaspoon baking powder
- ½ teaspoon baking soda
- 1 teaspoon table salt
- ¾ cup buttermilk
- 1 teaspoon vanilla extract
- 3 large eggs plus 1 large egg yolk, room temperature
- 2 cups (14 ounces) granulated sugar

GLAZE

- 2 cups (8 ounces) confectioners' sugar
- 2–3 tablespoons juice from 1 lemon
- 1 tablespoon buttermilk

1. FOR THE CAKE: Adjust an oven rack to the lower-middle position and heat the oven to 350 degrees. Stir together the 1 tablespoon melted butter and 1 tablespoon of the flour in a small bowl until a paste forms. Using a pastry brush, coat all the interior surfaces of a standard 12-cup Bundt pan. (If the mixture becomes too thick to brush on, microwave it for 10 to 20 seconds, or until warm and softened.) Mince the lemon zest to a fine paste (you should have about 2 tablespoons). Combine the zest and lemon juice in a small bowl; set aside to soften, 10 to 15 minutes.

2. Whisk the remaining 3 cups flour, the baking powder, baking soda, and salt in a large bowl. Combine the lemon juice mixture, buttermilk, and vanilla in a medium bowl. In a small bowl, gently whisk the eggs and yolk to combine. In a standing mixer fitted with the paddle attachment, beat the remaining 18 tablespoons butter and the granulated sugar at medium-high speed until pale and fluffy, about 3 minutes. Reduce to medium speed and add half of the eggs, mixing until incorporated, about 15 seconds; scrape down the bowl with a rubber spatula. Repeat with the remaining eggs; scrape down the bowl again. Reduce to low speed; add about one-third of the flour mixture, followed by half of the buttermilk mixture, mixing until just incorporated after each addition (about 5 seconds). Repeat using half of the remaining flour mixture and all of the remaining buttermilk mixture. Scrape down the bowl and add the remaining flour mixture; mix at medium-low speed until the batter is thoroughly combined, about 15 seconds. Transfer the batter to the prepared pan, smoothing the top with a rubber spatula. Lightly tap the pan against the countertop two or three times to settle the batter.

3. Bake until the top is golden brown and a toothpick inserted into the center comes out with no crumbs attached, 45 to 50 minutes, rotating the pan halfway through the baking time.

4. FOR THE GLAZE: While the cake is baking, whisk the confectioners' sugar, 2 tablespoons of the lemon juice, and the buttermilk until smooth, adding more lemon juice gradually as needed until the glaze is thick but still pourable. Cool the cake in the pan on a wire rack set over a baking sheet for 10 minutes, then invert the cake directly onto the rack. Pour half of the glaze over the warm cake and cool for 1 hour; pour the remaining glaze evenly over the top of the cake and continue to cool to room temperature, at least 2 hours. Cut into slices and serve.

LEMON POUND CAKE

WHY THIS RECIPE WORKS: Pound cakes often turn out spongy, rubbery, heavy, and dry—and lemon pound cakes often lack true lemon flavor. We wanted to produce a superior pound cake (fine-crumbed, rich, moist, and buttery) while making the process as simple and foolproof as possible.

After less-than-successful results with a standing mixer and a hand mixer, we turned to the food processor to mix our cake. It ensured a perfect emulsification of the eggs, sugar, and melted butter (we found that a blender worked, too). Cake flour produced a tender crumb, but our cake was still a bit heavy. We fixed matters with the addition of baking powder, which increased lift and produced a consistent, fine crumb. Finally, in addition to mixing lemon zest into the cake batter, we glazed the finished cake with lemon sugar syrup—but first we poked holes all over the cake to ensure that the tangy, sweet glaze infused the cake with a blast of bright lemon flavor.

Lemon Pound Cake

MAKES ONE 8-INCH LOAF, SERVING 8

You can use a blender instead of a food processor to mix the batter. To add the butter, remove the center cap of the lid so it can be drizzled into the whirling blender with minimal splattering. This batter looks almost like a thick pancake batter and is very fluid.

CAKE

- 16 tablespoons (2 sticks) unsalted butter, plus 1 tablespoon, softened, for the pan
- 1½ cups (6 ounces) cake flour, plus 1 tablespoon for the pan
- 1 teaspoon baking powder
- ½ teaspoon table salt
- 1¼ cups (8¾ ounces) sugar
- 2 tablespoons grated zest plus 2 teaspoons juice from 1 lemon
- 4 large eggs, room temperature
- 1½ teaspoons vanilla extract

GLAZE

- ½ cup (3½ ounces) sugar
- ¼ cup juice from 2 lemons

1. FOR THE CAKE: Adjust an oven rack to the middle position and heat the oven to 350 degrees. Grease an 8½ by 4½-inch loaf pan with 1 tablespoon of the softened butter; dust with 1 tablespoon of the flour, tapping out the excess. In a medium bowl, whisk together the remaining 1½ cups flour, the baking powder, and salt; set aside.

2. Melt the remaining 16 tablespoons butter in a small saucepan over medium heat. Whisk the melted butter thoroughly to reincorporate any separated milk solids.

3. In a food processor, pulse the sugar and zest until combined, about 5 pulses. Add the lemon juice, eggs, and vanilla; process until combined, about 5 seconds. With the machine running, add the melted butter through the feed tube in a steady stream (this should take about 20 seconds). Transfer the mixture to a large bowl. Sift the flour mixture over the egg mixture in three additions, whisking gently after each addition until just combined.

4. Pour the batter into the prepared pan and bake 15 minutes. Reduce the oven temperature to 325 degrees and continue to bake until deep golden brown and a toothpick inserted in the center comes out clean, about 35 minutes, rotating the pan halfway through the baking time. Cool in the pan for 10 minutes, then turn onto a wire rack. Poke the top and sides of the cake throughout with a toothpick. Cool to room temperature, at least 1 hour. (The cooled cake can be wrapped tightly in plastic wrap and stored at room temperature for up to 5 days.)

5. FOR THE GLAZE: While the cake is cooling, bring the sugar and lemon juice to a boil in a small saucepan, stirring occasionally to dissolve the sugar. Reduce the heat to low and simmer until thickened slightly, about 2 minutes. Brush the top and sides of the cake with the glaze and cool to room temperature.

APPLESAUCE CAKE

WHY THIS RECIPE WORKS: Applesauce cakes run the gamut from dense, chunky fruitcakes to gummy "health" cakes without much flavor. We wanted a moist and tender cake that actually tasted like its namesake.

It was easy to achieve the looser, more casual crumb that is best suited to a rustic snack cake. Since this texture is similar to that of quick breads and muffins, we used the same technique, i.e. mixing the wet ingredients separately and then gently adding the dry ingredients by hand. The harder challenge was to develop more apple flavor—simply adding more applesauce made for a gummy cake and fresh apples added too much moisture. But two other sources worked well. Apple cider, reduced to a syrup, contributed a pleasing sweetness and a slight tang without excess moisture. And plumping dried apples in the cider while it was reducing added even more apple taste without making the cake chunky. With such great apple flavor, we didn't want the cake to be too sweet or rich, so we rejected the idea of topping the cake with a glaze or frosting. But we found we liked the modicum of textural contrast provided by a simple sprinkling of spiced granulated sugar.

Applesauce Snack Cake

SERVES 9

This recipe can be easily doubled and baked in a 13 by 9-inch baking dish. If doubling the recipe, give the cider and dried apple mixture about 20 minutes to reduce, and bake the cake for about 45 minutes. The cake is very moist, so it is best to err on the side of overdone when testing its doneness. The test kitchen prefers the rich flavor of cider, but apple juice can be substituted.

> 1 **cup apple cider (see note)**
> ¾ **cup (2 ounces) dried apples, cut into ½-inch pieces**
> 1½ **cups (7½ ounces) unbleached all-purpose flour**
> 1 **teaspoon baking soda**
> ⅔ **cup (4⅔ ounces) sugar**
> ½ **teaspoon ground cinnamon**
> ¼ **teaspoon ground nutmeg**
> ⅛ **teaspoon ground cloves**
> 1 **cup unsweetened applesauce, room temperature**
> 1 **large egg, room temperature, lightly beaten**
> ½ **teaspoon table salt**
> 8 **tablespoons (1 stick) unsalted butter, melted and cooled slightly**
> 1 **teaspoon vanilla extract**

1. Adjust an oven rack to the middle position and heat the oven to 325 degrees. Cut a 16-inch length of parchment paper or foil and fold lengthwise to a 7-inch width. Grease an 8-inch square baking dish and fit the parchment into the dish, pushing it into the corners and up the sides; allow the excess to overhang the edges of the dish.

2. Bring the cider and dried apples to a simmer in a small saucepan over medium heat; cook until the liquid evaporates and the mixture appears dry, about 15 minutes. Cool to room temperature.

3. Whisk the flour and baking soda in a medium bowl to combine; set aside. In a second medium bowl, whisk the sugar, cinnamon, nutmeg, and cloves together. Measure 2 tablespoons of the sugar-spice mixture into a small bowl and set aside for the topping.

4. In a food processor, process the cooled dried-apple mixture and applesauce until smooth, 20 to 30 seconds, scraping down the sides of the bowl as needed; set aside. Whisk the egg and salt in a large bowl to combine. Add the sugar-spice mixture and whisk continuously until well combined and light colored, about 20 seconds. Add the butter in three additions, whisking after each addition. Add the applesauce mixture and vanilla and whisk to combine. Add the flour mixture to the wet ingredients; using a rubber spatula, fold gently until just combined and evenly moistened.

5. Transfer the batter to the prepared pan, smoothing the top with a rubber spatula. Lightly tap the pan against the countertop two or three times to settle the batter. Sprinkle the reserved 2 tablespoons sugar-spice mixture evenly over the batter. Bake until a toothpick inserted into the center comes out clean, 35 to 40 minutes, rotating the pan halfway through the baking time. Cool the cake to room temperature in the pan on a wire rack, about 2 hours. Remove the cake from the pan by lifting the parchment overhang and transfer to a cutting board. Cut the cake into squares and serve.

OATMEAL CAKE

WHY THIS RECIPE WORKS: While we (usually) love the broiled icing on this classic snack cake, we find that the cake itself is often dense, gummy, and bland. And the icing isn't always perfect, either; it can be saccharine sweet and tend toward greasiness. We wanted a moist, not dense, cake with buttery undertones topped by a broiled icing that features chewy coconut, crunchy nuts, and a butterscotch-like flavor.

We solved the problem of denseness by replacing some of the brown sugar with granulated sugar—less moist than brown sugar, granulated sugar lightened the cake's texture. We also reduced the proportion of flour to oats, using the minimum amount of flour needed to keep the cake from collapsing into crumbs. The cake was now sufficiently light, and its more moderate sweetness made it better suited to a sugary icing. We still had to tackle the gumminess, however, which was created partly by soaking the oats in water; the hydrated oats were a sticky mess when we stirred them into the batter. But simply folding in dried oats didn't work—they never fully hydrated during baking, and tasted raw and chewy in the finished cake. The answer proved to be soaking the oats in room-temperature rather than boiling water, minimizing the amount of released starch. As for the type of oats, quick-cooking worked best. Unlike the cake, the icing only required a few tweaks. Cutting back on the sugar brought the sweetness in line, using melted butter (rather than creaming the butter into the sugar) simplified the recipe, and adding a splash of milk made the icing more pliable. Keeping the cake about 9 inches from the heating element produced the "crun-chewy" texture we wanted.

Oatmeal Cake with Broiled Icing

SERVES 9

Do not use old-fashioned or instant oats for this recipe. Be sure to use a metal baking dish; glass pans are not recommended when broiling. If you have a drawer-style broiler (underneath the oven), position the rack as far as possible from the broiler element and monitor the icing carefully as it cooks in step 5. A vertical sawing motion with a serrated knife works best for cutting through the crunchy icing and tender crumb.

CAKE

- 1 cup (3 ounces) quick-cooking oats (see note)
- ¾ cup water, room temperature
- ¾ cup (3¾ ounces) unbleached all-purpose flour
- ½ teaspoon baking soda
- ½ teaspoon baking powder
- ½ teaspoon table salt
- ¼ teaspoon ground cinnamon
- ⅛ teaspoon ground nutmeg
- 4 tablespoons (½ stick) unsalted butter, softened
- ½ cup (3½ ounces) granulated sugar
- ½ cup packed (3½ ounces) light brown sugar
- 1 large egg, room temperature
- ½ teaspoon vanilla extract

BROILED ICING

- ¼ cup packed (1¾ ounces) light brown sugar
- 3 tablespoons unsalted butter, melted and cooled
- 3 tablespoons milk
- ¾ cup sweetened shredded coconut
- ½ cup (2½ ounces) pecans, chopped

1. FOR THE CAKE: Adjust an oven rack to the middle position and heat the oven to 350 degrees. Cut two 16-inch lengths of aluminum foil and fold both lengthwise to 5-inch widths. Grease an 8-inch square metal baking dish. Fit the foil pieces into the baking dish, one overlapping the other, pushing them into the corners and up the sides of the pan; allow the excess to overhang the pan edges. Spray the foil lightly with vegetable oil spray.

2. Combine the oats and water in a medium bowl and let sit until the water is absorbed, about 5 minutes. In a

second medium bowl, whisk the flour, baking soda, baking powder, salt, cinnamon, and nutmeg together.

3. In the bowl of a standing mixer fitted with the paddle attachment, beat the butter and sugars on medium speed until combined and the mixture has the consistency of damp sand, 2 to 4 minutes, scraping down the bowl with a rubber spatula halfway through mixing. Add the egg and vanilla; beat until combined, about 30 seconds. Add the flour mixture in two additions and mix until just incorporated, about 30 seconds. Add the soaked oats and mix until combined, about 15 seconds.

4. Give the batter a final stir with a rubber spatula to make sure it is thoroughly combined. Transfer the batter to the prepared pan and lightly tap it against the countertop two or three times to settle the batter; smooth the surface with the spatula. Bake the cake until a toothpick inserted into the center comes out with a few crumbs attached, 30 to 35 minutes, rotating the pan halfway through the baking time. Cool the cake slightly in the pan, at least 10 minutes.

5. FOR THE BROILED ICING: While the cake cools, adjust an oven rack about 9 inches from the broiler element and heat the broiler. In a medium bowl, whisk the brown sugar, melted butter, and milk together; stir in the coconut and pecans. Spread the mixture evenly over the warm cake. Broil until the topping is bubbling and golden, 3 to 5 minutes.

6. Cool the cake in the pan 1 hour. To remove the cake from the pan, pick up the overhanging edges of the foil and transfer the cake to a platter. Gently push the side of the cake with a knife and remove the foil, one piece at a time. Cut the cake into squares and serve.

APPLE UPSIDE-DOWN CAKE

WHY THIS RECIPE WORKS: Pineapple has become synonymous with upside-down cake ever since canned pineapple was introduced into this country in the early 1900s. But at one time, upside-down cakes were made with seasonal fruit, such as apples. We loved the idea of resurrecting apple upside-down cake. We wanted a rich buttery cake topped with tightly packed, burnished, sweet apples.

We started our testing with choosing the type of apple. Most apples turned mushy and watery and were simply too sweet, but crisp, tart Granny Smiths made the cut. Following the lead of recipes found in our research, we shingled the apples in the pan and poured the cake batter over the top. But once baked and inverted, our apple layer was shrunken and dry. The solution turned out to be

increasing the number of apples, for a hefty layer of fruit. This effort yielded better results, but we found the apples to be overcooked, so we turned to a method uncovered in our recipe for Deep-Dish Apple Pie (page 564)— we precooked half the apples by sautéing them on the stovetop then we cut the remainder thin, so they baked through evenly. For the butter cake, we tested milk, buttermilk, yogurt, and sour cream. Sour cream won hands down—its subtle tang balanced the sweetness of the cake and complemented the caramelized apples. And another addition—cornmeal—gave the cake a hint of earthy flavor and a pleasantly coarse texture. Our final discovery came when we attempted to release the cake cleanly from the pan. Typical recipes instruct a 5 to 10-minute cooling period, but we found that a full 20 minutes was required to allow the apple filling to set. And turning the cake out onto a rack to finish cooling let the bottom of the cake breathe, preventing sogginess, which is typical of so many upside-down cakes.

Apple Upside-Down Cake

SERVES 8

We like the slight coarseness that cornmeal adds to the cake, but it's fine to omit it. Golden Delicious apples can be substituted for the Granny Smiths. You will need a 9-inch nonstick cake pan with sides that are at least 2 inches high; anything shallower and the cake will overflow. Alternatively, a 10-inch ovenproof stainless steel skillet (don't use cast iron) can be used to both cook the apples and bake the cake, with the following modifications: Cook the apples in the skillet and set them aside while mixing the batter (it's OK if the skillet is still warm when the batter is added) and increase the baking time by 7 to 9 minutes. If you don't have either a 2-inch-high cake pan or an ovenproof skillet, use an 8-inch square pan.

TOPPING

- 4 **tablespoons (½ stick) unsalted butter, cut into 4 pieces, plus extra for the pan**
- 4 **Granny Smith apples (about 2 pounds), peeled and cored (see note)**
- ⅔ **cup packed (4⅔ ounces) light brown sugar**
- 2 **teaspoons juice from 1 lemon**

CAKE

- 1 **cup (5 ounces) unbleached all-purpose flour**
- 1 **tablespoon cornmeal (optional; see note)**
- 1 **teaspoon baking powder**
- ½ **teaspoon table salt**
- ¾ **cup (5¼ ounces) granulated sugar**
- ¼ **cup packed (1¾ ounces) light brown sugar**
- 2 **large eggs, room temperature**
- 6 **tablespoons (¾ stick) unsalted butter, melted and cooled slightly**
- ½ **cup sour cream**
- 1 **teaspoon vanilla extract**

1. FOR THE TOPPING: Butter the bottom and sides of a nonstick 9-inch-wide by 2-inch-high round cake pan; set aside. Adjust an oven rack to the lowest position and heat the oven to 350 degrees.

2. Halve the apples from pole to pole. Cut 2 apples into ¼-inch-thick slices; set aside. Cut the remaining 2 apples into ½-inch-thick slices. Melt the butter in a 12-inch skillet over medium-high heat. Add the ½-inch-thick apple slices and cook, stirring two or three times, until the apples begin to caramelize, 4 to 6 minutes. (Do not fully cook the apples.) Add the ¼-inch-thick apple slices, brown sugar, and lemon juice; continue cooking, stirring constantly, until the sugar dissolves and the apples are coated, about 1 minute longer. Transfer the apple mixture to the prepared pan and lightly press into an even layer. Set aside while preparing the cake.

3. FOR THE CAKE: Whisk the flour, cornmeal (if using), baking powder, and salt together in a medium bowl; set aside. Whisk the sugars and eggs together in a large bowl until thick and homogeneous, about 45 seconds. Slowly whisk in the butter until combined. Add the sour cream and vanilla; whisk until combined. Add the flour mixture and whisk until just combined. Pour the batter into the pan and spread evenly over the fruit. Lightly tap the pan against the countertop two or three times to settle the batter. Bake until the cake is golden brown and a toothpick inserted into the center comes out clean, 35 to 40 minutes, rotating the pan halfway through the baking time.

4. Cool the pan on a wire rack 20 minutes. Run a small knife around the sides of the cake to loosen. Place a wire rack over the cake pan. Holding the rack tightly, invert the cake pan and wire rack together; lift off the cake pan. Place the wire rack over a baking sheet or large plate to catch any drips. If any fruit sticks to the pan bottom, remove and position it on top of the cake. Cool the cake 20 minutes (or longer to cool it completely), then transfer it to a serving platter, cut into pieces, and serve.

Apple Upside-Down Cake with Almond

Follow the recipe for Apple Upside-Down Cake, combining ⅓ cup finely ground toasted almonds with the flour and adding 1 teaspoon almond extract with the sour cream and vanilla in step 3.

Apple Upside-Down Cake with Lemon and Thyme

Follow the recipe for Apple Upside-Down Cake, adding 1 teaspoon finely grated lemon zest and 1 teaspoon finely chopped fresh thyme leaves with the sour cream and vanilla in step 3.

CARROT CAKE

WHY THIS RECIPE WORKS: A relic of the health food craze, carrot cake was once heralded for its use of vegetable oil in place of butter and carrots as a natural sweetener. Sure, the carrots add some sweetness, but they also add a lot of moisture, which is why carrot cake is invariably soggy. And oil? It makes this cake dense and, well, oily. We didn't want a greasy cake. We wanted a moist, rich cake with a tight and tender crumb and balanced spice.

We started with all-purpose flour—cake flour proved too delicate to support the grated carrots that get mixed in. For lift, we liked a combination of baking soda and baking powder. Some carrot cakes use a heavy hand with the spices and taste too much like spice cake. We took a conservative approach and used modest amounts of cinnamon, nutmeg, and cloves. After trying varying amounts of grated carrots, we settled on 3 cups for a pleasantly moist texture. One and one-half cups of vegetable oil gave us a rich, but not greasy, cake. Cream cheese frosting is the perfect partner to carrot cake—we enriched our version with sour cream for extra tang and vanilla for depth of flavor.

Carrot Cake

SERVES 15 TO 18

You can serve the cake right out of the pan, in which case you'll only need 3 cups of frosting for the top of the cake.

- 2½ cups (12½ ounces) unbleached all-purpose flour
- 1¼ teaspoons ground cinnamon
- 1¼ teaspoons baking powder
- 1 teaspoon baking soda
- ½ teaspoon table salt
- ½ teaspoon ground nutmeg
- ⅛ teaspoon ground cloves
- 4 large eggs, room temperature
- 1½ cups (10½ ounces) granulated sugar
- ½ cup packed (3½ ounces) light brown sugar
- 1½ cups vegetable oil
- 1 pound carrots (about 6 medium), peeled and grated (about 3 cups)
- 4 cups Cream Cheese Frosting (recipe follows; see note)

1. Adjust an oven rack to the middle position and heat the oven to 350 degrees. Grease a 13 by 9-inch baking pan, then line the bottom with parchment paper. Whisk the flour, cinnamon, baking powder, baking soda, salt, nutmeg, and cloves together in a medium bowl.

2. In a large bowl, whisk the eggs and sugars together until the sugars are mostly dissolved and the mixture is frothy. Continue to whisk, while slowly drizzling in the oil, until thoroughly combined and emulsified. Whisk in the flour mixture until just incorporated. Stir in the carrots.

3. Give the batter a final stir with a rubber spatula to make sure it is thoroughly combined. Scrape the batter into the prepared pan, smooth the top, and lightly tap the pan against the countertop two or three times to settle the batter. Bake the cake until a toothpick inserted in the center comes out with a few moist crumbs attached,

35 to 40 minutes, rotating the pan halfway through the baking time.

4. Cool the cake completely in the pan, set on a wire rack, about 2 hours. Run a small knife around the edge of the cake and flip the cake out onto a wire rack. Peel off the parchment paper, then flip the cake right side up onto a serving platter. Spread the frosting evenly over the top and sides of the cake and serve.

Cream Cheese Frosting

MAKES ABOUT 4 CUPS

If the frosting becomes too soft to work with, let it chill in the refrigerator until firm.

- 2 (8-ounce) packages cream cheese, softened
- 10 tablespoons (1¼ sticks) unsalted butter, cut into chunks and softened
- 2 tablespoons sour cream
- 1½ teaspoons vanilla extract
- ¼ teaspoon table salt
- 2 cups (8 ounces) confectioners' sugar

1. Beat the cream cheese, butter, sour cream, vanilla, and salt together in a large bowl with an electric mixer on medium-high speed until smooth, 2 to 4 minutes.

2. Reduce the mixer speed to medium-low, slowly add the confectioners' sugar, and beat until smooth, 4 to 6 minutes. Increase the mixer speed to medium-high and beat until the frosting is light and fluffy, 4 to 6 minutes.

LIGHT CARROT CAKE

WHY THIS RECIPE WORKS: Although carrot cake sounds healthy, most versions tip the scales at 500 calories and 31 grams of fat per slice. We wanted to create a moist and rich carrot cake and we wanted the cake to be lighter in both calories and fat.

We made four significant changes to satisfy our goal of a tasty dessert we could enjoy more than once in a while. We reduced the amount of oil from 1½ cups to ½ cup and also reduced the number of eggs from four to three. We whipped air into the eggs to keep the cake from being dense and leaden. And, finally, we replaced the cream cheese and butter in the frosting with Neufchâtel reduced-fat cream cheese and mixed it by hand to prevent it from being runny. In the end, we reduced the calories to 350 and the fat grams to 13 and still had a cake that was tender, moist, and flavorful.

Light Carrot Cake

SERVES 16

You can use either the large holes of a box grater or the large-holed shredding disk in a food processor for grating the carrots. Use a metal cake pan, not a glass or Pyrex pan, for best results. This cake is terrific with our Light Cream Cheese Frosting (recipe follows) or a simple dusting of confectioners' sugar.

- 2½ cups (12½ ounces) all-purpose flour
- 1¼ teaspoons baking powder
- 1 teaspoon baking soda
- 1¼ teaspoons ground cinnamon
- ½ teaspoon ground nutmeg
- ½ teaspoon table salt
- ⅛ teaspoon ground cloves
- 3 large eggs, room temperature
- 1 cup packed (7 ounces) light brown sugar
- 1 cup (7 ounces) granulated sugar
- ½ cup vegetable oil
- 1 pound carrots (about 6 medium), peeled and grated (about 3 cups) (see note)

1. Adjust an oven rack to the middle position and heat the oven to 350 degrees. Grease a 13 by 9-inch cake pan, then line the bottom with parchment paper. Whisk the flour, baking powder, baking soda, cinnamon, nutmeg, salt, and cloves together in a medium bowl.

2. Beat the eggs, brown sugar, and granulated sugar together in a large bowl with an electric mixer on medium speed until the mixture turns thick and creamy, 1 to 3 minutes. Reduce the mixer speed to low and slowly beat in the oil until thoroughly combined and emulsified, 30 to 60 seconds.

3. Sift half the flour mixture over the batter and gently whisk in by hand. Repeat with the remaining flour mixture and continue to whisk the batter gently until most of the lumps are gone (do not overmix). Using a rubber spatula, gently stir in the carrots.

4. Pour the batter into the prepared pan and smooth the top. Bake until a wooden skewer inserted into the center of the cake comes out with a few moist crumbs attached, 35 to 40 minutes, rotating the pan halfway through the baking time.

5. Cool the cake completely in the pan, about 2 hours. Run a paring knife around the edge of the cake and flip the cake out onto a wire rack. Peel off the parchment paper, then flip the cake right side up onto a serving platter. If desired, spread the frosting (see note) evenly over the top and sides of the cake and serve.

Light Cream Cheese Frosting

MAKES ABOUT 2 CUPS

- 12 ounces Neufchâtel (⅓ less fat) cream cheese, softened
- 1 teaspoon vanilla extract
- 1½ cups (6 ounces) confectioners' sugar

Mix the cream cheese and vanilla together in a large bowl with a rubber spatula. Add the confectioners' sugar and stir until thoroughly combined and smooth.

SPICE CAKE

WHY THIS RECIPE WORKS: The problem with spice cakes? Spice. Some variations suffer spice overload, which makes them gritty and dusty. Others are so lacking in spice flavor that it seems as if a cinnamon stick has only been waved in their general direction. We wanted an old-fashioned, moist, and substantial spice cake with spices that were warm and bold without being overpowering, and a rich, but complementary cream cheese frosting.

We needed a less-than-tender cake, one with a substantial and open crumb that could stand up to the spices. We found that all-purpose flour, rather than cake flour, added volume and heft. Butter and eggs added richness. Simply adding more spices didn't lead to increased spiciness; the

spices simply smelled stronger than they tasted. Therefore, we needed to bloom the spices in butter, a process that intensified their aromas and gave the cake a heightened spice impact throughout. We used the classic mixture of cinnamon, cloves, cardamom, allspice, and nutmeg, but found that a tablespoon of grated fresh ginger and a couple of tablespoons of molasses gave the cake an extra zing. And reserving a little of the spice mixture to add to the cream cheese frosting united the frosting and the cake.

Spice Cake

SERVES 15 TO 18

Using fresh ginger instead of dried ground ginger gives this cake a brighter flavor. You can serve the cake right out of the pan, in which case you'll only need 3 cups of frosting for the top of the cake.

- 1 tablespoon ground cinnamon
- ¾ teaspoon ground cardamom
- ½ teaspoon ground allspice
- ½ teaspoon ground cloves
- ¼ teaspoon ground nutmeg
- 16 tablespoons (2 sticks) unsalted butter, cut into 16 pieces and softened
- 2¼ cups (11¼ ounces) all-purpose flour
- ½ teaspoon baking powder
- ½ teaspoon baking soda
- ½ teaspoon table salt
- 2 large eggs plus 3 large egg yolks, room temperature
- 1 teaspoon vanilla extract
- 1¾ cups (12¼ ounces) sugar
- 2 tablespoons light or mild molasses
- 1 tablespoon minced or grated fresh ginger (see note)
- 1 cup buttermilk, room temperature
- 4 cups Cream Cheese Frosting (page 494; see note)

1. Adjust an oven rack to the middle position and heat the oven to 350 degrees. Grease a 13 by 9-inch baking pan, then line the bottom with parchment paper.

2. Combine the cinnamon, cardamom, allspice, cloves, and nutmeg in a small bowl; reserve ½ teaspoon of the spice mixture for the frosting. Melt 4 tablespoons of the butter in a small skillet over medium heat and continue to cook, swirling the pan constantly, until the butter is light brown, 3 to 6 minutes. Stir in the spice mixture and cook until fragrant, about 15 seconds. Set the mixture aside to cool slightly.

3. In a medium bowl, whisk the flour, baking powder, baking soda, and salt together. In a small bowl, whisk the eggs, egg yolks, and vanilla together.

4. In a standing mixer fitted with the paddle attachment, beat the remaining 12 tablespoons butter, the sugar, and molasses on medium-high speed until light and fluffy, 3 to 6 minutes; scrape down the bowl with a rubber spatula. Beat in the ginger, cooled butter-spice mixture, and half of the egg mixture until combined, about 30 seconds. Beat in the remaining egg mixture until combined, about 30 seconds, and scrape down the bowl again.

5. Reduce the mixer speed to low and beat in one-third of the flour mixture, followed by half of the buttermilk. Repeat with half of the remaining flour mixture and the remaining buttermilk. Beat in the remaining flour mixture until just combined; scrape down the bowl.

6. Give the batter a final stir with a rubber spatula to make sure it is thoroughly combined. Scrape the batter into the prepared pan, smooth the top, and lightly tap the pan against the countertop two or three times to settle the batter. Bake the cake until a toothpick inserted in the center comes out with a few moist crumbs attached, 30 to 35 minutes, rotating the pan halfway through the baking time.

7. Cool the cake completely in the pan, set on a wire rack, about 2 hours. Run a small knife around the edge of the cake and flip the cake out onto a wire rack. Peel off the parchment paper, then flip the cake right side up onto a serving platter. Stir the reserved spice mixture into the frosting, spread the frosting evenly over the top and sides of the cake, and serve.

STRAWBERRY CREAM CAKE

WHY THIS RECIPE WORKS: What could possibly ruin the heavenly trio of cake, cream, and ripe strawberries? How about soggy cake, bland berries, and squishy cream? We wanted a sturdy cake, a firm filling, and strawberry flavor fit for a starring role—a cake that would serve a formal occasion better than a simple strawberry shortcake.

To start, we had to solve three crucial problems. First, we realized that tender butter cakes couldn't support a substantial strawberry filling, so we developed a chiffon-style cake that combined the rich flavor of a butter cake with the light-yet-sturdy texture of a sponge cake. Second, we made a flavorful berry "mash" with half of the berries and then reduced the macerated juice in a sauce-pan (with a little kirsch) to help concentrate and round out the flavor. We sliced the rest of the berries and placed them around the edges of the cake for visual appeal. Another problem arose when the cake was sliced: The filling squirted out and the layers fell apart. To correct the problem, we reduced the number of layers from four to three and fortified the whipped-cream filling with cream cheese. This filling stayed put and didn't mar the glorious layers of this spectacular summertime cake.

Strawberry Cream Cake

SERVES 8 TO 10

You will need a cake pan with straight sides that are at least 2 inches high.

CAKE

- 1¼ cups (5 ounces) cake flour, plus extra for the pan
- 1½ teaspoons baking powder
- ¼ teaspoon table salt
- 1 cup (7 ounces) sugar
- 5 large eggs (2 whole and 3 separated), room temperature
- 6 tablespoons (¾ stick) unsalted butter, melted and cooled slightly
- 2 tablespoons water
- 2 teaspoons vanilla extract

STRAWBERRY FILLING

- 2 pounds fresh strawberries (medium or large, about 2 quarts), washed, dried, and stemmed
- 4-6 tablespoons sugar
- 2 tablespoons kirsch
- Pinch salt

WHIPPED CREAM

- 8 ounces cream cheese, room temperature
- ½ cup (3½ ounces) sugar
- 1 teaspoon vanilla extract
- ⅛ teaspoon table salt
- 2 cups heavy cream

1. FOR THE CAKE: Adjust an oven rack to the lower-middle position and heat the oven to 325 degrees. Grease and flour a 9-inch-wide by 2-inch-high round cake pan or 9-inch springform pan and line it with parchment paper. Whisk the flour, baking powder, salt, and all but 3 table-spoons sugar in a mixing bowl. Whisk in 2 whole eggs and 3 yolks (reserving the whites), the butter, water, and vanilla; whisk until smooth.

2. In the clean bowl of a standing mixer fitted with the whisk attachment, beat the remaining 3 egg whites at medium-low speed until frothy, 1 to 2 minutes. With the machine running, gradually add the remaining 3 table-spoons sugar, increase the speed to medium-high, and

beat until soft peaks form, 60 to 90 seconds. Stir one-third of the whites into the batter to lighten; add the remaining whites and gently fold into the batter until no white streaks remain. Transfer the batter to the prepared pan,

BUILDING A STRAWBERRY CREAM CAKE

1. With a serrated knife, use a sawing motion to cut the cake into three layers, rotating the cake as you go.

2. Place sliced berries evenly around the edges (they will be visible once layers are assembled).

3. Cover the center of the cake completely with half of the pureed strawberries.

4. Spread one-third of the whipped cream over the berries, leaving a ½-inch border. Repeat the layering.

5. Press the last layer into place, spread with the remaining cream, and decorate with berries.

smoothing the top with a rubber spatula. Lightly tap the pan against the countertop two or three times to settle the batter. Bake until a toothpick inserted into the center comes out clean, 30 to 40 minutes, rotating the pan halfway through the baking time. Cool the cake in the pan on a wire rack for 10 minutes, then invert onto the wire rack and peel off the parchment. Invert the cake again and cool completely on the rack, about 2 hours.

3. FOR THE STRAWBERRY FILLING: Halve 24 of the best-looking berries and reserve. Quarter the remaining berries; toss with 4 to 6 tablespoons sugar (depending on the sweetness of the berries) in a medium bowl and let sit 1 hour, stirring occasionally. Strain the juices from the berries and reserve (you should have about ½ cup). In a food processor, give the macerated berries 5 pulses (you should have about 1½ cups). In a small saucepan over medium-high heat, simmer the reserved juices and the kirsch until syrupy and reduced to about 3 tablespoons, 3 to 5 minutes. Pour the reduced syrup over the processed, macerated berries, add the salt, and toss to combine. Set aside until the cake has cooled.

4. FOR THE WHIPPED CREAM: When the cake has cooled, place the cream cheese, sugar, vanilla, and salt in the clean bowl of a standing mixer fitted with the whisk attachment. Whisk at medium-high speed until light and fluffy, 1 to 2 minutes, scraping down the bowl with a rubber spatula as needed. Reduce the speed to low and add the heavy cream in a slow, steady stream; when almost fully combined, increase the speed to medium-high and beat until the mixture holds stiff peaks, 2 to 2½ minutes more, scraping down the bowl as needed (you should have about 4½ cups).

5. TO ASSEMBLE THE CAKE: Line the edges of a cake platter with strips of parchment paper to keep the platter clean. Following the photos on page 497, use a serrated knife to cut the cake into three even layers. Place the bottom layer on a the platter and arrange a ring of 20 strawberry halves, cut sides down and stem ends facing out, around the perimeter of the cake layer. Pour one-half of the pureed berry mixture (about ¾ cup) in the center, then spread to cover any exposed cake. Gently spread about one-third of the whipped cream (about 1½ cups) over the berry layer, leaving a ½-inch border from the edge. Place the middle cake layer on top and press down gently (the whipped cream layer should become flush with the cake edge). Repeat with 20 additional strawberry halves, the remaining berry mixture, and half of the remaining whipped cream; gently press the last cake layer on top. Spread the remaining whipped cream over the top; decorate with the remaining cut strawberries. Remove the parchment strips from the platter and serve.

COCONUT LAYER CAKE

WHY THIS RECIPE WORKS: Too often, a coconut cake is just plain white cake with plain white frosting sprinkled with shredded coconut, lacking any real coconut flavor. Coconut cake should be perfumed inside and out with the cool, subtle, mysterious essence of coconut. Its layers of snowy white cake should be moist and tender, with a delicate, yielding crumb, and the icing a silky, gently sweetened coat covered with a deep drift of downy coconut.

For this type of cake, we found a traditional butter cake to be best. To infuse this cake with maximum coconut flavor, we relied on coconut extract and cream of coconut in the cake and the buttercream icing. We also coated the cake with a generous amount of shredded coconut for more flavor and textural interest.

Coconut Layer Cake
SERVES 10 TO 12
Be sure to use cream of coconut (such as Coco López), and not coconut milk here. If you like, before decorating, toast the shredded coconut in a 350-degree oven, stirring often, until golden, about 10 minutes. Toasting the coconut, which is optional, adds a golden halo to the finished cake, as well as a nutty flavor.

CAKE
2¼ cups (9 ounces) cake flour, plus extra for the pans
 ¾ cup cream of coconut (see note)
  5 large egg whites plus 1 large egg, room temperature
 ¼ cup water
  1 teaspoon coconut extract
  1 teaspoon vanilla extract
  1 cup (7 ounces) granulated sugar
  1 tablespoon baking powder
 ¾ teaspoon table salt
 12 tablespoons (1½ sticks) unsalted butter, cut into 12 pieces and softened

FROSTING
  2 tablespoons heavy cream
  1 teaspoon coconut extract
  1 teaspoon vanilla extract
     Pinch table salt
 16 tablespoons (2 sticks) unsalted butter, cut into chunks and softened
 ¼ cup cream of coconut (see note)
  3 cups (12 ounces) confectioners' sugar
  2 cups sweetened shredded coconut (see note)

1. FOR THE CAKE: Adjust an oven rack to the middle position and heat the oven to 325 degrees. Grease and flour two 9-inch round cake pans, then line the bottoms with parchment paper. Whisk the cream of coconut, egg whites, egg, water, and extracts together in a medium bowl.

2. In a standing mixer fitted with the paddle attachment, mix the flour, granulated sugar, baking powder, and salt on low speed until combined, about 30 seconds. Increase the speed to medium and beat the butter into the flour mixture, one piece at a time, about 30 seconds. Continue to beat the mixture until it resembles moist crumbs, about 1 minute.

3. Beat in all but ½ cup of the cream of coconut mixture, then increase the mixer speed to medium and beat the batter until smooth, light, and fluffy, about 1 minute. Reduce the mixer speed to low and slowly beat in the remaining cream of coconut mixture until the batter is combined, about 30 seconds.

4. Scrape the batter into the prepared pans, smooth the tops, and lightly tap the pans against the countertop two or three times to settle the batter. Bake the cakes until a toothpick inserted in the center comes out with a few crumbs attached, 30 to 35 minutes, rotating the pans halfway through the baking time.

5. Cool the cakes in the pans for 10 minutes. Run a small knife around the edge of the cakes, then flip them out onto a wire rack. Peel off the parchment paper, flip the cakes right side up, and cool completely before frosting, about 2 hours.

6. FOR THE FROSTING: In a small bowl, stir the cream, extracts, and salt together. In a standing mixer fitted with the paddle attachment, beat the butter and cream of coconut together on medium-high speed until smooth, about 20 seconds. Reduce the mixer speed to medium-low and

gradually beat in the confectioners' sugar, then continue to beat until smooth, about 2 minutes. Beat in the cream mixture. Increase the mixer speed to medium-high and beat until the mixture is light and fluffy, about 4 minutes.

7. Line the edges of a cake platter with strips of parchment paper to keep the platter clean while you assemble the cake. Place one of the cake layers on the platter. Spread 1 cup of the frosting over the cake, right to the edges. Place the other cake layer on top and press lightly to adhere. Frost the cake with the remaining frosting. Press the coconut into the sides of the cake and sprinkle it over the top. Remove the parchment strips from the platter before serving.

LEMON LAYER CAKE

WHY THIS RECIPE WORKS: Most versions of lemon layer cake are poorly executed concoctions of heavy cake stacked with filling and frosting that taste more like butter than lemon. We wanted an old-fashioned cake in which tangy, creamy lemon filling divides layers of tender, delicate cake draped in sweet frosting—an ideal contrast of sweet and tart.

Most layer cakes are substantial butter cakes, but we suspected that the light, fresh flavor of lemon would be better served by something more ethereal. After trying a sponge cake and a classic yellow cake, we found that a white butter cake was the perfect compromise: a cake nicely flavored by butter yet light enough for our flavors, with a fine crumb and tender texture.

Lemon layer cake is often filled with lemon-scented buttercream, but this filling can mute the lemon flavor and make the cake far too rich. We preferred the brightness of lemon curd. We also wanted something lighter than buttercream for our frosting, eventually landing on an old-fashioned classic: seven-minute icing. We needed to make some adjustments, as the traditional version was a little too sweet, slightly thick, and required holding a hand-held mixer for longer than was comfortable. We cut back on the sugar and added a squeeze of lemon juice to solve the first two problems. After some trial and error, we learned that if we heated the mixture to at least 160 degrees and then transferred it to the standing mixer for whipping (rather than holding a hand mixer for seven minutes), the end result was just as billowy and shiny as the old-fashioned version.

Lemon Layer Cake with Fluffy White Icing

SERVES 10 TO 12

You will need a cake pan with straight sides that are at least 2 inches high. For neater slices, dip a knife into hot water before cutting the cake.

LEMON CURD FILLING
- 1 cup juice from about 6 lemons
- 1 teaspoon powdered gelatin
- 1½ cups (10½ ounces) sugar
- ⅛ teaspoon table salt
- 4 large eggs plus 6 large egg yolks (reserve the egg whites for the cake)
- 8 tablespoons (1 stick) unsalted butter, cut into ½-inch cubes and frozen

CAKE
- 2¼ cups (9 ounces) cake flour, plus extra for the pans
- 1 cup whole milk, room temperature
- 6 large egg whites, room temperature
- 2 teaspoons vanilla extract
- 1¾ cups (12¼ ounces) sugar
- 4 teaspoons baking powder
- 1 teaspoon table salt
- 12 tablespoons (1½ sticks) unsalted butter, cut into 12 pieces, softened but still cool

FLUFFY WHITE ICING
- 1 cup (7 ounces) sugar
- 2 large egg whites, room temperature
- ¼ cup water
- 1 tablespoon juice from 1 lemon
- 1 tablespoon corn syrup

1. FOR THE FILLING: Measure 1 tablespoon of the lemon juice into a small bowl; sprinkle the gelatin over the top. Heat the remaining lemon juice, the sugar, and salt in a medium saucepan over medium-high heat, stirring occasionally, until the sugar dissolves and the mixture is hot but not boiling. Whisk the eggs and yolks in a large bowl. Whisking constantly, slowly pour the hot lemon-sugar mixture into the eggs, then return the mixture to the saucepan. Cook over medium-low heat, stirring constantly with a heatproof spatula, until the mixture registers 170 degrees on an instant-read thermometer and is thick enough to leave a trail when the spatula is scraped along the pan bottom, 4 to 6 minutes. Immediately remove the pan from the heat and stir in the gelatin mixture until dissolved. Stir in the frozen butter until incorporated. Pour the filling through a fine-mesh strainer into a bowl (you should have 3 cups). Lay a sheet of plastic wrap directly on the surface and refrigerate until firm enough to spread, at least 4 hours.

2. FOR THE CAKE: Adjust an oven rack to the middle position and heat the oven to 350 degrees. Grease and flour two 9-inch-wide by 2-inch-high round cake pans and line with parchment paper. In a 2-cup liquid measure or medium bowl, whisk together the milk, egg whites, and vanilla.

3. In a standing mixer fitted with the paddle attachment, mix the flour, sugar, baking powder, and salt at low speed until combined, about 30 seconds. With the mixer running at low speed, add the butter one piece at a time; continue beating until the mixture resembles moist crumbs with no visible butter chunks. Add all but ½ cup of the milk mixture to the crumbs and beat at medium speed until the mixture is pale and fluffy, about 1½ minutes. With the mixer running at low speed, add the remaining ½ cup milk mixture; increase the speed to medium and beat for 30 seconds more. Stop the mixer and scrape the sides of the bowl. Return the mixer to medium speed and beat for 20 seconds longer. Divide the batter evenly between the pans, smoothing the tops with a rubber spatula. Lightly tap the pan against the countertop two or three times to settle the batter.

4. Bake until a toothpick inserted in the center of the cakes comes out clean, 23 to 25 minutes, rotating the pans halfway through the baking time. Cool the cakes in the pans on a wire rack for 10 minutes. Run a small knife around the edges of the cakes, then flip them out onto a wire rack. Peel off the parchment paper, flip the cakes right side up, and cool completely before frosting, about 2 hours.

5. TO ASSEMBLE: Line the edges of a cake platter with strips of parchment paper to keep the platter clean while you assemble the cake. Use a serrated knife to cut each cake horizontally into two even layers. Place the bottom layer of one cake on the platter. Using a spatula, spread 1 cup of the lemon filling evenly on the cake, leaving a

½-inch border around the edge. Carefully place the upper cake layer on top of the filling. Spread 1 cup of the filling on top; repeat using the remaining filling and cake layers. Smooth out any filling that has leaked from the sides of the cake; cover with plastic wrap and refrigerate while making the icing.

6. FOR THE ICING: Combine all the ingredients in the bowl of a standing mixer or a large heatproof bowl and set over a medium saucepan filled with 1 inch of barely simmering water (do not let the bowl touch the water). Cook, stirring constantly, until the mixture registers 160 degrees on an instant-read thermometer, 5 to 10 minutes. Remove the bowl from the heat and transfer the mixture to a standing mixer fitted with the whisk attachment. Beat on medium speed until soft peaks form, about 5 minutes. Increase the speed to medium-high and continue to beat until the mixture has cooled to room temperature and stiff peaks form, 5 minutes longer. Using a spatula, spread the frosting evenly over the top and sides of the cake. Remove the parchment strips from the platter and serve.

OLD-FASHIONED BIRTHDAY CAKE

WHY THIS RECIPE WORKS: White layer cakes have been the classic birthday cake for more than 100 years. White cake is simply a basic butter cake made with egg whites instead of whole eggs. The whites produce the characteristic color, and they are also supposed to make the cake soft and fine-grained—that's what we wanted. Unfortunately, the white cakes that we have baked over the years, though good enough, always fell short of our high expectations. They came out a little dry and chewy—one might say cottony—and we noticed that they were riddled with tunnels and small holes. What were we doing wrong?

Every traditional recipe for white cake calls for stiffly beaten egg whites folded into the batter at the end. We began to suspect that it was the beaten egg whites that were forming the large air pockets and those unsightly holes in the baked cakes. We solved this problem by mixing the egg whites with the milk before beating them into the flour-and-butter mixture. The results were fantastic. The cake was not only fine-grained and free from holes but, to our surprise, it was also larger and lighter than the ones we'd prepared with beaten whites. And the method couldn't be simpler, quicker, or more foolproof. To make this cake birthday-special, we iced it with an easy butter frosting and added a layer of raspberry jam and chopped toasted almonds.

Classic White Layer Cake with Butter Frosting and Raspberry-Almond Filling
SERVES 10 TO 12

There will be enough frosting left to pipe a border around the base and top of the cake; to decorate the cake more elaborately, you should make 1½ times the frosting recipe. If desired, finish the sides of the cake with 1 cup of sliced almonds.

CAKE
- 2¼ cups (9 ounces) cake flour, plus extra for the pans
- 1 cup whole milk, room temperature
- 6 large egg whites, room temperature
- 1 teaspoon vanilla extract
- 1 teaspoon almond extract
- 1¾ cups (12¼ ounces) granulated sugar
- 4 teaspoons baking powder
- 1 teaspoon table salt
- 12 tablespoons (1½ sticks) unsalted butter, cut into 12 pieces and softened

FROSTING AND FILLING
- 16 tablespoons (2 sticks) unsalted butter, softened
- 4 cups (1 pound) confectioners' sugar
- 1 tablespoon vanilla extract
- 1 tablespoon milk
- Pinch table salt
- ½ cup (2¼ ounces) blanched slivered almonds, toasted and chopped coarse
- ⅓ cup seedless raspberry jam

1. FOR THE CAKE: Adjust an oven rack to the middle position and heat the oven to 350 degrees. Grease and flour two 8- or 9-inch round cake pans, then line the bottoms with parchment paper. Whisk the milk, egg whites, and both extracts together in a small bowl.

2. In a standing mixer fitted with the paddle attachment, mix the flour, sugar, baking powder, and salt together on low speed until combined, about 30 seconds. Increase the speed to medium-low and beat the butter into the flour mixture, one piece at a time, about 30 seconds. Continue to beat the mixture until it resembles moist crumbs, about 1 minute.

3. Beat in all but ½ cup of the milk mixture, then increase the mixer speed to medium and beat until smooth, light, and fluffy, about 1 minute. Reduce the mixer speed to low and slowly beat in the remaining ½ cup milk mixture until the batter looks slightly curdled, about 15 seconds.

4. Give the batter a final stir with a rubber spatula to make sure it is thoroughly combined. Scrape the batter into the prepared pans, smooth the tops, and lightly tap the pans against the countertop two or three times to settle the batter. Bake the cakes until a toothpick inserted in the center comes out with a few crumbs attached, 20 to 25 minutes, rotating the pans halfway through the baking time.

5. Cool the cakes in the pans for 10 minutes. Run a small knife around the edge of the cakes, then flip them out onto a wire rack. Peel off the parchment paper, flip the cakes right side up, and cool completely before frosting, about 2 hours.

6. FOR THE FROSTING AND FILLING: In the bowl of a standing mixer fitted with the paddle attachment, beat the butter, confectioners' sugar, vanilla, milk, and salt on low speed until the sugar is moistened, about 30 seconds. Increase the speed to medium-high; beat, stopping twice to scrape down the bowl, until creamy and fluffy, about 1½ minutes.

7. Line the edges of a cake platter with strips of parchment to keep the platter clean while you assemble the cake. Place one cake layer on the platter. Combine ½ cup of the frosting with the almonds in a small bowl. Spread the almond frosting over the first layer. Carefully spread the jam on top, then cover with the second cake layer. Spread the remaining frosting evenly over the top and sides of the cake. Remove the parchment strips from the platter before serving.

CLASSIC YELLOW LAYER CAKE

WHY THIS RECIPE WORKS: Traditional yellow layer cake should melt in the mouth and taste of butter and eggs. But many recipes we tried came out crumbly, sugary, and hard. And the flavor? It tasted merely sweet. We wanted a yellow cake that was tender, buttery, and could stand up to a slathering of frosting, if desired.

Most versions of yellow layer cake rely on the 1–2-3–4 formula (1 cup butter, 2 cups sugar, 3 cups flour, and four eggs—plus milk, baking powder, vanilla, and salt) and follow the classic way of mixing together the ingredients—creaming the butter and sugar, adding the eggs one at a time, and finally adding the milk and dry ingredients alternately. This worked okay, but we wanted something easier for this cake. The two-stage method fit the bill. In this technique, the dry ingredients are combined and then two-thirds of the milk and eggs are added and beaten until thick and fluffy. Then in the second stage, the rest of the milk and eggs are poured in and the batter is beaten again. This technique is simpler and quicker, and produced a tender cake. The flavor still

needed some improvement. We tackled the proportions of the ingredients, increasing the butter, eggs, and sugar. This cake turned out fine-grained, soft, and meltingly rich—just what we wanted. As for the frosting, we chose a traditional vanilla buttercream. Rich with egg yolks, butter, sugar, and corn syrup for sheen, this supple frosting is the perfect complement to our cake.

Classic Yellow Layer Cake with Vanilla Buttercream

SERVES 8 TO 10

Cake flour gives this buttery yellow cake its tender crumb; do not substitute all-purpose flour. When making the buttercream, make sure that the sugar mixture is poured into the egg yolks while still hot. For a decorative finish, press toasted sliced almonds on the sides of the cake.

CAKE

- 1¾ cups (7 ounces) cake flour (see note), plus extra for the pans
- ½ cup whole milk, room temperature
- 4 large eggs, room temperature
- 2 teaspoons vanilla extract
- 1½ cups (10½ ounces) sugar
- 2 teaspoons baking powder
- ¾ teaspoon table salt
- 16 tablespoons (2 sticks) unsalted butter, cut into 16 pieces and softened

VANILLA BUTTERCREAM

- 6 large egg yolks, room temperature
- ¾ cup (5¼ ounces) sugar
- ½ cup light corn syrup
- 2½ teaspoons vanilla extract
- ¼ teaspoon table salt
- 4 sticks unsalted butter, cut into chunks and softened

1. FOR THE CAKE: Adjust an oven rack to the middle position and heat the oven to 350 degrees. Grease and flour two 8- or 9-inch round cake pans, then line the bottoms with parchment paper. Whisk the milk, eggs, and vanilla together in a small bowl.

2. In a standing mixer fitted with the paddle attachment, whisk the flour, sugar, baking powder, and salt together on low speed until combined, about 30 seconds. Increase the speed to medium-low and beat the butter into the flour mixture, one piece at a time, about 30 seconds. Continue to beat the mixture until it resembles moist crumbs, about 1 minute.

3. Beat in all but ½ cup of the milk mixture, then increase the mixer speed to medium and beat the batter until smooth, light, and fluffy, about 1 minute. Reduce the mixer speed to low and slowly beat in the remaining ½ cup milk mixture until the batter looks slightly curdled, about 15 seconds.

4. Give the batter a final stir with a rubber spatula to make sure it is thoroughly combined. Scrape the batter into the prepared pans and smooth the tops with a rubber spatula. Lightly tap the pans against the countertop two or three times to settle the batter. Bake the cakes until a toothpick inserted in the center comes out with a few crumbs attached, 20 to 25 minutes, rotating the pans halfway through the baking time.

5. Cool the cakes in the pans for 10 minutes. Run a small knife around the edge of the cakes, then flip them out onto a wire rack. Peel off the parchment paper, flip the cakes right side up, and cool completely before frosting, about 2 hours.

6. FOR THE FROSTING: Whip the egg yolks in a large bowl with an electric mixer on medium speed until slightly thickened and pale yellow, 4 to 6 minutes.

7. Meanwhile, bring the sugar and corn syrup to a boil in a small saucepan over medium heat, stirring occasionally to dissolve the sugar, about 3 minutes.

8. Without letting the hot sugar mixture cool off, turn the mixer to low and slowly pour the warm sugar syrup into the whipped egg yolks without hitting the side of the bowl or the beaters. Increase the mixer speed to medium-high and whip the mixture until it is light and fluffy and the bowl is no longer warm, 5 to 10 minutes.

9. Reduce the mixer speed to medium-low and add the vanilla and salt. Gradually add the butter, one piece at a time, until completely incorporated, about 2 minutes. Increase the mixer speed to medium-high and whip the buttercream until smooth and silky, about 2 minutes. (If the mixture looks curdled, wrap a hot wet towel around the bowl and continue to whip until smooth, 1 to 2 minutes.)

10. Line the edges of a cake platter with strips of parchment to keep the platter clean while you assemble the cake. Place one cake layer on the platter. Spread 1½ cups frosting evenly across the top of the cake with a spatula. Place the second cake layer on top, then spread the remaining frosting evenly over the top and sides of the cake. Remove the parchment strips from the platter before serving.

FLUFFY YELLOW CAKE

WHY THIS RECIPE WORKS: It's easy to create a supremely fluffy layer cake with additives, but most cakes made entirely from natural ingredients are either unpleasantly dense or too fragile to support layers of frosting. We wanted a frosted yellow layer cake with an ethereal texture and the great flavor of real butter and eggs.

Chiffon cakes are especially weightless, springy, and moist. But unlike butter cakes, they are too light to stand up to a serious slathering of frosting. We decided to blend the two types of cake. We adapted a chiffon technique (using a large quantity of whipped egg whites to get a high volume and light texture) to combine the ingredients from our butter cake recipe. This worked beautifully, creating a light, porous cake that was hefty enough to hold the frosting's weight. But the cake lacked moistness and some tenderness. To fix the problem, we used a combination of fats (butter plus vegetable oil), which kept the butter flavor intact while improving the moistness of the cake. For extra tenderness, we increased the sugar and substituted buttermilk for milk. The buttermilk not only introduced a new flavor dimension, but also allowed us to replace some of the baking powder with a little baking soda to ensure an even rise.

As for the frosting, a fluffy chocolate frosting is the perfect partner to this cake. A hefty amount of cocoa powder combined with melted chocolate gave the frosting a deep chocolate flavor. A combination of confectioners' sugar and corn syrup made it smooth and glossy. To keep the frosting from separating and turning greasy, we moved it out of the stand mixer and into the food processor. The faster machine minimized any risk of overbeating, as it blended the ingredients quickly without melting the butter or incorporating too much air. The result is a thick, fluffy chocolate frosting that spreads like a dream.

Fluffy Yellow Layer Cake with Milk Chocolate Frosting

SERVES 10 TO 12

Bring all the ingredients to room temperature before beginning. For the frosting, cool the chocolate to between 85 and 100 degrees before adding it to the butter mixture. The frosting can be made 3 hours in advance. For longer storage, refrigerate the frosting, covered, and let it stand at room temperature for 1 hour before using.

CAKE

- 2½ cups (10 ounces) cake flour, plus extra for the pans
- 1¾ cups (12¼ ounces) granulated sugar
- 1¼ teaspoons baking powder
- ¼ teaspoon baking soda
- ¾ teaspoon table salt
- 1 cup buttermilk, room temperature
- 10 tablespoons (1¼ sticks) unsalted butter, melted and cooled slightly
- 3 tablespoons vegetable oil
- 2 teaspoons vanilla extract
- 6 large egg yolks plus 3 large egg whites, room temperature

FROSTING

- 20 tablespoons (2½ sticks) unsalted butter, softened
- 1 cup (4 ounces) confectioners' sugar
- ¾ cup Dutch-processed cocoa powder
  Pinch table salt
- ¾ cup light corn syrup
- 1 teaspoon vanilla extract
- 8 ounces milk chocolate, melted and cooled slightly (see note)

1. FOR THE CAKE: Adjust an oven rack to the middle position and heat the oven to 350 degrees. Grease and flour two 9-inch-wide by 2-inch-high round cake pans and line with parchment paper. Whisk the flour, 1½ cups of the granulated sugar, the baking powder, baking soda, and salt together in a large bowl. In a 4-cup liquid measuring cup or medium bowl, whisk together the buttermilk, melted butter, oil, vanilla, and yolks.

2. In a standing mixer fitted with the whisk attachment, beat the egg whites at medium-high speed until foamy, about 30 seconds. With the machine running, gradually add the remaining ¼ cup granulated sugar; continue to beat until stiff peaks just form, 30 to 60 seconds (the whites should hold a peak but the mixture should appear moist). Transfer to a bowl and set aside.

3. Add the flour mixture to the now-empty mixing bowl. With the mixer still fitted with the whisk attachment, and running at low speed, gradually pour in the butter mixture and mix until almost incorporated (a few streaks of dry flour will remain), about 15 seconds. Stop the mixer and scrape the whisk and the sides of the bowl. Return the mixer to medium-low speed and beat until smooth and fully incorporated, 10 to 15 seconds.

4. Using a rubber spatula, stir one-third of the whites into the batter to lighten, then add the remaining whites and gently fold into the batter until no white streaks remain. Divide the batter evenly between the prepared pans, smoothing the tops with a rubber spatula. Lightly tap the pans against the countertop two or three times to settle the batter.

5. Bake until the cake layers begin to pull away from the sides of the pans and a toothpick inserted into the centers comes out clean, 20 to 22 minutes, rotating the pans halfway through the baking time. Cool the cakes in the pans on a wire rack for 10 minutes. Run a small knife around the edge of the cakes, then flip them out onto a wire rack. Peel off the parchment paper, flip the cakes right side up, and cool completely before frosting, about 2 hours.

6. FOR THE FROSTING: In a food processor, process the butter, sugar, cocoa, and salt until smooth, about 30 seconds, scraping down the sides of the bowl as needed. Add the corn syrup and vanilla and process until just combined, 5 to 10 seconds. Scrape down the sides of the bowl, then add the chocolate and process until smooth and creamy, 10 to 15 seconds. The frosting can be used immediately or held (see note).

7. Line the edges of a cake platter with strips of parchment to keep the platter clean while you assemble the cake. Place one cake layer on the platter. Spread 1½ cups of the frosting evenly across the top of the cake with a spatula. Place the second cake layer on top, then spread the remaining frosting evenly over the top and sides of the cake. Remove the parchment strips from the platter before serving.

NOTES FROM THE TEST KITCHEN

FROSTING A LAYER CAKE

1. Dollop a portion of frosting in the center of the cake and spread into an even layer right to the edge.

2. Lay the second layer on top. Brush away any large crumbs, dollop more frosting in the center, and spread slightly over the edge.

3. Gather a few tablespoons of frosting onto the top of the spatula, then gently smear it onto the side of the cake. Repeat to frost the sides completely.

4. For smooth sides, gently run the edge of the spatula around the cake. Or, to create billows in the frosting, press the back of a soup spoon into the frosting, then twirl the spoon as you lift it away.

OLD-FASHIONED CHOCOLATE LAYER CAKE

WHY THIS RECIPE WORKS: Over the years, chocolate cakes have become denser, richer, and squatter. Many contemporary cakes are so intense that just a few forkfuls satisfy. These cakes taste great—it's hard to imagine a bad chocolate cake—but sometimes we'd rather have a real piece of cake, not a fudge-like confection. We wanted an old-style, mile-high chocolate layer cake with a tender, airy, open crumb and a soft, billowy frosting.

The mixing method was the key to getting the right texture. After trying a variety of techniques, we turned to ribboning, a popular old-fashioned method used for cakes like genoise (a moist, light sponge cake). Ribboning involves whipping eggs with sugar until they double in volume, then adding the butter, dry ingredients, and milk. The egg foam aerated the cake, giving it both structure and tenderness. To achieve a moist cake with rich chocolate flavor, we once again looked to historical sources, which suggested using buttermilk and making a "pudding" with a mixture of chocolate, water, and sugar. We simply melted unsweetened chocolate and cocoa powder in hot water over a double boiler, then stirred in sugar until it dissolved. Turning to the frosting, we wanted to combine the best elements of classic chocolate frostings: the intense chocolate flavor of a ganache (a mixture of chocolate and cream) and the volume of a meringue or buttercream. The solution turned out to be a simple reversal of the conventional ganache procedure: We poured cold (rather than heated) cream into warm (rather than room-temperature) chocolate, waited for it to cool to room temperature, then whipped until fluffy.

Old-Fashioned Chocolate Layer Cake with Chocolate Frosting

SERVES 10 TO 12

For a smooth, spreadable frosting, use chopped semisweet chocolate, not chocolate chips—chocolate chips contain less cocoa butter than bar chocolate and will not melt as readily. As for other bar chocolate, bittersweet chocolate that is 60 percent cacao can be substituted but it will produce a stiffer, but still spreadable, frosting. Bittersweet chocolate with 70 percent cacao, however, should be avoided—it will produce a frosting that is crumbly and it will not spread. For best results, don't make the frosting until the cakes are cooled, and use the frosting as soon as it is ready. If the frosting gets too cold and stiff to spread easily, wrap the mixer bowl with a towel soaked in hot water and mix on low speed until the frosting appears creamy and smooth.

CAKE
- 1¾ cups (8¾ ounces) unbleached all-purpose flour, plus extra for the pans
- 4 ounces unsweetened chocolate, chopped coarse
- ¼ cup Dutch-processed cocoa powder
- ½ cup hot water
- 1¾ cups (12¼ ounces) sugar
- 1½ teaspoons baking soda
- 1 teaspoon table salt
- 1 cup buttermilk
- 2 teaspoons vanilla extract
- 4 large eggs plus 2 large egg yolks, room temperature
- 12 tablespoons (1½ sticks) unsalted butter, very soft

FROSTING
- 1 pound semisweet chocolate, chopped fine (see note)
- 8 tablespoons (1 stick) unsalted butter
- ⅓ cup (2⅓ ounces) sugar
- 2 tablespoons corn syrup
- 2 teaspoons vanilla extract
- ¼ teaspoon table salt
- 1¼ cups heavy cream, chilled

1. FOR THE CAKE: Adjust an oven rack to the middle position and heat the oven to 350 degrees. Grease and flour two 9-inch-wide by 2-inch-high round cake pans and line with parchment paper. Combine the chocolate, cocoa powder, and hot water in a medium heatproof bowl set over a saucepan filled with 1 inch of barely simmering water, stirring occasionally until smooth. Add ½ cup of the sugar to the chocolate mixture and stir until thick and glossy, 1 to 2 minutes. Remove the bowl from the heat and set aside to cool.

2. Whisk the flour, baking soda, and salt in a medium bowl. Combine the buttermilk and vanilla in a small bowl. In the bowl of a standing mixer fitted with the whisk attachment, whisk the eggs and yolks on medium-low speed until combined, about 10 seconds. Add the remaining 1¼ cups sugar, increase the speed to high, and whisk until fluffy and lightened in color, 2 to 3 minutes. Replace the whisk with the paddle attachment. Add the cooled chocolate mixture to the egg-sugar mixture and mix on medium speed until thoroughly incorporated, 30 to 45 seconds, pausing to scrape down the sides of the bowl with a rubber spatula as needed. Add the softened butter 1 tablespoon at a time, mixing about 10 seconds after each addition. Add about one-third of the flour mixture followed by half of the buttermilk mixture, mixing until incorporated after each addition (about 15 seconds). Repeat, using half of the remaining flour mixture and all of the remaining buttermilk mixture (the batter may appear separated). Scrape down the sides of the bowl and add the remaining flour mixture; mix at medium-low speed until the batter is thoroughly combined, about 15 seconds. Remove the bowl from the mixer and fold the batter once or twice with a rubber spatula to incorporate any remaining flour. Divide the batter evenly between the prepared pans, smoothing the tops with a rubber spatula. Lightly tap the pans against the countertop two or three times to settle the batter.

3. Bake the cakes until a toothpick inserted into the center comes out with a few crumbs attached, 25 to 30 minutes, rotating the pans halfway through the baking time. Cool the cakes in the pans on a wire rack for 15 minutes. Run a small knife around the edge of the cakes, then flip them out onto a wire rack. Peel off the parchment paper, flip the cakes right side up, and cool completely before frosting, about 2 hours.

4. FOR THE FROSTING: Melt the chocolate in a heatproof bowl set over a saucepan containing 1 inch of barely simmering water, stirring occasionally until smooth. Remove from the heat and set aside. Meanwhile, heat the butter in a small saucepan over medium-low heat until melted. Increase the heat to medium; add the sugar, corn syrup, vanilla, and salt and stir with a heatproof spatula until the sugar is dissolved, 4 to 5 minutes. Add the melted chocolate, butter mixture, and cream to the clean bowl of a standing mixer and stir to thoroughly combine.

5. Place the mixer bowl over an ice bath and stir the mixture constantly with a rubber spatula until the frosting is thick and just beginning to harden against the sides of the bowl, 1 to 2 minutes (the frosting should be at 70 degrees). Place the bowl on a standing mixer fitted with the paddle attachment and beat on medium-high speed until the frosting is light and fluffy, 1 to 2 minutes. Stir with a rubber spatula until completely smooth.

6. Line the edges of a cake platter with strips of parchment to keep the platter clean while you assemble the cake. Place one cake layer on the platter. Spread 1½ cups of the frosting evenly across the top of the cake with a spatula. Place the second cake layer on top, then spread the remaining frosting evenly over the top and sides of the cake. Remove the parchment strips from the platter before serving.

CHOCOLATE SHEET CAKE

WHY THIS RECIPE WORKS: Sheet cakes, for all their simplicity, can still turn out dry, sticky, or flavorless and, on occasion, can even sink in the middle. We wanted to find a simple, dependable recipe, one that delivered a moist yet also tender and chocolaty cake.

We started with the mixing method—testing everything from creaming butter to beating yolks, whipping whites, and gently folding together everything in the end. The best of the lot was the most complicated to make, so we took a step back. The simplest technique we tried was simply whisking all the ingredients together without beating, creaming, or whipping. The recipe needed work, but the approach was clearly a good match for the simple

all-purpose nature of a sheet cake. First we added buttermilk and baking soda to lighten the batter, since the original cake had been too dense. To increase the chocolate flavor, we reduced the sugar and flour, and decreased the butter. To further deepen the chocolate taste, we used semisweet chocolate in addition to the cocoa. We baked the cake at a low temperature for a long time—40 minutes—to produce a perfectly baked cake with a lovely flat top. Though this cake can be frosted with almost anything, we like a classic American milk chocolate frosting, which pairs well with the darker flavor of the cake.

Chocolate Sheet Cake with Easy Chocolate Frosting

SERVES 15 TO 18

We prefer Dutch-processed cocoa for the deeper chocolate flavor it gives the cake. The frosting needs about an hour to cool before it can be used, so begin making it when the cake comes out of the oven. You can also serve the cake lightly dusted with confectioners' sugar or with lightly sweetened whipped cream.

CAKE

- **12** tablespoons (1½ sticks) unsalted butter
- **¾** cup cocoa, preferably Dutch-processed (see note)
- **1¼** cups (6¼ ounces) unbleached all-purpose flour
- **½** teaspoon baking soda
- **¼** teaspoon table salt
- **8** ounces semisweet chocolate, chopped
- **4** large eggs, room temperature
- **1½** cups (10½ ounces) granulated sugar
- **1** teaspoon vanilla extract
- **1** cup buttermilk

FROSTING

- **½** cup heavy cream
- Pinch table salt
- **1** tablespoon light or dark corn syrup
- **10** ounces milk chocolate, chopped
- **½** cup (2 ounces) confectioners' sugar
- **8** tablespoons (1 stick) cold unsalted butter, cut into 8 pieces

1. FOR THE CAKE: Adjust an oven rack to the middle position and heat the oven to 325 degrees. Grease a 13 by 9-inch baking pan, then line the bottom with parchment paper.

2. Sift together the cocoa, flour, baking soda, and salt in a medium bowl; set aside. Melt the chocolate and butter in a heatproof bowl set over a saucepan filled with 1 inch of barely simmering water, stirring occasionally until smooth. Whisk together the eggs, sugar, and vanilla in a medium bowl. Whisk in the buttermilk until smooth.

3. Whisk the chocolate into the egg mixture until combined. Whisk in the dry ingredients until the batter is smooth and glossy. Pour the batter into the prepared pan; bake until firm in the center when lightly pressed and a toothpick inserted in the center comes out clean, about 40 minutes, rotating the pan halfway through the baking time. Let the cake cool completely in the pan, set on a wire rack, about 2 hours. Run a small knife around the cake and flip the cake out onto a wire rack. Peel off the parchment paper, then flip the cake right side up onto a serving platter.

4. FOR THE FROSTING: Heat the cream, salt, and corn syrup in a microwave-safe measuring cup on high power until simmering, about 1 minute, or bring to a simmer in a small saucepan over medium heat.

5. Place the chocolate in a food processor. With the machine running, gradually add the hot cream mixture through the feed tube; process 1 minute after the cream has been added. Stop the machine; add the confectioners' sugar and process to combine, about 30 seconds. With the machine running, add the butter through the feed tube one piece at a time; process until incorporated and smooth, about 20 seconds longer.

6. Transfer the frosting to a medium bowl and cool at room temperature, stirring frequently, until thick and spreadable, about 1 hour. Spread the frosting evenly over the top and sides of the cake and serve.

GERMAN CHOCOLATE CAKE

WHY THIS RECIPE WORKS: Most German chocolate cake recipes are similar, if not identical, to the one on the German's Sweet Chocolate box. Our tasters found several shortcomings in this recipe. It produced a cake that was too sweet, with chocolate flavor that was too mild, and with a texture so listless that the filling and cake together formed a soggy, sweet mush. We wanted a cake that was less sweet and more chocolaty than the original, but we didn't want to sacrifice the overall blend of flavors and textures that makes German chocolate cake so appealing in the first place.

The first order of business was to scale back the recipe by one quarter, which allowed us to fit the batter into two cake pans, thereby producing a cake with four thinner layers rather than three thicker layers. After testing, we discovered that the texture of the cake actually improved when we used whole eggs instead of laboriously separating the eggs, beating the whites, and folding them into the batter. We increased chocolate flavor with a combination of cocoa powder and good-quality semisweet or bittersweet chocolate. By adjusting the level and proportions of the sugar (both brown and white) and butter in the cake and filling, as well as toasting the pecans, we finished the necessary adjustments to create a definitely easier-to-make cake, with better texture and flavor than the original.

German Chocolate Cake

SERVES 12 TO 16

When you assemble the cake, the filling should be cool or cold. To be time-efficient, first make the filling, then use the refrigeration time to prepare, bake, and cool the cakes. For an accurate measurement of boiling water, bring a kettle of water to a boil, then measure out the desired amount. Note that the toasted pecans are stirred into the filling just before assembly to keep them from becoming soft and soggy.

FILLING

- 4 large egg yolks, room temperature
- 1 (12-ounce) can evaporated milk
- 1 cup (7 ounces) granulated sugar
- ¼ cup packed (1¾ ounces) light brown sugar
- 6 tablespoons (¾ stick) unsalted butter, cut into 6 pieces
- ⅛ teaspoon table salt
- 2 teaspoons vanilla extract
- 2⅓ cups sweetened shredded coconut
- 1½ cups (6 ounces) finely chopped pecans, toasted (see note)

CAKE

- 4 ounces semisweet or bittersweet chocolate, chopped fine
- ¼ cup Dutch-processed cocoa powder
- ½ cup boiling water (see note)
- 2 cups (10 ounces) unbleached all-purpose flour, plus extra for the pans
- ¾ teaspoon baking soda
- 12 tablespoons (1½ sticks) unsalted butter, softened
- 1 cup (7 ounces) granulated sugar
- ⅔ cup packed (4⅔ ounces) light brown sugar
- ¾ teaspoon table salt
- 4 large eggs, room temperature
- 1 teaspoon vanilla extract
- ¾ cup sour cream, room temperature

1. FOR THE FILLING: Whisk the yolks in a medium saucepan; gradually whisk in the evaporated milk. Add the sugars, butter, and salt and cook over medium-high heat, whisking constantly, until the mixture is boiling, frothy, and slightly thickened, about 6 minutes. Transfer the mixture to a bowl, whisk in the vanilla, then stir in the coconut. Cool until just warm, cover with plastic wrap, and refrigerate until cool or cold, at least 2 hours or up to 3 days. (The pecans are stirred in just before cake assembly.)

2. FOR THE CAKE: Adjust an oven rack to the lower-middle position; heat the oven to 350 degrees. Combine the chocolate and cocoa in a small bowl; pour the boiling water over and let stand to melt the chocolate, about 2 minutes. Whisk until smooth; set aside until cooled to room temperature.

3. Meanwhile, grease and flour two 9-inch-wide by 2-inch-high round cake pans and line with parchment paper. Sift the flour and baking soda into a medium bowl or onto a sheet of parchment or waxed paper.

4. In a standing mixer fitted with the paddle attachment, beat the butter, sugars, and salt at medium-low speed until the sugar is moistened, about 30 seconds. Increase the speed to medium-high and beat until the mixture is light and fluffy, about 4 minutes, scraping down the bowl with a spatula halfway through. With the mixer running at medium speed, add the eggs one at a time, beating well after each addition and scraping down the bowl halfway through. Beat in the vanilla; increase the speed to medium-high and beat until light and fluffy, about 45 seconds. With the mixer running at low speed, add the chocolate mixture, then increase the speed to medium and beat until combined, about 30 seconds, scraping down the bowl once (the batter may appear curdled). Add about

one-third of the flour mixture, followed by half of the sour cream, mixing until just incorporated after each addition (about 5 seconds). Repeat using half of the remaining flour mixture and all of the remaining sour cream. Scrape down the bowl and add the remaining flour mixture; mix at medium-low speed until the batter is thoroughly combined, about 15 seconds. Divide the batter evenly between the prepared cake pans, smoothing the tops with a rubber spatula. Lightly tap the pans against the countertop two or three times to settle the batter.

5. Bake the cakes until a toothpick inserted into the centers comes out clean, about 30 minutes, rotating the pans halfway through the baking time. Cool the cakes in the pans on a wire rack for 10 minutes. Run a small knife around the edges of the cakes, then flip them out onto a wire rack. Peel off the parchment, flip the cakes right side up, and cool completely before frosting, about 2 hours.

6. TO ASSEMBLE: Stir the toasted pecans into the chilled filling. Line the edges of a cake platter with strips of parchment paper to keep the platter clean while you assemble the cake. Use a serrated knife to cut each cake into two even layers. Place one bottom layer on the platter. Spread about 1 cup of the filling evenly across the top of the cake with a spatula. Carefully place the upper cake layer on top of the filling; repeat using the remaining filling and cake layers. Remove the parchment strips before serving.

CHOCOLATE CUPCAKES

WHY THIS RECIPE WORKS: Cupcakes shouldn't be complicated, but homemade versions can take a lot of time and store-bought mixes don't deliver good chocolate flavor. We wanted the consummate chocolate cupcake—one with a rich, buttery flavor, a light, moist, cakey texture, and just the right amount of sugar—but we wanted it to be almost as quick and easy to make as the cupcakes that come from a box.

For the mixing method, we found that the melted-butter method often used for mixing muffins, quick breads, and brownies—a method that requires no mixer and no time spent waiting for butter to soften—worked best. The same procedure won out over the more conventional creaming method for our cupcakes, delivering a light texture with a tender, fine crumb. Moving on to tackle our desire for deep chocolate flavor, we found that a combination of cocoa powder and bittersweet chocolate delivered deep chocolate flavor and that mixing the cocoa powder with the butter and chocolate as they melted (rather than adding the cocoa to the dry ingredients) made the chocolate flavor even stronger and richer. Sour cream gave our cupcakes moistness and a little tang, while just the right amounts of baking soda and baking powder helped them rise to a gently domed shape that was perfect for frosting.

Dark Chocolate Cupcakes

MAKES 12 CUPCAKES

Store leftover cupcakes (frosted or unfrosted) in the refrigerator, but let them come to room temperature before serving.

- **8 tablespoons (1 stick) unsalted butter, cut into 4 pieces**
- **2 ounces bittersweet chocolate, chopped**
- **½ cup cocoa powder, preferably Dutch-processed**
- **¾ cup (3¾ ounces) unbleached all-purpose flour**
- **¾ teaspoon baking powder**
- **½ teaspoon baking soda**
- **2 large eggs, room temperature**
- **¾ cup (5¼ ounces) sugar**
- **1 teaspoon vanilla extract**
- **½ teaspoon table salt**
- **½ cup sour cream**
- **1 recipe Easy Vanilla Bean Buttercream, Easy Chocolate Buttercream, or Easy Coffee Buttercream (recipes follow)**

1. Adjust an oven rack to the lower-middle position and heat the oven to 350 degrees. Line a standard-sized muffin pan with baking cup liners.

2. Melt the butter, chocolate, and cocoa in a medium heatproof bowl set over a saucepan filled with 1 inch of barely simmering water, stirring occasionally. Set aside to cool until just warm to the touch.

3. Whisk the flour, baking powder, and baking soda in a small bowl to combine.

4. Whisk the eggs in a medium bowl to combine; add the sugar, vanilla, and salt and whisk until fully incorporated. Add the cooled chocolate mixture and whisk until combined. Sift about one-third of the flour mixture over the chocolate mixture and whisk until combined; whisk in the sour cream until combined, then sift the remaining flour mixture over the batter and whisk until homogeneous and thick.

5. Divide the batter evenly among the muffin cups. Bake until a toothpick or wooden skewer inserted into the center of the cupcakes comes out clean, 18 to 20 minutes, rotating the pan halfway through the baking time.

6. Cool the cupcakes in the pan on a wire rack until cool enough to handle, about 15 minutes. Carefully lift each cupcake from the muffin pan and set on a wire rack. Cool to room temperature before icing, about 30 minutes. To frost: Mound about 2 tablespoons of icing on the center of each cupcake. Using a small spatula or butter knife, spread the icing to the edge of the cupcake, leaving a slight mound in the center.

Easy Vanilla Bean Buttercream

MAKES ABOUT 1½ CUPS, ENOUGH TO FROST 12 CUPCAKES

If you prefer to skip the vanilla bean, increase the extract to 1½ teaspoons. Any of the buttercream frostings can be made ahead and refrigerated; if refrigerated, however, the frosting must stand at room temperature to soften before use. If using a hand-held mixer, increase mixing times significantly (by at least 50 percent).

- **10 tablespoons (1¼ sticks) unsalted butter, softened**
- **½ vanilla bean, halved lengthwise (see note)**
- **1¼ cups (5 ounces) confectioners' sugar**
  Pinch table salt
- **1 tablespoon heavy cream**
- **½ teaspoon vanilla extract**

In a standing mixer fitted with the whisk attachment, beat the butter at medium-high speed until smooth, about 20 seconds. Using a paring knife, scrape the seeds from the vanilla bean into the butter and beat the mixture at medium-high speed to combine, about 15 seconds. Add the confectioners' sugar and salt and beat at medium-low speed until most of the sugar is moistened, about 45 seconds. Scrape down the bowl and beat at medium speed until the mixture is fully combined, about 15 seconds. Scrape down the bowl, add the heavy cream and vanilla extract, and beat at medium speed until incorporated, about 10 seconds, then increase the speed to medium-high and beat until light and fluffy, about 4 minutes, scraping down the bowl once or twice.

Easy Chocolate Buttercream

Follow the recipe for Easy Vanilla Bean Buttercream, omitting the vanilla bean and heavy cream and reducing the sugar to 1 cup. After beating in the vanilla extract, reduce the speed to low and gradually beat in 4 ounces melted and cooled semisweet or bittersweet chocolate.

Easy Coffee Buttercream

Follow the recipe for Easy Vanilla Bean Buttercream, omitting the vanilla bean and dissolving 1½ teaspoons instant espresso powder in the heavy cream and vanilla extract.

FLOURLESS CHOCOLATE CAKE

WHY THIS RECIPE WORKS: While all flourless chocolate cake recipes share common ingredients (chocolate, butter, and eggs), the techniques used to make them vary, as do the results. You can end up with anything from a fudge brownie to a bittersweet chocolate soufflé. We wanted something dense, moist, and ultra-chocolaty, but with some textural finesse.

We started with the type of chocolate. A cake made with unsweetened chocolate was neither smooth nor silky enough for this kind of cake. Bittersweet or semisweet chocolate each won out—both delivered deep chocolate flavor and a smooth texture. Next we turned to the eggs—we compared cakes made with room temperature whole eggs and whole eggs taken straight from the fridge. The batter made with chilled eggs produced a denser foam and the resulting cake boasted a smooth, velvety texture. And the gentle, moist heat of a water bath further preserved the cake's lush texture.

Flourless Chocolate Cake

SERVES 12 TO 16

This cake is best enjoyed when baked a day ahead to mellow its flavor. Even though the cake may not look done, pull it from the oven when an instant-read thermometer registers 140 degrees. (Make sure not to let the tip of the thermometer hit the bottom of the pan.) It will continue to firm up as it cools. If you use a 9-inch springform pan instead of the preferred 8-inch pan, reduce the baking time to 18 to 20 minutes. See page 607 for our top-rated brands of chocolate.

> 8 large eggs, chilled
> 1 pound bittersweet or semisweet chocolate, chopped
> ½ pound (2 sticks) unsalted butter, cut into ½-inch chunks
> ¼ cup strong coffee
> Confectioners' sugar or cocoa powder, for decoration

1. Adjust an oven rack to the lower-middle position and heat the oven to 325 degrees. Grease an 8-inch springform pan, then line the bottom with parchment paper. Wrap the outside of the pan with two 18-inch-square pieces of heavy-duty foil; set the springform pan in a roasting pan. Bring a kettle of water to a boil.

2. In a standing mixer fitted with the whisk attachment, beat the eggs at medium speed until doubled in volume, about 5 minutes.

3. Meanwhile, melt the chocolate and butter in a large heatproof bowl set over a saucepan filled with 1 inch of barely simmering water until smooth, stirring once or twice; stir in the coffee. Using a large rubber spatula, fold one-third of the egg mixture into the chocolate mixture until only a few streaks of egg are visible; fold the remaining egg mixture, in two additions, until the batter is totally homogeneous.

4. Scrape the batter into the prepared pan and smooth the surface with the spatula. Set the roasting pan on the oven rack and pour in enough boiling water to come about halfway up the sides of the pan. Bake until the cake has risen slightly, the edges are just beginning to set, a thin glazed crust (like a brownie) has formed on the surface, and an instant-read thermometer inserted halfway through the center of the cake registers 140 degrees, 22 to 25 minutes. Remove the pan from the water bath and set on a wire rack; cool to room temperature. Cover and refrigerate overnight to mellow the flavors. (The cake can be covered and refrigerated for up to 4 days.)

5. About 30 minutes before serving, remove the springform pan sides, then flip the cake out onto the wire rack. Peel off the parchment and flip the cake right side up onto a serving platter. Lightly dust the cake with confectioners' sugar or unsweetened cocoa powder, if desired, and serve.

HOT FUDGE PUDDING CAKE

WHY THIS RECIPE WORKS: Those who have eaten hot fudge pudding cake know its charms: unpretentious, moist, brownie-like chocolate cake sitting on a pool of thick, chocolate pudding–like sauce, baked together in one dish, as if by magic. Served warm with vanilla ice cream, this cake has a flavor that more than makes up for its homespun looks. But some recipes lack decent chocolate flavor; texture can be a problem, too. Instead of providing enough spoon-coating sauce to accompany the cake, some are dry, with a disproportionate amount of cake, while others are soupy, with a wet, sticky, underdone cake. We set out to master this humble dessert.

Pudding cake is made by sprinkling brownie batter with a mixture of sugar and cocoa, then pouring hot water on top, and baking. To bump up the chocolate flavor, we used a combination of Dutch-processed cocoa and bittersweet chocolate. We also added instant coffee to the water that is poured over the batter to cut the sweetness of the cake. We baked the cake slow and low to promote a good top crust and a silky sauce. And we found that letting the cake rest for 20 to 30 minutes before eating allows the sauce to become pudding-like and the cake brownie-like.

Hot Fudge Pudding Cake
SERVES 8

If you have cold brewed coffee on hand, it can be used in place of the instant coffee and water, but to make sure it isn't too strong, use 1 cup of cold coffee mixed with ½ cup of water. Serve the cake warm with vanilla or coffee ice cream.

2	teaspoons instant coffee powder (see note)
1½	cups water
1	cup (7 ounces) granulated sugar
⅔	cup Dutch-processed cocoa
⅓	cup packed (2⅓ ounces) brown sugar
6	tablespoons (¾ stick) unsalted butter
2	ounces bittersweet or semisweet chocolate, chopped
¾	cup (3¾ ounces) unbleached all-purpose flour
2	teaspoons baking powder
⅓	cup whole milk
1	tablespoon vanilla extract
¼	teaspoon table salt
1	large egg yolk, room temperature

1. Adjust an oven rack to the lower-middle position and heat the oven to 325 degrees. Lightly grease an 8-inch square glass or ceramic baking dish. Stir the instant coffee into the water; set aside to dissolve. Stir together ⅓ cup of the granulated sugar, ⅓ cup of the cocoa, and the brown sugar in a small bowl, breaking up large clumps with your fingers; set aside. Melt the butter, the remaining ⅓ cup cocoa, and the chocolate in a small bowl set over a saucepan filled with 1 inch of barely simmering water; whisk until smooth and set aside to cool slightly. Whisk the flour and baking powder in a small bowl to combine; set aside. Whisk the remaining ⅔ cup granulated sugar, the milk, vanilla, and salt in a medium bowl until combined; whisk in the egg yolk. Add the chocolate mixture and whisk to combine. Add the flour mixture and whisk until the batter is evenly moistened.

2. Pour the batter into the prepared baking dish and spread evenly to the sides and corners. Sprinkle the cocoa-sugar mixture evenly over the batter (the cocoa mixture should cover the entire surface of the batter); pour the coffee mixture gently over the cocoa mixture. Bake until the cake is puffed and bubbling and just beginning to pull away from the sides of the baking dish, about 45 minutes, rotating the pan halfway through the baking time. (Do not overbake.) Cool the cake in the dish on a wire rack about 25 minutes and serve.

Individual Hot Fudge Pudding Cakes

Follow the recipe for Hot Fudge Pudding Cake, heating the oven to 400 degrees and lightly greasing eight 6 to 8-ounce ramekins; set the ramekins on a baking sheet. Divide the batter evenly among the ramekins (about ¼ cup per ramekin) and level with the back of a spoon; sprinkle about 2 tablespoons cocoa-sugar mixture over the batter in each ramekin. Pour 3 tablespoons coffee mixture over the cocoa-sugar mixture in each ramekin. Bake until puffed and bubbling, about 20 minutes. (Do not overbake.) Cool the pudding cakes about 15 minutes before serving (the cakes will fall as they cool).

BITTERSWEET CHOCOLATE ROULADE

WHY THIS RECIPE WORKS: A chocolate roulade can be a baker's nightmare—a hard-to-roll cake with a dry texture and a filling that squirts out the sides instead of staying put. We wanted a recipe for a true showcase roulade, a cake with a velvety texture and deep chocolate flavor, a thick, rich filling that stays put, and a decadent icing that covers it all.

We used bitter- or semisweet chocolate for maximum chocolate flavor. Six eggs gave our cake great support.

A combination of cocoa and flour provided further structural support and extra chocolate flavor. Once the cake was baked, we cooled it briefly in the pan on a cooling rack, then unmolded it onto a kitchen towel rubbed with cocoa to prevent sticking. While the cake was still warm, we rolled it up with the towel inside, cooled it briefly, and then unrolled the cake—this method gave the cake a "memory" so it could be filled and re-rolled. For the filling, we made a simple espresso-flavored cream with just four ingredients, including the lush Italian cream cheese, mascarpone. Mascarpone provided both structural support and rich flavor. For the icing, we chose dark chocolate ganache, made with bittersweet chocolate and cognac for sophisticated flavor.

Bittersweet Chocolate Roulade

SERVES 8 TO 10

We suggest that you make the filling and ganache first, then make the cake while the ganache is setting up. Or, if you prefer, the cake can be baked, filled, and rolled—but not iced—then wrapped in plastic wrap and refrigerated for up to 24 hours. If serving this cake in the style of a holiday yule log, make wood-grain striations in the ganache with a fork. The roulade is best served at room temperature.

- ¼ cup (1¼ ounces) unbleached all-purpose flour, plus extra for the pan
- 6 ounces bittersweet or semisweet chocolate, chopped fine
- 2 tablespoons cold unsalted butter, cut into 2 pieces
- 2 tablespoons cold water
- ¼ cup Dutch-processed cocoa, sifted, plus 1 tablespoon for unmolding
- ⅛ teaspoon table salt
- 6 large eggs, room temperature and separated
- ⅓ cup (2⅓ ounces) sugar
- 1 teaspoon vanilla extract
- ⅛ teaspoon cream of tartar
- 1 recipe Espresso-Mascarpone Cream (recipe follows)
- 1 recipe Dark Chocolate Ganache (recipe follows)

1. Adjust an oven rack to the upper-middle position and heat the oven to 400 degrees. Spray a 17½ by 12-inch rimmed baking sheet with vegetable oil spray, cover the pan bottom with parchment paper, and spray the parchment with vegetable oil spray; dust with flour and tap out the excess.

2. Heat the chocolate, butter, and water in a small heat-proof bowl set over a saucepan filled with 1 inch of barely simmering water, stirring occasionally until smooth. Set aside to cool slightly. Sift ¼ cup of the cocoa, the flour, and salt together into a small bowl and set aside.

3. In a standing mixer fitted with the whisk attachment, beat the egg yolks at medium-high speed until just combined, about 15 seconds. With the mixer running, add half of the sugar. Continue to beat, scraping down the sides of the bowl as necessary, until the yolks are pale yellow and the mixture falls in a thick ribbon when the whisk is lifted, about 8 minutes. Add the vanilla and beat to combine, scraping down the bowl once, about 30 seconds. Turn the mixture into a medium bowl; wash and dry the mixer bowl and whisk attachment.

4. In the clean bowl with the clean whisk attachment, beat the whites and cream of tartar at medium speed until foamy, about 30 seconds. With the mixer running, add about 1 teaspoon more sugar; continue beating until soft peaks form, about 40 seconds. Gradually add the remaining sugar and beat until the whites are glossy and hold stiff peaks when the whisk is lifted, about 1 minute longer. Do not overbeat.

5. Stir the chocolate mixture into the egg yolks. With a rubber spatula, stir one-quarter of the egg whites into the chocolate mixture to lighten it. Fold in the remaining whites until almost no streaks remain. Sprinkle the cocoa-flour mixture over the top and fold in quickly but gently.

6. Pour the batter into the prepared pan; using a spatula and working quickly, even the surface and smooth the batter into the pan corners. Lightly tap the pan against the countertop two or three times to settle the batter. Bake until the center of the cake springs back when touched with a finger, 8 to 10 minutes, rotating the pan halfway through the baking time. Cool the cake in the pan on a wire rack for 5 minutes.

7. While the cake is cooling, lay a clean kitchen towel over the work surface and sift the remaining 1 tablespoon cocoa over the towel; rub the cocoa into the towel. Run a small knife around the baking sheet to loosen the cake. Flip the cake onto the towel and peel off the parchment.

8. Roll the cake, towel and all, into a jellyroll shape. Cool for 15 minutes, then unroll the cake and towel. Using a spatula, immediately spread the filling evenly over the cake, almost to the edges. Roll up the cake gently but snugly around the filling. Set a large sheet of parchment paper on an overturned rimmed baking sheet and set the roulade, seam side down, on top. Trim both ends on the diagonal. Spread the ganache evenly over the roulade. Use a fork to make wood-grain striations, if desired, on the surface of

the ganache before the icing has set. Refrigerate the cake, on the baking sheet, uncovered, to slightly set the icing, about 20 minutes.

9. Carefully slide two wide metal spatulas under the cake and transfer the cake to a serving platter. Cut into slices and serve.

Espresso-Mascarpone Cream
MAKES ABOUT 2½ CUPS

Mascarpone is a fresh Italian cheese. Its flavor is unique—mildly sweet and refreshing. It is sold in small containers in some supermarkets as well as most gourmet stores, cheese shops, and Italian markets.

½   cup heavy cream
2   teaspoons espresso powder or instant coffee
6   tablespoons confectioners' sugar
16½ ounces mascarpone cheese (generous 2 cups)

1. Bring the cream to a simmer in a small saucepan over high heat. Off the heat, stir in the espresso and confectioners' sugar; cool slightly.

2. With a spatula, beat the mascarpone in a medium bowl until softened. Gently whisk in the cooled cream mixture until combined. Cover with plastic wrap and refrigerate until ready to use.

Dark Chocolate Ganache
MAKES ABOUT 1½ CUPS

If your kitchen is cool and the ganache becomes too stiff to spread, set the bowl over a saucepan of simmering water, then stir briefly until it is smooth and icing-like.

¾   cup heavy cream
2   tablespoons unsalted butter
6   ounces high-quality bittersweet or semisweet chocolate, chopped
1   tablespoon cognac

Microwave the cream and butter in a microwave-safe measuring cup on high power until bubbling, about 1½ minutes. (Alternatively, bring to a simmer in a small saucepan over medium-high heat.) Place the chocolate in a food processor. With the machine running, gradually add the hot cream mixture and cognac through the feed tube and process until smooth and thickened, about 3 minutes. Transfer the ganache to a medium bowl and let stand at room temperature 1 hour, until spreadable (the ganache should have the consistency of soft icing).

TRIPLE-CHOCOLATE MOUSSE CAKE

WHY THIS RECIPE WORKS: Triple chocolate mousse cake is a truly decadent dessert. Most times, though, the mousse texture is exactly the same from one layer to the next and the flavor is so overpoweringly rich it's hard to finish more than a few forkfuls. We set out to tweak this showy confection. By finessing one layer at a time, starting with the dark chocolate base and building to the top white chocolate tier, we aimed to create a triple-decker that was incrementally lighter in texture—and richness.

For simplicity's sake, we decided to build the whole dessert, layer by layer, in the same springform pan. For a base layer that had the heft to support the upper two tiers, we chose flourless chocolate cake instead of the typical mousse. Folding egg whites into the batter helped lighten the cake without affecting its structural integrity. For the middle layer, we started with a traditional chocolate mousse, but the texture seemed too heavy when combined with the cake, so we removed the eggs and cut back on the chocolate a bit—this resulted in the lighter, creamier layer we desired. And for the crowning layer to our cake, we made an easy white chocolate mousse by folding whipped cream into melted white chocolate—and to prevent the soft mousse from oozing during slicing, we added a little gelatin to the mix.

Triple-Chocolate Mousse Cake

SERVES 12 TO 16

This recipe requires a springform pan at least 3 inches high for all three layers to fit. It is imperative that each layer is made in sequential order. Cool the base completely before topping with the middle layer. We recommend Ghirardelli Bittersweet Chocolate Baking Bar for the base and middle layers; our other recommended brand of chocolate, Callebaut Intense Dark L-60–40NV, may be used but will produce drier, slightly less sweet results. Our preferred brand of white chocolate is Guittard Choc-Au-Lait White Chips. For best results, chill the mixer bowl before whipping the heavy cream. For neater slices, clean the knife thoroughly between slices.

BASE LAYER

- 6 tablespoons (¾ stick) unsalted butter, cut into 6 pieces
- 7 ounces bittersweet chocolate, chopped fine (see note)
- ¾ teaspoon instant espresso powder
- 4 large eggs, room temperature and separated
- 1½ teaspoons vanilla extract
  Pinch table salt
- ⅓ cup packed (2⅓ ounces) light brown sugar, crumbled with fingers to remove lumps

MIDDLE LAYER

- 5 tablespoons hot water
- 2 tablespoons cocoa powder, preferably Dutch-processed
- 7 ounces bittersweet chocolate, chopped fine (see note)
- 1½ cups heavy cream, chilled
- 1 tablespoon granulated sugar
- ⅛ teaspoon table salt

TOP LAYER

- ¾ teaspoon powdered gelatin
- 1 tablespoon water
- 6 ounces white chocolate, chopped fine (see note)
- 1½ cups heavy cream, chilled
  Shaved chocolate or cocoa powder for serving (optional)

1. FOR THE BASE LAYER: Adjust an oven rack to the middle position and heat the oven to 325 degrees. Grease the bottom and sides of a 9-inch-wide by 3-inch-high round springform pan. Melt the butter, chocolate, and espresso powder in a large heatproof bowl set over a saucepan filled with 1 inch of barely simmering water, stirring occasionally until smooth. Remove from the heat and cool the mixture slightly, about 5 minutes. Whisk in the egg yolks and vanilla; set aside.

2. In a standing mixer fitted with the whisk attachment, beat the egg whites and salt at medium speed until frothy, about 30 seconds. Add half of the brown sugar and beat until combined, about 15 seconds. Add the remaining brown sugar and beat at high speed until soft peaks form when the whisk is lifted, about 1 minute longer, scraping down the sides halfway through. Using a whisk, fold one-third of the beaten egg whites into the chocolate mixture to lighten. Using a rubber spatula, fold in the remaining egg whites until no white streaks remain. Carefully transfer the batter to the prepared pan, gently smoothing the top with a spatula.

3. Bake until the cake has risen, is firm around the edges, and the center has just set but is still soft (the center of the cake will spring back after pressing gently with a finger), 13 to 18 minutes. Transfer the cake to a wire rack to cool completely, about 1 hour. (The cake will collapse as it cools.) Do not remove the cake from the pan.

4. FOR THE MIDDLE LAYER: Combine the hot water and cocoa powder in a small bowl; set aside. Melt the chocolate in a large heatproof bowl set over a saucepan filled with 1 inch of barely simmering water, stirring occasionally until smooth. Remove from the heat and cool slightly, 2 to 5 minutes.

5. In the clean bowl of a standing mixer fitted with the whisk attachment, whip the heavy cream, sugar, and salt at medium speed until it begins to thicken, about 30 seconds. Increase the speed to high and whip until soft peaks form when the whisk is lifted, 15 to 60 seconds. Whisk the cocoa powder mixture into the melted chocolate until smooth. Using a whisk, fold one-third of the whipped cream mixture into the chocolate mixture to lighten. Using a rubber spatula, fold in the remaining whipped cream mixture until no white streaks remain. Spoon the mousse into the springform pan over the cooled cake and lightly tap the pan against the countertop two or three times to settle the mousse; gently smooth the top with a spatula. Wipe the inside edge of the pan with a damp cloth to remove any drips. Refrigerate the cake at least 15 minutes while preparing the top layer.

6. FOR THE TOP LAYER: In a small bowl, sprinkle the gelatin over the water; let stand at least 5 minutes. Place the white chocolate in a medium bowl. Bring ½ cup of the cream to a simmer in a small saucepan over medium-high heat. Remove from the heat; add the gelatin mixture and stir until fully dissolved. Pour the cream mixture over the white chocolate and whisk until the chocolate is melted

and the mixture is smooth, about 30 seconds. Cool to room temperature, stirring occasionally, 5 to 8 minutes (the mixture will thicken slightly).

7. In the bowl of a standing mixer fitted with the whisk attachment, whip the remaining 1 cup cream at medium speed until it begins to thicken, about 30 seconds. Increase the speed to high and whip until soft peaks form when the whisk is lifted, 15 to 60 seconds. Using a whisk, fold one-third of the whipped cream into the white chocolate mixture to lighten. Using a rubber spatula, fold the remaining whipped cream into the white chocolate mixture until no white streaks remain. Spoon the white chocolate mousse into the pan over the bittersweet chocolate mousse layer. Smooth the top with a spatula. Return the cake to the refrigerator and chill until set, at least 2½ hours.

8. TO SERVE: Garnish the top of the cake with chocolate curls or dust with cocoa (if using). Run a thin knife between the cake and sides of the springform pan; remove the sides of the pan. Run the cleaned knife along the outside of the cake to smooth the sides. Serve.

CHOCOLATE VOLCANO CAKES WITH ESPRESSO ICE CREAM

WHY THIS RECIPE WORKS: A common restaurant dessert, volcano cake, or molten chocolate cake, is an intensely chocolate cake that boasts a warm, liquid center. In addition to its great flavor and alluring contrasting textures, the cake can often be made ahead and baked just before serving. The make-ahead appeal of such a cake inspired us to master this dessert for the home cook.

The initial recipes we tried revealed a host of problems with this cake—unbalanced chocolate flavor and a soggy or dry texture were just a few issues we faced. After testing various chocolates, we settled on a combination of bittersweet chocolate and unsweetened chocolate—this gave us maximum chocolate flavor. Chocolate alone seemed a little flat, so we added Grand Marnier for another layer of flavor. Whole eggs and egg yolks contributed richness and cornstarch helped make the batter remarkably stable. To help the cakes fall right out of the ramekins without a struggle, we buttered and sugared the ramekins before pouring in the batter. The cakes alone were great, but we felt they were even better when accompanied by a cold, creamy scoop of doctored "espresso" ice cream.

Chocolate Volcano Cakes with Espresso Ice Cream

SERVES 8

Use a bittersweet bar chocolate in this recipe, not chips—the chips include emulsifiers that will alter the cakes' texture. The cake batter can be mixed and portioned into the ramekins, wrapped tightly with plastic wrap, and refrigerated up to 24 hours in advance. The cold cake batter should be baked straight from the refrigerator.

ESPRESSO ICE CREAM

- 2 pints coffee ice cream, softened
- 1½ tablespoons finely ground espresso beans

CAKES

- 10 tablespoons (1¼ sticks) unsalted butter, cut into ½-inch pieces, plus extra for the ramekins
- 1½ cups (10½ ounces) granulated sugar, plus extra for the ramekins
- 8 ounces bittersweet chocolate, chopped fine (see note)
- 2 ounces unsweetened chocolate, chopped fine
- 2 tablespoons cornstarch
- 3 large eggs plus 4 large egg yolks, room temperature
- 2 teaspoons Grand Marnier (or other orange-flavored liqueur)
  Confectioners' sugar, for dusting the cakes

1. FOR THE ICE CREAM: Transfer the ice cream to a medium bowl and, using a rubber spatula, fold in the ground espresso until incorporated. Press a sheet of plastic wrap directly on the ice cream to prevent freezer burn and return it to the freezer. (The ice cream can be prepared up to 24 hours ahead.)

2. FOR THE CAKES: Lightly coat eight 4-ounce ramekins with butter. Dust with sugar, tapping out any excess, and set aside.

3. Melt the bittersweet and unsweetened chocolates and the 10 tablespoons butter in a large heatproof bowl set over a pan filled with 1 inch of barely simmering water, stirring occasionally, until smooth. In a large bowl, whisk the 1½ cups sugar and cornstarch together. Add the chocolate mixture and stir to combine. Add the eggs, egg yolks, and Grand Marnier and whisk until fully combined. Using a ½-cup measure, scoop the batter into each of the prepared ramekins. (The ramekins can be covered tightly with plastic wrap and refrigerated for up to 24 hours.)

4. Adjust an oven rack to the upper-middle position and heat the oven to 375 degrees. Place the filled ramekins on a rimmed baking sheet and bake until the tops of the cakes are set, have formed shiny crusts, and are beginning to crack, 16 to 20 minutes.

5. Transfer the ramekins to a wire rack and cool slightly, about 2 minutes. Run a small knife around the edge of each cake. Using a towel to protect your hand from the hot ramekins, invert each cake onto a small plate, then immediately invert again right side up onto eight individual plates. Sift confectioners' sugar over each cake. Remove the ice cream from the freezer and scoop a portion next to each cake. Serve immediately.

TIRAMISÙ

WHY THIS RECIPE WORKS: There's a reason restaurant menus (Italian or not) offer tiramisù. Delicate ladyfingers soaked in a spiked coffee mixture layered with a sweet, creamy filling make an irresistible combination. Preparing tiramisù, however, can be labor intensive and the dessert is not without its problems. Some versions are overly rich and the ladyfingers, which should be moist, sometimes turn soggy to the point of mush. We wanted to avoid these issues and find a streamlined approach—one that highlights the luxurious combination of flavors and textures that have made this dessert so popular.

Instead of hauling out a double boiler to make the fussy custard-based filling (called *zabaglione*), we instead simply whipped egg yolks, sugar, salt, rum (our preferred spirit), and mascarpone together. Salt is not traditional, but we found that it heightened the filling's subtle flavors. And to lighten the filling, we chose whipped cream instead of egg whites. For the coffee soaking mixture, we combined strong brewed coffee and espresso powder (along with more rum). To moisten the ladyfingers so that they were neither too dry nor too saturated, we dropped them one at a time into the spiked coffee mixture and, once they were moistened, rolled them over to moisten the other side for just a couple of seconds. For best flavor and texture, we discovered that it was important to allow the tiramisù to chill in the refrigerator for at least six hours.

Tiramisù

SERVES 10 TO 12

Brandy and even whiskey can stand in for the dark rum. The test kitchen prefers a tiramisù with a pronounced rum flavor; for a less potent rum flavor, halve the amount of rum added to the coffee mixture in step 1. Do not allow the mascarpone to warm to room temperature before using it; it has a tendency to break if allowed to do so.

2½ cups strong brewed coffee, room temperature
9 tablespoons dark rum (see note)
1½ tablespoons instant espresso powder
6 large egg yolks, room temperature
⅔ cup (4⅔ ounces) sugar
¼ teaspoon table salt
1½ pounds mascarpone (generous 3 cups) (see note)
¾ cup heavy cream, chilled
14 ounces (42 to 60, depending on size) dried ladyfingers
3½ tablespoons cocoa powder, preferably Dutch-processed
¼ cup grated semisweet or bittersweet chocolate (optional)

1. Stir together the coffee, 5 tablespoons of the rum, and the espresso powder in a wide bowl or baking dish until the espresso dissolves; set aside.

2. In a standing mixer fitted with the whisk attachment, beat the yolks at low speed until just combined. Add the sugar and salt and beat at medium-high speed until pale yellow, 1½ to 2 minutes, scraping down the sides of the bowl with a rubber spatula once or twice. Add the remaining 4 tablespoons rum and beat at medium speed until just combined, 20 to 30 seconds; scrape the bowl. Add the mascarpone and beat at medium speed until no lumps remain, 30 to 45 seconds, scraping down the sides

of the bowl once or twice. Transfer the mixture to a large bowl and set aside.

3. In the now-empty mixer bowl (no need to clean the bowl), beat the cream at medium speed until frothy, 1 to 1½ minutes. Increase the speed to high and continue to beat until the cream holds stiff peaks, 1 to 1½ minutes longer. Using a rubber spatula, fold one-third of the whipped cream into the mascarpone mixture to lighten, then gently fold in the remaining whipped cream until no white streaks remain. Set the mascarpone mixture aside.

4. Working one at a time, drop half of the ladyfingers into the coffee mixture, roll, remove, and transfer to a 13 by 9-inch glass or ceramic baking dish. (Do not submerge the ladyfingers in the coffee mixture; the entire process should take no longer than 2 to 3 seconds for each cookie.) Arrange the soaked cookies in a single layer in the baking dish, breaking or trimming the ladyfingers as needed to fit neatly into the dish.

5. Spread half of the mascarpone mixture over the ladyfingers; use a rubber spatula to spread the mixture to the sides and into the corners of the dish and smooth the surface. Place 2 tablespoons of the cocoa in a fine-mesh strainer and dust the cocoa over the mascarpone.

6. Repeat the dipping and arrangement of the ladyfingers; spread the remaining mascarpone mixture over the ladyfingers and dust with the remaining 1½ tablespoons cocoa. Wipe the edges of the dish with a dry paper towel. Cover with plastic wrap and refrigerate for 6 to 24 hours. Sprinkle with the grated chocolate (if using); cut into pieces and serve chilled.

Tiramisù with Cooked Eggs

This recipe involves cooking the yolks in a double boiler, which requires a little more effort and makes for a slightly thicker mascarpone filling, but the results are just as good as with our traditional method. You will need an additional ⅓ cup heavy cream.

Follow the recipe for Tiramisù through step 1. In step 2, add ⅓ cup cream to the yolks after the sugar and salt; do not whisk in the rum. Set the bowl with the yolks over a medium saucepan containing 1 inch gently simmering water; cook, constantly scraping along the bottom and sides of the bowl with a heatproof spatula, until the mixture coats the back of a spoon and registers 160 degrees on an instant-read thermometer, 4 to 7 minutes. Remove from the heat and stir vigorously to cool slightly, then set aside to cool to room temperature, about

15 minutes. Whisk in the remaining 4 tablespoons rum until combined. Transfer the bowl to a standing mixer fitted with the whisk attachment, add the mascarpone, and beat at medium speed until no lumps remain, 30 to 45 seconds. Transfer the mixture to a large bowl and set aside. Continue with the recipe from step 3, using the full amount of cream specified (¾ cup).

NEW YORK–STYLE CHEESECAKE

WHY THIS RECIPE WORKS: The ideal New York cheesecake should be a tall, bronze-skinned, and dense affair. At the core, it should be cool, thick, smooth, satiny, and creamy. The flavor should be pure and minimalist, sweet and tangy, and rich. But many recipes fall short—going wrong in a number of ways—with textures that range from fluffy to rubbery and leaden, and flavors that are starchy or overly citrusy. We wanted to find the secret to perfect New York cheesecake.

After trying a variety of crusts, we settled on the classic graham cracker crust—a simple combination of graham crackers, butter, and sugar. For the filling, cream cheese, boosted by the extra tang of a little sour cream, delivered the best flavor. A little lemon juice and vanilla added just the right sweet, bright accents without calling

attention to themselves. A combination of eggs and egg yolks yielded a texture that was dense but not heavy. We found that the New York method worked better for this cheesecake than the typical water bath—baking the cake in a hot oven for 10 minutes then in a low oven for a full 90 minutes yielded the satiny texture we were after.

New York Cheesecake

SERVES 12

For neater slices, clean the knife thoroughly between slices. Serve as is or with Strawberry Topping (recipe follows).

CRUST

- 8 **whole graham crackers, broken into 1-inch pieces**
- 7 **tablespoons unsalted butter, melted and cooled**
- 3 **tablespoons sugar**

FILLING

- 2½ **pounds cream cheese, cut into chunks and softened**
- 1½ **cups (10½ ounces) sugar**
- ⅛ **teaspoon table salt**
- ⅓ **cup sour cream**
- 2 **teaspoons juice from 1 lemon**
- 2 **teaspoons vanilla extract**
- 6 **large eggs plus 2 large egg yolks, room temperature**

1. FOR THE CRUST: Adjust an oven rack to the middle position and heat the oven to 325 degrees. Process the graham cracker pieces in a food processor to fine, even crumbs, about 30 seconds. Sprinkle 6 tablespoons of the melted butter and the sugar over the crumbs and pulse to incorporate. Sprinkle the mixture into a 9-inch springform pan. Press the crumbs firmly into an even layer using the bottom of a measuring cup. Bake the crust until fragrant and beginning to brown, 10 to 15 minutes. Cool the crust to room temperature, about 30 minutes.

2. FOR THE FILLING: Meanwhile, increase the oven temperature to 500 degrees. In the bowl of a standing mixer fitted with the paddle attachment, beat the cream cheese on medium-low speed until smooth, 1 to 3 minutes. Scrape down the bowl and beaters as needed.

3. Beat in half of the sugar and salt until incorporated, 1 to 3 minutes. Beat in the remaining sugar until incorporated, 1 to 3 minutes. Beat in the sour cream, lemon juice, and vanilla until incorporated, 1 to 3 minutes. Beat in the eggs and egg yolks, two at a time, until combined, 1 to 3 minutes.

4. Being careful not to disturb the baked crust, brush the inside of the prepared springform pan with the remaining 1 tablespoon melted butter. Set the pan on a rimmed baking sheet. Carefully pour the filling into the pan. Bake the cheesecake for 10 minutes.

5. Without opening the oven door, reduce the oven temperature to 200 degrees and continue to bake until the center of the cheesecake registers 150 degrees on an instant-read thermometer, about 1½ hours.

6. Transfer the cheesecake to a wire rack and run a knife around the edge of the cake. Cool the cheesecake until just barely warm, 2½ to 3 hours, running a knife around the edge of the cake every hour or so. Wrap the pan tightly in plastic wrap and refrigerate until cold, about 3 hours.

7. To unmold the cheesecake, wrap a wet, hot kitchen towel around the cake pan and let sit for 1 minute. Remove the sides of the pan and carefully slide the cake onto a cake platter. Let the cheesecake sit at room temperature for 30 minutes before serving.

Strawberry Topping

MAKES ABOUT 6 CUPS

This accompaniment to cheesecake is best served the same day it is made.

    2 pounds fresh strawberries, cleaned, hulled, and cut
       lengthwise into ¼ to ⅛-inch slices
    ½ cup (3½ ounces) sugar
       Pinch table salt
    1 cup strawberry jam
    2 tablespoons juice from 1 lemon

1. Toss the berries, sugar, and salt in a medium bowl; let stand until the berries have released their juices and the sugar has dissolved, about 30 minutes, tossing occasionally to combine.

2. Process the jam in a food processor until smooth, about 8 seconds; transfer to a small saucepan. Bring the jam to a simmer over medium-high heat; simmer, stirring frequently, until dark and no longer frothy, about 3 minutes. Stir in the lemon juice; pour the warm liquid over the strawberries and stir to combine. Let cool, then cover with plastic wrap and refrigerate until cold, at least 2 hours or up to 12 hours. To serve, spoon a portion of topping over each slice of cheesecake.

LIGHT CHEESECAKE

WHY THIS RECIPE WORKS: Of all the desserts that people long for in low-fat form, cheesecake is probably the most popular—but it's also the most difficult to lighten. Why? One modest slice of cheesecake boasts nearly 600 calories and about 40 grams of fat. Start removing the fat and sugar in the cake and flavor and texture can suffer terribly, as evidenced by the light recipes we tried. These cheesecakes were simply inedible—rubbery, gummy, and chock-full of artificial flavors. We set out to develop a light cheesecake worth eating.

Three key steps produced our desired results. We replaced full-fat cream cheese and sour cream with a combination of light cream cheese, low-fat cottage cheese, and low-fat yogurt cheese. And to ensure a firm, not loose, filling, we drained the cottage cheese—this rid it of excess moisture. We cut the fat further by using a reduced number of whole eggs instead of whole eggs and yolks. And, finally, we pureed the filling in a food processor for an ultrasmooth texture. The result? A rich, creamy cheesecake with about half the calories and three-quarters less fat than the original.

Light New York Cheesecake

SERVES 12

You can buy low-fat yogurt cheese (also called labne) or make your own with low-fat yogurt—allow at least 10 hours for the yogurt to drain. To make 1 cup yogurt cheese, line a fine-mesh strainer with 3 paper coffee filters or a double layer of cheesecloth. Spoon 2 cups of plain low-fat yogurt into the lined strainer, cover, and refrigerate for 10 to 12 hours (about 1 cup of liquid will have drained out of the yogurt to yield 1 cup yogurt cheese). Serve as is, or with Strawberry Topping (at left).

CRUST
    9 whole graham crackers, broken into 1-inch pieces
    4 tablespoons (½ stick) unsalted butter, melted
    1 tablespoon sugar

FILLING
    1 pound 1 percent cottage cheese
    1 pound light cream cheese, cut into chunks and softened
    8 ounces (1 cup) low-fat yogurt cheese (see note)
    1½ cups (10½ ounces) sugar

1 **tablespoon vanilla extract**

1 **teaspoon grated zest from 1 lemon**

¼ **teaspoon table salt**

3 **large eggs, room temperature**

1. FOR THE CRUST: Adjust an oven rack to the middle position and heat the oven to 325 degrees. Process the graham cracker pieces in a food processor to fine, even crumbs, about 30 seconds. Mix the cracker crumbs, melted butter, and sugar together, then pour into a 9-inch springform pan. Press the crumbs firmly into an even layer using the bottom of a measuring cup. Bake the crust until fragrant, 10 to 15 minutes. Cool on a wire rack, about 30 minutes.

2. FOR THE FILLING: Meanwhile, increase the oven temperature to 500 degrees. Line a medium bowl with a clean dish towel or several layers of paper towels. Spoon the cottage cheese into the bowl and let drain for 30 minutes.

3. Process the drained cottage cheese in a food processor until smooth and no visible lumps remain, about 1 minute, scraping down the bowl as needed. Dollop the cream cheese and yogurt cheese into the food processor and continue to process until smooth, 1 to 2 minutes, scraping down the bowl as needed. Add the sugar, vanilla, lemon zest, and salt and continue to process until smooth, about 1 minute. With the processor running, add the eggs one at a time and continue to process until smooth.

4. Being careful not to disturb the baked crust, spray the insides of the springform pan with vegetable oil spray. Set the pan on a rimmed baking sheet. Pour the processed cheese mixture into the cooled crust and bake for 10 minutes.

5. Without opening the oven door, reduce the oven temperature to 200 degrees and continue to bake until the center of the cheesecake registers 150 degrees on an instant-read thermometer, about 1 hour and 30 minutes.

6. Transfer the cake to a wire rack and run a paring knife around the edge of the cake. Cool until barely warm, 2½ to 3 hours, running a paring knife around the edge of the cake every hour or so. Wrap the pan tightly in plastic wrap and refrigerate until cold, about 3 hours.

7. To unmold the cheesecake, wrap a wet, hot kitchen towel around the springform pan and let stand for 1 minute. Remove the sides of the pan. Blot any excess moisture from the top of the cheesecake with paper towels and slide onto a cake platter. Let the cheesecake stand at room temperature about 30 minutes before slicing.

PUMPKIN CHEESECAKE

WHY THIS RECIPE WORKS: Those who suffer from pumpkin pie ennui embrace pumpkin cheesecake as "a nice change," but the expectations are low. Undoubtedly, pumpkin cheesecake can be good in its own right, though it rarely is. Textures run the gamut from dry and dense to wet, soft, and mousse-like. Flavors veer from far too cheesy and tangy to pungently overspiced to totally bland. We wanted a creamy pumpkin cheesecake with a velvety smooth texture that tasted of sweet, earthy pumpkin as well as tangy cream cheese, that struck a harmonious spicy chord, and, of course, that had a crisp, buttery, cookie-crumb crust.

For a cookie crust that complemented the earthy, warm flavors of pumpkin, we spiced up a graham cracker crust with ginger, cinnamon, and cloves. For a smooth and creamy texture, we blotted canned pumpkin puree with paper towels to remove excess moisture—this solved the sogginess issue. For dairy, we liked heavy cream, not sour cream, for added richness. We also preferred white sugar to brown, which tended to overpower the pumpkin flavor. Whole eggs, vanilla, salt, lemon juice, and a moderate blend of spices rounded out our cake. And for a smooth, velvety texture, we baked the cheesecake in a water bath in a moderate oven.

Spiced Pumpkin Cheesecake
SERVES 12

Be sure to buy unsweetened canned pumpkin, not pumpkin pie filling, which is preseasoned and sweetened. For neater slices, clean the knife thoroughly between slices.

CRUST

8 whole graham crackers, broken into 1-inch pieces

7 tablespoons unsalted butter, melted and cooled

3 tablespoons sugar

½ teaspoon ground ginger

½ teaspoon ground cinnamon

¼ teaspoon ground cloves

FILLING

1 (15-ounce) can pumpkin puree (see note)

1⅓ cups (9⅓ ounces) sugar

1 teaspoon ground cinnamon

½ teaspoon ground ginger

¼ teaspoon ground nutmeg

¼ teaspoon ground cloves

¼ teaspoon ground allspice

½ teaspoon table salt

1½ pounds cream cheese, cut into chunks and softened

1 tablespoon juice from 1 lemon

1 tablespoon vanilla extract

5 large eggs, room temperature

1 cup heavy cream

1. FOR THE CRUST: Adjust an oven rack to the middle position and heat the oven to 325 degrees. Process the graham cracker pieces in a food processor to fine, even crumbs, about 30 seconds. Sprinkle 6 tablespoons of the melted butter, sugar, and spices over the crumbs and pulse to incorporate. Sprinkle the mixture into a 9-inch springform pan. Press the crumbs firmly into an even layer using the bottom of a measuring cup. Bake the crust until fragrant and beginning to brown, 10 to 15 minutes. Let the crust cool to room temperature, about 30 minutes. Once cool, wrap the outside of the pan with two sheets of heavy-duty foil and set in a large roasting pan lined with a dish towel. Bring a kettle of water to a boil.

2. FOR THE FILLING: Pat the pumpkin puree dry with several layers of paper towels. Whisk the sugar, spices, and salt together in a small bowl.

3. In a standing mixer fitted with the paddle attachment, beat the cream cheese on medium-low speed until smooth, about 1 minute. Scrape down the bowl and beaters as needed.

4. Beat in half of the sugar mixture until incorporated, about 1 minute. Beat in the remaining sugar mixture until incorporated, about 1 minute. Beat in the dried pumpkin,

lemon juice, and vanilla until incorporated, about 1 minute. Beat in the eggs, one at a time, until combined, about 1 minute. Beat in the heavy cream until incorporated, about 1 minute.

5. Being careful not to disturb the baked crust, brush the inside of the springform pan with the remaining 1 tablespoon of melted butter. Carefully pour the filling into the pan. Set the roasting pan, with the cheesecake, on the oven rack and pour the boiling water into the roasting pan until it reaches about halfway up the sides of the pan. Bake the cheesecake until the center registers 150 degrees on an instant-read thermometer, about 1½ hours.

6. Cool the cheesecake in the roasting pan for 45 minutes, then transfer to a wire rack and cool until barely warm, 2½ to 3 hours, running a knife around the edge of the cake every hour or so. Wrap the pan tightly in plastic wrap and refrigerate until cold, about 3 hours.

7. To unmold the cheesecake, wrap a wet, hot kitchen towel around the cake pan and let sit for 1 minute. Remove the sides of the pan and carefully slide the cake onto a cake platter. Let the cheesecake sit at room temperature for 30 minutes before serving.

LEMON CHEESECAKE

WHY THIS RECIPE WORKS: Cheesecake is decadently rich. We love it in its unadulterated form, but sometimes the fresh flavor of citrus can take cheesecake to a refreshing new level. We aimed to develop a creamy cheesecake with a bracing but not overpowering lemon flavor.

Graham crackers, our usual cookie for cheesecakes, were too overpowering for the filling's lemon flavor. Instead, we turned to biscuit-type cookies, such as animal crackers, for a mild-tasting crust that allowed the lemon flavor of the cheesecake to shine. For maximum lemon flavor, we ground lemon zest with a portion of the sugar. This released its flavorful oils dramatically. Grinding the zest also improved the filling's texture (minced lemon zest baked up into fibrous bits in the cake). Heavy cream, in addition to cream cheese, provided richness, and vanilla rounded out the flavors. For ultimate creaminess, we baked the cake in a water bath. And finally, for an additional layer of bright lemon flavor, we topped off the cake with lemon curd.

Lemon Cheesecake

SERVES 12

Be sure to zest the lemons before juicing them. For neater slices, clean the knife thoroughly between slices.

CRUST

- **5** ounces Nabisco Barnum's Animal Crackers or Social Tea Biscuits
- **7** tablespoons unsalted butter, melted and cooled
- **3** tablespoons sugar

FILLING

- **1¼** cups (8¾ ounces) sugar
- **1** tablespoon grated zest from 1 lemon
- **1½** pounds cream cheese, cut into chunks and softened
- **¼** teaspoon table salt
- **¼** cup juice from 2 lemons
- **2** teaspoons vanilla extract
- **4** large eggs, room temperature
- **½** cup heavy cream

CURD

- **⅓** cup juice from 2 lemons
- **½** cup (3½ ounces) sugar
- Pinch table salt
- **2** large eggs plus 1 large egg yolk
- **2** tablespoons unsalted butter, cut into ½-inch pieces and frozen
- **1** tablespoon heavy cream
- **¼** teaspoon vanilla extract

1. FOR THE CRUST: Adjust an oven rack to the middle position and heat the oven to 325 degrees. Process the cookies in a food processor to fine, even crumbs, about 30 seconds. Sprinkle 6 tablespooons of the melted butter and sugar over the crumbs and pulse to incorporate. Sprinkle the mixture into a 9-inch springform pan. Press the crumbs firmly into an even layer using the bottom of a measuring cup. Bake the crust until fragrant and beginning to brown, 10 to 15 minutes. Let the crust cool to room temperature, about 30 minutes. Once cool, wrap the outside of the pan with two sheets of heavy-duty foil and set in a large roasting pan lined with a dish towel. Bring a kettle of water to a boil.

2. FOR THE FILLING: Process ¼ cup of the sugar and lemon zest in a food processor until the sugar is yellow and the zest is very fine, about 15 seconds. Pulse in the remaining 1 cup sugar to combine.

3. In a standing mixer fitted with the paddle attachment, beat the cream cheese on medium speed until smooth, about 1 minute. Scrape down the bowl and beaters as needed.

4. Beat in half of the lemon sugar and salt until incorporated. Beat in the remaining lemon sugar until incorporated, about 1 minute. Beat in the lemon juice and vanilla until incorporated, about 1 minute. Beat in the eggs, one at a time, until combined, about 1 minute. Beat in the heavy cream until incorporated, about 1 minute.

5. Being careful not to disturb the baked crust, brush the inside of the prepared springform pan with the remaining 1 tablespoon melted butter. Carefully pour the filling into the pan. Set the roasting pan, with the cheesecake, on the oven rack and pour the boiling water into the roasting pan until it reaches about halfway up the sides of the springform pan. Bake the cheesecake until the center registers 150 degrees on an instant-read thermometer, about 1½ hours.

6. Cool the cheesecake in the roasting pan for 45 minutes, then transfer to a wire rack and cool until barely warm, 2½ to 3 hours, running a knife around the edge of the cake every hour or so. Wrap the pan tightly in plastic wrap and refrigerate until cold, about 3 hours.

7. FOR THE CURD: Meanwhile, cook the lemon juice, sugar, and salt together in a small saucepan over medium-high heat until the sugar dissolves and the mixture is hot (do not boil). In a medium bowl, whisk the eggs and egg yolk together until combined, then slowly whisk in the hot lemon mixture to temper. Return the mixture to the saucepan and cook over medium-low heat, stirring constantly, until the mixture is thickened and a spatula scraped along the bottom of the pan leaves a trail (170 degrees on an instant-read thermometer), 2 to 4 minutes.

8. Off the heat, stir in the frozen butter until melted and incorporated, then stir in the cream and vanilla. Strain the curd through a fine-mesh strainer into a small bowl. Press plastic wrap directly on the surface of the curd and refrigerate until needed.

9. TO FINISH THE CAKE: When the cheesecake is cold, spoon the lemon curd over the top of the cake and spread into an even layer. Wrap the pan tightly in plastic wrap and refrigerate until the curd and cake have set, at least 5 hours.

10. To unmold the cheesecake, wrap a wet, hot kitchen towel around the cake pan and let sit for 1 minute. Remove the sides of the pan and carefully slide the cake onto a cake platter. Let the cheesecake sit at room temperature for 30 minutes before serving.

CHAPTER 23

PUDDINGS AND SOUFFLÉS

Stovetop Rice Pudding   526

Coconut Rice Pudding   526

Panna Cotta   527

   Raspberry Coulis

Classic Crème Brûlée   528

Espresso Crème Brûlée   529

Classic Crème Caramel   529

Chocolate Pots de Crème   530

Milk Chocolate Pots de Crème   531

Dark Chocolate Mousse   531

Chocolate-Orange Mousse   532

Chocolate-Raspberry Mousse   532

Premium Dark Chocolate Mousse   532

Grand Marnier Soufflé   533

Grand Marnier Soufflé with Grated Chocolate   534

Chilled Lemon Soufflé   534

Chilled Lemon Soufflé with White Chocolate   535

Individual Chilled Lemon Soufflés   535

Make-Ahead Chocolate Soufflés   536

Make-Ahead Mocha Soufflés   536

Skillet Lemon Soufflé   537

Skillet Chocolate-Orange Soufflé   537

STOVETOP RICE PUDDING

WHY THIS RECIPE WORKS: At its best, rice pudding is lightly sweet and tastes of its primary component, rice. At its worst, the rice flavor is lost to cloying sweetness, over-cooked milk, and a pasty, leaden consistency. We wanted a rice pudding with intact, tender grains bound loosely in a subtly sweet, creamy pudding.

For simple, straightforward rice flavor, we avoided aromatic rices like basmati and jasmine. Arborio rice, used for risotto, was stiff and gritty. Overall, medium-grain rice produced the best texture (with long-grain rice a close second). We found that cooking the rice in water rather than milk left its flavor intact. After the rice absorbed the water, we added sugar and equal amounts of milk and half-and-half, which delivered the proper degree of richness; the eggs and butter found in other recipes were just too overpowering. When we cooked the rice in water with the lid on the pan, then removed the lid while the rice simmered in the milk mixture, we got the results we wanted: distinct, tender grains of rice in a milky, subtly sweet sauce.

Stovetop Rice Pudding
SERVES 6 TO 8
We prefer pudding made with medium-grain rice, but long-grain rice works, too.

- 2 cups water
- 1 cup medium-grain rice (see note)
- ¼ teaspoon table salt
- 2½ cups whole milk
- 2½ cups half-and-half
- ⅔ cup (4⅔ ounces) sugar
- ½ cup raisins
- 1½ teaspoons vanilla extract
- 1 teaspoon ground cinnamon

1. Bring the water to a boil in a large saucepan. Stir in the rice and salt, cover, and simmer over low heat, stirring once or twice, until the water is almost fully absorbed, 15 to 20 minutes.

2. Stir in the milk, half-and-half, and sugar. Increase the heat to medium-high and bring to a simmer, then reduce the heat to maintain a simmer. Cook, uncovered and stirring frequently, until the mixture starts to thicken, about 30 minutes. Reduce the heat to low and continue to cook, stirring every couple of minutes to prevent sticking and scorching, until a spoon is just able to stand up in the pudding, about 15 minutes longer.

3. Remove from the heat and stir in the raisins, vanilla, and cinnamon. Serve warm, at room temperature, or chilled. (To store, press plastic wrap directly onto the surface of the pudding and refrigerate for up to 2 days. If serving at room temperature or chilled, stir in up to 1 cup warm milk, 2 tablespoons at a time, as needed to loosen before serving.)

Coconut Rice Pudding

To toast the coconut, spread it out on a rimmed baking sheet and toast it in a 325-degree oven, stirring often, until light golden, 10 to 15 minutes.

Follow the recipe for Stovetop Rice Pudding, substituting coconut milk for the whole milk and garnishing with 1 cup shredded sweetened coconut, toasted, before serving.

PANNA COTTA

WHY THIS RECIPE WORKS: Though its name is lyrical, the literal translation of panna cotta, "cooked cream," does nothing to suggest its ethereal qualities. In fact, panna cotta is not cooked at all. Neither is it complicated with eggs, as is a custard. Instead, sugar and gelatin are melted in cream and milk, and the whole mixture is then turned into individual ramekins and chilled. Panna cotta is more often found on restaurant menus, but we wanted a version for the home cook—one that would guarantee a pudding with the rich flavor of cream and vanilla and a delicate texture.

After trying several different recipes, we concluded that we needed a higher proportion of cream to milk to achieve the creamiest flavor and texture. The amount of gelatin proved critical—too much turned the panna cotta rubbery; it needs to be just firm enough to unmold, so we used a light hand. And because gelatin sets more quickly at cold temperatures, we minimized the amount of heat by softening the gelatin in cold milk, then heating it very briefly until it was melted. To avoid premature hardening, we gradually added cold vanilla-infused cream to the gelatin mixture and stirred everything over an ice bath to incorporate the gelatin. Chilled until set and served with a raspberry sauce, our panna cotta was creamy, smooth, and light.

Panna Cotta

SERVES 8

A vanilla bean gives the panna cotta the deepest flavor, but 2 teaspoons of vanilla extract can be used instead. If you like, you can omit the Raspberry Coulis and simply serve the panna cotta with lightly sweetened berries. Though traditionally unmolded, panna cotta may be chilled and served in wine glasses and sauced on top. If you would like to make the panna cotta a day ahead, decrease the amount of gelatin to 2½ teaspoons, and chill the filled wine glasses or ramekins for 18 to 24 hours.

- 1 **cup whole milk**
- 2¾ **teaspoons gelatin (see note)**
- 3 **cups heavy cream**
- 1 **vanilla bean, halved lengthwise (see note)**
- 6 **tablespoons sugar**
   Pinch table salt
   Raspberry Coulis (recipe follows)

1. Pour the milk into a medium saucepan; sprinkle the surface evenly with the gelatin and let stand for 10 minutes. Meanwhile, turn the contents of two ice cube trays (about 32 cubes) into a large bowl; add 4 cups cold water. Pour the cream into a large measuring cup or pitcher. With a paring knife, scrape the vanilla seeds into the cream; place the pod in the cream along with the seeds and set the mixture aside. Set eight 4-ounce ramekins on a rimmed baking sheet.

2. Heat the milk and gelatin mixture over high heat, stirring constantly, until the gelatin is dissolved and the mixture registers 135 degrees on an instant-read thermometer, about 1½ minutes. Off the heat, add the sugar and salt; stir until dissolved, about 1 minute.

3. Stirring constantly, slowly pour the cream with the vanilla into the saucepan containing the milk, then transfer the mixture to a medium bowl and set the bowl over the ice water bath. Stir frequently until thickened to the consistency of eggnog and the mixture registers 50 degrees on an instant-read thermometer, about 10 minutes. Strain the mixture into a large measuring cup or pitcher, then distribute evenly among the ramekins. Cover the baking sheet with plastic wrap, making sure that the plastic does not mar the surface of the cream; refrigerate until just set (the mixture should wobble when shaken gently), about 4 hours.

4. To serve, spoon a portion of the raspberry coulis onto eight individual serving plates. Pour 1 cup boiling water into a small wide-mouthed bowl, dip a ramekin filled with panna cotta into the water for 3 seconds and lift the ramekin out of the water. With a moistened finger, press lightly on the periphery of the panna cotta to loosen the edges. Dip the ramekin back into the hot water for another 3 seconds. Invert the ramekin over your palm and loosen the panna cotta by cupping your fingers between the panna cotta and the edges of the ramekin. Gently lower the panna cotta onto a serving plate with the coulis. Repeat the process with the remaining ramekins of panna cotta. Serve.

Raspberry Coulis

MAKES ABOUT 1½ CUPS

- 24 **ounces (about 5 cups) frozen raspberries**
- ⅓ **cup (2⅓ ounces) sugar**
- ¼ **teaspoon juice from 1 lemon**
   Pinch table salt

1. Place the frozen raspberries in a 4-quart saucepan. Cover and simmer over medium-high heat, stirring occasionally, for 10 to 12 minutes. Add the sugar and increase the heat to high. Boil for 2 minutes.

2. Strain the berries through a fine-mesh strainer into a bowl, using a rubber spatula to push the berries through the strainer; discard the seeds. Stir in the lemon juice and salt. Cover and refrigerate until chilled, at least 2 hours or up to 3 days.

CRÈME BRÛLÉE

WHY THIS RECIPE WORKS: Crème brûlée is all about the contrast between the crisp sugar crust and the silky custard underneath. But too often the crust is either stingy or rock-hard and the custard is heavy and tasteless. Because crème brûlée requires so few ingredients, we knew that finding just the right technique would be key in creating the quintessential version of this elegant dessert.

The texture of the custard should not be firm but rather soft and supple. The secret, we found, is using eggs yolks—and lots of them—rather than whole eggs. Heavy cream gave the custard a luxurious richness. Sugar, a vanilla bean, and a pinch of salt were the only other additions. Despite instructions in many recipes to use scalded cream, we found that this technique was more likely to result in overcooked custard, so we thought we would leave the ingredients cold. The downside, however, was that we needed heat to extract flavor from the vanilla bean and dissolve the sugar. Our compromise was to heat only half of the cream with the sugar and vanilla bean and add the remaining cream cold, which worked perfectly. For the crust, we used crunchy turbinado sugar, which was easy to spread on the baked and chilled custards. A propane or butane torch worked better than the broiler for caramelizing the sugar, and because the blast of heat inevitably warms the custard beneath the crust, we chilled our crèmes brûlées once more before serving.

Classic Crème Brûlée
SERVES 8

Separate the eggs and whisk the yolks after the cream has finished steeping; if left to sit, the surface of the yolks will dry and form a film. A vanilla bean gives the custard the deepest flavor, but 2 teaspoons of vanilla extract, whisked into the yolks in step 4, can be used instead. The best way to judge doneness is with an instant-read thermometer. For the caramelized sugar crust, we recommend turbinado or Demerara sugar. Regular granulated sugar will work, too, but use only 1 scant teaspoon on each ramekin or 1 teaspoon on each shallow fluted dish. It's important to use 4 to 5-ounce ramekins.

- 4 cups heavy cream, chilled
- ⅔ cup (4⅔ ounces) granulated sugar
  Pinch table salt
- 1 vanilla bean, halved lengthwise (see note)
- 12 large egg yolks (see note)
- 8–12 teaspoons turbinado or Demerara sugar (see note)

1. Adjust an oven rack to the lower-middle position and heat the oven to 300 degrees.

2. Combine 2 cups of the cream, the sugar, and salt in a medium saucepan. With a paring knife, scrape the seeds from the vanilla bean into the pan, submerge the pod in the cream, and bring the mixture to a boil over medium heat, stirring occasionally to ensure that the sugar dissolves. Take the pan off the heat and let steep for 15 minutes.

3. Meanwhile, place a kitchen towel in the bottom of a large baking dish or roasting pan and arrange eight 4- or 5-ounce ramekins (or shallow fluted dishes) on the towel (making sure they do not touch). Bring a kettle or large saucepan of water to a boil.

4. After the vanilla bean has steeped, stir in the remaining 2 cups cream to cool down the mixture. Whisk the yolks in a large bowl until broken up and combined. Whisk about 1 cup of the cream mixture into the yolks until loosened and combined; repeat with 1 cup more cream. Add the remaining cream and whisk until evenly colored and thoroughly combined. Strain the mixture through a fine-mesh strainer into a large measuring cup or pitcher (or clean medium bowl); discard the solids in the strainer. Pour or ladle the mixture into the ramekins, dividing it evenly among them.

5. Carefully place the baking dish with the ramekins on the oven rack; pour the boiling water into the dish, taking care not to splash water into the ramekins, until the water reaches two-thirds of the way up the sides of the ramekins. Bake until the centers of the custards are just barely set and are no longer sloshy and register 170 to 175 degrees on an instant-read thermometer, 30 to 35 minutes (25 to 30 minutes for shallow fluted dishes). Begin checking the temperature about 5 minutes before the recommended time.

6. Transfer the ramekins to a wire rack and cool to room temperature, about 2 hours. Set the ramekins on a rimmed baking sheet, cover tightly with plastic wrap, and refrigerate until cold, at least 4 hours or up to 4 days.

7. Uncover the ramekins; if condensation has collected on the custards, blot the moisture with a paper towel. Sprinkle each with about 1 teaspoon turbinado sugar (1½ teaspoons for shallow fluted dishes); tilt and tap each ramekin for even coverage. Ignite a torch and caramelize the sugar. Refrigerate the ramekins, uncovered, to rechill, 30 to 45 minutes (but no longer); serve.

Espresso Crème Brûlée

Place ¼ cup espresso beans in a zipper-lock bag and crush lightly with a rolling pin or meat pounder until coarsely cracked. Follow the recipe for Classic Crème Brûlée, substituting the cracked espresso beans for the vanilla bean and whisking 1 teaspoon vanilla extract into the yolks in step 4 before adding the cream.

CRÈME CARAMEL

WHY THIS RECIPE WORKS: This simple, classic French dessert is essentially a baked custard, but what makes it really stand out is the caramel sauce. We found that making the caramel is relatively simple; what we needed to address was the custard, which should be silky smooth, modestly sweet, and firm but not rubbery.

We discovered that the proportion of egg whites to yolks in the custard was critical for the texture. Too many whites caused the custard to solidify too much, and too few left it almost runny. We settled on a formula of three whole eggs and two yolks. Light cream and milk for the dairy component provided the proper amount of richness. For contrast with the sweet caramel, we kept the amount of sugar in the custard to a minimum. The caramel comes together quickly; sugar is dissolved in water and cooked until caramel-colored. Baking the ramekins in a water bath was essential for even cooking and ensured a delicate custard; a dish towel on the bottom of the pan stabilized the ramekins and prevented the bottoms of the custards from overcooking. When we unmolded our crème caramel on serving plates, the sweet caramel sauce bathed the rounds of perfectly cooked custard.

Classic Crème Caramel

SERVES 8

You can vary the amount of sugar in the custard to suit your taste. Most tasters preferred the full ⅔ cup, but you can reduce that amount to as little as ½ cup to create a greater contrast between the custard and the caramel. Cook the caramel in a pan with a light-colored interior, since a dark surface makes it difficult to judge the color of the syrup. Caramel can leave a real mess in a pan, but it is easy to clean. Simply boil water in the pan for 5 to 10 minutes to loosen the hardened caramel.

CARAMEL

- ⅓ cup water
- 2 tablespoons light corn syrup
- ¼ teaspoon juice from 1 lemon
- 1 cup (7 ounces) sugar

CUSTARD

- 1½ cups whole milk
- 1½ cups light cream
- 3 large whole eggs, plus 2 large egg yolks
- ⅔ cup (4⅔ ounces) sugar (see note)
- 1½ teaspoons vanilla extract
  Pinch table salt

1. FOR THE CARAMEL: Combine the water, corn syrup, and lemon juice in a 2 to 3-quart saucepan. Pour the sugar into the center of the saucepan, taking care not to let the sugar granules touch the sides of the pan. Gently stir with a clean spatula to moisten the sugar thoroughly. Bring to a boil over medium-high heat and cook, without stirring, until the sugar is completely dissolved and the liquid is clear, 6 to 10 minutes. Reduce the heat to medium-low and continue to cook (swirling occasionally) until the caramel darkens to a honey color, 4 to 5 minutes longer. Remove the pan immediately from the heat and, working quickly but carefully (the caramel is above 300 degrees and will burn if it touches your skin), pour a portion of the caramel into each of eight ungreased 6-ounce ramekins. Allow the caramel to cool and harden, about 15 minutes. (The caramel-coated ramekins can be covered with plastic wrap and refrigerated for up to 2 days; return to room temperature before adding the custard.)

2. FOR THE CUSTARD: Adjust an oven rack to the middle position and heat the oven to 350 degrees. Heat the milk and cream in a medium saucepan over medium heat, stirring occasionally, until steam appears and/or the mixture registers 160 degrees on an instant-read thermometer, 6 to 8 minutes; remove from the heat. Meanwhile, gently whisk the eggs, yolks, and sugar in a large bowl until just combined. Off the heat, gently whisk the warm milk mixture, vanilla, and salt into the eggs until just combined but not at all foamy. Strain the mixture through a fine-mesh strainer into a large measuring cup or pitcher (or clean medium bowl); set aside.

3. Bring a kettle or large saucepan of water to a boil. Meanwhile, place a kitchen towel in the bottom of a large baking dish or roasting pan. Arrange the ramekins on the towel (making sure they do not touch). Divide the reserved custard mixture among the ramekins and carefully place the baking dish on the oven rack. Pour the boiling water into the dish, taking care not to splash water into the ramekins, until the water reaches halfway up the sides of the ramekins; cover the entire pan loosely with aluminum foil. Bake until a paring knife inserted halfway between the center and the edge of the custards comes out clean, 35 to 40 minutes. Transfer the custards to a wire rack and cool to room temperature. (The custards can be covered with plastic wrap and refrigerated for up to 2 days.)

4. To unmold, slide a paring knife around the perimeter of each ramekin, pressing the knife against the side of the dish. Hold a serving plate over the top of the ramekin and invert; set the plate on a work surface and shake the ramekin gently to release the custard. Repeat with the remaining ramekins and serve.

CHOCOLATE POTS DE CRÈME

WHY THIS RECIPE WORKS: Classic pots de crème can be finicky and laborious, requiring a hot water bath that threatens to splash the custards every time the pan is moved. In addition, the individual custards don't always cook at the same rate. We wanted a user-friendly recipe that delivered a decadent dessert with a satiny texture and intense chocolate flavor.

First we moved the dish out of the oven, concentrating on an unconventional approach in which the custard is cooked on the stovetop in a saucepan, then poured into ramekins. Our next challenge was developing the right amount of richness and body, which we did by choosing a combination of heavy cream and half-and-half, along with egg yolks only, for maximum richness. For intense chocolate flavor, we focused on bittersweet chocolate—and a lot of it. Our chocolate content was at least 50 percent more than in any other recipe we had encountered.

Chocolate Pots de Crème
SERVES 8

We prefer pots de crème made with 60 percent bittersweet chocolate (our favorite brands are Ghirardelli Bittersweet Chocolate and Callebaut Intense Dark Chocolate), but 70 percent bittersweet chocolate can also be used. If using a 70 percent bittersweet chocolate, reduce the amount of chocolate to 8 ounces. An instant-read thermometer is the most reliable way to judge when the custard has reached the proper temperature. However, you can also judge the progress of the custard by its thickness. Dip a wooden spoon into the custard and run your finger across the back. The custard is ready when it coats the spoon and a line drawn maintains neat edges. The pots de crème (minus the whipped cream garnish) can be covered tightly with plastic wrap and refrigerated for up to 3 days.

POTS DE CRÈME

- **10** ounces bittersweet chocolate, chopped fine (see note)
- **5** large egg yolks
- **5** tablespoons sugar
- **¼** teaspoon table salt
- **1½** cups heavy cream
- **¾** cup half-and-half
- **1** tablespoon vanilla extract
- **½** teaspoon instant espresso powder mixed with 1 tablespoon water

WHIPPED CREAM AND GARNISH

- **½** cup heavy cream, chilled
- **2** teaspoons sugar
- **½** teaspoon vanilla extract

  Cocoa, for dusting (optional)

  Chocolate shavings, for sprinkling (optional)

1. FOR THE POTS DE CRÈME: Place the chocolate in a medium heatproof bowl; set a fine-mesh strainer over the bowl and set aside.

2. Whisk the yolks, sugar, and salt together in a medium bowl until combined, then whisk in the heavy cream and half-and-half. Transfer the mixture to a medium saucepan. Cook the mixture over medium-low heat, stirring constantly and scraping the bottom of the pot with a wooden spoon, until it is thickened and silky and registers 175 to 180 degrees on an instant-read thermometer, 8 to 12 minutes. (Do not let the custard overcook or simmer.)

3. Immediately pour the custard through the strainer over the chocolate. Let the mixture stand to melt the chocolate, about 5 minutes. Whisk gently until smooth, then whisk in the vanilla and dissolved espresso. Divide the mixture evenly among eight 5-ounce ramekins. Gently tap the ramekins against the counter to remove any air bubbles.

4. Cool the pots de crème to room temperature, then cover with plastic wrap and refrigerate until chilled, at least 4 hours or up to 3 days. Before serving, let the pots de crème stand at room temperature for 20 to 30 minutes.

5. FOR THE WHIPPED CREAM AND GARNISH: Using an electric mixer, whip the cream, sugar, and vanilla on medium-low speed until small bubbles form, about 30 seconds. Increase the speed to medium-high and continue to whip the mixture until it thickens and forms stiff peaks, about 1 minute. Dollop each pot de crème with about 2 tablespoons of the whipped cream and garnish with cocoa and/or chocolate shavings (if using). Serve.

Milk Chocolate Pots de Crème

Milk chocolate behaves differently in this recipe than bittersweet chocolate, and more of it must be used to ensure that the custard sets. And because of the increased amount of chocolate, it's necessary to cut back on the amount of sugar so that the custard is not overly sweet.

Follow the recipe for Chocolate Pots de Crème, substituting 12 ounces milk chocolate for the 10 ounces bittersweet chocolate. Reduce the amount of sugar to 2 tablespoons and proceed as directed.

CHOCOLATE MOUSSE

WHY THIS RECIPE WORKS: Rich, creamy, and dense, chocolate mousse can be delicious but too filling after a few mouthfuls. On the other hand, light and airy mousse usually lacks deep chocolate flavor. We wanted chocolate mousse with both a light, meltingly smooth texture and a substantial chocolate flavor.

To start, we addressed the mousse's dense, heavy texture. Most recipes for chocolate mousse contain butter. Could we do without it? We eliminated the butter and found that our mousse tasted less heavy. We further lightened the mousse's texture by reducing the number of egg whites and yolks. To make up for the lost volume of the eggs, we whipped the cream to soft peaks before adding it to the chocolate.

Next we tackled the mousse's flavor. We maximized the chocolate flavor with a combination of bittersweet chocolate and cocoa powder. And to further deepen the chocolate flavor, we found that a small amount of instant espresso powder, salt, and brandy did the trick.

Dark Chocolate Mousse

SERVES 6 TO 8

When developing this recipe, we used our winning brands of dark chocolate, Ghirardelli Bittersweet Chocolate and Callebaut Intense Dark Chocolate, which each contain about 60 percent cacao. If you want to use a chocolate with a higher percentage of cacao, see our variation, Premium Dark Chocolate Mousse (page 532). If you choose to make the mousse a day in advance, let it sit at room temperature for 10 minutes before serving. Serve with very lightly sweetened whipped cream and chocolate shavings, if desired.

8   ounces bittersweet chocolate, chopped fine (see note)
5   tablespoons water
2   tablespoons cocoa powder, preferably Dutch-processed
1   tablespoon brandy
1   teaspoon instant espresso powder
2   large eggs, separated
1   tablespoon sugar
⅛   teaspoon table salt
1   cup plus 2 tablespoons heavy cream, chilled

1. Melt the chocolate, water, cocoa powder, brandy, and espresso powder in a medium heatproof bowl set over a saucepan filled with 1 inch of barely simmering water, stirring frequently until smooth. Remove from the heat.

2. Whisk the egg yolks, 1½ teaspoons of the sugar, and the salt in a medium bowl until the mixture lightens in color and thickens slightly, about 30 seconds. Pour the melted chocolate into the egg mixture and whisk until combined. Cool until just warmer than room temperature, 3 to 5 minutes.

3. Using an electric mixer, whip the egg whites at medium-low speed until frothy, 1 to 2 minutes. Add the remaining 1½ teaspoons sugar, increase the mixer speed to medium-high, and whip until soft peaks form when the whisk is lifted, about 1 minute. Whisk the last few strokes by hand, making sure to scrape any unbeaten whites from the bottom of the bowl. Using the whisk, stir about one-quarter of the whipped egg whites into the chocolate mixture to lighten it; gently fold in the remaining egg whites with a rubber spatula until a few white streaks remain.

4. In the now-empty bowl, whip the heavy cream at medium speed until it begins to thicken, about 30 seconds. Increase the speed to high and whip until soft peaks form when the whisk is lifted, about 15 seconds more. Using a rubber spatula, fold the whipped cream into the

mousse until no white streaks remain. Spoon the mousse into six to eight individual serving dishes or goblets. Cover with plastic wrap and refrigerate until set and firm, at least 2 hours or up to 24 hours. Serve.

Chocolate-Orange Mousse

For best flavor, the orange zest needs to steep in the heavy cream overnight, so plan accordingly. Garnish each serving of mousse with a thin strip of orange zest, if desired.

Follow the recipe for Dark Chocolate Mousse with the following changes: Start by bringing the heavy cream to a simmer in a medium saucepan. Remove from the heat and transfer to a liquid measuring cup; add 3 strips orange zest (each about 2 inches long and ½ inch wide). Cool until just warm, cover, and refrigerate overnight. Remove and discard the zest; add more heavy cream, if necessary, to equal 1 cup plus 2 tablespoons. Continue with step 1, reducing the amount of water to 4 tablespoons and omitting the brandy. Once the chocolate is melted, stir in 2 tablespoons Grand Marnier and proceed as directed in step 2.

Chocolate-Raspberry Mousse

Chambord is our preferred brand of raspberry-flavored liqueur for this recipe. Serve the mousse with fresh raspberries, if desired.

Follow the recipe for Dark Chocolate Mousse, reducing the amount of water to 4 tablespoons, omitting the brandy, and, once the chocolate is melted at the end of step 1, stirring in 2 tablespoons raspberry-flavored liqueur.

Premium Dark Chocolate Mousse

This recipe is designed to work with a boutique chocolate that contains a higher percentage of cacao than the Ghirardelli or Callebaut chocolate recommended for our Dark Chocolate Mousse.

Follow the recipe for Dark Chocolate Mousse, replacing the bittersweet chocolate (containing about 60 percent cacao) with an equal amount of bittersweet chocolate containing 62 to 70 percent cacao. Increase the amount of water to 7 tablespoons, add 1 egg (for a total of 3 eggs), and increase the amount of sugar to 3 tablespoons (adding the extra 2 tablespoons sugar to the chocolate mixture in step 1).

GRAND MARNIER SOUFFLÉ

WHY THIS RECIPE WORKS: Home cooks are wary of attempting soufflés, which have the reputation of being difficult and temperamental and so are relegated to being eaten only in restaurants. The reality, however, is that they are relatively easy to make. To prove the point, we set out to develop a reliable recipe for a classic Grand Marnier soufflé.

The best soufflés have a crusty top layer above the rim of the dish and a contrasting rich, creamy, almost-fluid center, so we needed to produce height without making the entire dish foamy. For the base we began with a *bouillie*—a paste of flour and milk. Butter kept the egginess at bay, and increasing the usual amount of flour prevented the frothiness we wanted to avoid. An equal number of egg whites and yolks was the right proportion for rise versus richness. Adding a little sugar and some cream of tartar to the whites while we whipped them stabilized the whites so that they would hold their structure. We discovered that the sugar must be added gradually and partway through the beating process, not at the beginning, or the soufflé will not rise properly and will taste too sweet. We also found it important to remove the soufflé from the oven while the center was still loose and moist to prevent overcooking. With a luxuriously creamy interior and crusty top, our foolproof soufflé is an impressive dessert that can easily be made at home.

Grand Marnier Soufflé

SERVES 6 TO 8

Make the soufflé base and immediately begin beating the whites before the base cools too much. Once the whites have reached the proper consistency, they must be used at once. Do not open the oven door during the first 15 minutes of baking time; as the soufflé nears the end of its baking, you may check its progress by opening the oven door slightly. (Be careful here; if your oven runs hot, the top of the soufflé may burn.) A quick dusting of confectioners' sugar is a nice finishing touch, but a soufflé waits for no one, so be ready to serve it immediately.

SOUFFLÉ DISH PREPARATION
- 1 tablespoon unsalted butter, softened
- ¼ cup sugar
- 2 teaspoons sifted cocoa

SOUFFLÉ
- 5 tablespoons unbleached all-purpose flour
- ½ cup (3½ ounces) sugar
- ¼ teaspoon table salt
- 1 cup whole milk
- 2 tablespoons unsalted butter, room temperature
- 5 large eggs, separated
- 1 tablespoon grated zest from 1 orange
- 3 tablespoons Grand Marnier
- ⅛ teaspoon cream of tartar

1. Adjust an oven rack to the upper-middle position and heat the oven to 400 degrees. Grease a 1½-quart porcelain soufflé dish with the butter, making sure to coat all of the interior surfaces. Stir the sugar and cocoa together in a small bowl; pour into the buttered soufflé dish and shake to coat the bottom and sides with a thick, even coating. Tap out the excess and set the dish aside.

2. FOR THE SOUFFLÉ: Whisk the flour, ¼ cup of the sugar, and the salt in a small saucepan. Gradually whisk in the milk, whisking until smooth and no lumps remain. Bring the mixture to a boil over high heat, whisking constantly, until thickened and the mixture pulls away from the sides of the pan, about 3 minutes. Scrape the mixture into a medium bowl; whisk in the butter until combined. Whisk in the yolks until incorporated; stir in the orange zest and Grand Marnier.

3. Using an electric mixer, whip the egg whites, cream of tartar, and 1 teaspoon more sugar at medium-low speed until combined, about 10 seconds. Increase the speed to medium-high and whip until frothy and no longer translucent, about 2 minutes. With the mixer running, sprinkle in half of the remaining sugar; continue whipping until the whites form soft, billowy peaks, about 30 seconds. With the mixer still running, sprinkle in the remaining sugar and whip until just combined, about 10 seconds. The whites should form soft peaks when the beater is lifted but should not appear Styrofoam-like or dry.

4. Using a rubber spatula, immediately stir one-quarter of the beaten whites into the soufflé base to lighten until almost no white streaks remain. Scrape the remaining whites into the base and fold in the whites with a balloon whisk until the mixture is just combined, gently flicking the whisk after scraping up the sides of the bowl to free any of the mixture caught in the whisk. Gently pour the mixture into the prepared dish and run your index finger through the mixture, tracing the circumference about ½ inch from the side of the dish, to help the soufflé rise properly. Bake until the surface of the soufflé is deep brown, the center jiggles slightly when shaken, and the soufflé has risen 2 to 2½ inches above the rim of the dish, 20 to 25 minutes. Serve immediately.

Grand Marnier Soufflé with Grated Chocolate

A rotary cheese grater is the perfect tool for grating the chocolate, though a box grater works well, too.

Finely grate ½ ounce bittersweet chocolate (you should have about ⅓ cup). Follow the recipe for Grand Marnier Soufflé, folding the grated chocolate into the soufflé base along with the beaten whites.

CHILLED LEMON SOUFFLÉ

WHY THIS RECIPE WORKS: "Chilled lemon soufflé" can be interpreted in many ways, from cooled baked pudding cake to lemony, eggy foam. But no matter what the desired outcome, what typically results is a dense, rubbery mass or a mouthful of tart egg white foam. The delicate balance of ingredients is hard for home cooks to get right. We wanted to perfect the unusual marriage of cream and foam, sweet and sour, high lemony notes and rich custard.

A starting point of egg whites, gelatin, sugar, and lemon juice had none of the creaminess we desired, so we cooked a custard base of milk, egg yolks, and sugar, adding a little cornstarch to prevent the yolks from curdling. To our custard we then added lemon juice and gelatin (to stabilize the mixture so it would set up while chilling). Because this was to be a soufflé, not a pudding, we lightened the custard with whipped cream and beaten egg whites. The egg yolks and dairy tended to mute the lemon flavor, so for more citrus punch we included grated lemon zest. Now we had the balance of flavor and texture that we sought: a satisfying but light custard with bright lemon flavor.

Chilled Lemon Soufflé

SERVES 4 TO 6

To make this lemon soufflé "soufflé" over the rim of the dish, use a 1-quart soufflé dish and, following the photo on page 536, make a foil collar for it before beginning the recipe. For those less concerned about appearance, this dessert can be served from any 1½-quart serving bowl. For the best texture, serve the soufflé after 1½ hours of chilling. It may be chilled for up to 6 hours; though the texture will stiffen slightly because of the gelatin, it will taste just as good.

½	cup juice plus 2½ teaspoons grated zest from 3 lemons
1	(¼-ounce) package gelatin
1	cup whole milk
¾	cup (5¼ ounces) sugar
5	large egg whites plus 2 large yolks, room temperature
¼	teaspoon cornstarch
	Pinch cream of tartar
¾	cup heavy cream
	Mint, raspberries, confectioners' sugar, or finely chopped pistachios, for garnish (optional)

1. Place the lemon juice in a small bowl; sprinkle the gelatin over and set aside.

2. Heat the milk and ½ cup of the sugar in a medium saucepan over medium-low heat, stirring occasionally, until steaming and the sugar is dissolved, about 5 minutes. Meanwhile, whisk the yolks, 2 tablespoons more sugar, and the cornstarch in a medium bowl until pale yellow and thickened. Whisking constantly, gradually add the hot milk to the yolks. Return the milk-egg mixture to the saucepan and cook, stirring constantly, over medium-low heat until the foam has dissipated to a thin layer and the mixture thickens to the consistency of heavy cream and registers 185 degrees on an instant-read thermometer, about 4 minutes. Pour the mixture through a fine-mesh strainer into a medium bowl; stir in the lemon juice mixture and zest. Set the bowl with the custard in a large bowl of ice water; stir occasionally to cool.

3. While the custard mixture is chilling, use an electric mixer to whip the egg whites and cream of tartar on medium speed until foamy, about 1 minute. Increase the speed to medium-high; gradually add the remaining 2 tablespoons sugar and continue to whip until glossy and the whites hold soft peaks when the beater is lifted, about 2 minutes longer. Do not overwhip. Remove the bowl containing the custard mixture from the ice water bath; gently whisk in about one-third of the egg whites, then fold in the remaining whites with a large rubber spatula until almost no white streaks remain.

4. In the same mixer bowl, whip the cream on medium-high speed until soft peaks form when the beater is lifted, 2 to 3 minutes. Fold the cream into the custard and egg-white mixture until no white streaks remain.

5. Pour into a 1½ quart soufflé dish or bowl (see note). Chill until set but not stiff, about 1½ hours; remove the foil collar, if using, and serve, garnishing if desired.

Chilled Lemon Soufflé with White Chocolate

The white chocolate in this variation subdues the lemony kick.

Follow the recipe for Chilled Lemon Soufflé, adding 2 ounces chopped white chocolate to the warm custard before adding the lemon juice mixture and the zest. Stir until melted and fully incorporated.

Individual Chilled Lemon Soufflés

Follow the recipe for Chilled Lemon Soufflé, dividing the batter equally among eight ¾-cup ramekins (filled to the rim) or six 6-ounce ramekins with foil collars (see page 536).

MAKE-AHEAD CHOCOLATE SOUFFLÉS

WHY THIS RECIPE WORKS: A chocolate soufflé is a grand dessert to serve dinner guests, but most cooks wouldn't risk the anxiety of all the last-minute preparation when entertaining. It seemed a shame to cross this dessert off the list of possibilities for a dinner party, so we challenged ourselves to find a way to make it in advance.

First we needed to perfect the soufflé recipe itself. We wanted the chocolate to be front and center, so we used a base of egg yolks beaten with sugar, with no flour or milk to mute the chocolate flavor. Instead of the equal number of egg yolks and whites that worked for our Grand Marnier Soufflé (page 533), two extra whites were necessary to lighten and lift our chocolaty base. Now that we had the flavor and texture we wanted, it was time to address the problem of making the soufflés ahead of time. To our amazement, the answer was simple: freezing. Adding a little confectioners' sugar to the egg whites helped stabilize them so they held up better in the freezer, and individual ramekins produced better results than a single large soufflé dish. Now we could make our dinner party dessert ahead of time, confident that we could pull perfectly risen, rich chocolate soufflés from the oven at the end of the meal.

Make-Ahead Chocolate Soufflés

SERVES 6 TO 8

The yolk whipping time in step 3 depends on the type of mixer you use; a standing mixer will take about 3 minutes, and a handheld mixer will take about 8 minutes. If using 6-ounce ramekins, reduce the cooking time to 20 to 22 minutes. See our tip (following recipe) for making a collar for the ramekins.

RAMEKIN PREPARATION
- 2 tablespoons unsalted butter, softened
- 2 tablespoons granulated sugar

SOUFFLÉS
- 8 ounces bittersweet or semisweet chocolate, chopped coarse
- 4 tablespoons (½ stick) unsalted butter, cut into ½-inch pieces
- 1 tablespoon Grand Marnier
- ½ teaspoon vanilla extract
- ⅛ teaspoon table salt
- 6 large egg yolks plus 8 large egg whites
- ⅓ cup (2⅓ ounces) granulated sugar
- ¼ teaspoon cream of tartar
- 2 tablespoons confectioners' sugar

1. FOR THE RAMEKINS: Grease the inside of eight 8-ounce ramekins with the softened butter, then coat the inside of each dish evenly with the granulated sugar.

2. FOR THE SOUFFLÉS: Melt the chocolate and butter together in a medium heatproof bowl set over a saucepan filled with 1 inch of barely simmering water, stirring frequently until smooth. Remove from the heat and stir in the Grand Marnier, vanilla, and salt; set aside.

3. Using an electric mixer, whip the yolks and granulated sugar at medium speed until the mixture triples in volume and is thick and pale yellow, 3 to 8 minutes (see note). Fold the yolk mixture into the chocolate mixture. Thoroughly clean and dry the mixing bowl and the beaters.

4. Using the clean beaters, whip the egg whites at medium-low speed until frothy, 1 to 2 minutes. Add the cream of tartar, increase the mixer speed to medium-high, and whip until soft peaks form when the beaters are lifted, 1 to 2 minutes. Add the confectioners' sugar and continue to whip until stiff peaks form, 2 to 4 minutes (do not overwhip). Whisk the last few strokes by hand, making sure to scrape any unwhipped whites from the bottom of the bowl.

5. Vigorously stir one-quarter of the whipped egg whites into the chocolate mixture. Gently fold the remaining whites into the chocolate mixture until just incorporated. Carefully spoon the mixture into the prepared ramekins almost to the rim, wiping the excess filling from the rims with a wet paper towel. If making a foil collar for the ramekins, see below for instructions. (To serve right away, bake as directed in step 7, reducing the baking time to 12 to 15 minutes.)

6. TO STORE: Cover each ramekin tightly with plastic wrap and then foil and freeze for at least 3 hours or up to 1 month. (Do not thaw before baking.)

7. TO BAKE AND SERVE: Adjust an oven rack to the lower-middle position and heat the oven to 400 degrees. Unwrap the ramekins and spread them out on a baking sheet. Bake the soufflés until fragrant, fully risen, and the exterior is set but the interior is still a bit loose and creamy, about 25 minutes. (To check the interior, use two spoons to pull open the top of one and peek inside.) Serve immediately.

Make-Ahead Mocha Soufflés

Follow the recipe for Make-Ahead Chocolate Soufflés, adding 1 tablespoon instant coffee or espresso powder dissolved in 1 tablespoon hot water to the melted chocolate with the vanilla in step 2.

NOTES FROM THE TEST KITCHEN

MAKING A FOIL COLLAR

Baking our individual chocolate soufflés from the freezer gives them a high rise and a domed top, just as we like them. But placing a collar around the ramekins yields an even higher rise with an iconic, perfectly flat top.

Secure a strip of foil that has been sprayed with vegetable oil spray around each ramekin so that it extends 2 inches above the rim (do this after the ramekins have been filled). You can tape the foil collar to the dish to prevent it from slipping.

SKILLET SOUFFLÉ

WHY THIS RECIPE WORKS: Having taken the mystique out of soufflé making and even developing a recipe for making soufflés ahead of time, we wondered if we could take our expertise one step further. If we could make a soufflé in a skillet, we would guarantee that this great dessert was in the realm of everyday cooking.

We theorized that the heat on the stovetop would activate the batter and ensure an even rise from the egg whites. To determine what to use for the soufflé base, we pitted the bases used in our other soufflés—béchamel and bouillie—against a simpler base of whipped egg yolks. All tasted fine, but the whipped egg yolks were so much less complicated that we decided to start there. A little flour added to the yolks kept the soufflé creamy rather than foamy. We decided that lemon would be the best flavoring, since it would shine through the eggy base well; lemon juice and zest provided bright, natural citrus flavor. We beat the egg whites separately, adding sugar partway through, folded them into the egg-lemon base, and poured the mixture into a buttered ovensafe skillet. After a few minutes on the stovetop the soufflé was just set around the edges and on the bottom (and the crust that eventually formed on the bottom was a bonus our tasters applauded), so we moved the skillet to the oven to finish. A few minutes later our soufflé was puffed, golden on top, and creamy in the middle—a successful transformation from fussy to easy.

Skillet Lemon Soufflé

SERVES 6

Don't open the oven door during the first 7 minutes of baking, but do check the soufflé regularly for doneness during the final few minutes in the oven. Be ready to serve the soufflé immediately after removing it from the oven. Using a 10-inch traditional (not nonstick) skillet is essential to getting the right texture and height in the soufflé.

- 5 large eggs, separated
- ¼ teaspoon cream of tartar
- ⅔ cup (4⅔ ounces) granulated sugar
- ⅛ teaspoon table salt
- ⅓ cup juice plus 1 teaspoon grated zest from 2 lemons
- 2 tablespoons unbleached all-purpose flour
- 1 tablespoon unsalted butter
  Confectioners' sugar, for dusting

1. Adjust an oven rack to the middle position and heat the oven to 375 degrees. Using an electric mixer, whip the egg whites and cream of tartar together on medium-low speed until foamy, about 1 minute. Slowly add ⅓ cup of the granulated sugar and the salt, then increase the mixer speed to medium-high, and continue to whip until stiff peaks form, 3 to 5 minutes. Gently transfer the whites to a clean bowl and set aside.

2. Using an electric mixer (no need to wash the mixing bowl), whip the yolks and the remaining ⅓ cup granulated sugar together on medium-high speed until pale and thick, about 1 minute. Whip in the lemon juice, zest, and flour until incorporated, about 30 seconds.

3. Fold one-quarter of the whipped egg whites into the yolk mixture until almost no white streaks remain. Gently fold in the remaining egg whites until just incorporated.

4. Melt the butter in a 10-inch ovensafe skillet over medium-low heat. Swirl the pan to coat it evenly with the melted butter, then gently scrape the soufflé batter into the skillet and cook until the edges begin to set and bubble slightly, about 2 minutes.

5. Transfer the skillet to the oven and bake the soufflé until puffed, the center jiggles slightly when shaken, and the surface is golden, 7 to 11 minutes. Using a potholder (the skillet handle will be hot), remove the skillet from the oven. Dust the soufflé with the confectioners' sugar and serve immediately.

Skillet Chocolate-Orange Soufflé

Grating the chocolate fine is key here; we find it easiest to use either a rasp grater or the fine holes of a box grater.

Follow the recipe for Skillet Lemon Soufflé, substituting 1 tablespoon grated zest from 1 orange for the lemon zest and ⅓ cup orange juice for the lemon juice. Gently fold 1 ounce finely grated bittersweet chocolate (about ½ cup) into the soufflé batter after incorporating all of the whites in step 3.

CHAPTER 24

CLASSIC FRUIT DESSERTS

Strawberry
Shortcakes 540

Sour Cherry Cobbler 541

Fresh Sour Cherry
Cobbler 542

Blueberry Cobbler 542

Peach Crisp 544

Peach Crisp for a
Crowd 544

Simple Raspberry
Gratin 544

Individual Fresh
Berry Gratins with
Zabaglione 545

Individual Fresh Berry
Gratins with Lemon
Zabaglione 546

Skillet Apple Brown
Betty 546

Easy Apple Strudel 548
    Tangy Whipped Cream

Skillet Apple Pie 549

Bananas Foster 550

Crêpes Suzette 551

Individual Summer
Berry Puddings 552

Large Summer Berry
Pudding 553

Caramelized Pears with
Blue Cheese and
Black Pepper–Caramel
Sauce 554

Strawberries with
Balsamic Vinegar 554

Rhubarb Fool 555

Strawberry-Rhubarb
Fool 555

STRAWBERRY SHORTCAKES

WHY THIS RECIPE WORKS: While some cooks like to spoon strawberries over pound cake, sponge cake, and even angel food cake, our idea of strawberry shortcake definitely involves a biscuit. We wanted a juicy strawberry filling and mounds of freshly whipped cream sandwiched in between a lightly sweetened, tender biscuit.

While eggs are not traditional, we found that one whole egg and one egg yolk gave our biscuits a light, tender texture. And we used just enough dairy (half-and-half or milk) to bind the dough together. A modest amount of sugar yielded a lightly sweetened biscuit. For the strawberries, we wanted to avoid both a mushy puree and dry chunks of fruit. We found our solution in a compromise—mashing a portion of the berries and slicing the rest for a chunky, juicy mixture that didn't slide off the biscuit. And lightly sweetened whipped cream, flavored with vanilla, provided a cool, creamy contrast to the berries and biscuits.

Strawberry Shortcakes

SERVES 6

Start the recipe by preparing the fruit, then set the fruit aside while preparing the biscuits to allow the juices to become syrupy.

FRUIT
- **8 cups (40 ounces) strawberries, hulled**
- **6 tablespoons sugar**

SHORTCAKE
- **2 cups (10 ounces) unbleached all-purpose flour, plus extra for the work surface and biscuit cutter**
- **5 tablespoons sugar**
- **1 tablespoon baking powder**
- **½ teaspoon table salt**
- **8 tablespoons (1 stick) unsalted butter, cut into ½-inch pieces and chilled**
- **½ cup plus 1 tablespoon half-and-half or milk**
- **1 large egg, lightly beaten**
- **1 large egg white, lightly beaten**

WHIPPED CREAM
- **1 cup heavy cream, chilled**
- **1 tablespoon sugar**
- **1 teaspoon vanilla extract**

1. FOR THE FRUIT: Crush 3 cups of the strawberries in a large bowl with a potato masher. Slice the remaining 5 cups of berries and stir them into the crushed berries along with the sugar. Set aside until the sugar has dissolved and the berries are juicy, at least 30 minutes and up to 2 hours.

2. FOR THE SHORTCAKE: Adjust an oven rack to the lower-middle position and heat the oven to 425 degrees. Line a large baking sheet with parchment paper. Pulse the flour, 3 tablespoons of the sugar, the baking powder, and salt in a food processor until combined. Sprinkle the butter pieces over the top and pulse until the mixture resembles coarse meal, about 15 pulses. Transfer the mixture to a large bowl.

3. Whisk the half-and-half and lightly beaten whole egg together in a small bowl, then stir into the flour mixture with a rubber spatula until large clumps form. Turn the dough onto a lightly floured work surface and knead lightly until it comes together.

4. Pat the dough into a 9 by 6-inch rectangle, about ¾ inch thick. Do not overwork the dough. Using a floured 2¾-inch biscuit cutter, cut out six dough rounds. Arrange the shortcakes on the prepared baking sheet, spaced about 1½ inches apart. Brush the tops with the lightly beaten egg white and sprinkle evenly with the remaining 2 tablespoons sugar. (The unbaked shortcakes can be covered with plastic wrap and refrigerated for up to 2 hours.)

5. Bake until the shortcakes are golden brown, 12 to 14 minutes, rotating the sheet halfway through the baking time. Transfer the sheet to a wire rack and cool the shortcakes until warm, about 10 minutes.

6. FOR THE WHIPPED CREAM: In a medium bowl, whip the cream, sugar, and vanilla with an electric mixer on medium-low speed until frothy, about 1 minute. Increase the speed to high and continue to whip until the cream forms soft peaks, 1 to 3 minutes.

7. TO ASSEMBLE: When the shortcakes have cooled slightly, split them in half horizontally. Place each short-cake bottom on an individual plate, spoon a portion of the berries over each bottom, dollop with whipped cream, and cap with the shortcake tops. Serve immediately.

CHERRY COBBLER

WHY THIS RECIPE WORKS: Most cherry cobblers are no more than canned pie filling topped with dry, heavy biscuits. We wanted a filling that highlighted the unique, sweet-tart flavor of sour cherries and, on top, we wanted a tender, feather-light biscuit crust.

Because fresh sour cherries are so hard to find most of the year, we picked jarred Morello cherries—easy to find and available year-round. Embellishing the cherries with cherry juice, cinnamon, and vanilla was a step in the right direction but the filling still tasted a bit flat, so we switched out some of the juice for red wine and replaced the vanilla with almond extract. The resulting sauce was better, but a little thin. A small amount of cornstarch thickened the filling nicely. As for the biscuits, we favored

buttermilk biscuits, which have a light and fluffy texture. To ensure nicely browned biscuits that didn't become soggy over the filling, we parbaked them on their own ahead of time, then slid the biscuits over the warm cherry filling and put it in the oven to finish cooking.

Sour Cherry Cobbler

SERVES 12

Use the smaller amount of sugar in the filling if you prefer your fruit desserts on the tart side and the larger amount if you like them sweet. Serve with vanilla ice cream or lightly sweetened whipped cream.

BISCUIT TOPPING

- 2 cups (10 ounces) unbleached all-purpose flour
- ½ cup (3½ ounces) sugar
- ½ teaspoon baking powder
- ½ teaspoon baking soda
- ½ teaspoon table salt
- 6 tablespoons (¾ stick) unsalted butter, cut into ½-inch pieces and chilled
- 1 cup buttermilk

FILLING

- 8 cups jarred Morello cherries from 4 (24-ounce) jars, drained, 2 cups juice reserved
- ¾–1 cup (5¼ to 7 ounces) sugar (see note)
- 3 tablespoons plus 1 teaspoon cornstarch
  Pinch table salt
- 1 cup dry red wine
- 1 (3-inch) cinnamon stick
- ¼ teaspoon almond extract

1. Adjust an oven rack to the middle position and heat the oven to 425 degrees. Line a large baking sheet with parchment paper.

2. FOR THE BISCUIT TOPPING: Pulse the flour, 6 table-spoons of the sugar, the baking powder, baking soda, and salt in a food processor until combined. Sprinkle the butter pieces over the top and pulse until the mixture resembles coarse meal, about 15 pulses. Transfer the mixture to a large bowl; add the buttermilk and stir with rubber spat-ula until combined. Using a greased ¼-cup measure ice cream scoop, scoop 12 biscuits onto the prepared baking sheet, spacing them 1½ inches apart. Sprinkle the biscuits evenly with the remaining 2 tablespoons sugar and bake until lightly browned, about 15 minutes, rotating the sheet halfway through baking. (Do not turn the oven off.)

3. FOR THE FILLING: Meanwhile, arrange the drained cherries in an even layer in a 13 by 9-inch glass baking dish. Combine the sugar, cornstarch, and salt in a medium saucepan. Stir in the reserved cherry juice and wine and add the cinnamon stick; cook over medium-high heat, stirring frequently, until the mixture simmers and thickens, about 5 minutes. Discard the cinnamon stick, stir in the almond extract, and pour the hot liquid over the cherries in the baking dish.

4. TO BAKE: Arrange the hot biscuits in three rows of four biscuits over the warm filling. Bake the cobbler until the filling is bubbling and the biscuits are deep golden brown, about 10 minutes. Transfer the baking dish to a wire rack and cool 10 minutes; serve.

Fresh Sour Cherry Cobbler

Morello or Montmorency cherries can be used in this cobbler made with fresh sour cherries. Do not use sweet Bing cherries. If the cherries do not release enough juice after 30 minutes in step 1, add cranberry juice to make up the difference.

1¼	cups (8¾ ounces) sugar
3	tablespoons plus 1 teaspoon cornstarch
	Pinch table salt
8	cups (4 pounds) fresh sour cherries, pitted, juice reserved (see note)
1	cup dry red wine
	Cranberry juice, as needed
1	recipe Biscuit Topping (see page 541)
1	(3-inch) cinnamon stick
¼	teaspoon almond extract

1. Whisk the sugar, cornstarch, and salt together in a large bowl; add the cherries and toss well to combine. Pour the wine over the cherries; let stand 30 minutes. Drain the cherries in a colander set over a medium bowl. Combine the drained and reserved juices (from pitting the cherries); you should have 3 cups (if not, add cranberry juice to make this amount).

2. Meanwhile, prepare and bake the biscuit topping.

3. Arrange the drained cherries in an even layer in a 13 by 9-inch glass baking dish. Bring the juices, wine, and cinnamon stick to a simmer in a medium saucepan over medium-high heat, stirring frequently, until the mixture thickens, about 5 minutes. Discard the cinnamon stick, stir in the almond extract, and pour the hot juices over the cherries in the baking dish.

4. Arrange the hot biscuits in three rows of four biscuits over the warm filling. Bake the cobbler until the filling is bubbling and the biscuits are deep golden brown, about 10 minutes. Transfer the baking dish to a wire rack and cool 10 minutes; serve.

BLUEBERRY COBBLER

WHY THIS RECIPE WORKS: Too often, blueberry cobbler means a filling that is too sweet, overspiced, and unappealingly thick. We wanted a not-too-thin, not-too-thick filling where the blueberry flavor would be front and center. And over the fruit, we wanted a light, tender biscuit topping that could hold its own against the fruit filling, with an ingredient list simple enough to allow the blueberries to play a starring role.

We prepared a not-too-sweet filling using 6 cups of fresh berries and less than a cup of sugar. Cornstarch worked well as a thickener—it thickened the fruit's juice without leaving a starchy texture behind. A little lemon and cinnamon were all that were needed to enhance the filling without masking the blueberry flavor. For the topping, ease of preparation was our guiding principle, so we made light, rustic drop biscuits enriched with a little cornmeal. Adding the biscuit topping to the cobbler after the filling had baked on its own allowed the biscuits to brown evenly and cook through. A sprinkling of cinnamon sugar on the dropped biscuit dough added a pleasing sweet crunch.

Blueberry Cobbler

SERVES 6 TO 8

While the blueberries are baking, prepare the ingredients for the topping, but do not stir the wet ingredients into the dry ingredients until just before the berries come out of the oven. A standard or deep-dish 9-inch pie plate works well; an 8-inch square baking dish can also be used. Vanilla ice cream or lightly sweetened whipped cream is the perfect accompaniment. To reheat leftovers, put the cobbler in a 350-degree oven for 10 to 15 minutes, until heated through.

FILLING

½ cup (3½ ounces) sugar
1 tablespoon cornstarch
  Pinch ground cinnamon
  Pinch table salt
6 cups (30 ounces) fresh blueberries, rinsed and
  picked over
1½ teaspoons grated zest plus 1 tablespoon juice from
  1 lemon

BISCUIT TOPPING

1 cup (5 ounces) unbleached all-purpose flour
¼ cup (1¾ ounces) plus 2 teaspoons sugar
2 tablespoons stone-ground cornmeal
2 teaspoons baking powder
¼ teaspoon baking soda
¼ teaspoon table salt
4 tablespoons (½ stick) unsalted butter, melted
⅓ cup buttermilk
½ teaspoon vanilla extract
⅛ teaspoon ground cinnamon

1. Adjust an oven rack to the lower-middle position and heat the oven to 375 degrees.

2. FOR THE FILLING: Whisk the sugar, cornstarch, cinnamon, and salt together in a large bowl. Add the berries and mix gently with a rubber spatula until evenly coated; add the lemon zest and juice and mix to combine.

Transfer the berry mixture to a 9-inch glass pie plate, place the pie plate on a rimmed baking sheet, and bake until the filling is hot and bubbling around the edges, about 25 minutes.

3. FOR THE BISCUIT TOPPING: Meanwhile, whisk the flour, ¼ cup of the sugar, the cornmeal, baking powder, baking soda, and salt together in a large bowl. Whisk the melted butter, buttermilk, and vanilla together in a small bowl. Mix the remaining 2 teaspoons sugar with the cinnamon in a second small bowl and set aside. One minute before the berries come out of the oven, add the wet ingredients to the dry ingredients; stir with a rubber spatula until just combined and no dry pockets remain.

4. TO ASSEMBLE AND BAKE: Remove the berries from the oven; increase the oven temperature to 425 degrees. Divide the biscuit dough into eight equal pieces and place them on the hot berry filling, spacing them at least ½ inch apart (they should not touch). Sprinkle each mound of dough evenly with the cinnamon sugar. Bake until the filling is bubbling and the biscuits are golden brown on top and cooked through, 15 to 18 minutes. Transfer the cobbler to a wire rack; cool 20 minutes and serve.

PEACH CRISP

WHY THIS RECIPE WORKS: There is seldom anything crisp about most crisps. This simple fruit dessert usually comes out of the oven with a soggy, mushy topping—quite a letdown from the ideal of a warm, fruity filling covered in a crunchy, sweet topping. We set out to make peach crisp that wouldn't disappoint, one with the perfect balance of nicely thickened filling and a lightly sweetened, crisp topping.

We tried everything from Grape-Nuts to cookie crumbs and found the ideal topping mixture to be chopped nuts, butter, and flour. Cutting the butter into the flour is crucial for creating a crisp topping, and we found that a food processor was ideally suited to producing a mixture that resembles crumbly wet sand. Another issue to tackle was sugar: what kind and how much. White sugar alone was too bland, while brown sugar on its own was too strong tasting. A 50-50 mix of the two proved to be the perfect combination. We decided not to use too much sugar in the fruit filling so there would be some contrast with the topping. And we nixed the idea of a thickener—the filling without one had a nicely bright fresh fruit flavor and the topping remained crisp whether we used one or not.

Peach Crisp

SERVES 4 TO 6

Lightly sweetened whipped cream or vanilla ice cream is the perfect accompaniment, especially if serving the crisp warm. A standard or deep-dish 9-inch pie plate works well; an 8-inch square baking dish can also be used.

TOPPING

- 6 tablespoons unbleached all-purpose flour
- ¼ cup packed (1¾ ounces) light brown sugar
- ¼ cup (1¾ ounces) granulated sugar
- ¼ teaspoon ground cinnamon
- ¼ teaspoon ground nutmeg
- ¼ teaspoon table salt
- 5 tablespoons unsalted butter, cut into ½-inch pieces and chilled
- ¾ cup (about 4 ounces) coarsely chopped pecans, walnuts, or almonds

FILLING

- 3 pounds peaches (6 to 8 medium), peeled, pitted, and cut into ½-inch slices
- ¼ cup (1¾ ounces) granulated sugar
- ½ teaspoon grated zest plus 1½ tablespoons juice from 1 lemon

1. FOR THE TOPPING: Pulse the flour, sugars, cinnamon, nutmeg, and salt in a food processor until combined. Sprinkle the butter pieces over the top and pulse until the mixture resembles coarse meal, about 15 pulses. Add the nuts and pulse until the mixture clumps together and resembles wet sand, about 5 pulses; do not overmix. Transfer the mixture to a bowl and refrigerate while preparing the filling, at least 15 minutes.

2. FOR THE FILLING: Adjust an oven rack to the lower-middle position and heat the oven to 375 degrees.

Combine the peaches, sugar, zest, and juice in a large bowl and toss gently to combine. Transfer the peach mixture to a 9-inch glass pie plate, place the pie plate on a rimmed baking sheet, and sprinkle the chilled topping evenly over the top.

3. Bake for 40 minutes. Increase the oven temperature to 400 degrees and continue to bake until the filling is bubbling and the topping is deep golden brown, about 5 minutes longer. Serve warm.

Peach Crisp for a Crowd

SERVES 10

Follow the recipe for Peach Crisp, doubling all the ingredients and using a 13 by 9-inch baking dish. Increase the baking time to 55 minutes and bake at 375 degrees without increasing the oven temperature.

RASPBERRY GRATIN

WHY THIS RECIPE WORKS: Quicker than a crisp and dressier than a shortcake, a gratin is a layer of fresh fruit piled into a shallow baking dish, dressed up with bread crumbs, and run under a broiler. The topping browns and the fruit is warmed just enough to release a bit of juice. We wanted to find the quickest, easiest route to this pleasing dessert.

We started with perfect raspberries: ripe, dry, unbruised, and clean. Tossing the sweet-tart berries with just a bit of sugar and kirsch (a clear cherry brandy; vanilla extract can be substituted) provided enough additional flavor and sweetness. For the topping, we combined soft white bread, brown sugar, cinnamon, and butter in the food processor and topped the berries with the fluffy crumbs. Instead of broiling the gratin, which can produce a crust that's burnt in spots, we simply baked it. We found that a moderately hot oven gave the berries more time to soften and browned the crust more evenly.

Simple Raspberry Gratin

SERVES 4 TO 6

If you prefer, you can substitute blueberries, blackberries, or strawberries for part or all of the raspberries. If using strawberries, hull them and slice them in half lengthwise if small or into quarters if large. Later in the summer season, ripe, peeled peaches or nectarines, sliced, can be used in combination with the blueberries or raspberries.

- 4 cups (20 ounces) fresh or frozen (not thawed) raspberries (see note)
- 1 tablespoon granulated sugar
- 1 tablespoon kirsch or vanilla extract (optional)
  Pinch table salt
- 3 slices high-quality white sandwich bread, torn into quarters
- ¼ cup packed (1¾ ounces) light or dark brown sugar
- 2 tablespoons unsalted butter, softened
  Pinch ground cinnamon

1. Adjust an oven rack to the lower-middle position and heat the oven to 400 degrees. Gently toss the raspberries, granulated sugar, kirsch (if using), and salt in a medium bowl. Transfer the mixture to a 9-inch glass pie plate.

2. Pulse the bread, brown sugar, butter, and cinnamon in a food processor until the mixture resembles coarse crumbs, about 10 pulses. Sprinkle the crumbs evenly over the fruit and bake until the crumbs are deep golden brown, 15 to 20 minutes. Transfer to a wire rack; cool 5 minutes and serve.

FRESH BERRY GRATIN

WHY THIS RECIPE WORKS: Gratins can be very humble, as in our Simple Raspberry Gratin (page 544), where the topping is little more than sweetened bread crumbs. Or they can be a bit more sophisticated, as when they are topped with the foamy Italian custard called *zabaglione*. Zabaglione is made with just three simple ingredients—egg yolks, sugar, and alcohol—but it requires constant watching so that the mixture doesn't overcook. It also needs to be whisked just long enough to transform the egg yolks to the ideal thick, creamy texture. We were after a foolproof method for this topping for a gratin that could serve as an elegant finale to a special summer meal.

We chose to make individual gratins—perfect for entertaining—and settled on raspberries, strawberries, blueberries, and blackberries. We tossed the berries with sugar and a pinch of salt to draw out their juices and let the mixture sit while we worked on the custard. To prevent scrambled eggs, we kept the heat low; for the right texture, we didn't stop whisking when soft peaks formed—instead we waited until the custard became slightly thicker. As for flavor, tasters thought that zabaglione made with the traditional Marsala wine was a bit sweet and cloying on top of the berries. We switched to a crisp, dry Sauvignon Blanc and found that its clean flavor allowed the berries to shine. However, with that

change, our zabaglione was almost runny. After trying to thicken it with cornstarch and gelatin (with disappointing results), we turned to whipped cream. After carefully folding a few tablespoons of whipped cream into the cooked and slightly cooled zabaglione base, we spooned it over the berries. Finally, we sprinkled the custard with a mixture of brown and white sugar before broiling for a crackly, caramelized crust.

Individual Fresh Berry Gratins with Zabaglione
SERVES 4

When making the zabaglione, make sure to cook the egg mixture in a glass bowl over water that is barely simmering; glass conducts heat more evenly and gently than metal. If the heat is too high, the yolks around the edges of the bowl will start to scramble. Constant whisking is required. Do not use frozen berries for this recipe. You will need four shallow 6-inch gratin dishes, but a broiler-safe pie plate or gratin dish can be used instead. To prevent scorching, pay close attention to the gratins when broiling.

BERRY MIXTURE
- 3 cups (about 15 ounces) mixed berries (raspberries, blueberries, blackberries, and strawberries; strawberries hulled and halved lengthwise if small, quartered if large), room temperature (see note)
- 2 teaspoons granulated sugar
  Pinch table salt

ZABAGLIONE
- **3 large egg yolks**
- **3 tablespoons granulated sugar**
- **3 tablespoons dry white wine, such as Sauvignon Blanc**
- **2 teaspoons light brown sugar**
- **3 tablespoons heavy cream, chilled**

1. FOR THE BERRY MIXTURE: Toss the berries, sugar, and salt together in a medium bowl. Divide the berry mixture evenly among four shallow 6-ounce gratin dishes set on a rimmed baking sheet; set aside.

2. FOR THE ZABAGLIONE: Whisk the egg yolks, 2 tablespoons plus 1 teaspoon of the granulated sugar, and the wine together in a medium glass bowl until the sugar is dissolved, about 1 minute. Set the bowl over a saucepan of barely simmering water and cook, whisking constantly, until the mixture is frothy. Continue to cook, whisking constantly, until the mixture is slightly thickened, creamy, and glossy, 5 to 10 minutes (the mixture will form loose mounds when dripped from the whisk). Remove the bowl from the saucepan and whisk constantly for 30 seconds to cool slightly. Transfer the bowl to the refrigerator and chill until the egg mixture is completely cool, about 10 minutes.

3. Meanwhile, adjust an oven rack 6 inches from the broiler element and heat the broiler. Combine the brown sugar and the remaining 2 teaspoons granulated sugar in a small bowl.

4. Whisk the heavy cream in a large bowl until it holds soft peaks, 30 to 90 seconds. Using a rubber spatula, gently fold the whipped cream into the cooled egg mixture. Spoon the zabaglione over the berries and sprinkle the sugar mixture evenly on top; let stand at room temperature for 10 minutes, until the sugar dissolves.

5. Broil the gratins until the sugar is bubbly and caramelized, 1 to 4 minutes. Serve immediately.

Individual Fresh Berry Gratins with Lemon Zabaglione

Follow the recipe for Individual Fresh Berry Gratins with Zabaglione, replacing 1 tablespoon of the wine with 1 tablespoon juice from 1 lemon and adding 1 teaspoon grated zest from 1 lemon to the yolk mixture in step 2.

APPLE BROWN BETTY

WHY THIS RECIPE WORKS: In its most basic form, apple brown betty contains only four ingredients: apples, bread crumbs, sugar, and butter. Sadly, this simple combination inevitably results in a soggy, mushy mess of a dessert—not the classic Colonial dish of tender, lightly spiced chunks of apple topped with buttery toasted bread crumbs. We decided it was time to give "Betty" a serious makeover.

For a lightly sweetened, crisp crumb topping, we toasted white sandwich bread crumbs with butter and a bit of sugar. The sweet/tart combination of Granny Smith and Golden Delicious apples made a not-too-sweet apple filling. Instead of baking the dessert, we prepared it in a skillet on the stovetop and cooked the apples in two batches to ensure even cooking. After preparing the bread crumbs, we removed them from the pan and caramelized the apples. Adding brown sugar to the apples along with ginger and cinnamon gave the dessert a deepened, lightly spiced flavor. The addition of apple cider to the fruit brought moisture and a further dimension of apple flavor; a bit of lemon juice brightened the filling. For a thicker filling, we added a portion of the toasted bread crumbs to the apples and reserved the remainder for sprinkling over the top.

Skillet Apple Brown Betty
SERVES 6 TO 8

If your apples are especially tart, omit the lemon juice. If, on the other hand, your apples are exceptionally sweet, use the full amount. Leftovers can be refrigerated in an airtight container; topped with vanilla yogurt, they make an excellent breakfast.

BREAD CRUMBS

- **4** slices high-quality white sandwich bread, torn into quarters
- **3** tablespoons unsalted butter, cut into 4 pieces
- **2** tablespoons packed light brown sugar

FILLING

- **¼** cup packed (1¾ ounces) light brown sugar
- **¼** teaspoon ground ginger
- **¼** teaspoon ground cinnamon
  Pinch table salt
- **3** tablespoons unsalted butter
- **1½** pounds Granny Smith apples (about 3 large), peeled, cored, and cut into ½-inch cubes (about 4 cups)
- **1½** pounds Golden Delicious apples (about 3 large), peeled, cored, and cut into ½-inch cubes (about 4 cups)
- **1¼** cups apple cider
- **1–3** teaspoons juice from 1 lemon (see note)

1. FOR THE BREAD CRUMBS: Pulse the bread, butter, and sugar in a food processor until coarsely ground, 5 to 7 pulses. Transfer the bread crumbs to a 12-inch skillet and toast over medium heat, stirring constantly, until they are deep golden brown, 8 to 10 minutes. Transfer to a paper towel–lined plate; wipe out the skillet.

2. FOR THE FILLING: Combine the sugar, spices, and salt in a small bowl. Melt 1½ tablespoons of the butter in the now-empty skillet over high heat. Stir in the Granny Smith apples and half of the sugar mixture. Distribute the apples in an even layer and cook, stirring two or three times, until medium brown, about 5 minutes; transfer to a medium bowl. Repeat with the remaining butter, the Golden Delicious apples, and the remaining sugar mixture, returning the first batch of apples to the skillet when the second batch is done.

3. Add the apple cider to the skillet and scrape the bottom and sides of the pan with a wooden spoon to loosen the browned bits; cook until the apples are tender but not mushy and the liquid has reduced and is just beginning to thicken, 2 to 4 minutes.

4. Remove the skillet from the heat; stir in the lemon juice (if using) and ⅓ cup of the toasted bread crumbs. Using a wooden spoon, lightly flatten the apples into an even layer in the skillet and evenly sprinkle with the remaining toasted bread crumbs. Spoon the warm betty into individual bowls and serve with vanilla ice cream, if desired.

EASY APPLE STRUDEL

WHY THIS RECIPE WORKS: Apple strudel, lightly spiced apples in a thin, flaky pastry, is meant to be savored by the forkful, preferably with a strong cup of coffee. We wanted all the flavor and charm of this apple dessert, but we didn't want to bother with the hours of preparation the paper-thin dough requires. So, chucking the notion of homemade strudel dough, we started with a simpler option—store-bought phyllo dough—and set out to simplify this classic dessert while keeping the rich apple filling and as much of the crisp, flaky texture as possible.

Replacing homemade strudel dough with purchased phyllo dough made for a crust with crisp, flaky layers in a fraction of the time. We brushed the phyllo sheets with melted butter to keep them crisp and flaky. A combination of Golden Delicious and McIntosh apples, sliced thin, gave us a filling with layered apple flavor and just the right texture. A small amount of bread crumbs, browned in butter, thickened the filling without weighing it down. Golden raisins, plumped on the stove with Calvados (apple brandy), added a sophisticated, fruity dimension to the apple filling; for brightness and to lighten the filling, we added in some fresh lemon juice. We found that the phyllo on most strudels, including this one, curled and shattered as it cooled; sprinkling sugar between the layers of phyllo "glued" them together in the oven and prevented this problem.

Easy Apple Strudel

SERVES 6

The best ways to thaw the phyllo are in the refrigerator overnight or at room temperature for 3 to 4 hours; it doesn't defrost well in the microwave. Make sure that the phyllo sheets you use for the strudel are not badly torn. If they have small cuts or tears in the same location (sometimes an entire package sustains cuts in the same spot), when forming the strudel, flip alternating

NOTES FROM THE TEST KITCHEN

ASSEMBLING STRUDEL

1. Brush 1 sheet of phyllo with melted butter and sprinkle with sugar. Place another sheet of phyllo next to it, overlapping the sheets. Brush with more butter and sprinkle with sugar. Repeat this process four times.

2. Mound the filling along the bottom edge of the phyllo, leaving a 2½-inch border on the bottom and a 2-inch border on the sides.

3. Fold the dough on the sides over the apples. Fold the dough on the bottom over the apples and continue to roll the dough around the filling to form the strudel.

4. After the strudel has been assembled and rolled, gently lay it seam side down on the prepared baking sheet.

layers so that the cuts will not line up, thereby creating a weak spot that can cause the strudel to burst during baking. To make the fresh bread crumbs, process one slice of high-quality white sandwich bread in a food processor until fine, 20 to 30 seconds. Serve the strudel warm with Tangy Whipped Cream (recipe follows) or regular whipped cream; if you choose to make the tangy whipped cream, make it before starting the strudel because it must stand at room temperature for about 1½ hours before serving.

½   cup golden raisins
2   tablespoons Calvados or apple cider
8   tablespoons (1 stick) unsalted butter, melted and cooled
¼   cup fresh bread crumbs (see note)
1   pound Golden Delicious apples (about 2 large), peeled, cored, and sliced ¼ inch thick
1   medium McIntosh apple, peeled, cored, and sliced ¼ inch thick
¼   cup (1¾ ounces) plus 2 tablespoons granulated sugar
⅓   cup finely chopped walnuts (optional), toasted
¼   teaspoon ground cinnamon
⅛   teaspoon table salt
1   teaspoon juice from 1 lemon
10   (14 by 9-inch) sheets phyllo, thawed (see note)
1½   teaspoons confectioners' sugar

1. Adjust an oven rack to the lower-middle position and heat the oven to 475 degrees. Line a large baking sheet with parchment paper. Bring the raisins and Calvados to a simmer in a small saucepan over medium heat. Cover, remove from the heat, and let stand until needed.

2. Combine 1 tablespoon of the butter and the bread crumbs in a small skillet and cook over medium heat, stirring frequently, until golden brown, about 2 minutes. Transfer the bread crumbs to a small bowl and set aside.

3. Drain off and discard any remaining liquid from the raisins. Toss the apples, raisins, bread crumbs, ¼ cup of the granulated sugar, the walnuts (if using), cinnamon, salt, and lemon juice in a large bowl to combine.

4. Melt the remaining 7 tablespoons butter. Place a large sheet of parchment paper horizontally on a work surface. Following the photos, lay 1 sheet of phyllo on the left side of the sheet of parchment paper, then brush with melted butter and sprinkle with ½ teaspoon more of the granulated sugar. Place another sheet of phyllo on the right side of the parchment, overlapping the sheets by 1 inch, then brush with more butter and sprinkle with sugar. Repeat this process with the remaining 8 sheets of phyllo, more butter, and more sugar. Mound the filling along the bottom edge of the phyllo, leaving a 2½-inch border on the bottom and a 2-inch border on the sides. Fold the dough on the sides over the apples. Fold the dough on the bottom over the apples and continue to roll the dough around the filling to form the strudel.

5. Place the strudel, seam side down, on the prepared baking sheet; brush with the remaining butter and sprinkle with the remaining 1 teaspoon sugar. Cut four 1-inch crosswise vents into the top of the strudel and bake until golden brown, 15 minutes. Transfer the baking sheet to a wire rack and cool until warm, about 40 minutes.

6. Dust the strudel with the confectioners' sugar before serving; slice with a serrated knife and serve warm or at room temperature.

Tangy Whipped Cream

MAKES ABOUT 2 CUPS

Adding sour cream to whipped cream mimics the pleasantly tart flavor of the rich French-style whipped cream, crème fraîche.

- 1 **cup heavy cream**
- ½ **cup sour cream**
- 1 **tablespoon sugar**
- 1 **teaspoon vanilla extract**

Whip the heavy cream and sour cream in a large bowl with an electric mixer on medium-low speed until frothy, about 1 minute. Add the sugar and vanilla. Increase the mixer speed to high and continue to whip until the cream forms soft peaks, 1 to 3 minutes.

APPLE PANDOWDY

WHY THIS RECIPE WORKS: Apple pandowdy harks back to Colonial-era New England—the dessert takes a more rustic approach to apple pie in that it features just one pastry crust, placed on top of a lightly sweetened apple filling. During or after baking, the pastry is broken and pushed into the filling—a technique known as "dowdying." We found the idea of an easier approach to apple pie very appealing—no fussy crimping and only one piece of pastry dough to roll out, so we set out to make our own version—one with a flaky crust and tender, juicy apples.

For a juicy apple filling with bright fruit flavor, we added cider to the apples and sweetened the filling with maple syrup—the tart intensity of the cider deepened the apple flavor and maple syrup's rich character added the right degree of sweetness. Both additions also made for a pleasantly saucy filling. Parcooking the apples in a skillet until caramelized before adding the other ingredients helped to deepen their flavor. For the crust, we cut a standard pie crust into squares after rolling it over the fruit right in the skillet—this encouraged a multitude of crispy edges that contrast nicely with the tender fruit and recall (in a less dowdy way) the broken-up crusts of a traditional pandowdy.

Skillet Apple Pie

SERVES 6 TO 8

If your skillet is not ovensafe, precook the apples and stir in the cider mixture as instructed, then transfer the apples to a 13 by 9-inch baking dish. Roll out the dough to a 13 by 9-inch rectangle and cut the crust and bake the pandowdy as instructed. If you do not have apple cider, reduced apple juice may be used as a substitute; simmer 1 cup apple juice in a small saucepan over medium heat until reduced to ½ cup (about 10 minutes). Serve the pandowdy warm or at room temperature with vanilla ice cream or whipped cream. Use a combination of sweet, crisp apples such as Golden Delicious and firm, tart apples such as Cortland or Empire.

CRUST

- 1 cup (5 ounces) unbleached all-purpose flour, plus extra for the work surface
- 1 tablespoon sugar
- ½ teaspoon table salt
- 2 tablespoons vegetable shortening, chilled
- 6 tablespoons (¾ stick) unsalted butter, cut into ¼-inch pieces and chilled
- 3–4 tablespoons ice water

FILLING

- ½ cup apple cider
- ⅓ cup maple syrup
- 2 tablespoons juice from 1 lemon
- 2 teaspoons cornstarch
- ⅛ teaspoon ground cinnamon (optional)
- 2 tablespoons unsalted butter
- 2½ pounds sweet and tart apples (about 4 large), peeled, cored, and cut into ½-inch-thick wedges (see note)
- 1 large egg white, lightly beaten
- 2 teaspoons sugar

1. FOR THE CRUST: Pulse the flour, sugar, and salt in a food processor until combined, about 4 pulses. Add the shortening and pulse until the mixture has the texture of coarse sand, about 10 pulses. Sprinkle the butter pieces over the flour mixture and pulse until the mixture is pale yellow and resembles coarse crumbs, with the butter bits no larger than small peas, about 10 pulses. Transfer the mixture to a medium bowl.

2. Sprinkle 3 tablespoons of the ice water over the mixture. With a rubber spatula, use a folding motion to mix, pressing down on the dough until the dough is slightly tacky and sticks together, adding up to 1 tablespoon more ice water if the dough does not come together. Flatten the dough into a 4-inch disk. Wrap the disk in plastic wrap and refrigerate at least 1 hour or up to 2 days. Let the dough stand at room temperature for 15 minutes before rolling.

3. FOR THE FILLING: Adjust an oven rack to the upper-middle position (between 7 and 9 inches from the heating element) and heat the oven to 500 degrees. Whisk the cider, syrup, lemon juice, cornstarch, and cinnamon (if using) together in a medium bowl until smooth. Melt the butter in a 12-inch ovensafe skillet over medium–high heat. Add the apples and cook, stirring two or three times, until the apples begin to caramelize, about 5 minutes. (Do not fully cook the apples.) Remove the pan from the heat, add the cider mixture, and gently stir until the apples are well coated. Set aside to cool slightly.

4. TO ASSEMBLE AND BAKE: Roll the dough out on a lightly floured work surface to an 11-inch circle. Roll the dough loosely around the rolling pin and unroll over the apple filling. Brush the dough with the egg white and sprinkle with the sugar. With a sharp knife, gently cut the dough into six pieces by making one vertical cut followed by two evenly spaced horizontal cuts (perpendicular to the first cut). Bake until the apples are tender and the crust is a deep golden brown, about 20 minutes, rotating the skillet halfway through the baking time. Cool for 15 minutes and serve.

BANANAS FOSTER

WHY THIS RECIPE WORKS: Although the New Orleans dessert bananas Foster is quick and simple, with few ingredients (butter, brown sugar, rum, and bananas), things can go wrong. Sometimes the bananas are overcooked and mushy. Or the sauce can be too thin, overly sweet, or taste too strongly of alcohol. We wanted to fix these issues and come up with a quick, reliable dessert with tender bananas and a flavorful but not boozy sauce.

First we kept the amounts of butter and brown sugar in check—most recipes use a high ratio of butter to brown sugar, which makes for a thin, greasy sauce. For the rum, we found that a small amount was just enough to impart a definite rum flavor without turning the dessert into a cocktail. We decided to add some rum to the sauce and use the rest to flambé the bananas. We also enhanced the sauce with a little cinnamon and lemon zest, which added some complexity. As for the bananas, we cooked them in the sauce until soft, flipping them over halfway through cooking so they turned out tender, not mushy.

Bananas Foster

SERVES 4

While the bananas cook, scoop the ice cream into individual bowls so they are ready to go once the sauce has been flambéed. Before preparing this recipe, read "Tips for Fearless Flambé" on page 274.

- 4 tablespoons (½ stick) unsalted butter
- ½ cup packed (3½ ounces) dark brown sugar
- 1 (3-inch) cinnamon stick
- 1 (2-inch) strip zest from 1 lemon
- 4 tablespoons dark rum
- 2 large, firm, ripe bananas, peeled and quartered
- 1 pint vanilla ice cream, divided among four bowls

1. Combine the butter, sugar, cinnamon stick, zest, and 1 tablespoon of the rum in a 12-inch skillet. Cook over medium-high heat, stirring constantly, until the sugar dissolves and the mixture has thickened, about 2 minutes.

2. Reduce the heat to medium and add the bananas to the pan, spooning some sauce over each quarter. Cook until the bananas are glossy and golden on the bottom, about 1½ minutes. Flip the bananas; continue to cook until very soft but not mushy or falling apart, about 1½ minutes longer.

3. Off the heat, add the remaining 3 tablespoons rum and allow the rum to warm slightly, about 5 seconds. Wave a lit match over the pan until the rum ignites, shaking the pan to distribute the flame over the entire pan. When the flames subside (this will take 15 to 30 seconds), discard the cinnamon stick and zest and divide the bananas and sauce among the four bowls of ice cream. Serve.

CRÊPES SUZETTE

WHY THIS RECIPE WORKS: Classic French restaurants have mastered the fiery theatrics of this tableside treat—a sophisticated combination of crêpes, oranges, liqueur, and a showy flambé. We wanted to develop a recipe that would comfortably guide the home cook through the flambé process so this dessert could be prepared for an elegant dinner party.

For a foolproof flambé that didn't create a frightening fireball or, conversely, didn't burn at all, we ignited the alcohol (cognac) alone in the skillet before building the sauce. To build a delicate sauce with complex flavor, we enriched a reduction of butter, sugar, and fresh orange juice with additional orange juice, fresh orange zest, and triple sec (not the pricier Grand Marnier or Cointreau). For tender but sturdy crêpes that would stand up to the sauce without turning soggy, we skipped the usual resting of the batter, meant to relax the gluten, before cooking. Then, once the crêpes were cooked, we sprinkled them with sugar and ran them under the broiler for a sweet and crunchy coating.

Crêpes Suzette
SERVES 6

Note that it takes a few crêpes to get the heat of the pan right; your first two or three will almost inevitably be unusable. (To allow for practice, the recipe yields about 16 crêpes; only 12 are needed for the dish.) A dry measuring cup with a ¼-cup capacity is useful for portioning the batter. We prefer crêpes made with whole milk, but low-fat or skim milk can also be used. Before preparing this recipe, read "Tips for Fearless Flambé" on page 274.

CRÊPES

- 3 **large eggs**
- 1½ **cups whole milk (see note)**
- 1½ **cups (7½ ounces) unbleached all-purpose flour**
- ½ **cup water**
- 5 **tablespoons unsalted butter, melted, plus extra for brushing the pan**
- 3 **tablespoons sugar**
- 2 **tablespoons cognac**
- ½ **teaspoon table salt**

ORANGE SAUCE

- 4 **tablespoons cognac**
- 1¼ **cups juice plus 1 tablespoon finely grated zest from 3 to 4 large oranges**
- 6 **tablespoons (¾ stick) unsalted butter, cut into 6 pieces**
- ¼ **cup (1¾ ounces) sugar**
- 2 **tablespoons orange-flavored liqueur, preferably triple sec**

1. FOR THE CRÊPES: Combine the eggs, milk, flour, water, melted butter, sugar, cognac, and salt in a blender until a smooth batter forms, about 10 seconds. Transfer the batter to a medium bowl.

2. Using a pastry brush, brush the bottom and sides of a 10-inch nonstick skillet very lightly with melted butter and heat the skillet over medium heat. When the butter stops sizzling, tilt the pan slightly to the right and begin pouring in a scant ¼ cup batter. Continue to pour the batter in a slow, steady stream, rotating your wrist and twirling the pan slowly counterclockwise until the pan bottom is covered with an even layer of batter. Cook until the crêpe starts to lose its opaqueness and turns spotty light golden brown on the bottom, loosening the crêpe from the side of the pan with a heatproof rubber spatula, 30 seconds to 1 minute. To flip the crêpe, loosen the edge with the spatula and, with your fingertips on the top side, slide the spatula under the crêpe and flip. Cook until dry on the second side, about 20 seconds.

3. Place the cooked crêpe on a plate and repeat the cooking process with the remaining batter, brushing the pan very lightly with butter before making each crêpe. As they are done, stack the crêpes on a plate (you will need 12 crêpes). (The crêpes can be double-wrapped in plastic wrap and refrigerated up to 3 days; bring them to room temperature before making the sauce.)

4. FOR THE ORANGE SAUCE: Adjust an oven rack to the lower-middle position and heat the broiler. Add 3 tablespoons of the cognac to a broiler-safe 12-inch skillet; heat the pan over medium heat just until the vapors begin to rise from the cognac, about 5 seconds. Remove the pan from the heat and wave a lit match over the pan until the cognac ignites, shaking the pan until the flames subside, about 15 seconds; reignite if the flame dies too soon.

5. Add 1 cup of the orange juice, the butter, and 3 tablespoons of the sugar and simmer briskly over high heat, stirring occasionally, until many large bubbles appear and the mixture reduces to a thick syrup, 6 to 8 minutes (you should have just over ½ cup sauce). Transfer the sauce to a small bowl; do not wash the skillet. Stir the remaining ¼ cup orange juice, zest, liqueur, and the remaining 1 tablespoon cognac into the sauce; cover.

6. TO ASSEMBLE: Fold each crêpe in half, then in half again to form a wedge shape. Arrange nine folded crêpes around the edge of the now-empty skillet, with the rounded edges facing inward, overlapping as necessary to fit. Arrange the remaining three crêpes in the center of the pan. Sprinkle the crêpes evenly with the remaining 1 tablespoon sugar. Broil until the sugar caramelizes and the crêpes turn spotty brown, about 5 minutes. (Watch the crêpes constantly to prevent scorching; turn the pan as necessary.) Carefully remove the pan from the oven and pour half of the sauce over the crêpes, leaving some areas uncovered. Transfer the crêpes to individual serving dishes and serve immediately, passing the extra sauce separately.

SUMMER PUDDING

WHY THIS RECIPE WORKS: If any food speaks of summer, the English dessert called summer pudding does. Ripe, fragrant, lightly sweetened berries are gently cooked to coax out their juices and then packed into a bowl lined with slices of bread. The berry juices soak and soften the bread to make it meld with the fruit. We set out to master this summertime classic.

Instead of lining the mold with bread and then filling it with berries, we opted to layer bread (cut out with a biscuit cutter) and berries together in ramekins; this way, the layers of bread on the inside would almost melt into the fruit. Combining the berries—we used strawberries, raspberries, blueberries, and blackberries—with sugar and lemon juice, and gently cooking the mixture for just five minutes, released just the right amount of juice and offset the tartness of the berries. Fresh bread became too gummy in the pudding, but day-old bread had just the right consistency. We used potato bread; its even, tight-crumbed, tender texture and light sweetness was a perfect match for the berries (challah makes a good substitute). To ensure that the puddings would come together and hold their shape, we weighted and refrigerated them for at least eight hours.

Individual Summer Berry Puddings
SERVES 6

The bread should be dry to the touch but not brittle. If working with fresh bread, dry the slices by heating them on an oven rack in a single layer in a 200-degree oven about 1 hour, flipping them once halfway through the time. For this recipe, you will need six 6-ounce ramekins and a round cookie cutter of a slightly smaller diameter than the ramekins. If you don't have the right size cutter, use a paring knife and the bottom of a ramekin (most ramekins taper toward the bottom) as a guide for trimming the rounds. Challah will need to be cut into slices about ½ inch thick; if both potato bread and challah are unavailable, use high-quality white sandwich bread. Summer pudding can be made up to 24 hours before serving; held any longer, the berries begin to lose their freshness. Lightly sweetened whipped cream is the perfect accompaniment.

    4 cups (20 ounces) strawberries, hulled and sliced
    2 cups (about 10 ounces) raspberries
    1 cup (about 5 ounces) blueberries
    1 cup (about 5 ounces) blackberries
    ¾ cup (5¼ ounces) sugar
    2 tablespoons juice from 1 lemon
    12 slices stale potato bread, challah, or high-quality white
       sandwich bread (see note)

1. Cook the strawberries, raspberries, blueberries, blackberries, and sugar in a large saucepan over medium heat, stirring occasionally, until the berries begin to release their juice and the sugar has dissolved, about 5 minutes. Off the heat, stir in the lemon juice; cool to room temperature.

2. While the berries are cooling, spray six 6-ounce ramekins with vegetable oil spray and place on a rimmed baking sheet. Use a cookie cutter to cut out 12 bread rounds that are slightly smaller in diameter than the ramekins.

3. Using a slotted spoon, place ¼ cup of the fruit mixture in each ramekin. Lightly soak one bread round in the fruit juice in the saucepan and place on top of the fruit in a ramekin; repeat with five more bread rounds and the remaining ramekins. Diving the remaining fruit among the ramekins. Lightly soak one bread round in the juice and place on top of the fruit in a ramekin (it should sit above the lip of the ramekin); repeat with the remaining five bread rounds and the remaining ramekins. Pour the remaining fruit juice over the bread and cover the ramekins loosely with plastic wrap. Place a second baking sheet on top of the ramekins and weight it with heavy cans. Refrigerate the puddings for at least 8 hours and up to 24 hours.

4. Remove the cans and baking sheet and uncover the puddings. Loosen the puddings by running a paring knife around the edge of each ramekin, unmold into individual bowls, and serve immediately.

Large Summer Berry Pudding
SERVES 6 TO 8

You will need a 9 by 5-inch loaf pan for this recipe. Because there is no need to cut out rounds for this version, you will need only about 8 slices bread, depending on their size.

Follow the recipe for Individual Summer Berry Puddings through step 1. While the berries are cooling, spray a 9 by 5-inch loaf pan with vegetable oil spray, line it with plastic wrap, and place it on a rimmed baking sheet. Trim the crusts from the bread and trim the slices to fit in a single layer in the loaf pan (you will need about 2½ slices per layer; there will be three layers). Using a slotted spoon, spread about 2 cups of the fruit mixture evenly over the bottom of the prepared pan. Lightly soak enough bread slices for one layer in the fruit juice in the saucepan and place on top of the fruit. Repeat with two more layers of fruit and bread. Pour the remaining fruit juice over the bread and cover loosely with plastic wrap. Place a second baking sheet on top of the loaf pan and weight it with heavy cans. Refrigerate the pudding for at least 8 hours and up to 24 hours. Remove the cans and baking sheet and uncover the pudding. Invert the pudding onto a serving platter, remove the loaf pan and plastic wrap, slice, and serve.

CARAMELIZED PEARS

WHY THIS RECIPE WORKS: Pears and blue cheese are a classic combination, but we wanted to up the flavor ante with another component—caramel. We had encountered this triple play in restaurants, where a caramel sauce is draped over seared pears and a modest amount of pungent blue cheese, served alongside, provides a nice contrast to the dessert's sweetness. We decided to adapt this dish so it would be easy for the home cook, while still letting each ingredient shine (meaning no mushy pears and no sticky, overcooked caramel).

To streamline the recipe, we cooked the pears right in the caramel sauce, instead of separately, saving time and eliminating some dirty dishes. We brought water and sugar (the basis for caramel sauce) to a boil in a skillet and slid the pears into the hot mixture to cook in the browning caramel. We added cream to the pan to transform the sticky sugar syrup into a smooth sauce that clung lightly to the pears. After removing the pears, we were able to season the sauce left in the skillet with just the right amount of black pepper and salt. For an attractive presentation, we stood the pears upright on a plate (we had already trimmed the bottom off each pear for a flat base) and drizzled the caramel sauce around them, then added wedges of strong blue cheese—the perfect foil to the sweet caramel.

Caramelized Pears with Blue Cheese and Black Pepper-Caramel Sauce

SERVES 6

Any type of pear can be used in this recipe, but the pears must be firm to withstand the heat. If desired, the pears can be served upright on a large platter instead of on individual plates, with the warm caramel sauce and the blue cheese passed separately. Many pepper mills do not have a sufficiently coarse setting; in that case, crush peppercorns with the back of a heavy pan or a rolling pin. See page 589 for information on our top-rated pepper mill.

⅓ cup water
⅔ cup (4⅔ ounces) sugar
3 ripe, firm pears, halved, cored, and ¼ inch trimmed off the bottom (see note)
⅔ cup heavy cream
  Table salt
¼ teaspoon black peppercorns, crushed (see note)
3 ounces strong blue cheese (such as Stilton), cut into 6 wedges

1. Pour the water into a 12-inch nonstick skillet, then pour the sugar into the center of the pan, being careful not to let it hit the sides of the pan. Bring to a boil over high heat, stirring occasionally, until the sugar is fully dissolved and the liquid is bubbling. Add the pears to the skillet, cut side down, cover, reduce the heat to medium-high, and cook until the pears are almost tender and a paring knife inserted into the center of the pears meets slight resistance, 13 to 15 minutes.

2. Uncover, reduce the heat to medium, and cook until the sauce is golden brown and the cut sides of the pears are beginning to brown, 3 to 5 minutes. Pour the heavy cream around the pears and cook, shaking the pan until the sauce is a smooth, deep caramel color and the cut sides of the pears are golden brown, 3 to 5 minutes.

3. Off the heat, transfer the pears, cut side up, to a wire rack set over a rimmed baking sheet and cool slightly. Season the sauce left in the pan with salt to taste and the crushed peppercorns, then transfer it to a small bowl.

4. Carefully (the pears will still be hot) stand each pear half upright on an individual plate and arrange a wedge of the blue cheese beside it. Drizzle the caramel sauce over the plate and the pear. Serve immediately.

STRAWBERRIES WITH BALSAMIC VINEGAR

WHY THIS RECIPE WORKS: Strawberries with balsamic vinegar may sound a bit trendy, but this combination actually goes back in time—hundreds of years at least—to northern Italy. We wanted to pay homage to this time-honored tradition and create our own dessert, with the vinegar enhancing but not overwhelming the flavor of bright, summer berries.

We didn't want to pay big bucks for a super-pricey balsamic vinegar, so we opted to use an inexpensive vinegar. To coax big flavor out of our bargain balsamic, we simmered it with some sugar to approximate the syrupy texture of an aged vinegar. Next we tried to enhance the flavor with honey or vanilla, but these flavors were too overpowering; a squirt of fresh lemon juice brought just the right amount of brightness. We tossed the berries with light brown sugar—rather than the traditional granulated sugar—for the most complex flavor. Once we mixed the sliced berries and sugar together, it took about 15 minutes for the sugar to dissolve and the berries to release their juice; if the strawberries sat any longer than this, they continued to soften and became quite mushy.

Strawberries with Balsamic Vinegar

SERVES 6

If you don't have light brown sugar on hand, sprinkle the berries with an equal amount of granulated sugar. Serve the berries and syrup as is or with a scoop of vanilla ice cream or a dollop of lightly sweetened whipped cream.

⅓ cup balsamic vinegar
2 teaspoons granulated sugar
½ teaspoon juice from 1 lemon
6 cups (30 ounces) strawberries, hulled, sliced lengthwise ¼ inch thick if large, halved or quartered if small
¼ cup packed (1¾ ounces) light brown sugar (see note)
  Ground black pepper

1. Bring the vinegar, granulated sugar, and lemon juice to a simmer in a small saucepan over medium heat. Simmer until the syrup is reduced by half (about 3 tablespoons), about 3 minutes. Transfer to a small bowl and cool completely.

2. Gently toss the berries and brown sugar in a large bowl. Let stand until the sugar dissolves and the berries exude some juice, 10 to 15 minutes. Pour the vinegar syrup over the berries, add pepper to taste, and toss to combine. Serve immediately.

RHUBARB FOOL

WHY THIS RECIPE WORKS: A fool is a quick, everyday dessert that just so happens to have a quaint and quirky British name. When we decided to try our hand at this simple dessert—essentially cooked fruit with sweetened whipped cream folded in—we sided with tradition and used rhubarb as the foundation. Although fool is in itself no culinary feat, the challenges lie in the rhubarb, with its sometimes overpowering sourness and tendency to cook into a thick, drab gray mess. We knew that before we could finalize a fool, we would have to tame the rhubarb. We wanted the perfect balance in our fool—pinkish-red, sweet/tart, toothsome fruit mixed with light, sweet cream.

Baking, stewing, and sautéing the rhubarb all led to gray, mushy fruit. Eventually, we hit on soaking the rhubarb in cold water for 20 minutes—this removed some of the bitterness—and simmering it with orange juice. Its flavor was now round and full, and its color bright red. As for the whipped cream, we decided that a soft-to-medium peak gave the fool just enough body without making it sliceable and stiff. For the best presentation and flavor, we arranged the rhubarb and whipped cream in layers rather than folding the two elements together. The alternating texture of fruit and cream made for a pleasing contrast of color and flavor.

Rhubarb Fool

SERVES 8

For a more elegant presentation, use a pastry bag to pipe the whipped cream into individual glasses. To make one large fool, double the recipe and layer the rhubarb and whipped cream in a 12-cup glass bowl.

- 2¼ **pounds rhubarb, trimmed and cut into 6-inch lengths**
- ⅓ **cup juice from 1 large orange**
- 1 **cup (7 ounces) plus 2 tablespoons sugar**
  Pinch table salt
- 2 **cups heavy cream, chilled**

1. Soak the rhubarb in cold water for 20 minutes. Drain, pat dry with paper towels, and cut crosswise into ½-inch-thick pieces.

2. Bring the orange juice, ¾ cup of the sugar, and the salt to a boil in a medium saucepan over medium-high heat. Add the rhubarb and return to a boil, then reduce the heat to medium-low and simmer, stirring two or three times, until the rhubarb begins to break down and is tender, 7 to 10 minutes. Transfer the rhubarb to a large bowl, cool to room temperature, cover with plastic wrap, and refrigerate until cold, at least 1 hour or up to 24 hours.

3. Whip the cream and remaining 6 tablespoons sugar in a large bowl with an electric mixer on medium-low speed until frothy, about 1 minute. Increase the speed to high and continue to whip until the cream forms soft peaks, 1 to 3 minutes.

4. To assemble, spoon about ¼ cup rhubarb into each of eight 8-ounce glasses, then layer about ¼ cup whipped cream on top. Repeat, ending with a dollop of cream; serve. (The fools can be refrigerated, covered with plastic wrap, up to 6 hours.)

Strawberry-Rhubarb Fool

Follow the recipe for Rhubarb Fool, substituting 4 cups strawberries, hulled and quartered, for 1¼ pounds of the rhubarb and adding the strawberries to the saucepan with the rhubarb in step 2.

CHAPTER 25

KEEP YOUR FORK— THERE'S PIE!

Basic Double-Crust Pie Dough   558

Hand Mixed Basic Double-Crust Pie Dough   559

Basic Single-Crust Pie Dough   559

Hand Mixed Basic Single-Crust Pie Dough   559

Single-Crust Pie Dough for Custard Pies   559

All-Butter Double-Crust Pie Dough   560

Hand Mixed All-Butter Double-Crust Pie Dough   560

Foolproof Double-Crust Pie Dough   561

Graham Cracker Crust   562

Classic Apple Pie   563

Apple Pie with Crystallized Ginger   563

Apple Pie with Dried Fruit   563

Apple Pie with Fresh Cranberries   563

Deep-Dish Apple Pie   564

Lattice-Top Fresh Peach Pie   565

Blueberry Pie   567

Summer Berry Pie   569

Pumpkin Pie   569

Pecan Pie   570

Triple-Chocolate-Chunk Pecan Pie   571

Key Lime Pie   572

Lemon Meringue Pie   573

Coconut Cream Pie   574

Chocolate Cream Pie   575

Classic Tart Dough   576

Lemon Tart   577

Free-Form Summer Fruit Tart   577

Fresh Fruit Tart with Pastry Cream   579

Mixed Berry Tart with Pastry Cream   579

Apple Galette   580

Free-Form Apple Tart   581

30-Minute Tarte Tatin   582

Pear Tatin   582

BASIC PIE DOUGH

WHY THIS RECIPE WORKS: Basic pie dough often contains vegetable shortening, which makes the dough easier to handle and yields a crust that is remarkably flaky. The primary issue with vegetable shortening crusts, however, is that they lack flavor. We set out to master basic pie dough by determining the right fat, the right proportion of fat to flour, and the right method for combining them.

Flakiness is important to a crust, but so is flavor—and nothing beats butter. We experimented with a variety of combinations and ultimately settled on a proportion of 3 parts butter to 2 parts shortening as optimal for both flavor and texture. We also settled on a ratio of 2 parts flour to 1 part fat. This crust is relatively high in fat, but we found that the 2–1 proportion produces dough that is easier to work and a baked crust that is more tender and flavorful than any other. You can make this pie dough by hand, but the food processor is faster and easier and does the best job of cutting the fat into the flour.

Basic Double-Crust Pie Dough

MAKES ENOUGH FOR ONE 9-INCH PIE

The dough, wrapped tightly in plastic wrap, can be refrigerated for up to 2 days or frozen for up to 1 month. If frozen, let the dough thaw completely on the counter before rolling it out.

2½	**cups (12½ ounces) unbleached all-purpose flour, plus extra for the work surface**
2	**tablespoons sugar**
1	**teaspoon table salt**
½	**cup vegetable shortening, cut into ½-inch pieces and chilled**
12	**tablespoons (1½ sticks) unsalted butter, cut into ¼-inch pieces and chilled**
6–8	**tablespoons ice water**

1. Process the flour, sugar, and salt together in a food processor until combined. Scatter the shortening over the top and process until the mixture resembles coarse cornmeal, about 10 seconds. Scatter the butter pieces over the top and pulse the mixture until it resembles coarse crumbs, about 10 pulses. Transfer the mixture to a large bowl.

2. Sprinkle 6 tablespoons of the ice water over the mixture. Stir and press the dough together, using a stiff rubber

NOTES FROM THE TEST KITCHEN

ROLLING AND FITTING PIE DOUGH

1. Lay the disk of dough on a lightly floured work surface and roll the dough outward from its center into a 12-inch circle. Between every few rolls, give the dough a quarter turn to help keep the circle nice and round.

2. Toss additional flour underneath the dough as needed to keep the dough from sticking to the work surface.

3. Loosely roll the dough around the rolling pin, then gently unroll it over the pie plate.

4. Lift the dough and gently press it into the pie plate, letting the excess hang over the plate. For a double-crust pie, cover the crust lightly with plastic wrap and refrigerate for at least 30 minutes. To crimp a single-crust pie, see page 559.

spatula, until the dough sticks together. If the dough does not come together, stir in the remaining water, 1 tablespoon at a time, until it does.

3. Divide the dough into two even pieces. Turn each piece of dough onto a sheet of plastic wrap and flatten each into a 4-inch disk. Wrap each piece tightly in plastic wrap and refrigerate for 1 hour. Before rolling the dough out, let it sit on the counter to soften slightly, about 10 minutes.

Hand Mixed Basic Double-Crust Pie Dough

Freeze the butter in its stick form until very firm. Whisk the flour, sugar, and salt together in a large bowl. Add the chilled shortening and press it into the flour using a fork. Grate the frozen butter on the large holes of a box grater into the flour mixture, then cut the mixture together using two butter or dinner knives, until the mixture resembles coarse crumbs. Follow the recipe for Basic Double-Crust Pie Dough, adding the water as directed.

Basic Single-Crust Pie Dough

MAKES ENOUGH FOR ONE 9-INCH PIE

The dough, wrapped tightly in plastic wrap, can be refrigerated for up to 2 days or frozen for up to 1 month. If frozen, let the dough thaw completely on the counter before rolling it out.

- 1¼ **cups (6¼ ounces) unbleached all-purpose flour, plus extra for the work surface**
- 1 **tablespoon sugar**
- ½ **teaspoon table salt**
- 3 **tablespoons vegetable shortening, cut into ½-inch pieces and chilled**
- 5 **tablespoons unsalted butter, cut into ¼-inch pieces and chilled**
- 4–6 **tablespoons ice water**

1. Process the flour, sugar, and salt together in a food processor until combined. Scatter the shortening over the top and process until the mixture resembles coarse cornmeal, about 10 seconds. Scatter the butter pieces over the top and pulse the mixture until it resembles coarse crumbs, about 10 pulses. Transfer the mixture to a medium bowl.

2. Sprinkle 4 tablespoons of the ice water over the mixture. Stir and press the dough together, using a stiff rubber spatula, until the dough sticks together. If the dough does not come together, stir in the remaining water, 1 tablespoon at a time, until it does.

3. Turn the dough onto a sheet of plastic wrap and flatten into a 4-inch disk. Wrap the dough tightly in plastic wrap and refrigerate for 1 hour. Before rolling the dough out, let it sit on the counter to soften slightly, about 10 minutes.

4. Following the photos on page 558, roll the dough into a 12-inch circle and fit it into a pie plate. Following the photos at right, trim, fold, and crimp the edge of the dough. Wrap the dough-lined pie plate loosely in plastic wrap and place in the freezer until the dough is fully chilled and firm, about 30 minutes, before using.

Hand Mixed Basic Single-Crust Pie Dough

Freeze the butter in its stick form until very firm. Whisk the flour, sugar, and salt together in a medium bowl. Add the chilled shortening and press it into the flour using a fork. Grate the frozen butter on the large holes of a box grater into the flour mixture, then cut the mixture together using two butter or dinner knives, until the mixture resembles coarse crumbs. Follow the recipe for Basic Single-Crust Pie Dough, adding the water as directed.

Single-Crust Pie Dough For Custard Pies

We like rolling our single-crust dough in fresh graham cracker crumbs because it adds flavor and crisp textural appeal to many of our custard pies.

Crush 3 whole graham crackers to fine crumbs. (You should have about ½ cup crumbs.) Follow the recipe for Basic Single-Crust Pie Dough, dusting the work surface with the graham cracker crumbs instead of flour. Continue sprinkling the dough with the crumbs, both underneath and on top, as it is being rolled out.

NOTES FROM THE TEST KITCHEN

CRIMPING A SINGLE-CRUST PIE DOUGH

For a traditional single-crust pie, you need to make an evenly thick edge before crimping. Trim the pie dough so that it hangs over the pie plate by ½ inch, then tuck the dough underneath itself to form a tidy, even edge that sits on the lip of the pie plate.

FOR A FLUTED EDGE: Use the index finger of one hand and the thumb and index finger of the other to create fluted ridges perpendicular to the edge of the pie plate.

FOR A RIDGED EDGE: Press the tines of a fork into the dough to flatten it against the rim of the pie plate.

ALL-BUTTER PIE DOUGH

WHY THIS RECIPE WORKS: All-butter pie doughs possess great flavor, but they often fail to be flaky and are notoriously difficult to work with. We wanted an all-butter pie pastry that was easier to mix, handle, and roll, producing a pie crust with all the tenderness and flavor that the description "all-butter" promises.

We initially tried to make the dough easier to handle by reducing the amount of butter, but this resulted in bland flavor and dry texture. Rather than adding back the subtracted butter, we experimented with other forms of fat, including heavy cream, cream cheese, and sour cream. We found that sour cream not only added flavor but, because acid reduces gluten development, also helped keep the dough tender and flaky. And to mix the dough, we used a food processor, which brought the ingredients together quickly and evenly.

NOTES FROM THE TEST KITCHEN

MAKING ALL-BUTTER DOUBLE-CRUST PIE DOUGH

1. Pulse the butter and flour mixture together in a food processor until the butter is the size of large peas, about 10 pulses.

2. After adding the sour cream and water mixture, pinch the dough with your fingers. If the dough is dry and does not hold together, sprinkle 1 to 2 tablespoons ice water over the mixture and pulse 3 to 5 times.

3. Divide the dough into two pieces and flatten each into a 4-inch disk. Wrap the disks tightly in plastic wrap and refrigerate for 1 hour. Before rolling the dough out, let it sit on the counter to soften slightly, about 10 minutes.

All-Butter Double-Crust Pie Dough
MAKES ENOUGH FOR ONE 9-INCH PIE

Freezing the butter for 10 to 15 minutes is crucial to the flaky texture of this crust. If preparing the dough in a very warm kitchen, refrigerate all of the ingredients before making the dough. The dough, wrapped tightly in plastic wrap, can be refrigerated for up to 2 days or frozen for up to 1 month. If frozen, let the dough thaw completely on the counter before rolling it out.

- ⅓ **cup ice water, plus extra as needed**
- 3 **tablespoons sour cream**
- 2½ **cups (12½ ounces) unbleached all-purpose flour, plus extra for the work surface**
- 1 **tablespoon sugar**
- 1 **teaspoon table salt**
- 16 **tablespoons (2 sticks) unsalted butter, cut into ¼-inch pieces and frozen for 10 to 15 minutes (see note)**

1. Mix ⅓ cup of the ice water and the sour cream in a small bowl until combined. Process the flour, sugar, and salt together in a food processor until combined. Following the photos, scatter the butter pieces over the top and pulse the mixture until the butter is the size of large peas, about 10 pulses.

2. Pour half of the sour cream mixture over the flour mixture and pulse until incorporated, about 3 pulses. Repeat with the remaining sour cream mixture. Pinch the dough with your fingers; if the dough feels dry and does not hold together, sprinkle 1 to 2 tablespoons more ice water over the mixture and pulse until the dough forms large clumps and no dry flour remains, 3 to 5 pulses.

3. Divide the dough into two even pieces. Turn each piece of dough onto a sheet of plastic wrap and flatten each into a 4-inch disk. Wrap each piece tightly in plastic wrap and refrigerate for 1 hour. Before rolling the dough out, let it sit on the counter to soften slightly, about 10 minutes.

Hand Mixed All-Butter Double-Crust Pie Dough

Freeze the butter in its stick form until very firm. Whisk the flour, sugar, and salt together in a large bowl. Grate the frozen butter on the large holes of a box grater into the flour mixture, then cut the mixture together using two butter or dinner knives, until the mixture resembles coarse crumbs. Follow the recipe for All-Butter Double-Crust Pie Dough, adding the liquid as directed, stirring it with a rubber spatula.

FOOLPROOF PIE DOUGH

WHY THIS RECIPE WORKS: Unless you're a practiced pie baker, it's hard to get the same results every time. While we think our All-Butter Pie Dough (page 560) and Basic Pie Dough (page 558) are great, we wanted a recipe for pie dough that rolls out easily every time and produces a tender, flaky crust.

The first step was to determine the right fat. As with our basic dough, a combination of butter and shortening provided the best balance of flavor and tenderness. Once again, the best tool to cut the fat into the flour was the food processor. To ensure same-sized pieces of butter time after time, we eliminated the pieces entirely and made a paste instead. Rather than starting with all the flour in the processor, we put aside 1 cup of flour and processed the remaining 1½ cups with all of the fat until it formed a unified paste. We added the reserved flour to the bowl and pulsed it until it was just evenly distributed. Finally, we tackled the tenderness issue, which is partially determined by the amount of water added. In order to roll easily, dough needs a generous amount of water, but more water makes crusts tough. We found the answer in the liquor cabinet: vodka. While gluten (the protein that makes crust tough) forms readily in water, it doesn't form in ethanol, and vodka is 60 percent water and 40 percent ethanol. So adding ¼ cup of vodka produced a moist, easy-to-roll dough that stayed tender. (The alcohol vaporizes in the oven, so you won't taste it in the baked crust.)

Foolproof Double-Crust Pie Dough

MAKES ENOUGH FOR ONE 9-INCH PIE

Vodka is essential to the tender texture of this crust and imparts no flavor—do not substitute water. This dough is moister than most standard pie doughs and will require lots of flour to roll out (up to ¼ cup). The dough, wrapped tightly in plastic wrap, can be refrigerated for up to 2 days or frozen for up to 1 month. If frozen, let the dough thaw completely on the counter before rolling it out.

- 2½ cups (12½ ounces) unbleached all-purpose flour, plus extra for the work surface (see note)
- 2 tablespoons sugar
- 1 teaspoon table salt
- 12 tablespoons (1½ sticks) unsalted butter, cut into ¼-inch pieces and chilled
- ½ cup vegetable shortening, cut into 4 pieces and chilled
- ¼ cup vodka, chilled (see note)
- ¼ cup ice water

BEHIND THE SCENES

YOU CAN NEVER HAVE ENOUGH RECIPES FOR PIE DOUGH

Viewers of our television show and readers of our recipes may wonder why we revisit the same recipes (roast chicken, mashed potatoes, and pie dough, to name a few) and develop alternate versions of them. Simply put, personal choice is a big factor. Take pie dough. There are few recipes that divide the test kitchen like the humble pie crust. Some in the test kitchen are purists when it comes to pie dough—they wouldn't dream of using anything but an all-butter dough. The flavor of our All-Butter Pie Dough (page 560) is undeniably buttery and delicious, but let's face it—this dough can be difficult to work with and isn't quite as flaky as a pie dough made with vegetable shortening. Next are the cooks who prefer the ease of working with a dough made with vegetable shortening as well as butter, like our Basic Pie Dough (page 558). Vegetable shortening, such as Crisco, is made from vegetable oil that has been hydrogenated, a process in which hydrogen gas is pumped into vegetable oil so it solidifies. Adding vegetable shortening makes the dough easier to work with and it does a good job of lightening and tenderizing the dough. That said, this pie dough still takes some patience to roll out.

The problem is that most pie dough recipes are stingy with the water (and thus really hard to roll out). Adding more water may seem to help matters, but once baked, the resulting crust is tougher. So to solve this problem, we developed a third pie dough, based on our Basic Pie Dough but with an unlikely ingredient—vodka.

While gluten (the protein that makes crust tough) forms readily in water, it doesn't form in ethanol, and vodka is 60 percent water and 40 percent ethanol. So adding ¼ cup of vodka and ¼ cup of water produces a moist, easy-to-roll dough that stays tender because the alcohol vaporizes in the oven, leaving the final crust with only about 6 tablespoons of water. This dough bakes into a crust that is tender, flavorful, and that rolls out easily every time. For those in the test kitchen who demand an easy-to-roll pie dough, this is their dream recipe. (And for those who aren't practiced bakers and make a pie maybe once a year around the holidays, this dough makes a lot of sense.) Does that mean we're through developing pie doughs? Maybe, maybe not.

1. Process 1½ cups of the flour, the sugar, and salt together in a food processor until combined. Scatter the butter and shortening over the top and continue to process until incorporated and the mixture begins to form uneven clumps with no remaining floury bits, about 15 seconds.

2. Scrape down the workbowl and redistribute the dough evenly around the processor blade. Sprinkle the remaining 1 cup flour over the dough and pulse until the mixture has broken up into pieces and is evenly distributed around the bowl, 4 to 6 pulses.

3. Transfer the mixture to a medium bowl. Sprinkle the vodka and water over the mixture. Stir and press the dough together, using a stiff rubber spatula, until the dough sticks together.

4. Divide the dough into two even pieces. Turn each piece of dough onto a sheet of plastic wrap and flatten each into a 4-inch disk. Wrap each piece tightly in plastic wrap and refrigerate for 1 hour. Before rolling the dough out, let it sit on the counter to soften slightly, about 10 minutes.

GRAHAM CRACKER CRUST

WHY THIS RECIPE WORKS: Saving time is always a good idea—just as long as you're not sacrificing quality. But while store-bought graham cracker pie crusts are tempting (all you have to do is fill, chill, then serve), they taste stale and bland. We wanted a fresh-tasting homemade crust that wasn't too sweet, with a crisp texture.

Turns out, a classic graham cracker crust couldn't be easier to make: Combine crushed crumbs with a little butter and sugar to bind them, then use a measuring cup or flat-bottomed glass to pack the crumbs into the pie plate. And producing a perfect graham cracker crust has a lot to do with the type of graham crackers used. After experimenting with the three leading brands, we discovered subtle but distinct differences among them and found that these differences carried over into crumb crusts made with each kind of cracker. Here in the test kitchen, we prefer Nabisco Original Graham Crackers for their hearty molasses flavor.

Graham Cracker Crust
MAKES ENOUGH FOR ONE 9-INCH PIE
We don't recommend using store-bought graham cracker crumbs here as they can often be stale. Be sure to note whether the crust needs to be warm or cool before filling (the pie recipes will specify) and plan accordingly.

8 whole graham crackers, broken into 1-inch pieces
5 tablespoons unsalted butter, melted and cooled
3 tablespoons sugar

1. Adjust an oven rack to the middle position and heat the oven to 325 degrees. Process the graham cracker pieces in a food processor to fine, even crumbs, about 30 seconds. Sprinkle the butter and sugar over the crumbs and pulse to incorporate.

2. Sprinkle the mixture into a 9-inch pie plate. Following the photo, use the bottom of a measuring cup to press the crumbs into an even layer on the bottom and sides of the pie plate. Bake until the crust is fragrant and beginning to brown, 13 to 18 minutes. Following the particular pie recipe, use the crust while it is still warm or let it cool completely.

APPLE PIE

WHY THIS RECIPE WORKS: In the test kitchen, we have found that it's difficult to produce an apple pie with a filling that is tart as well as sweet and juicy. We wanted to develop a classic apple pie recipe—one with the clean, bright taste of apples that could be made year-round, based on apple types that are always available in the supermarket.

To arrive at the tartness and texture we were after, we had to use two kinds of apples in our pie, Granny Smith and McIntosh. The Grannies could be counted on for tartness and for keeping their shape during cooking; the Macs added flavor, and their otherwise frustrating tendency to become mushy was a virtue, providing a nice, juicy base for the harder Grannies. While many bakers add butter to their apple pie fillings, we found that it dulled the fresh taste of the apples and so did without it. Lemon juice, however, was essential, counterbalancing the sweetness of the apples. To give the apples the upper hand, we settled on quite modest amounts of cinnamon, nutmeg, and allspice.

Classic Apple Pie

SERVES 8

You can use All-Butter Double-Crust Pie Dough (page 560), Basic Double-Crust Pie Dough (page 558), or Foolproof Double-Crust Pie Dough (page 561) for this pie. The pie is best eaten when cooled to room temperature, or even the next day. Serve with vanilla ice cream or lightly sweetened whipped cream.

- 1 recipe double-crust pie dough (see note)
- 2 tablespoons unbleached all-purpose flour, plus extra for the work surface
- ¾ cup (5¼ ounces) plus 1 tablespoon sugar
- 1 teaspoon grated zest plus 1 tablespoon juice from 1 lemon
- ¼ teaspoon table salt
- ¼ teaspoon ground nutmeg
- ¼ teaspoon ground cinnamon
- ⅛ teaspoon ground allspice
- 2 pounds firm McIntosh apples (about 4 large), peeled, cored, and sliced ¼ inch thick
- 1½ pounds Granny Smith apples (about 3 large), peeled, cored, and sliced ¼ inch thick
- 1 large egg white, lightly beaten

1. Following the photos on page 558, roll one disk of dough into a 12-inch circle on a lightly floured work surface, then fit it into a 9-inch pie plate, letting the excess dough hang over the edge; cover with plastic wrap and refrigerate for 30 minutes. Roll the other disk of dough into a 12-inch circle on a lightly floured work surface, then transfer to a parchment-lined baking sheet; cover with plastic wrap and refrigerate for 30 minutes.

2. Adjust an oven rack to the lowest position, place a rimmed baking sheet on the rack, and heat the oven to 500 degrees.

3. Mix the flour, ¾ cup of the sugar, the zest, salt, nutmeg, cinnamon, and allspice together in a large bowl. Add the lemon juice and apples and toss until combined. Spread the apples with their juice into the dough-lined pie plate, mounding them slightly in the middle. Following the photos on page 565, loosely roll the second piece of dough around the rolling pin and gently unroll it over

the pie. Trim, fold, and crimp the edges, and cut four vent holes in the top. Brush the dough with the egg white and sprinkle with the remaining 1 tablespoon sugar.

4. Place the pie on the heated baking sheet, reduce the oven temperature to 425 degrees, and bake until the crust is golden, about 25 minutes. Reduce the oven temperature to 375 degrees, rotate the baking sheet, and continue to bake until the juices are bubbling and the crust is deep golden brown, 30 to 35 minutes longer. Cool the pie on a wire rack to room temperature, about 4 hours. Serve.

Apple Pie with Crystallized Ginger

Follow the recipe for Classic Apple Pie, adding 3 tablespoons chopped crystallized ginger to the apple mixture.

Apple Pie with Dried Fruit

Toss 1 cup raisins, dried sweet cherries, or dried cranberries with the lemon juice plus 1 tablespoon applejack, brandy, or cognac. Follow the recipe for Classic Apple Pie, adding the dried fruit and liquid to the apple mixture.

Apple Pie with Fresh Cranberries

Follow the recipe for Classic Apple Pie, increasing the sugar to 1 cup (7 ounces) and adding 1 cup fresh or frozen cranberries to the apple mixture.

DEEP-DISH APPLE PIE

WHY THIS RECIPE WORKS: The problem with deep-dish apple pie is that the apples are often unevenly cooked (some mushy, some crunchy) and the exuded juice leaves the apples swimming in an ocean of liquid, producing a bottom crust that is a pale, soggy mess. Then there is the gaping hole left between the apples (which are shrunken from the loss of all that moisture) and the arching top crust, making it impossible to slice and serve a neat piece of pie. We wanted our piece of deep-dish pie to be a towering wedge of tender, juicy apples, fully framed by a buttery, flaky crust.

Precooking the apples solved the shrinking problem, helped the apples hold their shape, and prevented a flood of juices from collecting in the bottom of the pie plate, thereby producing a nicely browned bottom crust. Why didn't cooking the apples twice (once on the stovetop and once in the oven) cause them to become insipid and mushy? We learned that when the apples are gently heated, their pectin is converted to a heat-stable form that keeps them from becoming mushy when cooked further in the oven. This allowed us to boost the quantity of apples to 5 pounds. All that was left to do was to choose the right combination of sweet and tart apples and stir in a little brown sugar, salt, lemon, and cinnamon, for flavor and sweetness.

Deep-Dish Apple Pie
SERVES 8

You can use All-Butter Double-Crust Pie Dough (page 560), Basic Double-Crust Pie Dough (page 558), or Foolproof Double-Crust Pie Dough (page 561) for this pie. Use a combination of tart and sweet apples for this pie. Good choices for tart are Granny Smiths, Empires, or Cortlands; for sweet we recommend Golden Delicious, Jonagolds, or Braeburns. Serve with vanilla ice cream or lightly sweetened whipped cream.

- 1 **recipe double-crust pie dough (see note)**
  Unbleached all-purpose flour, for the work surface
- 2½ **pounds firm tart apples (about 5 large), peeled, cored, and sliced ¼ inch thick (see note)**
- 2½ **pounds firm sweet apples (about 5 large), peeled, cored, and sliced ¼ inch thick (see note)**
- ½ **cup (3½ ounces) plus 1 tablespoon granulated sugar**
- ¼ **cup packed (1¾ ounces) light brown sugar**
- ½ **teaspoon grated zest plus 1 tablespoon juice from 1 lemon**
- ¼ **teaspoon table salt**
- ⅛ **teaspoon ground cinnamon**
- 1 **large egg white, lightly beaten**

1. Following the photos on page 558, roll one disk of dough into a 12-inch circle on a lightly floured work surface, then fit it into a 9-inch pie plate, letting the excess dough hang over the edge; cover with plastic wrap and refrigerate for 30 minutes. Roll the other disk of dough into a 12-inch circle on a lightly floured work surface, then transfer to a parchment-lined baking sheet; cover with plastic wrap and refrigerate for 30 minutes.

2. Toss the apples, ½ cup of the granulated sugar, the brown sugar, zest, salt, and cinnamon together in a Dutch oven. Cover and cook over medium heat, stirring frequently, until the apples are tender when poked with a fork but still hold their shape, 15 to 20 minutes. Transfer the apples and their juice to a rimmed baking sheet and cool to room temperature, about 30 minutes.

3. Adjust an oven rack to the lowest position, place a rimmed baking sheet on the rack, and heat the oven to 425 degrees. Drain the cooled apples thoroughly through a colander, reserving ¼ cup of the juice. Stir the lemon juice into the reserved ¼ cup of apple juice.

4. Spread the apples into the dough-lined pie plate, mounding them slightly in the middle, and drizzle with the lemon juice mixture. Following the photos on page 565, loosely roll the second piece of dough around the

MAKING A DOUBLE-CRUST PIE

1. Loosely roll the chilled top crust around the rolling pin, then gently unroll it over the filled pie crust bottom.

2. Using scissors, trim all but ½ inch of the dough over-hanging the edge of the pie plate.

3. Press the top and bottom crusts together, then tuck the edges underneath.

4. Crimp the dough evenly around the edge of the pie, using your fingers. Cut vent holes attractively in the center of the top crust with a paring knife (drier pies only require four vents, while very juicy pies require eight vents).

PEACH PIE

WHY THIS RECIPE WORKS: Fresh peach pies are often soupy or overly sweet, with a bottom crust that is soggy or undercooked. We wanted to create a filling that was juicy but not swimming in liquid, its flavors neither muscled out by spices nor overwhelmed by thickeners, and we wanted a crust that was well browned on the bottom.

We peeled and sliced the peaches and found that all they needed in the way of flavor was sugar, lemon juice, cinnamon, nutmeg, and a dash of salt. To thicken the juices, we used a little cornstarch, but still, we needed to do more. A lattice-top pie crust was our solution—while it requires a bit more work than making a regular double-crust pie, we found that it's worth the effort. Not only is it pretty and very traditional on peach pies, but it serves an important purpose: The structure of a lattice top allows for maximum evaporation while the pie cooks—the juices released by the fruit cook down slowly while baking so the filling isn't soupy. For easy assembly, we rolled and cut the dough, then froze it so the strips were firm and easy to handle.

Lattice-Top Fresh Peach Pie
SERVES 8

You can use All-Butter Double-Crust Pie Dough (page 560), Basic Double-Crust Pie Dough (page 558), or Foolproof Double-Crust Pie Dough (page 561) for this pie. A serrated peeler makes peeling peaches a whole lot easier and you can avoid the step of blanching the peaches. Serve with vanilla ice cream or lightly sweetened whipped cream.

rolling pin and gently unroll it over the pie. Trim, fold, and crimp the edges and cut four vent holes in the top. Brush the dough with the egg white and sprinkle with the remaining 1 tablespoon sugar.

5. Place the pie on the heated baking sheet and bake until the crust is golden, about 25 minutes. Reduce the oven temperature to 375 degrees, rotate the baking sheet, and continue to bake until the juices are bubbling and the crust is deep golden brown, 25 to 30 minutes longer. Cool the pie on a wire rack until the filling has set, about 2 hours; serve slightly warm or at room temperature.

1 recipe double-crust pie dough (see note)
  Unbleached all-purpose flour, for the work surface
2½ pounds ripe peaches (6 to 7 medium), peeled, pitted, and sliced ⅓ inch thick (see note)
1 cup (7 ounces) plus 1 tablespoon sugar
1 tablespoon cornstarch
1 tablespoon juice from 1 lemon
  Pinch ground cinnamon
  Pinch ground nutmeg
  Pinch table salt
1 large egg white, lightly beaten

1. Following the photos on page 558, roll one disk of dough into a 12-inch circle on a lightly floured work surface, then fit it into a 9-inch pie plate, letting the excess dough hang over the edge; cover with plastic wrap and refrigerate 30 minutes to 1 hour.

2. Roll the other disk of dough into a 13½ by 10½-inch rectangle, then transfer to a parchment-lined baking sheet. Trim the dough to a 13 by 10-inch rectangle with straight edges and slice it lengthwise into eight 13-inch-long strips. Separate the strips slightly, cover with plastic wrap, and freeze until very firm, about 30 minutes.

3. Toss the peaches and 1 cup of the sugar together in a large bowl and let sit, tossing occasionally, until the peaches release their juice, about 1 hour. Adjust an oven rack to the lowest position, place a rimmed baking sheet on the rack, and heat the oven to 425 degrees.

4. Drain the peaches thoroughly through a colander, reserving ¼ cup of the juice. In a large bowl, toss the drained fruit, the reserved juice, cornstarch, lemon juice, cinnamon, nutmeg, and salt together until well combined.

5. Spread the peaches into the dough-lined pie plate and, following the photos, weave the chilled strips of dough over the top into a lattice. Let the strips soften for 5 to 10 minutes, then trim, fold, and crimp the edges. Lightly brush the lattice with the egg white and sprinkle with the remaining 1 tablespoon sugar.

6. Place the pie on the heated baking sheet and bake until the top crust is golden, about 25 minutes. Reduce the oven temperature to 375 degrees, rotate the baking sheet, and continue to bake until the juices are bubbling and the crust is deep golden brown, 25 to 35 minutes longer. Let the pie cool on a wire rack until the filling has set, about 2 hours; serve slightly warm or at room temperature.

NOTES FROM THE TEST KITCHEN

MAKING A LATTICE TOP

Making a lattice-top pie crust is a bit more work than making a regular double-crust pie, but it is well worth the effort. Not only is it pretty and very traditional on fruit pies, but it also serves an important purpose: The structure of a lattice top allows for maximum evaporation while the pie cooks. This is especially important for stone fruit pies, such as cherry and peach, as it allows the juices released by the fruit to cook down slowly while baking so that the filling isn't too soupy.

1. Using the chilled strips of lattice, lay four parallel strips evenly over the filling. Weave a fifth strip in the opposite direction.

2. Continue to weave in the remaining three strips, one at a time, to create a lattice.

3. After letting the strips thaw and soften for a few minutes, trim the overhanging edges of the dough to ½ inch. Press the edges of the bottom crust and lattice strips together and fold underneath.

4. Crimp the dough evenly around the edges of the pie using your fingers. Crimping the dough gives the pie a decorative edge and an attractive, finished look.

BLUEBERRY PIE

WHY THIS RECIPE WORKS: If the filling in blueberry pie doesn't jell, a sliced wedge can collapse into a soupy puddle topped by a sodden crust. Too much thickener and the filling can be so dense that cutting into it is like slicing through gummi bears. We wanted a pie that had a firm, glistening filling full of fresh, bright flavor and still-plump berries.

To thicken the pie, we favored tapioca because it didn't mute the fresh yet subtle blueberry flavor as cornstarch and flour did. The back of the tapioca box recommended 6 tablespoons, but this produced a stiff, congealed mass. Cooking and reducing half of the berries helped us cut down on the tapioca required, but not enough. A second inspiration came from a peeled and grated Granny Smith apple. Apples are high in pectin, a type of carbohydrate that acts as a thickener when cooked. Combined with a modest 2 tablespoons of tapioca, the apple thickened the filling to a soft, even consistency that was neither gelatinous nor slippery. The crust posed a much simpler challenge. As with all of our fruit pies, baking on a preheated baking sheet on the bottom oven rack produced a crisp, golden bottom crust. And we found a fast, easy alternative to a lattice top in a small biscuit cutter, which we used to cut out circles in the top crust before transferring the dough onto the pie. The attractive, unusual-looking top crust vented the steam from the berries as successfully as a classic lattice top.

Blueberry Pie

SERVES 8

You can use All-Butter Double-Crust Pie Dough (page 560), Basic Double-Crust Pie Dough (page 558), or Foolproof Double-Crust Pie Dough (page 561) for this pie. This recipe was developed using fresh blueberries, but unthawed frozen blueberries (our favorite brands are Wyman's and Cascadian Farm) will work as well. In step 3, cook half the frozen berries over medium-high heat, without mashing, until reduced to 1¼ cups, 12 to 15 minutes. Grind the tapioca to a powder in a spice grinder or mini food processor. If using pearl tapioca, reduce the amount to 5 teaspoons. Serve with vanilla ice cream or lightly sweetened whipped cream.

1 recipe double-crust pie dough (see note)
Unbleached all-purpose flour, for the work surface
6 cups (30 ounces) fresh blueberries (see note)
1 Granny Smith apple, peeled, cored, and shredded on the large holes of a box grater
¾ cup (5¼ ounces) sugar
2 tablespoons instant tapioca, ground (see note)
2 teaspoons grated zest plus 2 teaspoons juice from 1 lemon
Pinch table salt
2 tablespoons unsalted butter, cut into ¼-inch pieces
1 large egg white, lightly beaten

1. Following the photos on page 558, roll one disk of dough into a 12-inch circle on a lightly floured work surface, then fit it into a 9-inch pie plate, letting the excess dough hang over the edge; cover with plastic wrap and refrigerate for 30 minutes.

2. Roll the other disk of dough into a 12-inch circle on a lightly floured work surface. Following the photo on page 568, use a 1¼-inch round biscuit cutter to cut a round from the center of the dough. Cut 6 more rounds from the dough, 1½ inches from the edge of the center

MAKING A CUT-OUT CRUST

1. Use a 1¼-inch biscuit cutter (or spice jar lid) to cut holes in the dough.

2. The cut-out crust vents the steam from the berry filling and is an easy alternative to a lattice-top pie.

hole and equally spaced around the center hole. Transfer the dough to a parchment-lined baking sheet; cover with plastic wrap and refrigerate for 30 minutes.

3. Place 3 cups of the berries in a medium saucepan and set over medium heat. Using a potato masher, mash the berries several times to release the juices. Continue to cook, stirring frequently and mashing occasionally, until about half of the berries have broken down and the mixture is thickened and reduced to 1½ cups, about 8 minutes. Cool slightly.

4. Adjust an oven rack to the lowest position, place a rimmed baking sheet on the rack, and heat the oven to 400 degrees.

5. Place the shredded apple in a clean kitchen towel and wring dry. Transfer the apple to a large bowl and stir in the cooked berries, remaining 3 cups uncooked berries, sugar, tapioca, lemon zest and juice, and salt until combined. Spread the mixture into the dough-lined pie plate and scatter the butter pieces over the top.

6. Following the photos on page 565, loosely roll the second piece of dough around the rolling pin and gently unroll it over the pie. Trim, fold, and crimp the edges. Brush the dough with the egg white.

7. Place the pie on the heated baking sheet and bake until the crust is golden, about 25 minutes. Reduce the oven temperature to 350 degrees, rotate the baking sheet,

and continue to bake until the juices are bubbling and the crust is deep golden brown, 30 to 40 minutes longer. Cool the pie on a wire rack to room temperature, about 4 hours. Serve.

SUMMER BERRY PIE

WHY THIS RECIPE WORKS: A fresh berry pie might seem like an easy-to-pull-off summer dessert, but most of the recipes we tried buried the berries in gluey thickeners or embedded them in bouncy gelatin. Our goal was to make a pie with great texture and flavor—and still keep it simple.

We started with the test kitchen's quick and easy homemade graham cracker crust. For the filling, we used a combination of raspberries, blackberries, and blueberries. After trying a few different methods, we found a solution that both bound the berries in the graham cracker crust and intensified their bright flavor. We processed a portion of berries in the food processor until they made a smooth puree, then we thickened the puree with cornstarch. Next, we tossed the remaining berries with warm jelly for a glossy coat and a shot of sweetness. Pressed gently into the puree, the berries stayed put and tasted great.

Summer Berry Pie

SERVES 8

Feel free to vary the amount of each berry as desired as long as you have 6 cups of berries total; do not substitute frozen berries here. Serve with lightly sweetened whipped cream.

> 2 cups (10 ounces) raspberries (see note)
> 2 cups (10 ounces) blackberries (see note)
> 2 cups (10 ounces) blueberries (see note)
> ½ cup (3½ ounces) sugar
> 3 tablespoons cornstarch
> ⅛ teaspoon table salt
> 1 tablespoon juice from 1 lemon
> 1 recipe Graham Cracker Crust (page 562), baked and cooled
> 2 tablespoons red currant or apple jelly

1. Gently toss the berries together in a large bowl. Process 2½ cups of the berries in a food processor until very smooth, about 1 minute (do not under-process). Strain the puree through a fine-mesh strainer into a small saucepan, pressing on the solids to extract as much puree as possible (you should have about 1½ cups); discard the solids.

2. In a small bowl, whisk the sugar, cornstarch, and salt together, then whisk into the strained puree. Bring the puree to a boil over medium heat, stirring constantly, and cook until it is as thick as pudding, about 7 minutes. Off the heat, stir in the lemon juice and set aside to cool slightly.

3. Pour the warm berry puree into the baked and cooled pie crust. Melt the jelly in a small saucepan over low heat, then pour over the remaining 3½ cups berries and toss to coat. Spread the berries evenly over the puree and lightly press them into the puree. Cover the pie loosely with plastic wrap and refrigerate until the filling is chilled and set, about 3 hours. Serve chilled or at room temperature.

PUMPKIN PIE

WHY THIS RECIPE WORKS: Too often, pumpkin pie appears at the end of a Thanksgiving meal as a grainy, overspiced, canned-pumpkin custard encased in a soggy crust. We wanted to create a pumpkin pie recipe destined to be a new classic: velvety smooth, packed with pumpkin flavor, and redolent of just enough fragrant spices.

Canned pumpkin contains moisture, which dilutes a pie's flavor. To maximize flavor, we concentrated this liquid by cooking the pumpkin with sugar and spices, then whisked in heavy cream, milk, and eggs. This improved the flavor and the hot filling let the custard firm up quickly in the oven, preventing it from soaking into the crust. For spices, we chose nutmeg, cinnamon, and, surprisingly, freshly grated ginger. Sugar and maple syrup sweetened things, but tasters still craved a more complex pie. On a whim, we added mashed roasted yams to the filling and tasters appreciated the deeper flavor. To streamline the recipe we switched to canned candied yams and cooked them with the pumpkin. To keep the custard from curdling, we started the pie at a high temperature for 10 minutes, followed by a reduced temperature for the remainder of the baking time. This cut the baking time to less than one hour and the dual temperatures produced a creamy pie fully and evenly cooked from edge to center.

Pumpkin Pie

SERVES 8

If candied yams are unavailable, regular canned yams can be substituted. When the pie is properly baked, the center 2 inches of the pie should look firm but jiggle slightly. The pie finishes cooking with residual heat; to ensure that the filling sets, cool it at room temperature and not in the refrigerator. The crust and filling must both be warm when the filling is added. Serve with lightly sweetened whipped cream.

NOTES FROM THE TEST KITCHEN

BLIND BAKING A PIE CRUST

1. Line the chilled pie shell with a double layer of aluminum foil, covering the edges to prevent burning.

2. Fill the shell with pie weights and bake until dry and light in color. After baking, carefully remove the weights and let the crust cool (for a partially baked crust) or continue to bake until deep golden brown (for a fully baked crust).

1 recipe Basic Single-Crust Pie Dough (see page 559), fitted into a 9-inch pie plate and chilled
1 cup heavy cream
1 cup whole milk
3 large eggs plus 2 large yolks
1 teaspoon vanilla extract
1 (15-ounce) can pumpkin puree
1 cup candied yams, drained (see note)
¾ cup (5¼ ounces) sugar
¼ cup maple syrup
2 teaspoons grated or minced fresh ginger
1 teaspoon table salt
½ teaspoon ground cinnamon
¼ teaspoon ground nutmeg

1. Adjust an oven rack to the lowest position, place a rimmed baking sheet on the rack, and heat the oven to 400 degrees. Following the photos on page 569, line the chilled pie shell with a double layer of foil and fill with pie weights.

2. Bake the pie shell on the heated baking sheet for 15 minutes. Remove the weights and foil and continue to bake the crust until golden brown and crisp, 5 to 10 minutes longer. Transfer the pie crust with the baking sheet to a wire rack. (The crust must still be warm when the filling is added.)

3. While the pie shell is baking, whisk the cream, milk, eggs, egg yolks, and vanilla together in a medium bowl. Bring the pumpkin puree, yams, sugar, maple syrup, ginger, salt, cinnamon, and nutmeg to a simmer in a large saucepan over medium heat and cook, stirring constantly and mashing the yams against the sides of the pot, until thick and shiny, 15 to 20 minutes.

4. Remove the pan from the heat and whisk in the cream mixture until fully incorporated. Strain the mixture through a fine-mesh strainer set over a medium bowl, using the back of a ladle or spatula to press the solids through the strainer. Whisk the mixture, then transfer to the warm prebaked pie crust.

5. Bake the pie on the baking sheet for 10 minutes. Reduce the oven temperature to 300 degrees and continue to bake until the edges of the pie are set and the center registers 175 degrees on an instant-read thermometer, 20 to 35 minutes longer. Cool the pie on a wire rack to room temperature, 2 to 3 hours, before serving.

PECAN PIE

WHY THIS RECIPE WORKS: Pecan pies can be overwhelmingly sweet, with no real pecan flavor. And they too often turn out curdled and separated. What's more, the weepy filling makes the bottom crust soggy and leathery. The fact that the crust usually seems underbaked to begin with doesn't help matters. We wanted to create a recipe for a not-too-sweet pie with a smooth-textured filling and a properly baked bottom crust.

We tackled this pie's problems by using brown sugar and reducing the amount, which helped bring out the pecan flavor. We also partially baked the crust, which kept it crisp. We found that it's important to add the hot filling to a warm pie crust as this helps keep the crust from getting soggy. In addition, we discovered that simulating a double boiler when you're melting the butter and making the filling is an easy way to maintain gentle heat, which helps ensure that the filling doesn't curdle.

Pecan Pie

SERVES 8

The crust must still be warm when the filling is added. To serve the pie warm, cool it thoroughly so that it sets completely, then warm it in a 250-degree oven for about 15 minutes and slice. Serve with vanilla ice cream or lightly sweetened whipped cream.

1 recipe Basic Single-Crust Pie Dough (page 559), fitted into a 9-inch pie plate and chilled
6 tablespoons (¾ stick) unsalted butter, cut into 1-inch pieces
1 cup packed (7 ounces) dark brown sugar
½ teaspoon table salt
3 large eggs
¾ cup light corn syrup
1 tablespoon vanilla extract
2 cups (8 ounces) pecans, toasted and chopped into small pieces

1. Adjust an oven rack to the middle position and heat the oven to 375 degrees. Following the photos on page 569, line the chilled pie shell with a double layer of foil and fill with pie weights. Bake until the pie dough looks dry and is light in color, 25 to 30 minutes. Transfer the pie plate to a wire rack and remove the weights and foil. Adjust the oven rack to the lower-middle position and reduce the oven temperature to 275 degrees. (The crust must still be warm when the filling is added.)

2. Melt the butter in a heatproof bowl set in a skillet of water maintained at just below a simmer. Remove the bowl from the skillet and stir in the sugar and salt until the butter is absorbed. Whisk in the eggs, then the corn syrup and vanilla until smooth. Return the bowl to the hot water and stir until the mixture is shiny, hot to the touch, and registers 130 degrees on an instant-read thermometer. Off the heat, stir in the pecans.

3. Pour the pecan mixture into the warm pie crust. Bake the pie until the filling looks set but yields like Jell-O when gently pressed with the back of a spoon, 50 to 60 minutes. Cool the pie on a wire rack until the filling has firmed up, about 2 hours; serve slightly warm (see note) or at room temperature.

Triple-Chocolate-Chunk Pecan Pie

SERVES 8

Use either just one type of chocolate listed or a combination of two or three types. See page 607 for information on our top-rated brands of chocolate. The crust must still be warm when the filling is added.

- **1** recipe Basic Single-Crust Pie Dough (page 559), fitted into a 9-inch pie plate and chilled
- **3** tablespoons unsalted butter, cut into 3 pieces
- **¾** cup packed (5¼ ounces) dark brown sugar
- **½** teaspoon table salt
- **2** large eggs
- **½** cup light corn syrup
- **1** teaspoon vanilla extract
- **1** cup (4 ounces) pecans, toasted and chopped coarse
- **6** ounces semisweet, milk, and/or white chocolate, chopped coarse (see note)

1. Adjust an oven rack to the middle position and heat the oven to 375 degrees. Following the photos on page 569, line the chilled pie shell with a double layer of foil and fill with pie weights. Bake until the pie dough looks dry and is light in color, 25 to 30 minutes. Transfer the pie plate to a wire rack and remove the weights and foil. Adjust the oven rack to the lower-middle position and reduce the oven temperature to 275 degrees. (The crust must still be warm when the filling is added.)

2. Melt the butter in a heatproof bowl set in a skillet of water maintained at just below a simmer. Remove the bowl from the skillet and stir in the sugar and salt until the butter is absorbed. Whisk in the eggs, then the corn syrup and vanilla until smooth. Return the bowl to the hot water and stir until the mixture is shiny, hot to the touch, and registers 130 degrees on an instant-read thermometer. Off the heat, stir in the pecans.

3. Pour the pecan mixture into the warm pie crust. Scatter the chocolate over the top and lightly press it into the filling with the back of a spoon. Bake the pie until the filling looks set but yields like Jell-O when gently pressed with the back of a spoon, 50 to 60 minutes. Cool the pie on a wire rack until the filling has firmed up, about 2 hours; serve slightly warm or at room temperature.

KEY LIME PIE

WHY THIS RECIPE WORKS: Some of us have been served Key lime pie in restaurants and found it disappointing, usually harsh and artificial tasting. We wanted a recipe for classic Key lime pie with a fresh flavor and silky filling. Traditional Key lime pie is usually not baked; instead, the combination of egg yolks, lime juice, and sweetened condensed milk firms up when chilled because the juice's acidity causes the proteins in the eggs and milk to bind.

Although we had suspected that the sweetened condensed milk was the party guilty of giving Key lime pies their "off" flavor, we found that the real culprit was the lime juice—bottled, reconstituted lime juice, that is. When we substituted the juice and zest from fresh limes, the pie became an entirely different experience: pungent and refreshing, cool and yet creamy, and very satisfying. We also discovered that while the pie filling will set without baking (most recipes call only for mixing and then chilling), it set much more nicely after being baked for only 15 minutes. We tried other, more dramatic, departures from the "classic" recipe—folding in egg whites, substituting heavy cream for condensed milk—but they didn't work. Just two seemingly minor adjustments to the recipe made all the difference in the world.

Key Lime Pie

SERVES 8

Despite this pie's name, we found that tasters could not tell the difference between pies made with regular supermarket limes (called Persian limes) and true Key limes. Since Persian limes are easier to find and juice, we recommend them. The timing here is different from other pies; you need to make the filling first, then prepare the crust.

PIE
- 4 large egg yolks
- 4 teaspoons grated zest plus ½ cup juice from 3 or 4 limes (see note)
- 1 (14-ounce) can sweetened condensed milk
- 1 recipe Graham Cracker Crust (page 562)

TOPPING (OPTIONAL)
- 1 cup heavy cream, chilled
- ¼ cup (1 ounce) confectioners' sugar

1. FOR THE PIE: Whisk the egg yolks and lime zest together in a medium bowl until the mixture has a light-green tint, about 2 minutes. Whisk in the condensed milk

until smooth, then whisk in the lime juice. Cover the mixture and set aside at room temperature until thickened, about 30 minutes.

2. Meanwhile, prepare and bake the crust. Transfer the pie plate to a wire rack and leave the oven at 325 degrees. (The crust must still be warm when the filling is added.)

3. Pour the thickened filling into the warm pie crust. Bake the pie until the center is firm but jiggles slightly when shaken, 15 to 20 minutes. Let the pie cool slightly on a wire rack, about 1 hour, then cover loosely with plastic wrap and refrigerate until the filling is chilled and set, about 3 hours.

4. FOR THE TOPPING, IF USING: Before serving, whip the cream and sugar together in a large bowl with an electric mixer on medium-low speed until frothy, about 1 minute. Increase the mixer speed to high and continue to whip until the cream forms soft peaks, 1 to 3 minutes. Spread the whipped cream attractively over the top of the pie and serve.

LEMON MERINGUE PIE

WHY THIS RECIPE WORKS: Most everybody loves lemon meringue pie—at least the bottom half of it. The most controversial part is the meringue. On any given day it can shrink, bead, puddle, deflate, burn, sweat, break down, or turn rubbery. We wanted a pie with a crisp, flaky crust and a rich filling that would balance the airy meringue, without blocking the clear lemon flavor. The filling should be soft but not runny; firm enough to cut but not stiff and gelatinous. Most important, we wanted a meringue that didn't break down and puddle on the bottom or "tear" on top.

We consulted a food scientist, who told us that the puddling underneath the meringue is from undercooking. The beading on top of the pie is from overcooking.

We discovered that if the filling is piping hot when the meringue is applied, the underside of the meringue will not undercook; if the oven temperature is relatively low, the top of the meringue won't overcook. Baking the pie in a relatively cool (325-degree) oven also produces the best-looking, most evenly baked meringue. To further stabilize the meringue and keep it from weeping (even on hot, humid days), we beat in a small amount of cornstarch.

Lemon Meringue Pie

SERVES 8

Make the pie crust, let it cool, and then begin work on the filling. As soon as the filling is made, cover it with plastic wrap to keep it hot and then start working on the meringue topping. You want to add hot filling to the pie crust, apply the meringue topping, and then quickly get the pie into the oven.

- 1 **recipe Single-Crust Pie Dough for Custard Pies (page 559), fitted into a 9-inch pie plate and chilled**

FILLING
- 1½ **cups water**
- 1 **cup (7 ounces) sugar**
- ¼ **cup (1 ounce) cornstarch**
- ⅛ **teaspoon table salt**
- 6 **large egg yolks**
- 1 **tablespoon grated zest plus ½ cup juice from 3 lemons**
- 2 **tablespoons unsalted butter, cut into 2 pieces**

MERINGUE
- ⅓ **cup water**
- 1 **tablespoon cornstarch**
- ½ **cup (3½ ounces) sugar**
- ¼ **teaspoon cream of tartar**
- 4 **large egg whites**
- ½ **teaspoon vanilla extract**

1. Adjust an oven rack to the middle position and heat the oven to 375 degrees. Following the photos on page 569, line the chilled pie shell with a double layer of foil and fill with pie weights. Bake until the pie dough looks dry and is light in color, 25 to 30 minutes. Remove the weights and foil and continue to bake the crust until deep golden brown, 10 to 12 minutes longer. Cool the crust to room temperature. Reduce the oven temperature to 325 degrees.

2. FOR THE FILLING: Bring the water, sugar, cornstarch, and salt to a simmer in a large saucepan over medium heat, whisking constantly. When the mixture starts to turn translucent, whisk in the egg yolks, 2 at a time. Whisk in the lemon zest and juice, and butter. Return the mixture to a brief simmer, then remove the pan from the heat. Lay a sheet of plastic wrap directly on the surface of the filling to keep warm and prevent a skin from forming.

3. FOR THE MERINGUE: Bring the water and cornstarch to a simmer in a small saucepan and cook, whisking occasionally, until thickened and translucent, 1 to 2 minutes. Set aside off the heat to cool slightly.

4. Combine the sugar and cream of tartar in a small bowl. In a large bowl, whip the egg whites and vanilla together with an electric mixer on medium-low speed until foamy, about 1 minute. Increase the mixer speed to medium-high, add the sugar mixture, 1 tablespoon at a time, and whip the whites until shiny and soft peaks form, 1 to 3 minutes. Add the cornstarch mixture, 1 tablespoon at a time, and continue to whip the meringue to stiff peaks, about 1 to 3 minutes longer.

5. Meanwhile, remove the plastic from the filling and return to very low heat during the last minute or so of beating the meringue (to ensure the filling is hot).

6. Pour the warm filling into the pie crust. Using a rubber spatula, immediately distribute the meringue evenly around the edge and then the center of the pie, attaching the meringue to the pie crust to prevent shrinking. Use the back of a spoon to create attractive swirls and peaks in the meringue. Bake until the meringue is golden brown, about 20 minutes. Cool the pie on a wire rack until the filling has set, about 2 hours. Serve.

COCONUT CREAM PIE

WHY THIS RECIPE WORKS: Most recipes for this diner dessert are nothing more than a redecorated vanilla cream pie. A handful of coconut shreds stirred into the filling or sprinkled on the whipped cream might be enough to give it a new name, but certainly not enough to give it flavor. We wanted a coconut cream pie with the exotic and elusive flavor of tropical coconut rather than a thinly disguised vanilla custard.

We found that using not-too-sweet graham crackers made a crust with a delicate, cookie-like texture that didn't overshadow the coconut filling. For the filling, we started with a basic custard, using a combination of unsweetened coconut milk and whole milk. For more coconut flavor, we stirred in unsweetened shredded coconut and cooked it so the shreds softened slightly in the hot milk. Lastly, we topped the pie with simple sweetened whipped cream and dusted it with crunchy shreds of toasted coconut.

Coconut Cream Pie

SERVES 8

Do not use low-fat coconut milk here because it does not have enough flavor. Also, don't confuse coconut milk with cream of coconut. The filling should be warm—neither piping hot nor room temperature—when poured into the cooled pie crust. To toast the coconut, place it in a small skillet over medium heat and cook, stirring frequently, 3 to 5 minutes. It burns quite easily, so keep a close eye on it.

FILLING

- 1 (14-ounce) can coconut milk (see note)
- 1 cup whole milk
- ½ cup (1¼ ounces) unsweetened shredded coconut
- ⅔ cup (4⅔ ounces) sugar
- ¼ teaspoon table salt
- 5 large egg yolks
- ¼ cup cornstarch
- 2 tablespoons unsalted butter, cut into 2 pieces
- 1½ teaspoons vanilla extract

- 1 recipe Graham Cracker Crust (page 562), baked and cooled

TOPPING

- 1½ cups heavy cream, chilled
- 1½ tablespoons sugar
- 1½ teaspoons dark rum (optional)
- ½ teaspoon vanilla extract
- 1 tablespoon unsweetened shredded coconut, toasted (see note)

1. FOR THE FILLING: Bring the coconut milk, whole milk, shredded coconut, ⅓ cup of the sugar, and the salt to a simmer in a medium saucepan over medium-high heat, stirring occasionally.

2. As the milk mixture begins to simmer, whisk the remaining ⅓ cup sugar, the egg yolks, and cornstarch together in a separate bowl. Slowly whisk 1 cup of the simmering coconut milk mixture into the yolk mixture to temper, then slowly whisk the tempered yolks back into the simmering saucepan. Reduce the heat to medium and cook, whisking vigorously, until the mixture is thickened and a few bubbles burst on the surface, about 30 seconds.

3. Off the heat, whisk in the butter and vanilla. Cool the mixture until just warm, stirring often, about 5 minutes.

4. Pour the warm filling into the baked and cooled pie crust. Lay a sheet of plastic wrap directly on the surface of the filling and refrigerate the pie until the filling is chilled and set, about 4 hours.

5. FOR THE TOPPING: Before serving, whip the cream, sugar, rum (if using), and vanilla together with an electric mixer on medium-low speed until frothy, about 1 minute. Increase the mixer speed to high and continue to whip until the cream forms soft peaks, 1 to 3 minutes. Spread the whipped cream attractively over the top of the pie and sprinkle with the toasted coconut.

CHOCOLATE CREAM PIE

WHY THIS RECIPE WORKS: Chocolate cream pies can look superb but are often gummy, gluey, overly sweet, and impossible to slice. We wanted a voluptuously creamy pie, with a well-balanced chocolate flavor somewhere between milkshake and melted candy bar, and a delicious, easy-to-slice crust.

After testing every type of cookie on the market, we hit on pulverized Oreos and a bit of melted butter for the tastiest, most tender, sliceable crumb crust. We found that the secret to perfect chocolate cream pie filling was to combine two different types of chocolate for a deeper, more complex flavor. Bittersweet or semisweet chocolate provides the main thrust of flavor and intensely flavored unsweetened chocolate lends depth. One ounce of unsweetened chocolate may not seem like much, but it gives this pie great flavor. We also discovered that the custard's texture depended upon carefully pouring the egg yolk mixture into simmering half-and-half, then whisking in butter.

Chocolate Cream Pie

SERVES 8

For the best chocolate flavor and texture, we recommend either Callebaut semisweet and unsweetened chocolates or Hershey's Special Dark and Hershey's unsweetened chocolates. Other brands of chocolate sandwich cookies may be substituted for the Oreos, but avoid any "double-filled" cookies because the proportion of cookie to filling won't be correct. Do not combine the yolks and sugar in advance of making the filling—the sugar will begin to break down the yolks, and the finished cream will be pitted.

CRUST
- 16 Oreo cookies, broken into rough pieces (see note)
- 4 tablespoons (½ stick) unsalted butter, melted and cooled

FILLING
- 2½ cups half-and-half
- ⅓ cup (2⅓ ounces) sugar
- Pinch table salt
- 6 large egg yolks
- 2 tablespoons cornstarch
- 6 tablespoons (¾ stick) unsalted butter, cut into 6 pieces
- 6 ounces semisweet or bittersweet chocolate, chopped fine (see note)
- 1 ounce unsweetened chocolate, chopped fine (see note)
- 1 teaspoon vanilla extract

TOPPING
- 1½ cups heavy cream, chilled
- 2 tablespoons sugar
- ½ teaspoon vanilla extract

1. FOR THE CRUST: Adjust an oven rack to the middle position and heat the oven to 350 degrees. Pulse the cookies in a food processor until coarsely ground, about 15 pulses, then continue to process to fine, even crumbs, about 15 seconds. Sprinkle the butter over the crumbs and pulse to incorporate.

2. Sprinkle the mixture into a 9-inch pie plate. Following the photo on page 562, use the bottom of a measuring cup to press the crumbs into an even layer on the bottom and sides of the pie plate. Bake until the crust is fragrant and looks set, 10 to 15 minutes. Transfer the crust to a wire rack and cool completely.

3. FOR THE FILLING: Bring the half-and-half, 3 tablespoons of the sugar, and the salt to a simmer in a medium saucepan over medium-high heat, stirring occasionally.

4. As the half-and-half mixture begins to simmer, whisk the egg yolks, cornstarch, and remaining sugar together in a medium bowl until smooth. Slowly whisk about 1 cup of the simmering half-and-half mixture into the yolk mixture to temper, then slowly whisk the tempered yolks back into the simmering saucepan. Reduce the heat to medium and cook, whisking vigorously, until the mixture is thickened and a few bubbles burst on the surface, about 30 seconds.

5. Off the heat, whisk in the butter and chocolates until completely smooth and melted. Stir in the vanilla. Pour the warm filling into the baked and cooled pie crust. Lay a sheet of plastic wrap directly on the surface of the filling and refrigerate the pie until the filling is chilled and set, about 4 hours.

6. FOR THE TOPPING: Before serving, whip the cream, sugar, and vanilla together with an electric mixer on medium-low speed until frothy, about 1 minute. Increase the mixer speed to high and continue to whip until the cream forms soft peaks, 1 to 3 minutes. Spread the whipped cream attractively over the top of the pie.

CLASSIC TART DOUGH

WHY THIS RECIPE WORKS: The problem with most tarts is the crust—it's usually either too tough or too brittle. While regular pie crust is tender and flaky, classic tart crust should be fine-textured, buttery-rich, crisp, and crumbly—it is often described as being shortbread-like. We set out in the test kitchen to achieve the perfect tart dough, one that we could use in several of our tart recipes.

We found that using a full stick of butter made tart dough that tasted great and was easy to handle, yet still had a delicate crumb. Instead of using the hard-to-find superfine sugar and pastry flour that many other recipes call for, we used confectioners' sugar and all-purpose flour to achieve a crisp texture. Rolling the dough and fitting it into the tart pan was easy, and we had ample dough to patch any holes.

Classic Tart Dough
MAKES ENOUGH FOR ONE 9-INCH TART

Tart crust is sweeter, crisper, and less flaky than pie crust—it is more similar in texture to a cookie. The dough, wrapped tightly in plastic wrap, can be refrigerated for up to 2 days or frozen for up to 1 month. If frozen, let the dough thaw completely on the counter before rolling out.

- 1 **large egg yolk**
- 1 **tablespoon heavy cream**
- ½ **teaspoon vanilla extract**
- 1¼ **cups (6¼ ounces) unbleached all-purpose flour**
- ⅔ **cup (2⅔ ounces) confectioners' sugar**
- ¼ **teaspoon table salt**
- 8 **tablespoons (1 stick) unsalted butter, cut into ¼-inch pieces and chilled**

1. Whisk the egg yolk, cream, and vanilla together in a small bowl. Process the flour, sugar, and salt together in a food processor until combined. Scatter the butter pieces over the top and pulse until the mixture resembles coarse cornmeal, about 15 pulses.

2. With the machine running, add the egg mixture through the feed tube and continue to process until the dough just comes together around the processor blade, about 12 seconds.

3. Turn the dough onto a sheet of plastic wrap and flatten into a 6-inch disk. Wrap the dough tightly in plastic wrap and refrigerate for 1 hour. Before rolling the dough out, let it sit on the counter to soften slightly, about 10 minutes.

NOTES FROM THE TEST KITCHEN

MAKING A TART SHELL

1. After rolling the dough out into an 11-inch circle on a lightly floured work surface, wrap it loosely around the rolling pin and unroll the dough over a 9-inch tart pan with a removable bottom.

2. Lifting the edge of the dough, gently ease the dough into the pan. Press the dough into the corners and fluted sides of the pan.

3. Run the rolling pin over the top of the tart pan to remove any excess dough and make a clean edge.

4. If parts of the edge are too thin, reinforce them by pressing in some of the excess dough. If the edge is too thick, press some of the dough up over the edge of the pan and trim it away.

LEMON TART

WHY THIS RECIPE WORKS: Despite its apparent simplicity, there is much that can go wrong with a lemon tart. It can slip over the edge of sweet into cloying; its tartness can grab at your throat; it can be gluey or eggy or, even worse, metallic-tasting. Its crust can be too hard, too soft, too thick, or too sweet. We wanted a proper tart, one in which the filling is baked with the shell. For us, that meant only one thing: lemon curd.

For just enough sugar to offset the acid in the lemons, we used 3 parts sugar to 2 parts lemon juice, plus a whopping ¼ cup of lemon zest. To achieve a curd that was creamy and dense with a vibrant lemony yellow color, we used a combination of whole eggs and egg yolks. We cooked the curd over direct heat, then whisked in cold butter. And for a smooth, light texture, we strained the curd, then stirred in heavy cream just before baking.

Lemon Tart

SERVES 8 TO 10

Once the lemon curd ingredients have been combined, cook the curd immediately; otherwise it will have a grainy finished texture. Dust with confectioners' sugar before serving, or serve with lightly whipped cream.

- 1 recipe Classic Tart Dough (page 576)
  Unbleached all-purpose flour, for the work surface
- 7 large egg yolks plus 2 large eggs
- 1 cup (7 ounces) sugar
- ¼ cup grated zest plus ⅔ cup juice from 4 to 5 lemons
  Pinch table salt
- 4 tablespoons (½ stick) unsalted butter, cut into 4 pieces
- 3 tablespoons heavy cream

1. Roll the dough out to an 11-inch circle on a lightly floured work surface and, following the photos on page 576, fit it into a 9-inch tart pan with a removable bottom. Set the tart pan on a large plate and freeze the tart shell for 30 minutes.

2. Adjust an oven rack to the middle position and heat the oven to 375 degrees. Set the tart pan on a large baking sheet. Press a double layer of foil into the frozen tart shell and over the edges of the pan and fill with pie weights. Bake until the tart shell is golden brown and set, about 30 minutes, rotating the baking sheet halfway through.

3. Carefully remove the weights and foil and continue to bake the tart shell until it is fully baked and golden, 5 to 10 minutes longer. Transfer the tart crust with the baking sheet to a wire rack and cool the tart shell slightly while making the filling.

4. Whisk the egg yolks and eggs together in a medium saucepan. Whisk in the sugar until combined, then whisk in the lemon zest and juice and salt. Add the butter and cook over medium-low heat, stirring constantly, until the mixture thickens slightly and registers 170 degrees on an instant-read thermometer, about 5 minutes. Immediately pour the mixture through a fine-mesh strainer into a bowl and stir in the cream.

5. Pour the lemon filling into the warm tart shell. Bake the tart on the baking sheet until the filling is shiny and opaque and the center jiggles slightly when shaken, 10 to 15 minutes. Let the tart cool completely on the baking sheet, about 1½ hours. To serve, remove the outer metal ring of the tart pan, slide a thin metal spatula between the tart and the tart pan bottom, and carefully slide the tart onto a serving platter or cutting board.

FREE-FORM FRUIT TART

WHY THIS RECIPE WORKS: Few things are better than a summer fruit pie, but that takes time (and skill). What we wanted was simple: a buttery, flaky crust paired with juicy summer fruit—a lazy recipe, one that produced both crust and fruit with half the work of a regular pie. A free-form tart—a single layer of buttery pie dough folded up around fresh fruit—seemed the obvious solution.

Without the support of a pie plate, tender crusts are prone to leak juice, and this results in soggy bottoms. For our crust, we used a high proportion of butter to flour, which provided the most buttery flavor and tender texture without compromising the structure. We then turned to a French technique in pastry making called *fraisage*. To begin, butter is only partially cut into the dry ingredients. Then, with the heel of the hand, the cook presses the barely mixed dough firmly against the counter. As a result, the chunks of butter are pressed into long, thin sheets that create lots of flaky layers when the dough is baked. We rolled the dough into a 12-inch circle, which produced a crust that was thick enough to contain a lot of fruit but thin enough to bake evenly and thoroughly. We placed the fruit in the middle, then lifted the dough up and back over the fruit (the center of the tart remained exposed) and pleated it loosely to allow for shrinkage. The bright summer fruit needed only the simple addition of sugar.

Free-Form Summer Fruit Tart

SERVES 6

The dough, wrapped tightly in plastic wrap, can be refrigerated for up to 2 days or frozen for up to 1 month. If frozen, let the dough thaw completely on the counter before rolling it out. Though we prefer a tart made with a mix of stone fruits and berries, you can use only one type of fruit if you prefer. Taste the fruit before adding sugar to it; use the lesser amount if the fruit is very sweet, more if it is tart. However much sugar you use, do not add it to the fruit until you are ready to fill and form the tart. Serve with vanilla ice cream, lightly sweetened whipped cream, or crème fraîche.

MIXING A FLAKY DOUGH

1. Starting at one end of the rectangular pile of dough, smear a small amount of the dough against the work surface with the heel of your hand. Repeat this process (called *fraisage*) until the rest of the buttery crumbs have been worked.

2. Gather the smeared bits into another rectangular pile and repeat the smearing process until all of the crumbs have been worked again. This second time won't take as long and will result in large flakes of dough.

RUSTIC TART DOUGH

- 1½ cups (7½ ounces) unbleached all-purpose flour, plus extra for the work surface
- ½ teaspoon table salt
- 10 tablespoons (1¼ sticks) unsalted butter, cut into ½-inch pieces and chilled
- 4–6 tablespoons ice water

FILLING

- 1 pound peaches, nectarines, apricots, or plums, pitted and sliced into ½-inch-thick wedges
- 1 cup (5 ounces) blueberries, raspberries, or blackberries
- 3–5 tablespoons plus 1 tablespoon sugar (see note)

1. FOR THE RUSTIC TART DOUGH: Process the flour and salt in a food processor until combined. Scatter the butter pieces over the top and pulse until the mixture resembles coarse bread crumbs and the butter pieces are about the size of small peas, about 10 pulses. Continue to pulse, adding the water through the feed tube 1 tablespoon at a time, until the dough begins to form small curds that hold together when pinched with your fingers (the dough will be crumbly), about 10 pulses.

2. Following the photos, turn the dough crumbs out onto a lightly floured work surface and gather into a rectangular-shaped pile. Starting at the farthest end, use the heel of your hand to smear a small amount of dough against the work surface. Continue to smear the dough

until all the crumbs have been worked. Gather the smeared crumbs together in another rectangular-shaped pile and repeat the process. Flatten the dough into a 6-inch disk, wrap it tightly in plastic wrap, and refrigerate for 1 hour. Before rolling the dough out, let it sit on the counter to soften slightly, about 10 minutes.

3. Roll the dough into a 12-inch circle between two large sheets of floured parchment paper. Slide the dough, still between the parchment sheets, onto a large baking sheet and refrigerate until firm, about 20 minutes.

4. FOR THE FILLING: Adjust an oven rack to the middle position and heat the oven to 375 degrees. Gently toss the fruit and sugar together in a large bowl. Remove the top sheet of parchment paper from the dough. Mound the fruit in the center of the dough, leaving a 2½-inch border around the edge. Following photo 2 on page 582, and being careful to leave a ½-inch border of dough around the fruit, fold the outermost 2 inches of dough over the fruit, pleating it every 2 to 3 inches as needed; gently pinch the pleated dough to secure, but do not press the dough into the fruit. Working quickly, brush the dough with water and sprinkle evenly with the additional 1 tablespoon sugar.

5. Bake the tart until the crust is deep golden brown and the fruit is bubbling, about 1 hour, rotating the baking sheet halfway through.

6. Cool the tart on the baking sheet on a wire rack for 10 minutes, then use the parchment paper to gently transfer the tart to a wire rack. Use a metal spatula to loosen the tart from the parchment and remove the parchment. Cool the tart on the rack until the juices have thickened, about 25 minutes. Serve warm or at room temperature.

FRESH FRUIT TART WITH PASTRY CREAM

WHY THIS RECIPE WORKS: Fresh fruit tarts usually offer little substance beyond their dazzling beauty, with rubbery or institutionalized pudding fillings, soggy crusts, and underripe, flavorless fruit. We set out to create a buttery, crisp crust filled with rich, lightly sweetened pastry cream, topped with fresh, glistening fruit.

We started with our classic tart dough as the crust and baked it until it was golden brown. We then filled the tart with pastry cream, made with half-and-half that was enriched with butter and thickened with just enough cornstarch to keep its shape without becoming gummy. For the fruit, we chose a combination of kiwi, which we peeled and sliced into half-moons, raspberries, and

blueberries. We found that it was important not to wash the berries, as washing causes them to bruise and bleed and makes for a less than attractive tart (buy organic if you're worried about pesticide residues). The finishing touch: a drizzle with a jelly glaze for a glistening presentation.

Fresh Fruit Tart with Pastry Cream

SERVES 8 TO 10

The pastry cream can be made a day or two in advance, but do not fill the prebaked tart shell until just before serving. Once filled, the tart should be topped with fruit, glazed, and served within half an hour or so. Don't wash the berries or they will lose their flavor and shape.

PASTRY CREAM

- 2 cups half-and-half
- ½ cup (3½ ounces) sugar
  Pinch table salt
- 5 large egg yolks
- 3 tablespoons cornstarch
- 4 tablespoons (½ stick) unsalted butter, cut into 4 pieces
- 1½ teaspoons vanilla extract

TART SHELL AND FRUIT

- 1 recipe Classic Tart Dough (page 576)
  Unbleached all-purpose flour, for the work surface
- 2 large kiwis, peeled, halved lengthwise, and sliced ⅜ inch thick
- 2 cups (10 ounces) raspberries (see note)
- 1 cup (5 ounces) blueberries (see note)
- ½ cup red currant or apple jelly

1. FOR THE PASTRY CREAM: Bring the half-and-half, 6 tablespoons of the sugar, and the salt to a simmer in a medium saucepan over medium-high heat, stirring occasionally.

2. As the half-and-half mixture begins to simmer, whisk the egg yolks, cornstarch, and remaining 2 tablespoons sugar together in a medium bowl until smooth. Slowly whisk about 1 cup of the simmering half-and-half mixture into the yolks to temper, then slowly whisk the tempered yolks back into the simmering saucepan. Reduce the heat to medium and cook, whisking vigorously, until the mixture is thickened and a few bubbles burst on the surface, about 30 seconds.

3. Off the heat, stir in the butter and vanilla. Transfer the mixture to a medium bowl, lay a sheet of plastic wrap directly on the surface, and refrigerate the pastry cream until chilled and firm, about 3 hours.

4. FOR THE TART SHELL AND FRUIT: Roll the dough out to an 11-inch circle on a lightly floured work surface and, following the photos on page 576, fit it into a 9-inch tart pan with a removable bottom. Set the tart pan on a large plate and freeze the tart shell for 30 minutes.

5. Adjust an oven rack to the middle position and heat the oven to 375 degrees. Set the tart pan on a large baking sheet. Press a double layer of foil into the frozen tart shell and over the edges of the pan and fill with pie weights. Bake until the tart shell is golden brown and set, about 30 minutes, rotating the baking sheet halfway through.

6. Carefully remove the weights and foil and continue to bake the tart shell until it is fully baked and golden, 5 to 10 minutes longer. Transfer the tart shell with the baking sheet to a wire rack and cool the tart shell completely, about 1 hour.

7. Spread the chilled pastry cream evenly over the bottom of the cooled tart shell. Shingle the kiwi slices around the edge of the tart, then arrange three rows of raspberries inside the kiwi. Finally, arrange a mound of blueberries in the center.

8. Melt the jelly in a small saucepan over medium-high heat, stirring occasionally to smooth out any lumps. Using a pastry brush, dab the melted jelly over the fruit. To serve, remove the outer metal ring of the tart pan, slide a thin metal spatula between the tart and the tart pan bottom, and carefully slide the tart onto a serving platter or cutting board.

Mixed Berry Tart with Pastry Cream

Follow the recipe for Fresh Fruit Tart with Pastry Cream, omitting the kiwi and adding 2 cups (10 ounces) extra berries (including blackberries or quartered strawberries). Combine the berries in a large plastic bag and toss them gently to mix. Carefully spread the berries in an even layer over the tart. Glaze and serve as directed.

FRENCH APPLE TART

WHY THIS RECIPE WORKS: The French tart known as an apple galette should have a flaky crust and a substantial layer of nicely shingled sweet caramelized apples. But it's challenging to make a crust strong enough to hold the apples and still be eaten out of hand—most recipes create a crust that is tough, cracker-like, and bland. Our ideal galette has the buttery flakiness of a croissant but is strong enough to support a generous layer of caramelized apples.

Choosing the right flour put us on the right track. All-purpose flour contains too much gluten for this dough; it made the pastry tough. Lower-protein pastry flour created a flaky, tender, and sturdy pastry. As pastry flour is hard to find, we created a practical alternative by mixing regular all-purpose flour with instant flour. Technique also proved to be important. We used the French fraisage method of blending butter into dough (see page 578 for more information). The apple topping was simple. We found that any thinly sliced apple would work, although we slightly preferred Granny Smith.

Apple Galette

SERVES 10 TO 12

The most common brands of instant flour are Wondra and Shake & Blend; they are sold in canisters in the baking aisle. The galette can be made without instant flour, using 2 cups unbleached all-purpose flour and 2 tablespoons cornstarch; however, you might have to increase the amount of ice water. The dough, wrapped tightly in plastic wrap, can be refrigerated for up to 2 days or frozen for up to 1 month. If frozen, let the dough thaw completely on the counter before rolling out. Serve with ice cream, whipped cream, or crème fraîche.

DOUGH

- 1½ cups (7½ ounces) unbleached all-purpose flour, plus extra for the work surface
- ½ cup (2½ ounces) instant flour (see note)
- ½ teaspoon table salt
- ½ teaspoon sugar
- 12 tablespoons (1½ sticks) unsalted butter, cut into ¼-inch pieces and chilled
- 7–9 tablespoons ice water

TOPPING

- 1½ pounds Granny Smith apples (about 3 large), peeled, cored, and sliced ⅛ inch thick
- 2 tablespoons unsalted butter, cut into ¼-inch pieces
- ¼ cup (1¾ ounces) sugar
- 3 tablespoons apple jelly

1. FOR THE DOUGH: Process the flours, salt, and sugar together in a food processor until combined. Scatter the butter pieces over the top and pulse until the mixture resembles coarse cornmeal, about 15 pulses. Continue to pulse, adding the water through the feed tube 1 tablespoon at a time until the dough begins to form small curds that hold together when pinched with your fingers (the dough will be crumbly), about 10 pulses.

2. Following the photos on page 578, turn the dough crumbs onto a lightly floured work surface and gather into a rectangular-shaped pile. Starting at the farthest end, use the heel of your hand to smear a small amount of dough against the work surface. Continue to smear the dough until all the crumbs have been worked. Gather the smeared crumbs together in another rectangular-shaped pile and repeat the process. Press the dough into a 4-inch square, wrap it tightly in plastic wrap, and refrigerate for 1 hour. Before rolling the dough out, let it sit on the counter to soften slightly, about 10 minutes.

3. Adjust an oven rack to the middle position and heat the oven to 400 degrees. Cut a piece of parchment to measure exactly 16 by 12 inches. Following the photos on page 581, roll the dough out over the parchment, dusting with flour as needed, until it just overhangs the parchment. Trim the edges of the dough even with the parchment. Roll the outer 1 inch of the dough up to create a ½-inch-thick border. Slide the parchment paper with the dough onto a large rimmed baking sheet.

4. FOR THE TOPPING: Starting in one corner of the tart, shingle the apple slices into the crust in tidy diagonal rows, overlapping them by a third. Dot with the butter and sprinkle evenly with the sugar. Bake the tart until the bottom is deep golden brown and the apples have caramelized, 45 to 60 minutes, rotating the baking sheet halfway through.

5. Melt the jelly in a small saucepan over medium-high heat, stirring occasionally to smooth out any lumps. Brush the glaze over the apples and let the tart cool slightly on the baking sheet for 10 minutes. Slide the tart onto a large platter or cutting board and slice the tart in half lengthwise, then crosswise into square pieces. Serve warm or at room temperature.

NOTES FROM THE TEST KITCHEN

PREPARING APPLE GALETTE

1. Cut a piece of parchment to measure exactly 16 by 12 inches, then roll the dough out on top of the parchment until it just over-hangs the edge and is about ⅛ inch thick.

2. Trim the dough so that the edges are even with the parchment paper. We use the parchment as a guide to cut a perfectly even rect-angle of dough from which we can make a large thin crust.

3. Roll up 1 inch of each edge to create a ½-inch-thick border. This border is decorative and helps keep the apple slices in place.

4. Slide the parchment and dough onto a rimmed bak-ing sheet. Starting in one corner, shingle the apple slices in tidy rows on the diagonal over the dough, overlapping each row by a third.

FREE-FORM APPLE TART

WHY THIS RECIPE WORKS: Apple tarts are easier to make than apple pie, but they have their problems: The filling can dry out owing to the lack of a top crust, and the dough can be limp and tacky. We wanted a simple free-form tart with moist, flavorful apples neatly contained by a flaky, easy-to-handle dough.

Off the bat, we decided to borrow the crust from our Free-Form Summer Fruit Tart recipe (see page 577)—it's sturdy yet flaky, with a great buttery flavor. As with our Classic Apple Pie (see page 563), we favored a combination of Granny Smith and McIntosh apples. To ensure that the apples cooked through in a short amount of time, we sliced them ¼ inch thick. All the apples needed in the way of flavor enhancement was lemon juice, sugar, and cinnamon.

Free-Form Apple Tart

SERVES 6

Serve with vanilla ice cream or lightly sweetened whipped cream.

- 1 **pound Granny Smith apples (about 2 large), peeled, cored, and sliced ¼ inch thick**
- 1 **pound McIntosh apples (about 2 large), peeled, cored, and sliced ¼ inch thick**
- ½ **cup (3½ ounces) plus 1 tablespoon sugar**
- 1 **tablespoon juice from 1 lemon**
- ⅛ **teaspoon ground cinnamon**
- 1 **recipe Rustic Tart Dough (page 576), rolled into a 12-inch circle and chilled**

1. Adjust an oven rack to the middle position and heat the oven to 375 degrees. Toss the apples, ½ cup of the sugar, lemon juice, and cinnamon together in a large bowl.

2. Remove the top sheet of parchment paper from the dough. Following the photos on page 582, stack some of the apples into a circular wall, leaving a 2½-inch border around the edge. Fill in the middle of the tart with the remaining apples. Being careful to leave a ½-inch border of dough around the fruit, fold the outermost 2 inches of dough over the fruit, pleating it every 2 to 3 inches as needed; gently pinch the pleated dough to secure, but do not press the dough into the fruit. Working quickly, brush the dough with water and sprinkle evenly with the remaining 1 tablespoon sugar.

3. Bake the tart on a large rimmed baking sheet until the crust is deep golden brown and the apples are tender, about 1 hour, rotating the baking sheet halfway through.

MAKING A FREE-FORM TART

1. Discard the top piece of parchment. Stack the apple slices into a circular wall, leaving a 2½–inch border of dough. Fill the center with the remaining apples.

2. Fold 2 inches of the dough up over the fruit, leaving a ½-inch border between the fruit and the edge of the tart shell. This ½-inch space helps prevent the tart juices from leaking through the folds in the shell.

4. Cool the tart on the baking sheet on a wire rack for 10 minutes, then use the parchment paper to gently transfer the tart to the wire rack. Use a metal spatula to loosen the tart from the parchment and remove the parchment. Cool the tart on the rack until the juices have thickened, about 25 minutes. Serve warm or at room temperature.

TARTE TATIN

WHY THIS RECIPE WORKS: Making a true tarte Tatin requires an investment of time and a certain amount of skill. Traditionally, the apples are cooked in a skillet until caramelized then topped with homemade pastry. Then the skillet is put in the oven to cook the pastry. Before serving, the tart is masterfully flipped out onto a serving platter. Yes, this version is great, but we wanted to simplify it enough for a weeknight dessert.

We first baked a sheet of store-bought puff pastry until it was beautifully golden brown. While the pastry baked, we cooked the apples in a skillet until they were caramelized and tender. We then spooned the apples over the pastry, arranging them in three even rows with a ½-inch border around the outside of the pastry. As a final touch, we created a simple sauce by adding heavy cream and Grand Marnier to the juices left behind after the apples were cooked.

30-Minute Tarte Tatin
SERVES 6 TO 8

To get this dessert on the table in 30 minutes, peel the apples while the oven preheats and the pastry thaws, and then bake the pastry while the apples are caramelizing. This dessert is especially good with Tangy Whipped Cream (page 549).

- 1 (9½ by 9-inch) sheet frozen puff pastry, thawed
- 8 tablespoons (1 stick) unsalted butter
- ¾ cup (5¼ ounces) sugar
- 2 pounds Granny Smith apples (about 4 large), peeled, quartered, and cored
- ¼ cup heavy cream
- 2 tablespoons Grand Marnier, spiced rum, or Calvados (optional)

1. Adjust an oven rack to the middle position and heat the oven to 400 degrees. Line a rimmed baking sheet with parchment paper. Unfold the puff pastry, lay it on the prepared baking sheet, and bake until golden brown and puffed, 15 to 20 minutes, rotating the baking sheet halfway through. Transfer the baked pastry sheet to a serving platter and press lightly to flatten if domed.

2. Meanwhile, melt the butter in a 12-inch nonstick skillet over high heat. Remove the pan from the heat and sprinkle evenly with the sugar. Lay the apples in the skillet, return the skillet to high heat, and cook until the juice in the pan turns a rich amber color and the apples are caramelized, about 15 minutes, turning the apples halfway through.

3. Remove the apples from the pan one at a time and arrange in three overlapping rows on the baked pastry sheet, leaving a ½-inch border. Spoon about half of the pan juice over the apples.

4. Whisk the cream and Grand Marnier (if using) into the remaining juice in the pan and bring to a simmer. Pour some sauce over the tart and serve, passing the remaining sauce separately.

Pear Tatin

We like to use Bosc or Bartlett pears here because they maintain their shape nicely when cooked. If you have it on hand, substitute Poire William (or other pear liqueur) for the Grand Marnier.

Follow the recipe for 30-Minute Tarte Tatin, substituting 2 pounds Bosc or Bartlett pears for the apples. Increase the cooking time by 5 or 10 minutes if necessary.

THE AMERICA'S TEST
KITCHEN SHOPPING GUIDE

SHOPPING FOR EQUIPMENT

With a well-stocked kitchen, you'll be able to take on any recipe. But there's so much equipment out there on the market, how do you figure out what's what? Price often correlates with design, not performance. Over the years, our test kitchen has evaluated thousands of products. We've gone through copious rounds of testing and have identified the most important attributes in every piece of equipment, so when you go shopping you'll know what to look for. And because our test kitchen accepts no support from product manufacturers, you can trust our ratings. Prices in this chart are based on shopping at online retailers and will vary.

KNIVES AND MORE	ITEM	WHAT TO LOOK FOR	TEST KITCHEN FAVORITES
MUST-HAVE ITEMS	CHEF'S KNIFE	• High-carbon stainless steel blade • Curved 8-inch blade • Lightweight • Comfortable grip and nonslip handle	**Victorinox Forschner Fibrox 8-Inch Chef's Knife** $29.95
	PARING KNIFE	• 3½- to 4-inch blade • Thin, flexible blade • Comfortable grip and nonslip handle	**Victorinox Forschner Fibrox 4-Inch Paring Knife** $12.95
	SERRATED KNIFE	• 10- to 12-inch blade • Long, rigid, slightly curved blade • Pointed serrations that are uniformly spaced and moderately sized • Comfortable grip and nonslip handle	**Wüsthof Classic 10-Inch Bread Knife** $89.95 Best Buy: **Victorinox Forschner Fibrox 10¼-Inch Bread Knife** $31.95
	SLICING KNIFE	• Tapered 12-inch blade for slicing large cuts of meat • Oval scallops (granton edge) carved into both sides of blade • Fairly rigid blade with rounded tip • Comfortable grip and nonslip handle	**Victorinox Forschner Fibrox 12-Inch Granton Edge Slicing Knife** $54.95
	STEAK KNIVES	• Super-sharp, straight-edge blade • Sturdy, not wobbly, blade • Comfortable grip and nonslip handle	**Victorinox Forschner Rosewood Straight Edge Steak Knife Set** $180 for a set of six Best Buy: **Cuisinart Steak Knife Set** $42 for a set of four
	SANTOKU KNIFE	• 6½-inch blade • Oval scallops (granton edge) carved into both sides of blade • Narrow, curved, and stubby blade • Comfortable grip and nonslip handle	**MAC Superior 6½-Inch Santoku Knife** $70

KNIVES AND MORE	ITEM	WHAT TO LOOK FOR	TEST KITCHEN FAVORITES
	BONING KNIFE	• 6-inch blade • Narrow, maneuverable, razor-sharp blade • Comfortable grip and nonslip handle	**Victorinox Forschner Fibrox 6-Inch Straight Boning Knife (Flexible)** $19.95
	MEAT CLEAVER	• Razor-sharp blade • Balanced weight between handle and blade • Comfortable grip and nonslip handle	**Global 6-Inch Meat Cleaver** $173.95 Best Buy: **LamsonSharp 7-Inch Meat Cleaver** $40
	MANDOLINE	• Hand guard to shield fingers • Gripper tongs to grasp food • Measurement-marked dial for precision cuts • Storage for extra blades	**OXO Good Grips V-Blade Mandoline Slicer** $39.99 Best Buy: **Kyocera Adjustable Ceramic Mandoline Slicer** $24.95
	CARVING BOARD	• Heavy, sturdy board • Deep, wide trench to trap juices • Central well to hold meat snugly	**Williams-Sonoma Medium Reversible Carving Board** $58
	CUT-RESISTANT GLOVE	• Tightly woven fabric for durability • Stretchy fabric for comfortable fit • Fits either right or left hand	**Microplane Specialty Series Cut Resistant Glove** $24.95
	CUTTING BOARD	• Lightweight board of 5 pounds or less • Durable bamboo or plastic board for resilient cutting surface	**Totally Bamboo Congo Cutting Board** $49.95 Best Buy: **Architec Gripper Nonslip Cutting Board** $14.99
	KNIFE SHARPENER	• Diamond sharpening material for electric sharpeners • Easy and comfortable to use • Clear instructions	Electric: **Chef's Choice Professional Sharpening Station 130** $159.99 Manual: **Accusharp Knife and Tool Sharpener** $12

MUST-HAVE ITEMS

POTS AND PANS	ITEM	WHAT TO LOOK FOR	TEST KITCHEN FAVORITES
	TRADITIONAL SKILLET	• Stainless steel interior and fully clad construction for even heat distribution • 12-inch diameter and flared sides • Comfortable, ovensafe handle welded or riveted to pan • Roomy interior (cooking surface of 9 inches or more) • Smaller sizes (8- or 10-inch) useful too	**All-Clad Stainless 12-Inch Frypan** $135
	NONSTICK SKILLET	• Dark, nonstick surface • 12-inch diameter and thick bottom • Comfortable, ovensafe handle welded or riveted to pan • Roomy interior (cooking surface of 9 inches or more) • Smaller sizes (8- or 10-inch) useful too	**Calphalon Simply Calphalon Nonstick 12-Inch Omelette Pan** $54.95
	CAST-IRON SKILLET	• Thick bottom and straight sides • Roomy interior (cooking surface of 9 inches or more) • Preseasoned	**Lodge Logic 12-Inch Skillet** $33.95
	ECO-FRIENDLY SKILLET	• PFOA-free surfaces are nonstick and more durable than silicone coatings • Roomy interior (cooking surface of 9 inches or more) • Balanced and not too heavy for easy maneuverability NOTE: We prefer our favorite traditional nonstick skillet for its superior performance and maneuverability.	**Scanpan Professional Fry Pan** $129.95
	DUTCH OVEN	• Enameled cast iron or stainless steel • Capacity of at least 6 quarts • Diameter of more than 9 inches • Tight-fitting lid • Sturdy handles	**Le Creuset 7¼-Quart Round French Oven** $269 **All-Clad Stainless 8-Quart Stockpot** $279 Best Buy: **Tramontina 6.5-Quart Cast Iron Dutch Oven** $40
	SAUCEPANS	• Large saucepan with 3- to 4-quart capacity and small nonstick saucepan with 2- to 2½-quart capacity • Tight-fitting lids • Thick bottom to prevent scorching • Long, comfortable, stay-cool handles welded or riveted to pan	Large: **All-Clad Stainless 4-Quart Saucepan** $199.95 Small: **Calphalon Contemporary Nonstick Short & Saucy 2½-Quart Shallow Saucepan with Cover** $39.95

MUST-HAVE ITEMS

POTS AND PANS	ITEM	WHAT TO LOOK FOR	TEST KITCHEN FAVORITES
MUST-HAVE ITEM	RIMMED BAKING SHEET	• Light-colored surface (heats and browns evenly) • Thick, sturdy construction • Dimensions of 18 by 13 inches • Buy at least two	**Lincoln Foodservice Half-Size Heavy Duty Sheet Pan (13-Gauge)** $16.49
	SAUTÉ PAN	• Stainless steel interior and fully clad construction for even heat distribution • Stainless steel handle • 10-inch diameter • Helper handle for easy lifting	**All-Clad Stainless 3-Quart Sauté Pan** $194.95
	OMELET PAN	• Gently sloped sides for easy turning and rolling of omelets • Nonstick finish • Heavy construction for durability and even heat distribution • 8-inch size for French omelets	**Original French Chef Omelette Pan** $139.95 Best Buy: **KitchenAid Gourmet Essentials Hard Anodized Nonstick 8-Inch Open French Skillet** $19.99
	STOCKPOT	• 12-quart capacity • Thick bottom to prevent scorching • Wide body for easy cleaning and storage • Flat or round handles that extend at least 1¾ inches	**All-Clad Stainless 12-Quart Stock Pot** $344.95 Best Buy: **Cuisinart Chef's Classic Stainless 12-Quart Stock Pot** $64.95
MUST-HAVE ITEM	ROASTING PAN	• Dimensions of at least 15 by 11 inches • Stainless steel interior with aluminum core for even heat distribution • Upright, riveted handles for easy gripping • Light interior for better monitoring of food	**Calphalon Contemporary Stainless Steel Roasting Pan (with V-Rack)** $129.99
	V-RACK	• Fixed, not adjustable, to provide sturdiness • Tall, vertical handles positioned on long side of rack	**All-Clad Nonstick Roasting Rack** $24.95
	COOKWARE SET	• Fully clad stainless steel with aluminum core for even heat distribution • Moderately heavy, durable construction • Lids included • The right mix of pans and sizes includes 12-inch skillet, 10-inch skillet, 2-quart saucepan, 4-quart saucepan, 8-quart stockpot	**All-Clad Stainless Steel 10-Piece Cookware Set** $699.95 Best Buy: **Tramontina 18/10 Stainless Steel TriPly-Clad Cookware Set** $144.97

HANDY TOOLS	ITEM	WHAT TO LOOK FOR	TEST KITCHEN FAVORITES
	KITCHEN SHEARS	• Take-apart scissors (for easy cleaning) • Slim blades • Slip-resistant, comfortable handles	Messermeister Take-Apart Shears $19.95 For Left-Handed Users: Wüsthof's Come-Apart Kitchen Shears $19.95
	TONGS	• Scalloped, not sharp and serrated, edges • Slightly concave pincers • Length of 12 inches (to keep your hand far from the heat)	OXO Good Grips 12-Inch Locking Tongs $10.95
	WOODEN SPOON	• Broad bowl • Thin edges for effective scraping • Strong, nonbulky handle	Mario Batali 13-Inch Wooden Spoon $4.95
MUST-HAVE ITEMS	SLOTTED SPOON	• Deep bowl • Long handle • Enough holes/slits for quick draining	OXO Good Grips Nylon Slotted Spoon $5.99
	ALL-AROUND SPATULA	• Wide blade with a thin edge • Long handle	Little difference among various brands
	SILICONE SPATULA	• Wide, stiff blade with a thin edge • Flexible enough to conform to the curve of a mixing bowl • Heatproof	Rubbermaid Professional 13½-Inch High Heat Scraper $11.48
	OFFSET SPATULA	• Flexible blade offset from handle • Useful to have a small spatula for icing cookies and cupcakes and a large one for layer cakes and sheet cakes	Large: Ateco Offset Spatula $5 Small: Wilton Angled Comfort Grip Spatula $4.50
MUST-HAVE ITEM	ALL-AROUND WHISK	• Skinny whisk to reach into corners of pan for making pan sauces and gravies • 10 to 12 inches in length	Best Manufacturers 12-Inch Standard French Whip $9.95
	BALLOON WHISK	• Balloon-shaped whisk with long, thin wires for beating egg whites and whipping cream • Lightweight design • Comfortable handle	OXO Steel 11-Inch Balloon Whisk $9.99

HANDY TOOLS	ITEM	WHAT TO LOOK FOR	TEST KITCHEN FAVORITES
	PEPPER MILL	• At least ½-cup capacity • Wide, unobstructed filler doors • Easy-to-adjust grind settings	**Unicorn Magnum Plus** $45
	LADLE	• Stainless steel • Hook handle • Pouring rim to prevent dripping • Handle 9 to 10 inches in length	**Rösle Ladle with Pouring Rim and Hook Handle** $29.95
	CAN OPENER	• Intuitive and easy to attach and detach • Smooth turning motions • Magnet for no-touch disposal of lid • Comfortable handle	**OXO Good Grips i-Series Can Opener** $19.95
	GARLIC PRESS	• Large capacity that holds multiple garlic cloves • Curved, comfortable handles • Long handle and short distance between pivot point and plunger	**Kuhn Rikon Easy-Squeeze Garlic Press** $20 Best Buy: **Trudeau Garlic Press** $11.99
	SERRATED FRUIT PEELER	• Sharp blade • Comfortable grip and nonslip handle • Lightweight	**Messermeister Serrated Swivel Peeler** $5.50
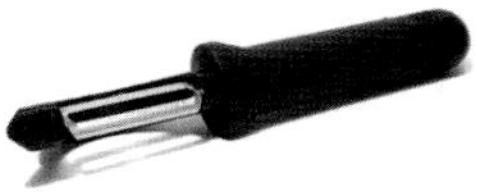	VEGETABLE PEELER	• Sharp blade • Comfortable grip and nonslip handle • Lightweight	**Messermeister Pro-Touch Swivel Peeler** $5.95
	RASP GRATER	• Sharp teeth (require little effort or pressure when grating) • Maneuverable over round or irregular shapes • Comfortable handle	**Microplane Grater/Zester** $14.95
	BOX GRATER	• Sharp teeth (require little effort or pressure when grating) • Clear container marked with cup measurements that snaps onto the bottom (for easy storage and cleaning) • Slim body and comfortable handle for easy use	**OXO Good Grips Box Grater** $17.95
	JUICER	• Hand-held squeezer with a comfortable handle • Sturdy, enameled aluminum construction • Sized specifically for limes, lemons, or oranges	**Amco Enameled Citrus Squeezer** $11.95 for the lime, $12.95 for the lemon, and $15.95 for the orange squeezer

(Left margin labels: MUST-HAVE ITEMS, MUST-HAVE ITEM, MUST-HAVE ITEM)

HANDY TOOLS	ITEM	WHAT TO LOOK FOR	TEST KITCHEN FAVORITES
	PORTION SCOOP	• Perfect half-sphere shape for easy portioning of batter and dough • Easy-to-squeeze handles to eject dough • Size number indicates how many portions per quart	Fante's Stainless Portion Scoop #16 (2-Ounce) $11.99
	ICE CREAM SCOOP	• Stainless steel • Comfortable handle • Thin bowl edge for easier scooping	Rösle Ice Cream Scoop $22.95
	MEAT POUNDER	• At least 1 pound in weight • Well-balanced offset handle • Large, flat disk shape	Norpro Meat Pounder $27.99
	BENCH SCRAPER	• Sturdy blade • Ruler marks (for easy measuring) • Comfortable handle with plastic, rubber, or nylon grip	OXO Good Grips Stainless Steel Multi-Purpose Scraper and Chopper $8.95
	BOWL SCRAPER	• Curved shape with comfortable grip • Contoured silicone covering with metal insert construction—rigid enough to move dough but flexible enough to scrape up batter • Thin, straight edge doubles as a dough cutter or bench scraper	iSi Basics Silicone Scraper Spatula $5.99
ROLLING PIN	• Wooden pin 20 inches in length with a diameter of at least 1½ inches • Tapered shape (makes it easy to roll dough to even thickness)	Fante's Large French Rolling Pin with Tapered Ends $6.99
MIXING BOWLS	• Good to have both stainless steel and glass • Microwave-safe (for glass) • Sets of 6–9 nesting, graduated bowls ranging in capacity from about 1¼ ounces to 4 quarts (for glass) and 2 cups to 8 quarts (for stainless steel)	Little difference among various brands
MINI PREP BOWLS	• Sturdy and somewhat heavy bowls with a stable base to prevent tipping • Roomy 6-ounce capacity is easier to scrape out with utensils • Glass bowls resist stains and don't absorb odors • Dishwasher- and microwave-safe	Pyrex 6-Ounce Dessert Dishes, Set of 4 $6.99
OVEN MITT	• 12- or 15-inch length (depending on hand size) • Machine washable • Flexible, heat-resistant material	Kool-Tek Protective Apparel $35.95, 12-Inch $40.95, 15-Inch Best Buy: Parvin Flameguard Oven Mitt $8.40

MUST-HAVE ITEMS

MUST-HAVE ITEM

HANDY TOOLS	ITEM	WHAT TO LOOK FOR	TEST KITCHEN FAVORITES
	COOKIE CUTTERS	• Metal cutters • Thin, sharp cutting edge and rounded or rubber-grip top • Depth of at least 1 inch	Little difference among various brands
	PASTRY BRUSH	• Thin silicone bristles (heat-resistant, durable, and easy to clean) • Perforated flaps (to trap liquid)	OXO Good Grips Silicone Pastry Brush $9.95
	SPLATTER SCREEN	• Diameter of at least 13 inches • Lollipop-shaped design • Tightly woven mesh face	Amco 13-Inch Splatter Screen $15.95
	CHINOIS	• Conical shape • Mesh-protecting steel band • Flexible fine-mesh screen	Little difference among various brands
	COLANDER	• 4- to 7-quart capacity • Stable base • Many holes for quick draining	Endurance Precision Pierced Stainless Steel Colander $29.99
	FINE-MESH STRAINER	• Stainless steel handle with rubber grip or ergonomic ridges for fingers • Deep bowl	OXO Steel 6½-Inch Strainer $24.95
	FOOD MILL	• Interchangeable disks for fine, medium, and coarse purees • Stainless steel • Easy-to-turn handle	Cuisipro Stainless Steel Food Mill $104.95
	FAT SEPARATOR	• Pitcher style • Plastic construction • 4-cup capacity	Trudeau Gravy Separator with Integrated Strainer $8.95
	POTATO MASHER	• Solid mashing disk with small holes • Comfortable grip	WMF Profi Plus Stainless Steel Potato Masher $17.99
	SALAD SPINNER	• Solid bottom for holding water to wash greens in bowl • Ergonomic and easy-to-operate hand pump	OXO Good Grips Salad Spinner $29.99

MUST-HAVE ITEMS

MUST-HAVE ITEMS

MEASURING EQUIPMENT	ITEM	WHAT TO LOOK FOR	TEST KITCHEN FAVORITES
MUST-HAVE ITEMS	DRY MEASURING CUPS	• Stainless steel cups (hefty and durable) or plastic cups (lightweight and comfortable) • Sets that include ⅔ and ¾ cups • Measurement markings that are visible even when the cup is full • Evenly weighted and stable • Long, flat handles level with cup so you can sweep across with blade for precise measurements	**OXO Good Grips Soft-Handled Measuring Cup Set (7 Pieces)** $7.95 **Amco Basic Ingredient 4-Piece Measuring Cup Set** $9.95
	LIQUID MEASURING CUPS	• Plastic or glass for easy viewing of liquids • Wide mouth • Range of easy-to-read gradation markings • Useful to have in a variety of sizes (1, 2, and 4 cups)	**Cuisipro Deluxe Liquid Measuring Cup** $7.95, 2-cup $10.95, 4-cup Best Buy: **Pyrex Prepware Liquid Measuring Cup** $3.99, 1-cup $4.99, 2-cup $5.99, 4-cup
	ADJUSTABLE MEASURING CUP	• Plungerlike bottom (with a tight seal between plunger and tube) that adjusts to correct measurement, with push-up bottom to cleanly extract sticky ingredients (such as shortening and peanut butter) • 1- or 2-cup capacity • Dishwasher-safe	**KitchenArt Pro Adjust-A-Cup** $11.95
MUST-HAVE ITEMS	MEASURING SPOONS	• Deep bowls (less spillage, easy to dip into a dry ingredient and sweep across the top for accurate measuring) • Oval shape fits into tall, narrow jars	**Cuisipro Stainless Steel Oval Measuring Spoons** $13.95
	KITCHEN RULER	• Stainless steel • 18 inches in length • Dishwasher-safe	**Little difference among various brands**
	DIGITAL SCALE	• Easy-to-read display unobstructed by weighing platform • Large weight range (0.05 ounces to 10 pounds) • Accessible buttons • Gram-to-ounce conversion feature	**OXO Digital Food Scale** $49.99 Best Buy: **Soehnle 65055 Digital Scale** $29.75

THERMOMETERS & TIMERS	ITEM	WHAT TO LOOK FOR	TEST KITCHEN FAVORITES
MUST-HAVE ITEM	INSTANT-READ THERMOMETER	• Digital model with automatic shut-off • Quick-response readings in 10 seconds or less • Wide temperature range (-40 to 450 degrees) • Long stem to reach interior of large cuts of meat	**ThermoWorks Super-Fast Thermapen** $89 Best Buy: **Maverick Redi-Chek Professional Chef's Digital Thermometer** $12.99

THERMOMETERS AND TIMERS	ITEM	WHAT TO LOOK FOR	TEST KITCHEN FAVORITES
MUST-HAVE ITEM	OVEN THERMOMETER	• Uncluttered face with large numbers and thin dial for easy readability • Stable base (to keep it in place and prevent it from being knocked over)	**CDN Multi-Mount Oven Thermometer** $7.99
	CANDY THERMOMETER	• Digital model • Easy-to-read console • Mounting clip (to attach probe to the pan)	**CDN Digital Cooking Thermometer and Timer** $24.95
	MEAT-PROBE THERMOMETER	• Long cord • Simple, single-function buttons	**ThermoWorks Original Cooking Thermometer/Timer** $19
	REFRIGERATOR/ FREEZER THERMOMETER	• Digital display • Wire probe for monitoring refrigerator and freezer simultaneously	**Maverick Cold-Chek Digital Refrigerator/Freezer Thermometer** $34.95
MUST-HAVE ITEM	KITCHEN TIMER	• Lengthy time range (1 second to at least 10 hours) • Ability to display two times simultaneously • Ability to count up after alarm goes off	**Polder Dual Timer/Stopwatch** $19.99

BAKEWARE	ITEM	WHAT TO LOOK FOR	TEST KITCHEN FAVORITES
MUST-HAVE ITEMS	GLASS BAKING DISH	• Dimensions of 13 by 9 inches • Large enough to hold casseroles and large crisps and cobblers • Handles	**Pyrex Bakeware 13 x 9-Inch Baking Dish** $8.95
	METAL BAKING PAN	• Dimensions of 13 by 9 inches • Straight sides • Nonstick coating for even browning and easy release of cakes and bar cookies • Handles	**Baker's Secret 13 x 9-Inch Nonstick Cake Pan** $3.99
	SQUARE BAKING PANS	• Straight sides • Light gold or dark nonstick surface for even browning and easy release of cakes • Useful to have both 9-inch and 8-inch square pans	**Williams-Sonoma 9-Inch Square Nonstick Goldtouch Cake Pan** $24 Best Buy: **Chicago Metallic Gourmetware 8-Inch Nonstick Square Cake Pan** $5.99
	ROUND CAKE PANS	• Straight sides • Nonstick coating for even browning and easy release of cakes • Useful to have a set of both 9-inch and 8-inch round pans	**Chicago Metallic Professional Lifetime 9-Inch Nonstick Round Cake Pan** $14.95

BAKEWARE	ITEM	WHAT TO LOOK FOR	TEST KITCHEN FAVORITES
	PIE PLATE	• Glass promotes even browning and allows progress to be monitored • ½-inch rim (makes it easy to shape decorative crusts) • Angled sides prevent crusts from slumping • Useful to have two	Pyrex Bakeware 9-Inch Pie Plate $2.99
	LOAF PAN	• Light gold or dark nonstick surface • Useful to have a set of both 8½ by 4½-inch and 9 by 5-inch pans	Williams-Sonoma 8½ x 4½-Inch Nonstick Goldtouch Loaf Pan $21 Best Buy: Baker's Secret 8½ x 4½-Inch Nonstick Loaf Pan $5
	SPRINGFORM PAN	• Rimless glass bottom allows you to monitor browning • Handles • Tight seal between band and bottom of pan (prevents leakage) • A 9-inch pan is standard, but multiple sizes are useful for frequent bakers	Frieling's Handle-It Glass Bottom 9-Inch Springform Pan $42.95
	MUFFIN TIN	• Dark nonstick surface for even browning and easy release • Generous lip (makes a convenient handle) • Cup capacity of ½ cup	Wilton Ultra-Bake 12-Cup Muffin Tin $10.99
	COOLING RACK	• Grid-style rack with tightly woven, heavy-gauge bars • Should fit inside a standard 18 by 13-inch rimmed baking sheet • Dishwasher safe	CIA Bakeware 17 x 12-Inch Cooling Rack $15.95 Best Buy: Libertyware Cross Wire Cooling Rack $5.95
	BISCUIT CUTTERS	• Sharp edges • A set with a variety of sizes	Ateco Plain Round Cutters (11-Piece Set) $13
	BUNDT PAN	• Thick, durable, cast aluminum with nonstick surface for even browning and easy release • Clearly defined ridges • 12-cup capacity	NordicWare Platinum Series 12-Cup Classic Bundt Pan $29.95 Best Buy: Baker's Secret Nonstick Fluted Tube Pan $9.99
	TART PAN	• Tinned steel for even browning and easy release • Removable bottom • A 9-inch pan is the most versatile choice, but multiple sizes are useful for frequent bakers	Kaiser Tinplate 9-Inch Quiche Pan $9

MUST-HAVE ITEMS

BAKEWARE	ITEM	WHAT TO LOOK FOR	TEST KITCHEN FAVORITES
	TUBE PAN	• Heavy durable metal with dark nonstick surface for even browning and easy release • 16-cup capacity • Feet on the rim	**Chicago Metallic Professional Angel Food Cake Pan** $19.95
	RAMEKINS	• Sturdy, high-fired porcelain (chip-resistant and safe for use in oven, broiler, microwave, and dishwasher) • For one all-purpose set, capacity of 6 ounces and diameter of 3 inches	**Apilco 6-Ounce Ramekins** $32 for a set of four
	BAKING STONE	• Dimensions of 16 by 14 inches • Smooth rimless edges (to easily slide items onto and off of the surface)	*The Baker's Catalogue* **Pizza Baking Stone** $52.95

SMALL APPLIANCES	ITEM	WHAT TO LOOK FOR	TEST KITCHEN FAVORITES
	FOOD PROCESSOR	• 12-cup capacity • Sharp and sturdy blades • Large feed tube • Should include basic blades and discs: steel blade, dough blade, shredding/slicing disc	**KitchenAid 12-Cup Food Processor** $199.95
	STANDING MIXER	• Planetary action (stationary bowl and single mixing arm) • Powerful motor • Bowl size of at least 4½ quarts • Tapered bowl • Should include basic attachments: paddle, dough hook, metal whisk	**Cuisinart 5.5-Quart Stand Mixer** $299 Best Buy: **KitchenAid Classic Plus Stand Mixer** $199.99
	HANDHELD MIXER	• Lightweight with comfortable handle • Simple digital controls • Separate button to eject beaters • Simple wire beaters	**Cuisinart Power Advantage 7-Speed Hand Mixer** $49.95
	BLENDER	• Tapered or serrated blades in asymmetrical positions • At least 6½-cup capacity • Comes apart for easy cleaning or dishwasher safe • Sturdy, tapered polycarbonate or glass jar with flutes (vertical ribs)	**KitchenAid 5-Speed Blender** $99.95 Best Buy: **Kalorik BL Blender** $49.99
	IMMERSION BLENDER	• Stainless steel shaft to prevent staining and for heat resistance • Removable blade for easy cleaning	**KitchenAid Immersion Blender** $99.95

MUST-HAVE ITEM

MUST-HAVE ITEMS

SMALL APPLIANCES	ITEM	WHAT TO LOOK FOR	TEST KITCHEN FAVORITES
	ELECTRIC EGG COOKER	• Boiling capacity of seven eggs • Well-fitting lid, not too tight, for safety • Pleasantly audible timer • Easy to use	**West Bend Automatic Egg Cooker** $24.99
	ELECTRIC GRIDDLE	• Large cooking area (about 21 by 12 inches) • Large grease trap • Nonstick surface for easy cleaning	**BroilKing Professional Griddle** $99.99 Best Buy: **West Bend Cool-Touch Nonstick Electric Griddle** $51.95
	JUICER, ELECTRIC	• Ideal for making a large amount of juice • Easy to operate, clean, and assemble, if necessary • Motorized reamer for efficient juicing • Pulp screen to strain seeds and pulp	**Breville Stainless Steel Juicer** $150 Best Buy: **Black & Decker CitrusMate Plus** $19.95
	COFFEE MAKER	• Thermal carafe that keeps coffee hot and fresh with capacity of at least 10 cups • Short brewing time (6 minutes is ideal) • Copper, not aluminum, heating element • Easy-to-fill water tank • Clear, intuitive controls	**Technivorm Moccamaster KBT 741 Coffeemaker** $239.95 Best Buy: **Bodum Chambord 8-Cup French Press** $39.95
	DEEP FRYER	• 1-gallon capacity for time-efficient frying • Wide, shallow basket for even cooking • Enclosed heating element is safer than stovetop frying NOTE: We prefer to deep-fry in a Dutch oven for superior temperature control and larger capacity, but a deep fryer can be useful for French fries and other low-temperature fried foods.	**Waring Professional Digital Deep Fryer** $139.95
	PORTABLE INDUCTION BURNERS	• Large cooking surface for even heating of pans • Basic push buttons and dial controls for ease of use	**Max Burton Induction Cook Top** $124.25
	PRESSURE COOKER	• 8-quart capacity • Wide base for even browning • Large quick-release valve	**Fagor Duo 8-Quart Pressure Cooker** $109.99

SMALL APPLIANCES	ITEM	WHAT TO LOOK FOR	TEST KITCHEN FAVORITES
	SLOW COOKER	• 6-quart capacity • Oval shape • Insert handles • Clear lid to allow monitoring of food • Dishwasher-safe crock and lid • "Keep warm" setting with timer	**All-Clad Stainless Steel Slow Cooker with Ceramic Insert** $179.95 Best Buy: **Hamilton Beach Programmable Slow Cooker with Probe** $59.95
	ICE CREAM MAKER	• Minimum 1½-quart capacity • Electric model • Revolving canister with mixing arm	**Cuisinart Automatic Frozen Yogurt–Ice Cream & Sorbet Maker** $49.95
	TOASTER	• Extra-wide slots to fit bagels and large slices of bread • Deep crumb trays that slide in and out easily	Two–Slice (shown): **Farberware FST200 Cool Touch Toaster** $26.99 Four–Slice: **Michael Graves Design Hamilton Beach 4-Slice Toaster** $34.99
	WAFFLE IRON	• Temperature-control gauge • Four-waffle capacity • Ready light	**Black & Decker Grill and Waffle Baker** $49.99

GRILLING EQUIPMENT	ITEM	WHAT TO LOOK FOR	TEST KITCHEN FAVORITES
	GAS GRILL	• Large grilling area (at least 350 square inches) • Built-in thermometer • Two or three burners for varying heat levels • Attached table • Fat drainage system	Two-Burner: **Weber Spirit E-210 Propane Grill** $399 Three-Burner: **Weber Spirit E-310 Propane Grill** $499
	CHARCOAL GRILL	• Large grilling area • Deep grill cover to fit large food items (such as a turkey) • Hinged grill grate so you can tend the fire • Ash catcher for easier cleanup	**Weber 22½-Inch One-Touch Gold Charcoal Grill** $139.33
	CHIMNEY STARTER	• 6-quart capacity • Holes in the canister so air can circulate around the coals • Sturdy construction • Heat-resistant handle • Dual handle for easy control	**Weber Rapid Fire Chimney Starter** $12.99

GRILLING EQUIPMENT	ITEM	WHAT TO LOOK FOR	TEST KITCHEN FAVORITES
	GRILL TONGS	• 16 inches • Scalloped, not sharp and serrated, edges	OXO Good Grips 16-Inch Locking Tongs $13.95
	GRILL BRUSH	• Long handle (about 14 inches) • Large woven-mesh detachable stainless steel scrubbing pad	Grill Wizard BBQ Brush $9.99
	BASTING BRUSH	• Silicone bristles • Angled brush head • Handle between 8 and 13 inches	Precision Grill Tools Super Silicone Angled BBQ Basting Brush $8.99
	SKEWERS	• Flat and metal • ³⁄₁₆-inch thick	Norpro's 12-Inch Stainless Steel Skewers $10 for a set of six
	OUTDOOR GRILL PAN	• Narrow slits or steel mesh construction allows maximum grill flavor with minimum food loss • Sturdy construction with handles for ease of use • Stainless steel composition for easy cleaning and maintenance	Weber Style 6435 Professional Grade Grill Pan $19.99 Williams-Sonoma Mesh Grill Top Fry Pan $29.95
	VERTICAL ROASTER	• Helps poultry cook evenly • 8-inch shaft keeps chicken above fat and drippings in pan • Attached basin catches drippings for pan sauce and doesn't require use of additional pan • Sturdy construction to support chicken and for easy cleaning	Norpro Vertical Roaster with Infuser $27.95 Best Buy: Elizabeth Karmel's Grill Friends Porcelain Chicken Sitter $11.99
SPECIALTY ITEMS	ITEM	WHAT TO LOOK FOR	TEST KITCHEN FAVORITES
	APPLE CORER	• Sharp teeth • Blade diameter greater than ¾ inch and length greater than 3½ inches • Comfortable grip	OXO Good Grips Corer $7.95
	APPLE SLICER	• Ability to cut 12 or 16 slices (better for baking than thicker pieces cut by 8-slice models) • Sharp, serrated corer with 1-inch diameter • Comfortable handle	Williams-Sonoma Dial-a-Slice/Adjustable Apple Divider $19.95
	CORN STRIPPER	• Removes kernels from cob with ease • Not as messy as using a chef's knife and safer too • Comfortable grip and sharp blade • Attached cup to catch kernels	OXO Good Grips Corn Stripper $11.99

SPECIALTY ITEMS	ITEM	WHAT TO LOOK FOR	TEST KITCHEN FAVORITES
	PIZZA CUTTER	• 4-inch wheel • Rubberized, nonslip handle • Thumb guard • Angled neck	OXO Good Grips 4-Inch Pizza Wheel $11.95
	PASTRY BAG	• Plastic-coated canvas pastry bag (for durability and easy cleaning) or disposable bags • Large bag (about 18 inches in length) for easier gripping and twisting • Accommodates standard-sized tips	Ateco 18-Inch Plastic-Coated Pastry Bag $5.95
	FISH SPATULA	• Strong but flexible • Tapered edges (to help slip beneath food) • Tip with an upward curve (to cradle food)	Wüsthof Gourmet 7.5-Inch Slotted Turner/Fish Spatula $34.95
	MORTAR AND PESTLE	• Cast-iron construction with a 2½- to 3-cup capacity • 7-inch-long pestle for efficient grinding • Rough interior to prevent food from sliding around for easier grinding	Fox Run Cast Iron Mortar and Pestle $29.99
	GRILL PRESS	• Cast-iron construction for heat retention, durability, and versatility (can be used on the stove or on the grill) • Comfortable handle • 4½- to 5-pound weight ensures even cooking and adequately pressed panini	Emerilware by All-Clad Cast-Iron Square Grill Press $27.95
	GRILL PAN	• Aluminum nonstick pan with generous cooking area (at least 11 inches wide) • Large ridges (5/16 inch or more) for better caramelization • Open indentations on pan bottom (not solid bottom) for better heat transfer	Simply Calphalon Nonstick 13-Inch Round Grill Pan $31.99
	STOVETOP GRIDDLE	• Lightweight anodized aluminum with nonstick coating • Heat-resistant loop handles • At least 17 by 9 inches (large enough to span two burners) • Pour spout for draining grease	Anolon Advanced Double Burner Griddle $48.95
	KITCHEN TORCH	• Easy one-hand operation • Triggered by thumb instead of forefinger (more comfortable) • Safety switch can easily be flicked off with thumb	Bernzomatic 3 in 1 Micro Torch (model ST2200T) $37.95
	MILK FROTHER	• Easy to use and clean • Immersion blender–style wand • Battery operated	Aerolatte Milk Frother $14.99

SPECIALTY ITEMS	ITEM	WHAT TO LOOK FOR	TEST KITCHEN FAVORITES
	OYSTER KNIFE	• Slightly angled pointed tip for easy penetration • Contoured handle for secure, comfortable grip	**OXO Good Grips Oyster Knife** $7.95
	POTATO RICER	• Large hopper that can hold 1¼ cups sliced potatoes • Interchangeable fine and coarse disks • Sturdy, ergonomic handles	**RSVP International Classic Kitchen Basics Potato Ricer** $11.99
	REVOLVING CAKE STAND	• Elevated rotating stand so you can hold the spatula steady for easy frosting	**Ateco Professional Icing Turntable** $62.99 Best Buy: **Ateco Revolving Cake Stand** $22.99
	SPICE/COFFEE GRINDER	• Electric, not manual, operation • Deep bowl to hold ample amount of coffee beans • Easy-to-adjust grind texture • Buy two, one each for coffee grinding and spice grinding	**Krups Fast-Touch Coffee Mill** $19.99
	TEAPOT	• Contained ultra-fine mesh strainer keeps tea leaf dregs separate • One-piece design for easy cleaning • Comfortable design for efficient and easy use	**Adagio Teas ingenuiTEA** $14.95
	WINE OPENER	• Lever-style design • Lever length of 6½ inches or more	**Screwpull Trigger** $79.95 Best Buy: **Wine Enthusiast Quicksilver Corkscrew** $29.99
	ELECTRIC WINE OPENER	• Sturdy corkscrew that moves slowly for adequate drilling into cork • Broad base to allow the device to rest firmly on the bottle • Quiet operation	**Waring Pro Professional Cordless Wine Opener** $39.95
	WINE AERATOR	• Eliminates standard wait for red wine to "breathe" by exposing wine to air as it is poured • Releases volatile compounds, making flavor fuller and smoother	**Nuance Wine Finer** $49.95

KITCHEN SUPPLIES	ITEM	WHAT TO LOOK FOR	TEST KITCHEN FAVORITES
	PARCHMENT PAPER	• Sturdy paper for heavy doughs • Easy release of baked goods • At least 14 inches wide	Reynolds Parchment Paper $3.39
	PLASTIC WRAP	• Clings tightly and resticks well • Packaging with sharp teeth that aren't exposed (to avoid snags on clothing and scratches on skin) • Adhesive pad to hold cut end of wrap	Glad Cling Wrap Clear Plastic $2.59
	LIQUID DISH DETERGENT	• Includes both vegetable- and petroleum-based cleaning agents	Method Go Naked Ultra Concentrated Dish Detergent $2.99 Best Buy: Ajax Lemon Super Degreaser $1.99
	SOAP-FILLED DISH BRUSH	• Handle for easy gripping and to keep hands dry • Tight seal to prevent soap from leaking	OXO Steel Soap Squirting Dish Brush $11.99
	POT SCRUBBER	• Open mesh of copper strands for abrasive scouring (for use on stainless steel only; may scratch aluminum and enamel finishes) • Compact and easy to grip	Chore Boy Copper Scouring Pad $1.29
	NONSCRATCH POT SCRUBBER	• Ribbonlike nylon mesh covering one side for gentle scrubbing • Smooth sponge on second side for all-purpose cleaning • Thin, rectangular scrubber to fit in tight corners	Chore Boy Scratch-Free Longlast Scrubber $1.19

MUST-HAVE ITEMS

SHOPPING FOR INGREDIENTS

Today, a trip to the supermarket can be a time-consuming and confusing task. Shelves are filled with a dizzying array of choices—and price does not equal quality. Over the past 10 years, the test kitchen's blind tasting panels have evaluated thousands of ingredients, brand by brand, side by side, plain and in prepared applications to determine which brands you can trust and which brands to avoid. In the chart that follows, we share the results, revealing our top-rated choices and the attributes that made them stand out among the competition. And because our test kitchen accepts no support from product manufacturers, you can trust our ratings.

	TEST KITCHEN FAVORITES	WHY WE LIKE IT	RUNNERS-UP
	ANCHOVIES **Ortiz Oil-Packed Spanish**	• Pleasantly fishy, salty flavor, not overwhelming or bland • Firm, meaty texture, not mushy • Already filleted and ready to use, unlike salt-packed variety	Flott Salt-Packed
	APPLESAUCE **Musselman's Lite**	• An unusual ingredient, sucralose, sweetens this applesauce without overpowering its fresh, bright apple flavor • Pinch of salt boosts flavor above weak, bland, and too-sweet competitors • Coarse, almost chunky texture, not slimy like applesauces sweetened with corn syrup	Musselman's Home Style
	BACON, SUPERMARKET **Farmland Hickory Smoked**	• Good balance of saltiness and sweetness • Smoky and full flavored, not one-dimensional • Very meaty, not too fatty or insubstantial • Crisp yet hearty texture, not tough or dry	Boar's Head Brand Naturally Smoked Sliced and Hormel Black Label Original
	BARBECUE SAUCE **Bull's-Eye Original**	• Spicy, fresh tomato taste • Good balance of tanginess, smokiness, and sweetness • Robust flavor from molasses • Sweetened with sugar and molasses, not high-fructose corn syrup which caramelizes and burns quickly	
	BEANS, CANNED CHICKPEAS **Pastene**	• Firm yet tender texture bests pasty and dry competitors • Clean chickpea flavor • Enough salt to enhance but not overwhelm the flavor	Goya
	BEANS, CANNED RED KIDNEY **Goya**	• Sweet with strong bean flavor • Beautiful red, plump beans • Smooth, creamy texture, not mushy, chalky, or too firm • Flavor boost from added sugar and salt	S&W
	BEANS, CANNED WHITE **Westbrae Organic Great Northern**	• Clean, earthy flavor • Smooth, creamy interior with tender skins • Not full of broken beans like some competitors	Progresso Cannellini

	TEST KITCHEN FAVORITES	WHY WE LIKE IT	RUNNERS-UP
	BREAD, WHITE SANDWICH **Arnold Country Classics**	• Subtle sweetness, not tasteless or sour • Perfect structure, not too dry or too soft	
	Pepperidge Farm **Farmhouse Hearty**	• Flavorful for white bread • Slightly sweet with a familiar taste • Good texture, not too dry or too soft NOTE: Pepperidge Farm brand bread is available only east of the Mississippi River.	
	BREAD, WHOLE-WHEAT **SANDWICH** **Pepperidge Farm 100%** **Natural Whole Wheat**	• Whole-grain, earthy flavor with wheaty nuttiness • Dense, chewy texture, not gummy or too soft • Not too sweet, contains no corn syrup and has low sugar level unlike competitors NOTE: Available only east of the Mississippi River.	Rudi's Organic Bakery Honey Sweet Whole Wheat and Arnold Natural 100% Whole Wheat
	BREAD CRUMBS **Ian's Panko**	• Crisp, with a substantial crunch • Not too delicate, stale, sandy, or gritty • Oil-free and without seasonings or undesirable artificial flavors	
	BROTH, BEEF **Redi-Base Beef Base**	• Deep, distinct beefiness with notes of onion and mushroom, not artificial, chickeny, or vegetal • Hearty, roasted flavor, not mild or metallic	Pacific
	BROTH, CHICKEN **Swanson Certified Organic** **Free Range**	• Strong chicken flavor, not watery, beefy, or vegetal • Hearty and pleasant aroma • Roasted notes, not sour, rancid, or salty like some competitors • Flavor-boosting ingredients include carrots, celery, and onions	Better Than Bouillon Chicken Base and Swanson Natural Goodness
	BROTH, VEGETABLE **Swanson Vegetarian**	• Balanced vegetable flavor with carrot and celery nuances • High concentration of vegetable product not found in competitors • High sodium content enhances vegetable flavors NOTE: Despite this broth's high concentration of artificial additives and salt, it is the only vegetable broth we found with acceptable flavor.	

	TEST KITCHEN FAVORITES	WHY WE LIKE IT	RUNNERS-UP
	BUNS, HAMBURGER **Pepperidge Farm** **Premium Bakery Rolls**	• Hearty texture stands up well to condiments • Wheaty, not too sweet flavor • Generous 4½-inch diameter big enough for burgers, unlike all other competitors NOTE: Available only east of the Mississippi River.	
	BUNS, HOT DOG **Pepperidge Farm** **Split Top**	• Pleasantly yeasty flavor • Sturdy bun with crusty exterior • Unusual split-top style holds hot dog and condiments securely NOTE: Available only east of the Mississippi River.	
	BUTTER, UNSALTED **Lurpak Imported Danish**	• Nutty, rich flavor • Not too tangy or too bland like some premium butters • Silky, creamy texture • Culturing process used to make this butter results in complex flavor	Vermont Butter & Cheese Company and Land O'Lakes
	CHEESE, AMERICAN, PRESLICED **Land O'Lakes**	• Strong cheesy flavor, unlike some competitors • Slightly rubbery but pleasantly gooey when melted • Higher content of cheese culture contributes to better flavor	Kraft Deli Deluxe White
	CHEESE, ASIAGO **BelGioioso**	• Sharp, tangy, and complex flavor, not mild • Firm and not too dry • Melts, shreds, and grates well	
	CHEESE, BLUE For dressings and dips: **Stella**	• Sweet, balanced, and mild flavor, not too pungent • Wet and extremely crumbly texture similar to feta	Danish Blue
	For eating out of hand: **Stilton**	• Balance of buttery, nutty, sweet, and salty flavors • Fairly firm with sliceable yet crumbly texture	Roquefort
	CHEESE, CHEDDAR, EXTRA-SHARP **Cabot Private Stock**	• Balance of salty, creamy, and sweet flavors • Considerable but well-rounded sharpness, not overwhelming • Firm, crumbly texture, not moist, rubbery, or springy • Aged a minimum of 12 months for complex flavor	Cabot Extra Sharp, Grafton Village Cheese Company Premium, Cabot Sharp, and Tillamook

	TEST KITCHEN FAVORITES	WHY WE LIKE IT	RUNNERS-UP
	CHEESE, CHEDDAR, PRESLICED **Tillamook Sharp**	• Slightly crumbly, not rubbery or processed, texture characteristic of block cheddar • Strong, tangy, and salty flavor, not bland or too mild	Cabot All Natural Sharp and Cracker Barrel Natural Sharp
	CHEESE, CHEDDAR, REDUCED-FAT **Cracker Barrel Reduced Fat Sharp**	• Ample creaminess • Strong cheesy flavor • Good for cooking, but didn't rate as well when eaten out of hand	Cabot 50% Light Sharp
	CHEESE, CHEDDAR, SHARP **Cabot Sharp Vermont**	• Sharp, clean, and tangy flavor • Firm, crumbly texture, not moist, rubbery, or springy • Aged a minimum of 12 months for complex flavor	Tillamook Sharp, Cracker Barrel Sharp White, and Grafton Village Cheese Company Cheddar
	CHEESE, COTTAGE **Hood Country Style**	• Rich, well-seasoned, and buttery flavor • Velvety, creamy texture • Pillowy curds	Friendship 4% California Style and Breakstone's 4% Small Curd
	CHEESE, CREAM **Philadelphia**	• Rich, tangy, and milky flavor • Thick, creamy texture, not pasty, waxy, or chalky	Organic Valley
	CHEESE, FETA **Athenos**	• Tangy, salty flavor • Moist and creamy texture • Soft and somewhat yielding, not hard or crumbly • Vacuum-sealed with small amount of brine for better preservation and flavor	
	CHEESE, FONTINA For eating out of hand: **Fontina Val d'Aosta** For cooking: **BelGioioso**	• Strong, earthy aroma • Somewhat elastic texture with small irregular holes • Grassy, nutty flavor—but can be overpowering in cooked dishes • Semisoft, super-creamy texture • Mildly tangy, nutty flavor • Melts well	
	CHEESE, GOAT **Vermont Butter & Cheese Company Chèvre**	• Buttery, tangy flavor with a clean taste, not overpowering • Creamy yet firm texture, not chalky, pasty, or too soft • No offensive flavors as in some competitors	Westfield Farm Capri and Belmont
	CHEESE, GRUYÈRE **Emmi Le Gruyère Reserve**	• Grassy, salty flavor, not bland or pedestrian • Creamy yet dry texture, not plasticky like some competitors • Aged a minimum of 10 months for strong and complex flavor • Melts especially well	Gruyère Salé

	TEST KITCHEN FAVORITES	WHY WE LIKE IT	RUNNERS-UP
	CHEESE, MONTEREY JACK **Cabot**	• Mild flavor with an acidic tang, mellows when melted • Smooth, creamy consistency, not grainy	
	CHEESE, MOZZARELLA Block cheese: **Dragone Whole Milk**	• Rich, tangy, and milky flavor • Creamy, smooth, and moist texture, not plasticky	
	Shredded cheese: **Kraft Shredded Part-Skim**	• Slightly mild, rich, fresh, and tangy flavor, not acidic or too salty • Not too chalky, pasty, or rubbery	
	CHEESE, PARMESAN **Boar's Head Parmigiano-Reggiano**	• Rich and complex flavor balances tanginess and nuttiness • Dry, crumbly texture yet creamy with a crystalline crunch, not rubbery or dense • Aged a minimum of 12 months for better flavor and texture	Il Villagio Parmigiano-Reggiano and BelGioioso
	CHEESE, PROVOLONE **Provolone Vernengo**	• Bold, nutty, and tangy flavor, not plasticky or bland • Firm, dry texture	BelGioioso Sliced Mild
	CHEESE, RICOTTA, PART-SKIM **Calabro**	• Clean, fresh flavor, not rancid or sour from addition of gums or stabilizers • Creamy texture with perfect curds unlike chalky, grainy, and soggy competitors	Freshly made ricotta cheese without gums or stabilizers
	CHEESE, SWISS For eating out of hand: **Emmenthaler**	• Subtle flavor with sweet, buttery, nutty, and fruity notes • Firm yet gently giving texture, not rubbery • Aged longer for better flavor, resulting in larger eyes • Mildly pungent yet balanced	For eating out of hand or cooking: Sargento Baby, Sargento Deli Style Aged, and Boar's Head Gold Label Premium Imported
	For cooking: **Jarlsberg**	• Creamy texture • Salty mildness preferable for grilled cheese sandwiches	
	CHICKEN, BREASTS, BONELESS SKINLESS **Empire Kosher**	• Nicely seasoned, buttery chicken flavor, not bland and no artificial or off-flavors • Moist and tender texture with not a hint of dryness • Slightly salty but superior flavor results from kosher processing	Springer Mountain Farms and Eberly's Free Range Young Organic
	Bell & Evans Naturally Raised	• Clean, rich chicken taste, not too bland and no artificial or off-flavors • Moist and tender texture	

	TEST KITCHEN FAVORITES	WHY WE LIKE IT	RUNNERS-UP
	CHICKEN, WHOLE **Empire Kosher Roasting**	• Natural and flavorful taste • Moist and juicy • Firm and tender texture • Kosher processing renders brining unnecessary	Bell & Evans Fresh Young
	CHILI POWDER **Spice Islands**	• Blend of chile peppers with added seasonings, not assertively hot, overly smoky, or one-dimensional • Balance of sweet and smoky flavors • Potent but not overwhelming	The El Paso Chile Company Chili Spices and Fixin's and Pendery's Top Hat Chile Blend
	CHOCOLATE, DARK **Callebaut Intense Dark L-60-40 NV (60% Cacao)**	• Creamy and thick texture, not grainy or chalky • Rich and earthy, complex flavor with notes of caramel, smoke, and espresso • Balance of sweetness and bitterness, not too sugary or sour	Ghirardelli Bittersweet Chocolate Baking Bar (60% Cacao)
	CHOCOLATE, MILK **Dove**	• Strong chocolate flavor with balanced sweetness; not too mild, too dark, or artificial-tasting like competitors • Creamy texture, not waxy, chalky, or grainy	Scharffen Berger and Lindt Excellence Extra Creamy
	CHOCOLATE, MILK CHIPS **Hershey's**	• Bold chocolate flavor outshines too-sweet, weak chocolate flavor of other chips • Complex with caramel and nutty notes • Higher fat content makes texture creamier than grainy, artificial competitors	
	CHOCOLATE, SEMISWEET CHIPS **Ghirardelli 60% Cacao Bittersweet**	• Intense, complex flavor beats one-dimensional flavor of competitors • Low sugar content allows chocolate flavor to shine • High amount of cocoa butter ensures creamy, smooth texture, not gritty and grainy • Wider, flatter shape and high percentage of fat helps chips melt better in cookies	Hershey's Special Dark Mildly Sweet
	CHOCOLATE, UNSWEETENED **Scharffen Berger Unsweetened Pure Dark**	• Complex profile with fruity and nutty notes and deep caramelized flavor, not acidic, dull, or scorched • Smooth and creamy texture results from conching process, not grainy or dry	Callebaut, Ghirardelli Baking Bar, and Valrhona Cacao Pâte Extra
	CHOCOLATE, WHITE CHIPS **Guittard Choc-Au-Lait**	• Creamy texture, not waxy or crunchy • Silky smooth meltability from high fat content • Complex flavor like high-quality real chocolate, no artificial or off-flavors	Guittard 31% Cacao Pure White Chocolate Wafers and Ghirardelli Premium Baking Chips Classic White

	TEST KITCHEN FAVORITES	WHY WE LIKE IT	RUNNERS-UP
	CINNAMON **Penzeys Extra Fancy** **Vietnamese Cassia**	• Warm, fragrant aroma with clove, fruity, and slightly smoky flavors • Mellow start with spicy finish • Strong yet not overpowering • Not harsh, bitter, dusty, or gritty NOTE: Available through mail order, Penzeys (800-741-7787, www.penzeys.com).	Durkee Ground, Smith and Truslow Freshly Ground Organic, and Adams Ground
	COCOA POWDER **Callebaut**	• Rich chocolate flavor • Perfectly balanced, lacking bitterness or off-flavors present in competitors • Floral, nutty, and smoky notes	Droste
	COCONUT MILK For savory recipes: **Chaokoh**	• Strong coconut flavor • Smooth and creamy texture superior to competitors • Not very sweet, ideal for savory recipes like soup and stir-fry	
	For sweet recipes: **Ka-Me**	• Rich, velvety texture, not too thin or watery • Fruity and complex flavor, not mild or bland • Ideal sweetness complementary, not saccharine, in desserts	
	COFFEE, WHOLE BEAN, SUPERMARKET Dark roast: **Millstone Colombian Supremo**	• Deep, complex, and balanced flavor without metallic, overly acidic, or otherwise unpleasant notes • Smoky and chocolaty with a bitter, not burnt, finish	Starbucks Coffee House Blend
	Lighter roast: **Green Mountain Coffee Our Blend**	• Soft, complex, and balanced flavor • Pleasantly acidic with notes of caramel and fruit	Eight O'Clock Coffee Original
	CORNMEAL **Arrowhead Mills Whole-Grain**	• Clean, pure corn flavor comes from using whole-grain kernels • Ideal texture resembling slightly damp, fine sand, not too fine or too coarse	
	CURRY POWDER **Penzeys Sweet**	• Balanced, neither too sweet nor too hot, with no off-flavors • Complex and vivid earthy flavor, not thin, bland, or one-dimensional NOTE: Available through mail order, Penzeys (800-741-7787, www.penzeys.com).	Durkee

	TEST KITCHEN FAVORITES	WHY WE LIKE IT	RUNNERS-UP
	FLOUR, ALL-PURPOSE **King Arthur Unbleached**	• Fresh, toasty flavor • No metallic or other off-flavors • Consistent results across recipes • Made tender, flaky pie crust, hearty biscuits, crisp cookies, and chewy, sturdy bread	Gold Medal Enriched Bleached Presifted, Gold Medal Unbleached, and Heckers/Ceresota Unbleached Enriched Presifted
	Pillsbury Unbleached Enriched	• Clean, toasty, and hearty flavor • No metallic or other off-flavors • Consistent results across recipes • Made flaky pie crust, chewy cookies, and tender biscuits, muffins, and cakes	
	HAM, SPIRAL-SLICED, HONEY-CURED **Cook's Spiral Sliced Hickory Smoked Honey**	• Good balance of smokiness, saltiness, and sweetness • Moist, tender yet firm texture, not dry or too wet • Clean, meaty ham flavor	
	HOISIN SAUCE **Kikkoman**	• Balances sweet, salty, pungent, and spicy flavors • Initial burn mellows into harmonious and aromatic blend without bitterness	
	HOT DOGS **Nathan's Famous Beef Franks**	• Meaty, robust, and hearty flavor, not sweet, sour, or too salty • Juicy but not greasy • Firm, craggy texture, not rubbery, mushy, or chewy	Johnsonville Stadium Style Beef Franks and Hebrew National Beef Franks
	HOT FUDGE SAUCE **Hershey's Hot Fudge Topping**	• True fudge flavor, not weak or overly sweet • Thick, smooth, and buttery texture	
	HOT SAUCE **Frank's RedHot Original**	• Bright and tangy flavor, not bitter • Potent but not searing heat doesn't mask other flavors • Luxurious body, not thin and watery	
	ICE CREAM, CHOCOLATE **Ben & Jerry's**	• Intense but not overwhelming chocolate flavor, not too sweet or light on chocolate taste • Creamy and smooth dense texture, not fluffy, grainy, or icy • Absence of off-flavors present in competitors	Edy's Grand (sold as Dreyer's Grand west of the Rockies)
	ICE CREAM, VANILLA **Turkey Hill All Natural**	• Subdued but clean vanilla flavor, not overpowering, synthetic, or boozy • Very creamy, gooey texture, not icy or gummy • Smooth, balanced taste	Häagen-Dazs Vanilla and Häagen-Dazs Vanilla Bean

	TEST KITCHEN FAVORITES	WHY WE LIKE IT	RUNNERS-UP
	KETCHUP Hunt's	• Fresh, tangy, and balanced flavor, not bland or dull • Smooth, thick texture, not watery, pasty, or chunky • Balance of sweetness and acidity	Heinz Organic and Annie's Naturals Organic
	LEMONADE Newman's Own Old Fashioned Roadside Virgin	• Natural-tasting lemon flavor, without artificial or off-notes • Perfect balance of tartness and sweetness, unlike many overly sweet competitors	Florida's Natural and Minute Maid Premium Frozen Concentrated
	MAPLE SYRUP Maple Grove Farms Grade A Dark Amber	• Clean yet rich maple flavor, not too mild, harsh, or artificial in flavor • Moderate sweetness bests overwhelmingly sugary competitors • Ideal consistency, neither too thin nor too thick like pancake syrups made from corn syrup	Highland Sugarworks Grade B (especially in baking) and Camp Grade A Dark Amber
	MAYONNAISE Hellmann's Real	• Bright, well-seasoned, and classic flavor • Good balance of tanginess, sweetness, and acidity • Light, creamy consistency NOTE: Hellmann's is known as Best Foods west of the Rockies.	Kraft Real
	MAYONNAISE, LIGHT Hellmann's Light	• Bright, balanced flavor close to full-fat counterpart, not overly sweet like other light mayos • Slightly pasty but acceptable texture NOTE: Hellmann's is known as Best Foods west of the Rockies.	Hellmann's Canola Cholesterol Free
	MIRIN (JAPANESE RICE WINE) Mitoku Organic Mikawa Mirin Sweet Rice Seasoning	• Subtle salty-sweet and balanced flavor with woodsy undertones • Smoky, maplelike aftertaste • Not astringent or too sweet	Eden Mirin Rice Cooking Wine, Sushi Chef Mirin Sweetened Sake, and Kikkoman Aji-Mirin Sweet Cooking Rice Seasoning
	MOLASSES Grandma's Original (mild)	• Potent and rich flavor without being overpowering • Pleasing, slightly bitter finish	Grandma's Robust, Brer Rabbit Mild, and Brer Rabbit Full
	MUSTARD, DIJON Grey Poupon	• Potent, bold, and very hot, not weak or mild • Good balance of sweetness, tanginess, and sharpness • Not overly acidic, sweet, or one-dimensional like competitors	Maille Dijon Originale Traditional and Roland Extra Strong

	TEST KITCHEN FAVORITES	WHY WE LIKE IT	RUNNERS-UP
	MUSTARD, WHOLE-GRAIN **Grey Poupon Harvest** **Coarse Ground**	• Spicy, tangy burst of mustard flavor • High salt content amplifies flavor • Contains no superfluous ingredients that mask mustard flavor • Big, round seeds add pleasant crunch • Just enough vinegar, not too sour or thin	Grey Poupon Country Dijon
	OATS, ROLLED For hot cereal: **Bob's Red Mill Organic** **Extra Thick**	• Rich oat flavor with nutty, barley, and toasty notes • Creamy, cohesive texture • Plump grains with decent chew	
	For baking: **Quaker Old-Fashioned**	• Plump, almost crunchy texture with a slight chew, not gluey or mushy • Hearty, oaty, and toasty flavor, not bland or cardboardlike • Subtly sweet with a natural taste	
	OATS, STEEL-CUT **Bob's Red Mill Organic**	• Rich and complex oat flavor with buttery, earthy, nutty, and whole-grain notes • Creamy yet toothsome texture • Moist but not sticky NOTE: Not recommended for baking.	Arrowhead Mills Organic Hot Cereal, Country Choice Organic, and Hodgson's Mill Premium
	OLIVE OIL, CALIFORNIA **California Olive Ranch** **Arbequina**	• Round and full, sweet olive flavor with little bitterness or pungency • Complex with fruity, nutty, and buttery notes and fresh, pure olive aftertaste NOTE: Available only through mail order, California Olive Ranch (916-239-2999, www.californiaoliveranch.com).	Sciabica's Sevillano Variety Fall Harvest
	OLIVE OIL, EXTRA-VIRGIN **Columela**	• Buttery flavor that is sweet and full with a peppery finish • Aromatic and fruity, not bland or bitter • Clean taste comparable to a fresh-squeezed olive outshines bland, greasy competitors	Lucini Italia Premium Select and Colavita
	OLIVE OIL, PURE **DaVinci 100% Pure**	• Peppery, fruity flavor, not too bland or mild like some competitors • Grassy and herbaceous notes, not boring or flavorless • Closest to extra-virgin olive oil among samples tasted although significantly more mild	Colavita and Filippo Berio
	ORANGE JUICE **Natalie's Orchid Island**	• Blend of Hamlin, Pineapple, and Valencia oranges • Fresh, sweet, and fruity flavor without overly acidic, sour, or from-concentrate taste • Gentler pasteurization helps retain fresh-squeezed flavor • Pleasant amount of light pulp	Tropicana Pure Premium 100% Pure and Natural with Some Pulp

	TEST KITCHEN FAVORITES	WHY WE LIKE IT	RUNNERS-UP
	PAPRIKA **The Spice House Hungarian Sweet**	• Complex flavor with earthy, fruity notes • Bright and bold, not bland and boring • Rich, toasty aroma NOTE: Available only through mail order, The Spice House (312-274-0378, www.thespicehouse.com).	Penzeys Hungary Sweet (available mail order, Penzeys, 800-741-7787, www.penzeys.com)
	PASTA, EGG NOODLES **Light 'n Fluffy Extra Wide**	• Balanced, buttery flavor with no off-flavors • Light and fluffy texture, just like name, not gummy or starchy	Black Forest Girl Extra Broad
	PASTA, ELBOW MACARONI **Barilla Elbows**	• Rich, wheaty taste with no off-flavors • Pleasantly hearty texture, not mushy or chewy • Ridged surface and slight twist in shape hold sauce especially well	Mueller's, Ronzoni Smart Taste, and Ronzoni
	PASTA, FARFALLE **Mueller's Bowties**	• Nutty, slightly sweet flavor, not bland or eggy • Ideal texture, not gummy, sticky, or rubbery	DeCecco
	PASTA, FRESH **Contadina Buitoni Fettuccine**	• Firm but yielding, slightly chewy texture, not too delicate, gummy, or heavy • Faint but discernible egg flavor with no chemical, plasticky, or otherwise unpleasant flavors • Rough, porous surface absorbs sauce better than dried pasta	Monterey Pasta Fettuccine
	PASTA, LASAGNA NOODLES, NO-BOIL **Ronzoni Oven Ready**	• Pleasing, lightly eggy flavor • Perfectly al dente texture, not limp or unevenly cooked	Pasta DeFino and Barilla
	PASTA, PENNE **Mueller's Penne Rigate**	• Hearty texture, not insubstantial or gummy • Wheaty, slightly sweet flavor, not bland	Benedetto Cavalieri Penne Rigate and DeCecco
	PASTA, SPAGHETTI **Ronzoni**	• Nutty, buttery flavor, not bland or eggy • Firm texture, neither too chewy nor too soft, not gritty or gummy	DeCecco, Mueller's, and Barilla
	PASTA, SPAGHETTI, WHOLE-WHEAT **Heartland Perfect Balance (21% Whole Grain)**	• Tender, smooth and chewy, not gummy or gritty • Subtle wheat flavor tastes similar to white pasta	Barilla PLUS Multigrain
	Bionaturae 100% Whole Wheat	• Chewy, firm and toothsome, not mushy or rubbery • Full and nutty wheat flavor	

	TEST KITCHEN FAVORITES	WHY WE LIKE IT	RUNNERS-UP
	PASTA SAUCE **Bertolli Tomato & Basil**	• Fresh-cooked, balanced tomato flavor, not overly sweet • Pleasantly chunky texture, not too smooth or pasty • Not overseasoned with dry herbs like competitors	Francesco Rinaldi Traditional Marinara, Prego Marinara Italian, and Barilla Marinara
	PEANUT BUTTER, CREAMY **Skippy**	• Balance of sweet and salty flavors • Strong nuttiness • Ideal texture, not too stiff, grainy, or oily	Jif and Reese's
	PEPPERCORNS, BLACK **Kalustyan's Indian** **Tellicherry**	• Enticing and fragrant, not musty, aroma with flavor to back it up • Fresh, complex flavor at once sweet and spicy, earthy and smoky, fruity and floral • Moderate rather than strong heat NOTE: Available only through mail order, Kalustyan's (800-352-3451, www.kalustyans.com).	Morton & Bassett Organic Whole (widely available)
	PEPPERS, ROASTED RED **Dunbars Sweet**	• Balance of smokiness and sweetness • Mild and pure, sweet and earthy red pepper flavor • Firm texture, not slimy or mushy • Packed in simple yet strong brine of salt and water without distraction of other strongly flavored ingredients	Cento
	PICKLES, **BREAD-AND-BUTTER** **Cascadian Farm**	• Good balance of sweet and tangy flavors • Pleasantly crunchy, not mushy • Organic with natural, not artificial, taste • Contains real sugar for flavor and as a preservative, unlike many competitors, which use high-fructose corn syrup	Bubbies
	PIE CRUST **Pillsbury Just Unroll!**	• Impressively flaky when baked • Flexible enough to successfully unroll and line a pie plate • Not overwhelmingly pasty and bland	
	PIZZA, CHEESE, FROZEN **California Pizza Kitchen** **Crispy Thin Crust** **Margherita**	• Pleasing combination of flavors and fresh taste with no offensive or off-flavors • Low in preservatives as compared to the competition • Chunks of tomato in place of sauce—avoids common pitfalls like dusty or overly sweet sauce	Freschetta Ultra Thin Golden Baked Crispy 5-Cheese, Tombstone Extra Cheese Original, and Amy's
	POTATO CHIPS **Lay's Kettle Cooked** **Original**	• Big potato flavor, no offensive or off-flavors • Perfectly salted • Slightly thick chips have some body, not too delicate or brittle • Not too greasy	Herr's Crisp 'N Tasty, Utz, and Kettle Chips Lightly Salted

	TEST KITCHEN FAVORITES	WHY WE LIKE IT	RUNNERS-UP
	PRESERVES, RASPBERRY Smucker's	• Clean, strong raspberry flavor, not too tart or sweet • Not overly seedy • Ideal, spreadable texture, not too thick, artificial, or over-processed	Trappist
	PRESERVES, STRAWBERRY Welch's	• Big, distinct strawberry flavor • Natural-tasting and not overwhelmingly sweet • Thick and spreadable texture, not runny, slimy, or too smooth	Smucker's and Smucker's Simply Fruit Spreadable Fruit
	RELISH, SWEET PICKLE Cascadian Farm	• Piquant, sweet flavor, lacks out-of-place flavors such as cinnamon and clove present in competitors • Fresh and natural taste, free of yellow dye #5 and high-fructose corn syrup • Good texture, not mushy like competitors	Heinz Premium
	RICE, ARBORIO RiceSelect	• Creamier than competitors • Smooth grains • Characteristic good bite of Arborio rice in risotto where al dente is ideal	Riso Baricella
	RICE, BASMATI Tilda Pure	• Very long grains expand greatly with cooking, a result of being aged for a minimum of one year, as required in India • Ideal, fluffy texture, not dry, gummy, or mushy • Nutty taste with no off-flavors • Sweet aroma	Kohinoor Super
	RICE, LONG-GRAIN WHITE Canilla Extra Long Grain Enriched (by Goya)	• Clean yet distinct flavor reminiscent of jasmine rice • Slightly sticky and natural-looking, not rubbery or round like converted rice	Carolina Extra Long Grain Enriched and Sem-Chi Organically Grown Florida Long Grain
	SALSA, HOT Pace Hot Chunky	• Good balance of bright tomato, chile, and vegetal flavors • Chunky, almost crunchy texture, not mushy or thin • Spicy and fiery but not overpowering	Frontera Hot Habanero Salsa with Roasted Tomatoes and Cilantro, Newman's Own All Natural Chunky Hot, and Herdez Hot Salsa Casera
	SALT Maldon Sea Salt	• Light and airy texture • Delicately crunchy flakes • Not so coarse as to be overly crunchy or gritty nor so fine as to disappear NOTE: We recommend reserving sea salt for a garnish and table salt for most cooking and baking applications.	Fleur de Sel de Camargue, Morton Coarse Kosher, and Diamond Crystal Kosher

	TEST KITCHEN FAVORITES	WHY WE LIKE IT	RUNNERS-UP
	SAUSAGE, BREAKFAST **Farmland Fully Cooked** **Pork Links**	• Big pork flavor, not bland or overly spiced • Good balance of saltiness and sweetness with pleasantly lingering spiciness • Tender, super-juicy meat, not rubbery, spongy, or greasy	Farmland Original Pork Links
	SOY SAUCE For cooking: **Lee Kum Kee Tabletop**	• Pleasantly salty yet sweet with high sodium and sugar content • Depth of flavor balances salty, sweet, roasted, and fruity notes • Aromatic in rice and teriyaki	
	For dipping: **Ohsawa Nama Shoyu** **Organic Unpasteurized**	• Lower sodium content allows clean, mellow taste to shine in uncooked applications • Rich and nuanced flavor with sweet, floral, and caramel notes resulting from traditional, slow-brewed production	
	SWEETENED CONDENSED MILK **Borden Eagle Brand** **Whole Milk**	• Made with whole milk; creamier in desserts and balances more assertive notes from other ingredients	Nestlé Carnation and Parrot
	TEA, BLACK For plain tea: **Twinings English Breakfast**	• Bright, bold, and flavorful yet not too strong • Fruity, floral, and fragrant • Smooth, slightly astringent profile preferred for tea without milk	PG Tips
	For tea with milk: **Tazo Awake**	• Clean, strong taste • Smoky and fruity with notes of clove, cinnamon, and vanilla • Aromatic but not overwhelming • Good balance of flavor and intensity • More astringent profile stands up to milk	Tetley Specialty English Breakfast
	TERIYAKI SAUCE **Annie Chun's All Natural**	• Distinct teriyaki flavor without offensive or dominant flavors, unlike competitors • Smooth, rich texture, not too watery or gluey	
	TOMATOES, CANNED CRUSHED **Tuttorosso in Thick Puree** **with Basil**	• Chunky texture, not pasty, mushy, or watery • Bright, fresh tomato taste reminiscent of tomatoes, not ketchup or bland puree • Balance of saltiness, sweetness, and acidity NOTE: Available only in New England, Mid-Atlantic region, and Florida.	Muir Glen Organic with Basil (widely available) and Hunt's Organic
	TOMATOES, CANNED DICED **Muir Glen Organic**	• Fresh, lively flavor, not stale, metallic, or stewed-tasting • Balance of sweetness and saltiness • Moderately firm texture, not mushy or mealy	S&W Ready-Cut Premium Peeled and Redpack Ready-Cut

	TEST KITCHEN FAVORITES	WHY WE LIKE IT	RUNNERS-UP
	TOMATOES, CANNED PUREED **Hunt's Tomato Puree**	• Full tomato flavor without any bitter, sour, or tinny notes • Pleasantly thick, even consistency, not watery or thin	Progresso, Cento, and Muir Glen
	TOMATOES, CANNED WHOLE **Progresso Italian-Style Peeled with Basil Packed in Juice**	• Good balance of acidity and fruitiness • Bright, lively flavor, not dull, stale, or metallic • Firm, fresh texture, not overcooked, mushy, or watery	Redpack Peeled in Thick Puree and Hunt's
	TOMATO PASTE **Amore**	• Fresh, full tomato taste, not overpowered by dried herbs • Deep and intense flavor, not weak or stale • Tube packaging avoids tinny aftertaste that plagues canned competition	Redpack
	TORTILLA CHIPS **Santitas Authentic Mexican Style White Corn**	• Mild and pleasantly salty flavor, not bland, artificial, or rancid • Sturdy yet crunchy and crisp texture, not brittle, stale, or cardboardlike	Tostitos 100% White Corn Restaurant Style, Green Mountain Gringo All Natural, and Tostitos Natural Yellow Corn Restaurant Style
	TORTILLAS, FLOUR **Tyson Mexican Original**	• Thin and flaky texture, not doughy or stale • Mild, pleasantly wheaty flavor without sour or off-flavors NOTE: Available only in the Northeast.	Mission
	TUNA, IN OLIVE OIL **Ortiz Bonito del Norte Ventresca (canned)**	• Silky, tender texture, not overprocessed • Full, clean, and fresh flavor with no bitter or unpleasant notes • Uses bonito tuna exclusively and seasoned only with olive oil and salt	Ortiz Bonito del Norte (canned) and Ortiz Bonito del Norte (jarred)
	TUNA, IN WATER **Chicken of the Sea Solid White Albacore (canned)**	• Pleasant, mild flavor with fresh, oceanlike taste, not overly fishy • Chunky with large flakes of meat, not overprocessed or mealy • Moist texture, not dry	Starkist Solid White Albacore (canned) and Starkist Premium Chunk White Albacore (in pouch)
	TURKEY, WHOLE **Empire Kosher**	• Moist and dense texture without being watery, chewy, or squishy • Meaty, full turkey flavor • Buttery white meat • Koshering process renders brining unnecessary	Good Shepherd Ranch Heritage (only available mail order, Good Shepherd Turkey Ranch Inc., 785-227-5149, www.reeseturkeys.net) and Butterball Frozen
	VANILLA EXTRACT **McCormick Pure**	• Strong, rich vanilla flavor where others are weak and sharp • Complex flavor with spicy, caramel notes and a sweet undertone	Rodelle Pure and Gold Medal Imitation (by C.F. Sauer Co.)

	TEST KITCHEN FAVORITES	WHY WE LIKE IT	RUNNERS-UP
	VINEGAR, APPLE CIDER **Maille**	• Deep, warm profile with sweet, mellow, and smooth cider flavor • Balance of richness and tanginess • Complex with notes of honey and caramel with clear apple taste	Spectrum Naturals Organic Unfiltered
	VINEGAR, BALSAMIC **Lucini Gran Riserva Balsamico**	• Sweet, nuanced flavor lacking any harshness or astringency • Smooth and thick like traditional balsamic, not too thin or light • Balance of tanginess and sweetness with complexity and a slight acidic zing	Monari Federzoni of Modena and Ortalli of Modena
	VINEGAR, RED WINE **Spectrum Naturals Organic**	• Smooth and full bodied with sweet, peppery flavor • Balance of fruitiness and acidity, not mild, bitter, or harsh • Fruity notes of lemons, berries, cherries, and grapes	Pompeian and Eden Selected
	VINEGAR, WHITE WINE For cooking: **Colavita Aged**	• Balance of tanginess and subtle sweetness, not overly acidic or weak • Fruity, bright, and perfumed	
	For vinaigrettes: **Spectrum Naturals Organic**	• Rich, dark flavor tastes fermented and malty, not artificial or harsh • Fruity flavor with caramel, earthy, and nutty notes	
	YEAST **SAF-Instant**	• Steady, predictable rise • Clean, clear aroma and flavor, not heady, strong, or otherwise off-tasting • Perfect crumb in yeasted coffee cake, airy crumb and crisp crust in baguettes	Red Star, Fermipan Instant, and Fleischmann's
	YOGURT, LOW-FAT STRAWBERRY **Dannon Fruit on the Bottom**	• Balance of tanginess and strawberry flavor, not too sweet, sour, or bland • Pleasantly thick, not watery or runny • No artificial, plasticky, or otherwise unwelcome flavors as in many competitors	Wallaby Organic Creamy Australian-Style and Fage 2% All Natural Greek Strained
	YOGURT, WHOLE-MILK **Brown Cow Cream Top Plain**	• Rich, well-rounded flavor, not too sour or bland • Especially creamy, smooth texture, not thin or watery • Higher fat content contributes to flavor and texture	Stonyfield Farm Organic Plain

CONVERSIONS AND EQUIVALENCIES

Some say cooking is a science and an art. We would say that geography has a hand in it, too. Flour milled in the United Kingdom and elsewhere will feel and taste different from flour milled in the United States. So, while we cannot promise that the loaf of bread you bake in Canada or England will taste the same as a loaf baked in the States, we can offer guidelines for converting weights and measures. We also recommend that you rely on your instincts when making our recipes. Refer to the visual cues provided. If the bread dough hasn't "come together in a ball," as described, you may need to add more flour—even if the recipe doesn't tell you so. You be the judge.

The recipes in this book were developed using standard U.S. measures following U.S. government guidelines. The charts below offer equivalents for U.S., metric, and Imperial (U.K.) measures. All conversions are approximate and have been rounded up or down to the nearest whole number.

EXAMPLE:

1 teaspoon = 4.929 milliliters, rounded up to 5 milliliters
1 ounce = 28.349 grams, rounded down to 28 grams

VOLUME CONVERSIONS

U.S.	METRIC
1 teaspoon	5 milliliters
2 teaspoons	10 milliliters
1 tablespoon	15 milliliters
2 tablespoons	30 milliliters
¼ cup	59 milliliters
⅓ cup	79 milliliters
½ cup	118 milliliters
¾ cup	177 milliliters
1 cup	237 milliliters
1¼ cups	296 milliliters
1½ cups	355 milliliters
2 cups	473 milliliters
2½ cups	592 milliliters
3 cups	710 milliliters
4 cups (1 quart)	0.946 liter
1.06 quarts	1 liter
4 quarts (1 gallon)	3.8 liters

WEIGHT CONVERSIONS

OUNCES	GRAMS
½	14
¾	21
1	28
1½	43
2	57
2½	71
3	85
3½	99
4	113
4½	128
5	142
6	170
7	198
8	227
9	255
10	283
12	340
16 (1 pound)	454

CONVERSIONS FOR INGREDIENTS COMMONLY USED IN BAKING

Baking is an exacting science. Because measuring by weight is far more accurate than measuring by volume, and thus more likely to achieve reliable results, in our recipes we provide ounce measures in addition to cup measures for many ingredients. Refer to the chart below to convert these measures into grams.

INGREDIENT	OUNCES	GRAMS
Flour		
1 cup all-purpose flour*	5	142
1 cup cake flour	4	113
1 cup whole wheat flour	5½	156
Sugar		
1 cup granulated (white) sugar	7	198
1 cup packed brown sugar (light or dark)	7	198
1 cup confectioners' sugar	4	113
Cocoa Powder		
1 cup cocoa powder	3	85
Butter†		
4 tablespoons (½ stick, or ¼ cup)	2	57
8 tablespoons (1 stick, or ½ cup)	4	113
16 tablespoons (2 sticks, or 1 cup)	8	227

* U.S. all-purpose flour, the most frequently used flour in this book, does not contain leaveners, as some European flours do. These leavened flours are called self-rising or self-raising. If you are using self-rising flour, take this into consideration before adding leavening to a recipe.

† In the United States, butter is sold both salted and unsalted. We generally recommend unsalted butter. If you are using salted butter, take this into consideration before adding salt to a recipe.

OVEN TEMPERATURES

FAHRENHEIT	CELSIUS	GAS MARK (imperial)
225	105	¼
250	120	½
275	130	1
300	150	2
325	165	3
350	180	4
375	190	5
400	200	6
425	220	7
450	230	8
475	245	9

CONVERTING TEMPERATURES FROM AN INSTANT-READ THERMOMETER

We include doneness temperatures in many of our recipes, such as those for poultry, meat, and bread. We recommend an instant-read thermometer for the job. Refer to the table above to convert Fahrenheit degrees to Celsius. Or, for temperatures not represented in the chart, use this simple formula:
Subtract 32 degrees from the Fahrenheit reading, then divide the result by 1.8 to find the Celsius reading.

EXAMPLE:

"Roast until the thickest part of the chicken thigh registers 175 degrees on an instant-read thermometer." To convert:

175° F – 32 = 143
143 ÷ 1.8 = 79° C (rounded down from 79.44)

2010 TV SHOW EPISODE DIRECTORY

EPISODE ONE
Triple-Chocolate Mousse Cake
Triple-Chocolate Mousse Cake 515

EPISODE TWO
Chicken Classics, Reinvented
Crisp-Skinned Roast Chicken 74
Hearty Chicken Noodle Soup 5

EPISODE THREE
Best Weekend Breakfast
Blueberry Muffins 431
French Omelet 417

EPISODE FOUR
Classic Beef Braises
Hungarian Beef Stew 52
Braised Beef Short Ribs 54

EPISODE FIVE
Two Ways with Pork
Oven-Roasted Pork Chops 118
Maple-Glazed Pork
Tenderloin 140

EPISODE SIX
The Cookie Jar
Classic Chocolate Chip
Cookies 461
Sablés (French Butter
Cookies) 472

EPISODE SEVEN
Saucy Italian Favorites
Pasta with Hearty Italian Meat
Sauce (Sunday Gravy) 206
Pasta with Tomato and Almond
Pesto (Pesto alla Trapanese) 198

EPISODE EIGHT
**Meat and Potatoes for
Company**
Roast Beef Tenderloin 131
French Mashed Potatoes with
Cheese and Garlic (Aligot) 258

EPISODE NINE
Rolls and Loaves
Rustic Dinner Rolls 445
Multigrain Bread 455

EPISODE TEN
Egg Dishes with an Accent
Spanish Tortilla 418
French Onion and Bacon Tart 253

EPISODE ELEVEN
Sensational Skillet Recipes
Stovetop Roast Chicken with
Lemon-Herb Sauce 77
Skillet Lemon Soufflé 537

EPISODE TWELVE
An Austrian Supper
Breaded Pork Cutlets
(Pork Schnitzel) 139
Austrian-Style Potato Salad 35

EPISODE THIRTEEN
Who Wants Pasta?
Baked Ziti 215
Garlicky Shrimp Pasta 204

EPISODE FOURTEEN
**An Old-Fashioned
Thanksgiving**
Slow-Roasted Turkey with
Gravy 91
Pumpkin Pie 569

EPISODE FIFTEEN
Coconut Layer Cake
Coconut Layer Cake 498

EPISODE SIXTEEN
Salmon—Indoors and Out
Oven-Roasted Salmon 155
Grilled Salmon Fillets 372

EPISODE SEVENTEEN
Italian Bread and Sauce
Ciabatta 453
Quick Tomato Sauce 194

EPISODE EIGHTEEN
Great Glazed Chicken
Glazed Roast Chicken 75
Roasted Broccoli 387

EPISODE NINETEEN
Chicken and Rice—Indian-Style
Tandoori Chicken 333
Rice Pilaf 406

EPISODE TWENTY
All-Time Cookie Favorites
Chocolate Cookies 463
Thin and Crispy Oatmeal
Cookies 468

EPISODE TWENTY-ONE
South-of-the-Border Supper
Mexican Pulled Pork
(Carnitas) 292
Mexican-Style Grilled Corn 383

EPISODE TWENTY-TWO
Best Burgers and Fries
Best Old-Fashioned Burgers 183
Easier French Fries 187

EPISODE TWENTY-THREE
The Italian Grill
Italian-Style Grilled Chicken 243
Grilled Stuffed Flank Steak 347

EPISODE TWENTY-FOUR
Classic Asian Appetizers
Shrimp Tempura 301
Thai Pork Lettuce Wraps 302

EPISODE TWENTY-FIVE
Turkey on the Grill
Grill-Roasted Boneless
Turkey Breast 102
Crispy Roasted Potatoes 401

EPISODE TWENTY-SIX
Old-Fashioned Fruit Desserts
Apple Upside-Down Cake 492
Individual Fresh Berry Gratins
with Zabaglione 545

INDEX

Note: Page references in *italics* indicate photographs.

A

All-Butter Double-Crust Pie Dough, 560
All-Purpose Corn Bread, 448–49
All-Purpose Turkey Gravy, 99, *99*
Almond(s)
  -Crusted Chicken with Wilted Spinach Salad, 24–25
  Green Beans Amandine, 392
  or Hazelnut Crescent Cookies, 476
  -Raspberry Filling and Butter Frosting, Classic White
    Layer Cake with, 501–2, *502*
  Spritz Cookies, 471
  Toasted, Meringue Cookies, 477
  and Tomato Pesto, Pasta with (Pesto alla Trapanese), *198,*
    198–99
  Vinaigrette, 373
Almost No-Knead Bread, 451–52
American Potato Salad with Hard-Cooked Eggs and
    Sweet Pickles, 34–35, *35*
Anchovies
  Pissaladière, 254–55, *255*
  Spaghetti Puttanesca, 196
Angel Food Cake, 486, *486*
Antipasto Pasta Salad, 32–33, *33*
Appetizers
  Beef Satay, 303
  Charcoal-Grilled Baba Ghanoush, 380–81
  Cheesy Nachos with Guacamole and Salsa, 279, *279*
  Creamy Herbed Spinach Dip, 394–95
  Frico, 229–30
  Gas-Grilled Baba Ghanoush, 381
  Potstickers with Scallion Dipping Sauce, *300,* 300–301
  Shrimp Cocktail, 163
  Shrimp Tempura, 301–2
  Spiced Pecans with Rum Glaze, 407
Apple Cider
  Cider and Brown Sugar Glaze, 146
  Cider-Glazed Pork Chops, *122,* 122–23
  Sauce, 138
Apple(s)
  Apple Cider Sauce, 138
  Applesauce Snack Cake, 490, *490*
  Bacon, Sage, and Caramelized Onions, Bread Stuffing with,
    90–91
  Brown Betty, Skillet, *546,* 546–47
  -Cranberry Filling, Charcoal-Grilled Pork Loin with, 358–59,
    359

Apple(s) *(cont.)*
  -Cranberry Filling, Gas-Grilled Pork Loin with, 359–60
  and Currants, Curried Tuna Salad with, 172
  -Ginger Chutney, 127
  Glaze, Spicy, Grilled Salmon with, 375
  Pancake, German, 424–25, *425*
  Pie
    Classic, 562–63, *563*
    with Crystallized Ginger, 563
    Deep-Dish, *564,* 564–65
    with Dried Fruit, 563
    with Fresh Cranberries, 563
    Skillet (Apple Pandowdy), *549,* 549–50
  Simple Applesauce, 386
  Strudel, Easy, *547,* 547–49
  Tarts
    Free-Form, 581–82
    French (Apple Galette), *580,* 580–81
    30-Minute Tarte Tatin, 582
  Upside-Down Cake, *492,* 492–93
    with Almond, 493
    with Lemon and Thyme, 493
Applesauce
  Simple, 386
  Snack Cake, 490, *490*
Appliances, small, buying guide, 595–97
Apricot and Corn Muffins with Orange Essence, 434
Argentinian-Style Fresh Parsley and Garlic Sauce
    (Chimichurri), 113
Arugula
  Asparagus, Walnuts, and Blue Cheese, Cavatappi with, 201
  and Flank Steak Sandwiches with Red Onion, 115
  Goat Cheese, and Sun-Dried Tomato Pesto, Campanelle with,
    199
  Salad with Figs, Prosciutto, Walnuts, and Parmesan, 22
Asparagus
  Arugula, Walnuts, and Blue Cheese, Cavatappi with, 201
  Basil, and Balsamic Glaze, Campanelle with, 200–201, *201*
  Broiled, 386
  Ham, and Gruyère Frittata, 420, *420*
  Pan-Roasted, 387
  Shrimp, and Yellow Pepper, Stir-Fried, with Lemon Sauce,
    312–13
  trimming tough ends, 200
Austrian-Style Potato Salad, 35

Avocado(s)
Chunky Guacamole, 280
dicing, 280
and Orange, Shrimp Salad with, 164
-Orange Salsa, 159
Salsa, 168

B

Baba Ghanoush, Charcoal-Grilled, 380–81
Baba Ghanoush, Gas-Grilled, 381
Bacon
Cheeseburgers, Well-Done Grilled, 345
and Onion Tart, French, 253–54
Oven-Fried, 413
Quiche Lorraine, *421,* 421–22
Spaghetti alla Carbonara, 212–13
Tomato, and Onion, Pasta with (Pasta all'Amatriciana), 197,
197
Warm, Dressing, Wilted Spinach Salad with, *22,* 22–23
Baked Manicotti, *216,* 216–17
Baked Ziti, *215,* 215–16
Bakeware, essential, buying guide, 593–95
Balsamic Vinegar, Strawberries with, 554
Banana(s)
Bread, *427, 427*
Foster, 550–51
frozen, uses for, 61
Barbecued Baby Back Ribs for a Charcoal Grill, 366–67, *367*
Barbecued Baby Back Ribs for a Gas Grill, 368
Barbecued Beef Brisket, Charcoal-Grilled, 354–55, *355*
Barbecued Beef Brisket, Gas-Grilled, 355
Barbecued Beef Ribs, Texas-Style, for a Charcoal Grill, *368,*
368–69
Barbecued Beef Ribs, Texas-Style, for a Gas Grill, 369
Barbecued Pulled Chicken for a Charcoal Grill, 337–39
Barbecued Pulled Chicken for a Crowd, 339
Barbecued Pulled Chicken for a Gas Grill, 339
Barbecued Pulled Pork for a Charcoal Grill, 360–61, *361*
Barbecued Pulled Pork for a Gas Grill, 361
Barbecued Salmon for a Charcoal Grill, 375–76
Barbecued Salmon on a Gas Grill, 376
Barbecue Glaze, 341–42
Barbecue Sauce
Eastern North Carolina, 362
Kansas City, 363–64
Quick, 366
for Texas-Style Beef Ribs, 369
Bars
Blondies, 478, *478*
Brownies
Chewy Fudgy Triple-Chocolate, 480, *480*
Classic, 479, *479*
Fudgy Low-Fat, 480–81
Triple-Chocolate Espresso, 480

Bars *(cont.)*
Chocolate-Cherry, with Hazelnuts, 475
Congo, 478
Key Lime, 482–83, *483*
Raspberry Squares, 482
Triple Citrus, 483
Basic Double-Crust Pie Dough, 558
Basic Polenta, 234, *234*
Basic Single-Crust Pie Dough, 559
Basic Spice Rub for Pork Chops, 357
Basic White Rice, 308
Basil
-Cherry Tomato Vinaigrette, Chunky, 158
Farfalle with Pesto, 197–98
Pasta Caprese, 193, *193*
Pasta Salad with Pesto, 32, *32*
Tomatoes, and Mozzarella, Deep-Dish Pizza with, *223,*
223–24
washing and storing, 21
Bean(s)
Barbecue, Smoky Kansas City, 364
Black, Soup, 282–83, *283*
Boston Baked, 390, *390*
Ham and Split Pea Soup, 14
Hearty Lentil Soup, 12–13
Indian-Style Curry with Potatoes, Cauliflower, Peas, and
Chickpeas, *331,* 331–32
Indian-Style Curry with Sweet Potatoes, Eggplant, Green
Beans, and Chickpeas, 332
Kidney, Beef Chili with, 293–94
Refried, 297
Skillet Tamale Pie, 42
see also Green Bean(s); White Bean(s)
Bean Sprouts
Pad Thai, *325,* 325–26
and Peas, Fried Rice with, 308
Beef
Braised in Barolo, *246,* 246–47
Brisket
Barbecued, Charcoal-Grilled, 354–55, *355*
Barbecued, Gas-Grilled, 355
Onion-Braised, 135–37, *136*
Burgers
Best Old-Fashioned, *183,* 183–84
Charcoal-Grilled Hamburgers, 343, *343*
Gas-Grilled Hamburgers, 344
Grilled Cheeseburgers, 344
Well-Done Charcoal-Grilled Hamburgers, *344,* 344–45
Well-Done Gas-Grilled Hamburgers, 345
Well-Done Grilled Bacon Cheeseburgers, 345
Chili Con Carne, 294–95, *295*
Chili with Kidney Beans, 293–94
Cincinnati Chili, *177,* 177–78
Classic Stuffed Bell Peppers, 182–83
Glazed All-Beef Meat Loaf, 180–81, *181*
Pasta and Slow-Simmered Tomato Sauce with Meat, 210

Beef *(cont.)*

Pot Roast, Simple, 50, *50*

Prime Rib, 134–35

prime rib, carving, 135

Ribs, Short

boning, 54

Braised, 53–54, *54*

Slow Cooker Beer-Braised, 55, *55*

Ribs, Texas-Style

Barbecued, for a Charcoal Grill, *368,* 368–69

Barbecued, for a Gas Grill, 369

Barbecue Sauce for, 369

Roast

resting, before carving, 134

Slow-Roasted, 130–31

Tenderloin, *131,* 131–32

Tenderloin with Caramelized Onion and Mushroom
Stuffing, *132,* 132–34

salting, effect of, 130

Satay, 303

Simple Italian-Style Meat Sauce, *207,* 207–8

Skillet Lasagna, 39–40, *40*

Skillet Tamale Pie, 42

Spaghetti and Meatballs, 210–11, *211*

Steak

au Poivre with Brandied Cream Sauce, 272–73

blade, trimming, 51

Chicken-Fried, 179

Diane, *273,* 273–74

Fajitas for a Charcoal Grill, 288

Fajitas for a Gas Grill, 288

Filet Mignon, Pan-Seared, 112–13, *113*

Filet Mignon, Pepper-Crusted, 114, *114*

Filets Mignons, Charcoal-Grilled, 351, *351*

Filets Mignons, Gas-Grilled, 351

Flank, and Arugula Sandwiches with Red Onion, 115

flank, butterflying, 348

Flank, Charcoal-Grilled Marinated, 345–46, *346*

Flank, Gas-Grilled Marinated, 346

Flank, Grilled Stuffed, for a Charcoal Grill, *347,* 347–48

Flank, Grilled Stuffed, for a Gas Grill, 348

Flank, Grilled Stuffed, with Spinach and Pine Nuts, 349

flank, stuffing, 348

Pan-Seared, 108

Pan-Seared Inexpensive, 111, *111*

Pan-Seared Thick-Cut, *109,* 109–10

searing two at same time, 110

Strip or Rib, Charcoal-Grilled, 350–51

Strip or Rib, Gas-Grilled, 351

Tacos, 285–86

Tips, Charcoal-Grilled, 349

Tips, Gas-Grilled, 349

Stew

Beer, and Onion, Belgian (Carbonnade à la Flamande), *51,*
51–52

Burgundy, 267–69

Beef, Stew *(cont.)*

Burgundy, Slow-Cooker, 269–70

Daube Provençal, *266,* 266–67

Hungarian, 52–53, *53*

Stir-Fried

and Broccoli with Oyster Sauce, *314,* 314–15

Tangerine, with Onion and Snow Peas, 316–17

Teriyaki, with Green Beans and Shiitakes, 315–16

Thai-Style, with Chiles and Shallots, *324,* 324–25

Stroganoff, Skillet, 43, *43*

Tacos, 284, *284*

Tenderloin

Grill-Roasted, for a Charcoal Grill, *352,* 352–53

Grill-Roasted, for a Gas Grill, 353

and Vegetable Soup, Quick, *6,* 6–7

see also Meat loaf mix

Beer-Braised Short Ribs, Slow Cooker, 55, *55*

**Beer Can Chicken, Grill-Roasted, for a Charcoal Grill,
339–40**

Beer Can Chicken, Grill-Roasted, for a Gas Grill, 340

Behind the Scenes

brining tips, 100

brining turkey, 87, 100

buying chicken, 68

chimney starters, 337

chopping onions, 251

cooking and serving pasta, 196

cooking in skillets, 41

cooking pork, 124

creating TV scripts and filming shows, 13

developing pie dough recipes, 561

equipment hall of shame, 397

essential kitchen tools, 230

flambéing food, 274

heating oil in skillets, 158

hiring test cooks, 173

kosher chicken, 119

making pan sauces with fond, 272

mincing garlic, 178, 219

mise en place, 269

natural pork, flavor of, 119

pasta cooking gadgets, 203

preventing food from sticking to grill, 374

rating equipment, 9, 353

reducing sauces and liquids, 112

resting meat before carving, 134

salting, or "dry-brining" meat, 130

sharpening knives, 403

stir-frying, 313

storing tomatoes, 191

taste testing ingredients, 25, 175

testing recipes, 338, 412, 460

test kitchen freezer items, 61

using rulers in cooking, 467

washing and storing greens, 21

weighing and measuring ingredients, 449

Belgian Beef, Beer, and Onion Stew (Carbonnade à la Flamande), *51,* 51–52
Belgian-Style Dipping Sauce, 187
Berry(ies)
    Fresh, Gratins, Individual, with Lemon Zabaglione, 546
    Fresh, Gratins, Individual, with Zabaglione, *545,* 545–46
    Mixed, Tart with Pastry Cream, 579
    Summer, Pie, *568,* 568–69
    Summer, Pudding, Large, 553
    Summer, Puddings, Individual, *552,* 552–53
    see also Blueberry(ies); Cranberry(ies); Raspberry(ies); Strawberry(ies)
Best Drop Biscuits, 444–45, *445*
Best Old-Fashioned Burgers, *183,* 183–84
Big and Chewy Oatmeal-Date Cookies, 468
Big and Chewy Oatmeal-Raisin Cookies, 467–68
Biscuits
    Best Drop, 444–45, *445*
    Cheddar, 444
    Cream, 444
    Cream, with Fresh Herbs, 444
Bittersweet Chocolate Roulade, *513,* 513–14
Black and White Spiral Cookies, 473
Black Bean(s)
    Skillet Tamale Pie, 42
    Soup, 282–83, *283*
Blanched Green Beans, 391
Blondies, 478, *478*
Blueberry(ies)
    Boy Bait, 435–36, *436*
    Cobbler, 542–43, *543*
    Honeydew, and Mango with Lime-Ginger Reduction, 441
    Muffins, *431,* 431–32
    Nectarines, and Raspberries with Champagne-Cardamom Reduction, 441
    Pancakes, 423–24, *424*
    Pie, *567,* 567–68
    Scones, 428–30, *429*
Blue Cheese–Chive Butter, 115
Bok Choy and Crispy Noodle Cake, Stir-Fried Chicken with, 310–11, *311*
Boston Baked Beans, 390, *390*
Braised Beef Short Ribs, 53–54, *54*
Brandied Cream Sauce, Steak au Poivre with, 272–73
Bran Muffins, 432–33, *433*
Breaded Chicken Cutlets, 64–65, *65*
Breaded Pork Cutlets (Pork Schnitzel), *139,* 139–40
Bread pudding. *See* Strata
Bread(s)
    Almost No-Knead, 451–52
    Banana, 427, *427*
    Cheese, Quick, 447–48, *448*
    Cheese, Quick, with Bacon, Onion, and Gruyère, 448
    Ciabatta, 452–54, *453*
    Country, Rustic, 450–51
    Croutons, Classic, 8–9

Bread(s) *(cont.)*
    Croutons, Garlic, 16
    Garlic, Cheesy, 229
    Garlic, Classic, 228–29
    Multigrain, 454–55, *455*
    Quick Cinnamon Buns with Buttermilk Icing, 436–37, *437*
    Rustic Dinner Rolls, 445–46, *446*
    Soda, Irish, 446–47
    Soda, Whole Wheat, 447
    Sticky Buns with Pecans, 437–39, *438*
    see also Biscuits; Corn Bread; Muffins; Scones
Bread stuffings and dressings
    Bread Stuffing with Bacon, Apples, Sage, and Caramelized Onions, 90–91
    Mushroom-Leek Bread Stuffing with Herbs, 80
    Sausage Dressing, 94–95, *96*
    stuffing into turkey, 90
Breakfast Strata with Sausage, Mushrooms, and Monterey Jack, 423
Breakfast Strata with Spinach and Gruyère, *422,* 422–23
Brining techniques, 87, 100
Broccoli
    and Beef, Stir-Fried, with Oyster Sauce, *314,* 314–15
    and Cheddar, Skillet Chicken and Rice with, 46
    Chicken, and Mushrooms, Thai Green Curry with, 322–23
    Chicken, and Ziti, Skillet, 38–39
    Roasted, *387,* 387–88
    Roasted, with Garlic, 388
Broccoli Rabe and Sausage, Orecchiette with, 202–3
Broiled Asparagus, 386
Broiled Salmon with Mustard and Crisp Dilled Crust, *153,* 153–54
Brown Betty, Skillet Apple, *546,* 546–47
Brownies
    Chewy, Fudgy Triple-Chocolate, 480, *480*
    Classic, 479, *479*
    Fudgy Low-Fat, 480–81
    Triple-Chocolate Espresso, 480
Brown Sugar Cookies, *458,* 458–59
Buffalo Wings, 82–83
Buns, Quick Cinnamon, with Buttermilk Icing, 436–37, *437*
Buns, Sticky, with Pecans, 437–39, *438*
Burgers
    Best Old-Fashioned, *183,* 183–84
    Charcoal-Grilled Hamburgers, 343, *343*
    Gas-Grilled Hamburgers, 344
    Grilled Cheeseburgers, 344
    Well-Done Charcoal-Grilled Hamburgers, *344,* 344–45
    Well-Done Gas-Grilled Hamburgers, 345
    Well-Done Grilled Bacon Cheeseburgers, 345
Burger Sauce, Classic, 184
Butter
    Blue Cheese–Chive, 115
    Chipotle and Garlic, with Lime and Cilantro, 132
    Chipotle-Garlic, with Lime and Cilantro, 158
    freezing, 61

Butter *(cont.)*

Lemon, Garlic, and Parsley, 352

Mustard-Garlic, with Thyme, 79

Roasted Red Pepper and Smoked Paprika, 352

Shallot and Parsley, 132

Thai Chili, 110

Buttercream, Easy

Chocolate, 511

Coffee, 511

Vanilla Bean, 510–11

Buttermilk

Coleslaw, Creamy, 29–30, *30*

Mashed Potatoes, 400–401, *401*

Waffles, 426, *426*

Butternut Squash Risotto, 235–36, *236*

Butternut Squash Soup, 11

C

Cabbage

Creamy Buttermilk Coleslaw, 29–30, *30*

Creamy Coleslaw, 29

Potstickers with Scallion Dipping Sauce, *300,* 300–301

Salad, Confetti, with Spicy Peanut Dressing, 30–31

shredding, 29

Cakes

Angel Food, 486, *486*

Applesauce Snack, 490, *490*

Apple Upside-Down, *492,* 492–93

with Almond, 493

with Lemon and Thyme, 493

Carrot, 493–94, *494*

Carrot, Light, 494–95

Chocolate

Bittersweet, Roulade, *513,* 513–14

Bundt, Rich, 487, *487*

Cupcakes, Dark, 509–10

Flourless, *511,* 511–12

German, *508,* 508–9

Hot Fudge Pudding, 512

Hot Fudge Pudding, Individual, 513

Layer, Old-Fashioned, with Chocolate Frosting, *505,* 505–7

Sheet, with Easy Chocolate Frosting, *507,* 507–8

Triple- , Mousse Cake, *515,* 515–16

Volcano, with Espresso Ice Cream, 516–17

Coconut Layer, 498–99, *499*

Lemon Bundt, 488

Lemon Layer, with Fluffy White Icing, 499–501, *500*

Lemon Pound, 489, *489*

Oatmeal, with Broiled Icing, *491,* 491–92

Spice, *495,* 495–96

Strawberry Cream, 496–98

Tiramisù, 517–18, *518*

Tiramisù with Cooked Eggs, 518–19

Cakes *(cont.)*

White Layer, Classic, with Butter Frosting and Raspberry-Almond Filling, 501–2, *502*

Yellow Layer, Classic, with Vanilla Buttercream, 502–3

Yellow Layer, Fluffy, with Milk Chocolate Frosting, 503–5, *504*

see also Cheesecakes; Coffee Cakes

Campanelle with Arugula, Goat Cheese, and Sun-Dried Tomato Pesto, 199

Campanelle with Asparagus, Basil, and Balsamic Glaze, 200–201, *201*

Candied Sweet Potato Casserole, 105, *105*

Caper(s)

-Lemon Sauce, 118

Salsa Verde, 354

-Tomato Pan Sauce, 111–12

Caramelized Pears with Blue Cheese and Black Pepper–Caramel Sauce, 553–54

Caramel Sauce, 425–26

Carbonnade à la Flamande (Belgian Beef, Beer, and Onion Stew), *51,* 51–52

Carrot(s)

Cake, 493–94, *494*

Glazed, 389

Mashed Potatoes and Root Vegetables, 399, *399*

Roasted, 388, *388*

Cassoulet, Simplified, with Pork and Kielbasa, 270–71

Cauliflower, Potatoes, Peas, and Chickpeas, Indian-Style Curry with, *331,* 331–32

Cavatappi with Asparagus, Arugula, Walnuts, and Blue Cheese, 201

Charcoal-grilled dishes. *See under* **Grilled dishes**

Cheddar Biscuits, 444

Cheese

Baked Manicotti, *216,* 216–17

Baked Ziti, *215,* 215–16

Baked Ziti, Skillet, 38, *38*

Blue, and Black Pepper–Caramel Sauce, Caramelized Pears with, 553–54

Blue, –Chive Butter, 115

Blue, Dressing, Rich and Creamy, Leafy Green Salad with, 20–21

Bread, Quick, 447–48, *448*

Cheesy Garlic Bread, 229

Cheesy Nachos with Guacamole and Salsa, 279, *279*

Eggplant Parmesan, 232–33

Espresso-Mascarpone Cream, 514

Fettuccine Alfredo, *213,* 213–14

Four- , Baked Pasta, Creamy, *214,* 214–15

Frico, 229–30

and Garlic, French Mashed Potatoes with (Aligot), *258,* 258–59

Goat, Herbed Baked, and Vinaigrette, Salad with, 23–24

Grilled, Sandwiches, Classic, 173–74

Grilled Cheeseburgers, 344

Lighter Chicken Parmesan, 237–38, *238*

Cheese (cont.)

Macaroni and, Classic, 174, *174*

Macaroni and, Light, 176

Macaroni and, Stovetop, 175

Omelet, Family-Sized, 416

Parmesan-Crusted Chicken Cutlets, 239–40

Pasta Caprese, 193, *193*

Quesadillas, 280–81

Spicy Jalapeño-Cheddar Corn Bread, 449

Tiramisù, 517–18, *518*

Tiramisù with Cooked Eggs, 518–19

Tomato and Mozzarella Tart, 227, 227–28

Well-Done Grilled Bacon Cheeseburgers, 345

see also Cream Cheese; Lasagna; Pizza

Cheesecakes

Lemon, 522–23

New York, *519*, 519–20

New York, Light, 520–21

Spiced Pumpkin, *521*, 521–22

Cherry(ies)

-Chocolate Bars with Hazelnuts, 475

Dried, and Pecans, Chocolate-Chunk Oatmeal Cookies with, *466*, 466–67

Dried, –Port Sauce with Onions and Marmalade, 142

Fresh Sour, Cobbler, 542

-Port Glaze, 147

-Port Reduction, 114–15

Sour, Cobbler, *541*, 541–42

Cherry Tomato Salad with Feta and Olives, 26–27, *27*

Chewy, Fudgy Triple-Chocolate Brownies, 480, *480*

Chicken

Almond-Crusted, with Wilted Spinach Salad, 24–25

Barbecued Pulled

for a Charcoal Grill, 337–39

for a Crowd, 339

for a Gas Grill, 339

Beer Can, Grill-Roasted, for a Charcoal Grill, 339–40

Beer Can, Grill-Roasted, for a Gas Grill, 340

Biryani, *328*, 328–29

Breasts

Bone-In, Charcoal-Grilled, 336, *336*

Bone-In, Gas-Grilled, 336–37

butterflying, 66

Pan-Roasted, with Sage-Vermouth Sauce, 70–71, *71*

Skillet-Roasted, with Potatoes, *44*, 44–45

split, trimming, 71

Stuffed, French-Style, *260*, 260–61

Broccoli, and Mushrooms, Thai Green Curry with, 322–23

Broccoli, and Ziti, Skillet, 38–39

buying, tips for, 68

Chili, White, 295–96

with 40 Cloves of Garlic, 263–65

Coq au Vin, 262–63, *263*

Cutlets

Breaded, 64–65, *65*

Parmesan-Crusted, 239–40

Chicken, Cutlets (cont.)

Sautéed, with Mustard-Cider Sauce, 64, *64*

Stuffed, with Ham and Cheddar, 65–66

and Dumplings, *56*, 56–57

Enchiladas Verdes, *290*, 290–91

Enchiladas with a Red Chili Sauce, 288–89, *289*

Fajitas for a Charcoal Grill, *286*, 286–87

Fajitas for a Gas Grill, 287

Francese, 240–41, *241*

Fried, Crispy, 80–81, *81*

Fried, Oven-, 81–82, *82*

Italian-Style Charcoal-Grilled, 242–43, *243*

Italian-Style Gas-Grilled, 243

Kiev, *67*, 67–68

kosher, flavor of, 119

Marsala, 237

Noodle Soup, Classic, 4

Noodle Soup, Hearty, *5*, 5–6

Orange-Flavored, 309–10, *310*

Oven-Barbecued, Sweet and Tangy, 68–69, *69*

Paella, *59*, 59–60

Parmesan, Lighter, 237–38, *238*

Piccata, 239

Picnic, Spice-Rubbed, 70, *70*

in a Pot, French, 262

Pot Pie, Skillet, with Biscuit Topping, 40–42

Provençal, *265*, 265–66

and Rice

Curried, 46

Latino-Style, *57*, 57–58

Latino-Style, with Bacon and Roasted Red Peppers, 58

Latino-Style, with Ham, Peas, and Orange, 58

Skillet, with Broccoli and Cheddar, 46

Skillet, with Peas and Scallions, 45

Roast

carving, 76

Crisp-Skinned, 74–75

Glazed, *75*, 75–76

High-Roast Butterflied, with Potatoes, 78–79

Lemon, Classic, 72–73, *73*

Simple, 72

Stovetop, with Lemon-Herb Sauce, 76–77, *77*

"Stuffed" Butterflied, *79*, 79–80

Saltimbocca, 242

Shredded, Sesame Noodles with, *306*, 306

Simplified Cassoulet with Pork and Kielbasa, 270–71

Skillet Jambalaya, 47

Soup, Thai-Style, 303–4, *304*

Stir-Fried, and Zucchini with Ginger Sauce, 312

Stir-Fried, with Bok Choy and Crispy Noodle Cake, 310–11, *311*

Tandoori, 332–33, *333*

Teriyaki, *308*, 308–9

Thai Grilled, on a Gas Grill, 327

Thai Grilled, with Spicy, Sweet, and Sour Dipping Sauce, 326–27, *327*

Chicken *(cont.)*
  Tikka Masala, *329,* 329–30
  Tortilla Soup, *281,* 281–82
  whole, cutting up, 264
  Wings, Buffalo, 82–83
  wings, cutting up, 83
Chicken-Fried Steaks, 179
Chile(s)
  Green Curry Paste, 323
  Red Curry Paste, 324
  Spicy Jalapeño-Cheddar Corn Bread, 449
  see also Chipotle
Chili
  Beef, with Kidney Beans, 293–94
  Chicken, White, 295–96
  Cincinnati, *177,* 177–78
  Con Carne, 294–95, *295*
Chili-Mustard Spice Rub, 358
Chilled Lemon Soufflé, 534–35
  Individual, 535
  with White Chocolate, 535
Chipotle
  Chile Sauce, Creamy, 167
  -Garlic Butter with Lime and Cilantro, 158
  and Garlic Butter with Lime and Cilantro, 132
  Garlic-Chile Wet Paste Marinade, 347
  -Orange Glaze, 337
Chive and Black Pepper Dipping Sauce, 187
Chocolate
  Blondies, 478, *478*
  Brownies
    Chewy, Fudgy Triple-Chocolate, 480, *480*
    Classic, 479, *479*
    Fudgy Low-Fat, 480–81
    Triple-Chocolate Espresso, 480
  Cakes
    Bittersweet, Roulade, *513,* 513–14
    Bundt, Rich, 487, *487*
    Cupcakes, Dark, 509–10
    Flourless, *511,* 511–12
    German, *508,* 508–9
    Hot Fudge Pudding Cake, 512
    Hot Fudge Pudding Cakes, Individual, 513
    Layer, Old-Fashioned, with Chocolate Frosting, *505,* 505–7
    Sheet, with Easy Chocolate Frosting, *507,* 507–8
    Triple-, Mousse, *515,* 515–16
    Volcano, with Espresso Ice Cream, 516–17
  -Cherry Bars with Hazelnuts, 475
  -sChunk, Triple-, Pecan Pie, 571
  Congo Bars, 478
  Cookies, *463,* 463–64
    Black and White Spiral, 473
    Chocolate Chip, Classic, 460–61, *461*
    Chocolate Chip, Thick and Chewy, 461–62
    Chocolate Chip, Thin and Crispy, 462–63

Chocolate, Cookies *(cont.)*
  Chocolate-Chunk Oatmeal, with Pecans and Dried Cherries, *466,* 466–67
  Double-Chocolate, Thick and Chewy, 464–65
  Meringue, 477
  Sablés, 472
  Sandwich, 473
  Triple-Chocolate, Thick and Chewy, 465
  Cream Pie, 575
  Cupcakes, Dark, 509–10
  -Dipped Triple-Coconut Macaroons, *469,* 470
  Ganache, Dark, 514
  Milk, Frosting, Fluffy Yellow Layer Cake with, 503–5, *504*
  Mousse
    Dark, 531–32, *532*
    Orange, 532
    Premium Dark, 532
    Raspberry, 532
  Pots de Crème, *530,* 530–31
  Pots de Crème, Milk Chocolate, 531
  Soufflés
    Grand Marnier, with Grated Chocolate, 534
    Make-Ahead, *535,* 535–36
    Make-Ahead Mocha, 536
    Skillet Chocolate-Orange, 537
    White, Chilled Lemon Soufflé with, 535
Chowder, New England Clam, 17, *17*
Chunky Cherry Tomato–Basil Vinaigrette, 158
Chunky Guacamole, 280
Chutney
  Cilantro-Mint, 332
  Ginger-Apple, 127
  Sweet-and-Sour, 153
Ciabatta, 452–54, *453*
Cider. *See* Apple Cider
Cilantro and Garlic Marinade with Garam Masala, 371
Cilantro-Mint Chutney, 332
Cincinnati Chili, *177,* 177–78
Cinnamon Buns, Quick, with Buttermilk Icing, 436–37, *437*
Clambake, Indoor, 169
Clam Chowder, New England, 17, *17*
Classic Apple Pie, 562–63, *563*
Classic Burger Sauce, 184
Classic Chicken Noodle Soup, 4
Classic Chocolate Chip Cookies, 460–61, *461*
Classic Cranberry Sauce, 103
Classic Cream of Tomato Soup, 7
Classic Crème Brûlée, *528,* 528–29
Classic Crème Caramel, *529,* 529–30
Classic Croutons, 8–9
Classic French Fries, 186
Classic French Onion Soup, *250,* 250–51
Classic Garlic Bread, 228–29
Classic Gazpacho, 16
Classic Greek Salad, 27–28
Classic Green Bean Casserole, *103,* 103–4

Classic Grilled Cheese Sandwiches, 173–74
Classic Macaroni and Cheese, 174, *174*
Classic Mashed Potatoes, 397
Classic Roast Lemon Chicken, 72–73, *73*
Classic Roast Stuffed Turkey, *89,* 89–90
Classic Roast Turkey, 86, *86*
Classic Stuffed Bell Peppers, 182–83
Classic Tart Dough, 576
Classic Tuna Salad, 172, *172*
Classic White Layer Cake with Butter Frosting and
    Raspberry-Almond Filling, 501–2, *502*
Classic Yellow Layer Cake with Vanilla Buttercream, 502–3
Cobblers
    Blueberry, 542–43, *543*
    Fresh Sour Cherry, 542
    Sour Cherry, *541,* 541–42
Coca-Cola Glaze with Lime and Jalapeño, 146
Cocktail Sauce, 163
Coconut
    Congo Bars, 478
    Cream Pie, 574, *574*
    German Chocolate Cake, *508,* 508–9
    Layer Cake, 498–99, *499*
    Oatmeal Cake with Broiled Icing, *491,* 491–92
    Rice Pudding, 526
    Snowballs, Lime-Glazed, 475
    Triple- , Macaroons, 469–70
    Triple- , Macaroons, Chocolate-Dipped, *469,* 470
Coffee
    Chocolate Volcano Cakes with Espresso Ice Cream, 516–17
    Espresso Crème Brûlée, 529
    Espresso-Mascarpone Cream, 514
    Make-Ahead Mocha Soufflés, 536
    Tiramisù, 517–18, *518*
    Tiramisù with Cooked Eggs, 518–19
Coffee Cakes
    Blueberry Boy Bait, 435–36, *436*
    New York–Style Crumb Cake, 434–35, *435*
    Sour Cream, with Brown Sugar–Pecan Streusel, *440,* 440–41
Coleslaw, Creamy, 29
Coleslaw, Creamy Buttermilk, 29–30, *30*
Confetti Cabbage Salad with Spicy Peanut Dressing, 30–31
Congo Bars, 478
Cookies
    Black and White Spiral, 473
    Brown Sugar, *458,* 458–59
    Butter, Glazed, 474
    Chocolate, *463,* 463–64
        Double- , Thick and Chewy, 464–65
        Sablés, 472
        Sandwich, 473
        Triple- , Thick and Chewy, 465
    Chocolate Chip
        Classic, 460–61, *461*
        Thick and Chewy, 461–62
        Thin and Crispy, 462–63

Cookies *(cont.)*
    Crescent, Almond or Hazelnut, 476
    Crescent, Pecan or Walnut, 476, *476*
    holiday rolled, 474–75
    holiday spritz, 470–71
    Jam Sandwiches, 474–75
    Lime-Glazed Coconut Snowballs, 475
    Meringue, 477, *477*
        Chocolate, 477
        Toasted Almond, 477
    Molasses Spice, 459–60
    Molasses Spice, with Dark Rum Glaze, 460
    Oatmeal
        Chocolate-Chunk, with Pecans and Dried Cherries, *466,* 466–67
        -Date, Big and Chewy, 468
        -Raisin, Big and Chewy, 467–68
        Salty Thin and Crispy, 469
        Thin and Crispy, *468,* 468–69
    Peanut Butter, *465,* 465–66
    Sablés (French Butter Cookies), 471–72
    Spritz, *470,* 470–71
        Almond, 471
        with Lemon Essence, 471
    Triple-Coconut Macaroons, 469–70
    Triple-Coconut Macaroons, Chocolate-Dipped, *469,* 470
    Vanilla Pretzel, 473
    see also Bars
Cool and Creamy Macaroni Salad, 31, *31*
Coq au Vin, 262–63, *263*
Corn
    Fritters, *389,* 389–90
    Mexican-Style Charcoal-Grilled, 383, *383*
    Mexican-Style Gas-Grilled, 383
Corn Bread
    All-Purpose, 448–49
    Golden, 96
    Sausage Dressing, 94–95, *96*
    Southern, 449–50
    Spicy Jalapeño-Cheddar, 449
Cornish Game Hens
    Grill-Roasted, for a Charcoal Grill, *341,* 341–42
    Grill-Roasted, for a Gas Grill, 342–43
Cornmeal
    All-Purpose Corn Bread, 448–49
    Basic Polenta, 234, *234*
    Corn and Apricot Muffins with Orange Essence, 434
    Corn Muffins, 433–34
    Golden Corn Bread, 96
    Skillet Tamale Pie, 42
    Southern Corn Bread, 449–50
    Spicy Jalapeño-Cheddar Corn Bread, 449
Corn Muffins, 433–34
    and Apricot, with Orange Essence, 434
Crab Cakes, Maryland, 166
Crab Towers with Avocado and Gazpacho Salsas, 167–68, *168*

Cranberry(ies)
    -Apple Filling, Charcoal-Grilled Pork Loin with,
        358–59, *359*
    -Apple Filling, Gas-Grilled Pork Loin with, 359–60
    Dried, and Pecans, Wild Rice Pilaf with, 406–7
    Fresh, Apple Pie with, 563
    Sauce, Classic, 103
Cream Biscuits, 444
    Cheddar, 444
    with Fresh Herbs, 444
Cream Cheese
    Frosting, 494
    Frosting, Light, 495
    Lemon Cheesecake, 522–23
    New York Cheesecake, *519,* 519–20
    New York Cheesecake, Light, 520–21
    Spiced Pumpkin Cheesecake, *521,* 521–22
Creamless Creamy Tomato Soup, 8, *8*
Cream Scones, 427–28
Creamy Baked Four-Cheese Pasta, *214,* 214–15
Creamy Buttermilk Coleslaw, 29–30, *30*
Creamy Chipotle Chile Sauce, 167
Creamy Coleslaw, 29
Creamy Herbed Spinach Dip, 394–95
Creamy Mashed Potatoes, 398
Creamy Mushroom Soup, *10,* 10–11
Creamy Pea Soup, 9–10
Crème Brûlée, Classic, *528,* 528–29
Crème Brûlée, Espresso, 529
Crème Caramel, Classic, *529,* 529–30
Creole-Style Shrimp and Sausage Gumbo, *60,* 60–61
Crêpes Suzette, *551,* 551–52
Crisp, Peach, 543–44, *544*
Crisp, Peach, for a Crowd, 544
Crisp-Skin High-Roast Butterflied Turkey with Sausage
        Dressing, 94–95
Crisp-Skinned Roast Chicken, 74–75
Crisp Thin-Crust Pizza, 222, *222*
Crispy Fried Chicken, 80–81, *81*
Crispy Roasted Potatoes, 401–2
Croutons, Classic, 8–9
Croutons, Garlic, 16
Crunchy Baked Pork Chops, 124–25, *125*
Crunchy Oven-Fried Fish, 150, *150*
Crust, Graham Cracker, 562
Cucumber(s)
    Classic Gazpacho, 16
    Gazpacho Salsa, 168
    and Pineapple Salsa with Mint, 378
    Relish, Spicy, 156
    Salad, Sesame Lemon, 28
Cupcakes, Dark Chocolate, 509–10
Curried dishes
    Curried Chicken and Rice, 46
    Curried Tuna Salad with Apples and Currants, 172
    Indian Curry, 330–31

Curried dishes *(cont.)*
    Indian-Style Curry with Potatoes, Cauliflower, Peas, and
        Chickpeas, *331,* 331–32
    Indian-Style Curry with Sweet Potatoes, Eggplant, Green
        Beans, and Chickpeas, 332
    Mulligatawny Soup, 14–15, *15*
    Thai Green Curry with Chicken, Broccoli, and Mushrooms,
        322–23
    Thai Red Curry with Shrimp, Pineapple, and Peanuts,
        323–24
    Thai-Style Chicken Soup, 303–4, *304*
Curry Paste, Green, 323
Curry Paste, Red, 324
Custards
    Chocolate Pots de Crème, *530,* 530–31
    Classic Crème Brûlée, *528,* 528–29
    Classic Crème Caramel, *529,* 529–30
    Espresso Crème Brûlée, 529
    Milk Chocolate Pots de Crème, 531

D

Dark Chocolate Cupcakes, 509–10
Dark Chocolate Ganache, 514
Dark Chocolate Mousse, 531–32, *532*
Date-Oatmeal Cookies, Big and Chewy, 468
Daube Provençal, *266,* 266–67
Deep-Dish Apple Pie, *564,* 564–65
Deep-Dish Pizza with Tomatoes, Mozzarella, and Basil, *223,*
        223–24
Denver Omelet, 414–15, *415*
Desserts
    cakes, 485–523
    cookies and bars, 457–83
    fruit desserts, 539–55
    pies and tarts, 557–82
    puddings and soufflés, 525–37
    see also specific dessert category
Diner-Style Home Fries, 414, *414*
Dips and spreads
    Belgian-Style Dipping Sauce, 187
    Charcoal-Grilled Baba Ghanoush, 380–81
    Chive and Black Pepper Dipping Sauce, 187
    Chunky Guacamole, 280
    Cocktail Sauce, 163
    Creamy Herbed Spinach Dip, 394–95
    Garlic Mayonnaise, 419
    Garlic-Soy Mayonnaise, 115
    Gas-Grilled Baba Ghanoush, 381
    One-Minute Salsa, 279
    Scallion Dipping Sauce, *300,* 300–301
    Spicy Peanut Dipping Sauce, 303
Dressing, Sausage, 94–95, *96*
Dried Cherry–Port Sauce with Onions and Marmalade,
        142

Drinks
    Fresh Margaritas, 278
    Sangria, 278–79
Dry Rub for Barbecue, 362

E

Easier French Fries, 187, *187*
Easiest Kansas City Sticky Ribs, 363
Eastern North Carolina Barbecue Sauce, 362
Easy Apple Strudel, *547,* 547–49
Easy Chocolate Buttercream, 511
Easy Coffee Buttercream, 511
Easy Vanilla Bean Buttercream, 510–11
Eggplant
    Charcoal-Grilled Baba Ghanoush, 380–81
    Gas-Grilled Baba Ghanoush, 381
    Parmesan, 232–33
    Pork, and Onion, Stir-Fried, with Garlic and Black Pepper,
        317–18
    Sweet Potatoes, Green Beans, and Chickpeas, Indian-Style
        Curry with, 332
Eggs
    Asparagus, Ham, and Gruyère Frittata, 420, *420*
    Fried, 412
    Hard-Cooked, and Sweet Pickles, American Potato Salad
        with, 34–35, *35*
    Hard-Cooked, Foolproof, 23
    Huevos Rancheros, 296–97
    Leek, Prosciutto, and Goat Cheese Frittata, 421
    Omelets
        Cheese, Family-Sized, 416
        Denver, 414–15, *415*
        French, *417,* 417–18
    Pad Thai, *325,* 325–26
    Poached, 413
    Scrambled
        with Bacon, Onion, and Pepper Jack Cheese, 410–11
        Fluffy, 410, *410*
        with Sausage, Sweet Pepper, and Cheddar Cheese, 411
    Spaghetti alla Carbonara, 212–13
    Spanish Tortilla with Chorizo and Scallions, 419
    Spanish Tortilla with Roasted Red Peppers and Peas, 418–19,
        419
    Wilted Spinach Salad with Warm Bacon Dressing, *22,* 22–23
    see also Soufflés
Enchiladas, Chicken, with a Red Chili Sauce, 288–89, *289*
Enchiladas Verdes, *290,* 290–91
Equipment, ratings of
    behind the scenes look at, 9, 353, 397
    essential bakeware, 593–95
    grilling equipment, 597–98
    handy tools, 588–91
    kitchen supplies, 601

Equipment, ratings of *(cont.)*
    knives and more, 584–85
    measuring equipment, 592
    pots and pans, 586–87
    small appliances, 595–97
    specialty items, 598–600
    thermometers and timers, 592–93
    useless equipment and gadgets, 397
Espresso
    Crème Brûlée, 529
    Ice Cream, Chocolate Volcano Cakes with, 516–17
    -Mascarpone Cream, 514

F

Fajitas
    Chicken, for a Charcoal Grill, *286,* 286–87
    Chicken, for a Gas Grill, 287
    Steak, for a Charcoal Grill, 288
    Steak, for a Gas Grill, 288
Family-Sized Cheese Omelet, 416
Farfalle with Pesto, 197–98
Farfalle with Tomatoes, Olives, and Feta, 194
Fettuccine Alfredo, *213,* 213–14
Fettuccine with Slow-Simmered Bolognese Sauce, 208
Figs, Prosciutto, Walnuts, and Parmesan, Arugula
        Salad with, 22
Fish
    and Chips, 151–52, *152*
    Halibut Steaks, Pan-Roasted, 156–57, *157*
    halibut steaks, trimming and serving, 157
    Meunière with Browned Butter and Lemon, 275, *275*
    Oven-Fried, Crunchy, 150, *150*
    Red Snapper, Charcoal-Grilled Blackened, *377,* 377–78
    Red Snapper, Gas-Grilled Blackened, 378
    see also Anchovies; Salmon; Shellfish; Tuna
Flambéed Pan-Roasted Lobster, 164–66
Flank Steak and Arugula Sandwiches with Red Onion, 115
Flour, weighing, 449
Flourless Chocolate Cake, *511,* 511–12
Fluffy Mashed Potatoes, 400
Fluffy Scrambled Eggs, 410, *410*
Fluffy Yellow Layer Cake with Milk Chocolate Frosting,
        503–5, *504*
Foil tray for a grill, creating, 375
Fool, Rhubarb, 555, *555*
Fool, Strawberry-Rhubarb, 555
Foolproof Double-Crust Pie Dough, 561–62
Foolproof Hard-Cooked Eggs, 23
Four-Cheese Lasagna, 217–18
Free-Form Apple Tart, 581–82
Free-Form Summer Fruit Tart, 577–78
French Apple Tart, *580,* 580–81
French Chicken in a Pot, 262

French Mashed Potatoes with Cheese and Garlic (Aligot), *258*, 258–59
French Omelets, *417*, 417–18
French Onion and Bacon Tart, 253–54
French Onion Soup, Classic, *250*, 250–51
French Onion Soup, Streamlined, 251–52
French Potato Salad, 252–53, *253*
French-Style Stuffed Chicken Breasts, *260*, 260–61
Fresh Fruit Tart with Pastry Cream, 578–79, *579*
Fresh Margaritas, 278
Fresh Sour Cherry Cobbler, 542
Fresh Tomato Relish, 156
Fresh Tomato Sauce with Feta and Olives, 380
Frico, 229–30
Fried Eggs, 412
Fried Rice with Peas and Bean Sprouts, 308
Fried Rice with Shrimp, Pork, and Shiitakes, 307, *307*
Frittata, Asparagus, Ham, and Gruyère, 420, *420*
Frittata, Leek, Prosciutto, and Goat Cheese, 421
Fritters, Corn, *389*, 389–90
Frostings
  Cream Cheese, 494
  Cream Cheese, Light, 495
  Dark Chocolate Ganache, 514
  Easy Chocolate Buttercream, 511
  Easy Coffee Buttercream, 511
  Easy Vanilla Bean Buttercream, 510–11
  see also specific cake recipes
Fruit
  Dried, Apple Pie with, 563
  Fresh, Tart with Pastry Cream, 578–79, *579*
  Salads, 440–41
  Summer, Tart, Free-Form, 577–78
  see also Fruit desserts; specific fruits
Fruit desserts
  Bananas Foster, 550–51
  Caramelized Pears with Blue Cheese and Black Pepper–
    Caramel Sauce, 553–54
  Cobblers
    Blueberry, 542–43, *543*
    Fresh Sour Cherry, 542
    Sour Cherry, *541*, 541–42
  Crêpes Suzette, *551*, 551–52
  Easy Apple Strudel, *547*, 547–49
  Gratins
    Individual Fresh Berry, with Lemon Zabaglione, 546
    Individual Fresh Berry, with Zabaglione, *545*, 545–46
    Simple Raspberry, 544–45
  Peach Crisp, 543–44, *544*
  Peach Crisp for a Crowd, 544
  Rhubarb Fool, 555, *555*
  Skillet Apple Brown Betty, *546*, 546–47
  Skillet Apple Pie (Apple Pandowdy), *549*, 549–50
  Strawberries with Balsamic Vinegar, 554
  Strawberry-Rhubarb Fool, 555

Fruit desserts *(cont.)*
  Strawberry Shortcakes, *540*, 540–41
  Summer Berry Pudding, Large, 553
  Summer Berry Puddings, Individual, *552*, 552–53
Fudgy Low-Fat Brownies, 480–81

G

Galette, Apple, *580*, 580–81
Garlic
  Bread, Cheesy, 229
  Bread, Classic, 228–29
  -Chile Wet Paste Marinade, 347
  and Cilantro Marinade with Garam Masala, 371
  Croutons, 16
  40 Cloves of , Chicken with, 263–65
  and Fresh Parsley Sauce, Argentinian-Style (Chimichurri), 113
  Garlicky Lime Sauce with Cilantro, 142
  Garlicky Shrimp Pasta, 203–4, *204*
  Garlicky Shrimp with Buttered Bread Crumbs, *161*, 161–62
  Ginger, and Soy Marinade, 350
  -Ginger-Sesame Wet Paste Marinade, 346
  Gremolata, 245–46
  Lemon, and Parsley Butter, 352
  -Lemon Sauce, Spicy, 380
  Mayonnaise, 419
  mincing, ahead of time, 219
  mincing, with garlic press, 178
  Oil, Spicy, 227
  and Oil, Pasta with, 190, *190*
  and Olive Oil Mashed Potatoes, 398–99
  and Rosemary, Charcoal-Grilled Potatoes with, *381*, 381–82
  and Rosemary, Gas-Grilled Potatoes with, 382
  -Shallot-Rosemary Wet Paste Marinade, 346
  Shrimp, Spanish-Style, 162, *162*
  Shrimp fra Diavolo, 204–5, *205*
  Shrimp Scampi, 247
  -Soy Mayonnaise, 115
  -Studded Roast Pork Loin, 144
  and Thyme Sauce, 120
Gas-grilled dishes. *See under* **Grilled dishes**
Gazpacho, Classic, 16
Gazpacho Salsa, 168
German Apple Pancake, 424–25, *425*
German Chocolate Cake, *508*, 508–9
Giblet Pan Gravy, 87
Giblet Pan Gravy for a Crowd, 88–89
Ginger
  -Apple Chutney, 127
  Crystallized, Apple Pie with, 563
  Garlic, and Soy Marinade, 350
  -Garlic-Sesame Wet Paste Marinade, 346
  -Soy Glaze, 337
  -Soy Sauce with Scallions, 159

Ginger (cont.)
 and Tangerine Relish, 156
 Warm-Spiced Parsley Marinade with, 370–71
Glazed All-Beef Meat Loaf, 180–81, *181*
Glazed Butter Cookies, 474
Glazed Carrots, 389
Glazed Maple-Pecan Oatmeal Scones, 431
Glazed Roast Chicken, *75*, 75–76
Glazed Spiral-Sliced Ham, 146–47, *147*
Glazes
 Barbecue, 341–42
 Cherry-Port, 147
 Cider and Brown Sugar, 146
 Coca-Cola, with Lime and Jalapeño, 146
 Maple-Orange, 147
 Orange, Cinnamon, and Star Anise, 146
 Orange-Chipotle, 337
 Pineapple-Ginger, Spicy, 146
 Soy-Ginger, 337
Golden Corn Bread, 96
Graham Cracker Crust, 562
Grains
 Bran Muffins, 432–33, *433*
 freezing, 61
 Multigrain Bread, 454–55, *455*
 see also Cornmeal; Oats; Rice
Grand Marnier Soufflé, *533*, 533–34
Grand Marnier Soufflé with Grated Chocolate, 534
Grapes
 and Balsamic Vinegar, Tuna Salad with, 172
 and Strawberries with Balsamic and Red Wine Reduction,
 440–41
Gratins
 Individual Fresh Berry, with Lemon Zabaglione, 546
 Individual Fresh Berry, with Zabaglione, *545*, 545–46
 Simple Raspberry, 544–45
Gravy
 All-Purpose, Quick, 127
 Pan, Giblet, 87
 Pan, Giblet, for a Crowd, 88–89
 Slow-Roasted Turkey with, *91*, 91–92
 Turkey, 96–97
 Turkey, All-Purpose, 99, *99*
Greek Salad, Classic, 27–28
Green Bean(s)
 Amandine, 392
 Blanched, 391
 Casserole, Classic, *103*, 103–4
 "Casserole," Quick, 104–5
 Pork, and Red Bell Pepper, Stir-Fried, with Gingery Oyster
 Sauce, 318, *318*
 Roasted, 392
 with Sautéed Shallots and Vermouth, 391, *391*
 and Shiitakes, Teriyaki Stir-Fried Beef with, 315–16
 Sweet Potatoes, Eggplant, and Chickpeas, Indian-Style Curry
 with, 332

Green Bean(s) *(cont.)*
 with Toasted Hazelnuts and Brown Butter, 391–92
 trimming quickly, 316
Green Curry Paste, 323
Greens
 Classic Greek Salad, 27–28
 Hearty Tuscan Bean Stew, 231–32, *232*
 Leafy Green Salad with Red Wine Vinaigrette, 20, *20*
 Leafy Green Salad with Rich and Creamy Blue Cheese
 Dressing, 20–21
 Pan-Seared Scallops with Wilted Spinach, Watercress, and
 Orange Salad, 25–26
 Salad with Herbed Baked Goat Cheese and Vinaigrette,
 23–24
 Simple Sautéed Swiss Chard, 395–96
 Spicy Salad with Mustard and Balsamic Vinaigrette, 21
 Thai Pork Lettuce Wraps, 302–3
 Tough, Quick-Cooked, 395
 washing and storing, 21
 see also Arugula; Cabbage; Spinach
Gremolata, 245–46
Grilled dishes (beef)
 Beef Brisket, Barbecued, Charcoal-Grilled, 354–55, *355*
 Beef Brisket, Barbecued, Gas-Grilled, 355
 Beef Ribs, Texas-Style Barbecued, for a Charcoal Grill, *368*,
 368–69
 Beef Ribs, Texas-Style Barbecued, for a Gas Grill, 369
 Beef Tenderloin, Grill-Roasted, for a Charcoal Grill, *352*,
 352–53
 Beef Tenderloin, Grill-Roasted, for a Gas Grill, 353
 Cheeseburgers, Bacon, Well-Done Grilled, 345
 Cheeseburgers, Grilled, 344
 Filets Mignons, Charcoal-Grilled, 351, *351*
 Filets Mignons, Gas-Grilled, 351
 Hamburgers, Charcoal-Grilled, 343, *343*
 Hamburgers, Gas-Grilled, 344
 Hamburgers, Well-Done Charcoal-Grilled, *344*, 344–45
 Hamburgers, Well-Done Gas-Grilled, 345
 Marinated Flank Steak, Charcoal-Grilled, 345–46, *346*
 Marinated Flank Steak, Gas-Grilled, 346
 Steak Fajitas for a Charcoal Grill, 288
 Steak Fajitas for a Gas Grill, 288
 Steak Tips, Charcoal-Grilled, 349
 Steak Tips, Gas-Grilled, 349
 Strip or Rib Steaks, Charcoal-Grilled, 350–51
 Strip or Rib Steaks, Gas-Grilled, 351
 Stuffed Flank Steak, Grilled, for a Charcoal Grill, *347*,
 347–48
 Stuffed Flank Steak, Grilled, for a Gas Grill, 348
 Stuffed Flank Steak, Grilled, with Spinach and Pine Nuts,
 349
Grilled dishes (lamb)
 Rack of Lamb, Charcoal-Grilled, 371–72
 Rack of Lamb, Gas-Grilled, 372
 Shish Kebabs, Charcoal-Grilled, 370
 Shish Kebabs, Gas-Grilled, 370

Grilled dishes (pizza)
  Grilled Tomato and Cheese Pizzas for a Charcoal Grill,
    225–26
  Grilled Tomato and Cheese Pizzas for a Gas Grill, 226
Grilled dishes (pork)
  Baby Back Ribs, Barbecued, for a Charcoal Grill, 366–67,
    367
  Baby Back Ribs, Barbecued, for a Gas Grill, 368
  Kansas City Sticky Ribs, Easiest, 363
  Kansas City Sticky Ribs for a Charcoal Grill, 362–63, *363*
  Kansas City Sticky Ribs for a Gas Grill, 363
  Pork Chops, Charcoal-Grilled, 356, *356*
  Pork Chops, Gas-Grilled, 356–57
  Pork Loin, Charcoal-Grilled, with Apple-Cranberry Filling,
    358–59, *359*
  Pork Loin, Gas-Grilled, with Apple-Cranberry Filling,
    359–60
  Pork Loin, Grill-Roasted, for a Charcoal Grill, *357*, 357–58
  Pork Loin, Grill-Roasted, for a Gas Grill, 358
  Pulled Pork, Barbecued, for a Charcoal Grill, 360–61, *361*
  Pulled Pork, Barbecued, for a Gas Grill, 361
Grilled dishes (poultry)
  Chicken, Barbecued Pulled, for a Charcoal Grill, 337–39
  Chicken, Barbecued Pulled, for a Crowd, 339
  Chicken, Barbecued Pulled, for a Gas Grill, 339
  Chicken, Beer Can, Grill-Roasted, for a Charcoal Grill,
    339–40
  Chicken, Beer Can, Grill-Roasted, for a Gas Grill, 340
  Chicken, Italian-Style Charcoal-Grilled, 242–43, *243*
  Chicken, Italian-Style Gas-Grilled, 243
  Chicken, Thai Grilled, on a Gas Grill, 327
  Chicken, Thai Grilled, with Spicy, Sweet, and Sour Dipping
    Sauce, 326–27, *327*
  Chicken Breasts, Bone-In, Charcoal-Grilled, 336, *336*
  Chicken Breasts, Bone-In, Gas-Grilled, 336–37
  Chicken Fajitas for a Charcoal Grill, *286*, 286–87
  Chicken Fajitas for a Gas Grill, 287
  Cornish Game Hens, Grill-Roasted, for a Charcoal Grill,
    341, 341–42
  Cornish Game Hens, Grill-Roasted, for a Gas Grill, 342–43
  Turkey, Grill-Roasted, on a Charcoal Grill, 100–101
  Turkey, Grill-Roasted, on a Gas Grill, 101
  Turkey Breast, Boneless, Charcoal Grill–Roasted, *101*,
    101–2
  Turkey Breast, Boneless, Gas Grill–Roasted, 102–3
Grilled dishes (seafood)
  Red Snapper, Blackened, Charcoal-Grilled, *377*, 377–78
  Red Snapper, Blackened, Gas-Grilled, 378
  Salmon, Barbecued, for a Charcoal Grill, 375–76
  Salmon, Barbecued, on a Gas Grill, 376
  Salmon, Glazed, Charcoal-Grilled, 374–75, *375*
  Salmon, Glazed, Gas-Grilled, 375
  Salmon, Grilled, with Orange-Sesame Glaze, 375
  Salmon, Grilled, with Spicy Apple Glaze, 375
  Salmon Fillets, Charcoal-Grilled, 372–73, *373*
  Salmon Fillets, Gas-Grilled, 373

Grilled dishes (seafood) *(cont.)*
  Shrimp Skewers, Charcoal-Grilled, 379, *379*
  Shrimp Skewers, Gas-Grilled, 379–80
Grilled dishes (vegetables)
  Baba Ghanoush, Charcoal-Grilled, 380–81
  Baba Ghanoush, Gas-Grilled, 381
  Beans, Barbecue, Smoky Kansas City, 364
  Corn, Mexican-Style Charcoal-Grilled, 383, *383*
  Corn, Mexican-Style Gas-Grilled, 383
  Potatoes with Garlic and Rosemary, Charcoal-Grilled, *381*,
    381–82
  Potatoes with Garlic and Rosemary, Gas-Grilled, 382
Grills
  chimney starters for, 337
  creating foil tray for, 375
  grilling equipment, buying guide, 597–98
  preventing food from sticking to, 374
Guacamole, Chunky, 280
Gumbo, Creole-Style Shrimp and Sausage, *60,* 60–61

H
Halibut Steaks
  Pan-Roasted, 156–57, *157*
  trimming and serving, 157
Ham
  Asparagus, and Gruyère Frittata, 420, *420*
  and Cheddar, Stuffed Chicken Cutlets with, 65–66
  Denver Omelet, 414–15, *415*
  Fresh, Roast, *145,* 145–46
  Fried Rice with Shrimp, Pork, and Shiitakes, 307, *307*
  Peas, and Orange, Latino-Style Chicken and Rice with, 58
  Spiral-Sliced, Glazed, 146–47, *147*
  and Split Pea Soup, 14
  see also Prosciutto
Hamburgers. *See* Burgers
Hand Mixed All-Butter Double-Crust Pie Dough, 560
Hand Mixed Basic Double-Crust Pie Dough, 559
Hand Mixed Basic Single-Crust Pie Dough, 559
Hazelnut(s)
  Chocolate-Cherry Bars with, 475
  or Almond Crescent Cookies, 476
  Toasted, and Brown Butter, Green Beans with, 391–92
Hearty Chicken Noodle Soup, *5,* 5–6
Hearty Lentil Soup, 12–13
Hearty Tuscan Bean Stew, 231–32, *232*
Herb(s)
  and Caper Vinaigrette, Poached Salmon with, *154,* 154–55
  freezing, 61
  Fresh, Cream Biscuits with, 333
  and Fresh Tomatoes, Pasta with, 190–91
  Herbed Roast Turkey, *97,* 97–98
  see also specific herbs
High-Roast Butterflied Chicken with Potatoes, 78–79
Home-Fried Taco Shells, 284

Honeydew, Mango, and Blueberries with Lime-Ginger
    Reduction, 441
Horseradish
    Cocktail Sauce, 163
    Cream Sauce, 131
    Cream Sauce with Chives, 376
    and Lime, Tuna Salad with, 172
Hot and Sour Soup, 304–5, *305*
Hot Fudge Pudding Cake, 512
Hot Fudge Pudding Cakes, Individual, 513
Huevos Rancheros, 296–97
Hungarian Beef Stew, 52–53, *53*

I

Ice Cream, Espresso, Chocolate Volcano Cakes with, 516–17
Indian Curry, 330–31
Indian-Style Curry with Potatoes, Cauliflower, Peas, and
    Chickpeas, *331,* 331–32
Indian-Style Curry with Sweet Potatoes, Eggplant, Green
    Beans, and Chickpeas, 332
Individual Chilled Lemon Soufflés, 535
Individual Fresh Berry Gratins with Lemon Zabaglione, 546
Individual Fresh Berry Gratins with Zabaglione, *545,* 545–46
Individual Hot Fudge Pudding Cakes, 513
Individual Summer Berry Puddings, *552,* 552–53
Indoor Clambake, 169
Ingredients, tastings of
    behind the scenes look at, 25, 175
    shopping guide, 602–17
Irish Soda Bread, 446–47
Italian-Style Charcoal-Grilled Chicken, 242–43, *243*
Italian-Style Gas-Grilled Chicken, 243

J

Jambalaya, Skillet, 47
Jam Sandwiches, 474–75

K

Kansas City Barbecue Beans, Smoky, 364
Kansas City Barbecue Sauce, 363–64
Kansas City Sticky Ribs
    for a Charcoal Grill, 362–63, *363*
    Easiest, 363
    for a Gas Grill, 363
Key Lime Bars, 482–83, *483*
Key Lime Pie, 572, *572*
Kitchen supplies, buying guide, 601
Knives, buying guide, 584–85
Knives, sharpening, 403
Kung Pao Shrimp, *320,* 320–21

L

Lamb
    Indian Curry, 330–31
    Rack of
        Charcoal-Grilled, 371–72
        Gas-Grilled, 372
        trimming fat from, 372
    Shish Kebabs, Charcoal-Grilled, 370
    Shish Kebabs, Gas-Grilled, 370
Large Summer Berry Pudding, 553
Lasagna
    Four-Cheese, 217–18
    with Hearty Tomato-Meat Sauce, 218–19
    Skillet, 39–40, *40*
Latino-Style Chicken and Rice, 57, **57–58**
    with Bacon and Roasted Red Peppers, 58
    with Ham, Peas, and Orange, 58
Lattice-Top Fresh Peach Pie, *565,* 565–66
Leafy Green Salad with Red Wine Vinaigrette, 20, *20*
Leafy Green Salad with Rich and Creamy Blue Cheese
    Dressing, 20–21
Leek, Prosciutto, and Goat Cheese Frittata, 421
Leek-Potato Soup, Rustic, 12, *12*
Lemon grass, cutting, 323
Lemon(s)
    Bundt Cake, 488
    -Caper Sauce, 118
    Cheesecake, 522–23
    Chicken Francese, 240–41, *241*
    Chicken Piccata, 239
    Essence, Spritz Cookies with, 471
    Fresh Margaritas, 278
    Garlic, and Parsley Butter, 352
    -Garlic Sauce, Spicy, 380
    Gremolata, 245–46
    -Herb Sauce, Stovetop Roast Chicken with, 76–77, *77*
    Layer Cake with Fluffy White Icing, 499–501, *500*
    Meringue Pie, 572–73, *573*
    Pound Cake, 489, *489*
    Roast Chicken, Classic, 72–73, *73*
    Salsa Verde, 354
    Soufflé
        Chilled, 534–35
        Chilled, Individual, 535
        Chilled, with White Chocolate, 535
        Skillet, 537, *537*
    Tart, 576–77
    Triple Citrus Bars, 483
Lentil Soup, Hearty, 12–13
Lettuce Wraps, Thai Pork, 302–3
Light Carrot Cake, 494–95
Light Cream Cheese Frosting, 495
Lighter Chicken Parmesan, 237–38, *238*
Light Macaroni and Cheese, 176
Light New York Cheesecake, 520–21

Lime(s)
    Fresh Margaritas, 278
    -Glazed Coconut Snowballs, 475
    Key, Bars, 482–83, *483*
    Key, Pie, 572, *572*
    Triple Citrus Bars, 483
Lobster
    Flambéed Pan-Roasted, 164–66
    Indoor Clambake, 169
Lo Mein, Pork, 318–20, *319*

M

Macaroni
    and Cheese, Classic, 174, *174*
    and Cheese, Light, 176
    and Cheese, Stovetop, 175
    Salad, Cool and Creamy, 31, *31*
Macaroons, Triple-Coconut, 469–70
Macaroons, Triple-Coconut, Chocolate-Dipped, *469,* 470
Madeira Pan Sauce with Mustard and Anchovies, 113
Make-Ahead Chocolate Soufflés, *535,* 535–36
Make-Ahead Mocha Soufflés, 536
Mango, Honeydew, and Blueberries with Lime-Ginger
        Reduction, 441
Maple
    -Glazed Pork Roast, 142–43, *143*
        with Orange Essence, 143
        with Rosemary, 143
        with Smoked Paprika, 143
        with Star Anise, 143
    -Glazed Pork Tenderloin, *140,* 140–41
    -Mustard Sauce, 138
    -Orange Glaze, 147
Margaritas, Fresh, 278
Marinades
    Garlic, Ginger, and Soy, 350
    Garlic and Cilantro, with Garam Masala, 371
    Garlic-Chile Wet Paste, 347
    Garlic-Ginger-Sesame Wet Paste, 346
    Garlic-Shallot-Rosemary Wet Paste, 346
    Parsley, Warm-Spiced, with Ginger, 370–71
    Southwestern, 350
Marinara Sauce, *195,* 195–96
Maryland Crab Cakes, 166
Mascarpone
    -Espresso Cream, 514
    Tiramisù, 517–18, *518*
    Tiramisù with Cooked Eggs, 518–19
Mashed Potatoes
    Buttermilk, 400–401, *401*
    Classic, 397
    Creamy, 398
    Fluffy, 400
    French, with Cheese and Garlic (Aligot), *258,* 258–59

Mashed Potatoes *(cont.)*
    Garlic and Olive Oil, 398–99
    and Root Vegetables, 399, *399*
Mashed Sweet Potatoes, 405–6
Mayonnaise, Garlic, 419
Mayonnaise, Garlic-Soy, 115
Measuring equipment, buying guide, 592
Meat
    resting, before carving, 134
    salting, effect of, 130
    see also Beef; Lamb; Pork; Veal
Meatballs
    Pasta with Hearty Italian Meat Sauce (Sunday Gravy), 205–7
    Spaghetti and, 210–11, *211*
Meat Loaf
    All-Beef, Glazed, 180–81, *181*
    with Brown Sugar–Ketchup Glaze, 181–82
Meat loaf mix
    Fettuccine with Slow-Simmered Bolognese Sauce, 208
    Lasagna with Hearty Tomato-Meat Sauce, 218–19
    Meat Loaf with Brown Sugar–Ketchup Glaze, 181–82
    Pasta with Hearty Italian Meat Sauce (Sunday Gravy), 205–7
    Pasta with Weeknight Bolognese Sauce, 208–10, *209*
    Skillet Lasagna, 39–40, *40*
Meringue Cookies, 477, *477*
    Chocolate, 477
    Toasted Almond, 477
Mexican Pulled Pork (Carnitas), *291,* 291–92
Mexican Rice, 292–93, *293*
Mexican-Style Charcoal-Grilled Corn, 383, *383*
Mexican-Style Gas-Grilled Corn, 383
Mid–South Carolina Mustard Sauce, 362
Milk Chocolate Pots de Crème, 531
Mise en place, meaning of, 269
Mixed Berry Tart with Pastry Cream, 579
Mocha Soufflés, Make-Ahead, 536
Molasses Spice Cookies, 459–60
Molasses Spice Cookies with Dark Rum Glaze, 460
Mousse
    Chocolate-Orange, 532
    Chocolate-Raspberry, 532
    Dark Chocolate, 531–32, *532*
    Premium Dark Chocolate, 532
Muffins
    Blueberry, *431,* 431–32
    Bran, 432–33, *433*
    Corn, 433–34
    Corn and Apricot, with Orange Essence, 434
Mulligatawny Soup, 14–15, *15*
Multigrain Bread, 454–55, *455*
Mushroom(s)
    -Leek Bread Stuffing with Herbs, 80
    –Red Wine Pan Sauce, 110
    Risotto, 234–35
    Sautéed, and Thyme, Pasta with, 202, *202*
    Soup, Creamy, *10,* 10–11

Mushroom(s) *(cont.)*
  Stir-Fried Portobellos with Ginger-Oyster Sauce, 321–22, *322*
  Stir-Fried Portobellos with Sweet Chili-Garlic Sauce, 322
  Wild, Sautéed, 11
Mustard
  -Chili Spice Rub, 358
  -Cream Pan Sauce, 112
  -Dill Sauce, 376
  -Garlic Butter with Thyme, 79
  -Maple Sauce, 138
  Sauce, Mid–South Carolina, 362
  -Shallot Sauce with Thyme, 144

N

Nachos, Cheesy, with Guacamole and Salsa, 279, *279*
Nectarines, Blueberries, and Raspberries with Champagne-Cardamom Reduction, 441
New England Clam Chowder, 17, *17*
New York Cheesecake, *519,* 519–20
New York Cheesecake, Light, 520–21
New York–Style Crumb Cake, 434–35, *435*
Noodle(s)
  Cake, Crispy, and Bok Choy, Stir-Fried Chicken with, 310–11, *311*
  Classic Chicken Noodle Soup, 4
  Hearty Chicken Noodle Soup, *5,* 5–6
  Pad Thai, *325,* 325–26
  Pork Lo Mein, 318–20, *319*
  Sesame, with Shredded Chicken, 306, *306*
  Skillet Beef Stroganoff, 43, *43*
Nut(s)
  Almond or Hazelnut Crescent Cookies, 476
  Chocolate-Cherry Bars with Hazelnuts, 475
  freezing, 61
  Green Beans with Toasted Hazelnuts and Brown Butter, 391–92
  Toasted, and Parsley Pesto, Penne with, 199–200
  see also Almond(s); Pecan(s); Walnut(s)

O

Oatmeal Cake with Broiled Icing, *491,* 491–92
Oatmeal Scones, *430,* 430–31
Oats
  Big and Chewy Oatmeal-Date Cookies, 468
  Big and Chewy Oatmeal-Raisin Cookies, 467–68
  Chocolate-Chunk Oatmeal Cookies with Pecans and Dried Cherries, *466,* 466–67
  Glazed Maple-Pecan Oatmeal Scones, 431
  Oatmeal Cake with Broiled Icing, *491,* 491–92
  Oatmeal Scones, *430,* 430–31
  Raspberry Squares, 482

Oats *(cont.)*
  Salty Thin and Crispy Oatmeal Cookies, 469
  Thin and Crispy Oatmeal Cookies, *468,* 468–69
Oil. *See* Olive Oil
Old-Fashioned Chocolate Layer Cake with Chocolate Frosting, *505,* 505–7
Olive Oil
  and Garlic Mashed Potatoes, 398–99
  Spicy Garlic Oil, 227
Olive(s)
  Pesto, Spaghetti with, 200
  Pissaladière, 254–55, *255*
  Spaghetti Puttanesca, 196
  Vinaigrette, 373
Omelets
  Cheese, Family-Sized, 416
  Denver, 414–15, *415*
  French, *417,* 417–18
One-Minute Salsa, 279
Onion(s)
  and Bacon Tart, French, 253–54
  Beef, and Beer Stew, Belgian (Carbonnade à la Flamande), *51,* 51–52
  -Braised Beef Brisket, 135–37, *136*
  chopping, without tears, 251
  Pickled, Sweet and Spicy, 286
  Pissaladière, 254–55, *255*
  Potatoes Lyonnaise, 259, *259*
  Relish, 332
  Rings, Oven-Fried, *184,* 184–85
  Smothered Pork Chops, *123,* 123–24
  Soup, Classic French, *250,* 250–51
  Soup, Streamlined French, 251–52
  Sweet-and-Sour Chutney, 153
Orange(s)
  and Avocado, Shrimp Salad with, 164
  -Avocado Salsa, 159
  -Chipotle Glaze, 337
  -Chocolate Soufflé, Skillet, 537
  Cinnamon, and Star Anise Glaze, 146
  Crêpes Suzette, *551,* 551–52
  -Flavored Chicken, 309–10, *310*
  Olives, and Almonds, Rice Salad with, 33–34, *34*
  Sangria, 278–79
  segmenting, 167
  -Sesame Glaze, Grilled Salmon with, 375
  Triple Citrus Bars, 483
Orecchiette with Broccoli Rabe and Sausage, 202–3
Osso Buco, 245–46
Oven-Barbecued Spareribs, *365,* 365–66
Oven-Fried Bacon, 413
Oven-Fried Chicken, 81–82, *82*
Oven-Fried Onion Rings, *184,* 184–85
Oven-Roasted Pork Chops, 118
Oven-Roasted Salmon, 155–56, *156*

P

Pad Thai, *325,* 325–26
Paella, *59,* 59–60
Pancake, German Apple, 424–25, *425*
Pancakes, Blueberry, 423–24, *424*
Pandowdy, Apple, *549,* 549–50
Panna Cotta, 526–27
Pan-Roasted Asparagus, 387
Pan-Roasted Chicken Breasts with Sage-Vermouth Sauce, 70–71, *71*
Pan-Roasted Halibut Steaks, 156–57, *157*
Pan-Seared Filet Mignon, 112–13, *113*
Pan-Seared Inexpensive Steaks, 111, *111*
Pan-Seared Oven-Roasted Pork Tenderloins, 141
Pan-Seared Salmon, 152–53
Pan-Seared Scallops with Wilted Spinach, Watercress, and Orange Salad, 25–26
Pan-Seared Sesame-Crusted Tuna Steaks, 158–59, *159*
Pan-Seared Shrimp, 159–60, *160*
    with Chipotle-Lime Glaze, 160
    with Garlic-Lemon Butter, 160
    with Ginger-Hoisin Glaze, 160
Pan-Seared Steaks, 108
Pan-Seared Thick-Cut Pork Chops, 119–20, *120*
Pan-Seared Thick-Cut Steaks, *109,* 109–10
Paprika, Smoked, and Roasted Red Pepper Butter, 352
Parmesan-Crusted Chicken Cutlets, 239–40
Parsley
    Fresh, and Garlic Sauce, Argentinian-Style (Chimichurri), 113
    Gremolata, 245–46
    Lemon, and Garlic Butter, 352
    Marinade, Warm-Spiced, with Ginger, 370–71
    Salsa Verde, 354
    and Shallot Butter, 132
    and Toasted Nut Pesto, Penne with, 199–200
Pasta
    Campanelle with Arugula, Goat Cheese, and Sun-Dried Tomato Pesto, 199
    Campanelle with Asparagus, Basil, and Balsamic Glaze, 200–201, *201*
    Caprese, 193, *193*
    Cavatappi with Asparagus, Arugula, Walnuts, and Blue Cheese, 201
    cooking, 196
    cooking gadgets, note about, 203
    with Creamy Tomato Sauce, *192,* 192–93
    draining and serving, 196
    e Fagioli, 230–31, *231*
    Farfalle with Pesto, 197–98
    Farfalle with Tomatoes, Olives, and Feta, 194
    Fettuccine Alfredo, *213,* 213–14
    Fettuccine with Slow-Simmered Bolognese Sauce, 208
    Four-Cheese, Creamy Baked, *214,* 214–15
    with Fresh Tomatoes and Herbs, 190–91
    and Fresh Tomato Sauce with Garlic and Basil, 191–92

Pasta *(cont.)*
    with Garlic and Oil, 190, *190*
    with Hearty Italian Meat Sauce (Sunday Gravy), 205–7
    Lasagna
        Four-Cheese, 217–18
        with Hearty Tomato-Meat Sauce, 218–19
        Skillet, 39–40, *40*
    Macaroni
        and Cheese, Classic, 174, *174*
        and Cheese, Light, 176
        and Cheese, Stovetop, 175
        Salad, Cool and Creamy, 31, *31*
    Manicotti, Baked, *216,* 216–17
    Orecchiette with Broccoli Rabe and Sausage, 202–3
    Penne with Toasted Nut and Parsley Pesto, 199–200
    Penne with Vodka Sauce (Penne alla Vodka), 212, *212*
    Pork Lo Mein, 318–20, *319*
    Salad
        Antipasto, 32–33, *33*
        Macaroni, Cool and Creamy, 31, *31*
        with Pesto, 32, *32*
    Sauces
        Marinara, *195,* 195–96
        Meat, Simple Italian-Style, *207,* 207–8
        Tomato, Quick, *194,* 194–95
    with Sautéed Mushrooms and Thyme, 202, *202*
    Shrimp, Garlicky, 203–4, *204*
    Shrimp fra Diavolo, 204–5, *205*
    and Slow-Simmered Tomato Sauce with Meat, 210
    with Tomato, Bacon, and Onion (Pasta all'Amatriciana), 197, *197*
    with Tomato and Almond Pesto (Pesto alla Trapanese), *198,* 198–99
    with Weeknight Bolognese Sauce, 208–10, *209*
    Ziti
        Baked, *215,* 215–16
        Chicken and Broccoli, Skillet, 38–39
        Skillet Baked, 38, *38*
    see also Noodle(s); Spaghetti
Pastry Cream, Fresh Fruit Tart with, 578–79, *579*
Peach
    Crisp, 543–44, *544*
    Crisp for a Crowd, 544
    Fresh, Pie, Lattice-Top, *565,* 565–66
Peanut Butter
    Confetti Cabbage Salad with Spicy Peanut Dressing, 30–31
    Cookies, *465,* 465–66
    Sesame Noodles with Shredded Chicken, 306, *306*
    Spicy Peanut Dipping Sauce, 303
Pears, Caramelized, with Blue Cheese and Black Pepper–Caramel Sauce, 553–54
Pear Tatin, 582
Pea(s)
    and Bean Sprouts, Fried Rice with, 308
    and Scallions, Skillet Chicken and Rice with, 45

Pea(s) *(cont.)*

Snow, and Onion, Tangerine Stir-Fried Beef with, 316–17

Snow, Tofu, and Red Onion, Stir-Fried, with Hot and Sour Sauce, 313–14

Soup, Creamy, 9–10

Pecan(s)

Blondies, 478, *478*

–Brown Sugar Streusel, Sour Cream Coffee Cake with, *440,* 440–41

Candied Sweet Potato Casserole, 105, *105*

Congo Bars, 478

and Dried Cherries, Chocolate-Chunk Oatmeal Cookies with, *466,* 466–67

and Dried Cranberries, Wild Rice Pilaf with, 406–7

German Chocolate Cake, *508,* 508–9

Glazed Maple-Pecan Oatmeal Scones, 431

Oatmeal Cake with Broiled Icing, *491,* 491–92

or Walnut Crescent Cookies, 476, *476*

Pie, 570–71, *571*

Pie, Triple-Chocolate-Chunk, 571

Raspberry Squares, 482

Spiced, with Rum Glaze, 407

Sticky Buns with, 437–39, *438*

Penne with Toasted Nut and Parsley Pesto, 199–200

Penne with Vodka Sauce (Penne alla Vodka), 212, *212*

Pepper-Crusted Filet Mignon, 114, *114*

Pepper(s)

Bell, Classic Stuffed, 182–83

Classic Gazpacho, 16

Gazpacho Salsa, 168

Roasted Red, and Smoked Paprika Butter, 352

Sweet, and Vinegar, Pork Chops with, *244,* 244–45

Pesto

Farfalle with, 197–98

Olive, Spaghetti with, 200

Pasta Salad with, 32, *32*

Sun-Dried Tomato, Arugula, and Goat Cheese, Campanelle with, 199

Toasted Nut and Parsley, Penne with, 199–200

Tomato and Almond, Pasta with (Pesto alla Trapanese), *198,* 198–99

Pickled Onions, Sweet and Spicy, 286

Pie Dough

All-Butter Double-Crust, 560

All-Butter Double-Crust, Hand Mixed, 560

Basic Double-Crust, 558

Basic Double-Crust, Hand Mixed, 559

Basic Single-Crust, 559

Basic Single-Crust, Hand Mixed, 559

blind-baking, 569

Foolproof Double-Crust, 561–62

recipes for, behind the scenes, 561

rolling and fitting, 558

single-crust, crimping, 559

Single-Crust, For Custard Pies, 559

Pies

Apple

Classic, 562–63, *563*

with Crystallized Ginger, 563

Deep-Dish, *564,* 564–65

with Dried Fruit, 563

with Fresh Cranberries, 563

Skillet (Pandowdy), *549,* 549–50

blind-baking crust for, 569

Blueberry, *567,* 567–68

Chocolate Cream, 575

Coconut Cream, 574, *574*

double-crust, forming, 565

Key Lime, 572, *572*

Lemon Meringue, 572–73, *573*

Peach, Fresh, Lattice-Top, *565,* 565–66

Pecan, 570–71, *571*

Pecan, Triple-Chocolate-Chunk, 571

Pumpkin, 569–70, *570*

Summer Berry, *568,* 568–69

see also Tarts (dessert)

Pies, Skillet

Apple (Apple Pandowdy), *549,* 549–50

Tamale, 42

Pineapple

and Cucumber Salsa with Mint, 378

–Ginger Glaze, Spicy, 146

Shrimp, and Peanuts, Thai Red Curry with, 323–24

Pissaladière, 254–55, *255*

Pizza

Bianca, 224–25, *225*

Deep-Dish, with Tomatoes, Mozzarella, and Basil, *223,* 223–24

Quick Tomato Sauce for, 223

Thin-Crust, Crisp, 222, *222*

Tomato and Cheese, Grilled, for a Charcoal Grill, 225–26

Tomato and Cheese, Grilled, for a Gas Grill, 226

Poached Eggs, 413

Poached Salmon with Herb and Caper Vinaigrette, 154, **154–55**

Polenta, Basic, 234, *234*

Pommes Anna, *257,* 257–58

Pork

Chops

Basic Spice Rub for, 357

Charcoal-Grilled, 356, *356*

Cider-Glazed, *122,* 122–23

cooking tip, 122

Crunchy Baked, 124–25, *125*

Gas-Grilled, 356–57

Oven-Roasted, 118

Pan-Seared Thick-Cut, 119–20, *120*

Skillet-Barbecued, 120–21, *121*

Smothered, *123,* 123–24

Stuffed, 125–27

with Vinegar and Sweet Peppers, *244,* 244–45

Pork *(cont.)*

Cutlets, Breaded (Pork Schnitzel), *139,* 139–40

Hot and Sour Soup, 304–5, *305*

internal cooking temperatures, 124

and Kielbasa, Simplified Cassoulet with, 270–71

Lettuce Wraps, Thai, 302–3

Loin

with Apple-Cranberry Filling, Charcoal-Grilled, 358–59, *359*

with Apple-Cranberry Filling, Gas-Grilled, 359–60

cutting open and stuffing, 360

Grill-Roasted, for a Charcoal Grill, *357,* 357–58

Grill-Roasted, for a Gas Grill, 358

Roast, Garlic-Studded, 144

Lo Mein, 318–20, *319*

natural versus enhanced, 119

Pasta with Hearty Italian Meat Sauce (Sunday Gravy), 205–7

Potstickers with Scallion Dipping Sauce, *300,* 300–301

Pulled, Mexican (Carnitas), *291,* 291–92

Pulled Barbecued, for a Charcoal Grill, 360–61, *361*

Pulled Barbecued, for a Gas Grill, 361

Ribs

Barbecued Baby Back, for a Charcoal Grill, 366–67, *367*

Barbecued Baby Back, for a Gas Grill, 368

Kansas City Sticky, Easiest, 363

Kansas City Sticky, for a Charcoal Grill, 362–63, *363*

Kansas City Sticky, for a Gas Grill, 363

Oven-Barbecued Spareribs, *365,* 365–66

Roast

Maple-Glazed, 142–43, *143*

Maple-Glazed, with Orange Essence, 143

Maple-Glazed, with Rosemary, 143

Maple-Glazed, with Smoked Paprika, 143

Maple-Glazed, with Star Anise, 143

salting, effect of, 130

Stir-Fried, Eggplant, and Onion with Garlic and Black Pepper, 317–18

Stir-Fried, Green Beans, and Red Bell Pepper with Gingery Oyster Sauce, 318, *318*

Tenderloin

Maple-Glazed, *140,* 140–41

Medallions, Thick-Cut, 137, *138*

medallions, tying, 138

Pan-Seared Oven-Roasted, 141

tail end, tying into medallion, 137

see also Bacon; Ham; Meat loaf mix; Sausage(s)

Port

-Cherry Glaze, 147

-Cherry Reduction, 114–15

–Dried Cherry Sauce with Onions and Marmalade, 142

Potato(es)

Crispy Roasted, 401–2

Diner-Style Home Fries, 414, *414*

Fish and Chips, 151–52, *152*

Potato(es) *(cont.)*

Fries

French, Classic, 186

French, Easier, 187, *187*

Steak, *185,* 185–86

with Garlic and Rosemary, Charcoal-Grilled, *381,* 381–82

with Garlic and Rosemary, Gas-Grilled, 382

High-Roast Butterflied Chicken with, 78–79

-Leek Soup, Rustic, 12, *12*

Lyonnaise, 259, *259*

Mashed

Buttermilk, 400–401, *401*

Classic, 397

Creamy, 398

Fluffy, 400

French, with Cheese and Garlic (Aligot), *258,* 258–59

Garlic and Olive Oil, 398–99

and Root Vegetables, 399, *399*

Pommes Anna, *257,* 257–58

Salad

American, with Hard-Cooked Eggs and Sweet Pickles, 34–35, *35*

Austrian-Style, 35

French, 252–53, *253*

Scalloped, 403

skewering, for the grill, 382

Skillet-Roasted, 402, *402*

Skillet-Roasted Chicken Breasts with, *44,* 44–45

Smashed, 396

Spanish Tortilla with Chorizo and Scallions, 419

Spanish Tortilla with Roasted Red Peppers and Peas, 418–19, *419*

Twice-Baked, 404

see also Sweet Potato(es)

Pot Pie, Skillet Chicken, with Biscuit Topping, 40–42

Pots and pans

best, for stir-fries, 313

buying guide, 586–87

heating oil in skillets, 158

skillets, versatility of, 41

Pots de Crème, Chocolate, *530,* 530–31

Pots de Crème, Milk Chocolate, 531

Potstickers with Scallion Dipping Sauce, *300,* 300–301

Poultry

Grill-Roasted Cornish Game Hens for a Charcoal Grill, *341,* 341–42

Grill-Roasted Cornish Game Hens for a Gas Grill, 342–43

see also Chicken; Turkey

Premium Dark Chocolate Mousse, 532

Prime Rib, 134–35

Prosciutto

Chicken Saltimbocca, 242

Figs, Walnuts, and Parmesan, Arugula Salad with, 22

Grilled Stuffed Flank Steak for a Charcoal Grill, *347,* 347–48

Grilled Stuffed Flank Steak for a Gas Grill, 348

Leek, and Goat Cheese Frittata, 421

Puddings
  Panna Cotta, 526–27
  Rice, Coconut, 526
  Rice, Stovetop, 526, *526*
  Summer Berry, Individual, *552,* 552–53
  Summer Berry, Large, 553
  see also Custards; Mousse
Puddings, bread. *See* Strata
Pumpkin Cheesecake, Spiced, *521,* 521–22
Pumpkin Pie, 569–70, *570*

Q

Quesadillas, 280–81
Quiche Lorraine, *421,* 421–22
Quick All-Purpose Gravy, 127
Quick Barbecue Sauce, 366
Quick Beef and Vegetable Soup, *6,* 6–7
Quick Cheese Bread, 447–48, *448*
Quick Cheese Bread with Bacon, Onion, and Gruyère, 448
Quick Cinnamon Buns with Buttermilk Icing, 436–37, *437*
Quick-Cooked Tough Greens, 395
Quick Green Bean "Casserole," 104–5
Quick Roasted Acorn Squash with Brown Sugar, 404–5, *405*
Quick Tomato Sauce, *194,* 194–95
Quick Tomato Sauce for Pizza, 223

R

Raisins
  Big and Chewy Oatmeal-Raisin Cookies, 467–68
  Golden, and Almonds, Sautéed Baby Spinach with, 393–94
Raspberry(ies)
  Coulis, 527
  Gratin, Simple, 544–45
  Nectarines, and Blueberries with Champagne-Cardamom
    Reduction, 441
Raspberry jam
  Jam Sandwiches, 474–75
  Raspberry Squares, 482
Red Curry Paste, 324
Red Snapper, Charcoal-Grilled Blackened, *377,* 377–78
Red Snapper, Gas-Grilled Blackened, 378
Red Wine
  Beef Braised in Barolo, *246,* 246–47
  Beef Burgundy, 267–69
  Beef Burgundy, Slow-Cooker, 269–70
  Coq au Vin, 262–63, *263*
  Daube Provençal, *266,* 266–67
  –Mushroom Pan Sauce, 110
  Pan Sauce, 108
  Sangria, 278–79
  Sauce Base for Steak Diane, 274

Refried Beans, 297
Relish
  Cucumber, Spicy, 156
  Onion, 332
  Tangerine and Ginger, 156
  Tomato, Fresh, 156
Rémoulade, 378
Rhubarb Fool, 555, *555*
Rhubarb-Strawberry Fool, 555
Rice
  Butternut Squash Risotto, 235–36, *236*
  Chicken and
    Curried, 46
    Latino-Style, *57,* 57–58
      with Bacon and Roasted Red Peppers, 58
      with Ham, Peas, and Orange, 58
     Skillet, with Broccoli and Cheddar, 46
     Skillet, with Peas and Scallions, 45
  Chicken Biryani, *328,* 328–29
  Classic Stuffed Bell Peppers, 182–83
  Fried, with Peas and Bean Sprouts, 308
  Fried, with Shrimp, Pork, and Shiitakes, 307, *307*
  Mexican, 292–93, *293*
  Mushroom Risotto, 234–35
  Paella, *59,* 59–60
  Pilaf, 406
  Pudding, Coconut, 526
  Pudding, Stovetop, 526, *526*
  Salad with Oranges, Olives, and Almonds, 33–34, *34*
  Skillet Jambalaya, 47
  White, Basic, 308
  Wild, Pilaf with Pecans and Dried Cranberries, 406–7
Rich Chocolate Bundt Cake, *487,* 487
Risotto, Butternut Squash, 235–36, *236*
Risotto, Mushroom, 234–35
Roast Beef Tenderloin, *131,* 131–32
Roast Beef Tenderloin with Caramelized Onion and
  Mushroom Stuffing, *132,* 132–34
Roasted Broccoli, *387,* 387–88
Roasted Broccoli with Garlic, 388
Roasted Carrots, 388, *388*
Roasted Green Beans, 392
Roast Fresh Ham, *145,* 145–46
Roast Salted Turkey, *92,* 92–94
Roast Turkey for a Crowd, 88
Rolls, Rustic Dinner, 445–46, *446*
Rosemary
  -Garlic-Shallot Wet Paste Marinade, 346
  Pizza Bianca, 224–25, *225*
Rubs
  Dry, for Barbecue, 362
  Spice, 341
  Spice, Basic, for Pork Chops, 357
  Spice, Chili-Mustard, 358
  Spicy Chili, 355

Rustic Country Bread, 450–51
Rustic Dinner Rolls, 445–46, *446*
Rustic Potato-Leek Soup, 12, *12*

S

Sablés, 471–72
Sablés, Chocolate, 472
Salad dressings. *See specific salad recipes*
Salads
    Arugula, with Figs, Prosciutto, Walnuts, and Parmesan, 22
    Cabbage, Confetti, with Spicy Peanut Dressing, 30–31
    Cherry Tomato, with Feta and Olives, 26–27, *27*
    Creamy Buttermilk Coleslaw, 29–30, *30*
    Creamy Coleslaw, 29
    Cucumber, Sesame Lemon, 28
    Fruit, 440–41
    Greek, Classic, 27–28
    with Herbed Baked Goat Cheese and Vinaigrette, 23–24
    Leafy Green, with Red Wine Vinaigrette, 20, *20*
    Leafy Green, with Rich and Creamy Blue Cheese Dressing, 20–21
    Macaroni, Cool and Creamy, 31, *31*
    Pasta, Antipasto, 32–33, *33*
    Pasta, with Pesto, 32, *32*
    Potato
        American, with Hard-Cooked Eggs and Sweet Pickles, 34–35, *35*
        Austrian-Style, 35
        French, 252–53, *253*
    Rice, with Oranges, Olives, and Almonds, 33–34, *34*
    Shrimp, 163–64, *164*
        with Avocado and Orange, 164
        with Roasted Red Pepper and Basil, 164
    Spicy, with Mustard and Balsamic Vinaigrette, 21
    Thai Pork Lettuce Wraps, 302–3
    Tuna
        with Balsamic Vinegar and Grapes, 172
        Classic, 172, *172*
        Curried, with Apples and Currants, 172
        with Lime and Horseradish, 172
    Wilted Spinach
        Almond-Crusted Chicken with, 24–25
        with Warm Bacon Dressing, *22,* 22–23
        Watercress, and Orange, Pan-Seared Scallops with, 25–26
Salmon
    Barbecued, for a Charcoal Grill, 375–76
    Barbecued, on a Gas Grill, 376
    Broiled, with Mustard and Crisp Dilled Crust, *153,* 153–54
    fillet, skinning, 155
    Fillets, Charcoal-Grilled, 372–73, *373*
    Fillets, Gas-Grilled, 373
    Glazed, Charcoal-Grilled, 374–75, *375*
    Glazed, Gas-Grilled, 375

Salmon *(cont.)*
    Grilled, with Orange-Sesame Glaze, 375
    Grilled, with Spicy Apple Glaze, 375
    Oven-Roasted, 155–56, *156*
    Pan-Seared, 152–53
    Poached, with Herb and Caper Vinaigrette, *154,* 154–55
Salsas
    Avocado, 168
    Avocado-Orange, 159
    Gazpacho, 168
    One-Minute, 279
    Pineapple and Cucumber, with Mint, 378
Salsa Verde, 354
Salted Roast Turkey, *92,* 92–94
Salty Thin and Crispy Oatmeal Cookies, 469
Sandwiches
    Flank Steak and Arugula, with Red Onion, 115
    Grilled Cheese, Classic, 173–74
    Tuna Salad
        with Balsamic Vinegar and Grapes, 172
        Classic, 172, *172*
        Curried, with Apples and Currants, 172
        with Lime and Horseradish, 172
    see also Burgers
Sangria, 278–79
Satay, Beef, 303
Sauces
    Apple Cider, 138
    Barbecue
        Eastern North Carolina, 362
        Kansas City, 363–64
        Quick, 366
        for Texas-Style Beef Ribs, 369
    Bolognese, Slow-Simmered, Pasta with, 208
    Bolognese, Weeknight, Pasta with, 208–10, *209*
    Burger, Classic, 184
    Caramel, 425–26
    Chipotle Chile, Creamy, 167
    Cranberry, Classic, 103
    Dipping
        Belgian-Style, 187
        Chive and Black Pepper, 187
        Cocktail, 163
        Scallion, *300,* 300–301
        Spicy Peanut, 303
    Dried Cherry–Port, with Onions and Marmalade, 142
    Fresh Parsley and Garlic, Argentinian-Style (Chimichurri), 113
    Garlic and Thyme, 120
    Garlicky Lime, with Cilantro, 142
    Ginger-Soy, with Scallions, 159
    Horseradish Cream, 131
    Horseradish Cream, with Chives, 376
    Lemon-Caper, 118
    Lemon-Garlic, Spicy, 380

Sauces *(cont.)*

Madeira Pan, with Mustard and Anchovies, 113
Maple-Mustard, 138
Marinara, *195,* 195–96
Meat, Hearty Italian (Sunday Gravy), Pasta with, 205–7
Meat, Simple Italian-Style, *207,* 207–8
Mustard, Mid–South Carolina, 362
Mustard-Cream Pan, 112
Mustard-Dill, 376
Mustard-Shallot, with Thyme, 144
pan, using fond for, 272
Port-Cherry Reduction, 114–15
Raspberry Coulis, 527
reducing, tip for, 112
Red Wine–Mushroom Pan, 110
Red Wine Pan, 108
Rémoulade, 378
Salsa Verde, 354
Sauce Base for Steak Diane, 274
Shallot Butter, 109
Tartar, Sweet and Tangy, 151
Tomato
  -Caper Pan, 111–12
  Marinara, *195,* 195–96
  Quick, *194,* 194–95
  Quick, for Pizza, 223
  Simple, 238
  Slow-Simmered, with Meat, Pasta and, 210
Vodka, Penne with (Penne alla Vodka), 212, *212*
see also Gravy; Salsas

Sausage(s)

Antipasto Pasta Salad, 32–33, *33*
and Broccoli Rabe, Orecchiette with, 202–3
Dressing, 94–95, *96*
Mushrooms, and Monterey Jack, Breakfast Strata with, 423
Paella, *59,* 59–60
Pasta with Hearty Italian Meat Sauce (Sunday Gravy), 205–7
and Shrimp Gumbo, Creole-Style, *60,* 60–61
Simplified Cassoulet with Pork and Kielbasa, 270–71
Skillet Jambalaya, 47
Spanish Tortilla with Chorizo and Scallions, 419
Sweet Pepper, and Cheddar Cheese, Scrambled Eggs with, 411

Sautéed Baby Spinach with Almonds and Golden Raisins, 393–94
Sautéed Chicken Cutlets with Mustard-Cider Sauce, 64, *64*
Sautéed Garlic-Lemon Spinach, 393, *393*
Sautéed Wild Mushrooms, 11
Scallion Dipping Sauce, *300,* 300–301
Scalloped Potatoes, 403
Scallops, Pan-Seared, with Wilted Spinach, Watercress, and Orange Salad, 25–26
Scones

Blueberry, 428–30, *429*
Cream, 427–28

Scones *(cont.)*

Oatmeal, *430,* 430–31
Oatmeal, Glazed Maple-Pecan, 431

Scrambled Eggs

with Bacon, Onion, and Pepper Jack Cheese, 410–11
Fluffy, 410, *410*
with Sausage, Sweet Pepper, and Cheddar Cheese, 411

Sesame oil

Garlic-Ginger-Sesame Wet Paste Marinade, 346
Grilled Salmon with Orange-Sesame Glaze, 375

Sesame seeds

Sesame-Crusted Pan-Seared Tuna Steaks, 158–59, *159*
Sesame Lemon Cucumber Salad, 28
Sesame Noodles with Shredded Chicken, 306, *306*

Shallot(s)

Butter Sauce, 109
-Garlic-Rosemary Wet Paste Marinade, 346
-Mustard Sauce with Thyme, 144
and Parsley Butter, 132
Sautéed, and Vermouth, Green Beans with, 391, *391*

Shellfish

Crab Towers with Avocado and Gazpacho Salsas, 167–68, *168*
Flambéed Pan-Roasted Lobster, 164–66
Indoor Clambake, 169
Maryland Crab Cakes, 166
New England Clam Chowder, 17, *17*
Paella, *59,* 59–60
Pan-Seared Scallops with Wilted Spinach, Watercress, and Orange Salad, 25–26
see also Shrimp

Shish Kebabs, Charcoal-Grilled, 370
Shish Kebabs, Gas-Grilled, 370
Shortcakes, Strawberry, *540,* 540–41
Shrimp

Cocktail, 163
deveining, 160
fra Diavolo, 204–5, *205*
Garlic, Spanish-Style, 162, *162*
Garlicky, with Buttered Bread Crumbs, *161,* 161–62
Kung Pao, *320,* 320–21
Pad Thai, *325,* 325–26
Paella, *59,* 59–60
Pan-Seared, 159–60, *160*
  with Chipotle-Lime Glaze, 160
  with Garlic-Lemon Butter, 160
  with Ginger-Hoisin Glaze, 160
Pasta, Garlicky, 203–4, *204*
Pineapple, and Peanuts, Thai Red Curry with, 323–24
Pork, and Shiitakes, Fried Rice with, 307, *307*
Salad, 163–64, *164*
  with Avocado and Orange, 164
  with Roasted Red Pepper and Basil, 164
and Sausage Gumbo, Creole-Style, *60,* 60–61
Scampi, 247
skewering, for the grill, 380

Shrimp *(cont.)*
 Skewers, Charcoal-Grilled, 379, *379*
 Skewers, Gas-Grilled, 379–80
 Skillet Jambalaya, 47
 Stir-Fried, Asparagus, and Yellow Pepper with Lemon Sauce, 312–13
 Tempura, 301–2
Simple Applesauce, 386
Simple Italian-Style Meat Sauce, *207,* 207–8
Simple Pot Roast, 50, *50*
Simple Raspberry Gratin, 544–45
Simple Roast Chicken, 72
Simple Sautéed Swiss Chard, 395–96
Simple Tomato Sauce, 238
Simplified Cassoulet with Pork and Kielbasa, 270–71
Single-Crust Pie Dough For Custard Pies, 559
Skillet Apple Brown Betty, *546,* 546–47
Skillet Apple Pie (Apple Pandowdy), *549,* 549–50
Skillet Baked Ziti, 38, *38*
Skillet-Barbecued Pork Chops, 120–21, *121*
Skillet Beef Stroganoff, 43, *43*
Skillet Chicken, Broccoli, and Ziti, 38–39
Skillet Chicken and Rice with Broccoli and Cheddar, 46
Skillet Chicken and Rice with Peas and Scallions, 45
Skillet Chicken Pot Pie with Biscuit Topping, 40–42
Skillet Jambalaya, 47
Skillet Lasagna, 39–40, *40*
Skillet-Roasted Chicken Breasts with Potatoes, *44,* 44–45
Skillet-Roasted Potatoes, 402, *402*
Skillet Soufflé, Chocolate-Orange, 537
Skillet Soufflé, Lemon, 537, *537*
Skillet Tamale Pie, 42
Slow-Cooker Beef Burgundy, 269–70
Slow Cooker Beer-Braised Short Ribs, 55, *55*
Slow-Roasted Beef, 130–31
Slow-Roasted Turkey with Gravy, *91,* 91–92
Smashed Potatoes, 396
Smoked Paprika and Roasted Red Pepper Butter, 352
Smoky Kansas City Barbecue Beans, 364
Smothered Pork Chops, *123,* 123–24
Soda Bread, Irish, 446–47
Soda Bread, Whole Wheat, 447
Soufflés
 Chilled Lemon, 534–35
  Individual, 535
  with White Chocolate, 535
 Grand Marnier, *533,* 533–34
 Grand Marnier, with Grated Chocolate, 534
 Make-Ahead Chocolate, *535,* 535–36
 Make-Ahead Mocha, 536
 making foil collars for, 536
 Skillet Chocolate-Orange, 537
 Skillet Lemon, 537, *537*
Soups
 Beef and Vegetable, Quick, *6,* 6–7

Soups *(cont.)*
 Black Bean, 282–83, *283*
 Butternut Squash, 11
 Chicken, Thai-Style, 303–4, *304*
 Chicken Noodle, Classic, 4
 Chicken Noodle, Hearty, *5,* 5–6
 Classic Gazpacho, 16
 French Onion, Classic, *250,* 250–51
 French Onion, Streamlined, 251–52
 Ham and Split Pea, 14
 Hearty Tuscan Bean Stew, 231–32, *232*
 Hot and Sour, 304–5, *305*
 Lentil, Hearty, 12–13
 Mulligatawny, 14–15, *15*
 Mushroom, Creamy, *10,* 10–11
 New England Clam Chowder, 17, *17*
 Pasta e Fagioli, 230–31, *231*
 Pea, Creamy, 9–10
 Potato-Leek, Rustic, 12, *12*
 Tomato, Classic Cream of, 7
 Tomato, Creamless Creamy, 8, *8*
 Tortilla, *281,* 281–82
 see also Stews
Sour Cherry Cobbler, *541,* 541–42
Sour Cream Coffee Cake with Brown Sugar–Pecan Streusel, *440,* 440–41
Southern Corn Bread, 449–50
Southwestern Marinade, 350
Soy (sauce)
 Garlic, and Ginger Marinade, 350
 -Ginger Glaze, 337
 -Ginger Sauce with Scallions, 159
Spaghetti
 alla Carbonara, 212–13
 Cincinnati Chili, *177,* 177–78
 and Meatballs, 210–11, *211*
 with Olive Pesto, 200
 Pasta with Garlic and Oil, 190, *190*
 Puttanesca, 196
 Turkey Tetrazzini, 176–77
Spanish-Style Garlic Shrimp, 162, *162*
Spanish Tortilla with Chorizo and Scallions, 419
Spanish Tortilla with Roasted Red Peppers and Peas, 418–19, *419*
Spice Cake, *495,* 495–96
Spiced Pecans with Rum Glaze, 407
Spiced Pumpkin Cheesecake, *521,* 521–22
Spice Rub, 341
 Basic, for Pork Chops, 357
 Chili-Mustard, 358
Spice-Rubbed Picnic Chicken, 70, *70*
Spicy Chili Rub, 355
Spicy Cucumber Relish, 156
Spicy Garlic Oil, 227
Spicy Jalapeño-Cheddar Corn Bread, 449

Spicy Lemon-Garlic Sauce, 380
Spicy Peanut Dipping Sauce, 303
Spicy Pineapple-Ginger Glaze, 146
Spicy Salad with Mustard and Balsamic Vinaigrette, 21
Spinach
    Baby, Sautéed, with Almonds and Golden Raisins, 393–94
    Dip, Creamy Herbed, 394–95
    and Gruyère, Breakfast Strata with, *422,* 422–23
    and Pine Nuts, Grilled Stuffed Flank Steak with, 349
    Sautéed Garlic-Lemon, 393, *393*
    Wilted, Salad, Almond-Crusted Chicken with, 24–25
    Wilted, Salad with Warm Bacon Dressing, *22,* 22–23
    Wilted, Watercress, and Orange Salad, Pan-Seared Scallops
        with, 25–26
Split Pea and Ham Soup, 14
Spreads. *See* Dips and spreads
Spritz Cookies, *470,* 470–71
    Almond, 471
    with Lemon Essence, 471
Squash
    Acorn, Quick Roasted, with Brown Sugar, 404–5, *405*
    Butternut, Risotto, 235–36, *236*
    Butternut, Soup, 11
    Pumpkin Pie, 569–70, *570*
    Spiced Pumpkin Cheesecake, *521,* 521–22
    Stir-Fried Chicken and Zucchini with Ginger Sauce, 312
    Summer Vegetable Gratin, *256,* 256–57
Steak, beef. *See under* Beef
Steak Fries, *185,* 185–86
Stews
    Bean, Hearty Tuscan, 231–32, *232*
    Beef, Beer, and Onion, Belgian (Carbonnade à la Flamande),
        51, 51–52
    Beef, Hungarian, 52–53, *53*
    Beef Burgundy, 267–69
    Beef Burgundy, Slow-Cooker, 269–70
    Daube Provençal, *266,* 266–67
Sticky Buns with Pecans, 437–39, *438*
Stir-fries
    best pans for, 313
    Kung Pao Shrimp, *320,* 320–21
    Pad Thai, *325,* 325–26
    Pork Lo Mein, 318–20, *319*
    Stir-Fried Beef and Broccoli with Oyster Sauce, *314,* 314–15
    Stir-Fried Chicken and Zucchini with Ginger Sauce, 312
    Stir-Fried Chicken with Bok Choy and Crispy Noodle Cake,
        310–11, *311*
    Stir-Fried Pork, Eggplant, and Onion with Garlic and Black
        Pepper, 317–18
    Stir-Fried Pork, Green Beans, and Red Bell Pepper with
        Gingery Oyster Sauce, 318, *318*
    Stir-Fried Portobellos with Ginger-Oyster Sauce, 321–22,
        322
    Stir-Fried Portobellos with Sweet Chili-Garlic Sauce, 322
    Stir-Fried Shrimp, Asparagus, and Yellow Pepper with Lemon
        Sauce, 312–13

Stir-fries *(cont.)*
    Stir-Fried Thai-Style Beef with Chiles and Shallots, *324,*
        324–25
    Stir-Fried Tofu, Snow Peas, and Red Onion with Hot and
        Sour Sauce, 313–14
    Tangerine Stir-Fried Beef with Onion and Snow Peas,
        316–17
    Teriyaki Stir-Fried Beef with Green Beans and Shiitakes,
        315–16
Stovetop Macaroni and Cheese, 175
Stovetop Rice Pudding, 526, *526*
Stovetop Roast Chicken with Lemon-Herb Sauce, 76–77, *77*
Strata, Breakfast, with Sausage, Mushrooms, and Monterey
        Jack, 423
Strata, Breakfast, with Spinach and Gruyère, *422,* 422–23
Strawberry(ies)
    with Balsamic Vinegar, 554
    Cream Cake, 496–98
    and Grapes with Balsamic and Red Wine Reduction, 440–41
    -Rhubarb Fool, 555
    Shortcakes, *540,* 540–41
    Topping, 520
Streamlined French Onion Soup, 251–52
Strudel, Easy Apple, *547,* 547–49
Stuffed Chicken Cutlets with Ham and Cheddar, 65–66
Stuffed Pork Chops, 125–27
"Stuffed" Roast Butterflied Chicken, *79,* 79–80
Stuffings and dressings
    Bread Stuffing with Bacon, Apples, Sage, and Caramelized
        Onions, 90–91
    inserting into turkey, 90
    Mushroom-Leek Bread Stuffing with Herbs, 80
    Sausage Dressing, 94–95, *96*
Sugar, Brown, Cookies, *458,* 458–59
Summer Berry Pie, *568,* 568–69
Summer Vegetable Gratin, *256,* 256–57
Sweet-and-Sour Chutney, 153
Sweet and Spicy Pickled Onions, 286
Sweet and Tangy Oven-Barbecued Chicken, 68–69, *69*
Sweet and Tangy Tartar Sauce, 151
Sweet Potato(es)
    Casserole, Candied, 105, *105*
    Eggplant, Green Beans, and Chickpeas, Indian-Style Curry
        with, 332
    Mashed, 405–6
Swiss Chard, Simple Sautéed, 395–96

T

Tacos, Beef, 284, *284*
Tacos, Steak, 285–86
Taco Shells, Home-Fried, 284
Tamale Pie, Skillet, 42
Tandoori Chicken, 332–33, *333*
Tangerine and Ginger Relish, 156

Tangerine Stir-Fried Beef with Onion and Snow Peas, 316–17
Tangy Whipped Cream, 549
Tartar Sauce, Sweet and Tangy, 151
Tart Dough, Classic, 576
Tarts (dessert)
  Apple, Free-Form, 581–82
  Apple, French (Apple Galette), *580,* 580–81
  Fresh Fruit, with Pastry Cream, 578–79, *579*
  Lemon, 576–77
  Mixed Berry, with Pastry Cream, 579
  Pear Tatin, 582
  preparing shell for, 576
  Summer Fruit, Free-Form, 577–78
  30-Minute Tarte Tatin, 582
Tarts (savory)
  Onion and Bacon, French, 253–54
  Pissaladière, 254–55, *255*
  Tomato and Mozzarella, *227,* 227–28
Tequila
  Fresh Margaritas, 278
Teriyaki Stir-Fried Beef with Green Beans and Shiitakes, 315–16
Texas-Style Barbecued Beef Ribs for a Charcoal Grill, *368,* 368–69
Texas-Style Barbecued Beef Ribs for a Gas Grill, 369
Thai Chili Butter, 110
Thai Green Curry with Chicken, Broccoli, and Mushrooms, 322–23
Thai Grilled Chicken on a Gas Grill, 327
Thai Grilled Chicken with Spicy, Sweet, and Sour Dipping Sauce, 326–27, *327*
Thai Pork Lettuce Wraps, 302–3
Thai Red Curry with Shrimp, Pineapple, and Peanuts, 323–24
Thai-Style Chicken Soup, 303–4, *304*
Thermometers, buying guide, 592–93
Thick and Chewy Chocolate Chip Cookies, 461–62
Thick and Chewy Double-Chocolate Cookies, 464–65
Thick and Chewy Triple-Chocolate Cookies, 465
Thick-Cut Pork Tenderloin Medallions, 137, *138*
Thin and Crispy Chocolate Chip Cookies, 462–63
Thin and Crispy Oatmeal Cookies, *468,* 468–69
30-Minute Tarte Tatin, 582
Timers, kitchen, buying guide, 592–93
Tiramisù, 517–18, *518*
Tiramisù with Cooked Eggs, 518–19
Tofu
  Hot and Sour Soup, 304–5, *305*
  Stir-Fried, Snow Peas, and Red Onion with Hot and Sour Sauce, 313–14
Tomatillos
  Enchiladas Verdes, *290,* 290–91
Tomato(es)
  and Almond Pesto, Pasta with (Pesto alla Trapanese), *198,* 198–99

Tomato(es) *(cont.)*
  and Cheese Pizza, Grilled, for a Charcoal Grill, 225–26
  and Cheese Pizzas, Grilled, for a Gas Grill, 226
  Cherry, –Basil Vinaigrette, Chunky, 158
  Cherry, Salad with Feta and Olives, 26–27, *27*
  Classic Gazpacho, 16
  Crisp Thin-Crust Pizza, 222, *222*
  Fresh, and Herbs, Pasta with, 190–91
  Fresh, Relish, 156
  Gazpacho Salsa, 168
  Huevos Rancheros, 296–97
  Mozzarella, and Basil, Deep-Dish Pizza with, *223,* 223–24
  and Mozzarella Tart, *227,* 227–28
  Olives, and Feta, Farfalle with, 194
  One-Minute Salsa, 279
  Pasta Caprese, 193, *193*
  Penne with Vodka Sauce (Penne alla Vodka), 212, *212*
  Sauce
    Creamy, Pasta with, *192,* 192–93
    Fresh, with Feta and Olives, 380
    Fresh, with Garlic and Basil, Pasta with, 191–92
    Marinara, *195,* 195–96
    Quick, *194,* 194–95
    Quick, for Pizza, 223
    Simple, 238
    Tomato-Caper Pan, 111–12
  Shrimp fra Diavolo, 204–5, *205*
  Soup, Classic Cream of, 7
  Soup, Creamless Creamy, 8, *8*
  Spaghetti Puttanesca, 196
  storing, 191
Tools, handy, buying guide, 588–91
Tools, specialty, buying guide, 598–600
Tortilla, Spanish, with Chorizo and Scallions, 419
Tortilla, Spanish, with Roasted Red Peppers and Peas, 418–19, *419*
Tortilla(s)
  Beef Tacos, 284, *284*
  Cheesy Nachos with Guacamole and Salsa, 279, *279*
  Chicken Enchiladas with a Red Chili Sauce, 288–89, *289*
  Home-Fried Taco Shells, 284
  Huevos Rancheros, 296–97
  Quesadillas, 280–81
  Soup, *281,* 281–82
  Steak Tacos, 285–86
  see also Fajitas
Triple-Chocolate-Chunk Pecan Pie, 571
Triple-Chocolate Espresso Brownies, 480
Triple-Chocolate Mousse Cake, *515,* 515–16
Triple Citrus Bars, 483
Triple-Coconut Macaroons, 469–70
Triple sec
  Fresh Margaritas, 278
  Sangria, 278–79
Tuna
  Salad, Classic, 172, *172*

Tuna (cont.)

Salad, Curried, with Apples and Currants, 172

Salad with Balsamic Vinegar and Grapes, 172

Salad with Lime and Horseradish, 172

Steaks, Pan-Seared Sesame-Crusted, 158–59, *159*

Turkey

Breast

Boneless, Charcoal Grill–Roasted, *101,* 101–2

Boneless, Gas Grill–Roasted, 102–3

carving, 99

deboning, 102

brining, 87

Grill-Roasted, on a Charcoal Grill, 100–101

Grill-Roasted, on a Gas Grill, 101

how to butterfly, 95

inserting stuffing into, 90

Roast

Classic, 86, *86*

Classic Stuffed, *89,* 89–90

Crisp-Skin High-Roast Butterflied, with Sausage Dressing, 94–95

for a Crowd, 88

Herbed, *97,* 97–98

Salted, *92,* 92–94

Slow-Roasted, with Gravy, *91,* 91–92

Tetrazzini, 176–77

Turkey Gravy, 96–97

All-Purpose, 99, *99*

Giblet Pan, 87

Giblet Pan, for a Crowd, 88–89

Slow-Roasted Turkey with, *91,* 91–92

Twice-Baked Potatoes, 404

V

Vanilla Pretzel Cookies, 473

Veal

Osso Buco, 245–46

see also Meat loaf mix

Vegetable(s)

and Beef Soup, Quick, *6,* 6–7

Root, and Potatoes, Mashed, 399, *399*

Summer, Gratin, *256,* 256–57

see also specific vegetables

Vinaigrettes

Almond, 373

Cherry Tomato–Basil, Chunky, 158

Olive, 373

Vinegar

Eastern North Carolina Barbecue Sauce, 362

and Sweet Peppers, Pork Chops with, *244,* 244–45

Vodka Sauce, Penne with (Penne alla Vodka), 212, *212*

W

Waffles, Buttermilk, 426, *426*

Walnut(s)

Asparagus, Arugula, and Blue Cheese, Cavatappi with, 201

Figs, Prosciutto, and Parmesan, Arugula Salad with, 22

or Pecan Crescent Cookies, 476, *476*

Warm-Spiced Parsley Marinade with Ginger, 370–71

Watercress, Wilted Spinach, and Orange Salad, Pan-Seared Scallops with, 25–26

Well-Done Charcoal-Grilled Hamburgers, *344,* 344–45

Well-Done Gas-Grilled Hamburgers, 345

Well-Done Grilled Bacon Cheeseburgers, 345

Whipped Cream, Tangy, 549

White Bean(s)

Boston Baked Beans, 390, *390*

Hearty Tuscan Bean Stew, 231–32, *232*

Pasta e Fagioli, 230–31, *231*

Simplified Cassoulet with Pork and Kielbasa, 270–71

White Chicken Chili, 295–96

White Chicken Chili, 295–96

Whole Wheat Soda Bread, 447

Wild Rice Pilaf with Pecans and Dried Cranberries, 406–7

Wilted Spinach Salad with Warm Bacon Dressing, *22,* 22–23

Wine

Chicken Marsala, 237

Madeira Pan Sauce with Mustard and Anchovies, 113

see also Port; Red Wine

Z

Zabaglione, Individual Fresh Berry Gratins with, *545,* 545–46

Zucchini

and Chicken, Stir-Fried, with Ginger Sauce, 312

Summer Vegetable Gratin, *256,* 256–57